# Lecture Notes in Computer Science 13555

More information about this series at https://link.springer.com/bookseries/558

Vijayalakshmi Atluri · Roberto Di Pietro ·
Christian D. Jensen · Weizhi Meng (Eds.)

# Computer Security – ESORICS 2022

27th European Symposium
on Research in Computer Security
Copenhagen, Denmark, September 26–30, 2022
Proceedings, Part II

Springer

*Editors*
Vijayalakshmi Atluri ⒾⒹ
Rutgers University
Newark, NJ, USA

Roberto Di Pietro ⒾⒹ
Hamad Bin Khalifa University
Doha, Qatar

Christian D. Jensen ⒾⒹ
Technical University of Denmark
Kongens Lyngby, Denmark

Weizhi Meng ⒾⒹ
Technical University of Denmark
Kongens Lyngby, Denmark

ISSN 0302-9743            ISSN 1611-3349 (electronic)
Lecture Notes in Computer Science
ISBN 978-3-031-17145-1        ISBN 978-3-031-17146-8 (eBook)
https://doi.org/10.1007/978-3-031-17146-8

# Preface

The 27th European Symposium on Research in Computer Security (ESORICS 2022) was held together with the affiliated workshops during the week of September 26–30, 2022. Due to the COVID-19 pandemic, the conference and the workshops took place in a hybrid mode. The virtual and in-person attendance was hosted and managed by the Technical University of Denmark.

ESORICS is a flagship European security conference. The aim of ESORICS is to advance the research in computer security and privacy by establishing a European forum, bringing together researchers in these areas, and promoting the exchange of ideas with developers, standardization bodies, and policy makers, as well as by encouraging links with researchers in related fields.

Continuing the model introduced in 2021, this year ESORICS also offered two review cycles: a winter cycle and a spring cycle. We believe that such an approach sports great advantages. On the one hand, it is more convenient for the authors and, on the other hand, it also increases the number of submissions, thus securing high-quality papers. In response to the call for papers, which covered a few new topics, we received a record-high number of papers: 562. This is a testimony of the growth and vitality of the computer security field, the expansion of the research community in this field, and the growing importance of ESORICS itself.

These papers were peer-reviewed and subsequently discussed based on the quality of their scientific contribution, novelty, and impact by the members of the Program Committee. The submissions were single-blind, and in almost all cases there were vivid discussions among the members of the Program Committee to decide the merit of reviewed papers.

The submission of the papers and the review process was carried out using the Easy-Chair platform. Based on the reviews and the discussion, 104 papers were selected for presentation at the conference, resulting in an acceptance rate of 18.5%. The most tangible result of this whole process was that ESORICS had an exciting scientific program covering timely and interesting security and privacy topics in theory, systems, networks, and applications.

The papers that were selected for presentation at ESORICS 2022 have been published in a three-volume set of proceedings: LNCS 13554, LNCS 13555, and LNCS 13556.

Aside from the paper presentations, we were honored to have four outstanding keynote speakers: Giuseppe Ateniese, Paulo Esteves-Verissimo, Ahmad Reza Sadeghi, and Ravi Sandhu. Their talks provided interesting insights and research directions in important research areas.

The Program Committee (PC) consisted of 180 members. We would like to thank the members of the PC and the external referees for their hard work in supporting the review process, as well as everyone who supported the organization of ESORICS 2022. In particular, the exceptional number of submissions put quite a burden on the reviewers (over the two cycles of submission, an average of 12 papers were reviewed by each reviewer).

We are grateful to the general co-chairs, Christian D. Jensen and Weizhi Meng; the workshops chairs, Mauro Conti and Jianying Zhou, and all of the workshop co-chairs; the poster chair, Joaquin Garcia-Alfaro; the publicity co-chair's Cristina Alcaraz and Wenjuan Li; the web chair, Wei-Yang Chiu; and the ESORICS Steering Committee and its chair, Sokratis Katsikas.

We are also grateful to BlockSec for supporting the organization of ESORICS 2022.

Finally, we would like to provide a heartfelt thank you to the authors for submitting their papers to ESORICS 2022. It is their efforts that, in the end, decided the success of ESORICS 2022, confirmed ESORICS as a top-notch security conference, planted the seeds for future successes, and advanced science.

We hope that the proceedings will promote research and facilitate future work in the exciting, challenging, and evolving field of security.

September 2022                                            Roberto Di Pietro
                                                         Vijayalakshmi Atluri

# Organization

## General Chairs

Christian D. Jensen      Technical University of Denmark, Denmark
Weizhi Meng      Technical University of Denmark, Denmark

## Program Committee Chairs

Vijayalakshmi Atluri      Rutgers University, USA
Roberto Di Pietro      Hamad Bin Khalifa University, Qatar

## Steering Committee

Sokratis Katsikas (Chair)      NTNU, Norway
Joachim Biskup      University of Dortmund, Germany
Véronique Cortier      CNRS, France
Frédéric Cuppens      Polytechnique Montréal, Canada
Sabrina De Capitani di Vimercati      Università degli Studi di Milano, Italy
Joaquin Garcia-Alfaro      Institut Polytechnique de Paris, France
Dieter Gollmann      Hamburg University of Technology, Germany
Kutylowski Mirek      Wroclaw University of Technology, Poland
Javier Lopez      Universidad de Malaga, Spain
Jean-Jacques Quisquater      University of Louvain, Belgium
Peter Ryan      University of Luxembourg, Luxembourg
Pierangela Samarati      Università degli Studi di Milano, Italy
Einar Snekkenes      NTNU, Norway
Michael Waidner      ATHENE, Germany

## Program Committee

Abu-Salma, Ruba      King's College London, UK
Afek, Yehuda      Tel-Aviv University, Israel
Akiyama, Mitsuaki      NTT, Japan
Albanese, Massimiliano      George Mason University, USA
Alcaraz, Cristina      University of Malaga, Spain
Allman, Mark      International Computer Science Institute, USA
Alrabaee, Saed      United Arab Emirates University, UAE
Asif, Hafiz      Rutgers University, USA

| | |
|---|---|
| Ayday, Erman | Case Western Reserve University, USA, and Bilkent University, Turkey |
| Bai, Guangdong | University of Queensland, Australia |
| Bakiras, Spiridon | Singapore Institute of Technology, Singapore |
| Bardin, Sebastien | CEA LIST, France |
| Batra, Gunjan | Kennesaw State University, USA |
| Bertino, Elisa | Purdue University, USA |
| Blasco, Jorge | Royal Holloway, University of London, UK |
| Blundo, Carlo | Università degli Studi di Salerno, Italy |
| Bonaci, Tamara | Northeastern University, USA |
| Camtepe, Seyit | CSIRO Data61, Australia |
| Ceccato, Mariano | Università di Verona, Italy |
| Chakraborti, Anrin | Stony Brook University, USA |
| Chan, Aldar C-F. | University of Hong Kong, Hong Kong |
| Chen, Bo | Michigan Technological University, USA |
| Chen, Xiaofeng | Xidian University, China |
| Chen, Liqun | University of Surrey, UK |
| Chen, Rongmao | National University of Defense Technology, China |
| Chen, Yu | Shandong University, China |
| Chow, Sherman S. M. | The Chinese University of Hong Kong, Hong Kong |
| Chowdhury, Omar | University of Iowa, USA |
| Conti, Mauro | Università di Padova, USA |
| Coull, Scott | Mandiant, USA |
| Crispo, Bruno | University of Trento, Italy |
| Cukier, Michel | University of Maryland, USA |
| Cuppens, Frédéric | Polytechnique Montréal, Canada |
| Cuppens-Boulahia, Nora | Polytechnique Montréal, Canada |
| Damiani, Ernesto | University of Milan, Italy |
| Daza, Vanesa | Universitat Pompeu Fabra, Spain |
| De Capitani di Vimercati, Sabrina | Università degli Studi di Milano, Italy |
| Debar, Hervé | Télécom SudParis, France |
| Desmedt, Yvo | University of Texas at Dallas, USA |
| Diao, Wenrui | Shandong University, China |
| Dimitriou, Tassos | Kuwait University, Kuwait |
| Domingo-Ferrer, Josep | Universitat Rovira i Virgili, Spain |
| Dong, Changyu | Newcastle University, UK |
| Ferrara, Anna Lisa | University of Bristol, UK |
| Ferrer-Gomila, Jose-Luis | University of the Balearic Islands, Spain |
| Fila, Barbara | INSA Rennes, IRISA, France |
| Fischer-Hübner, Simone | Karlstad University, Sweden |

| | |
|---|---|
| Gadyatskaya, Olga | Leiden University, The Netherlands |
| Gao, Debin | Singapore Management University, Singapore |
| Garcia-Alfaro, Joaquin | Institut Polytechnique de Paris, France |
| Garg, Siddharth | New York University, USA |
| Giacinto, Giorgio | University of Cagliari, Italy |
| Gollmann, Dieter | Hamburg University of Technology, Germany |
| Gong, Neil | Duke University, USA |
| Gope, Prosanta | University of Sheffield, UK |
| Gosain, Devashish | Max Planck Institute for Informatics, Germany |
| Gritzalis, Stefanos | University of Piraeus, Greece |
| Gu, Zhongshu | IBM, USA |
| Gulmezoglu, Berk | Iowa State University, USA |
| Haines, Thomas | Queensland University of Technology, Australia |
| He, Xinlei | CISPA Helmholtz Center for Information Security, Germany |
| Hernández-Serrano, Juan | Universitat Politècnica de Catalunya, Spain |
| Hong, Yuan | Illinois Institute of Technology, USA |
| Huang, Xinyi | Fujian Normal University, China |
| Jager, Tibor | Bergische Universität Wuppertal, Germany |
| Jeon, Yuseok | Ulsan National Institute of Science and Technology, South Korea |
| Ji, Shouling | Zhejiang University, China |
| Jonker, Hugo | Open University of the Netherlands, The Netherlands |
| Karame, Ghassan | NEC Laboratories Europe, Germany |
| Katsikas, Sokratis | NTNU, Norway |
| Kim, Hyoungshick | Sungkyunkwan University, South Korea |
| Klai, Kais | Sorbonne University, France |
| Kremer, Steve | Inria, France |
| Krotofil, Marina | Kudelski Security, Switzerland |
| Kruegel, Christopher | University of California, Santa Barbara, USA |
| Lambrinoudakis, Costas | University of Piraeus, Greece |
| Landau Feibish, Shir | The Open University of Israel, Israel |
| Lee, Adam | University of Pittsburg, USA |
| Leita, Corrado | VMware, UK |
| Li, Shujun | University of Kent, UK |
| Li, Zitao | Purdue University, USA |
| Liang, Kaitai | TU Delft, The Netherlands |
| Lin, Zhiqiang | Ohio State University, USA |
| Liu, Xiangyu | Alibaba Inc., China |
| Liu, Peng | Pennsylvania State University, USA |
| Livraga, Giovanni | University of Milan, Italy |

| | |
|---|---|
| Schinzel, Sebastian Münster | Münster University of Applied Sciences, Germany |
| Schneider, Steve | University of Surrey, UK |
| Schroeder, Dominique | Friedrich-Alexander-Universiät Erlangen-Nürnberg, Germany |
| Schwarz, Michael | CISPA Helmholtz Center for Information Security, Germany |
| Schwenk, Joerg | Ruhr-Universität Bochum, Germany |
| Sciancalepore, Savio | Eindhoven University of Technology, The Netherlands |
| Shahandashti, Siamak | University of York, UK |
| Sharma, Piyush Kumar | Indraprastha Institute of Information Technology Delhi, India |
| Shulman, Haya | Fraunhofer SIT, Germany |
| Sinanoglu, Ozgur | New York University Abu Dhabi, UAE |
| Sklavos, Nicolas | University of Patras, Greece |
| Snekkenes, Einar | NTNU, Norway |
| Somorovsky, Juraj | Paderborn University, Germany |
| Strufe, Thorsten | Karlsruhe Institute of Technology, Germany |
| Sural, Shamik | IIT Kharagpur, India |
| Susilo, Willy | University of Wollongong, Australia |
| Tang, Qiang | University of Sydney, Australia |
| Tang, Qiang | Luxembourg Institute of Science and Technology, Luxembourg |
| Tapiador, Juan Manuel | Universidad Carlos III de Madrid, Spain |
| Tian, Dave | Purdue University, USA |
| Torrey, Jacob | Thinkst Applied Research, USA |
| Trachtenberg, Ari | Boston University, USA |
| Treharne, Helen | University of Surrey, UK |
| Trieu, Ni | Arizona State University, USA |
| Tripunitara, Mahesh | University of Waterloo, Canada |
| Tsohou, Aggeliki | Ionian University, Greece |
| Urban, Tobias | Institute for Internet Security, Germany |
| Esteves-Verissimo, Paulo | KAUST, Saudi Arabia |
| Viganò, Luca | King's College London, UK |
| Visconti, Ivan | University of Salerno, Italy |
| Voulimeneas, Alexios | KU Leven, Belgium |
| Waidner, Michael | ATHENE, Germany |
| Wang, Cong | City University of Hong Kong, Hong Kong |
| Wang, Tianhao | Purdue University, USA |
| Wang, Di | State University of New York at Buffalo, USA |
| Wang, Haining | University of Delaware, USA |

| Wang, Lingyu | Concordia University, Canada |
| Wool, Avishai | Tel Aviv University, Israel |
| Xenakis, Christos | University of Piraeus, Greece |
| Xiang, Yang | Swinburne University of Technology, Australia |
| Xu, Jun | University of Utah, USA |
| Yang, Jie | Florida State University, USA |
| Yang, Kang | State Key Laboratory of Cryptology, China |
| Yang, Guomin | University of Wollongong, Australia |
| Yeun, Chan | Khalifa University, Abu Dhabi, UAE |
| Yi, Xun | RMIT University, Australia |
| Yu, Yu | Shanghai Jiao Tong University, China |
| Yuen, Tsz | University of Hong Kong, Hong Kong |
| Zhang, Zhikun | CISPA Helmholtz Center for Information Security, Germany |
| Zhang, Yuan | Fudan University, China |
| Zhang, Kehuan | The Chinese University of Hong Kong, Hong Kong |
| Zhao, Yunlei | Fudan University, China |
| Zhou, Jianying | Singapore University of Technology and Design, Singapore |
| Zhu, Rui | Indiana University, USA |
| Zhu, Sencun | Pennsylvania State University, USA |

## Workshops Chairs

| Conti Mauro | University of Padua, Italy |
| Zhou Jianying | Singapore University of Technology and Design, Singapore |

## Poster Chair

| Garcia-Alfaro Joaquin | Institut Polytechnique de Paris, France |

## Publicity Chairs

| Alcaraz Cristina | University of Malaga, Spain |
| Li Wenjuan | Hong Kong Polytechnic University, Hong Kong |

## Web Chair

| Chiu Wei-Yang | Technical University of Denmark, Denmark |

# Posters Program Committee

| | |
|---|---|
| Atluri, Vijay | Rutgers University, USA |
| de Fuentes, Jose M. | Universidad Carlos III de Madrid, Spain |
| Di Pietro, Roberto | Hamad Bin Khalifa University, Qatar |
| González Manzano, Lorena | Universidad Carlos III de Madrid, Spain |
| Hartenstein, Hannes | Karlsruhe Institute of Technology, Germany |
| Kikuchi, Hiroaki | Meiji University, Japan |
| Matsuo, Shin'Ichiro | Georgetown University, USA |
| Navarro-Arribas, Guillermo | Universitat Autonoma de Barcelona, Spain |
| Nespoli, Pantaleone | Universidad de Murcia, Spain |
| Ranise, Silvio | University of Trento and Fondazione Bruno Kessler, Italy |
| Saint-Hilarire, Kéren | Institut Polytechnique de Paris, France |
| Signorini, Matteo | Nokia Bell Labs, France |
| Vasilopoulos, Dimitrios | IMDEA Software Institute, Spain |
| Zannone, Nicola | Eindhoven University of Technology, The Netherlands |

# Additional Reviewers

Abadi, Aydin
Abbadini, Marco
Ahmadi, Sharar
Akand, Mamun
Akbar, Yousef
Alrahis, Lilas
Ameur Abid, Chiheb
Amine Merzouk, Mohamed
Anagnostopoulos, Marios
Angelogianni, Anna
Anglés-Tafalla, Carles
Apruzzese, Giovanni
Arapinis, Myrto
Arriaga, Afonso
Arzt, Steven
Avitabile, Gennaro
Avizheh, Sepideh
Bag, Arnab
Bagheri, Sima
Bampatsikos, Michail
Battarbee, Christopher
Baumer, Thomas
Benaloh, Josh

Berger, Christian
Berrang, Pascal
Blanco-Justicia, Alberto
Böhm, Fabian
Bolgouras, Vaios
Botta, Vincenzo
Bountakas, Panagiotis
Brighente, Alessandro
Bursuc, Sergiu
C. Pöhls, Henrich
Cachin, Christian
Cai, Cailing
Cao, Chen
Casolare, Rosangela
Chen, Xihui
Chen, Niusen
Chen, Min
Chen, Jinrong
Chen, Chao
Chen, Long
Chen, Zeyu
Chu, Hien
Ciampi, Michele

Cicala, Fabrizio
Cinà, Antonio
Coijanovic, Christoph
Costantino, Gianpiero
Craaijo, Jos
Crochelet, Pierre
Cui, Hui
Cui, Handong
Dai, Tianxiang
Damodaran, Aditya
Daniyal Dar, Muhammad
Das Chowdhury, Partha
Daudén-Esmel, Cristòfol
Davies, Peter
Davies, Gareth
de Ruck, Dairo
Debant, Alexandre
Debnath, Joyanta
Degani, Luca
Demetrio, Luca
Deuber, Dominic
Dexheimer, Thomas
Diemert, Denis
Dodd, Charles
Dragan, Constantin Catalin
Driouich, Youssef
Du, Changlai
Du, Linkang
Du, Minxin
Duman, Onur
Duong, Dung
Dutta, Priyanka
Dutta, Sabyasachi
Dutta, Moumita
Duttagupta, Sayon
Ebrahimi, Ehsan
Echeverria, Mitziu
Ehsanpour, Maryam
Eichhammer, Philipp
Ekramul Kabir, Mohammad
Empl, Philip
Eyal, Ittay
Facchinetti, Dario
Fadavi, Mojtaba
Fallahi, Matin

Farao, Aristeidis
Fauzi, Prastudy
Feng, Hanwen
Feng, Qi
Feng, Shuya
Fisseha Demissie, Biniam
Fournaris, Apostolos
Fraser, Ashley
Friedl, Sabrina
Friess, Jens
Friolo, Daniele
Gao, Jiahui
Gardiner, Joseph
Garfatta, Ikram
Gattermayer, Tobias
Gellert, Kai
George, Dominik
Gerault, David
Gerhart, Paul
Ghadafi, Essam
Gholipourchoubeh, Mahmood
Gil-Pons, Reynaldo
Glas, Magdalena
Golinelli, Matteo
Gong, Junqing
Grisafi, Michele
Groll, Sebastian
Große-Kampmann, Matteo
Guan Tan, Teik
Guo, Xiaojie
Haffar, Rami
Haffey, Preston
Hallett, Joseph
Hammad Mazhar, M.
Han, Jinguang
Handirk, Tobias
Hao, Xuexuan
Hao, Shuai
Hasan Shahriar, Md
Heftrig, Elias
Heitjohann, Raphael
Henry Castellanos, John
Herranz, Javier
Hirschi, Lucca
Hlavacek, Tomas

Hobbs, Nathaniel
Hong, Hanbin
Horne, Ross
Horváth, Máté
Hu, Zhenkai
Hu, Lijie
Hu, Yan
Huang, Jianwei
Huso, Ingrid
Iadarola, Giacomo
Ioannidis, Thodoris
Iovino, Vincenzo
Ising, Fabian
Jacobs, Adriaan
Jebreel, Najeeb
Jeitner, Philipp
Jensen, Meiko
Jesús A., Zihang
Jin, Lin
Kailun, Yan
Kaiser, Fabian
Kaplan, Alexander
Karim, Imtiaz
Karyda, Maria
Katsis, Charalampos
Kavousi, Alireza
Kelarev, Andrei
Kempinski, Stash
Kermabon-Bobinnec, Hugo
Kern, Sascha
Khalili, Mojtaba
Khandpur Singh, Ashneet
Khin Shar, Lwin
Knechtel, Johann
Kokolakis, Spyros
Krumnow, Benjamin
Ksontini, Rym
Kulkarni, Tejas
Lai, Jianchang
Lee, Hyunwoo
Léger, Marc-André
Li, Jinfeng
Li, Rui
Li, Shaoyu
Li, Yanan

Li, Shuang
Li, Guangpu
Liang, Yuan
Likhitha Mankali, Lakshmi
Limbasiya, Trupil
Lin, Chao
Lin Aung, Yan
Liu, Lin
Liu, Xiaoning
Liu, Bingyu
Liu, Guannan
Liu, Xiaoyin
Liu, Jiahao
Liu, Zhen
Liu, Xueqiao
Liu, Xiaoyuan
Lu, Yun
Lucchese, Marco
Luo, Junwei
Lv, Chunyang
Lyu, Lin
Lyvas, Christos
Ma, Wanlun
Ma, Mimi
Maiorca, Davide
Maitra, Sudip
Makriyannis, Nikolaos
Manjón, Jesús A.
Martinez, Sergio
Mccarthy, Sarah
Mei, Qian
Menegatos, Andreas
Meng, Long
Mercaldo, Francesco
Merget, Robert
Mestel, David
Meyuhas, Bar
Michalas, Antonis
Mirdita, Donika
Mizera, Andrzej
Mohammadi, Farnaz
Mohammed, Ameer
Morillo, Paz
Morrison, Adam
Mujeeb Ahmed, Chuadhry

Nabi, Mahmudun
Neal, Christopher
Nguyen, Son
Niehues, David
Nixon, Brian
Oldani, Gianluca
Oqaily, Momen
Oqaily, Alaa
Osliak, Oleksii
P. K. Ma, Jack
Pan, Shimin
Pan, Jianli
Pang, Chengbin
Pang, Bo
Panja, Somnath
Paolo Tricomi, Pier
Paspatis, Ioannis
Peng, Hui
Pitropakis, Nikolaos
Polato, Mirko
Pryvalov, Ivan
Pu, Sihang
Puchta, Alexander
Putz, Benedikt
Qian, Chen
Qin, Baodong
Qin, Xianrui
Rabhi, Mouna
Radomirovic, Sasa
Ramokapane, Kopo M.
Rangarajan, Nikhil
Ravi, Divya
Rawat, Abhimanyu
Raza, Ali
Román-García, Fernando
Rossi, Matthew
Rovira, Sergi
S. M. Asadujjaman, A.
Saatjohann, Christoph
Sadighian, Alireza
Saha, Rahul
Samanis, Emmanouil
Sarathi Roy, Partha
Sarkar, Pratik
Schiff Agron, Shir

Schlette, Daniel
Schmidt, Carsten
Sentanoe, Stewart
Sha, Zeyang
Shao, Jun
Shi, Shanghao
Shibahara, Toshiki
Shioji, Eitaro
Shojafar, Mohammad
Shreeve, Benjamin
Silde, Tjerand
Singh, Animesh
Singh Sehrawat, Vipin
Sinha, Sayani
Siniscalchi, Luisa
Skrobot, Marjan
Sohrabi, Nasrin
Sollomoni, Avi
Song, Shang
Sotgiu, Angelo
Souid, Nourelhouda
Soumelidou, Katerina
Sun, Shihua
Tabatabaei, Masoud
Tabiban, Azadeh
Taha Bennani, Mohamed
Talibi Alaoui, Younes
Tang, Lihong
Tao, Youming
Tedeschi, Pietro
Terrovitis, Manolis
Tian, Guohua
Tian, Yangguang
Turrin, Federico
Umayya, Zeya
Vinayagamurthy, Dhinakaran
Visintin, Alessandro
Vollmer, Marcel
von der Heyden, Jonas
Voudouris, Anastassios
W. H. Wong, Harry
Wagner, Benedikt
Wang, Han
Wang, Ning
Wang, Kailong

Wang, Xiuhua
Wang, Yalan
Wang, Shu
Wang, Jiafan
Wang, Haizhou
Wang, Zhilong
Wang, Xiaolei
Wang, Yunling
Wang, Qin
Wang, Yu
Wang, Cheng-Long
Wang, Weijia
Wang, Xinyue
Wang, Yi
Wang, Yuyu
Wang, Yangde
Watanabe, Takuya
Wu, Huangting
Wu, Yulian
Wu, Chen
Wu, Mingli
Wu, Qiushi
Xiang, Zihang
Xiao, Yang
Xiao, Jidong
Xie, Shangyu
Xu, Shengmin
Yadav, Tarun
Yan, Di
Yang, Zhichao
Yang, Shishuai

Yang, Xu
Yang, S. J.
Yang, Xuechao
Yang, Junwen
Yin Chan, Kwan
You, Weijing
Yu, Hexuan
Yurkov, Semen
Zeng, Runzhi
Zhang, Sepideh
Zhang, Min
Zhang, Yanjun
Zhang, Zicheng
Zhang, Cong
Zhang, Lan
Zhang, Yuchen
Zhang, Xinyu
Zhang, Kai
Zhang, Tao
Zhang, Yunhang
Zhang, Xiaoyu
Zhang, Zidong
Zhang, Rongjunchen
Zhao, Yongjun
Zhao, Shujie
Zhao, Lingchen
Zheng, Xiang
Zhou, Xiaotong
Zhu, Fei
Zikas, Vassilis
Zou, Qingtian

# Contents – Part II

## Access Control

## Authentication

## Digital Signatures

# Anonymity

# A Machine Learning Approach to Detect Differential Treatment of Anonymous Users

Isabel Wagner(✉)

Cyber Technology Institute, De Montfort University, Leicester, UK
isabel.wagner@unibas.ch

**Abstract.** Anonymous Internet use is essential to safeguard against mass surveillance and to protect privacy online. Tor Browser and the Tor anonymity network provide an effective and convenient way to browse the Internet anonymously. However, many websites make browsing inconvenient for anonymous users either by blocking access entirely, by blocking access to some functionality, or by using CAPTCHAs to make access more difficult. Prior work has relied on heuristics to study the extent to which anonymous users are treated differently. However, these heuristics either underestimated blocking or required extensive manual labeling. To address these shortcomings, here we propose a machine learning approach to detect when anonymous users are treated differently. We train binary and multi-class classifiers based on six feature sets and find that they perform very well on our test data (F1 scores 100%–94% for binary and 97%–84% for multi-class classifiers). Applying these classifiers to data collected from browsing 1,000 sites, including visits to subsites and executing search functionality, via 100 Tor exit nodes we find that 16.7% of landing pages inconvenience anonymous users, compared with 15.2% of subsites and 3.8% of search result pages. In particular, we find that websites hosted by Akamai, EdgeCast, and Cloudflare have significantly higher block rates than average, and that blocking of search results is dominated by Google which displays a block page or CAPTCHA for 39.8% of search result pages.

**Keywords:** Tor · Anonymous communication · Tor exit blocking · Machine learning · CAPTCHA

## 1 Introduction

Anonymity is the property that individual users of a communication systems are not identifiable [17]. The most well-known anonymity system for the Internet is The Onion Router (Tor) [7]. Proposed in 2004, Tor is now available as Tor Browser, which makes it as easy to use as other browsers. However, people who want to use the Internet anonymously are subject to more restrictions and inconveniences than regular Internet users. For example, some websites categorically deny access to users of Tor browser, while some make Tor users solve

© The Author(s), under exclusive license to Springer Nature Switzerland AG 2022
V. Atluri et al. (Eds.): ESORICS 2022, LNCS 13555, pp. 3–23, 2022.
https://doi.org/10.1007/978-3-031-17146-8_1

CAPTCHAs before allowing access. This differential treatment of Tor users is not always aimed specifically at Tor users. Instead, the IP addresses of Tor exit nodes can be labeled as suspicious because many Tor users share the same exit node [22]. However, regardless of the technical reason for blocking of Tor users, anonymous users are experiencing inconvenience and disadvantage as a result.

Prior work has studied the nature of Tor exit node blocking [22] and how the network and application layer contribute to the discrimination against Tor users [9]. These studies have also estimated the prevalence of Tor exit blocking based on a sample of the top 500 or 1,000 websites. However, these studies have relied on heuristics and manual labeling to identify which websites are blocking Tor users.

In this paper we use machine learning to classify when websites are blocked because (1) heuristics can be imprecise, in particular, we show in Sect. 3.1 that heuristics do not perform well when predicting which websites are blocked; (2) existing heuristics do not distinguish between blocked websites and websites that show a CAPTCHA; and (3) manual labeling does not scale well. Based on our machine learning classifiers, we then estimate the prevalence of Tor exit blocking, taking into account visits to subsites in addition to landing pages as well as searches and visits to search result pages. Specifically, we make the following contributions[1]:

- We engineer six feature sets based on paired visits to websites with Firefox and Tor Browser, including features extracted from HTTP requests and responses, HTML source code, and screenshots. Each feature set restricts the number of features it uses to allow for classification when only limited data collection can be performed.
- We train binary (blocked/unblocked) and multi-class (blocked/CAPTCHA/unblocked) classifiers for each feature set and evaluate classifier performance. We find that the classifiers perform very well on our test data, with F1 scores of 100%–94% for binary and 97%–84% for multi-class classifiers.
- We estimate the prevalence of Tor exit blocking and analyze to what extent block and CAPTCHA rates depend on the visit type, characteristics of Tor exit nodes, and characteristics of the websites, based on data collected from 998 websites and a sample of 101 exit nodes. We find average block rates of 16.7% for landing pages, 15.2% for subsites, and 3.8% for searches. The characteristics of exit nodes have no statistically significant influence on block or CAPTCHA rates, whereas significant differences can be observed depending on a website's hosting provider and category. Specifically, websites hosted on Akamai, Cloudflare, and EdgeCast have higher block rates than average, and websites from Fashion/Beauty (51%) and Finance/Banking (29%) have the highest block rates.

The remainder of this paper is organized as follows: we present related work in Sect. 2, explain the methodology for feature selection and engineering, as well as classifier training and performance evaluation in Sect. 3, and evaluate the

---

[1] Code and data for this paper are available at https://gitlab.com/iwagner/tor-inconvenience.

prevalence of Tor exit blocking in Sect. 4. We discuss limitations of our work in Sect. 5 and conclude in Sect. 6.

## 2  Related Work

The main areas of relevant related work are (1) work that studies Tor and Internet censorship, and (2) work on Internet measurement and associated methods.

Tor is an overlay network that routes user traffic over three intermediate hops or relays [7]. Routing information including source and destination is encrypted in onion layers so that none of the relays can link the identity of the user to the identity of the visited web service, thereby providing anonymity to the user. Although Tor is often portrayed as a tool that provides anonymity to criminals, most of its 8 million daily users [10] likely rely on Tor for safe, privacy-friendly, and uncensored Internet access. This point is underpinned by the fact that less than 4% of traffic on Tor visits onion services [10] which include the dark web (but also anonymous access to regular websites such as search engines). In addition, it has been shown that Wikipedia edits made by Tor users are of similar quality as edits made by non-anonymous users [25].

The characteristics and performance of Tor, as well as attacks against the Tor network, have been studied extensively. For example, researchers have proposed machine learning classifiers to distinguish Tor traffic from other Internet traffic [5,8,23], as well as traffic fingerprinting techniques to identify search terms in encrypted Tor traffic [15]. The two studies most similar to our work are [9, 22]. Both studies used heuristics to determine when Tor users are blocked from accessing a website, based on HTTP status codes [9] and perceptual hashes of screenshots [22], respectively. We describe these heuristics in detail in Sect. 3.1. The main limitations of these studies are their reliance on heuristics and their selection of websites which does not consider subsites, i.e., internal pages that are not a domain's front- or landing page.

Another group of related work studies Internet censorship [13] and geoblocking [12]. Like our work, they are concerned with detecting when access to certain websites is available and when it is not. However, they focus on differences related to the vantage point, i.e., which country a website is accessed from, whereas we focus on access via Tor. The heuristics proposed in [12,13] are nevertheless useful for detecting blocking, and we integrate some of them as features into our machine learning classifiers.

Many Internet measurement studies have been published in the last decade. We follow the commonly used method of automated website crawls followed by statistical data analysis [27]. Websites are usually selected from a toplist, such as Alexa or Tranco [18], which rank the most popular websites. Measurement studies increasingly recognize that it is important to study subsites in addition to landing pages because subsites have been found, for example, to include more advertising [2] and more trackers [26]. To the best of our knowledge, the only toplist that currently includes subsites is Hispar [2] which consists of around 2,000 websites with 50 subsites each.

Machine learning is often used in the context of measurement studies to overcome the limitations of heuristics. For example, machine learning has been proposed to discover privacy leaks in mobile network traffic [19], to automate the detection of trackers [20], or to categorize the advertisements served to users [21]. To the best of our knowledge, machine learning has not yet been used to detect when access to websites is restricted.

## 3   Methodology

To create classifiers that can detect when Tor users are treated differently from non-anonymous users, we follow three steps: (1) we collect and label training data; (2) we define and select features; and (3) we train and tune the classifiers.

### 3.1   Collection and Labeling of Training Data

Our training data consists of paired website visits, once with Tor Browser and once with Firefox. We automate Firefox and Tor Browser with Selenium and tor-browser-selenium [1], respectively. For each website visit, we record the HTML source, a screenshot, and a HAR archive of HTTP requests and responses using the browser add-on HAR Export Trigger [14]. We select two Tor exit nodes for half of the visits so that we acquire two pairs of visits for every three website loads. In addition, before data collection we manually verify that traffic from the two exit nodes results in some blocking behavior. Specifically, we verify that we obtain CAPTCHAs when searching on google.com and when visiting zillow.com. By doing this, we increase the number of block pages in our data set and thereby reduce the amount of training data we have to label manually.

We visit a total of 600 websites: the top 150 sites from the Tranco toplist [18], 100 sites sampled uniformly at random from ranks 150–500, 50 sites sampled from ranks 1000–1500 (two exit nodes each), and 300 sites sampled from the Hispar toplist (one exit node) [2]. In addition, we visit three subsites for each website. For sites from the Tranco list, we sample three links from the website's landing page, and for sites from the Hispar list, we sample three subsites from the published list. The subsites are sampled prior to data collection to ensure that they are consistent between all visits. The rationale for including subsite visits is that they may trigger more blocking behaviors than landing pages, similar to them including more advertising and tracking [2,26]. We use the Tranco and Hispar lists instead of Alexa to improve reproducibility. In particular, the Alexa list does not allow to cite specific list versions, does not include subsites, and will be discontinued in 2022. Tranco aggregates rankings from different sources which makes the ranking more consistent and less open to manipulation [18].

To trigger additional blocking behaviors, similar to [22], we detect search boxes on each website and submit one search query per detected search box. However, in contrast to prior work, we did not attempt to log into websites: creating a fresh account for each website would have been too time-consuming, and the method of authenticating with Google OAuth credentials used by Singh et al. in 2017 [22] did not work anymore because Google now blocks logins when the browser is controlled by automated software.

In total, we collect 3,409 paired visits, covering 509 topsites, 1,350 subsites, and 535 searches. The number of successfully visited topsites is smaller than 600 because some domains, such as highly-ranked windowsupdate.com, do not serve HTML pages. The final distribution of ranks in our training data, according to Tranco, is shown in Fig. 1.

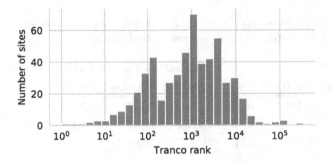

| Label | Count |
|-------|-------|
| same | 2837 |
| block | 257 |
| captcha | 44 |
| missing | 44 |
| slow | 110 |
| nocookie | 18 |
| cookie | 4 |
| other | 95 |

**Fig. 1.** Rank distribution of 509 sites in training data

**Fig. 2.** Label distribution in training data set.

**Labeling.** We created a Python GUI for labeling the collected data (see Fig. 8 in Appendix B). The GUI presents the two screenshots from a paired visit and allows the creation of eight labels, indicating whether the visit from Tor Browser shows *no substantial differences*, a *block page*, a *captcha*, missing elements such as login buttons or search functions, missing elements due to timeouts, a cookie banner where Firefox shows none, no cookie banner where Firefox shows one, or other substantial differences such as localization. To clean our data set for training, we include only visits with the first three labels and disregard visits with the other labels. Figure 2 shows the number of visits for each label.

**Heuristics vs Manual Labels.** We compare three previously proposed heuristics[2] to our manual labels. These heuristics classify paired visits into *blocked* and *not blocked*. We use our *same* label for the *not blocked* case, and compare two options for the *blocked* case: (1) using only our *block* label, and (2) combining the visits with *block* and *captcha* labels.

The first heuristic, labeled *Khattak1* in Table 1, classifies visits as blocked if Firefox receives a 200 (OK) status code, but Tor Browser receives a non-200 level status code [9]. The *Khattak2* heuristic classifies visits as blocked if Firefox is unblocked while Tor Browser is blocked, where a visit counts as blocked if the request timed out, was rejected, or received an HTTP response status code 400 or

---

[2] For convenience of referring to them, we name each heuristic after the first author of the corresponding paper.

higher [9]. Finally, the *Singh* heuristic relies on perceptual hashing of screenshots [22]. Perceptual hashing maps images to hashes such that the hashes are similar if the images are similar. Visits are classified as blocked if the difference between perceptual hashes is higher than a threshold (0.75 in [22]), or when Firefox receives a 200 status code but Tor Browser receives a status code indicating an error (400 or higher). Visits are classified as not blocked if the perceptual hash difference is below a threshold of 0.4. The remaining visits remain unclassified; [22] manually label these cases.

**Table 1.** Performance of three heuristics on our manually labeled data set, showing the F1 scores for each heuristic predicting *blocked* and *not blocked* labels.

| Heuristic | "Blocked" = *block* | | | "Blocked" = *block+captcha* | | |
|---|---|---|---|---|---|---|
| | Khattak1 | Khattak2 | Singh | Khattak1 | Khattak2 | Singh |
| Blocked | 0.253 | 0.374 | 0.729 | 0.249 | 0.371 | 0.744 |
| Not blocked | 0.934 | 0.938 | 0.935 | 0.927 | 0.932 | 0.934 |
| Support | 3094 | 3094 | 724 | 3138 | 3138 | 735 |

Table 1 shows the performance of these heuristics in terms of their F1 scores, assuming our manual labels as ground truth. The performance of the *Singh* heuristic depends on the perceptual hashing algorithm and its parameters. Here, we use the Python ImageHash library[3] [4]. The number of cases for the *Singh* heuristic is lower because we omit all cases that, according to the heuristic, would have to be labeled manually. As a result, we expect that the Singh heuristic combined with a manual labeling step would perform better than what Table 1 indicates. However, manual labeling is costly, which is why a machine learning approach is desirable.

Table 1 shows that all heuristics are very good at predicting the *not blocked* label (F1 scores of 93–94%), but have significant weaknesses in predicting the *blocked* label (F1 scores of 25–74%). In practice, this means that the heuristics are likely to underestimate the number of blocked cases. Overall, this comparison indicates that if a machine learning approach can improve on the prediction of the *blocked* label, it can enable more accurate and fully automated labeling of the differential treatment of Tor users.

### 3.2   Feature Selection

We use three main sources of features for our classifiers: the HTML source code, HTTP requests and responses, and screenshots. Based on these feature groups, we construct six feature sets: unrestricted (F1); all feature groups without features based on differences between Firefox and Tor Browser (F2); only features from HTML source code and screenshots (F3); only features from HTTP requests and responses (F4); only features from HTML and screenshots without differences (F5); and only HTTP features without differences (F6).

---

[3] Parameter settings: hash size = 32, high frequency factor = 10.

**Screenshot-Based Features.** For screenshot-based features, we take inspiration from [22] and compute perceptual hashes[4] and wavelet hashes[5] for each screenshot. We also compute the differences between hashes for paired visits. Because we use machine learning, we do not have to select manual thresholds for these hashes. In total, we use 14 screenshot-based features.

**HTML-Based Features.** We extract four groups of features from the HTML source. First, we focus on the size of the HTML source. Because block pages are often shorter than non-blocked websites [12], we compute the byte size of the HTML source and the absolute and relative differences between sources sizes. In addition, we compute a unified diff between the sources of paired visits and count the number of differences.

Second, we focus on HTML tags. Differences in tag frequencies can indicate differences in page structure, which can indicate presence of a block page or CAPTCHA. We therefore extract HTML tag frequencies for all tags, specifically the number of and difference between tags present in HTML sources [12].

Third, we focus on JavaScript inclusions. This can help detect CAPTCHAs that are served from the same included JavaScript. Accordingly, we extract the sources, domains, and paths of included JavaScript as well as their differences. We then convert each set of JavaScript information (i.e., sources, domains, paths, and their differences) into a bag-of-words representation using the CountVectorizer from scikit-learn. The bag-of-words representation results in a matrix of token counts which indicates which pieces of JS information were present for each visit.

Fourth, we focus on the website text. We extract the website's text from the HTML source and compute the textual similarity for paired visits [13]. To do this, we construct a list of the words contained in each visit and estimate the Jaccard similarity between the two lists using the MinHash algorithm [3] implemented in the Python datasketch library [28]. We then compute the difference in website text as the list of words that appear in the Tor Browser visit, but not in Firefox. We use website text and text differences to construct page signatures [12], i.e., term frequency–inverse document frequency [24] feature vectors with 1- and 2-grams. In total, we use 4 features based on HTML source size, 1,410 features based on HTML tags, 18,159 features from JavaScript information in bag-of-words representation, and 478,945 features from website text in Tf-Idf representation.

**HTTP-Based Features.** For features from HTTP requests and responses, we first focus on status codes and extract the first received status code [9], the number and percent difference in received 200-level, 300-level, and 500-level status codes, and the frequencies of all received status codes as well as their differences. Next, we extract the number of and difference in sent requests and received responses, the number of requests that contain a (previously set) cookie

---

[4] Parameter settings for perceptual hash sizes and high frequency factors: (8,4), (16,8), (32,10), and (32,16).

[5] Parameter settings for wavelet hash sizes: 8, 16, 32.

value, and the number of responses that set a cookie. This results in a total of 73 HTTP-based features.

### 3.3 Classifier Training and Tuning

We pursue three goals when training our classifiers: (1) we expect our binary classifiers to exceed the performance of the three heuristics; (2) we expect our multi-class classifiers to accurately separate block pages from CAPTCHAs; and (3), we expect the classifiers to perform well on restricted feature sets, in particular: on HTML-only features (F3) because these features are easier to record than HTTP requests and responses; on features that do not include differences (F2, F5, F6) because this reduces the reliance on paired samples; and on HTTP-only features (F4) because this would enable classification of paired samples from the Open Observatory of Network Interference (OONI) [16].

A challenge for the training phase is that our training data is imbalanced: we have 11x more non-blocked samples than samples of block pages, and 64x more non-blocked samples than CAPTCHAs. To address this challenge, we select algorithms that are insensitive to imbalanced training data, such as decision trees and ensemble methods. Specifically, we use most of the algorithms implemented in the sklearn.tree and sklearn.ensemble modules: DecisionTreeClassifier, ExtraTreesClassifier, RandomForestClassifier, AdaBoostClassifier, and GradientBoostingClassifier. In addition, we apply appropriate metrics to evaluate the performance of the classifiers, i.e., F1 scores instead of accuracy. We report macro F1 scores to give equal weight to each label, irrespective of the number of samples.

To select the parameter settings for each classifier, we perform a grid search with 10-fold cross-validation for each algorithm. In addition, we use recursive feature elimination and tree-based feature elimination to train classifiers that rely on a smaller number of features. For each feature set, we then select the algorithm, hyperparameter settings, and feature elimination method that results in the best classifier performance. We train classifiers on a stratified sample of 70% of our data set and reserve 30% as a test set to evaluate classifier performance.

Tables 2 and 3 show the classifier performance for binary and multi-class classification, respectively (detailed performance results are in Appendix A). Overall, classifier performance is very satisfactory and clearly meets the three goals set out above. We can see that binary classification always performs better than multi-class classification, and that classification performance decreases with increasingly restricted feature sets. In addition, we note that performance for prediction of the *same* label is almost always better than for the *block* and *captcha* labels. This may be caused by the comparatively small number of training samples with the *block* and *captcha* labels. All of our classifiers perform better than the three heuristics introduced in Sect. 3.1.

## 4   Results: Differential Treatment of Tor Users

We now apply these classifiers to a large data set of paired samples collected in October–December 2021 (Sect. 4.1). For binary classification, we present results

**Table 2.** Performance of best classifiers for binary classification on *test* data set

| Feature set | F1 | F2 | F3 | F4 | F5 | F6 |
|---|---|---|---|---|---|---|
| classifier | Random Forest | Decision Tree | Random Forest | Ada Boost | Gradient Boosting | Extra Trees |
| feature elimination | Recursive | Tree | recursive | – | recursive | tree |
| number of features | 10 | 4573 | 131 | 81 | 45 | 10 |
| block+captcha | 1.000 | 0.979 | 1.000 | 0.971 | 0.978 | 0.882 |
| same | 1.000 | 0.998 | 1.000 | 0.997 | 0.998 | 0.988 |
| macro F1 | 1.000 | 0.988 | 1.000 | 0.984 | 0.988 | 0.935 |

**Table 3.** Performance of best classifiers for multi-class classification on *test* data set

| Feature set | F1 | F2 | F3 | F4 | F5 | F6 |
|---|---|---|---|---|---|---|
| classifier | Ada Boost | Decision Tree | Ada Boost | Gradient Boosting | Ada Boost | Gradient Boosting |
| feature elimination | tree | tree | recursive | – | recursive | – |
| number of features | 3549 | 4624 | 131 | 81 | 683645 | 41 |
| block | 1.000 | 0.941 | 1.000 | 0.967 | 0.876 | 0.894 |
| captcha | 0.900 | 0.900 | 0.900 | 0.842 | 0.842 | 0.625 |
| same | 0.998 | 0.993 | 0.998 | 0.996 | 0.988 | 0.988 |
| macro F1 | 0.966 | 0.945 | 0.966 | 0.935 | 0.902 | 0.836 |

using feature set F1 (all features) with recursive feature elimination (Sects. 4.2, 4.3 and 4.4). For multi-class classification, we present results using feature set F5 (HTML features and screenshots, no features based on differences) because the classification results matched best with a sample of manually labeled instances (Sect. 4.5). Importantly, the statistically significant effects described below are present in classifiers based on all six feature sets, even though the precise block rates predicted by each classifier vary slightly.

## 4.1 Data Collection

To collect this data set, we use the same methods as described in Sect. 3.1, with the exception of the selection of sites and the selection of Tor exit nodes.

To make our selection of subsites reproducible, we use the Hispar toplist [2] and select 1,000 sites with five subsites each. In addition, we attempt to find search boxes following the heuristics in [22] and execute one search for each search box. Overall, we successfully collected data for 998 topsites, a total of 3,992 subsites, and 1,574 searches executed on 587 different topsites.

Similar to prior work [22], we sample 101 Tor exit nodes (~8%). However, in contrast [22], we add a purposive element to our sampling. Specifically, we analyze the countries where exit nodes are located and sample one exit node per country (52 countries corresponding to 52 nodes). Then we sample one additional node from every country with at least 5 exits (23 additional nodes), 15 exits (14 nodes), 25 exits (6 nodes), 50 exits (4 nodes), and 100 exits (2 nodes). As a result, the two countries with more than 100 exit nodes (US and the Netherlands) are each represented with 6 nodes. We ensure that all sampled exit nodes come from a unique Autonomous System (AS).

Two exit nodes stopped offering exit node services during the data collection. One was replaced with another node from the same country, while the other was removed because it was the only node from its country.

## 4.2    Block Rates by Visit Type

We distinguish three types of visits to websites: a visit to the front page or landing page, a visit to a subsite, and a visit to a search result page after having submitted a search query. To analyze differential treatment of Tor users, we focus on the *block rate*, i.e., the fraction of visits that appear blocked to the user. On average across all visits to landing pages, subsites, and searches, we observe a block rate of 12.9%.

**Landing Pages.** For landing pages, we find that 16.7% of visits are blocked. This is less than the 20% reported by Singh et al. in 2017 [22], but more than the 6.8% reported by Khattak et al. in 2016 [9]. It is likely that the heuristic used in [9] underestimates the block rate, as has already been argued by [22]. Singh's heuristic, due to its reliance on manual labeling, is less likely to under- or overestimate the block rate. Our lower estimate may instead be due to a change in block rates over the last 5 years, a difference in which sites were sampled ([22] used the top 500 from Alexa), or a difference in the sampled exit nodes.

Figure 3 shows the 100 landing pages that block the most Tor exit nodes. In 2016, the site with the highest block rate blocked ~70% of exit nodes, and 1.6% of sites blocked more than 60% of exit nodes [9]. In contrast, we find that the highest block rate is 99%, indicating that sites have become better at blocking all visits from Tor. In addition, 7.2% of sites in our sample block more than 60% of exit nodes.

**Subsites.** Compared to landing pages, we observe a slightly lower block rate for visits to subsites (15.2%). This is contrary to our expectation that subsites would be blocked at higher rates. However, we note that our data collection method is slightly different to how a real user would browse because we visited subsites directly, from a prior list of subsites, instead of clicking on a link on the landing page. This means that our crawler may be able to visit subsites that ordinarily would be hidden behind a blocked landing page. As a result, the block rates for subsites experienced by real users would be at least as high as the block rate for landing pages. This may indicate that some sites have only implemented blocking for visitors to their landing page, but have not rolled out the blocking logic on direct visits to subsites.

**Searches.** We observed a very low block rate for search result pages (3.8%). It is important to note that our crawler could only find search boxes and submit queries on pages that were not blocked. As a result, the real block rate for searches is the block rate for landing pages plus the observed 3.8% block rate for searches. This increment of 3.8% in blocking for search pages is almost exactly what [22] found in 2017.

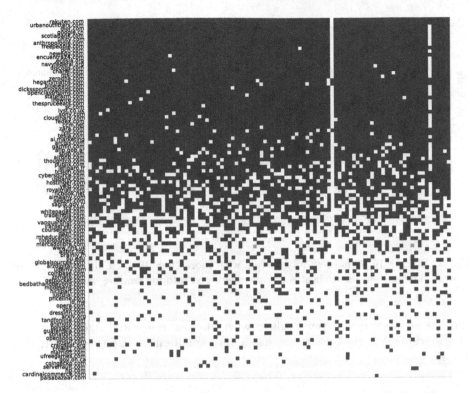

**Fig. 3.** 100 *landing pages* that block the most Tor exit nodes. Each column represents one exit node. Blue squares indicate when a landing page has blocked an exit node. The white vertical lines represent the two exit nodes that disappeared during data collection. Heat maps for subsites and searches are in Appendix C.

### 4.3   Block Rates by Characteristics of Tor Exit Nodes

We analyze whether block rates differ depending on characteristics of Tor exit nodes, in particular the country, exit probability, age, bandwidth, and number of open ports. We compute correlation coefficients using the Pearson correlation coefficient $r$ and find that all correlations with exit probability ($r = 0.16$, $p = 0.10$), age ($r = -0.016$, $p = 0.88$), bandwidth ($r = 0.10$, $p = 0.31$), and number of open ports ($r = 0.06$, $p = 0.55$) are statistically not significant. This finding is consistent with results reported in 2017 [22].

Analyzing these correlations separately depending on a website's hosting provider, focusing on the four large hosters Akamai, Amazon, Cloudfront, and Cloudflare, we do not find any significant correlations. This is in contrast to prior work which found that block rates for Amazon-hosted sites are higher when the exit node has higher bandwidth [22].

We did find statistically significant differences in block rates depending on the exit node's country. However, all differences have small effect sizes according to Cohen's $d$. For example, the difference between the two countries with highest

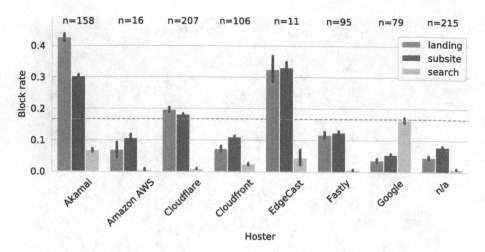

**Fig. 4.** Block rate by hoster (only hosters with more than 10 sites in our sample are shown). The dashed line indicates the average block rate for landing pages (16.7%).

and lowest block rates (New Zealand with 14.5% average and Azerbaijan with 11.4% average) is significant, but has a very small effect size ($p < 0.001$, $d = 0.093$).

## 4.4 Block Rates by Characteristics of Web Sites

Finally, we analyze whether block rates differ depending on characteristics of the visited websites, specifically the hosting provider, website category, and rank. To identify the hosting provider for each visited site, we use the findCDN library [6]. We use McAfee's URL categorization service [11] to identify website categories, and the Tranco toplist [18] from 2021-05-11 for website ranks. For all our results on statistical significance, we apply the Bonferroni correction to offset the problem of multiple comparisons.

**Block Rates by Hosting Provider.** Figure 4 shows the block rates we observe for the seven most common hosters in our data set, split by block rates for landing pages, subsites, and searches. We find that Akamai (28%, $d = 0.46$), EdgeCast (31%, $d = 0.45$), and Cloudflare (15%, $d = 0.089$) have block rates that are significantly higher than average (all $p < 0.001$). Especially Akamai and Cloudflare, because they are used by many sites, drive up the overall block rate. Block rates for the other hosters are significantly lower than the average. The lowest block rate is observed for websites with an unidentified hoster, which only block 5.8% of visits ($n/a$ in the figure, $d = 0.3$).

In addition, we find that Google-hosted sites block significantly more searches than any other hosting provider (16% compared to the average of 3.8%, $d = 0.51$).

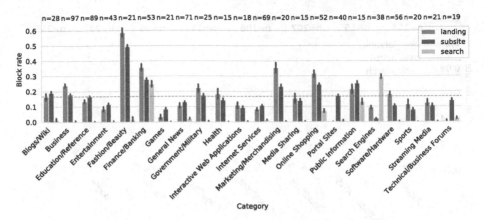

**Fig. 5.** Block rate by website category (only categories with at least 15 sites in our sample are shown). The dashed line indicates the average block rate for landing pages (16.7%).

**Block Rates by Category.** Figure 5 shows the block rate by website category. Overall, five categories of websites block landing pages and subsites with a significantly higher than average rate and at least a small effect size (all $p < 0.001$, $d > 0.2$): *Fashion/Beauty* (51%, $d = 0.85$), *Finance/Banking* (35%, $d = 0.35$), *Marketing/Merchandising* (25%, $d = 0.25$), *Online Shopping* (25%, $d = 0.27$), and *Public Information* (24%, $d = 0.23$). Conversely, three categories have significantly lower block rates: *Games* (7.4%, $d = 0.25$), *Search Engines* (3.6%, $d = 0.43$), and *Sports* (8.2%, $d = 0.22$).

Analyzing whether block rates on landing pages and subsites differ by category, we find only few cases with statistically significant differences and at least small effect sizes: websites in *Marketing/Merchandising*, *Search Engines*, and *Software/Hardware* block landing pages at higher rates, where as *Games*, *Portal* sites and *Technical/Business Forums* block subsites at higher rates. These findings indicate that our expectation that subsites are blocked at a much higher rate than landing pages is likely incorrect.

Finally, we observe that searches are blocked with a high rate by websites in the *Search Engines* category. This block rate is caused almost entirely by Google's "unusual traffic" CAPTCHA: Google blocks 39.7% of searches by Tor users, whereas other search engines only block 1%.

**Block Rates by Rank.** Analyzing block rates by website rank, we find that the correlation coefficients for landing pages, subsites, and searches are all negative but very small ($r$ between $-0.02$ and $-0.05$), indicating a slightly lower block rate for lower-ranked websites. However, none of the correlations are statistically significant.

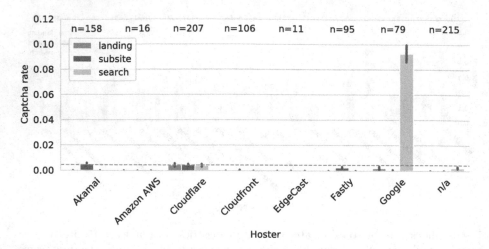

**Fig. 6.** Captcha rate by hoster. The dashed line indicates the average captcha rate (0.4%).

### 4.5 CAPTCHA Rates

To analyze the results from our multi-class classifiers, we analyze CAPTCHA rates in addition to block rates, i.e., the fraction of website visits that asked the user to solve a CAPTCHA before permitting access. We only evaluate the presence of a CAPTCHA, but not its difficulty[6].

We observe that CAPTCHA rates on average are much lower than block rates: 0.15% for landing pages, 0.23% for subsites, and 1.2% for searches. Similar to the results for block rates, we did not find significant correlations with exit node characteristics including age, bandwidth, open ports, and exit probability. CAPTCHA rates differ significantly between the countries with highest and lowest rates (Italy with 0.08% average and the Netherlands with 1% average), but the effect size is very small ($d = 0.13$).

Figure 6 shows the CAPTCHA rates by hosting provider. We can see that the overall largest contributor to CAPTCHA rates is searches performed on Google-hosted sites. The CAPTCHA rates for all hosters except Cloudflare and Akamai differ significantly from the average rate: Google has a significantly higher rate ($d = 0.18$), whereas all others have lower rates.

Analyzing CAPTCHA rates by website category (Fig. 7), we find that four categories have significantly higher than average CAPTCHA rates: *Blogs/Wiki* (1.3%, $d = 0.1$), *Finance/Banking* (1%, $d = 0.08$), *Games* (1.4%, $d = 0.1$) and *Search Engines* (3.6%, $d = 0.25$). We find no significant correlations between CAPTCHA rate and website rank.

---

[6] Anecdotally, CAPTCHAs given to anonymous users are more difficult than for other users, however, we leave the measurement of this effect and its analysis for future work.

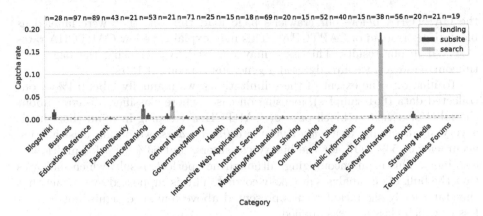

**Fig. 7.** Captcha rate by website category. The dashed line indicates the average CAPTCHA rate (0.4%).

In the analyses by hoster and by category, Google stands out because it shows CAPTCHAs to anonymous users who perform a search, but not on the landing page or other subsites. However, we note that Google is over-represented in our data set because it is present with several of its localized domains (76 Google domains among our 998 topsites, or 7.6%). This slightly skews the results for block and CAPTCHA rates for searches and for Google-hosted sites. However, the finding that Google serves block pages or CAPTCHAs for searches from anonymous users in almost 40% of cases remains. To an individual user, this means that 2 out of 5 Google searches may fail, which may be frustrating enough to discourage Tor users from using Google.

## 5    Limitations

The main limitations of our study relate to the collection and labeling of training data. First, our training data is unbalanced. In particular, the number of CAPTCHA samples is very small compared to samples of block pages, which negatively impacts multi-class classification. We have addressed this limitation mainly on the algorithm-level. Other promising ways to address this limitation would be to include more samples from known CAPTCHA-serving websites in the training data, to use data-level approaches such as over-/under-sampling or SMOTE, and to use other metrics including the receiver operating characteristic curve (ROC).

Second, our set of labels does not account for cases when both Firefox and Tor Browser show a CAPTCHA to the user (they have been labeled as *same*). This makes it more difficult for classifiers to correctly label CAPTCHA cases. It may be better to exclude these cases from the training data. Third, CAPTCHAs are often slow to load. For example, they are often hidden behind a timed "checking your browser" page. In cases where these pages did not proceed to show the CAPTCHA before our crawler's page load timeout, they were labeled as block pages instead of CAPTCHAs. This may explain the low CAPTCHA rates observed in our results. This issue may be fixed by increasing the page load timeout, however, we already used a generous timeout of 120 s.

To illustrate the extent of these limitations, we manually label 0.1% of our collected data (661 samples), focusing on cases where classifiers disagree about the label of a visit as block page or CAPTCHA. Keeping in mind that this is a very small sample that *only contains difficult cases*, we obtain classification accuracies of 54%–90% for the binary classifiers, and 63%–79% for multi-class classifiers. This is an encouraging, although not perfect, result, which indicates that the bulk of our analyses are likely correct. This is supported by the fact that the statistically significant results presented above remained significant regardless of which classifier was applied.

We use a limited set of features for JavaScript inclusions and screenshots, namely, the domain names, paths, and files names of the JS inclusions and the perceptual hashes of screenshots. It is possible that including features based on JS code and full image classification could improve the performance of our classifiers. In addition, we only evaluate the effect of feature groups on classifier performance, but not the effect of individual features.

Our study does not investigate *why* websites discriminate against Tor users. This would be an interesting extension that ultimately may help websites to better distinguish between malicious and benign traffic, and thereby reduce discrimination.

## 6    Conclusion

In this paper, we have presented machine learning classifiers to detect when websites block anonymous visitors from Tor Browser, and we have evaluated the prevalence of Tor exit blocking based on a large-scale data collection. We find that on average, one in six websites (16.7%) are inaccessible when browsing with Tor. In addition, Google's high block/CAPTCHA rate for anonymous users who perform searches is notable. Compared to studies published in 2016/17 [9,22], we find that the prevalence of blocking has not changed much, but that websites have become better at blocking all visits coming from Tor if they so wish (indicated by several websites with near 100% block rates in our sample).

Future work may improve on our results, especially for CAPTCHA rates, by expanding the training data collection with more CAPTCHA samples and fine-tuning the labeling approach. Promising avenues for future work include the evaluation of CAPTCHA difficulty (e.g., based on the CAPTCHA type, the number of sets that users have to complete, or the server-side time delays in the CAPTCHA solving process), and the measurement of the time cost imposed on Tor users for solving CAPTCHAs.

**Acknowledgements.** We thank the anonymous reviewers and our shepherd Kui Ren for their valuable feedback and Matthew Ford for contributions to an early prototype of our crawler and data analysis.

# A    Classifier Performance

(See Tables 4, 5, 6, 7, 8, 9, 10, 11, 12, 13, 14, 15).

**Table 4.** Performance of binary classifier for feature set F1

|  | Precision | Recall | F1-score | Support |
|---|---|---|---|---|
| block+captcha | 1.000 | 1.000 | 1.000 | 70.000 |
| same | 1.000 | 1.000 | 1.000 | 646.000 |
| accuracy | 1.000 | 1.000 | 1.000 | 1.000 |
| macro avg | 1.000 | 1.000 | 1.000 | 716.000 |

**Table 5.** Performance of binary classifier for feature set F2

|  | Precision | Recall | F1-score | Support |
|---|---|---|---|---|
| block+captcha | 0.972 | 0.986 | 0.979 | 70.000 |
| same | 0.998 | 0.997 | 0.998 | 646.000 |
| accuracy | 0.996 | 0.996 | 0.996 | 0.996 |
| macro avg | 0.985 | 0.991 | 0.988 | 716.000 |

**Table 6.** Performance of binary classifier for feature set F3

|  | Precision | Recall | F1-score | Support |
|---|---|---|---|---|
| block+captcha | 1.000 | 1.000 | 1.000 | 70.000 |
| same | 1.000 | 1.000 | 1.000 | 646.000 |
| accuracy | 1.000 | 1.000 | 1.000 | 1.000 |
| macro avg | 1.000 | 1.000 | 1.000 | 716.000 |

**Table 7.** Performance of binary classifier for feature set F4

|  | Precision | Recall | F1-score | Support |
|---|---|---|---|---|
| block+captcha | 0.971 | 0.971 | 0.971 | 70.000 |
| same | 0.997 | 0.997 | 0.997 | 646.000 |
| accuracy | 0.994 | 0.994 | 0.994 | 0.994 |
| macro avg | 0.984 | 0.984 | 0.984 | 716.000 |

**Table 8.** Performance of binary classifier for feature set F5

|  | Precision | Recall | F1-score | Support |
|---|---|---|---|---|
| block+captcha | 0.985 | 0.957 | 0.971 | 70.000 |
| same | 0.995 | 0.998 | 0.997 | 646.000 |
| accuracy | 0.994 | 0.994 | 0.994 | 0.994 |
| macro avg | 0.990 | 0.978 | 0.984 | 716.000 |

**Table 9.** Performance of binary classifier for feature set F6

|  | Precision | Recall | F1-score | Support |
|---|---|---|---|---|
| block+captcha | 0.909 | 0.857 | 0.882 | 70.000 |
| same | 0.985 | 0.991 | 0.988 | 646.000 |
| accuracy | 0.978 | 0.978 | 0.978 | 0.978 |
| macro avg | 0.947 | 0.924 | 0.935 | 716.000 |

**Table 10.** Performance of multi-label classifier for feature set F1

|  | Precision | Recall | F1-score | Support |
|---|---|---|---|---|
| BLOCK | 1.000 | 1.000 | 1.000 | 59.000 |
| CAPTCHA | 1.000 | 0.818 | 0.900 | 11.000 |
| SAME | 0.997 | 1.000 | 0.998 | 646.000 |
| accuracy | 0.997 | 0.997 | 0.997 | 0.997 |
| macro avg | 0.999 | 0.939 | 0.966 | 716.000 |

**Table 11.** Performance of multi-label classifier for feature set F2

|  | Precision | Recall | F1-score | Support |
|---|---|---|---|---|
| BLOCK | 0.933 | 0.949 | 0.941 | 59.000 |
| CAPTCHA | 1.000 | 0.818 | 0.900 | 11.000 |
| SAME | 0.992 | 0.994 | 0.993 | 646.000 |
| accuracy | 0.987 | 0.987 | 0.987 | 0.987 |
| macro avg | 0.975 | 0.920 | 0.945 | 716.000 |

**Table 12.** Performance of multi-label classifier for feature set F3

|         | Precision | Recall | F1-score | Support |
|---------|-----------|--------|----------|---------|
| BLOCK   | 0.983     | 1.000  | 0.992    | 59.000  |
| CAPTCHA | 1.000     | 0.818  | 0.900    | 11.000  |
| SAME    | 0.997     | 0.998  | 0.998    | 646.000 |
| accuracy| 0.996     | 0.996  | 0.996    | 0.996   |
| macro avg| 0.993    | 0.939  | 0.963    | 716.000 |

**Table 13.** Performance of multi-label classifier for feature set F4

|         | Precision | Recall | F1-score | Support |
|---------|-----------|--------|----------|---------|
| BLOCK   | 0.951     | 0.983  | 0.967    | 59.000  |
| CAPTCHA | 1.000     | 0.727  | 0.842    | 11.000  |
| SAME    | 0.995     | 0.997  | 0.996    | 646.000 |
| accuracy| 0.992     | 0.992  | 0.992    | 0.992   |
| macro avg| 0.982    | 0.902  | 0.935    | 716.000 |

**Table 14.** Performance of multi-label classifier for feature set F5

|         | Precision | Recall | F1-score | Support |
|---------|-----------|--------|----------|---------|
| BLOCK   | 0.851     | 0.966  | 0.905    | 59.000  |
| CAPTCHA | 1.000     | 0.727  | 0.842    | 11.000  |
| SAME    | 0.994     | 0.986  | 0.990    | 646.000 |
| accuracy| 0.980     | 0.980  | 0.980    | 0.980   |
| macro avg| 0.948    | 0.893  | 0.912    | 716.000 |

**Table 15.** Performance of multi-label classifier for feature set F6

|         | Precision | Recall | F1-score | Support |
|---------|-----------|--------|----------|---------|
| BLOCK   | 0.859     | 0.932  | 0.894    | 59.000  |
| CAPTCHA | 1.000     | 0.455  | 0.625    | 11.000  |
| SAME    | 0.988     | 0.989  | 0.988    | 646.000 |
| accuracy| 0.976     | 0.976  | 0.976    | 0.976   |
| macro avg| 0.949    | 0.792  | 0.836    | 716.000 |

# B     Labeling

**Fig. 8.** Screenshot of GUI for manual labeling of training data

## C    Block Rates for Subsites and Searches

(See Figs. 9 and 10).

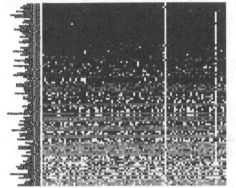
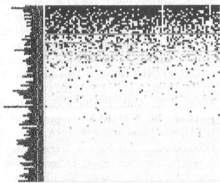

**Fig. 9.** Subsites that block the most Tor exit nodes. Each column represents one exit node.

**Fig. 10.** Sites that block the most Tor exit nodes when performing a search.

## References

1. Acar, G., Juarez, M.: Individual contributors: Tor-browser-selenium - Tor Browser automation with Selenium (2020). https://github.com/webfp/tor-browser-selenium
2. Aqeel, W., Chandrasekaran, B., Feldmann, A., Maggs, B.M.: On landing and internal web pages: the strange case of Jekyll and Hyde in web performance measurement. In: Proceedings of the ACM Internet Measurement Conference, IMC 2020, pp. 680–695. Association for Computing Machinery, Pittsburgh, PA, USA, October 2020
3. Broder, A.Z.: Identifying and Filtering Near-Duplicate Documents. In: Giancarlo, R., Sankoff, D. (eds.) Combinatorial Pattern Matching. pp. 1–10. Lecture Notes in Computer Science, Springer, Berlin, Heidelberg (2000)
4. Buchner, J.: ImageHash, January 2022. https://github.com/JohannesBuchner/imagehash
5. Cuzzocrea, A., Martinelli, F., Mercaldo, F., Vercelli, G.: Tor traffic analysis and detection via machine learning techniques. In: 2017 IEEE International Conference on Big Data (Big Data), pp. 4474–4480, December 2017
6. Cybersecurity and Infrastructure Security Agency: FindCDN. Cybersecurity and Infrastructure Security Agency, January 2022. https://github.com/cisagov/findcdn
7. Dingledine, R., Mathewson, N., Syverson, P.: Tor: the second-generation onion router. In: 13th USENIX Security Symposium (USENIX Security 2004). USENIX Association, San Diego, CA, USA, August 2004
8. Gurunarayanan, A., Agrawal, A., Bhatia, A., Vishwakarma, D.K.: Improving the performance of machine learning algorithms for Tor detection. In: 2021 International Conference on Information Networking (ICOIN), pp. 439–444, January 2021

9. Khattak, S., et al.: Do You See What I See? Differential treatment of anonymous users. In: Proceedings 2016 Network and Distributed System Security Symposium. Internet Society, San Diego, CA (2016)
10. Mani, A., Wilson-Brown, T., Jansen, R., Johnson, A., Sherr, M.: Understanding Tor usage with privacy-preserving measurement. In: Proceedings of the Internet Measurement Conference 2018, IMC 2018, pp. 175–187. Association for Computing Machinery, Boston, MA, USA, October 2018
11. McAfee, LLC: Customer URL Ticketing System for McAfee Web Gateway (2022). https://www.trustedsource.org/
12. McDonald, A., et al.: 403 forbidden: a global view of CDN geoblocking. In: Proceedings of the Internet Measurement Conference 2018, IMC 2018, pp. 218–230. ACM, Boston, MA, USA (2018)
13. Niaki, A.A., et al.: ICLab: a global, longitudinal internet censorship measurement platform. In: 2020 IEEE Symposium on Security and Privacy (S&P), pp. 214–230. IEEE, San Francisco, CA, USA, May 2020
14. Odvarko, J.: HAR Export Trigger, May 2018. https://addons.mozilla.org/en-US/firefox/addon/har-export-trigger/
15. Oh, S.E., Li, S., Hopper, N.: Fingerprinting keywords in search queries over Tor. Proc. Privacy Enhancing Technol. **2017**(4), 251–270 (2017)
16. OONI: Open Observatory of Network Interference (2022). https://ooni.org/
17. Pfitzmann, A., Hansen, M.: A terminology for talking about privacy by data minimization: anonymity, unlinkability, undetectability, unobservability, pseudonymity, and identity management. Technical report, August 2010. http://dud.inf.tu-dresden.de/literatur/Anon_Terminology_v0.34.pdf
18. Pochat, V.L., van Goethem, T., Joosen, W.: Rigging research results by manipulating top websites rankings. In: 26th Annual Network and Distributed System Security Symposium. Internet Society, San Diego, CA, USA, February 2019
19. Ren, J., Rao, A., Lindorfer, M., Legout, A., Choffnes, D.: ReCon: revealing and controlling PII leaks in mobile network traffic. In: Proceedings of the 14th Annual International Conference on Mobile Systems, Applications, and Services, MobiSys 2016, pp. 361–374. ACM, Singapore (2016)
20. Shuba, A., Markopoulou, A.: NoMoATS: towards automatic detection of mobile tracking. Proc. Privacy Enhancing Technol. **2020**(2), 45–66 (2020)
21. Silva, M., Santos de Oliveira, L., Andreou, A., Vaz de Melo, P.O., Goga, O., Benevenuto, F.: Facebook ads monitor: an independent auditing system for political ads on Facebook. In: Proceedings of The Web Conference 2020, WWW 2020, pp. 224–234. ACM, Taipei, Taiwan, April 2020
22. Singh, R., et al.: Characterizing the nature and dynamics of Tor exit blocking. In: 26th USENIX Security Symposium (USENIX Security 2017), pp. 325–341. USENIX Association, Vancouver, BC, August 2017
23. Soleimani, M.H.M., Mansoorizadeh, M., Nassiri, M.: Real-time identification of three Tor pluggable transports using machine learning techniques. J. Supercomputing **74**(10), 4910–4927 (2018). https://doi.org/10.1007/s11227-018-2268-y
24. Spärck Jones, K.: A statistical interpretation of term specificity and its application in retrieval. Journal of Documentation **28**(1), 11–21 (1972)
25. Tran, C., Champion, K., Forte, A., Hill, B.M., Greenstadt, R.: Are anonymity-seekers just like everybody else? An analysis of contributions to Wikipedia from Tor. In: 2020 IEEE Symposium on Security and Privacy (S&P), pp. 974–990. IEEE, San Francisco, CA, USA, May 2020

26. Urban, T., Degeling, M., Holz, T., Pohlmann, N.: Beyond the front page: measuring third party dynamics in the field. In: Proceedings of The Web Conference 2020, WWW 2020, pp. 1275–1286. ACM, Taipei, Taiwan, April 2020
27. Wagner, I.: Auditing Corporate Surveillance Systems: Research Methods for Greater Transparency. Cambridge University Press, Cambridge (2022)
28. Zhu, E.: Datasketch: Big Data Looks Small, January 2022. https://github.com/ekzhu/datasketch

# Utility-Preserving Biometric Information Anonymization

Bill Moriarty[1], Chun-Fu (Richard) Chen[1], Shaohan Hu[1(✉)], Sean Moran[1],
Marco Pistoia[1], Vincenzo Piuri[2], and Pierangela Samarati[2]

[1] JPMorgan Chase Bank, N.A., New York, NY, USA
{william.r.moriarty,richard.cf.chen,shaohan.hu,sean.j.moran,
marco.pistoia}@jpmorgan.com
[2] Università degli Studi di Milano, Milan, Italy
{vincenzo.piuri,pierangela.samarati}@unimi.it

**Abstract.** The use of biometrics such as fingerprints, voices, and images are becoming increasingly more ubiquitous through people's daily lives, in applications ranging from authentication, identification, to much more sophisticated analytics, thanks to the recent rapid advances in both the sensing hardware technologies and machine learning techniques. While providing improved user experiences and better business insights, the use of biometrics has raised serious privacy concerns, due to their intrinsic sensitive nature and the accompanying high risk of leaking personally identifiable and private information.

In this paper, we propose a novel utility-preserving biometric anonymization framework, which provides a method to anonymize a biometric dataset without introducing artificial or external noise, with a process that retains features relevant for downstream machine learning-based analyses to extract interesting attributes that are valuable to relevant services, businesses, and research organizations. We carried out a thorough experimental evaluation using publicly available visual and vocal datasets. Results show that our proposed framework can achieve a high level of anonymization, while at the same time retain underlying data utility such that subsequent analyses on the anonymized biometric data could still be carried out to yield satisfactory accuracy.

## 1 Introduction

As sensing technologies get increasingly adopted into commodity electronic devices that people use in their daily lives, biometrics have become more accessible and appealing as an information source, for example to enable seamless authentication without manual password input [1]. What's more, the latest sensing technologies have gone way beyond just targeting more traditional biometrics such as fingerprints, whose sole usage is arguably authentication only. Today's sensing devices can collect rich biometrics such as facial imagery, voice, and even posture/gait, iris, and neural signal data. With the help of the recent rapid advances in machine learning techniques, a wide range of interesting analytics

V. Atluri et al. (Eds.): ESORICS 2022, LNCS 13555, pp. 24–41, 2022.
https://doi.org/10.1007/978-3-031-17146-8_2

can then be performed on the rich biometric data [2], for example, to infer or extract information such as age, gender, dialect, sentiment, emotion, focus level, medical condition, etc., which could then enable vast opportunities in various relevant services and business interests.

Despite the high potential value of biometric information, one major concern preventing its universal collection and utilization is its linkage to personal identity and potential privacy violation [3–5]. For example, a user might enjoy the convenience of Face Unlock on their personal electronic devices, but likely would not appreciate having their facial features and identity information collected and used for targeted advertisements. Similarly, businesses have deployed Voice ID authentication in their automated phone system to streamline their customer service call experience. It would be deeply problematic if a business extracts information such as age, gender, and race from the voice data and uses it to profile each of their individual customers for preferential treatments.

It is therefore our goal to devise a data transformation mechanism to resolve this conflict between the value of biometric data and the potential identity disclosure. The problem of de-identification has been studied for the past decades [6]. Ideally for our particular case of biometrics, a successful anonymization should transform the data such that no identity information could be recovered, but at the same time other interesting attributes are left intact. Such a biometric anonymization mechanism would be tremendously valuable across a multitude of use cases. For example, a marketing firm that has recruited a focus group to study people's preference towards different products by presenting to them series of images of new products and taking pictures of their facial reactions for analysis might want to anonymize their collected facial imagery data and transfer it to a technology company focusing on developing computer vision algorithms and software. Or, an international medical research institute that has collected detailed biometric records from a large population might have completed their study of a particular disease and would like to release an anonymized version of the dataset publicly so other medical researchers could carry out their own studies on the dataset and potentially make discoveries that are related, or even orthogonal, to the data's original purpose.

To make the data release and reuse possible, the key challenge lies in the high dimensionality of biometric data as well as in the intrinsic probabilistic nature of machine learning-based analytics performed on top of it. In comparison, for traditional tabular data where the useful information associated with each data record is simply the textual content itself (e.g., date of birth, zip code, etc.), a rich body of literature exists that provides promising anonymization results. For biometric data, on the other hand, each data record on itself (e.g., facial image, voice audio clip, etc.) is essentially just a blob of bits, and does not show its useful information without either manual labeling or automated machine learning-based analyses, which by nature is probabilistic. Even though from a philosophical point of view, our goal of preserving interesting attributes and removing identities might seem self-contradicting in that any features preserved could potentially be used for re-identification, we argue that our problem at hand around biometrics is far from being binary. On the contrary, the high dimensionality of the data itself and the probabilistic nature of machine learning-based analytics introduce a high degree of uncertainty that we can take advantage of to achieve retention of interesting attributes while performing anonymization.

In this paper we introduce a novel biometric data transformation framework that aims at accomplishing this exact goal, namely anonymize raw biometric data to prevent/minimize identity breaching in a manner that retains other data characteristics for successful subsequent analytics. Our contribution is three-fold:

- To the best of our knowledge, our proposed framework is the first one to introduce the concept of *utility preservation under the context of ML-based analytics with general biometric information anonymization.*
- We introduce a novel anonymization technique that uses a dynamically assembled random set and task-oriented machine learning models to help guide a selective weighted-mean based transformation to anonymize biometric records.
- We demonstrate the effectiveness of our method's identity protection and utility preservation via a thorough experimental evaluation using publicly available multi-modal datasets.

## 2   Basic Concepts and Problem Statement

Since our objective is to transform a private biometric dataset for public release such that personal identities cannot be recovered but data utility is preserved as much as possible, we would like to define a few terms we use as well as making a clear problem statement for our proposed utility-preserving data anonymization task, just so we are on level ground going forward with our discussion.

### 2.1   Basic Concepts

Regarding the utility of a biometric dataset, we define *attribute of interest* and *additional attributes*, as follows.

- *Attribute of Interest.* An individual's biometric data contains features that can be used to predict certain attributes about them. An *attribute of interest* is an attribute detectable from biometric data, whose value must be protected. For example, the sentiment states displayed in a set of facial images could be considered as an attribute of interest due to their potential uses in computer vision studies or business applications. Therefore, in anonymizing such a facial dataset, we want to preserve the discoverability of sentiment states of the images.
- *Additional Attribute.* Features detectable from the biometric data, in addition to the *attribute of interest*, are denoted *additional attributes*. For example, from a voice dataset, information such as age group and dialect can be extracted by analyzing each audio clip. If the age group information is the sole attribute of interest, the dialect information is considered an additional attribute. Preserving the dialect as well as the age group information while anonymizing the voice dataset could be desirable for the expanded potential usages of a public release.

## 2.2   Problem Statement

Due to the high dimensionality of biometric data and the high uncertainty of ML-based analytics, we argue it is impossible to formulate a provable security guarantee for our biometric anonymization problem at hand. Therefore, in this paper we propose a purely *data-driven* approach so that the level of utility preservation and the level of anonymization can both be quantified, experimentally through measurements.

For an original biometric dataset $\mathbb{D}$, suppose it has an attribute of interest $p$ and a set of $n$ additional attributes $\{q_n\}$, with their corresponding recognition models $\mathcal{P}(\cdot)$ and $\{\mathcal{Q}_n(\cdot)\}$ all trained from the original dataset $\mathbb{D}$. Suppose $\mathbb{D}$ has an identity classification model $\mathcal{I}(\cdot)$, also trained from the original dataset. Then, for any data transformation $\mathcal{T}(\cdot)$, we can represent the *Utility* $U(\cdot)$ of the transformed data as the collective attribute recognition accuracy

$$U(\mathcal{T}(\mathbb{D})) = \mathcal{P}(\mathcal{T}(\mathbb{D})) + \sum_{i=1}^{n} \alpha_i \mathcal{Q}_i(\mathcal{T}(\mathbb{D})),$$

and what we call *Identity Mixture* $M(\cdot)$ the degree to which the trained identity classification model is confused by the transformed data

$$M(\mathcal{T}(\mathbb{D})) = 1 - \mathcal{I}(\mathcal{T}(\mathbb{D})).$$

In the formulas, $\mathcal{T}(\mathbb{D})$ is the transformed biometric dataset, $\{\alpha_n\}$ are user input weights for the additional attributes. Each of the attribute recognition models $\mathcal{P}(\cdot)$ and $\{\mathcal{Q}_n(\cdot)\}$, as well as the identity classification model $\mathcal{I}(\cdot)$, takes as input an entire dataset and outputs its accuracy. Intuitively, to find the best anonymization for a biometric dataset $\mathbb{D}$ is to find the optimal $\mathcal{T}^*(\cdot)$ that maximizes both $U$ and $M$ (or achieves a good trade-off between them), which is to say that the corresponding transformed data thoroughly confuses the identity classification model but can still be used to reliably extract interesting attributes.

## 2.3   Attack Model

From our problem statement, we would like to make an important observation on the identity classification model $\mathcal{I}(\cdot)$: Only the data owner knows the ground-truth identity correspondence between the original data $\mathbb{D}$ and the transformed data $\mathcal{T}(\mathbb{D})$. Therefore, only the data owner can compute the accuracy $\mathcal{I}(\mathcal{T}(\mathbb{D}))$. Any attacker who tries to use an identity classifier $\mathcal{I}'(\cdot)$ would not be able to recover any identities because of the apparent lack of ground-truth identity correspondence between $\mathbb{D}$ and $\mathcal{T}(\mathbb{D})$. Therefore, even if the attacker's model $\mathcal{I}'(\cdot)$ correctly classified $x\%$ of the hidden identities in $\mathcal{T}(\mathbb{D})$, the attacker would not be able to tell which $x\%$ in $\mathcal{T}(\mathbb{D})$ the model $\mathcal{I}'(\cdot)$ got correctly. Thus, their attempted re-identification attack is reduced to random guess.

Additionally, we argue that it is reasonable to assume the data owner's model is always more powerful than the attacker's model, $\forall \mathbb{D} : \mathcal{I}(\mathbb{D}) \geq \mathcal{I}'(\mathbb{D})$, because the data owner and the attacker can both select the latest and most powerful identity classification algorithm, but the data owner has the advantage of having access to the original unanonymized data, which the attacker does not have. Therefore, if we let the attacker's model be the same as its upper bound, $\mathcal{I}'(\cdot) = \mathcal{I}(\cdot)$, we can treat the data owner's measured identity mixture $M$, to be the lower bound of what the attacker can possibly experience. In other words, *the already hidden identity in the anonymized data would appear even more mixed to an attacker*. Therefore, in our discussion, we assume that *i)* the data owner only releases the final anonymized data, and nothing else, and *ii)* the identity classification model used by the attacker is effectively the same as the model used by the data owner.

Our attack model gives us a solid ground for our subsequent discussions We believe that, in practice, our data-driven approach can bring value to a wide range of application scenarios.

## 3    Rationale of Approach

To achieve our objective of utility-preserving anonymization for biometrics, the high dimensionality of the data and the uncertainty of ML-based analytics need to be accounted for. For each data record **d** we aim to anonymize, we dynamically assemble a random set containing **d** and perform a selective weighted-mean-based operation, where the weighting is only applied to the most important features, as guided by task-specific machine learning models. We intend to make our data transformation retain as much truthfulness as possible, hence our particular design follows the intuition of only utilizing information from the original biometric dataset, and purposefully avoiding external artificial noise. Therefore, the transformation step $\mathcal{T}(\cdot)$ randomly assembles a short-lived, parameter-driven (such parameters include desired set size, attribute purity, etc., which are discussed in detail in Sect. 4.1) set of feature vectors with which to calculate the weighted-mean for each of the target feature vectors being anonymized.

Under our proposal, each data record becomes different from its original form. Also, due to the high dimensional nature of biometrics, it is also unlikely for any anonymized data record to have an exact match in the original dataset, or vice versa. As will be demonstrated in Sect. 5.2, regardless of the particular attack method of choice—be it a direct distance measure between two data records or via a trained ML model to compute the probability of a match—the likelihood of an attacker being able to link any anonymized data record to its true corresponding original record is reduced to a random guess on the entire dataset. In other words, an anonymized record is equally likely to be the closest, or the farthest, or anywhere in between, to its true match, as far as re-identification is concerned. Hence, the attacker is unable to reliably recover any identities from the anonymized biometric dataset.

## 4    Methodology

In this section, we discuss our proposed framework for performing utility-preserving anonymization on biometric data. Our proposal is generally applicable to all types of biometrics, and not restricted to any particular data modalities or feature extraction methods. For example, as demonstrated in Sect. 5, our method is evaluated on both facial image-based and voice audio-based datasets, where multiple different feature extraction methods are used, including no feature extraction at all (e.g., raw image pixels).

## 4.1  Dynamically Assembled Random Set

Regardless of the particular preprocessing and feature extraction, each biometric data record is essentially a feature vector, which we transform through a series of operations, starting with dynamically assembling a random set of other data records from the dataset to be anonymized. For each target data record $\mathbf{d}$ in the original dataset $\mathbb{D}$, we assemble a set $F$ of $g$ data records ($g$ can be roughly interpreted as the size of the crowd that $\mathbf{d}$ is hiding in, and can be determined experimentally, as demonstrated in Sect. 5), where $\mathbf{d} \in F$, and the rest $g - 1$ of the data records, $F \setminus \{\mathbf{d}\}$, are selected from $\mathbb{D}$ based on their attribute-of-interest values, according to a *purity* parameter

$$t = \frac{|\{\mathbf{f} \in F | p_{\mathbf{f}} = p_{\mathbf{d}}\}|}{g},$$

where $p_{\mathbf{f}}$ denotes the value of $\mathbf{f}$'s attribute of interest. For example, if $t = 1$, then all $g$ elements in $F$ share the same attribute-of-interest value as $\mathbf{d}$; if $t = \frac{|\{k \in \mathbb{D} | p_k = p_{\mathbf{d}}\}|}{|\mathbb{D}|}$, which is the proportion of $p_{\mathbf{d}}$ in the entire population $\mathbb{D}$, then all of $F$'s elements are to be uniformly randomly selected from $\mathbb{D}$ regardless of their attribute-of-interest values; if $t = \frac{1}{g}$, then all other elements in $F$ are selected to be of different attribute-of-interest values than $\mathbf{d}$. This way of assembling the set $F$ is inspired by the $k$-anonymity, $\ell$-diversity, and $t$-closeness methods, but differs in that our approach was designed with the main objective of preserving the attribute of interest, while also including mechanisms for trading off between attribute preservation and identity mixture, in the form of different set sizes $g \in \mathbb{Z}^+$ and purity levels $t \in \left[\frac{1}{g}, 1\right]$.

## 4.2  Selective Weighted Mean-Based Transformation

After dynamically assembling a random set $F$, we transform the target biometric record $\mathbf{d}$ by computing its weighted mean with the rest of $F$'s elements $F \setminus \{\mathbf{d}\}$. In order to preserve $\mathbf{d}$'s attributes, we want to protect its corresponding features by assigning them a higher *weight* such that they do not get completely buried when $\mathbf{d}$ is averaged with the rest of $F$. The higher weight, the more we anchor $\mathbf{d}$'s features in place during averaging.

One caveat of the weighting is that on one hand it protects the target's features, but on the other hand, it could potentially weaken the identity mixing effect of the averaging. For example, for $g \equiv |F| = 10$, a high weight $w = 1000$, would virtually completely anchor a target in place, rendering the transformation almost trivial. To mitigate this problem, we modify the weighting strategy such that the weights are only applied to selective "important" features of each biometric record as derived from the task-specific machine learning model for the attribute of interest. For example, a sentiment classifier on facial features might

---

**Algorithm 1.** Utility Preserving Biometric Anonymization

---

**Inputs:**

$\mathbb{D}$ : the set of original biometric data feature vectors to be anonymized

$\mathcal{P}(\cdot)$ : the classifier trained on $\mathbb{D}$ for the attribute of interest

$\{\mathcal{Q}_n(\cdot)\}$ : the classifiers trained on $\mathbb{D}$ for the additional attributes

$c_p$ : number of features to retain for attribute of interest

$\{c_{q_n}\}$ : numbers of features to retain for each of the additional attributes

$g$ : size of random set for anonymization

$t$ : purity of the random set's attribute-of-interest value

$w$ : weight parameter for computing weighted mean

**Output:**

$\mathbb{D}'$ : the set of anonymized biometric data feature vectors

---

1: $I_p \leftarrow$ list of feature indices in descending order of importance from $\mathcal{P}(\cdot)$
2: $\{I_{q_n}\} \leftarrow$ lists of feature indices in descending order of importance from $\{\mathcal{Q}_n(\cdot)\}$
3: $I \leftarrow I_p[0:c_p] \cup \{\cup_{i \in \{n\}} I_{q_i}[0:c_{q_i}]\}$
4: $X_I \leftarrow$ indicator vector s.t. $X_I[j] = \begin{cases} 1, \text{ if } j \in I \\ 0, \quad \text{o.w.} \end{cases}$
5: $\mathbb{D}' \leftarrow \emptyset$
6: **for each** $\mathbf{d} \in \mathbb{D}$ **do**
7:     Randomly select $F \subseteq \mathbb{D}$ s.t. $\mathbf{d} \in F$, $|F| = g$, and $\frac{|\{\mathbf{f} \in F | p_{\mathbf{f}} = p_{\mathbf{d}}\}|}{g} = t$
8:     $\mathbf{d}' \leftarrow \frac{1}{w} \cdot \text{mean}(F) + \frac{(w-1)}{w} \cdot X_I \odot \mathbf{d}$
9:     $\mathbb{D}' \leftarrow \mathbb{D}' \cup \{\mathbf{d}'\}$
10: **end for**
11: **return** $\mathbb{D}'$

---

pay more attention to features around the mouth. Our weighted mean calculation would therefore apply nontrivial weights to the target $\mathbf{d}$'s mouth features, and use $w = 1$ for other non-important features like the hair. This way, the weighting helps protect biometric attributes without running the risk of largely fixing target biometric records unchanged and causing low identity mixtures.

Note that not only can the attribute of interest be preserved by the weighting, so can any additional attributes. For example, in addition to the sentiment attribute of interest, the data owner of a facial image dataset might also want to preserve gaze directions as an additional attribute. In that case, they would query their gaze detector for a set of relevant features, which most likely are around the eyes. And these eye features would then be added to the list of features that nontrivial weights are applied to.

The algorithm pseudo-code is shown in Algorithm 1. Line 1 through 4 collect the set of important features from the corresponding task-specific ML models. Line 7 prepares the dynamically assembled random set as discussed in Sect. 4.1. The selective weighted mean as discussed in Sect. 4.2 is computed on Line 8, where $\odot$ is the component-wise multiplication operator. Please note that even though we only use a single weight $w$ here, the algorithm can be easily extended to incorporate multiple weights, one per attribute for example, by modifying the indicator-vector preparation on Line 4 and/or the averaging computation on Line 8. Lastly, each iteration of the for-loop in Line 6 through 10 is independent from the rest, leading to highly parallelizable and efficient computation in practice.

# 5    Experimental Evaluation

In this section, we experimentally evaluate our biometric anonymization technique using publicly available datasets. First, we describe the characteristics of the datasets we use, and the experimental settings. Next, we report the results of the various sets of experiments where we compare the effects of parameters in our proposed technique by examining its capabilities of identity mixture and biometric attribute preservation under various experimental settings.

## 5.1    Experimental Setup

**Datasets.** Our framework enables the preservation of multiple attributes of biometric data while performing anonymization. Thus, an ideal dataset for us to use to demonstrate this capability would be one that contains ground-truth label information for multiple interesting attributes. We curated two publicly available datasets that fitted our requirement for testing our method.

The first one is the facial image FER-2013 dataset [7], which contains grayscale images of human faces with associated ground-truth sentiment label information, and thus suits our purpose. A round of manual inspection was performed on the original dataset to remove problematic images that were duplicates, non-photographic, or of poor resolution, etc. We treat *sentiment* as an example biometric attribute of interest in our experiments. Moreover, we augment FER-2013 with the *mouth-slightly-open* attribute using a model pre-trained on the CelebFaces Attributes (CelebA) dataset [8] as an additional attribute. As a result, the final in-use FER-2013 dataset has 8,470 training images, 978 validation images and 1,060 testing images, and it has 4 classes for the sentiment attribute and two classes for the mouth-slightly-open attribute.

The other one is the voice AudioMNIST [9] dataset, which contains the waveform signal of different people speaking digits. We use *spoken digit* as the attribute of interest in our experiments. We sub-sampled the dataset to rebalance the difference classes since the original class distributions were highly skewed. We ended up with 7,200 training audios, 2,400 validation audios, and 2,400 testing audios. The dataset contains 24 speaker identities and has 10 classes for the spoken digit. For both datasets, the training and validation splits are used to train the classifiers and we use the testing split to evaluate our proposed method.

**Data Preprocessing.** For FER-2013, we experimented with multiple feature extraction methods as the representation for each data records: *i)* FaceGraph, which is the fully-connected graph built on facial landmarks extracted from each facial image (using the Swift Vision Library [10]); *ii)* Pixel, which simply uses the raw pixel values of an image as the feature vector; *iii)* Eigenface [11], which is the projection of an facial image onto the eigenspace computed from all facial images; and *iv)* Vggfeats, which is the feature of the final layer of the facenet [12] neural network. For AudioMNIST, on the other hand, we extract the embeddings by using HuBERT [13] on the voice signal and then average the embeddings of each token as our final data representation.

**Evaluation Protocol.** We use the *classification on attribute of interest* as a driving example for our experiments. Each classification task itself, however, is *not* necessarily our focus—our goal is not to find the model that achieves absolutely the best accuracy for a classification test; rather, we are mostly interested in demonstrating that a model trained on the original biometric data can continue to successfully perform classification tasks even on the version of the biometric data transformed by our anonymization method. Therefore, we simply experimented with a few well-known classification algorithms and empirically picked the one that struck a balance between classification performance and training speed. We ended up picked the off-the-shelf Random-Forest [14] classifier from scikit-learn [15] for our experiments for attribute classification. It provided good accuracy on both the attribute of interest and the additional attribute on FER-2013 as well as AudioMNIST.

The evaluation protocol is setup as follows. First, to evaluate the preserved attribute of interest, we train and test a random-forest classifier on the original unanonymized data. We then apply this classifier on the anonymized data to check the level of preservation on the attribute of interest. We also evaluate the level of identity mixture on the anonymized data. Since the FER-2013 dataset does not come with identity information, when evaluating the level of identity mixture, we simply consider each image as a different identity and then measure the *cosine distance* between each anonymized data record to all originals to find the closest one as the potential match. AudioMNIST, on the other hand, does include the identity information. So, we employ an ML-based method to measure the level of identity mixture, where we train a multi-layer perceptron (MLP) over the identity labels using the original dataset and then evaluate its performance on the anonymized dataset.

**Feature Ranking.** In our proposed method, we need to rank all data features in order to decide which ones to retain. There are existing feature ranking methods that determine the importance of each feature [16,17]. The random-forest classifier also ranks each feature upon building its decision trees, which we directly use as our metrics to gauge the importance of each feature.

**Parameter Settings.** We carried out a thorough scan through the parameter space in order to uncover all interesting trends and crucial regions in our experiments. For the sake of presentation brevity, we report in Sect. 5.2 only the representative results, under the following parameter settings:

- Set attribute purity $t$: ranges from 0.0 to 1.0 with step size 0.1;
- Set size: $g = 8, 32, 128$;
- Feature retention ratio $r_p = c_p/|\mathbf{d}|$ for the attribute of interest:
  $r_p = 0.1\%, 1\%, 10\%, 50\%, 100\%$;
- Feature retention ratio $r_q = c_q/|\mathbf{d}|$ for the additional attributes:
  $r_q = 0\%, 0.1\%, 1\%, 10\%, 50\%$;
- Weight: $w = 10, 100, 1000$,

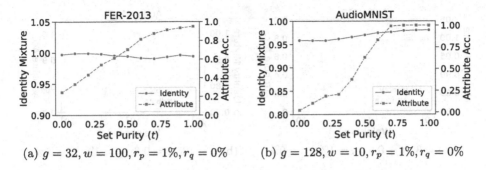

(a) $g = 32, w = 100, r_p = 1\%, r_q = 0\%$     (b) $g = 128, w = 10, r_p = 1\%, r_q = 0\%$

**Fig. 1.** Varying set purity $t$. Higher $t$ leads to better attribute-of-interest recognition accuracy as each original data record **d** is combined with more records sharing **d**'s attribute value.

where $c_p$, $c_q$, and **d** are as defined in Algorithm 1. After we explored these parameters (see Fig. 1 through 4), we used $t = 0.6$, $g = 32$, $r_p = 1\%$, $w = 100$ for FER-2013, and $t = 0.8$, $g = 128$, $r_p = 1\%$, $w = 10$ for AudioMNIST.

## 5.2  Results

We organize our results as follows. First, we report the attribute recognition accuracies on the original unanonymized dataset as baselines. Next, we perform ablation studies on the parameters of our method and discuss the result. We then take a closer examination of the quality of the anonymization achieved by our method. Please note that all these above results on FER-2013 are obtained by using the FaceGraph feature representation. So lastly, we experiment with applying our method on all four different feature representations on FER-2013, as discussed in Sect. 5.1, and report our findings.

**Performance on Unanonymized Data.** Before any discussion on the anonymized biometric data, we first establish a reference point by obtaining the accuracy of the classification model for the attribute of interest on original un-anonymized data. We expect this classification result to be reasonably accurate because otherwise it would be difficult to assess the level of utility preservation if the original biometric dataset already had low utility to begin with. For the attributes of interest on FER-2013 and AudioMNIST, the random-forest classifier achieved 77% and 90.6% recognition accuracy, respectively.

**Effects of Parameters.** Figures 1 through 4 show how each parameter affects the data transformation's identity mixture and preservation of the attribute of interest. In each of these experiments, we tune a single parameter while keeping the rest fixed at the optimal configuration we obtained empirically.

First, we examined the influence of the set purity $t$, which determines the percentage of the data records sharing the same attribute value as the target in each random set, as defined in Sect. 4.1. As shown in Fig. 1, the set purity and

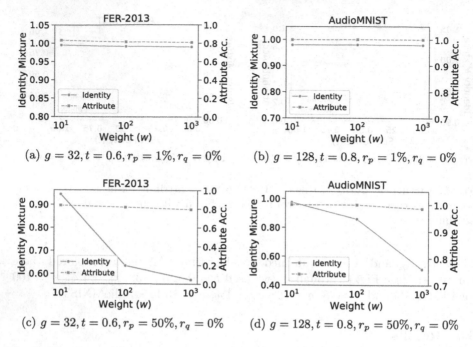

(a) $g = 32, t = 0.6, r_p = 1\%, r_q = 0\%$      (b) $g = 128, t = 0.8, r_p = 1\%, r_q = 0\%$

(c) $g = 32, t = 0.6, r_p = 50\%, r_q = 0\%$      (d) $g = 128, t = 0.8, r_p = 50\%, r_q = 0\%$

**Fig. 2.** Varying weight $w$. Under $r_p = 1\%$, our method works well regardless of the weight since only 1% of features are retrained. On the other hand, with $r_p = 50\%$, the identity mixture decreases when $w$ increases because the anonymized data record is now much closer to the original one because of the large portion of features being retained via a higher $r_p$ and anchored in place via a higher $w$.

the recognition accuracy of the attribute of interest on the anonymized data is positively correlated, which demonstrates that our method can indeed preserve the attribute of interest effectively. On the other hand, varying the purity level does not affect the level of identity mixtures.

The weight $w$ controls how much a data record is anchored in place during transformation in terms of its retained features. Its other features would still be blended with the other data records. As shown in Fig. 2, when we set the feature retention to only keep $r_p = 1\%$ of features, even with very small weight, we can still achieve high recognition accuracy for the attribute of interest and high identity mixture on anonymized data. On the other hand, when we retain $r_p = 50\%$ features, the larger weight $w$ results in lower identity mixture as the anonymized data is now much too similar to the original data.

The set size $g$ is related to the size of the population each data record is to be mixed with. Therefore, a larger $g$ would lead to a more diverse set for our method to increase the level of identity mixture. On the other hand, as we can control the set purity $t$, the result set will affect identity mixture more than it does the attribute of interest. As shown in Fig. 3, identity mixture improves when set size increases, whereas the recognition accuracy of the attribute of interest remains relatively unchanged.

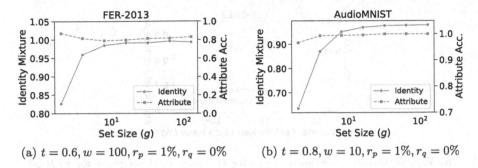

(a) $t = 0.6, w = 100, r_p = 1\%, r_q = 0\%$     (b) $t = 0.8, w = 10, r_p = 1\%, r_q = 0\%$

**Fig. 3.** Varying set size $g$. With larger set size, identity mixture increases as mixing more data leads to better anonymization without affecting the recognition of the attribute of interest.

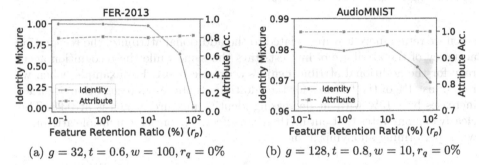

(a) $g = 32, t = 0.6, w = 100, r_q = 0\%$     (b) $g = 128, t = 0.8, w = 10, r_q = 0\%$

**Fig. 4.** Varying feature retention ratio $r_p$. Retaining more features increases the similarity between the original and anonymized data. Therefore, it helps increase attribute recognition accuracy, but lead to lower identity mixture. Hence, a trade-off needs to be made here.

For the feature retention ratio $r_p$ for the attribute of interest, retaining more features would lead to smaller difference between the original data record and its anonymized version, resulting in lower identity mixture, as can be observed in Fig. 4. On the other hand, thanks to feature ranking, even if only $r_p = 1\%$ of features are retained, the recognition accuracy of the attribute of interest remains unaffected even though the identity mixture drops significantly. As we expect identity mixture to be high in an anonymized dataset, we can use such experimental parameter space exploration to help locate desirable configuration. For example, for the feature retention ratio in the range $r_p \in [0.1\%, 10\%]$, we observe, for both FER-2013 and AudioMNIST, both high levels of identity mixture and high attribute recognition accuracy—both are desirable characteristics for utility-preserving anonymization.

**Additional Attribute.** We next demonstrate, using FER-2013, the preservation of not only the attribute of interest, but also an additional attribute, while performing anonymization. The results are shown in Fig. 5. It can be seen that

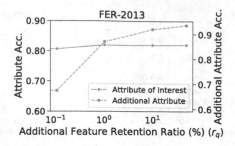

**Fig. 5.** Varying feature retention ratio $r_q$ for the additional attribute for FER-2013 ($g = 32, t = 0.6, w = 100, r_p = 1\%$). The corresponding identity mixtures are 0.99, 0.99, 0.97, 0.70, from left to right. Again, a trade-off can be made here that achieves good recognition accuracy for both the attribute of interest and the additional attribute, as well as a high degree of identity mixture.

when we retain more features related to the additional attribute, the recognition accuracy of the attribute of interest stays the same while the recognition accuracy for the additional attribute enjoys a drastic boost. For example, when we retain just 1% of the features for the addition attribute, its recognition accuracy increases by ∼15% without decreasing identity mixture, which is at 0.99. This clearly demonstrates that our method can effectively preserve multiple attributes when performing anonymization.

**Anonymization Quality.** We have so far been judging the quality of anonymization via identity mixture. While an informative metric, identity mixture does not paint the whole picture, as it is based only on the binary hit-or-miss results of identity classification models. A "perfect" anonymization would reduce an attacker's re-identification attempts to random guesses, which means the attacker gains zero information with the attacks. Therefore, we use two methods to take a deeper look into the anonymization quality achieved by our proposed approach, with different set sizes. *i)* The level of identity mixture over top-$k$ predictions, and *ii)* The KL divergence between the predicted probability and that of random guesses. Results are shown in Fig. 6 and Fig. 7.

The level of identity mixture over top-$k$ prediction means that a re-identification attack is considered successful if the true identity is contained in the attacker's top $k$ candidate matches. As shown in Fig. 6, if the curve is below and close to that of the random guess, it implies that the data are anonymized in a way that the attacker can only achieve random guess in re-identification attacks. Moreover, if the curve is above the random guess, it means the anonymized data can actually fool the attacker better than random guess, in which case the attacker might as well try guessing randomly.

We also measure how far the predicted distribution deviates from that of random guesses. A value close to zero means that the attacker won't be able to do better than random guess. We compute each KL divergence from random guess for each data record and then average across the whole dataset. Results

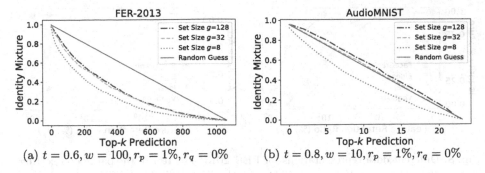

**Fig. 6.** The level of identity mixture over top-$k$ predictions, where a re-identification attack is considered successful if the true identity is contained in the attacker's top $k$ candidate matches. The straight lines correspond to random guesses.

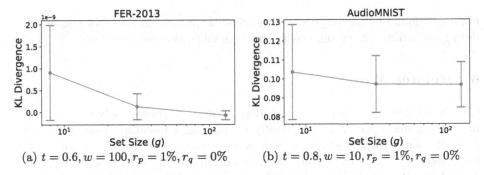

**Fig. 7.** KL Divergence from random guess at different set size. For FER-2013, the KL divergence from random guess is almost 0, whereas the overall KL divergence remain very small for AudioMNIST.

are shown in Fig. 7, where we observe that $i)$ the overall KL divergence values are already close to zero, indicating good anonymization qualities, and $ii)$ with larger set size, re-identification attempts tend to behave increasingly more like random guesses.

**Different Data Representations.** Lastly, we experiment with multiple different biometric feature extractions and data representations. Results are shown in Fig. 8. First, it can be observed that our method is applicable to different data representations. For example, when setting the feature retention ratio to $r_p \in [0.1\%, 1\%]$, good identity mixture is observed for all different data representations, even though they do show varying recognition accuracies for the attribute of interest. In this particular example, our FaceGraph representation happens to give the best result among all. We also observe that the Vggfeats performs the worst, likely due to the low resolution of the images and the fact that the domain of images is different from that of the pretrained model. In general, the optimal data representation as well as parameter configuration can

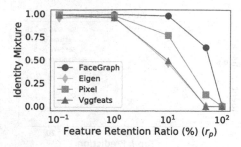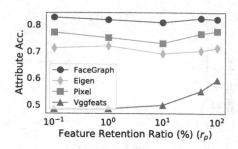

**Fig. 8.** Different data representations for FER-2013. The rest of the parameter setting is $g = 32, t = 0.6, w = 100, r_q = 0\%$. Our method is applicable to different data representations, and with only 1% features, the method can increase the identity mixture to almost 1.0 while retaining good accuracy on the attribute of interest.

always be found by our empirical data-driven approach, to tailor for the specific data type, utility-preserving needs, and anonymization requirements.

## 6   Related Work

Closely related research can be considered those efforts to apply or adapt the data truthfulness preserving anonymity techniques, for example $k$-anonymity, $\ell$-diversity, and $t$-closeness to various data sources, ranging from categorical data that might appear in for example relational database tables, to location data and biometric data. Typically, most applications seek to find that balance between anonymizing the data effectively while also retaining utility to some degree [18, 19]. The fundamental difference of our proposed method from these existing techniques is that *we do not generalize*, as each transformed biometric data record remains different from the others, which opens up the possibility of more interesting attributes being preserved through anonymization. Next, we briefly survey these techniques.

Categorical data was one of the first sources for application of $k$-anonymity [20] and $\ell$-diversity [21]. $k$-Anonymity, which our dynamically assembling a random set technique is inspired by, is a property induced in the data by generalization and suppression, which means each record is indistinguishable from $k-1$ other records. $\ell$-Diversity addresses the weakness of $k$-anonymity with regards to attribute disclosure, by demanding that there are at least $\ell$ well-represented values of the attribute within each group of indistinguishable records (equivalence class). Achieving the property of $k$-anonymity in a database can be a challenging task. In fact, Bayardo and Agrawal [22] highlight that achieving optimal $k$-anonymity on a database is an NP-hard computational problem and they propose an optimization technique to achieve a given level of $k$-anonymity automatically. $t$-Closeness extends the protection of $k$-anonymity by requiring that the distribution of a sensitive attribute in an equivalence class be similar to the global attribute distribution, so no information is leaked by a potentially altered cluster-specific distribution, which is another concept we borrowed when dynamically assembling a random set in our proposed pipeline.

Biometric image data is most relevant to the contribution in this paper. Initially obfuscation of image data was achieved by blurring, blacking out or pixelating salient regions of the face [23]. While these methods achieve admirable anonymization of the biometric data, they do not retain any degree of utility. Anonymization of facial image biometric data while retraining utility has been addressed by several prior studies [11, 24–26], which introduced the $k$-same family of algorithms. In general, this family of algorithms work as follows with different variations: Firstly, the biometric data in the database is partitioned into clusters, usually with $k$ individuals per cluster, for the required level of $k$-anonymity. The centroids of the clusters are computed and the $k$ individuals in a cluster are replaced by their corresponding cluster centroid. In this way every individual in the cluster shares the same de-identified face (i.e., the centroid). The algorithms vary in how individuals are assigned to clusters, e.g., using label information or not, and in what space the analysis is performed, e.g., pixel space, parameter space. The $k$-same family of algorithms were not extended to enforce $\ell$-diversity in attributes that could be considered sensitive. Furthermore, many of the instantiations of $k$-same operate in pixel-space, leading to degradation in the utility of the anonymity representations, e.g., via excessive blurring induced by the centroid computation. Recent works have explored more advanced anonymization models such as neural networks for face de-identification [27–29]. While showing impressive clarity in generating fake faces for replacing real faces, these techniques require large amounts of training data and are also difficult to interpret or reason about, making it difficult to audit the models for industrial applications. It is also in question as to whether the focus should be on accurate reproduction of life-like anonymized images in pixel-space or a focus on generating highly anonymized abstract representations that can retain utility for other tasks, we follow the latter approach in this paper. The survey article [23] has further related work on face de-identification for the interested reader.

## 7  Conclusions

In this paper we introduce a biometric data anonymizing transformation framework that aims at stripping away personally identifiable information while at the same time preserving the utility of the biometrics by leaving intact its other characteristics such that downstream tasks such as machine learning-based analytics could still extract useful and valuable attributes from the anonymized biometric data. We present our end-to-end algorithm design, which uses dynamically assembled random set and selective weighted-mean to transform biometrics. We experimentally evaluated our method using publicly available facial image and voice audio datasets and observed that our proposed method could effectively anonymize the different modalities of biometrics, while at the same time successfully preserve other interesting attributes for downstream analytics.

# Disclaimer

This paper was prepared for information purposes by the teams of researchers from the various institutions identified above, including the Global Technology Applied Research group of JPMorgan Chase Bank, N.A. This paper is not a product of the Research Department of JPMorgan Chase Bank, N.A. or its affiliates. Neither JPMorgan Chase Bank, N.A. nor any of its affiliates make any explicit or implied representation or warranty and none of them accept any liability in connection with this paper, including, but limited to, the completeness, accuracy, reliability of information contained herein and the potential legal, compliance, tax or accounting effects thereof. This document is not intended as investment research or investment advice, or a recommendation, offer or solicitation for the purchase or sale of any security, financial instrument, financial product or service, or to be used in any way for evaluating the merits of participating in any transaction.

# References

1. Rui, Z., Yan, Z.: A survey on biometric authentication: toward secure and privacy-preserving identification. IEEE Access **7**, 5994–6009 (2018)
2. Ortiz, N., Hernández, R.D., Jimenez, R., Mauledeoux, M., Avilés, O.: Survey of biometric pattern recognition via machine learning techniques. Contemp. Eng. Sci. **11**(34), 1677–1694 (2018)
3. Barni, M., Donida Labati, R., Genovese, A., Piuri, V., Scotti, F.: Iris deidentification with high visual realism for privacy protection on websites and social networks. IEEE Access **9**, 131995–132010 (2021). 2169-3536
4. Datta, P., Bhardwaj, S., Panda, S.N., Tanwar, S., Badotra, S.: Survey of security and privacy issues on biometric system. In: Gupta, B.B., Perez, G.M., Agrawal, D.P., Gupta, D. (eds.) Handbook of Computer Networks and Cyber Security, pp. 763–776. Springer, Cham (2020). https://doi.org/10.1007/978-3-030-22277-2_30
5. Labati, R.D., Piuri, V., Scotti, F.: Biometric privacy protection: guidelines and technologies. In: Obaidat, M.S., Sevillano, J.L., Filipe, J. (eds.) ICETE 2011. CCIS, vol. 314, pp. 3–19. Springer, Heidelberg (2012). https://doi.org/10.1007/978-3-642-35755-8_1
6. Garfinkel, S.: De-identification of Personal Information: US Department of Commerce, National Institute of Standards and Technology (2015)
7. Goodfellow, I.J., et al.: Challenges in representation learning: a report on three machine learning contests. In: NIPS (2013)
8. Liu, Z., Luo, P., Wang, X., Tang, X.: Deep learning face attributes in the wild. In: ICCV (2015)
9. Becker, S., Ackermann, M., Lapuschkin, S., Müller, K.-R., Samek, W.: Interpreting and explaining deep neural networks for classification of audio signals. CoRR, vol. abs/1807.03418 (2018)
10. Apple, "Vision framework: Apply computer vision algorithms to perform a variety of tasks on input images and video" (2021). https://developer.apple.com/documentation/vision
11. Newton, E.M., Sweeney, L., Malin, B.: Preserving privacy by de-identifying face images. In: IEEE TKDE (2005)

12. Schroff, F., Kalenichenko, D., Philbin, J.: FaceNet: a unified embedding for face recognition and clustering. In: Proceedings of the IEEE Conference on Computer Vision and Pattern Recognition (CVPR), June 2015
13. Hsu, W.-N., Bolte, B., Tsai, Y.-H.H., Lakhotia, K., Salakhutdinov, R., Mohamed, A.: HuBERT: self-supervised speech representation learning by masked prediction of hidden units. IEEE/ACM Trans. Audio Speech Lang. Process. **29**, 3451–3460 (2021)
14. Breiman, L.: Random forests. Mach. Learn. **45**, 5–32 (2001)
15. Pedregosa, F., et al.: Scikit-learn: machine learning in Python. J. Mach. Learn. Res. **12**, 2825–2830 (2011)
16. Roffo, G., Melzi, S., Cristani, M.: Infinite feature selection. In: IEEE International Conference on Computer Vision (ICCV) 2015, pp. 4202–4210 (2015)
17. Gu, Q., Li, Z., Han, J.: Generalized fisher score for feature selection. In: Proceedings of the Twenty-Seventh Conference on Uncertainty in Artificial Intelligence, ser. UAI 2011, Arlington, Virginia, USA, pp. 266–273. AUAI Press (2011)
18. De Capitani, S., di Vimercati, S., Foresti, G.L., Samarati, P.: Data privacy: definitions and techniques. Int. J. Uncertain. Fuzziness Knowl.-Based Syst. **20**(6), 793–817 (2012)
19. Ciriani, V., De Capitani di Vimercati, S., Foresti, S., Samarati, P.: k-Anonymity. In: Yu, T., Jajodia, S. (eds.) Secure Data Management in Decentralized Systems. Springer, Cham (2007)
20. Samarati, P.: Protecting respondents' identities in microdata release. IEEE Trans. Knowl. Data Eng. (TKDE) **13**(6), 1010–1027 (2001)
21. Machanavajjhala, A., Kifer, D., Gehrke, J., Venkitasubramaniam, M.: $\ell$-diversity: privacy beyond $k$-anonymity. In: ACM TKDD (2007)
22. Bayardo, R.J., Agrawal, R.: Data privacy through optimal $k$-anonymization. In: ICDE (2005)
23. Ribaric, S., Ariyaeeinia, A., Pavesic, N.: De-identification for privacy protection in multimedia content. Image Commun. **47**, 131–151 (2016)
24. Gross, R., Airoldi, E., Malin, B., Sweeney, L.: Integrating utility into face de-identification. In: PET (2005)
25. Gross, R., Sweeney, L., de la Torre, F., Baker, S.: Semi-supervised learning of multi-factor models for face de-identification. In: CVPR (2008)
26. Sun, Z., Meng, L., Ariyaeeinia, A.: Distinguishable de-identified faces. In: FG (2015)
27. Meden, B., Emersic, Z., Struc, V., Peer, P.: $\kappa$-Same-Net: neural-network-based face deidentification. In: IWOBI (2017)
28. Pan, Y.-L., Haung, M.-J., Ding, K.-T., Wu, J.-L., Jang, J.-S.: K-Same-Siamese-GAN: K-same algorithm with generative adversarial network for facial image de-identification with hyperparameter tuning and mixed precision training. In: AVSS (2019)
29. Li, T., Lin, L.: AnonymousNet: natural face de-identification with measurable privacy. In: CVPR Workshops (2019)

# Anonymous Traceback for End-to-End Encryption

Erin Kenney[1(✉)], Qiang Tang[2], and Chase Wu[1]

[1] New Jersey Institute of Technology, Newark, NJ 07102, USA
clk8@njit.edu
[2] The University of Sydney, Sydney, NSW 2006, Australia

**Abstract.** As secure messaging services become ubiquitous, the need for moderation tools that can function within these systems without defeating their purpose becomes more and more pressing. There are several solutions to deal with moderation on a local level, handling harassment and personal-scale issues, but handling wider-scale issues like disinformation campaigns narrows the field; traceback systems are designed for this, but most are incompatible with anonymity.

In this paper, we present Anonymous Traceback, a traceback system capable of functioning within anonymous secure messaging systems. We carefully model security properties, provide two provably secure and simple constructions, with the most practical construction able to preserve anonymity for all but the original source of a reported abusive message. Our implementation shows integration to messaging systems such as Signal is feasible, with client-side overhead smaller than Signals' sealed sender system, and low overhead overall.

## 1 Introduction

End-to-End Encrypted (E2EE) messaging services have become ubiquitous. People want to claw back some privacy from the nature of the internet, to communicate with actual peace of mind. However, they also open up many problems, a key one being: how do we moderate a messaging system where all messages are hidden? Message Franking [3,5] for instance, allows a receiver of an abusive message to report it and prove the identity of the one who sent it to them. In many cases, just blocking the immediate sender may be insufficient; attackers may abuse E2EE systems through viral messages and misinformation campaigns, which have become a major issue on various online platforms. Such campaigns have spread disinformation about vaccines [1,2], attempted to interfere with elections [14], and even resulted in deaths [9]. To deal with those issues, [13] initiated the study of source tracing in E2EE systems, which enables the server (with the assistance of a reporting client) to follow the path of a forwarded message through the network and locate the original sender of a reported abusive message. A core challenge of traceback is to maintain security of messages as much as possible until a valid report is made to the tracing server.

However, traceback in its original form has several limitations. On one hand, [13] focused on preserving message confidentiality without considering

© The Author(s), under exclusive license to Springer Nature Switzerland AG 2022
V. Atluri et al. (Eds.): ESORICS 2022, LNCS 13555, pp. 42–62, 2022.
https://doi.org/10.1007/978-3-031-17146-8_3

anonymity. Their first "path traceback" construction reveals the identities of the whole forwarding chain, while their second "tree traceback" scheme further reveals every user involved with the message. Since the purpose is to reduce the spread of viral misinformation while maintaining user security/privacy as much as possible, identifying much more information beyond the originator of the reported message should be unnecessary. In addition, it is incompatible with (partially) anonymous E2EE messaging systems such as Signal; for the tracing algorithms in [13] to work, it is necessary that the platform logs who is talking to who. Attackers could still abuse an anonymous E2EE system, to spread viral misinformation where traceback cannot be applied.

## 1.1  Our Contributions

For those reasons, we introduce Anonymous Traceback. We carefully formulate and define the problem and give 2 constructions capable of maintaining the useful core feature of locating the source of a reported (potentially abusive) message, while working within a partially or even fully anonymous messaging system.

**Formulating Anonymous Traceback.** We take the basic structure of traceback, and rework it to function in an anonymous system. While the general structure of algorithms remains similar to the original traceback [13], several subtleties need to be taken care of, since tracing the source while preserving anonymity may seem to be antagonistic goals. We first alter the existing security property of trace unforgeability to *anonymous trace unforgeability* to account for the larger scope of actions the adversary can take, and introduce new notions for anonymity. Specifically, *pre-trace anonymity* which keeps a user's identity hidden until a trace is made on a message they are involved with, and *post-trace anonymity* which lasts even after a trace is made. We afford originators and forwarders different levels of anonymity as is feasible.

**Constructing Anonymous Traceback.** We design two constructions, stressing on simplicity for minimal overhead, and compatibility to existing systems.

The first is *"anonymous path traceback"*. As we mentioned above, the path traceback in [13] requires explicitly the identity information of each user for the tracing algorithm. Simply encrypting the information renders it trivial to frame innocent users, as the server cannot verify that information during tracing; some means of ensuring the accuracy of the hidden information is necessary. This somewhat naturally leads towards tools such as zero knowledge proofs, which still incur significant overhead. While those would work in theory, we prefer to create a more efficient solution with minimal overhead. We first observe that we can take advantage of the message recipient's position to place responsibility for verifying critical information on them; if the receiver fails to properly check this information, we consider them corrupted and a valid result for tracing.

There is one more subtle threat: that an adversary may try to launch a "delayed replay attack": the adversary sends an abusive message and corrupts one user $A$ in the forwarding chain. $A$ receives the message from a forwarder $B$, and then later sends a copy of that message to himself pretending $B$ is the original sender. This is possible due to limited storage space putting a lifespan on previous send information. We observe that the conventional wisdom of adding timestamps resolves this issue. Here we do not need precise synchronization of all the clocks, just roughly close.

Although anonymous path traceback achieves *pre-tracing anonymity*, it cannot manage *post-tracing anonymity*. In an anonymous messaging system, revealing the whole tracing path *also reveals second and more order connections*, which can be used to identify social groups on the platform. This is fairly troublesome: targeted advertising can be considered invasive, and far worse are the possibilities of a hate group identifying a community to target, or a government cracking down on dissent. Even if you trust the messaging platform, that does not mean that data could not end up in the wrong hands regardless.

To preserve more anonymity, we next construct *anonymous source traceback*, capable of retaining anonymity for *all users except the original source* (or an intentional malicious forwarder). However, current tracing method is a step-by-step process, each message's tracing information pointing backwards to the previous message in the forwarding chain. At each step the tracing information is verified, including the sender's identity, meaning the entire path becomes known in the process of finding the original source. To escape this limitation, we observe that the identity information needs to be decoupled from the tracing information. We realize this by separating the platform into a message server and a tracing server. The former is only in charge of regular messaging functionality and maintains identity-related metadata (still preserves anonymity), while the latter stores relevant tracing information. During tracing, the two servers could jointly "emulate" the step-by-step tracing process as before, until an identity is considered as output of the tracing algorithm. We note this two-server architecture is comparable to other work in the literature, and could have several plausible instantiations in practice, see Sect. 4 for more discussion.

**Implementation and Evaluations.** We implement and benchmark our constructions' cryptographic components and compare them to benchmarks of lib-signal, showing that our computational overhead is practical to integrate into a large-scale messaging application - and is in fact less overhead than Signal's sealed sender system currently uses. While it would be additional overhead on top of sealed sender, that still indicates it is low enough to work at scale. In addition, we also provide an estimate of necessary storage space for tracing data compared to the original traceback paper's metrics, which while larger also appears practical.

## 1.2   Related Work

There have been an increasing number of studies into accountability in encrypted messaging recently. The moderation tool that began this trend is Message Franking [3,5], which is the baseline tool many others, including traceback, expand upon. To the best of our knowledge, the original traceback [13] is the first instance of a system capable of following a message's forwarding trail to find the original source. In addition to the path traceback capability we replicate here in anonymous path

**Table 1.** Comparison of tracing systems. $\triangle$, $\blacktriangle$, and $\blacktriangle$ represent degrees of pre-trace anonymity, while ● represents full post-trace anonymity. Hecate does not require the moderator and platform to be separate and non-colluding, but has a similar issue as FACTS when a user is out of tokens otherwise.

|  | Original [13] | [8] | FACTS [7] | Hecate [6] | Anon path | Anon source |
|---|---|---|---|---|---|---|
| Traces | Path/Tree | Source | Source | Source | Path | Source |
| Origin Anon. | N/A | N/A | $\triangle$ | $\blacktriangle$ | $\blacktriangle$ | $\blacktriangle$ |
| Forwarder Anon. | N/A | N/A | $\triangle$ | ● | $\blacktriangle$ | ● |
| Deniability | Likely | Yes | Likely | Yes | No | No |
| Server count | 1 | 1 | 1 | 2* | 1 | 2 |
| Storage Reqs | Moderate | Small | Small | Small | Large | Large |

traceback, their second construction, tree traceback, could recover the entire forwarding tree branching out from the initial source.

Peale, Eskandarian, and Boneh [8] also develop a tracing method they call Source Tracking, which improves upon traceback with two constructions capable of tracing to the original sender without needing to store information for each message on the server, or revealing forwarders. However, the more efficient of these constructions loses the property they call "tree unlinkability", which corresponds to some of the original traceback's *user trace confidentiality* property, and both are incompatible with any form of anonymity, as they require senders to identify themselves to the platform.

FACTS [7] improves upon traceback both by finding only the original source, as in our latter construction and source tracking, and also with threshold reporting; FACTS will only allow a message to be traced after it has been reported by a sufficiently large number of users. This is a step towards preventing the abuse of tracing systems by focusing them on the large-scale misinformation they are meant for. However, FACTS is not fully compatible with anonymous messaging systems either. While FACTS could theoretically function on top of sealed sender, it requires that senders request a token and signature from the server prior to sending their message, making anonymity guarantees fragile at best.

Hecate [6] aims to provide tracing within an anonymous system as we do, though they make different trade-offs. Hecate is derived from Asymmetric Message Franking [11] and so achieves deniability where we do not. However, they achieve tracing through each user generating tokens ahead of time with the moderator, one token consumed with each message sent makes them identifiable to the moderator when reported. This carries a key issue: the tokens cannot be generated directly before use or the anonymity guarantees are significantly weakened, similar to [7]. This means users who leave their phones off, or simply send large volumes of messages at once, are not getting the full anonymity guarantee (Table 1).

Orca [12] also works towards accountability in metadata private messaging systems, approached from the opposite end; where we focus on identifying the original source of forwarded messages, ORCA focuses on more personal-scale issues, enabling users to block people harassing them directly without needing moderator intervention. Orca is a complement to our own work; it allows users to stop harassment directly without needing the intermediary of the platform, while keeping the platform as a whole clean is left to systems like ours.

**Ethics of Source Tracing.** The ethics of moderation systems will always be a tricky topic. If used without care they can be abused to harass a userbase or silence criticism, and revealing anonymous identities could lead to legal consequences. At the same time, they have undeniable utility in dealing with toxic behavior. We recommend extensive care in using these systems, and would generally not recommend using our first construction; while it is an important theoretical stepping stone, it reveals more information than we are comfortable with. Further discussion on ethics is present in the full version [4].

## 2    Definitions and Security Models

Our goal is to create a variant of the traceback system that can function within an Anonymous messaging system and avoid compromising that Anonymity.

**Cryptographic Primitives.** We will use standard cryptographic tools including symmetric key encryption, hash functions, digital signatures and collision resistant pseudorandom functions (which is a pseudorandom function with an extra collision resistance property taking both the key and PRF input as function input, see [13]). The collision resistant PRF function will be referred to as $F$, but we omit further details due to the page limit.

**The Messaging System.** For the most part we treat the underlying E2EE Messaging system our systems are built on top of as a black box, but there are a few key assumptions we make about that system:

- There exists a PKI (Public Key Infrastructure) system in place, such that each user $U$ has an associated public key and private key, as well as a certificate $cert_U$ binding their public key to their identity. We make use of these long-term keys as $LTPK_U$ and $LTSK_U$, to sign and verify our primary digital signature and also as an identifier.
- That for anonymous messages, analogous to Signal's Sealed Sender, the sender includes in their encrypted message a certificate $cert_{U_s}$ for recipient to verify their identity, we input it to our RecMsg function in our first two constructions as a confirmation that we and the underlying platform are in agreement on the identity of the sender.

**Notations in Anonymous Traceback.** Now the following will explain notation for various elements within the constructions:

- **Users** are denoted by $U_i$, where $i$ is an identification number unique to that user. $U_s$ and $U_r$ indicate the user sending and receiving a message respectively.
- $mid$ is the **message id** value, it is generated by the PRF and used as a key to store trace information in the platform's database.

- $tt_s$, $tt_r$, and $tt_p$ represent the **tracing tags** for the sender, receiver, and platform respectively. They contain each party's view of the trace information. When moving to the split server construction, $tt_p$ is split into $tt_{ms}$ and $tt_{ts}$ for the message server and tracing server respectively.
- $C_K, C_{PK}, C_{sig}$ are the **ciphertexts** containing a **tracing key, long-term public key**, and **signature** respectively.
- $k_i$ represents the (symmetric) tracing key for the $i$'th message in a trace, and $\hat{k}_i$ is the hashed version, to use as the PRF key.
- $DB$ is the **database** of path tracing information, stored as a key: value system with each entry structured as $(mid : C_K, C_{PK}, C_{sig}, ts)$.
- $pk_{eph}$ and $sk_{eph}$ are **asymmetric keys** generated for an **ephemeral signature** used in the second construction, with $sig_{eph}$ representing that signature.
- $MDB$ and $TDB$ are the two halves of the $DB$ **database**, used when the servers are split for the Message Server and Tracing Server respectively. $MDB$ entries are structured $(mid : C_{PK}, C_{sig}, ts, pk_{eph}, sig_{eph})$ and $TDB$ entries are structured $(mid : C_k, pk_{eph})$.

## 2.1 Anonymous Traceback Syntax

The basic structure of an anonymous traceback scheme is similar to that of the original traceback schemes [13], consisting of the following components:

**TagGen**$(U_s, m, td_g) \rightarrow k, tt_s$: This algorithm generates the tracing key $k$ and the tracing tag $tt_s$. The input $td_g$ is a catch-all for the data relevant to tracing necessary for tag generation, which varies by construction but always includes the previous tracing key $k_{prev}$ if available. When delivering the message, $k$ is encrypted alongside the message plaintext $m$ for the recipient to access. Compared to the original, we remove the requirement of providing the recipient's identity as we want to keep as few identities involved in each operation as possible.

**Svr-Process**$(st_{plat}, tt_s, U_r) \rightarrow (mid, tt_p), tt_r$: This protocol is used to verify incoming tracing information from a sender $(tt_s)$ prior to delivering the message and logs information into the platform's state $st_{plat}$. The output comes in two parts: first the Message ID $mid$ and platform tracing information $tt_p$, typically used to update the database(s) with $mid$ as the key pointing to $tt_p$, and second the tracing information that is passed on to the recipient, $tt_r$, which they use for their own verification in **RecMsg**.

**RecMsg**$(k, U_s, U_r, m, tt_r) \rightarrow td_r$: The recipient runs this algorithm to verify the tag $tt_r$ they receive along with the message $m$, prior to accepting the message. The output catch-all $td_r$ includes cryptographic data identifying the message, for use in submitting a tracing request later. Usually, for **RecMsg** $td$ is simply $k$. In our constructions, rather than just the identity $U_s$, we typically use that user's PKI certificate, as is delivered with messages in Sealed Sender.

**Svr-Trace**$(st_{plat}, m, k, td_t) \rightarrow trace$: The protocol that performs the actual tracing operations, utilizing a message $m$, associated key $k$, the platform's state and additional data represented as $td_t$. The result, *trace*, varies by construction in what information it reveals, but the minimum requirement is enough information to penalize the original source of the message.

One change worth noting is that we remove the **NewMsg** algorithm here, combining its functionality into **TagGen** for readability; while useful as an abstraction in security games, in practice it is only called immediately prior to calling **TagGen** with all of its output. Having **TagGen** check the $td$ for a previous key and generate one if absent simplifies things. **Svr-Process** and **Svr-Trace** are now protocols to be executed by different components of a platform working in concert. We take full advantage of this in our latter two constructions by splitting the server into two halves, a Message Server and Tracing Server, each with their own database.

## 2.2  Security Model

Our overall goals are to maintain the ability of tracing to find the original source of the message, and at the same time preserve as much anonymity as possible. This leads to the following properties.

**Anonymity.** Retaining anonymity despite the presence of a tracing system is the primary goal of this paper, so we aim to make these definitions as strong as possible. Origin Anonymity defines anonymity for the original source of a specific message, while Forwarder Anonymity defines anonymity for those who forward a different message. Due to lack of space, we briefly explain the high-level intuitions, detailed security games can be found in the full version [4], represented in the *OriginAnon* and *ForwarderAnon* games respectively. In addition, our constructions achieve different degrees of anonymity for these two groups, represented by changing oracles: *post-trace anonymity* is the preferred result, where even after a message is traced identities remain hidden, while *pre-trace anoynmity* maintains anonymity until a trace is made (more explanations below).

We give the adversary complete control outside of the context of the challenge message; able to cause message sends, traces, and read from the database both before and after the challenge message is sent. For the challenge, the adversary chooses the message sent, the recipient user, and in *ForwarderAnon* they even choose the initial sender of the message. Only at the time of message delivery must the two possible senders/forwarders and the recipient be honest, and otherwise the adversary has free reign to corrupt. This also means our anonymity definitions have forward and backward security; unlimited corruptions are allowed both before and after the challenge message, it is only tracing the message that is disallowed, and only for pre-trace anonymity.

They are formulated by allowing the adversary access to multiple oracles: **Send**, to send or forward messages, **Trace**, to perform traces, and **DB** to query the server's database. The primary differences between pre-trace and post-trace anonymity are that for pre-trace anonymity the challenge message and its forwards are flagged so the tracing oracle will refuse to trace them, while post-trace anonymity oracles have no such restriction. In addition, for anonymous source traceback the **DB** oracle gives access to only the message server's database, since the two servers cannot collude. We choose the message server's database as it is the more useful of the two, containing the encrypted identity information.

It is worth noting that these properties apply on a message-by-message basis. As none of the tracing information (aside from the signature, which is encrypted) derives from identity or is re-used, an originator whose message is traced in a system that guarantees only pre-trace anoynmity loses anonymity for that specific message, but any other messages they have sent or will send in the future remain anonymous until and unless those specific messages are traced.

*Limitations of Sender Anonymity.* We note that there is an inherent limitation to sender anonymity. As the recipient's identity is known, a curious server could choose to log each recipient and associate them to the message IDs that they receive. This may reveal the identity of the 'first' recipient of each message that is traced, the one who received it from the originator. This leakage cannot be avoided and so excluded in our models.

However, should the system be built on top of a messaging service that has both sender and receiver anonymity, this leak would disappear. No modification of our constructions is needed, as we at no point require the recipient's identity. While there is a decent amount of evidence that Signal would not take advantage of this leak [10], the same cannot be said of all messaging services. In the long run it would be best to build anonymous traceback on top of systems with stronger anonymity guarantees to avoid this leak.

**Anonymous Trace Unforgeability.** We borrow the basic structure from trace unforgeability in [13], but careful modifications are needed to accommodate the new complications of introducing *anonymity*, and the adversary's additional capabilities. This property ensures that when a trace is performed, an honest user who (a) is not the original source of the message and (b) did not deliberately partition the trace, cannot be framed. We consider the adversary here to be any group of colluding users; as the point of tracing functionality is to assist the platform in moderation we assume the platform will follow our algorithm. In addition, if the platform wants to punish a user they have the authority to do so regardless of a tracing result. Due to page limit, we explain the high-level idea here, for detailed security games, we refer to the full version [4].

Overall, the adversary is allowed to create a database state through the oracles available to them, and then perform a trace of their choosing. They succeed if any of four (two in the case of anonymous source traceback) possible failure conditions arise in that trace: Either a completely empty trace result, an honest user is misidentified as the original source, the reporter never received the message they are reporting, or an honest user is misidentified as a forwarder.

The **Send** and **SendMal** oracles allow causing honest and dishonest users to send messages, respectively. **SendMal** in particular has been expanded upon, and allows further deviation from the protocol and usage of adversarially chosen values where **Send** behaves honestly. The **NewMsg** oracle allows honestly generating information for a new 'original' message, and is required by the honest **Send** oracle when authoring a new message.

We also add the **ClearDB** oracle to allow an attacker to simulate waiting for the database sliding window to advance, clearing the trace data, to allow attempting delayed replay attacks.

As the adversary succeeds when the game returns true, the advantage expression for *anonymous trace unforgeability* given a specific construction TB is:

$$\mathbf{Adv}_{TB}^{AnonTrUNF}(\mathcal{A}) = Pr[AnonTrUNF_{TB}^{A} \Rightarrow true]$$

We remark that *Trace Partitioning* is a potential attack where a malicious forwarder purposefully breaks the tracing information to appear to be the original sender themselves. Similar to the original [13] we cannot actually prevent this from happening; even if we were to include text matching software to convert copy & paste into forwards (which likely should be done to prevent the non-tech-savvy from accidentally partitioning a trace by missing the forward button or another similar misunderstanding), this would not stop those who modify their client software from having the capability to break the path and become a 'new' originator. Still, even if someone does this, the end result of a trace will still be a bad actor: the one who deliberately broke the path to the originator. Regardless of which occurs, a single bad actor will be removed from the platform, so while imperfect this still allows traceback to fulfill its purpose.

**Trace Confidentiality.** A property we carry over from [13] that aims to keep message path information hidden from both the user and the platform until and unless a trace is performed. It can be split into two separate properties: *platform trace confidentiality* and *user trace confidentiality*, defining the ability to hide information from the Platform (prior to tracing) and Users respectively.

The goal is simply to keep information about a message's path hidden unless that message is being traced. In practice this comes down to ensuring that from both the user's and platform's view it is impossible to tell whether a given message is a forward or new; if it is not even known whether a message is a forward to begin with, it is of course impossible to determine information such as previous forwarders or the original sender.

We inherit this property from [13] largely unchanged, including the security games; the adversary is given access to tracing information appropriate to either the platform or a receiving user, and succeeds if able to distinguish between a newly authored message (or random string) and a forwarded message.

## 3    Warm-Up: Anonymous Path Traceback

The original traceback [13] algorithm has a fairly simple core. When messages are sent, a message ID (*mid*) is generated via the PRF F using a freshly generated symmetric key, $k$. When delivering a message the server uses *mid* as a key to store tracing metadata: sender and receiver identities and an encryption of the previous key if forwarded (garbage if an originator). Later a report can be made to the server by sending the plaintext and key, used to generate a $mid$ value. This $mid$ is looked up, the previous key decrypted, used to generate a new $mid$, and so on. When a lookup fails, a garbage previous key was used, and so the message's originator has been found.

Attempting to introduce anonymity to this system quickly creates issues, however. The original system relies heavily on communications being authenticated; should the sender not authenticate to the server, there is no way to ensure that the information on the sender is correct. The need to authenticate anonymously reminds us of anonymous credentials, but while that would work fine to verify that the sender is "allowed to message", it would not ensure that the identity could be accurately revealed later during the tracing procedure. Adding a zero knowledge proof to be verified by the platform could ensure a message would not be sent without a guarantee that a valid signature existed matching the identity that will be recovered later. However, this solution had a significant drawback: compared to secure messaging systems that support a massive scale of users, it was significantly less efficient. We strive for an extremely *simple* solution with minimal overhead.

A key observation of the trust model used for traceback provided our solution - the idea of partitioning a trace. In traceback, the linked-list nature of the tracing information means that a dishonest user can break the connection to previous messages at any time, essentially choosing to become the new "original source" and take responsibility for a message they forward. This is referred to as "partitioning the trace", and is an inherent part of traceback's security model; they cannot be stopped from taking the blame if they choose but either way a bad actor is detected. This ties in nicely with one of the properties of an anonymous communication system: while the server has no information on the sender's identity, the receiver knows it. Therefore, we may pass the responsibility (which is lightweight) to check that the tracing information corresponds to the correct person to the recipient.

The end result of this is our addition of a digital signature. We assume the underlying messaging system already makes use of a PKI, and so use the existing long term keys to sign the tracing information to be certain the sender's identity is accurate. We sign on $mid$, the encryption of the previous tracing key from original traceback ($C_K$), as well as an encryption of the public key ($C_{PK}$) used both to verify the signature and identify the sender. Passing the signature along in the clear creates a problem of its own: the server could brute-force attempt to verify the signature with all known public keys to identify the sender, so it is encrypted as well, to be verified by the server only during tracing. Meanwhile, the recipient is expected to verify the signature, and reject messages if they fail. If they accept a bad signature, when it fails to verify the server will know the recipient accepted an untraceable message.

However, there is one subtle issue remaining. While in theory we can treat the database of tracing information as infinite, in practice that is unsustainable. [13] recommends using a sliding window, where database entries are removed after a certain period of time. However, that leaves recipients with valid tags and signatures that will no longer be rejected for duplicate $mid$. These could be used to recreate that message without the previous entries, framing the sender as the originator of the message's second life even if they only forwarded the original. Thankfully, the solution to this Delayed Replay Attack could be again simple: by adding a timestamp to the values signed on and checking for recentness when the server delivers a message, this exploit is closed off.

## 3.1   Construction Details

We follow the same general structure here as the original path traceback construction [13], creating a database of trace information keyed by a unique message id value generated via a collision resistant PRF.

**TagGen**$(U_s, m, k_{prev}, LTSK_{U_s}) \rightarrow (k_i, tt_s, sig)$:
1. Randomly generate a new tracing key $k_i$. If no $k_{prev}$ is provided, also generate a false previous key, for a new message.
2. Generate the timestamp $ts$.
3. Use a hash to generate $\tilde{k}_i$ from $k_i$, to separate the key used for the PRF F from the key used in encryption.
4. Calculate the message ID, $mid$, as $F_{\tilde{k}_i}(m)$.
5. Using $k_i$, encrypt $k_{prev}$ and the sender's long term public key $LTPK_{U_s}$ as $C_K$ and $C_{PK}$ respectively.
6. Using $LTSK_{U_s}$, generate a digital signature, $sig$, on the combined information $(mid, C_K, C_{PK}, ts)$.
7. Encrypt $sig$ using $k_i$ as $C_{sig}$.
8. Create the tracing tag $tt_s$ as $(mid, C_K, C_{PK}, ts, C_{Sig})$, to be delivered to the server when sending the associated message. (The tracing key $k_i$ is encrypted with the message, to be delivered to the recipient only.)

**Svr-Process**$(DB, U_r, tt_s) \rightarrow ((mid, tt_p), tt_r)$:
1. Check the database $DB$ for an existing entry under $mid$. If one exists, reject the message.
2. Check that the timestamp is recent, if not reject the message.
3. Add the current tracing information to $DB$, with $mid$ as the key value.
4. Copy $tt_s$ to create the tracing tag for the recipient, $tt_r$.

**RecMsg**$(k_i, cert_{U_s}, U_r, m, tt_r) \rightarrow k_i$:
1. Verify that the $mid$ in $tt_r$ can be generated using the received message $m$ and tracing key $k_i$ with the PRF. If not reject the message.
2. Decrypt $C_{PK}$ and verify that the public key $LTPK_{U_S}$ matches the sending user's certificate, $cert_{U_s}$. If not reject the message.
3. Decrypt and verify the signature within $C_{sig}$ using the information from $tt_r$, if verification fails reject the message.
4. If all verification succeeds, display the message. Output $k_i$ can be used to report the message for tracing.

**Svr-Trace**$(DB, U, m, k) \rightarrow Tr$:
1. Initialize a list $Tr$ of tracing information, beginning with the reporter.

2. Use the supplied $m$ and $k$ to generate $mid = \mathsf{F}_{\tilde{k}}(m)$.
3. Look up the generated $mid$ within $DB$, and retrieve the relevant tracing information. If the lookup fails, the trace has concluded.
4. Decrypt $C_{PK}$ to identify the sender with $LTPK_{U_s}$.
5. Decrypt $sig$ from $C_{sig}$ and verify, if it fails the trace has concluded.
6. Add the user's identity $U_s$ and message ID $mid$ to $Tr$.
7. Decrypt $C_K$ to retrieve the next tracing key, replacing $k$, and calculate a new $mid$ using the new $k$ and the reported message $m$.
8. Repeat steps 3–7 until a lookup fails (indicating the original sender) or a signature fails to verify (indicating a bad signature was knowingly accepted). Tr will now contain the user identities and associated $mid$ values (for reference) in reverse order.

**Security Analysis.** Our Anonymous Path Traceback construction achieves trace confidentiality, anonymous trace unforgeability, and pre-trace anonymity for both originators and forwarders of a given message. Proof sketches are in the appendix, the complete proofs are left to the full version [4].

## 4   Anonymous Source Traceback

Path traceback is inherently limited when our goals include maintaining as much anonymity as possible within the system, so with the basics ironed out we turn towards preserving the anonymity of the links along the chain. This is called source traceback, which reveals *only* the original source's identity.

The primary obstacle to achieving source traceback based on our existing construction is the structure of our database itself. As we follow the trail of message IDs, at each and every step we verify the signature at that entry, revealing the identity of the person who sent or forwarded it. This is unavoidable with a step-by-step method and identity information present.

We solve this by splitting the server in half, passing the identity-related information to a message server that delivers the messages and giving necessary tracing information to a tracing server which follows the chain of $mid$ evaluations and lookups to its end. When tracing, the tracing server passes its result along to the message server, who can then verify the signature and learn the identity. Splitting the database is the only option to continue with the current structure of the system, where traces are made one step at a time. There has to be information in the trace capable of revealing the user's identity, and no real way to prevent the platform from recovering it when performing a trace, since it is necessary to find the source.

*Technical Challenges:* There are challenges in building an *extremely simple* two-party protocol for source traceback in our split server model. The main challenge is how to deal with a failed signature verification. The message server can only verify the signature of the final result, so what happens if that fails? It must go back to the tracing server for more information. So the tracing server must retain information on its most recent traces and respond to the message server when it needs help. However, this creates another problem: what is stopping the message server from simply asking for all the information whether they need it or not, reverting to path traceback? Assuming the tracing server is unwilling to collude with the message server, we can solve this issue by introducing an extra signature. This signature, made using ephemeral one-use keys to sign the tracing data entry that the message server handles, can be used to prove to the tracing server that the failed signature justifying its request is legitimate.

Additionally, the two servers need to ensure that the tracing information for any message is present on both servers; the opposite half of the tracing information must be guaranteed to exist on the other server. This manifests in the form of a small amount of communication to allow the message server to reject messages that have no corresponding information in the tracing server. Aside from this, the split also creates a theoretical issue; no longer can the encryption of the previous key, $C_K$, be verified, which opened a few interesting questions that are answered in the full version's [4] security proof.

In this way we can maintain the efficiency and the simplicity of the first construction while achieving anonymity for all but the reporter and the "source", if the underlying messaging system's anonymity is strong enough. With only sender anonymity as mentioned before we leak only the first recipient's identity.

*Benefits and Instantiations of Split Servers:* The split server construction does have benefits of its own as well. For example, prior to this construction a user colluding with someone who has access to the server's database could reveal an entire forwarding path; in essence making a report that will definitely result in a trace. With the message server and tracing server as distinct entities this collusion becomes more difficult. Access to just the tracing server's database cannot reveal identities, while the message server's database would reveal the identity of the immediate sender, but tracing to the originator would be impossible. In addition, we can allow more privacy to originators: the tracing server learns only the message, not their identity, and the message server learns only the identity without the message. Passing the message to the message server is a trivial change that does not affect any of the security properties, but it is an extra layer of privacy available due to the split.

As for instantiation, there are several possible options for the two non-colluding servers needed to maintain our anonymity properties, including trusted hardware on the messaging server, or having one server run by an independent entity such as an NGO or non-profit. We also remark that the other relevant solution, Hecate [6], implicitly requires a similar structure; while their moderator and server can technically be separate, doing so would reduce their anonymity guarantee for token-less originators similar to [7].

## 4.1  Construction Details

Compared to the anonymous path traceback construction, while we add an amount of communication overhead, the primary effect is splitting the server-side work between the message server and the tracing server.

Where originally a database entry contained a $mid$ as a key pointing to $C_K, C_{cert}, C_{sig}, k_T$, and the recipient's identity, these are now split. The tracing server's database contains only the information necessary to follow a chain of entries, $mid$ and $C_K$, while as the message server delivers the message to the recipient, its database carries information related to the signature, $mid, C_{cert}, C_{sig}, ts$, and $k_T$. In addition to splitting the old information, both servers store the new ephemeral public key, $pk_{eph}$, and the message server stores the signature it verifies, $sig_{eph}$. One new wrinkle is that, as the message server's database no longer contains $C_K$, it can no longer be signed on by the signature. This will be covered in more detail in the security proofs, but during analysis it will be shown that $C_K$ actually does not need to be verified by the signature.

The client-side algorithms contain only minor modifications:

**TagGen**$(U_s, m, k_p rev, LTSK_{U_s}) \rightarrow (k_i, tt_{ms}, tt_{ts}, sig)$:
1. Follow steps 1–7 from the Anonymous Path Traceback version of TagGen.
2. Generate an ephemeral asymmetric key pair $pk_{eph}$ and $sk_{eph}$.
3. Generate $sig_{eph}$ by signing on $(mid, C_{PK}, ts, C_{sig})$ with $sk_{eph}$.
4. Create the message server's tracing tag $tt_{ms}$ as $(mid, C_{PK}, ts, C_{Sig}, pk_{eph}, sig_{eph})$, and the tracing server's tracing tag $tt_{ts}$ as $(mid, C_K, pk_{eph})$.

**RecMsg**$(k_i, cert_{U_s}, U_r, m, tt_r) \rightarrow k_i$:
1. Act as Anonymous Path Traceback's RecMsg. The only difference is removing $C_K$ from the signature verification.

The server-side algorithms however, have split into two, and add **TSvr-Req**, to handle the message server's requests for additional information:

**TSvr-Process**$(TDB, tt_{ts}) \rightarrow mid$:
1. Check the database $TDB$ for an existing entry under $mid$. If one exists, reject the message.
2. Add the information within $tt_{ts}$ to $TDB$, with $mid$ as the key.
3. Pass $mid$ along to the message server to notify that the tracing server's half of the tracing data has been received for that message.

**MSvr-Process**$(MDB, U_r, tt_{ms})$:
1. Check the database $MDB$ for an existing entry under $mid$. If one exists, reject the message.
2. Check that the timestamp $ts$ is recent. If not reject the message.
3. Verify $sig_{eph}$, reject the message if this fails.
4. Add the information within $tt_{ms}$ to $MDB$, with $mid$ as the key.
5. Create the tracing tag $tt_r$ as $(mid, C_{PK}, ts, C_{Sig})$, for the recipient.

**TSvr-Trace**$(TDB, TLOG, m, k) \rightarrow (mid, k, tid)$:
1. Initialize a list $Tr$ of tracing information.
2. Use the supplied $m$ and $k$ to generate $mid = F_{\tilde{k}}(m)$.
3. Look up the generated $mid$ within $TDB$, and retrieve the tracing information. If the lookup fails, the trace has concluded.
4. Add the $mid$ and associated key $k$ to $Tr$.
5. Decrypt $C_K$ to retrieve the next tracing key, replacing $k$, and calculate a new $mid$ using the new $k$ and the reported message $m$.

6. Repeat steps 3–5 until a lookup fails. Tr will now contain the $mid$ values and associated keys of the message chain in reverse order.
7. Store the full trace information $Tr$ in $TLOG$ to be referenced later if needed, generating a trace ID $tid$ as the key.
8. Return the end result $mid$ and key to the message server along with $tid$.

**MSvr-Trace**$(MDB, mid, k, tid) \rightarrow U_s$:

1. Look up the provided $mid$ value in $MDB$, then decrypt $sig$ from the associated $C_{sig}$ and verify.
2. If the signature fails to verify, request the next $mid$ in the trace from the tracing server using TSvr-Req, and repeat step 1.
3. When the signature verifies, either the original source or a user who purposely accepted a bad signature has been identified.

**TSvr-Req**$(TDB, TLOG, mid, k, tid, tt_{ms}) \rightarrow (mid, k_{prev}, tid)$:

1. Look up the provided $mid$ value in $TDB$ and verify that the provided $tt_{ms}$ matches, $sig_{eph}$ verifies, and $sig$ within $C_{sig}$ does not verify to prove the message server requires additional information. If this fails, reject the request.
2. Look up the provided $tid$ in $TLOG$, and return the next $mid$ value in the trace to the message server.

**Security Analysis.** Our Anonymous Source Traceback construction achieves trace confidentiality from both user and platform, anonymous trace unforgeability, pre-trace anonymity for message originators, and post-trace anonymity for message forwarders; leaving forwarders unknown even after a successful trace of a message they forwarded. For further details and proof sketches see the appendix, the complete proofs are left to the full version [4].

# 5   Implementation and Performance

Our implementation focused on testing the cryptographic overhead our constructions cause on the clients and servers of an E2EE system. The implementation was programmed in C, using the libsodium cryptographic libary. While there does exist an implementation of the original traceback [13], one of its dependencies no longer exists and the successor has a different API, rendering the original implementation immeasurable, so we started from scratch. For the hash function H and PRF F, we use the Blake2b algorithm, encryption uses the XChaCha20 algorithm, for signatures we used EdDSA. We also make use of the libsignal-client general purpose Signal library as a point of comparison; its session and sealed sender benchmarks can estimate the overhead of the double-ratchet and sealed sender. All tests were run on an Intel i7-11800H processor with turbo disabled, meaning the processor was locked to its base clock speed of 2.3 Ghz.

**Table 2.** Average cryptographic overhead for client-side. In order: baseline Signal overhead, then additional overhead from Sealed Sender, then further additional overhead from [13] or from our own constructions. Compared to Hecate [6], who tested with a stronger processor, our anonymous source traceback construction's sending overhead is comparable to their combined token generation and sending overhead, with our recipient overhead much lower.

|                  | Signal  | Sealed sender | [13]     | Anon path | Anon source |
|------------------|---------|---------------|----------|-----------|-------------|
| Sending ($\mu s$)   | 7.0958  | 198.69        | +1.569   | +34.7775  | +96.5644    |
| Receiving ($\mu s$) | 204.15  | 174.42        | +0.6075  | +80.992   | +80.992     |

**Performance Results.** Looking at the client-side overhead in Table 2, there is obviously an overhead with our constructions compared to the non-anonymous traceback [13], however even in the worst case we remain under 1 ms on average. Compared to the overhead Signal users already face, this is definitely feasible.

Server-side processing overhead is workable as well. In our anonymous path traceback construction we use no additional cryptography, so we only see an increase in overhead when verifying the ephemeral key signature in our anonymous source traceback construction, which costs on average 79.82 μs. While this may sound like a large performance hit compared to no cryptographic overhead at all, on average it can be calculated 12,528 times in a second. Given that we are testing with a single thread on a CPU locked to its base clock speed, in a data center this number will scale to a much higher figure.

Overhead during tracing is also worth discussing. In anonymous path traceback every signature in a trace must be verified so overhead scales directly with the length of the trace (approx. 81.919463 μs per forward). In anonymous source traceback only the original's overhead occurs per forward (approx. 1.338296 μs) while signature verifications are conditional; only if the message server's initial verification fails must the tracing server and message server perform further verifications, costing approximately 80.552661 μs to the message server and 160.840751 μs to the tracing server per bad signature. Most traces will not contain many bad signatures, so on average there should be much less overhead in anonymous path traceback. Though it is worth considering the possibility of purposefully chaining garbage signatures as a denial of service attack.

To examine our space efficiency we use the same estimation as [13]: a messaging service that uses a 1-month window and sees 1 billion messages per day. In anonymous path traceback a database entry is 136 bytes, leading to a requirement of ≈4.08 TB, while for anonymous source traceback entries in the tracing database are 96 bytes, requiring ≈2.88 TB, and message database entries are 232 bytes, requiring ≈6.96 TB. Compared to the original's figures [13] of ≈600 GB for path traceback and ≈2 TB for tree traceback, we do take up quite a bit more space. However, while the results are not exciting, they are still likely feasible for a large service, and our implementation uses conservatively high key sizes, so there's room to reduce while maintaining security.

**Implementation Concerns.** One thing the original [13] leaves unexamined is the sliding window approach they recommend for databases when implementing their system. This puts a cap on storage costs, but it creates a surprising number of problems in the process. Previously discussed in more detail is the delayed replay attack, though that is only an issue due to anonymity.

A general issue for traceback-style systems that use a sliding window is behavior when a message trace is called for after the original source has timed out of the database. A lookup failure indicates that the original source has been found, but if lookup fails because an entry no longer exists, the trace could penalize the wrong person. Using a sliding window thus requires care. At the very least, a 2-part window that first flags an entry as timed out, then deletes after a second time window would avoid misattribution of blame, though the trace still would not find the source.

It is worth considering preventing forwards client-side after the window has passed, but this may do more harm than good. The likelihood of a user just copy-pasting is high, and the alternative of a confirmation prompt warning that they will be held responsible may not prevent it. Overall, the limitations of the sliding window should be kept in mind.

**Acknowledgements.** The authors were partially supported by NSF CNS #1801491. Qiang is also partially supported by gifts from Ethereum Foundation, Protocol Labs, Stellar Foundation, and Algorand Foundation.

# 6    Proof Sketches

## 6.1    Anonymous Path Traceback

**Trace Confidentiality.** For *trace confidentiality*, both user and platform, we can refer back to [13] for their original proofs, as we add no additional information that could be used to distinguish forwarded messages from original messages. This is fairly straightforward to see, while we add (depending on the system), a Signature, Timestamp, and/or Anonymous Blacklisting Authentication Token, these components do not vary between original or forwarded messages. The only difference remains the value of the previous key encrypted as $C_K$, just as it was in the original Traceback paper, and so we can inherit their security here.

**Theorem 1.** *With APT as the anonymous path traceback scheme defined in Sect. 3.1: For any AnonTrUNF adversary $\mathcal{A}$, there are corresponding adversaries $\mathcal{B}$ and $\mathcal{C}$ running in the same time as $\mathcal{A}$ such that:*

$$\mathbf{Adv}_{APT}^{AnonTrUNF}(\mathcal{A}) \leq \mathbf{Adv}_F^{cr}(\mathcal{B}) + \mathbf{Adv}_{Sig}^{forge}(\mathcal{C})$$

*For any PreAnon adversary $\mathcal{A}$, there is a corresponding adversary $\mathcal{B}$ running in the same time as $\mathcal{A}$ such that:*

$$\mathbf{Adv}_{APT}^{PreAnon}(\mathcal{A}) \leq \mathbf{Adv}_{ENC}^{cpa}(\mathcal{B})$$

**Trace Unforgeability.** As seen in Theorem 1, the adversary's advantage against *anonymous trace unforgeability* is a sum of the advantage against the PRF's collision resistance and the advantage for forging a signature. This means their advantage should be negligible, as otherwise the probability of breaking one of the two secure building block schemes would be non-negligible.

**Proof Sketch.** For *anonymous trace unforgeability*, the same four failure cases still form the basis of the proof:

- Case 1: An empty trace.
- Case 2: The identified honest original sender never sent the message.
- Case 3: The reporter never received the message they reported.
- Case 4: An honest user identified as a forwarder did not forward the message.

However, we must also account for the adversary's additional capabilities; specifically, it is no longer guaranteed that the identity stored matches the identity of the user who actually sent the message. To model this the **SendMal** Oracle now allows much more freedom to the adversary. In addition, we model the possibility of a change in the sliding window with the **ClearDB** oracle.

To account for the adversary's new capabilities we add a game transition; **SendMal** sets *BadSend* when the sender identity does not match the tag. This separates out the situations where the original traceback security proof's assumptions fail. Regardless of why the identities do not match, for the message to have been accepted means a signature must have been forged.

The remaining failure cases are handled as they are in the original [13] proof, with one exception. Cases 1 and 3 are impossible because they require an honest user to report a message they never received; the **Send** and **SendMal** oracles both set WasRec. Case 2, $U_j$ falsely identified as original source for a message they did not send, cannot happen in absence of signature forgeries due to PRF collision resistance: a trace for a different plaintext or key must result in the same *mid* as a different message $U_j$ sent.

Case 4 is similar to Case 2, $U_j$ is falsely identified as a forwarder, and in absence of signature forgery this also requires a PRF collision. Either in the exact same manner as Case 2, or in a special case where $U_j$ is actually the original source. In the original proof this is designated "problematic" and several game transitions are used to isolate it, but on second inspection this is still the result of a PRF collision between the plaintext and fake $k_{prev}$ with some unrelated message and key.

**Pre-trace Anonymity.** Anonymous path traceback aims for *pre-trace anonymity* for both the originators and forwarders of its messages, therefore in both cases the **Send** oracle tracks forwards of the challenge message and **Trace** oracles disallow tracing those messages.

**Proof Sketch.** For both *OriginAnon* and *ForwarderAnon* the proofs are nearly identical. In both cases security is guaranteed by encryption; the only useful information the adversary has is the server's view of the challenge messages.

When looking at that view, all relevant information is encrypted, so breaking encryption is necessary to learn the sender's identity. There is one extra wrinkle for *ForwarderAnon*; the adversary can choose the key that will be encrypted by $U_b$ as their $C_K$ value, which the adversary has access to through the **DB** oracle. However, attempting to recover the key in this way corresponds to a chosen plaintext attack, which would also break the encryption's security.

## 6.2   Anonymous Source Traceback

**Theorem 2.** *With AST as the anonymous source traceback scheme defined in Sect. 4.1: For any AnonTrUNF adversary $\mathcal{A}$, there are corresponding adversaries $\mathcal{B}$ and $\mathcal{C}$ running in the same time as $\mathcal{A}$ such that:*

$$\mathbf{Adv}_{AST}^{AnonTrUNF}(\mathcal{A}) \leq \mathbf{Adv}_F^{cr}(\mathcal{B}) + \mathbf{Adv}_{Sig}^{forge}(\mathcal{C})$$

*For any FPostAnon adversary $\mathcal{A}$, there are corresponding adversaries $\mathcal{B}$ and $\mathcal{C}$ running in the same time as $\mathcal{A}$ such that:*

$$\mathbf{Adv}_{AST}^{FPostAnon}(\mathcal{A}) \leq \mathbf{Adv}_{ENC}^{cpa}(\mathcal{B}) + \mathbf{Adv}_{Sig}^{forge}(\mathcal{C})$$

**Originator Pre-trace Anonymity.** This aims for *pre-trace anonymity* for originators, so as in path traceback, the **Send** oracle tracks forwards of the challenge message and **Trace** oracles disallow tracing those messages.

**Proof Sketch.** As the amount of information in the hands of the adversary has slightly shrunk as compared to anonymous path traceback, things remain largely the same as the previous *pre-trace anonymity* proof.

Just as before, the only useful things here are $C_{PK}$ and $C_{sig}$, which must be decrypted to utilize, and whose key is unavailable and generated independent of any other information. Therefore, breaking the encryption remains necessary.

**Theorem 3.** *With AST as the Anonymous Source Traceback scheme defined in Sect. 4.1, for any OPreAnon adversary $\mathcal{A}$, there is a corresponding adversary $\mathcal{B}$ running in the same time as $A$ such that:*

$$\mathbf{Adv}_{AST}^{OPreAnon}(\mathcal{A}) \leq \mathbf{Adv}_{ENC}^{cpa}(\mathcal{B})$$

**Forwarder Post-trace Anonymity.** Anonymous source traceback aims to give forwarders *post-trace anonymity*, so unlike the previous anonymity definitions, the **Send** and **Trace** oracles do not limit tracing in any way. However, to account for the new avenue the message server has in gathering information, we also add the **Request** oracle to allow querying the tracing server.

**Proof Sketch.** The new **Request** oracle allows the adversary to attempt to gain information on forwarders of a message after a trace is complete, however to do so would require forging the ephemerally keyed signature meant to ensure the Message Server's honesty. We use a game transition to isolate this possibility. Outside of that new possibility, the adversary cannot learn path information from the Tracing Server. While we now allow tracing messages downstream from the forwarder whose identity we want to protect, this gives no real advantage without the path information, so breaking encryption is still required to learn the forwarder's identity.

**Anonymous Trace Unforgeability.** The primary difference from the anonymous path traceback proof is that no tracing information can be verified at the time of tracing aside from the final result's. For most of that information, there is no real benefit to providing bad entries; the signature will fail to verify and honest recipients will drop the message. The one interesting case is $C_K$, which is no longer included in the signature. If $C_K$ could be chosen properly, it would redirect a trace in a completely different direction, but that still requires violating the collision resistance property of the PRF. As we no longer have to worry about the full message path remaining accurate, only two failure conditions remain: an empty trace, and a misidentified source. These reduce in the same way as the previous unforgeability proof; if the identities mismatch a signature was forged, and otherwise a PRF collision occurred.

# References

1. Bond, S.: Just 12 people are behind most vaccine hoaxes on social media, research shows. NPR (2021). https://www.npr.org/2021/05/13/996570855/disinformation-dozen-test-facebooks-twitters-ability-to-curb-vaccine-hoaxes
2. For Countering Digital Hate, C.: The disinformation dozen (2021). https://www.counterhate.com/disinformationdozen
3. Dodis, Y., Grubbs, P., Ristenpart, T., Woodage, J.: Fast message franking: from invisible salamanders to encryptment. Cryptology ePrint Archive, Report 2019/016 (2019). https://ia.cr/2019/016
4. Anonymous traceback for end to end encryption. https://drive.google.com/file/d/1uDBndw3dvAK2Ep_ocwovSzabPl1wXLrT/view?usp=sharing
5. Grubbs, P., Lu, J., Ristenpart, T.: Message franking via committing authenticated encryption. Cryptology ePrint Archive, Report 2017/664 (2017). https://ia.cr/2017/664
6. Issa, R., AlHaddad, N., Varia, M.: Hecate: abuse reporting in secure messengers with sealed sender. Cryptology ePrint Archive, Report 2021/1686 (2021). https://ia.cr/2021/1686
7. Liu, L., Roche, D.S., Theriault, A., Yerukhimovich, A.: Fighting fake news in encrypted messaging with the fuzzy anonymous complaint tally system (facts). Cryptology ePrint Archive, Report 2021/1148 (2021). https://ia.cr/2021/1148

8. Peale, C., Eskandarian, S., Boneh, D.: Secure complaint-enabled source-tracking for encrypted messaging. In: Proceedings of the 2021 ACM SIGSAC Conference on Computer and Communications Security, CCS 2021, pp. 1484–1506. Association for Computing Machinery, New York, NY, USA (2021). https://doi.org/10.1145/3460120.3484539
9. Samuels, E.: How misinformation on whatsapp led to a mob killing in India. The Washington Post (2020). https://www.washingtonpost.com/politics/2020/02/21/how-misinformation-whatsapp-led-deathly-mob-lynching-india/
10. Government requests. https://signal.org/bigbrother/
11. Tyagi, N., Grubbs, P., Len, J., Miers, I., Ristenpart, T.: Asymmetric message franking: content moderation for metadata-private end-to-end encryption. In: Boldyreva, A., Micciancio, D. (eds.) CRYPTO 2019. LNCS, vol. 11694, pp. 222–250. Springer, Cham (2019). https://doi.org/10.1007/978-3-030-26954-8_8
12. Tyagi, N., Len, J., Miers, I., Ristenpart, T.: Orca: blocklisting in sender-anonymous messaging. Cryptology ePrint Archive, Report 2021/1380 (2021). https://ia.cr/2021/1380
13. Tyagi, N., Miers, I., Ristenpart, T.: Traceback for end-to-end encrypted messaging. Cryptology ePrint Archive, Report 2019/981 (2019). https://ia.cr/2019/981
14. Vasilogambros, M.: Disinformation may be the new normal, election officials fear. PEW (2021). https://www.pewtrusts.org/en/research-and-analysis/blogs/stateline/2021/09/21/disinformation-may-be-the-new-normal-election-officials-fear

# Cloud Security

# Public Cloud Data Auditing Revisited: Removing the Tradeoff Between Proof Size and Storage Cost

Willy Susilo[1] , Yannan Li[1(✉)] , Fuchun Guo[1] , Jianchang Lai[2] , and Ge Wu[2]

[1] Institute of Cybersecurity and Cryptology, School of Computing and Information Technology, University of Wollongong, Wollongong, NSW 2522, Australia
{wsusilo,yannan,fuchun}@uow.edu.au
[2] School of Cyber Science and Engineering, Southeast University, Nanjing, China
jl967@uowmail.edu.au, gewu@seu.edu.cn

**Abstract.** Public cloud data auditing allows any third party to check the integrity of data stored on untrusted cloud servers without retrieving the data. The challenge is how to audit the proof of storage with efficient communications. In ACM CCS 2007, Ateniese *et al.* described the first practical public cloud data auditing scheme based on RSA, in which the proof of storage consists of one RSA element and one hash value and the storage cost for generating the proof can be as short as 1% of the stored file. Soon after, in Asiacrypt 2008, Shacham and Waters gave another public cloud data auditing scheme based on bilinear pairing, in which the generated proof of storage can be as short as 320 bits for 80-bit security (71% less compared to Ateniese *et al.*'s scheme). However, Shacham and Waters' scheme must trade off the storage cost, where the storage overhead for generating the proof of storage must be 100% of the stored file. Surprisingly, until today, the tradeoff between the proof size (namely proof of storage) and the storage cost (namely storage overhead) in cloud data auditing remains an open problem.

In this paper, we introduce a completely new public cloud data auditing mechanism. The proof of storage is not computed from block tags directly, but from evolution tags that are still unforgeable and evolved from bunch tags. We propose a concrete public cloud data auditing scheme based on this mechanism, in which the proof size is 240 bits for 80-bit security (25% less compared to Shacham and Waters' scheme) and the storage cost can be as efficient as Ateniese *et al.*'s scheme. The core of our technique is the feasibility of tag aggregations within this new mechanism. Our scheme is provably secure in the random oracle model.

**Keywords:** Cloud data auditing · Proof of storage · Data aggregation

## 1 Introduction

Storing a large amount of data (document files) on remote cloud servers can dramatically reduce the burden of data owners. However, it leads to security concerns and cloud data integrity is one of the most distressing problems. This is because cloud data owners have lost physical possession and full control of the outsourced data. Aiming at guaranteeing data integrity, public cloud data auditing enables anyone to request proof from

ⓒ The Author(s), under exclusive license to Springer Nature Switzerland AG 2022
V. Atluri et al. (Eds.): ESORICS 2022, LNCS 13555, pp. 65–85, 2022.
https://doi.org/10.1007/978-3-031-17146-8_4

the cloud server to prove the integrity of outsourced data. Without the need of retrieving original and large data from the cloud server, the verifier can be convinced via the proof that the data is intact on the cloud server.

In ACM CCS 2007, Ateniese *et al.* [3] proposed the first practical public cloud data auditing scheme named Provable Data Possession (PDP) based on RSA. In their design, a file is divided into many blocks and each block is associated with a block tag. Each block can be any arbitrary bit string while each tag is a variant of an RSA-type signature. Any verifier can audit the integrity of a file by sending some challenge, and the response (namely the proof of storage) generated by the cloud server is constant-size and composed of one RSA element and one hash value, which have about 1184 (1024+160) bits for 80-bit security.

In Asiacrypt 2008, Shacham and Waters [22] proposed another public cloud data auditing scheme with a compact proof of storage based on bilinear pairing. A file is also divided into blocks to generate block tags. Each block is an element from $Z_p$ and each tag is a BLS-type signature [8]. When a verifier audits the integrity of a file by sending some challenge, the response generated by the cloud server is compact and composed of one integer in $Z_p$ and one group element, which can be 320 (160 + 160) bits only for 80-bit security.

## 1.1 Motivation

Since the seminal papers by Ateniese *et al.* [3] in 2007 and by Shacham and Waters [22] in 2008, there have been a significant number of research papers working on cloud data auditing with different motivations (see Sect. 2). Most of them were based on the auditing schemes in [3,22]. There is no other secure public cloud data auditing scheme with a shorter proof of storage in the literature. That is, the proof of storage with two elements giving 320 bits by Shacham and Waters is the minimal size that the existing auditing schemes can achieve in the public cloud data auditing scenario.

The research motivation of this work is inspired by the tradeoff between the auditing scheme by Ateniese *et al.* [3] and by Shacham and Waters [22].

- In Ateniese *et al.*'s [3] scheme, the proof of storage must be 1184 bits for 80-bit security, and the rate of block size and tag size can be $s : 1$ for any reasonably-large parameter $s$ such that the storage cost on the cloud is $\frac{|M|}{s}$ for the file $M$.
- On the other hand, in Shacham and Waters' scheme [22], the proof of storage is compact with 320 bits for 80-bit security, but the rate of block size and tag size must be $1 : 1$ such that the storage cost on the cloud is $|M|$.

Even when $s = 100$, we can see that the storage cost is just 1% of the stored file in Ateniese *et al.*'s scheme [3] compared to 100% of the stored file in Shacham and Waters' scheme [22]. Although Shacham and Waters has shown how to reduce the storage cost to $\frac{|M|}{s}$ in [22], the proof of storage is no longer compact and is linear in the number of $s$. The inherent question is:

*Can we remove the tradeoff between*
*the compact proof of storage and the light storage cost?*

Unfortunately, no existing work in the literature can solve this problem since 2008. The motivation has been studied before but the existing schemes proposed in the literature have been shown insecure (See Sect. 2).

## 1.2  Our Contributions

We develop a completely new mechanism in public cloud data auditing constructions. In all previous cloud data auditing schemes, the proof of storage is generated based on block tags, which is originally computed by the file blocks. We circumvent this mechanism and propose the concept of evolution tags that are unforgeable and evolved from bunch tags. The proof of storage will be computed from evolution tags instead of block tags.

Based on the proposed mechanism, we can design a novel public cloud data auditing scheme that has addressed the tradeoff between Ateniese *et al.*'s scheme[3] and Shacham and Waters' scheme [22].

- We first propose a basic public cloud data auditing scheme that can be seen as a variant of Shacham and Waters' scheme. In our basic scheme, a file is also split into blocks in $Z_p$ for tag generation. The proof of storage in our scheme is composed of only one element from $Z_p$ and one hash value from $Z_p$, and the storage cost is still 100% of the stored file. That is, our scheme is as efficient as Shacham and Waters' scheme, while the proof of storage and the verification are based on evolution tags.
- Then we show how to reduce the storage cost of our basic scheme. With the aggregation idea, data owners are able to aggregate $n$ tags into a bunch tag, which is as short as a normal tag. The corresponding storage overhead for a file $M$ is therefore reduced from $|M|$ to $\frac{|M|}{n}$. When $n$ is chosen the same as the parameter $s$ in Ateniese *et al.*'s scheme [3], the storage cost in our construction is as efficient as [3]. Most importantly, the evolution tags are still extractable from bunch tags and the aggregation will not change the size of proof of storage.

Therefore, the proof of storage (proof size) in our second scheme is as efficient as Shacham and Waters' scheme and the storage cost in our scheme is as efficient as Ateniese *et al.*'s scheme. The comparison of the schemes is shown in Table 1.

We stress that the proof size in our schemes can be further reduced compared to Shacham and Waters' scheme. In our cloud data auditing schemes, the proof of storage is composed of one element from $Z_p$ and one hash value from $Z_p$. Let $\kappa$ be the security level. For security consideration, we must have $|p| = 2\kappa$ and therefore the proof size is $4\kappa$ bits. The hash value can be computed from the stored file and block tags by the cloud server, or from the $Z_p$ element and a secret known by the verifier for verification. There is no need to send the whole hash value to the verifier but we can truncate it into half. The error probability is still negligible as small as $\frac{1}{2^\kappa}$. The final proof size therefore is $3\kappa$ bits only. We note that the truncated idea is also available for Ateniese *et al.*'s scheme but not for Shacham and Waters' scheme.

Our cloud data auditing schemes also support the proofs of retrievability (POR) with the same techniques in Shacham and Waters' scheme, where POR allows data owners to extract their files with the proof of storage generated by cloud servers. Our schemes are provably secure in the random oracle model under the $n$-GDHE hardness assumption.

**Table 1.** The comparison of our public cloud data auditing scheme under 80-bit security ($n = s = 100$).

| Schemes | Public key | Storage cost | Proof size |
|---|---|---|---|
| Ateniese *et al.* [3] | $O(1)$ | 1% of the file | 1104 bits |
| Shacham and Waters [22] | $O(1)$ | 100% of the file | 320 bits |
| Ours | $O(n)$ | 1% of the file | 240 bits |

The price to pay for our cloud data auditing schemes is the computational inefficiency and the increase of public key size compared to Shacham and Waters' scheme. The public key in our scheme is linear with the number of parameter $n$ for tag aggregation. Our cloud data auditing scheme is at most $n$ times slower due to the need for tag extractions from the aggregate one.

**Our Approach.** It is quite natural to consider tag aggregation in order to reduce the storage cost when block size and tag size is $1 : 1$. The challenge is how to extract tags from the aggregate tag in order to generate the proof of storage by the cloud server. The tag of each block must be an unforgeable signature and each aggregate tag can be seen as an aggregate signature. Actually, Boneh *et al.* in [7] have proved that extracting BLS signatures [8] from an aggregate BLS signature is equivalent to solving a computationally hard problem. Therefore, to be able to aggregate tags without affecting the generation of proof of storage, we must somehow bypass the impossibility result given in [7].

In this paper, we solve this problem or bypass the difficulty by relaxing the need of extracting original signatures from the aggregate signature, or extracting normal tags from the aggregate tag to generate the proof of storage. Our observations are as follows.

- When a cloud data owner generates a normal block tag $t_i$ for a file block $m_i$ and multiple tags are aggregated, it is not necessary for the cloud server to extract the normal tag $t_i$ but one kind of evolution tag $etag$ denoted by $e_i$, as long as $e_i$ is unforgeable without the secret key and $e_i$ can be used in generating the proof of storage.
- The aggregation-extraction mechanism only needs to work in the way that tags $(t_1, t_2, \cdots, t_n)$ generated for file blocks $(m_1, m_2, \cdots, m_n)$ are aggregated into one constant-size bunch tag $T_1$. Then the evolution tags $(e_1, e_2, \cdots, e_n)$ can be extracted from the bunch tag $T_1$ and file blocks $(m_1, m_2, \cdots, m_n)$ without the need of secret key.

The diagram in Fig. 1 shows how our idea works.

Next we show how to construct such a public cloud data auditing scheme. Let $(G_1, G_2, G_T, g_1, g_2, p, e)$ be an asymmetric pairing and $H : \{0,1\}^* \to G_1$ be a cryptographic hash function.

The public key of the data onwer is $pk = (g_1, h_2, h_2^\alpha, h_2^{\alpha^2}, \cdots, h_2^{\alpha^n}, h_2^{\alpha^{n+1}}, \cdots, h_2^{\alpha^{2n}})$, and the secret key is $\alpha \in Z_p$. Here, $h_2$ is another random group element.

Let $f$ be the name of a file $M = (m_1, m_2, m_3, \cdots, )$ to be stored on the cloud. In our cloud data auditing scheme, the tag $t_i$ for message $m_i$ is computed as

$$t_i = \left( H(f\|i)g_1^{m_i} \right)^{\alpha^k},$$

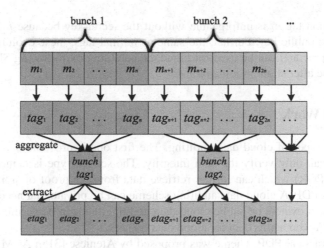

**Fig. 1.** The high-level idea of our cloud data auditing scheme with evolution tags.

where $k \in [1, n]$ is an integer satisfying $i = j \cdot n + k$ for some integer $j$. The tags to be aggregated are computed with different exponents. For example, if $i = n + 2$, then $j = 1$ and $k = 2$; if $i = 2n + 3$, then $j = 2$ and $k = 3$.

Without the loss of generality, we show how to handle tags from $t_1$ to $t_{2n}$ for file blocks from $m_1$ to $m_{2n}$, where the tags $(t_1, t_2, \cdots, t_n)$ will be aggregated into a bunch tag $T_1$ and the tags $(t_{n+1}, t_{n+2}, \cdots, t_{n+n})$ will be aggregated into a bunch tag $T_2$. The corresponding bunch tags are aggregated as follows.

$$T_1 = \prod_{\nu=1}^{n} \left( H(f\|\nu) g_1^{m_\nu} \right)^{\alpha^\nu}, \quad T_2 = \prod_{\nu=n+1}^{2n} \left( H(f\|\nu) g_1^{m_\nu} \right)^{\alpha^{\nu-n}}.$$

To audit the data, we assume a TPA (third-party auditor) to perform cloud data auditing for cloud data owners. Before auditing, the TPA will generate another key pair based on $pk$, namely $tpk = (h_2^\beta, h_2^{\alpha\beta}, h_2^{\alpha^2\beta}, \cdots, h_2^{\alpha^n\beta}, h_2^{\alpha^{n+2}\beta}, \cdots, h_2^{\alpha^{2n}\beta})$ and $tsk = h_2^{\beta\alpha^{n+1}}$ with a random number $\beta \in Z_p$. The TPA can pre-generate this key pair and store $tpk$ on the cloud server before cloud data auditing. Since $tpk$ and $tsk$ can be generated from $pk$, anyone can perform the data auditing.

With the public key $tpk$ and bunch tags, cloud server can compute the evolution tags $(e_1, e_2, \cdots, e_n)$ from $T_1$ defined as

$$e_i = e\left( H(f\|i) g_1^{m_i}, \ h_2^{\beta\alpha^{n+1}} \right).$$

For example, $e_1$ is computed as

$$\frac{e(T_1, h_2^{\beta\alpha^n})}{\prod_{\nu=2}^n e(H(f\|\nu) g_1^{m_\nu}, h_2^{\beta\alpha^{n+\nu}})} = \frac{e(\prod_{\nu=1}^n \left( H(f\|\nu) g_1^{m_\nu} \right)^{\alpha^\nu}, h_2^{\beta\alpha^n})}{\prod_{\nu=2}^n e(H(f\|\nu) g_1^{m_\nu}, h_2^{\beta\alpha^{n+\nu}})} = e\left( H(f\|1) g_1^{m_1}, h_2^{\beta\alpha^{n+1}} \right).$$

The evolution tag $e_i$ is unforgeable without the secret key because $h_2^{\beta \alpha^{n+1}}$ is not provided in the public key. Further, the same as normal tags, these evolution tags are still homomorphic and can be used for cloud data auditing by following Shacham and Waters' scheme after slight modification.

## 2    Related Work

There are two types of cloud data auditing. The first one is provable data possession (PDP) which can only verify the data integrity. The second type is named proofs of retrievability (POR) which can further retrieve data from the proof of storage besides the function of PDP. A cloud data auditing scheme can be private that needs the secret key of cloud data owners or public cloud data auditing that can be verified by anyone such as the TPA who audits data for cloud data owners.

The first practical PDP scheme was proposed by Ateniese [3] in ACM CCS 2007. The concept of POR was first proposed by Juels and Kaliski [16] in ACM CCS 2007 too, but it supports a bounded number of auditing. Shacham and Waters in Asiacrypt 2008 [22] proposed two POR schemes. The first one is a private cloud data auditing based on pseudorandom functions (PRF) [17], and the second one is public cloud data auditing based on BLS short signatures [8].

We now review other cloud data auditing schemes with additional features that meet specific motivations proposed in the literature.

**Privacy-Preserving Public Cloud Data Auditing.** The public cloud data auditing schemes are to verify the data integrity without privacy-preserving on data. Anyone who audits data can learn the information of data from the proof of storage. Wang *et al.* [26,27] achieved cloud data auditing with privacy against TPA by random masking techniques. Yu *et al.* [33] realized zero-knowledge privacy against TPA in the public cloud data auditing.

**Dynamic Operations.** How to realize cloud data auditing that can efficiently support the update of stored data was also studied in the literature. Ateniese *et al.* [4] first considered scalable PDP with data update. Later in ACM CCS 2009, Erway *et al.* [14] proposed a dynamic PDP with fully dynamic operations based on authenticated dictionaries that allow cloud data owners to insert, modify, and delete the blocks on the cloud. In EUROCRYPT 2013, Cash *et al.* [10] proposed the first POR with dynamic storage based on oblivious RAM. It supports arbitrary reads and writes anywhere of the data. More works with dynamic operations on cloud data can be found in [11,13,25] with different techniques including rank-based MHT, skip lists and status table.

**Multi-replicas.** In order to increase the probability of retrieving the cloud data, cloud data auditing with multi-replicas was proposed [12]. In this notion, we consider the scenario that cloud data owners prefer to store multiple copies of the same file but the cloud server just wants to store only one copy of the file to save the storage. Curtmola *et al.* [12] proposed the first construction with a PRF to generate multi-replicas. The proof of storage is almost as efficient as that of a single copy in data auditing. In 2016, Armknecht *et al.* [1] proposed Mirror, a scheme to prove data replicas and retrievability on cloud using a tunable puzzle-based replication scheme, which reduces computational costs of cloud data owners.

**Key Management.** The aforementioned cloud data auditing schemes are all based on public-key infrastructure (PKI). Yu *et al.* [33] proposed identity-based cloud data auditing scheme with provable security, where cloud data owners' public keys are their identities and their private keys are computed by a trusted third party. More identity-based cloud data auditing schemes with different motivations were studied in [24,28,35]. Li *et al.* [19] proposed a fuzzy identity-based cloud data auditing scheme, which can use biometric information as the identity to generate private keys for auditing. Later, the concept of attribute-based cloud data auditing was proposed in [15,34], which supports the use of attribute keys in tag generation and auditing.

**Lattice-Based Cloud Data Auditing.** Secure cloud data auditing schemes against quantum computer attacks were also studied in the literature. Li *et al.* [18] proposed a lattice-based cloud data auditing with privacy-preserving and forward-secure properties. Zhang *et al.* [39] proposed a lattice-based certificateless cloud data auditing scheme with multiple replicas. Liu *et al.* [20] designed an identity-based cloud data auditing scheme from lattice.

**Online/Offline Auditing.** Some cloud data auditing schemes focused on the computational efficiency of processing the data. For instance, Wang *et al.* [29] proposed an online/offline PDP to efficiently preprocess the data before uploading to the cloud. In their construction, the computation is divided into offline and online computations, where the offline one can be precomputed and the online computations are very fast.

**Delegatable Auditing.** In private cloud data auditing, only verifiers with a secret key can audit the data. Delegatbale auditing was studied in the literature to support cloud data auditing by a wider range of verifiers. Shen and Tzeng [23] proposed a delegatable provable data possession, in which the data owner can control who can audit the cloud data. The construction is efficient in terms of communication costs. Xu *et al.* [30,31] proposed delegatable proofs of storage with lightweight tag generations. In their construction, there is no exponentiation in tag generation and the size of response is constant without sacrificing storage cost.

**POR with Bounded-Use Auditing.** Some researches focused on POR that supports a limited number times of auditing, besides the first scheme by Juels and Kaliski [16]. In ESORICS 2014, Azraoui *et al.* [5] proposed StealthGuard, which is a sentinel-based POR with some random blocks called watchdogs. The performance of the scheme outperforms [16]. In [9], Bowers *et al.* proposed a modified POR upon Juels and Kaliski [16]. They employed a new encoding technique of arbitrary error-correcting code (ECC). The storage cost and proof size are related to the outer code of ECC, which can be much smaller than [16,22].

**POR with Reliability of the TPA.** In ACM CCS 2014, Armknecht *et al.* [2] proposed a new concept named outsourced proofs of retrievability (OPOR) based on POR. In their new model, they considered TPA reliability and included the cloud data auditing of the TPA in the security model.

**Public Cloud Data Auditing with Improved Efficiency.** Our motivation towards compact proof of storage with reduced overhead has been paid attention already in the literature. For example, the schemes proposed by Yuan and Yu in [36,37] and Yang and Jia in [32]. Unfortunately, those schemes have been found insecure in [38] and [21], respectively.

## 3   Definitions of Public (Third-Party) Auditing

A public cloud data auditing scheme consists of three entities, namely cloud data owners, a cloud server, and a TPA (we assume that the TPA will perform data auditing for all cloud data owners, and anyone can perform as the TPA in auditing data.

In all previous public cloud data auditing schemes, the TPA will run challenge-response algorithms with cloud server directly using the public key of cloud data owner. There is no need for the TPA to generate any other key pairs. We change the definitions in order to have efficient constructions. More precisely, the TPA also needs to generate a key pair $(tpk, tsk)$ during the cloud data auditing. The key pair can be generated based on the cloud data owner's public key. The $tpk$ is used in the generation of proof of storage and the $tsk$ is used for verification. Therefore, this definition does not affect the public cloud data auditing because anyone can generate such a key pair. The only inconvenience is that the TPA should send $tpk$ to cloud server first before auditing data under $pk$ for data owners.

A public cloud data auditing scheme is defined as follows.

- KeyGen$(1^\lambda, n) \to (pk, sk)$: This algorithm is a probabilistic algorithm run by the cloud data owner. On input a security parameter $\lambda$ and a scheme parameter $n^1$, the algorithm generates a public and secret key pair $(pk, sk)$.
- T.KeyGen$(pk) \to (tpk, tsk)$: This algorithm is a probabilistic algorithm run by the TPA. On input the cloud data owner's public key $pk$, the algorithm generate a public and secret key pair $(tpk, tsk)$ used by the TPA.
- TagGen$(sk, M) \to (t)$: This algorithm is a probabilistic algorithm run by the cloud data owner. On input secret key $sk$ and a file $M$ to be stored on the cloud, this algorithm outputs tags $t$. The file and tags will be stored on the cloud server.
- Challenge$(l) \to (chal)$: This algorithm is a probabilistic algorithm run by the TPA. On input the number of challenged blocks $l$, this algorithm outputs the challenge set $chal$.
- T.Response$(tpk, M, t, chal) \to (T.resp)$: This algorithm is a deterministic algorithm run by the cloud server. On input the public key $tpk$, the stored file $M$, the tags $t$, and the challenge $chal$, this algorithm outputs a proof $T.resp$.
- T.Verify$(tsk, T.resp, chal) \to (0/1)$: This algorithm is a deterministic algorithm run by the TPA. On input the secret key $tsk$, the proof $T.resp$, and the challenge $chal$, this algorithm outputs 1 meaning that data is intact. Otherwise, it outputs 0.

**Correctness.** The correctness of a public cloud data auditing scheme requires that for any public and secret key pairs $(pk, sk)$ generated by KeyGen$(1^\lambda, n)$, for any public

---

$^1$ The parameter $n$ is related to the number of tags that will be aggregated into a constant one.

and secret key pairs $(tpk, tsk)$ generated by T.KeyGen($pk$), for any file $M$, for all tags $t$ generated by TagGen($sk, M$), for any challenges $chal$ generated by Challenge($l$), and the proof $T.resp$ generated by T.Reponse($tpk, M, t, chal$), we have,

$$\Pr\left[\text{T.Verify}(tsk, T.resp, chal) = 1\right] = 1.$$

**Security.** The security of a public cloud data auditing scheme requires the holding of soundness. More precisely, if any cheating prover can generate valid proof that passes the T.Verify($tsk, T.resp, chal$) algorithm, it is actually storing the challenged file. That is to say, there is no adversary who does not store the file can produce a valid proof of the challenged data. To depict the soundness described above, an extractor is defined to recover the file from the proof. Following the idea by Ateniese *et al.* [3], we give the security model described as follows.

**Setup.** The challenger $\mathcal{C}$ runs the KeyGen algorithm to compute $(pk, sk)$ and runs the T. KeyGen algorithm to compute $(tpk, tsk)$. Then it forwards $(pk, tpk)$ to the adversary $\mathcal{A}$ and keeps $(sk, tsk)$ to itself. The secret key $sk$ is used for tag generation and $tsk$ is used for verification.

**Query.** The adversary $\mathcal{A}$ is allowed to make queries to the TagGen oracle. Specifically, $\mathcal{A}$ chooses some file $M$ on its own and $\mathcal{C}$ runs TagGen($sk, M$) and returns the tags $t$ to the adversary.

**ProofGen.** For the file $M$ that has been queried in the Query phase, the adversary $\mathcal{A}$ can interact with $\mathcal{C}$ by following the challenge-response algorithms. The challenger $\mathcal{C}$ runs Challenge($l$) and forwards the output $chal$ to $\mathcal{A}$. The adversary $\mathcal{A}$ then runs T.Response($tpk, M, t, chal$) to generate a proof $T.resp$. At the end of each interaction, $\mathcal{A}$ is provided with the output of T.Verify($tsk, T.resp, chal$).

**Challenge.** The challenger generates a challenge $chal^*$.

**Output.** Finally, the adversary $\mathcal{A}$ outputs a proof $T.resp^*$ and wins the game if the algorithm T.Verify($tsk, T.resp^*, chal^*$) returns 1.

**Definition 1.** *We say a public cloud data auditing scheme is sound and secure if for any probabilistic polynomial-time (P.P.T.) adversary the probability that the adversary wins the game is negligibly close to the probability that the challenger can extract file blocks from the proof.*

## 4   Our Constructions

Let $G_1, G_2, G_T$ be three pairing groups of prime order $p$, $g_1$ be a generator of $G_1$, $g_2$ be a generator of $G_2$, and $e : G_1 \times G_2 \rightarrow G_T$ denote an asymmetric bilinear map. The scheme needs two cryptographic hash functions $H : \{0, 1\}^* \rightarrow G_1$ and $H_1 : G_T \rightarrow Z_p$. We first give a basic public cloud data auditing scheme without tag aggregation, then show how to reduce the storage cost by aggregation. Our cloud data auditing schemes are shown as follows.

## 4.1   Basic Public Cloud Data Auditing Scheme

Our construction is based on but slightly different from Shacham and Waters' scheme [22]. Similarly, a file $M$ to be stored on the cloud will be split into blocks $M = (m_1, m_2, m_3, \cdots)$ where each $m_i$ is in the message space $Z_p$. Each block file has a corresponding block tag.

KeyGen($1^\lambda, n$): On input a security parameter $\lambda$ and scheme parameter $n$, the algorithm chooses a random $\alpha \in Z_p$ and another generator $h_2 \in G_2$. The public key is defined as

$$pk = \begin{pmatrix} g_1, \\ h_2, h_2^\alpha, h_2^{\alpha^2}, \cdots, h_2^{\alpha^n}, h_2^{\alpha^{n+1}}, h_2^{\alpha^{n+2}}, \cdots, h_2^{\alpha^{2n}} \end{pmatrix}$$

and the secret key is $sk = \alpha$. Here, the number $n$ decides the maximum number of tags to be aggregated.

T.KeyGen($pk$): On input the cloud data owner's public key $pk$, the TPA chooses a random $\beta \in Z_p$ and computes

$$tpk = (h_2^\beta, h_2^{\beta\alpha}, h_2^{\beta\alpha^2}, \cdots, h_2^{\beta\alpha^n}, \quad h_2^{\beta\alpha^{n+2}}, \cdots, h_2^{\beta\alpha^{2n}}).$$

The $tsk$ is set as $h_2^{\beta\alpha^{n+1}} = (h_2^{\alpha^{n+1}})^\beta$.

TagGen($sk, M$): On input a file $M$ to be stored on the cloud, the cloud data owner first chooses a file name $f^2$, and then splits the file into blocks in $Z_p$, namely

$$M = (m_1, m_2, m_3, \cdots) : \ m_i \in Z_p.$$

The tag $t_i$ for the $i$-th block message $m_i$ is computed as

$$t_i = \left( H(f\|i) \cdot g_1^{m_i} \right)^{\alpha^k},$$

where $k \in [1, n]$ is the integer defined as $k = i - j \cdot n$ for some integer $j$. For example, if $i = n + 2$, then $j = 1$ and $k = 2$. After all tags are generated, forward the file $M$ and all block tags $t = \{t_i\}$ to the cloud server.

Challenge($l$): On input a set $L$ of $l$ challenged blocks, for each $i \in L$, generate a random number $r_i \in Z_p$. Forward the set $chal = \{i, r_i\}$ to the cloud server.

T.Response($tpk, M, t, chal$): Suppose the $i$-th block is challenged. The cloud server is not to use tag $t_i$ in computing the response. Instead, the cloud server will first compute an evolution tag, denoted by $e_i$, from $t_i$ and the public key $tpk$ as follows

$$e_i = e\left( t_i, h_2^{\beta\alpha^{n+1-k}} \right) = e\left( H(f\|i)g_1^{m_i}, h_2^{\beta\alpha^{n+1}} \right),$$

which can be computed from the block tags $t = \{t_i\}$ and $tpk$.

---

[2] A secure signature scheme is needed for $f$ stored on the cloud server. This part is omit to make the scheme neat. The techniques to generate the signature on the file can be referred to [22].

Then the cloud server computes the proof $T.resp = (H_1(E), \mu) \in Z_p^2$ where

$$E = \prod_{(i,r_i) \in chal} (e_i)^{r_i} \in G_T, \quad \mu = \sum_{(i,r_i) \in chal} m_i r_i \mod p,$$

which are set as the proof of storage and forwarded to the verifier.

T.Verify($tsk, T.resp, chal$): Upon receiving the proof $T.resp = (H_1(E), \mu)$, the TPA computes

$$\widehat{E} = e \left( \prod_{(i,r_i) \in chal} H(f\|i)^{r_i} \cdot g_1^{\mu}, \; h_2^{\beta \alpha^{n+1}} \right)$$

and accepts the proof if $H_1(\widehat{E}) = H_1(E)$.

The correctness holds here because we have

$$E = \prod_{(i,r_i) \in chal} e_i^{r_i}$$

$$= \prod_{(i,r_i) \in chal} e \left( H(f\|i) g_1^{m_i}, h_2^{\beta \alpha^{n+1}} \right)^{r_i}$$

$$= e \left( \prod_{(i,r_i) \in chal} H(f\|i)^{r_i} g_1^{m_i r_i}, \; h_2^{\beta \alpha^{n+1}} \right)$$

$$= e \left( \prod_{(i,r_i) \in chal} H(f\|i)^{r_i} \cdot g_1^{\mu}, \; h_2^{\beta \alpha^{n+1}} \right) = \widehat{E}.$$

In our basic scheme, the proof of storage is composed of two elements from $Z_p$ only. Furthermore, if the proof $(H_1(E), \mu)$ is correct, the TPA can compute the first element from the second element and the secret key $tsk$. Therefore, the first element is really the proof of storage in the front of $\mu$. We truncate the first element into half to further reduce the proof of storage, as long as it is hard for the cloud server to compute $E$ without storing file and block tags. This is because the probability of correctly guessing the truncated $H_1(E)$ is $\frac{1}{\lceil 2^{\kappa} \rceil} = \frac{1}{2^{80}}$ for 80-bit security when the output of hash function is uniformly random (in the random oracle model). For $\kappa$-bit security, $p$ must have at least $2\kappa$ bits. Therefore, the proof of storage in our scheme has $3\kappa$ bits only for $\kappa$-bit security.

The storage on the cloud is $2 \cdot |M|$ if $|t_i| = |m_i|$ which is possible using the asymmetric pairing the same as [22] because $|g_1| = |p|$. The storage cost in our basic scheme is therefore $|M|$, meaning that the size of file and the size of block tags are the same. In the next subsection, we show how to reduce the size of tags by aggregation where computing the proof $T.resp$ is still feasible by the cloud server.

## 4.2   Public Cloud Data Auditing Scheme with Reduced Storage Cost

The high-level idea of how to reduce the cloud storage is already given in Fig. 1 in the introduction. Here we show how to achieve this in detail.

Before sending all tags to the cloud, the cloud data owner will group each $n$ tags and compute an aggregate tag called *bunch tag*. All bunch tags denoted by $\{T_i\}$ will be forwarded to the cloud instead of all tags $t = \{t_i\}$, while the cloud server can still extract each evolution tag from the bunch tag.

Next we describe how to aggregate tags into a bunch tag, and then extract evolution tags from the bunch tag in response phase.

**TagGen**$(sk, M)$: On input a file $M = (m_1, m_2, m_3, \cdots)$ to be stored on the cloud, the cloud data owner first computes all block tags $\{t_i\}$ following the basic scheme.

Then the data owner groups each $n$ tags sequentially into a bunch as

| | |
|---|---|
| bunch 1: | $(t_{0+1}, t_{0+2}, \cdots, t_{0+n})$ |
| bunch 2: | $(t_{n+1}, t_{n+2}, \cdots, t_{n+1,n})$ |
| | $\vdots$ |
| bunch $j$: | $(t_{(j-1)n+1}, t_{(j-1)n+2}, \cdots, t_{(j-1)n+n})$ |
| | $\vdots$ |

The cloud data owner computes a bunch tag $T_j$ from all tags in the $j$-th bunch by simple group operations as

$$T_j = t_{(j-1)n+1} \cdot t_{(j-1)n+2} \cdots t_{(j-1)n+n} = \prod_{\nu=1}^{n} \left( H(f\|(j-1)n + \nu) \cdot g_1^{m_{(j-1)n+\nu}} \right)^{\alpha^\nu}.$$

In particular, we have $T_1 = \prod_{\nu=1}^{n} (H(f\|\nu)g_1^{m_\nu})^{\alpha^\nu}$. Finally, the cloud data owner forwards the file $M$ and all file bunch tags $t = \{T_j\}$ to the cloud server.

This completes the new algorithm of tag generation. The challenge phase is the same as the basic scheme, while the response phase is described as follows.

**T.Response**$(tpk, M, t, chal)$: Suppose the $i$-th block is challenged. Given the file $M$ and all file bunch tags $t = \{T_j\}$, the cloud server can follow the basic scheme to generate the proof as long as the evolution tag $e_i$ is extractable from the file bunch tags.

Without loss of generality, we assume $i \in [1, n]$ and show how to compute $e_i$ from $T_1 = \prod_{\nu=1}^{n} (H(f\|\nu)g_1^{m_\nu})^{\alpha^\nu}$. We have $i = 0 \cdot n + k$. The cloud server computes the evolution tag $e_i = e(H(f\|i)g_1^{m_i}, h_2^{\beta\alpha^{n+1}})$ by

$$e_i = \frac{e(T_1, h_2^{\beta\alpha^{n+1-k}})}{\prod_{\nu=1, \nu\neq k}^{n} e(H(f\|\nu)g_1^{m_\nu}, h_2^{\beta\alpha^{n+1-k+\nu}})}$$

$$= \frac{e(\prod_{\nu=1}^{n} (H(f\|\nu)g_1^{m_\nu})^{\alpha^\nu}, h_2^{\beta\alpha^{n+1-k}})}{\prod_{\nu=1, \nu\neq k}^{n} e(H(f\|\nu)g_1^{m_\nu}, h_2^{\beta\alpha^{n+1-k+\nu}})}$$

$$= e\left( H(f\|i)g_1^{m_i}, h_2^{\beta\alpha^{n+1}} \right).$$

The above extraction is available by the cloud server because the group elements $h_2^{\beta\alpha^{n+1-k}}$ and $h_2^{\beta\alpha^{n+1-k+\nu}}$ are both available from the public key for any $k, \nu \in [1, n]$ as long as $k \neq \nu$. Therefore, all evolution tags can be extracted from the file bunch tags.

This completes the description of our public cloud data auditing scheme with reduced storage cost. When $|t_i| = |m_i|$, it is easy to see that the cloud storage is reduced from $2|M|$ to $|M| + \frac{|M|}{n}$ because $n$ tags are aggregated into a bunch tag, while the proof of storage is not changed.

## 5    Proof of Security

From the view of cloud server, the cloud data owners do not provide more information to the cloud when the file bunch tags $\{T_j\}$ are forwarded instead of normal tags $\{t_i\}$ because the bunch tags are computed from the normal tags. Therefore, our cloud data auditing scheme with reduced storage is secure as long as our basic scheme is secure. In this section, we prove that our basic public cloud data auditing scheme achieves the soundness, as long as the $n$-General Diffie-Hellman Exponent ($n$-GDHE) Problem is hard. That is to say, if a cloud server generates a valid response for a challenge of the file, it must store the file with an overwhelming probability; otherwise, we can solve the $n$-GDHE hard problem.

**Definition 2 ($n$-General Diffie-Hellman Exponent Problem).** *The $n$-GDHE problem [6] is to compute* $e(h_1, h_2)^{a^{n+1}bc}$ *from the following given instance*

$$h_1, h_1^c \in G_1$$
$$h_2, h_2^b \in G_2$$
$$h_1^a, h_1^{a^2}, \cdots, h_1^{a^n} \in G_1$$
$$h_2^{a^1}, h_2^{a^2}, \cdots, h_2^{a^n}, h_2^{a^{n+1}}, h_2^{a^{n+2}}, \cdots, h_2^{a^{2n}} \in G_2$$
$$h_2^{a^1 b}, h_2^{a^2 b}, \cdots, h_2^{a^n b}, \qquad , h_2^{a^{n+2}b}, \cdots, h_2^{a^{2n}b} \in G_2.$$

*We say that the $n$-GDHE problem is hard if every P.P.T. adversary has only a negligible probability of computing* $e(h_1, h_2)^{a^{n+1}bc}$ *from the given problem instance, where the probability is a negligible function in the security parameter of generating problem instance.*

The proof of hardness of the $n$-GDHE problem is given in the appendix which shows that it is within the hard problem defined in [6].

**Theorem 1.** *If the $n$-GDHE problem is hard in bilinear groups, in the random oracle model where $H$ and $H_1$ are modeled as random oracles, our basic public cloud data auditing scheme is sound and secure.*

*Proof.* Upon receiving the challenge $chal$ on $(M, t)$, the prover (cloud server) should generate a proof $T.resp$. Suppose that the prover will always return the proof $T.resp$ from the algorithm T.Response($tpk, M, t, chal$). It is easy to see that we can extract block file from the proof. Without loss of generality, let $chal_1 =$

$\{(1, r_1), (2, r_2), (4, r_4)\}$ and $chal_2 = \{(1, r_1'), (2, r_2), (4, r_4)\}$ where $r_1 \neq r_1'$. With these two challenges, the prover should respond with

$$(H_1(E_1), \mu_1), \quad (H_1(E_2), \mu_2).$$

In particular, we have

$$\mu_1 = m_1 r_1 + m_2 r_2 + m_4 r_4 \quad \mod p.$$

$$\mu_2 = m_1 r_1' + m_2 r_2 + m_4 r_4 \quad \mod p.$$

We then can extract $m_1$ by computing

$$m_1 = \frac{\mu_2 - \mu_1}{r_1' - r_1} \quad \mod p.$$

Therefore, the soundness proof for our scheme is going to prove that given the same challenge $chal$ on $(M, t)$, the response from the prover must be identical to T.Response$(tpk, M, t, chal)$ except with negligible probability. In the following, we prove this by reduction showing that breaking this identical output can be reduced to solve the $n$-GDHE problem. More precisely, if the response is different from the output T.Response$(tpk, M, t, chal)$, we can solve the hard problem.

The simulator $\mathcal{S}$ is given as input the problem instance of the $n$-GDHE problem and the goal is to output $e(h_1, h_2)^{a^{n+1}bc}$.

**Setup.** The simulator sets $\alpha = a$ and $\beta = b$, and also sets $g_1 = h_1^c$. Then the public key $pk$ is set as

$$pk = \begin{pmatrix} h_1^c, \\ h_2, h_2^a, h_2^{a^2}, \cdots, h_2^{a^n}, h_2^{a^{n+1}}, h_2^{a^{n+2}}, \cdots, h_2^{a^{2n}} \end{pmatrix}.$$

The simulator sets $tpk$ as

$$tpk = (h_2^b, h_2^{ab}, h_2^{a^2b}, \cdots, h_2^{a^n b}, \quad h_2^{a^{n+2}b}, \cdots, h_2^{a^{2n}b}).$$

It is easy to see that the elements in $pk$ and $tpk$ are available from the problem instance.

**Hash-Query.** The simulator creates a list $\mathcal{L}$ to record all hash queries to the random oracle $H$ and a list $\mathcal{L}_1$ to record all hash queries to the random oracle $H_1$.

Upon receiving a hash query $x$ to $H$, if the query has already been made and there exists a pair $(x, y)$ in the hash list $\mathcal{L}$, the simulator responds to the query with $y$. Otherwise, $x$ is a new query and the simulator randomly chooses $y \in G_1$ and sets as the response, namely $y = H(x)$. The pair $(x, y)$ is added into the hash list $\mathcal{L}$.

Upon receiving a hash query $x$ to $H_1$, the response is exactly the same as that by the random oracle $H$ except that $y$ is randomly chosen from $Z_p$ if $x$ is a new hash query.

**Query.** The adversary can adaptively choose any file $M$ for query its tags. Suppose the file $M$ is split into $M = (m_1, m_2, m_3, \cdots)$. The simulator chooses a file name $f$ and computes the tags $\{t_i\}$ for the adversary as follows for each block.

- Choose a random $d_i$ and set $H(f\|i) = h_1^{d_i} g_1^{-m_i}$. That is, the simulator will add one pair to the hash list $\mathcal{L}$

$$(x, y) = (f\|i, \ h_1^{d_i} g_1^{-m_i}),$$

where $d_i$ is also stored as additional secret in $\mathcal{L}$ and linked to this pair.
- Compute $t_i$ as

$$t_i = (H(f\|i) g_1^{m_i})^{\alpha^k} = \left( h_1^{d_i} g_1^{-m_i} \cdot g_1^{m_i} \right)^{\alpha^k} = (h_1^{\alpha^k})^{d_i},$$

which is computable with $h_1^a, h_1^{a^2}, \cdots, h_1^{a^n}$ from the problem instance and $d_i$ because $k \in [1, n]$.

All block tags $\{t_i\}$ can be computed in the similar way by the simulator and then are forwarded to the adversary.

**ProofGen.** Suppose the file $M$ has been queried and the adversary asks to run auditing schemes. The simulator runs the challenge algorithm to generate the challenge $chal$. Suppose the proof from the adversary is $T.resp$. The simulator is asked to output $T.\mathsf{Verify}(tsk, T.resp, chal)$

In our simulation, the simulator does not know $sk$ or $tsk$ and therefore cannot perform the corresponding verification directly. However, according to our basic public cloud data auditing scheme, the proof for the same challenge is deterministic. Since the simulator can simulate all tags $\{t_i\}$ in the above phase, it can use them to compute the proof by itself. If the computed proof is equal to the queried $T.resp$, the algorithm $T.\mathsf{Verify}(tsk, T.resp, chal)$ must return 1. Otherwise, it returns 0. Therefore, the simulator can simulate the output $T.\mathsf{Verify}(tsk, T.resp, chal)$ correctly for the adversary.

**Challenge.** The simulator generates a challenge $chal^*$.

**Output.** Finally, the adversary $\mathcal{A}$ outputs a proof $T.resp^*$ and wins the game if the algorithm $T.\mathsf{Verify}(tsk, T.resp^*, chal^*)$ returns 1.

Let $T.resp^* = (Y, \mu)$. According to our scheme, if the response is correct, we should have $H_1(X) = Y$ where

$$X = e\left( \prod_{(i,r_i) \in chal^*} H(f\|i)^{r_i} \cdot g_1^{\mu}, \ h_2^{\beta \alpha^{n+1}} \right).$$

That is, the adversary must ever query $X$ to the random oracle $H_1$. Therefore, the simulator has successfully received $(X, \mu)$ from the adversary.

On the other hand, the simulator can simulate all tags $\{t_i\}$ and therefore can also generate $(\widehat{E^*}, \mu^*)$ satisfying

$$\widehat{E^*} = e\left( \prod_{(i,r_i) \in chal^*} H(f\|i)^{r_i} \cdot g_1^{\mu^*}, \ h_2^{\beta \alpha^{n+1}} \right),$$

where $(H_1(\widehat{E^*}), \mu^*)$ is equal to the output returned from $T.\mathsf{Response}(tpk, M, t, chal^*)$. In particular, we have

$$\mu^* = \sum_{(i,r_i) \in chal^*} m_i r_i \mod p.$$

With the pair $(X, \mu)$ from the adversary and the pair $(\widehat{E^*}, \mu^*)$ generated by the simulator, we can see that $(X, \mu) = (\widehat{E^*}, \mu^*)$ if $\mu = \mu^*$. Therefore, if the response generated by the adversary is different from the response $(\widehat{E^*}, \mu^*)$, the returned pair must satisfy $\mu \neq \mu^*$. We can deduct that

$$
\frac{X}{\widehat{E^*}} = \frac{e\left(\prod_{(i,r_i)\in chal^*} H(f\|i)^{r_i} \cdot g_1^{\mu}, h_2^{\beta\alpha^{n+1}}\right)}{e\left(\prod_{(i,r_i)\in chal^*} H(f\|i)^{r_i} \cdot g_1^{\mu^*}, h_2^{\beta\alpha^{n+1}}\right)}
$$
$$
= e(g_1, h_2^{\beta\alpha^{n+1}})^{\mu-\mu^*}.
$$

Since $g_1 = h_1^c, \alpha = a, \beta = b$, we have

$$
e(h_1, h_2)^{a^{n+1}bc} = \left(\frac{X}{\widehat{E^*}}\right)^{\frac{1}{\mu-\mu^*}},
$$

which is the solution to the problem instance.

This completes the simulation and the solution. The simulation of public keys $(pk, tpk)$ are random and independent because $(a, b, c)$ are random integers from the problem instance. The simulation of random oracles is indistinguishable because all responses are random and independent. In particular, for each response $H(f\|i)$, the simulator chooses a random $d_i$ in computing the response.

Our reduction shows that the response $T.resp^*$ returned from the adversary must be equal to the output from T.response$(tpk.M, t, chal^*)$. Otherwise, the simulator is able to solve the $n$-GDHE problem. This completes the proof of the theorem.     □

## 6     Implementation Results

We provide evaluation results to show the efficiency of our construction. The implementation was conducted on a laptop with Intel(R) Core (TM) i7-8550U CPU 2.13 GHz and a 8.0 GB RAM. All the algorithms were implemented with C++ language with Visual Studio 2019 compiler and MIRACL library. We used the asymmetric bilinear pairing $e : G_1 \times G_2 \rightarrow G_T$ with 80-bit security. The Cock-Pinch curve as $y^2 = x^3 - 3x + B(\mod p)$ is chosen with ate pairing, where $p$ is a prime of 160 bits. To test the efficiency, we fix the file to be uploaded with 5,000 blocks and change the number of blocks $n$ in a bunch. Each time we challenge 1% of the total blocks, which is 50 blocks. For each algorithm, we run 50 times to get the average running time. The implementation results are shown in the following figures.

The result of key generation is shown in Fig. 2. We first test the time consumption of KeyGen and T.KeyGen with the increase of $n$, the number of blocks in a bunch. We can see that the time cost is linear in $n$. This matches our theoretical analysis, since the public key $pk$ and $tpk$ are both $\mathcal{O}(n)$ large. The time cost of KeyGen is two times more than that in T.KeyGen, since more parameters are generated in KeyGen.

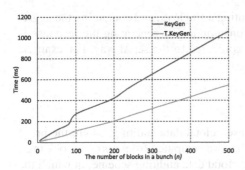

**Fig. 2.** Time cost of KeyGen &T.KeyGen

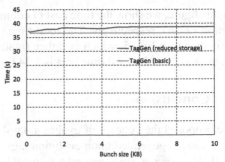

**Fig. 3.** Time cost of TagGen

The result of tag generations is shown in Fig. 3. We test the time cost of TagGen in both our basic construction 4.1 and our construction with reduced storage 4.2. The time costs of both algorithms are almost constant with the growing of the bunch size. Since the total number blocks are fixed in the experiments, the total number of exponentiation in group $G_1$ is determined accordingly, which is the dominant operation in TagGen. It is also easy to see from Fig. 3 that, the TagGen in reduced storage does not lead to too much additional cost compared with that in the basic construction.

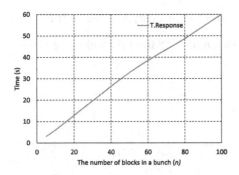

**Fig. 4.** Time cost of T.Response

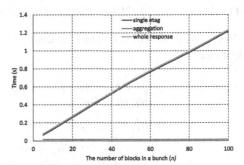

**Fig. 5.** T.Response in parallel

The result of response by the cloud server is shown in Fig. 4. We test the consumption for T.Response with the growing number of blocks in a bunch $n$. We can see that the time cost is linear in $n$. This is reasonable since each evolution tag $e_i'$ in the challenged block set is extracted from a bunch, which needs $n$ pairing computations at most. Our test is based on the worst case that each evolution tag has to be extracted from a different bunch tag. We note that the time cost can be dramatically reduced if the evolution tags can be extracted in parallel. It is reasonable for cloud server, which is assumed to enjoy adequate computation and storage resources, to perform paralleled computation. The time cost to evaluate T.Response in this way is shown in Fig. 5.

In this figure, we show the time cost of computing a single $e_i$, and computing the aggregation $(E, \mu)$, respectively. The total time consumption of generating the response is also shown in Fig. 5, which is rather small compared to the serial way. For example when $n = 100$, the total time cost is 1.243 s.

## 7 Conclusion

We proposed the concept of evolution tag-based cloud data auditing, where the proof of storage is generated upon evolution tags that are computed from normal block tags. With this concept, we proposed a new public cloud data auditing scheme, in which the proof size is even smaller than the state-of-the-art scheme by Shacham and Waters and the storage cost is as efficient as the scheme by Ateniese *et al.* We have successfully removed the tradeoff between the proof size and storage cost that has existed since 2008. The price to pay is the computational overhead and the generation of another key pair before auditing.

**Acknowledgment.** This paper is partially supported by National Natural Science Foundation of China (No. 61902191, No. 62002058) and Natural Science Foundation of Jiangsu Province (No. BK20200391).

## Appendix A

**Theorem 2.** *The $n$-GDHE problem fulfils the intractability analysis stated in [6].*

*Proof.* The $n$-GDHE problem is to compute $e(h_1, h_2)^{a^{n+1}bc}$ from the following given instance

$$h_1, h_1^c \in G_1$$
$$h_2, h_2^b \in G_2$$
$$h_1^a, h_1^{a^2}, \cdots, h_1^{a^n} \in G_1$$
$$h_2^{a^1}, h_2^{a^2}, \cdots, h_2^{a^n}, h_2^{a^{n+1}}, h_2^{a^{n+2}}, \cdots, h_2^{a^{2n}} \in G_2$$
$$h_2^{a^1 b}, h_2^{a^2 b}, \cdots, h_2^{a^n b}, \quad, h_2^{a^{n+2}b}, \cdots, h_2^{a^{2n}b} \in G_2.$$

The $n$-GDHE problem instance can be reformulated as

$$P_1 = \begin{pmatrix} 1, \, c, \\ a, \, a^2, \cdots, \, a^n, \end{pmatrix},$$

$$P_2 = \begin{pmatrix} 1, \, b \\ a, \, \cdots, \, a^n, \, a^{n+1}, \, a^{n+2}, \, \cdots, \, a^{2n} \\ ab, \cdots, \, a^n b, \quad\quad a^{n+2}b, \, \cdots, \, a^{2n}b \end{pmatrix},$$

$$Q = 1,$$
$$F = a^{n+1}bc.$$

Here, $P_1$ refers to the set of exponents with $h_1$ as the base in all group elements in $G_1$ in the problem instance. $P_2$ refers to the set of exponents with $h_2$ as the base in all group elements in $G_2$ in the problem instance. $Q$ refers to the set of exponents with $e(h_1, h_2)$ as the base in all group elements in $G_T$ in the problem instance.

We need to show that $F$ is independent of $(P_1, P_2, Q)$, i.e. that no coefficients $x_i, y_j$ and $z$ exist such that $a^{n+1}bc = F = \sum x_i d_i y_j d_j + z$, where $d_i \in P_1, d_j \in P_2$. In order to satisfy this equation, the multiplication of any element from $P_1$ and any element from $P_2$ must contain $abc$ only. By making all possible multiplications listed in $F'$ as follows

$$F' = \begin{pmatrix} ab \cdot c, \ a^2b \cdot c, \ \cdots, \ a^nb \cdot c, \\ a^{n+2}b \cdot c, \ \cdots, \ a^{2n}b \cdot c \end{pmatrix}.$$

we want to prove that no linear combination among the polynomials from the list $F'$ below leads to $F$.

Any such linear combination associated with $abc$ can be written as $a^{n+1}bc = A(a)abc + B(a)a^{n+2}bc$, where $A(a)$ and $B(a)$ are polynomials with $0 \leq degA(a) \leq n - 1$ and $0 \leq degB(a) \leq n - 2$. By cancelling out $abc$ in both sides, we can simplify the above equation as

$$a^n(1 - aB(a)) = A(a).$$

Since $A(a)$ has the degree less than $n$ and $a^n | A(a)$, we have $1 - aB(a) = A(a) = 0$. That is, $aB(a) = 1$ for any $a$. On the other hand, we have $0 \cdot B(0) = 0$. Therefore, there does not exist coefficients $x_i, y_j$ and $z$ such that $F = \sum x_i d_i y_j d_j + z$ holds. Hence, the defined $n$-GDHE problem is one of the intractable GDHE problems. This completes the proof. □

# References

1. Armknecht, F., Barman, L., Bohli, J.M., Karame, G.O.: Mirror: enabling proofs of data replication and retrievability in the cloud. In: Holz, T., Savage, S. (eds.) USENIX Security Symposium 2016, pp. 1051–1068. USENIX Association (2016)
2. Armknecht, F., Bohli, J.M., Karame, G.O., Liu, Z., Reuter, C.A.: Outsourced proofs of retrievability. In: Ahn, G., Yung, M., Li, N. (eds.) CCS 2014, pp. 831–843. ACM (2014)
3. Ateniese, G., et al.: Provable data possession at untrusted stores. In: Ning, P., di Vimercati, S.D.C., Syverson, P.F. (eds.) CCS 2007, pp. 598–609. ACM (2007)
4. Ateniese, G., Di Pietro, R., Mancini, L.V., Tsudik, G.: Scalable and efficient provable data possession. In: Levi, A., Liu, P., Molva, R. (eds.) SecureComm 2008, pp. 1–10. ACM (2008)
5. Azraoui, M., Elkhiyaoui, K., Molva, R., Önen, M.: StealthGuard: proofs of retrievability with Hidden Watchdogs. In: Kutyłowski, M., Vaidya, J. (eds.) ESORICS 2014. LNCS, vol. 8712, pp. 239–256. Springer, Cham (2014). https://doi.org/10.1007/978-3-319-11203-9_14
6. Boneh, D., Boyen, X., Goh, E.-J.: Hierarchical identity based encryption with constant size ciphertext. In: Cramer, R. (ed.) EUROCRYPT 2005. LNCS, vol. 3494, pp. 440–456. Springer, Heidelberg (2005). https://doi.org/10.1007/11426639_26
7. Boneh, D., Gentry, C., Lynn, B., Shacham, H.: Aggregate and verifiably encrypted signatures from bilinear maps. In: Biham, E. (ed.) EUROCRYPT 2003. LNCS, vol. 2656, pp. 416–432. Springer, Heidelberg (2003). https://doi.org/10.1007/3-540-39200-9_26
8. Boneh, D., Lynn, B., Shacham, H.: Short signatures from the weil pairing. In: Boyd, C. (ed.) ASIACRYPT 2001. LNCS, vol. 2248, pp. 514–532. Springer, Heidelberg (2001). https://doi.org/10.1007/3-540-45682-1_30

9. Bowers, K.D., Juels, A., Oprea, A.: Proofs of retrievability: theory and implementation. In: Sion, R., Song, D. (eds.) CCSW 2009, pp. 43–54. ACM (2009)
10. Cash, D., Küpçü, A., Wichs, D.: Dynamic proofs of retrievability via oblivious RAM. In: Johansson, T., Nguyen, P.Q. (eds.) EUROCRYPT 2013. LNCS, vol. 7881, pp. 279–295. Springer, Heidelberg (2013). https://doi.org/10.1007/978-3-642-38348-9_17
11. Cash, D., Küpçü, A., Wichs, D.: Dynamic proofs of retrievability via oblivious ram. J. Cryptol. **30**(1), 22–57 (2017)
12. Curtmola, R., Khan, O., Burns, R., Ateniese, G.: Mr-pdp: multiple-replica provable data possession. In: ICDCS 2008, pp. 411–420. IEEE Computer Society (2008)
13. Erway, C.C., Kupcu, A., Papamanthou, C., Tamassia, R.: Dynamic provable data possession. ACM Trans. Inf. Syst. Sec. (TISSEC) **17**(4), 1–29 (2015)
14. Erway, C., Küpçü, A., Papamanthou, C., Tamassia, R.: Dynamic provable data possession. In: Al-Shaer, E., Jha, S., Keromytis, A.D. (eds.) CCS 2009, pp. 213–222. ACM (2009)
15. Gudeme, J.R., Pasupuleti, S.K., Kandukuri, R.: Attribute-based public integrity auditing for shared data with efficient user revocation in cloud storage. J. Ambient. Intell. Humaniz. Comput. **12**(2), 2019–2032 (2020). https://doi.org/10.1007/s12652-020-02302-6
16. Juels, A., Kaliski Jr, B.S.: Pors: proofs of retrievability for large files. In: Ning, P., di Vimercati, S.D.C., Syverson, P.F. (eds.) CCS 2007, pp. 584–597. ACM (2007)
17. Katz, J.: Digital signatures. Springer Science & Business Media (2010)
18. Li, H., Liu, L., Lan, C., Wang, C., Guo, H.: Lattice-based privacy-preserving and forward-secure cloud storage public auditing scheme. IEEE Access **8**, 86797–86809 (2020)
19. Li, Y., Yu, Y., Min, G., Susilo, W., Ni, J., Choo, K.K.R.: Fuzzy identity-based data integrity auditing for reliable cloud storage systems. IEEE Trans. Dependable Secure Comput. **16**(1), 72–83 (2017)
20. Liu, Z., Liao, Y., Yang, X., He, Y., Zhao, K.: Identity-based remote data integrity checking of cloud storage from lattices. In: BigCom 2017, pp. 128–135. IEEE Computer Society (2017)
21. Ni, J., Yu, Y., Mu, Y., Xia, Q.: On the security of an efficient dynamic auditing protocol in cloud storage. IEEE Trans. Parallel Distrib. Syst. **25**(10), 2760–2761 (2013)
22. Shacham, H., Waters, B.: Compact proofs of retrievability. In: Pieprzyk, J. (ed.) ASIACRYPT 2008. LNCS, vol. 5350, pp. 90–107. Springer, Heidelberg (2008). https://doi.org/10.1007/978-3-540-89255-7_7
23. Shen, S.-T., Tzeng, W.-G.: Delegable provable data possession for remote data in the clouds. In: Qing, S., Susilo, W., Wang, G., Liu, D. (eds.) ICICS 2011. LNCS, vol. 7043, pp. 93–111. Springer, Heidelberg (2011). https://doi.org/10.1007/978-3-642-25243-3_8
24. Shen, W., Qin, J., Yu, J., Hao, R., Hu, J.: Enabling identity-based integrity auditing and data sharing with sensitive information hiding for secure cloud storage. IEEE Trans. Inf. Forensics Secur. **14**(2), 331–346 (2018)
25. Stefanov, E., van Dijk, M., Juels, A., Oprea, A.: Iris: A scalable cloud file system with efficient integrity checks. In: Zakon, R.H. (ed.) ACSAC 2012, pp. 229–238. ACM (2012)
26. Wang, C., Chow, S.S., Wang, Q., Ren, K., Lou, W.: Privacy-preserving public auditing for secure cloud storage. IEEE Trans. Comput. **62**(2), 362–375 (2011)
27. Wang, C., Wang, Q., Ren, K., Lou, W.: Privacy-preserving public auditing for data storage security in cloud computing. In: INFOCOM 2010, pp. 525–533. IEEE (2010)
28. Wang, Y., Wu, Q., Qin, B., Shi, W., Deng, R.H., Hu, J.: Identity-based data outsourcing with comprehensive auditing in clouds. IEEE Trans. Inf. Forensics Secur. **12**(4), 940–952 (2016)
29. Wang, Y., Wu, Q., Qin, B., Tang, S., Susilo, W.: Online/offline provable data possession. IEEE Trans. Inf. Forensics Secur. **12**(5), 1182–1194 (2017)
30. Xu, J., Yang, A., Zhou, J., Wong, D.S.: Lightweight delegatable proofs of storage. In: Askoxylakis, I., Ioannidis, S., Katsikas, S., Meadows, C. (eds.) ESORICS 2016. LNCS, vol. 9878, pp. 324–343. Springer, Cham (2016). https://doi.org/10.1007/978-3-319-45744-4_16

31. Yang, A., Xu, J., Weng, J., Zhou, J., Wong, D.S.: Lightweight and privacy-preserving delegatable proofs of storage with data dynamics in cloud storage. IEEE Trans. Cloud Comput. **9**(1), 212–225 (2018)

32. Yang, K., Jia, X.: An efficient and secure dynamic auditing protocol for data storage in cloud computing. IEEE Trans. Parallel Distrib. Syst. **24**(9), 1717–1726 (2012)

33. Yu, Y., et al.: Identity-based remote data integrity checking with perfect data privacy preserving for cloud storage. IEEE Trans. Inf. Forensics Secur. **12**(4), 767–778 (2016)

34. Yu, Y., Li, Y., Yang, B., Susilo, W., Yang, G., Bai, J.: Attribute-based cloud data integrity auditing for secure outsourced storage. IEEE Trans. Emerg. Top. Comput. **8**(2), 377–390 (2017)

35. Yu, Y.: Cloud data integrity checking with an identity-based auditing mechanism from rsa. Futur. Gener. Comput. Syst. **62**, 85–91 (2016)

36. Yuan, J., Yu, S.: Proofs of retrievability with public verifiability and constant communication cost in cloud. In: Sun, X., Shi, E., Ren, K. (eds.) SCC@ASIACCS 2013, pp. 19–26. ACM (2013)

37. Yuan, J., Yu, S.: Pcpor: public and constant-cost proofs of retrievability in cloud1. J. Comput. Secur. **23**(3), 403–425 (2015)

38. Zhang, J.H., Tang, W.J.: Security analysis on a public por scheme in cloud storage. Appli. Mech. Mater. **556–562**, 5395–5399 (2014)

39. Zhang, Y., Sang, Y., Xi, Z., Zhong, H.: Lattice based multi-replica remote data integrity checking for data storage on cloud. In: Shen, H., Sang, Y. (eds.) PAAP 2019. CCIS, vol. 1163, pp. 440–451. Springer, Singapore (2020). https://doi.org/10.1007/978-981-15-2767-8_39

# DEKS: A Secure Cloud-Based Searchable Service Can Make Attackers Pay

Yubo Zheng[1], Peng Xu[1(✉)], Wei Wang[2], Tianyang Chen[1], Willy Susilo[3], Kaitai Liang[4], and Hai Jin[1]

[1] National Engineering Research Center for Big Data Technology and System, Services Computing Technology and System Lab, Hubei Engineering Research Center on Big Data Security, School of Cyber Science and Engineering, Huazhong University of Science and Technology, Wuhan 430074, China
{zhengyubo,xupeng,chentianyang,hjin}@mail.hust.edu.cn
[2] Cyber-Physical-Social Systems Lab, School of Computer Science and Technology, Huazhong University of Science and Technology, Wuhan 430074, China
viviawangwei@hust.edu.cn
[3] Institute of Cybersecurity and Cryptology, School of Computing and Information Technology, University of Wollongong, Wollongong, Australia
wsusilo@uow.edu.au
[4] Faculty of Electrical Engineering, Mathematics and Computer Science, Delft University of Technology, Delft, The Netherlands
Kaitai.Liang@tudelft.nl

**Abstract.** Many practical secure systems have been designed to prevent real-world attacks via maximizing the attacking cost so as to reduce attack intentions. Inspired by this philosophy, we propose a new concept named delay encryption with keyword search (DEKS) to resist the notorious keyword guessing attack (KGA), in the context of secure cloud-based searchable services. Avoiding the use of complex (and unreasonable) assumptions, as compared to existing works, DEKS optionally leverages a *catalyst* that enables one (e.g., a valid data user) to easily execute encryption; without the *catalyst*, any unauthenticated system insiders and outsiders take severe time consumption on encryption. By this, DEKS can overwhelm a KGA attacker in the encryption stage before it obtains any advantage. We leverage the repeated squaring function, which is the core building block of our design, to construct the first DEKS instance. The experimental results show that DEKS is practical in thwarting KGA for both small and large-scale datasets. For example, in the Wikipedia, a KGA attacker averagely takes 7.23 years to break DEKS when the delay parameter $T = 2^{24}$. The parameter $T$ can be flexibly adjusted based on practical needs, and theoretically, its upper bound is infinite.

**Keywords:** Delay encryption with keyword search · Keyword guessing attack · Security · Privacy

© The Author(s), under exclusive license to Springer Nature Switzerland AG 2022
V. Atluri et al. (Eds.): ESORICS 2022, LNCS 13555, pp. 86–104, 2022.
https://doi.org/10.1007/978-3-031-17146-8_5

# 1  Introduction

To date, an increasing number of individuals and companies choose to outsource their personal and business data to remote cloud. Combining with encryption technique, cloud-based searchable service, like CipherCloud [2], bitglass [1], and MVISION Cloud [3], provide privacy-preserving data query and retrieval for cloud users without violating data security. The secure service enables a data searcher to put, say a keyword, into a search query, and after that, the cloud server performs searching and returns matching files without knowing the information of the keyword and the files. This searchability can be captured by the use of *searchable symmetric-key encryption* (SSE) [36], in a single-sender scenario but with complex key distribution for multiple senders, or *searchable public-key encryption* (SPE) [10] (also well known as *public-key encryption with keyword search*, PEKS), in a multi-sender scenario.

In PEKS, each sender generates keyword-searchable ciphertexts with a target receiver's public key. The key is public so that any sender can generate a PEKS ciphertext without pre-communication with the receiver. The receiver can keep off-line, after publishing his public key, till he wants to retrieve the ciphertexts of an expected keyword. Upon getting a keyword search delegation of the receiver, the cloud server finds all matching ciphertexts and then returns them. However, many PEKS schemes suffer from *keyword guessing attack* (KGA).

KGA seriously threatens the security of PEKS. This is due to the intrinsic design of PEKS [27]. Boneh *et al.* [11] concluded that it is a challenge to resist KGA unless the target keyword is sufficiently unpredictable. Figure 1 shows two types of KGA categorized as their interactive pattern, namely, off-line KGA [13] and on-line KGA [41]. Specifically, an off-line KGA attacker guesses the keyword in a unique search request without interaction with the cloud server, for example, the malicious server itself and other attackers launch KGA locally. An attacker can exhaust all possible keywords, generate the corresponding PEKS ciphertexts, and guess the target keyword by testing if a given ciphertext matches the trapdoor. As for on-line KGA, attackers, like malicious senders, need public injecting guessing ciphertexts into the cloud server. They can upload all possible PEKS ciphertexts to the server, eavesdrop the search results to determine which ciphertext corresponds to which trapdoors, and reveal the target keyword.

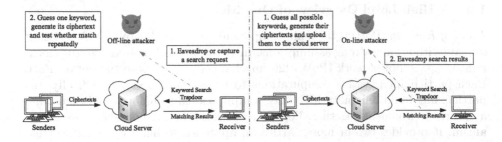

**Fig. 1.** Off-line and on-line KGA overview.

## 1.1    Motivation

Many research works have contributed to resisting KGA. We analyze and categorize them into the following types based on the core techniques they use. Note we here briefly introduce the types and will present a detailed review later.

- Type-I: The schemes, in [21,22,33,34], suppose that server is trusted. The receiver can designate that only trusted server can perform keyword search. Thus, KGA can be easily excluded.
- Type-II: The schemes, in [15,39,42], require that both senders and receiver know the distribution of all possible keywords, and the distribution is static. This facilitates the receiver to constrain the malicious server's search capability only to fuzzy keyword search. Thus, the server cannot guess the accurate target keyword.
- Type-III: The schemes, in [17,38], make good use of two non-colluding servers. The receiver can split a complete search procedure into two phases and delegate the phases to the two non-colluding servers, respectively. Neither of the servers can guess the target keyword independently.
- Type-IV: Those works, in [25,29–32,37], assume that the receiver can always identify if senders are trusted. The receiver may only search over these trusted senders' ciphertexts. Thus, on-line KGA may be easily prevented.
- Type-V: The solutions, in [16,43], requires a trusted server interactively to assist senders in generating ciphertexts (but does not launch on-line KGA). No sender can generate ciphertexts without the server. Thus, the server can limit the capability of malicious senders to launch on-line KGA.

We find that all the aforementioned solutions are valid only if some additional and strong assumptions (or unreasonable constraints) hold. These assumptions are hard to be captured in real-world scenarios, and they even deviate from the original PEKS. Specifically, the assumptions of the Type-I and Type-V solutions are too ideal in practice. The assumption of the Type-IV solutions limits the application of secure searchability, to some degree. The Type-II and Type-III solutions also restrict the scalability of PEKS. Note the comprehensive analyses will be given in Sect. 2. Without using the above assumptions, we make efforts to investigate a brand new design idea for KGA-resistant design.

## 1.2    A High-Level Overview of Our Idea

*Proof of Honesty* (PoH) is the main component we use to design a KGA-resistant scheme without any strong assumptions. Inspired by blockchain consensus mechanism, e.g., proof of work (PoW) [26] mechanism, we propose the notion PoH. Each participant pays his computations to prove his honesty. Specifically, the participants build reliability with only computational techniques and then build a secure environment together. PoH is a self-constructing honesty-aware mechanism. It provides two or more parties an approach to build up essential trust in fewer conversations, even non-interactively. Based on PoH, we successfully let attackers pay severe time consumption mandatorily in encryption. It results that a KGA attacker may lose intention or must pay a huge cost for attack. A considerable amount of cost overweighs the attacker's benefits such that KGA may be meaningless. Our approach does not yield complex interactions and expensive computational costs; meanwhile, it does not introduce any extra assumptions.

## 1.3   Our Contributions

This work aims at constructing a practical KGA-resistant scheme for cloud-based searchable service via the use of you-attack-then-you-pay philosophy. Our contributions are described as follows.

We investigate the existing KGA-resistant works and categorize them into five types according to their technical features. After comprehensively analyzing, we notice that we can design a KGA-resistant scheme in the PoH approach, to open a new vision in this research line. To this end, we propose a new scheme named *delay encryption with keyword search* (DEKS). DEKS allows the receiver to define the time cost of generating a keyword-searchable ciphertext when initializing his public key. With the receiver's public key, no sender can generate a ciphertext with a time cost less than the receiver's requirement, even when the sender is malicious. In other words, DEKS can delay the generation of ciphertext as the request of the receiver. Note such a delay process is non-interactive. Moreover, DEKS allows the receiver to initialize a *catalyst*, which enables the receiver to generate a keyword search trapdoor efficiently (without any delay). In application, the receiver optionally can give the *catalyst* to honest senders (e.g., top contacts of the email system who usually are the receiver's close friends or business partners) and speed up the generation of a ciphertext. In terms of security, the sender cannot leverage the *catalyst* to forge any legal search trapdoor.

We apply repeated squaring and bilinear mapping to realize a DEKS instance. In DEKS, we have four phases, namely, **Setup**, **DEKS**, **Trapdoor**, and **Test**. In **Setup**, the receiver generates his public-and-private keys and a *catalyst*. The public key contains a delay parameter $T$, which means the mandatory number of executing squaring modulo operations to generate a ciphertext in **DEKS**. However, the honest senders (like top contacts) can fast generate ciphertexts when getting the *catalyst* from the receiver. In **Trapdoor**, the receiver efficiently generates a trapdoor for an expected keyword with both the *catalyst* and the private key. We prove that if the generation of a ciphertext without the *catalyst* does not satisfy the above mandatory time limitation, the trapdoor is ineffective in testing the ciphertext even if they have the same keyword in the **Test** phase. We also prove that DEKS is semantically secure.

Finally, we evaluate DEKS through comprehensive experiments. We take the *Enron* mail data and *Wikipedia* article data to examine the practical security of DEKS for resisting KGA, respectively. DEKS is valid for both small and large-scale datasets. As the delay parameter $T$ increases, an attacker's average consumed time to complete a successful KGA climbs exponentially. For example, for the Wikipedia dataset, when $T = 2^{24}$, it takes 7.23 years for an attacker to complete a successful KGA. And, the average time cost to break a traditional PEKS is less than $51\,\mathrm{h}$. As for the small-scale dataset Enron, DEKS can also give a better performance on resisting KGA by increasing the value of $T$. At last, we consider the case where attackers are equipped with parallel computing ability. For mitigating the effect of parallel computing, the receiver can slightly increase the value of $T$. $T$ belongs to a large set and does have an infinite upper bound. It, thus, can be a factor to properly limit the KGA ability.

**Discussions.** To the best of our knowledge, the repeated squaring function is a unique technique to construct DEKS, which is also implied in [12]. From the technical viewpoint, our DEKS is different from the scheme in [12]. Furthermore, we cannot construct DEKS from their design because they delay the generation of a private key instead of ciphertext. Besides, the following delay techniques cannot be used to construct DEKS either. The password-based key-derivation function is used to mitigate dictionary attacks on password [40]. It delays deriving keys so that the workload of key search attacks significantly increases. But it cannot be used to delay encryption. Both PoW [26] and proof of sequential work (PoSW) [19] can mandatorily assign the time cost of finding a valid proof of a work. However, they require many valid proofs for a given task, and the receiver cannot securely delegate a semi-trust server to verify different proofs. This approach may not be feasible for us. The verifiable delay function (VDF) [9], which is not based on the repeated squaring function, is also ineffective in constructing DEKS. Such a kind of component cannot achieves either the non-interactive delay and verification functions or the *catalyst*-optional delay function, which is similar to the non-interactive VDF in [23], failing to achieve the optional *short-cut* to speed up finding a delay proof. We note that the *short-cut* (or the *catalyst*) is a must for guaranteeing a DEKS is friendly to the receiver and honest senders.

## 2   KGA Revisited

Table 1 shows the comparisons among the aforementioned five types of existing schemes and our proposed DEKS. We here separately consider insiders and outsiders in off-line and on-line KGA. Outside attackers are eavesdroppers and malicious senders. Semi-trusted servers perform as insider attackers. Our comprehensive analyzations as follows.

**Type-I.** The Type-I solutions suppose a trusted server performs all keyword search tasks while any other entity cannot. Baek *et al.* [6] first proposed this idea and designed a secure channel-free PEKS, but their work cannot resist KGA. Rhee *et al.* [34] applied this idea to construct the first PEKS instance resisting outside off-line KGA. Some following works, like [21,22,33], also applied this

**Table 1.** Comparisons among existing and our works.

| Type | Off-line KGA-resistant | | On-line KGA-resistant | | The particular required Assumption | Other disadvantages |
|------|---------|--------|---------|--------|------|------|
| | Outside | Inside | Outside | Inside | | |
| Type-I | √ | Omitted | √ | Omitted | A trusted server to implement keyword searches | Make PEKS useless in practice |
| Type-II | √ | √ | √ | √ | The distribution of keywords is known | Additional cost to filter out the redundant ciphertexts |
| Type-III | √ | √ | × | × | Two non-colluding servers to implement keyword searches cooperatively | The communication cost between two servers |
| Type-IV | √ | √ | √ | √ | The receiver can always identify if senders are trusted | The size of a keyword trapdoor is linear with the count of senders |
| Type-V | √ | Omitted | √ | Omitted | A trusted server to assist the generation of ciphertexts and trapdoors | The assistant server is needed and could be a performance bottleneck |
| DEKS | √ | √ | √ | √ | No above assumptions | No above disadvantages |

idea to resist outside off-line KGA. Generally, the Type-I solutions can be easily extended to resist outside on-line KGA by requesting the trusted server returns the encrypted search results to the receiver, as in [18]. However, supposing a trusted server is too ideal to realize in real-world scenarios. This assumption leads the Type-I solutions to omit inside off-line and on-line KGAs. Moreover, this assumption also makes PEKS meaningless in practice. A trusted server is allowed to search keywords directly over plaintexts while maintaining the confidentiality of keywords by applying a traditional secure communication technique.

**Type-II.** The Type-II solutions suppose that the distribution of keywords is known and public and allows the server only to implement fuzzy keyword search. Both the server and the malicious sender cannot know the accurate keyword that the receiver requests. Thus, the Type-II solutions can resist off-line and on-line KGAs. Xu *et al.* [39] proposed the first Type-II solution. Some following works utilize the same idea and achieve new properties, such as the works in [15,42]. However, it is difficult to know the distribution of keywords. In practice, different applications have different distributions of keywords. Moreover, the distribution of keywords can be dynamic due to the character of data. In addition, the Type-II solutions return many redundant ciphertexts to the receiver, and the receiver must pay an additional time cost to filter out these ciphertexts.

**Type-III.** The Type-III solutions suppose two non-colluding servers and split a search task into two parts, and these servers each implement a part. This idea first appeared in work [38]. However, if a single server is malicious, it can still launch the inside off-line KGA. Chen *et al.* overcame this limitation and designed a new Type-III solution [17]. However, it is not easy to guarantee that these two servers do not collude in practice. Moreover, the additional interaction between these two servers increases the communication cost and decreases the search performance.

**Type-IV.** The Type-IV solutions suppose the receiver can always identify if senders are trusted, and the receiver generates a trapdoor for each trusted sender to realize a keyword search over these senders' ciphertexts. Huang and Li [25] proposed the first and specific Type-IV solution to resist off-line and on-line KGAs. Some subsequent works applied the same idea to resist KGA, such as works in [29–32,37]. However, the Type-IV solutions limit the application of PEKS to some individual scenarios, such as the receiver knows all trusted senders in advance. Indeed, in such a scenario, SSE is more convenient than PEKS for achieving keyword searches over ciphertexts. In addition, the receiver has to generate many trapdoors for searching a keyword, and the count of trapdoors increases linearly with the count of trusted senders.

**Type-V.** The Type-V solutions suppose a trusted server to assist PEKS in generating its ciphertexts and trapdoors. Chen *et al.* [16] first proposed the Type-V solution. It designed a particular trusted keyword server to compute the hash values of keywords when senders encrypt these keywords or the receiver generates these keywords' trapdoors. Since this trusted server does not help the untrusted server and malicious senders generate the ciphertext, the Type-V solutions can resist the outside off-line and on-line KGAs. In addition, to resist the on-line KGA, the trusted server intentionally limits the speed to generate ciphertexts. Later, Zhang *et al.* [43] used multiple servers to avoid the single-point-of-failure problem. However, the Type-V solutions omit the case that the assistant server could be an inside attacker. Besides, the assistant server could be a performance bottleneck if many senders connect with the server simultaneously.

**DEKS.** As the first of its type, it avoids the unreasonable assumptions used in the previous types, and it can resist all kinds of KGAs. DEKS allows the receiver to non-interactively constrain the minimum time cost of generating a keyword-searchable ciphertext. Neither the malicious sender nor the untrusted server can break this constraint. Thus, launching a successful KGA will take a considerable time cost such that the cost could be beyond the benefits obtained by a successful attack. Compared with existing works, DEKS provides the best performance in all metrics, except encryption. But DEKS has a negligible impact on encryption throughput, and honest senders who hold a *catalyst* could generate ciphertexts efficiently. DEKS also does not affect testing throughput.

In summary, all previous KGA-resistant works rely on some particular assumptions. These assumptions are either difficult to realize or restrict the application of PEKS to some individual scenarios. In contrast, DEKS adopts the novel idea of delaying the encryption performance to resist KGA without any particular assumption. Any sender can independently achieve the encryption, but no one can avoid the mandatory encryption delay without a *catalyst*, even if the sender is malicious.

## 3   System Definition and Model

### 3.1   System Overview

A DEKS system contains three participants: receiver, sender, and server, and they work as follows, shown in Fig. 2.

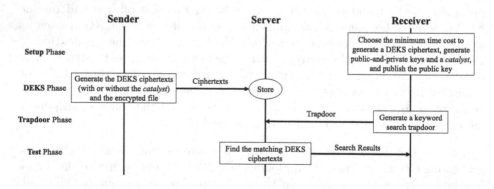

**Fig. 2.** The workflow of DEKS.

- *Receiver*. In **Setup**, a receiver chooses the minimum time cost to generate a DEKS ciphertext, generates his public-and-private keys and a *catalyst*, and then publishes his public key. In **Trapdoor**, the receiver chooses an expected keyword and delegates the corresponding keyword trapdoor to the server. The receiver optionally could give the *catalyst* to the honest senders (such as top contacts in the email system) for accelerating encryption.
- *Sender*. In **DEKS**, each sender abstracts keywords from the to-upload file, then gets the corresponding ciphertexts by encrypting these keywords with a receiver's public key, and finally uploads these ciphertexts and the encrypted file to a semi-trusted server. With the *catalyst*, the honest senders can encrypt keywords fast. Other senders without the *catalyst* can only encrypt with a mandatory and slow speed.
- *Server*. In **DEKS**, the server stores the uploaded ciphertexts from senders. In **Test**, once getting a keyword search delegation from a receiver, the server finds and returns all matching ciphertexts to the receiver. Note that the server is honest in implementing a keyword search; however, meanwhile, the server is curious about the keywords that the receiver desires to search.

### 3.2 Definition of DEKS

The main difference between PEKS and DEKS appears in the definitions of the encryption algorithm and correctness or consistency. The encryption algorithm of DEKS has an optional input parameter. When the optional input parameter is a *catalyst*, the encryption algorithm performs fast; otherwise, the performance is relatively slow. In addition to the search correctness, we define the correctness for delaying the generation of a DEKS ciphertext. The proposed correctness guarantees that everyone must take a fixed minimum time to generate a ciphertext without a *catalyst* - even for the malicious parties.

**Definition 1 (DEKS).** *A DEKS scheme* $\mathcal{DEKS}$ *contains four algorithms,* **Setup, DEKS, Trapdoor,** *and* **Test,** *as shown below.*

- $(PK, SK, \pi) \leftarrow$ **Setup**$(k, t)$: *Take as inputs a security parameter* $k$ *and a minimum time constraint* $t$ *and probabilistically output a pair of public-and-private keys* $(PK, SK)$ *and a catalyst* $\pi$.
- $C_w \leftarrow$ **DEKS**$(PK, w, opt)$: *Take as inputs the public key* $PK$, *a keyword* $w$ *and an optional input parameter* $opt$, *probabilistically output a DEKS ciphertext* $C_w$ *of keyword* $w$ *with a high speed if the optional input parameter* $opt = \pi$; *Otherwise, slowly output a probabilistical DEKS ciphertext* $C_w$ *of keyword* $w$.
- $T_{w'} \leftarrow$ **Trapdoor**$(SK, \pi, w')$: *Take as inputs the private key* $SK$, *the catalyst* $\pi$, *and a keyword* $w'$, *output a keyword search trapdoor* $T_{w'}$ *of keyword* $w'$.
- *"0" or "1"*$\leftarrow$ **Test**$(T_{w'}, C_w)$: *Take as inputs a keyword search trapdoor* $T_{w'}$ *and a DEKS ciphertext* $C_w$, *output "1" if trapdoor* $T_{w'}$ *and ciphertext* $C_w$ *contain the same keyword (namely, the representation* $w = w'$ *holds); otherwise, output "0".*

*In addition,* $\mathcal{DEKS}$ *must be correct or consistent in the following senses:*

- *Search Correctness:* For any two keywords $w$ and $w'$, given the corresponding ciphertext $C_w \leftarrow$ **DEKS**$(PK, w, opt)$ and the corresponding trapdoor $T_{w'} \leftarrow$ **Trapdoor**$(SK, \pi, w')$, scheme $\mathcal{DEKS}$ always has that algorithm **Test**$(T_{w'}, C_w)$ outputs "1" if $w = w'$ holds and "0" otherwise, except with a negligible probability.
- *Delay Correctness:* For any keyword $w$, no one can generate a valid DEKS ciphertext with a time cost less than parameter $t$ if it is the first time to encrypt the keyword $w$ without the catalyst $\pi$. A valid DEKS ciphertext means that the ciphertext can satisfy the above search correctness.

**Remark.** In practice, suppose a receiver determines that a sender is honest. The former optionally can help the latter to accelerate ciphertext generation by giving the *catalyst* $\pi$ securely, so that the time cost may decrease significantly. Beyond that, the sender cannot use the *catalyst* $\pi$ to harm the scheme, like recovering a valid keyword search trapdoor.

### 3.3  SS-CKA Security

Semantic security is recognized as a strong enough guarantee in the public-key setting, especially with simple assumptions. The semantic security of DEKS is the same as that of PEKS. It is also defined as the *semantic security under chosen keyword attacks* (SS-CKA). The SS-CKA security is distinct from the security under KGA. The former focuses on if a ciphertext leaks its keyword under the assumption that the keyword's trapdoor is unknown; while the latter captures if a trapdoor leaks its keyword, which implies that the KGA adversary knows the target trapdoor. We briefly review SS-CKA security below. More details can be found in reference [10].

**Definition 2 (SS-CKA).** *A DEKS scheme $\mathcal{DEKS}$ is SS-CKA secure if any probabilistically polynomial time (PPT) adversary $\mathcal{A}$ wins the following SS-CKA game with only a negligible advantage:*

- **Setup**: *A challenger sets the public-and-private keys and the* catalyst *of $\mathcal{DEKS}$ and publishes the public key (and the* catalyst*) to adversary $\mathcal{A}$.*
- **Query Phase 1**: *Adversary $\mathcal{A}$ adaptively requests the expected keywords' trapdoors.*
- **Challenge**: *Adversary $\mathcal{A}$ chooses two challenge keywords and issues them to the challenger. The challenger randomly picks one of those keywords to generate the challenge ciphertext.*
- **Query Phase 2**: *Same as* **Query Phase 1**. *Noting that adversary $\mathcal{A}$ cannot request the trapdoors of the challenge keywords in* **Query Phase 1 and 2**.
- **Guess**: *Adversary $\mathcal{A}$ guesses which challenge keyword is contained in the challenge ciphertext. Adversary $\mathcal{A}$ wins this game if the guess is correct.*

# 4    A Concrete Construction for DEKS

## 4.1    Mathematical Tools

**Bilinear Mapping Function** [14]. Let $\mathbb{G}_1$, $\mathbb{G}_2$ and $\mathbb{G}_T$ be three multiplicative groups with the same prime order $q$. Let $g_1$ and $g_2$ denote generators of group $\mathbb{G}_1$ and $\mathbb{G}_2$, respectively. The bilinear mapping function is defined as an efficient function $\hat{e} : \mathbb{G}_1 \times \mathbb{G}_2 \to \mathbb{G}_T$ with the property that equation $\hat{e}(g_1^u, g_2^v) = \hat{e}(g_1, g_2)^{uv}$ holds for $\forall u, v \in \mathbb{Z}_q^*$.

**Repeated Squaring Function** [35]. Let $P$ and $Q$ be two special primes having the same binary size. We say that primes $P$ and $Q$ are special if equations $P = 2P_1 + 1$, $P_1 = 2P_2 + 1$, $Q = 2Q_1 + 1$, and $Q_1 = 2Q_2 + 1$ hold and $P_1, P_2, Q_1$, and $Q_2$ are also primes [8]. Without loss of generality, suppose $P_2$ is less than $Q_2$. Let $N = P \cdot Q$ and $\varphi(\cdot)$ denote Euler's totient function. Given $\forall \varpi \in \mathbb{Z}_N^*$ and $T < P_2$, a repeated squaring function is defined to compute $\varpi^{2^T} \bmod N$.

With Euler number $\varphi(N)$, it is very efficient to compute $\varpi^{2^T} \bmod N$ by computing $2^T \bmod \varphi(N)$ first and then computing $\varpi^{2^T \bmod \varphi(N)} \bmod N$. In contrast, without Euler number $\varphi(N)$, we usually have to repeatedly compute $\varpi = \varpi^2 \bmod N$ $T$ times.

## 4.2    The Construction

We apply the repeated squaring function (RSF) to delay the time cost of ciphertext generation. Instead of directly generating a searchable ciphertext for a keyword, we take the keyword as input to implement the RSF and then compute the ciphertext from the resulting output. We state that no practical method can accelerate the implementation of the RSF without a *catalyst*. We also use a similar idea to efficiently generate a keyword search trapdoor (with the *catalyst*). Due to the delay capability, anyone who does not know the *catalyst* must take a mandatory time to generate a ciphertext. And this capability does not affect the search performance. The details of our instance are described below.

- **Setup**$(k, t, \mathcal{W})$: Take as inputs the security parameter $k$, the minimum time constraint $t$, and the keyword space $\mathcal{W}$ and implement the steps below:
  1. Generate parameters $(q, \mathbb{G}_1, \mathbb{G}_2, \mathbb{G}_T, g_2, \hat{e})$ of the bilinear mapping function according to the security parameter $k$;
  2. Pick parameters $(P, Q, N, T)$ of the repeated squaring function, such that for any randomly chosen $\varpi \in \mathbb{Z}_N^*$, the time cost to compute $\varpi^{2^T} \bmod N$ is more than the minimum time constraint $t$ without $\varphi(N)$;
  3. Set $\pi = 2^T \bmod \varphi(N)$, randomly pick $\sigma \in \mathbb{Z}_q^*$, and set $\eta = g_2^\sigma$;
  4. Choose three cryptographic hash functions $H_1 : \mathcal{W} \to \mathbb{Z}_N^*$, $H_2 : \mathbb{Z}_N^* \to \mathbb{G}_1$, and $H_3 : \mathbb{G}_T \to \{0, 1\}^k$;
  5. Output public key $PK = (q, \mathbb{G}_1, \mathbb{G}_2, \mathbb{G}_T, g_2, \eta, \hat{e}, \mathcal{W}, N, T, H_1, H_2, H_3)$, private key $SK = \sigma$, and *catalyst* $\pi$.
- **DEKS**$(PK, w, opt)$: Take as inputs public key $PK$, a keyword $w \in \mathcal{W}$, and an optional parameter $opt \in \{Null, \pi\}$ and execute the steps below:

1. Take the hash value $H_1(w)$ as input to compute its repeated squaring, where directly compute $\Delta = H_1(w)^\pi \mod N$ if $opt = \pi$, and otherwise, get the same result slowly by computing $\Delta = H_1(w)^{2^T} \mod N$;
2. Randomly pick $r \in \mathbb{Z}_q^*$ and compute $C_1 = g_2^r$ and $C_2 = H_3(\hat{e}(H_2(\Delta)^r, \eta))$;
3. Output the DEKS ciphertext $C_w = (C_1, C_2)$ of keyword $w$.
- **Trapdoor**$(SK, \pi, w')$: Take as inputs private key $SK$, catalyst $\pi$, and a keyword $w' \in \mathcal{W}$, compute the repeated squaring $\Delta' = H_1(w')^\pi \mod N$ of the hash value $H_1(w')$, and finally output the keyword search trapdoor $T_{w'} = H_2(\Delta')^\sigma$.
- **Test**$(T_{w'}, C_w)$: Take as inputs a keyword search trapdoor $T_{w'}$ and a DEKS ciphertext $C_w = (C_1, C_2)$, output "1" if $H_3(\hat{e}(T_{w'}, C_1)) = C_2$, and otherwise, output "0".

### 4.3   Correctness and Security Proof

Theorem 1 and 2 separately guarantee the search correctness and delay correctness of our DEKS instance. Due to the limit of space, we provide the proofs of these two theorems in the full version of this paper.

**Theorem 1.** *Suppose that hash functions $H_1, H_2$, and $H_3$ are random oracles. DEKS can maintain search correctness, except for a negligible probability.*

**Theorem 2.** *Given two special primes $P$ and $Q$ having $P \neq Q$, $N = P \cdot Q$, and a positive integer $T < P_2$; suppose that $N$ is an n-bit composite number. The time cost to generate a DEKS ciphertext is at least $t = \mathcal{S}_n \cdot T$ without catalyst $\pi$, where $\pi = 2^T \mod \varphi(N)$, $\varphi(N) = (P-1)(Q-1)$, and $\mathcal{S}_n$ is the time cost to compute squaring modulo $N$.*

The SS-CKA security relies on the *computational bilinear Diffie-Hellman* (CBDH) assumption. According to the security parameter $k$, given parameters $(q, \mathbb{G}_1, \mathbb{G}_2, \mathbb{G}_T, g_1, g_2, \hat{e})$ of the bilinear mapping function and parameters $(g_2^a, g_2^b, g_1^c)$, the CBDH problem is to compute the value of $\hat{e}(g_1, g_2)^{abc}$, where $(a, b, c)$ are randomly sampled from $\mathbb{Z}_q^*$. Let $\text{Adv}_{\mathcal{B}}^{\text{CBDH}}(k)$ denote the advantage of solving the CBDH problem by algorithm $\mathcal{B}$. The CBDH assumption holds if $\text{Adv}_{\mathcal{B}}^{\text{CBDH}}(k)$ is negligible.

In the proof, we show that a specially constructed algorithm can solve the CBDH problem if a PPT adversary can break the SS-CKA security of our DEKS instance. Formally, we have Theorem 3 below. Since the CBDH assumption holds in practice, Theorem 3 guarantees that no one can break the SS-CKA security. Due to the limit of space, we provide the proof in the full version of this paper.

**Theorem 3.** *Model hash functions $H_1$, $H_2$, and $H_3$ as three random oracles $\mathcal{Q}_{H_1}(\cdot)$, $\mathcal{Q}_{H_2}(\cdot)$, and $\mathcal{Q}_{H_3}(\cdot)$, respectively. Suppose a PPT adversary $\mathcal{A}$ wins with advantage $\text{Adv}_{\text{DEKS}, \mathcal{A}}^{\text{SS-CKA}}$ in the SS-CKA game of our DEKS instance, in which $\mathcal{A}$ makes at most $q_1$ queries to $\mathcal{Q}_{H_1}(\cdot)$, at most $q_2$ queries to $\mathcal{Q}_{H_2}(\cdot)$, at most $q_3$ queries to $\mathcal{Q}_{H_3}(\cdot)$, and at most $q_t$ queries to $\mathcal{Q}_{trapdoor}(\cdot)$. Then, the probability of a PPT algorithm $\mathcal{B}$ to solve the CBDH problem in parameters $(q, \mathbb{G}_1, \mathbb{G}_2, \mathbb{G}_T, g_1, g_2, \hat{e}, g_2^a, g_2^b, g_1^c)$ is $\text{Adv}_{\mathcal{B}}^{\text{CBDH}}(k) \geq \frac{2}{e^2 q_t^2 q_3} \text{Adv}_{\text{DEKS}, \mathcal{A}}^{\text{SS-CKA}}$, where $e$ denotes the base of the natural logarithm.*

# 5  Evaluation

We evaluate practical schemes in terms of computation and communication. And we experimentally compare DEKS with the two most-efficient schemes. We also leverage the *Enron* mail data [20] and *Wikipedia* article dataset [24] to evaluate the security of our DEKS under KGA.

## 5.1  Complexity Analysis

In terms of complexity, we compare DEKS with six classic PEKS instances. These schemes include the first PEKS (BC'04 [10]) and different types of KGA-resistant PEKS (RS'09 [34], XJ'13 [39], CM'16 [17], HL'17 [25], and CMY'16 [16]). For each of them, we analyze the efficiency in three algorithms: ciphertext generation, trapdoor computation, and test if a ciphertext matches. And we also analyze the size for the main public and private parameters. Moreover, we evaluate the number of expensive cryptographic operations implemented in those algorithms. The expensive operations mainly include the computations of exponentiation, multiplication, division, and bilinear mapping in different algebraic groups. To make the comparison simple and clear, Table 2 defines the symbols which we use later.

Compared with RS'09, XJ'13, CM'16, HL'17, and CMY'16, DEKS is much efficient in trapdoor generation and test stage. But DEKS is more complicated in ciphertext generation than others. We choose to use this tricky and subtle way to resist KGA. Further, both DEKS and BC'04 are most efficient in terms of communication complexity. If honest senders are given the *catalyst*, the complexity of encryption reduces significantly which could be quite close to the performance of BC'04. Besides, DEKS still performs well in terms of parameter size.

In summary, BC'04 has great performance in terms of the complexity and the interaction pattern but cannot thwart KGA. Under some particular assumptions, others may resist KGA while sacrificing some complexity and communication price. DEKS maintains analogous complexity and the same interaction pattern as BC'04, while merely sacrificing the efficiency of encryption.

**Table 2.** Theoretical comparison among DEKS and existing works in efficiency.

| Instance | Computation complexity | | | Communication Cost | | | Parameter Size | | Type |
|---|---|---|---|---|---|---|---|---|---|
| | Ciphertext | Trapdoor | Testing | Ciphertext | Trapdoor | Testing | Public | Private | |
| BC'04 [10] | $2 \times E_1 + B$ | $E_1$ | $B$ | $G+k$ | $G$ | $\Omega$ | $2 \times G$ | $\mathbb{Z}_q^*$ | Original |
| RS'09 [34] | $2 \times E_1 + B$ | $3 \times E_1 + M_1$ | $2 \times E_1 + D + B$ | $G+k$ | $2 \times G$ | $\Omega$ | $3 \times G$ | $2 \times \mathbb{Z}_q^*$ | Type-I |
| XJ'13 [39] | $4 \times E_1 + 2 \times B$ | $2 \times E_1$ | $2 \times B$ | $2 \times G + 2 \times k$ | $G$ | $2 \times \Omega$ or $3 \times \Omega$ | $2 \times G$ | $\mathbb{Z}_q^*$ | Type-II |
| CM'16 [17] | $4 \times E_1 + 2 \times M_1$ | $4 \times E_1 + D + M_1$ | $7 \times E_1 + D + 5 \times M_1$ | $6 \times G$ | $3 \times G$ | $\Omega$ | $2 \times G$ | $4 \times \mathbb{Z}_q^*$ | Type-III |
| HL'17 [25] | $3 \times E_1 + M_1$ | $\theta \times (E_1 + B)$ | $M_2 + B$ | $2 \times G$ | $\theta \times G_T$ | $\Omega$ | $2 \times G$ | $2 \times \mathbb{Z}_q^*$ | Type-IV |
| CMY'16 [16] | $2 \times E_1 + 2 \times E_2 + 2 \times M_3 + B$ | $E_1 + 2 \times E_2 + 2 \times M_3$ | $B$ | $2 \times \mathbb{Z}_N^* + G + k$ | $2 \times \mathbb{Z}_N^* + G$ | $\Omega$ | $2 \times G + 2 \times \mathbb{Z}_N^*$ | $\mathbb{Z}_q^* + \mathbb{Z}_N^*$ | Type-V |
| DEKS | $2 \times E_1 + T \times M_3 + B$ or $2 \times E_1 + E_2 + B$ | $E_1 + E_2$ | $B$ | $G+k$ | $G$ | $\Omega$ | $2 \times G + \mathbb{Z}_N^*$ | $\mathbb{Z}_q^* + \mathbb{Z}_N^*$ | New |

Notations*:
$E_1$ and $E_2$ separately denote the exponentiation operation in groups G and $\mathbb{Z}_N^*$;
$\theta$ denotes the number of possible senders; $\Omega$ denotes the size of matching ciphertexts;
$T$ denotes the delay parameter in our DEKS instance; $k$ denotes the security parameter;
$B$ denotes the bilinear mapping operation; $D$ denotes the division operation in group G;
$M_1$, $M_2$, and $M_3$ separately denote the multiplication operation in groups G, $G_T$, and $\mathbb{Z}_N^*$.

*Without loss of generality, we use G denote $G_1$ or $G_2$.

## 5.2   Experimental Analysis

We design two kinds of experiments to evaluate DEKS's performance, and further compare it with two efficient works, namely, BC'04 and CMY'16. The first experiment codes the above three instances. It compares their time costs in the aforementioned three algorithms. The second experiment tests the capability of DEKS in resisting KGA. It separately compares the time costs in launching KGA on DEKS and BC'04 in order to show that DEKS can make attackers cost massively. Further, we evaluate the average time cost on one guessing attempt for attackers equipped with parallel computing supports. The results show that our DEKS still makes attackers suffer well. Our experimental source codes are available on https://github.com/HustSecurityLab/DEKS_Exp, and the interested readers can use the codes to reproduce the results.

**Table 3.** Experimental environment.

| Hardware & operation system | 4 × Intel Xeon CPU E5-2630 v3 @ 2.40 GHz and 48 GB RAM; Ubuntu 20.04LTS |
|---|---|
| Compiler & interpreter | GCC v9.3.0 and Python v3.6 |
| Program library | GMP v6.1.2, PBC v0.5.14, and NLTK v3.5 |
| Dataset | Enron dataset [20] and Wikipedia dataset [24] |
| Elliptic curve $y^2 = x^3 + b$ with Embedding Degree 12 (unit: decimal) | |
| Base field | 16283262548997601220198008118239886027035269286659395419233331082106632227801 |
| Group order | 162832625489976012201980081182398860269076633990640343451383740756301306087801 |
| $b$ | 7322757890651446833342173470888950103129198494728585151431956701557392549679 |
| Repeated Squaring Function $y = x^{2^T}$ mod $N$ with $N = P \cdot Q$; both $P, Q$ are special primes (unit: hexadecimal) | |
| $P$ | DD848D47E193DCF0F57DD9256ABF10B5869C2D5D600C21A4D36C29659C062542B5CDCB6CF1002D7177D720472078AFC0 193BAD7E0FCE7C07CABC83526F71CF2881993188748C07C52CF73D1A09BF38F22163909A7EBAEEC9A9D9019F6CE919AE F18BCD995F80E7823370D500B53DC85D169F4FBA383C9A2E7DA2393A11A9B171C86957B82E8115F9FB19670466155E50 E41ADF91FB392EBC53614A475F58F9959972E56346993923991BD15110D2393513243DFEB2C28FCDFA067535E7A8A4DF |
| $Q$ | F9CE5FD04C169FC42F3C24C9E149EDCA7513A02648628C9AB80A9E9CE6F1FCD7EF4EA0FBC5AD4BE3E2B199A99969B749 01B46BAF632A3B653A2E0FDC37D9D44646247C104EAB0A38027725886DCCAC682A3E71A84F57E5CE3FAF8C6DD7DEA272 07AD6B3FBDDD51A4898884FB9C4853826C2836987179D4359122308CC6D44987562800D136BFB01CB3611E66B0F862EF A0E3769BE3795A9A75CA36A69E60851111849F8F0B8D46C5ACE50FCA7157B48B991C5AE30BC7B4198C464302C477CD0F |

- **Experimental Environment.** Table 3 shows the experimental platform, including the hardware and software, the elliptic curve for realizing the bilinear mapping function, and the parameters of the repeated squaring function. We use the GNU Multiple Precision Arithmetic (GMP) library and the Pairing-Based Cryptography (PBC) library to implement BC'04, CMY'16, and DEKS. We produce the instances in the same bilinear-mapping-friendly elliptic curve [7] that offers efficient exponentiation operations. The elliptic curve and the composite number $N$ both provide the same security level as AES-128. To test the performance, as in [28], we apply the Enron and Wikipedia and extract their keywords to generate a small-scale dataset and a large-scale dataset separately.
- **Performance Comparison.** This part shows the experimental results of the three instances BC'04, CMY'16, and DEKS. For Algorithm **Test, Trapdoor**, and **DEKS**, we choose the delay parameter $T$ with values $2^0, 2^{12}$, and $2^{24}$

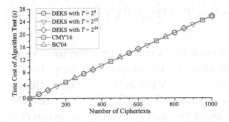

**Fig. 3.** Time cost: algorithm **Test**.

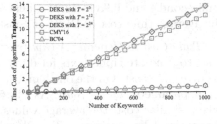

**Fig. 4.** Time cost: algorithm **Trapdoor**.

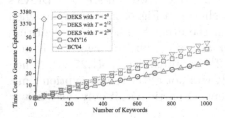

**Fig. 5.** Time cost: generate ciphertexts.

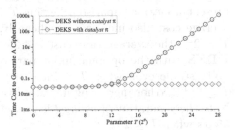

**Fig. 6.** DEKS time cost: generate a ciphertext with an increase in parameter $T$.

to clearly show the relations between the value of $T$ and algorithms' performance. Meanwhile, we set a test size of 1,000 to clearly show the average time cost in each figure. Moreover, we present the average encryption time of DEKS with different delay parameters. Without lose generality, we use $T = 2^i (i \in [0, 28])$ to show the experimental results clearly. We let the delay parameter $T < 2^{28}$ since it is sufficient for us to practically resist KGA (which can be seen later).

*Time Cost of Algorithm* **Test**. Table 2 concludes that instances BC'04, CMY'16, and DEKS have the same complexity in testing a ciphertext. The experimental results, as shown in Fig. 3, also confirm this conclusion. Given different numbers of ciphertexts, we test the total time cost to find the matching ciphertexts and compute the average time to test a ciphertext. In summary, the above three instances have the same average time cost, which is approximately 25.55 milliseconds, in testing a ciphertext.

*Time Cost of Algorithm* **Trapdoor**. For each instance, we test the total time costs to generate the corresponding trapdoors for different numbers of keywords and compute the average cost. The numerical results, which is described in Fig. 4, imply that DEKS takes more time than BC'04 in trapdoor generation, and the time cost of DEKS is slightly higher than that of CMY'16. For example, the average time cost of BC'04, CMY'16, and DEKS are 0.96 milliseconds, 12.24

milliseconds, and 0.98 to 13.71 milliseconds (for $T \in [2^0, 2^{24}]$), respectively. And the average time cost of DEKS is constant for $T \geq 2^{12}$.

*Time Cost to Generate A Ciphertext.* For each instance, we test the total time costs to generate ciphertexts for different numbers of keywords and compute the average time cost. On the one hand, we test algorithm **DEKS** with the optional input parameter $opt = Null$. As Fig. 5 shows, when $T = 2^0$, DEKS and BC'04 take a similar cost, the average values are 28.63 ms and 28.47 ms, respectively. When the delay parameter $T = 2^{12}$, the average of DEKS and CMY'16 change to 45.11 ms and 39.87 ms, respectively. Note for the case where $T = 2^{24}$, we only present the result of 50 keywords in Fig. 5. We note that is sufficient to present a clear comparison. Setting $T$ from $2^0$ to $2^{28}$, we can see that DEKS's average cost also increases significantly, as shown in Fig. 6. For example, when $T = 2^{20}$, the average time cost is 4.25 s. On the other hand, we test algorithm **DEKS** with the optional input parameter $opt = \pi$. The average cost is now quite stable even when $T$ is increased to $2^{12}$, approximately 41.27 ms. When $T \geq 2^{12}$, further increasing its value, we say, will not affect the encryption time. Note the generation of *catalyst* is very efficient, in particular, it only takes nearly 55 μs when $T \leq 2^{28}$.

- **Testing DEKS's Capability Against KGA**. We take the *Enron* mail data and *Wikipedia* article dataset as examples and test the average time cost on launching a successful KGA on DEKS and BC'04. First, we remove the wiki syntax from the entire *Wikipedia* article dataset using Wikipedia Extractor [5], then extract keywords using the PorterStemmer tool provided by the NLTK library [4] and remove stop words. Thus, we extract 6,756,439 different keywords from the *Wikipedia*. Similarly, we extract 400,087 keywords from the *Enron*.

Suppose a KGA attacker desires to know the keyword underlying a given keyword search trapdoor. The attacker picks a keyword from the keyword space, generates the keyword's searchable ciphertext, and tests if the searchable ciphertext matches the given trapdoor. If the test outputs a yes, the attacker successfully guesses the keyword and stops the attack. Otherwise, it chooses a new keyword and repeats the above steps.

Note BC'04 always provides fixed time cost w.r.t. ciphertext generation and keyword testing; and given a fixed $T$, DEKS also maintains fixed cost. Thus, it is feasible for us to compute the time cost to launch a successful KGA for a given trapdoor. For example, let $\mathcal{T}^{\mathrm{Gen}}$ and $\mathcal{T}^{\mathrm{Test}}$ be the time costs to generate and test a ciphertext, respectively. Suppose that the KGA attacker can get the keyword in a target trapdoor after guessing $num$ keywords. Then, the time cost of the KGA attacker is equal to $num \cdot (\mathcal{T}^{\mathrm{Gen}} + \mathcal{T}^{\mathrm{Test}})$.

According to the above methods, we compute the time costs of launching a successful KGA, for each keyword. Then, we compute these costs' arithmetic mean, which is equal to the sum of them divided by the total count of distinct keywords. Table 4 and 5 present the results on launching KGA on DEKS (with some different delay parameters) and BC'04, with Wikipedia and Enron datasets.

**Table 4.** Time cost: launch KGA on DEKS and BC'04 with Wikipedia.

| Instance | Arithmetic mean of time cost | | | | | | | | | |
|---|---|---|---|---|---|---|---|---|---|---|
| | $T$ | Time | $T$ | Time | $T$ | Time | $T$ | Time | $T$ | Time |
| DEKS | $2^{10}$ | 54.76 h | $2^{11}$ | 58.90 h | $2^{12}$ | 65.99 h | $2^{13}$ | 3.39 days | $2^{14}$ | 4.69 days |
| | $2^{15}$ | 7.27 days | $2^{16}$ | 12.51 days | $2^{17}$ | 22.74 days | $2^{18}$ | 43.42 days | $2^{19}$ | 84.85 days |
| | $2^{20}$ | 167.18 days | $2^{21}$ | 340.10 days | $2^{22}$ | 1.81 yrs | $2^{23}$ | 3.63 yrs | $2^{24}$ | 7.23 yrs |
| BC'04 | 50.69 h | | | | | | | | | |

**Table 5.** Time cost: launch KGA on DEKS and BC'04 with Enron.

| Instance | Arithmetic mean of time cost | | | | | | | | | |
|---|---|---|---|---|---|---|---|---|---|---|
| | $T$ | Time | $T$ | Time | $T$ | Time | $T$ | Time | $T$ | Time |
| DEKS | $2^{10}$ | 194.57 min | $2^{11}$ | 209.28 min | $2^{12}$ | 234.48 min | $2^{13}$ | 4.82 h | $2^{14}$ | 6.67 h |
| | $2^{15}$ | 10.33 h | $2^{16}$ | 17.78 h | $2^{17}$ | 32.32 h | $2^{18}$ | 61.70 h | $2^{19}$ | 5.02 days |
| | $2^{20}$ | 9.89 days | $2^{21}$ | 20.14 days | $2^{22}$ | 39.22 days | $2^{23}$ | 78.44 days | $2^{24}$ | 156.29 days |
| | $2^{25}$ | 312.84 days | $2^{26}$ | 1.71 yrs | $2^{27}$ | 3.44 yrs | $2^{28}$ | 6.86 yrs | | |
| BC'04 | 180.09 min | | | | | | | | | |

We find that the attack works quite well on BC'04 for both small and large-scale datasets. But, with the increase of $T$, DEKS can make attackers' time cost jump exponentially. For instance, for the Wikipedia, when $T = 2^{10}$, we make attackers take 54.76 h; when $T = 2^{17}$, the cost jumps to 22.74 days; and further $T = 2^{24}$, it exponentially increases to 7.23 years. As for the small-scale dataset, Enron, the time cost of the attacker also reaches 6.86 years, along with the increase of $T$.

In practice, a KGA attacker may guess and test possible keywords in parallel so as to enhance attack performance. To simulate this setting, we experimentally test the average time cost of one guessing attempt (namely, generating and testing a DEKS ciphertext), with different delay parameters and various degrees of parallelism. Figure 7 presents the main results. From the results, it can be seen that even a tiny increase of $T$ may effectively mitigate the influence of parallel attacks. For instance, given $T = 2^{19}$, the attacker with 16 cores CPU can reduce the time cost of one attempt from 2.17 s to 0.17 s. If we put $T$ to $2^{23}$, the cost bounces back to 2.61 s. We state that DEKS resists KGA by adaptively increasing the time cost of generating a ciphertext. And this increase is unavoidable for any PPT adversary. According to the specific application, we can choose an

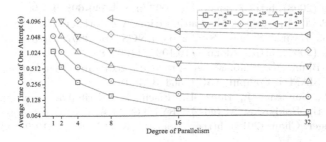

**Fig. 7.** DEKS average time cost: guess and test possible keywords in parallel.

appropriate value of $T$ to increase the attack difficulty, so that the intaken cost of attack is far beyond the benefit attackers achieve.

## 6    Conclusion

To resist KGA on secure cloud-based searchable service, we propose a new scheme DEKS, which allows receivers to constrain the minimum time cost of a keyword-searchable ciphertext generation, in a non-interactive way. No sender who generates the ciphertext can break the time constraint without a *catalyst*. We apply both the RSF and bilinear mapping function to construct the first DEKS instance and prove its unique encryption delay capability. Compared with existing works, DEKS provides good performance and simple interaction pattern as the original PEKS, except that the time cost of ciphertext generation may go beyond the minimum constraint. Our experimental results show that our design can practically resist KGA in small and large-scale datasets.

**Acknowledgements.** We would like to thank our shepherd Anrin Chakraborti and the anonymous reviewers for their insightful comments and valuable suggestions. This work was partly supported by the National Key Research and Development Program of China under Grant No. 2021YFB3101304, the Wuhan Applied Foundational Frontier Project under Grant No. 2020010601012188, the National Natural Science Foundation of China under Grant No. 61872412, the Guangdong Provincial Key Research and Development Plan Project under Grant No. 2019B010139001, and the European Union's Horizon 2020 Research and Innovation Programme under Grant Agreement No. 952697 (ASSURED) and No. 101021727 (IRIS).

## References

1. Bitglass. https://www.bitglass.com/cloud-encryption
2. CipherCloud. https://www.ciphercloud.com/encryption-and-tokenization/
3. MVISION cloud. https://www.mcafee.com/enterprise/en-us/products/mvision-cloud/salesforce.html
4. Natural Language Toolkit (2020). http://www.nltk.org/
5. Attardi, G.: WikiExtractor (2015). https://github.com/attardi/wikiextractor
6. Baek, J., Safavi-Naini, R., Susilo, W.: Public key encryption with keyword search revisited. In: Gervasi, O., Murgante, B., Laganà, A., Taniar, D., Mun, Y., Gavrilova, M.L. (eds.) ICCSA 2008. LNCS, vol. 5072, pp. 1249–1259. Springer, Heidelberg (2008). https://doi.org/10.1007/978-3-540-69839-5_96
7. Barreto, P.S.L.M., Naehrig, M.: Pairing-friendly elliptic curves of prime order. In: Preneel, B., Tavares, S. (eds.) SAC 2005. LNCS, vol. 3897, pp. 319–331. Springer, Heidelberg (2006). https://doi.org/10.1007/11693383_22
8. Blum, L., Blum, M., Shub, M.: A simple unpredictable pseudo-random number generator. SIAM J. Comput. **15**(2), 364–383 (1986)
9. Boneh, D., Bonneau, J., Bünz, B., Fisch, B.: Verifiable delay functions. In: Shacham, H., Boldyreva, A. (eds.) CRYPTO 2018. LNCS, vol. 10991, pp. 757–788. Springer, Cham (2018). https://doi.org/10.1007/978-3-319-96884-1_25

10. Boneh, D., Di Crescenzo, G., Ostrovsky, R., Persiano, G.: Public key encryption with keyword search. In: Cachin, C., Camenisch, J.L. (eds.) EUROCRYPT 2004. LNCS, vol. 3027, pp. 506–522. Springer, Heidelberg (2004). https://doi.org/10.1007/978-3-540-24676-3_30

11. Boneh, D., Raghunathan, A., Segev, G.: Function-private identity-based encryption: hiding the function in functional encryption. In: Canetti, R., Garay, J.A. (eds.) CRYPTO 2013. LNCS, vol. 8043, pp. 461–478. Springer, Heidelberg (2013). https://doi.org/10.1007/978-3-642-40084-1_26

12. Burdges, J., De Feo, L.: Delay encryption. In: Canteaut, A., Standaert, F.-X. (eds.) EUROCRYPT 2021. LNCS, vol. 12696, pp. 302–326. Springer, Cham (2021). https://doi.org/10.1007/978-3-030-77870-5_11

13. Byun, J.W., Rhee, H.S., Park, H.-A., Lee, D.H.: Off-line keyword guessing attacks on recent keyword search schemes over encrypted data. In: Jonker, W., Petković, M. (eds.) SDM 2006. LNCS, vol. 4165, pp. 75–83. Springer, Heidelberg (2006). https://doi.org/10.1007/11844662_6

14. Chatterjee, S., Menezes, A.: On cryptographic protocols employing asymmetric pairings - the role of $\Psi$ revisited. Discret. Appl. Math. **159**(13), 1311–1322 (2011)

15. Chen, H., Cao, Z., Dong, X., Shen, J.: SDKSE-KGA: a secure dynamic keyword searchable encryption scheme against keyword guessing attacks. In: Meng, W., Cofta, P., Jensen, C.D., Grandison, T. (eds.) IFIPTM 2019. IAICT, vol. 563, pp. 162–177. Springer, Cham (2019). https://doi.org/10.1007/978-3-030-33716-2_13

16. Chen, R., et al.: Server-aided public key encryption with keyword search. IEEE Trans. Inf. Forensics Secur. **11**(12), 2833–2842 (2016)

17. Chen, R., Mu, Y., Yang, G., Guo, F., Wang, X.: Dual-server public-key encryption with keyword search for secure cloud storage. IEEE Trans. Inf. Forensics Secur. **11**(4), 789–798 (2016)

18. Chen, Y.: SPEKS: secure server-designation public key encryption with keyword search against keyword guessing attacks. Comput. J. **58**(4), 922–933 (2015)

19. Cohen, B., Pietrzak, K.: Simple proofs of sequential work. In: Nielsen, J.B., Rijmen, V. (eds.) EUROCRYPT 2018. LNCS, vol. 10821, pp. 451–467. Springer, Cham (2018). https://doi.org/10.1007/978-3-319-78375-8_15

20. Cohen, W.W.: Enron Email Dataset (2015). https://www.cs.cmu.edu/./enron/

21. Emura, K., Ito, K., Ohigashi, T.: Secure-channel free searchable encryption with multiple keywords: a generic construction, an instantiation, and its implementation. J. Comput. Syst. Sci. **114**, 107–125 (2020)

22. Fang, L., Susilo, W., Ge, C., Wang, J.: Public key encryption with keyword search secure against keyword guessing attacks without random oracle. Inf. Sci. **238**, 221–241 (2013)

23. De Feo, L., Masson, S., Petit, C., Sanso, A.: Verifiable delay functions from supersingular isogenies and pairings. In: Galbraith, S.D., Moriai, S. (eds.) ASIACRYPT 2019. LNCS, vol. 11921, pp. 248–277. Springer, Cham (2019). https://doi.org/10.1007/978-3-030-34578-5_10

24. Foundation, W.: Wikimedia downloads (2020). https://dumps.wikimedia.org/enwiki/20201120/enwiki-20201120-pages-articles.xml.bz2

25. Huang, Q., Li, H.: An efficient public-key searchable encryption scheme secure against inside keyword guessing attacks. Inf. Sci. **403**, 1–14 (2017)

26. Jakobsson, M., Juels, A.: Proofs of work and bread pudding protocols (extended abstract). In: Preneel, B. (ed.) Secure Information Networks. ITIFIP, vol. 23, pp. 258–272. Springer, Boston, MA (1999). https://doi.org/10.1007/978-0-387-35568-9_18

27. Jeong, I.R., Kwon, J.O., Hong, D., Lee, D.H.: Constructing PEKS schemes secure against keyword guessing attacks is possible? Comput. Commun. **32**(2), 394–396 (2009)
28. Kim, K.S., Kim, M., Lee, D., Park, J.H., Kim, W.: Forward secure dynamic searchable symmetric encryption with efficient updates. In: CCS 2017, pp. 1449–1463 (2017)
29. Lu, Y., Li, J.: Lightweight public key authenticated encryption with keyword search against adaptively-chosen-targets adversaries for mobile devices. IEEE Trans. Mob. Comput. (2021). https://doi.org/10.1109/TMC.2021.3077508
30. Lu, Y., Li, J., Zhang, Y.: Secure channel free certificate-based searchable encryption withstanding outside and inside keyword guessing attacks. IEEE Trans. Serv. Comput. **14**(6), 2041–2054 (2021)
31. Miao, Y., Tong, Q., Deng, R.H., Choo, K.K.R., Liu, X., Li, H.: Verifiable searchable encryption framework against insider keyword-guessing attack in cloud storage. IEEE Trans. Cloud Comput. **10**(1), 835–848 (2022)
32. Qin, B., Chen, Y., Huang, Q., Liu, X., Zheng, D.: Public-key authenticated encryption with keyword search revisited: security model and constructions. Inf. Sci. **516**, 515–528 (2020)
33. Rhee, H.S., Park, J.H., Susilo, W., Lee, D.H.: Trapdoor security in a searchable public-key encryption scheme with a designated tester. J. Syst. Softw. **83**(5), 763–771 (2010)
34. Rhee, H.S., Susilo, W., Kim, H.: Secure searchable public key encryption scheme against keyword guessing attacks. IEICE Electron. Exp. **6**(5), 237–243 (2009)
35. Rivest, R.L., Shamir, A., Wagner, D.A.: Time-lock puzzles and timed-release crypto. Technical report, MIT/LCS/TR-684 (1996). https://people.csail.mit.edu/rivest/pubs/RSW96.pdf
36. Song, D.X., Wagner, D.A., Perrig, A.: Practical techniques for searches on encrypted data. In: S&P 2000, pp. 44–55 (2000)
37. Sun, L., Xu, C., Zhang, M., Chen, K., Li, H.: Secure searchable public key encryption against insider keyword guessing attacks from indistinguishability obfuscation. Sci. China Inf. Sci. **61**(3), 1–3 (2017). https://doi.org/10.1007/s11432-017-9124-0
38. Wang, C., Tu, T.: Keyword search encryption scheme resistant against keyword-guessing attack by the untrusted server. J. Shanghai Jiaotong Univ. (Sci.) **19**(4), 440–442 (2014). https://doi.org/10.1007/s12204-014-1522-6
39. Xu, P., Jin, H., Wu, Q., Wang, W.: Public-key encryption with fuzzy keyword search: a provably secure scheme under keyword guessing attack. IEEE Trans. Comput. **62**(11), 2266–2277 (2013)
40. Yao, F.F., Yin, Y.L.: Design and analysis of password-based key derivation functions. IEEE Trans. Inf. Theory **51**(9), 3292–3297 (2005)
41. Yau, W., Phan, R.C., Heng, S., Goi, B.: Keyword guessing attacks on secure searchable public key encryption schemes with a designated tester. Int. J. Comput. Math. **90**(12), 2581–2587 (2013)
42. Yousefipoor, V., Ameri, M.H., Mohajeri, J., Eghlidos, T.: A secure attribute based keyword search scheme against keyword guessing attack. In: IST 2016, pp. 124–128 (2016)
43. Zhang, Y., Xu, C., Ni, J., Li, H., Shen, X.S.: Blockchain-assisted public-key encryption with keyword search against keyword guessing attacks for cloud storage. IEEE Trans. Cloud Comput. **9**(4), 1335–1348 (2021)

# Lighter is Better: A Lighter Multi-client Verifiable Outsourced Computation with Hybrid Homomorphic Encryption

Xingkai Wang[1] (ID), Zhenfu Cao[2]([⊠]) (ID), Zhen Liu[1,4] (ID), and Kaitai Liang[3] (ID)

[1] Shanghai Jiao Tong University, Shanghai, China
{starshine87,liuzhen}@sjtu.edu.cn
[2] East China Normal University, Shanghai, China
zfcao@sei.ecnu.edu.cn
[3] Delft University of Technology, Delft, The Netherlands
kaitai.liang@tudelft.nl
[4] Shanghai Qizhi Institute, Shanghai, China

**Abstract.** Gordon et al. (TCC 2015) systematically studied the security of Multi-client Verifiable Computation (MVC), in which a set of computationally-weak clients outsource the computation of a general function $f$ over their private inputs to an untrusted server. They introduced the universally composable (UC) security of MVC and proposed a scheme achieving UC-security, where the protocol remains secure after arbitrarily composed with other UC-secure instances. However, the clients in their scheme have to undertake the heavy computation overhead caused by fully homomorphic encryption (FHE) and further, the plaintext size is linear to the function input size.

In this work, we propose a more efficient UC-secure multi-client privacy-preserving verifiable computation protocol, called MVOC, that sharply reduces amortized overheads for clients, in both semi-honest and malicious settings. In particular, our protocol achieves stronger *outsourcability* by outsourcing more computation to the server, so that it may be more friendly to those lightweight clients. More specifically, we revisit the definition of garbling scheme, and propose a novel garbled circuit protocol whose circuit randomness is non-interactively provided by multiple parties. We also realize the idea of hybrid homomorphic encryption, which makes the FHE plaintext size independent of the input size. We present the detailed proof and analyze the theoretical complexity of MVOC. We further implement our protocol and evaluate the performance, and the results show that, after adopting our new techniques, the computation and communication overheads during input phase can be decreased by 55.15%–68.05% and 62.55%–75% respectively.

**Keywords:** Verifiable computation · Outsourced computation · Hybrid homomorphic encryption

V. Atluri et al. (Eds.): ESORICS 2022, LNCS 13555, pp. 105–125, 2022.
https://doi.org/10.1007/978-3-031-17146-8_6

# 1   Introduction

The technique of verifiable computation (VC) [12] and multi-client verifiable computation (MVC) [7,17] are proposed to allow computationally weak clients to delegate the computation of a function $f$ on private inputs to a remoted server, achieving privacy, soundness and efficiency in the single and multi-client context. Specifically, privacy requires the protocol not to disclose sensitive data including input and output, soundness ensures the validity of the result provided by the server, and efficiency guarantees that the cost of the client during outsourcing should be much lower than that of computing the function by itself.

Gennaro et al. [12] introduced the definition of verifiable computation (VC). Its primary goal is to achieve privacy and soundness against malicious server, assuming that the client is honest. Their protocol achieves efficiency amortizedly. They combined garbled circuit [20] with a fully homomorphic encryption (FHE) scheme [14]. More precisely, after generating a garbled circuits, the client is allowed to use FHE to encrypt the circuit along with encoded input labels. Due to IND-CPA security of the FHE scheme, the client can reuse the same circuit without loss of soundness and hence the computational cost for the client is bounded in amortized sense. Choi et al. [7] later extended single-client VC to the multiple clients to yield a MVC protocol. In such a setting, $n$ clients intend to compute some function $f$ over a series of joint input $\{(x_1^{(\mathsf{ssid})}, ..., x_n^{(\mathsf{ssid})})\}_{\mathsf{ssid}}$. They adopted a new primitive *proxy oblivious transfer* (POT) constructed from a non-interactive key-exchange (NIKE) scheme. This new primitive is able to keep clients' input private from each other and from the server. But their protocol cannot guarantee the security in the context of either client-client corruption or the existence of malicious clients. Gordon et al. [17] systematically studied MVC in the universally composable (UC) model. The UC security captures selective failure attack and adaptive soundness, and considers the participation of malicious clients, which may be seen as a stronger notion than the prior definitions. They also proposed a protocol that satisfies the "stronger" security, with a new primitive *attribute-hiding multi-sender attribute-based encryption* (ah-mABE), constructed by a two-outcome ABE scheme with local encoding, an FHE scheme and a POT protocol. They eventually pointed out the impossibility of achieving the security when client-server collusion exists.

There are many studies that have been proposed to achieve verifiable computation since Gennaro et al.'s VC protocol [12]. A similar approach is to apply succincct functional encryption (FE) technique, which was introduced by Goldwasser et al. [16]. Later, Goldwasser et al. [15] extended the former definition to multi-input functional encryption (MIFE), which implies an efficient MVC protocol. However, neither ABE nor indistinguishable obfuscation (iO), especially the latter, is a cost-effective building block. Moreover, iO introduces a strong assumption, which makes the protocol less practical.

Another method to achieve private verifiable computation is to prove after computing, rather than to prove with computing. Fiore et al. [9] proposed a protocol on verifiable delegation of computation on encrypted data, by developing a novel homomorphic hashing technique that may significantly reduce overhead.

The core idea is to use a VC to prove the correctness of homomorphic evaluation on ciphertext, and the new technique solves the difficulty of dealing with FHE ciphertext expansion. Later, Fiore et al. [11] and Bois et al. [2] extended the protocol of [9]. The former supported public verifiability, and extended the degree of delegated function from two to any constant value, using well-designed zk-SNARKs for polynomial rings. While the latter increases the efficiency of HE scheme by allowing flexible choices of HE parameters. However, the incurred extra time cost on verification for client may not be applicable to computation-restricted devices.

Gennaro et al. [13] proposed a new primitive denoted as fully homomorphic message authenticators (HA), which allows the receiver to verify the computation result, constructed with FHE. Almost at the same time, Catalano et al. [5] proposed a new construction of HA by much more efficient building blocks, while sacrificing the maximum size of delegated circuit. In multi-client scenario, Fiore et al. [10] proposed several constructions of multi-key homomorphic authenticator. But the time cost of verifying a result for client is not less than executing the computation. An idea to avoid this overhead for client could be to outsource the verification function to the server. However, the implemented solutions either cause extra communication complexity which break the non-interactive property, or introduce SNARG-like proof system. None of the solutions so far is efficient enough for practical use.

**Possible Limitations.** In the constructions of both [7] and [17], the clients remain using FHE to encrypt labels proportional to their input size, where FHE is a bottleneck in efficiency, compared to other building blocks in their protocols.

Although outsourcability has been initially achieved, most of existing FHE-based protocols still cannot avoid heavy client-side overheads. This is so because the messages to be fully homomorphic encrypted for client is proportion to the size of function input. *How to make such complexity independent to the input size is an interesting long-lasting problem in the research line.*

Besides the cost of FHE, a POT-based MVC scheme needs $O(n^2)$ instances of functionality during a single online phase of outsourced computation, where $n$ is the number of clients. The overhead caused by POT rises substantially as the number of users increases in both communication and computation. Furthermore, the first client always needs to take over most of the computation, since it has to encrypt "twice" the actual length of input labels in an instance of POT, which may lead to imbalance in the overall overheads. Thus, *a cost-effective and efficiency-balance protocol in multi-client context is worthy being considered, especially when $n$ is sufficiently large.*

**Contribution.** We propose a new multi-client verifiable computation scheme MVOC. The proposed scheme has lower communication complexity and is more efficient for clients than existing works, while still satisfying strong security guarantees in both semi-honest and malicious model. Our contributions is summarized as follows:

- We revisit the definition of garbling scheme, and design a new primitive *Multi-client Outsourced Garbled Circuit* (MOGC). Its encoding function is generated by all clients in a distributed way. Clients, who do not generate circuits, can learn the garbled input wires without using OT or proxy OT, so that we can significantly reduce the communication overhead from $O(n^2 l)$ to $O(nl)$. We further show that a secure MOGC protocol implies a UC-secure one-time MVC.

- We adopt the technique of hybrid homomorphic encryption to the MOGC to construct a UC-secure MVC protocol against malicious server or semi-honest client-client collusion . We further improve the outsourcability of MVC protocol by reducing the FHE overhead from $O(l)$ to $O(\kappa)$, which is independent to the input size, where $\kappa$ is the security parameter. We also show the possibility to construct a secure MVC against the corruption of malicious client by adopting a zero-knowledge compiler.

- We implement the proposed MVOC with Yao's Garbled Circuit and the most efficient hybrid homomorphic encryption scheme, and make a comparison on clients' overhead in both computation and communication. The experimental results show that the proposed scheme provides a significant advantage in efficiency over other existing FHE-based works.

**Table 1.** Comparison of privacy-preserving verifiable computation

| Schemes | Security model | Collusion | UC | Multi-client | Communication | Computation |
|---------|---------------|-----------|-----|--------------|---------------|-------------|
| Gennaro et al. [12] | Semi-honest | ✗ | ✗ | ✗ | – | $O(dl\kappa)$ |
| Choi et al. [7] | Semi-honest | ✗ | ✗ | ✔ | $O(n^2 l)$ | $O(dl\kappa)$ |
| Gordon et al. [17] | Malicious | ✔ | ✔ | ✔ | $O(n^2 l)$ | $O(dl\kappa)$ |
| MVOC | malicious | ✔ | ✔ | ✔ | $O(nl)$ | $O(d\kappa) + O(l)$ |

\* We denote $d$ as the expansion rate of complexity caused by FHE.

**Technical Roadmap.** Since it is impossible to achieve input privacy when the server colludes with any client [17], we may assume the client-server collusion does not exist. We divide our technical roadmap into two steps.

*Multi-client Outsourced Garbled Circuit.* The garbled circuit in a garbling scheme is mostly generated by a single party. This feature causes the inconvenience of providing the corresponding garbled labels for other parties. Specifically, in Yao's secure two-party computation protocol, after Alice generates the garbled circuit, the second participant Bob obtains the garbled labels by oblivious transfer (OT). Essentially, OT transfers the randomness from Alice to Bob. Bob is not allowed to learn the garbled labels that is not related to his input, since Bob also plays the role of circuit executor, and he may benefit from this extra information.

We notice that, if we separate the role of circuit executor from data provider, the above concern will be tackled. Briefly, we introduce a (not necessarily trusted) third party, the server, who dedicates to executing the computation, and the client provides his own randomness for garbled circuit. In this case, OT may be no longer needed, since client could generate its corresponding garbled labels using its own randomness.

According to the above observation, we propose a new primitive named *Multi-client Outsourced Garbled Circuit* (MOGC), and construct a secure MOGC protocol from Yao's Garbled Circuit. We also claim that a secure MOGC protocol implies a one-time MVC protocol. The proposed MOGC protocol solves the problem of transferring randomness from circuit generator to data provider, plays the role of OT in secure 2PC and the role of POT in MVC, where POT is the crux of unbalance problem.

*Multi-client Verifiable Outsourced Computation.* Similar to the approach of constructing VC from the one-time VC intuitively implied from Yao's Garbled Circuit, we use FHE to provide circuit privacy. In order to avoid heavy overhead caused by FHE, we adopt the philosophy of hybrid encryption: firstly using symmetric key encryption (SKE) scheme to encipher message, and then FHE to encapsulate the symmetric key. This KEM-DEM-like technique is able to offload the heavy FHE overhead to the server. More concretely, after the generator generates the garbled circuit $F$ for a function $f$ by MOGC in offline phase, each client $\mathsf{P}_i$ uses its own encoding function share to obtain garbled input $X_i^{\mathsf{ssid}}$ corresponding to its private input $x_i^{\mathsf{ssid}}$. After that, the generator executes FHE setup to acquire FHE key pair $(\mathsf{pk_{FHE}}, \mathsf{sk_{FHE}})$. Each client computes the hybrid ciphertext, which comprises of an FHE and a SKE ciphertext. The server can recover the FHE ciphertext of garbled input wire from the hybrid ciphertext sent by each client, and computes on the garbled circuit as in MOGC. The correctness of FHE and MOGC ensures the result is verifiable. As long as there is a secure channel for transmitting FHE ciphertext of the hybrid, the protocol also achieves privacy against clients.

## 2  Multi-client Verifiable Computation

### 2.1  Syntax

We first revise the notion of non-interactive multi-client verifiable computation (MVC). Let $\kappa$ denote the security parameter. Suppose there are $n$ clients $\mathsf{P}_1, ..., \mathsf{P}_n$ intending to delegate some computation on an $n$-ary function $f : \mathcal{X}^n \to \mathcal{Y}^n$ to a remote server $\mathsf{Serv}$ for multiple times, and to require the validity of their answers. The length of input and output message space are polynomial in $\kappa$.

Briefly speaking, a MVC protocol can be divided into three phases:

1. In setup phase, each participant is allowed to access an initial setup $\mathcal{G}$.
2. In offline phase, each client is allowed to send a message to every other clients respectively, and also needs to send a message to the server $\mathsf{Serv}$.
3. During online phase, there might be multiple subsessions in which clients are delegating some computations on the same function with different inputs. In a subsession, each client is allowed to send a single message to $\mathsf{Serv}$, and to receive an output from $\mathsf{Serv}$.

The detailed definition is given as follows.

**Definition 1 (non-interactive Multi-client Verifiable Computation).** *Let $\kappa$ be the security parameter, $n$ be the number of clients. A non-interactive multi-client verifiable computation comprises the following three phases:*

**Setup Phase:** *All participants have access to a setup $\mathcal{G}$. Each party $P_i$ obtains $(pk_i, sk_i)$ and the server Serv obtains $(pk_S, sk_S)$.*

**Offline Phase:** *After the delegated function $f$ is chosen, each client $P_i$ receives from each other client $P_j$ the corresponding encoding mapping $e_{j,i}$, and sends a garbled version of $f$ to Serv, noted as $F_i$.*

**Online Phase:** *During a single subsession indexed by ssid, after input $(\text{ssid}, x_i^{\text{ssid}})$ provided by $P_i$ is determined, the client computes $(\xi_i^{\text{ssid}}, \tau_i^{\text{ssid}})$. The first value will be sent to the server while the second one is kept private by $P_i$. After receiving information from all clients, the server Serv computes and sends the result $(\text{ssid}, \omega_i^{\text{ssid}})$ to each client $P_i$. Each client then decodes the encrypted result and obtains $y_i^{\text{ssid}} \backslash \perp$, where $\perp$ indicates that the client is not convinced by the server's result, and will no longer continue executing the protocol unless restarting from Setup Phase.*

*Remark 1.* Compared with [17], our definition is different in two aspects. In offline phase, we allow each client to send a message to others. This does not increase communication complexity amortizedly, since offline phase would be executed only once before multiple computation queries being carried out. After receiving a failure result from Serv, our clients will no longer trust the server and abandon the present protocol. Clients may re-select another trusted outsourcer or rollback to the setup phase, in order to obtain a new trusted environment.

## 2.2 Security Definition

We follow the UC framework in [3]. We formally define the ideal functionality for MVC in Table 2, which captures the correctness and privacy, but also adaptive soundness and selective failure attack. The server and clients are either semi-honest or malicious in our model. In any circumstances, the server is not allowed to collude with any client; otherwise input privacy will be never guaranteed [17].

*Remark 2.* We note our security definition is different from [17] in the behavior of server S. Since we do not allow client-server collusion, we claim that there is no difference between the behavior of a corrupted and an uncorrupted server S. This may be seen as a special case of the origin definition in [17], which does not show contradiction. Because the indices set of corrupted clients is always empty, no information will gained from the blackbox oracle where the simulation could query on function $f$ for different inputs provided by corrupted clients.

**Definition 2 (Universal composability [3]).** *A protocol $\Pi$ UC-realizes ideal functionality $\mathcal{F}$ if for any PPT adversary $\mathcal{A}$ there exists a PPT simulator $S$ such that, for any PPT environment $\mathcal{E}$, the ensembles $\text{EXEC}_{\Pi, \mathcal{A}, \mathcal{E}}$ and $\text{EXEC}_{\text{IDEAL}_{\mathcal{F}}, S, \mathcal{E}}$ are indistinguishable.*

**Definition 3 (UC-security of MVC).** *A protocol MVC is UC-secure if MVC UC-realizes $\mathcal{F}_{\text{MVC}}$, against malicious server and clients, without client-server collusion.*

**Table 2.** Ideal functionality of multi-client verifiable computation

---

### Multi-client Verifiable Computation

The functionality $\mathcal{F}_{\mathsf{MVC}}$ is parameterized with an $n$-ary function $f : \mathcal{X}^n \to \mathcal{Y}^n$. The functionality $\mathcal{F}_{\mathsf{MVC}}$ interacts with $n$ clients $P_1$, ..., $P_n$, a remote server Serv and a simulator S.

• *Initialization:*

Upon receiving (**Init**) from client $P_i$, send (**Init**, $P_i$) to notify the simulator S. After S returns (**Init**, $P_i$), send (**Init**, $P_i$, $\Phi(f_i)$) to the server Serv, and send (**Init**, $P_i$) to each other client $P_j$ where $j \neq i$. After receiving all responces (**Init**, $P_i$) from client $P_j$ for all $j \neq i$ and all responses (**Init**, Serv, $P_i$) for all $i \in [n]$ from server, send (**Init**, Serv) to notify the simulator S.

• *Outsourcing:*

Upon receiving (**Input**, sid, $x_i$) from client $P_i$, send (ssid, $P_i$) to notify S. After S returns (ssid, $P_i$), store (ssid, $x_i$) and send a notification (**Input**, ssid, $P_i$) to Serv. Upon receiving (**Input**, ssid) from Serv, retrieve (ssid, $x_i$) for all $i \in [n]$. If some (ssid, $x_i$) has not been stored yet, send (**Output**, ssid, **FAIL**) to the server and all clients.

Compute $(y_1, ..., y_n) \leftarrow f(x_1, ..., x_n)$. Upon receiving (ssid, $P_i$, $\phi$) from the simulator S, if $\phi = $ **OK** then send (**Output**, ssid, $y_i$) to $P_i$; otherwise send (**Output**, ssid, **FAIL**) to $P_i$. Later when S returns (ssid, $P_i$, $\phi$), send (**Output**, ssid, $y_i$) to client $P_i$ if $\phi = $ **OK**, else send (**Output**, ssid, **FAIL**) if $\phi = $ **FAIL** to client $P_i$.

---

**Adaptive Soundness Against Selective Failure.** There are multiple sub-sessions in our definition, which enables the functionality to capture adaptive soundness. We allow clients to report the output to environment and thus, the definition captures security against selective failure attacks.

**Static Malicious Corruption.** We assume a static corruption model, with malicious corrupted participants. In such a model, the adversary can only corrupt parties at the beginning of protocol execution, instead of corrupting any party once the protocol has been executed. A malicious corrupted party may arbitrarily deviate the original protocol.

**Communication Model.** We assume that all of the communication channels among clients are controlled by the adversary, while the channels between clients and server are secure. We can implement such channels with the ideal functionality $\mathcal{F}_{\mathsf{STP}}$ [3]. All of the protocols are described assuming in $\mathcal{F}_{\mathsf{STP}}$-hybrid world.

**Outsourcability.** The *oursourcability* defines the improvements of client efficiency brought by outsourcing tasks to servers (i.e., how much computational and storage costs could be offloaded to servers). It is described in such to guarantee the overheads of clients in the online phase should be less that the costs incurred by a client-side self execution. We later will focus on discussing online efficiency for the clients in terms of time and communication costs. For the former, as FHE is an expensive component in MVC, we should require that the plaintext of FHE is independent of the input size in an outsourcable MVC protocol. As for the latter, we may require the communication size to be constraint to at most proportional to the input size, in particular when there exists a relatively large client number.

## 3    Building Blocks

### 3.1    Garbling Scheme

The technique of garbled circuits was first proposed by Yao [20]. We first follow the well-designed definition in [1] culled out by Bellare et al. The garbled circuit is generated by a single party named *garbler*. We will later discuss a new case where the randomness of garbled circuit is provided by multiple parties.

**Definition 4 (Garbling Schemes [1]).** *A garbling scheme for a family of functions $\mathcal{F}$ whose arbitrary element $f$ is a mapping that can efficiently compute, comprises five algorithms* $\mathsf{Gb} = \mathsf{Gb}.\{\mathsf{Gb}, \mathsf{En}, \mathsf{De}, \mathsf{Ev}, \mathsf{ev}\}$. *The first algorithm is probabilistic and the others are deterministic. Specifically,*

- $(F, e, d) \leftarrow \mathsf{Gb}(1^\kappa, f)$. *Taking as input the security parameter $\kappa$ and a object function $f$, output the garbled circuit $F$, encoding function $e$ and decoding function $d$.*
- $X = \mathsf{Ev}(e, x)$. *Taking as input the encoding function $e$ and input $x$, output garbled input $X$.*
- $y = \mathsf{De}(d, Y)$. *Taking as input the decoding function $d$ and garbled output $Y$, obtain the final output $y$.*
- $Y = \mathsf{Ev}(F, X)$. *Taking as input a garbled circuit $F$ and garbled input $X$, obtain the garbled output $Y$.*
- $y = \mathsf{ev}(f, x)$. *Taking as input the origin function $f$ and input $x$, obtain the plaintext output $y$.*

We require a garbling scheme satisfying several properties. The correctness ensures that the final output decoded from the result of garbled circuit is the exact function value, i.e. $f = e \circ F \circ d$. The obliviousness ensures that a party acquiring $(F, X)$, but not $d$, should not learn anything about $f$, $x$, or $y$. The authenticity means that a party acquiring $(F, X)$ should not be able to produce a valid garbled output $Y' \neq F(X)$ such that $De(d, Y') \neq \perp$. The formal definition of authenticity is shown as follows.

**Definition 5 (Authenticity of Garbling Schemes [1]).** *For a garbling scheme $GS = \mathsf{Gb}.(\mathsf{Gb}, \mathsf{En}, \mathsf{De}, \mathsf{Ev}, \mathsf{ev})$, and for any PPT adversary $\mathcal{A}$, consider the following experiment:*    $\boldsymbol{Exp}_\mathcal{A}^{\mathrm{Aut}}[GS, \kappa]$ :

$(F, e, d) \leftarrow \mathsf{Gb}(1^\kappa, f); \; X \leftarrow \mathsf{En}(e, x); \; Y' \leftarrow \mathcal{A}(F, X); \; r \leftarrow \mathsf{De}(Y');$

*If $r \neq \perp$ and $Y' \neq \mathsf{Ev}(F, X)$, output 1, else 0.*

*Garbling scheme $GS$ is authentic, if for any PPT adversary $\mathcal{A}$, there is a negligible function negl such that* $\Pr[\boldsymbol{Exp}_\mathcal{A}^{\mathrm{Aut}}[GS, \kappa]] \leq negl(\kappa)$.

**Side-Information Function.** It is unable to achieve absolute privacy for a garbling scheme. The information we expected to reveal is captured by a *side-information function* $\Phi$, which is a deterministic mapping from a function $f$ to a side-information set $\phi = \Phi(f)$. Specifically, in this paper, we allow the server to obtain the circuit size, including input and output size. In other words, we regard our protocol as a multi-client version of private function evaluation (PFE), rather than secure function evaluation (SFE). One could extend the definition to SFE version of MVC, by assigning $\Phi(f) = f$.

## 3.2 Fully Homomorphic Encryption

After Gentry [14] gave the first construction of FHE, Canetti et al. [4] proposed concrete implements of IND-CCA1-secure FHE. We don't need the security to be as strong as the one against CCA1 in our scheme. We show the syntax and define the security of IND-CPA as follows.

**Syntax.** For a permitted circuit set $\mathcal{C}$, a fully homomorphic encryption scheme FHE comprises of four PPT algorithms:

- $(pk, sk) \leftarrow \text{Gen}(1^\kappa)$. The key generation algorithm which outputs public-private key pair of FHE.
- $c \leftarrow \text{Enc}(pk, m)$. The encryption algorithm which takes message $m$ as input and outputs ciphertext $c$.
- $m := \text{Dec}(sk, c)$. The decryption algorithm which takes ciphertext $c$ as input and outputs plaintext message $m \in \mathcal{M}$.
- $c_{\text{eval}} := \text{Eval}(C, \{c_i\})$. The evaluation algorithm which executes the circuit $C \in \mathcal{C}$ on ciphertext input collection $\{c_i\}$, and outputs ciphertext result $c_{\text{eval}}$.

**Properties.** The *Correctness* of FHE is defined as key pair generated by Gen allows the output of Dec which takes the ciphertext of Enc on some message $m$ is identical to $m$. The *Homomorphic correctness* is defined as the output of Eval decrypts to the result of applying $C$ on plaintext inputs $\{m_i\}$. The *Compactness* means that the size of homomorphic ciphertext should be independent of the size, depth value or number of inputs to $C$, and less than $\text{poly}(\kappa)$.

**Definition 6 (IND-CPA Security of FHE).** *For a fully homomorphic encryption scheme* FHE = (Gen, Enc, Dec, Eval), *and for any PPT adversary* $\mathcal{A}$, *consider the following experiment:*

$\text{Exp}_{\mathcal{A}}^{CPA}[\text{FHE}, \kappa]$ :

$(pk, sk) \leftarrow \text{Gen}(1^\kappa); \ (m_0, m_1, \tau) \leftarrow \mathcal{A}^{\text{Enc}(pk, \cdot)};$

$b \xleftarrow{\$} \{0, 1\}; \ c_b \leftarrow \text{Enc}(pk, m_b); \ \hat{b} \leftarrow \mathcal{A}(\tau, c_b);$

*If* $\hat{b} = b$, *output 1, else 0;*

*Note* $\mathcal{A}$ *has access to* Dec($sk, \cdot$) *as an oracle. We define its advantage in the experiment above as:* $\text{Adv}_{\mathcal{A}}^{CPA}(\text{FHE}, \kappa) = \left| 2\Pr[\text{Exp}_{\mathcal{A}}^{CPA}[\text{FHE}, \kappa] = 1] - 1 \right|.$

*The* FHE *is CPA-secure, if for any PPT adversary* $\mathcal{A}$, *there is a negligible function* negl *such that:* $\text{Adv}_{\mathcal{A}}^{CPA}(\text{FHE}, \kappa) \leq \text{negl}(\kappa).$

## 4    Multi-client Outsourced Garbled Circuits

In this section, we revisit the definition of Garbling Scheme [1], and introduce a new primitive called *Multi-client Outsourced Garbled circuits* (MOGC).

In conventional Yao's garbled circuits protocol for two-party computation [20], there are two parties, Alice and Bob, intending to execute a computation of function $f$ over their private inputs $x_a$ and $x_b$ respectively. Specifically, Alice generates a garbled circuit $F$ from the function $f$, and further sends it to Bob, along with her garbled version of private input $X_a$. Then Alice and Bob execute an OT protocol to enable Bob to learn the garbled version of his private input $X_b$ without: (i) revealing information about $b$ to Alice, and (ii) allowing Bob to know any garbled input except $X_b$. Bob then carries out the computation on $F$ and obtains the garbled result $Y$. After receiving $Y$ from Bob, Alice knows the final result $y = f(x_a, x_b)$.

We extend the previous definition to multi-client scenarios. In an MOGC protocol, the computation is carried out by a third party who does not provide any input. Specifically, there is a *generator*, a *server* and at least one *collaborator*. The generator and the collaborator(s) outsource the computation of a function $f$ on their input data $\vec{x}$, and the generator learns the output $f(\vec{x})$. We require the protocol to be non-interactive, which indicates that each party could only send a single message to another party in an instance of the protocol. This means that we cannot trivially use the OT technique, and the randomness of the garbled circuits should be provided by all data providers.

We will first give the syntax of MOGC, construct a secure MOGC protocol from a Yao's protocol, and then shows that a MOGC protocol implies a one-time multi-client verifiable computation.

### 4.1    Syntax of MOGC

**Definition 7 (Multi-client Outsourced Garbled Circuits).** *An MOGC for a family of function $\mathcal{F}$ whose arbitrary element $f$ is a mapping that can efficiently compute, comprises six algorithms* $\mathsf{MOGC} = \mathsf{MOGC}.\{\mathsf{Gb_C}, \mathsf{Gb_G}, \mathsf{En}, \mathsf{De}, \mathsf{Ev}, \mathsf{ev}\}$. *The first two algorithms are probabilistic and the rest are deterministic.*

- $e_c \leftarrow \mathsf{Gb_C}(1^\kappa, f)$. *The collaborator generates his corresponding part of encoding functions.*
- $(F, e_g, d) \leftarrow \mathsf{Gb_G}(1^\kappa, f, \vec{e_c})$. *The generator generates his part of encoding and decoding function, computes the garbled circuits along with other parts of encoding functions.*
- $X_{c/g} = \mathsf{En}(e_{c/g}, x_{c/g})$. *The generator or the collaborator obtains the garbled input from private input via the corresponding encoding function.*
- $Y = \mathsf{Ev}(F, \vec{X})$. *The server carries out the computation on garbled circuits and obtains the encoded output.*
- $y = \mathsf{De}(d, Y)$. *The generator recovers the final output using decoding function.*
- $y = \mathsf{ev}(f, \vec{x})$. *An auxiliary function that carries out the original function $f$.*

Our definition is defined in semi-honest model, so that all participants could gather information as much as they could without deviating from the original protocol. We do not allow client-server corruption, but the corruptions between clients are permitted. We assume that there exists secure communication channels between client and server.

A secure MOGC protocol should satisfy several properties. The *Correctness* ensures the final output is identical to the result of function evaluation. The *Privacy* guarantees that each client's input is kept private from other client and the server. And the *Authenticity* requires that the server could not provide a wrong result that could be decoded by the generator.

Before proceeding to an MOGC construction, we analyze how Yao's garbled circuits can achieve secure two-party computation. Alice and Bob who have private inputs respectively want to compute a function on their inputs. Alice generates the garbled circuit while Bob carries out the exact computation. The privacy against Bob is guaranteed by the randomness of circuit generation, which is provided by the generator Alice. Meanwhile, the privacy against Alice is guaranteed by OT protocol, which delivers the randomness from Alice to Bob. A trivial observation is that the circuit executor should not be the circuit generator, since authenticity is protected by the randomness of encoded values, and that is the reason why the same garbled circuit should not be used twice. Fortunately, the circuit execution is taken over by a third party "server", which is independent of data providers. Hence there is no concern of such an authentic crisis. Moreover, if the encoding function is *separable*, which means that the randomness of the encoding function can be regarded as separately provided by each client correspondingly, we may construct a protocol without adopting OT. More precisely, after acquiring each client's encoding function share, the generator computes the garbled circuit with those encoding information. We give the definition of *separability* as follows.

**Definition 8 (Separability of Garbling Scheme).** *We say that a garbling scheme is separable if the garbling algorithm* Gb *can be equivalently regarded as the following, where there are* $|\mathcal{I}|$ *input wires indexed by* $[|\mathcal{I}|]$, *with* $\mathcal{I}$ *being the set of all input wires and two sub-algorithm* ran *and* garb:

1. *randomly select* $|\mathcal{I}|$ *randomness* $r_1, ..., r_{|\mathcal{I}|}$;
2. *compute* $e_i \leftarrow \mathsf{ran}(f, r_i)$ *for* $i \in [|\mathcal{I}|]$, *set* $e = (e_1, ..., e_{|\mathcal{I}|})$;
3. *compute* $d \leftarrow \mathsf{ran}(f, r_1)$;
4. *compute* $F \leftarrow \mathsf{garb}(f, e, d)$;

**Theorem 1.** *Assuming the existence of a separable garbling scheme, there exists a correct, private and authenticate multi-client outsourced garbled circuit protocol.*

*Proof.* We prove the theorem by construction. For $\mathsf{Gb_C}$, on input $f$ the collaborator executes Step 1 and 2 in the above definition. For $\mathsf{Gb_G}$, on input $f$ and all encoding function shares $\vec{e_c}$ from collaborators, the generator executes Step 2, 3 and 4 in the above definition. The remaining algorithms are identical to the original garbling scheme respectively.

The construction of MOGC and a garbling scheme is merely slightly different in the generation of encoding function $e$. The definitions of correctness, privacy (including obliviousness), and authenticity are irrelevant to how $e$ is generated. These properties can easily be inherited from those of a garbling scheme.  □

### 4.2  Construction of MOGC

We define a protocol for MOGC from conventional Yao's Garbled Circuits. Yao's circuits include garbled gates corresponding to the circuit gates. Suppose $x_a, x_b$ be the input wires of a gate, and $x_c$ be the output wire. The generator Alice first randomly chooses six values for each gate, $w_t^b$ where $t \in \{a, b, c\}$ and $b \in \{0, 1\}$, represents 0 and 1 values of three wires respectively. Each of garbled gates contains four ciphertexts $\gamma_{ij} = E_{w_a^i}(E_{w_b^j}(w_c)^{g(i,j)})$, where $i, j \in \{0, 1\}$ and $E$ is a well-designed symmetric encryption scheme.

It is intuitive that Yao's Garbled Circuits protocol is a separable garbling scheme. Instead of generating $|\mathcal{I}|$ encoded values by the same randomness $r$, we use $|\mathcal{I}|$ different randomness $r_1, ..., r_{|\mathcal{I}|}$ to obtain the encoded values. A PPT adversary cannot distinguish between two sets of the random values with merely different randomness. Hence we achieve the separability.

Moreover, we separate the $|\mathcal{I}|$ input wires into $n$ buckets. When generating the encoded values for input wires, we use the same randomness for inputs in the same bucket, and use variant randomnesses for inputs in different buckets. A PPT adversary also cannot distinguish the random values from the encoding values of Yao's protocol.

We define our protocol as follows. For each input wire that is relevant to the client $C_i$'s input, we let $C_i$ choose two random values of this wire using his own randomness $r_i$ and then handle the values to the generator. Then, the generator chooses random values which are relevant to his own input and other non-input wires, and computes the garbled circuit $F$ using those values. After acquiring $F$ and all encoded inputs from clients, the server carries on the computation on $F$ and obtains the encoded output, and handles it to the generator. The generator finally checks the output wire and recovers the final result. Since Yao's protocol is separable, our protocol is a secure MOGC according to Theorem 1.

## 5  Construction

We present our construction for MVC and give the proof for its UC-security. We start the construction from designing one-time MVC protocol from MOGC. We define the ideal functionality of one-time MVC named $\mathcal{F}_{\text{OT-MVC}}$, and show that the proposed protocol UC-realizes the functionality. Then we construct an MVOC scheme that UC-realizes $\mathcal{F}_{\text{MVC}}$ in the $\mathcal{F}_{\text{OT-MVC}}$-hybrid world.

Without loss of generality, we only consider one case in the following construction: when only client $P_1$ may obtain the output. We could simply executing the protocol in parallel to achieve output-retrieving for every client. Similar approaches also can be seen in [7, 17].

## 5.1   One-Time Multi-client Verifiable Computation (OT-MVC)

There are $n$ clients and a server participating in an OT-MVC protocol. All clients are reached consensus on the function $f$ to be computed. Each client $P_i$ provides a private input $x_i$ respectively. The goal is to enable the client $P_1$ to obtain the function result $f(x_1, ..., x_n)$, while the server only knows the legal side-information $\Phi(f)$. The client participants behave semi-honestly while the server behaves maliciously, and client-server collusion is not allowed in our model. The ideal functionality $\mathcal{F}_{OT\text{-}MVC}$ is the same as $\mathcal{F}_{MVC}$ except that the outsourcing phase is only executed once. The formal definition of the ideal functionality $\mathcal{F}_{OT\text{-}MVC}$ is shown in Table 3.

**Table 3.** Ideal functionality of one-time multi-client verifiable computation

| One-Time Multi-client Verifiable Computation |
|---|
| The functionality $\mathcal{F}_{OT\text{-}MVC}$ is parameterized with an $n$-ary function $f$ : $\mathcal{X}^n \to \mathcal{Y}^n$, and interacts with $n$ clients $P_1$, ..., $P_n$, a remote server Serv and a simulator S. <br><br> Upon receiving (**Init**) from client $P_i$, send (**Init**, $P_i$) to notify the simulator S. After S returns (**Init**, $P_i$), send (**Init**, $P_i$, $\Phi(f_i)$) to the server Serv, and send (**Init**, $P_i$) to each client $P_j$ where $j \neq i$. After receiving all responces (**Init**, $P_i$) from client $P_j$ for all $j \neq i$ and all responses (**Init**, Serv, $P_i$) for all $i \in [n]$ from server, send (**Init**, Serv) to notify the simulator S. <br><br> Upon receiving (**Input**, $x_i$) from client $P_i$, send ($P_i$) to notify S. After S returns ($P_i$), store ($x_i$) and send a notification (**Input**, $P_i$) to Serv. Upon receiving (**Input**) from Serv, retrieve ($x_i$) for all $i \in [n]$. If some ($x_i$) has not been stored yet, send (**Output**, **FAIL**) to the server and all clients. Compute $(y_1, ..., y_n) \leftarrow f(x_1, ..., x_n)$. Upon receiving ($P_i$, $\phi$) from the simulator S, if $\phi = $ **OK** then send (**Output**, $y_i$) to $P_i$; otherwise send (**Output**, **FAIL**) to $P_i$. Later when S returns ($P_i$, $\phi$), send (**Output**, $y_i$) to client $P_i$ if $\phi = $ **OK**, else send (**Output**, **FAIL**) if $\phi = $ **FAIL** to client $P_i$. |

We give a construction of $\mathcal{F}_{OT\text{-}MVC}$ from a secure MOGC protocol. Let $f$ : $(\{0,1\}^l)^n \to \{0,1\}^l$ be the outsourced function, $P_1$ be the generator, $P_2, ..., P_n$ be the collaborators, and Serv be the server. The parties work as follows:

- Collaborators $P_2, ..., P_n$ execute the algorithm $Gb_C$ to generate encoding function shares $e_2, ..., e_n$ respectively, and send the shares to $P_1$.
- The generator $P_1$ executes the algorithm $Gb_G$ to generate his encoded function share $e_1$, the garbled circuit $F$ and the decoding function $d$. Then $P_1$ sends $F$ to the server.
- All clients $P_1, ..., P_n$ execute the algorithm En on their own private inputs $x_1, ..., x_n$ respectively to obtain the garbled input $X_1, ..., X_n$, and send the garbled inputs to the server.
- The server Serv executes the algorithm Ev on encoded inputs to obtain the encoded output $Y$, and sends the result to the generator $P_1$.

– The generator $P_1$ executes the algorithm De on encoded output $Y$ to recover the final result. If $Y$ is a valid value, it accepts and outputs the final result $y$; otherwise rejects and outputs $\perp$.

**Theorem 2.** *The above protocol UC-realizes $\mathcal{F}_{OT\text{-}MVC}$ against semi-honest corruption of any fixed subset of clients, or against malicious server corruption.*

*Proof.* Let $\Pi$ represent the above protocol. We intend to construct a simulator S for any PPT environment $\mathcal{E}$, such that for any PPT adversary $\mathcal{A}$ who is allowed to corrupt the server maliciously and to corrupt a fixed subset of clients semi-honestly, the two ensembles $\mathsf{EXEC}_{\Pi,\mathcal{A},\mathcal{E}}$ and $\mathsf{EXEC}_{\mathcal{F}_{OT\text{-}MVC},S,\mathcal{E}}$ are indistinguishable. Upon receiving an input from the environment $\mathcal{E}$, the simulator S writes the input on $\mathcal{A}$'s input tape. Upon obtaining an output value from the adversary $\mathcal{A}$, the simulator S writes the output on $\mathcal{E}$'s output tape.

*Case 1: Honest Server and Client.* Since we assume the channel is private, the simulator S could use the ciphertext of a random string to simulate the communication script. Because the server and all the clients are honest, the communication script is the only thing that the simulator S should simulate.

*Case 2: Honest Server and Partially Corrupted (Semi-honest) Clients.* Besides the communication script, the simulator S needs to simulate the view of all corrupted clients, which contains the encoded function share and the encoded input for each client. The simulator S randomly chooses two strings as the encoded input wires for a label, and sets the encoded input to the exact string corresponding to the input. The adversary cannot tell the difference between the encoded input wires in the encoding function and the newly generated random strings.

*Case 3: Corrupted (Malicious) Server and Honest Clients.* Besides the communication script, the simulator S needs to simulate the server Serv's view, including $(F, \{X\}_n)$. The simulator S randomly chooses the encoded input wires which are not chosen by clients, denoted as $\{\bar{X}\}_n$. Then S merges the two sets into the universal encoding function. Concretely speaking, encoded wires in $\{X\}_n$ and $\{\bar{X}\}_n$ are regarded as the encoded wires of 0's and 1's, respectively. After randomly choosing the encoded intermediate and output values, the simulator S generates the garbled circuit $F'$, and sets the decoding function to $d'$. If there exists a distinguisher that could distinguish $(F, \{X\}_n)$ from $(F', \{\bar{X}\}_n)$, then we can construct an adversary $\mathcal{B}$ that uses $(f, f', \{x\}_n, \{\vec{0}\}_n)$ as input to break the obliviousness of MOGC.

In conclusion, the two ensembles $\mathsf{EXEC}_{\Pi,\mathcal{A},\mathcal{E}}$ and $\mathsf{EXEC}_{\mathcal{F}_{OT-MVC},S,\mathcal{E}}$ are indistinguishable in all cases. $\qquad\square$

## 5.2    Construction of MVOC

We give a construction that UC-realizes $\mathcal{F}_{MVC}$ from a secure MOGC scheme, a fully homomorphic encryption scheme FHE and a symmetric-key encryption scheme SKE. The protocol is in the $(\mathcal{F}_{SMT}, \mathcal{G}^{FHE})$-hybrid world, where $\mathcal{G}^{FHE}$ serves as a self-registered PKI which allows $P_1$ to generate FHE key pair and register the public key, and $\mathcal{F}_{\mathsf{SMT}}$ is the functionality of Secure Message Transmission [3]. It returns $\mathsf{pk}_{\mathsf{FHE}}$ when the server or any other party queries it. The construction is described as follows. For simplicity, we omit the superscript ssid of the variables in online phase.

1. Collaborators $P_2, ..., P_n$ execute the algorithm MOGC.Gb$_C$ to generate encoding function shares $e_2, ..., e_n$ respectively, and send the shares to $P_1$.
2. The generator $P_1$ executes the algorithm MOGC.Gb$_G$ to generate his encoded function share $e_1$, the garbled circuit $F$ and the decoding function $d$. Then $P_1$ sends $F$ to the server.
3. The generator $P_1$ interacts with $\mathcal{G}_{\mathsf{FHE}}$ and acquires a new FHE key pair $(\mathsf{pk}_{\mathsf{FHE}}, \mathsf{sk}_{\mathsf{FHE}})$. Then $P_1$ obtains $X_1$ by executing the algorithm MOGC.En on its own private input $x_1$, randomly chooses a symmetric key $k_1 \leftarrow \mathcal{K}_{\mathsf{SKE}}$, and computes $m_{11} = \mathsf{SKE.Enc}(k_1, X_1)$ and $m_{12} = \mathsf{FHE.Enc}(\mathsf{pk}_{\mathsf{FHE}}, k_1)$. $P_1$ finally sends $m_1 = (m_{11}, m_{12})$ to the server Serv.
4. For $i \in [n]\backslash\{1\}$, the collaborator $P_i$ interacts with $\mathcal{G}_{\mathsf{FHE}}$ and acquires the current FHE public key $\mathsf{pk}_{\mathsf{FHE}}$. Similarly, $P_i$ obtains $X_i$ by executing the algorithm MOGC.En on its own private input $x_i$, randomly chooses a symmetric key $k_i \leftarrow \mathcal{K}_{\mathsf{SKE}}$, and computes $m_{i1} = \mathsf{SKE.Enc}(k_i, X_i)$ and $m_{i2} = \mathsf{FHE.Enc}(\mathsf{pk}_{\mathsf{FHE}}, k_i)$. $P_i$ finally sends $m_i = (m_{i1}, m_{i2})$ to the server Serv.
5. After parsing $m_i = (m_{i1}, m_{i2})$, Serv computes $\hat{X}_i = \mathsf{SKE.Dec}(m_{i1}, \mathsf{FHE.Enc}(m_{i2}))$, for $i \in [n]$. Then Serv executes the algorithm MOGC.Ev on $\{\hat{X}_i\}_n$, obtains a circuit result $\hat{Y}$, and sends it to the generator $P_1$.
6. The generator $P_1$ computes $Y = \mathsf{FHE.Dec}(\mathsf{sk}_{\mathsf{FHE}}, \hat{Y})$, and recovers the final result by executing the algorithm MOGC.De. If $Y$ is a valid value, then $P_1$ accepts and outputs the final result $y$. Otherwise, $P_1$ rejects and outputs $\bot$.

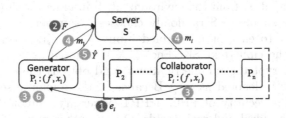

**Fig. 1.** Construction of MVOC

As shown in Fig. 1, Step 1 and 2 are in offline phase, and the rest are online. Step 3 and 6 are locally executed by each client and the generator respectively with no data transmission between participants. After Step 6 is executed without the result being $\bot$, the protocol comes back to Step 3; otherwise, it terminates. This abortion makes the advantage that the server gained from providing incorrect result cannot be carried over to the next sub-session.

**Theorem 3.** *Suppose FHE is an IND-CPA secure public-key fully homomorphic encryption scheme, SKE is a semantically secure symmetric-key encryption scheme, and MOGC is a secure multi-client outsourced garbled circuit protocol, then the aforementioned protocol UC-realizes $\mathcal{F}_{MVC}$ against semi-honest corruption of any fixed subset of clients, or against malicious server corruption.*

*Proof.* Let $\Pi$ represents the above protocol. We intend to construct a simulator S for any PPT environment $\mathcal{E}$, such that for any PPT adversary $\mathcal{A}$ who is allowed to corrupt the server maliciously and to corrupt a fixed subset of clients semi-honestly, the two ensembles $\mathsf{EXEC}_{\Pi,\mathcal{A},\mathcal{E}}$ and $\mathsf{EXEC}_{\mathcal{F}_{MVC},S,\mathcal{E}}$ are indistinguishable. Upon receiving an input from the environment $\mathcal{E}$, the simulator S writes the input on $\mathcal{A}$'s input tape. Upon obtaining an output value from the adversary $\mathcal{A}$, the simulator S writes the output on $\mathcal{E}$'s output tape.

*Case 1: Honest Server and Client.* Since we assume the channel is private, the simulator S could use the ciphertext of a random string to simulate the communication script. Because the server and all the clients are honest, the communication script is the only thing that the simulator S should simulate.

*Case 2: Honest Server and Partially Corrupted (Semi-honest) Clients.* Besides the communication script, the simulator S needs to simulate the view of all corrupted clients, which contains an FHE public key, the encoded function share and the message sent to the server for each client. Concretely speaking, if the generator $P_1$ is not corrupted, the view in the real world contains $(\mathsf{pk}_{\mathsf{FHE}})$ and $(e_i, k_i, m_{i1}, m_{i2})$ for each client $P_i$. It is intuitive that all the above variables could be reproduced by the same way as in the protocol, since all the collaborators only send messages to others and do not receive any message from other parties. Specifically, the simulator S randomly chooses the encoded wires for simulating the encoding function share, noted as $e_i'$. Then in each online phase, after acquiring input $x_i$ from the environment, S interacts with $\mathcal{G}_{\mathsf{FHE}}$ to obtain $\mathsf{pk}_{\mathsf{FHE}}$. Next, the simulator S randomly chooses a symmetric key $k_i' \leftarrow \mathcal{K}_{\mathsf{SKE}}$, and uses the key to encrypt its garbled input $X_i' = e_i'(x_i)$ corresponding to $x_i$ and obtains the ciphertext $\mathsf{SKE.Enc}(k_i', X_i')$, denoted as $m_{i2}'$. After that, S uses $\mathsf{pk}_{\mathsf{FHE}}$ to encrypt the symmetric key $k_i'$ and obtains the encapsulated key $\mathsf{FHE.Enc}(\mathsf{pk}_{\mathsf{FHE}}, k_i')$, denoted as $m_{i1}'$. Because of the semantic security of SKE and the IND-CPA security of FHE, a PPT adversary cannot distinguish the views between the ideal and real worlds. On the other hand, if the generator $P_1$ is corrupted, the view contains $(\mathsf{pk}_{\mathsf{FHE}}, \mathsf{sk}_{\mathsf{FHE}}, d, F)$ and $(e_i, k_i, m_{i1}, m_{i2})$ for each client $P_i$. The only difference from the above case is that the generator $P_0$ needs to simulate the circuit $F$ along with its decoding function $d$. Actually he could reproduce these values by first randomly generating the decoding function $d'$ and its encoding function share $e_1'$, and then randomly choosing intermediate garbled wires, and computing a circuit $F'$ using the garbled wires above. These new variables are chosen randomly, since the adversary still cannot distinguish the views between the two worlds.

*Case 3: Corrupted (Malicious) Server and Honest Clients.* Besides the communication script, S needs to simulate the server Serv's view, including $(F, \mathsf{pk}_{\mathsf{FHE}}, \hat{Y})$, and $(m_{i1}, m_{i2})$ for each $i \in [n]$. Upon receiving $\Phi(f)$, the simulator randomly generates a circuit $F'$ with the circuit structure information revealed by $\Phi(f)$. During online phase, the simulator interacts with $\mathcal{G}_{\mathsf{FHE}}$ to obtain the public key $\mathsf{pk}_{\mathsf{FHE}}$. Then, for each $i \in [n]$, the simulator chooses two random strings $s_1$ and $s_2$ of length $k$ and $w$ respectively, where $k$ is the length of a valid SKE key and $w$ is the length of a valid garbled wire. S computes $\mathsf{SKE.Enc}(s_1, s_2)$ and $\mathsf{FHE.Enc}(\mathsf{pk}_{\mathsf{FHE}}, s_1)$, denoted as $m'_{i1}$ and $m'_{i2}$ respectively. If there exists a distinguisher that could tell the views of the ideal and real worlds, it either distinguishes $F$ from $F'$, or distinguishes $(m_{i1}, m_{i2})$ from $m'_{i1}$ and $m'_{i2}$. If the former happens, then we can construct an adversary $\mathcal{B}$ using $(f, f', \{x\}_n, \{\vec{0}\}_n)$ as input to break the obliviousness of MOGC. If the latter happens, we can construct an adversary $\mathcal{B}$ that uses $(m_{i1}, m'_{i1})$ and $(m_{i2}, m'_{i2})$ as input to break the semantic security of SKE and IND-CPA security of FHE, respectively.

Thus $\mathsf{EXEC}_{\Pi, \mathcal{A}, \mathcal{E}}$ and $\mathsf{EXEC}_{\mathcal{F}_{\mathsf{MVC}}, \mathcal{S}, \mathcal{E}}$ are indistinguishable in all cases.    □

## 5.3   From Semi-honest Clients to Malicious Clients

We inherit the approach in [17] to upgrade an MVC protocol that is secure against semi-honest clients to the one against malicious clients. The theorem in [17] indicates that, if an MVC protocol which is secure against semi-honest client corruptions satisfies *perfect privacy*, then there exists an MVC protocol which is secure against malicious client corruptions, in the ZK and self-registered PKI setup hybrid world. We will give the definition as follows.

**Definition 9. (Perfect Privacy of MVC [17]).** *An MVC protocol which is secure against semi-honest client corruptions is perfectly private if for all inputs $x_1, ..., x_n$, for an adversary $\mathcal{A}$ that semi-honestly corrupts some subset of the parties with index set $\mathcal{I}$ where $\mathcal{I} \subset [n]$, and for every random tape $r_{\mathcal{A}}$ belonging to $\mathcal{A}$, there exists a simulator $S$ such that the two distributions $\mathsf{View}_{\Pi(x_1, ..., x_n), \mathcal{A}}$ and $S(\{x_i, y_i\}_{i \in \mathcal{I}}, r_{\mathcal{A}})$ are identical.*

We then show our previous MVOC construction satisfying perfect privacy.

*Claim.* If MOGC, FHE and SKE in the aforementioned MVOC construction are perfectly correct, then MOVC satisfies perfect privacy.

*Proof.* Since all the collaborators in our protocol do not receive any message, their view could be easily simulated by executed the protocol honestly. Hence we only need to simulate the view of the generator $\mathsf{P}_1$ in the case of $1 \in \mathcal{I}$, without loss of generality. The view $\mathsf{View}_{\Pi(x_1, ..., x_n), \mathcal{A}}$ for $\mathsf{P}_1$ contains $(F, e_1, d)$ and $\hat{Y}$ for each online phase. During the protocol $\mathsf{P}_1$ uses randomness $r$ to obtain $e_1, d$, and randomness $r_{\mathsf{sid}}$ to obtain $k_1, m_{11}, m_{12}$. S could use $r_{\mathsf{sid}}$ to compute the current encoded result by encrypting the encoded wire of $y_1$ using FHE, producing a view which is identical to $\hat{Y}$. Thus S can simulate a perfect identical view.

# 6    Evaluation

## 6.1    Efficiency Analysis

As we discussed before, *outsourcability* may be seen as an efficiency improvement for client side. We make a comparison between our scheme and Choi et al.'s [7] in terms of efficiency performance, since [7] is a general solution in the multi-client settings, which is theoretically more efficient than the general UC-secure solution [17]. We analyze the cost in the offline and online phases separately. Because the final result could only be obtained by the generator, for average consideration, we aggregate a total complexity by executing the protocol for $n$ times in a single computing period, during which each client acts as the generator once and as the collaborator $n - 1$ times, where $n$ is the number of clients.

- In offline phase, the clients together generate the whole garbled circuit. The total computational complexity is $O(\Phi(f))$. For communication, each collaborator sends a message of size $O(l)$ to the generator, and the generator sends an $O(\Phi(f))$-size circuit to server.
- In online phase, the generator runs an FHE key generation algorithm. Then each client executes a symmetric key encryption with size $O(l\kappa)$, and executes a fully homomorphic encryption with size $O(\kappa)$. During result recovering, the generator executes a fully homomorphic decrypting algorithm with plaintext size $O(l\kappa)$. For communication, each client sends the ciphertext generated above.

## 6.2    Implementation and Evaluation

We implement our protocol, and run all the experiments on an Ubuntu Server with Intel i7-10700 CPU (2.9 GHz) and 80 GB DDR4 2133 MHz RAM. We focus on simulating the execution of clients. We adopt TinyGarble [19] as the implement of garbling scheme, which is mature and uses several most recent optimization on GC protocol. The computation benchmark we choose is the AES encryption algorithm. For simplicity, we set the number of clients be 2. One client provides a 128-bit key, and the other uses a 128-bit plaintext. There are 6,400 non-XOR gates in the circuit, and the total size of the garbled circuit is $2.1 \times 10^6$ bits. We use TFHE [6] as the FHE scheme, since it supports the encryption of boolean values and can be optimized for fast gate bootstrapping. For symmetric encryption scheme, we deploy two schemes, a 4-round algorithm AGRASTA [8] and a 6-round DASTA [18]. The former provides small key size while the latter is efficient in encrypting. Both schemes are well compatible with TFHE. We note that one may use more efficient SKE schemes (which could be less compatible with FHE) but relatively huge overhead may be incurred in the server side.

We set security parameter $\kappa$ be 128. Specifically, the key-size of AGRASTA and DASTA are 129 and 351 respectively. All the experiments are executed in single-thread mode. We compare our implement with [7], and the result is shown in Table 4. As we claimed previously, the more number of client we set, the larger scale of input will be, and thus the more outsourcability our protocol provides. Our implement is the least advantageous in this situation, where there are only two clients and the input length is only 128 for each client, which is almost as little as the ciphertext extension rate of FHE. Under such circumstances, we increase the communication efficiency by at least 2.67x and the time cost by at least 2.24x, as compared to [7]. As the data size increases, the improvement ratio of efficiency converges to a ratio proportion to the throughput rate of the two schemes. According to our evaluation, the slowest SKE throughput is 72.98 bit/ms by AGRASTA, while TFHE offers 46.57 bit/ms. Hence, with large input scale, our efficiency improvement comes to 4x and 3.13x respectively.

It is worth noting that the evaluation of the efficiency improvement is based on the worst case, in which the number of non-server participants is 2. As shown in Table 1, a larger $n$ brings higher efficiency improvements.

**Table 4.** Overheads for Clients

| Schemes | Offline phase | | Input phase | |
|---|---|---|---|---|
| | Time (ms) | Communication (kbits) | Time (ms) | Communication (kbits) |
| Choi et al. [7] | 73.756 | 2099.2 | 1055.434* | 147.456 |
| MVOC (DASTA) | 73.756 | 2131.968 | 65.22 | 55.232 |
| MVOC (AGRASTA) | 73.756 | 2131.968 | 480.695 | 41.024 |

* This time cost is underestimated, since it does not include the time consumed by POT, which is not a component in our implement.

## 7  Conclusion

We proposed a lighter multi-client privacy-preserving verifiable outsourced computation scheme. To adopt garbled circuit in multi-client scenario, we developed a new primitive MOGC based on garbling scheme. We further showed that a secure MOGC protocol implies a one-time multi-client verifiable computation. To construct an efficient MVOC protocol, we used hybrid encryption technique to avoid expensive overheads from FHE. We proved the UC security of the proposed protocol. We made a theoretical analysis on efficiency and implemented our scheme. The results demonstrate that the proposed protocol can enhance the efficiency of input phase by 2.67-4x and 2.24-3x in communication and computation cost, respectively.

**Acknowledgements.** This work was supported by the National Key Research and Development Program of China (Grant No. 2020YFA0712300), the National Natural Science Foundation of China (No. 62132013, 62072305, 62132005, 62172162), European Union's Horizon 2020 research and innovation programme under grant agreement No. 952697 (ASSURED) and No. 101021727 (IRIS), and Shanghai Technology Innovation Centre of Distributed Privacy-Preserving Artificial Intelligence.

# References

1. Bellare, M., Hoang, V.T., Rogaway, P.: Foundations of garbled circuits. In: ACM CCS 2012, pp. 784–796 (2012)
2. Bois, A., Cascudo, I., Fiore, D., Kim, D.: Flexible and efficient verifiable computation on encrypted data. In: Garay, J.A. (ed.) PKC 2021. LNCS, vol. 12711, pp. 528–558. Springer, Cham (2021). https://doi.org/10.1007/978-3-030-75248-4_19
3. Canetti, R.: Universally composable security: a new paradigm for cryptographic protocols. In: FOCS 2001, pp. 136–145 (2001)
4. Canetti, R., Raghuraman, S., Richelson, S., Vaikuntanathan, V.: Chosen-ciphertext secure fully homomorphic encryption. In: Fehr, S. (ed.) PKC 2017. LNCS, vol. 10175, pp. 213–240. Springer, Heidelberg (2017). https://doi.org/10.1007/978-3-662-54388-7_8
5. Catalano, D., Fiore, D.: Practical homomorphic MACs for arithmetic circuits. In: Johansson, T., Nguyen, P.Q. (eds.) EUROCRYPT 2013. LNCS, vol. 7881, pp. 336–352. Springer, Heidelberg (2013). https://doi.org/10.1007/978-3-642-38348-9_21
6. Chillotti, I., Gama, N., Georgieva, M., Izabachène, M.: TFHE: fast fully homomorphic encryption over the torus. J. Cryptol. **33**(1), 34–91 (2020)
7. Choi, S.G., Katz, J., Kumaresan, R., Cid, C.: Multi-client non-interactive verifiable computation. In: Sahai, A. (ed.) TCC 2013. LNCS, vol. 7785, pp. 499–518. Springer, Heidelberg (2013). https://doi.org/10.1007/978-3-642-36594-2_28
8. Dobraunig, C., et al.: Rasta: a cipher with low ANDdepth and few ANDs per bit. In: Shacham, H., Boldyreva, A. (eds.) CRYPTO 2018. LNCS, vol. 10991, pp. 662–692. Springer, Cham (2018). https://doi.org/10.1007/978-3-319-96884-1_22
9. Fiore, D., Gennaro, R., Pastro, V.: Efficiently verifiable computation on encrypted data. In: ACM CCS 2014, pp. 844–855 (2014)
10. Fiore, D., Mitrokotsa, A., Nizzardo, L., Pagnin, E.: Multi-key homomorphic authenticators. IET Inf. Secur. **13**(6), 618–638 (2019)
11. Fiore, D., Nitulescu, A., Pointcheval, D.: Boosting verifiable computation on encrypted data (2020)
12. Gennaro, R., Gentry, C., Parno, B.: Non-interactive verifiable computing: outsourcing computation to untrusted workers. In: Rabin, T. (ed.) CRYPTO 2010. LNCS, vol. 6223, pp. 465–482. Springer, Heidelberg (2010). https://doi.org/10.1007/978-3-642-14623-7_25
13. Gennaro, R., Wichs, D.: Fully homomorphic message authenticators. In: Sako, K., Sarkar, P. (eds.) ASIACRYPT 2013. LNCS, vol. 8270, pp. 301–320. Springer, Heidelberg (2013). https://doi.org/10.1007/978-3-642-42045-0_16
14. Gentry, C.: Fully homomorphic encryption using ideal lattices. In: STOC 2009, pp. 169–178 (2009)
15. Goldwasser, S., et al.: Multi-input functional encryption. In: Nguyen, P.Q., Oswald, E. (eds.) EUROCRYPT 2014. LNCS, vol. 8441, pp. 578–602. Springer, Heidelberg (2014). https://doi.org/10.1007/978-3-642-55220-5_32
16. Goldwasser, S., Kalai, Y., Popa, R.A., Vaikuntanathan, V., Zeldovich, N.: Reusable garbled circuits and succinct functional encryption. In: STOC 2013, pp. 555–564 (2013)
17. Gordon, S.D., Katz, J., Liu, F.-H., Shi, E., Zhou, H.-S.: Multi-client verifiable computation with stronger security guarantees. In: Dodis, Y., Nielsen, J.B. (eds.) TCC 2015. LNCS, vol. 9015, pp. 144–168. Springer, Heidelberg (2015). https://doi.org/10.1007/978-3-662-46497-7_6

18. Hebborn, P., Leander, G.: Dasta-alternative linear layer for Rasta. IACR Trans. Sym. Cryptol., 46–86 (2020)
19. Songhori, E.M., Hussain, S.U., Sadeghi, A.R., Schneider, T., Koushanfar, F.: Tiny-Garble: highly compressed and scalable sequential garbled circuits. In: S&P 2015, pp. 411–428 (2015)
20. Yao, A.C.C.: How to generate and exchange secrets. In: FOCS 1986, pp. 162–167 (1986)

# Verifying the Quality of Outsourced Training on Clouds

Peiyang Li[1,2], Ye Wang[1,2], Zhuotao Liu[1,2], Ke Xu[1,2], Qian Wang[3], Chao Shen[4], and Qi Li[1,2(✉)]

[1] Tsinghua University & BNRist, Beijing, China
{lpy20,wangye22}@mails.tsinghua.edu.cn,
{zhuotaoliu,xuke,qli01}@tsinghua.edu.cn
[2] Zhongguancun Lab, Beijing, China
[3] Wuhan University, Wuhan, China
qianwang@whu.edu.cn
[4] Xi'an Jiaotong University, Xi'an, China
chaoshen@mail.xjtu.edu.cn

**Abstract.** Deep learning training is often outsourced to clouds due to its high computation overhead. However, clouds may not perform model training correctly due to the potential violations on Service Level Agreement (SLA) and attacks, incurring low quality of outsourced training. It is challenging for customers to understand the quality of outsourced training on clouds. They cannot measure the quality by simply testing the trained models because the testing performance is impacted by various factors, e.g., the quality of training and testing data. In order to address these issues, in this paper, we propose a novel framework that allows customers to verify the quality of outsourced training without modifying the processes of model training. Particularly, our framework achieves black-box verification by utilizing an extra training task that can be learned by the model only after the model converges on the original training task. We construct well-designed extra training tasks according to the original tasks, and develop a training quality verification method to measure the model performance on the extra task with a hypothesis testing-based threshold. The experiment results show that the models passing the quality verification achieve at least 96% of their best performance with negligible accuracy loss, i.e., less than 0.25%.

**Keywords:** Outsourced deep learning services · Verification

## 1 Introduction

Deep learning has been widely used for a variety of tasks, such as image recognition [10] and sentiment classification [24]. Despite achieved classification performances, the training of these models requires both substantial computational resources and deep learning expertise. Outsourced training on clouds, such as Amazon SageMaker [2], Google Vertex AI [3], and Microsoft Azure [4], can liberate customers from the heavy lifting of training deep learning models. Namely,

V. Atluri et al. (Eds.): ESORICS 2022, LNCS 13555, pp. 126–144, 2022.
https://doi.org/10.1007/978-3-031-17146-8_7

the customer only needs to upload the training data. The cloud will conduct the training algorithm and return a well trained model which is convergent on the training data.

However, the outsourced training is typically invisible to customers. A customer is unable to make sure whether the model returned by the cloud is well trained due to various reasons. For example, cloud providers may have financial incentives to stealthily violate Service Level Agreements (SLAs) [16,35,36]. Model training may be stopped before the models are well trained, e.g., in order to save their computing resources and reap economic benefits. Moreover, adversaries may directly perform malicious operations to interfere with model training on clouds [8,11,29]. All these issues will incur low quality of outsourced training on clouds, leading to inaccurate model inferences.

A number of existing methods have been developed to verify outsourced inference. Nevertheless, they are unable to efficiently verify the quality of outsourced training. They either utilize verifiable computing techniques [11,14,21,36], or enable verifiability for deployed models [16,31]. The former incurs significant model training overhead, while the latter can only ensure the integrity of deployed models. In order to ensure the quality of outsourced training, we need to address the following challenges: (i) It is infeasible to monitor the status of outsourced training. We cannot simply use the results of training loss and validation accuracy because they can be easily disturbed. (ii) Besides the training quality, the performance of a model is also impacted by various factors, such as the quality of training set and testing set, which is hard to measure. Thus, a customer can hardly predict the model performance of a well trained model so as to verify the quality of training.

In this paper, we take the first step towards the verification of outsourced training. To overcome the challenges above, we propose a novel and effective framework to achieve black-box verification on outsourced training using a carefully designed extra task. Specifically, by utilizing the over-parameterization property of deep learning models, we make the model learn an extra task that is semantically different from the original task specified by the customer. We propose to construct an extra task which will only be learned by the model after the model converges to the original task. The customers can verify the training quality by measuring the model performance on the extra task. Note that, since we only generate a small number of training samples in the extra task, the extra task incurs a negligible impact on the model performance on the original task and negligible computational overhead. In summary, we make the following contributions:

- To the best of our knowledge, we are the first one to propose a framework for verifying the training quality of an outsourced model.
- We develop a method to construct the extra training task according to the original task, and develop a training quality verification method.
- We conduct a comprehensive evaluation on various datasets with different models to demonstrate that our proposed framework is effective and has a negligible impact on the performance of the model.

## 2　Background and Problem Statement

### 2.1　Background

*Deep Learning.* Deep learning model aims to build a function $f_\theta$ that maps the input $X$ to the output $Y$, where $f$ represents the model structure and $\theta$ represents the model parameters. Generally, $\boldsymbol{x} \in X$ is a $d$-dimensional feature vector and $y \in Y$ is a discrete label.

To make $f_\theta$ best capture the relationship between $X$ and $Y$, training process is performed on a set of labeled data, called training data, $\mathcal{D} = \{(\boldsymbol{x}_i, y_i)_{i=1}^n\}$ to find a set of optimal parameters $\theta$. The optimality of $\theta$ can be measured by a loss function $\mathcal{L}$. The trainer generally uses the gradient descent based algorithm [27] to minimize $\mathcal{L}$ on the training data. Specifically, gradient descent is an iterative method where in each step the trainer computes the gradient of the loss function with respect to $\theta$ and updates $\theta$ based on this gradient. As the iteration progresses, the model gets convergent. The trainer regularly check the model according to certain rules, e.g., the testing accuracy does not go up over a substantial amount of iterations [33], to determine whether the model has been convergent.

*Outsourced Deep Learning Services.* Development of deep learning requires both substantial computing resources and deep learning expertise. Numerous cloud service providers offer outsourced deep learning services to make it convenient for customers, such as Amazon SageMaker [2], Google Vertex AI [3], Microsoft Azure [4]. There are two main types of services: model training and model deploying [17,18]. The model training services support customers without the knowledge of algorithm details and hardware devices (e.g., GPU) training a deep learning model easily. The customer uploads a training dataset to the cloud. The cloud then performs model training and returns the resulting model to the customer. Generally, the cloud provides a variety of model structures for customers to choose from and even provides an algorithm market [1] which allow third parties to provide model to meet the demands for different scenarios.

The model deploying services help customers with limited resources publish their models for end-users to query. The customer uploads a trained model to the cloud. The cloud allocates the resources to host the model and releases APIs. The cloud is responsible for availability and scalability of deployed models.

### 2.2　Problem Statement

We consider a scenario in which a customer desires to develop a deep learning model by outsourced training. The customer can choose a training set, upload it to the cloud and specify a model type for model training. The cloud will conduct a training algorithm based on the training set and then return the resulting model (or the model's API) to the customer. The outsourced training is a black-box to the customer.

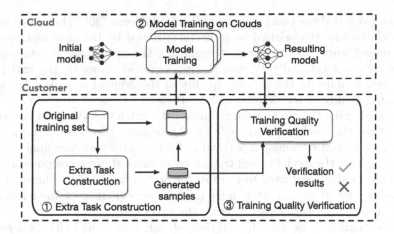

**Fig. 1.** The overall workflow of our framework.

Normally, to achieve the best model performance, the resulting model should be *well trained* by the cloud to be convergent on the training set (i.e., additional training will not improve the model performance). However, the resulting model may be not well trained due to various reasons. For example, cloud service providers have a financial incentive to stop training before the model is well trained [16,35,36]. Moreover, adversaries may directly perform malicious operations to cause the programs executed in the cloud to terminate unexpectedly [8,11,29]. We do not consider the scenario where the cloud compromises the integrity of training data, e.g., the cloud trains a model using a subset of the training data, which can be addressed by combining the model partition techniques with TEE within limited time consumption [13]. We also do not consider the compromise of the model structure, e.g., a simpler model with fewer parameters is trained to replace the model specified by the customer. The assumption is rational since the customer can easily observe whether the structure of the resulting model is correct.

Our goal is to design a method $S$ for customers to verify the quality of outsourced training, i.e., verify whether the resulting model $f_\theta$ is well trained on the training set $\mathcal{D}$. Formally,

$$S(f_\theta, \mathcal{D}) \rightarrow \{0, 1\}, \tag{1}$$

where 0 means $f_\theta$ is well trained using $\mathcal{D}$ and 1 means otherwise.

## 3 System Framework

We design a framework that allows customers to verify the quality of outsourced training. The framework is motivated by the over-parameterization property of deep learning models, that is, a deep learning model has parameter redundancy for a task [7,34]. With parameter redundancy, a model can learn multiple tasks at a time even if these tasks are semantically different [30]. Therefore, in our framework, besides the original task that is specified by the customer, we also let the model learn an extra task. Specifically, the extra task is semantically different from the original task, and the model performance on the extra task can be used to indicate the training quality of the original task. We can verify the training quality of the original task by the extra task.

Note that using the model performance of the extra task does not contradict the fact that the model performance on the original task cannot be used to verify the quality of training. In particular, for the extra task, our goal is not to measure whether the model is well trained on it. Instead, we focus on evaluating whether the model has started to learn it (see Sect. 4 for details). Therefore, it is not necessary for us to accurately infer the best performance on the extra task, which is also the critical benefit of using the extra task.

Figure 1 outlines the overall workflow of our framework with two parties involved, a customer and a cloud. The framework consists of the following three steps.

- **Extra Task Construction.** The customer collects an original training set that corresponds to his original task and constructs an extra task by manipulating his original training set. Then he uploads the modified training set to the cloud for model training and specifies the model type.
- **Model Training on Clouds.** The cloud gets a model type and a training set from the customer as input. It trains the specific model based on the training set and outputs the resulting model to the customer.
- **Training Quality Verification.** The customer downloads the resulting model from the cloud. He uses the extra task to verify whether the resulting model has been well trained or not. If the resulting model passes the verification, the customer accepts the resulting model and ends the entire process. Otherwise, the customer rejects the resulting model and an exception is raised.

Note that, our framework considers outsourced training as a black-box. This has two benefits: (i) for the customer, the verification can be performed without accessing the outsourced training in the cloud and (ii) for the cloud, no modification in the training pipeline is required and the behaviour of clouds can be the same as the standard one. Thus it is easy and practical to deploy our framework.

## 4    Design Details

### 4.1    Extra Task Construction

To enable verification on the quality of outsourced training, we extend the training set to let the deep learning model learn an extra task during the model training. The extra task is carefully designed, which aims to indicate the training quality of the resulting model without degrading the model performance on the original task.

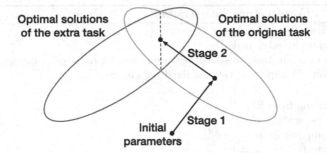

**Fig. 2.** The extra task can be used to verify the training quality of original task. Parameters trajectories during training are illustrated in the simplified parameter space. In stage 1, only the original task will be optimized. In stage 2, extra task will be optimized after the model converges to an optimal solution of the original task.

As shown in Fig. 2, we intend to design an extra task that will only be learned after the model converges to an optimal solution of the original task. Based on the different generalizability of deep learning model for cleanly labeled samples and randomly labeled samples [7], we can have the following theorem. The detailed proof of this theorem is provided in the Appendix.

**Theorem 1:** *Given a training set which contains the training samples of clean labels $\mathcal{D}_c$ and training samples of random labels $\mathcal{D}_r$ such that $|\mathcal{D}_c| > |\mathcal{D}_r|$, consider training a model $f_\theta$ using a loss function $\mathcal{L}$, if the model does not converge to an optimal solution of $\mathcal{D}_c$, then we have:*

$$\|\nabla_\theta \mathcal{L}(\mathcal{D}_c, f_\theta)\| \gg \|\nabla_\theta \mathcal{L}(\mathcal{D}_r, f_\theta)\|. \qquad (2)$$

According to the theorem, we can see that, when the model is not convergent, training samples of clean labels have a larger norm of gradients than training samples of random labels. Therefore, it is possible to let the model learn tasks in a specific order since parameters will be first updated to optimize samples with a larger norm of gradients. However, we cannot simply generate random labels or features for the extra task. Specifically, if we randomly select samples from the original training set and assign them random labels, their random labels will conflict with the clean labels in the original training set and thus the model performance will degrade significantly. Moreover, although random samples whose features and labels are both random can avoid conflict with the original training set, which have a very small norm of gradients, they may be learned by the model before the model converges on the original task because they are very sparse in the vast random feature space [39].

To overcome the limitations above, we propose a novel method that constructs extra tasks by utilizing a fixed region in the feature space of the extra task. The fixed region ensures effectiveness of the sample, while effectively reducing the size of random feature spaces. Algorithm 1 presents the extra task construction algorithm. Let $d$ denote the number of dimensions in the feature space.

---

**Algorithm 1.** Constructing the extra task

---

**Function** Extra_Task_Cons($\mathcal{D}, d, C, \eta, s$)

**Output**: Samples in extra task $\mathcal{D}_E$.

/* $\mathcal{D}$: samples in origin task; $d$: size of feature space; $C$: number of categories; */
/* $\eta$: proportion of samples; $s$: ratio of fixed region;*/

1: $\mathcal{D}_E \leftarrow \emptyset$;
2: $x_f \leftarrow$ Sampling from $\mathbb{R}^{\lfloor s \times d \rfloor}$;
3: **while** $|\mathcal{D}_E| < \eta \times |\mathcal{D}|$ **do**
4:    $x_r \leftarrow$ Sampling from $\mathbb{R}^{d - \lfloor s \times d \rfloor}$;
5:    $x \leftarrow$ Concatenate($x_f, x_r$);
6:    $y \leftarrow$ Sampling from $[0, C-1]$;
7:    $\mathcal{D}_E \leftarrow \mathcal{D}_E \cup \{(x, y)\}$;
8: **end while**
9: **return** $\mathcal{D}_E$

---

We use a ratio $s$ to control the size of fixed region in the feature space, i.e., the $d$-dimensional feature space $\mathbb{R}^d$ is divided into an $\lfloor s \times d \rfloor$-dimensional fixed region and a $\lfloor (1-s) \times d \rfloor$-dimensional random region. We first randomly sample features $x_f$ from the fixed region $\mathbb{R}^{\lfloor s \times d \rfloor}$ (line 2). For each sample, we randomly sample features $x_r$ from the random region $\mathbb{R}^{d - \lfloor s \times d \rfloor}$ (line 4). Features of each sample are the concatenation of identical features $x_f$ and different features $x_r$ (line 5). We also randomly sample a label for each sample (line 7). Note that, the number of samples in the extra task is determined by the proportion $\eta$ of samples in the original task $\mathcal{D}$ (line 3).

For simplicity, we use two typical training tasks (i.e., image and text tasks) to illustrate how we construct extra tasks. Note that our method is not only applicable to these two fields and it can be extended to other fields easily.

(i) On image task. Given an image $x \in \mathbb{R}^{w \times h \times 3}$, where $w$ and $h$ are the image width and height respectively, we define the rectangular region bounded by the first $\lfloor (\sqrt{1-s}) \times h \rfloor$ rows and the first $\lfloor (\sqrt{1-s}) \times w \rfloor$ columns as random regions and the rest as fixed regions. Both fixed and random regions are pseudorandom images that can be generated by using any pseudorandom functions chosen by the customer.

(ii) On text task. Suppose that the max length of the text documents is $m$, we define the first $\lfloor (1-s) \times m \rfloor$ words as random regions and the rest words as fixed regions. The words can be generated by enumerating the words from the vocabulary of the original training set [30].

In practice, the extra task construction algorithm is not sensitive to the hyper-parameters $\eta$ and $s$, which allow us to easily find a common setting. We illustrate it in Sect. 5.

---

**Algorithm 2.** Verifying the training quality

---
**Function** Train_Quality_Veri($\mathcal{M}, \mathcal{D}_E, C, \alpha, \epsilon$)
**Output**: verification results $\{0,1\}$.
/* $\mathcal{M}$: resulting model; $\mathcal{D}_E$: samples in extra task;     $C$: number of categories; */
/* $\alpha$: significance level;   $\epsilon$: compensation;     */
1: $acc \leftarrow$ Comp_Accuracy $(\mathcal{M}, \mathcal{D}_E)$;
2: Compute $p$ according to $C$, $\epsilon$, Equation 3;
3: Compute $T$ according to $p$, $\alpha$, Equation 4 and 5;
4: **if** $acc > T$ **then**
5:   **return** 0
6: **else**
7:   **return** 1
8: **end if**

---

## 4.2   Training Quality Verification

We now describe the training quality verification. Given a resulting model returned by the cloud, we use extra tasks to verify whether resulting models are well trained. Recall that our extra task is learned after the model converges on the original task. Thus, if the model starts learning the extra task, we can infer that the model has been well trained on the original task.

We use the accuracy of the extra task to determine whether the model has started learning the extra task. Specifically, we compute the accuracy $acc = N_c/N$, where $N$ denotes the number of samples in the extra task and $N_c$ the number of samples in the extra task that are correctly predicted by the resulting model. A higher accuracy $acc$ indicates that the resulting model has a higher probability of starting learning the extra task. We compare $acc$ with an accuracy threshold $T$. The resulting model with $acc > T$ is considered well trained.

We design a hypothesis testing -based approach to find $T$. Our null hypothesis is that "the model has not converged on the original task". Formally, let $C$ be the total number of categories and a compensation $\epsilon$ be the probability that a sample in the extra task will be learned by the model before the model converges to an optimal solution of the original task. If the null hypothesis is valid, each sample in the extra task will be correctly predicted with a probability $p$ such that:

$$p = \epsilon \cdot 1 + (1 - \epsilon) \cdot \frac{1}{C}, \tag{3}$$

where 1 and $1/C$ are the probabilities of correct prediction of a learned sample and a not learned sample, respectively. Since the prediction of each sample is independent of each other, the number of correctly predicted samples $N_c$ subjects to a binomial distribution. The probability of correctly predicting at most $N_c$ samples is:

$$F(N_c) = \sum_{x \leq N_c} C_N^x p^x (1 - p)^{N-x}. \tag{4}$$

Thus, let $\alpha$ indicate the significance level, we compute the accuracy threshold $T$ to reject the null hypothesis by solving

$$1 - F(T \cdot N) = \alpha. \tag{5}$$

Intuitively, $T$ satisfies that a not well trained model has an accuracy $acc \geq T$ with a probability $\alpha$ under the null hypothesis.

Algorithm 2 summarizes how we verify the training quality. Given the resulting model and samples in the extra task, we first compute the accuracy (line 1). Then we find a accuracy threshold (line 2–3). We compare $acc$ with $T$, and the resulting model with $acc > T$ is considered well trained and otherwise not well trained (line 4–8).

*Discussion.* In this paper, we focus on measuring training of supervised deep learning models, i.e., training data contains labels. Theoretically, our method can also be applied to any model that uses the gradient descent based algorithm as an optimizer. Thus, we can extend it for unsupervised deep learning models. In the extra task construction step, we can only generate samples whose features are the concatenation of identical features in the fixed region and different features in the random region due to the fact that samples in unsupervised learning have no labels. Thus, we can omit the random sampling of a label (i.e., line 6 in Algorithm 1). In the training quality verification step, depending on the supervisory signals leveraged by different models, we use different metrics to determine whether the model has started learning the extra task. For instance, the unsupervised autoencoder [6,25] learns to represent samples and reconstruct samples using their representation, and hence we can use reconstruction error as the metric.

## 5   Evaluation

In this section, we evaluate our method to answer the following questions.

**Q1.** How effectively can our method detect models with low training quality?
**Q2.** How does the extra task affect the performance of models on the original task?
**Q3.** How does extra task construction affect the performance of our method?

### 5.1   Experiment Setup

Experiments are conducted on a GPU server. Its hardware environment and software environment are configured as NVIDIA 2080Ti and Ubuntu 18.04.3 LTS. The deep learning algorithms are implemented in Python 3.7 and PyTorch 1.6. For each experiment, we run it three times with different random seeds and report the average values.

*Baseline.* We use an accuracy-based verification method as the baseline. Given a pre-defined accuracy threshold, if the accuracy of the resulting model is larger than the threshold, the method outputs "0", i.e., the resulting model passes the verification. Otherwise, the method outputs "1". For a comprehensive comparison, we choose the thresholds from 60% to 90%, which covers the accuracy of our selected models.

**Table 1.** Datasets and models in our evaluation. # Ns is the number of training samples, # Cs is the number of categories, # params is the number of parameters of the models, Test acc is the testing set accuracy on the baseline models.

| Dataset | # Ns | # Cs | Model | # Params | Test acc |
|---------|------|------|-------|----------|----------|
| CIFAR10 (C10) | 50K | 10 | RES | 21.29M | 92.23 |
|  |  |  | VGG | 9.75M | 89.20 |
| CIFAR100 (C100) | 50K | 100 | RES | 21.34M | 70.19 |
|  |  |  | VGG | 9.80M | 60.44 |
| IMDB (IM) | 25K | 2 | TCNN | 1.12M | 88.82 |
|  |  |  | A-BL | 1.63M | 89.99 |
| AGNews (AG) | 120K | 4 | TCNN | 1.12M | 92.58 |
|  |  |  | A-BL | 1.63M | 92.21 |

*Datasets and Models.* Table 1 summarizes the datasets and models we use in the evaluation. We evaluate our method on four publicly available datasets, including CIFAR10 (C10) [20], CIFAR100 (C100) [20], IMDB (IM) [24] and AGNews[1] (AG). CIFAR10 and CIFAR100 are image datasets about object classification. IMDB and AGNews are text datasets, where IMDB is about sentiment classification and AGNews is about news topic classification. For C10 and C100, we use a 34-layer ResNet (RES) [15] and a 11-layer VGG [28]. For IM and AG, we use a TextCNN (TCNN) with 100 filters [19] and an ATT-BLSTM (A-BL) model with the hidden size of 128 [38]. Our setting covers various tasks, datasets and model structures.

*Evaluation Metrics.* We define the following two metrics to evaluate the performance of our method. (1) To measure the ability of our method to detect models with low training quality, we calculate the *critical training quality* (CQ), that is, suppose the accuracy of the original task on a well trained model is $acc_{max}$, models with an accuracy lower than CQ $\times$ $acc_{max}$ will be detected as not well trained. The greater CQ is, the higher the training quality is guaranteed. We can compute CQ following the equation below:

$$CQ = \frac{acc_t}{acc_{max}}, \tag{6}$$

where $acc_t$ is the accuracy of the original task when the accuracy of the extra task exceeds the threshold in our proposed method, or is the accuracy threshold in the baseline method. Notice that, it is a false positive if the methods judge the well trained model as not well trained, i.e., the accuracy of the extra task on the well trained model is lower than the threshold in our method, or $acc_{max}$ is lower than the accuracy threshold in the baseline method. (2) To measure the impact of the extra task on the original task, we define the *performance loss* as

---

[1] http://groups.di.unipi.it/~gulli/AG_corpus_of_news_articles.html.

**Table 2.** CQ (%) of our method and the accuracy-based verification on different datasets and models. Acc-X means the accuracy-based verification where the accuracy threshold is set to be X%. The missing value represents a false positive case.

| Dataset | Model | Ours | Acc-60 | Acc-70 | Acc-80 | Acc-90 |
|---------|-------|------|--------|--------|--------|--------|
| C10 | RES | **98.70** | 65.05 | 75.90 | 86.74 | 97.58 |
|     | VGG | **98.10** | 67.26 | 78.48 | 89.69 | – |
| C100 | RES | 97.63 | 85.48 | **99.73** | – | – |
|      | VGG | 98.19 | **99.27** | – | – | – |
| IM | TCNN | **96.43** | 67.55 | 78.81 | 90.07 | – |
|    | A-BL | **97.43** | 66.67 | 77.79 | 88.90 | – |
| AG | TCNN | **99.40** | 64.81 | 75.61 | 86.41 | 97.21 |
|    | A-BL | **98.40** | 65.07 | 75.91 | 86.76 | 97.60 |

**Table 3.** Performance loss (%) of our method on different datasets and models. A negative number means the accuracy increase.

| Dataset | C10 | | C100 | | IM | | AG | |
|---------|-----|-----|------|-----|------|------|------|------|
| Model | RES | VGG | RES | VGG | TCNN | A-BL | TCNN | A-BL |
| Performance loss | 0.06 | 0.12 | -0.55 | -0.43 | 0.19 | 0.25 | 0.01 | 0.07 |

the difference in accuracy of the original task on the well trained model before and after adding the extra task.

*Hyper-Parameters.* In our method, we set the proportion $\eta$ to be 0.8%, the ratio $s$ of fixed region size to be 0.75, significance level $\alpha$ to be 1% and compensation $\epsilon$ to be 3%.

## 5.2 Results

*Our Method is Effective.* We compare our method with the baseline in Table 2. It can be seen that our method significantly outperforms the accuracy-based verification in most cases. Our method effectively ensures that the resulting models achieve high training quality in all settings and introduces no false positive. The values of CQ exceed 98% on C10 and AG, 97% on C100 and 96% on IMDB. However, the performance of accuracy-based verification is highly dependent on the selection of thresholds. Low thresholds do not guarantee the high training quality, e.g., C10-RES, and high thresholds may cause false positives, e.g., C100-VGG. This is because the accuracy of a well trained model is related to many factors, such as the quality of training data. It is difficult to choose a universal threshold for accuracy-based verification.

*Impact on the Original Task.* We report the performance loss in Table 3. The extra task in our method has limited impact on the model performance on

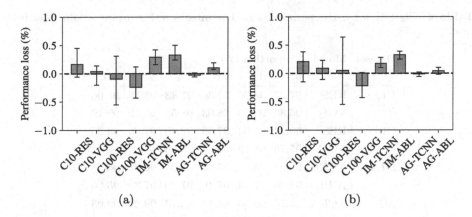

(a)                                         (b)

**Fig. 3.** Performance loss comparisons (a) when the proportion $\eta$ is changed from 0.4% to 4.0% and (b) when the ratio $s$ is changed from 0.35 to 0.85. A negative number means the accuracy increases after adding the extra task.

the original task for all settings. For example, the performance loss is at most 0.25%, i.e., the accuracy drops by 0.25%. Note that the accuracy sometimes even increases, e.g., the performance losses are −0.55% and −0.43% on C100. This is because the extra task introduces minor randomness in the training process. Existing research also makes a similar observation [34,37].

*Impact of the Number of Samples in the Extra Task.* We change the proportion $\eta$ from 0.4% to 4.0% and report the results of performance loss and CQ in Fig. 3a and Table 4, respectively. First, the performance of the models is stable when $\eta$ changes. As shown in Fig. 3a, testing accuracy drops less than 1.0% in all settings. Second, a larger proportion may cause false positive. The false positives occur in the setting of C100-VGG and AG-ALSTM when $\eta$ is greater than 3%. This is because it will be increasingly difficult to learn the extra task as the number of samples gets larger [39]. Third, a smaller proportion may cause the CQ drops. The CQ drops occasionally when $\eta$ is 0.4%. This is mainly because too few samples introduce randomness into model prediction, resulting in unreliable results.

*Impact of the Fixed Region Size.* We change the ratio $s$ from 0.85 to 0.35 and report the results of performance loss and CQ in Fig. 3b and Table 5, respectively. First, the choice of fixed region size has a small impact on the performance of original tasks. The results shown in Fig. 3b are similar to those in Fig. 3a. The accuracy of original task drops by less than 1.0% in all settings. Second, we observe that the small fixed region size may cause the CQ drops. The value of CQ is high and stable when the ratio $s$ is greater than 0.5, but it tends to drop when $s$ is lower than 0.5 in some cases, e.g., the setting of C10-VGG. This validates our design in Sect. 4.1, i.e., the large random feature space may not ensure that extra tasks are learned only after the original task converges.

**Table 4.** CQ (%) w.r.t. the proportion $\eta$. The missing value means a false positive case.

| Dataset | Model | Proportion (%) $\eta$ | | | | | |
|---------|-------|------|------|------|------|------|------|
| | | 0.4 | 0.8 | 1.6 | 2.4 | 3.2 | 4.0 |
| C10 | RES | 97.26 | 98.70 | 97.36 | 97.43 | 98.30 | 98.06 |
| | VGG | 96.30 | 98.10 | 98.03 | 98.53 | 98.50 | 99.10 |
| C100 | RES | 98.33 | 97.63 | 97.66 | 97.40 | 97.66 | 93.20 |
| | VGG | 95.76 | 98.19 | 98.23 | 98.96 | – | – |
| IM | TCNN | 95.93 | 96.43 | 96.13 | 95.30 | 96.83 | 96.43 |
| | A-BL | 91.36 | 97.43 | 97.46 | 97.20 | 97.39 | 95.96 |
| AG | TCNN | 99.70 | 99.40 | 99.13 | 98.73 | 99.20 | 99.03 |
| | A-BL | 98.33 | 98.40 | 98.06 | 99.10 | 99.03 | – |

**Table 5.** CQ (%) w.r.t. the ratio $s$. The missing value means a false positive case.

| Dataset | Model | Ratio $s$ | | | | | |
|---------|-------|------|------|------|------|------|------|
| | | 0.85 | 0.75 | 0.65 | 0.55 | 0.45 | 0.35 |
| C10 | RES | 98.26 | 98.70 | 98.10 | 98.60 | 97.53 | 96.59 |
| | VGG | 98.36 | 98.10 | 97.93 | 98.16 | 94.83 | 93.80 |
| C100 | RES | 98.36 | 97.63 | 97.63 | 97.40 | 97.83 | 97.16 |
| | VGG | 98.60 | 98.19 | 97.37 | 97.30 | 97.07 | 97.20 |
| IM | TCNN | 96.00 | 96.43 | 96.23 | 96.86 | 95.93 | 96.36 |
| | A-BL | 96.59 | 97.43 | 96.80 | 96.53 | 95.70 | 95.30 |
| AG | TCNN | 99.63 | 99.40 | 99.53 | 99.53 | 99.23 | 99.36 |
| | A-BL | 98.03 | 98.40 | 97.93 | 98.16 | 97.73 | 98.00 |

*The Choice of Extra Task Construction.* We compare the performance loss between our extra task construction method and a naive extra task construction method. In this naive extra task construction, we select some samples in the testing set and assign them random labels. Figure 4 shows the results on C10 and C100. We can observe that the overall performance loss using the naive method is greater, and the difference between the performance loss of two methods becomes more obvious when the proportion of samples increases. This is because samples in the naive method and samples in the original task follow a similar distribution in the feature space, and thus random labels will conflict with labels in the original training set.

## 5.3 Visualizing Training Examples

In order to illustrate how the extra task works, we visualize the gradient similarity between the training samples. We first visualize the similarity between

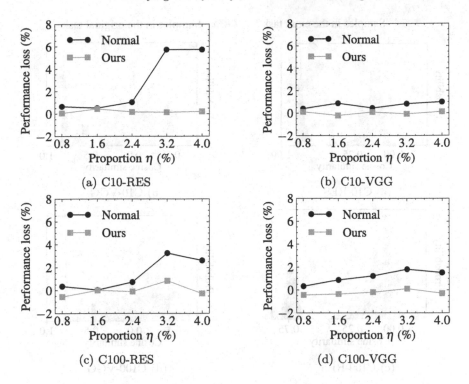

**Fig. 4.** Performance loss comparisons using different extra tasks.

training samples in the same task. We divide samples in the original task and in the extra task into 25 chunks, respectively, and show the cosine similarity of the gradient of parameters for each chunk. Figure 5 shows the results on C10 and C100. We can see that the cosine similarity between samples in the extra task is smaller than between samples in the original task, which implies the correlation between samples in our extra task is weaker than between samples in the original task. Optimizing a chunk of samples in the original task contributes to optimizing other chunks, while optimizing a chunk of samples in the extra task has almost no contribution to other chunks.

We further visualize the similarity between training samples in two types of tasks. Figure 6 shows the cosine similarity of gradients between samples in the original training set and in the modified training set (i.e., samples in both original and extra tasks). At the beginning of training, the gradient of samples in the modified training set is almost the same as the gradient of samples in the original training set, which is empirical evidence of Eq. 2, as well as a reason for selecting a small $\epsilon$. Moreover, as the training goes on, the similarity tends to drop. This is because the model tends to converge on the original task and the influence of the gradient of the samples in the extra task becomes larger among the gradient of all samples.

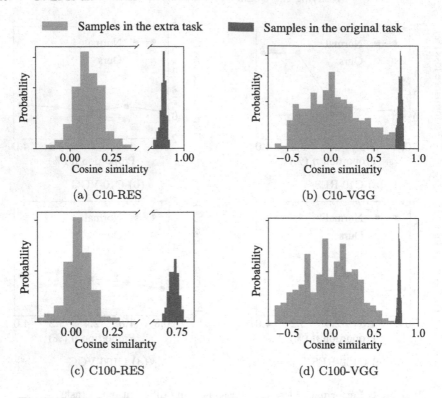

**Fig. 5.** PDF of cosine similarity of gradients between the training samples.

## 6   Related Work

*Verifying the Outsourced Deep Learning Services.* Many works proposes methods to verify the outsourced deep learning services. These methods can be grouped into two categories, one of which is based on verifiable computing techniques, and the other enables verifiability based on deep learning properties. Most methods utilize verifiable computing techniques. SafetyNets [11] verifies the deep learning inference based on an interactive proof protocol, to prevent clouds from using a simple model with low accuracy to perform inference. VeriML [36] constructs a circuit to ensure that the resource consumption claimed by the clouds equals to the actual workload. Occlumency [21] leverages the trusted execution environment to protect the computation of inference in outsourced deep learning services. However, all these methods introduce large overhead, thus are unacceptable in practice especially for training a deep learning model. Although Slalom [31] harmonizes GPU with trusted execution environment to eliminate the overhead, this technique cannot be extended to outsourced training. Few works enable verifiability by exploiting properties of deep learning. He et al. [16] propose the concept of sensitive-samples to verify whether the cloud violates the SLA in a black-box setting. However, their method can only be applied in the

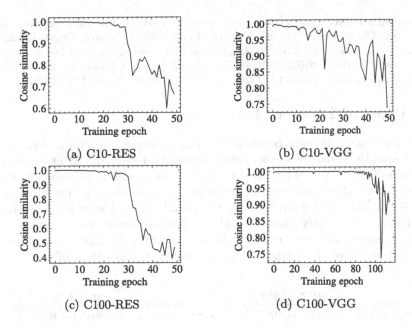

**Fig. 6.** Cosine similarity of gradients between the original training samples and the modified training samples.

deep learning inference. To the best of our knowledge, our work is the first work to verify the quality of outsourced training.

*Over-Parameterization for Security.* In security field, over-parameterization of deep learning has been widely exploited. Recent works use over-parameterization to protect the intellectual property of models. Without affecting the performance of models, some proposals embed the watermark message into the parameters of the model [9,26,32] or the predicted labels [5,22]. In contrast, over-parameterization has also been used for backdoor attacks [12,23]. In these attacks, the model learns two task at a time, where the first one is the original task and the second task is for identifying the malicious input data and triggering the malicious behaviors. In this work, we utilize the over-parameterization and propose a framework to accurately verify the quality of outsourced training.

# 7 Conclusion

In this paper, we propose a novel framework for verifying the quality of outsourced training. Our framework achieves black-box verification by utilizing the over-parameterization property of deep learning models. We design a method to construct extra training tasks according to the original tasks, and develop a verification method that verifies training quality by measuring the model performance on extra tasks. Experiments on both image and text tasks demonstrate the effectiveness of our framework.

**Acknowledgement.** This work is supported in part by the National Key R&D Project of China under Grant 2021ZD0110502, NSFC under Grant 62132011, U20B2049, U21B2018, and 62161160337, Beijing Outstanding Young Scientist Program under Grant BJJWZYJH01201910003011, China National Funds for Distinguished Young Scientists under Grant 61825204, and BNRist under Grant BNR2020RC01013.

# A    Proof of Theorem 1

*Proof:* The main difference between the cleanly labeled samples and randomly labeled samples is that the former can be generalized while the latter can only be "memorized" by the model [7]. Specifically, the gradients for optimizing a cleanly labeled sample also contribute to optimize the other cleanly labeled samples, when the model is not convergent on the cleanly labeled samples. In contrast, optimizing any randomly labeled sample has almost no contribution to the other randomly labeled samples or cleanly labeled samples. In other words, the gradient correlation of clean label samples is much stronger than of gradients of random label samples:

$$\underset{x_i \in D_c, x_j \in D_c, x_i \neq x_j}{\text{average}} \frac{g(x_i) \cdot g(x_j)}{\|g(x_i)\| \|g(x_j)\|} \gg \underset{x_i \in D_r, x_j \in D_r, x_i \neq x_j}{\text{average}} \frac{g(x_i) \cdot g(x_j)}{\|g(x_i)\| \|g(x_j)\|}, \quad (7)$$

where $g(x)$ denote the gradient of $x$, i.e., $g(x) := \nabla_\theta \mathcal{L}(x, f_\theta)$. The norm of the gradient of a individual sample can be approximated to a constant $C$ since the direction of gradients has a more important effect than the norm of gradients. Then, we have:

$$\underset{x_i \in D_c, x_j \in D_c, x_i \neq x_j}{\text{average}} g(x_i) \cdot g(x_j) \gg \underset{x_i \in D_r, x_j \in D_r, x_i \neq x_j}{\text{average}} g(x_i) \cdot g(x_j). \quad (8)$$

Suppose there are $n_c$ and $n_r$ samples in $\mathcal{D}_c$ and $\mathcal{D}_r$ respectively, i.e., $D_c = \{(x_i, y_i)_{i=1}^{n_c}\}$ and $D_r = \{(x_i, y_i)_{i=n_c+1}^{n_c+n_r}\}$. The left term of Eq. 2 can be rewritten as:

$$\|\nabla_\theta \mathcal{L}(\mathcal{D}_c, \theta)\|^2 = \left\| \sum_{i=1}^{n_c} g(x_i) \right\|^2 \quad (9)$$

$$= \sum_{i=1}^{n_c} \|g(x_i)\|^2 + 2 \sum_{\substack{j=1 \\ j \neq i}}^{n_c} \sum_{i=1}^{n_c} g(x_i) \cdot g(x_j) \quad (10)$$

$$= n_c \cdot C + 2 \sum_{\substack{j=1 \\ j \neq i}}^{n_c} \sum_{i=1}^{n_c} g(x_i) \cdot g(x_j). \quad (11)$$

Similarly, for the right term of Eq. 2, we have:

$$\|\nabla_\theta \mathcal{L}(\mathcal{D}_r, \theta)\|^2 = n_r \cdot C + 2 \sum_{\substack{j=n_c+1 \\ j \neq i}}^{n_c+n_r} \sum_{i=n_c+1}^{n_c+n_r} g(x_i) \cdot g(x_j). \quad (12)$$

Since $|\mathcal{D}_r| > |\mathcal{D}_c|$, we have $n_c > n_r$. Then the conclusion can be deductively reasoned from Eq. 11, 12 and 8.    $\square$

# References

1. Algorithmia (2022). https://algorithmia.com/
2. Amazon sagemaker (2022). https://aws.amazon.com/sagemaker/
3. Google vertex AI (2022). https://cloud.google.com/vertex-ai/
4. Microsoft azure (2022). https://azure.microsoft.com/en-us/services/machine-learning/
5. Adi, Y., Baum, C., Cisse, M., Pinkas, B., Keshet, J.: Turning your weakness into a strength: watermarking deep neural networks by backdooring. In: USENIX (2018)
6. An, J., Cho, S.: Variational autoencoder based anomaly detection using reconstruction probability. Spec. Lect. IE **2**(1), 1–18 (2015)
7. Arpit, D., et al.: A closer look at memorization in deep networks. In: ICML (2017)
8. Bugiel, S., Nürnberger, S., Pöppelmann, T., Sadeghi, A.R., Schneider, T.: Amazonia: when elasticity snaps back. In: CCS (2011)
9. Chen, H., Rohani, B.D., Koushanfar, F.: Deepmarks: A digital fingerprinting framework for deep neural networks. arXiv preprint arXiv:1804.03648 (2018)
10. Deng, J., et al.: ImageNet: a large-scale hierarchical image database. In: CVPR (2009)
11. Ghodsi, Z., Gu, T., Garg, S.: SafetyNets: verifiable execution of deep neural networks on an untrusted cloud. In: NeurIPS (2017)
12. Gu, T., Dolan-Gavitt, B., Garg, S.: BadNets: identifying vulnerabilities in the machine learning model supply chain. arXiv preprint arXiv:1708.06733 (2017)
13. Gu, Z., et al.: Securing input data of deep learning inference systems via partitioned enclave execution. arXiv preprint arXiv:1807.00969 (2018)
14. Hashemi, H., Wang, Y., Annavaram, M.: DarKnight: an accelerated framework for privacy and integrity preserving deep learning using trusted hardware. In: MICRO (2021)
15. He, K., Zhang, X., Ren, S., Sun, J.: Deep residual learning for image recognition. In: CVPR, pp. 770–778 (2016)
16. He, Z., Zhang, T., Lee, R.: Sensitive-sample fingerprinting of deep neural networks. In: CVPR (2019)
17. He, Z., Zhang, T., Lee, R.B.: VeriDeep: verifying integrity of deep neural networks through sensitive-sample fingerprinting. arXiv preprint arXiv:1808.03277 (2018)
18. Hunt, T., Song, C., Shokri, R., Shmatikov, V., Witchel, E.: Chiron: privacy-preserving machine learning as a service. arXiv preprint arXiv:1803.05961 (2018)
19. Kim, Y.: Convolutional neural networks for sentence classification. In: EMNLP. ACL (2014)
20. Krizhevsky, A., Hinton, G., et al.: Learning multiple layers of features from tiny images (2009)
21. Lee, T., et al.: Occlumency: privacy-preserving remote deep-learning inference using SGX. In: MobiCom (2019)
22. Li, Z., Hu, C., Zhang, Y., Guo, S.: How to prove your model belongs to you: a blind-watermark based framework to protect intellectual property of DNN. In: ACSAC (2019)
23. Liu, Y., et al.: Trojaning attack on neural networks. In: NDSS (2018)
24. Maas, A., et al.: Learning word vectors for sentiment analysis. In: ACL (2011)

25. Mirsky, Y., Doitshman, T., Elovici, Y., Shabtai, A.: Kitsune: an ensemble of autoencoders for online network intrusion detection. arXiv preprint arXiv:1802.09089 (2018)
26. Nagai, Y., Uchida, Y., Sakazawa, S., Satoh, S.: Digital watermarking for deep neural networks. Int. J. Multimedia Inf. Retr. **7**(1), 3–16 (2018). https://doi.org/10.1007/s13735-018-0147-1
27. Ruder, S.: An overview of gradient descent optimization algorithms. arXiv preprint arXiv:1609.04747 (2016)
28. Simonyan, K., Zisserman, A.: Very deep convolutional networks for large-scale image recognition. arXiv preprint arXiv:1409.1556 (2014)
29. Somorovsky, J., Heiderich, M., Jensen, M., Schwenk, J., Gruschka, N., Lo Iacono, L.: All your clouds are belong to us: security analysis of cloud management interfaces. In: SCC@ASIACCS (2011)
30. Song, C., Ristenpart, T., Shmatikov, V.: Machine learning models that remember too much. In: SIGSAC (2017)
31. Tramer, F., Boneh, D.: Slalom: fast, verifiable and private execution of neural networks in trusted hardware. In: ICLR (2018)
32. Uchida, Y., Nagai, Y., Sakazawa, S., Satoh, S.: Embedding watermarks into deep neural networks. In: ICMR (2017)
33. Yao, Y., Rosasco, L., Caponnetto, A.: On early stopping in gradient descent learning. Constr. Approx. **26**(2), 289–315 (2007)
34. Zhang, C., Bengio, S., Hardt, M., Recht, B., Vinyals, O.: Understanding deep learning requires rethinking generalization. In: ICLR (2017)
35. Zhang, X., Li, F., Zhang, Z., Li, Q., Wang, C., Wu, J.: Enabling execution assurance of federated learning at untrusted participants. In: IEEE INFOCOM (2020)
36. Zhao, L., et al.: VeriML: enabling integrity assurances and fair payments for machine learning as a service (2019)
37. Zhong, Z., Zheng, L., Kang, G., Li, S., Yang, Y.: Random erasing data augmentation. In: AAAI (2020)
38. Zhou, P., et al.: Attention-based bidirectional long short-term memory networks for relation classification. In: ACL, pp. 207–212 (2016)
39. Zhu, J., Gibson, B., Rogers, T.T.: Human rademacher complexity. In: NeurIPS (2009)

# SecQuant: Quantifying Container System Call Exposure

Sunwoo Jang[1], Somin Song[1], Byungchul Tak[1(✉)], Sahil Suneja[2],
Michael V. Le[2], Chuan Yue[3], and Dan Williams[4]

[1] Kyungpook National University, Daegu, Republic of Korea
{swjang,sominsong,bctak}@knu.ac.kr
[2] IBM TJ Watson Research Center, Yorktown Heights, NY, USA
{suneja,mvle}@us.ibm.com
[3] Colorado School of Mines, Golden, CO, USA
chuanyue@mines.edu
[4] Virginia Tech, Blacksburg, VA, USA
djwillia@vt.edu

**Abstract.** Despite their maturity and popularity, security remains a
critical concern in container adoption. To address this concern, secure
container runtimes have emerged, offering superior guest isolation, as well
as host protection, via system call *policing* through the surrogate kernel
layer. Whether or not an adversary can bypass this protection depends
on the effectiveness of the system call policy being enforced by the container runtime. In this work, we propose a novel method to quantify this
container system call exposure. Our technique combines the analysis of a
large number of exploit codes with comprehensive experiments designed
to uncover the syscall pass-through behaviors of container runtimes. Our
exploit code analysis uses information retrieval techniques to rank system calls by their risk weights. Our study shows that secure container
runtimes are about 4.2 to 7.5 times more secure than others, using our
novel quantification metric. We additionally uncover changing security
trends across a 4.5 year version history of the container runtimes.

**Keywords:** Secure container runtime · Security quantification ·
System call · Container escape · Exploit code analysis

## 1 Introduction

Container technology has firmly established itself as an essential component
of modern cloud platforms. All major cloud providers offer various kinds of
container-based services either in the form of directly usable container instances,
orchestrated container environment services, or as an underlying layer for serverless computing engines [5,16,19,31]. However, the foremost concern of adopting
containers in production firmly remains security [26]. Examples of some infa-
mous vulnerabilities affecting containers include Dirty COW (CVE-2016-5195),

S. Jang and S. Song—Contributed equally.

RunC Container Escape (CVE-2019-5736), and Kubernetes container escape via eBPF (CVE-2021-31440).

To address the security concerns, there have been recent efforts to design secure container runtimes such as gVisor [17], Kata [20], Nabla [32], Firecracker [4,13], and Unikernels [21,22,29], amongst others. These focus on limiting a containerized application's system call access to the host kernel, to minimize the possibility of an exploit. The main principle is the employment of a 'surrogate or proxy kernel'. This kernel can take the form of a user-space kernel, a library OS, or a light-weight virtual machine (VM) guest kernel, which lies in front of the actual host kernel being protected, effectively sandboxing the containerized applications and preventing them from interfacing directly with the host. The role of this surrogate kernel is to handle most of the system calls directly and allow only a reduced subset of system calls to reach the host kernel.

Most claims about the security guarantees offered by the secure container runtime techniques are qualitative at best [11,26,36,39]. What is missing is a metric that reflects the quantitative measures of their 'secureness', which can be a useful tool as container technologies continue to evolve. First, it can be used to track and guide the security hardening processes across the development iterations of the container runtimes [25]. Second, it enables a direct comparison of the security strengths of different, and in some cases competing, secure container runtime alternatives. Lastly, a quantification methodology that reflects the up-to-date state of vulnerabilities enables observing score changes due to external factors such as time-varying trends of threats.

Our goal in this work is to measure how well the secure container runtimes fair at policing or filtering the application-invoked system calls. One approach for a security metric could be to use the specification of the secure container runtimes, in terms of the set of system calls allowed to reach the host. However, the number of system calls in the set alone is not an accurate and sufficient metric of security. This is because the usefulness or importance of system calls in exploits differs, and changes over time. Also, it is unclear how to correctly compare sets not in a proper subset relationship with each other. So the challenge exists in translating the presence or absence of system calls into a numeric score.

In this paper, we present a novel approach for quantifying the system call exposure of container runtimes. Our technique, called SecQuant, consists of two parts: SCAR(*System Call Assessment of Risk*) and SCED(*System Call Exposure Discovery*). In SCAR, SecQuant produces numerical risk weights of system calls by analyzing existing exploit codes, and applying a variant of the information retrieval technique—TF-IDF—customized and extended for the security quantification task. In SCED, SecQuant performs comprehensive system call tests inside the target containers using a purpose-built test suite. It generates one-to-many mappings between container-invoked system calls and the ones appearing on the host in response. The outputs from SCAR and SCED are combined to produce system call exposure scores for the different container runtimes.

Analyzing the container runtimes with our quantification methodology reveals several interesting findings. First, secure container runtimes offer 4.2

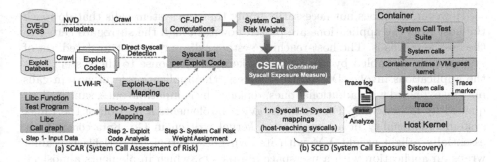

**Fig. 1.** SecQuant architecture for quantifying container system call exposure

to 7.5 times improved (i.e., reduced) system call exposure than their general-purpose counterparts. Second, in addition to a non-negligible number of *pass-through* system calls reaching the host kernel, the secure container runtimes also generate a significant number of *derived* system calls, appearing consistently in response to the ones invoked by the application. This presents an indirect avenue of exposure which we account for in our metric. Third, their exposure scores change across a 4.5 year version history, showing both increasing and decreasing trends across different runtimes.

## 2    Secure Containers and Threat Model

In the overall container security landscape, we limit the scope of this work to the specific case of system call access restriction to the host. Our analysis targets primarily the host kernel vulnerabilities, which an adversary inside a container wishes to exploit via possibly crafted system calls. We approach the security problem from the host perspective, in terms of the reachability of critical system calls. For example, if the container runtime uses light-weight virtualization instead of containerization, then the system call pass-through policy will get accounted towards the container runtime's exposure score.

We assume an untrustworthy guest container, either instantiated directly by an adversary, or compromised to gain control by them. The goal of the adversary is then to attack the host, or other colocated guests, from within this guest container, for malicious gains such as privilege escalation, denial of service, data corruption, information leak, and service theft, amongst others [18].

We set the scope of our analysis to exploits which leverage vulnerabilities exposed by system calls. For example, the exploits targeting the Dirty COW vulnerability (CVE-2016-5195) abuse a race condition in the kernel by rapidly calling `madvise` system call and `write` system call on `/proc/self/mem` for privilege escalation. One way in which secure container runtimes protect against such attacks is by policing system call invocations made from the guest. This is typically achieved by employing a *surrogate* kernel to handle a majority of the system calls and allowing only a few necessary ones to reach the host.

However, this does not necessarily imply that the system calls that do reach the host from the applications are passed down through the surrogate kernel to the host kernel as-is. The host-reaching system calls may be a 'translated' set of system calls assembled by the surrogate kernel in response to the system calls the applications invoke. During this process, the application-level system calls may be extended with additional ones, replaced by compatible ones, sanitized, or queued up for batching. For example, gVisor implements a portion of the Linux system functionality in an application kernel written in Go. Kata containers is essentially a light-weight VM with its own guest kernel. And Nabla container wraps an application with a userspace library OS, which implements almost all of the system call functionality tailored to the application.

Depending upon the system call policy enforced by a secure container runtime, an adversarial guest may succeed in its attack. For example, Kata containers have been shown to be vulnerable to the buffer overflow exploits [35]. In this work, we quantify this system call exposure of the different secure container runtimes. We trust the host system's integrity and assume that it is not already compromised. We base our measurements on publicly available exploit codes, assuming they are representative of real-world attacks.

## 3    Design of SecQuant

Figure 1 shows the overall architecture of our SecQuant approach to quantify system call (or *syscall*, used interchangeably) exposure of container runtimes. It consists of two independent components: (i) SCAR: System Call Assessment of Risk, and (ii) SCED: System Call Exposure Discovery. SCAR is container-independent and determines the *risk weights* associated with system calls by analyzing existing exploit codes. These per-syscall risk weights are generated by employing static code analysis as well as dynamic experiments, in conjunction with information retrieval techniques. SecQuant's second component, SCED, examines the system call reachability and host-kernel *pass-through* behavior for a given container runtime. By using a systematic exploration of syscall-level access via a custom test suite, it emits a 1:n mapping between a syscall made at the application-level to the syscalls reached the host-level. Finally, the output of the two components, per-syscall risk weights and syscalls-per-container, are combined together to produce an overall Container System call Exposure Measure (CSEM) for the container runtime. This CSEM metric essentially quantifies how well the container runtime fairs at policing the application-invoked system calls. We use it to (i) compare the security posture across different container runtime alternatives, and (ii) analyze evolution across different versions (Sect. 5).

### 3.1    SCAR: System Call Assessment of Risk

The goal of SecQuant's SCAR component is to determine a *risk weight* associated with each syscall. The intuition is to convert the occurrence frequencies of different system calls in existing exploit codes, into a numerical measure encapsulating the importance of each syscall in attacking the host. Figure 1(a) shows the steps involved in extracting syscall risk weights, described as follows.

**Step 1- Input Data:** SecQuant ingests three different types of input data:

1. **Exploit codes:** From ExploitDB [1], Project-Zero [2], and a few other standalone git repositories, we collected 298 exploit codes written in C and targeting the Linux kernel.
2. **Exploit Metadata:** The exploit codes extracted from the aforementioned vulnerability databases are augmented with metadata such as their CVE-ID, release date, and CVSS scores from NVD, wherever applicable.
3. **Library function Call Graph:** To facilitate the extraction of syscalls from the library functions used in an exploit, we use the library function call graphs from CONFINE [14] and refine it.

**Step 2- Exploit Code Analysis:** The objective of this step is to build a complete set of system calls being used by each exploit code. While it is possible to put efforts into directly running the exploits to uncover the syscalls used [26], such an approach can be challenging to properly set up and difficult to automate. Hence, we rely mostly on a static analysis approach. Since high-level code rarely invokes system calls directly, relying instead on library functions, we need to discover syscalls being invoked indirectly by these library calls. To collect the syscall set for each exploit code, we first identify the library functions it uses, and then use a mapping between the library functions and the corresponding syscalls being employed underneath. The specific details are described next.

1. **Exploit-to-Libc Mapping:** Instead of directly parsing the C syntax of the exploit codes, we use the LLVM Intermediate Representation (IR) to identify the library functions in the codes. LLVM IR uses the prefix character '@' for library functions, making it easier to recognize them.

2. **Libc-to-Syscall Mapping:** The next step is to identify the reachable system calls for different library functions extracted from the exploit codes. We use the state-of-the-art for such libc-to-syscall mapping, CONFINE, which uses static code analysis to build a function call graph from the libc source code, terminating with system calls at the leaves. The challenge, however, is the accuracy of the call graph, especially in the case of function pointers, which results in either missing system calls or reporting a bloated set as reachable. We found certain errors in CONFINE's libc-to-syscall mapping, in both over and under estimating the reachable system calls, especially when the mapping is not 1:1. In such cases, we use a custom test suite to call the corresponding library functions and collect the system calls reaching the host kernel using ftrace. Using such refinement over CONFINE, we are able to map almost 90% of the libc functions to at-most two system calls each. We limit our scope to only the libc functions and their corresponding arguments appearing in our exploit codes, and not the entire 2000+ APIs. Linking the exploit codes with another C library such as musl would possibly change the system call mappings. We leave this comparison for the future exploration. In addition to the libc, we also extract system calls from functions of other libraries used in the exploits, e.g. `libfuse`, `libecryptfs`, `libpcap`, `libaio`, etc.

**3. Direct Syscall Detection:** In some exploit codes, we observe direct invocations of system calls through INT or SYSCALL instructions, which bypass the libc library. Such carefully crafted system call invocations are likely to be key to the intended attack in the exploit codes. We directly parse such inline assembly codes to identify the syscalls being employed.

**Step 3- System Call Risk Weight Assignment:** After extracting the syscalls being used by the exploit codes, the next step is to assign a *risk weight* to each syscall based on its importance to the exploits. One approach is to use the proportion of exploit codes a syscall appears in, as an indicator of its associated risk. However, this may not appropriately capture its degree of risk. A syscall may appear in many exploit codes simply because it is part of a commonly used initialization procedure. On the other hand, it may appear in only a few exploit codes, but be critical to successfully exploit the corresponding vulnerabilities.

To address this challenge, we adopt a popular technique, TF-IDF, used in the Information Retrieval (IR) domain to compute the relevance of words to a particular topic across documents. TF, the Term Frequency, captures the idea that the more frequently appearing terms are likely more important to the content of the document. IDF, the Inverse Document Frequency, penalizes the term weights if they appear in many documents since it implies that such words are common and carry less relevance to any specific topic. Adopting TF-IDF to our security context, the *term* is mapped to a *system call*, while *document* is mapped to the *exploit code*. However, we observe that such naïve translation is insufficient. While the rationale of IDF holds true in our setting, the rationale of TF may not necessarily hold. Specifically, adhering to the IDF rationale, a syscall widely used across many exploit codes is less likely to be a syscall playing a key role in the attack logic. The observation that the most used system calls in exploit code are close, brk, exit and nanosleep also supports this. However, in contrast to the TF rationale, just because a syscall appears frequently within an exploit code (i.e., used repeatedly in a single type of attack), it does not necessarily mean that it is more important to the attack than less frequent ones.

Thus, we introduce another component—*Class Frequency* (CF)—to replace the role of TF. We define CF as the proportion of exploit codes a particular syscall appears in within a *class*. A *class* is defined as a subset of exploit codes grouped by common characteristics, such as the vulnerability being leveraged, or the attack methodology, amongst others. The intuition is that if a syscall consistently appears across the exploit codes within the same *class*, then it presumably plays a key role to the attack logic for that class. Note the contrast to IDF which considers a syscall with more appearances across the entire exploit codes as less relevant. If a syscall is indeed crucial to a specific class of exploits, it will render the CF value high. At the same time, this value will be countered by IDF if the syscall appears frequently throughout other exploit codes as well. The information we currently use to realize the *class* concept is the CVE-ID [12] associated with each exploit code.

**Metric Formulation:** Our metric to calculate system call risk weights is denoted as **CF-IDF**, obtained by combining the two components. Formally, let $s$, $e$ and $E$ denote a system call, an exploit code and the set of all exploit codes, respectively. We use $C_e$ to indicate the class, subset of $E$, of which $e$ is a member. The smallest size of $C_e$ is 1. That is, an exploit code can be the sole member of a class. Also, the set of syscalls used in a specific exploit code $e$ is denoted as $\sigma_e$.

The IDF component is represented as a vector, computed using the generic IR formulation as:

$$idf(s, E) = log_{|E|} \left( \frac{|E|}{|\{e|s \in \sigma_e\}| + 1} \right) \qquad (1)$$

Note that we use the size of $E$ as the base of log in order to keep the IDF value within 0 and 1 as well. The term $\{e|s \in \sigma_e\}$ is the set of exploit codes within which $s$ exists. Equation 1 gives us a lower value as the system call appears in a larger number of exploit codes.

The CF component is represented as the fraction of exploit codes which contain the syscall $s$ amongst all exploit codes belonging to the class $C_e$. It can be viewed as a DF (Document Frequency) metric for each class. It also contains the normalized CVSS score (to [0,1] range) to reflect the vulnerability severity of the CVE that the exploit code belongs to. Formally, CF is represented as:

$$cf(s, C_e) = \frac{1}{10} CVSS_e \times \frac{|\{e|s \in \sigma_e, e \in C_e, C_e \subseteq E\}|}{|C_e| + 1} \qquad (2)$$

The overall CF-IDF value (V) is computed by multiplying both components, and represented as 2D data consisting of syscalls and exploit codes, as:

$$V(s, e) = cf(s, C_e) \times idf(s, E) \qquad (3)$$

Finally, a per-syscall risk weight (W) is calculated by averaging its CF-IDF values across all exploit codes, as:

$$W_s = \frac{\sum_e V(s, e)}{|\{e|s \in \sigma_e\}|} \qquad (4)$$

### 3.2   SCED: System Call Exposure Discovery

While SecQuant's SCAR component computes risk weights for different system calls, SCED determines which of these system calls are *accessible* under the different container runtimes (Fig. 1(b)). This information is gathered by executing test programs within a given container runtime, and observing which syscalls reach the host-kernel. We developed our own test programs instead of using existing tools such as LTP [28] or Syzkaller [37]. Their focus is somewhat different (e.g. stress testing), which made the cost of extending them significantly greater than rewriting. Their heavy use of library calls, instead of direct syscall invocations, made it difficult to add necessary modifications. We thus created a custom test suite limited to the 185 syscalls found in the exploit codes we collected.

**System Call Tracing:** Depending upon how a container runtime handles the application-invoked system calls, different behavior can be observed on the host:

- No system calls whatsoever seen at the host kernel
- Identical system call arriving at the host kernel
- Syscalls arriving at the host kernel including the application-invoked syscall
- Syscalls arriving at the host kernel without the application-invoked syscall

We use the ftrace mechanism to detect these cases, while running our test suite inside the container(s) to exercise all target system calls. We tightly enclose all syscall statements inside the test programs with the ftrace's *trace-marker* write actions, to accurately pinpoint the begin and end markers in the ftrace logs. Then, the host-reaching syscall set is identified by locating the sys_enter events within these markers. We also set the event-fork option to include all the child processes that may be spawned along the way.

Even with the use of the *trace-marker* to narrow down the exact time range, the ftrace logs can contain syscalls from other parallel threads, which can incorrectly inflate the derived syscall set. We use domain knowledge specific to the container runtimes to identify the relevant threads, and filter the logs accordingly to collect only the syscall events triggered by the original syscall of the test program.

The *trace-marker* approach works for most container runtimes we experiment with, except Kata, sysbox, and LXC. In case of Kata, mounting the tracefs filesystem inside the container (VM, technically) is problematic. As a marker for Kata, we instead use the fsync syscall (repeated fixed number of times as a signature), which we found to be a stable and immediately responsive pass-through syscall. getpgid syscall similarly serves as a marker for sysbox and LXC.

**Traced System Call Types:** We further categorize the system calls that reach the host kernel into the following groups:

- *Pass-through*: These include the application-level system calls which eventually end up reaching the host kernel, either as-is or after any argument sanitization. We additionally include a notion of *equivalent* system calls for this category—system calls with different syscall numbers but sharing the same kernel function for execution (Appendix Table 8). If a syscall results in triggering such equivalent syscalls, it is considered a pass-through.
- *Derived*: It refers to the system calls generated by the container runtime (and reaching the host kernel) in response to an application-invoked system call, excluding the pass-through if any. These can be differentiated into:
  - *Workload-dependent*: The set of system calls necessary to carry out an application-invoked system call. One application-invoked syscall may be translated, replaced or converted into a sequence of multiple syscalls.
  - *Architecture-dependent*: The set of system calls that are consistently generated and reached the host kernel for every application-invoked syscall, owing to the container runtime's architectural characteristics. It may be, for example, due to the specific syscall interception mechanism used, or from the auxiliary components for the container management.

**Table 1.** Example host-reaching syscall data for open as an output of SCED

| runsc-ptrace | | | | kata-qemu | | |
|---|---|---|---|---|---|---|
| Observed syscalls | Count | Caller process | | Observed syscalls | Count | Caller process |
| futex | 20 | gofer, sandbox | | futex | 6 | pool, virtiofsd |
| ptrace | 10 | sandbox | | write | 3 | pool |
| openat | 4 | gofer | | read | 3 | virtiofsd |
| newfstat | 4 | gofer | | ppoll | 3 | virtiofsd |
| wait4 | 2 | sandbox | | openat | 3 | pool |
| fcntl | 2 | gofer | | setresuid | 2 | pool |
| sendmsg | 1 | gofer | | setresgid | 2 | pool |
| recvmsg | 1 | sandbox | | newfstatat | 1 | pool |
| dup | 1 | gofer | | geteuid | 1 | pool |
| close | 1 | gofer | | getegid | 1 | pool |

SCED results in host-reachability data for each system call for a given container runtime. Table 1 shows an example for the open system call for two container runtimes—gVisor and Kata. The output contains a list of observed syscalls with the occurrence count and the originating process name. As can be seen, calling open inside the containers results in a large number of derived system calls, together with its pass-through equivalent—openat.

### 3.3  Container Syscall Exposure Measure

The complementary information gathered and computed by SecQuant's SCAR and SCED components, in terms of risk-weights-per-syscall and syscalls-per-container respectively, are finally combined together to generate the overall container system call exposure measure—CSEM. Formally, let $S$ be the complete list of known system calls. Computing CSEM requires three inputs: (i) from SCAR: the per-syscall risk weight vector $W = \{W_i | i \in S\}$ (ii) from SCED: the entire list of observed system call sets, $D$, in which $D_s$ refers to a single set of system calls observed to be induced from a system call $s$, and (iii) a reduction ratio $r$ ($0 \leq r \leq 1$), controlling the risk-weight contribution of the derived system calls. Pass-through system calls are given the whole risk weight values from $W_s$ if $s$ exists in $D_s$. Derived system calls are applied the reduction ratio and averaged over the set size of $D_s$. Finally, CSEM is defined as:

$$CSEM(W, D, r) = \sum_s \sum_{d \in D_s} \left( W_s \cdot I(s, d) + \frac{W_d \cdot r}{|D_s|} (1 - I(s, d)) \right) \quad (5)$$

where I is an indicator function selecting the correct terms while going through syscalls in $D_s$, testing if two given syscalls are identical or not, as:

$$I(s, d) = \begin{cases} 1 & if \ s = d \\ 0 & otherwise \end{cases} \quad (6)$$

**Table 2.** CF-IDF correctly capturing similarity within exploit code groups. Similarity scores are against the first exploit code in each group.

| Group | Grouping Criteria | Exploit-ID (source) | CVE-ID | Similarity |
|---|---|---|---|---|
| G-I | Same CVE | 40003 (exploit-db) | CVE-2016-0728 | – |
| | Keyring object reference mishandling with crafted keyctl PrivEsc, DoS | 39277 (exploit-db) | | 1.0 |
| | | 2016-0728A (git) | | 1.0 |
| | | 2016-0728B (git) | | 1.0 |
| G-II | Same CVE | 33589 (exploit-db) | CVE-2013-2094 | – |
| | Incorrect integer data type via crafted perf_even_open PrivEsc | 26131 (exploit-db) | | 1.0 |
| | | 25444 (exploit-db) | | 1.0 |
| G-III | Different CVE but same vulnerability type | 35403 (exploit-db) | CVE-2011-1083 | – |
| | Improper traversal via crafted epoll_create and epoll_ctl. DoS | 35404 (exploit-db) | CVE-2011-1082 | 0.764533 |
| G-IV | Different CVE but same vulnerability type | 2021-31440A (git) | CVE-2021-31440 | - |
| | Lack of validation with bpf PrivEsc | 2020-8835A (git) | CVE-2020-8835 | 1.0 |
| | | 2020-8835B (git) | | 1.0 |
| | | 2021-3490A (git) | CVE-2021-3490 | 0.975811 |

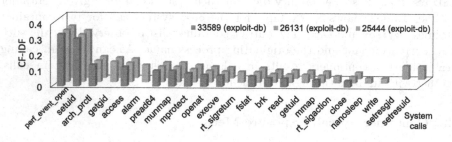

**Fig. 2.** Comparison of risk weight vectors of exploits in Group II showing visually very similar signatures for all three group members (Table 2). The key system call, `perf_event_open` is identified correctly to have the highest weight.

## 4   System Call Analysis Results

### 4.1   Verification of CF-IDF Metric

We first provide empirical justification supporting the soundness of the CF-IDF metric we use to assign risk weights to system calls. The CF-IDF scores in its 2D form, which is the collection of vectors with the length equal to the number of syscalls, can be considered as signatures that represent the characteristic of exploit codes. If our assumptions and intuitions behind CF-IDF are valid, it would generate similar signatures (i.e., vector of risk weights) for the exploit codes that are *truly similar* in their nature. We analyzed all exploits using domain knowledge and classified them as similar groups if the vulnerability was located in the same kernel component or the method for triggering the vulnerability was similar. We present such a similarity comparison in Table 2. It shows four example groups each containing similar kinds of exploit codes. Column 5 shows the similarity scores generated using cosine similarity between our risk weight vectors for the different exploit codes. As can be seen, the generated similarity scores are high within each group. This can also be seen in Fig. 2's vector distribution, which is very similar for all exploits within a group (and different across

**Table 3.** Partial (top-70) ranked list of system calls by the risk weights obtained from the SCAR process. Full list given in Appendix Table 7.

| Rank | Syscall | Weight | Rank | Syscall | Weight | Rank | Syscall | Weight | Rank | Syscall | Weight |
|---|---|---|---|---|---|---|---|---|---|---|---|
| 1 | capset | 0.439551 | 19 | futimesat | 0.30329 | 37 | shmget | 0.244536 | 55 | pwrite64 | 0.21538 |
| 2 | add_key | 0.409431 | 19 | inotify_rm_watch | 0.30329 | 37 | shmat | 0.244536 | 55 | set_mempolicy | 0.21538 |
| 3 | recvmmsg | 0.392371 | 19 | inotify_init1 | 0.30329 | 37 | sigaltstack | 0.244536 | 55 | readv | 0.21538 |
| 4 | getresuid | 0.388023 | 19 | restart_syscall | 0.30329 | 37 | setxattr | 0.244536 | 55 | sched_getaffinity | 0.21538 |
| 4 | sendfile | 0.388023 | 19 | utimensat | 0.30329 | 41 | symlink | 0.244057 | 55 | shmdt | 0.21538 |
| 4 | io_uring_reg | 0.388023 | 24 | clock_nanosleep | 0.303143 | 42 | getcwd | 0.244007 | 60 | mremap | 0.212287 |
| 7 | shutdown | 0.335366 | 25 | umount2 | 0.295618 | 43 | fchmod | 0.240128 | 61 | inotify_init | 0.210391 |
| 8 | settimeofday | 0.334059 | 26 | chown | 0.286681 | 44 | modify_ldt | 0.237571 | 62 | sched_yield | 0.206736 |
| 9 | rename | 0.329819 | 27 | link | 0.284955 | 44 | clock_gettime | 0.237571 | 63 | recvmsg | 0.205074 |
| 10 | creat | 0.329663 | 28 | dup3 | 0.272522 | 46 | process_vm_readv | 0.237358 | 64 | getegid | 0.204785 |
| 11 | keyctl | 0.32028 | 29 | eventfd2 | 0.269163 | 47 | writev | 0.235578 | 65 | fallocate | 0.202194 |
| 12 | fchown | 0.316477 | 30 | msgsnd | 0.267191 | 48 | getdents | 0.234431 | 65 | _sysctl | 0.202194 |
| 12 | flock | 0.316477 | 31 | sched_setscheduler | 0.264745 | 49 | sendmmsg | 0.232625 | 65 | move_pages | 0.202194 |
| 12 | mknod | 0.316477 | 32 | inotify_add_watch | 0.261581 | 50 | syslog | 0.232287 | 68 | shmctl | 0.200075 |
| 12 | mq_notify | 0.316477 | 32 | waitid | 0.261581 | 51 | mount | 0.226888 | 69 | msgctl | 0.199029 |
| 12 | io_setup | 0.316477 | 34 | msgget | 0.254518 | 52 | rmdir | 0.224417 | 70 | dup | 0.197707 |
| 12 | io_submit | 0.316477 | 35 | pipe2 | 0.25433 | 53 | getgroups | 0.219776 | ... | ... | ... |
| 12 | kcmp | 0.316477 | 36 | chmod | 0.248783 | 54 | select | 0.216088 | 185 | close | 0.026151 |

groups; shown in Appendix Fig. 5). This corroborates the effectiveness of our CF-IDF metric in being able to capture the unique characteristics of different exploit (groups) in terms of system call composition and risk weights.

## 4.2    System Call Risk Weights

Table 3 shows the output of SecQuant's SCAR component, in terms of a ranking of syscalls by their risk weights computed using the CF-IDF metric (partial list shown due to space constraints; full list in Appendix Table 7). As per SCAR's analysis, the capset system call gets assigned the highest weight, while close gets ranked the last. The high weight assignment to capset is owing to the exceptionally high CVSS score (10/10) of the only CVE that it belongs to—CVE-2000-0506. Appendix B uses concrete examples to show how the various interdependent factors—CVSS scores, number of exploits, and CVE class size—affect the system call risk weights.

Note that the last syscall in the list should not be interpreted as a *harmless* syscall because, although ranked the last, it is given a rank because it played a part in composing the attack logic in some of the exploit codes. The fact that it is on this list already implies a substantial degree of utility to the attacks. Similarly, it is not always the case that a syscall with a higher rank is always riskier than nearby syscalls with slightly lower risk weights. This is because the final risk weight of a syscall is an average of values of a vector across exploit codes as expressed in Eq. 4.

## 4.3    Pass-Through System Calls Across Containers

Table 4 shows the output of SecQuant's SCED component, in terms of the syscall handling behavior of different container runtimes. As expected, the trace results of general-purpose container runtimes (runc, crun, sysbox, and lxc) contain mostly pass-through syscalls and a small number of derived syscalls. On the

**Table 4.** Number of pass-through/non-pass-through system calls

| Container runtime | # of Pass-through syscalls | # of Non-pass-through syscalls | # of Tested syscalls |
|---|---|---|---|
| runc | 176 (93.6%) | 12 (6.4%) | 188 |
| runsc-ptrace | 37 (19.5%) | 153 (80.5%) | 190 |
| runsc-kvm | 35 (18.6%) | 153 (81.4%) | 188 |
| kata-qemu | 43 (22.5%) | 148 (77.5%) | 191 |
| kata-clh | 44 (22.2%) | 154 (77.8%) | 198 |
| crun | 181 (95.8%) | 8 (4.2%) | 189 |
| sysbox | 181 (91.9%) | 16 (8.1%) | 197 |
| lxc | 187 (94.9%) | 10 (5.1%) | 197 |

**Table 5.** Pass-through system calls for `runsc` and `kata` runtimes. Equivalent system calls are shown as X→Y. SCAR rank is given in parenthesis.

| runsc-ptrace (weight rank) | kata-qemu (weight rank) |
|---|---|
| utimensat(23), futimesat(19) → utimensat(23), fchmod(43), chmod(36) → fchmod(43), pwrite64(55), write(173) → pwrite64(55), getdents64(76), getdents(48) → getdents64(76), ptrace(86), tgkill(103), ftruncate(133), wait4(157), pread64(171), munmap(172), nanosleep(174), openat(179), open(175) → openat(179), creat(10) → openat(179), fstatfs, statfs(90) → fstatfs, fstat(180) → fstatfs, renameat, rename(9) → renameat, mkdirat, mkdir(75) → mkdirat, linkat, link(27) → linkat, readlinkat, readlink(107) → readlinkat, fchownat, fchown(12) → fchownat, chown(26) → fchownat, symlinkat, symlink(41) → symlinkat, unlinkat, lchown, fsync | utimensat(23), futimesat(19) → utimensat(23), fallocate(65), getdents64(76), getdents(48) → getdents64(76), futex(89), ftruncate(133), connect(150), renameat2(166), write(173), openat(179), open(175) → openat(179), creat(10) → openat(179), close(185), pwritev2, pwritev, writev(47) → pwritev, fchmodat, chmod(36) → fchmodat, fchmod(43) → fchmodat, fstatfs, statfs(90) → fstatfs, mknodat, mknod(14) → mknodat, renameat, rename(9) → renameat, mkdirat, mkdir(75) → mkdirat, linkat, link(27) → linkat, readlinkat, readlink(107) → readlinkat, fchownat, fchown(12) → fchownat, chown(26) → fchownat, symlinkat, symlink(41) → symlinkat, unlinkat, unlink(128) → unlinkat, lchown, fsync |

contrary, Kata containers and gVisor generate a large number of derived syscalls, passing only about 20% of application-side syscalls through the runtime layer.

Table 5 shows a list of *pass-through* syscalls we captured from gVisor and Kata containers runtimes. The gVisor and Kata containers runtimes pass through different set of system calls, the risk weights of which eventually impact the overall exposure measure for the container runtimes (Sect. 5.1). In determining the *pass-through* system calls, we use the concept of system call *equivalence*. If a container invokes a system call X (e.g., open), and we observe a system call Y (e.g., openat), they are not a *pass-through* in a strict sense. However, if X and Y share the code at the function level in the kernel, we view them as identical and, thus, *pass-through*. Arrows in Table 5 and 6 indicate these relationships. Note the ranking order of the lists with some syscalls out of place, e.g., `getdents` and `creat`. These syscalls get assigned the weights of their *equivalent* syscall counterparts (Sect. 3.2), which they are always replaced with by the container runtime.

A large part of pass-through syscalls are file I/O related since the data has to physically travel in and out of the container runtime. This holds true even for the Kata containers which is a light-weight VM with its own guest kernel.

## 5    Container Runtime Security Analysis

In this section, we analyze the security posture of container runtimes using our CSEM metric. We use LXC, runc, crun, and sysbox as baseline container runtimes,

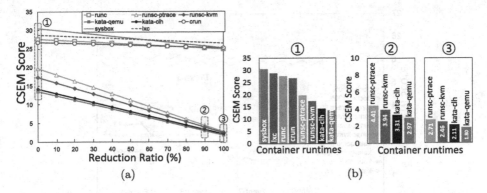

**Fig. 3.** CSEM score comparison of container runtimes. Lower is better. (a) Across all reduction ratios. (b) Selected reduction ratios ①, ② and ③ from (a).

and gVisor and Kata containers as secure alternatives. The gVisor runsc uses a userspace surrogate kernel, intercepting application-level syscalls using either ptrace (runsc-ptrace) or KVM (runsc-kvm). Kata uses a light-weight VM to run the user application, relying on either QEMU (kata-qemu), Firecracker [13][1] or Cloud Hypervisor (kata-clh) [10] as VM hypervisors. Host and container runtime version information can be found in Appendix C. We do not include unikernel-inspired container runtimes such as Nabla [32] in our study, since they require varying degrees of effort to make general applications (including our test suite) run on them—a by-product of their generality vs. security trade-off.

## 5.1 Container Syscall Exposure Measure Scores

Figure 3(a) compares the CSEM scores of different container runtimes. The graph shows the change of CSEM scores as we vary the *reduction ratio* on the x-axis. Recall that the reduction ratio governs how much the weights of the *derived* system calls contribute to the final CSEM score. A reduction ratio of 0% means that the derived system calls are given the full risk weights as determined by the SCAR analysis. On the other hand, the reduction ratio of 100% implies derived system calls are ignored, and only the *pass-through* system calls are taken into account towards CSEM scoring. Overall, as expected, gVisor and Kata have much lower CSEM scores than the baseline container runtimes, and exhibit higher sensitivity to the changes in reduction ratio owing to a higher proportion of derived system calls, as shown in Table 4.

Given that the value of the *ideal* reduction ratio is subjective, Fig. 3(b) shows the CSEM score differences at three spots chosen from Fig. 3(a). Spot ① is the CSEM score where derived system calls are treated equally to the pass-through system calls. This is only a theoretical configuration, not conforming to any expected practical setting. This is especially disadvantageous for the container

---

[1] Firecracker unsupported in Kata 2.x as of conducting this study.

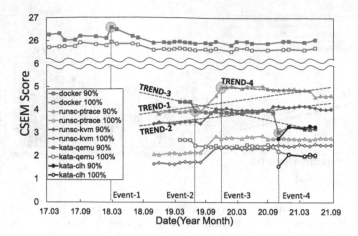

**Fig. 4.** CSEM score changes by container runtime versions. Two reduction ratios, 90% and 100% (latter for reference only; theoretical lower bound), are applied to 5 runtimes. Y-axis is abridged to reduce the gap.

runtimes that tend to generate many derived system calls as the CSEM score of gVisor (runsc-ptrace) shows. On the other extreme, CSEM score at Spot ③ is where only the *pass-through* system calls are used in the calculation. The assumption here is that the derived system calls are not useful or easily craftable for an adversarial attack, which seems unlikely as well.

Spot ② considers a more reasonable setting of reducing risk weights of derived system calls by 90%. This reflects the intuition that derived system calls can also likely, albeit with some difficulty, be exploited and hence deserve some, but smaller, risk weights. Figure 6 in Appendix shows the contribution of each system call types to the CSEM score. A majority of the derived system calls turn out to be architecture-dependent rather than application workload-dependent.

## 5.2 Historical Trends Across Versions

We now present a case study of using our CSEM metric to analyze the changing trends of the security posture of container runtimes. Across a 4.5 year history, we track 31, 35 and 22 versions of runc, gVisor and Kata respectively. Figure 4 shows the trends of the changing CSEM scores for the different container runtimes:

- runc(Docker): Steady for the whole measurement period.
- runsc-ptrace: Exhibits an increasing trend in the long-term (TREND-1), but a decreasing trend in the short-term (TREND-4).
- runsc-kvm: Has a slightly increasing trend (TREND-2).
- Kata-qemu: Has a decreasing long-term trend (TREND-3).
- Kata-clh: Insufficient data points for trend analysis.

**Table 6.** Differences of *pass-through* system calls between the first and the last versions of container runtimes

| Runtime | Version | Count | Syscalls unique to this version (Risk weight rank) |
|---|---|---|---|
| runsc-ptrace | 20180610 | 33 | getrandom, sched_setaffinity(96) |
| | 20210906 | 37 | utimensat(23), futimesat(19) → utimensat(23), openat(179), munmap(172), nanosleep(174), fstat(180) → fstatfs |
| kata-qemu | 1.5.4 | 46 | gettimeofday(102), newfstatat(no rank), recvmsg(63), sendmsg(114) |
| | 2.1.1 | 44 | connect(150), fallocate(65), nanosleep(174), renameat2(166), unlink(128) → unlinkat |

Overall, the observations from the previous Section hold across time–both of Kata and gVisor naturally being better than runc. The increasing trend of gVisor and the decreasing trend in Kata can be explained by analyzing the changes in their pass-through system calls (bigger contribution to CSEM scores—Appendix Fig. 6) across versions. This can be seen in Table 6, comparing the system calls between two opposite ends of the version history. For gVisor, the syscall count has increased over time, and the risk weights of newly added syscalls are higher than the ones removed. For Kata, the risk-weight ranks of recent version decrease and the syscall count decreases as well.

Additionally, we identify four places of interest in the figure which exhibit a sudden change of CSEM scores, labeled as Event-1 through Event-4:

- **Event-1:** Our tracking tests resulted in a weight increase in 53 syscalls in Docker v18.03.0. This was mostly because of the appearances of epoll_wait and futex syscalls. Docker release notes mentioned a version bump-up for runc, containerd and golang, which we believe to be the cause of changes in the derived syscall sets. The pass-through sets were unchanged.
- **Event-2:** The score drop in Kata v1.8.0 is due to the disappearance of write and futex from the derived syscall set, which otherwise contribute significantly to the overall CSEM score (18% and 9% respectively). On cross-verification with the release notes, this was a result of QEMU upgrade in Kata.
- **Event-3:** Starting with runsc-ptrace v20191210, one architecture-dependent derived syscall disappeared—getcpu. It makes the CSEM score larger by causing the denominator smaller in the Eq. 5 for all syscalls. This can be traced to getcpu being replaced by a golang API, as per the gVisor patch note.
- **Event-4:** A second score drop in Kata, this time in v1.12.0, is due to the disappearance of gettimeofday and clock_gettime, leading to a further reduction in derived system calls from 5 to 3.

Historical analysis presented in this section, made possible by SecQuant, demonstrates the important utility of quantifying the syscall exposure. It enables us to compare the degree of syscall exposure between container runtimes and uncover hidden trends. Associating the score changes with production events provides us with deeper insights.

# 6   Related Work

**Attack Surface and Risk Metrics.** Existing research proposes ways to measure the attack surface of a host kernel and how to quantify its security risk. Kurmus et al. [23] define attack surfaces of a kernel as a set of entry functions, the associated call graphs, and a set of barrier functions. Williams et al. [40,41] use ftrace-based system call coverage as a proxy for attack surface. Li et al. [24] developed a risk metric based on popular paths through the kernel to evaluate their LibOS based scheme for securing privileged kernels. These works do not discuss how to assess the risks of system calls with respect to how they are used by exploits. Nayak et al. [33] utilize a large collection of real-world exploits as a basis for their analysis on the vulnerabilities of systems and their attack surfaces. Cheng et al. [9] developed three security metrics: the vulnerable host percentage, CVSS severity score, and compromised host percentage to evaluate the general security of an enterprise network based on vulnerability assessment. However, these works do not offer a methodology to statistically analyze the risk of system calls. Bernaschi et al. [7] presented a system call classification based on function and threat level. However, their analysis is limited to buffer overflow-based attacks, and their 4-level threat classification method is difficult to expand and update due to subjective criteria.

**Measuring Container Security.** Works that attempt to evaluate the security mechanisms of containers and their runtimes by analyzing the design and architecture of the respective containerization technology also exist [6,34]. Other researchers have deployed known vulnerabilities and exploits to assess the isolation and security promises of containers and their runtimes [26,30,42]. For example, Lin et al. [26] deployed 88 known exploits to measure and analyze how Docker containers fare against them. This collection of exploits includes attacks against both the applications in the container as well as the host kernel. Wu et al. [42] evaluated five cloud-based container offerings against selected attacks that were chosen to exploit specific security mechanisms that were identified to be lacking in those particular offerings. However, none of these works developed a methodology for scoring the risks of system call usage found in exploits and their associated effects on the security of container runtimes.

**System Call Extraction.** We build upon works that devise mechanisms for extracting system calls from programs for the purpose of debloating/specializing the kernel or automatically generating seccomp profiles. Ghavamnia et al. [14,15] have used static analysis to build out system call mappings for libc and target applications as well as whole containers create tight seccomp policies. They evaluated the security benefit of their works using a list of critical system calls derived from exploit programs as well as system calls linked to CVEs. Unfortunately, they do not specify the methodology in which the criticality of the system calls was derived nor do they provide any ranking among the security-critical/affected system calls. Similarly, works from Abubakar et al. [3] and Olufogorehan et al. [38] generate system call lists from target applications using a static analysis approach. Bulekov et al. [8] build a mapping between system calls and PHP APIs. Lopes et al. [27] perform dynamic analysis by running the target application and using unit testing combined with fuzzing to come up with their system call list. These works all have common elements with our work in how we extract the system call list.

# 7  Considerations for Improvements

As this is the first attempt, to the best of our knowledge, to quantify the syscall behavioral aspect of secure containers, there are several promising improvements and challenges yet to be addressed. Although each topic may lead to in-depth discussion, we only briefly outline them here due to space constraints.

- *Benign application*: Incorporating known benign applications into the syscall analysis can further improve the validity of our syscall risk weights. For example, if some system calls are found to be used heavily in exploit codes, but not in benign applications, this may be a ground to increase the risk weights. However, the challenge is to select benign applications that are *representative*.
- *Argument checking of system call tracing and the need for systematic argument fuzzing*: Current SCED process for testing the syscall path-through behavior can be made more accurate and comprehensive by extending test cases with systematic argument fuzzing. Our experience suggested that syscall pass-through behaviors can vary by syscall argument values. In addition, we need to enhance our implementation to better observe argument values and how one syscall translates into another while passing through the proxy kernel.
- *Validity of using exploit codes publicly available*: Exploit codes we used are all publicly available ones. This may raise a concern that some of these *open* exploit codes may not resemble the *real, unknown* ones. Our current assumption is that the core part of the attack logic remains similar since they are based on the same principle. However, as we find more exploit codes, we can easily incorporate them into our automated analysis and adjust scores.

# 8   Conclusion

In this work, we presented a novel syscall exposure quantification technique, Sec-Quant, for secure container runtimes. SecQuant works by combining the system call risk weights obtained from IR-based analysis on a large set of exploit codes, and the system call pass-through/filter behavior of runtimes through extensive experimentation. Our analysis revealed several interesting syscall pass-through behaviors with varying types and numbers of syscalls reaching the host kernel. According to our metric, secure container runtimes have 4.2 to 7.5 times smaller syscall exposure. We have also found that there exist both increasing and decreasing trends in syscall exposures of container runtimes. SecQuant can further be improved by employing more accurate syscall-to-exploit mapping techniques and more general and accurate pass-through test platforms in the future. Especially, a technique for comparing the arguments of application and host-arrived syscalls can enable more sophisticated quantification.

**Acknowledgement.** This work was supported by the National Research Foundation of Korea(NRF) grant funded by the Korea government(MSIT) (No. NRF-2021R1A5A1021944). Authors S. Jang and S. Song contributed equally to this work.

# A   Complete Ranking of System Calls by Risk Weights

We provide a complete list of system calls ranked by the risk weights calculated by our CF-IDF methodology in Table 7 .

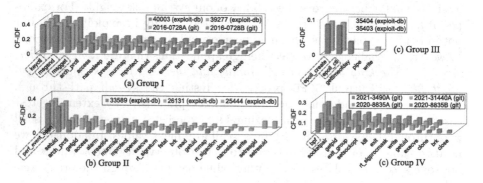

**Fig. 5.** Visual comparison of the similarity between risk weight vectors of exploits within different groups

**Table 7.** List of syscalls ranked by risk weights obtained by SCAR

| Rank | System call | Weight | Rank | System call | Weight | Rank | System call | Weight | Rank | System call | Weight | Rank | System call | Weight |
|---|---|---|---|---|---|---|---|---|---|---|---|---|---|---|
| 1 | capset | 0.439551 | 37 | shmat | 0.244536 | 75 | mkdir | 0.193169 | 112 | pipe | 0.139035 | 149 | setgid | 0.104811 |
| 2 | add_key | 0.409431 | 37 | sigaltstack | 0.244536 | 76 | getdents64 | 0.188096 | 113 | getppid | 0.138948 | 150 | connect | 0.103625 |
| 3 | recvmmsg | 0.392371 | 37 | setxattr | 0.244536 | 77 | _llseek | 0.187949 | 114 | sendmsg | 0.136639 | 151 | prlimit64 | 0.101779 |
| 4 | getresuid | 0.388023 | 41 | symlink | 0.244057 | 77 | getpriority | 0.187949 | 115 | setresgid | 0.136633 | 152 | seccomp | 0.101097 |
| 4 | sendfile | 0.388023 | 42 | getcwd | 0.244007 | 79 | setns | 0.187368 | 116 | uselib | 0.136261 | 153 | stat | 0.100942 |
| 4 | io_uring_register | 0.388023 | 43 | fchmod | 0.240128 | 80 | msgrcv | 0.185928 | 116 | msync | 0.136261 | 154 | setitimer | 0.092306 |
| 7 | shutdown | 0.335366 | 44 | modify_ldt | 0.237571 | 81 | getsockname | 0.184515 | 116 | mincore | 0.135555 | 155 | setsockopt | 0.091907 |
| 8 | settimeofday | 0.334059 | 44 | clock_gettime | 0.237571 | 82 | setrlimit | 0.175967 | 119 | uname | 0.135125 | 156 | lseek | 0.087384 |
| 9 | rename | 0.329819 | 46 | process_vm_readv | 0.237358 | 83 | getrlimit | 0.175651 | 120 | pause | 0.134133 | 157 | wait4 | 0.084849 |
| 10 | creat | 0.329663 | 47 | writev | 0.235578 | 83 | sync | 0.175651 | 121 | vmsplice | 0.130688 | 158 | exit_group | 0.080511 |
| 11 | keyctl | 0.32028 | 48 | getdents | 0.234431 | 85 | splice | 0.174387 | 122 | alarm | 0.128849 | 159 | getpid | 0.078393 |
| 12 | fchown | 0.316477 | 49 | sendmmsg | 0.232625 | 86 | ptrace | 0.169211 | 123 | setresuid | 0.128281 | 160 | ioctl | 0.077965 |
| 12 | flock | 0.316477 | 50 | syslog | 0.232287 | 87 | setpriority | 0.167943 | 124 | gettid | 0.128004 | 161 | arch_prctl | 0.073672 |
| 12 | mknod | 0.316477 | 51 | mount | 0.226888 | 88 | userfaultfd | 0.167438 | 125 | epoll_create1 | 0.126591 | 162 | rt_sigaction | 0.072893 |
| 12 | mq_notify | 0.316477 | 52 | rmdir | 0.224417 | 89 | futex | 0.166319 | 125 | setgroups | 0.126591 | 163 | kill | 0.069353 |
| 12 | io_setup | 0.316477 | 53 | getgroups | 0.219776 | 90 | statfs | 0.165307 | 125 | umask | 0.126591 | 164 | access | 0.068628 |
| 12 | io_submit | 0.316477 | 54 | select | 0.216088 | 91 | dup2 | 0.164186 | 128 | unlink | 0.126579 | 165 | exit | 0.06426 |
| 12 | kcmp | 0.316477 | 55 | pwrite64 | 0.21538 | 92 | accept | 0.164048 | 129 | time | 0.123122 | 166 | renameat2 | 0.063323 |
| 19 | futimesat | 0.30329 | 55 | set_mempolicy | 0.21538 | 93 | perf_event_open | 0.163461 | 130 | socketpair | 0.122321 | 167 | sysinfo | 0.061537 |
| 19 | inotify_rm_watch | 0.30329 | 55 | readv | 0.21538 | 94 | poll | 0.15674 | 131 | geteuid | 0.121388 | 167 | setreuid | 0.061537 |
| 19 | inotify_init1 | 0.30329 | 55 | sched_getaffinity | 0.21538 | 95 | getsockopt | 0.15602 | 132 | setuid | 0.120857 | 169 | socket | 0.059526 |
| 19 | restart_syscall | 0.30329 | 55 | shmdt | 0.21538 | 96 | sched_setaffinity | 0.155237 | 133 | ftruncate | 0.1204 | 170 | rt_sigprocmask | 0.058141 |
| 19 | utimensat | 0.30329 | 60 | mremap | 0.212287 | 97 | timerfd_create | 0.154563 | 134 | mlock | 0.119328 | 171 | pread64 | 0.055834 |
| 24 | clock_nanosleep | 0.303143 | 61 | inotify_init | 0.210391 | 97 | timerfd_settime | 0.154563 | 135 | setsid | 0.119298 | 172 | munmap | 0.055819 |
| 25 | umount2 | 0.295618 | 62 | sched_yield | 0.206736 | 99 | unshare | 0.153808 | 136 | epoll_ctl | 0.116779 | 173 | write | 0.055482 |
| 26 | chown | 0.286681 | 63 | recvmsg | 0.205074 | 100 | fcntl | 0.153628 | 137 | sendto | 0.115332 | 174 | nanosleep | 0.055054 |
| 27 | link | 0.284955 | 64 | getegid | 0.204785 | 101 | madvise | 0.152935 | 138 | setpgid | 0.113589 | 175 | open | 0.05293 |
| 28 | dup3 | 0.272522 | 65 | fallocate | 0.202194 | 102 | gettimeofday | 0.151181 | 139 | getgid | 0.113317 | 176 | getuid | 0.052282 |
| 29 | eventfd2 | 0.269163 | 65 | _sysctl | 0.202194 | 103 | tgkill | 0.150511 | 140 | setresgid | 0.113173 | 177 | mprotect | 0.049306 |
| 30 | msgsnd | 0.267191 | 65 | move_pages | 0.202194 | 104 | personality | 0.150292 | 140 | adjtimex | 0.113173 | 178 | execve | 0.04722 |
| 31 | sched_setscheduler | 0.264745 | 68 | shmctl | 0.200075 | 105 | listen | 0.148191 | 140 | timer_create | 0.113173 | 179 | openat | 0.043193 |
| 32 | inotify_add_watch | 0.261581 | 69 | msgctl | 0.199029 | 106 | prctl | 0.146587 | 140 | memfd_create | 0.113173 | 180 | fstat | 0.040249 |
| 32 | waitid | 0.261581 | 70 | dup | 0.197707 | 107 | readlink | 0.144822 | 144 | epoll_wait | 0.108171 | 181 | clone | 0.035285 |
| 34 | msgget | 0.254518 | 71 | io_uring_enter | 0.194227 | 108 | chroot | 0.142477 | 145 | set_tid_address | 0.107822 | 182 | brk | 0.034785 |
| 35 | pipe2 | 0.25433 | 71 | io_uring_setup | 0.194227 | 109 | bpf | 0.142335 | 145 | set_robust_list | 0.107822 | 183 | read | 0.032339 |
| 36 | chmod | 0.248783 | 73 | chdir | 0.19396 | 110 | recvfrom | 0.140137 | 147 | bind | 0.106639 | 184 | mmap | 0.03019 |
| 37 | shmget | 0.244536 | 74 | iopl | 0.193403 | 111 | epoll_create | 0.139559 | 148 | rt_sigreturn | 0.1059 | 185 | close | 0.026151 |

# B    Break-down of Sample Risk Weights

To gain better understanding of ranks and scores presented in Sect. 4.2, we provide four sample system calls shmdt, capset, add_key and io_uring_register with details of how the scores are computed.

The first example shows the impact of CVSS scores for the same CVE class size. Although both shmdt and capset appear only in one exploit code each (CVE-2019-15666 and CVE-2000-0506, respectively), they have very different risk-weight rankings—55 vs 1. For shmdt, the IDF value is 0.88, but the CF is only 0.245 because of the low CVSSv2 score 4.9. On the other hand, capset has the same IDF value but CF of 0.5 because of the high CVSSv2 score 10.

In the case of add_key and io_uring_register, the size of the class affected the rank (2 vs. 4) following the Eq. 2. Since add_key appear in three exploit codes belonging to CVE-2016-8655 and io_uring_register appear in two exploit codes belonging to CVE-2020-29534, it grants the IDF score of about 0.76 to add_key and about 0.81 to io_uring_register. The CVEs of add_key and io_uring_register have the same CVSS score (7.2) but the class size (3 vs. 2) is different. Thus, 0.75 and 0.67 are multiplied by the normalized CVSS score. Eventually, io_uring_register has a higher IDF score than add_key, but the total weight is lower.

## C    Experiment Setup

runc v1.0.0-rc10. gVisor v20210906. Kata v2.1.0. Host: Ubuntu 20.04 / Linux 5.11. For historical trends, running older versions of container runtimes required setup of compatible environments including older OS versions, e.g. Ubuntu 16.04 / Linux 4.4 for Docker. glibc v2.33 used for extracting libc-to-syscall mapping.

**Table 8.** System call groups that share kernel functions

| Syscall Group | Shared Kernel Fxn | Syscall Group | Shared Kernel Fxn |
|---|---|---|---|
| open, openat, creat | do_sys_open | unlink, unlinkat | do_unlinkat |
| link, linkat | do_linkat | chmod, fchmod, fchmodat | chmod_common |
| mkdir, mkdirat | do_mkdirat | statfs, fstatfs | do_statfs_native |
| mknod, mknodat | do_mknodat | utimensat, utime | do_utimes |
| symlink, symlinkat | do_symlinkat | utimes, futimesat | |
| readlink, readlinkat | do_readlinkat | fchownat, chown | chown_common |
| read, pread64 | vfs_read | lchown, fchown | |
| readv, preadv, preadv2 | vfs_readv | write, pwrite64, | vfs_write |
| rename, renameat | do_renameat2 | writev, pwritev, pwritev2 | vfs_writev |
| renameat2 | | clone, fork | kernel_clone |

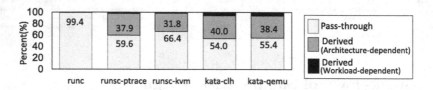

**Fig. 6.** CSEM score break-down by system call types at 90% reduction ratio

## References

1. Exploit Database. https://www.exploit-db.com. (Accessed 12 Oct 2021)
2. Project Zero. https://bugs.chromium.org/p/project-zero/issues/list. (Accessed 12 Oct 2021)
3. Abubakar, M., Ahmad, A., Fonseca, P., Xu, D.: Shard: Fine-grained kernel specialization with context-aware hardening. In: USENIX Security Symposium (2021)
4. Agache, A., et al.: Firecracker: Lightweight virtualization for serverless apps. In: NSDI 2020 (2020)
5. AWS: Lambda (2014). https://aws.amazon.com/ko/lambda/. (Accessed Oct 2021)
6. Babar, A., Ramsey, B.: Understanding container isolation mechanisms for building security-sensitive private cloud. Technical Report CREST (2017)
7. Bernaschi, M., Gabrielli, E., Mancini, L.V.: Operating system enhancements to prevent the misuse of system calls. In: Proceedings of the 7th ACM Conference on Computer and Communications Security, p. 174–183 (2000)
8. Bulekov, A., Jahanshahi, R., Egele, M.: Saphire: sandboxing php applications with tailored system call allowlists. In: 30th USENIX Security Symposium (2021)

9. Cheng, Y., Deng, J., Li, J., DeLoach, S.A., Singhal, A., Ou, X.: Metrics of security. In: Kott, A., Wang, C., Erbacher, R.F. (eds.) Cyber Defense and Situational Awareness. AIS, vol. 62, pp. 263–295. Springer, Cham (2014). https://doi.org/10.1007/978-3-319-11391-3_13

10. Cloud Hypervisor. https://github.com/cloud-hypervisor/cloud-hypervisor. (Accessed 12 Oct 2021)

11. Combe, T., Martin, A., Di Pietro, R.: To docker or not to docker: a security perspective. IEEE Cloud Comput. 3(5), 54–62 (2016)

12. CVE. https://cve.mitre.org. (Accessed 12 Oct 2021)

13. Firecracker. https://firecracker-microvm.github.io. (Accessed 22 June 2022)

14. Ghavamnia, S., Palit, T., Benameur, A., Polychronakis, M.: Confine: automated system call policy generation for container attack surface reduction. In: The 23rd International Symposium on Research in Attacks, Intrusions and Defenses (2020)

15. Ghavamnia, S., Palit, T., Mishra, S., Polychronakis, M.: Temporal system call specialization for attack surface reduction. In: USENIX Security Symposium (2020)

16. Google: Cloud Function (2016). https://cloud.google.com/functions. (Accessed 10 Oct 2021)

17. gVisor. https://github.com/google/gvisor/. (Accessed 17 May 2022)

18. Hunt, P., Hansman, S.: A taxonomy of network and computer attack methodologies. Comput. Secur. 24(1), 31–43 (2003)

19. IBM: IBM Cloud Functions (2016). https://cloud.ibm.com/functions/. (Accessed 10 Oct 2021)

20. Kata Containers. https://katacontainers.io/. (Accessed 17 May 2022)

21. Kuenzer, S., et al.: Unikraft: fast, specialized unikernels the easy way. In: EuroSys (2021)

22. Kuo, H.C., Williams, D., Koller, R., Mohan, S.: A linux in unikernel clothing. In: EuroSys (2020)

23. Kurmus, A., et al.: Attack surface metrics and automated compile-time os kernel tailoring. In: NDSS (2013)

24. Li, Y., Dolan-Gavitt, B., Weber, S., Cappos, J.: Lock-in-pop: securing privileged operating system kernels by keeping on the beaten path. In: USENIX ATC (2017)

25. Lie, D., Satyanarayanan, M.: Quantifying the strength of security systems. In: USENIX HOTSEC (2007)

26. Lin, X., Lei, L., Wang, Y., Jing, J., Sun, K., Zhou, Q.: A measurement study on linux container security: Attacks and countermeasures. In: ACSAC (2018)

27. Lopes, N., Martins, R., Correia, M.E., Serrano, S., Nunes, F.: Container hardening through automated seccomp profiling. In: Proceedings of the 2020 6th International Workshop on Container Technologies and Container Clouds, pp. 31–36 (2020)

28. LTP: Linux Test Project. https://github.com/linux-test-project/ltp. (Accessed 12 Oct 2021)

29. Manco, F., et al.: My vm is lighter (and safer) than your container. In: Proceedings of the 26th Symposium on Operating Systems Principles (2017)

30. Martin, A., Raponi, S., Combe, T., Pietro, R.D.: Docker ecosystem - vulnerability analysis. In: Computer Communications, vol. 122, pp. 30–43 (2018)

31. Microsoft: Azure Function. https://azure.microsoft.com/en-us/services/functions/

32. Nabla Containers: A new approach to Container Isolation. https://nabla-containers.github.io/. (Accessed 12 Oct 2021)

33. Nayak, K., Marino, D., Efstathopoulos, P., Dumitraş, T.: Some vulnerabilities are different than others. In: Workshop on Recent Advances in Intrusion Detection 2014 (2014)

34. Reshetova, E., Karhunen, J., Nyman, T., Asokan, N.: Security of os-level virtualization technologies: Technical report. Secure IT Systems (2014)
35. Suneja, S.: The choices we make: Impact of using host filesystem interface for secure containers (2018). https://nabla-containers.github.io/2018/11/28/fs/
36. Sultan, S., Ahmad, I., Dimitriou, T.: Container security: issues, challenges, and the road ahead. IEEE Access **7**, 52976–52996 (2019)
37. Syzkaller: Kernel Fuzzer. https://github.com/google/syzkaller. (Accessed Oct 2021)
38. Tunde-Onadele, O., Lin, Y., He, J., Gu, X.: Self-patch: Beyond patch tuesday for containerized applications. In: IEEE ACSOS (2020)
39. Viktorsson, W., Klein, C., Tordsson, J.: Security-performance trade-offs of kubernetes container runtimes. In: IEEE MASCOTS (2020)
40. Williams, D., Koller, R., Lucina, M., Prakash, N.: Unikernels as processes. In: Proceedings of the ACM Symposium on Cloud Computing, pp. 199–211 (2018)
41. Williams, D., Koller, R., Lum, B.: Say goodbye to virtualization for a safer cloud. In: 10th USENIX Workshop on Hot Topics in Cloud Computing (2018)
42. Wu, Y., Lei, L., Wang, Y., Sun, K., Meng, J.: Evaluation on the security of commercial cloud container services. In: ISC (2020)

# Robust and Scalable Process Isolation
# Against Spectre in the Cloud

Martin Schwarzl[1(✉)], Pietro Borrello[2], Andreas Kogler[1], Kenton Varda[3],
Thomas Schuster[1], Michael Schwarz[4], and Daniel Gruss[1]

[1] Graz University of Technology, Graz, Austria
`martin.schwarzl@iaik.tugraz.at`
[2] Sapienza University of Rome, Rome, Italy
[3] Cloudflare Inc., San Francisco, USA
[4] CISPA Helmholtz Center for Information Security, Saarbrücken, Germany

**Abstract.** In the quest for efficiency and performance, edge-computing providers replace process isolation with sandboxes, to support a high number of tenants per machine. While secure against software vulnerabilities, microarchitectural attacks can bypass these sandboxes.

In this paper, we present a Spectre attack leaking secrets from co-located tenants in edge computing. Our remote Spectre attack, using amplification techniques and a remote timing server, leaks 2 bit/min. This motivates our main contribution, *DyPrIs*, a scalable process-isolation mechanism that only isolates suspicious worker scripts following a lightweight detection mechanism. In the worst case, DyPrIs boils down to process isolation. Our proof-of-concept implementation augments real-world cloud infrastructure used in production at large scale, *Cloudflare Workers*. With a false-positive rate of only 0.61 %, we demonstrate that DyPrIs outperforms strict process isolation while statistically maintaining its security guarantees, fully mitigating cross-tenant Spectre attacks.

## 1 Introduction

With the recent discovery of transient-execution attacks [7], such as Spectre [34] or Meltdown [37], attackers even leak data, not only meta-data. As most transient-execution attacks work across logical CPUs, *i.e.*, hyperthreads, many cloud providers do not assign logical CPUs to different tenants. With the introduction of edge computing [2,9], where resources are dynamically provided on a machine that is close to the customer, virtualization-based security was replaced by more efficient solutions. Cloud providers either rely on strict process isolation [2,42], *i.e.*, one process per tenant, or language-level isolation [9,16,17], *i.e.*, code is written in a sandboxed language such as JavaScript. While language-level isolation has the least overhead [10], it does not protect against Spectre within the same process [30,34,41,57], necessitating process or site isolation [48]. To avoid these costly countermeasures, *Cloudflare Workers* rely on a modified JavaScript sandbox [9] that disables all known timers and primitives that can be abused to build timers [22,54]. A similar design using language-level isolation WebAssembly is

© The Author(s), under exclusive license to Springer Nature Switzerland AG 2022
V. Atluri et al. (Eds.): ESORICS 2022, LNCS 13555, pp. 167–186, 2022.
https://doi.org/10.1007/978-3-031-17146-8_9

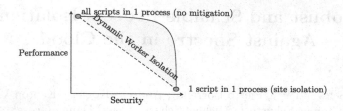

**Fig. 1.** Strict process isolation choses the security and performance trade-off via the number of scripts inside one process (dashed line). DyPrIs improves this trade-off while never being worse than strict process isolation.

used by Fastly [17]. As *Cloudflare* is one of the top three edge computing providers, with millions of requests daily, this raises the following scientific question:

*Can edge computing without strict process isolation, as is already deployed and widely used today, offer the same security levels with respect to microarchitectural attacks as edge computing with strictly isolated processes?*

This paper has an offensive and a defensive contribution: First, we demonstrate that it is possible to steal secrets on *Cloudflare Workers* with 2 bit/min using an amplified Spectre attack [58] relying on an external time server. This proof-of-concept attack shows that language-level isolation is insufficient.

Second, we propose, *DyPrIs (Dynamic Process Isolation)*, a technique that relies on a probabilistic Spectre detection and process-isolates suspicious workloads. DyPrIs is a middle ground between the two extremes of strict process isolation and language-level isolation. Hence, DyPrIs keeps the performance benefits of language-level isolation for the majority of benign workloads and provides the security guarantees of process isolation against malicious workloads. Even if every workload was classified as Spectre, DyPrIs only boils down to strict process isolation with a the small overhead of 2 % for the detection, but on average, it results in far higher performance (cf. Fig. 1).

Our detection uses hardware performance counters (HPC) for mispredicted and retired branches. We show that HPC usage, as suggested in prior work [32, 43, 46, 70] has too much overhead for efficiency-driven edge systems. However, we demonstrate that even with a limited set of performance counters, we detect running Spectre attacks with a small performance overhead of 2 %.

We evaluated DyPrIs in a production environment in the cloud. Our result is a false-positive rate of 0.61 %, while detecting all attack attempts with all state-of-the-art techniques. DyPrIs blocks our attack without interrupting any of our own or other workloads.

**Contributions.** The main contributions of this work are:

1. We demonstrate a remote Spectre attack on the restricted *Cloudflare Workers*, showing that current mitigations are insufficient.
2. We propose a novel, low-overhead probabilistic detection for Spectre attacks.
3. We introduce DyPrIs, a technique with, on average, lower overhead than state-of-the-art strict process isolation.

## 2  Background and Related Work

In modern processors, instructions are divided into multiple micro-operations ($\mu$OPs) that are executed out of order. To improve the performance of branch instructions, CPUs leverage speculative execution. For example, the branch prediction unit (BPU) tries to predict whether a branch is taken or not using different data structures, e.g., the Pattern History Table (PHT) [34]. If the prediction was correct, the results of the execution are retired. Otherwise, the speculatively executed instructions are discarded, and the correct code path is executed. Mistakenly executed instructions are called *transient instructions* [7,37]. They still have an effect on the microarchitecture, e.g., measurable timing differences in the cache that can be extracted with cache attacks [7,34,37]. Cache attacks are even possible in JavaScript [44].

Spectre attacks [34] exploit speculative execution. Spectre-PHT [7] (also known as Spectre V1) exploits the Pattern History Table, which predicts the outcome of a conditional branch [34]. A typical Spectre-PHT gadget is a bounds check, e.g., if (x < array1_size) y = array2[array1[x] * 4096];. The attacker controls the index x, which is bounds-checked. By mistraining the branch prediction with in-bounds values, speculation follows the in-bounds path with out-of-bounds values, allowing out-of-bounds reads. Spectre variants exploit different prediction mechanisms, e.g., the Branch Target Buffer, memory disambiguation, or the Return-Stack Buffer [29,34,35,38] and have been demonstrated over the network [55] and in JavaScript [34,41,57].

Many cache side-channel defenses have been proposed, e.g., focusing on *detection* using HPCs [8,28,32,46,66,67,70,71]. To detect Spectre-type attacks, static code analysis and patching, taint tracking, symbolic execution, and detection via HPCs were proposed [13,25–27,40,43,65]. However, these proposals focus on attack detection but do not propose and evaluate mechanisms to respond to detected attacks. Detection methods suffer from false positives but terminating a detected attack is not acceptable for *Cloudflare Workers*.

*Cloudflare Workers* is an edge computing service to intercept web requests and modify their content using JavaScript, handling millions of HTTP requests per second across tens of thousands of web sites. *Cloudflare Workers* support multiple thousand workers from up to 2000 tenants running inside the same process. Each worker is single-threaded and stateless. This design leads to a high-performant solution based on language-level isolation. To impede microarchitectural attacks, *Cloudflare Workers* restricts the available JavaScript timing functions to only update after a request is performed. Additionally, JavaScript worker threads are disabled to prevent counting threads [22,34,54].

## 3  Remote Spectre Attacks on *Cloudflare Workers*

In this section, we show that the single-address-space design of *Cloudflare Workers* enables remote Spectre attacks. First, we define the Spectre building blocks and overview how a remote adversary can mount a Spectre attack. Since

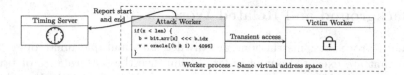

**Fig. 2.** Overview of the *Cloudflare Workers* remote Spectre attack.

there is no local timing primitive, a common requirement for microarchitectural attacks [18,53], we have to resort to a remote timing primitive. Our proof-of-concept implementation running on *Cloudflare Workers* leaks 2 bit/min, even if address space layout randomization (ASLR) is active.

### 3.1   Threat Model and Attack Overview

In our threat model, the attacker can run *Cloudflare Workers* executing JavaScript code but no native code. Furthermore, the attacker controls a remote server to record high-resolution timestamps, e.g., using rdtsc, and a low-latency network connection. We also assume a powerful attacker with a worker co-located with the victim worker, e.g., by spawning multiple *Cloudflare Workers* and detecting co-location. An attacker spawning its instances close in time to the victim's one can maximize the probability of co-location [49]. *Cloudflare Workers* architecture aims to serve the same application from every location. A high number of tenants per machine is possible. Physical co-location of the attacker server is not required. However, this leads to the strongest possible attacker. We assume no exploitable software bugs, e.g., memory safety violations, in the JavaScript engine and no sandbox escapes. Thus, *architectural* exploits to leak data from other tenants or processes are not possible.

The typical requirements for state-of-the-art Spectre attacks on the timer and memory are listed in Table 1, showing the differences to our attack. Figure 2 provides an overview of our attack. In the *Cloudflare Workers* setup, each worker runs in the same process, and thus, shares the virtual address space. The attacker runs a malicious JavaScript file containing a self-crafted Spectre-PHT gadget that performs a Spectre attack on its own process. As the victim and attacker share the same process, the attacker can leak sensitive data from a victim worker, without having an existing Spectre gadget in the victim.

Spectre attacks in JavaScript rely on speculative out-of-bounds accesses of objects. Assuming the attacker can either trigger a victim worker's secret allocation, delay it, or just manages to execute before the victim, we can use heap-grooming techniques [21] to bring the process memory into a predictable state before both the leaking object and the victim data are allocated. Alternatively, the attacker worker can predict the offset between the leaking object and the victim worker's data, target a certain range of the virtual memory, e.g., regions where V8 places similar objects [61], or break ASLR using speculative probing [19]. Hence, ASLR does not mitigate the attack. Furthermore, Agarwal [1] demonstrated that it is possible to leak over the full address space using a JavaScript Spectre attack in the V8 engine.

**Table 1.** Requirements and leakage rate of Spectre attacks.

| Spectre attack (variant) | Gadget | Native | HR Timer | Memory | Leakage Rate | Error | Channel |
|---|---|---|---|---|---|---|---|
| Kocher et al. [34] (PHT) | Yes | Yes | Yes (ns) | 2.40 MB | 4420.46 B/s ± 6.75 % | 0.07 % | Cache-L3 |
| Canella et al. [7] (PHT) | Yes | Yes | Yes (ns) | 3.54 MB | 3.13 B/s ± 113.79 % | 0.00 % | Cache-L3 |
| Safeside [20] (PHT) | Yes | Yes | Yes (ns) | 7.00 MB | 4384.03 B/s ± 7.75 % | 0.00 % | Cache-L3 |
| Canella et al. [7] (BTB) | Yes | Yes | Yes (ns) | 6.91 MB | 0.71 B/s ± 2.43 % | 0.00 % | Cache-L3 |
| SafeSide [20] (BTB) | Yes | Yes | Yes (ns) | 7.01 MB | 269.53 B/s ± 0.85 % | 0.00 % | Cache-L3 |
| Canella et al. [7] (STL) | Yes | Yes | Yes (ns) | 3.54 MB | 14.37 B/s ± 211.95 % | 0.00 % | Cache-L3 |
| Safeside [20] (STL) | Yes | Yes | Yes (ns) | 7.00 MB | 272.46 B/s ± 0.22 % | 0.00 % | Cache-L3 |
| Canella et al. [7] (RSB) | Yes | Yes | Yes (ns) | 20.08 MB | 30.67 B/s ± 195.59 % | 0.00 % | Cache-L3 |
| Safeside [20] (RSB) | Yes | Yes | Yes (ns) | 7.00 MB | 116.70 B/s ± 0.58 % | 0.00 % | Cache-L3 |
| Google [57] (PHT) | No | No | Yes (μs) | 15.00 MB | 335.02 B/s ± 23.50 % | 0.26 % | Cache-L1 |
| Google [57] (PHT) | No | No | Yes (ms) | 15.00 MB | 9.46 B/s ± 31.40 % | 2.71 % | Cache-L1 |
| Agarwal et al. [1] (PHT) | No | No | Yes (μs) | N/A | 533.00 B/s ± N/A | 0.32 % | Cache-L3 |
| Schwarz et al. [55] (PHT) | Yes | Yes | No | N/A | 7.50 B/h ± N/A | 0.58 % | AVX unit |
| **Our work (PHT)** | **No** | **No** | **No** | 27.54 MB | 15.00 B/h ± 2.67 % | 0.00 % | Cache-L3 |

Gadget: Spectre gadget must be in victim;   Native: native code execution;   HR Timer: High-resolution timer

For our attack, we rely on a Spectre-PHT [34] gadget, as this is the simplest gadget to introduce in JIT-compiled code. Moreover, Spectre-BTB [34] can be prevented by the JIT compiler [59]. In contrast to the original Spectre attack [34], we do not encode the data bytewise but bitwise. The advantage of such a *binary Spectre gadget* is that it is easier to distinguish two states compared to 256 states using a side channel [4,55]. While such a gadget might not be commonly *found* in real applications, it is easy to *introduce*.

As there are no high-resolution timers to distinguish microarchitectural states directly, we have to amplify the timing difference between a cache hit and a miss, *i.e.*, between a leaked '0' and '1' bit. We combine the amplification techniques by McIlroy et al. [41] with the remote measurement methods by Schwarz et al. [55]. With this semi-remote Spectre attack, we show that it is indeed feasible to leak data from co-located *Cloudflare Workers* in such a restricted setting. Our Spectre attack is the only one not requiring native code execution, a local timer, or an existing gadget. Moreover, microcode cannot prevent it (cf. Table 1).

## 3.2   Building Blocks

As our attack uses the cache as the covert-channel part of the Spectre attack, we require building blocks for measuring the timing of cache accesses in JavaScript. While this can be done using a high-resolution timer in some browsers [34], the required primitives are not available on *Cloudflare Workers*. Hence, in addition to a different timing primitive with a lower resolution, we have to amplify the signal such that we can reliably distinguish '0' and '1' bits.

**Remote Timer.** On *Cloudflare Workers*, there are no local timers or known primitives to build timers [54]. We verified that, indeed, no technique from Schwarz et al. [54] resulted in a timer with a resolution higher than 100 ms. Thus, there is no possibility to accurately measure the time directly in JavaScript, and, therefore, it is not possible to perform a local Spectre attack [34].

```
if (secret_bit) { read A; } else { read B; } //transiently leak bit
read A; //perform architectural access
```

**Listing 1.1.** Amplified Spectre-PHT gadget [41].

In this setup, the attacker sends a network request to a remote server to start a timing measurement. The remote server stores a local high-resolution timestamp, e.g., using `rdtsc`, associated with the request. To stop the timing measurement and receive the time delta, the attacker sends another request to the remote server, which sends back the time difference from the current to the stored timestamp. Hence, the attacker has a high-resolution time difference that is only impacted by the network latency between the attacker's worker and the remote server. We evaluated this timing primitive on *Cloudflare Workers*. For the best case, *i.e.*, same physical machine, we achieve a resolution of 0.47 ns on a 2.1 GHz CPU, with a jitter of 1.67 %. With a resolution of 0.47 ns, we can distinguish a cache hit from a miss for the cache covert channel. However, this case is unlikely in reality, as the latency is typically in the microsecond range [63].

**Amplification.** In our attack scenario, the attacker has no high-resolution timer but full control over the Spectre gadget. Hence, to mount a successful attack with the remote timer, we have to rely on amplification techniques that amplify the latency between a cache hit and miss [41]. One such technique is to transiently access multiple cache lines for a single bit instead of a single cache line and probe over these to increase the latency between a cache hit and a miss. However, this technique is quite memory-consuming and limited by the number of cache lines.

A way to arbitrarily amplify the latency between cache hits and misses is to either access a memory location which encodes a '0' or '1' bit transiently and then accesses the memory location for a '1' again architecturally [58]. Listing 1.1 illustrates an *arbitrary amplification* [58] gadget. If the Spectre gadget is optimal in terms of mistraining, we have twice as many cache misses for a '0' bit as for a '1' bit. With a loop over the gadget, we can create arbitrarily large timing differences between hits and misses. We evaluate the amplification idea on an Intel Xeon Silver 4208, running Ubuntu 20.04 (kernel 5.4.0) in native code. We increase the number of amplification iterations and run each iteration 1000 times to get stable results. This leads to a linear growth with the increase of the number of loop iterations (amplification factor). Depending on how much runtime is given to the worker, it is possible to arbitrarily increase the delay. Hence, we can also see that there are no strict requirements for the resolution of the remote timer. For lower resolutions, we can increase the amplification, resulting in a reduced leakage rate, no prevention of the attack, as also shown in related work [57].

**Eviction.** To repeat our amplification and reset the cache state, cache eviction is required. One way to evict certain addresses from the cache is by building eviction sets [23,44,64]. While a targeted eviction set leads to a fast eviction, building the eviction set is costly. Even with a local timer, the currently fastest approach takes more than 100 ms [64]. In our remote scenario, this would require a lot of network requests to find the eviction set for our encoding oracle, as building the eviction set requires constant timing measurements. Furthermore, eviction sets cannot be reused due to address-space-layout randomization on each run. Instead of using eviction sets, we iterate over a large eviction array (multiple MB, depending on the cache size) in cache-line steps (64 byte) and access the values. If enough addresses are accessed, the cached value is evicted [23,34].

We evaluate the eviction directly on the V8 engine used in *Cloudflare Workers* on an Intel Xeon Silver 4208, running Ubuntu 20.04 (kernel 5.4.0). We access a certain index $v$ of a large array to cache it, iterate over the eviction set, and verify if $v$ is still cached. We observe that an eviction array of 2 MB always evicts $v$ on our Intel Xeon Silver 4208 ($n = 1000$).

Note that address randomization can be deterministically circumvented using engineering. Göktas et al. [19] introduced the concept of a speculative probing primitive that leverages Spectre to break classical and fine-grained ASLR. Gras et al. [22], Schwarz et al. [51], and Lipp et al. [36] demonstrated that microarchitectural attacks in JavaScript can break memory randomization.

### 3.3    Attack on *Cloudflare Workers*

Using the building blocks, we mount an attack on *Cloudflare Workers* to extract secret bits from a worker at a known location to estimate the best possible attack. For that, we send an initial request with a sequence number to a timing server. The timing server stores a local, high-resolution timestamp on this request. We perform a Spectre attack on a target address and send another request to the server. The timing server computes the delta between the current and the stored timestamp to distinguish between a cache hit or miss. As the attacker controls both the attacking worker and the timing server, there is no need to send the leaked information back to the worker.

There are different challenges when creating a JavaScript Spectre PoC, as the V8 JIT compiler optimizes code based on assumptions. If such assumptions are invalidated, the function is de-optimized. We thus avoid triggering any de-optimization points in our generated code, as that ruins the training achieved. Therefore, we place the out-of-bound access behind a mispredicted guard branch, preventing the JIT compiler from de-optimizing the code when detecting out-of-bound accesses. Moreover, during the garbage collection phase, objects move between different heap spaces of the same worker to reduce the memory footprint. By forcing garbage collection phases, we stabilize an object's location.

**Evaluation.** To develop and evaluate a proof-of-concept attack, we obtained a local developer copy of *Cloudflare Workers* to not interfere with any worker of other customers. We ensured that the configuration on our local system is identical to the configuration running on the cloud. As *Cloudflare Workers* mostly use server CPUs, we also focus our attack on an Intel server CPU, specifically an Intel Xeon Silver 4208, running Ubuntu 20.04 (kernel 5.4.0).

We create a Spectre-PHT PoC that leaks bits from a victim `ArrayBuffer` by transiently reading out-of-bounds. We describe the technical implementation details for optimal leakage in the extended version [56] (Appendix B).

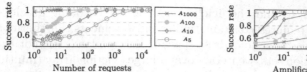
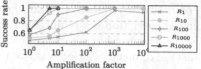

(a) Success over the number of requests per number of amplification factor.

(b) Success of different amplification factors for different number of requests.

**Fig. 3.** Success of different amplification factors for different number of requests.

We call the function performing a Spectre attack 10 000 times and repeat the experiment 1000 times, observing a success rate of 54.31 % ($n = 1000$, $\sigma = 23.16\%$). We assume that the attacker is capable of creating a stable exploit with 100 % success rate. From now on, we evaluate our metrics with a 100 % success rate to estimate the best possible attack, where the attacker knows where the secret array is located.

We evaluate a set of different amplification factors (number of loop iterations) in native code between 1 and 1000, and sample each loop length 100 000. We implement the box test [14] to determine the number of required requests [6,14,63]. Figure 3a illustrates the number of requests required to achieve a certain success rate for different amplification factors. The higher the amplification factor is, the fewer requests are required to achieve high success rates. As Fig. 3b illustrates, with small amplification factors but enough requests, we can also achieve a high success rate of more than 95 %. We refer to the work of Van Goethem et al. [63] and Schwarz et al. [55] for the required requests in a network with multiple hops.

We evaluate our attack locally, *i.e.*, with a timing server on the same machine. We first evaluate an optimal attack in native code. Ideally, an attacker chooses the number with the highest success rate and the lowest number of requests required, minimizing the execution time. We choose a random 16-bit secret. As amplification factor, we choose 100 000 loop iterations and perform just one request. With this setup, leaking one bit takes on average 2.5 s ($n = 100$, $\sigma_{\bar{x}} = 0.05\%$). We repeat the experiment 100 times and observe a leakage rate of 23 bit/s ($n = 100$, $\sigma_{\bar{x}} = 2.8\%$). Using an outlier filter, this error can be reduced towards 0. As these values are from a native-code attack, we consider these numbers as the maximum achievable leakage rate for JavaScript. A JavaScript attacker is more restricted in terms of evicting certain addresses from the cache and thus requires additional time for the eviction. Furthermore, the code is JIT-compiled, requiring a warmup to stabilize the JIT-compiled code. We evaluate the amplification in JavaScript in the V8 engine with an amplification factor of 250 000, a native timestamp counter to measure the response times, and a random 16 bit secret. One script execution takes about 30 s, which is the maximum execution time for *Cloudflare Workers* [12]. All evaluated numbers are shown in Table 2 in the extended version [56] (Appendix A). With a success rate of 100 % we determine an optimal leakage rate of 2 bit/min leading to a leakage rate of 120 bit/h.

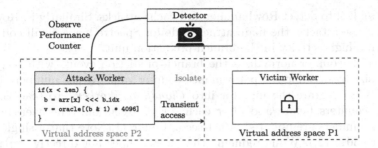

**Fig. 4.** DyPrIs isolating a malicious worker based on performance counters.

## 4   DyPrIs

In this section, we present an approach to dynamically isolate malicious *Cloud-flare Workers* to benefit both from the security of process isolation and the performance of language-level isolation. The basic idea is to use HPCs to detect potential Spectre attacks and isolate suspicious *Cloudflare Workers* using process isolation (Fig. 4). While a detection mechanism typically suffers from false positives, DyPrIs can cope even with high false-positive rates. In the worst case, a Spectre attack is detected for every worker, leading to the worst-case scenario of one worker per process, *i.e.*, strict process isolation, as currently used in browsers plus the 2 % detection overhead. As workers are stateless, they can also be suspended or migrated at any time. Thus, even if many worker are considered malicious, the resources of *Cloudflare* are not exhausted. Every false-positive rate below 100 % performs better than strict process isolation.

We discuss how to reliably detect Spectre attacks using performance counters (cf. Sect. 4.1). We integrate our approach into *Cloudflare Workers* and measure the performance overhead of reading performance counters on a real-world cloud system (cf. Sect. 4.2). We show that there is a small performance overhead of 2 % for reading performance counters.

### 4.1   Detecting Spectre Attacks

In this section, we discuss the detection of Spectre attacks using HPCs. While the common use of HPCs is finding bottlenecks, researchers used HPCs for detecting malware, rootkits, CFI violations, ROP, Rowhammer, or cache-side channel attacks [5,8,24,28,39,68,69,73].

**Detecting Attacks Using Normalized Performance Counters.** Our second approach tries to detect Spectre attacks using normalized performance counters. At first we collect data from different performance counters. We collect the following hardware events (PERF_COUNT_HW_*): CACHE_iTLB, BRANCH_MISSES, BRANCH_INSTRUCTIONS, CACHE_REFERENCES, CACHE_MISSES, CACHE_L1D/READ_MISSES and CACHE_L1D/READ_ACCESSES. We normalize the values using iTLB performance counters (iTLB accesses) which was also used by

Gruss et al. [24] to detect Rowhammer and cache attacks. Similarly to Rowhammer and cache attacks, the main attack code for Spectre has a small code footprint with a high activity in the branch-prediction unit.

The iTLB counter normalizes the branch-prediction events with respect to the code size by dividing the performance counter value by the number of iTLB accesses. We integrate the monitor into *Cloudflare Workers*, to read the performance counters before and after each script execution. The averaged per-execution numbers are updated in a 1-second interval (Note that a single script runs up to 30 s [12]). While reducing the interval does not directly impact the performance of a worker, it potentially leads to more false positives as outliers are not filtered. We collect data from the benign workload and compare it to a worker executing a Spectre attack. Based on the performance numbers, we find a threshold to distinguish between an attack and normal workload. We evaluate this approach in Sect. 5.1.

### 4.2  Process Isolation

For DyPrIs, we fundamentally rely on process isolation. A well-known implementation of process isolation is site isolation, where every page in a browser runs in its own process to prevent memory safety violations as well as Spectre attacks [48]. However, in contrast to full site isolation, we only isolate potentially malicious *Cloudflare Workers* if the Spectre detection mechanism flags them. Hence, DyPrIs only falls back to full site isolation in the worst case, while reducing the overhead caused by process isolation in the average case.

Related work proposes efficient in-process isolation mechanisms using Intel Memory Protection Keys (MPK) [45,50,62]. However, Intel MPK is only available on selected CPUs since Skylake-SP, limited to 16 protection keys and thus not practical for *Cloudflare Workers* [62], running multiple thousand workers per process. Furthermore, the threat model of these approaches does not include side-channel or transient-execution attacks. For DyPrIs, we modify the *Cloudflare Workers* software to isolate a potentially malicious worker, *i.e.*, a worker that was flagged by the performance-counter-based detection, into a separate process. We implement process isolation in *Cloudflare Workers* from scratch (cf. Fig. 5). For that, we start process sandboxes by forking from a zygote process, and talk to the new process over an RPC protocol [3,11]. All communication between the main process and the isolated process are over this RPC connection, communications between the process sandbox and the outside have to go through the main process. Since the runtime of a worker is, on average, less than 1 ms, the isolation must not introduce a high performance overhead. Thus, one instance of a worker frequently reads out the performance counters per script execution and computes a moving average. From our results in Sect. 5, we observed that the normalized iTLB performance provides the best detection tradeoff in terms of performance overhead and accuracy. We first run an attack and collect its performance-counter data. Additionally, we collect anonymized per-CPU-core performance-counter data of real scripts running in production. Based on our evaluation in Sect. 5.1, we use a threshold of 4096 retired branches

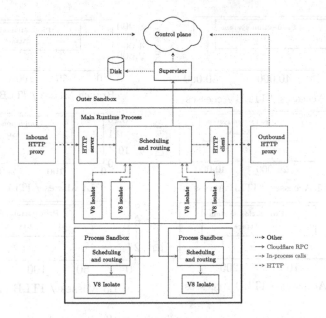

**Fig. 5.** DyPrIs overview.

per iTLB access to distinguish between a suspicious and a benign script. If a script exceeds this threshold, we flag it as a potential Spectre attack and isolate it into a separate process. In contrast to, e.g., browser tabs, worker are stateless. Thus, a worker can simply be migrated. Isolating instead of terminating ensures that the worker can continue running, e.g., in case the detection was a false positive, while it cannot access data of any other worker.

## 5 Evaluation

In this section, we evaluate the accuracy and performance overhead of our detection methodology. We choose a threshold of 4096 branch accesses per iTLB access, which allows distinguishing a Spectre attack from a benign script. We use a large set of different programs to sample the number of mispredicted and retired branches. For our set, we observe that out of 141 programs, which includes the 13 Spectre gadgets from Kocher [33], we cannot distinguish 4 benign programs from a Spectre gadget, resulting in a false-positive rate of 2.83 % with a small performance overhead of 2 %. Using our normalized counters approach, we observe a negligible overhead of 2 % in our production environment.

### 5.1 Normalized Performance Counters

We evaluated our approach on 5 Intel Xeon server CPUs (Broadwell, Skylake 4116, Skylake 6162, Skylake 6162, Cascade Lake 6262) and one AMD Epyc Rome

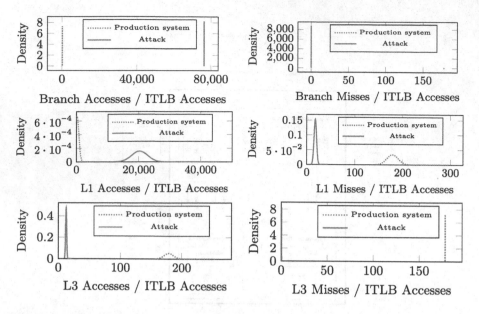

**Fig. 6.** Performance counters of average *Cloudflare Workers* and a Spectre attack on the production system.

CPU. To decide whether a script is susceptible or not, we collect performance data from the production system running our Spectre attack. We recorded the performance counters on the production environment and sampled over 50 000 times as a baseline. Figure 6 shows the normalized performance counters of our cloud machines. For last-level-cache accesses, misses, and branch misses, the numbers of the attack script are below the average script. For the number of L1-cache accesses and retired branches, we can clearly distinguish average script from attack. Especially for the retired branches, the distance between an attack script and the average regular script is 34 times the standard deviation of a benign script. We collected our numbers from real-world worker production machines to calculate the false-positive rate. We choose the number of normalized retired branch instructions as an indicator for a Spectre attack and run it on our cloud machines. First, we run a Spectre attack to verify whether their number is in a similar range on each test machine. We then evaluate different threshold boundaries for the number of normalized retired branch instructions and report the number of false positives. Figure 7 shows the number of false positives depending on the threshold on our cloud machines in the production environment. For a strict threshold, *i.e.*, 1024, the false-positive rate is 21.41 %. However, this threshold is set higher to reduce the number of false positives. The numbers of false positives are in a similar range on each of the tested machines. Setting the threshold to 4096, results in an average false positive rate of 0.61 % on our devices. For a threshold of 8192 the average false-positive rate decreases to 0.26 %, and at a threshold of 65 536, we do not observe any false positives.

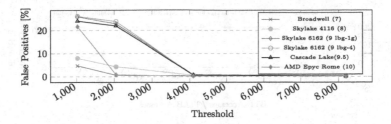

**Fig. 7.** Number of false positives depending on the normalized iTLB threshold.

Next, we look at the performance overhead of our attack when the attacker tries to get below the detection thresholds. Getting below this threshold requires the attacker to significantly slow down the amplified Spectre attack. Since the attacker cannot get rid of the cache eviction, the number of amplification iterations has to be reduced. Consequently, if the number of amplification iterations is reduced, more requests, *i.e.*, samples, are required to clearly distinguish cache hits and misses (cf. Fig. 3a and 3b). We evaluate the best possible attacker in native code who only mistrains one branch. By omitting amplification or with a small factor of 10, we can reduce the number of retired branch instructions/iTLB accesses on our test devices to 604.71 and 3492.41, respectively, which is in the ranges of an average script. However, with the latter, the leakage rate is 1 bit/h. Thus, we set the threshold to 4096 and receive an average false positive rate of 0.61 % on our tested devices. Figure 8 illustrates the decrease in leakage if the attack degrades from an amplified Spectre attack to a sequential attack. Using a non-amplified approach, about 250 000 requests are required (Sect. 3.3). We achieve a leakage of 1 bit/h in a local-network scenario. Hence, as an additional security margin, we limit the number of subsequent requests per worker to 10 000 on the same machine. If more than 10 000 requests are issued, we redirect the request to a different machine. Thus, we can still prevent leakage from a slowed-down attack using our threshold-based approach. We assume that there are no attacks running on the production system, thus we cannot measure the number of false negatives. Our own attack is detected by the threshold, as well as the 15 Spectre samples provided by Kocher [33]. In addition, we evaluated and analyzed the new and larger Spectre-PHT gadgets generated by FastSpec [60]. The gadgets are based on the 15 variants, and we observe that the generated gadgets are quite similar. We evaluated 100 random gadgets from FastSpec and did not observe any false negatives with our detection. As the mistraining for those gadgets is similar, the branch accesses per iTLB access are in a similar range. We also evaluated the detection on the Spectre JavaScript PoC from Röttger and Janc [57]. Even with the low amplification factor of 4 000 in this PoC, we reliably detect the attack ($n = 500$, $\mu = 19\,253.73$).

*Spectre-BTB, Spectre-RSB and Spectre-STL.* In addition to Spectre-PHT we also run our performance counter analysis on other Spectre variants exploiting the branch-target buffer (BTB), return-stack buffer (RSB) and store-to-load

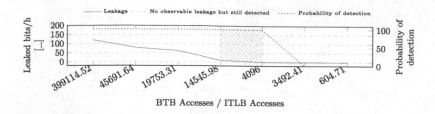

**Fig. 8.** Branch accesses/iTLB accesses and the corresponding leakage rate.

(STL) forwarding. We create native code proof-of-concepts for these variants executing each gadget 10 000 times on a Xeon Silver 4208. We ran the PoCs 500 times and collected the number of branch and iTLB accesses. The numbers for Spectre-BTB and RSP are an order of magnitude lower than for Spectre-PHT ($\mu_{\overline{btb}} = 423171.54$). However, they are still detected with the same metric ($n = 500$): Spectre-BTB ($\mu_{\overline{btb}} = 23401.20$), Spectre-RSB ($\mu_{\overline{rsb}} = 38369.17$), Spectre-STL ($\mu_{\overline{stl}} = 982.20$). The metric for Spectre-STL is far below the threshold of 4096. However, the values for `memory_disambiguation.history_reset` are significantly higher on average if the store-to-load logic is exploited in Spectre-STL ($n = 500$, $\mu_{\overline{stl}} = 8993.98$, $\mu_{\overline{nostl}} = 2644.73$). Thus, we also use this counter to detect potential Spectre-STL attacks.

## 5.2 DyPrIs

We integrate DyPrIs in *Cloudflare Workers*, which requires modifications of 6459 lines of code, not including the Spectre detection mechanism. As with any isolation technology, the performance overhead varies depending on the workload [48]. *Cloudflare Workers* is an environment where typical guest workloads use very little memory and spend very little CPU time responding to any particular event. As a result, in this environment, DyPrIs's overhead is expected to be large compared to the underlying workload. In a first test, we evaluate the overhead for a test script by increasing the number of isolated processes, *i.e.*, the number of sandboxed V8 isolates, up to 500. We measure the overhead in terms of executed scripts per second, *i.e.*, the requests executed per second from the localhost and the total amount of consumed main memory. The execution is repeated 10 times per isolation level with 2000 requests ($n = 20000$, $\sigma_{\overline{rps}} = 3.87\%$, $\sigma_{\overline{mem}} = 0.23\%$). Figure 9 shows the requests per second and the total memory consumption based on the number of isolated V8 processes. As expected, we observe a linear decrease in the possible number of requests per second and a linear increase in the memory consumption. Further, we performed a load test of *Cloudflare Workers* runtime using a selection of sample guest workers simulating a heavy-load machine. They mostly respond to I/O in under a millisecond and allocate little memory. By forcing process isolation on the workers, the memory overhead of each guest was 2x–5x higher, and CPU time was 8x higher, compared to a worker using a single process. We performed

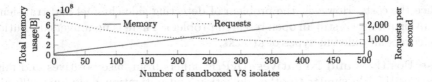

**Fig. 9.** Requests per second and memory consumption of process isolation.

a second test using a real-world worker known to be unusually resource hungry in both CPU and memory usage. In this case, memory overhead is 20 %–70 % worse with DyPrIs, and CPU time about 60 % worse. These numbers appear to be high, but when only 0.61 % of workers are isolated, the overhead is negligible. As our proof of concept was not optimized, it still has big potential for optimizations. For example, it currently uses an RPC protocol [3] to communicate between processes, but does so over a Unix domain socket. This protocol is designed in such a way that it could be communicated in shared memory, reducing communication overhead. The implementation could also use OS primitives for faster context switching, such as the FUTEX_SWAP feature proposed by Google. However, while especially the CPU overhead could be reduced, there is always a significant cost incurred by context switching and marshalling to communicate between processes. The total overhead on all machines can only be estimated as it depends on the workload. The detection overhead is 2 %. In the worst case, we are slightly worse than full process isolation due to the 2 % detection overhead.

## 6  Discussion

**Comparison Between *Cloudflare Workers* and Competing Approaches.** The main challenge of edge computing is to run various applications of numerous tenants efficiently. Approaches like AWS Lambda and Azure Functions rely on containers to achieve this [2,42]. While their design strictly prevents Spectre attacks on other tenants, the performance overhead is higher for the use case of edge computing than *Cloudflare Workers* [10]. The *Cloudflare Workers* architecture is stateless in a sense that every worker in any data centre can process any request, *i.e.*, the request is processed by the worker with the lowest latency. *Cloudflare Workers* rely on a single-process architecture with language-level isolation to isolate their tenants architecturally. However, as we showed, this design leads to potential Spectre attacks. A similar design with language-level isolation of WebAssembly code from different tenants is used by Fastly [17]. Therefore, Fastly also needs to consider Spectre attacks within the same process by either applying DyPrIs or switching to full isolation via processes or containers.

**Mitigation versus Detection.** Especially in high-performance scenarios, such as cloud systems, Spectre mitigations [7,31,34] result in high power consumption. Hence, instead of paying the constant costs of mitigations, dectecing attack can reduce the costs. However, the problem of detecting side-channel and transient-execution attacks is still an open research problem. There is no universal solution that covers all different types of attacks.

**False Positives and Negatives.** DyPrIs suffers from false positives and false negatives [15,72], similar to other detection and mitigation techniques [25,65]. False positives only impact the performance and not the security. False negatives occur when slowing down attacks to 1 bit/h (cf. Table 2 in Appendix A in the extended version [56]). Therefore, the maximum execution time is restricted to 30 s, far from 1 h. Using the machine learning approach of Gulmezoglu [26], the false positive rate could be reduced further. However, this approach would require a re-training with real-world data of *Cloudflare Workers* and a frequent re-updating of the training set. Adding additional code pages also allows getting below the thresholds. To "hide" the native attack, we access 125 additional code pages (500 KB) per bit to get the branch accesses/iTLB accesses below the threshold (cf. Fig. 10 in Appendix A in the extended version [56]). While feasible in native code, the resulting code size causes V8 to abort the optimization phase, stopping the attack.

**Comparison to Existing Detections.** Besides full site isolation, prior work discusses detection but not how to stop attacks once they are detected. Existing static analysis approaches [13,27] on binaries are not applicable to the use case of *Cloudflare Workers*. Approaches that perform taint tracking and fuzzing on binaries to dynamically detect gadgets [25,47,52,65] are infeasible for the high-performance requirements of *Cloudflare Workers*. The approach of Mambretti et al. [40] does not evaluate real-world workloads and cannot distinguish the different workloads of *Cloudflare Workers* from an external process.

**Reliability of HPCs in DyPrIs.** As Zhou et al. [72] and Das et al. [15] discuss, using HPCs for detection of cache attacks can lead to flaws caused by non-determinism and overcounting. We showed that in our statistical approach both only marginally reduce the performance of DyPrIs not the security.

**Alternative Spectre JS Attacks.** Concurrent work [57] has demonstrated a Spectre exploit on V8, leaking up to 60 B/s using timers with a precision of 1 ms or worse through a L1 covert channel. Similarly to our PoC, it uses a Spectre-PHT gadget to read out-of-bound from a JavaScript TypedArray, giving an attacker access to the entire address space. The PoC uses small-sized TypedArrays for which the backing store is allocated in the isolate itself. Thus, it leaks data inside the same isolate. In concurrent work, Agarwal et al. [1] has extended the PoC from Röttger and Janc [57] to leak data using 64-bit addresses using a local timing source. They use speculative type confusion between an ArrayBuffer and a custom object that should be properly aligned across two cache lines.

# 7   Conclusion

In this paper, we presented DyPrIs, a practical low-overhead solution to actively detect and mitigate Spectre attacks. We first presented an amplified JavaScript remote attack on *Cloudflare Workers*, which leaks 2 bit/min, *i.e.*, 1 bit per worker invocation. We proposed a practical approach for actively detecting and mitigating Spectre attacks. We show that it is still possible to efficiently detect Spectre attacks using performance counters with a false-positive rate of 0.61 % at the cost of 2 % overhead for the detection. We demonstrate that conditionally applying process isolation based on a detection mechanism has a better performance than full process isolation, under the same security guarantees.

**Acknowledgments.** We want to thank our anonymous reviewers and in particular our shepherds Roberto Di Pietro and Vijayalakshmi Atluri. This work was supported by generous gifts from Cloudflare. We want to especially thank Harris Hancock, Claudio Canella and Moritz Lipp for valueable feedback on this work. Any opinions or recommendations expressed in this work are those of the authors and do not necessarily reflect the views of the funding parties.

# References

1. Agarwal, A., et al.: Spook.js: attacking chrome strict site isolation via speculative execution. In: S&P (2022)
2. Amazon, AWS Lambda@Edge (2019). https://aws.amazon.com/lambda/edge/
3. Anonymous. Anonymized for Double Blind Submission (2019)
4. Bhattacharyya, A., et al.: SMoTherSpectre: exploiting speculative execution through port contention. In: CCS (2019)
5. Briongos, S., Irazoqui, G., Malagón, P., Eisenbarth, T.: Detecting cache attacks through self-observation. In: CODASPY, Cacheshield (2018)
6. Brumley, D., Boneh, D.: Remote timing attacks are practical. Comput. Netw. **48**(5), 701–716 (2005)
7. Canella, C.: A systematic evaluation of transient execution attacks and defenses. In: USENIX Security Symposium. Extended classification tree and PoCs at (2019). https://transient.fail/
8. Chiappetta, M., Savas, E., Yilmaz, C.: Real time detection of cache-based side-channel attacks using hardware performance counters. ePrint 2015/1034 (2015)
9. Cloudflare. Cloudflare Workers (2019). https://www.cloudflare.com/products/cloudflare-workers/
10. Cloudflare. Cloudflare Workers (2019). https://blog.cloudflare.com/cloud-computing-without-containers/
11. Cloudflare. Anonymized for Double Blind Submission (2020)
12. Cloudflare. Limits - Cloudflare Workers (2021). https://developers.cloudflare.com/workers/platform/limits
13. Corbet, J.: Finding Spectre vulnerabilities with smatch, April 2018. https://lwn.net/Articles/752408/
14. Crosby, S.A., Wallach, D.S., Riedi, R.H.: Opportunities and limits of remote timing attacks. ACM Trans. Inf. Syst. Sec. (TISSEC) **12**(3), 17 (2009)

15. Das, S., Werner, J., Antonakakis, M., Polychronakis, M., Monrose, F.: Sok: the challenges, pitfalls, and perils of using hardware performance counters for security. In: S&P (2019)
16. Deno, A.: Globally Distributed JavaScript VM (2021). https://deno.com/deploy
17. Fastly. Serverless Compute Environment - Fastly Compute@Edge (2021). https://www.fastly.com/products/edge-compute/serverless
18. Ge, Q., Yarom, Y., Cock, D., Heiser, G.: A Survey of microarchitectural timing attacks and countermeasures on contemporary hardware. J. Crypt. Eng. **8**, 1–27 (2016)
19. Göktaş, E., Razavi, K., Portokalidis, G., Bos, H., Giuffrida, C.: Hacking Blind in the Spectre Era. In: CCS, Speculative Probing (2020)
20. Google. SafeSide: Understand and mitigate software-observable side-channels (2019). https://github.com/google/safeside
21. Google Project Zero. What is a "good" memory corruption vulnerability? (2015). https://googleprojectzero.blogspot.com/2015/06/what-is-good-memory-corruption.html
22. Gras, B., Razavi, K., Bosman, E., Bos, H., Giuffrida, C.: Practical Cache Attacks on the MMU. In: NDSS, ASLR on the Line (2017)
23. Gruss, D., Maurice, C., Mangard, S.: Rowhammer.js: a remote software-induced fault Attack in JavaScript. In: DIMVA (2016)
24. Gruss, D., Maurice, C., Wagner, K., Mangard, S.: Flush+Flush: a fast and stealthy cache attack. In: DIMVA (2016)
25. Guarnieri, M., Köpf, B., Morales, J.F., Reineke, J., Sánchez, A.: Principled detection of speculative information flows. In: S&P, SPECTECTOR (2020)
26. Gulmezoglu, B., Moghimi, A., Eisenbarth, T., Sunar, B.: FortuneTeller: predicting microarchitectural attacks via unsupervised deep learning. arXiv:1907.03651 (2019)
27. Hat, R.: Spectre and Meltdown Detector (2018). https://access.redhat.com/labsinfo/speculativeexecution
28. Herath, N., Fogh, A.: These are not your grand daddys CPU performance counters - CPU hardware performance counters for security. In: Black Hat Briefings (2015)
29. Horn, J.: speculative execution, variant 4: speculative store bypass (2018)
30. Intel. Intel Analysis of Speculative Execution Side Channels (2018). Revision 4.0
31. Intel. Speculative Execution Side Channel Mitigations (2018). Revision 3.0
32. Irazoqui, G., Eisenbarth, T., Sunar., B.: Preventing microarchitectural attacks before distribution. In: CODASPY, Mascat (2018)
33. Kocher, P.: Spectre Mitigations in Microsoft's C/C++ Compiler (2018)
34. Kocher, P., et al.: Exploiting Speculative Execution. In: S&P, Spectre Attacks (2019)
35. Koruyeh, E.M., Khasawneh, K., Song,C., Abu-Ghazaleh, N.: Spectre returns! speculation attacks using the Return Stack Buffer. In: WOOT (2018)
36. Lipp, M., Hadžić, V., Schwarz, M., Perais, A., Maurice, C., Gruss, D.: Exploring the security implications of AMD's cache way predictors. In: AsiaCCS, Take a Way (2020)
37. Lipp, M., et al.: Reading kernel memory from user space. In: USENIX Security Symposium, Meltdown (2018)
38. Maisuradze, G., Rossow, C.: ret2spec: speculative execution using return stack buffers. In: CCS (2018)
39. Malone, C., Zahran, M., Karri, R.: Are hardware performance counters a cost effective way for integrity checking of programs. In: STC (2011)

40. Mambretti,A., Neugschwandtner, M., Sorniotti, A., Kirda, E., Robertson, W., Kurmus, A.: Speculator: a tool to analyze speculative execution attacks and mitigations. In: ACM ACSAC (2019)
41. Mcilroy, R., Sevcik, J., Tebbi, T., Titzer, B.L., Verwaest, T.: Spectre is here to stay: an analysis of side-channels and speculative execution. arXiv:1902.05178 (2019)
42. Microsoft. Azure serverless computing (2019). https://azure.microsoft.com/en-us/overview/serverless-computing/
43. Mushtaq, M., et al.: WHISPER: a tool for run-time detection of side-channel attacks. IEEE Access **8**, 83871–83900 (2020)
44. Oren, Y., Kemerlis, V.P., Sethumadhavan, S., Keromytis, A.D.: The spy in the sandbox: practical cache attacks in javaScript and their implications. In: CCS (2015)
45. Park, S., Lee, S., Xu, W., Moon, H., Kim, T.: libmpk: software abstraction for intel memory protection keys. arXiv:1811.07276 (2018)
46. Payer, M.: HexPADS: a platform to detect "stealth" attacks. In: ESSoS (2016)
47. Qi, Z., et al.: Speculative taint analysis for discovering spectre gadgets. In: NDSS, Spectaint (2021)
48. Reis, C., Moshchuk, A., Oskov, N.: Site isolation: process separation for web sites within the browser. In: USENIX Security Symposium (2019)
49. Ristenpart, T., Tromer, E., Shacham, H., Savage, S.: Exploring information leakage in third party compute clouds. In: CCS, Hey, You, Get Off of My Cloud (2009)
50. Schrammel, D.: Domain keys-efficient in-process isolation for RISC-V and x86. In: USENIX Security Symposium (2020)
51. Schwarz, M., Canella, C., Giner, L., Gruss, D.: Store-to-leak forwarding: leaking data on meltdown-resistant CPUs. arXiv:1905.05725 (2019)
52. Schwarz, M., Lipp, M., Canella, C., Schilling, R., Kargl, F., Gruss, D.: A generic approach for mitigating spectre. In: NDSS, ConTExT (2020)
53. Schwarz, M., Lipp, M., Gruss, D.: Real JavaScript and zero side-channel attacks. In: NDSS, JavaScript Zero (2018)
54. Schwarz, M., Maurice, C., Gruss, D., Mangard, S.: High-resolution microarchitectural attacks in javaScript. In: FC, Fantastic Timers and Where to Find Them (2017)
55. Schwarz, M., Schwarzl, M., Lipp, M., Masters, J., Gruss, D.: Read arbitrary memory over network. In: ESORICS, NetSpectre (2019)
56. Schwarzl, M.: Robust and scalable process isolation against Spectre in the cloud (extended version) (2022). https://martinschwarzl.at/media/files/robust_extended.pdf
57. Roettger, S., Janc, A.: A Spectre proof-of-concept for a Spectre-proof web (2021). https://security.googleblog.com/2021/03/a-spectre-proof-of-concept-for-spectre.html
58. Titzer, b.: What spectre means for language implementers (2019). https://pliss2019.github.io/ben_titzer_spectre_slides.pdf
59. Titzer, B.L., Sevcik, J.: A year with Spectre: a V8 perspective (2019). https://v8.dev/blog/spectre
60. Tol, M.C., Yurtseven, K., Gulmezoglu, B., Sunar, B.: FastSpec: scalable generation and detection of Spectre gadgets using neural embeddings. arXiv:2006.14147 (2020)
61. v8 developer blog (2020). https://v8.dev/blog/v8-release-83
62. Vahldiek-Oberwagner, A., Elnikety, E., Garg, D., Druschel, P.: ERIM: secure and efficient in-process isolation with memory protection keys. I: USENIX Security Symposium (2019)

63. Van Goethem, T., Pöpper, C., Joosen, W., Vanhoef, M.: Timeless timing attacks: exploiting concurrency to leak secrets over remote connections. In: USENIX Security Symposium (2020)
64. Vila, P., Köpf, B., Morales, J.: Theory and practice of finding Eviction sets. In: S&P (2019)
65. Wang, G., Chattopadhyay, S., Gotovchits, I., Mitra, T., Roychoudhury, A.: oo7: low-overhead Defense against Spectre attacks via Program Analysis. Trans. Softw. Eng. **47**, 2504–2519 (2019)
66. Wang, H., Sayadi, H., Sasan, A., Rafatirad, S., Homayoun, H.: Hybrid-shield: accurate and efficient cross-layer countermeasure for run-time detection and mitigation of cache-based side-channel attacks. In: ICCAD (2020)
67. Wang, H., Sayadi, H., Sasan, A., Rafatirad, S., Mohsenin, T., Homayoun, H.: Comprehensive evaluation of machine learning countermeasures for detecting microarchitectural side-channel attacks. In: GLSVLSI (2020)
68. Wang, X., Karri, R.: Numchecker: detecting kernel control-flow modifying rootkits by using hardware performance counters. In: DAC (2013)
69. Xia, Y., Liu, Y., Chen, H., Zang, B. Detecting violation of control flow integrity using performance counters. In: DSN, CFIMon (2012)
70. Zhang, T., Zhang, Y., Lee, R.B.: CloudRadar: a real-time side-channel attack detection system in clouds. In: RAID (2016)
71. Zhang, Z.: Detecting malware in SGX enclaves with SGX-Bouncer. In: AsiaCCS, See through Walls (2021)
72. Zhou, B., Gupta, A., Jahanshahi, R., Egele, M., Joshi, A.: Hardware performance counters can detect malware: Myth or fact? In: AsiaCCS (2018)
73. Zhou, H., Xin, W., Shi, W., Yuan, J., Liang, B.: Detecting rop attacks using performance monitoring counters. In: ISPEC, Hdrop (2014)

# Access Control

# Administration of Machine Learning Based Access Control

Mohammad Nur Nobi[1]([✉]), Ram Krishnan[2]([✉]), Yufei Huang[3],
and Ravi Sandhu[4]

[1] Department of Computer Science, Institute for Cyber Security (ICS),
The University of Texas at San Antonio (UTSA), San Antonio, TX 78249, USA
mohammadnur.nobi@my.utsa.edu
[2] Department of Electrical and Computer Engineering, ICS,
NSF Center for Security and Privacy Enhanced Cloud Computing (C-SPECC),
UTSA, San Antonio, TX 78249, USA
ram.krishnan@utsa.edu
[3] Department of Medicine, University of Pittsburgh, and UPMC Hillman Cancer
Center, Pittsburgh, PA 15260, USA
yuh119@pitt.edu
[4] Department of Computer Science, ICS, C-SPECC, UTSA,
San Antonio, TX 78249, USA
ravi.sandhu@utsa.edu

**Abstract.** When the access control state of a system is complex, Machine learning (ML)-based access control decision engines have demonstrated advantages of accuracy and generalizability. This field is emerging with multiple efforts where an ML model is trained based on either existing access control state or historic access logs; the trained model then makes access control decisions. This paper explores ML-based access control's administration problem, focusing on capturing changes in the access control state. We investigate this problem in a simulated system with Random Forest (RF) method from a symbolic ML class and the ResNet method from a non-symbolic one. Both classes have their respective advantages and disadvantages for issues such as insufficient learning of new changes and forgetting existing access information while updating the ML model. Our experimental results show that the non-symbolic approaches perform better than the symbolic ones while adjusting for continual (or incremental) changes in the access control state.

**Keywords:** Access control · Administration · Machine learning

## 1 Introduction

Machine Learning (ML) is used in the field of access control for different purposes such as policy mining [1], attribute engineering [3] and role mining [26]. In traditional access control systems such as RBAC [31] and ABAC [15], the access control decision engine decides accesses based on a written policy (or role assignments, in the case of RBAC). In recent years, researchers have proposed utilizing a trained

© The Author(s), under exclusive license to Springer Nature Switzerland AG 2022
V. Atluri et al. (Eds.): ESORICS 2022, LNCS 13555, pp. 189–210, 2022.
https://doi.org/10.1007/978-3-031-17146-8_10

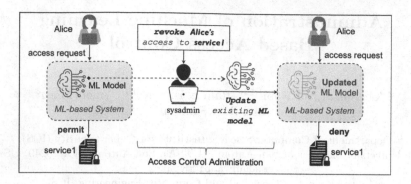

**Fig. 1.** Administration problem in ML-based access control system.

ML model to make access control decisions, possibly supplementing or even eventually replacing rule-based access control systems. We refer to such systems as machine learning based access control (MLBAC) [9,10,19,22,28,35]. We briefly discuss these methods in related work Sect. 2.2. These works have demonstrated that, for a given ground truth of an access control state represented in the form of authorization tuples, MLBAC models could capture that access control state with significantly higher accuracy than the traditional access control models such as ABAC. In addition, some works also demonstrate that MLBAC generalizes better than traditional approaches [9,10,19,28]. (Note that generalization is the ability of a model to make accurate decisions on users and resources not explicitly seen during policy mining or ML model training.) Even if MLBAC does not replace traditional forms of access control in practice, it could serve as an effective approach for access control monitoring/auditing or operate in tandem with traditional systems [24,28,38].

However, access control systems are not static—changes in access control state are inevitable. A user may be granted new permissions, or some of her current permissions could get revoked. As shown in Fig. 1, 'Alice' has access to the 'service1' resource. To revoke her access, the learned access control state in MLBAC will need to be correspondingly updated such that it can react accordingly to the applied change. This problem is referred to as *access control administration* in the access control domain [30]. Evidently, administration problems have been thoroughly investigated for traditional approaches [18,30,36], but the issue remains entirely unexplored for MLBAC.

Administration challenges could vary from model to model, but the problem's importance remains unchanged. In the case of RBAC, administration activities include assigning/removing permission to/from a role, creating a new role, and managing role hierarchy [30]. For ABAC, administration activities include updating user/resource attributes and policy modification [33]. In such traditional approaches, the changes are accomplished by modifying existing configurations such as written access control policies, and attribute and role assignments. However, in MLBAC, there is no notion of a human-readable written policy to update. If an access control state change is to be made, it requires modification of existing model. Such a modification is complicated as, in most cases, an ML model is a highly complex function, a tree, or even a black-box that a human user can not directly access and modify. Often, to capture changes, one must go through a process similar to the initial training process.

In this paper, we investigate the administration problem of MLBAC. In particular, we consider the situations where a trained ML could be either from *symbolic* (e.g., RF) or *non-symbolic* (e.g., neural network) types. The symbolic ML methods represent knowledge in the form of logic or a tree that distinguishes them from non-symbolic ones, either statistical or neural [9]. To the best of our knowledge, our proposed method is the first work towards administration in an ML-based access control system. We summarize our contributions as follows.

- We define MLBAC administration problem and propose a methodology to automate and systematize the MLBAC administration process.
- We develop two prototypes of administration in a system where access control decisions are made based on either symbolic or non-symbolic ML approaches.
- We thoroughly evaluate both prototypes for the efficacy of symbolic and non-symbolic ML approaches from an access control administration perspective.
- We demonstrate that administration in an MLBAC poses additional challenges and propose different techniques to overcome them.

The rest of the paper is organized as follows. Section 2 discusses related work. Section 3 presents an overview of the MLBAC administration, its requirements, and the administration methodology. In Sect. 4, we implement two MLBAC administration prototypes in a simulated system and evaluate those prototypes in Sect. 5. Finally, Sect. 6 concludes the paper.

## 2    Related Work

This section discusses works where ML algorithms are proposed in the context of an access control decision engine. One body of work in this category apply ML for the policy administration in traditional access control system [2,6,12]. Another body of work proposes an ML model (MLBAC) in place of traditional access control policies [9,10,19,22,28,35].

### 2.1    ML for Administration of Policy-Based Access Control

Researchers exploit the power of ML to administer changes in traditional policy-based access control systems. The authors in [2] develop an adaptive access control framework for the IoT domain using RF and Neural Networks. The proposed framework dynamically refines the access policies based on the access behaviors of the IoT devices. Argento et al. [6] propose an ML-based approach that identifies policy misconfigurations and adjusts policies at run-time. Gumma et al. [12] propose PAMMELA, an ML-based ABAC policy administration method that creates new rules for the proposed changes and extends existing policy.

## 2.2   MLBAC

In MLBAC, an ML model makes an access control prediction, which is then interpreted into a permit or deny decision. We briefly discuss them below.

Cappelletti et al. [9] train ML models based on user/resource attribute values and access request logs that subsequently decide access permissions. Specifically, the authors build a Decision Tree [29] and RF [8] classifier from the symbolic ML class and Support Vector Machines (SVM) [11] and Multi-Layer Perceptron (MLP) [32] from non-symbolic ones. The empirical results suggest that if the underlying access control state is complex, a symbolic ML approach could perform better. The authors highlight that a system is *complex* if the data (e.g., access logs) are not easily separable according to PCA and t-SNE visualization.

Chang et al. [10] propose an ML-based time-constraint access control where access policies are associated with the time (e.g., a user may only have access to a resource during office hours). The authors train an SVM using each user's login time and a password. For any access request, the trained SVM classifies the users into their respective groups (e.g., department) and provides desired security access right during that period.

Karimi et al. [19] develop an ABAC-RL framework to map between access requests and the access decisions (permit or deny). For deciding accesses, the ABAC-RL trains a reinforcement learning (RL) *agent* that adapts an ABAC policy via a feedback control loop by interacting with users and administrators.

Liu et al. [22] propose EPDE-ML transforming the access control 'permission decision' problem into an 'ML classification' problem that allows or denies accesses. EPDE-ML uses an RF to construct a vector decision classifier to establish a permission decision engine for making access decisions.

Our prior work [28] develops DLBAC using user/resource metadata and the existing access control state as authorization tuples. We build multiple deep neural networks, including ResNet [14], DenseNet [17], etc., that make more generalized and accurate access decisions than ABAC and other ML-based methods.

Srivastava et al. [35] develop risk adaptive access control (RAdAC) for dynamic access decisions (changes in accesses during run-time). For any access request, the RAdAC determines the genuineness of the user, measures the risk, and then provides access accordingly. The framework considers many dynamic attributes such as access time, location, user history, resource sensitivity, etc., and experiments using a neural network and an RF algorithm.

While developing MLBAC using either symbolic [9,22,35] or non-symbolic approaches [9,10,19,28,35], the administration problem is not investigated. In this work, we develop an administrative framework for MLBAC.

## 3   MLBAC Administration

Figure 2 illustrates the overview of MLBAC administration. As depicted in the figure, the *Admin Engine*, the administrative framework, takes a change request as the input, which we refer to as a *Task*. We aim to incorporate the requested Task in MLBAC administration. We assume that the Admin Engine has access to

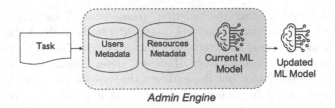

**Fig. 2.** Overview of MLBAC administration.

the user and resource metadata databases and the ML model, which is currently being used for decision making. We refer to this ML model as *Current ML Model* and denote as $\mathbb{F}_{current}$. The objective of administration in MLBAC is to modify $\mathbb{F}_{current}$ to capture the requested Task and generate an updated model. We also refer to this updated model as *Updated ML Model* and designate as $\mathbb{F}_{updated}$.

## 3.1   Requirements

For the purpose of this paper, we generalize MLBAC as follows. An MLBAC model is trained using the existing access control state of a system, along with various pieces of available metadata values such as those of users and objects. Since the decision engine in MLBAC is an ML model, modifying its access control state is not as obvious as that of, say, ABAC, where a rule is typically adjusted to grant or deny existing accesses. It is often required to modify the model itself to accommodate any authorization-related changes. Consequently, the administrative tasks in MLBAC are somewhat simplified since we no longer need to worry about policy and attribute updates. In this paper, we focus on basic administrative tasks for MLBAC, including granting/revoking the access of one or multiple users to one or more resources.

Over time, by learning from proposed changes and observing the metadata of users and objects, MLBAC could intelligently adjust other "similar" accesses in the system. We believe smarter access control administration is one of the most significant benefits of MLBAC in practice, hence the focus of this work.

## 3.2   Problem Statement and Approach

In an ML model, to modify a piece of learned information, it is required to iteratively update the weights of its neurons (in the case of neural network) or parameters (for classical ML) starting with random initialization [37]. Consequently, we state the MLBAC administration problem as:

*'Given an administrative task, update the MLBAC model's weights and/or parameters such that the updated model captures the desired changes in the access control state.'*

By desired changes, we mean both the given administrative task and additional administrative tasks that are similar to the given task. The challenge specifically, then, is: what is the best approach to accurately learn to accommodate the given task and perform additional changes that are *similar* to the proposed task while keeping the existing access control state unchanged for all other users and resources that are vastly dissimilar? We indicate similar changes as changing access to other users and resources similar to the user and resource given in the proposed task. However, determining whether two users (or resources) are similar or not depends on the *type* of their metadata. If the metadata is real-valued (e.g., age, salary, etc.), it is possible to automatically determine other similar users and resources using distance measurement or clustering approaches [41]. This is also applicable for ordinal categorical values, where there is a notion of *order* among its values (e.g., degrees, clearances, job roles, etc.). However, in the case for nominal categorical values (e.g., department, expertise, etc.), there is no notion of order among them, and therefore one could only perform an equality check based on their values.

In practice, one could anticipate a mix of real-valued, ordinal categorical, and nominal categorical data. The model would automatically find additional similar administrative tasks for real-valued and ordinal categorical metadata values. For nominal categorical metadata values, we seek input from the system administrator (sysadmin) to determine the similarity between the user(resource) involved in the proposed task and other users(resources) in the system. We assume sysadmin will provide some 'similarity measurement criteria' in terms of user and resource metadata, which we refer to as *Criteria*. We further illustrate its syntax in Sect. 3.3.

### 3.3   Terminologies

This section introduces some terminologies that we repeatedly use for the explanation of administration in MLBAC.

– **Authorization Tuple.** An Authorization Tuple is user-permissions tuple $\langle user, resource, permissions \rangle$ that specifies the permissions of a *user* to a *resource*. For example, an Authorization Tuple $\langle u1, r1, \{op1, op3\} \rangle$ indicates that a user $u1$ has operations $op1$ and $op3$ access to a resource $r1$.
– **Task.** A Task is a change request which is expressed through a tuple of four elements $\langle user, resource, operation, access \rangle$, where the *access* could be either permit or deny. For example, a Task $\langle u1, r1, op3, deny \rangle$ is a request to revoke the $op3$ access of the user $u1$ to the resource $r1$.
– **AAT (Admin Authorization Tuple).** AAT is an updated Authorization Tuple generated from an existing one based on a Task. For example, $\langle u1, r1, \boldsymbol{op3}, \boldsymbol{deny} \rangle$ is a given *Task*. Suppose that the existing Authorization Tuple in the system for user $u1$ and resource $r1$ is $\langle u1, r1, \{op1, \boldsymbol{op3}, op4\} \rangle$. The AAT with respect to the given Task would be $\langle u1, r1, \{op1, op4\} \rangle$. AAT, in effect, is the change that the admin seeks to make.
– **Criteria.** Criteria is defined as a tuple of user metadata name and value pairs and resource metadata name and value pairs that is expressed as:

$$\Big\langle \{umeta_0 \in \{val_0, \ldots, val_i\}, \ldots, umeta_m \in \{val_0, \ldots, val_j\}\},$$

$$\{rmeta_0 \in \{val_0, \ldots, val_k\}, \ldots, rmeta_n \in \{val_0, \ldots, val_l\}\}\Big\rangle$$

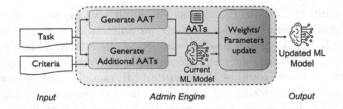

**Fig. 3.** Administration process flow in MLBAC.

where $\{umeta_0, \ldots, umeta_m\}$ is a set of user metadata names, $\{rmeta_0, \ldots, rmeta_n\}$ is a set of resource metadata names, and $\{val_0, \ldots\}$ indicates possible values for respective metadata. For example, a sample Criteria could be $\langle umeta1 \in \{val_0, val_1\}, rmeta4 \in \{val_2\}\rangle$. In this Criteria, the possible values of $umeta1$ are $val_0$ and $val_1$, and the possible value of $rmeta4$ is $val_2$.

- **Additional AAT.** The Additional AAT is a set of *similar* AAT determined based on users and resources similar to the user and resource in the Task. This paper determines similar users/resources based on the input Criteria. Section 3.4 discusses Additional AAT generation.
- **OATs (Other Authorization Tuples).** The OAT is a set of Authorization Tuples in the access control system that excludes AAT and Additional AAT.

### 3.4 Methodology

As shown in Fig. 3, the Admin Engine generates an Admin Authorization Tuple (AAT) for the given Task as described in Sect. 3.3. The AAT is the Authorization Tuple that we aim to integrate into the current ML model, $\mathbb{F}_{current}$. Next, the Admin Engine generates Additional AAT based on the Task and Criteria. Both AAT and Additional AAT are independent of each other hence it is not required to maintain any specific order for their generation.

We generate Additional AAT based on a set of *similar* users and resources determined using Criteria, as discussed in Sect. 3.2. The Criteria consist of user and resource metadata names and value pairs. For each user, we compare their metadata values with respective metadata values stipulated in the Criteria. If it matches, we call the corresponding user as the *similar user*. Eventually, we determine all the similar users and follow the same approach for finding similar resources. These similar users and resources are the candidate users and resources for the Additional AAT generation. Next, we iterate over the list of candidate users and candidate resources to make user-resource pairs and determine a list of operations for each pair that the user has access to the resource and *update* their access according to the given Task. The user-resource pair with their updated access operation is an Additional AAT. Eventually, we obtain all the Additional AAT for the given Task and Criteria by repeating the same process. (Appendix A illustrates the pseudo-code of Additional AAT generation.) Collectively both AAT and Additional AAT are stored in a set that we refer to as **AATs**. Note that the 'size of AATs' indicates the number of elements in the set.

At this point, the Admin Engine has the input (AATs) to accommodate in its $\mathbb{F}_{current}$ model and adjust the weights/ parameters to react accordingly for the newly added changes and produce the $\mathbb{F}_{updated}$ model. This accommodation is not straightforward, and there are multiple underlying challenges. A naive solution to this problem could be to *retrain* an ML model based on newly generated AATs and original training data that we used to train the $\mathbb{F}_{current}$. While this approach has its benefits, there are multiple shortcomings. For example, to retrain an ML model, one always has to maintain the original training dataset and the AATs of each administration. Also, retraining is expensive in terms of training time and resource consumption. Therefore, it might not be practical nor feasible for many systems to retrain an ML model to accommodate new changes.

A potential solution could be to update the weights/parameters of the $\mathbb{F}_{current}$. However, the process of updating the weights/parameter values in an ML model has a direct correlation with the type of model in question. Suppose the underlying model is a classical ML algorithm such as SVM and Ensemble Methods. In that case, an incremental machine learning (a.k.a online learning) technique could be a prospective solution [7]. If the model is a neural network, a possible technique could be to use *fine-tuning* [20]. Fine-tuning performs internal adjustments to a trained neural network's (e.g., $\mathbb{F}_{current}$ in MLBAC) weight based on a set of given examples (AATs in the case of MLBAC).

## 4    MLBAC Administration Prototype

This section implements two prototypes of MLBAC administration using ML models from symbolic and non-symbolic classes. We experiment with MLBAC administration to assess how well it reacts to the administrative changes. We apply MLBAC administration in a synthetically generated extensive system with thousands of users and resources. The following sections briefly introduce the simulated system, the ML models, and different administration strategies.

### 4.1    System for MLBAC Administration Experimentation

Access control administration is a continuous process where one could expect many change requests during the life of a system. A limited number of real-world access control-related datasets are available from Amazon [4,5]. These datasets have been used extensively in the literature for ML model training and ABAC policy mining and evaluating how accurately the trained model or mined policy can decide accesses [1,9,27,28]. For any access control administration experiment, we need a system where we will have continuous change requests during the system's life. The Amazon datasets in themselves do not provide such administrative tasks. Our prior work [28] provides a dataset[1] named *u5k-r5k-auth12k* for a simulated access control system. We created the dataset using the data generation algorithm proposed by Xu et al. [39] (see Appendix B). The simulated

---

[1] https://github.com/dlbac/DlbacAlpha/tree/main/dataset/synthetic.

system has around five thousand users and five thousand resources. Also, there are eight user and eight resource metadata for each user and resource, respectively, and four operations. The dataset contains *nominal* categorical metadata values, as integers, of which each value denotes a category. (Section 3.2 briefly discussed nominal and ordinal categorical data.) When visualizing the dataset using t-SNE [23], we found that the samples overlap significantly and are not easily separable, indicating the simulated system is fairly complex [9,28] (see Appendix C). We train ML models for MLBAC using this dataset.

### 4.2 Symbolic and Non-symbolic ML Models

Among symbolic approaches, the RF algorithm got special attention in the access control domain due to its expressiveness of a decision in the form of a rule [9, 22,35]. RF can achieve excellent performance in capturing the access control state of a system. However, if the access control state of the underlying system is complicated, a non-symbolic method such as a neural network-based system shows superior performance compared to the symbolic ones [9,28]. In this work, we develop an MLBAC administration prototype with an RF from the symbolic class to determine its efficiency from an administration perspective, which we refer to as RF-MLBAC. We also investigate another prototype with the neural network from the non-symbolic type. In particular, we consider ResNet [14] as our candidate neural network and refer to it as ResNet-MLBAC. We note that one could use other neural networks, including MLP [32], DenseNet [17], etc., although we do not anticipate any significant changes in our results.

Both RF and ResNet in MLBAC take user/resource metadata values as input to make corresponding access control decisions. Since the metadata values in our dataset are categorical, we encode them before applying them to the model [13]. Our experiment's ResNet architecture has a depth of 8, and the RF has 100 estimators (decision trees in the forest). As the dataset has four different operations, both models output the *probability* of granting the permission for a related operation. Given a feature vector $x$ of the user and resource metadata, the ML model is defined as a prediction function $f$: $\hat{y} = f(x)$, where $\hat{y}$ is the predicted label or permission (grant (1) or deny (0)) of the operation $op$, obtained from comparing the probability of granting the permission from the output of the ML model with a *threshold*. We consider a threshold of 0.5 for our experiment.

### 4.3 Administration Strategies in MLBAC

We follow multiple strategies for accommodating a given Task in MLBAC. From a Task perspective, we propose single-Task and multi-Task administration approaches. Also, we examine two learning strategies that include retraining and sequential learning. We discuss them below.

**Single-Task Administration.** We administer each Task individually and replace the current ML model ($\mathbb{F}_{current}$) with the updated model ($\mathbb{F}_{updated}$).

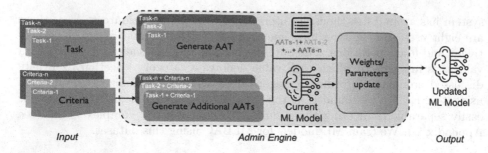

**Fig. 4.** Multi-task administration process flow in MLBAC.

In this case, we simulate that the sysadmin updates the underlying ML model after receiving any new Task. For single-Task administration, the Admin Engine determines AATs (i.e., both AAT and Additional AAT) for the given Task and then apply the generated AATs for the administration. Figure 3 is an illustration of single-Task administration.

**Multi-task Administration.** In practice, sysadmin may receive multiple unique Tasks together, or they may wait for additional Tasks to accumulate before initiating an administration. To simulate this, we investigate administrations with multiple simultaneous Tasks in MLBAC, which we refer to *multi-Task administration*. In this case, Admin Engine determines AATs for each Task individually and combines them. Then, the combined AATs are used for the administration. We use the term *Task count* to refer to the number of Tasks we consider for a multi-Task administration. Figure 4 illustrates the multi-Task administration process for n-Tasks. We experiment with 2-Tasks, 3-Tasks, and 6-Tasks administration for multi-Task administration with Task counts 2, 3, and 6.

**Retraining.** A naive solution to the administration problem could be to *retrain* an ML model based on newly generated AATs and initial training data that we used to train the $\mathbb{F}_{current}$. The idea is to train a fresh model from scratch with the dataset that combines both initial training data and the samples generated for the respective Task (AATs in case of MLBAC)), as shown in Fig. 5 (left). The trained model will replace the existing $\mathbb{F}_{current}$ model.

Retraining may not be feasible or practical for many systems due to some reasons. For instance, this process requires storing the *entire* initial training data for future administration. Also, retraining is expensive in terms of computation time and resource consumption. Model training is one of the most time-consuming parts of ML-based applications. One needs to spend the same amount of time to accommodate any new change in an existing system. Besides, retraining an ML model produces a new model that does not hold any previous history of access change and only portrays the data provided during training.

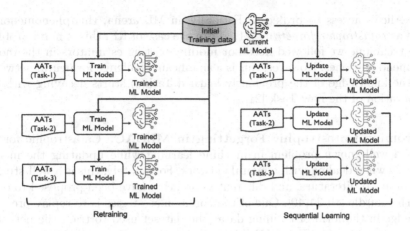

**Fig. 5.** Retraining (left) vs. sequential learning (right) strategies.

**Sequential Learning.** Sequentially learning Tasks is vital for developing an autonomous system. It reflects how a human learner identifies the materials to be learned [16,25]. We also embrace this learning phenomenon to administer MLBAC, as illustrated in Fig. 5 (right). As shown, for Task-1, the Admin Engine utilizes the $\mathbb{F}_{current}$ and AATs of Task-1 to update the existing model and generate $\mathbb{F}_{updated}$ model. This $\mathbb{F}_{updated}$ model replaces the $\mathbb{F}_{current}$ model for deciding accesses and acts as input for the Task-2 administration.

**Sequential Learning Process and Its Effect.** For sequential administration in RF, we append additional estimators that learn new changes while keeping existing estimators untouched. Even though this method is not as efficient as incremental learning in other classical approaches, we did not find any better strategy for RF in the literature. For each single-Task administration, we append two estimators in the RF model. We append 5, 8, and 10 estimators for 2-Tasks, 3-Tasks, and 6-Tasks administration, respectively. Note that we performed trial and error with more estimators; however, increasing this number of estimators was efficient in performance and model size. On the other hand, for ResNet, we employ the *fine-tuning* technique (discussed in Sect. 3.4) to incrementally learn new changes and update the network's weights accordingly.

However, one of the major challenges of sequential learning is maintaining the existing access control state unchanged. An ML model could *forget* previous knowledge while learning new information. For example, Alice has read and write access to a resource projectA, and Bob has only read access to another resource projectB. Sysadmin received a Task '*to permit Bob with the write access to projectB*'. After administering the requested Task, the system correctly updates the access control state such that Bob has both read and write access to the projectB. However, there might be a case that the updated system could not make the correct access decision for Alice to the projectA. In other words, the system *forgot* Alice's access to projectA. Formally, in ML arena, this phenomenon is known as *catastrophic forgetting* [21,40]. In the case of RF, this is not a problem as the technique we followed does not modify existing estimators in the model but append new ones. However, this is a significant challenge for neural networks since the knowledge of the previously learned Task(s) starts decaying with the incorporation of the new Task [21].

**Overcoming Catastrophic Forgetting in MLBAC.** Catastrophic forgetting is a well-known problem in machine learning while updating the model, especially when dealing with a neural network. Fortunately, this is a well-studied problem in ML literature, and different approaches have been proposed to overcome this hurdle [16,34,40]. One of the common strategies is to replay previous knowledge in the form of training data (the dataset used to train the network) with new samples (AATs in MLBAC) during fine-tuning [34]. It may not be practical to store the training data in many applications if the samples are too large (e.g., image, video, etc.). However, this is not an issue for MLBAC as it works based on numerical user and resource metadata and attributes values. In our simulated system, each training sample is a *vector* of user and resource numerical metadata. Other real-world datasets [27] are also similar, which indicates the feasibility of storing the prior training data for MLBAC. To minimize the required storing space, we reserve a quarter of all the original training samples instead of keeping the entire training dataset, which we refer to as *Replay Data*. The Admin Engine can access the Replay Data and add them during administration along with AATs for the correspondent Task. After performing an administration, we append a quarter of AATs to the Replay Data, which reflects the current task's information during the next administration. Admin Engine ensures that the AATs and Replay Data are *mutually exclusive*.

## 5    Evaluation

This section measures the performance for our simulated system to determine the feasibility and efficacy of the proposed strategies for MLBAC administration.

### 5.1    Evaluation Methodology

We experiment and evaluate administration performance in RF-MLBAC and ResNet-MLBAC prototypes on *u5k-r5k-auth12k* dataset. The dataset has around twelve thousand samples (Authorization Tuples). We use 80% of the samples for training and 20% for testing the ML models. After initial training, the trained models' (RF and ResNet) performances are above 99% for the test samples, respectively, implying that $F_{current}$ is highly accurate in making access decisions.

We create a set of Tasks to simulate that the sysadmin received all those Tasks one by one during the system's life span. To that extent, we randomly

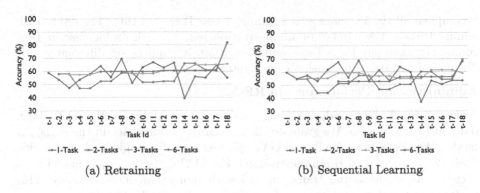

(a) Retraining                    (b) Sequential Learning

**Fig. 6.** AATs performance in RF-MLBAC. (Color figure online)

construct eighteen distinct Tasks from the $u5k$-$r5k$-$auth12k$ dataset with different kinds of Criteria (Appendix D). For example, the Task Id $t$-$1$ indicates the first Task and a Task: $\langle uid = 259, rid = 112, op3, permit \rangle$ means a user with $uid = 259$ needs $op3$ access to a resource with $rid = 112$. Also, the Criteria: $\langle umeta0 \in \{9\}, umeta6 \in \{6\}, rmeta0 \in \{9\}, rmeta3 \in \{46\} \rangle$ specifies the user whose $umeta0$ and $umeta6$ metadata values are 6 and 9, respectively, could have $op3$ access to resources with $rmeta0$ and $rmeta3$ metadata values 9 and 46, respectively. Besides, based on the Task and Criteria, the number of generated Additional AAT is 42, and combining the AAT gives an AATs of size 43. We ensure that every Task is independent concerning its change request and purpose. While updating the model, we use 80% of the AATs for training and 20% for testing the updated ML model. We have created a repository on GitHub consisting of the source code, dataset, and respective AATs, OATs, and ReplayData for each Task.[2]

We evaluate the administration performance in terms of accuracy. We define the *accuracy* as the measure (in percentage) of correct access authorization for a user to a resource with respect to the actual access control state (ground truth).

## 5.2   Results

To evaluate the administration performance in RF-MLBAC and ResNet-MLBAC, we assess how accurately the $\mathbb{F}_{\mathbf{updated}}$ model can capture the AATs (both AAT and Additional AAT). We also evaluate how well it can preserve the access control state of all other users and resources (OATs as described in Sect. 3.3).

We experiment and evaluate the performance for all eighteen Tasks with single-Task and multi-Task administrations. For multi-Task administration, we consider 2-Tasks, 3-Tasks, and 6-Tasks. For example, a 3-Tasks administration indicates, we use three different Tasks together for an administration. In the single-Task administration, it requires *eighteen* different administration to

---

[2] https://github.com/dlbac/MLBAC-Administration.

accomplish all the 18 Tasks as it administer one Task at a time. For multi-Task administration, the number of administration reduces with an increase in Task count. For example, for 3-Tasks administration, it requires six different multi-Task administrations to finish all the eighteen Tasks.

## Administration Performance in RF-MLBAC

**Retraining.** As discussed, retraining is a naive approach and inefficient for both data and computation. We evaluate the retraining performance in the $\mathbb{F}_{updated}$ model. We assess both AATs and OATs performance for single-Task and multi-Task (2, 3, and 6 Tasks) administrations. For OATs, the $\mathbb{F}_{updated}$ model is as accurate as of the initial trained model with more than 99% accuracy. This performance is consistent across all the single and multi-Tasks administrations. However, in the case of AATs, as demonstrated in Fig. 6a, the accuracy range is 40% to 80%. In almost all the circumstances, the accuracy is inconsistent except for six-Tasks administration that shows a better and more persistent result across administrations with 60% accuracy. Overall, the low AATs performance indicates that the RF model can capture only a portion of new changes while accommodating the proposed Task.

**Sequential Learning.** We perform the same evaluation for sequential learning and apply both single and multi-Tasks administrations. Similar to retraining, the OATs performance is over 99% across administrations and consistent, indicating that the RF model could preserve the existing access control state better. This excellent result indicates that the RF model did not forget the initial access control state. This result is anticipated because RF-MLBAC appends new estimators to comprehend proposed changes instead of modifying their existing estimators while learning new changes.

However, we see a very opposite scenario in AATs performance. As shown in Fig. 6b, the accuracy of AATs varies in the range of 40% to 70%. For single-Task and two-Tasks administrations (green and orange lines in the figure), the AATs performance seems highly inconsistent compared to what we see for six-Tasks administration (blue line). However, the accuracy of six-Tasks administration is about 55%, which indicates that considering many Tasks together for a single administration may not provide a better result. On the contrary, the three-Tasks administration shows a consistent performance with around 60% accuracy across Tasks, suggesting an RF model's multi-Tasks administration with around three Tasks could be a potential administration to consider.

## Administration performance in ResNet-MLBAC

**Sequential Learning.** Training a neural network from scratch is computationally costly, which is neither efficient nor feasible in access control. As a result, we did not take the naive (retraining) approach for this prototype. To begin with administration in ResNet-MLBAC, we administer the first three Tasks (t-1 to t-3) as a single-Task administration without providing any Replay Data to see the impact of sequential learning in the existing access control state. As

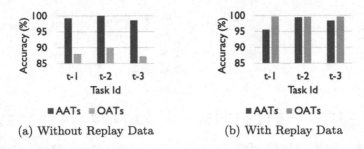

(a) Without Replay Data               (b) With Replay Data

**Fig. 7.** Administration Performance in ResNet-MLBAC for Sequential Learning.

shown in Fig. 7a, the updated network captures the authorization for AATs with excellent accuracy, as opposed to what we observed in RF-MLBAC. However, for OATs, we see a lower accuracy (below 90%) in all three cases, indicating the network forgot (catastrophic forgetting) the access control state of a good amount of existing users and resources while learning new information. To overcome that, we apply Replay Data (as discussed in Sect. 4.3) along with AATs during administration. Figure 7b illustrates that combining Replay Data with AATs helps ResNet-MLBAC administration to significantly reduce the catastrophic forgetting. As shown in the figure, the accuracy of OATs is now above 99% across all three Tasks. Such a significant increase in OAT performance implies the remarkable impact of Replay Data in overcoming catastrophic forgetting.

Further, we experiment with all eighteen Tasks for single and multi-Task administrations. Figure 8a and Fig. 8b demonstrate the performance of AATs and OATs, respectively. As illustrated, the AATs performance range is 96% to 99% accuracy, significantly better than what we observed in the RF-MLBAC. As we see in the figures, for both AATs and OATs, the performance of 6-Tasks administration is low compared to other multi-Task administrations. Such inferior results indicate the infeasibility of using many Tasks under a multi-Task administration in ResNet-MLBAC administration. Similarly, the performance of AATs in single-Task administration is inconsistent across all the Tasks, which signifies that using single-Task administration in ResNet-MLBAC may produce very unstable performance. However, for both 2-Tasks and 3-Tasks multi-Task administrations, the result is persistent and progressing for both AATs and OATs, thereby proving feasible and better for ResNet-MLBAC administration.

**Summary of Performance in RF-MLBAC and ResNet-MLBAC.** Based on AATs and OATs performance in both prototypes, it is evident that the RF-MLBAC shows better results in preserving the existing access control state. It was expected as we did not change the estimators of the initial RF model. However, the AATs performance in RF-MLBAC is extremely low, indicating it could not well capture proposed changes. Besides, it has other drawbacks from model size and optimization perspectives. The size of the trained model gradually grows with the addition of new estimators in it. Also, each administration needs trial

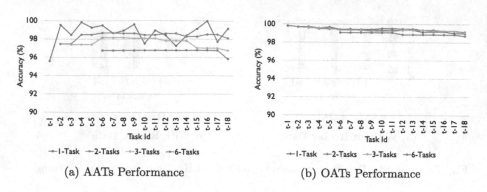

(a) AATs Performance              (b) OATs Performance

**Fig. 8.** Performance in ResNet-MLBAC.

and error to determine an optimal number of new estimators to append that correlates with how many Task one consider for a multi-Task administration. On the other hand, ResNet-MLBAC administration shows a better accuracy for AATs and comparable performance in OATs, indicating it could better capture proposed changes while retaining the existing access control state intact.

**Administration Cost Evaluation in RF-MLBAC and ResNet-MLBAC**
We evaluate administration costs for both administration prototypes concerning computation time for an administration. We observe that RF-MLBAC administration generally takes less than a second to complete an administration (considering a maximum of 18 Tasks for an administration). On the contrary, ResNet-MLBAC administration is slower than RF-MLBAC and varies with the increase of Tasks count for each administration, as depicted in Fig. 9. We measure the computation cost of single-Task and multi-Task administrations in ResNet-MLBAC to identify how administration time varies with the increase in *Task count* and how many Tasks are feasible for a single administration. We consider different sizes (1, 3, 6, 9, 12, 15, and 18 Tasks) multi-Task administration.

As shown in Fig. 9, it needs 10 s for a single-Task administration, which is the same for 3, 6, and 9-Tasks administrations, and becomes double for 12, 15, and 18-Tasks administrations. From a performance perspective, for 3 and 6-Tasks administrations, we see a balanced accuracy in AATs and OATs. Such results suggest the feasibility of using multi-Task administration in ResNet-MLBAC. However, considering many Tasks together (e.g., 12 or 15-Tasks administration) decreases the OATs performance, justifying the infeasibility of administering too many Tasks together under a single administration.

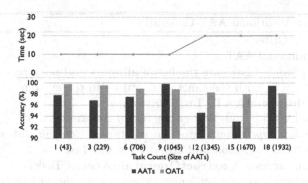

**Fig. 9.** Administration cost in ResNet-MLBAC for sequential learning.

# 6   Conclusion

This paper explores the access control administration problem for MLBAC. We review administration requirements in the same context and propose an administrative framework for MLBAC administration. We implement two prototypes, RF-MLBAC and ResNet-MLBAC, on a simulated system applying ML algorithms from symbolic and non-symbolic classes. Due to the uniqueness of the MLBAC administration problem, there are many underlying challenges, such as insufficient learning of the proposed changes and forgetting existing access information. We propose different strategies to overcome them. Also, we thoroughly evaluate both prototypes. Our empirical results summarize that the non-symbolic approach performs better than the symbolic one while adjusting for new changes in MLBAC administration.

**Acknowledgements.** We would like to thank the CREST Center For Security And Privacy Enhanced Cloud Computing (C-SPECC) through the National Science Foundation (NSF) (Grant Award #1736209) and the NSF Division of Computer and Network Systems (CNS) (Grant Award #1553696) for their support and contributions to this research.

# A   Additional AAT Generation

We depict the pseudo-code of Additional AAT generation in Algorithm 1.

# B   Data Generation

In our earlier work [28], we simulate a system using the data generation approach proposed by Xu et al. [39]. The algorithm generates a set of attributes for users and resources and a set of *rules* based on those attributes. Each *rule* is a tuple of the form $\langle UAE, RAE, OP, C \rangle$, where $UAE$ is the user attribute expression, $RAE$ is the resource attribute expression, $C$ is the set of constraints, and $OP$ is a set

---

**Algorithm 1:** Additional AAT Generation

---

**inputs:** Task, Criteria
**output:** Additional AAT
**data:** uList[ ] and rList[ ] are the list of all users and resources,
       respectively, with their metadata values in the system
**generateAdditionalAAT** (Task, Criteria)
   | additionalAAT[ ] = $\emptyset$ //An empty list of Additional AAT
   | //The extractOperationAccess is a utility function that takes a Task,
   | //and returns operation and access from the Task
   | $operation_t$, $access_t$ = **extractOperationAccess**(Task)
   | //getSimilarUsers and getSimilarResources are the utility functions
   | //that take list of all users and resources, respectively,
   | //and the Criteria, and return similar users and resources
   | candidateUsers[ ] = **getSimilarUsers**(uList, Criteria)
   | candidateResources[ ] = **getSimilarResources**(rList, Criteria)
   | //getAccessOperations is a utility function that takes a user and
   | //resource, returns user's set of access operations to the resource
   | **foreach** $user_c$ **in** candidateUsers **do**
   |   | **foreach** $resource_c$ **in** candidateResources **do**
   |   |   | $Op_c$[ ] = **getAccessOperations**($user_c$, $resource_c$)
   |   |   | **if** $Op_c \neq \emptyset$ **then**
   |   |   |   | **if** ($access_t$ = permit AND $operation_t$ **not in** $Op_c$) OR
   |   |   |   | ($access_t$ = deny AND $operation_t$ **in** $Op_c$) **then**
   |   |   |   |   | cAAT [ ] = $\emptyset$
   |   |   |   |   | cAAT.append($user_c$)
   |   |   |   |   | cAAT.append($resource_c$)
   |   |   |   |   | **if** $access_t$ = permit **then**
   |   |   |   |   |   | $Op_c$.append($operation_t$)
   |   |   |   |   | **else**
   |   |   |   |   |   | $Op_c$.remove($operation_t$)
   |   |   |   |   | **end**
   |   |   |   |   | cAAT.append($Op_c$)
   |   |   |   |   | additionalAAT.append(cAAT)
   |   |   |   | **end**
   |   |   | **end**
   |   | **end**
   | **end**
   | **return** additionalAAT

---

of operations. The attribute expressions express the sets of users and resources to which a rule applies. A user will be authorized to operate on a resource if the user satisfies the UAE, the resource satisfies the RAE, and both the user and resource meet the constraint stated in the rule. For each rule, the algorithm generates a set of users that satisfy the rule and then generates resources where for each resource, there is at least one user available to satisfy the rule.

Finally, we create (or update if it already exists) an Authorization Tuple with a new operation for each generated user, resource, and operation combination that satisfies a rule. Each user and resource has eight user metadata and eight resource metadata in the simulated system. Also, there are four different operations (*op1, op2, op3, op4*) in the system, where a user could have access to one or more operations to a resource. For example, an Authorization Tuple for a user with uid = 101 and a resource with rid = 212 with {op1, op3} access is mapped in the dataset as ⟨101|212|*3 9 2 6 13 19 30 55* | *10 21 78 3 9 13 29 23* |⟨*1 0 1 0*⟩⟩, where *3 9 2 6 13 19 30 55* and *10 21 78 3 9 13 29 23* represents user's and resource's eight metadata values, respectively.

## C    Dataset Visualization

We visualize the *u5k-r5k-auth12k* dataset using the t-SNE plot [23]. We project 16 user-resource metadata to 2-dimensional feature space and plot them in Fig. 10. The plot's samples (represented by dots) overlap significantly. Users with similar metadata values have different access and are not easily separable.

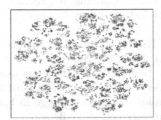

**Fig. 10.** t-SNE visualization of the *u5k-r5k-auth12k* Dataset.

## D    List of Simulated Task and Criteria

We simulate eighteen distinct Tasks from the *u5k-r5k-auth12k* dataset with different kinds of Criteria and report them in Table 1.

**Table 1.** List of task and criteria.

| Task Id | Task | Criteria | Size of AATs |
|---|---|---|---|
| t-1 | $\langle uid = 259, rid = 112, op3, permit \rangle$ | $\langle umeta0 \in \{9\}, umeta6 \in \{6\}, rmeta0 \in \{9\}, rmeta3 \in \{46\} \rangle$ | 43 |
| t-2 | $\langle uid = 4624, rid = 4634, op4, deny \rangle$ | $\langle umeta2 \in \{58, 49\}, umeta3 \in \{39\}, rmeta3 \in \{39\} \rangle$ | 94 |
| t-3 | $\langle uid = 1992, rid = 1858, op1, permit \rangle$ | $\langle umeta2 \in \{11\}, rmeta2 \in \{11\}, rmeta3 \in \{48, 91\} \rangle$ | 92 |
| t-4 | $\langle uid = 5049, rid = 5177, op4, permit \rangle$ | $\langle umeta1 \in \{6\}, umeta4 \in \{47, 71\}, rmeta1 \in \{6\} \rangle$ | 215 |
| t-5 | $\langle uid = 2034, rid = 2041, op2, deny \rangle$ | $\langle umeta4 \in \{10\}, rmeta1 \in \{6, 10\}, rmeta4 \in \{10\} \rangle$ | 75 |
| t-6 | $\langle uid = 1348, rid = 1083, op2, permit \rangle$ | $\langle umeta3 \in \{46, 50, 53\}, umeta5 \in \{13\}, rmeta3 \in \{46, 50, 53\}, rmeta5 \in \{13\} \rangle$ | 187 |
| t-7 | $\langle uid = 1345, rid = 1092, op4, permit \rangle$ | $\langle umeta0 \in \{24, 64\}, umeta6 \in \{7\}, rmeta0 \in \{24, 64\}, rmeta6 \in \{7\} \rangle$ | 139 |
| t-8 | $\langle uid = 442, rid = 580, op3, permit \rangle$ | $\langle umeta3 \in \{49\}, umeta5 \in \{47, 111\}, rmeta5 \in \{47, 111\}, rmeta7 \in \{49\} \rangle$ | 134 |
| t-9 | $\langle uid = 2599, rid = 2593, op1, permit \rangle$ | $\langle umeta0 \in \{11\}, umeta1 \in \{17\}, rmeta0 \in \{11\}, rmeta1 \in \{17\} \rangle$ | 66 |
| t-10 | $\langle uid = 4112, rid = 1241, op2, permit \rangle$ | $\langle umeta1 \in \{18\}, rmeta1 \in \{18\}, rmeta3 \in \{45, 47, 113\} \rangle$ | 75 |
| t-11 | $\langle uid = 2135, rid = 4875, op3, deny \rangle$ | $\langle umeta2 \in \{13\}, umeta4 \in \{71, 96\}, rmeta2 \in \{13\}, rmeta4 \in \{71, 96\} \rangle$ | 118 |
| t-12 | $\langle uid = 660, rid = 560, op1, permit \rangle$ | $\langle umeta3 \in \{88\}, umeta5 \in \{48, 111\}, rmeta5 \in \{48, 111\}, rmeta7 \in \{88\} \rangle$ | 107 |
| t-13 | $\langle uid = 2019, rid = 2056, op2, permit \rangle$ | $\langle umeta4 \in \{12\}, rmeta1 \in \{78, 82\}, rmeta4 \in \{12\} \rangle$ | 121 |
| t-14 | $\langle uid = 1228, rid = 1088, op1, permit \rangle$ | $\langle umeta2 \in \{11, 63\}, umeta5 \in \{20\}, rmeta5 \in \{20\} \rangle$ | 97 |
| t-15 | $\langle uid = 2825, rid = 3044, op2, permit \rangle$ | $\langle umeta6 \in \{8\}, rmeta1 \notin \{6, 10\}, rmeta2 \in \{61, 62\}, rmeta6 \in \{8\} \rangle$ | 107 |
| t-16 | $\langle uid = 965, rid = 861, op4, permit \rangle$ | $\langle umeta3 \in \{45\}, umeta7 \in \{20\}, rmeta3 \in \{45\}, rmeta6 \in \{20\} \rangle$ | 63 |
| t-17 | $\langle uid = 3745, rid = 3843, op3, permit \rangle$ | $\langle umeta0 \in \{31\}, umeta6 \in \{2, 5, 9, 18\}, umeta7 \in \{4, 13\}, rmeta0 \in \{31\} \rangle$ | 83 |
| t-18 | $\langle uid = 2488, rid = 2495, op3, permit \rangle$ | $\langle umeta1 \in \{58\}, rmeta1 \in \{58\}, rmeta2 \in \{58, 61\} \rangle$ | 116 |

# References

1. Abu Jabal, A., et al.: Polisma - a framework for learning attribute-based access control policies. In: Chen, L., Li, N., Liang, K., Schneider, S. (eds.) ESORICS 2020. LNCS, vol. 12308, pp. 523–544. Springer, Cham (2020). https://doi.org/10.1007/978-3-030-58951-6_26

2. Alkhresheh, A., Elgazzar, K., Hassanein, H.S.: Adaptive access control policies for IoT deployments. In: IEEE IWCMC (2020)

3. Alohaly, M., Takabi, H., Blanco, E.: A deep learning approach for extracting attributes of ABAC policies. In: ACM SACMAT (2018)

4. Amazon, K.: Amazon employee access challenge in Kaggle (2013). https://www.kaggle.com/c/amazon-employee-access-challenge/

5. Amazon, U.: Amazon access samples data set (2011). http://archive.ics.uci.edu/ml/datasets/Amazon+Access+Samples

6. Argento, L., Margheri, A., Paci, F., Sassone, V., Zannone, N.: Towards adaptive access control. In: Kerschbaum, F., Paraboschi, S. (eds.) DBSec 2018. LNCS, vol. 10980, pp. 99–109. Springer, Cham (2018). https://doi.org/10.1007/978-3-319-95729-6_7

7. Benczúr, A.A., et al.: Online machine learning in big data streams. arXiv (2018)

8. Breiman, L.: Random forests. Mach. Learn. **45**, 5–32 (2001). https://doi.org/10.1023/A:1010933404324

9. Cappelletti, L., Valtolina, S., Valentini, G., et al.: On the quality of classification models for inferring ABAC policies from access logs. In: IEEE Big Data (2019)

10. Chang, C.C., Lin, I.C., Liao, C.T.: An access control system with time-constraint using support vector machines. Int. J. Netw. Secur. **2**(2), 150–159 (2006)

11. Cortes, C., Vapnik, V.: Support-vector networks. Mach. Learn. **20**, 273–297 (1995). https://doi.org/10.1007/BF00994018

12. Gumma, V., Mitra, B., Dey, S., Patel, P.S., Suman, S., Das, S.: PAMMELA: policy administration methodology using machine learning. arXiv (2021)

13. Hancock, J.T., Khoshgoftaar, T.M.: Survey on categorical data for neural networks. J. Big Data **7**(1), 1–41 (2020). https://doi.org/10.1186/s40537-020-00305-w

14. He, K., et al.: Deep residual learning for image recognition. In: IEEE CVPR (2016)
15. Hu, V.C., Ferraiolo, D., et al.: Guide to attribute based access control (ABAC) definition and considerations (draft). NIST Special Publication (2013)
16. Hu, W., et al.: Overcoming catastrophic forgetting for continual learning via model adaptation. In: ICLR (2018)
17. Huang, G., Liu, Z., Van Der Maaten, L., Weinberger, K.Q.: Densely connected convolutional networks. In: IEEE CVPR (2017)
18. Jha, S., Sural, S., Atluri, V., Vaidya, J.: An administrative model for collaborative management of ABAC systems and its security analysis. In: IEEE CIC (2016)
19. Karimi, L., Abdelhakim, M., Joshi, J.: Adaptive ABAC policy learning: a reinforcement learning approach. arXiv (2021)
20. Kaya, A., et al.: Analysis of transfer learning for deep neural network based plant classification models. Comput. Electron. Agric. **158**, 20–29 (2019)
21. Kirkpatrick, J., Pascanu, R., Rabinowitz, N., Veness, J., et al.: Overcoming catastrophic forgetting in neural networks. National Academy of Sciences (2017)
22. Liu, A., Du, X., Wang, N.: Efficient access control permission decision engine based on machine learning. Secur. Commun. Netw. **2021** (2021)
23. Van der Maaten, L., Hinton, G.: Visualizing data using t-SNE. JMLR **9**(11)(2008)
24. Martin, E., Xie, T.: Inferring access-control policy properties via machine learning. In: IEEE POLICY (2006)
25. McCloskey, M., Cohen, N.J.: Catastrophic interference in connectionist networks: the sequential learning problem. In: Psychology of Learning and Motivation (1989)
26. Ni, Q., Lobo, J., Calo, S., Rohatgi, P., Bertino, E.: Automating role-based provisioning by learning from examples. In: ACM SACMAT (2009)
27. Nobi, M.N., Gupta, M., Praharaj, L., Abdelsalam, M., Krishnan, R., Sandhu, R.: Machine learning in access control: a taxonomy and survey. arXiv (2022)
28. Nobi, M.N., Krishnan, R., Huang, Y., Shakarami, M., Sandhu, R.: Toward deep learning based access control. In: ACM CODASPY (2022)
29. Safavian, S.R., Landgrebe, D.: A survey of decision tree classifier methodology. IEEE Trans. Syst. Man Cybern. **21**, 660–674 (1991)
30. Sandhu, R., Munawer, Q.: The ARBAC99 model for administration of roles. In: IEEE ACSAC (1999)
31. Sandhu, R.S., et al.: Role-based access control models. Computer **29**, 38–47 (1996)
32. Schmidhuber, J.: Deep learning in neural networks: an overview. Neural Netw. **61**, 85–117 (2015)
33. Servos, D., Osborn, S.L.: Current research and open problems in attribute-based access control. ACM Comput. Surv. (CSUR) **49**, 1–45 (2017)
34. Shin, H., et al.: Continual learning with deep generative replay. arXiv (2017)
35. Srivastava, K., Shekokar, N.: Machine learning based risk-adaptive access control system to identify genuineness of the requester. In: Gunjan, V.K., Zurada, J.M., Raman, B., Gangadharan, G.R. (eds.) Modern Approaches in Machine Learning and Cognitive Science: A Walkthrough. SCI, vol. 885, pp. 129–143. Springer, Cham (2020). https://doi.org/10.1007/978-3-030-38445-6_10
36. Stoller, S.D.: An administrative model for relationship-based access control. In: Samarati, P. (ed.) DBSec 2015. LNCS, vol. 9149, pp. 53–68. Springer, Cham (2015). https://doi.org/10.1007/978-3-319-20810-7_4
37. Tajbakhsh, N., Shin, J.Y., et al.: Convolutional neural networks for medical image analysis: full training or fine tuning? IEEE Trans. Med. Imaging **35**, 1299–1312 (2016)
38. Xiang, C., Wu, Y., Shen, B., Shen, M., et al.: Towards continuous access control validation and forensics. In: CCS. ACM (2019)

39. Xu, Z., Stoller, S.D.: Mining attribute-based access control policies. TDSC **12**, 533–545 (2014)
40. Yoon, J., Yang, E., Lee, J., Hwang, S.J.: Lifelong learning with dynamically expandable networks. arXiv (2017)
41. Zhang, Y., Cheung, Y.M.: An ordinal data clustering algorithm with automated distance learning. In: AAAI Conference on Artificial Intelligence (2020)

# Real-Time Policy Enforcement with Metric First-Order Temporal Logic

François Hublet[✉][iD], David Basin[iD], and Srđan Krstić[iD]

Institute of Information Security, Department of Computer Science, ETH Zürich,
Zurich, Switzerland
{francois.hublet,basin,srdan.krstic}@inf.ethz.ch

**Abstract.** Correctness and regulatory compliance of today's software systems are crucial for our safety and security. This can be achieved with policy enforcement: the process of monitoring and possibly modifying system behavior to satisfy a given policy. The enforcer's capabilities determine which policies are enforceable.

We study the enforceability of policies specified in metric first-order temporal logic (MFOTL) with enforcers that can cause and suppress different system actions in real time. We consider an expressive safety fragment of MFOTL and show that a policy from that fragment is enforceable if and only if it is equivalent to a policy in a simpler, syntactically defined MFOTL fragment. We then propose an enforcement algorithm for all monitorable policies from the latter fragment, and show that our EnfPoly enforcer outperforms state-of-the-art tools.

## 1 Introduction

Modern software systems are increasingly complex, ubiquitous and intransparent. In this context, allowing individuals to scrutinize and control the systems that affect their daily lives is an important technical and societal challenge. To achieve this goal it is crucial to develop systems that can *monitor* and *control* other target systems, by enforcing *policies* that describe the acceptable target system's behaviors.

Policy enforcement [54], depicted in Fig. 1, is a form of execution monitoring where a system, called an *enforcer*, observes a target system's actions, *detects* attempted policy violations, and reacts to *prevent* them. In contrast, policy monitoring (or runtime verification) [7,26] provides *monitors* that only passively detect policy violations by the target system. Both problems have offline and online variants: the former considers a trace of recorded target system actions, while the latter observes the target system in real time.

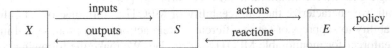

An enforcer $E$ observes actions in a target system $S$ and reacts (e.g., causes or suppresses some actions in $S$) to ensure policy compliance. $S$ interacts with an environment $X$, which $E$ cannot control.

**Fig. 1.** Policy enforcement

The original version of this chapter was revised: figure-1 was corrected. The correction to this chapter is available at https://doi.org/10.1007/978-3-031-17146-8_36

V. Atluri et al. (Eds.): ESORICS 2022, LNCS 13555, pp. 211–232, 2022.
https://doi.org/10.1007/978-3-031-17146-8_11

Policy enforcement has been studied in different communities (Sect. 2) like controller synthesis [1,46,47], security [4,54], and operating systems [51,52], each defining and solving the problem in a different, specialized context.

Schneider [54] studied the general form of the policy enforcement problem in the context of security. He proposed security automata as enforcers that, when composed with the target system, prevent policy violations by simply terminating it. Schneider, and later others [11], identified classes of policies that were *enforceable* using such an enforcer. As policy enforceability depends on the enforcer's powers over the target system (e.g., its ability to suppress, cause, or delay system's actions), other enforceable policy classes have been suggested [9].

Automata and temporal logic are popular formalisms for policy specification. Existing security policy enforcers typically focus on propositional policies expressed as variants of (security, edit, or timed) automata [27]. In contrast, controller synthesis tools [6] also enforce specifications expressed in LTL [16] or in (fragments of) metric temporal logics [17,19,32,40]. However, automata and propositional temporal logic are limited in their expressiveness: they regard system actions as atomic and thus cannot formulate dependencies between the data values coming from an infinite domain that the actions may carry as parameters. For instance, a data value may contain personally identifiable information, and then each system action that uses the value should be preceded by an action that receives a consent for the value's particular use [5]. To the best of our knowledge, there is no tool that supports enforcement for first-order logic specifications.

In this paper, we consider the online policy enforcement (Sect. 3) of policies expressed in metric first-order temporal logic (MFOTL) [20], which extends LTL with metric constraints and first-order quantification (Sect. 4). To enforce MFOTL policies, our enforcer can observe the target system in real time, actively cause or suppress different types of actions, and only observe other actions of the target system. As enforcer must react in real time, policies must be such that their satisfaction does not depend on future information. All actions, caused either by the enforcer or the target system, are instantaneous and tagged with a timestamp.

We therefore consider two "well-behaved" fragments of MFOTL: (1) we study enforceability of $\mathrm{MFOTL}_{\Box}^{\mathcal{F}}$, a safety fragment of MFOTL comprising closed formulae of the form $\Box\varphi$ ("always $\varphi$") where $\varphi$'s satisfaction does not depend on future information; and (2) we design an efficient enforcement algorithm for *monitorable* and enforceable $\mathrm{MFOTL}_{\Box}^{\mathcal{F}}$ formulae. Violations of monitorable formulae [12] can be detected by manipulating only finite sets of satisfying valuations. As these sets are always finite, we can use simple, yet efficient, data structures and reuse the existing, highly-optimized monitoring algorithm for monitorable MFOTL formulae [13].

Overall, we characterize the enforceability of $\mathrm{MFOTL}_{\Box}^{\mathcal{F}}$ formulae by an enforcer with the ability to suppress or cause different system actions, and propose and implement an enforcer for monitorable $\mathrm{MFOTL}_{\Box}^{\mathcal{F}}$ formulae. We make the following contributions:

- For an enforcer with the ability to suppress or cause (disjoint sets of) actions, we characterize enforceability of $\mathrm{MFOTL}_{\Box}^{\mathcal{F}}$ formulae. We show that it is undecidable whether an $\mathrm{MFOTL}_{\Box}^{\mathcal{F}}$ formula is enforceable and propose an expressively complete syntactical approximation (Sect. 5).

- We develop an enforcement algorithm for monitorable MFOTL$_\Box^{\mathcal{F}}$ formulae and prove its correctness (Sect. 6).
- Finally, we describe our enforcer's implementation (Sect. 7) and evaluate its time and memory usage against other state-of-the-art tools (Sect. 8).

The proofs of all lemmas and theorems can be found in our extended report [35].

## 2  Related Work

We group related work into conceptual approaches and those that implement enforcers.

*Theory.* The policy enforcement problem was studied by Schneider and Erlingsson in the context of security [24,54]. Schneider defined security automata, a class of Büchi automata, as enforcers. Violations were prevented by terminating the system. Bauer *et al.* [14] extended Schneider's work by considering enforcers that can suppress and cause events. Basin *et al.* [11] distinguished between suppressable and (only-)observable events and refined Schneider's enforceability accordingly, but only discussed enforcement via suppression. Falcone *et al.* [25] later studied the enforcement of propositional timed policies by suppressing and delaying events. Recently, Aceto *et al.* [2] proposed *bidirectional* enforcers that treat input and output system actions differently. We see this distinction as a more refined event type partition (Sect. 3).

Policy enforcement is closely related to the controller synthesis problem [46], where a controller ($\approx$ enforcer) wants to ensure compliance of a plant ($\approx$ system) with a specification ($\approx$ policy). Specification *realizability* corresponds to enforceability, while controller synthesis (i.e., generating an automaton from a specification) corresponds to generating an enforcement algorithm tailored to a particular specification. Our enforcer does not explicitly generate code for a specific policy, but rather takes the policy directly as input. Early work by Pnueli, Rosner and Abadi [1,46,47] studied LTL realizability and LTL (controller) synthesis. More efficient approaches later emerged [29,39,53], as well as techniques for timed automata [6] and metric extensions of LTL [17,19,32,40].

*Tools.* Policy enforcement approaches typically rely on different classes of automata both as enforcers and as policies [11,14,21,24,25,27,28,41,42,45,49,50,54]. A recent survey [26] listed three enforcement tools: GREP [49], Proactive Libraries [50], and TiPEX [45]. Both GREP and TiPEX use timed automata as a specification language, and could thus support propositional temporal logics like MITL [3] via conversion to timed automata [18,43]. They do not, however, natively support temporal logic.

The state-of-the-art MonPoly tool [13] can detect violations of monitorable MFOTL policies [12]. Other tools for first-order temporal logics include Verimon [8,38,55] and DejaVu [30,31], none of which supports enforcement to prevent violations.

Many controller synthesis tools have been developed for LTL like Lily [36], Unbeast [23], Acacia+ [16] and SSyft [56]. Other tools synthesize controllers for systems described by timed automata to comply with specifications written in TCTL [15, 44], MTL [32], or its fragment MTL$_{0,\infty}$ [40]. BluSTL [22,48] is a MATLAB toolbox for generating controllers from signal temporal logic (STL) specifications. None of these tools supports first-order logic.

# 3   Policy Enforcement

We fix a signature $\Sigma = (\mathbb{D}, \mathbb{E}, a)$, containing an infinite set $\mathbb{D}$ of constant symbols, a finite set of *event names* $\mathbb{E}$, and an arity function $a : \mathbb{E} \to \mathbb{N}$. An *event* is a pair $(e, (d_1, \ldots, d_{a(e)})) \in \mathbb{E} \times \mathbb{D}^{a(e)}$ of an event name $e$ and $a(e)$ arguments.

Events model system actions *observable* by the enforcer. While some of these observable events can also be controlled (i.e., suppressed or caused) by the enforcer, others can *only* be observed. To capture these different cases, we partition $\mathbb{E}$ into two sets: a set of controllable event names, and a set of only-observable event names. Among the controllable event names, we further distinguish between *suppressable* event names $\mathsf{Sup} \subseteq \mathbb{E}$ and *causable* event names $\mathsf{Cau} \subseteq \mathbb{E}$. The set of only-observable event names is $\mathsf{Obs} = (\mathbb{E} \setminus \mathsf{Sup}) \setminus \mathsf{Cau}$. In general, some controllable events might be both suppressable and causable. However, we will assume that no such events exist, i.e. $\mathsf{Sup} \cap \mathsf{Cau} = \emptyset$. Our reason for this will become apparent when we consider MFOTL policy enforcement (Sect. 6), and we will discuss ways in which this assumption can be relaxed.

*Example 1.* As a running example, consider the signature $(\mathbb{N}, \{\mathtt{Open}, \mathtt{Close}, \mathtt{Knock}\}, a)$, where $a(\cdot) = 1$, $\mathsf{Sup} = \{\mathtt{Open}\}$, and $\mathsf{Cau} = \{\mathtt{Close}\}$. The target system controls a set of doors indexed by integers, which an enforcer can mechanically close or keep closed, but not hold open. Each door $i$ is equipped with a sensor that causes a $\mathtt{Knock}(i)$ event whenever a human knocks on the door. $\mathtt{Knock}$ events are only-observable ($\mathsf{Obs} = \{\mathtt{Knock}\}$), since they reflect the environment's behavior.

Given a signature $\Sigma$, we define the set of *(event) databases* $\mathbb{DB}^*$ as $2^{\{(e,d) \mid e \in \mathbb{E}, \, d \in \mathbb{D}^{a(e)}\}}$. Databases represent structures over $\Sigma$. We restrict ourselves to considering *automatic* databases, i.e., databases that can be represented by a collection of finite automata [37]. This setup is the most general one used for MFOTL monitoring in [12].

**Definition 1 (Automatic Event Database).** *An event database $D$ is automatic iff for all $e \in \mathbb{E}$, $D \cap \{(e,d) \mid d \in \mathbb{D}^{a(e)}\}$ is a regular set. $\mathbb{DB}$ is the set of automatic event databases.*

Finally, for any $E \subseteq \mathbb{E}$, we denote by $\mathsf{Ev}(E)$ the set of all databases with event names in $E$ only, i.e. $\mathsf{Ev}(E) := \{D \in \mathbb{DB} \mid \forall (e, (d_1, \ldots, d_{a(e)})) \in D. \, e \in E\}$.

*Traces* are finite or infinite sequences $\sigma = (\tau_i, D_i)_{1 \leq i \leq k}$, $k \in \mathbb{N} \cup \{\infty\}$, where $\tau_i \in \mathbb{N}$ are nondecreasing timestamps, and $D_i \in \mathbb{DB}$ are databases. The smallest timestamp of a trace $\sigma$ is denoted by $\mathsf{sts}(\sigma) = \tau_1 \in \mathbb{N}$, its largest timestamp is denoted by $\mathsf{lts}(\sigma) = \sup_{1 \leq i \leq k} \tau_i \in \mathbb{N} \cup \{\infty\}$. The empty trace is denoted by $\varepsilon$, the set of traces by $\mathbb{T}$, and the set of finite traces by $\mathbb{T}_f = \{\sigma \in \mathbb{T} \mid |\sigma| < \infty\}$. If $\sigma, \sigma'$ are two traces such that $\sigma$ is finite, $\sigma \cdot \sigma'$ denotes the concatenation of $\sigma$ and $\sigma'$. A *(trace) property* is a subset $P \subseteq \mathbb{T}$. For all $\sigma, \sigma' \in \mathbb{T}$, we write $\sigma \preceq \sigma'$ iff $\sigma$ is a prefix of $\sigma'$, and denote by $\mathsf{pre}(\sigma)$ the set of all prefixes of $\sigma$. The *limit closure* of a set $A \subseteq \mathbb{T}$, denoted by $\mathsf{cl}(A)$, contains all traces whose finite prefixes are all in $A$, i.e., $\mathsf{cl}(A) = \{\sigma \in \mathbb{T} \mid \forall \sigma' \in \mathsf{pre}(\sigma). \, |\sigma'| < \infty \Rightarrow \sigma' \in A\}$. The *truncation* of $A$ is $\mathsf{trunc}(A) = \{\sigma \in A \mid \mathsf{pre}(\sigma) \subseteq A\}$, the largest prefix-closed subset of $A$.

Finite databases $\mathbb{DB}^\dagger \subseteq \mathbb{DB}$ are a specific type of automatic databases. We also consider traces with finite databases $\mathbb{T}^\dagger \subseteq \mathbb{T}$, and finite traces with finite databases $\mathbb{T}^\dagger_f$. We now extend the definition of enforceability [11] to support causable events.

**Definition 2 (Enforceability).** *A property $P \subseteq \mathbb{T}$ is enforceable iff there is a deterministic Turing machine (TM) $\mathcal{M}$ accepting a set of finite traces $S$ such that*

*(i)* $\mathsf{cl}(\mathsf{trunc}(S)) = P$;
*(ii)* $\mathcal{M}$ *accepts* $\varepsilon$;
*(iii)* *For all* $\sigma \in \mathsf{trunc}(S)$, $\tau \geq \mathsf{lts}(\sigma)$, *and* $D \in \mathbb{DB}$, $\mathcal{M}$ *halts on* $\sigma \cdot ((\tau, D))$; *and*
*(iv)* *For all* $\sigma \in \mathsf{trunc}(S)$, $\tau \geq \mathsf{lts}(\sigma)$, *and* $D \in \mathbb{DB}$, *there exists* $S \in \mathsf{Ev}(\mathsf{Sup})$ *and* $C \in \mathsf{Ev}(\mathsf{Cau})$ *such that* $\mathcal{M}$ *accepts* $\sigma \cdot ((\tau, (D \setminus S) \cup C))$.

Properties are sets of infinite traces, while enforcers (that do not know the system's implementation) can only observe finite traces. Hence, an enforceable property must be checked "prefix-wise": a trace is in a property iff an enforcer accepts all of its prefixes. Enforceable properties must hold on the empty trace, i.e., the system must initially comply with the property. For any extension of a (non-violating) prefix, the enforcer must be able to decide on its compliance to the property. Whenever a valid prefix is extended with an additional database, there must exist sets of suppressable and causable events which the enforcer can respectively suppress and cause to ensure satisfaction of the property.

Our notion of enforceability implies safety:

**Lemma 1.** *Any enforceable property $P \subseteq \mathbb{T}$ is a safety property.*

The converse is not true: a safety property that requires that no Knock event ever happens is not enforceable, as Knock events are only-observable and cannot be suppressed.

An *enforcer* can be seen as a Turing machine that, given a finite trace, returns a pair of sets of events to be respectively suppressed and caused in the last database of the trace, with the additional requirement that events to be suppressed (resp. caused) should be suppressable (resp. causable) and present (resp. not already present) in this database.

**Definition 3 (Enforcer).** *An* enforcer *is a computable function* $\mu : \mathbb{T}_f \to \mathbb{DB} \times \mathbb{DB}$ *such that for all* $\sigma \in \mathbb{T}_f$, $\tau \geq \mathsf{lts}(\sigma)$, $D \in \mathbb{DB}$, *and* $(B, C) = \mu(\sigma \cdot ((\tau, D)))$:

*(i)* *For all* $(e, d) \in B$, $e \in \mathsf{Sup}$ *and* $(e, d) \in D$; *and*
*(ii)* *For all* $(e, d) \in C$, $e \in \mathsf{Cau}$ *and* $(e, d) \notin D$.

An enforcer $\mu$ is correct with respect to a property $P$ if, for all $\sigma \in P$, any trace $\sigma'$ obtained by adding a single database at the end of $\sigma$ and then updating it (to some $\sigma''$) according to $\mu$ ensures $\sigma'' \in P$.

**Definition 4 (Correct Enforcement).** *An enforcer $\mu$ is called* correct with respect to a *property $P \subseteq \mathbb{T}$ and a set of databases $\Delta \subseteq \mathbb{DB}$ if for all $\sigma \in P \cap \mathbb{T}_f$, $\tau \geq \mathsf{lts}(\sigma)$, $D \in \Delta$, and $(B, C) = \mu(\sigma \cdot ((\tau, D)))$, we have $\sigma \cdot ((\tau, (D \setminus B) \cup C)) \in P$.*

*Transparent* enforcers [10] do not to alter traces that belong to the enforced property:

$v, i \models_\sigma r(t_1, ..., t_n)$ iff $(r, (v(t_1), ..., v(t_n))) \in D_i$    |    $v, i \models_\sigma \neg\varphi$    iff $v, i \not\models_\sigma \varphi$

$v, i \models_\sigma \exists x. \varphi$    iff $v[x \mapsto d], i \models_\sigma \varphi$ for $d \in \mathbb{D}$    |    $v, i \models_\sigma \varphi \vee \psi$ iff $v, i \models_\sigma \varphi$ or $v, i \models_\sigma \psi$

$v, i \models_\sigma \bullet_I \varphi$    iff $i > 1$ and $v, i-1 \models_\sigma \varphi$ and $\tau_i - \tau_{i-1} \in I$    |    $v, i \models_\varepsilon \varphi$

$v, i \models_\sigma \bigcirc_I \varphi$    iff $i+1 \leq |\sigma|$ and $v, i+1 \models_\sigma \varphi$, and $\tau_{i+1} - \tau_i \in I$

$v, i \models_\sigma \varphi S_I \psi$    iff $v, j \models_\sigma \psi$ for some $j \leq i, \tau_i - \tau_j \in I$, and $v, k \models_\sigma \varphi$ for all $k, j < k \leq i$

$v, i \models_\sigma \varphi U_I \psi$    iff $v, j \models_\sigma \psi$ for some $|\sigma| \geq j \geq i, \tau_j - \tau_i \in I$, and $v, k \models_\sigma \varphi$ for all $k, j > k \geq i$

**Fig. 2.** MFOTL semantics

**Definition 5 (Transparent Enforcement).** *An enforcer $\mu$ is called* transparent *with respect to a property $P \subseteq \mathbb{T}$ and a set of databases $\Delta \subseteq \mathbb{DB}$ if for all $\sigma \in P \cap \mathbb{T}_f$, $\tau \geq \mathsf{lts}(\sigma)$, $D \in \Delta$, we have $\sigma \cdot ((\tau, D)) \in P \Longrightarrow \mu(\sigma \cdot ((\tau, D))) = (\emptyset, \emptyset)$.*

Given $A \subseteq \mathbb{T}$ and $B, C \subseteq \mathbb{E}$, $\mathsf{extend}(A, B, C)$ is the set of all traces $\sigma \cdot (\tau, D)$ obtained by appending to any trace $\sigma \in A$ the pair $(\tau, D \cup D')$ with $\tau \geq \mathsf{lts}(\sigma)$, $D \in 2^{B \times \mathbb{D}^*}$ and $D' = \{(c, d) \mid c \in C, d \in \mathbb{D}^{a(c)}\}$. Intuitively, set $\mathsf{extend}(A, B, C)$ is obtained from the set $A$ by appending *some* events from $B$ and *all* events from $C$ to $A$. We have:

**Lemma 2.** *Let $P \subseteq \mathbb{T}$ such that $P$ is enforceable. Then there exists a correct and transparent enforcer with respect to $P$ and $\mathbb{DB}$.*

## 4   Metric First-Order Temporal Logic

Metric first-order temporal logic (MFOTL) extends first-order logic with the metric temporal operators "previous" ($\bullet_I$), "next" ($\bigcirc_I$), "since" ($S_I$), and "until" ($U_I$). We write $\mathbb{I}$ for the set of intervals over $\mathbb{N}$ and $\mathbb{V}$ for a countable set of variables. MFOTL formulae over a signature $\Sigma$ are defined by the grammar

$$\varphi ::= r(t_1, ..., t_{a(r)}) \mid \neg\varphi \mid \varphi \vee \varphi \mid \exists x. \varphi \mid \bullet_I \varphi \mid \bigcirc_I \varphi \mid \varphi S_I \varphi \mid \varphi U_I \varphi,$$

where $t_1, ..., t_{a(r)} \in \mathbb{V} \cup \mathbb{D}$, $r \in \mathbb{E}$, and $I \in \mathbb{I}$. We define shorthands $\top := p \vee \neg p$, $\bot := \neg\top$, $\varphi \Rightarrow \psi := \neg\varphi \vee \psi$, and the operators "once" ($\blacklozenge_I \varphi := \top S_I \varphi$), "eventually" ($\lozenge_I \varphi := \top U_I \varphi$), "always" ($\square_I \varphi := \neg\lozenge_I \neg\varphi$), and "historically" ($\blacksquare_I \varphi := \neg\blacklozenge_I \neg\varphi$). Temporal operators with no interval have $[0, \infty)$ instead. Predicates are formulae of the form $r(t_1, ..., t_{a(r)})$.

We extend the domain of *valuation* $v : \mathbb{V} \to \mathbb{D}$ to $\mathbb{D}$ by setting $v(d) = d$ for all $d \in \mathbb{D}$. We write $v[x \mapsto d]$ for the mapping equal to $v$, except that $v(x)$ is $d$. We use $\mathsf{fv}(\varphi)$ for the set of $\varphi$'s free variables. For $k \in \mathbb{N}$, a trace $\sigma = ((\tau_i, D_i))_{1 \leq i \leq k}$, a timepoint $1 \leq i \leq |\sigma|$, a valuation $v$, and a formula $\varphi$, satisfaction relation $\models$ is defined in Fig. 2. Note that $\models$ is well-defined for both finite and infinite traces. We write $v \models_\sigma \varphi$ for $v, 1 \models_\sigma \varphi$.

We say that two MFOTL formulae $\varphi$ and $\psi$ are *equivalent*, written $\varphi \equiv \psi$, iff for all $v, \sigma \in \mathbb{T}$, $1 \leq i \leq |\sigma|$, we have $v, i \models_\sigma \varphi \Leftrightarrow v, i \models_\sigma \psi$.

If $\varphi$ is closed, i.e., $\mathsf{fv}(\varphi) = \emptyset$, $\varphi$'s satisfaction does not depend on $v$. We then write $\models_\sigma \varphi$ as shorthand for $\forall v. v \models_\sigma \varphi$. Given a closed formula $\varphi$, we denote by $\mathcal{L}(\varphi) \subseteq \mathbb{T}$ the set of all traces that satisfy $\varphi$, i.e., $\mathcal{L}(\varphi) := \{\sigma \in \mathbb{T} \mid \models_\sigma \varphi\}$. Finally, we denote by $\mathcal{L}_f(\varphi)$ the set of finite traces in $\mathcal{L}(\varphi)$, i.e., $\mathcal{L}_f(\varphi) = \{\sigma \in \mathcal{L}(\varphi) \mid |\sigma| < \infty\}$. Extending the previous terminology, we say that a formula $\varphi$ is enforceable iff $\mathcal{L}(\varphi)$ is enforceable.

If the truth value of a formula only depends on the trace content in the past or present, an enforcer can compute satisfactions for each trace prefix, and react timely.

**Definition 6 (Future-Free Formulae).** *An MFOTL formula $\varphi$ is called* future-free *iff for all $\sigma \in \mathbb{T}$, valuation $v$, and $\sigma' \preceq \sigma$ such that $|\sigma'| = i$, we have $v, i \models_\sigma \varphi \Leftrightarrow v, i \models_{\sigma'} \varphi$.*

For instance, formulae without future operators ($U_I$, $O_I$, $\Diamond_I$, $\Box_I$) are future-free, but also some that have these operators nested in appropriate past operators.

*Example 2.* The formula $\varphi_1 = \blacklozenge_{[3,4]}(\exists x. \texttt{Close}(x))$ uses no future temporal operators, and is therefore future-free. The formula $\varphi_2 = \blacklozenge_{[3,4]}(\exists x. \texttt{Close}(x) \wedge \Diamond_{[1,2]}\texttt{Open}(x))$ contains a future operator, but is still future-free, since the future operator $\Diamond_{[1,2]}$ (looking at most 2 time units into the future) is nested in a $\blacklozenge_{[3,4]}$ operator that is always evaluated at least 3 time units in the past. The formula $\varphi_3 = \Diamond_{[1,2]}\texttt{Open}(x)$ is not future-free: its truth value depends on events happening up to 2 time units in the future.

In the rest of this paper, we consider the fragment $\text{MFOTL}^{\mathcal{F}}_{\Box}$ that contains all closed formulae of the form $\Box\varphi$, where $\varphi$ is future-free. Given the correctness of the monitoring algorithm [12] for MFOTL formulae of the form $\Box\varphi$, where all future operators in $\varphi$ have bounded intervals and the fact that future-free formulae are a subset of the algorithm's supported formulae, we have:

**Lemma 3.** *For any $\varphi \in \text{MFOTL}^{\mathcal{F}}_{\Box}$, there exists a TM that decides $\mathcal{L}_f(\varphi)$.*

In fact, the algorithm determines without delay whether a future-free formula is satisfied.

## 5  MFOTL Enforceability

In this section, we characterize the enforceability of $\text{MFOTL}^{\mathcal{F}}_{\Box}$ formulae with an enforcer as described in Sect. 3. Our first result is negative: a reduction, presented in our extended report [35], shows that the enforceability of $\text{MFOTL}^{\mathcal{F}}_{\Box}$ formulae in undecidable.

**Theorem 1.** *Assume that* Sup *contains at least one event of arity at least 2 and* Obs $\neq \emptyset$. *The set $\mathcal{E} = \{\varphi \in \text{MFOTL}^{\mathcal{F}}_{\Box} \mid \varphi$ is enforceable$\}$ is not computable.*

The proof relies on the undecidability of universal validity in FOL. Therefore, it is sensible to ask whether some syntactical characterization of enforceability can be recovered by reasoning *modulo equivalence of formulae*. Is there a decidable and enforceable fragment of $\text{MFOTL}^{\mathcal{F}}_{\Box}$ that contains all enforceable policies modulo equivalence? If so, such a fragment would not only provide a sound approximation of enforceable $\text{MFOTL}^{\mathcal{F}}_{\Box}$ formulae, but also an approximation that is *expressively complete*. All enforceable $\text{MFOTL}^{\mathcal{F}}_{\Box}$ policies could be expressed using the fragment via an appropriate (manual) rewriting. Rather surprisingly, such a fragment exists. Consider the following:

**Definition 7 (GMFOTL).** *Guarded MFOTL (GMFOTL) is defined inductively by:*

$$\psi ::= \bot \mid s(t_1, \ldots, t_n) \mid \neg c(t_1, \ldots, t_n) \mid \psi \wedge \varphi \mid \psi \vee \psi \mid \exists x.\, \psi$$

*where $s \in$ Sup, $c \in$ Cau, and $\varphi$ is an MFOTL formula.*

In GMFOTL, all subformulae (and, in particular, all temporal subformulae) are *guarded* by an instance of a predicate $r(t_1, \ldots, t_n)$ with $r$ being suppressable, or by an instance of a negated predicate $\neg r(t_1 \ldots, t_n)$ with $r$ being causable. In the following, we call such a (possibily negated) predicate a *guard*. The presence of a guard ensures that, when an GMFOTL formula is satisfied with respect to a trace prefix, it can always be made false by suppressing or causing appropriate events in the last database of the prefix.

*Example 3.* Consider the formula $\varphi_4 = \neg\texttt{Close}(x) \land \psi$, with an arbitrary future-free formula $\psi$ and $\text{fv}(\psi) = \{x\}$. For $\varphi_4$ to be satisfied with respect to a trace prefix $\sigma$, it must hold for some valuation of $x$ and $\{(\texttt{Close}, (a)) \mid v, |\sigma| \models_\sigma \psi, v(x) = a\}$ must not be in the last database of $\sigma$. Hence, $\varphi_4$ can be falsified by causing the appropriate $\texttt{Close}$ events.

It can be shown that all closed formulae of the form $\Box\neg\psi$ with $\psi \in$ GMFOTL and future-free are enforceable. Since enforceability is defined in terms of the language recognized by a given formula, we obtain that all MFOTL$_\Box^\mathcal{F}$ formulae equivalent to some $\Box\neg\psi$, with $\psi \in$ GMFOTL closed and future-free, are enforceable. In fact, the converse is also true: all future-free MFOTL$_\Box^\mathcal{F}$ formulae are equivalent to a formula of the above form. We have thus obtained an expressively complete fragment of enforceable MFOTL$_\Box^\mathcal{F}$. Formally:

**Theorem 2.** *A formula* $\Box\varphi \in$ MFOTL$_\Box^\mathcal{F}$ *is enforceable iff there exists* $\psi \in$ GMFOTL *such that* $\Box\varphi \equiv \Box\neg\psi$.

*Example 4.* Consider the formula $\varphi_5 = \Box\forall x. (\texttt{Open}(x) \Rightarrow \neg\blacklozenge_{[2,5]}\texttt{Open}(x))$. This formula is enforceable: $\texttt{Open}$ events that lead to a violation (i.e., those occurring 2 to 5 time units after a previous $\texttt{Open}$ event with the same argument) can always be suppressed. The formula $\varphi_5$ is equivalent to $\Box\neg\psi$ where $\psi \in$ GMFOTL is

$$(\exists x. \texttt{Open}(x)) \land \neg(\forall x. (\texttt{Open}(x) \Rightarrow \neg\blacklozenge_{[2,5]}\texttt{Open}(x))).$$

## 6   MFOTL Enforcement in the Finite Case

In the previous section, we have presented GMFOTL, a syntactic class of MFOTL that is expressively complete for enforceable MFOTL$_\Box^\mathcal{F}$ formulae. Lemma 2 implies the existence of an enforcer for such formulae. However, the naive enforcer constructed in the lemma's proof may be inefficient—in fact, it may cause an infinite number of new events.

In this section, we focus on traces with finite databases and MFOTL formulae from the intersection of enforceable MFOTL$_\Box^\mathcal{F}$ formulae with monitorable MFOTL formulae [12]. We show that, in this case, we can exhibit a correct and transparent enforcer that produces only a finite number of events to be suppressed or caused.

## 6.1 Monitoring MFOTL Formulae

Basin *et al.* [12] describe an algorithm that efficiently monitors monitorable MFOTL formulae. Variants of this algorithm and the fragment it supports are used in several state-of-the-art tools [13,55]. We now briefly recall the algorithm and some of its properties.

The algorithm encodes each database $D \in \mathbb{DB}^\dagger$ as a finite set of tables, one for each event name in the database. The row $d$ is in the table corresponding to the event name $e$ if $(e,d) \in D$. The set of satisfying valuations of a formula can similarly be encoded as a table whose rows represent valuations restricted to the domain of the formula's free variables.

The algorithm computes the table of satisfying valuations for a monitorable MFOTL formula bottom-up, using well-known table operations like join, anti-join, union, and projection. The syntactic monitorable fragment ensures that table operations always produce finite tables. In the rest of the section, we assume that this algorithm is available as a subroutine $\text{SAT}(\varphi, \sigma) = \{v \mid v, |\sigma| \models_\sigma \varphi\}$ that returns the set of satisfying valuations of a monitorable MFOTL formula $\varphi$ with respect to finite trace $\sigma \in \mathbb{T}^\dagger$ and timepoint $|\sigma|$.

The monitorable MFOTL fragment [55] also ensures that for any valuation $v$ satisfying a formula $\varphi$ from the fragment with respect to a finite trace $\sigma$ and a time point $1 \le i \le |\sigma|$, for every $x \in \text{fv}(\varphi)$ the value $v(x) \in \mathbb{D}$ is contained in some event argument in a database in $\sigma$ or a constant term in $\varphi$. Formally:

**Lemma 4.** *For all monitorable $\varphi \in$ MFOTL, valuation $v$, trace $\sigma \in \mathbb{T}^\dagger$, and timepoint $1 \le i \le |\sigma|$, assuming $v, i \models_\sigma \varphi$, we have*

$$\forall x \in \text{fv}(\varphi). \exists 1 \le j \le |\sigma|. (e,d) \in D_j, 1 \le k \le a(e). d_k = v(x) \vee d_k \in \text{cst}(\varphi)$$

*where $\text{cst}(\varphi) \subset \mathbb{D}$ denotes the (finite) set of constant terms that appear in $\varphi$.*

We will use this lemma, as well as the termination of the subroutine $\text{SAT}$ [12], to prove the termination of our enforcer.

---

**Algorithm 1.** Function enf

---

**function** $\text{enf}(\varphi, \sigma, v)$
  **if** $\varphi = r(t_1, \ldots, t_n), r \in \text{Sup}$ **then**
    **return** $(\{(r, (v(t_1), \ldots, v(t_n)))\}, \emptyset)$
  **else if** $\varphi = \neg r(t_1, \ldots, t_n), r \in \text{Cau}$ **then**
    **return** $(\emptyset, \{(r, (v(t_1), \ldots, v(t_n)))\})$
  **else if** $\varphi = \varphi_1 \wedge \varphi_2$ **then**
    **return** $\text{enf}(\varphi, \sigma, v)$
  **else if** $\varphi = \varphi_1 \vee \varphi_2$ **then**
    **return** $\text{FIXPOINT}(\sigma, \text{enf}_{\text{or}, \varphi_1, \varphi_2, v})$
  **else if** $\varphi = \exists x. \varphi_1$ **then**
    **return** $\text{FIXPOINT}(\sigma, \text{enf}_{\text{ex}, \varphi_1, v})$

**function** $\text{enf}_{\text{or}, \varphi_1, \varphi_2, v}(\sigma)$
  $(D^-, D^+) \leftarrow (\emptyset, \emptyset)$
  **if** $v \in \text{SAT}(\varphi_1, \sigma)$ **then**
    $(D^-, D^+) \leftarrow (D^-, D^+) \uplus \text{enf}(\varphi_1, \sigma, v)$
  **if** $v \in \text{SAT}(\varphi_2, \sigma)$ **then**
    $(D^-, D^+) \leftarrow (D^-, D^+) \uplus \text{enf}(\varphi_2, \sigma, v)$
  **return** $(D^-, D^+)$

**function** $\text{enf}_{\text{ex}, \varphi_1, v}(\sigma)$
  $(D^-, D^+) \leftarrow (\emptyset, \emptyset)$
  **for** $v \in \mathbb{D}$ s.t. $v[x \mapsto v] \in \text{SAT}(\varphi_1, \sigma)$ **do**
    $(D^-, D^+) \leftarrow (D^-, D^+) \uplus \text{enf}(\varphi_1, \sigma, v[x \mapsto v])$
  **return** $(D^-, D^+)$

---

## 6.2  Enforcer

Given $\sigma \in \mathbb{T}_f$, $\tau \geq \mathsf{lts}(\sigma)$, and $D, D^-, D^+ \in \mathbb{DB}$, we first define the function update as

$$\mathsf{update}(\sigma \cdot ((\tau, D)), (D^-, D^+)) := \sigma \cdot ((\tau, (D \cup D^+) \setminus D^-)).$$

Namely, update returns the trace obtained by adding all events from $D^+$ and removing all events from $D^-$ in the last database of $\sigma$.

For any $\sigma \in \mathbb{T}_f$ and enforcer $\mu$, we define $\ell_\mu(\sigma) \in \mathbb{T}_f$ as the limit of the sequence $(u_i)_{i \in \mathbb{N}} \in \mathbb{T}_f^{\mathbb{N}}$ defined by $u_0 = \sigma$ and for all $i \in \mathbb{N}$, $u_{i+1} = \mathsf{update}(u_i, \mu(u_i))$. This limit is always well-defined [35], and if $u_{i+1} = u_i$ for some $i \in \mathbb{N}$, we have $\ell_\mu(\sigma) = u_i$. This allows us to define a routine FIXPOINT$(\sigma, \mu)$ that iteratively computes $u_0, u_1, \ldots, u_i, \ldots$, returns $\ell_\mu(\sigma) = u_i$ as soon as $(u_i)_{i \in \mathbb{N}}$ reaches a fixpoint $u_{i+1} = u_i$, and does not terminate otherwise. We will later show that, in our setup, this procedure always terminates.

Our enforcer relies on the function enf described in Algorithm 1, which takes as an input a future-free and monitorable GMFOTL formula $\varphi$, a finite trace $\sigma$, and a valuation $v$ such that $v, |\sigma| \models_\sigma \varphi$, and returns a pair of sets of events to be respectively suppressed and caused at the last timepoint in $\sigma$ in order to obtain some new trace $\sigma'$ such that $v, |\sigma| \not\models_{\sigma'} \varphi$. For notational convenience, we denote by $\uplus$ the elementwise union of pairs of sets $(A, B) \uplus (C, D) = (A \cup C, B \cup D)$.

The intuition behind enf is as follows. If the formula $\varphi$ is reduced to an atom $r(t_1, \ldots, t_n)$ or $\neg r(t_1, \ldots, t_n)$, we can make it false by suppressing or causing a single event. If $\varphi$ is of the form $\varphi_1 \wedge \varphi_2$ with $\varphi \in \mathsf{GMFOTL}$, it is sufficient to make $\varphi_1$ false to make $\varphi$ false: enf looks for events to be suppressed or caused in $\varphi_1$.

For formulae of the form $\varphi_1 \vee \varphi_2$, additional care is needed. At first glance, the strategy used for $\wedge$ seems applicable, modulo a simple case distinction: if both $\varphi_1$ and $\varphi_2$ are satisfied by a given pair of a trace and a valuation, we need to find events to suppress or cause in *both* subformulae; if only one conjunct is satisfied, we look for events to suppress or cause in this subformula only. But such a one-step strategy is insufficient.

*Example 5.* Consider the formula $\varphi_6 = \mathtt{Open}(1) \vee (\neg \mathtt{Close}(2) \wedge \neg \mathtt{Open}(1)) \in$ GMFOTL and the trace $\sigma_6 = ((0, \{(\mathtt{Open}, (1))\}))$. Only the left disjunct is satisfied. Hence, applying the above strategy would produce the trace $\sigma_6' = ((0, \emptyset))$, which again satisfies $\varphi_6$ as it satisfies the right disjunct now. Hence, after having suppressed $(\mathtt{Open}, (1))$ we must check for satisfaction of $\varphi_6$ again, and, if necessary, select additional events to be suppressed or caused, here causing $(\mathtt{Close}, (2))$ suffices. This results in the trace $\sigma_6'' = ((0, \{(\mathtt{Close}, (2))\}))$, which now does not satisfy $\varphi_6$.

The above iterative approach, which performs a fixpoint computation, is formalized as a call to FIXPOINT$(\sigma, \mathsf{enf}_{\mathrm{or}, \varphi_1, \varphi_2, v})$, where $\mathsf{enf}_{\mathrm{or}, \varphi_1, \varphi_2, v}$ performs the above case distinction for a fixed valuation $v$ satisfying $\varphi_1 \vee \varphi_2$.

The same problem arises with existentially quantified formulae of the form $\exists x. \varphi_1$. For fixed $v$, function $\mathsf{enf}_{\mathrm{ex}, \varphi_1, v}$ identifies events that must be suppressed or caused to prevent the satisfaction of $\varphi_1$ using any valuation $v'$ extending $v$, and a call to FIXPOINT$(\sigma, \mathsf{enf}_{\mathrm{ex}, \varphi_1, v})$ computes the corresponding fixpoint.

Finally, for any closed, monitorable and future-free $\varphi \in$ GMFOTL, we define our tentative enforcer for $\square \neg \varphi$ as

$$\hat{\mu}_\varphi(\rho) = \begin{cases} \mathsf{enf}(\varphi, \rho, \emptyset) & \text{if } |\sigma| \models_\rho \varphi \\ (\emptyset, \emptyset) & \text{otherwise.} \end{cases}$$

*Example 6.* Consider the GMFOTL monitorable formula

$$\varphi_7 = \underbrace{(\exists x. \, \mathsf{Open}(x) \wedge \blacklozenge_{[0,5]} \mathsf{Close}(x))}_{\varphi_7^1} \vee \underbrace{(\exists y. \, \neg \mathsf{Close}(y) \wedge \neg \mathsf{Close}(y) \, \mathsf{S}_{[5,\infty)} \, \mathsf{Open}(y))}_{\varphi_7^2},$$

which is satisfied whenever an $(\mathsf{Open}, (\mathsf{x}))$ event follows a $(\mathsf{Close}, (\mathsf{x}))$ within 5 time units for some $\mathsf{x} \in \mathbb{D}$, or there is a $(\mathsf{Close}, (\mathsf{y}))$ event for some $\mathsf{y} \in \mathbb{D}$ that is not followed by any $(\mathsf{Close}, (\mathsf{y}))$ event within 5 time units. Consider the following trace:

$$\sigma_7 = ((0, \{(\mathsf{Open}, (1))\}), (1, \{(\mathsf{Close}, (2))\}), (5, \{(\mathsf{Open}, (2))\})).$$

We have $\models_{\sigma_7} \varphi_7$: events $(\mathsf{Close}, (2))$ and $(\mathsf{Open}, (2))$ at timestamps 1 and 5 satisfy the left disjunct, while the $(\mathsf{Open}, (1))$ event at timestamp 0 and the lack of a $(\mathsf{Close}, (1))$ event between timestamps 0 and 5 satisfies the right disjunct. As $\varphi_7$ is closed, the set of valuations satisfying it is $\{\emptyset\}$, where $\emptyset$ denotes the empty application. We compute $\mathsf{enf}(\varphi_7, \sigma_7, \emptyset) = \mathrm{FIXPOINT}(\sigma_7, \mathsf{enf}_{\mathsf{or}, \varphi_7^1, \varphi_7^2}, \emptyset)$.

Since $\sigma_7$ satisfies both $\varphi_7^1$ and $\varphi_7^2$, we get:

$$\begin{aligned}
\mathsf{enf}_{\mathsf{or}, \varphi_7^1, \varphi_7^2, \emptyset}(\sigma_7) &= \mathsf{enf}(\varphi_7^1, \sigma_7, \emptyset) \uplus \mathsf{enf}(\varphi_7^2, \sigma_7, \emptyset) \\
&= \mathsf{enf}(\mathsf{Open}(x) \wedge \blacklozenge_{[0,5]} \mathsf{Close}(x), \sigma_7, \{x \mapsto 2\}) \uplus \\
&\quad \mathsf{enf}(\neg \mathsf{Close}(y) \wedge \neg \mathsf{Close}(y) \, \mathsf{S}_{[5,\infty)} \, \mathsf{Open}(y), \sigma_7, \{y \mapsto 1\}) \\
&= \mathsf{enf}(\mathsf{Open}(x), \sigma_7, \{\{x \mapsto 2\}\}) \uplus \mathsf{enf}(\neg \mathsf{Close}(y), \sigma_7, \{\{y \mapsto 1\}\}) \\
&= (\{(\mathsf{Open}, (2))\}, \emptyset) \uplus (\emptyset, \{(\mathsf{Close}, (1))\}) \\
&= (\{(\mathsf{Open}, (2))\}, \{(\mathsf{Close}, (1))\}).
\end{aligned}$$

We then update $\sigma_7$:

$$\begin{aligned}
\sigma_7' &= \mathsf{update}(\sigma_7, \mathsf{enf}_{\mathsf{or}, \varphi_7^1, \varphi_7^2, \emptyset}(\sigma_7)) \\
&= ((\{0, \mathsf{Open}, (1)\}), (1, \{\mathsf{Close}, (2)\}), (5, \{\mathsf{Close}, (1)\}))
\end{aligned}$$

and check that $\sigma_7' = \mathsf{update}(\sigma_7', \mathsf{enf}_{\mathsf{or}, \varphi_7^1, \varphi_7^2, \emptyset}(\sigma_7'))$, i.e., that $\not\models_{\sigma_7'} \varphi_7$.

Hence, we finally get $\hat{\mu}_{\varphi_7}(\sigma_7) = \mathsf{enf}(\varphi_7, \sigma_7, \emptyset) = (\{(\mathsf{Open}, (2))\}, \{(\mathsf{Close}, (1))\})$.

## 6.3   Correctness and Transparency

For any monitorable, future-free and closed $\varphi \in$ GMFOTL and finite $\sigma \in \mathbb{T}^\dagger$, the enforcer $\hat{\mu}_\varphi$ always terminates. Termination is a consequence of Lemma 4 above; the corresponding proofs are given in our extended report [35]. Having established termination, we can prove that our enforcer is correct and transparent:

**Theorem 3.** *Let* $\varphi \in$ GMFOTL *be closed, monitorable and future-free. Then* $\hat{\mu}_\varphi$ *is a correct and transparent enforcer with respect to* $\mathcal{L}(\Box\neg\varphi) \cap \mathbb{T}^\dagger$ *and* $\mathbb{DB}^\dagger$.

At this point, it is worth reflecting on the effect that the assumption $\text{Sup} \cap \text{Cau} = \emptyset$ has on the correctness of our enforcer. In general, dropping this assumption results in some non-enforceable formula being equivalent to some formula $\Box\neg\psi$ with $\psi \in$ GMFOTL; thus, Theorem 2 no longer holds. For example, a formula such as $\varphi_7 = \Box\neg(C \lor \neg C)$ where $C \in \text{Sup} \cap \text{Cau}$ and $a(C) = 0$ is not enforceable: given an initially empty trace—on which, by convention, $\varphi_7$ is satisfied—adding any first timepoint makes the formula unsatisfiable, since $\neg(C \lor \neg C) \equiv \bot$. This rules out enforceability, which requires that appending only-observable events to a valid trace does not lead to a violation.

To understand why we need to assume $\text{Sup} \cap \text{Cau} = \emptyset$ for the above algorithm to be correct, consider the behavior of $\hat{\mu}_{\varphi_7}$ for the (non-enforceable) formula $\varphi_7$ above on the trace $\sigma_7 = ((\{C\}, 0))$. The enforcer calls $\text{FIXPOINT}(\sigma_7, \text{enf}_{\text{or}, C, \neg C, \emptyset})$, which itself calls $\text{enf}_{\text{or}, C, \neg C, \emptyset}(\sigma_7)$. This routine determines that only the left disjunct $C$ is satisfied, and returns the actions $(D^-, D^+) = (\{C\}, \emptyset)$. We get $\sigma_7' = ((0, \emptyset))$ and call $\text{enf}_{\text{or}, C, \neg C}(\sigma_7)$ again to find a fixpoint. Now, the second disjunct is not satisfied, leading to the actions $(D^-, D^+) = (\emptyset, \{C\})$ and to the updated trace $\sigma_7'' = ((0, \{C\})) = \sigma_7$. The same process repeats indefinitely.

When $\text{Sup} \cap \text{Cau} = \emptyset$, such a behavior is avoided. Since only suppressable events are suppressed and causable events caused, and since suppressable and causable events are disjoint, the algorithm will never try to suppress (resp. cause) an event that it has previously caused (resp. suppressed). Hence, the sets of caused and suppressed events can only grow during the fixpoint computation. This ensures termination, as any new iteration except the last one must compute at least one new event to cause or suppress.

Note that the assumption $\text{Sup} \cap \text{Cau} = \emptyset$ can be relaxed if we additionally require each suppressable *and* causable event to appear only with, or only without, a negation in the formula. In the definition of enf, each element from $\text{Sup} \cap \text{Cau}$ can then be considered to belong to Sup or Cau only.

## 7   Implementation

We have implemented our enforcer in the EnfPoly tool [34], which extends the MonPoly tool [13] with ca. 500 lines of OCaml code. Users can specify suppressable and causable events by adding "-" or "+" after the corresponding event description in the signature.

*Example 7.* The example signature $\Sigma$ can be specified as:

```
Open(int)- Close(int)+ Knock(int)
```

Events that are both enforceable and causable can be specified, e.g. as SomeE+-. In this case, for each formula to be enforced, a simple constraint-solving procedure is used to determine whether each such event can be considered only enforceable or only causable in the context of the current formula.

*Strictly Relative-Past MFOTL.* Note that Algorithm 1 takes as input a monitorable and enforceable MFOTL$_\Box^{\mathcal{F}}$ formula. Monitorability and enforcability can be syntactically approximated, but determining whether an MFOTL formula is future-free is undecidable [35]. Therefore, we have also developed a syntactical approximation of future-free formulae, called *strictly relative-past* formulae, which EnfPoly uses in practice. We formally define the fragment in our extended report [35]. Intuitively, all formulae that use only past temporal operators (i.e. *past-only MFOTL*) are strictly relative-past. Additionally, the strictly relative-past fragment contains many non-past formulae, for which one can statically verify that they do not depend on the future. For example, $\varphi_8 = \blacklozenge_{[5,+\infty)}(\texttt{Close}(2)\ \mathsf{U}_{[0,5)}\ \texttt{Open}(3))$ is strictly relative-past, but not past-only. Observe that the intervals of the temporal operators of $\varphi_8$ ensure that its truth value does not depend on future events: the evaluation of $\varphi_8$ at timestamp $\tau$ uses $\texttt{Close}$ events from timestamps $\leq \tau - 5$, and $\texttt{Open}$ from timestamps $< \tau - 5 + 5 = \tau$, which all lie in the past.

To enforce a formula of the form $\Box\neg\varphi$, EnfPoly checks if $\varphi$ is closed, in GMFOTL, and strict relative-past. Associative and commutative rewriting is used to relax the GMFOTL membership conditions in conjuncts. Then, the enforcement loop starts. At every timepoint, the enforcer reacts either with OK, if there is no violation, or with a set of events to cause and a set of events to suppress, otherwise.

*Example 8.* The output of EnfPoly when enforcing formulae $\Box\neg\varphi_6$ and $\Box\neg\varphi_7$ (from Examples 5 and 6) on traces $\sigma_6$ and $\sigma_7$, respectively, is shown in the table below.

| Formula: $\Box\neg\varphi_6$, Trace: $\sigma_6$ | Formula: $\Box\neg\varphi_7$, Trace: $\sigma_7$ |
| --- | --- |
| @0 Open(1); | @0 Open(1); |
| [Enforcer] Suppress: Open(1) | [Enforcer] OK. |
| [Enforcer] Cause: Close(2) | @1 Close(2); |
| [Enforcer] OK. | [Enforcer] OK. |
| | @5 Open(2); |
| | [Enforcer] Suppress: Open(2) |
| | [Enforcer] Cause: Close(1) |
| | [Enforcer] OK. |

Timestamped databases (prefixed with @) of a trace are incrementally input to EnfPoly, while its output (prefixed with [Enforcer]) is shown chronologically interleved with the input. When enforcing $\Box\neg\varphi_6$ on $\sigma_6$, the enforcer immediately reacts to the the first database $\{(\texttt{Open},(1))\}$ at timestamp 0 with two actions: it suppresses the event $(\texttt{Open},(1))$ and causes the event $(\texttt{Close},(2))$. Finally, it indicates that it has finished enforcing the formula by emitting OK. For $\Box\neg\varphi_7$, EnfPoly processes three timestamped databases. The first two do not violate the policy and hence there is no reaction other than OK from the enforcer. The third database causes a violation and the enforcer suppresses event $(\texttt{Open},(2))$ and causes event $(\texttt{Close},(1))$ to satisfy the policy.

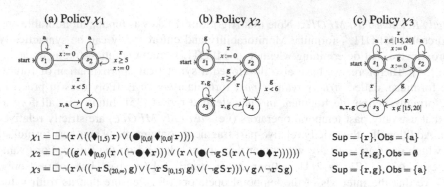

$$\chi_1 = \Box \neg (r \wedge ((\blacklozenge_{[1,5)} r) \vee (\bullet_{[0,0]} \blacklozenge_{[0,0]} r))))$$

$$\chi_2 = \Box \neg ((g \wedge \blacklozenge_{[0,6)} (r \wedge (\neg \bullet \blacklozenge r))) \vee (r \wedge (\bullet (\neg g S (r \wedge (\neg \bullet \blacklozenge r))))))$$

$$\chi_3 = \Box \neg (r \wedge ((\neg r S_{(20,\infty)} g) \vee (\neg r S_{[0,15)} g) \vee (\neg g S r))) \vee g \wedge \neg r S g)$$

$\text{Sup} = \{r\}, \text{Obs} = \{a\}$

$\text{Sup} = \{r,g\}, \text{Obs} = \emptyset$

$\text{Sup} = \{r,g\}, \text{Obs} = \{a\}$

**Fig. 3.** Policies used to compare EnfPoly to GREP

# 8   Evaluation

We now compare our enforcer with other state-of-the-art tools. As our tool is the first one to support the enforcement of first-order temporal policies, comparison is only possible with (1) *propositional* temporal enforcers or (2) first-order temporal *monitors*.

Note that when there are no causable events in the signature, online monitoring tools can be used as online enforcers in the following way. First, before the events of every timepoint are sent to the monitor, save the monitor's internal state. Then, have the monitor process the timepoint. If the monitor does not detect a violation, save the monitor's state again and proceed with the next timepoint. If a violation is detected, restore the previous saved state and re-read *only the only-observable events* from the timepoint that led to a violation, suppressing all suppressable events from the last timepoint. When the formula to monitor is enforceable and there are no causable events in the signature, this construction always provides a valid enforcer. This approach has been used recently [33] to perform MFOTL enforcement with MonPoly.

Our evaluation aims to answer the following research questions:

RQ1. Does EnfPoly show better performance than existing propositional enforcers?
RQ2a. Given an MFOTL formula, how much overhead does EnfPoly's enforcement cause compared to MonPoly's monitoring of the same formula?
RQ2b. Does EnfPoly show better performance in enforcing formulae over a signature with no causable events than MonPoly adapted to be an online enforcer?

For RQ1, we focus on runtime enforcement tools, which use a setup similar to ours in terms of enforcement capabilities. We compare EnfPoly to GREP [49]. The tool GREP, along with TiPEX and Proactive Libraries, is one of three tools referenced in a recent survey paper [26]. GREP has been shown to outperform TiPEX by up to two orders of magnitude [49], and, unlike Proactive Libraries, it comes with an publicly available implementation. For RQ2, we compare EnfPoly to MonPoly [13].

In all experiments, we measure the enforcers' memory using Python's psutil. We also measure enforcers' total runtime, as well as their latency, i.e., the time spent waiting for an enforcer to compute its output, which we normalize by the number of events in the trace. The speedup of our tool with respect to a tool $t$ is computed as the difference between $t$'s and our tool's runtime divided by $t$'s runtime. All experiments are run on an 2.4 GHz Intel Core i5-1135G7 QuadCore CPU with 32 GB RAM.

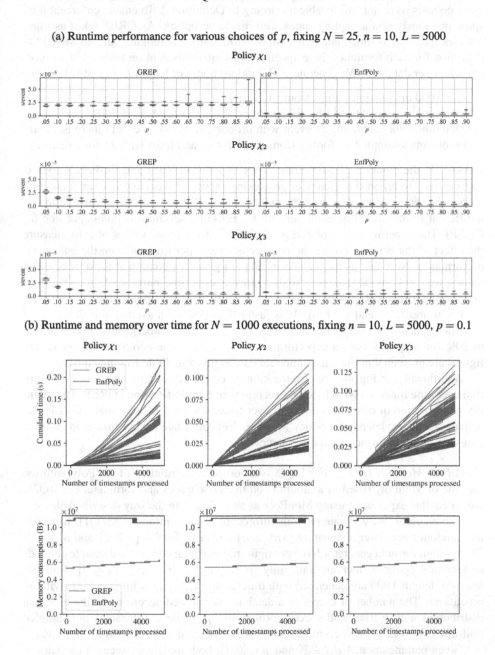

(a) Runtime performance for various choices of $p$, fixing $N = 25$, $n = 10$, $L = 5000$

(b) Runtime and memory over time for $N = 1000$ executions, fixing $n = 10$, $L = 5000$, $p = 0.1$

**Fig. 4.** Runtime and memory consumption of EnfPoly and GREP

*EnfPoly vs GREP (RQ1).*   To compare the performance of the two enforcers, we consider the three policies presented on Fig. 3, which are slight adaptations of the three benchmark examples used in [45, 49] to evaluate GREP and TiPEX. The original benchmark policies were not enforceable according to Definition 2. To enable enforceability, some previously non-accepting states were made accepting. As GREP takes as input policies specified as timed automata, we provide both an automaton and an MFOTL$_\square^\mathcal{F}$ definition for each formula. These specifications are equivalent on traces with at most one event per database. We generate such random traces of length $L \cdot n = 50\,000$ with

- $L = 5\,000$ unique timestamps from $\{1,\ldots,L\}$;
- timestamps $\tau_i$ equal to $\lceil \frac{i}{n} \rceil$ for timepoint $i \in \{1\ldots L \cdot n\}$, where $n = 10$;
- each timepoint containing an event with probability $p$ and no event otherwise; and
- event names sampled uniformly from $\{a,r\}$ for $\chi_1$ and from $\{a,g,r\}$ for $\chi_2$ and $\chi_3$.

For GREP, the duration of a time unit is set to 1 ms. GREP's and EnfPoly's code is instrumented to report the latency of processing inputs (i.e., excluding communication costs). Communication costs were excluded since GREP and EnfPoly receive inputs in a different format (one timepoint per line for EnfPoly, several timepoints per line for GREP). The experiment is repeated $N = 25$ times for various values of $p$ to measure the effect of the *event rate* (i.e., the number of events per time unit) on the enforcers' performance. Note that as the signatures of $\chi_1$, $\chi_2$, and $\chi_3$ contain at most three event names, we can keep the maximal number of events per timestamp small, fixing $n = 10$ and varying $p$ only. GREP is run in online mode with the "fast" option (flag -f) activated.

For formulae $\chi_1$ and $\chi_2$, EnfPoly is faster than GREP on average for all values of $p$, with a speedup between 40% and 90%. For $\chi_3$, GREP outperforms EnfPoly by up to 20% for $p \geq 0.55$, but underperforms it for $p < 0.55$. The corresponding summary figures are presented in Fig. 4a. Numerical data is given in Table 1 in the Appendix.

Additionally, in Fig. 4b, we plot the cumulated latency and the memory consumption over time for $N = 100$ individual executions of both EnfPoly and GREP. The memory consumption of our tool is constant over time, while GREP's is linear. GREP also displays quadratic latency for policy $\chi_1$, while EnfPoly's latency is constant in all three cases, resulting in linear cumulative latency.

*EnfPoly vs MonPoly (RQ2).*   For RQ2a, we compare the runtime of EnfPoly with the runtime of MonPoly (used as a monitor) on the same traces and formulae. For RQ2b, we repeat this experiment using MonPoly as an enforcer, in the way described above.

In both cases, we generate random enforceable and monitorable MFOTL formulae and random traces over a signature $(\texttt{int}, \mathbb{E}, a)$ with $\mathbb{E} = \mathsf{Sup} = \{\texttt{A},\texttt{B},\texttt{C}\}$ and $a(\cdot) = 1$. The random formula generator has a configurable maximal depth $d$ and samples bounds of temporal operator intervals uniformly from $\{(i,j) \in \{0,\ldots,I\}^2 \mid i \leq j\}$. Random traces of length $1\,000$ are generated with timestamps $1,2,\ldots,L$ with $L = 1\,000$ with no repetitions. The number of events in a database is sampled according to the binomial distribution with $n$ trials and success probability $p$, while event names are sampled uniformly from $\mathbb{E}$. Finally, event's arguments are sampled uniformly from $\{1,\ldots,A\}$.

Given parameters $n, A, d, I \in \mathbb{N}$ and $p \in [0,1]$, both tools are executed on pairs of independently generated random traces and enforceable and monitorable MFOTL$_\square^\mathcal{F}$ formulae with the same combinations of parameters, repeated $N = 25$ times.

For all values of the parameters, enforcement with EnfPoly adds up to 50% runtime overhead on top of the costs of monitoring with MonPoly, and does not affect memory consumption. On the other hand, using EnfPoly for enforcement is still 4 to 20 times faster than using MonPoly as an enforcer, working in the way described above, and with a comparable memory consumption. Most of the overhead of MonPoly used as an enforcer is due to loading and saving the (complete) monitor state at each iteration, which EnfPoly avoids. Average runtime costs are under 0.1 ms per event, with most averages under 10 μs. In individual executions, both tools display constant time and memory consumption. Detailed numerical results can be found in Table 1 in the Appendix (for RQ2b), as well as in our extended report [35] (for RQ2a).

*Discussion.* The above experiments show that EnfPoly, despite supporting a much larger specification language, displays a runtime and memory performance at least as good as GREP's. Our enforcer's performance is less sensitive to the choice of the input formula and consumes a constant amount of memory over time. Compared to using MonPoly as an MFOTL enforcer, EnfPoly provides a speedup of one order of magnitude. Runtime and memory consumption per event processed is stable or decreasing when more events occur simultaneously, and is not affected by longer trace sizes.

# 9 Conclusion

We have presented both the theory and practice of enforcing metric first-order temporal logic (MFOTL) formulae with disjoint sets of causable and suppressable events. We have characterized enforceability for MFOTL for such enforcers and proposed an efficient enforcement algorithm. Our enforcer EnfPoly extends the MonPoly monitoring tool and it is the first tool for first-order temporal logic enforcement. We have evaluated EnfPoly and showed that although it supports a more expressive language it can still outperform state-of-the-art enforcers.

As future work, we plan to generalize our approach to allow events that are both suppressable and causable. Currently, it remains open whether enforceability can be characterized syntactically modulo equivalence (as in Theorem 2) when this assumption is lifted. But even if no such characterization exists, in practice one could develop enforcement algorithms for larger (syntactical) fragments of enforceable policies.

**Acknowledgments.** We thank Dmitriy Traytel and three anonymous ESORICS reviewers for their helpful comments. François Hublet is supported by the Swiss National Science Foundation grant "Model-driven Security & Privacy" (204796).

# A  Evaluation Data

Table 1 shows the raw evaluation data produced by our experiments. The table on the left contains the data obtained when answering RQ1, while the data in the table on the right is obtained when answering RQ2. In the former we use three policies $\chi_1, \chi_2$, and $\chi_3$, while in the latter we generate random enforceable and monitorable MFOTL formulae.

**Table 1.** Mean runtime performance (standard deviation) for various parameter values

### RQI. EnPoly vs. GREP: $N = 25$, $n = 10$, $L = 5000$

| | $x_1$ | | | | $x_2$ | | | | $x_3$ | | |
|---|---|---|---|---|---|---|---|---|---|---|---|
| p | GREP s/event | EnPoly s/event | Speedup % | p | GREP s/event | EnPoly s/event | Speedup % | p | GREP s/event | EnPoly s/event | Speedup % |
| .05 | 1.86e-05 (1.01e-06) | 4.16e-06 (4.14e-07) | 77.7% (2.0%) | .05 | 2.60e-05 (2.01e-06) | 5.56e-06 (4.45e-07) | 78.5% (2.3%) | .05 | 3.03e-05 (2.51e-06) | 7.18e-06 (4.70e-07) | 76.1% (2.5%) |
| .10 | 1.95e-05 (1.05e-06) | 3.21e-06 (3.48e-07) | 83.6% (1.6%) | .10 | 1.55e-05 (1.25e-06) | 3.63e-06 (3.14e-07) | 76.3% (3.1%) | .10 | 1.68e-05 (1.09e-06) | 5.20e-06 (1.64e-07) | 69.0% (2.4%) |
| .15 | 1.94e-05 (1.18e-06) | 2.90e-06 (2.34e-07) | 85.1% (1.1%) | .15 | 1.24e-05 (1.97e-06) | 3.58e-06 (1.47e-06) | 71.5% (8.1%) | .15 | 1.25e-05 (7.15e-07) | 4.76e-06 (3.80e-07) | 61.8% (4.0%) |
| .20 | 1.93e-05 (7.45e-07) | 2.82e-06 (2.79e-07) | 85.3% (1.5%) | .20 | 1.01e-05 (1.53e-06) | 3.18e-06 (1.09e-06) | 68.7% (6.7%) | .20 | 1.05e-05 (5.64e-07) | 4.50e-06 (2.33e-07) | 57.0% (3.5%) |
| .25 | 1.99e-05 (2.02e-06) | 2.72e-06 (1.33e-07) | 86.2% (1.4%) | .25 | 8.66e-06 (1.07e-06) | 3.00e-06 (6.34e-07) | 65.5% (4.9%) | .25 | 8.87e-06 (4.87e-07) | 4.54e-06 (3.08e-07) | 48.7% (4.2%) |
| .30 | 1.95e-05 (1.07e-06) | 2.74e-06 (2.90e-07) | 86.0% (1.5%) | .30 | 8.37e-06 (1.34e-06) | 3.10e-06 (9.00e-07) | 63.3% (6.1%) | .30 | 8.14e-06 (3.74e-07) | 4.49e-06 (2.35e-07) | 44.7% (4.2%) |
| .35 | 1.98e-05 (1.51e-06) | 2.66e-06 (1.94e-07) | 86.5% (1.2%) | .35 | 7.28e-06 (8.33e-07) | 2.83e-06 (8.38e-07) | 61.3% (6.6%) | .35 | 7.60e-06 (1.14e-06) | 4.83e-06 (1.32e-06) | 37.0% (8.8%) |
| .40 | 1.99e-05 (1.10e-06) | 2.77e-06 (2.92e-07) | 86.0% (1.8%) | .40 | 6.88e-06 (1.25e-06) | 3.04e-06 (9.51e-07) | 56.4% (6.6%) | .40 | 6.76e-06 (2.77e-07) | 4.34e-06 (2.30e-07) | 35.7% (3.6%) |
| .45 | 2.04e-05 (1.51e-06) | 2.63e-06 (1.16e-07) | 87.1% (1.0%) | .45 | 6.78e-06 (1.02e-06) | 3.29e-06 (9.20e-07) | 51.9% (8.5%) | .45 | 6.53e-06 (8.48e-07) | 4.68e-06 (1.09e-06) | 28.7% (9.0%) |
| .50 | 2.08e-05 (1.78e-06) | 2.65e-06 (1.71e-07) | 87.2% (1.1%) | .50 | 6.57e-06 (1.18e-06) | 3.17e-06 (9.69e-07) | 52.2% (8.5%) | .50 | 6.00e-06 (1.08e-06) | 4.76e-06 (1.44e-06) | 21.3% (12.9%) |
| .55 | 2.06e-05 (2.12e-06) | 2.69e-06 (2.80e-07) | 86.8% (1.8%) | .55 | 6.05e-06 (1.09e-06) | 2.95e-06 (9.52e-07) | 51.8% (8.7%) | .55 | 5.34e-06 (1.28e-06) | 5.43e-06 (1.88e-06) | -0.4% (15.6%) |
| .60 | 2.10e-05 (1.75e-06) | 2.68e-06 (1.86e-07) | 87.2% (1.2%) | .60 | 6.19e-06 (1.57e-06) | 3.17e-06 (1.21e-06) | 49.6% (7.0%) | .60 | 4.65e-06 (7.65e-07) | 4.76e-06 (1.23e-06) | -1.9% (14.6%) |
| .65 | 2.32e-05 (4.84e-06) | 2.98e-06 (7.76e-07) | 87.2% (1.4%) | .65 | 6.06e-06 (1.88e-06) | 3.29e-06 (1.46e-06) | 46.5% (13.2%) | .65 | 4.46e-06 (7.68e-07) | 4.74e-06 (1.38e-06) | -5.6% (17.7%) |
| .70 | 2.11e-05 (2.04e-06) | 2.70e-06 (1.76e-07) | 87.1% (1.5%) | .70 | 5.15e-06 (8.15e-07) | 3.05e-06 (8.90e-07) | 41.9% (9.0%) | .70 | 4.33e-06 (7.80e-07) | 5.09e-06 (1.82e-06) | -15.6% (21.6%) |
| .75 | 2.06e-05 (1.23e-06) | 2.62e-06 (1.33e-07) | 87.3% (1.0%) | .75 | 5.63e-06 (1.87e-06) | 3.32e-06 (1.90e-06) | 41.4% (27.7%) | .75 | 4.16e-06 (6.60e-07) | 4.61e-06 (1.16e-06) | -10.3% (14.5%) |
| .80 | 2.22e-05 (4.37e-06) | 2.92e-06 (8.19e-07) | 86.9% (1.4%) | .80 | 5.77e-06 (1.94e-06) | 3.50e-06 (1.58e-06) | 40.2% (13.6%) | .80 | 4.05e-06 (7.03e-07) | 4.67e-06 (1.38e-06) | -14.5% (19.4%) |
| .85 | 2.19e-05 (3.68e-06) | 2.94e-06 (7.48e-07) | 86.6% (2.0%) | .85 | 5.69e-06 (1.58e-06) | 3.42e-06 (1.37e-06) | 40.8% (12.2%) | .85 | 3.91e-06 (8.13e-07) | 4.50e-06 (8.13e-07) | -16.5% (16.1%) |
| .90 | 2.74e-05 (8.95e-06) | 3.74e-06 (1.68e-06) | 86.5% (2.6%) | .90 | 5.01e-06 (1.06e-06) | 2.87e-06 (7.66e-07) | 42.7% (8.9%) | .90 | 3.77e-06 (5.52e-07) | 4.61e-06 (1.01e-06) | -21.8% (12.1%) |

### RQ2b. EnPoly vs. MonPoly used as an enforcer: $N = 25$, $n = 10$, $L = 1000$

$I = 50$, $A = 16$, $n = 10$, $p = .50$

| d | MonPoly s/event | EnPoly s/event | Speedup % |
|---|---|---|---|
| 2 | 3.44e-04 (2.50e-04) | 2.60e-06 (3.12e-06) | 94.3% (9.8%) |
| 3 | 3.15e-04 (2.17e-04) | 3.31e-06 (1.14e-06) | 95.1% (8.6%) |
| 4 | 2.28e-04 (2.55e-04) | 3.34e-06 (7.80e-07) | 88.2% (11.7%) |
| 5 | 2.68e-04 (2.49e-04) | 4.71e-06 (2.59e-06) | 90.3% (10.3%) |
| 6 | 2.59e-04 (2.79e-04) | 5.47e-06 (3.38e-06) | 88.0% (10.5%) |
| 7 | 1.91e-04 (2.39e-04) | 8.94e-06 (4.74e-06) | 84.3% (11.4%) |
| 8 | 2.48e-04 (2.81e-04) | 1.56e-05 (1.10e-05) | 82.7% (12.5%) |

$d = 5$, $I = 50$, $A = 16$, $n = 10$

| n | MonPoly s/event | EnPoly s/event | Speedup % |
|---|---|---|---|
| 1 | 3.39e-04 (5.57e-04) | 2.32e-05 (2.82e-06) | 82.4% (7.8%) |
| 2 | 4.61e-04 (6.81e-04) | 1.35e-05 (3.74e-06) | 86.0% (10.7%) |
| 5 | 2.37e-04 (3.83e-04) | 6.92e-06 (2.78e-06) | 83.3% (10.6%) |
| 10 | 2.68e-04 (2.49e-04) | 4.71e-06 (2.59e-06) | 90.3% (10.3%) |
| 20 | 1.38e-04 (1.42e-04) | 2.98e-06 (1.07e-06) | 86.5% (13.1%) |
| 50 | 5.62e-04 (5.80e-05) | 2.57e-06 (1.53e-06) | 80.3% (17.4%) |
| 100 | 2.89e-04 (2.95e-05) | 2.45e-06 (1.74e-06) | 73.4% (21.4%) |
| 200 | 1.64e-05 (1.47e-05) | 2.52e-06 (2.98e-06) | 68.3% (22.8%) |

$d = 5$, $A = 16$, $n = 10$, $p = .50$

| I | MonPoly s/event | EnPoly s/event | Speedup % |
|---|---|---|---|
| 1 | 1.90e-04 (2.17e-04) | 3.36e-06 (5.58e-07) | 88.5% (11.8%) |
| 5 | 3.00e-04 (2.59e-04) | 4.06e-06 (9.41e-07) | 90.4% (12.2%) |
| 10 | 2.98e-04 (2.63e-04) | 4.08e-06 (1.16e-06) | 90.1% (12.6%) |
| 50 | 2.74e-04 (2.62e-04) | 4.42e-06 (1.56e-06) | 89.3% (12.7%) |
| 100 | 2.05e-04 (2.52e-04) | 7.16e-06 (1.22e-05) | 85.8% (15.6%) |
| 200 | 2.17e-04 (2.31e-04) | 5.65e-06 (4.12e-06) | 88.6% (10.1%) |
| 500 | 2.56e-04 (2.72e-04) | 1.82e-05 (5.21e-05) | 85.0% (14.1%) |

$d = 5$, $I = 50$, $A = 16$, $n = 10$

| p | MonPoly s/event | EnPoly s/event | Speedup % |
|---|---|---|---|
| 0.00 | 1.17e-04 (1.27e-04) | 3.31e-06 (1.19e-06) | 87.7% (11.5%) |
| 0.01 | 7.80e-04 (5.14e-04) | 1.06e-04 (1.31e-05) | 82.1% (7.5%) |
| 0.05 | 6.46e-04 (7.35e-04) | 2.47e-05 (5.20e-06) | 87.0% (10.5%) |
| 0.10 | 4.02e-04 (4.48e-04) | 1.23e-05 (2.22e-06) | 88.1% (9.8%) |
| 0.25 | 3.36e-04 (3.82e-04) | 8.33e-06 (9.35e-06) | 87.6% (11.0%) |
| 0.50 | 2.68e-04 (2.49e-04) | 4.71e-06 (2.59e-06) | 90.3% (10.3%) |
| 0.75 | 2.35e-04 (1.94e-04) | 3.62e-06 (1.57e-06) | 90.1% (10.5%) |
| 0.88 | 1.95e-04 (1.56e-04) | 3.22e-06 (7.72e-07) | 90.8% (11.2%) |

$d = 5$, $I = 50$, $n = 10$, $p = .50$

| A | MonPoly s/event | EnPoly s/event | Speedup % |
|---|---|---|---|
| 2 | 1.34e-04 (1.96e-04) | 3.32e-06 (5.24e-07) | 83.3% (10.8%) |
| 4 | 1.92e-04 (2.60e-04) | 3.54e-06 (7.41e-07) | 85.4% (11.5%) |
| 8 | 2.19e-04 (2.65e-04) | 4.09e-06 (9.88e-07) | 86.2% (11.8%) |
| 16 | 2.68e-04 (2.49e-04) | 4.71e-06 (2.59e-06) | 90.3% (10.3%) |
| 32 | 1.72e-04 (2.50e-04) | 5.41e-06 (4.38e-06) | 84.1% (10.4%) |
| 64 | 3.46e-04 (2.66e-04) | 6.69e-06 (4.97e-06) | 90.2% (11.8%) |
| 128 | 1.75e-04 (2.17e-04) | 5.50e-06 (4.46e-06) | 84.8% (12.0%) |
| 256 | 1.69e-04 (2.41e-04) | 5.37e-06 (4.13e-06) | 82.7% (11.8%) |

Parameter $d$ is the depth of the generated random formulae, while $I$ defines the sample space for the bounds of temporal operator intervals: $\{(i,j) \in \{0,\ldots,I\}^2 \mid i \leq j\}$.

Random traces have length $L \cdot n$ with timestamps $1,2,\ldots,L$, each repeated $n$ times. Event names are sampled uniformly from $\mathbb{E} = \{\text{A},\text{B},\text{C}\}$, while their arguments are sampled uniformly from $\{1,\ldots,A\}$. The number of events in a database is sampled according to the binomial distribution with $n$ trials and success probability $p$.

Given parameters $n, A, d, I \in \mathbb{N}$ and $p \in [0,1]$, both tools are executed on pairs of independently generated random traces and enforceable and monitorable $\text{MFOTL}_{\square}^{\mathcal{F}}$ formulae with the same combinations of parameters repeated $N$ times.

# References

1. Abadi, M., Lamport, L., Wolper, P.: Realizable and unrealizable specifications of reactive systems. In: Ausiello, G., Dezani-Ciancaglini, M., Della Rocca, S.R. (eds.) ICALP 1989. LNCS, vol. 372, pp. 1–17. Springer, Heidelberg (1989). https://doi.org/10.1007/BFb0035748
2. Aceto, L., Cassar, I., Francalanza, A., Ingólfsdóttir, A.: On bidirectional runtime enforcement. In: Peters, K., Willemse, T.A.C. (eds.) FORTE 2021. LNCS, vol. 12719, pp. 3–21. Springer, Cham (2021). https://doi.org/10.1007/978-3-030-78089-0_1
3. Alur, R., Feder, T., Henzinger, T.: The benefits of relaxing punctuality. J. ACM **43**(1), 116–146 (1996). https://doi.org/10.1145/227595.227602
4. Ames, S.R., Gasser, M., Schell, R.R.: Security kernel design and implementation: an introduction. Computer **16**(7), 14–22 (1983). https://doi.org/10.1109/MC.1983.1654439
5. Arfelt, E., Basin, D., Debois, S.: Monitoring the GDPR. In: Sako, K., Schneider, S., Ryan, P.Y.A. (eds.) ESORICS 2019. LNCS, vol. 11735, pp. 681–699. Springer, Cham (2019). https://doi.org/10.1007/978-3-030-29959-0_33
6. Asarin, E., Maler, O., Pnueli, A.: Symbolic controller synthesis for discrete and timed systems. In: Antsaklis, P., Kohn, W., Nerode, A., Sastry, S. (eds.) HS 1994. LNCS, vol. 999, pp. 1–20. Springer, Heidelberg (1995). https://doi.org/10.1007/3-540-60472-3_1
7. Bartocci, Ezio, Falcone, Yliès (eds.): Lectures on Runtime Verification. LNCS, vol. 10457. Springer, Cham (2018). https://doi.org/10.1007/978-3-319-75632-5
8. Basin, D., et al.: A formally verified, optimized monitor for metric first-order dynamic logic. In: Peltier, N., Sofronie-Stokkermans, V. (eds.) IJCAR 2020. LNCS (LNAI), vol. 12166, pp. 432–453. Springer, Cham (2020). https://doi.org/10.1007/978-3-030-51074-9_25
9. Basin, D., Debois, S., Hildebrandt, T.: In the nick of time: proactive prevention of obligation violations. In: Computer Security Foundations Symposium (CSF), pp. 120–134. IEEE (2016). https://doi.org/10.1109/CSF.2016.16
10. Basin, D., Debois, S., Hildebrandt, T.: Proactive enforcement of provisions and obligations. J. Comput. Secur. (to appear)
11. Basin, D., Jugé, V., Klaedtke, F., Zălinescu, E.: Enforceable security policies revisited. ACM Trans. Inf. Syst. Secur. **16**(1), 1–26 (2013). https://doi.org/10.1007/978-3-642-28641-4_17
12. Basin, D., Klaedtke, F., Müller, S., Zălinescu, E.: Monitoring metric first-order temporal properties. J. ACM **62**(2), 1–45 (2015). https://doi.org/10.1145/2699444
13. Basin, D., Klaedtke, F., Zalinescu, E.: The MonPoly monitoring tool. In: Reger, G., Havelund, K. (eds.) International Workshop on Competitions, Usability, Benchmarks, Evaluation, and Standardisation for Runtime Verification Tools (RV-CuBES), vol. 3, pp. 19–28. Kalpa (2017). https://doi.org/10.29007/89hs
14. Bauer, L., Ligatti, J., Walker, D.: More enforceable security policies. In: Workshop on Foundations of Computer Security (FCS). Citeseer (2002)

15. Behrmann, G., Cougnard, A., David, A., Fleury, E., Larsen, K.G., Lime, D.: UPPAAL-Tiga: time for playing games! In: Damm, W., Hermanns, H. (eds.) CAV 2007. LNCS, vol. 4590, pp. 121–125. Springer, Heidelberg (2007). https://doi.org/10.1007/978-3-540-73368-3_14

16. Bohy, A., Bruyère, V., Filiot, E., Jin, N., Raskin, J.-F.: Acacia+, a tool for LTL synthesis. In: Madhusudan, P., Seshia, S.A. (eds.) CAV 2012. LNCS, vol. 7358, pp. 652–657. Springer, Heidelberg (2012). https://doi.org/10.1007/978-3-642-31424-7_45

17. Bouyer, P., Bozzelli, L., Chevalier, F.: Controller synthesis for MTL specifications. In: Baier, C., Hermanns, H. (eds.) CONCUR 2006. LNCS, vol. 4137, pp. 450–464. Springer, Heidelberg (2006). https://doi.org/10.1007/11817949_30

18. Brihaye, T., Geeraerts, G., Ho, H.-M., Monmege, B.: MIGHTYL: a compositional translation from MITL to timed automata. In: Majumdar, R., Kunčak, V. (eds.) CAV 2017. LNCS, vol. 10426, pp. 421–440. Springer, Cham (2017). https://doi.org/10.1007/978-3-319-63387-9_21

19. Bulychev, P., David, A., Larsen, K., Li, G.: Efficient controller synthesis for a fragment of $MTL_{0,\infty}$. Acta Inf. **51**(3-4), 165–192 (2014). https://doi.org/10.1007/s00236-013-0189-z

20. Chomicki, J.: Efficient checking of temporal integrity constraints using bounded history encoding. ACM Trans. Database Syst. **20**(2), 149–186 (1995). https://doi.org/10.1145/210197.210200

21. Dolzhenko, E., Ligatti, J., Reddy, S.: Modeling runtime enforcement with mandatory results automata. Int. J. Inf. Secur. **14**(1), 47–60 (2014). https://doi.org/10.1007/s10207-014-0239-8

22. Donzé, A., Raman, V.: BluSTL: controller synthesis from signal temporal logic specifications. In: Frehse, G., Althoff, M. (eds.) International Workshop on Applied veRification for Continuous & Hybrid Systems (ARCH@CPSWeek). EPiC, vol. 34, pp. 160–168. EasyChair (2015). https://doi.org/10.29007/g39q

23. Ehlers, R.: Unbeast: symbolic bounded synthesis. In: Abdulla, P.A., Leino, K.R.M. (eds.) TACAS 2011. LNCS, vol. 6605, pp. 272–275. Springer, Heidelberg (2011). https://doi.org/10.1007/978-3-642-19835-9_25

24. Erlingsson, Ú., Schneider, F.: SASI enforcement of security policies: a retrospective. In: Kienzle, D., Zurko, M.E., Greenwald, S., Serbau, C. (eds.) Workshop on New Security Paradigms, pp. 87–95. ACM (1999). https://doi.org/10.1145/335169.335201

25. Falcone, Y., Jéron, T., Marchand, H., Pinisetty, S.: Runtime enforcement of regular timed properties by suppressing and delaying events. Sci. Comp. Program. **123**, 2–41 (2016). https://doi.org/10.1016/j.scico.2016.02.008

26. Falcone, Y., Krstić, S., Reger, G., Traytel, D.: A taxonomy for classifying runtime verification tools. Int. J. Softw. Tools Technol. Transfer **23**(2), 255–284 (2021). https://doi.org/10.1007/s10009-021-00609-z

27. Falcone, Y., Mounier, L., Fernandez, J., Richier, J.: Runtime enforcement monitors: composition, synthesis, and enforcement abilities. Form. Methods Syst. Des. **38**(3), 223–262 (2011). https://doi.org/10.1007/s10703-011-0114-4

28. Falcone, Y., Pinisetty, S.: On the runtime enforcement of timed properties. In: Finkbeiner, B., Mariani, L. (eds.) RV 2019. LNCS, vol. 11757, pp. 48–69. Springer, Cham (2019). https://doi.org/10.1007/978-3-030-32079-9_4

29. Filiot, E., Jin, N., Raskin, J.: Antichains and compositional algorithms for LTL synthesis. Form. Methods Syst. Des. **39**(3), 261–296 (2011). https://doi.org/10.1007/s10703-011-0115-3

30. Havelund, K., Peled, D., Ulus, D.: DejaVu: a monitoring tool for first-order temporal logic. In: Workshop on Monitoring and Testing of Cyber-Physical Systems (MT-CPS), pp. 12–13. IEEE (2018). https://doi.org/10.1109/MT-CPS.2018.00013

31. Havelund, K., Peled, D., Ulus, D.: First-order temporal logic monitoring with BDDs. Form. Methods Syst. Des. **56**(1), 1–21 (2020). https://doi.org/10.1007/s10703-018-00327-4

32. Hofmann, T., Schupp, S.: TACoS: a tool for MTL controller synthesis. In: Calinescu, R., Păsăreanu, C.S. (eds.) SEFM 2021. LNCS, vol. 13085, pp. 372–379. Springer, Cham (2021). https://doi.org/10.1007/978-3-030-92124-8_21

33. Hublet, F.: The Databank Model. Master's thesis, ETH Zürich (2021)

34. Hublet, F., Basin, D., Krstić, S.: EnfPoly's development repository (2022). https://gitlab.ethz.ch/fhublet/mfotl-enforcement

35. Hublet, F., Basin, D., Krstić, S.: Real-time policy enforcement with metric first-order temporal logic. Tech. rep., ETH Zürich, Extended Report (2022). https://gitlab.ethz.ch/fhublet/mfotl-enforcement/-/blob/main/paper/extended.pdf

36. Jobstmann, B., Bloem, R.: Optimizations for LTL synthesis. In: International Conference Formal Methods in Computer-Aided Design (FMCAD), pp. 117–124. IEEE (2006). https://doi.org/10.1109/FMCAD.2006.22

37. Khoussainov, B., Nerode, A.: Automatic presentations of structures. In: Leivant, D. (ed.) LCC 1994. LNCS, vol. 960, pp. 367–392. Springer, Heidelberg (1995). https://doi.org/10.1007/3-540-60178-3_93

38. Krstić, S., Schneider, J.: A benchmark generator for online first-order monitoring. In: Deshmukh, J., Ničković, D. (eds.) RV 2020. LNCS, vol. 12399, pp. 482–494. Springer, Cham (2020). https://doi.org/10.1007/978-3-030-60508-7_27

39. Kupferman, O., Vardi, M.Y.: Safraless decision procedures. In: Symposium on Foundations of Computer Science (FOCS), pp. 531–542. IEEE (2005). https://doi.org/10.1109/SFCS.2005.66

40. Li, G., Jensen, P., Larsen, K., Legay, A., Poulsen, D.: Practical controller synthesis for $mtl_{0,\infty}$. In: Erdogmus, H., Havelund, K. (eds.) ACM SIGSOFT International SPIN Symposium on Model Checking of Software, pp. 102–111. ACM (2017). https://doi.org/10.1145/3092282.3092303

41. Ligatti, J., Bauer, L., Walker, D.: Enforcing non-safety security policies with program monitors. In: di Vimercati, S.C., Syverson, P., Gollmann, D. (eds.) ESORICS 2005. LNCS, vol. 3679, pp. 355–373. Springer, Heidelberg (2005). https://doi.org/10.1007/11555827_21

42. Ligatti, J., Bauer, L., Walker, D.: Run-time enforcement of nonsafety policies. ACM Trans. Inf. Syst. Secur. **12**(3), 1–41 (2009). https://doi.org/10.1145/1455526.1455532

43. Maler, O., Nickovic, D., Pnueli, A.: From MITL to timed automata. In: Asarin, E., Bouyer, P. (eds.) FORMATS 2006. LNCS, vol. 4202, pp. 274–289. Springer, Heidelberg (2006). https://doi.org/10.1007/11867340_20

44. Peter, H.-J., Ehlers, R., Mattmüller, R.: Synthia: verification and synthesis for timed automata. In: Gopalakrishnan, G., Qadeer, S. (eds.) CAV 2011. LNCS, vol. 6806, pp. 649–655. Springer, Heidelberg (2011). https://doi.org/10.1007/978-3-642-22110-1_52

45. Pinisetty, S., Falcone, Y., Jéron, T., Marchand, H.: TiPEX: a tool chain for timed property enforcement during eXecution. In: Bartocci, E., Majumdar, R. (eds.) RV 2015. LNCS, vol. 9333, pp. 306–320. Springer, Cham (2015). https://doi.org/10.1007/978-3-319-23820-3_22

46. Pnueli, A., Rosner, R.: On the synthesis of a reactive module. In: ACM Symposium on Principles of Programming Languages (POPL), pp. 179–190. ACM (1989). https://doi.org/10.1145/75277.75293

47. Pnueli, A., Rosner, R.: On the synthesis of an asynchronous reactive module. In: Ausiello, G., Dezani-Ciancaglini, M., Della Rocca, S.R. (eds.) ICALP 1989. LNCS, vol. 372, pp. 652–671. Springer, Heidelberg (1989). https://doi.org/10.1007/BFb0035790

48. Raman, V., Donzé, A., Sadigh, D., Murray, R., Seshia, S.: Reactive synthesis from signal temporal logic specifications. In: Girard, A., Sankaranarayanan, S. (eds.) International Conference on Hybrid Systems: Computation & Control (HSCC), pp. 239–248. ACM (2015). https://doi.org/10.1145/2728606.2728628

49. Renard, M., Rollet, A., Falcone, Y.: GREP: games for the runtime enforcement of properties. In: Yevtushenko, N., Cavalli, A.R., Yenigün, H. (eds.) ICTSS 2017. LNCS, vol. 10533, pp. 259–275. Springer, Cham (2017). https://doi.org/10.1007/978-3-319-67549-7_16

50. Riganelli, O., Micucci, D., Mariani, L.: Policy enforcement with proactive libraries. In: International Symposium on Software Engineering for Adaptive and Self-Managing Systems (SEAMS), pp. 182–192. IEEE (2017). https://doi.org/10.1109/SEAMS.2017.9

51. Rushby, J.: Design and verification of secure systems. In: Howard, J., Reed, D. (eds.) Symposium on Operating System Principles (SOSP), pp. 12–21. ACM (1981). https://doi.org/10.1145/800216.806586

52. Rushby, J.: Kernels for safety. In: Safe and Secure Computing Systems, pp. 210–220 (1989)

53. Schewe, S., Finkbeiner, B.: Bounded synthesis. In: Namjoshi, K.S., Yoneda, T., Higashino, T., Okamura, Y. (eds.) ATVA 2007. LNCS, vol. 4762, pp. 474–488. Springer, Heidelberg (2007). https://doi.org/10.1007/978-3-540-75596-8_33

54. Schneider, F.: Enforceable security policies. ACM Trans. Inf. Syst. Secur. **3**(1), 30–50 (2000). https://doi.org/10.1145/353323.353382

55. Schneider, J., Basin, D., Krstić, S., Traytel, D.: A formally verified monitor for metric first-order temporal logic. In: Finkbeiner, B., Mariani, L. (eds.) RV 2019. LNCS, vol. 11757, pp. 310–328. Springer, Cham (2019). https://doi.org/10.1007/978-3-030-32079-9_18

56. Zhu, S., Tabajara, L.M., Li, J., Pu, G., Vardi, M.Y.: A symbolic approach to safety LTL synthesis. In: HVC 2017. LNCS, vol. 10629, pp. 147–162. Springer, Cham (2017). https://doi.org/10.1007/978-3-319-70389-3_10

# A Tale of Four Gates
## Privilege Escalation and Permission Bypasses on Android Through App Components

Abdulla Aldoseri[✉], David Oswald[✉], and Robert Chiper[✉]

University of Birmingham, Birmingham, UK
{axa1170,d.f.oswald}@bham.ac.uk, robert.chiper@pm.me

**Abstract.** Android apps interact and exchange data with other apps through so-called app components. Previous research has shown that app components can cause application-level vulnerabilities, for example leading to data leakage across apps. Alternatively, apps can (intentionally or accidentally) expose their permissions (e.g. for camera and microphone) to other apps that lack these privileges. This causes a confused deputy situation, where a less privileged app exposes its app components, which use these permissions, to the victim app. While previous research mainly focused on these issues, less attention has been paid to how app components can affect the security and privacy guarantees of Android OS. In this paper, we demonstrate two according vulnerabilities, affecting recent Android versions. First, we show how app components can be used to leak data from and, in some cases, take full control of other Android user profiles, bypassing the dedicated lock screen. We demonstrate the impact of this vulnerability on major Android vendors (Samsung, Huawei, Google and Xiaomi). Secondly, we found that app components can be abused by spyware to access sensors like the camera and the microphone in the background up to Android 10, bypassing mitigations specifically designed to prevent this behaviour. Using a two-app setup, we find that app components can be invoked stealthily to e.g. periodically take pictures and audio recordings in the background. Finally, we present Four Gates Inspector, our open-source static analysis tool to systematically detect such issues for a large number of apps with complex codebases. Our tool successfully identified exposed components issues in 34 out 5,783 apps with average analysis runtime of 4.3 s per app and, detected both known malware samples and unknown samples downloaded from the F-Droid repository. We responsibly disclosed all vulnerabilities presented in this paper to the affected vendors, leading to several CVE records and a currently unresolved high-severity issue in Android 10 and earlier.

**Keywords:** Android · Application components · Multi-user · Sensors

## 1 Introduction

App sandboxing and isolation on widely deployed mobile operating systems like Android have brought various security benefits with it. However, due to the

© The Author(s), under exclusive license to Springer Nature Switzerland AG 2022
V. Atluri et al. (Eds.): ESORICS 2022, LNCS 13555, pp. 233–251, 2022.
https://doi.org/10.1007/978-3-031-17146-8_12

need to exchange data across apps and to access system resources like sensors (camera, microphone, etc.), Android provides several externally accessible entry points into apps beyond the user interface. The four main entry points (activities, services, broadcast receivers and content providers) are called app components. Over the last few years, app components have received considerable attention from security researchers [16, 23, 37]. Numerous vulnerabilities have been found that led to, among others, privileges escalation and side-channel leakage of user data [16, 38]. However, less attention has been paid to how these components interact with Android-wide restrictions, e.g., the separation of user-profiles and the permission system. In this paper, we address this issue and show how exposed app components can be used in unintended ways to break Android's Multi-User (MU) feature, (mis)use permissions held by other apps, and conceive a construction that allows accessing the camera and microphone in the background on recent Android versions. Subsequently, we introduce Four Gates Inspector, an open-source static analysis tool that can aid developers in detecting and preventing certain issues discovered in this paper.

## 1.1    Contributions

In this paper, we systematically analyse exposed app components across system restrictions and multiple user profiles on the same device. Based on our analysis, we discover several vulnerabilities impacting user privacy and security. We first show that users with the INTERACT_ACROSS_USERS or ACCESS_CONTENT_PROVIDER _EXTERNALLY permissions can invoke app components belonging to other user profiles. As the adb shell user has this permission by default, an attacker with either physical or remote access via WebUSB can misuse those interfaces to install apps into another user's profile, grant arbitrary permissions, and then exfiltrate the data through app components. Notably, the shell user does not have read/write access to other user profiles through standard means (e.g., using filesystem commands like ls, cd). The attack bypasses the dedicated lockscreen of the target user profile.

Secondly, we show that app components allow adversaries to construct stealthy spyware that can access sensors like the camera and microphone in the background. This is achieved by installing two apps: one app exposes access to the sensors through app components, and a second (unprivileged) app repeatedly invokes this functionality in the background. This issue bypasses countermeasures against background spyware for recent Android versions up to Android 10, thus affecting all Android devices in use at the time of reporting (Sep, 2020) [31].

To mitigate the issues presented in this paper, we propose Four Gates Inspector, a static analysis tool to detect the usage of a given class or API (e.g., camera or microphone) by tracing the invocation of methods of each app component using graph-based analysis. Additionally, the tool aids in detecting confused deputy issues in exposed app components [22]. Our main contributions are:

– We perform a systematic and empirical analysis of app components, including communication across user profiles, visibility of the user, and restrictions.

- We analyse the main four implementations of the Android multi-user feature (Samsung secure folder, Huawei private space, Xiaomi second space, Google multi-user) and show how to bypass Android lock screen protection in them, giving full access to an adversary through app components.
- We show how spyware can use app components to stealthily access camera and microphone in the background, breaking the OS countermeasures against such techniques up to Android 10.
- We present Four Gates Inspector, our open-source static analysis tool to detect the use of specific APIs (e.g., sensor access) in app component handlers. We show that Four Gates Inspector can not only detect known samples of background spyware, but also identified confused deputy issues in 34 (benign) apps (out of a sample of 5,783) downloaded from F-Droid [18] with an average runtime of 4.3 s per app.

## 1.2  Responsible Disclosure

The vulnerabilities described in this paper have been responsibly disclosed through the proper channels. Samsung secure folder's issue was reported on August 18, 2020, assigned moderate severity, and can be tracked via CVE-2020-26606. The vulnerability of Huawei's private space was reported on August 18, 2020, assigned moderate severity, and can be tracked via CVE-2020-9119. We reported Xiaomi's second space issue on August 28, 2020. However, Xiaomi informed us that this issue had been reported in parallel by a third party and was fixed on August 31, 2020. Finally, we reported Google's multi-user feature issue on Sep 17, 2020. In contrast to the other vendors, Google considers this as intended behaviour as does not intend to deploy a fix.

The stealthy background access to camera and microphone issue was reported to Google on Sep 18, 2020, and assigned a high severity. Google then confirmed that the issue has been fixed in Android 11. Google did not assign a CVE to this issue, as our report coincided with the release of Android 11 and thus did not affect the latest Android OS. The issue can be tracked via id 175232797 on Google issue tracker We further explored the the respective changes in Android 11 and found that Google re-designed the permission system to specifically mitigate this issue [9].

To ensure the reproducibility of our work and to provide the community with a relevant sample of vulnerable apps for evaluating future attacks and defences, we provide our code, demo videos, including Four Gates Inspector at https://akaldoseri.github.io/a-tale-of-four-gates/ and a-tale-of-four-gates repository at github.com.

## 2  Background

We first give an overview of app components and their security aspects.

***App Components.*** Mobile apps are isolated and sandboxed by Android OS in a per-app Virtual Machine (VM). For app communication, Android offers mechanisms to share data between apps. Among them is app components where they serve as entry points allowing communication between apps. They are widely used in practice. Thus, we focus on this aspect. There are four types of app components: *activity, service, broadcast receiver* and *content provider*. An *activity* consist of a user interface and an executable code section. *Services* run in the background without user interface/interaction. *Broadcast receivers* respond, once registered, to broadcasted Android Intents. *Content providers* abstract the interaction with app data, e.g., files or SQLite databases [5].

App components are accessible to other apps if their respective `exported` attribute in the manifest is set. They can be restricted by assigning them app-specific (custom) permissions which provide a protection level from low (*normal*) to higher levels (*dangerous, signature*, and *signatureOrSystem*) [8].

*Multi-user Feature.* In addition to app isolation, Android also provides a multi-user feature that allows to set up several isolated user profiles on a single device. Each profile has a workplace to store data and install apps [27]. To prevent users (including the `shell` user) from accessing each other data, Users' data is stored in a separate virtual area in the internal storage [4]. Additionally, a user can lock their profile via Android Gatekeeper (e.g., through their PIN or fingerprint) [3]. Use cases for this include a device shared by family members or an on-call team.

## 3   Related Work

*Privileges Escalation on Custom Permissions.* Custom permissions have a unique name and protection level to ensure access protection for their allocated resources. Several issues have been reported in custom permissions related to OS and app updates: Xing et al. showed that one can claim ownership of resources (e.g., permissions, package names, etc.) by defining them in an app in an old Android OS before they are actually introduced in an OS update [34]. (e.g., a malicious app can obtain the system permission `ADD_VOICEMAIL`). Tuncay et al. showed that an adversary can obtain signature permissions from third-party apps without signature matching. For this, the adversary first installs two apps, where one defines the target permission and the other grants it. By uninstalling the first app and installing the victim app, the second app gains access to the victim app using its target permissions, regardless of signature mismatches. This is because Android OS does not revoke granted permissions by default [33]. Considering the properties of Android that caused these issues, Rui Li et al. proposed a fuzzer to detect such problems by evaluating custom permissions in randomly created apps installed on devices across different test cases, including system update and app update. Their work demonstrates several issues that allow adversaries to obtain sensitive permissions without user consent [25].

*Exposed App Components.* Confused deputy attacks [22] are vulnerabilities in which an (unprivileged) attacker misuses permissions granted to a higher privileged component due to missing checks in communication interfaces. In the context of mobile devices, it has been repeatedly shown that this problem can manifest in apps [15,20,28,33].

In most cases, the underlying reason was the exposure of app components to all apps on the device by setting their `exported` flag. For instance, as a consequence, a content provider that manages private app data may expose full read/write access to this data if no restrictions are imposed [38]. Therefore, researcher have focused on developing tools and methods to detect such issues. Zhou and Jiang systemically analysed 62,519 apps w.r.t. two different impacts: data leakage and denial of (some) Android services. Their analysis showed that 1,279 (2.0%) and 871 (1.4%) apps were vulnerable to those issues, respectively [38]. Heuser et al. propose DroidAuditor, an Android module that observes apps behaviour at runtime and generates a graph-based representation of access to sensitive resources (e.g., camera, SMS, etc.) to inspect collusion attacks and confused deputy attacks [23]. Similarly, Yang Xu et al. developed a framework to detect permission-based issues by collecting runtime app states and applying policies and capability-based access control to mitigate these issues at runtime [35]. Bugiel et al. implemented a detection tool that monitors IPC communication at runtime and uses heuristics as well as detection rules [14]. Reardon et al. proposes a detection tool for covert channels and side channels in apps by monitoring an app's runtime behaviour and network traffic, whereas the interaction with the apps was automated with a user interface fuzzer [28]. Felt et al. developed an IPC inspector tool that revokes permissions temporarily when apps communicate with each other. The revocation process keeps only the commonly granted permissions between the communicating apps [20]. As a limitation, these solutions require changes on the OS level and access to high-privilege services. Also, their dynamic analysis nature may leave some code paths unexplored if only triggered by specific inputs, e.g., on a login screen [28].

Alternatively, other researchers have proposed approaches based on static analysis. CHEX is a taint-based method to detect leakage in exposed components [26]. AppSealer follows CHEX' approach, which is based on Taint-Droid [17,36]. AppSealer additionally introduces a patch code generator to patch the detected issues. Zhong et al. utilise tainting to detect these issues between selected pairs of applications by comparing their permission and performing inter-application control flow analysis [37]. Finally, Elsabagh et al. propose FIRMSCOPE, a static analysis tool based on practical context-sensitive, flow-sensitive, field-sensitive, and partially object-sensitive taint analysis [16]. It detected several privilege escalation vulnerabilities in system apps, including code execution using exposed components. FIRMSCOPE achieves a better performance than its predecessors FlowDROID [13], AmandDroid, and Droidsafe. Overall, methods based on taint analysis are limited by their high performance costs, which make them less practical [35], and over-tainting problems that may lead to false positives.

To overcome these limitations, in Sect. 6, we propose a static analysis tool that detects (i) confused deputy issues and the potential bypass of system restrictions and constraints (e.g., using the camera in the background) and (ii) exposure of certain libraries (e.g., tracking and scoped storage). For (i), we noticed that [20] does not consider two apps that expose the use of the same permission (e.g., camera) and communicate with each other. However, in Sect. 5, we show that this can bypass Android OS restriction to access the camera in the background. For (ii), most previously proposed solutions rely on permission settings. Recently, noticeable operations like scoped storage [7] introduced in Android allow access to the internal storage for read/write without storage permission, which might not be detectable by existing tools. Finally, given that taint-based approaches are computationally costly, we decided to investigate the alternative approach of statically analysing the execution trace of app components in a graph-based representation and detecting issues on the level of Smali code.

*Compromising User Privacy.* Starting from Android 9, Android prevents background services from accessing the camera and the microphone, even if they have the necessary permissions. Apps with foreground services can still use the camera and microphone without the app being in focus, but only if they display a persistent notification to users [2]. Sutter and Tellenbach discovered a race condition in this functionality: quickly hiding the foreground service's notifications allowed them to create spyware that uses the camera and microphone without showing any visible notification [32]. In Android 11, the camera and microphone can be used only while the app is active and in use (*i.e.*, in the foreground) [11]. In our work, we bypass the restriction that prevents access to camera and microphone while the app is in the background. We achieve this by accessing these sensors via exposed components from another app, which the activity manager considers to have foreground visibility.

*Containers and Multi-user Feature.* The Android multi-user feature has received considerable attention from the research community: Ratazzi et al. performed a systematic security evaluation, considering a threat model where multiple users share the same device. They discovered several vulnerabilities, e.g., that secondary users can access the owner's services like VPN, network, backup and reset settings because they are exported publicly. OEM-specific functionality derived from the multi-user feature has suffered from several issues in the past: the security space service that manages Xiaomi's second space allowed an adversary to switch to the second space without user authentication [19]. This was because the service was publicly accessible, and an adversary could start it with a crafted intent to bypass the authentication process. Kanonov and Wool reported several issues in Samsung Knox containers, including a man-in-the-middle vulnerability in the VPN service and data leakage from the Knox clipboard [24]. We demonstrate an issue that allows extracting data from either multi-user or OEM-specific spaces, bypassing the dedicated lock through the shell user permissions.

## 4    Analysis of App Components Across User Profiles

Starting from Android 5, Android supports a multi-user feature that allows adding additional users to the device so that a device can be shared by multiple people [4]. Regarding the security guarantees provided by the multi-user functionality, the relevant documentation states that "each user gets a workspace to install and place apps" and "No user has access to the app data of another user" [4]. Technically, as discussed in Sect. 2, each user's data is stored in a separate virtual area to prevent accessing the data of other users. Users can lock their profile via Android Gatekeeper [3]. However, apps can interact with each other using app components. Thus, the question arises if it is (i) possible to invoke app components of an app in one user profile from another profile, and (ii) if this can be used to bypass the user-specific lock screen.

***Accessing App Components with Different Users.*** We experimentally investigated interactions between an app residing in one profile and another one in another profile. We started by creating two users, "adversary" and "victim", and two apps in each profile: A callee app with four exposed app components (activity, service, background, and receiver), and a caller app to invoke the victim app components. Our initial analysis showed that apps can only interact with each other if they are in the same profile. Debugging the caller to send messages via adb using the activity manager am, and content tools showed that messages target apps in the same profile by default. Yet, we found that both tools accept a --user flag to specify the user ID of the target profile unlike their equivalent Java API. Specifying a user ID (obtained via the package manager pm) in the messages results in a permission denied exception from the UserCont roller class. We thus confirmed that apps cannot communicate across profiles by default.

***Underlying Permission.*** After analysing the exception, we found that UserC ontroller class manages multi-user functionality for am and, a user can interact with app components from other profiles if it has INTERACT_ACROSS_USERS_FULL, I NTERACT_ACROSS_USERS permissions for Android intents, and ACCESS_CONTENT_PROV IDER_EXTERNALLY permission for content providers.

These permissions are granted only for system apps with signature protection level (*i.e.*, apps signed with the system image certificate) [6]. An accessible user is the shell user (implemented by com.android.shell). We analysed its respective APK file and found that the shell package has all these permissions. Utilising du mpsys, we confirmed that the shell user is effectively granted these permissions.

By default, the shell user does not have read/write access to other users' profiles. Using commands like ls or cd to access them leads to insufficient permission errors. Therefore, we focus on exploiting these permissions. We sent both an intent and a content query using the shell, specifying the victim's user id, and noticed that sending an intent to an activity does trigger the lockscreen protection (Gatekeeper). However, for services, broadcast receivers and content providers, this is not the case, as they do not have a visible user interface. We thus could successfully bypass the Gatekeeper protection and interact with apps from a different profile. (e.g., a secondary user able to extract information from Owner user). Yet, practically exploiting this either requires a vulnerable app in the target profile, or the ability to install specific apps (e.g., an app that exposes user information through an app component) into the victim profile.

***Threat Model.*** Ratazzi et al. consider a threat model based on physical access to the device where a single device is shared by multiple users to show data leakage issues in the multi-user feature [27]. Such a model applies to our issue. However, we also consider a more generic threat model, where a victim uses a service that requires access to ADB (e.g., Vysor, GenyMobile, MirrorGo, ApowerMirror). These services are widely used for screen mirroring, operate on desktops or browsers via WebUSB, and have over 12M users in total. Because ADB gives the service access to potentially sensitive data in the user profile, we further assume that the user has created a second profile to limit the information accessible via ADB. Clearly, this threat model may be seen as specific and may require additional social engineering or similar circumstances. It does not require knowledge of PIN or fingerprint of the target profile or rooting the device and is thus applicable to Android devices where rooting is detectable, e.g., through a warranty bit [29] or where PIN/fingerprint are protected by secure hardware.

***Data Extraction Across User Profiles.*** To demonstrate a proof-of-concept of data extraction from another user profile (e.g., private profile or secure space), we first observed that the package manager system binary `pm` also accepts a `--u ser` flag, similar to `am` and `content`. `pm` exposes a range of app management operations, including app installation and granting of arbitrary permissions. Thus, a combination of `am`, `pm`, and `content` allows to fully bypass the isolation between user profiles for a `shell` adversary. Concretely, the attack proceeds as follows:

- The victim visits an adversary-controlled website with ADB support (e.g., disguised as a screen mirroring service) and connects their device to it via WebUSB.
- The adversary's website silently installs a malicious app into the victim's other user profile (e.g., one created to separate sensitive data from a profile used for screen mirroring) through `pm`.

  ```
  $ pm install com.app.malicious.apk --user 2
  ```

- Using `pm`, the adversary grants the malicious app read access to the victim user space's internal storage (e.g., `READ_EXTERNAL_STORAGE`) (or other permissions).

  ```
  $ pm grant com.app.malicious READ_EXTERNAL_STORAGE --user 2
  ```

- Finally, the adversary use the `shell` user to either send an intent or a content query to the malicious app to communicate with its app's components (service, broadcast receiver, or content provider) and instruct it to upload data (e.g., pictures and content of the internal storage) to a server under attacker control.

  ```
  $ content query --uri content://com.app.malicious/cp --user 2
  ```

- To hide the attack's traces, the malicious app can finally be removed via `pm`.

Alternatively, the above attack can also be carried out by an adversary with physical access to the device and a user profile, e.g., an abusive partner or family member of the victim. Apart from that, an adversary can also perform other actions using the system's Media Content Provider, which abstracts the interaction with a user's gallery. This includes: (i) reading all images from the victim user profile, (ii) placing own images into the victim user profile, possibly with incriminating content, and (iii) Denial-of-service (or ransomware-like) attack by deleting data (or threatening to do so) inside the victim user profile.

*Vendor-Specific Multi-user Implementations.* The above issue was demonstrated for the multi-user feature of Google devices. Other vendors chose to apply modifications to this functionality and refer to it with their names: Samsung's secure folder, Huawei's private space, and Xiaomi's second space, which all provide similar features to the default Android multi-user mode. However, some of these variants have been enhanced with protections to prevent access in case of rooting the device e.g., through Samsung Knox [29,30] or while the device is in debug mode for Huawei.

We thus analysed to what extent those implementations suffer from the same issues as the default multi-user function. For all tested variants, an `adb` shell provided a user with the required `INTERACT_ACROSS_USERS` or `ACCESS_CONTENT_PRO VIDER_EXTERNALLY` permission. We further found that, depending on the vendor, some restrictions were imposed on the `pm`, `am`, and `content` binaries. Table 1 in Appendix A summarises our findings.

Apart from Samsung secure folder, all implementations allowed installing apps in the victim profile and were thus vulnerable to the above attack, and also exposed full access to the gallery through the Media Content Provider. For Samsung, we compared to version of secure folder (1.2.32 for older devices below Android 9 and 1.4.06 for new devices). In both cases, installing apps was prevented, however, the Media Content Provider exposed full image data (for 1.2.32) or at least metadata (for 1.4.06), e.g., timestamps and geolocation.

Samsung and Huawei assessed the respective vulnerability as "moderate". For those vendors, the issue can be tracked via CVE-2020-26606 and CVE-2020-9119, respectively. Xiaomi was already aware of this issue at the time of our report and rolled out a fix shortly thereafter. Google regarded the issue as intended behaviour and thus does not plan to release mitigations.

## 5    Analysis of Sensor Background Access

Based on Sect. 2, we determined that app components are capable to be started by any other app with appropriate permissions. Also, app components like services, broadcast receivers and content providers are invisible to the user (no notifications), but can nevertheless access certain Android APIs, including sensors like camera and microphone (if the app has the required permissions). Since Android 9, the OS prevents apps to access those sensors in the background, even if the app has the required sensor access permissions [2] to ensure user privacy.

This restriction applies unless a foreground service displays a persistent notification to the user indicating its activity [11]. This raises the question of how Android distinguishes between "foreground" and "background" at a technical level, and especially how invocations of app components like content providers and services are handled w.r.t. to this aspect.

*Importance of App Components.* To answer this question, we developed a test app with four app components (activity, service, broadcast receiver, and content provider). Each component then dumps the current "importance" of the app. This importance refers to a numerical value that precisely specifies the visibility and foreground/background state of the app [1]. Generally, the foreground is given an importance of 100, while larger values indicated states increasingly in the background.

We noticed that the app has an importance of 100 (foreground) when it is visible to the user, regardless of any app components used. When the app is minimised and stopped, the observed importances range from 125 (foreground service) over 200 (visible) to 300 (service). Using the activity manager's start-fo reground-service option, background services can be run as foreground services and be assigned their respective importance, even if they are not developed as foreground services [11]. This highlights that "background" in Android OS does not refer to a single state, but actually a range of importances. As Android prevents access to the camera and microphone in the "background", it is important to determine for which importance this block is actually active.

To determine this, we developed two apps: the first app has three app components (service, broadcast receiver and content provider). We exclude the activity because it always runs in the foreground and thus visible to the user. We granted access to the microphone and the camera to the app and intentionally exposed these functions through all three app components. The second app then invokes the app components of the first app. We configured the intent for accessing the broadcast receiver and the service with FLAG_INCLUDE_STOPPED_PACKAGES, allowing it to invoke stopped apps. Crucially, we found that *all three app components were capable to access the camera with the first app in the background*, while the microphone was accessible from the service and content provider. No notification is shown to the user, making exploitation of this issue stealthy. Yet, in the initial proof-of-concept, the second (invoking) app was in the foreground, making practical exploitation obvious. To avoid this, we next consider how to invoke the respective app components from a background app.

## 5.1 Stealthy Background Spyware

Android provides several services (e.g., Timer, JobSchedule, AlarmManage and Runnable) for an app to persist in the background after it has been closed. While direct access to the camera and microphone is blocked in the context of these services by Android to prevent background spyware, app components can be invoked using these methods. As the timer class provides a minimum invocation interval of 1 s, it represents the best choice for an adversary to frequently capture camera images and audio through a second app's components.

Combining the caller app running in the background with a callee app that exposes sensor access through app components, stealthy, persistent spyware can be devised. Concretely, the attack proceeds as follows:

- The adversary installs (or tricks the user into installing) a *sensor app* that exposes a suitable app components (service, broadcast receiver, or content provider). This app must be granted sufficient permission to access the respective device sensors (*i.e.*, camera and microphone).
- The adversary then installs (or tricks the user into installing) the second *spyware service app* ①. This app has a single background service that starts a timer. This timer periodically communicates with the app component of the sensor app to record images and audio ②, and e.g., then upload them to a remote server under adversary control. The spyware app does not require any permissions and its service can run in the background ③.

The spyware app periodically communicates with the app component of the sensor app in the background. This will bring the sensor app temporarily to importances of 125, 200, and 300 (foreground service, visible, service), enabling access to all device sensors. While the pair of our attacker apps are running, there are no user-visible indications or notifications. Because the service app does not consume substantial device resources, after 3–5 s of running, Android will white-list it and consider it a cache process, which will not be terminated. The cache process can hence remain active for a long time—in our tests, it ran continuously for more than two hours until we force stopped it. The attack works regardless of using other apps, using the camera, or locking the phone.

Reviewing the source code [21] of Android 10 shows that the camera and microphone rely on the activity manager to determine if the calling app is active (not idle or in the background) by checking its proc state. The proc state value is a numeric value convertible to an importance. The activity manager implementation translates the observed importance of 125, 200, and 300 into the proc states of foreground service, foreground, and service, which are all considered not to be in the background and thus allow bypassing sensor access restrictions.

***Threat Model.*** We consider the "two-app setup" threat model widely used in the literature [15,20,28,33]. We assume an adversary that can install two apps on the target device (instead of one for "classical" spyware). This adversary model is realistic for spyware, where the attacker (e.g., an abusive partner) might have temporary access to the device or might be able to social-engineer a victim into installing apps disguised as harmless software (e.g., games or other apps by the same developer). Additionally, we consider the threat model of [38], where a benign app exposes access to sensors via exposed components: a malicious app can scan for such vulnerable app components and thus "inherit" their permissions. According to our experiments, the issue affects all devices running Android 10 and earlier. It does not replicate on Android 11 due to changes in the permission system as discussed in Sect. 7. Our attack does not require root or a `db shell` access and hence also applies to devices where no root exploit exists or where rooting leaves traces. As we detail further in Sect. 6, we found instances of this issue in real-world apps.

# 6    Evaluation

In this section, we evaluate the discovered issues to assess their impact and provide a detection mechanism for security researchers and mobile developers. First, the multi-user issues only affect OEM devices and are somewhat limited. Therefore, debugging the device using the *pm* and *am* binaries as discussed in Sect. 4 is sufficient for detection. A limitation of this approach might be that some devices do not have developer options or the shell user is inaccessible.

Conversely, the background spyware issue affects mobile apps and requires analysing the app to detect it. Therefore, we designed Four Gates Inspector to systematically discover corresponding issues and resolve limitations of existing solutions. Security researchers and mobile developers can use our tool to detect possible malicious apps. This is especially relevant when vendors pre-install third-party apps as part of system images. In the following, we discuss the design, implementation and practical results obtained with Four Gates Inspector.

## 6.1    Four Gates Inspector

As discussed in Sect. 3, runtime analysis tools previously proposed in the literature might not reach code paths that require specific input, e.g., login screens [28] and require changes to the OS, which makes them less practical. Additionally, taint-based solutions suffer from non-negligible computational cost and over-tainting that may lead to false positives [35]. To overcome this limitation, we investigate the potential of developing a static analysis tool that aids in the detection these issues. We designed Four Gates Inspector to statically analyse apps and detect confused deputy issues based on the usage of given classes and methods. Our tool is based on analysing the execution trace of the decompiled Smali code of app components. Four Gates Inspector offers a filter list that limits the scope of the analysis (e.g., camera usage, storage leakage, GPS). It provides fine-grained control over the analysis scope on the class level, compared to the permission level used by Bugiel et al. 's framework [14]. This allows us to trace issues related to non-permission classes, e.g., scoped storage in Android 11 [7].

*Design and Implementation.* Four Gates Inspector focuses on the execution trace of method invocation of app components, in contrast to taint-based solutions that trace the input and may introduce over-tainting [35]. We thus avoid false positives (e.g., due to usage of sensors unrelated to app components) and can also detect attempts to hide sensor use (e.g., through nested calls). Our tool is implemented in Python and requires apktool [12] to decompile mobile apps and untangle to parse XML files. Four Gates Inspector consist of four main modules: *Smali Handler*, *Manifest handler*, *APK handler* and *Component inspector*.

Overall, Four Gates Inspector implements the basic flow shown in Fig. 1 to analyse an app. First, the *Component inspector*, which controls the flow of the tool, starts by loading the application file (APK) and the filter list ①. The *APK handler* unpacks the app to extract the Smali code and Android manifest

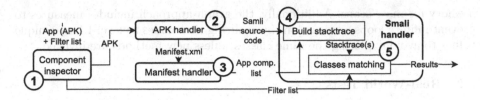

**Fig. 1.** Flow of Four Gates Inspector for analysis of app components.

②. The *Manifest handler* parses the app's Android manifest to detect app components and the use of specific classes and APIs (e.g., camera, microphone or storage) ③. To this end, the *Smali handler* initiates static analysis. It receives the component name from the Android manifest, builds a stack trace of all invoked methods and their classes for each component by parsing their Smali source code, and explores the stack trace for the usage of filter list ④.

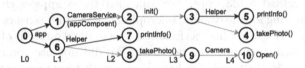

**Fig. 2.** Stack trace tree generated by Four Gates Inspector.

The stack trace (Fig. 2) is a tree-structured graph G(N,V): each app component has its G(N,V) tree, where N is a set of nodes that represent the invoked classes/methods in the execution trace, and V is a set of vertices that represent the invocation sequence between nodes. Figure 2 shows an example of the generated stack trace tree of an app that uses the camera through a CameraS ervice component via a custom Helper class. The graph starts with the single root node n0 for the app package class. Node n1 at level 1 represents an app component class. The *Smali handler* starts by identifying method and class invocation within n1. The top-level invoked methods in n1 (e.g., constructor, etc.) are added as children to n1. Then, each method at level 2 is analyzed to find further invocations to be added to the tree at level 3. The level 3 nodes might have an invocation to external classes and methods. These external invocations are added as child nodes to the root node n0. The process is repeated, starting with the Smali handler, for the new level 1 nodes, until all code has been traced. Once the stack trace is complete, the Smali handler performs tree traversal for each stack trace to detect the use of certain classes/methods. This is repeated for each component. Finally, Four Gates Inspector produces a summary report, containing detailed information about the inspected issues, class usage, stack traces, (custom) permissions and exported flags for each usage of the filtered APIs ⑤. Each stack trace of an app component is generated independently and reported to allow partial processing of apps, which avoids exhausting the memory for mass scans. Additionally, the graph approach includes measures to prevent infinite loops or recursions by ensuring that nodes at level 1 have unique values to avoid exploring the same classes unless new methods are invoked.

## 6.2 Real-World Tests

We evaluated the correctness and effectiveness of the tool using two test samples:

**Known samples test:** We analysed two known samples for use of the camera in the background. The first sample is the proof-of-concept for CVE-2019-2219, utilizing a race condition in a foreground service to use the camera in the background [32]. The second sample is our own proof-of-concept from Sect. 5.

**Unknown samples test:** To detect unknown instances, we downloaded 6,687 apps from F-Droid, a repository of free and open-source apps [18]. The apps are from multiple categories including navigation, development, graphics and system apps. We also considered multiple versions of an app to detect issues that were fixed (or introduced) with new versions. After eliminating duplicates, this yielded 5,783 apps. We analysed these apps with Four Gates Inspector, filtering for the camera, microphone, hardware sensors (accelerometer/gyro) and GPS use. This was followed by a manual analysis of the detected issues to confirm they are true positives. We did not use commercial apps, e.g., from Google Play, to avoid legal issues with terms and conditions that prohibit reverse engineering—this decision was taken because manual screening of the terms of thousands of apps is infeasible.

## 6.3 Evaluation and Results

In the known sample test, as expected, Four Gates Inspector successfully detected both spyware samples and indicated the exact instruction where camera and microphone are used. In the unknown sample test, the tool successfully generated reports for all 5,783 apps. Of these, 151 apps used sensors. Filtering for exported components apps yielded 34 apps with 43 components using sensors. We evaluated the correctness of the tool by manually analysing the Smali code of all those 34 cases of sensor use. We found that all the 43 cases were true positives and Four Gates Inspector correctly identified sensor usages.

In terms of performance overhead, we measured the execution time for analysis of each app under Ubuntu 16 on an i7 with 16 GB RAM. We calculated the average runtime of over 5,783 apps to be 4.3 s, which is reasonable for mass analysis, especially considering that our tool can be run in parallel. Comparing our tool to existing solutions, Four Gates Inspector is faster than other tools: AppSealer and FIRMSCOPE report 1–3 min and 7 min on average, respectively, to process an app. Note that the authors of AppSealer used a machine similar to ours (Intel i7 with 8 GB RAM), while FIRMSCOPE ran on a high-performance server (Intel Xeon 40-core processor with 150 GB RAM).

Remarkably, Four Gates Inspector found two instances of confused deputy issues in the tested apps, highlighting the practical relevance of our approach: `com.commonslab.commonslab` and `org.wikimedia.commons.wikimedia`, both used to access Wikimedia Commons, expose the audio recording permission to any unprivileged app on the same device.

We did not find instances of clearly malicious spyware in our sample collection, indicating that this type of malware is not common on open platforms like F-Droid. Comparing our results to Zhou and Jiang's study from 2012 [38], we observe a clear improvement in the adoption of proper security practices: most apps disabled the `exported` flag for their app components. Additionally, our tool can correctly distinguish between vulnerable and secure versions of apps. For instance, only version 9.1 of `net.majorkernelpanic.spydroid` had a component using a sensor, but not earlier and the later versions.

## 6.4 Limitations

Four Gates Inspector has certain limitations: while it handles inner classes, interfaces, extended classes, and case-sensitive naming (tested by considering different versions of the apps). However, the tool cannot detect overridden methods unless their invocation can be traced (e.g., within the app component). This is because Smali code does not label them, which makes detection difficult especially for event-based (e.g., `onStopped`, `onResume`, etc.) and native classes not shipped as part of the app package. Secondly, our tool does not detect runtime-evaluated code, which includes dynamically-registered broadcast receivers, reflection, `eval()`, and similar. To overcome this issue, the Smali handler would need to be changed to semantically analyse such instructions and then process them using the usual flow. We leave this for future work and welcome improvements from the community.

## 7    Discussion and Mitigation

*Multi-user Feature.* The vulnerabilities in multi-user functionalities (Sect. 4) allow an adversary with *shell* access (remotely via WebUSB or physically) to the device to bypass the dedicated Gatekeeper protection and extract data from other user profiles. We conclude that this issue is caused by granting the INTERACT _ACROSS_USERS and ACCESS_CONTENT_PROVIDER_EXTERNALLY permissions to the `shell` user. In addition, services, broadcast receivers and content providers do not have a user interface, hence Gatekeeper protection is not being invoked when such app components are accessed across profiles. We suggest the following mitigations:

**Removing the permission from the shell user:** Not granting these permissions to the `shell` user would resolve the issue for both the default Android implementation and vendor-specific variants.

**Sanitise the user flag of system binaries:** Alternatively, system binaries that allow access across profiles (`am`, `pm` and `content`) could blacklist user IDs of other profiles. This is especially applicable to vendor-specific implementations, as they provide a single secure space with fixed user ID. In contrast, Android's multi-user feature allows creating several users with different user IDs. Instead of blacklisting certain IDs, a whitelisting approach might be applicable.

Samsung seems applied the second approach, blocking the user ID of their secure spaces for `am`, `pm`, and `content`. While Huawei's patch include verifying the password of private space when the developer mode is enabled and inform the users about the developer mode's risks when the developed mode is enabled and entered. The mitigations taken by Xiaomi are unclear, as a parallel disclosure led them to not engage further during the patching process. As mentioned, Google regards the problem as intended behaviour and does not plan to roll out a fix. Thus, the issue does not apply to the latest version Android 11. We note that users of affected devices (e.g., Google and Android One like Xiaomi and Nokia) might not be aware of the threat model assumed by Google internally and use multi-user with wrong assumptions about its security guarantees.

*Background Access to Restricted Sensors.* The root causes of this issue is the definition of "background" in Android. We suggest the following mitigations:

**Restrict sensor access from app components:** Background services, broadcast receivers, and content providers should generally not have access to restricted sensors when the app is invisible. However, applying such a change old existing Android version might obviously break app functionality.

**Restrict sensors access when an app is not in use:** This would require redesigning the camera and microphone permissions to ensure that sensors are only accessible when the app is visible in the foreground and in use. Based on our understanding and testing of the behaviour of Android 11, we noticed that it relies on the "AppOpsService" [10] to mitigate this issue. The service tracks the app's proc state (importance) using mainly two modes, `MODE_ALLOWED` to allow and `MODE_IGNORED` to suppress access. The service receives the current proc state of an app and capability updates from ActivityManagerService, indicating "while in use" permissions. This restricts sensor access as follows: If the app is in the foreground, the mode is `MODE_ALLOWED` and behaves normally. When the app goes into the background, this changes to `MODE_IGNORED`, preventing sensor access. Note that `MODE_IGNORED` does not revoke the granted permission.

Google assigned a high severity to our issue and consider it fixed in Android 11 only since our report of the issue coincided with the release of Android 11 (Sept 2020). However, in practice, the privacy impact on users of older versions might be substantial: Many—especially non tech-savvy—users might not choose or be able to upgrade their devices to Android 11. As of Jan 2022 (two years after the Android 11 release), the majority of Android users (64.63%) still use Android 10 and below [31], without any easily available mitigations.

# 8    Conclusion

In this paper, we demonstrated how app components on Android can be abused to break some of the system's security and privacy guarantees. We show that they can be accessed across user profile boundaries, leading to data exfiltration for a range of vendors. We demonstrate how spyware can bypass Android's mitigations against background access to the camera and microphone by splitting the process into two apps that communicate over certain app components. Finally, we present our tool Four Gates Inspector that can automatically detect such issues through static analysis. Using the tool, we e.g., found issues in apps that expose the microphone to any unprivileged app on the same device.

**Acknowledgemen.** We thank Ali Darwish, ElMuthana Mohamed, Hamad Salmeen, Abdulla Subah and Zhuang Xu for participating in mobile testing.

This research was partially funded by the Engineering and Physical Sciences Research Council (EPSRC) under grants EP/R012598/1 and EP/V000454/1. Abdulla Aldoseri is supported by a stipend from the University of Bahrain.

# 9    Appendix

**Table 1.** MU attacks across vendor implementation. (●) exploited; (○) N/A; (◑) untested

| Vendors | | Google Multi-user | Samsung Folder 1.2 | Samsung Folder 1.4 | Huawei Xiaomi |
|---|---|---|---|---|---|
| Activity Manager | #1 Access broadcast receiver/service | ● | ● | ● | ◑ |
| Content Provider | #2 Access Content provider | ● | ● | ● | ● |
| Media Content Provider | #3 List images | ● | ● | ● | ● |
| | #4 Insert images | ● | ● | ● | ● |
| | #5 Delete images | ● | ● | ● | ● |
| | #5 Read images | ● | ● | ○ | ● |
| | #6 Write images | ● | ○ | ○ | ● |
| Package Manager (PM) | #9 List applications | ● | ● | ● | ● |
| | #10 Uninstall applications | ● | ● | ● | ● |
| | #11 Pull applications | ● | ● | ● | ● |
| | #12 Install applications | ● | ○ | ○ | ● |
| | #13 Grant/Revoke permissions | ● | ● | ● | ● |

# References

1. Android: ActivityManager.RunningAppProcessInfo. https://developer.android.com/reference/android/app/ActivityManager.RunningAppProcessInfo (2020). Accessed 17 Sept 2020
2. Android: Behavior changes: all apps. https://developer.android.com/about/versions/pie/android-9.0-changes-all (2020). Accessed 13 Sept 2020
3. Android: Gatekeeper. https://source.android.com/security/authentication/gatekeeper (2020). Accessed 11 Jan 2020

4. Android: Supporting multiple users. https://source.android.com/devices/tech/admin/multi-user/ (2020). Accessed 11 Jan 2020
5. Android: Application Fundamentals – Android Developers, May 2021. https://developer.android.com/guide/components/fundamentals. Accessed 05 May 2021
6. Android: Building multiuser-aware apps, May 2021. https://source.android.com/devices/tech/admin/multiuser-apps. Accessed 05 May 2021
7. Android: Data and file storage overview – Android developers, June 2021. https://developer.android.com/training/data-storage. Accessed 25 Jun 2021
8. Android: Permission – Android developers, May 2021. https://developer.android.com/guide/topics/manifest/permission-element. Accessed 05 May 2021
9. Android: Permissions updates in Android 11 – Android developers, September 2021. https://developer.android.com/about/versions/11/privacy/permissions. Accessed 19 Sept 2021
10. Android: App-ops, April 2022. https://android.googlesource.com/platform/frameworks/base/+/refs/heads/android11-d1-b-release/core/java/android/app/AppOps.md#foreground. Accessed 27 Apr 2022
11. Android: Foreground services – Android developers, April 2022. https://developer.android.com/guide/components/foreground-services. Accessed 14 Apr 2022
12. Apktool: Apktool–a tool for reverse engineering 3rd party, closed, binary Android apps, May 2021. https://ibotpeaches.github.io/Apktool/. Accessed 05 May 2021
13. Arzt, S., et al.: FlowDroid: precise context, flow, field, object-sensitive and lifecycle-aware taint analysis for Android apps. ACM SIGPLAN Not. **49**(6), 259–269 (2014)
14. Bugiel, S., Davi, L., Dmitrienko, A., Fischer, T., Sadeghi, A.R., Shastry, B.: Towards taming privilege-escalation attacks on Android. In: NDSS, San Diego, California, USA, vol. 17, p. 19 (2012)
15. Davi, L., Dmitrienko, A., Sadeghi, A.-R., Winandy, M.: Privilege escalation attacks on Android. In: Burmester, M., Tsudik, G., Magliveras, S., Ilić, I. (eds.) ISC 2010. LNCS, vol. 6531, pp. 346–360. Springer, Heidelberg (2011). https://doi.org/10.1007/978-3-642-18178-8_30
16. Elsabagh, M., Johnson, R., Stavrou, A., Zuo, C., Zhao, Q., Lin, Z.: {FIRMSCOPE}: automatic uncovering of {Privilege-Escalation} vulnerabilities in {Pre-Installed} apps in android firmware. In: 29th USENIX Security Symposium, USENIX Security 2020, pp. 2379–2396 (2020)
17. Enck, W., et al.: TaintDroid: an information-flow tracking system for realtime privacy monitoring on smartphones. ACM Trans. Comput. Syst. (TOCS) **32**(2), 1–29 (2014)
18. F-Droid: F-Droid - free and open source Android app repository. https://f-droid.org/. Accessed 05 Nov 2022
19. F-secure Labs: Xiaomi Redmi 5 Plus second space password bypass, May 2021. https://labs.f-secure.com/advisories/xiaomi-second-space/. Accessed 05 May 2021
20. Felt, A.P., Wang, H.J., Moshchuk, A., Hanna, S., Chin, E.: Permission re-delegation: attacks and defenses. In: USENIX Security Symposium, San Francisco, CA, USA, vol. 30, p. 88. USENIX (2011)
21. Google: IActivityManager source code, May 2021. https://android.googlesource.com/platform/frameworks/native/+/refs/heads/android10-c2f2-release/libs/binder/IActivityManager.cpp#82. Accessed 16 May 2022
22. Hardy, N.: The confused deputy (or why capabilities might have been invented). ACM SIGOPS Operating Syst. Rev. **22**(4), 36–38 (1988)
23. Heuser, S., Negro, M., Pendyala, P.K., Sadeghi, A.-R.: DroidAuditor: forensic analysis of application-layer privilege escalation attacks on Android (short paper). In:

Grossklags, J., Preneel, B. (eds.) FC 2016. LNCS, vol. 9603, pp. 260–268. Springer, Heidelberg (2017). https://doi.org/10.1007/978-3-662-54970-4_15

24. Kanonov, U., Wool, A.: Secure containers in Android: the Samsung Knox case study. In: Proceedings of the 6th Workshop on Security and Privacy in Smartphones and Mobile Devices, Vienna, Austria, pp. 3–12. ACM (2016)

25. Li, R., Diao, W., Li, Z., Du, J., Guo, S.: Android custom permissions demystified: from privilege escalation to design shortcomings. In: 2021 IEEE Symposium on Security and Privacy (SP), pp. 70–86. IEEE (2021)

26. Lu, L., Li, Z., Wu, Z., Lee, W., Jiang, G.: CHEX: statically vetting android apps for component hijacking vulnerabilities. In: Proceedings of the 2012 ACM Conference on Computer and Communications Security, pp. 229–240 (2012)

27. Ratazzi, P., Aafer, Y., Ahlawat, A., Hao, H., Wang, Y., Du, W.: A systematic security evaluation of Android's multi-user framework. arXiv preprint arXiv:1410.7752 1(1), 1–10 (2014)

28. Reardon, J., Feal, Á., Wijesekera, P., On, A.E.B., Vallina-Rodriguez, N., Egelman, S.: 50 ways to leak your data: an exploration of apps' circumvention of the Android permissions system. In: 28th USENIX Security Symposium, USENIX Security 2019, Santa Clara, CA, USA, pp. 603–620. USENIX (2019)

29. Samsung Knox: Root of trust, May 2021. https://docs.samsungknox.com/admin/whitepaper/kpe/hardware-backed-root-of-trust.htm. Accessed 06 May 2021

30. Samsung Knox: Secure folder – Samsung Knox, May 2021. https://www.samsungknox.com/en/solutions/personal-apps/secure-folder. Accessed 06 May 2021

31. Stats, S.G.: Mobile & tablet Android version market share worldwide – statcounter global stats. https://gs.statcounter.com/android-version-market-share/mobile-tablet/worldwide/#monthly-202006-202009. Accessed 20 Aug 2021

32. Sutter, T., Tellenbach, B.: Simple spyware: Androids invisible foreground services and how to (ab)use them. In: Black Hat Europe, London, 2–5 Dezemeber 2019, p. 27. Black Hat Europe, London, UK (2019)

33. Tuncay, G.S., Demetriou, S., Ganju, K., Gunter, C.: Resolving the predicament of android custom permissions. In: Network and Distributed System Security Symposium, vol. 1, no. 1, pp. 1–15 (2018)

34. Xing, L., Pan, X., Wang, R., Yuan, K., Wang, X.: Upgrading your Android, elevating my malware: privilege escalation through mobile OS updating. In: 2014 IEEE Symposium on Security and Privacy, Berkeley, CA, USA, pp. 393–408. IEEE (2014)

35. Xu, Y., Wang, G., Ren, J., Zhang, Y.: An adaptive and configurable protection framework against android privilege escalation threats. Futur. Gener. Comput. Syst. 92, 210–224 (2019)

36. Zhang, M., Yin, H.: AppSealer: automatic generation of vulnerability-specific patches for preventing component hijacking attacks in Android applications. In: NDSS (2014)

37. Zhong, X., Zeng, F., Cheng, Z., Xie, N., Qin, X., Guo, S.: Privilege escalation detecting in android applications. In: 2017 3rd International Conference on Big Data Computing and Communications (BIGCOM), pp. 39–44. IEEE (2017)

38. Zhou, Y., Jiang, X.: Detecting passive content leaks and pollution in android applications. In: Proceedings of the 20th Network and Distributed System Security Symposium (NDSS), Bangalore India, pp. 1–16. Association for Computing Machinery, New York (2013)

# Authentication

# Sequential Digital Signatures for Cryptographic Software-Update Authentication

Bertram Poettering[1] and Simon Rastikian[1,2(✉)]

[1] IBM Research Europe – Zurich, Rüschlikon, Switzerland
sra@zurich.ibm.com
[2] ETH Zurich, Zurich, Switzerland

**Abstract.** Consider a computer user who needs to update a piece of software installed on their computing device. To do so securely, a commonly accepted ad-hoc method stipulates that the old software version first retrieves the update information from the vendor's public repository, then checks that a cryptographic signature embedded into it verifies with the vendor's public key, and finally replaces itself with the new version. This updating method seems to be robust and lightweight, and to reliably ensure that no malicious third party (e.g., a distribution mirror) can inject harmful code into the update process. Unfortunately, recent prominent news reports (SolarWinds, Stuxnet, TikTok, Zoom, . . . ) suggest that nation state adversaries are broadening their efforts related to attacking software supply chains. This calls for a critical re-evaluation of the described signature based updating method with respect to the real-world security it provides against particularly powerful adversaries.

We approach the setting by formalizing a cryptographic primitive that addresses specifically the secure software updating problem. We define strong, rigorous security models that capture forward security (stealing a vendor's key today doesn't allow modifying yesterday's software version) as well as a form of self-enforcement that helps protecting vendors against coercion attacks in which they are forced, e.g. by nation state actors, to misuse or disclose their keys. We note that the common signature based software authentication method described above meets neither the one nor the other goal, and thus represents a suboptimal solution. Hence, after formalizing the syntax and security of the new primitive, we propose novel, efficient, and provably secure constructions.

## 1 Introduction

In August 2020, the US president signed an executive order requiring TikTok, a social media app of Chinese origin, to either be made unavailable on the US market or to be transferred to a new non-Chinese owner. The corresponding press statement reports that "credible evidence" indicates that the original producer of the app "might take action that threatens to impair the national security of

Please find the full version of this article at https://ia.cr/2022/995.

the United States".[1] Four months later, the US Department of Justice publicly accused an executive of the company behind the telecommunication service Zoom to have, on behalf of the Chinese government, misused the Zoom app to "willingly commit crimes [... and ...] unlawful conspiracy [...] against US-based individuals", and concluded that "no company with significant business interests in China is immune from the coercive power of the Chinese Communist Party".[2] Opinions on the appropriateness of the press statements, and the actions taken, may be split, but the steps make a recent tendency of nation states evident, namely to question the harmlessness and innocence of software originating from other countries. The main perceived threat seems to be that another country's government might coerce its legitimate software vendors to embed backdoors or hidden espionage tools into their products that could be used against the own country. Without going into details, we mention two more attacks (with different configurations of attacking and attacked countries) where users received manipulated software over seemingly regular distribution channels: The well-known Stuxnet attack was conducted by manipulating the driver distribution scheme of the Windows operating system,[3] and the recently uncovered SolarWinds attacks centrally and explicitly involved the malicious manipulation of a software supply chain.[4]

The above events indicate that re-evaluating the security of current software distribution methods against particularly powerful adversaries is a necessary and timely task. Some academics suggest that *advanced code-signing* primitives might ameliorate the situation.[5] In this article we focus on such a primitive.

STATE OF THE ART. An established approach to the authentic distribution of software updates builds on digital signature schemes. If a software version $S_i$ is updated to the next version $S_{i+1}$, the update information is signed by the original vendor so that its authenticity can be checked by the user before installing the update. This prevents malicious modifications by outsiders, including software repositories, Internet providers, etc. Unfortunately, the method provides little resilience against insider attacks in which, for instance, the vendor is coerced by a government agency to authenticate not only the legitimate $S_i \rightarrow S_{i+1}$ update, but in addition also a malicious $S_i \rightarrow S'_{i+1}$ update. If the malicious update is distributed to only a small set of high-value targets (while regular users continue to receive the legitimate version), it is unlikely that the attack is ever noticed by the victim or picked up by security researchers. The wording of the US Department of Justice, when stating that few international vendors are immune to governmental coercion attempts, suggests that such attacks are highly realistic.

---

[1] https://home.treasury.gov/system/files/136/EO-on-TikTok-8-14-20.pdf.

[2] https://www.justice.gov/usao-edny/pr/china-based-executive-us-telecommunications-company-charged-disrupting-video-meetings.

[3] https://www.welivesecurity.com/media_files/white-papers/Stuxnet_Under_the_Microscope.pdf.

[4] https://www.fireeye.com/blog/products-and-services/2020/12/global-intrusion-campaign-leverages-software-supply-chain-compromise.html.

[5] https://www.scmagazine.com/perspective/encryption/can-advanced-code-signing-help-end-supply-chain-attacks.

OUR APPROACH. We challenge the assumption that standard signature schemes are the right tool to securely distribute software updates, and we develop a signature variant that, we argue, is better suited for the task. We start with the observation that software versions are strictly ordered (suggesting our notation $S_1 \rightarrow S_2 \rightarrow S_3 \rightarrow \ldots$), meaning that any update $S_i \rightarrow S_{i+1}$ occurs in the context of all prior updates. This sequential property is not matched by standard signature schemes which allow signing and verifying in arbitrary order. This mismatch has at least two problematic consequences: (a) Even if the signer authenticates software versions in the correct order, precautions have to be taken to avoid that a verifier accepts updates in a wrong order (e.g., $S_1 \rightarrow S_2 \rightarrow S_3 \rightarrow S_2$), for instance in the context of a software downgrade attack; and (b) The solution does not provide forward security: If the signer first authenticates $S_1 \rightarrow S_2 \rightarrow S_3$ and is then coerced to reveal its key material to an adversary, the latter can use the key material to authenticate false updates $S_1 \rightarrow S_2'$ or $S_1 \rightarrow S_3'$. A solution that provides forward security (like ours, see below) would ensure that the adversary is limited to forging on succeeding versions.

Even a signature variant that requires strictly sequential operations and provides forward security is not sufficient to protect software supply chains against state actors that coerce signers early. In the extreme case, if the signer has to reveal its keys before authenticating the very first software version, the adversary can forge on *any* (because 'following') software version. We address this by proposing a public self-enforcement mechanism: We expect of a secure solution that from any two conflicting authentications $S_i \rightarrow S_{i+1}$ and $S_i \rightarrow S_{i+1}'$ the key material that was current after authenticating $S_i$ can be recovered by invoking an efficient extraction algorithm. That is, if both $S_1 \rightarrow S_2$ and $S_1 \rightarrow S_2'$ validate correctly, then *everybody* gets into the position to also authenticate $S_1 \rightarrow S_2''$ for any $S_2''$. From the perspective of both the software vendor and the coercing state actor, getting into this situation has to be avoided by all means. (The state actor would transfer its unique privilege on to everybody else, including to competing governments, thus not only losing the priviledge but also putting its own citizens at risk.) Concretely, our mechanism (1) strongly *incentivizes a benign signer* to make its implementation as secure and robust as possible, e.g., by out-sourcing the signing operations into a Hardware Security Module; (2) strongly *disincentivizes a tempted signer* to selectively forge signatures to its own advantage; and (3) strongly *disincentivizes state actors* to coerce honest signers to reveal their keys. These properties are not met by the classic signature based software distribution method (even when enhanced by an auxiliary "detection mechanism").

**Contributions and Structure.** We introduce, in Sect. 4, a new cryptographic primitive—a *sequential digital signature* (SDS) scheme—as a solution in the context of software authentication. We rigorously define suitable security properties (unforgeability with forward security, double-signing key extractability, . . . ), using game based models. Then, in Sect. 5, we propose generic constructions of SDS from a loosely related, simpler type of signature scheme (*strictly one-time signature*, SOT-DS, Sect. 3.2) that appeared in prior work. We implemented, tested, and evaluated our SDS scheme, and report on its efficiency in Sect. 6.

We paid special attention to ensuring that our construction can serve as a long-term solution for the secure software distribution problem. This included ensuring that it promises security also against quantum adversaries. Our SDS offers this type of security, but only if its building block, the SOT-DS scheme, does as well. Unfortunately, we found that all SOT-DS constructions proposed in prior work are based on number-theoretic assumptions like DLP and are thus *not* quantum resilient. Thus, in Sect. 5.1, as an additional contribution we construct a novel SOT-DS that is built solely from hash functions and thus represents the only known quantum-resilient candidate. We note that Germany's Federal Office for Information Security (BSI), with similar arguments, suggests prioritizing hash-based signatures for firmware authentication [8, Sect. 6.7].

**Related Work.** Digital signature schemes were first proposed in the late 70's, and since then, hundreds of flavours enriched the cryptographic literature. Regular signature schemes allow the secret key owners to sign arbitrary messages in arbitrary order. In the following we discuss publications that put forward signature variants that limit this freedom and require specific relations between the signed messages to hold.

Some digital signature schemes come with self-enforcement properties. For instance, in the *e-cash* setting, the anonymous cryptocurrency users should not be allowed to spend the same coin twice by signing two different transactions. As a countermeasure, Chaum, Fiat and Naor [10] proposed a scheme that penalizes such act by automatically revealing the identity of a double-spending user.

Analogously, in a public-key infrastructure (PKI) setting, certificate authorities (CAs) generate certificates that bind keys and identities together. However, law enforcement agencies or nation states can intimidate CAs to secretly issue certificates that bind unauthentic keys to the same identities, opening the path for impersonation attacks. Poettering and Stebila proposed a self-enforcement scheme that defends against such attacks [18]. Specifically, their scheme provides the double-authentication-preventing (DAP) security property that allows certifying pairs of identities and keys, and penalizes the CA if it ever certifies different keys for the same identity. This notion was followed by later publications proposing new schemes and improving the state of the art [5,7,12,13,16,19,20].

We note that DAP signatures (from [18]) and SDS (this work) are similar in spirit in the sense that both are self-enforcing signature schemes that penalize malicious signers by leaking their key. However, SDS are strictly sequential (which fits the linearity of software updates) where DAP signatures are 'random access' (which fits the PKI application). By consequence also the security guarantees given by the two primitives are crucially different. (E.g., there cannot be forward security for DAP signatures.) Construction-wise it seems that neither are DAP signatures implied by SDS (how to remove the sequentiality?) nor are SDS implied by DAP signatures (how to add forward security?).

While the negative effects of an injection of a fraudulent software update can be of any kind, once successful, smart adversaries might have an interest in remaining undetected as long as possible. One way to permanently yet undetectably harm the security of cryptographic implementations is via algorithm substitution attacks, as explored for instance in [1–4,11].

## 2   Notation

We write $\mathbf{T}$ and $\mathbf{F}$ for the two Boolean constants. We formalize correctness and security properties with games written in pseudo-code. The game body invokes an adversary $\mathcal{A}$ and provides it with access to zero or more oracles. A game terminates when executing a Stop with $C$ instruction, where $C$ is a Boolean expression. The truth value of $C$ is taken as the output of the game. We write $\Pr[G(\mathcal{A})]$ for the probability that game $G$ invoked with adversary $\mathcal{A}$ outputs $\mathbf{T}$. We assume three conditional game-terminating macros: If $C$ is a Boolean expression, the game instruction Require $C$ expands to 'If not $C$: Stop with $\mathbf{F}$', the instruction Reward $C$ expands to 'If $C$: Stop with $\mathbf{T}$', and the instruction Promise $C$ expands to 'If not $C$: Stop with $\mathbf{T}$'. The reader will appreciate how the macros' names correspond with their semantics in the games, where the macros are used to require a specific behaviour of the adversary, to reward the adversary for triggering a specific event, or to ensure that a specific promised property is indeed met by the scheme.

Game variables with attached brackets represent associative arrays (i.e., the dictionary data structure). For instance, the instruction '$B[4] \leftarrow 2$' assigns the value 2 to the element indexed by 4 in the array $B$, and the expression '$B[\cdot] \leftarrow 2$' initializes the entries at *all* indices to the value 2. If $X, Y$ are set variables we write $X \xleftarrow{\cup} Y$ shorthand for $X \leftarrow X \cup Y$, and if $x, y$ are vector variables we write $x \xleftarrow{\shortparallel} y$ shorthand for $x \leftarrow x \shortparallel y$, where $\shortparallel$ is the append operation. We assume the $\#$ function returns the length of a vector; for instance, if $v = (7, 8, 9)$ then $\#v = 3$.

To keep our games compact, we use the alias-creating operator $:=$ where convenient. The instruction '$A := B$' introduces $A$ as a symbolic alias for the expression $B$. (This crucially differs from $A \leftarrow B$ which is an assignment that evaluates expression $B$ and stores the result in variable $A$.) For instance, if $B[\,]$ is an array and $B[7]$ an integer entry, and an alias is created as per $A := B[7]$, then the instruction $A \leftarrow A + 1$ expands to $B[7] \leftarrow B[7] + 1$ and thus modifies the value of $B[7]$ (while $A$ itself is not a variable).

Some of the schemes that we formalize have stateful algorithms. A generic notation for the stateful execution of an algorithm $\alpha$ is $(\rho, y) \leftarrow \alpha(\rho, x)$ where $x$ is the algorithm's input, $y$ is the algorithm's output, and $\rho$ is the state that is updated by the execution (and thus both input and output). For compactness we use the notation $y \leftarrow \alpha\langle\rho\rangle(x)$ as a shortcut for the $(\rho, y) \leftarrow \alpha(\rho, x)$ instruction.

## 3   Stateless Signatures

We recall core principles of digital signature (DS) schemes. Our definitions are equivalent to those of prior work, but employ a slightly non-standard notation for algorithms and games. (For instance, we specify our games with an explicit verification oracle.) This will allow for an easier comparison with our definitions of stateful signatures in Sect. 4.

## 3.1 Digital Signatures: DS

SYNTAX. A *digital signature* (DS) scheme $S$ for a message space $\mathcal{M}$ consists of a signing key space $\mathcal{SK}$, a verification key space $\mathcal{VK}$, a signature space $\mathcal{S}$, and three efficient algorithms *gen*, *sig*, *ver* as follows. The key generation algorithm *gen* takes no input and outputs a signing key $sk \in \mathcal{SK}$ and a verification key $vk \in \mathcal{VK}$. The signing algorithm *sig* is parameterized by a signing key $sk \in \mathcal{SK}$, takes a message $m \in \mathcal{M}$ on input, and outputs a signature $\sigma \in \mathcal{S}$. The verification algorithm *ver* is parameterized by a verification key $vk \in \mathcal{VK}$, takes a message $m \in \mathcal{M}$ and a signature $\sigma \in \mathcal{S}$ on input, and outputs a Boolean value $v \in \{\mathbf{T}, \mathbf{F}\}$. Depending on whether algorithm *ver* outputs $\mathbf{T}$ or $\mathbf{F}$ we say that it accepts or rejects. Written more compactly, a DS has the following API.

$$gen \xrightarrow{\text{out}} \mathcal{SK} \times \mathcal{VK}$$
$$\mathcal{M} \xrightarrow{\text{in}} sig(\mathcal{SK}; \cdot) \xrightarrow{\text{out}} \mathcal{S}$$
$$\mathcal{M} \times \mathcal{S} \xrightarrow{\text{in}} ver(\mathcal{VK}; \cdot, \cdot) \xrightarrow{\text{out}} \{\mathbf{T}, \mathbf{F}\}.$$

CORRECTNESS. For $T \in \mathbb{N} \cup \{\infty\}$ we define the $T$-time correctness of a DS scheme via the game COR-DS in Fig. 1 (top), where lines 00,05,07 formalize the requirement that the signer issues at most $T$ signatures and lines 01,08,11,12 formalize the promise that all authentic signatures be accepted. Intuitively, DS scheme $S$ is *$T$-time correct* if the advantage $\mathrm{Adv}_S^{\text{cor-ds}}(\mathcal{A}) := \Pr[\text{COR-DS}(\mathcal{A})]$ is negligible for all efficient adversaries $\mathcal{A}$.

| Game COR-DS$(\mathcal{A})$ | Oracle $Sig(m)$ | Oracle $Ver(m, \sigma)$ |
|---|---|---|
| 00 $t \leftarrow 0$ | 05 Require $t < T$ | 10 $v \leftarrow ver(vk; m, \sigma)$ |
| 01 $\text{AC} \leftarrow \emptyset$ | 06 $\sigma \leftarrow sig(sk; m)$ | 11 If $(m, \sigma) \in \text{AC}$: |
| 02 $(sk, vk) \leftarrow gen$ | 07 $t \leftarrow t + 1$ | 12    Promise $v$ |
| 03 $\mathcal{A}(vk)$ | 08 $\text{AC} \xleftarrow{\cup} \{(m, \sigma)\}$ | 13 Return $v$ |
| 04 Stop with $\mathbf{F}$ | 09 Return $\sigma$ | |
| **Game SUF-DS$(\mathcal{A})$** | **Oracle $Sig(m)$** | **Oracle $Ver(m, \sigma)$** |
| 14 $t \leftarrow 0$ | 19 Require $t < T$ | 24 $v \leftarrow ver(vk; m, \sigma)$ |
| 15 $\text{AC} \leftarrow \emptyset$ | 20 $\sigma \leftarrow sig(sk; m)$ | 25 If $(m, \sigma) \notin \text{AC}$: |
| 16 $(sk, vk) \leftarrow gen$ | 21 $t \leftarrow t + 1$ | 26    Reward $v$ |
| 17 $\mathcal{A}(vk)$ | 22 $\text{AC} \xleftarrow{\cup} \{(m, \sigma)\}$ | 27 Return $v$ |
| 18 Stop with $\mathbf{F}$ | 23 Return $\sigma$ | |

**Fig. 1.** Games COR-DS and SUF-DS for defining the correctness and strong unforgeability, respectively, of a DS scheme. Set AC indicates the authentic message-signature pairs.

UNFORGEABILITY. With respect to security we define what it means for a DS scheme to provide ($T$-time) strong unforgeability. A scheme meets this property if all valid signatures that an adversary can come up with are replays of signatures priorly generated by the signer. This is formalized via the game SUF-DS in Fig. 1 (bottom), where lines 15,22,25,26 reward the adversary if it delivers a message-signature pair that is accepted despite being non-authentic. Intuitively, DS scheme $S$ is $T$-*time strongly unforgeable* if the advantage $\text{Adv}_S^{\text{suf-ds}}(\mathcal{A}) := \Pr[\text{SUF-DS}(\mathcal{A})]$ is negligible for all efficient adversaries $\mathcal{A}$.

## 3.2   Strictly One-Time Digital Signatures: SOT-DS

If more than $T$ messages are signed with a $T$-time signature scheme instance, then the instance is not anymore guaranteed to be secure. However, this does not imply that the instance's security collapses completely, i.e., that forging signatures on arbitrary messages suddenly becomes easy. In the following we recall the definition of a stronger form of DS that for the special case of one-time signatures guarantees that signing twice unavoidably leads to a maximum loss of security: A *strictly one-time digital signature* (SOT-DS, [16]) scheme is a 1-time DS scheme where any two signatures created with the same signing key immediately fully expose that signing key and thus enable universal forging. Note that [16] provides SOT-DS constructions that leverage on zero-knowledge proof systems over number-theoretic assumptions (like DLP). In Sect. 5.1 we specify two novel constructions that are based on hash functions.

SYNTAX. A SOT-DS scheme [16, Sect. 3.2] consists of the algorithms *gen, sig, ver* of a regular DS scheme, plus an additional key extraction algorithm that recovers the signing key from any two valid signatures. Precisely, the *ext* algorithm is parameterized by a verification key $vk \in \mathcal{VK}$, takes two message-signature pairs $(m^0, \sigma^0), (m^1, \sigma^1) \in \mathcal{M} \times \mathcal{S}$ on input, and outputs a signing key $sk \in \mathcal{SK}$. More compactly,

$$(\mathcal{M} \times \mathcal{S}) \times (\mathcal{M} \times \mathcal{S}) \xrightarrow{\text{in}} ext(\mathcal{VK}; \cdot, \cdot) \xrightarrow{\text{out}} \mathcal{SK}.$$

EXTRACTABILITY. The key extractability feature of a SOT-DS is formalized via the game KEX-DS in Fig. 2. In the game, a malicious signer that outputs two message-signature pairs (line 01) such that both signatures are valid (lines 02,03) yet the message-signature pairs are different (line 04) is rewarded if the key extraction (line 05) recovers a wrong key (line 06). Intuitively, SOT-DS scheme $S$ is *(one-time) key extractable* if the advantage $\text{Adv}_S^{\text{kex-ds}}(\mathcal{A}) := \Pr[\text{KEX-DS}(\mathcal{A})]$ is negligible for all efficient adversaries $\mathcal{A}$.

## 4   Sequential Digital Signatures: SDS

A sequential digital signature (SDS) is a variant of a regular digital signature (DS) where both the signer and the verifier are stateful. In SDS, message-signature pairs have to be verified in the same order as they are generated. This restriction of functionality is paired with a strengthening of security, and we argue that the latter makes the option of replacing a DS by an SDS, in applications where this is possible, attractive. In particular, we argue that using an SDS is advantageous over using a DS for the purpose of authenticating program code.

$$
\boxed{
\begin{array}{l}
\textbf{Game KEX-DS}(\mathcal{A}) \\
\texttt{00}\;\; (sk, vk) \leftarrow gen \\
\texttt{01}\;\; (m^0, \sigma^0), (m^1, \sigma^1) \leftarrow \mathcal{A}(sk, vk) \\
\texttt{02}\;\; \text{Require } ver(vk; m^0, \sigma^0) = \mathbf{T} \\
\texttt{03}\;\; \text{Require } ver(vk; m^1, \sigma^1) = \mathbf{T} \\
\texttt{04}\;\; \text{Require } (m^0, \sigma^0) \neq (m^1, \sigma^1) \\
\texttt{05}\;\; sk^* \leftarrow ext(vk; m^0, \sigma^0, m^1, \sigma^1) \\
\texttt{06}\;\; \text{Reward } sk^* \neq sk \\
\texttt{07}\;\; \text{Stop with } \mathbf{F}
\end{array}
}
$$

**Fig. 2.** Game KEX-DS for defining the key extractability of a SOT-DS scheme. Adversary $\mathcal{A}$ takes the role of a malicious signer and thus, in line 01, receives direct access to the signing key. (A consequence of this is that the game doesn't need to provide a signing oracle.)

This is both because an SDS provides forward security (i.e., maintains, after a signing key corruption, as much security as possible) and because an SDS may come with a self-enforcement mechanism that penalizes a signer that offends the rule of signing strictly sequentially.

In the following we formalize the SDS notion. We took efforts to align the syntax of DS and SDS as much as possible, and to also let the security notions and games correspond to each other. (This explains why in Sect. 3 we decided to use the slightly non-standard notation.)

SYNTAX. A *sequential digital signature* (SDS) scheme $S$ for a message space $\mathcal{M}$ consists of a signing state space $\mathcal{SST}$, a verification state space $\mathcal{VST}$, a signature space $\mathcal{S}$, and three efficient algorithms $gen, sig, ver$ as follows. The initialization algorithm $gen$ takes no input and outputs an initial signing state $sst \in \mathcal{SST}$ and an initial verification state $vst \in \mathcal{VST}$. The signing algorithm $sig$ depends on a signing state $sst \in \mathcal{SST}$ which it may update, takes a message $m \in \mathcal{M}$ on input, and outputs a signature $\sigma \in \mathcal{S}$. The verification algorithm $ver$ depends on a verification state $vst \in \mathcal{VST}$ which it may update, takes a message $m \in \mathcal{M}$ and a signature $\sigma \in \mathcal{S}$ on input, and outputs a Boolean value $v \in \{\mathbf{T}, \mathbf{F}\}$. Depending on whether algorithm $ver$ outputs $\mathbf{T}$ or $\mathbf{F}$ we say that it accepts or rejects. More compactly, using the state-update notation from Sect. 2,

$$
\begin{aligned}
gen &\xrightarrow{\text{out}} \mathcal{SST} \times \mathcal{VST} \\
\mathcal{M} \xrightarrow{\text{in}} sig\langle\mathcal{SST}\rangle(\cdot) &\xrightarrow{\text{out}} \mathcal{S} \\
\mathcal{M} \times \mathcal{S} \xrightarrow{\text{in}} ver\langle\mathcal{VST}\rangle(\cdot, \cdot) &\xrightarrow{\text{out}} \{\mathbf{T}, \mathbf{F}\}.
\end{aligned}
$$

Before proceeding with defining the correctness and security properties of SDS, we introduce the notions of signing history and verification history, explain why useful security definitions for SDS have to consider the existence of multiple independent verifiers, and indicate how our models capture forward security.

SIGNING/VERIFICATION HISTORY. Once an initial SDS signing state $sst$ was created, a series $m_1, m_2, \ldots$ of messages can be authenticated by iteratively invoking $\sigma_i \leftarrow sig\langle sst\rangle(m_i)$ (where each invocation of $sig$ may update $sst$). By the sequentiality of this process, the signing state $sst$ can be assumed to always reflect, explicitly or implicitly, the *signing history* $(m_1, \sigma_1)$ ‖ $(m_2, \sigma_2)$ ‖ $\ldots$ processed so far. Similarly, a *verification history* consists of the messages and signatures that a verifier accepted as authentic when iteratively invoked as per $v_i \leftarrow ver\langle vst\rangle(m_i, \sigma_i)$. (If $ver$ is invoked with a message-signature pair that is rejected, this pair is *not* recorded in the verification history.[6]) In our SDS games, the *Sig* and *Ver* oracles record signing and verification histories by appending generated or accepted message-signature pairs to game variables $sh$ and $vh$, respectively.

MULTIPLE VERIFIERS. A real-world characteristic of (stateless or stateful) signature schemes is that signers are typically matched by multiple independent verifiers that check their signatures. However, as in the stateless case there is no component that could individualize different verifiers (all verifiers receive the same input and cannot memorize anything), when formalizing the correctness and security of such schemes it is sufficient, without loss of generality, to consider a single verifier. The same is not possible for SDS where verifiers that are exposed to different sequences of valid or invalid message-signature pairs may end up in different states.[7] Our games hence explicitly model a setup where a single signer is matched by an unlimited number of independent verifiers. This is implemented by requiring the adversary to explicitly indicate, for each of its *Ver* queries, the identifier $id$ of the verifier instance that is meant to process the provided message-signature pair. We use the array variable VST[·] (see Sect. 2) to store the states of all verifiers so that its entry VST[$id$] represents the state of the verifier with identifier $id$. Similarly our games use the variable VH[·] to store the verification histories of all verifiers so that entry VH[$id$] represents the verification history of verifier $id$. Note that the values of $id$ are chosen at the discretion of the adversary. The identifiers are only used to implement the game logics while the SDS algorithms themselves will never learn them.

FORWARD SECURITY. Our models capture the forward security aspect by giving the adversary the option to *corrupt* the signer by invoking a dedicated oracle that returns a copy of the signer's current state.[8] Intuitively, before such a corruption happens, exclusively the signer is able to create valid signatures, i.e., is the only *authoritative* party. However, by invoking the *Corrupt* oracle also the adversary gets into the position to craft valid signatures (by applying the regular signing

---

[6] This does not preclude that information about the rejected message-signature pair is reflected in $vst$ which can be updated even if the verification fails.

[7] If an SDS verification algorithm is randomized then the verification states of different verifiers might diverge even when provided with the same sequence of message-signature pairs.

[8] Our verification oracles return copies of the verifier states right away, fully removing the need of having to think about also adding a corruption oracle for verifiers.

algorithm to the retrieved state), making the signer lose its authoritativeness. The notion of authoritativeness will appear explicitly in our security games.

**Correctness of SDS.** For $T \in \mathbb{N} \cup \{\infty\}$ we define the $T$-time correctness of an SDS scheme via the game COR-SDS in Fig. 3, where lines 00,09,11 formalize the requirement that the signer issues at most $T$ signatures and lines 01,13,19,20 formalize the promise that all authentic signing histories be accepted. Intuitively, SDS scheme $S$ is $T$-*time correct* if the advantage $\text{Adv}_S^{\text{cor-sds}}(\mathcal{A}) :=$ $\Pr[\text{COR-SDS}(\mathcal{A})]$ is negligible for all efficient adversaries $\mathcal{A}$.

| **Game** COR-SDS($\mathcal{A}$) | **Oracle** $Sig(m)$ | **Oracle** $Ver(id, m, \sigma)$ |
|---|---|---|
| 00 $t \leftarrow 0$ | 09 Require $t < T$ | 16 $vh := \text{VH}[id]$ |
| 01 $\text{AC} \leftarrow \emptyset$ | 10 $\sigma \leftarrow sig\langle sst\rangle(m)$ | 17 $vst := \text{VST}[id]$ |
| 02 $sh \leftarrow \epsilon$ | 11 $t \leftarrow t + 1$ | 18 $v \leftarrow ver\langle vst\rangle(m, \sigma)$ |
| 03 $\text{VH}[\cdot] \leftarrow \epsilon$ | 12 $sh \stackrel{\shortmid\shortmid}{\leftarrow} (m, \sigma)$ | 19 If $vh \shortmid\shortmid (m, \sigma) \in \text{AC}$: |
| 04 $(sst_0, vst_0) \leftarrow gen$ | 13 $\text{AC} \stackrel{\cup}{\leftarrow} \{sh\}$ | 20     Promise $v$ |
| 05 $sst \leftarrow sst_0$ | 14 Return $\sigma$ | 21 If $v$: $vh \stackrel{\shortmid\shortmid}{\leftarrow} (m, \sigma)$ |
| 06 $\text{VST}[\cdot] \leftarrow vst_0$ | | 22 Return $v, vst$ |
| 07 $\mathcal{A}(vst_0)$ | **Oracle** *Corrupt* | |
| 08 Stop with **F** | 15 Return $sst$ | |

**Fig. 3.** Game COR-SDS for defining the correctness of an SDS scheme. Set AC indicates the authentic signing histories. Vector $sh$ indicates the (signer's) signing history. For any verifier identity $id$, vector VH[$id$] indicates that verifier's verification history and VST[$id$] represents its verification state. (Recall from Sect. 2 that the instructions in lines 03,06 assign the same initial value to all array entries while the instructions in lines 16,17 create symbolic aliases.)

**Unforgeability of SDS.** Our security models capture forward security. Corrupting a signer unavoidably brings the adversary into the position to forge signatures on messages associated with points in time following the corruption, but if a scheme is forward secure then signatures for points in time preceding the corruption remain unforgeable. We start with making the concepts of the past and the future of a signer more precise.

In the correctness game of Fig. 3, a signing history is represented by a string $sh \in \mathcal{X}^*$ over the alphabet $\mathcal{X} = \mathcal{M} \times \mathcal{S}$ which is the universe of all message-signature pairs. Given a signing history $sh$, its past Past($sh$) consists of the signing histories that it developed from, and its future Future($sh$) consists of the signing histories that it could develop into. Formally, if $\prec$ denotes the (anti-reflexive) is-prefix-of relation on strings in $\mathcal{X}^*$, we let:

$$\text{Past}(sh) = \{sh' \in \mathcal{X}^* : sh' \prec sh\}$$
$$\text{Future}(sh) = \{sh' \in \mathcal{X}^* : sh \prec sh'\}$$

Note that we have Past($\epsilon$) = $\emptyset$ and Future($\epsilon$) = $\mathcal{X}^+$. ("Not having a past means having all options for the future.")

Recalling the concept of authoritativeness discussed above, let us now observe that (1) initially, until a signer is corrupted, it is authoritative for its entire future; and (2) corrupting a signer means that its authoritativeness is revoked for what follows the corruption. In our security games for SDS, game variable AE indicates for which signing histories the signer is authoritative. We implement the two observations by (1) starting the games with $AE = \text{Future}(\epsilon) = \mathcal{X}^+$; and (2) letting $AE \leftarrow AE \setminus \text{Future}(sh)$ whenever a corruption query is posed.

We are now ready to state our unforgeability definition for SDS schemes. For $T \in \mathbb{N} \cup \{\infty\}$ we define the $T$-time strong unforgeability of an SDS scheme via the game SUF-SDS in Fig. 4, where lines 02,16 implement the tracking of the signer's authoritativeness and lines 01,14,21,22 reward the adversary if it makes a verifier accept a non-authentic verification history, and this happens for a point where the signer should be authoritative. Intuitively, SDS scheme $S$ is $T$-time strongly unforgeable (with forward security) if the advantage $\text{Adv}_S^{\text{suf-sds}}(\mathcal{A}) := \Pr[\text{SUF-SDS}(\mathcal{A})]$ is negligible for all efficient adversaries $\mathcal{A}$.

| **Game** SUF-SDS($\mathcal{A}$) | **Oracle** $Sig(m)$ | **Oracle** $Ver(id, m, \sigma)$ |
|---|---|---|
| 00 $t \leftarrow 0$ | 10 Require $t < T$ | 18 $vh := \text{VH}[id]$ |
| 01 $AC \leftarrow \emptyset$ | 11 $\sigma \leftarrow sig\langle sst\rangle(m)$ | 19 $vst := \text{VST}[id]$ |
| 02 $AE \leftarrow \text{Future}(\epsilon)$ | 12 $t \leftarrow t+1$ | 20 $v \leftarrow ver\langle vst\rangle(m, \sigma)$ |
| 03 $sh \leftarrow \epsilon$ | 13 $sh \overset{\shortmid\shortmid}{\leftarrow} (m, \sigma)$ | 21 If $vh \shortmid\shortmid (m, \sigma) \in AE \setminus AC$: |
| 04 $\text{VH}[\cdot] \leftarrow \epsilon$ | 14 $AC \overset{\cup}{\leftarrow} \{sh\}$ | 22 $\quad$ Reward $v$ |
| 05 $(sst_0, vst_0) \leftarrow gen$ | 15 Return $\sigma$ | 23 If $v$: $vh \overset{\shortmid\shortmid}{\leftarrow} (m, \sigma)$ |
| 06 $sst \leftarrow sst_0$ | | 24 Return $v, vst$ |
| 07 $\text{VST}[\cdot] \leftarrow vst_0$ | **Oracle** $Corrupt$ | |
| 08 $\mathcal{A}(vst_0)$ | 16 $AE \leftarrow AE \setminus \text{Future}(sh)$ | |
| 09 Stop with $\mathbf{F}$ | 17 Return $sst$ | |

**Fig. 4.** Game SUF-SDS for defining the strong unforgeability of an SDS scheme. Set AE indicates the signing histories for which the signer is authoritative. See the caption of Fig. 3 for the meaning of other variables and symbols.

**Extractability of SDS.** We formalize two self-enforcement properties for SDS: double-signature forgeability and double-signature extractability. Observe that, assuming regular operations, for the verification histories $vh_1, vh_2$ of any two verifiers we have either $vh_1 \preceq vh_2$ or $vh_2 \preceq vh_1$, that is, the verification histories are identical modulo one of them possibly lagging behind. We refer to verification histories that don't follow this pattern as 'conflicting'.

**Definition 1.** *Two verification histories $vh_1, vh_2 \in \mathcal{X}^+$ are* conflicting *if they diverge, i.e., if $vh_1 = vh' \shortmid\shortmid P_1 \shortmid\shortmid vh''$ and $vh_2 = vh' \shortmid\shortmid P_2 \shortmid\shortmid vh'''$ where $vh' \in \mathcal{X}^*$ is a (possibly empty) common prefix, $P_1 = (m_1, \sigma_1) \in \mathcal{X}$ and $P_2 = (m_2, \sigma_2) \in \mathcal{X}$ are different message-signature pairs, and $vh'', vh''' \in \mathcal{X}^*$ are arbitrary (possibly empty) suffixes.*

In the following we consider irregular operations, i.e., the case where conflicting verification histories do emerge in the games. Reasons for conflicting histories include that the signer is not honest or is impersonated after being corrupted. Our aim is to disincentivize irregular behavior as much as possible, and we do this by demanding that from any conflicting pair of verification histories it be possible to forge signatures on arbitrary (future) messages with the same ease as if the forger knew the correct keys.

The security goal of double-signature forgeability (DSF) demands that from any conflicting pair of verification histories one can forge signatures using a dedicated algorithm *forge* with the following API:

$$\mathcal{VST} \times \mathcal{X}^* \times \mathcal{X} \times \mathcal{X} \times \mathcal{M}^+ \xrightarrow{\text{in}} forge \xrightarrow{\text{out}} \mathcal{S}^+.$$

Using the notation from the above definition, if *forge* is invoked as $\bar{\sigma} \leftarrow forge(vst_0, vh', P_1, P_2, \bar{m}_1 \parallel \ldots \parallel \bar{m}_l)$, where $vst_0$ is the initial verification key, then the signatures in $\bar{\sigma} = \bar{\sigma}_1 \parallel \ldots \parallel \bar{\sigma}_l$ shall be valid in the sense that $vh^* = vh' \parallel (\bar{m}_1, \bar{\sigma}_1) \parallel \ldots \parallel (\bar{m}_l, \bar{\sigma}_l)$ is a verification history accepted by any verifier.

For $T \in \mathbb{N} \cup \{\infty\}$ we define the $T$-time double-signature forgeability of an SDS scheme via the game DSF-SDS in Fig. 5, where lines 00–08 prepare the inputs for the *forge* algorithm and lines 10–15 declare the *forge*-crafted signatures to be as authentic as real ones by adding them to the set AC (so that they can be tested in the *Ver* oracle). Intuitively, SDS scheme $S$ is *T-time double-signature forgeable* if the advantage $\mathrm{Adv}_S^{\text{dsf-sds}}(\mathcal{A}) := \Pr[\text{DSF-SDS}(\mathcal{A})]$ is negligible for all efficient adversaries $\mathcal{A}$.

| **Game** DSF-SDS($\mathcal{A}$)<br>  as in Fig. 3 | **Oracle** *Forge*($id_1, id_2, \bar{m}$) |
|---|---|
| | 00  $H_1 := \text{VH}[id_1]$   →  08  Require $\#H + \#\bar{m} \le T$ |
| **Oracle** *Sig*($m$) | 01  $H_2 := \text{VH}[id_2]$   09  $\bar{\sigma} \leftarrow forge(vst_0, H, P_1, P_2, \bar{m})$ |
|   as in Fig. 3 | 02  Require $H_1 \not\preceq H_2$   10  Promise $\#\bar{m} = \#\bar{\sigma}$ |
| | 03  Require $H_2 \not\preceq H_1$   11  $\bar{m}_1 \ldots \bar{m}_l \leftarrow \bar{m}$ |
| **Oracle** *Corrupt* | 04  Find $H, P_1, P_2$ s.t.   12  $\bar{\sigma}_1 \ldots \bar{\sigma}_l \leftarrow \bar{\sigma}$ |
|   as in Fig. 3 | 05  - $H \parallel P_1 \preceq H_1$   13  For $i \leftarrow 1$ to $l$: |
| | 06  - $H \parallel P_2 \preceq H_2$   14  $H \overset{\shortparallel}{\leftarrow} (\bar{m}_i, \bar{\sigma}_i)$ |
| **Oracle** *Ver*($id, m, \sigma$) | 07  - $P_1 \ne P_2$   15  AC $\overset{\cup}{\leftarrow} \{H\}$ |
|   as in Fig. 3 | 16  Return $\bar{\sigma}_1, \ldots, \bar{\sigma}_l$ |

**Fig. 5.** Game DSF-SDS for defining the double-signature forgeability of an SDS scheme. See also the caption of Fig. 3 for the meaning of game variables.

Our second security goal of double-signature extractability (DSE) is strictly stronger than DSF and demands that from any conflicting pair of verification histories the signing state that was current when the double-signing happened can be extracted. Specifically, we demand that an extraction algorithm *ext* exists with the following API:

$$\mathcal{VST} \times \mathcal{X}^* \times \mathcal{X} \times \mathcal{X} \xrightarrow{\text{in}} ext \xrightarrow{\text{out}} \mathcal{SST}.$$

For instance, if in the above example we have $vh' = \epsilon$ then invoking $sst' \leftarrow ext(vst_0, vh', P_1, P_2)$ shall extract $sst' = sst_0$. It is easy to see that extractability implies forgeability. Demanding that *the* signing state is extracted makes sense only if there is at most one possible candidate. While not every SDS scheme meets this requirement (e.g., if the *sig* algorithm is randomized), our constructions from Sect. 5 do. We will thus analyze them in the stronger model (DSE).

For $T \in \mathbb{N} \cup \{\infty\}$ we define the $T$-time double-signature extractability of an SDS scheme via the game DSE-SDS in Fig. 6, where lines 00–08 prepare the inputs for the *ext* algorithm and lines 10–14 test that the extracted state is correct. Intuitively, SDS scheme $S$ is $T$-*time double-signature extractable* if the advantage $\mathrm{Adv}_S^{\mathrm{dse\text{-}sds}}(\mathcal{A}) := \Pr[\mathrm{DSE\text{-}SDS}(\mathcal{A})]$ is negligible for all efficient adversaries $\mathcal{A}$.

| Game DSE-SDS($\mathcal{A}$) | Oracle $Ext(id_1, id_2)$ | |
| --- | --- | --- |
| as in Fig. 3 | 00 $H_1 := \mathrm{VH}[id_1]$ | 09 $sst^* \leftarrow ext(vst_0, H, P_1, P_2)$ |
| | 01 $H_2 := \mathrm{VH}[id_2]$ | 10 $(m_1, \sigma_1) \ldots (m_l, \sigma_l) \leftarrow H$ |
| Oracle $Sig(m)$ | 02 Require $H_1 \not\preceq H_2$ | 11 $sst' \leftarrow sst_0$ |
| as in Fig. 3 | 03 Require $H_2 \not\preceq H_1$ | 12 For $i \leftarrow 1$ to $l$: |
| | 04 Find $H, P_1, P_2$ s.t. | 13 $\_ \leftarrow sig\langle sst' \rangle(m_i)$ |
| Oracle $Corrupt$ | 05 - $H \parallel P_1 \preceq H_1$ | 14 Promise $sst^* = sst'$ |
| as in Fig. 3 | 06 - $H \parallel P_2 \preceq H_2$ | |
| | 07 - $P_1 \neq P_2$ | |
| Oracle $Ver(id, m, \sigma)$ | 08 Require $\#H < T$ | |
| as in Fig. 3 | | |

**Fig. 6.** Game DSE-SDS for defining the double-signature extractability of an SDS scheme. The notation in line 13 means that the output of *sig* is ignored. See also the caption of Fig. 3 for the meaning of game variables.

## 5 Constructions

We construct an SDS that provably fulfills the security properties defined in Sect. 4. The scheme leverages on a strictly one-time digital signature scheme (SOT-DS, see Sect. 3.2) as a building block. Prior work [16] succeeded with constructing SOT-DS, and any of these constructions can be used in our context. However, as they are based on number-theoretic assumptions like the DLP, which are known not to withstand quantum adversaries, we also propose two variants of a novel SOT-DS construction that is based solely on hash functions.

### 5.1 Hash Function Based SOT-DS

Recall the classic hash function based (one-time) signature scheme by Lamport [15] where the signing key is a matrix $(x_i^b)_{b \in \{0,1\}, 1 \leq i \leq n}$ of randomly picked hash function pre-images $x_i^b$, the verification key is the matrix $(y_i^b)_{b \in \{0,1\}, 1 \leq i \leq n}$ of hash function images $y_i^b = H(x_i^b)$, and signing the $n$-bit message $m = m_1 \ldots m_n$

corresponds with releasing the pre-images $(x_i^{m_i})_{1 \leq i \leq n}$ as the signature. Recall further from Sect. 3.2 that a SOT-DS scheme is a one-time signature scheme where double-signing, i.e., signing two different messages with the same key, implies losing the signing key to the public by means of a dedicated *ext* algorithm. While Lamport's scheme releases key components as part of the signing process, and double-signing revokes its existential unforgeability property, double-signing does not release enough information to create signatures on arbitrary messages. The scheme is thus not a SOT-DS instance.

We propose to turn Lamport's scheme into a SOT-DS as follows. The first step is to generate the $b = 0$ half of the pre-images $x_i^b$ deterministically from a seed $k$ using a pseudo-random generator (PRG), i.e., we let $(x_1^0, \ldots, x_n^0) \leftarrow G(k)$.[9] Instead of choosing the $b = 1$ half uniformly distributed as well (either by random assignment or by using a PRG), we assign the $x_i^1$ values such that any pair $(x_i^0, x_i^1)$ allows extracting the seed $k$. Concretely we let $x_i^1 \leftarrow k \oplus x_i^0$ for all $i$, where $\oplus$ denotes XOR. Double-signing in Lamport's scheme corresponds with releasing, for at least one index $i$, the preimage $x_i^0$ in the one signature and the preimage $x_i^1$ in the other signature. That is, if we consider $k$ the signing key of the scheme, the extractability goal is attained. We still need to confirm that the scheme also provides unforgeability, but an analysis in the random oracle model for $G, H$ will show that this is indeed the case.

We derive two different yet closely-related SOT-DS constructions from the above intuition. The difference between the schemes is how verification keys and signatures are represented. The sizes of signing keys, verification keys, and signatures are 1, $2n$, and $n$ elements, respectively, for our first SOT-DS scheme, and are 1, 1, $2n$, respectively, for the second. That is, the latter has considerably smaller verification keys at the cost of a doubled signature length.

| **Algo** *gen* | **Algo** *sig*$(sk; m)$ | **Algo** *ver*$(vk; m, \sigma)$ |
|---|---|---|
| 00 $k \leftarrow \$(\{0,1\}^l)$ | 09 $m_1, \ldots, m_n \leftarrow m$ | 17 $m_1, \ldots, m_n \leftarrow m$ |
| 01 $(sk_1^0, \ldots, sk_n^0) \leftarrow G(k)$ | 10 $(sk_1^0, \ldots, sk_n^0) \leftarrow G(k)$ | 18 For $i \in \{1, \ldots, n\}$: |
| 02 For $i \in \{1, \ldots, n\}$: | 11 For $i \in \{1, \ldots, n\}$: | 19 $b \leftarrow m_i$ |
| 03 $sk_i^1 \leftarrow k \oplus sk_i^0$ | 12 $sk_i^1 \leftarrow k \oplus sk_i^0$ | 20 If $vk_i^b \neq H_i^b(\sigma_i)$: |
| 04 For $b \in \{0,1\}$: | 13 $b \leftarrow m_i$ | 21 Reject |
| 05 $vk_i^b \leftarrow H_i^b(sk_i^b)$ | 14 $\sigma_i \leftarrow sk_i^b$ | 22 Accept |
| 06 $sk := k$ | 15 $\sigma := (\sigma_i)_i$ | |
| 07 $vk := (vk_i^b)_{b,i}$ | 16 Return $\sigma$ | |
| 08 Return $sk, vk$ | | |

**Fig. 7.** First SOT-DS construction. We write $k \leftarrow \$(\{0,1\}^l)$ for randomly sampling an $l$-bit seed $k$. We write $H_i^b(x)$ shorthand for $H(b, i, x)$. We write Accept for Return **T** and Reject for Return **F**. The extraction algorithm is in Fig. 10 (left), in Appendix A.

---

[9] Other hash-based signature schemes like SPHINCS$^+$ use similar techniques [6,9].

DETAILS OF FIRST CONSTRUCTION This scheme is defined for a message space $\mathcal{M} = \{0,1\}^n$ and a security parameter $l \in \mathbb{N}$ (think of $l = 256$). Let $\mathcal{SK} = \{0,1\}^l$ and $\mathcal{VK} = \{0,1\}^{2 \times n \times l}$ and $\mathcal{S} = \{0,1\}^{n \times l}$. Let $G\colon \{0,1\}^l \to \{0,1\}^{n \times l}$ be a PRG and $H\colon \{0,1\} \times \{1,\dots,n\} \times \{0,1\}^l \to \{0,1\}^l$ a hash function. Both $G$ and $H$ will be modeled as random oracles and can be easily constructed from, say, SHA256. Our SOT-DS algorithms $gen, sig, ver, ext$ are then defined as in Fig. 7 and Fig. 10 (left, in Appendix A).

It is straightforward to verify that the scheme provides correctness and extractability by the definitions of Sect. 3. With respect to (one-time, strong) unforgeability, observe that all employed cryptographic primitives are random oracles, that is, the security argument will be combinatoric in nature. To get an idea of the proof, note that any strong forgery $(m^*, \sigma^*)$ that the adversary can come up with includes at least one fresh pre-image $x$ such that $H_i^b(x) = vk_i^b$, for some $b, i$. Finding such a pre-image from the random oracle alone is effectively infeasible: each attempt succeeds with probability $2^{-l}$. The other approach would involve guessing value $k$ (given just random oracle images), and again this succeeds only with probability $2^{-l}$ per attempt. Even if the adversary makes polynomially many queries to the random oracles, the resulting security bound will be of the type $p/2^{-l}$, for a polynomial $p$, which is negligible. A full proof will be provided in the full version [17].

DETAILS OF SECOND CONSTRUCTION. Our second construction is very much like the first but it has $\mathcal{VK} = \{0,1\}^l$ and $\mathcal{S} = \{0,1\}^{2 \times n \times l}$. It is based on the observation that the $sk_i^b$ components included in the signatures of Fig. 7 allow the verifier to recover the $vk_i^b$ components of the verification key. The idea is thus to replace the verification key $vk$ by a value $H^{\#}(vk)$, where $H^{\#}\colon \{0,1\}^{2 \times n \times l} \to \{0,1\}^l$ is an auxiliary collision resistant hash function, to include in each signature the verification key components missing to recover the complete verification key, and to then recover the key and verify it based on the present hash value. The algorithms of our scheme appear in Fig. 8 and Fig. 10 (center, in Appendix A). The security arguments are analogues of the ones given above, with the collision resistance of $H^{\#}$ added to the list of assumptions. A full proof will be provided in the full version [17].

## 5.2 SDS from SOT-DS

We use a SOT-DS scheme as a building block to construct a sequential digital signature (SDS) scheme that fulfills the security properties defined in Sect. 4. In the following we use the notation $\overline{gen}, \overline{sig}, \overline{ver}, \overline{ext}$ for SOT-DS algorithms and $gen, sig, ver, ext$ for SDS algorithms. For $\overline{gen}$ we assume that its randomness space is $\{0,1\}^l$ for some $l \in \mathbb{N}$. Our construction works by chaining multiple SOT-DS instances together. It supports a maximum of $T$ periods for a configurable $T \in \mathbb{N}$ and generates a total of $T$ SOT-DS instances as follows: While the first SOT-DS is generated regularly by invoking $\overline{gen}$ with fresh randomness, the remaining $T-1$ instances are generated by invoking $\overline{gen}$ with explicitly specified randomness that is derived with a random oracle $H\colon \bar{\mathcal{S}} \to \{0,1\}^l$ from the preceding SOT-DS signing key: If $(sk_i, vk_i)$ is the SOT-DS key pair of the $i$-th epoch,

| **Algo** $gen$ | **Algo** $sig(sk; m)$ | **Algo** $ver(vk; m, \sigma)$ |
|---|---|---|
| 00 $k \leftarrow \$(\{0,1\}^l)$ | 10 $m_1, \ldots, m_n \leftarrow m$ | 20 $m_1, \ldots, m_n \leftarrow m$ |
| 01 $(sk_1^0, \ldots, sk_n^0) \leftarrow G(k)$ | 11 $(sk_1^0, \ldots, sk_n^0) \leftarrow G(k)$ | 21 For $i \in \{1, \ldots, n\}$: |
| 02 For $i \in \{1, \ldots, n\}$: | 12 For $i \in \{1, \ldots, n\}$: | 22 $\quad b \leftarrow m_i$ |
| 03 $\quad sk_i^1 \leftarrow k \oplus sk_i^0$ | 13 $\quad sk_i^1 \leftarrow k \oplus sk_i^0$ | 23 $\quad d \leftarrow 1 - m_i$ |
| 04 $\quad$ For $b \in \{0,1\}$: | 14 $\quad b \leftarrow m_i$ | 24 $\quad (sk_i^b, vk_i^d) \leftarrow \sigma_i$ |
| 05 $\quad\quad vk_i^b \leftarrow H_i^b(sk_i^b)$ | 15 $\quad d \leftarrow 1 - m_i$ | 25 $\quad vk_i^b \leftarrow H_i^b(sk_i^b)$ |
| 06 $vk' \leftarrow (vk_i^b)_{b,i}$ | 16 $\quad vk_i^d \leftarrow H_i^d(sk_i^d)$ | 26 $vk' \leftarrow (vk_i^b)_{b,i}$ |
| 07 $sk := k$ | 17 $\quad \sigma_i \leftarrow (sk_i^b, vk_i^d)$ | 27 If $vk \neq H^\#(vk')$: |
| 08 $vk \leftarrow H^\#(vk')$ | 18 $\sigma := (\sigma_i)_i$ | 28 $\quad$ Reject |
| 09 Return $sk, vk$ | 19 Return $\sigma$ | 29 Accept |

**Fig. 8.** Second SOT-DS construction. We denote with $H^\#$ an auxiliary collision-resistant hash function. The extraction algorithm is in Fig. 10 (center), in Appendix A. See also the caption of Fig. 7.

then the SOT-DS key pair $(sk_{i+1}, vk_{i+1})$ of the next epoch is derived by letting $k \leftarrow H(sk_i)$ and $(sk_{i+1}, vk_{i+1}) \leftarrow \overline{gen}[k]$, where the bracket notation means the algorithm uses the explicitly specified randomness $k$.[10] The SDS signing state of the first epoch is $(sk_1, 1)$. The signing state deterministically evolves by one position after each signing operation. To achieve forward security, switching to the next SDS epoch also involves securely erasing the old SOT-DS signing key. The SDS verification state is the vector of all SOT-DS verification keys, plus an indication of the current epoch. (We also clear verification state elements that become redundant over time, but this is for efficiency and not for security.) The explicit specification of the scheme algorithms is in Fig. 9.

| **Algo** $gen_T$ | **Algo** $sig_T \langle sst \rangle (m)$ | **Algo** $ver_T \langle vst \rangle (m, \sigma)$ |
|---|---|---|
| 00 $k \leftarrow \$(\{0,1\}^l)$ | 08 $(sk_t, t) \leftarrow sst$ | 16 $(vk, t) \leftarrow vst$ |
| 01 For $t \leftarrow 1$ to $T$: | 09 Require $1 \leq t \leq T$ | 17 Require $1 \leq t \leq T$ |
| 02 $\quad (sk_t, vk_t) \leftarrow \overline{gen}[k]$ | 10 $\sigma \leftarrow \overline{sig}(sk_t; m)$ | 18 $v \leftarrow \overline{ver}(vk_t; m, \sigma)$ |
| 03 $\quad k \leftarrow H(sk_t)$ | 11 $k \leftarrow H(sk_t)$ | 19 Require $v$ |
| 04 $sst \leftarrow (sk_1, 1)$ | 12 Securely erase $sk_t$ | 20 $vk_t \leftarrow \bot$ |
| 05 $vk := (vk_1, \ldots, vk_T)$ | 13 $(sk_{t+1}, \_) \leftarrow \overline{gen}[k]$ | 21 $vst \leftarrow (vk, t+1)$ |
| 06 $vst \leftarrow (vk, 1)$ | 14 $sst \leftarrow (sk_{t+1}, t+1)$ | 22 Return $v$ |
| 07 Return $(sst, vst)$ | 15 Return $\sigma$ | |

**Fig. 9.** SDS construction. Parameter $T \in \mathbb{N}$ indicates the number of supported epochs and can be fixed arbitrarily. In line 02, $\overline{gen}$ is invoked with explicit randomness. The extraction algorithm is in Fig. 10 (right), in Appendix A.

---

[10] The random oracle $H$ used here should of course be independent of the random oracle with the same name of Sect. 5.1.

The correctness of the SDS scheme follows immediately from the correctness of the SOT-DS scheme. The (strong) unforgeability is easily reduced to the SOT-DS unforgeability: If the verifier's initial state is authentic, then any SDS forgery immediately translates to an SOT-DS forgery *or* the evaluation of the random oracle $H$ on input the previous signing key (in which case the reduction goes to the unforgeability of the previous SOT-DS instance). By the strict sequentiality of the construction, the forward security basically comes for free. Let's finally consider the extractability property. Two conflicting SDS verification histories translate immediately to two conflicting SOT-DS message-signature pairs, allowing for the recovery of the SOT-DS signing key of that epoch. The latter is precisely the SDS signing state that is to be recovered. A full proof will be provided in the full version [17].

# 6  Implementation and Evaluation

In order to experimentally evaluate our SDS construction from Sect. 5.2, we implemented its algorithms in the C programming language. We made experiments using both SOT-DS candidates from Sect. 5.1 as underlying building blocks. We tested the performance of our implementations on an Intel Core i7 8th generation CPU, using the hash functions SHA-2, SHA-3, and HARAKA [14].[11] Table 1 shows the time consumption of the different algorithms.

**Table 1.** Efficiency of SDS (Fig. 9) based on two different SOT-DS (left: Fig. 7; right: Fig. 8) using three different hash functions. The entries indicate the number of $\mu s$ per algorithm invocation, for a setting with $T = 100$ epochs.

|       | SHA-2 | SHA-3 | HARAKA |       | SHA-2 | SHA-3 | HARAKA |
|-------|-------|-------|--------|-------|-------|-------|--------|
| *gen* | 67834 | 78227 | 80166  | *gen* | 75341 | 84401 | 88193  |
| *sig* | 528   | 557   | 545    | *sig* | 643   | 699   | 664    |
| *ver* | 82    | 117   | 120    | *ver* | 147   | 186   | 124    |
| *ext* | 162   | 276   | 239    | *ext* | 283   | 373   | 239    |

When comparing the results associated with the two underlying SOT-DS schemes, the extra costs caused by the additional hash function operations of the second SOT-DS construction are clearly visible. Beyond that, we see that using SHA-2 is more efficient than using SHA-3. As HARAKA is specifically designed for handling fixed-length short inputs, it should be well suited for our application. However, HARAKA is also designed for modern platforms that support the AES-NI instruction set for AES [14]. Our implementation is generic and doesn't make

---

[11] We borrowed the hash function code from the NIST Post-Quantum competition repository, see https://csrc.nist.gov/CSRC/media/Projects/Post-Quantum-Cryptography/documents/example-files/api-notes.pdf.

use of such instructions, which makes it slower than our SHA-based candidates. We expect, however, that HARAKA will clearly outperform SHA-2 and SHA-3 with specifically optimized implementations.

**Acknowledgments.** We thank the anonymous reviewers for their valuable comments.

## A    Extractors

In Fig. 10 we specify extractors for our two SOT-DS constructions (left, center) and for our SDS construction (right). See Sect. 5 for details.

| **Alg** $ext(vk; m^0, \sigma^0, m^1, \sigma^1)$ | **Alg** $ext(vk; m^0, \sigma^0, m^1, \sigma^1)$ | **Alg** $ext_T(vst_0; vh', P_1, P_2)$ |
|---|---|---|
| 00 Require $m^0 \neq m^1$ | 09 Require $m^0 \neq m^1$ | 18 $(vk, 1) \leftarrow vst_0$ |
| 01 $m_1^0, \ldots, m_n^0 \leftarrow m^0$ | 10 $m_1^0, \ldots, m_n^0 \leftarrow m^0$ | 19 $t \leftarrow \#vh' + 1$ |
| 02 $m_1^1, \ldots, m_n^1 \leftarrow m^1$ | 11 $m_1^1, \ldots, m_n^1 \leftarrow m^1$ | 20 $sk_t \leftarrow \overline{ext}(vk_t; P_1, P_2)$ |
| 03 Find $i$ s.t. $m_i^0 \neq m_i^1$ | 12 Find $i$ s.t. $m_i^0 \neq m_i^1$ | 21 $sst \leftarrow (sk_t, t)$ |
| 04 Wlog $m_i^0 = 0 \wedge m_i^1 = 1$ | 13 $(sk_i^0, \_) \leftarrow \sigma_i^0$ | 22 Return $sst$ |
| 05 $sk_i^0 \leftarrow \sigma_i^0; sk_i^1 \leftarrow \sigma_i^1$ | 14 $(sk_i^1, \_) \leftarrow \sigma_i^1$ | |
| 06 $k \leftarrow sk_i^1 \oplus sk_i^0$ | 15 $k \leftarrow sk_i^0 \oplus sk_i^1$ | |
| 07 $sk := k$ | 16 $sk := k$ | |
| 08 Return $sk$ | 17 Return $sk$ | |

**Fig. 10.** Extractors. **Left:** Extractor for the first SOT-DS construction of Fig. 7. The algorithm assumes for its inputs that $ver(vk; m^0, \sigma^0) = \mathbf{T}$ and $ver(vk; m^1, \sigma^1) = \mathbf{T}$ and $(m^0, \sigma^0) \neq (m^1, \sigma^1)$, as it is promised by lines 02,03,04 of Fig. 2. As the third condition effectively implies $m^0 \neq m^1$ if $H$ is collision resistant, the algorithm will not abort in line 00 and the instruction of line 03 is guaranteed to succeed. **Center:** Extractor for the second SOT-DS construction of Fig. 8. **Right:** Extractor for the SDS construction of Fig. 9. The algorithm assumes for its inputs $P_1, P_2$ what it is promised by the DSE game in Fig. 6.

## References

1. Armour, M., Poettering, B.: Substitution attacks against message authentication. IACR Trans. Symm. Cryptol. **2019**(3), 152–168 (2019). https://doi.org/10.13154/tosc.v2019.i3.152-168
2. Armour, M., Poettering, B.: Subverting decryption in AEAD. In: Albrecht, M. (ed.) IMACC 2019. LNCS, vol. 11929, pp. 22–41. Springer, Cham (2019). https://doi.org/10.1007/978-3-030-35199-1_2
3. Armour, M., Poettering, B.: Algorithm substitution attacks against receivers. Int. J. Inf. Secur., 1–24 (2022). https://doi.org/10.1007/s10207-022-00596-5
4. Bellare, M., Paterson, K.G., Rogaway, P.: Security of symmetric encryption against mass surveillance. In: Garay, J.A., Gennaro, R. (eds.) CRYPTO 2014, Part I. LNCS, vol. 8616, pp. 1–19. Springer, Heidelberg (2014). https://doi.org/10.1007/978-3-662-44371-2_1

5. Bellare, M., Poettering, B., Stebila, D.: Deterring certificate subversion: efficient double-authentication-preventing signatures. In: Fehr, S. (ed.) PKC 2017, Part II. LNCS, vol. 10175, pp. 121–151. Springer, Heidelberg (2017). https://doi.org/10.1007/978-3-662-54388-7_5

6. Bernstein, D.J., Hülsing, A., Kölbl, S., Niederhagen, R., Rijneveld, J., Schwabe, P.: The SPHINCS$^+$ signature framework. In: Cavallaro, L., Kinder, J., Wang, X., Katz, J. (eds.) ACM CCS 2019, pp. 2129–2146. ACM Press, November 2019. https://doi.org/10.1145/3319535.3363229

7. Boneh, D., Kim, S., Nikolaenko, V.: Lattice-based DAPS and generalizations: self-enforcement in signature schemes. In: Gollmann, D., Miyaji, A., Kikuchi, H. (eds.) ACNS 2017. LNCS, vol. 10355, pp. 457–477. Springer, Cham (2017). https://doi.org/10.1007/978-3-319-61204-1_23

8. BSI: Quantum-safe cryptography - Fundamentals, current developments and recommendations. Technical report, Bundesamt für Sicherheit in der Informationstechnik (2022). https://www.bsi.bund.de/SharedDocs/Downloads/EN/BSI/Publications/Brochure/quantum-safe-cryptography.html

9. Buchmann, J., Dahmen, E., Szydlo, M.: Hash-based digital signature schemes. In: Bernstein, D.J., Buchmann, J., Dahmen, E. (eds.) Post-Quantum Cryptography, pp. 35–93. Springer, Heidelberg (2009). https://doi.org/10.1007/978-3-540-88702-7_3

10. Chaum, D., Fiat, A., Naor, M.: Untraceable electronic cash. In: Goldwasser, S. (ed.) CRYPTO 1988. LNCS, vol. 403, pp. 319–327. Springer, New York (1990). https://doi.org/10.1007/0-387-34799-2_25

11. Degabriele, J.P., Farshim, P., Poettering, B.: A more cautious approach to security against mass surveillance. In: Leander, G. (ed.) FSE 2015. LNCS, vol. 9054, pp. 579–598. Springer, Heidelberg (2015). https://doi.org/10.1007/978-3-662-48116-5_28

12. Derler, D., Ramacher, S., Slamanig, D.: Homomorphic proxy re-authenticators and applications to verifiable multi-user data aggregation. Cryptology ePrint Archive, Report 2017/086 (2017). https://eprint.iacr.org/2017/086

13. Derler, D., Ramacher, S., Slamanig, D.: Short double- and $N$-times-authentication-preventing signatures from ECDSA and more. In: 2018 IEEE European Symposium on Security and Privacy, EuroS&P 2018, London, United Kingdom, April 24–26, 2018, pp. 273–287. IEEE (2018). https://doi.org/10.1109/EuroSP.2018.00027

14. Kölbl, S., Lauridsen, M.M., Mendel, F., Rechberger, C.: Haraka v2 - efficient short-input hashing for post-quantum applications. IACR Trans. Symm. Cryptol. **2016**(2), 1–29 (2016). https://doi.org/10.13154/tosc.v2016.i2.1-29. https://tosc.iacr.org/index.php/ToSC/article/view/563

15. Lamport, L.: Constructing digital signatures from a one-way function. Technical report SRI-CSL-98, SRI International Computer Science Laboratory, October 1979

16. Poettering, B.: Shorter double-authentication preventing signatures for small address spaces. In: Joux, A., Nitaj, A., Rachidi, T. (eds.) AFRICACRYPT 2018. LNCS, vol. 10831, pp. 344–361. Springer, Cham (2018). https://doi.org/10.1007/978-3-319-89339-6_19

17. Poettering, B., Rastikian, S.: Sequential digital signatures for cryptographic software-update authentication. Cryptology ePrint Archive, Paper 2022/995 (2022). https://eprint.iacr.org/2022/995

18. Poettering, B., Stebila, D.: Double-authentication-preventing signatures. In: Kutyłowski, M., Vaidya, J. (eds.) ESORICS 2014. LNCS, vol. 8712, pp. 436–453. Springer, Cham (2014). https://doi.org/10.1007/978-3-319-11203-9_25

19. Poettering, B., Stebila, D.: Double-authentication-preventing signatures. Int. J. Inf. Secur. **16**(1), 1–22 (2015). https://doi.org/10.1007/s10207-015-0307-8
20. Ruffing, T., Kate, A., Schröder, D.: Liar, liar, coins on fire!: Penalizing equivocation by loss of Bitcoins. In: Ray, I., Li, N., Kruegel, C. (eds.) ACM CCS 2015, pp. 219–230. ACM Press, October 2015. https://doi.org/10.1145/2810103.2813686

# On Committing
# Authenticated-Encryption

John Chan$^{(\boxtimes)}$ and Phillip Rogaway

Department of Computer Science, University of California, Davis, USA
jmachan@ucdavis.edu, rogaway@cs.ucdavis.edu

**Abstract.** We provide a strong definition for *committing* authenticated-encryption (cAE), as well as a framework that encompasses earlier and weaker definitions. The framework attends not only to *what* is committed but also the extent to which the adversary knows or controls keys. We slot into our framework strengthened cAE-attacks on GCM and OCB. Our main result is a simple and efficient construction, CTX, that makes a nonce-based AE (nAE) scheme committing. The transformed scheme achieves the strongest security notion in our framework. Just the same, the added computational cost (on top of the nAE scheme's cost) is a single hash over a short string, a cost independent of the plaintext's length. And there is *no* increase in ciphertext length compared to the base nAE scheme. That such a thing is possible, let alone easy, upends the (incorrect) intuition that you can't commit to a plaintext or ciphertext without hashing one or the other. And it motivates a simple and practical tweak to AE-schemes to make them committing.

**Keywords:** AEAD · Authenticated encryption · Committing encryption · Key-robustness

## 1 Introduction

A natural misconception about authenticated encryption (AE) is the belief that a ciphertext produced by encrypting a plaintext with a key, nonce, and associated data (AD) effectively *commits* to those things: decrypting it with some *other* key, nonce, or AD will usually fail, the transmission deemed invalid. And why not? One wouldn't expect to successfully open a lock when using an incorrect key. The intuition is even memorialized in the name *authenticated* encryption: things aren't just private, the name implies, but authentic.

Yet Farshim, Orlandi, and Roşie [9] (FOR17) point out that AE provides no such guarantee—not if the adversary can select any keys. Subsequent work demonstrated that just *knowing* the keys suffices to construct a ciphertext that decrypts into different valid messages [7,11]. A variety of work has also made clear just how wrong things can go when designers implicitly and incorrectly assume that their encryption *is* committing [2,7,13].

We call the event of a ciphertext being "explained" in multiple and valid ways a *misattribution*. The cited works offer definitions and schemes that seek

© The Author(s), under exclusive license to Springer Nature Switzerland AG 2022
V. Atluri et al. (Eds.): ESORICS 2022, LNCS 13555, pp. 275–294, 2022.
https://doi.org/10.1007/978-3-031-17146-8_14

to protect against misattribution. But these definitions are mostly incomparable, weak, and fold in aims beyond avoiding misattribution.

DEFINITIONAL FRAMEWORK. To begin, we revisit definitions for committing AE. We offer a definitional framework that unifies and strengthens previous definitions targeting misattribution. We call the security goals *committing-AE* (cAE). The framework applies to schemes for *nonce-based AE with associated data* (nAE). Encryption takes in a key $K$, a nonce $N$, an associated data $A$, and a message $M$, and outputs a ciphertext $C$. Under our framework, an adversary succeeds in an attack when it creates a misattribution. That happens when $C$ results from known and distinct tuples $(K, N, A, M)$ and $(K', N', A', M')$ for valid messages $M, M'$. We say "results from" because $C$ could be output by encryption *or* input to decryption—anything that results in adversarial knowledge of the pair $(K, N, A, M)$, $(K', N', A', M')$.

Previous definitions consider only some forms of misattribution. For example, the *full robustness* and *key-commitment* notions [2,9] require that the keys differ, $K \neq K'$, but ignore the possibility of misattribution under the same key. Our framework can encompass all possible types of misattribution. That said, we regard the desired target as the *strongest* definition, AE that is *fully committing*, where the adversary wins if it manages *any* form of misattribution.

Our framework attends also to the status of keys held by parties. To model different levels of adversarial activity, we include a definitional parameter t. This two-character string dictates what types of keys the adversary might employ for a misattribution to occur. Keys are either: *honest* (represented by the character 0), meaning they are generated uniformly at random and remain unknown to the adversary; *revealed* (represented by a 1), meaning they were honestly generated, but the adversary knows their value; or *corrupted* (an X), meaning the adversary itself chose the key. This gives rise to six different definitions. This "knob" is useful for describing and understanding attacks. The weakest of these notions models when both keys are honest. We show that ordinary nAE-security implies this notion assuming the adversaries do not repeat nonces for the same key. Many applications that require cAE security would work just fine with 0X-security, and stronger quantitative bounds might be obtained for this case.

MAIN CONSTRUCTION. Our main result is a method to convert an arbitrary (tag-based) nAE scheme into a similarly efficient cAE scheme. We set high bars for security and efficiency. Security is with respect to the strongest form of commitment: $K$, $N$, $A$, and $M$ must all be "fixed" by a ciphertext, even if the adversary controls all keys.

Our CTX construction is extremely simple. Starting from an nAE scheme whose encryption algorithm $\mathcal{E}(K, N, A, M)$ produces a ciphertext $\mathcal{C} = C \parallel T$ consisting of a ciphertext core $C$ (with $|C| = |M|$) and a tag $T$ (with $|T| = \tau$), just replace the tag $T$ with an alternative tag $T^* = H(K, N, A, T)$ (this tag of length $\mu$). Decryption does the obvious, verifying $T^*$. The function $H$ is a cryptographic hash function that, in the security proofs, is modeled as a random oracle. The remarkable fact is that this extremely simple tweak to the nAE scheme not only works to commit to $K$, $N$, and $A$, but also to the underlying message $M$. This ultimately follows from the injectivity of the map from the ciphertext core $C$ to the plaintext $M$ when $K$, $N$, and $A$ are all fixed.

The CTX construction is computationally efficient insofar as the work on top of the base nAE scheme is a hash computation over a string that does not grow with the plaintext or ciphertext. And the nAE scheme's minimal ciphertext expansion is preserved, going from the $\tau$ (typically 128) extra bits that are needed to provide authenticity to the $\mu$ (typically 160) extra bits that are needed to provide authenticity *and* the binding (commitment) of all inputs.

ATTACKS ON GCM AND OCB. Previous misattribution attacks on GCM were mounted with adversarial control of the keys [7,11]. It is mentioned by those same authors that knowledge of the keys is sufficient. Under our terminology, this would be a $CAE_{xx}$-attack and a $CAE_{11}$-attack respectively.

We present a new attack on GCM for a weaker adversary, a $CAE_{01}$-attack. That is, the adversary can create a misattribution knowing just one key. For any ciphertext $C$ generated under a perfectly honest key, one can find a valid decryption for it under a known key. The attack strategy involves computing an AD that validates the decryption of the ciphertext. Intuitively, for any key, nonce, message, and ciphertext, there are an infinite number of ADs that validly decrypt the ciphertext—we only need to find one of them. The strategy extends to mounting a $CAE_{01}$-attack on OCB as well. These attacks demonstrate that nAE-security is insufficient for even $CAE_{01}$-security.

RELATED WORK. Prior work has been leading towards a definition for fully committing AE (the cAE-xx notion), but didn't quite get there. There has also been movement towards efficient schemes for this end.

The notion of committing encryption goes back to 2003 with Gertner and Herzberg [10], who consider the problem in both the symmetric and asymmetric settings. The authors do not look at deterministic or authenticated encryption.

Abdalla, Bellare, and Neven give definitions for what they call *robustness* [1] in the asymmetric setting. Their notion requires an adversary to produce a ciphertext that validly decrypts under two different keys. It encompasses keys that are honestly generated. Later, Farshim, Libert, Paterson, and Quaglia observe that, for some applications, robustness against adversarially-chosen keys is critical [8]. They then strengthen Abdalla et al.'s notion accordingly.

Farshim, Orlandi, and Roşie (FOR17) [9] contextualized Abdalla et al.'s robustness in the AE setting, initializing the study of what we call committing AE. Shortly after, Grubbs, Lu, and Ristenpart (GLR17) [11] defined a variant of committing AE with the goal of constructing schemes that support *message franking*. Dodis, Grubbs, Ristenpart, and Woodage (DGRW18) [7] also target message franking and further develop GLR17's definitions. These two works have goals beyond preventing misattributions. We are after simpler aims, with the syntax of classical nAE. Albertini, Duong, Gueron, Kölbl, Luykx, and Schmieg (ADGKLS20) [2] observe the possibility of mitigating the attacks described by GLR17 and DGRW18 under a weaker form of misattribution prevention. Their observation led them to develop a more efficient construction—one that avoids additional passes over the message.

Bellare and Hoang (BH22), in a contemporary work, offer a range of committing AE definitions, with starting points of both standard nAE and misuse-resistant AE [5]. The strongest of their definitions, like ours, requires that the ciphertext commit to *everything*– the key, nonce, AD, and plaintext. They also consider *multi-input committing security*, where an adversary is required to create misattributions of more than just two valid explanations.

Len, Grubbs, and Ristenpart demonstrate password-recovery attacks on non-committing password-based AEAD schemes [13]. Their attacks are built on efficiently creating ciphertexts that successfully decrypt under many keys.

A more detailed comparison of some of the cited works is in Sect. 6.

## 2 Preliminaries

COLLISION-RESISTANT HASH FUNCTIONS. A *hash function* $H\colon \mathcal{D} \to \{0,1\}^h$ maps strings from some domain $\mathcal{D} \subset \{0,1\}^*$ to strings of length $h$. Informally, a hash function is collision-resistant if it is difficult for an adversary $\mathcal{A}$ to find two unique inputs that map to the same output. This notion is captured by a collision resistance game CR where $\mathcal{A}$ is ran and outputs a pair $(M, M')$. The game outputs true if $H(M) = H(M')$ and $M \neq M'$. The adversary $\mathcal{A}$'s advantage against $H$ is then quantified as $\mathbf{Adv}_H^{\mathrm{col}}(\mathcal{A}) = \Pr[\mathrm{CR}_H^{\mathcal{A}} \Rightarrow \mathrm{true}]$. This definition of collision-resistance of unkeyed hash functions follows the human-ignorance approach of [17].

NONCE-BASED AE. An nAE scheme, or a *nonce-based authenticated encryption-scheme supporting associated data (AD)* is a pair of functions $(\mathcal{E}, \mathcal{D})$. The former, the *encryption algorithm*, is a deterministic function $\mathcal{E}\colon \mathcal{K} \times \mathcal{N} \times \mathcal{A} \times \mathcal{M} \to \mathcal{C}$ that takes in a key, a nonce, an AD, and a message, and outputs a ciphertext. The latter $\mathcal{D}$, the *decryption algorithm*, is a deterministic function $\mathcal{D}\colon \mathcal{K} \times \mathcal{N} \times \mathcal{A} \times \mathcal{C} \to \mathcal{M} \times \{\perp\}$. We sometimes write $\mathcal{E}_K^{N,A}(M)$ and $\mathcal{D}_K^{N,A}(C)$ to denote $\mathcal{E}(K, N, A, M)$ and $\mathcal{D}(K, N, A, C)$. An nAE scheme is *correct* if $\mathcal{D}_K^{N,A}(\mathcal{E}_K^{N,A}(M)) = M$ for all $K, N, A, M$. A notable property of correct schemes is how encryption is injective from $\mathcal{M}$ to $\mathcal{C}$ when $K, N, A$ are fixed. $K \in \mathcal{K}, N \in \mathcal{N}, A \in \mathcal{A}, M \in \mathcal{M}$ and $\mathcal{D}_K^{N,A}(C) = \perp$ otherwise. We assume that the message space $\mathcal{M} \subseteq \{0,1\}^*$ is a set of strings where $M \in \mathcal{M}$ implies $\{0,1\}^{|M|} \in \mathcal{M}$. We insist of an nAE scheme that there is an associated value, its *expansion*, which is a constant $\tau$ such that $|\mathcal{E}_K^{N,A}(M)| = |M| + \tau$ for all $K, N, A, M$.

A customary formulation of nAE security asks an adversary attacking the nAE scheme $\Pi = (\mathcal{E}, \mathcal{D})$ to distinguish between a pair of oracles [16]. The "real" oracles use $\Pi$'s algorithms while the "ideal" or "fake" oracles only give bogus responses. For an adversary $\mathcal{A}$ attacking $\Pi$, its advantage is defined as follows:

$$\mathbf{Adv}_\Pi^{\mathrm{nae}}(\mathcal{A}) = \Pr[K \leftarrow \mathcal{K};\ \mathcal{A}^{E_K(\cdot,\cdot,\cdot), D_K(\cdot,\cdot,\cdot)} \Rightarrow 1]$$
$$- \Pr[\mathcal{A}^{\$(\cdot,\cdot,\cdot), \perp(\cdot,\cdot,\cdot)} \Rightarrow 1].$$

Its interaction with the $E_K$ and $D_k$ oracles, the "real" oracles, begins with the uniformly random sampling of a key $K$. An oracle query then $E_K(N, A, M)$

returns $\mathcal{E}_K(N, A, M)$, while an oracle query $D_K(N, A, C)$ returns $\mathcal{D}_K(N, A, C)$. In contrast, an "ideal" oracle query of $\$(N, A, M)$ returns a uniformly random string of length $|M| + \tau$, while $\perp(N, A, C)$ always returns $\perp$.

The adversary is forbidden from querying its decryption oracles with $N, A, C$ if it acquired $C$ from its encryption oracles using $N, A$ as doing so would allow it to trivially win. Similarly, the definition demands that adversaries are *nonce-respecting*, meaning that they never repeat a nonce in its encryption queries.

We will find it useful to define a variant of nAE security that directly models multiple keys, which was first formalized in [6]. In this variant, an infinite number of keys are uniformly randomly generated for the real oracles at the initialization of the security game. Each oracle takes in an additional parameter, an index, that the adversary uses to specify which key to use for its query. Its advantage notion in this game is:

$$\mathbf{Adv}_\Pi^{\mathrm{nae}*}(\mathcal{A}) = \Pr[K \twoheadleftarrow \mathcal{K}^\infty; \ \mathcal{A}^{E_K(\cdot,\cdot,\cdot,\cdot),\, D_K(\cdot,\cdot,\cdot,\cdot)} \Rightarrow 1]$$
$$- \Pr[\mathcal{A}^{\$(\cdot,\cdot,\cdot,\cdot),\, \perp(\cdot,\cdot,\cdot,\cdot)} \Rightarrow 1].$$

Similarly, the adversary is restricted from querying $(i, N, A, C)$ to its decryption oracle if $C$ is the result of some $(i, N, A, M)$. The adversary is nonce-respecting in this case if it never repeats the same nonce for the same key when querying the encryption oracle.

## 3   Committing AE

COMMITTING AE. Informally, we call an nAE scheme a *committing AE scheme* (cAE) if it commits to any of the elements used to produce a ciphertext. We are primarily interested in cAE schemes that commit to all of these elements. By the definition of nAE in Sect. 2, those elements would be the key, nonce, AD, and message. The CAE game that captures this property is presented in Fig. 1.

An adversary attacking the CAE-security of an nAE scheme $\Pi$ aims to produce a ciphertext $C$ that has two distinct valid "explanations." That is, ciphertext $C$ could decrypt to a messages $M$ using $(K_i, N, A)$, or it could decrypt to a message $M'$ using $(K_j, N', A')$ such that $(K_i, N, A, M) \neq (K_j, N', A', M')$ and $M, M' \neq \perp$. When either of these occur, we say that the ciphertext is *misattributed*. We sometimes refer to $C$ as the *colliding ciphertext* and the $(K, N, A, M)$ associated to it as one of its attributions. In the game code, we write $S \xleftarrow{\cup} \{x\}$ as shorthand for $S \xleftarrow{\cup} S \cup \{x\}$, adding $x$ to the set $S$.

The adversary initializes the game with the Initialize procedure, which generates an infinite number of uniformly random keys indexed by the natural numbers. Several sets are also initialized, one of which is the set $S$ which keeps track of $(K, N, A, M, C)$ tuples that constitute encryption and decryption queries and responses made by the adversary. The game terminates with the Finalize procedure, which checks the tuples of $S$ in a pairwise fashion for an adversarial win. That is, it searches for a pair of tuples where the ciphertexts are equivalent and that the explanations are distinct and valid. There is an additional condition checked that pertains to the function chk that we describe later.

There are four other game procedures surfaced to the adversary: ENC, DEC, REV, COR. These are the encryption, decryption, reveal, and corruption oracles. The first two oracles let the adversary use $\Pi$'s encryption and decryption algorithms using a key specified by an index $i$. Any ciphertext or message generated by the call to $\Pi$'s algorithms is stored alongside the queried $K_i, N, A, M$ (or $C$) are stored in the set S. The reveal oracle allows the adversary to query an index $i$ and learn the key $K_i$. For the corruption oracle, the adversary queries an index $i$ and a key $K$ and supplants $K_i$ with $K$. Keys that are affected by these two oracles are added to the sets $\mathsf{K_r}$ and $\mathsf{K_c}$ respectively.

Note that ENC queries are restricted to be *nonce-respecting* for honest keys. That is, an adversary cannot repeat nonces for its encryption queries to an honest key $K_i$. This is reflected in the game code. The purpose of this is to prevent possibilities of an adversary in learning an honest key through abuse of the nonce as this would otherwise blur the distinction between revealed and honest keys.

When the adversary yields a colliding ciphertext with two distinct valid explanations, there is one more condition to check before the adversary is considered to have won. That is, the chk function is ran on the keys of the explanations. This function is the *collision check* function and relies on a parameter of the CAE game, t, which we refer to as the *collision type*. For any key $K_i$ in the game, the key can either be *corrupted, revealed,* or *honest*. A key is corrupted when it is added to the game through the corruption oracle COR and thus part of the set $\mathsf{K_c}$. A key is revealed when the adversary learns of it through the reveal oracle REV and thus part of the set $\mathsf{K_r}$. If the key is part of neither set, meaning it was chosen uniformly at random and unaffected by the adversary, then it is considered honest. Whether keys are corrupted, revealed, and honest are represented by X, 1, and 0 bits respectively. Six different types of collisions arise from these types of keys. The parameter t is a two-bit string that describes the kind of collision the adversary may win with.

Finally, the advantage of an adversary $\mathcal{A}$ attacking the CAE-security of an nAE scheme $\Pi$ in regards to a collision type t is quantified as $\mathbf{Adv}_{\Pi,t}^{\mathrm{cae}}(\mathcal{A}) = \Pr[\mathrm{CAE}_{\Pi,t}^{\mathcal{A}} \to 1]$. When discussing CAE-security with a specific type of collision, we denote the collision with a subscript i.e. $\mathrm{CAE_{XX}}$-security.

OTHER COMMITTING NOTIONS. Most other committing AE definitions focused on cases where the adversary has control over both keys when creating a colliding ciphertext, which would be a corrupted-corrupted (or t = XX) collision [2,7,11]. Farshim et al. consider one definition of key-robustness, called *semi-full robustness*, where the adversary is asked to come up with a ciphertext that decrypts under an honest key and a key that it knows (what we would call a 01-collision) [9]. Bellare gives another robustness notion for randomized symmetric encryption called *random-key robustness* in [4] that is comparable to the $\mathrm{CAE_{00}}$ notion and shows that authenticity implies random-key robustness. Our definitional framework can be tuned to consider these collisions and more, allowing flexibility when using the definition to model real systems.

---

$\underline{\text{CAE}_{\Pi,t}}$

**procedure** Initialize()
00  **for** $i \in \mathbb{N}$ **do** $K_i \leftarrow \mathcal{K}$; $N_i \leftarrow \emptyset$
01  S, K$_c$, K$_r$ $\leftarrow \emptyset$

**procedure** Finalize()
10  **ret** $\exists (K_i, N, A, M, C), (K_j, N', A', M', C') \in$ S s.t.
11     $(M \neq \bot \wedge M' \neq \bot)\wedge$
12     $(C = C')\wedge$
13     $(K_i, N, A, M) \neq (K_j, N', A', M')\wedge$
14     $(\text{chk}(K_i, K_j) \vee \text{chk}(K_j, K_i))$

$\underline{\text{chk}(K_i, K_j)}$
16  **if** $t = 00 \wedge K_i \notin$ K$_c \cup$ K$_r \wedge K_j \notin$ K$_c \cup$ K$_r$, **then ret** 1
17  **if** $t = 01 \wedge K_i \notin$ K$_r \cup$ K$_c \wedge K_j \notin$ K$_c$ **then ret** 1
18  **if** $t = 0X \wedge K_i \notin$ K$_r \cup$ K$_c$ **then ret** 1
19  **if** $t = 11 \wedge K_i \notin$ K$_c \wedge K_j \notin$ K$_c$ **then ret** 1
1A  **if** $t = 1X \wedge K_i \notin$ K$_c$ **then ret** 1
1B  **if** $t = XX$ **then ret** 1
1C  **ret** 0

**procedure** ENC$(i, N, A, M)$
20  **if** $K_i \notin$ K$_r \cup$K$_c \wedge N \in \boldsymbol{N}_i$
21     **then ret** $\bot$
22  $C \leftarrow \Pi.\mathcal{E}(K_i, N, A, M)$
23  S $\overset{\cup}{\leftarrow} \{(K_i, N, A, M, C)\}$
24  **ret** $C$

**procedure** DEC$(i, N, A, C)$
30  $M \leftarrow \Pi.\mathcal{D}(K_i, N, A, C)$
31  S $\overset{\cup}{\leftarrow} \{(K_i, N, A, M, C)\}$
32  **ret** $M$

**procedure** REV$(i)$
40  K$_r$ $\overset{\cup}{\leftarrow} \{K_i\}$; **ret** $K_i$

**procedure** COR$(i, K)$
50  $K_i \leftarrow K$; K$_c$ $\overset{\cup}{\leftarrow} \{K_i\}$

---

**Fig. 1. The** CAE-**security game.** The encryption, decryption, reveal, and corruption oracles are on the right. On the left, the game finalization procedure depends on the collision check function chk, which in turn relies on the collision type parameter t of the game. This function places restrictions on the keys that the adversary may win with.

Our definition considers the strongest level of misattributions. That is, we require that $(K_i, N, A, M) \neq (K_j, N', A', M')$. This means the adversary wins as long as one of the inputs to encryption differ when creating the colliding ciphertext. We call a cAE scheme that attends to all encryption inputs *fully committing*.

Most other works only consider sub-tuples. For example, the notion of key commitment from Albertini et al. only requires that $K_i \neq K_j$ from the adversary when it creates a collision [2]. They show that key commitment is important for several real world systems. Nonetheless, this definition does not capture colliding ciphertexts that are generated under the same key. In Sect. 4, we give a transform as efficient as theirs while protecting against misattributions over the entire tuple of encryption inputs. (In a way, our transform is more efficient as it does not need to re-key every encryption call).

Contemporary work from Bellare and Hoang considers fully committing cAE schemes as well as sub-tuples [5]. Their argument for fully committing schemes is to provide ease of use. Prior definitions required different inputs to be committed to achieve the different security goals demanded by their relevant applications. The designer of an application may not know exactly what they need to be committed. So, if full commitment is inexpensive, then one should aim to do so.

Nonetheless, we provide an alternative CAE-security game that considers weaker misattributions, which we present explicitly give in the full paper. It uses an additional parameter allowing the specification of which encryption inputs are important when considering misattributions. However, we do note our construction CTX presented in Sect. 4 achieves full commitment efficiently.

RELATIONSHIP WITH nAE SECURITY. Previously, DGRW18 show how to construct a ciphertext for AES-GCM in such a way that it decrypts validly under two different keys [7]. This shows that nae-secure schemes do not achieve $\text{CAE}_{\text{xx}}$-security. In fact, the attack presented by DGRW18 does not require the adversary to have full control over the keys; it is possible to do the attack with only knowledge of the keys, which means nae-secure schemes do not achieve $\text{CAE}_{11}$-security either.

We show that nAE schemes that are nae-secure in the multi-key sense—nae*-secure, are already $\text{CAE}_{00}$-secure. That is, when an adversary may not affect the keys in any way, it is already difficult to find colliding ciphertexts for nae-secure schemes.

**Theorem 1.** *Any authenticated encryption scheme $\Pi$ that is nae*-secure is also $\text{CAE}_{00}$-secure. That is, for any adversary $\mathcal{A}$ attacking the $\text{CAE}_{00}$-security of $\Pi$, there exists an adversary $\mathcal{B}$ against the nae*-security of $\Pi$ such that*

$$\mathbf{Adv}_{\Pi}^{\text{cae}-00}(\mathcal{A}) \leq 3 \cdot \mathbf{Adv}_{\Pi}^{\text{nae}*}(\mathcal{B}) + \frac{q_e^2}{2^{\tau+1}}$$

*where $q_e$ is the number of encryption queries made by $\mathcal{A}$ and $\tau$ is the expansion of the scheme $\Pi$. Furthermore, $\mathcal{B}$ makes the same number of encryption and decryption queries that $\mathcal{A}$ makes. That is, $\mathcal{B}$ makes $\Theta(q_e)$ encryption queries and $\Theta(q_d)$ decryption queries where $q_d$ is the number of decryption queries made by $\mathcal{A}$.*

*Proof.* Let $\mathcal{A}$ be an adversary attacking the $\text{CAE}_{00}$-security of $\Pi$. We assume that $\mathcal{A}$ is nonce-respecting and that it does not query output of encryption to decryption as it would already know the answers of those queries and those queries would not help $\mathcal{A}$ in obtaining a win. We also assume that $\mathcal{A}$ never calls the reveal or corruption oracles as it can only win with a collision on a pair of honest keys. We can construct an adversary $\mathcal{B}$ attacking the nae-security of $\Pi$ as follows. Adversary $\mathcal{B}$ sets up the CAE game as described in Fig. 1, maintaining its own set S to keep track of query and response tuples. Whenever $\mathcal{A}$ makes encryption or decryption queries, $\mathcal{B}$ queries its own encryption and decryption oracles to provide a response for $\mathcal{A}$. When $\mathcal{A}$ terminates, $\mathcal{B}$ checks S to see if

$\mathcal{A}$ has created a colliding ciphertext. If it has, then $\mathcal{B}$ returns 1. Otherwise, it returns 0.

Consider the three different ways that $\mathcal{A}$ can add a winning ciphertext and its associated explanations to S. Either they were added through two decryption queries, an encryption and a decryption query, or two encryption queries. Let $E_1, E_2, E_3$ be the events that those yielded $\mathcal{A}$ a win respectively. As these three events are all the ways to win, $\mathcal{A}$'s advantage is upper-bounded by the sum of the probabilities that each of these occur.

We bound the probabilities of each event by examining what happens when $\mathcal{B}$'s oracles are real or fake. For $E_1$ it is impossible for a winning tuple to be added to S when $\mathcal{B}$'s decryption oracle is fake as that oracle only ever returns $\perp$ and a winning tuple must have a valid message. As such, $\mathcal{B}$ only ever returns 0. However, if $\mathcal{B}$'s oracle is real, then $\mathcal{B}$ will return 1. Hence, $\Pr[E_1] \leq \mathbf{Adv}_{\mathcal{B}}^{\mathrm{nae}}$.

For $E_2$ a fake decryption oracle for $\mathcal{B}$ makes winning through this event impossible by the same reasoning as that of $E_1$, meaning $\mathcal{B}$ only returns 0 here as well. Similarly, $\mathcal{B}$ will return 1 if its oracles are real in this event. As such, the probability follows: $\Pr[E_2] \leq \mathbf{Adv}_{\mathcal{B}}^{\mathrm{nae}}$.

For $E_3$, $\mathcal{B}$ can return 1 with a fake encryption oracle so long as $\mathcal{A}$ gets a collision through its encryption queries. We can get the probability that this occurs by a birthday bound on the number of encryption queries made by $\mathcal{A}$. The birthday bound is over the random ciphertexts generated by the fake encryption oracle. With a real encryption oracle, $\mathcal{B}$ always returns 1. This gives the probability $\Pr[E_3] \leq \mathbf{Adv}_{\mathcal{B}}^{\mathrm{nae}} + \frac{q_e^2}{2^{\tau+1}}$. $\qquad\qquad\square$

## 4  The CTX Construction

THE CTX SCHEME. Recall that a cAE scheme is *fully committing* if it commits to the key, nonce, AD, and message and not some subset of them. We say that a scheme is *efficient* if its cost of getting cAE security on top of nAE security is independent of the message length. We call a scheme *strong* if it achieves $\mathrm{CAE_{xx}}$ security. Our CTX construction is fully committing, efficient, and strong.

Let $\Pi = (\mathcal{E}, \mathcal{D})$ be a tag-based nAE scheme. That is, ciphertexts it outputs consist of a ciphertext core $C$ and an authentication tag $T$. We assume that the encryption algorithm $\mathcal{E}$ can be split into two independent algorithms $\mathcal{E}_1$ and $\mathcal{E}_2$ such that on inputs $K, N, A, M$, $\mathcal{E}_1$ produces the core $C$ and $\mathcal{E}_2$ outputs the tag $T$. The core $C$ is the same length as $M$. As such, $\mathcal{E}_1$ is bijective when $K, N, A$ are fixed. The inverse of $\mathcal{E}_1$ is then decryption's subroutine $\mathcal{D}_1$, which takes in $K, N, A$ and just the core $C$, and outputs $M$. That is, $\mathcal{D}_1(K, N, A, \mathcal{E}_1(K, N, A, M)) = M$. Common schemes like GCM and OCB satisfy these structural demands.

From such an nAE scheme $\Pi$ and a collision-resistant hash function $H$, we can construct a $\mathrm{CAE_{xx}}$-secure cAE scheme, CTX$[\Pi, H]$. CTX's main mechanism is hashing the authentication tag $T$ along with $K, N, A$ into a new tag $T^*$. This effectively makes $T^*$ function as the nAE authenticity check and a commitment to $K, N, A$. The name CTX captures the scheme's ciphertext structure, which is

| CTX.$\mathcal{E}(K, N, A, M)$ | CTX.$\mathcal{D}(K, N, A, \mathcal{C})$ |
|---|---|
| 20  $C \leftarrow \Pi.\mathcal{E}_1(K, N, A, M)$ | 30  $C \parallel T \leftarrow \mathcal{C}$ |
| 21  $T \leftarrow \Pi.\mathcal{E}_2(K, N, A, M)$ | 31  $M \leftarrow \Pi.\mathcal{D}_1(K, N, A, C)$ |
| 22  $T^* \leftarrow H(K, N, A, T)$ | 32  $T' \leftarrow \Pi.\mathcal{E}_2(K, N, A, M)$ |
| 23  **ret** $C \parallel T^*$ | 33  **if** $T \neq H(K, N, A, T')$ **then ret** $\perp$ |
| | 34  **ret** $M$ |

**Fig. 2.** A $\text{CAE}_{\text{xx}}$-secure cAE scheme $\text{CTX}[\Pi, H]$ built from a tag-based nAE scheme $\Pi$ and a collision-resistant hash function $H$. The nAE encryption and decryption algorithms can be broken down into $\mathcal{E}_1, \mathcal{E}_2$, and $\mathcal{D}_1$. These create the ciphertext core, create the authentication tag, and recover the message from the core respectively.

a ciphertext core followed by a modified tag. The 'X' in the name suggests the scheme's XX-security level. The scheme is presented in Fig. 2.

We claim that CTX is $\text{CAE}_{\text{xx}}$-secure as long as $H$ is collision-resistant.

**Theorem 2.** *Let* $\Pi = (\mathcal{E}, \mathcal{D})$ *be a tag-based nAE scheme and let* $H$ *be a collision-resistant hash function. Let* $\mathcal{E}_1, \mathcal{E}_2, \mathcal{D}_1$ *be the algorithms used by* $\Pi$ *to encrypt messages into ciphertext cores, create authentication tags, and decrypt cores into messages respectively. Let* $\text{CTX}[\Pi, H]$ *be an nAE scheme constructed from* $\Pi$ *and* $H$ *as described in Fig. 2. Then, for any adversary* $\mathcal{A}$ *attacking the* $\text{CAE}_{\text{xx}}$*-security of* $\Pi'$, *there exists an adversary* $\mathcal{B}$, *explicitly given in the proof of this theorem and depending only on* $\mathcal{A}$ *as a black-box, such that*

$$\mathbf{Adv}_{\text{CTX}}^{\text{cae-XX}}(\mathcal{A}) \leq \mathbf{Adv}_H^{\text{col}}(\mathcal{B}).$$

We give the proof for Theorem 2 in the full paper.

DISCUSSION. From Theorem 2, we see that the $\text{CAE}_{\text{xx}}$-security of CTX is bounded by the collision-resistance of the hash function it employs. One can break this with about $2^{\mu/2}$ operations doing a birthday-attack, which is why we recommend having CTX tag length be 160-bits over, say, 128-bits. This raises a question: Can one lower the security requirement (something weaker than $\text{CAE}_{\text{xx}}$) and avoid the birthday bound?

The answer is that with CTX, you cannot unless there are further assumptions made of the nAE scheme $\Pi$ that it uses. There exists an attack on the $\text{CAE}_{\text{ox}}$-security of CTX using a birthday attack under standard assumptions on $\Pi$. We explicitly describe this attack in the full paper.

It remains to show that CTX remains nAE-secure after its transform. We do so in the random oracle model (ROM), denoting CTX as $\text{CTX}[\Pi]$ (as opposed to $\text{CTX}[\Pi, H]$) when it is in the ROM. The privacy and authenticity notions in Theorem 3 can be attained by breaking the nAE security notion in 2 apart and can be found in [18]. We prove Theorem 3 in the full paper.

**Theorem 3.** *Let* $\Pi = (\mathcal{E}, \mathcal{D})$ *be a tag-based nAE scheme with an expansion of* $\tau$. *Let* $\mathsf{CTX}[\Pi]$ *be the scheme described in Fig. 2. Fix an integer* $\delta \geq 0$. *Then, in the random oracle model, for any adversary* $\mathcal{A}_1$ *attacking the privacy of* $\mathsf{CTX}$, *we can construct nonce-respecting (explicitly given) adversaries* $\mathcal{B}_1$ *and* $\mathcal{B}_2$ *attacking the privacy of* $\Pi$ *such that*

$$\mathbf{Adv}^{\mathrm{priv}}_{\mathsf{CTX}[\Pi]}(\mathcal{A}_1^H) \leq \mathbf{Adv}^{\mathrm{priv}}_{\Pi}(\mathcal{B}_1) + \mathbf{Adv}^{\mathrm{priv}}_{\Pi}(\mathcal{B}_2) + \frac{q_{\mathsf{H}}}{2^{\delta + \tau}}$$

*where* $q_{\mathsf{H}}$ *is the number of random oracle queries made by* $\mathcal{A}_1$. *Let* $q_e$ *be the number of encryption queries made by* $\mathcal{A}_1$. *Then* $\mathcal{B}_1$ *also makes* $q_e$ *queries to its own encryption oracle and* $\mathcal{B}_2$ *makes* $q_e + 1$ *such queries.*

*Furthermore, for any adversary* $\mathcal{A}_2$ *attacking the authenticity of* $\mathsf{CTX}$, *there exists adversary* $\mathcal{B}_3$ *attacking the authenticity of* $\Pi$ *with advantage*

$$\mathbf{Adv}^{\mathrm{auth}}_{\mathsf{CTX}[\Pi]}(\mathcal{A}_2^H) \leq \mathbf{Adv}^{\mathrm{auth}}_{\Pi}(\mathcal{B}_3) + \frac{1}{2^{\mu}}$$

*where* $\mu$ *is the output length of the random oracle. We give* $\mathcal{B}_3$ *explicitly in the proof. If* $\mathcal{A}_2$ *makes* $q_e$ *encryption oracle queries, then* $\mathcal{B}_3$ *makes* $q_e + 1$ *queries to its own oracle.*

Note that the last term in the privacy bound $\frac{q_{\mathsf{H}}^2}{2^{\delta + \tau}}$ can be made small by choice of $\delta$, so it will not result in much loss.

## 5   Commitment Security of GCM and OCB

Prior work from GLR17 and DGRW18 has shown that it is possible to construct a colliding ciphertext with GCM when the attacker has control of both keys [7,11]. DGRW18 mentions that with their attack, control over the keys is not necessary, only knowledge of the keys is. Here, we show that it is possible for an attacker to create a colliding ciphertext with knowledge of only one key. That is, there exists an attack that violates the $\mathrm{CAE}_{01}$-security of GCM. As GCM is nae-secure, this attack means that nae-security does not imply $\mathrm{CAE}_{01}$-security.

A SIMPLE NAE SCHEME. Before we present the attack, consider a simple nAE scheme $\mathrm{NAE}[G, H]$ built on a PRG $G$ and a MAC $H$. The definition of $\mathrm{NAE}[G, H]$ is given in Fig. 3. In our pseudocode, we write $S[0..n]$ to denote a substring of the bitstring $S$ starting from the 0th bit to the $n$th bit.

However, NAE is vulnerable to a variety of CAE attacks given that the MAC $H$ is *targetable*. Suppose that the key $K$ used for computing $H$ is known and there exists an arbitrary target tag $T$ that an adversary is interested in producing. We call $H$ targetable if there exists a target function target that takes in $K$ and $T$ and outputs a message $M$ such that $H(K, M) = T$. We say that $H$ is *prefix-targetable* if there exists a prefixed target function may also take in an additional argument $C$, a prefix, such that $H(K, C \parallel M) = T$. GHASH, the MAC used by GCM, is prefix-targetable, and we will show how shortly.

| NAE.$\mathcal{E}(K, N, A, M)$ | NAE.$\mathcal{D}(K, N, A, C)$ |
|---|---|
| 00  $K_1 \parallel K_2 \leftarrow K$; $P \leftarrow G(K_1, N)$ | 10  $K_1 \parallel K_2 \leftarrow K$; $C \parallel T \leftarrow C$ |
| 01  $C \leftarrow M \oplus P[0..|M|-1]$ | 11  **if** $H(K_2, C \parallel A) \neq T$ **then ret** $\perp$ |
| 02  $T \leftarrow H(K_2, C \parallel A)$ | 12  $P \leftarrow G(K_1, N)$ |
| 03  **ret** $C \parallel T$ | 13  $M \leftarrow C \oplus P[0..|M|-1]$; **ret** $M$ |

**Fig. 3.** A simple nAE scheme given a PRG $G$ and a MAC $H$. GCM has a comparable structure if one considers the counter-mode operations as the PRG and GHASH as the MAC.

ATTACK ON GCM. The simple nAE scheme described has structure similar to GCM. For concreteness, we assume the blockcipher GCM employs $E$ has a block size of 128 bits. GCM uses $E$ in counter mode with the nonce as part of the initial counter in order to generate a one-time pad. This acts like the PRG that the simple scheme uses. For a key $K$, GCM uses $K' = E_K(0^{128})$ when computing its MAC, GHASH. For a ciphertext $C$, the tag $T = H(K', A, C) \oplus E_K(N \parallel 0^{31}1)$ where $A$ is the AD, $C$ is the ciphertext, $N$ is the nonce and $H$ is the GHASH function. We follow the GCM specification of [14,15].

GHASH works by computing a polynomial over the field $\mathrm{GF}(2^{128})$ using $E_{K'}(0^{128})$ as the variable and the ciphertext and AD blocks as coefficients. By block, we mean blocks of $b$ bits that can be used as input into a blockcipher. If the last block isn't a full 128 bits, GCM pads it with zeroes until it is. Let there be $c$ ciphertext blocks and $a$ AD blocks in the ciphertext and AD. Let len be a function where given some input, it outputs a 64-bit representation of said input. Let $P = E_{K'}(0^{128})$. Then GHASH is computed as follows (addition and multiplication done over $\mathrm{GF}(2^{128})$):

$$\mathrm{GHASH}(K', A, C) = \left[\sum_{i=1}^{a} A_i \cdot P^{a+c+2-i}\right] + \left[\sum_{i=1}^{c} C_i \cdot P^{c+2-i}\right] + (\mathrm{len}(A) \parallel \mathrm{len}(C)) \cdot P \quad (1)$$

And the tag $T$ is finalized as:

$$T = \mathrm{GHASH}(K', A, C) \oplus E_{K'}(N \parallel 0^{31}1) \quad (2)$$

where $N$ is the nonce.

Observe that the entire MAC is prefix-targetable as if one knows $K'$ and $T$, one can compute $A = \mathrm{ptarget}(K', T, C)$ for a ciphertext $C$ by evaluating the polynomial. Explicitly, we can solve for a single block AD $A$ as follows:

$$A = \left[T \oplus E_{K'}(N \parallel 0^{31}1) + (\mathrm{len}(A) \parallel \mathrm{len}(C)) \cdot P \right.$$
$$\left. + \left[\sum_{i=1}^{c} C_i \cdot P^{c+2-i}\right]\right] \cdot (P^{c+2})^{-1} \quad (3)$$

Once we can compute $A$ with the prefix-targeting function, we have an $CAE_{01}$ attack, call it adversary $\mathcal{A}$, as follows: $\mathcal{A}$ selects an arbitrary nonce $N$ and AD $A$; $\mathcal{A}$ queries its encryption oracle, asking for the encryption of a string of 0's of length $m$ under $K_0$, $N$, and $A$, and receives $C \parallel T$ back; $\mathcal{A}$ uses its reveal oracle to learn $K_1$; $\mathcal{A}$ computes a one-time pad $P$ in the style of GCM using $K_1$ and the nonce $N$; $\mathcal{A}$ computes a message $M'$ as the xor of $P$ and $C$; $\mathcal{A}$ uses the prefix-target function $\mathrm{ptarget}(K', T, C)$ as shown in Eq. 3 where $K'$ is the blockcipher $E$ applied to $0^{128}$ with $K_1$ (how GHASH is keyed) and acquires an AD $A'$; $\mathcal{A}$ queries its encryption oracle with $K_1, N, A', M'$ and receives a winning collision on $C \parallel T$. This attack on GCM prove that nae-security does not imply even $CAE_{01}$-security as GCM is nae-secure.

While Eq. 3 computes a single AD block that allows us to obtain a target tag, this is actually not restrictive. An attack can use an arbitrary AD $A$, perhaps with actually relevant header information, and search for a single block $A'$ that they can add to that AD to satisfy the equation. To capture this in terms of prefix-targeting, one would compute $A' = \mathrm{ptarget}(K', T, A \parallel C)$ instead of $\mathrm{ptarget}(K', T, C)$. Keep in mind that the dummy block can be placed anywhere in $A$, but we limit our description to prepending for simplicity.

ATTACK ON OCB. We now turn to performing a $CAE_{01}$ attack on OCB. We follow the specification of OCB as described in [12].

During encryption, OCB computes an offset $\Delta$ for each message block using the key and the nonce. This offset is xor-ed with each message block before being processed by a blockcipher under the key. The output of the blockcipher is then xor-ed with the offset again, finalizing a ciphertext block. Since the adversary has a revealed key $K_j$ and a nonce of its choice $N$, it can freely compute the offsets for each block. This allows it to decrypt the target colliding ciphertext $C \parallel T$, where $C$ is the ciphertext core and $T$ is the authentication tag, into some message $M$. The next step requires the adversary to ensure that $T$ verifies for $M$ under $K_j$ and $N$. In OCB, tag $T$ is generated first with a checksum that consists of an xor over all message blocks. The adversary can do this over the bogus message $M$ it got from decryption. This checksum is then xor-ed with a special offset, again computable with knowledge of key and nonce, before being processed by the blockcipher. This output, $F$, is xor-ed with a block called "$auth$" which finalizes the tag $T$.

The adversary then needs $auth = F \oplus T$ for $T$ to that remain valid with $K_j, N, M, C$ To do so, it has a choice of AD $A$. OCB computes $auth$ by computing offsets for each block of AD, xor-ing the offsets and blocks together, and applying the blockcipher on the results (a process identical to how the message blocks are processed with the exception of how the offsets are initialized). Each of these blocks are then xor-ed with each other, finalizing a single block $auth$. To acquire an $A$ that finishes the attack, the adversary deciphers $F \oplus T$ with the blockcipher, xors the result with the appropriate offset, and uses that for its final query $\mathrm{ENC}(j, N, A, M)$. The attack is described in code in Fig. 4.

$$\mathcal{A}_{\text{OCB},01}^{\text{CAE}}$$

20  $N \twoheadleftarrow \mathcal{N}$; $M \twoheadleftarrow \{0,1\}^m$; $C \parallel T \leftarrow \text{ENC}(0, N, \varepsilon, M)$

21  $C_1 \parallel C_2 \parallel \dots \parallel C_n \leftarrow C$ **where** $|C_i| = b$ for all $i \in [1..n]$

22  $K \leftarrow \text{REV}(1)$; $\Delta \leftarrow \text{init}(K, N)$

23  **for** $i = 1$ **to** $n$ **do**

24    $\Delta \leftarrow \text{incr}_i(\Delta)$

25    $P \leftarrow C_i \oplus \Delta$; $M_i' \leftarrow E_K^{-1}(P) \oplus \Delta$

26  $chk \leftarrow M_1' \oplus M_2' \oplus \dots \oplus M_n'$

27  $F \leftarrow chk \oplus \text{incr}_\$(\Delta)$; $F \leftarrow E_K(F)$

28  $\Delta \leftarrow \text{incr}_1(0^{128})$

29  $auth \leftarrow T \oplus F$; $A \leftarrow E_K^{-1}(auth) \oplus \Delta$

2A  $\text{ENC}(1, N, A, M_1' \parallel \dots \parallel M_n')$

**Fig. 4.** An $\text{CAE}_{01}$ attack on OCB. For simplicity, this attack assumes that the length of the ciphertext is a multiple of the blockcipher $E$'s block size $b$.

Like the attack on GCM, it should be noted that the attack is not limited to a single AD block. An adversary may select an arbitrary AD $A'$ that it wants to use to mount the attack. It can then compute a single dummy block $B'$ to append to the end of $A'$ to create an AD that validates decryption. Specifically, the adversary first computes $F$ as described above. Then it computes a value $auth'$ over the blocks of $A'$. The value $B = auth' \oplus F \oplus T$ will then be the "enciphered" AD block corresponding to $B'$. So the adversary only needs to decipher $B$ and apply the appropriate offset to compute $B'$. The final AD it uses is $A = A' \parallel B'$.

# 6    Other Committing AE Notions

Here we describe the committing AE notions of previous authors and highlight their differences. A summary of each of their definitions can be found in Table 1. The first to study committing encryption in the AE setting was Farshim, Orlandi, and Roşie (FOR17) [9]. Calling the property *key-robustness*, FOR17 give a set of definitions capturing different adversarial behaviors that can result in the misattribution of a ciphertext. Their strongest notion, *full robustness*, requires an adversary to produce two keys and a ciphertext $(K, K', C)$ such that $C$ decrypts validly under both keys. It needs to be noted that FOR17 study randomized AE without AD support.

**Table 1.** A comparison of the subtly different definitions in CAE literature.

| Paper | AE Variant | Committing AE Definition |
|---|---|---|
| FOR17 [9] | Probabilistic AE, No AD support | *Full robustness* - $\mathcal{A}$ finds $(K, K', C)$ s.t. decryption of $C$ with both keys is successful |
| GLR17 [11] | Probabilistic and deterministic AEAD | *Receiver-binding* - $\mathcal{A}$ finds $((K, A, M), (K', A', M'), C)$ s.t. decryption of $C$ with both sub-tuples is successful and $(A, M)) \neq (A', M')$ |
| DGRW18 [7] | Probabilistic AEAD | *Strong Receiver-binding* - Same as receiver-binding except $(K, A, M) \neq (K', A', M')$ |
| ADGKLS20 [2] | Deterministic AEAD | *Key-commitment* - $\mathcal{A}$ finds $((K, N, A, M), (K', N, A', M'), C)$ through ENC, DEC queries s.t. $K \neq K'$ and $M, M' \neq \perp$ |
| BH22 [5] | Deterministic AEAD + misuse-resistant AE | $CMT(D)_s$-$\ell$ *security* - $\mathcal{A}$ finds $(K_1, N_1, A_1, M_1), ..,$ $(K_s, N_s, A_s, M_s)$ such that what is committed from each tuple is distinct. The parameter $\ell$ specifies "what is committed." |
| This Paper | Deterministic AEAD | $CAE_t$-*security* - $\mathcal{A}$ finds $((K, N, A, M), (K', N', A', M'), C)$ through ENC, DEC queries s.t. $(K, N, A, M) \neq (K', N', A', M')$ and $M, M' \neq \perp$. The parameter t specifies how $\mathcal{A}$ interacts with the keys |

An interesting result from FOR17 is that security for such AE schemes implies *semi-full robustness*. In this notion, two keys are generated uniformly at random and one of them is shown to the adversary. With the help of encryption and decryption oracles for the hidden key, the adversary must find a ciphertext that validly decrypts under both keys. This definition is comparable to our $CAE_{01}$ notion, where the adversary must find a misattribution with a revealed and an honest key. One of our results is the existence of $CAE_{01}$-attacks against AES-GCM and OCB, which implies that nAE security does not grant 01-security. This seemingly contradicts FOR17's result of semi-full robustness because their analysis is for AE schemes without AD support.

In the same year as FOR17, Grubbs, Lu, and Ristenpart (GLR17) study message franking, which as they describe it, is the *verifiable* reporting of abusive messages in encrypted messaging systems [11]. To accomplish this goal, they use committing AE, focusing on randomized AE with AD support (AEAD) as it is more applicable to current encrypted messaging systems. In their model, there is a sender, a receiver, and a third party that verifies abuse reports. Every ciphertext comes with a commitment tag that serves as a commitment to the message and AD. Decryption produces an opening for the commitment alongside recovering the message. Their committing AE notion adds an additional verification algorithm as it is the third party's role to verify the commitment using that opening. We conflate their decryption and verification algorithms for ease of discussion and comparison to other notions.

There are several parts of their committing AE notion that make it difficult to compare as they tend to other things besides preventing misattributions. The part that attends to misattributions is their notion of *receiver binding*. This notion asks the adversary to find a ciphertext $C$ and two tuples

$(K, A, M), (K', A', M')$ such that decrypting $C$ with those keys and ADs results in those (valid) messages. The adversary must do so in a way such that $(A, M) \neq (A', M')$. This definition does not prevent the possibility of an adversary finding two keys that can validly decrypt $C$ into $M$ using $A$.

Dodis, Grubbs, Ristenpart, and Woodage (DGRW18) [7] extend GLR17's receiver binding to *strong receiver binding*. This notion accounts for the key to address the way receiver binding does not. One can argue that strong receiver binding commits to all encryption inputs for randomized AEAD. As a building block for cAE, DGRW18 introduce a new primitive *encryptment* that serves as a one-time use, deterministic encryption and commitment of a message.

One goal that GLR17 and DGRW18 consider that other works do not (including ours) is that of *multiple-opening security*. This security notion allows different ciphertexts encrypted under the same key to be "opened" and verified without jeopardizing the security of unopened ciphertexts. This is particularly useful in the message franking context as it allows a receiver to report a ciphertext to the verifying party without having to reveal the secret key, which would ruin the security of all other ciphertexts sent under that key.

Working with deterministic AEAD, Albertini, Duong, Gueron, Kölbl, Luykx, and Schmieg (ADGKLS20) [2] define their security goal as *key-commitment*. The adversary, in this notion, is tasked with finding a ciphertext $C$ and two "explanations" $(K, N, A, M), (K', N, A', M')$ such that the messages are valid and $K \neq K'$.

Bellare and Hoang (BH22), in a contemporary work, target fully committing schemes [5]. They attend to deterministic AEAD as well as misuse-resistant AE with encryption inputs $K, N, A, M$. Their committing security notion is $\mathrm{CMT(D)_s}\text{-}\ell$ where $s$ is an integer and $\ell \in \{1, 3, 4\}$. The presence or absence "D" denotes whether adversary is tasked with finding multiple decryption inputs that validly decrypt the same ciphertext or multiple encryption inputs that encrypt to the same ciphertext. The parameter $\ell$ determines what is committed: $\ell = 1$ denotes just the key, $\ell = 3$ denotes everything but the plaintext, and $\ell = 4$ denotes full commitment. Comparatively, our cAE definition presented in Sect. 3 does not allow for tweaking for commitments of sub-tuples of inputs, but the alternative framework described in the full paper does. The $s$ parameter generalizes their definition to capture misattributions with more than two valid explanations—what they call *multi-input committing security*. That is, $s$ is the number of distinct $(K, N, A, M)$ tuples the adversary needs to find that encrypt to the same $C$. While $s = 2$ implies all $s \geq 2$, Bellare and Hoang motivate this dimension of their definition by giving schemes where bounds on adversarial advantage improve as $s$ grows. They are the first to study misuse-resistant AE and multi-input committing security in the cAE space.

CONSTRUCTIONS. We describe a number of selected constructions from the above works. These constructions, each satisfying the committing AE notion defined in the work of their origin, are presented in Table 2.

Recall that FOR17 are in the probabilistic AE setting without associated data. Their construction $\mathrm{EtM}[\mathcal{E}, H]$ creates a tag that provides authenticity while

**Table 2.** A comparison of selected constructions targeting their respective cAE security goals. *Not a committing AE scheme, but closely related.

| Construction | Description |
|---|---|
| EtM[$\mathcal{E}, H$] [9] | $\mathcal{E}$ is AE scheme, $H$ is CR MAC. <br> Encrypt $M$ w/ $\mathcal{E}$ under key $K_e$ to get $C$. <br> Get $T$ by using MAC w/ key $K_h$ on $(C, K_e)$. <br> Output $C \parallel T$ |
| CEP[$G, F, F^{\mathrm{cr}}$] [11] | $G$ is PRG. $F, F^{\mathrm{cr}}$ are PRFs. $F^{\mathrm{cr}}$ is CR <br> Use $G$ w/ $K$ and $N$ to get $K_0, K_1, P$. <br> Use $P \oplus M$ to get $C_1$. Use $F^{\mathrm{cr}}$ w/ $K_0$ on $A, M$ for $C_2$. <br> Use $F$ w/ $K_1$ on $C_2$ to get $T$. Output $C_1 \parallel T \parallel C_2$ |
| HFC* [7] | HFC is an *encryptment* scheme built <br> from a compression function and a padding scheme. <br> DGRW18 show a simple transform that promotes <br> an encryption scheme into a cAE scheme |
| CommitKey$_{IV}$ [2] | $\mathcal{E}$ is nAE scheme. $F_0, F_1$ are independent CR PRFs. <br> Get $K_e$ from using $F_0$ w/ $K$ on nonce $N$. <br> Get $K_c$ from using $F_1$ w/ $K$ on nonce $N'$. <br> Use $\mathcal{E}$ on $N, A, M$ to get $C$. Output $C \parallel K_c$ |
| UtC[$\mathcal{E}, \mathsf{F}$] [5] | $\mathcal{E}$ is nAE scheme. $\mathsf{F}$ is *committing* PRF. <br> Get $(P, L)$ from $\mathsf{F}(K, N)$. Get $C$ from $\mathcal{E}(L, N, A, M)$. <br> Output $P \parallel C$ |
| HtE[$\mathcal{E}, H$] [5] | $\mathcal{E}$ is a <u>CMT-1</u> nAE scheme. $H$ is a CR function. <br> Get $L$ from $H(K, (N, A))$. Output $\mathcal{E}(L, N, \varepsilon, M)$ |

serving as a commitment to the encryption key as well. This is comparable to how CTX's tag provides authenticity while committing to all of $K, N, A, T$.

The scheme CEP[$G, F, F^{\mathrm{cr}}$] is the deterministic AEAD construction from GLR17. It makes two passes over the message—one to encrypt it one-time-pad-style using output from the PRG $G$ and the other to commit to the message and AD using the collision-resistant PRF $F^{\mathrm{cr}}$. The ciphertext output is expanded by both a tag for authenticity and a commitment—the output lengths of the two PRFs. Comparatively, our CTX construction requires no passes over the message and would typically expand ciphertexts from a 128-bit authentication tag to a 160-bit hash function output that gives both cAE security and nAE authenticity. An advantage of CEP is that one can verify the commitment without revealing the encryption key. One only needs to reveal $K_0$ to do so. This is in line with GLR17's additional goal of multiple opening security.

DGRW18 had similar goals to GLR17 as they both investigated committing AE for the purpose of message franking. They propose a new primitive, encryptment, that we do not describe in detail here. Encryptment is a a primitive that simultaneously encrypts and commits a message and is one-time use. They give a concrete encryptment scheme HFC that uses a compression function and a padding scheme. They give a simple transform that builds a cAE scheme out of an encryptment scheme and a probabilistic nAE scheme. We note that HFC requires a pass over the message to apply encrypt and commit it.

The CommitKey scheme from ADGKLS20 comes in four flavors. We describe the variant CommitKey$_{IV}$ here. It consists of an nAE scheme and two independent collision-resistant PRFs, On encryption, the PRFs are used on the nonce to generate an encryption key and a "key-commitment." The encryption key is then used to perform routine nAE encryption on the message, producing a ciphertext. Encryption returns both the ciphertext and the key-commitment. It commits only to the key and as such, does not require any passes over the plaintext. With this scheme, it is possible to find a misattribution where different AD lead to valid decryptions.

One can argue that this kind of misattribution may not be impactful to real-world systems. But CTX protects against these misattributions as well and without giving up efficiency. In fact, CTX enjoys the efficiency benefit of not having the re-key with each message encrypted.

That argument is specious, in any case. It is difficult for designers of systems to know exactly what needs to be committed to achieve their security goals. GLR17 and DGRW18 showed message franking requires the commitment of the header and message. ADGKLS20 found that various real-world systems (key management services, envelope encryption, and Subscribe with Google [3]) had potential vulnerabilities from lack of key commitment. It is not always clear what exactly needs to be committed, so a scheme that can inexpensively commit to everything would provide a way to cover all bases for application designers.

Bellare and Hoang give a fully committing cAE construction that builds off of one that only commits to a key. Their UtC construction only commits to the key (CMT-1 secure going by their notions). It uses a primitive they call a *committing PRF* which informally outputs a commitment to the key and the PRF input along with the conventional PRF output. They describe an efficient committing PRF in their paper.

To promote a CMT-1 secure scheme to a fully committing (CMT-4) one, BH22 give the HtE transform. Like our CTX construction, the application of HtE to UtC commits to everything without having to make a pass over the plaintext beyond encrypting it. The ciphertext expansion of BH22's transform however is expected to be at least 128-bits—the block length of the blockcipher that their committing PRF employs. On the other hand, CTX is expected to replace a conventional nAE tag, say 128-bits, to a 160-bit tag that provides both nAE authenticity and the commitment to all encryption inputs. This would be a 32-bit expansion compared to the expansion by a full block.

**Acknowledgements.** The authors gratefully acknowledge insightful input from Mihir Bellare and Tom Shrimpton. Thanks to Mihir specifically for the discussion on CTX's security level with notions weaker than CAE$_{xx}$-security as well as CTX's privacy and authenticity.

This work was funded by NSF grant CNS 1717542. Many thanks to the NSF for their years of support.

# References

1. Abdalla, M., Bellare, M., Neven, G.: Robust encryption. In: Micciancio, D. (ed.) TCC 2010. LNCS, vol. 5978, pp. 480–497. Springer, Heidelberg (2010). https://doi.org/10.1007/978-3-642-11799-2_28

2. Albertini, A., Duong, T., Gueron, S., Kölbl, S., Luykx, A., Schmieg, S.: How to abuse and fix authenticated encryption without key commitment. Cryptology ePrint Archive, Report 2020/1456 (2020). https://eprint.iacr.org/2020/1456

3. Albrecht, J.: Introducing subscribe with google, March 2018. https://blog.google/outreach-initiatives/google-news-initiative/introducing-subscribe-google/

4. Bellare, M.: A concrete-security analysis of the apple PSI protocol, July 2021. https://www.apple.com/child-safety/pdf/Alternative_Security_Proof_of_Apple_PSI_System_Mihir_Bellare.pdf

5. Bellare, M., Hoang, V.T.: Efficient schemes for committing authenticated encryption. In: Dunkelman, O., Dziembowski, S. (eds.) EUROCRYPT 2022, Part II. LNCS, vol. 13276, pp. 845–875. Springer, Cham (2022). https://doi.org/10.1007/978-3-031-07085-3_29

6. Bellare, M., Tackmann, B.: The multi-user security of authenticated encryption: AES-GCM in TLS 1.3. In: Robshaw, M., Katz, J. (eds.) CRYPTO 2016, Part I. LNCS, vol. 9814, pp. 247–276. Springer, Heidelberg (2016). https://doi.org/10.1007/978-3-662-53018-4_10

7. Dodis, Y., Grubbs, P., Ristenpart, T., Woodage, J.: Fast message franking: from invisible salamanders to encryptment. In: Shacham, H., Boldyreva, A. (eds.) CRYPTO 2018, Part I. LNCS, vol. 10991, pp. 155–186. Springer, Cham (2018). https://doi.org/10.1007/978-3-319-96884-1_6

8. Farshim, P., Libert, B., Paterson, K.G., Quaglia, E.A.: Robust encryption, revisited. In: Kurosawa, K., Hanaoka, G. (eds.) PKC 2013. LNCS, vol. 7778, pp. 352–368. Springer, Heidelberg (2013). https://doi.org/10.1007/978-3-642-36362-7_22

9. Farshim, P., Orlandi, C., Roşie, R.: Security of symmetric primitives under incorrect usage of keys. Cryptology ePrint Archive, Report 2017/288 (2017). https://eprint.iacr.org/2017/288

10. Gertner, Y., Herzberg, A.: Committing encryption and publicly-verifiable signcryption. Cryptology ePrint Archive, Report 2003/254 (2003). https://eprint.iacr.org/2003/254

11. Grubbs, P., Lu, J., Ristenpart, T.: Message franking via committing authenticated encryption. In: Katz, J., Shacham, H. (eds.) CRYPTO 2017, Part III. LNCS, vol. 10403, pp. 66–97. Springer, Cham (2017). https://doi.org/10.1007/978-3-319-63697-9_3

12. Krovetz, T., Rogaway, P.: The software performance of authenticated-encryption modes. In: Joux, A. (ed.) FSE 2011. LNCS, vol. 6733, pp. 306–327. Springer, Heidelberg (2011). https://doi.org/10.1007/978-3-642-21702-9_18

13. Len, J., Grubbs, P., Ristenpart, T.: Partitioning oracle attacks. Cryptology ePrint Archive, Report 2020/1491 (2020). https://eprint.iacr.org/2020/1491

14. McGrew, D., Viega, J.: The Galois/counter mode of operation (GCM). submission to NIST Modes of Operation Process, vol. 20, pp. 0278–0070 (2004)

15. McGrew, D.A., Viega, J.: The security and performance of the Galois/counter mode (GCM) of operation. In: Canteaut, A., Viswanathan, K. (eds.) INDOCRYPT 2004. LNCS, vol. 3348, pp. 343–355. Springer, Heidelberg (2004). https://doi.org/10.1007/978-3-540-30556-9_27

16. Namprempre, C., Rogaway, P., Shrimpton, T.: Reconsidering generic composition. In: Nguyen, P.Q., Oswald, E. (eds.) EUROCRYPT 2014. LNCS, vol. 8441, pp. 257–274. Springer, Heidelberg (2014). https://doi.org/10.1007/978-3-642-55220-5_15

17. Rogaway, P.: Formalizing human ignorance. In: Nguyen, P.Q. (ed.) VIETCRYPT 2006. LNCS, vol. 4341, pp. 211–228. Springer, Heidelberg (2006). https://doi.org/10.1007/11958239_14

18. Rogaway, P., Bellare, M., Black, J., Krovetz, T.: OCB: a block-cipher mode of operation for efficient authenticated encryption. In: Reiter, M.K., Samarati, P. (eds.) ACM CCS 2001: 8th Conference on Computer and Communications Security, Philadelphia, PA, USA, 5–8 November 2001, pp. 196–205. ACM Press

# Quantum-Resistant Password-Based Threshold Single-Sign-On Authentication with Updatable Server Private Key

Jingwei Jiang[1], Ding Wang[2,3]([✉]), Guoyin Zhang[1], and Zhiyuan Chen[1]

[1] College of Computer Science and Technology, Harbin Engineering University, Harbin 150001, China
[2] College of Cyber Science, Nankai University, Tianjin 300350, China
wangding@nankai.edu.cn
[3] Tianjin Key Laboratory of Network and Data Security Technology, Nankai University, Tianjin 300350, China

**Abstract.** Passwords are the most prevalent authentication mechanism, and proliferate on nearly every new web service. As users are overloaded with the tasks of managing dozens even hundreds of passwords, accordingly password-based single-sign-on (SSO) schemes have been proposed. In password-based SSO schemes, the authentication server needs to maintain a sensitive password file, which is an attractive target for compromise and poses a single point of failure. Hence, the notion of password-based threshold authentication (PTA) system has been proposed. However, a static PTA system is threatened by perpetual leakage (e.g., the adversary perpetually compromises servers). In addition, most of the existing PTA schemes are built on the intractability of conventional hard problems, and become insecure in the quantum era.

In this work, we first propose a threshold oblivious pseudorandom function (TOPRF) to harden the password so that PTA schemes can resist offline password guessing attacks. Then, we employ the threshold homomorphic aggregate signature (THAS) over lattices to construct the first quantum-resistant password-based threshold single-sign-on authentication scheme with the updatable server private key. Our scheme resolves various issues arising from user corruption and server compromise, and it is formally proved secure against quantum adversaries. Comparison results show that our scheme is superior to its counterparts.

**Keywords:** Password · Single-sign-on · Threshold authentication · Oblivious pseudorandom function · Lattice

## 1 Introduction

Password-based authentication is the most prevalent mechanism for validating users. Passwords have various advantages of being memorable, convenient, and regeneration, and it is unlikely to be replaced in the near future [1,2]. However, recent research reveals that each user has 80∼100 password accounts on

© The Author(s), under exclusive license to Springer Nature Switzerland AG 2022
V. Atluri et al. (Eds.): ESORICS 2022, LNCS 13555, pp. 295–316, 2022.
https://doi.org/10.1007/978-3-031-17146-8_15

average [3,4]. The management of such an amount of usernames and passwords for diverse applications is challenging, and would lead to insecure behaviors like reuse and writing down [5,6]. Single-sign-on (SSO) reduces this burden [7]. Specifically, password-based SSO verifies the username and password through a trusted identity server and generates an access token for the authenticated user [8]. The user can access *various* application servers within a specified period of time through the access token without showing them the password [9].

An inherent limitation of password-based SSO is that the server may become a single point of failure. On the one hand, when the server is compromised, an overwhelming fraction of users' passwords will be exposed, even if passwords are properly stored in salted-hash or memory-hard functions [10,11]. On the other hand, the adversary can obtain the master secret key and forge arbitrary tokens that enable access to arbitrary resources and information in the system [12].

A viable solution to this single point of failure is to employ threshold cryptography where a distributed protocol executes on $N$ servers. This is a widely applied idea in threshold password-authenticated key exchange [13,14] and threshold password-authenticated secret sharing [15,16]. Agrawal et al. [12] proposed a framework of password-based threshold authentication (PTA) scheme, called PASTA, which employs the threshold oblivious pseudorandom function (TOPRF) [17] to ensure password security. However, its inability to actively update the server's private key makes it vulnerable to perpetual leakage. Categorically, the adversary will continuously try to compromise servers and collect more than threshold shares over a long period of time. Consequently, the adversary will forge authentication tokens or even take control of the entire system.

There are various dynamic PTA schemes [18–20] to solve the perpetual leakage [21]. More concretely, Zhang et al. [18] use a key technique to require all identity servers to share 0 in a distributed way. Each server can renew the master secret share by adding the additional share of 0. Baum et al. [19] add a backup key to derive a new master private key based on using 0 sharing. Rawat et al. [20] extend the function of PASTA and add the function of password update. As we know, most of the existing PTA schemes are built on RSA-based or pairing-based cryptosystems. Unfortunately, with quantum computers' continuous development and progress [22,23], all those PTA schemes, which are based on traditionally intractable problems (e.g., large integer factorization problems and discrete logarithm problems), are vulnerable to quantum attacks.

In the study of quantum-resistant schemes, lattice-based schemes are regarded as the most promising general-purpose algorithms for public-key encryption by NIST [24,25]. Many quantum-resistant password-only [26,27] and authenticated key exchange schemes [28,29] have been proposed over lattices. Inspired by these lattice-based schemes, we believe that the lattice-based scheme is a promising choice for PTA. However, to the best of our knowledge, there is a lack of mature components for constructing PTA schemes over lattices, including the TOPRF for resisting offline password guessing attacks and the threshold homomorphism aggregation signature (THAS) for building threshold token generation (TGG). Thus, our main goal is to answer the following questions:

*Is it possible to design a quantum-resistant dynamic password-based threshold SSO authentication scheme with TOPRF and THAS over lattices?*

Our answer to the above question is affirmative. Next, we overview the concrete results and necessary contributions, showing the high-level ideas and components used throughout quantum-resistance PTA schemes.

## 1.1 Motivation

The large-scale quantum computers can execute Shor's [30], and Grover's [31] algorithms, which will greatly threaten the traditional cryptography system. Group-based and pair-based cryptographic schemes will no longer be secure. The standards organizations (e.g., IEEE, IETF, and NIST) have begun to prepare for the collection of quantum-resistant algorithms. According to the plan of NIST [24,25], the standard of post-quantum cryptography will be available in 2022–2024. In the status report on the third round of the NIST post-quantum cryptography standardization process [32], the lattice-based algorithm is the most popular quantum-resistant algorithm (five of the seven algorithms officially selected for the third round belonged to lattice cryptography).

The advantages of lattice-based cryptography include i) The worst-case to average-case reductions; ii) Both public key encryption and digital signatures are taken into consideration; iii) The ability to construct complex cryptographic primitives (e.g., fully homomorphic encryption). With these advantages, we believe that a quantum-resistant password-based threshold single-sign-on authentication scheme can be constructed on the lattice.

In addition, PASTA [12] as the round-optimal PTA scheme reduces the interaction to two flows on the network. If the user enters the correct username/password, the user can recover the authentication token locally after the interaction. However, servers do not know the login result of the user, and the scheme is vulnerable to online dictionary attacks. (Although online password guessing attacks can be prevented by limiting the login times of a single user, it is unrealistic to restrict the login times of all users at the same time). A feasible scheme is to give up the round optimization and calculate the token information on servers to improve security, such as the scheme of Zhang et al. [18].

Furthermore, to deal with potential threats in SSO, *the PTA scheme needs to use a series of essential components, including distributed key generation, TTG, TOPRF, and proactive secret renewal.* These components have been widely studied under the conventional hard problems and can be handily applied to PTA [12,18–20]. However, the lattice-based homomorphic group encryption provides no support for password re-randomization. In addition, threshold aggregation magnifies noise on the lattice that may cause users to derive different authentication information based on a password. These mature research results are challenging to construct quantum-resistant PTA schemes directly. It is necessary to use or design lattice-based components.

## 1.2 Contributions

The above motivations prompt us to design a two-round password-based threshold single-sign-on authentication on the lattice, consisting of registration, login and authentication, password update and server private key renewal. To summarize, we make the following key contributions.

- We design a threshold homomorphism aggregation signature to construct a threshold token generation (TTG) protocol. To address the fact that no mature tool like the BLS [33] over lattices can directly construct TTG, we use the universal thresholdizer [34] to add a threshold to a lattice-based aggregate signature, and propose an unforgeable TTG over lattices.
- We improve the oblivious pseudorandom function (OPRF) of Albrecht et al. [35], and design a new threshold OPRF (TOPRF) on the lattice for the first time. We show the threshold constraints for TOPRF to maintain correctness on the lattice. Furthermore, we prove that unpredictability and obliviousness are satisfied between the password and the derived authentication information. It means that the adversary can neither obtain the corresponding password through the authentication information, nor predict the authentication information derived from any password.
- We propose the first password-based threshold single-sign-on authentication scheme on the lattice, based on our TTG and TOPRF constructed above. Our scheme supports the feature that users update passwords and servers update private keys. No user assistance is required when the server updates the private key, and the generated authentication token is not invalidated after the private key is updated. We evaluate the security of our scheme under two parameter settings, and make a rigorous security proof based on the Bellare-Pointcheval-Rogaway (BPR)-like model [36] by the sequences of games. In addition, we show the computational overhead of each part in our scheme under different security levels. Comparison results show that our scheme is superior to its counterparts [9,12,18–20].

## 2 Preliminaries

**Notions.** For any integer $q$, there is a polynomial $R_q := \mathbb{Z}_q[X]/\langle X^n + 1 \rangle$ in the power-of-two cyclotomic ring. Let upper-case letter $A$ and lower-case bold letter $\mathbf{x}$ denote matrices and vectors, respectively. $\lfloor \cdot \rfloor$ indicates that a rational number is rounded to the nearest natural number. We write $x \xleftarrow{\$} \mathcal{D}$ to denote the sampling of $x$ according to distribution $\mathcal{D}$. We write $x \xleftarrow{R} S$ to indicate sampling uniformly at random from a finite set S. The notation $\approx_c$ denotes computationally indistinguishable. Finally, $\kappa$ denotes the security parameter.

## 2.1   Lattices, SIS, and DRLWE

For an $m$-dimensional lattice $\Lambda = \{As | s \in \mathbb{Z}^n\}$ with $A \in \mathbb{Z}^{m \times n}$ for $m \geq n\lceil log_2 q \rceil$ and the Gaussian distribution as $exp(-\pi \frac{(x-c)^2}{\sigma^2})$, where $c$ is a centre parameter, we call a distribution $\chi$ is $(B, \delta)$-bounded if $Pr[x \xleftarrow{\$} \chi || x| \geq B] \leq \delta$.

**Definition 1 ($SIS_{q,m,n,\sigma}$).** *Let $q, m, n, \sigma > 0$ depend on $\kappa$. The $SIS_{q,m,n,\sigma}$ problem is to find a nonzero vector $\mathbf{v} \in R_q$ of norm $\|\mathbf{v}\| \leq \delta$ such that $A\mathbf{v} = 0 \in R_q$. More formally, for any probabilistic polynomial-time (PPT) adversary $\mathcal{A}$, we define the advantage $Adv_{\mathcal{A}}^{SIS}(\kappa) = |Pr[\mathcal{A}(\mathbf{v} \leq \delta : A\mathbf{v} = 0 \in R_q)]| \leq \varepsilon(\kappa)$.*

**Definition 2 ($DRLWE_{q,m,n,\sigma}$, [37]).** *Let $q, m, n, \sigma > 0$ depend on $\kappa$. The $DRLWE_{q,m,n,\sigma}$ problem is to distinguish between $(A, A \cdot s + e_i)_{i \in [m]} \in (R_q)^2$ and $(A, r_i)_{i \in [m]} \in (R_q)^2$ for $A, r_i \xleftarrow{R} R_q$; $s, e_i \xleftarrow{R} R(\chi_\sigma)$. For any PPT $\mathcal{A}$, we define that $Adv_{\mathcal{A}}^{DRLWE}(\kappa) = |Pr[\mathcal{A}(q, m, n, \sigma, A, s)] - Pr[\mathcal{A}(q, m, n, \sigma, A, r_i)]| \leq \varepsilon(\kappa)$.*

## 2.2   Distributed Key Generation Protocol Over Lattices

Since lattice is an infinite additive group, it can not be directly combined with Shamir secret sharing scheme [38]. We can share elements of a finite abelian quotient group $\mathbb{G}$ with identity element 0 by $(t, N)$-threshold secret sharing [39]. Let $e(\mathbb{G})$ denotes exponent of $\mathbb{G}$ and $s \in \mathbb{G}$. Set $k \geq \log_p(n + 1)$, where $p$ is the smallest prime divisor of $e(\mathbb{G})$, we can share $s \in \mathbb{G}$ among $N$ servers using shares in $\mathbb{G}^k$. By [39], we can use $R = \mathbb{Z}_{e}(\mathbb{G})[X]/F(X)$ for any monic degree-k polynomial $F(X) = \sum_{i=0}^{k} F_i X^i \in \mathbb{Z}_e(\mathbb{G})$ that is irreducible modulo every prime dividing $e(\mathbb{G})$. We write $[s]^i$ to denote $i$-th server's share and the tuple of all shares by $[s]$. By employing integer sampling and MPC, a distributed server key generation without the trusted center is as follows:

**Definition 3.** *The distributed key generation $\mathcal{F}_{KG}$ must contain the following two polynomial algorithms:*

- $[s_i] \leftarrow$ Genshare$(\mathbb{Z}_e(\mathbb{G}), \mathbb{Z}_q)$ *is a probabilistic algorithm that sample a series of polynomials $F_i \xleftarrow{\$} \mathbb{Z}_e(\mathbb{G})$ and generates a series of shares $[s_i] \xleftarrow{R} \mathbb{Z}_q$.*
- $sk_j \leftarrow$ Genkey$(i, j, [s_i]^j)$ *is a deterministic algorithm that generates secret key $sk_j = \sum_{i=1}^{N}[s_i]^j$ by receiving n tuple of $(i, j, [s_i]^j)$. After receiving n numbers of $[s_i]^j$, $S_j$ computes $sk_j = \sum_{i=1}^{N}[s_i]^j$.*

*An unknown master secret key $msk = \sum_{j=1}^{t}[s]_j^0$ that cannot be recovered unless at least $t$ malicious servers collude.*

## 2.3   Threshold Homomorphic Aggregate Signatures Over Lattices

In a PTA scheme, servers generate an authentication token for the user (also called the client) by executing threshold token generation (TTG). We can construct a TTG by a threshold aggregate signature. Jing et al. [40] propose a lattice-based homomorphic aggregate signature (HAS) but without a threshold. Dan et al. [34] design a new concept, called a universal thresholdizer (UT), from which many threshold systems over lattices are possible (More details on UT technology can be found in Sect. 7 of [34]). By employing the UT technology and HAS, we can realize a threshold HAS (THAS) protocol as follows:

**Definition 4 (THAS).** *A THAS protocol contains four algorithms:*

- $(sk_i, pk_i) \leftarrow$ Setup$(1^\kappa, N)$. *Input the security parameter $1^\kappa$ and the maximum number of servers $N$. $\mathcal{F}_{KG}$ output a private key $sk_i$ for each server $S_i$, $i \in [1, N]$. Then, $S_i$ generates and publish the public key $pk_i$.*
- $Sign_i \leftarrow$ PartSign$(id, \mathbf{m}_i, sk_i)$. *For the $j$-th server, input a message $\mathbf{m}_i$ of subspace id and $sk_j$. The $j$-th server outputs the signature $Sign_i$ on $\mathbf{m}_i$.*
- $Sign \leftarrow$ Combine$(id, PK, \{\lambda_i, \mathbf{m}_i, Sign_i\}_{i=1}^t)$. *For $t$ $(t \leq N)$ pairs of message sharing the same id and the corresponding signature $Sign_i$, output the aggregate signature $Sign = \sum_{i=1}^t \lambda_i Sign_i$ on message $\mathbf{m} = \sum_{i=1}^t \lambda_i \mathbf{m}_i$.*
- $(1, 0) \leftarrow$ Verify$(id, PK, \mathbf{m}, Sign)$. *Given the id, public key $PK = \{pk_1 \parallel \ldots \parallel pk_t\}$, the aggregate message $\mathbf{m}$, and the aggregate signature $Sign$. If $PK \cdot Sign = h(\mathbf{m})$ and $\|Sign\| \leq n\sigma\sqrt{tm}$, the client output 1 or 0.*

*Remark 1.* Notably, the Lagrange coefficients $\lambda_i \in \mathbb{R}$ in the Combine of THAS. We can use "clear out their denominators" [34,41] to limit the Lagrange coefficients to integer. For $N$ servers, give $t$ $(t \leq N)$ numbers $I_1, \ldots, I_t \in [1, N]$. Define the Lagrange coefficients $\lambda_i = \prod_{i \neq j}^t \frac{-I_i}{(I_j - I_i)}$. Let the secret space is $\mathbb{Z}_p$ for a series of prime $p$ with $(N!)^3 \leq p$. Then, for every $1 \leq j \leq t$, the integer Lagrange coefficients $\lambda_j = (N!)^2 \cdot \prod_{i \neq j}^t \frac{-I_i}{(I_j - I_i)}$ is bounded $\lambda_j \leq (N!)^3$.

**Correctness.** For any message $m_i$, Verify$(id, PK, \mathbf{m}, Sign)$ outputs 1 with overwhelming probability, if $S_i$ strictly implement $(sk_i, pk_i) \leftarrow$ Setup$(1^\kappa, N)$, $Sign_i \leftarrow$ PartSign$(id, m_i, sk_i)$, and $Sign \leftarrow$ Combine$(id, PK, \{\lambda_i, \mathbf{m}_i, Sign_i\}_{i=1}^t)$. **Security.** A THAS is secure if the advantage of any PPT $\mathcal{A}$ without knowing more than $t$ secret keys $sk_i$ to forge a signature $Sign^*$ is that $Adv_{\mathcal{A}}^{\mathsf{SIS}}(\kappa) \leq \varepsilon(\kappa)$. According to Dan et al. [34], $\mathcal{A}$ cannot get $Sign$ by only executing Combine$(id, PK, \{\lambda_i, \mathbf{m}_i, Sign_i\}_{i=1}^t)$. For the aggregate signature $Sign$ on $M$, $\mathcal{A}$ can outputs a list of query messages $M = \{m_1, \ldots, m_Q\}$, then query $Sign_i \leftarrow$ PartSign$(id, m_i, sk_i)$ to obtain at least a $Sign_i$. By [40,42], the HAS meets unforgeability and binding. It means that $\mathcal{A}$ cannot get the signature $Sign_i$ of the server $S_i$ for message $m_i$ unless $\mathcal{A}$ knows the server-side secret key $sk_i$.

### 2.4 Oblivious Pseudorandom Function Over Lattices

Let $\ell = \lceil \log_2 q \rceil$. Define $G : R_q^{\ell \times \ell} \rightarrow R_q^{1 \times \ell}$ to be the linear operation corresponding to left multiplication by $(1, 2, \ldots, 2^{\ell-1})$ and the inverts $G^{-1} : R_q^{1 \times \ell} \rightarrow R_q^{\ell \times \ell}$. Fix an array of $\mathbf{a}_0, \mathbf{a}_1 \xleftarrow{R} R_q^{1 \times \ell}$. $G^{-1}(\mathbf{a})$ can be regarded as the bit decomposition operation of $\mathbf{a}$ into binary polynomials. For any $\mathbf{x} = (x_1, \ldots, x_L) \in \{0, 1\}^L$ subject to $\mathbf{a}_x := \mathbf{a}_{x_1} \cdot G^{-1}\left(\mathbf{a}_{x_2} \cdot G^{-1}\left(\ldots \left(\mathbf{a}_{x_{L-1}} \cdot G^{-1}\left(\mathbf{a}_{x_L}\right)\right)\right)\right) \in R_q^{1 \times \ell}$.

**Lemma 1 (PRF, [43]).** *Sample* $k \xleftarrow{\$} \mathbb{Z}_q$, *the function* $F_k(\mathbf{x}) = \lfloor \frac{p}{q} \cdot \mathbf{a}_x \cdot k \rceil$ *is a PRF over the* $DRLWE_{q,n,\sigma}$ *if* $q \gg p \cdot \sigma \cdot n \cdot \ell \cdot \sqrt{L}$.

**Lemma 2 (Bound on errors, [35]).** *Let* $x \in \{0,1\}^L$, $\ell = \lfloor \log_2 q \rceil$ *and* $n = poly(\kappa)$. *Sample from the probability distribution space of error* $\varepsilon_\sigma$ *have infinity norm at most* $L \cdot \ell \cdot \sigma \cdot n^{3/2}$ *with all but negligible probability.*

TOPRF can assist the PTA scheme to hide the password. Multi-servers assist the client in computing the PRF value on the input, but learning nothing about the client's input to prevent offline password guessing attacks. The main goal of our work in this section is to build a TOPRF, and declare a provably secure structure in the MPC model. We define an ideal functionality $\mathcal{F}_{\mathsf{TOPRF}}$ in Fig. 1.

Each server executes $\mathcal{F}_{KG}$ (Definition 3) to obtain a secret $sk_i$, and assist the client entering $\mathbf{x}$ to generate $F_k(x)$. To the best of our knowledge, it is challenging to construct programmable random oracle under the QROM model [44]. Therefore, we employ the MPC model [35] instead of the UC model [17] to define the security of TOPRF.

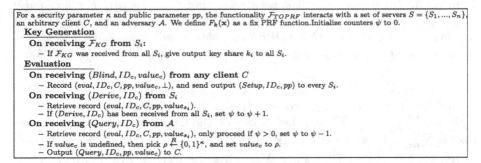

**Fig. 1.** The ideal functionality $\mathcal{F}_{\mathsf{TOPRF}}$.

**Definition 5 ( [35]).** *Let* $\mathcal{K}$ *denote the key distribution. The set of servers* $\mathbb{S}$ *and clients* $\mathbb{C}$ *are two parties of TOPRF protocol* $\Pi$. *For* $k \xleftarrow{\$} \mathcal{K}$, *there is* $\mathsf{real}_{\Pi,\mathcal{A},\mathbb{C}}(\mathbf{x}, \mathcal{K}, 1^\kappa)$ *to denote the joint output distribution of* $\mathcal{A}(\mathbf{x})$ *and* $\mathbb{S}(k)$. *Sim is a PPT simulator. A protocol* $\Pi$ *is a TOPRF if the following holds:*

- **Correctness** : *For every inputs* $(\mathbf{x}, k_i)$, $\Pr[\,\Pi\,(\mathbf{x}, k) \neq F_k(\mathbf{x})] \leq \varepsilon(\kappa)$.
- **Malicious client security(obliviousness)** : *For any PPT* $\mathcal{A}$ *corrupting* $t' \leq t$ *server, there exists a PPT simulator Sim such that for every pair of inputs* $(\mathbf{x}, k)$: $\mathsf{ideal}_{\mathcal{F}_{\mathsf{TOPRF}},Sim,\mathcal{A},\mathbb{S}}(\mathbf{x}, k, 1^\kappa) \approx_c \mathsf{real}_{\Pi,\mathcal{A},\mathbb{S}}(\mathbf{x}, k, 1^\kappa)$.
- **Average case malicious server security(unpredictability)** : *For any PPT* $\mathcal{A}$ *corrupting a client, there exists a PPT simulator Sim such that for all clients input* $x$, $\mathsf{ideal}_{\mathcal{F}_{\mathsf{TOPRF}},Sim,\mathcal{A},\mathbb{C}}(\mathbf{x}, \mathcal{K}, 1^\kappa) \approx_c \mathsf{real}_{\Pi,\mathcal{A},\mathbb{C}}(\mathbf{x}, \mathcal{K}, 1^\kappa)$ *And if* $\mathcal{A}$ *correctly outputs* $F_k(\mathbf{x})$ *with all but negligible probability over the choice* $k \leftarrow \mathcal{K}$ *when interacting directly with* $\mathbb{S}(k)$ *using* $\Pi$, *then* $\mathcal{A}$ *also outputs* $F_k(\mathbf{x})$ *with all but negligible probability when interacting via Sim.*

For a particular function $\mathbf{a}^F : \{0,1\}^L \rightarrow R_q^{1 \times L}$, we employ a bottom PRF is essentially the a particular instantiation of the PRF [43] $F_k(\mathbf{x}) = \lfloor \frac{p}{q} \cdot \mathbf{a}^F(\mathbf{x}) \cdot k \rceil$. All servers execute $\mathcal{F}_{KG}$, which is introduced in the Definition 3, to generate the secret key $k_i$ for $S_i$ and these secret key $k_i$ correspond to a master private key $msk$. For a public matrix $A \in R_q^{m \times n}$, each server $S_i$ publishes their public key $pk_i := A \cdot k_i + e_i$, where $e_i \overset{R}{\leftarrow} \mathcal{X}^{m \times 1}$. For $e, e_i, e_i' \leq \sigma\sqrt{n}$ and $e'' = msk \cdot e + \sum_{i=1}^{n} \lambda_{i,j} e_i' - \sum_{i=1}^{n} e_i \leq L \cdot \ell \cdot \sigma \cdot n^{3/2}$, a details of $\Pi_{\text{TOPRF}}$ is in Fig. 2.

---

**Oblivious Computation of PRF $F_k(\mathbf{x})$ between client C and server S**

1. On input $\mathbf{x}$, $C$ chooses $s \overset{R}{\leftarrow} Z_q^{n \times 1}$ and $e \overset{R}{\leftarrow} \mathcal{X}^{m \times 1}$; sends $\mathbf{x}^* = A \cdot s + e + \mathbf{a}^F(\mathbf{x})$ to each $S_i$.
2. $S_i$ chooses $e_i' \overset{R}{\leftarrow} \mathcal{X}^{m \times 1}$ responds with $\mathbf{x}_{k_i}^* = \mathbf{x}^* \cdot k_i + e_i'$.
3. $C$ computes $PK = \sum_{i=1}^{t} \lambda_{i,j} \cdot pk_i$, and output
$F_{msk}(\mathbf{x}) = \lfloor \frac{p}{q}(\sum_{i=1}^{t} \lambda_{i,j} \cdot \mathbf{x}_{sk_i}^* - PK \cdot s)\rceil \approx \lfloor \frac{p}{q} \cdot \mathbf{a}^F(\mathbf{x}) \cdot msk \rceil$.

---

**Fig. 2.** The basic scheme architecture.

**Lemma 3.** *Let $q, m, n, \sigma > 0$ depend on $\kappa$ and $\ell = \lceil \log_2 q \rceil$. For any noise $e \leq \sigma\sqrt{n}$, the $\mathbf{x}$ entered by the client is converted into binary and write as $\mathbf{x} = (x_1, ..., x_L) \in \{0,1\}^L$. Our TOPRF can obtain indistinguishable outputs for the same input with a reasonable choice of parameters, if $N \leq \frac{1}{4} \log_2 \frac{L \cdot \ell \cdot n - \sigma\sqrt{n}}{\sigma\sqrt{n}-1}$.*

*Proof.* $C$ chooses $s \overset{R}{\leftarrow} \mathbb{Z}_q^{n \times 1}$ and $e \overset{R}{\leftarrow} \mathcal{X}^{m \times 1}$. Each $S_i$ chooses $e_i, e_i' \overset{R}{\leftarrow} \mathcal{X}^{m \times 1}$. Both sides of the interaction execute $\Pi_{\text{TOPRF}}$ and $C$ output $F_{msk}(\mathbf{x})$. Let $e'' = msk \cdot e + \sum_{i=1}^{t} \lambda_i e_i' - \sum_{i=1}^{t} e_i$, Let $\lambda_i$ denote the Lagrange coefficient such that $msk = \sum_{i=1}^{t} \lambda_i k_i$, we have: $F_{msk}(\mathbf{x}) = \lfloor \frac{p}{q}(\sum_{i=1}^{t} \lambda_i \cdot x_{k_i}^* - PK \cdot s)\rceil = \lfloor \frac{p}{q}(((A \cdot s + e + \mathbf{a}^F(\mathbf{x})) \cdot \sum_{i=1}^{t} \lambda_i k_i + \sum_{i=1}^{t} \lambda_i e_i') - \sum_{i=1}^{t} (A \cdot k_i + e_i) \cdot s)\rceil = \lfloor \frac{p}{q}(\mathbf{a}^F(\mathbf{x}) \cdot msk + e'')\rceil$.

By Lemma 1, we know that the function $\lfloor \frac{p}{q} \cdot \mathbf{a}_x \cdot k \rceil$ is a PRF over the DRLWE$_{q,n,\sigma}$ when $q \gg p \cdot \sigma \cdot n \cdot \ell \cdot \sqrt{L}$. That means $\lfloor \frac{p}{q} \cdot \mathbf{a}_x \cdot k \rceil \approx_c \lfloor \frac{p}{q} u \rceil$, where $u$ is uniform in $R_q^{1 \times \ell}$. From Lemma 2, let $e'' \leq L \cdot \ell \cdot \sigma \cdot n^{3/2}$, we have $F_{msk}(\mathbf{x}) \approx \lfloor \frac{p}{q} \mathbf{a}^F(\mathbf{x}) \cdot msk \rceil \approx_c \lfloor \frac{p}{q} u \rceil$. Next, we analyze $e''$. We take the maximum value of each term in $e''$ and $|e''| = |\sigma^2 \cdot n + N(N!)^3 \cdot \sigma\sqrt{n} - N(N!)^3 \cdot \sigma^2 \cdot n| \leq L \cdot \ell \cdot \sigma \cdot n^{3/2}$. The fact that $(N!)^3 \leq (N)^{3N} \leq 2^{4N}$, thus $|e''| \leq |\sigma^2 \cdot n + 2^{4N+1}(\sigma\sqrt{n} - \sigma^2 \cdot n)| \leq L \cdot \ell \cdot \sigma \cdot n^{3/2}$. We have $N \leq \frac{1}{4} \log_2 \frac{L \cdot \ell \cdot n - \sigma\sqrt{n}}{\sigma\sqrt{-1}}$. To sum up, let $q \gg p \cdot \sigma \cdot n \cdot \ell \cdot \sqrt{L}$ and $N \leq \frac{1}{4} \log_2 \frac{L \cdot \ell \cdot n - \sigma\sqrt{n}}{\sigma\sqrt{-1}}$, the PRF $F_{msk}(\mathbf{x}) = \lfloor \frac{p}{q} \mathbf{a}^F(\mathbf{x}) \cdot msk \rceil$. □

**Security.** Our TOPRF inherits the security properties of the Definition 5 and satisfies quantum security, unpredictability, and obliviousness. Quantum security ensures that no adversary with any quantum capability can access the hidden secrets by cracking the encryption algorithm. Unpredictability and obliviousness mean that the value of the PRF is independent of the input secret. Unpredictability corresponds to average case malicious server security, and obliviousness corresponds to malicious client security in Definition 5. These ensure TOPRF against offline password guessing attacks. More details on security are in Appendix A.

# 3  Basic Scheme Architecture and Security Model

## 3.1  Password-Based Threshold SSO Authentication

We propose a password-based threshold SSO authentication architecture, as shown in Fig. 3, including the following two entities.

- **Client.** The client (denoted by $C$) registers with identity servers using the $ID_c$ and a human-memorable password $psw_c$. When the client enters the correct password $psw_c$ login corresponding to the $ID_c$, an authentication token can be obtained from identity servers.
- **Identity Servers.** There is a set of identity servers (denoted by $IS = \{IS_1, ..., IS_N\}$) that provide authentication tokens to the client. Each server stores a portion of the registration information independent of the client's password and generates an authentication token for the authenticated client.

**Fig. 3.** The TOPRF algorithm $\Pi_{\text{TOPRF}}$ .

Our scheme mainly focuses on the interaction between the client and a series of identity servers, including the interaction in the registration and login authentication phase. In addition, we add two dynamic update functions: password and server private key update, which further improves the security of the scheme. The formal definition of the functionality of our scheme is as follows.

**Definition 6.** *The quantum-resistant password-based threshold SSO authentication scheme over lattices includes the following five polynomial algorithms:*

- *$pp \leftarrow \text{Setup}(1^{\kappa})$. The algorithm generates the set of system parameters $pp$ by input a security parameter $\kappa$, including hash algorithm, common matrix, discrete Gaussian sampling parameters, etc., for $C$ and $IS$. $IS_i(i \in [1, n])$ calculates the public-private key pair $(sk_i, pk_i)$ and publishes $pk_i$. (The $sk_i$ is generated by $F_{KG}$ in Definition 3).*
- *Register is a registration protocol executed between the client $C$ and a set of servers $IS$ according to the following specification:*
  *$\{0, 1\} \leftarrow \text{RegC}(pp, ID_c, psw_c, IS_i)$. $C$ interacts with multiple servers to register by $psw_c$ and $ID_c$. If the registration aborts, the algorithm outputs 0. Otherwise it output 1.*
  *$\{0, 1\} \leftarrow \text{RegS}(pp, ID_c, sk_i)$. $IS_i(i \in [1, N])$ helps $C$ to get a server-derived key $sd_i$ and hold it. If the registration fails, the algorithm outputs 0. Otherwise it outputs 1 and stores the user's identity information.*

- *Login is a login and authentication protocol executed between the client $C$ and a set of servers $IS$ according to the following specification:*
  $AutToken \leftarrow$ LoginC$(pp, ID_c, psw_c, IS_i)$. *$C$ logins with $psw_c$ and $ID_c$ from the registration phase. Then, $C$ verifies $Aut_i$ from $IS_i$ and aggregates $t$ valid $Aut_i$ to generate an authentication token $AutToken$.*
  $Aut_i \leftarrow$ LoginS$(pp, ID_c, sk_i)$. *$IS_i$ assists $C$ to generate $sd'_i$ and compare it with $sd_i$ stored in the registration phase. If $sd'_i \neq sd_i$, login aborts. Otherwise, $IS_i$ generates $Aut_i =$ THAS.$PartSgin(ID_c, H(Token), sk_i)$ for $C$, where Token represents the client's message with client attributes, service validity time, access control policy, and other auxiliary information.*
- *PswUpdate is a password update protocol executed between the client $C$ and a set of servers $IS$ according to the following specification:*
  $\{0, 1\} \leftarrow$ PswUpdate$(pp, ID_c, psw_c^{old}, psw_c new, IS_i)$. *$C$ interacts with multiple servers to modify the password. $C$ generates $sd_i^{old}$ and $sd_i^{new}$ for $psw_c^{old}$ and $psw_c^{new}$, respectively, by interacting with $IS_i$ and sending them to $IS_i$. If password update fails, the algorithm outputs 0. Otherwise it output 1.*
  $\{0, 1\} \leftarrow$ PswUpdate$(pp, ID_c, sk_i)$. *$IS_i$ assists $C$ to generate $sd_i^{old}$ and $sd_i^{new}$. $IS_i$ compares $sd_i^{old}$ with $sd_i$ stored in the registration phase. If $sd_i^{old} \neq sd_i$, login aborts and output 0. Otherwise, $IS_i$ stores $sd_i^{new}$ and return 1.*
- $(0, 1) \leftarrow$ SkUpdate$(sk_i, Q)$. *Each $IS_i$ periodically updates $sk_i$ to resist permanent corruption attacks. $IS$ can update the private key by the update polynomial $Q$ without client participation. The generated authentication tokens are not invalidated after the complete update.*

**Correctness.** The correctness of our scheme above means that $C$ can obtain vaild authentication token *Token* if $C$ inputs the $psw_c$ consistent with the registration phase in the login phase. Formally, for any honest $C$, the probability $Pr[AutToken \leftarrow$ LoginC$(pp, ID_c, psw_c, IS_i)] = 1$ iff $\{0, 1\} \leftarrow$ RegC$(pp, ID_c, psw_c, IS_i)$, $\{0, 1\} \leftarrow$ RegS$(pp, ID_c, sk_i)$, $Aut_i \leftarrow$ LoginS$(pp, ID_c, sk_i)$.

## 3.2 Security Model

We consider an adversary with quantum computing power and controlling $t' \leq t$ servers in an epoch[1]. The adversary executes both online and offline guessing attacks to capture the authentication information of the honest client. We assume that the adversary needs to be profitable to launch an attack, as in [12, 18, 20].

Concretely, our single sign-on system assumes that the adversary's goal is to obtain an authentication token. There are two attack ways for the adversary, i.e., i) guessing the user's password and obtaining the authentication token by the login; ii) obtaining a sufficient number (greater than the threshold $t$) of server-side keys and thus forging the authentication token. This implies that a malicious server will not intentionally execute the protocol incorrectly to cause the user to generate the wrong authentication token since this is not profitable

---

[1] To cope with perpetual leakage [21], each server renews its secret key in a fixed time interval, called an epoch.

for the adversary. But it is more desirable if the computational legitimacy of the scheme can be verified. We leave this as our future work.

We employ the *Bellare-Pointcheval-Rogaway* (BPR)-like model [36] to analyze the security of our password-based scheme. Let $L$ denote a maintained list by the experiments. $sid_i$ denote $i$-th session. We define the following experiment:

> **Experiment** $Exp_{PTA,\mathcal{A}}^{Auth}(\kappa)$ :
> $sd_i \leftarrow \emptyset; sid_j \leftarrow 0; pp \leftarrow Setup(1^\kappa);$
> $(sid_{i*}, ID^*, psw^*) \leftarrow \mathcal{A}^{oracle(\cdot)}(pp);$
> $Aut_i \leftarrow \mathsf{LoginS}(sid_{i*}, ID^*, psw^*);$
> $(sid_{i*}, ID^*, psw^*) \notin L \wedge (psw^* \in |D|)$ return 1
> else rutrun 0

where the experiment uses the following oracles:

- Challenge$(c, sid_i, ID_c)$: The oracle aborts if $(sid_{i*} \geq 0) \vee (sid_i \geq sid_j) \vee ((sid_i, ID_c) \in L)$. Otherwise, it set $sid_{i*} \leftarrow sid_i$ and access oracle $\mathsf{LoginC}$.
- Registration$(i)$ The experiment randomly picks $psw$ satisfy $(sid_i, psw, i) \notin L$. At this point, $\mathcal{A}$ interacts with the honest client and server (oracle) as the corrupted server. After access, the experiment records $L[sid_i] \leftarrow (i, psw, sd_i)$, delivers $j$ to $\mathcal{A}$ and set $j \leftarrow j + 1$.
- RegistrationS$(sid_i)$: The oracle aborts if $sid_i \geq sid_j$. Otherwise, it gets $(i, psw, sd_i) \leftarrow L[sid_i]$. $\mathcal{A}$ interacts with the honest server (oracle) as the corrupted server.
- LoginC$(sid_i, ID, psw)$: The oracle aborts if $sid_i \geq sid_j$. Otherwise, it gets $(i, psw, sd_i) \leftarrow L[sid_i]$. $\mathcal{A}$ interacts with the honest client and server (oracle) as the corrupted server. In authentication experiment, the oracle additionally computes $L \leftarrow L \cup (sid_i, ID, psw)$.
- LoginS$(sid_i)$: The oracle aborts if $sid_i \geq sid_j$. Else, it gets $(i, psw, sd_i) \leftarrow L[sid_i]$. $\mathcal{A}$ interacts with the honest server (oracle) as the corrupted server.

The password update can be considered as combining a login algorithm without issuing a token and a registration algorithm. Consequently, we mainly focus on the registration and login phase. Notably, it has been shown that passwords follow the CDF-Zipf distribution [45]. We recommend using the accurate Zipf-based formulation for our password-based threshold SSO authentication scheme.

**Definition 7.** *Assuming that a PPT $\mathcal{A}$ executes at most $q_{send}$ online attacks, the advantage of $\mathcal{A}$ denoted $C' \cdot q_{send}^{s'}(\kappa) + \varepsilon(\kappa)$ where $C'$ and $s'$ are the Zipf parameters for all dictionary sizes $|\mathcal{D}|$ in the Zipf-law [45]. Following the experiment $Exp_{PTA,\mathcal{A}}^{Auth}(\kappa)$, the advantage of our scheme holds that $Adv_{PTA,\mathcal{A}}^{Auth}(\kappa) = Pr[1 \leftarrow Exp_{PTA,\mathcal{A}}^{Auth}(\kappa)] \leq C' \cdot q_{send}^{s'}(\kappa) + \varepsilon(\kappa)$.*

**Definition 8.** *To the best of our knowledge, the Grover algorithm [31], which is currently the most efficient for symmetric cryptosystems under the quantum computing model, only reduces the effective length of the key to half of the original one. Hence AES-256 still has 128-bit security in quantum attacks. For any PPT $\mathcal{A}$, we define the advantage $Adv_{\mathcal{A}}^{AES}(\kappa) \leq \varepsilon(\kappa)$.*

# 4   Quantum-Resistant Password-Based Threshold Single-Sign-On Authentication with Secret Update

The quantum-resistant password-based threshold SSO authentication scheme focus on the interaction between a client $C$, and a set of servers $IS = \{IS_1, ..., IS_N\}$. The details of the interaction part in our protocol are shown in Fig. 4. We highlight how clients can register, login, and password update by interacting with the server based on the TOPRF and THAS on the lattice. In the Setup, with the security parameter $\kappa$, the system generates public parameters $A \in R_q^{1\times\ell}$, $\sigma > 0$, and $c \in R_q$. Set $m > c\kappa log_2(q)$ and $q \geq poly(\kappa)(\sqrt{log_2\kappa})$. $H$ is a family of collision-resistant hash functions that preserve homomorphism property for verification [46]. Let $\mu$ be an upper limit that a client fails to pass $IS_i$ authentication, and an upper limit $\nu$ is the number of authentication token requests issued by a client in an epoch. $E$ is a secure symmetric key encryption algorithm (e.g., AES-256), and $D$ denotes the corresponding decryption algorithm. $N$ is the total number of servers, and $t$ is the threshold number.

Notice that in the threshold oblivious pseudorandom function, if the final calculation of the client is a PRF value, it is necessary to limit the size of the noise coefficient $e$. The only variable in the noise factor is the number of thresholds (more details of the conclusions' derivation and the noise's limits in Lemma 3). Hence, the noise can be effectively reduced by grouping users and using a server-side master key for each group of users. In addition, grouping users and limiting the number of logins within a group in an epoch (without grouping, it is unrealistic to restrict the number of logins for all users [12]) can effectively weaken the impact of online dictionary attacks and reduce the computational cost of the client, and the storage cost of the server [18].

Concretely, in the registration phase, after receiving the $ID_c$, the server determines whether the ID is a duplicate. If not, it stores the ID and assigns it a group. If no group can receive the client, a new group is generated for it. And settle the new server private key through the $F_{KG}$. In Login, if THAS.Verify output 1, $C$ uses $AutToken = \{Aut, Token, I\}$ as an authentication token, where $I$ is the set of signature servers' identifiers. The service provider can check the validity of $AutToken$ by executing $(1, 0) \leftarrow \text{Verify}(id, PK, Token, Aut)$ in Definition 4.

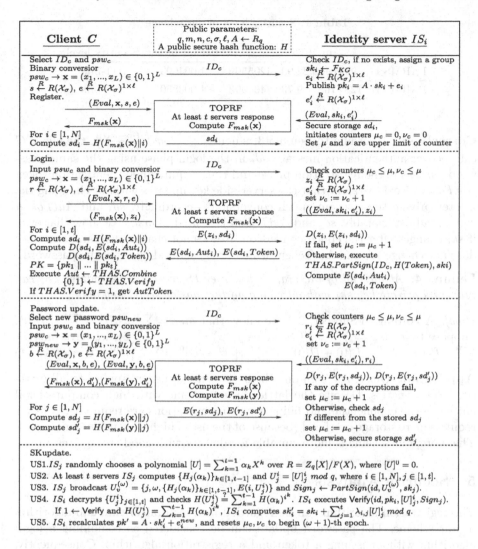

**Fig. 4.** The registration, login, and update phases of our scheme.

To cope with perpetual leakage [21], each $IS_i$ should update $sk_i$ at the end of an epoch. We describe SkUpdate at the end of the $\omega$-th epoch in Fig. 4. Notably, PartSign is actually a linearly homomorphic signature [42] in US3. Furthermore, the correctness of the equation $H(U_j^i) = \sum_{k=1}^{t-1} H(\alpha_k)^{i^k}$ can be found in Lemma 3 of [46] in US4. Finally, the $\mathsf{Verify}(id, pk_i, [U]_j^i, Sign_j)$ in US4 can be seen as Combine phase signature and message aggregation with 0.

**Table 1.** Security level of our scheme

|          | $\kappa$ | m   | $\sigma$ | q       | Hermit factor | Security level |
|----------|------|-----|-------|---------|---------------|----------------|
| PARMS I  | 95   | 512 | 22.93 | 4205569 | 1.004693      | 111-bits       |
| PARMS II | 128  | 768 | 9.73  | 8404993 | 1.003850      | 138-bits       |

**Correctness.** According to Lemma 3, when $N \leq \frac{1}{4} log_2 \frac{L \cdot \ell \cdot n - \sigma \sqrt{n}}{\sigma \sqrt{n} - 1}$, the client $C$ can recover authentication message $sd_i$ in the login phase using the same password $psw_c$ as in the registration phase and thus acquire an authentication token $AutToken$. Next, we show that the server-side key updates without changing the master private key after an epoch conversion. Accordingly, $sd_i$ and $AutToken$ will not adjust. Notably, $sd_i$ and $AutToken$ is related to $msk$. We show that even if $sk_i$ changes after the epoch conversion, it does not change $msk$ and therefore does not change $sd_i$ and AutToken, which are generated by the same password.

**Lemma 4.** *At the end of the era, each server $IS_i$ executes* SkUpdate. *$IS_i$ can renew its private key $sk_i$ without changing the master secret key $msk$.*

*Proof.* According to Subsect. 2.2, we know that $msk = \sum_{i=1}^{n}[S]_i^0 = \sum_{i=1}^{n} f_i(0)$. Suppose that $msk' = \sum_{i=1}^{n} f_i'(0)$. Since $f_i'(x) = f_i(x) + U_i(x)$, we have $msk' = \sum_{i=1}^{n} f_i'(0) = \sum_{i=1}^{n} f_i(0) + U_i(0) = \sum_{i=1}^{n}[s]_i^0 + [U]_i^0 = \sum_{i=1}^{n}[s]_i^0 + 0 = msk.$ □

**Application.** Our single sign-on scheme is general, i.e., it applies to all existing SSO scenarios. Despite the lattice-based scheme with high computational efficiency (no exponential and bilinear pairing operations are required), however requires more storage overhead (because of the use of high-dimensional matrices). Therefore, our scheme is more suitable for devices with good storage resources.

## 5   Security Analysis

The registration algorithm can be regarded as a login algorithm sub-algorithm in our scheme. The password update can be considered as combining a login algorithm without issuing a token and a registration algorithm. Consequently, we mainly focus on the login phase. Furthermore, we are concerned about the security of the server-side secret key update algorithm. See the full version paper[2] for the complete formal proofs of the following three theorems.

**Theorem 1 (Quantum Security).** *Let $\kappa = 128, n = 768$, $log\ q = 23$, our password-based threshold SSO authentication scheme in Fig. 4 is quantum security. For any PPT $\mathcal{A}$, the advantage holds that $Adv_{\mathcal{A}}^{Quantum}(\kappa) = Adv_{\mathcal{A}}^{DRLWE}(\kappa) + Adv_{\mathcal{A}}^{SIS}(\kappa) + Adv_{\mathcal{A}}^{AES}(\kappa) \leq \varepsilon(\kappa)$.*

*Proof.* Our scheme is based on DRLWE with quantum resistance under reasonable parameter settings. The detailed proof can be found in Appendix B.

□

---

[2] For a full version of this paper, see https://eprint.iacr.org/2022/989/.

**Theorem 2 (Resist Corrupt Attacks).** *Assuming that $\mathcal{A}$ cannot corrupt more than $t$ servers in an epoch, $\mathcal{A}$ cannot obtain msk of IS.*

**Table 2.** The computation overhead of each phase in our scheme

|              | PARMS I     |             | PARMS II    |             |
| ------------ | ----------- | ----------- | ----------- | ----------- |
|              | Client side | Server side | Client side | Server side |
| Registration | 0.627 ms    | 0.043 ms    | 1.582 ms    | 0.109 ms    |
| Login        | 0.805 ms    | 0.069 ms    | 2.003 ms    | 0.179 ms    |
| PswUpdate    | 0.585 ms    | 0.089 ms    | 1.455 ms    | 0.223 ms    |
| SkUpdate     | 0           | 0.773 ms    | 0           | 1.969 ms    |

**Table 3.** Comparison of the main OPRF protocol [17,48] with our work.

| For L = 64 | Jarecki et al. [17] | Everspaugh et al. [48] | Our TOPRF |
| ---------- | ------------------- | ---------------------- | --------- |
| Client     | 1.431 ms            | 5.227 ms               | 0.641 ms  |
| Server     | 0.572 ms            | 1.211 ms               | 0.049 ms  |

**Theorem 3 (Authentication).** *In our scheme, let $\mathcal{A}$ can get pp and access client-side oracle and server-side oracle $q_u$ times and $q_s$ times, respectively. For any PPT $\mathcal{A}$, the advantage of disrupting authentication that $Adv_{PTA,\mathcal{A}}^{Auth}(\kappa) \leq 2C' \cdot q_s^{s'}(\kappa) + (q_s + 2)Adv_{\mathcal{A}}^{DLWE}(\kappa) + Adv_{\mathcal{A}}^{SIS}(\kappa) + Adv_{\mathcal{A}}^{AES}(\kappa) + \varepsilon(\kappa).$*

## 6 Efficiency Analysis and Protocol Comparison

Our work is a single sign-on scheme constructed based on the lattice hardness problem. To meet the requirements of scheme quantum security, we employ the "lwe-estimator" scripts[3] to analyze the security level of our scheme under two different parameter settings. As shown in Table 1, our scheme can achieve 111-bit and 138-bit security, respectively.

Next, we estimate the computational cost by basic cryptographic operations. Let $T_M, T_A, T_H, T_S, T_E$ denote the time complexity for multiplication, addition, hash, Gaussian sampling, and symmetric encryption/decryption, respectively. In the registration phase, the computation overhead of the client-side is $(2t + 6)T_M + (2t+1)T_A + NT_H$, and a server's computation overhead is $T_M + T_A$. In the login phase, the computation overhead of the client-side is $(3t + 7)T_M + 3tT_A + (t + 1)T_H + 2tT_E$ and a server's computation overhead is $T_M + T_A + T_S + 2T_E$. In the password update phase, the computation overhead of the client-side is $(4t - 2)T_M + 4tT_A + 2NT_H + 2NT_M$, and a server's computation overhead is $2T_M + 2T_A + 2T_E$. The private key update phase requires no client participation

---
[3] The "lwe-estimator" scripts are available at https://bitbucket.org/malb/lwe-estimator/src/master.

and the computational overhead per server is $(Nt - N + 2t + 1)T_M + (Nt - 2N + 2t - 1)T_A + (N + t - 1)T_H + (2N - 2)T_E + (N - 1)T_S$.

Based on the above analysis, our C language reference implementation[4] is predicated on the q-TESLA 2.9 [47], and the measurement is obtained on a laptop with an AMD Ryzen 7-5800H running at 3.20 GHz. By Lemma 3, we set $L = 64$, $\ell = 256$, $N = 4$ and $t = 3$. The computational overhead of each phase in our scheme is shown in Table 2 for PARMS I and PARMS II. The time shown is calculated as the average of 1000 operations (Fig. 5).

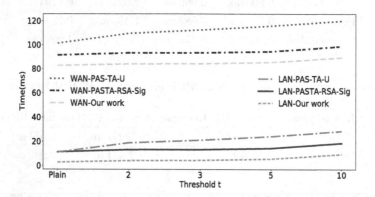

**Fig. 5.** Comparing the total time of current state-of-the-art $(t, N)$ PTA-SSO schemes [12,20] with our work. Set $N = 10$, and the round-trip latency of WAN is 80 ms. The Plain setting is the direct connection without the threshold setting.

We compare the widely used PRF protocol [17,48] with our work (at Sect. 2.4) in Table 3. Jarecki et al. [17] first constructed the 2HashDH-based TOPRF in ACNS17, which is widely used in various PTA schemes [12,19,20]. The 2HashDH-based TOPRF requires more computational overhead since group-based cryptographic primitives need exponential power operations. Everspaugh et al. [48] proposed the Pythia PRF in USENIX15, which is employed in the PTA scheme of Zhang et al. [18]. The additional computational overhead of Pythia PRF arises from the power exponential and bilinear pair operations.

Form Table 4, we compare the schemes of Jones et al. [9], Agrawal et al. [12], Baum et al. [19], Zhang et al. [18], and Rawat et al. [20] with our scheme. Through comparative analysis, except for the scheme of Jones et al. [9], other schemes use multiple identity servers to authenticate the client and issue authentication tokens to prevent a single point of server failure. In addition, these protocols employ various PRF constructs to resist offline dictionary attacks. The schemes of Baum et al. [19], Zhang et al. [18], and our scheme meet active security, which can resist perpetual leakage by updating the server-side key adaptively.

In terms of the number of protocol rounds in the login phase, compared with a round of the interaction of the schemes of Jones et al. [9], Agrawal et al.

---

[4] https://anonfiles.com/xauel4kayb/QSSO_zip.

[12], and Rawat et al. [20], our scheme needs two rounds of interaction, but the increased interaction is meaningful. It can prevent malicious clients from obtaining authentication tokens that do not belong to them through impersonation attacks. In addition, only partial multiplication and addition are added to the increased number of rounds, and the protocol can still run efficiently. Finally, by comparing the exponential operation, and bilinear pair operation performed by the client and server in the login phase, we can get the conclusion consistent, i.e., exponential and bilinear pair operation is not used in our scheme, which can make up for the computational overhead of symmetric encryption partly.

**Table 4.** Comparison among the schemes of Jones et al. [9], Agrawal et al. [12], Baum et al. [19], Zhang et al. [18], Rawat et al. [20] and our work.

| | Jones et al. [9] | Agrawal et al. [12] | Baum et al. [19] | Zhang et al. [18] | Rawat et al. [20] | Our Work |
|---|---|---|---|---|---|---|
| Threshold | $(1,1)$ | $(t,N)$ | $(N,N)$ | $(t,N)$ | $(t,N)$ | $(t,N)$ |
| Server Corruption | – | static | adaptive | adaptive | static | Adaptive |
| Server $sk$ | $O(1)$ | $O(C)$ | $O(n)$ | $O(G)$ | $O(C)$ | $O(G)$ |
| Password Update | × | × | × | × | ✓ | ✓ |
| Security Proactive | × | × | ✓ | ✓ | × | ✓ |
| Offline Att. Resist. | × | ✓ | ✓ | ✓ | ✓ | ✓ |
| Online Att. Resist. | ✓ | ✓ | ✓ | ✓ | ✓ | ✓ |
| Quantum secure | × | × | × | × | × | ✓ |
| Rounds | 1 | 1 | 2 | 2 | 1 | 2 |
| Efficiency Server | $1exe$ | $2exe$ | $4exe+1p$ | 0 | $2exe$ | 0 |
| Efficiency Client | 0 | $2exe$ | $5exe$ | $4p$ | $2exe$ | 0 |

† Att. Resist.=Attack resistance; Server $sk$ =Secret keys per server.
‡ $C$ denotes the number of clients. $G$ denotes the number of groups in the server.
∗ To compare the efficiency, we consider the most expensive operations, i.e., exponentiations (denoted by $exe$) and pairings (denoted by $p$).

# 7    Conclusion and Future Work

In this paper, we propose a secure and effective password-based threshold single-sign-on authentication scheme over lattices. The proposal adopts multiple identity servers to authenticate the client, and issues authentication tokens to prevent a single point of server failure. It also supports servers to update the private key against perpetual leakage. Moreover, our scheme allows the client to update the password. Considering password guessing attacks in the identity authentication scheme, we propose a threshold oblivious pseudorandom function over lattices to resist offline password guessing attacks. We use a grouping structure to mitigate the harm caused by online password guessing attacks. We also employ UT [34] to construct a threshold homomorphism aggregation signature protocol to distribute authentication tokens. In addition, the design of the component in our scheme is based on lattice-based intractable problems against quantum attacks. Finally, we provide security proof to show that our scheme is secure and robust under various attacks and can deal with the adversary of quantum computing power. Our scheme is efficient and has comprehensive functions through efficiency analysis and comparison with five authentication schemes.

For future work, we will investigate how to reduce the impact of noise accumulation further to increase the allowable range of thresholds so that the threshold authentication system is scalable. In addition, it is meaningful to verify the validity of the computation during the interaction. However, zero-knowledge proofs are too heavy for authentication systems, and verification schemes similar to BLS [33] face the exact impact of noise accumulation during aggregation. We note that a series of prior art [49] uses the smooth projective hash function to generate strong session keys without further validation in authenticated key exchange schemes. Accordingly, a smooth projective hash function to construct a password-based threshold authentication scheme may be feasible.

**Acknowledgment.** We are grateful to the anonymous reviewers for their invaluable comments. Ding Wang is the corresponding author. This research was supported by the National Natural Science Foundation of China (NSFC) under Grant No.62172240 by Natural Science Foundation of Tianjin, China under Grant No.21JCZXJC00100, and by Fundamental Research Funds for the Central Universities No.2122021385.

## A    Security of TOPRF

We prove the stored secret information $sd_i$ only depends on server-side secrets $sk_i$ by introducing unpredictability and obliviousness.

**Unpredictability.** $F_{msk}(\mathbf{x})$ is unpredictability, which means that the adversary $\mathcal{A}$ uses $\mathbf{x}$ to interacte with a set of servers and cannot predict the value of $F_{msk}(\mathbf{x})$, even if the adversary $\mathcal{A}$ can corrupt $t' < t$ servers. Unpredictability corresponds to average-case malicious client security in Definition 5. We describe a simulation Sim that communicates with malicious client $C^*$ and $\mathcal{F}_{TOPRF}$. Specifically, $Sim$ carries out the following steps:

- In the initialization phase, $\mathcal{A}$ and uniform $pk_{\mathcal{A}} \xleftarrow{R} R_q^{1 \times \ell}$ are generated. Send public parameters $pp$ and $pk_i$ to $\mathcal{A}$. Initialise an empty list $\mathbf{Q}$.
- During the query stage, for each message $pk_i$, do: $\mathcal{A}$ extracts $\mathbf{x}_{\mathcal{A}}, e_{\mathcal{A}}$, and sends the queries $\mathbf{x}$ to the functionality $\mathcal{F}_{TOPRF}$. If $\mathcal{F}_{TOPRF}$ returns $F_{msk}(\mathbf{x}) \in R_p^{1 \times \ell}$ and $F_{msk}(\mathbf{x}) \notin \mathbf{Q}$, sample $\mathbf{F}_q \xleftarrow{\$} R_q^{1 \times \ell} \cap \left(\frac{q}{p}\mathbf{y} + R_{\leq \frac{q}{2p}}^{1 \times \ell}\right)$ and add $(\mathbf{x}, \mathbf{F}_q)$ into $\mathbf{Q}$. Return $\mathbf{F}_q$ to $\mathcal{A}$. If $\mathcal{F}_{TOPRF}$ returns $F_{msk}(\mathbf{x}) \in R_p^{1 \times \ell}$ and $F_{msk}(\mathbf{x}) \in \mathbf{Q}$, set $\mathbf{F}_q = F_{msk}(\mathbf{x}) \in R_p^{1 \times \ell}$. Choose $e_i^* \xleftarrow{R} \chi_{\sigma'}$ and send $\mathbf{x}_{k_i}^* = pk \cdot k_i + e_i^* + \mathbf{F}_q$ to $\mathcal{A}$. Each round of queries uses different errors sampled from $R(\chi_{\sigma'}^{1 \times \ell})$. In a real protocol, if the adversary $\mathcal{A}$ can calculate the correct $\mathbf{F}_q$, it can perform the same operation on the message received from the simulator. $\mathbf{F}_q$ is sampled by Sim and the corresponding value $\mathbf{x}_{k_i}^*$. Let $e_{[1]} := \mathbf{y}_q - (q/p) \cdot \mathbf{y} \in R_{\leq \frac{q}{2p}}^{1 \times \ell}$, we have $\lfloor \frac{p}{q}(\sum_{i=1}^{N} \lambda_i \cdot \mathbf{x}_{k_i}^* - PK \cdot s) \rceil = \lfloor \frac{p}{q}(\mathbf{a}^F(\mathbf{x}) \cdot msk + e_{[1]} + e'') \rceil$, where $e'' \leq L \cdot \ell \cdot \sigma \cdot n^{3/2}$. Let $T = L \cdot \ell \cdot \sigma \cdot n^{3/2}$, there is $\|e_{[1]}\| < q/(2p) - T$. Thus, $\|msk \cdot e + \sum_{i=1}^{N} \lambda_i e_i' - \sum_{i=1}^{N} e_i\| \leq \frac{1}{2}$.

**Obliviousness.** $F_{msk}(\mathbf{x})$ is obliviousness, which means that even if $\mathcal{A}$ gets the value of $F_{msk}(\mathbf{x})$, it also cannot learn anything about the input $\mathbf{x}$, even if $\mathcal{A}$

knows $k_i$. Obliviousness corresponds to average-case malicious server security in Definition 5. We describe a simulation Sim that communicates with $\mathcal{A}$ and the functionality $\mathcal{F}_{TOPRF}$. In the initialization phase, $\mathcal{A}$ plays malicious server $S^*$. $S^*$ computes $pk^*$ from $k^*$ and publishes it, where $k_i \leq \sigma \cdot \sqrt{n}$. In the query phase, Sim randomly selected $r \xleftarrow{R} R_q^{1 \times \ell}$ and send to $S^*$ . Waiting for a response of $\mathbf{x}_{k_i}^*$ from $S^*$. Finally, the honest client $C$ send $F_{msk}(\mathbf{x})$ to adversary $\mathcal{A}$.

In real protocol, $\mathbf{x}^*$ generated by the honest client $C$. The secret value $\mathbf{x}$ is hidden by the encryption algorithm based on DRLWE. Thus, $\mathcal{A}$ cannot distinguish a real $\mathbf{x}^*$ from $r$. Let $\mathbf{x} \xleftarrow{R} R(\chi_\sigma)$ and $e \xleftarrow{R} R(\chi_\sigma)^{1 \times \ell}$ are sampled by $C$. For $C$ interacting with $\mathcal{F}_{TOPRF}$, and computes $F_{msk}(\mathbf{x}) = \lfloor \frac{p}{q}(\sum_{i=1}^{N} \lambda_i \cdot \mathbf{x}_{k_i}^* - PK \cdot s) \rceil = \lfloor \frac{p}{q}(\mathbf{a}^F(\mathbf{x}) \cdot msk + e'') \rceil$, where $e'' = msk \cdot e + \sum_{i=1}^{N} \lambda_i e_i' - \sum_{i=1}^{N} e_i$. If $N \leq \frac{1}{4}log_2 \frac{L \cdot \ell \cdot n - \sigma\sqrt{n}}{\sigma\sqrt{n}-1}$, the coefficient of $\frac{p}{q} \cdot \mathbf{a}^F(\mathbf{x}) \cdot msk$ is further than $e''$ away from $\mathbb{Z} + \frac{1}{2}$. According to $Adv_{\mathcal{A}}^{\mathsf{DRLWE}}(\kappa) \leq \varepsilon(\kappa)$, $\mathcal{A}$ can learn nothing about $\mathbf{x}$.

# B    Proof of Theorem 1

The security of lattice-based hardness problem is reduced to the hardness of finding a relatively short vector over lattices. $\mathcal{A}$ can execute the block-korkinzolotarev (BKZ) algorithm [30] to find the short vectors in the n-dimensional lattice. Alkim et al. [50] proved that DRLWE can effectively resist quantum attacks (primal attack and dual attack) based on the BKZ algorithm. The login phase of the scheme is divided into two main protocols: $i$) The client and multiple servers execute the *Oblivious Pseudo-Random Function* (TOPRF) to generate server-derived keys for authentication; and $ii$) the *Threshold Homomorphic Aggregate Signature* (THAS) protocol generates authentication tokens for authenticated clients. Proving that our protocols are quantum security comes down to proving that both components are quantum-resistant. The security of our TOPRF protocol is based on the DRLWE hardness assumption.

From Fig. 3, the messages sent in the first step and the second part are encrypted by RLWE. If $\mathcal{A}$ can recover the random number through the first step or the server private key through the second part, they can solve the RLWE problem. From the proof of Lemma 3, it can be seen that $\mathcal{A}$ can solve the DRLWE problem if they can compute the server master private key or recover the user password by the message in the third step. Applying the "estimator" [51] with the quantum-security model [19] and $\kappa = 128, n = 768, log\ q = 23$, our TOPRF protocol can provide 138-bit security with $N \leq \frac{1}{4}log_2 \frac{L \cdot \ell \cdot n - \sigma\sqrt{n}}{\sigma\sqrt{n}-1}$. According to Definition 2, for any PPT $\mathcal{A}$, the advantage holds that: $Adv_{\mathcal{A}}^{\mathsf{DRLWE}}(\kappa) \leq \varepsilon(\kappa)$.

According to the unforgeability analysis in [40,42], if $\mathcal{A}$ can forge a signature, they can solve the SIS problem. Thus, the advantage of any PPT $\mathcal{A}$ holds that: $Adv_{\mathcal{A}}^{\mathsf{SIS}}(\kappa) \leq \varepsilon(\kappa)$. According to the Definition 8, the advantage of $\mathcal{A}$ to obtain $sd_i$ by brutally cracking the symmetric encryption $E(z_i, sd_i)$ is $Adv_{\mathcal{A}}^{\mathsf{AES}}(\kappa) \leq \varepsilon(\kappa)$. In summary, our scheme can provide 128-bit security, and the advantage of any PPT $\mathcal{A}$ holds that: $Adv_{PTA,\mathcal{A}}^{\mathsf{Quantum}}(\kappa) = Adv_{\mathcal{A}}^{\mathsf{DRLWE}}(\kappa) + Adv_{\mathcal{A}}^{\mathsf{SIS}}(\kappa) + Adv_{\mathcal{A}}^{\mathsf{AES}}(\kappa) \leq \varepsilon(\kappa)$.

$\square$

# References

1. Bonneau, J., Herley, C., Oorschot, P., Stajano, F.: The quest to replace passwords: a framework for comparative evaluation of web authentication schemes. In: Proceedings of the IEEE S&P 2012, pp. 553–567 (2012)
2. Bonneau, J., Herley, C., van Oorschot, P., Stajano, F.: Passwords and the evolution of imperfect authentication. Commun. ACM **58**(7), 78–87 (2015)
3. Hanamsagar, A., Woo, S., Kanich, C., Mirkovic, J.: Leveraging semantic transformation to investigate password habits and their causes. In: Proceedings of the CHI, pp. 1–12 (2018)
4. Spadafora, A.: Struggling with password overload? You're not alone (2020). https://www.techradar.com/news/most-people-have-25-more-passwords-than-at-the-start-of-the-pandemic. Accessed 21 Oct 2020
5. Wang, D., Zhang, Z., Wang, P., Yan, J., Huang, X.: Targeted online password guessing: an underestimated threat. In Proceedings of the ACM CCS 2016, pp. 1242–1254 (2016)
6. Pal, B., Daniel, T., Chatterjee, R., Ristenpart, T.:. Beyond credential stuffing: password similarity models using neural networks. In Proceedings of the IEEE S&P, pp. 417–434 (2019)
7. Armando, A., Carbone, R., Compagna, L., Cuellar, J., Tobarra, L.: Formal analysis of SAML 2.0 web browser single sign-on: breaking the SAML-based single sign-on for google apps. In: Proceedings of the FMSE 2008, pp. 1–10 (2008)
8. Neuman, B., Ts'o, T.: Kerberos: an authentication service for computer networks. IEEE Commun. Mag. **32**(9), 33–38 (1994)
9. Jones, M., Bradley, J., Sakimura, N.: JSON Web Tokens. https://jwt.io/. Accessed 15 Dec 2021
10. Wang, D., Wang, P.: Offline dictionary attack on password authentication schemes using smart cards. In: Proceedings of the ISC 2013, pp. 221–237 (2013)
11. Alwen, J., Chen, B., Pietrzak, K., Reyzin, L., Tessaro, S.: Scrypt is maximally memory-hard. In: Proceedings of the Eurocrypt 2017, pp. 33–62 (2017)
12. Agrawal, S., Miao, P., Mohassel, P., Mukherjee, P.: PASTA: password-based threshold authentication. In: Proceedings of the ACM CCS 2018, pp. 2042–2059 (2018)
13. MacKenzie, P., Shrimpton, T., Jakobsson, M.: Threshold password-authenticated key exchange. In: Proceedings of the CRYPTO 2002, pp. 385–400 (2002)
14. Rabin, T.: A simplified approach to threshold and proactive RSA. In: Proceedings of the CRYPTO 1998, pp. 89–104 (1998)
15. Bagherzandi, A., Jarecki, S., Saxena, N., Lu, Y.: Password-protected secret sharing. In: Proceedings of the ACM CCS 2011, pp. 433–444 (2011)
16. Jarecki, S., Kiayias, A., Krawczyk, H.: Round-optimal password-protected secret sharing and T-PAKE in the password-only model. In: Proceedings of the ASIACRYPT, pp. 233–253 (2014)
17. Jarecki, S., Kiayias, A., Krawczyk, H., Xu, J.: TOPPSS: cost-minimal password-protected secret sharing based on threshold OPRF. In: Proceedings of the ACNS, pp. 39–58 (2017)
18. Zhang, Y., Xu, C., Li, H., Yang, K., Cheng, N., Shen, X.: PROTECT: efficient password-based threshold single-sign-on authentication for mobile users against perpetual leakage. IEEE Trans. Mob. Comput. **20**(6), 2297–2312 (2020)
19. Baum, C., Frederiksen, T., Hesse, J., Lehmann, A., Yanai, A.: PESTO: proactively secure distributed single sign-on, or how to trust a hacked server. In: Proceedings of the EuroS&P 2020, pp. 587–606 (2020)

20. Rawat, R., Jhanwar, M.: PAS-TA-U: PASsword-based threshold authentication with password update. In: Proceedings of the SPACE 2020, pp. 25–45 (2020)
21. Herzberg, A., Jarecki, S., Krawczyk, H., Yung, M.: Proactive secret sharing or: how to cope with perpetual leakage. In: Proceedings of the CRYPTO 1995, pp. 339–352 (1995)
22. Ladd, T., Jelezko, F., Laflamme, R., Nakamura, Y., Monroe, C., OBrien, J.: Quantum computers. Nature **464**(7285), 45–53 (2010)
23. Mavroeidis, V., Vishi, K., Zych, M., Jøsang, A.: The impact of quantum computing on present cryptography. Int. J. Adv. Comput. Sci. Appl. **9**(3), 405–414 (2018). IEEE Trans. Mob. Comput. **20**(6), 2297–2312 (2020)
24. Alagic, G., et al.: Status report on the first round of the NIST post-quantum cryptography standardization process (2019). https://nvlpubs.nist.gov/nistpubs/ir/2019/NIST.IR.8240.pdf
25. Alagic, G., et al.: Status report on the second round of the NIST post-quantum cryptography standardization process. Status Report on the Second Round of the NIST Post-quantum Cryptography Standardization Process. NIST, Tech. Rep. (2020)
26. Ding, J., Alsayigh, S., Lancrenon, J., Saraswathy, R., Snook, M.: Provably secure password authenticated key exchange based on RLWE for the post-quantum world. In: Proceedings of the CT-RSA 2017, pp. 183–204 (2017)
27. Li, Z., Wang, D.: Two-round PAKE protocol over lattices without NIZK. In: Proceedings of the INSCRYPT 2018, pp. 138–159 (2018)
28. Bos, J.W., Costello, C., Naehrig, M., Stebila, D.: Post-quantum key exchange for the TLS protocol from the ring learning with errors problem. In: Proceedings of the IEEE S&P 2015, pp. 553–570 (2015)
29. Zhang, J., Zhang, Z., Ding, J., Snook, M., Dagdelen, O.: Authenticated key exchange from ideal lattices. In: Proceedings of the EUROCRYPT 2015, pp. 719–751 (2015)
30. Schnorr, C., Euchner, M.: Lattice basis reduction: improved practical algorithms and solving subset sum problems. Math. Program. **66**(1), 181–199 (1994)
31. Grover, L.: A fast quantum mechanical algorithm for database search. In: Proceedings of the STOC 1996, pp. 212–219 (1996)
32. Alagic, G., et al.: Status Report on the Third Round of the NIST Post-Quantum Cryptography Standardization Process. National Institute of Standards and Technology, Gaithersburg (2022)
33. Boneh, D., Lynn, B., Shacham, H.: Short signatures from the Weil pairing. In: Proceedings of the ASIACRYPT 2001, pp. 514–532 (2001)
34. Boneh, D., et al.: Threshold cryptosystems from threshold fully homomorphic encryption. In: Proceedings of the CRYPTO 2018, pp. 565–596 (2018)
35. Albrecht, M., Davidson, A., Deo, A., Smart, N.: Round-optimal verifiable oblivious pseudorandom functions from ideal lattices. In: Proceedings of the PKC 2021, pp. 261–289 (2021)
36. Bellare, M., Pointcheval, D., Rogaway, P.: Authenticated key exchange secure against dictionary attacks. In: Proceedings of the EUROCRYPT 2000, pp. 139–155 (2000)
37. Lyubashevsky, V., Peikert, C., Regev, O.: On ideal lattices and learning with errors over rings. J. ACM **60**(6), 1–35 (2013)
38. Shamir, A.: How to share a secret. ACM Commun. **22**(11), 612–613 (1979)
39. Bendlin, R., Krehbiel, S., Peikert, C.: How to share a lattice trapdoor: threshold protocols for signatures and (H) IBE. In: Proceedings of the ACNS 2013, pp. 218–236 (2013)

40. Jing, Z.: An efficient homomorphic aggregate signature scheme based on lattice. Math. Probl. Eng. **2014**(1), 1–9 (2014)
41. Agrawal, S., Boyen, X., Vaikuntanathan, V., Voulgaris, P., Hoeteck, W.: Functional encryption for threshold functions (or fuzzy IBE) from lattices. In: Proceedings of the PKC 2012, pp. 280–297 (2012)
42. Wang, F.H., Hu, Y.P., Wang, B.C.: Lattice-based linearly homomorphic signature scheme over binary field. Sci. China Inf. Sci. **56**(11), 1–9 (2012). https://doi.org/10.1007/s11432-012-4681-9
43. Banerjee, A., Peikert, C.: New and improved key-homomorphic pseudorandom functions. In: Proceedings of the CRYPTO 2014, pp. 353–370 (2014)
44. Boneh, D., Dagdelen, Ö., Fischlin, M., Lehmann, A., Schaffner, C., Zhandry, M.: Random oracles in a quantum world. In: Proceedings of the ASIACRYPT 2011, pp. 41–69 (2011)
45. Wang, D., Cheng, H., Wang, P., Huang, X., Jian, G.: Zipf's law in passwords. IEEE Trans. Inf. Foren. Sec. **12**(11), 2776–2791 (2017)
46. Rajabi, B., Eslami, Z.: A verifiable threshold secret sharing scheme based on lattices. Inf. Sci. **501**, 655–661 (2019)
47. Alkim, E., Barreto, P., Bindel, N., Krämer, J., Longa, P., Ricardini, J.: The lattice-based digital signature scheme qTESLA. In: Proceedings of the ACNS 2020, pp. 441–460 (2020)
48. Everspaugh, A., Chaterjee, R., Scott, S., Juels, A., Ristenpart, T.: The Pythia PRF service. In: Proceedings of the USENIX SEC 2015, pp. 547–562 (2015)
49. Li, Z., Wang, D., Morais, E.: Quantum-safe round-optimal password authentication for mobile devices. IEEE Trans. Depend. Secur. Comput. **19**(3), 1885–1899 (2020)
50. Alkim, E., Ducas, L., Poppelmann, T., Schwabe, P.: Post-quantum key exchange a new hope. In: Proceedings of the USENIX SEC 2016, pp. 327–343 (2016)
51. Albrecht, M.R., Player, R., Scott, S.: On the concrete hardness of learning with errors. J. CRYPTOL **9**(3), 169–203 (2015)

# The Revenge of Password Crackers: Automated Training of Password Cracking Tools

Alessia Michela Di Campi, Riccardo Focardi[ID], and Flaminia L. Luccio[✉][ID]

Ca' Foscari University, Venice, Italy
{alessia.dicampi,focardi,luccio}@unive.it

**Abstract.** Passwords are stored in the form of salted one-way hashes so that attacks on servers cannot leak them in the clear. However, humans tend to select passwords that are easy to remember, and a motivated attacker may attempt to hash quite large sets of *easy* passwords until a match is found with the target hash. Password cracking tools such as hashcat and john the ripper do this job very efficiently, using different forms of attacks that, for example, try passwords with a certain syntactic structure or passwords taken from a dictionary and mangled through appropriate rules. Recent work on password guessing has shown that machine learning can, in principle, outperform existing cracking tools in terms of success rate, by generating sophisticated password models. In this paper, we give password cracking tools a second chance, by exploring automated training techniques that aim to effectively improve the success rate. To achieve this ambitious goal, we carry out a systematic and in-depth analysis of various cracking strategies, and we propose a new combination of techniques that we train and test on a dataset of more than 700M real passwords. Our results show that, with this new approach, we can almost double the success rate, returning the primacy to password cracking tools. The techniques are general, repeatable and publicly available up to ethical constraints, providing a new benchmark for future research on password guessing.

**Keywords:** Passwords · Cracking tools · Automated training

## 1 Introduction

Password-based authentication is the most common form of identification but it is subject to a well known dilemma: passwords should be easy to remember but complex to guess. Over the years it has been seen that humans tend to use passwords that are mere variations of known words, and even when there are password policies that mandate the use of particular characters, the patterns used by users to satisfy the policies are quite predictable. Passwords are saved on

This work has been partially supported by the POR FESR project SAFE PLACE: "Sistemi IoT per ambienti di vita salubri e sicuri".

servers in the form of salted one-way hashes to prevent that the leak of a password file provides the attacker with all the passwords in cleartext. However, once the password file is obtained, the attacker can compute the hash of a (large) set of passwords, combining it with the random salts, until a match is found, resulting in a password leak. There have been numerous attacks of this type in recent years which have caused billions of passwords to be leaked. Also considering the fact that users tend to reuse passwords across multiple accounts, these leaks have devastating effects [8,10].

hashcat [1] and john the ripper [2] are two very popular password recovery tools. They can recover a password from its salted hash using various techniques that aim to reduce a pure brute force attack to a smarter and more targeted search. For example, they can use masks that define the syntactic form of a password, dictionaries of commonly used words, and rules that apply simple password transformation schemes. These tools are highly optimized and take full advantage of the parallelism given by multi-core processors and GPUs. As it often happens in IT security, these tools are used by both security analysts and attackers. In fact, one could imagine that a system administrator periodically checks the quality of her users' passwords by trying to crack them. Interestingly, services such as haveibeenpwned.com [15,16] were created just for this purpose as they allow to check if a password has been leaked in the past and blacklist it. In order to enforce honest use of the service, leaked passwords are only available in hash form, so that it is easy to check if a password belongs to the set but, to get the passwords in the clear, it is in fact necessary to crack the hashes.

Attempting to crack a password to verify its strength requires a lot of resources and hardly emulates the skills of a motivated and experienced attacker. In recent years, several papers have proposed models and techniques for measuring the strength of a password, in terms of how complex it is for an attacker to guess it efficiently, without resorting to an actual cracking. This is very appealing for providing real-time feedback to users and forcing or guiding them in selecting strong enough passwords (see, e.g., [14,17–21,25,28,30]). These so called password guessability models are often compared with cracking tools such as hashcat and john the ripper in order to assess their accuracy. However, it has been noticed that these comparisons are often performed using off-the-shelf default tool configurations that do not reflect the actual capabilities of an experienced attacker [27,31], who selects suitable dictionaries, masks, rules and adapts the attack based on intermediate results and cracking success rate. In other words, there is a gap between automated cracking with default configurations, and advanced semi-automated cracking based on professional expertise.

In this paper, we try to reduce this gap by investigating automated training techniques that aim to improve the success rate of cracking tools. To achieve this ambitious goal, we carry out a systematic and in-depth analysis of various cracking strategies, and we propose a new combination of techniques that we train and test on a dataset of more than 700M real passwords. Our results show that, with this new approach, we can nearly double the success rate compared to off-the-shelf configurations, achieving success rates of more than 70% in just $10^{12}$ guesses, that is comparable to what is achieved through proprietary rules from experts [31]. The techniques are general, repeatable and publicly available up to ethical constraints, providing a new benchmark for future research on password guessing.

*Contributions.* We summarize our main contributions below:

- We build a plaintext dataset of 723M well-formed real passwords with associated frequencies which, to the best of our knowledge, is the biggest one ever analyzed in the literature. For ethical issues, we do not make this database publicly available but we describe its construction in detail and provide statistics about its data (cf. Sect. 3);
- We perform experiments using popular hashcat off-the-shelf rules, best64 and generated2, used in other studies, and we demonstrate how a dictionary composed of the most frequent real passwords outperforms both natural language dictionaries and randomly-selected password dictionaries. This suggests that users tend to select passwords similar to other popular passwords and not necessarily passwords that are variations of natural language words (cf. Sect. 4);
- We use the statsgen tool [5] to build masks from our training data and we introduce an efficient algorithm to simulate mask attacks without resorting to actual cracking. We show that the trained masks are very accurate on test data and, quite surprisingly, give results very similar to rule-based attacks with off-the-shelf rules which, as we discussed, are often used as baseline for password guessability models. To the best of our knowledge, our algorithm provides the first password guessability model based on masks (cf. Sect. 5);
- We provide a general method for constructing a set of rules from existing ones, with associated frequencies, and we show that they outperform the initial rule sets. We experiment by varying the length of the dictionary and the set of rules, with a fixed overall number of guesses (our *guessing budget*), and we find out that the best success rate is achieved by using the entire password dictionary with about a thousand rules. This seems to contradict the tendency to create a very broad set of rules (e.g., [3,4]) (cf. Sect. 6);
- We finally combine mask-based and rule-based attacks and, while we improve the success rate slightly, we also observe a huge overlap in the generated passwords. We optimize the attack by training masks on passwords that have not been cracked by the rule-based attack, in order to reduce the overlap, achieving our best cracking rate of 72.67% which significantly outperforms the 41.94% success rate of the off-the-shelf configurations (cf. Sect. 6).

We make masks and rules available together with an implementation of simulation algorithm and a script to compute password guessability [11]. For ethical and legal issues, we do not make plaintext passwords available.

## 2   Background and Related Work

In this section we summarize the state of the art of guessing attacks by highlighting several known approaches. First, we introduce password guessing attacks and then we discuss different techniques ranging from brute-force attacks, to probabilistic context-free grammars, Markov models, Neural Networks and GAN approaches, highlighting the differences with respect to our work.

*Password Guessing Attacks.* They include both offline and online guessing attacks. In *offline guessing attacks*, the attacker in principle has no limitations on the amount of time she can use to guess passwords. This typically occurs when a hashed password database is stolen and the attack amounts to hashing passwords generated in various ways (discussed below) until matches are found. This is what happened, e.g., to the `rockyou` database in 2009 [10], and to LinkedIn in 2012 [8]. The consequences of this kind of attacks are devastating and are amplified by the bad habit of reusing the same password for multiple accounts. This is what happened, e.g., in 2016 when hackers collected 99 million usernames and passwords from different websites and reused them to attack Taobao accounts using the Alibaba's cloud computing platform accessing more than 20 million accounts [12]. One way to limit this attack, is to guide users to create unpredictable, and hopefully also usable, passwords. In the recent years, a lot of work has been done in this direction by adding to the systems password meters whose aim is to provide users a visual feedback on the password strength. This approach can help both users who would tend to choose passwords that are easy to remember, and those who are unsure of the strength of a specific password. These password meters are based, e.g., on basic heuristics [9,30], or on artificial neural networks approaches [21,29].

In *online attacks*, instead, the attacker attempts to guess a password while logging into the system. A standard way to mitigate these attacks is to slow down the login process or even lock it after a certain number of wrong attempts. In this paper we focus on offline attacks.

*Mask and Rule-Based Attacks.* The search for a password in a password *brute-force attack* is done by exhaustively trying every possible combination of letters, numbers and symbols. Instead, *mask attacks* consist of only searching passwords that match a specific pattern [1]. Mask attacks are more efficient because the number of passwords to try is limited by the specific shape of the mask. For instance, if we know that a password in composed of 5 lowercase characters and 3 digits at the end, it is sufficient to use a mask that places any combination of 3 digits after 5 lowercase characters, i.e., only $26^5 \cdot 10^3$ possible passwords. In this paper we show that mask attacks can be trained and we study their performance alone and when used in combination with other attacks.

First proposed by Morris and Thompson in 1979 [24], one of the most commonly used attacks is the *dictionary attack* that consists of using dictionaries of popular words as a base for predictable passwords. Modern dictionary attacks often combine wordlists with mangling rules, i.e., rules that modify words and produce other likely passwords. A *mangled wordlist attack* consists in using both a file of commonly known words and often also passwords from other data leaks, and a file of rules that are applied to the wordist generating a set of possible password guesses that are applied to a password file to be cracked. Typical mangling rules involve operations such as capitalizing the first letter, adding digits and replacing characters (e.g., replace 's' with '$' and append a digit), or even more complex operations [1,2].

*Password Recovery Tools and their Analysis.* john the ripper [2] and hashcat [1] are the two most popular password recovery tools that support the attacks discussed above and are used extensively by both security analysts and real world attackers. Our work is based on hashcat but, even if there are differences with respect to john the ripper (see, e.g., [19]), we believe that our methods and results would apply to any tool supporting mask and rule-based attacks. The reason why we opted for hashcat is the availability of many advanced rule sets (e.g. [3,4]), and the existence of tools such as pack [5] which produce hashcat-style input files. For example, the rule sets made available in [3,4] have been optimized and tested over particular data sets producing very interesting cracking results. In Sect. 6 we will use part of these rule sets to train a more efficient and flexible set of rules that can be cut at different sizes, depending on the size of the available dictionary. hashcat is extremely optimized and can process millions of hashes using huge dictionaries, and very big numbers of masks and rules. It exploits multi-core and GPU hardware but in this study, as typically done in the literature, we present our results in terms of number of guesses and cracking success rate, independently of the actual cracking time. The intent is to make the results as much as possible independent of the available hardware.

In [19] Liu et al. propose a technique to reason, analytically, about rule-based attacks in hashcat and john the ripper. The proposed technique can be used, server-side, to check the strength of a password by estimating the number of guesses required to crack it. The tool is based on a rule inversion module that computes the preimage set for a rule given a password, i.e., the set of dictionary words that produce the target password when the rule is applied. This is very appealing and we tried to use it in our analysis. Unfortunately, the tool is quite resource intensive (cf. Sect. VII.B of [19]), and it did not terminate on our data sets due to their extensive size. The paper also studies reordering of rules and dictionaries to improve how quickly password are guessed. The idea is that using more efficient words and rules first would crack many passwords earlier. We exploit similar ideas but for a different purpose: we show that ordering is important to optimize attacks for a given budget of guesses by suitable cutting (sorted) dictionaries and rule sets. We additionally study how to train mask attacks by generating sorted lists of masks that, as for rules, can be cut in order to fit into a budget of guesses. It is also worth noticing that, contrary to [19], our study does not require any sophisticated ad-hoc software as all the training and tests are done directly using the latest version of hashcat. This makes it easily repeatable and portable to other password recovery tools.

*Password Guessability Models.* Weir et al. in [32] discuss a method that, starting from the probability distribution of user passwords, generates password patterns in order of decreasing probability. They create a probabilistic context-free grammar (PCFG) based upon a training set of previously disclosed passwords which generates word mangling rules, and from them, password guesses to be used in password cracking. This technique has been extended to compute *password guessability*, i.e., the number of guesses that is required by a cracking algorithm with particular training data to guess a password (see, e.g., [17,30]). The guessing efficiency of the technique has been improved by Komanduri in [18] and made more usable for practical purposes by Hranický et al. in [14]. The Markov model, first introduced by Narayanan and Shmatikov in [25] and further improved, e.g., by Ma et al. in [20], is based on the idea of local relevance, i.e., the model predicts the probability of a character based on the previous $n$ characters or context characters.

In [31], Segreti et al. compare password guessability models with password recovery tools. The authors found that each approach was highly dependent on its configuration. Interestingly, they show that it is dangerous to measure password guessability based on a single algorithm, and it is more accurate to run various algorithms and choose the minimum, more conservative value. The authors show that default configurations for john the ripper and hashcat perform poorly and for hashcat, in particular, they resort to an expert user and professional password researcher, who shared his proprietary mangling rules for the purpose of the analysis. Our work investigates exactly this line of research in order to better understand how the configuration of tools like hashcat can be improved using systematic, automated approaches, without necessarily resorting to professional experts. Our methods and results provide a more accurate baseline for comparison with respect to existing, off-the-shelf, approaches. Interestingly, our best success rate is similar to the best one achieved in [31], where the proprietary rules are tested over the simplest password set considered in the paper, named Basic. Our passwords, instead, are variegate and potentially much more complex than the one in Basic (cf. Sect. 3).

*Neural Networks and GANs.* Melicher et al. proposed neural networks to guess passwords [21]. The use of neural networks, like Markov models, assesses the likelihood of a future character in a candidate password depending on the preceding characters. Authors use hashcat and john the ripper using a rather simple configuration that we use in our paper as a baseline reference for comparison. We will show that our best configuration will significantly improve the success rate passing from 41.94% to 72.67%. In [13] Hitaj et al. propose PassGAN, an approach that uses a Generative Adversarial Network (GAN) to autonomously learn the distribution of real passwords from actual password leaks, and to generate high-quality password guesses without any knowledge on passwords structures. Recently, Pasquini et al. [28] proposed a deep generative learning approach for password guessing that improves the training process of PassGAN. Similarly to [21], the authors of these papers use hashcat and john the ripper with off-the-shelf suboptimal rules that are outperformed by our proposed methods. In a recent work [27] Pasquini et al. introduce an interesting technique to improve attacks based on two ideas: an adaptive mangling rule attack, that selects the most suitable mangling rule for each world in the dictionary, and a dynamic guessing strategy that incorporates cracked passwords in the dictionary to improve the success rate and make the attack less sensitive to the initial configuration. Authors have modified the CPU legacy version of hashcat to provide a proof-of-concept implementation of the first strategy. In our work, we do not consider it, as we focus on the official hashcat version without any changes. As for the second strategy, we do not consider it in our study as we always set a fixed guessing budget but its effectiveness can be justified in terms of performance increase with large dictionaries (cf. Sect. 6).

*Experimental Setup.* Our experiments have been done on a server equipped with an Intel(R) Xeon(R) E5-2699 v4 @ 2.20 GHz with 88 CPUs and 256G of RAM. We did not use GPUs. Time for each experiment varied from 1 to 8 h.

## 3    Building a Reliable Password Dataset

In this section we analyse existing datasets of real passwords, in order to select the most appropriate one for our study. This task is really challenging from various perspectives: (*i*) password datasets are related to real leaks and in many cases remain available for a limited amount of time; (*ii*) password datasets cannot be made available for reproducing research results because of ethical and legal issues; (*iii*) a single dataset could be biased in various ways due, e.g., to the specific password policy adopted, the language and background of the users, the type of application it belongs to. Items (*i*) and (*ii*) are particularly problematic from a scientific point of view, as they make very difficult, if not impossible, to compare new results with previous literature. As a matter of fact, when we started this research, we soon realized that many datasets used in previous work were in fact unavailable.

It is worth noticing that password datasets can be used to reject, very efficiently, passwords that have been already leaked in the past, forcing users to select stronger ones. So, it could be debated whether making available these datasets, with no information about associated users, is actually ethical or not. In fact, attacker probably have these lists anyway, and honest users might select a trivial-to-break password without having the opportunity of comparing it with these datasets. Interestingly, NIST recommends comparing passwords chosen by users against a *blacklist* of unacceptable passwords which should include passwords from previous breaches [26, Sect. A.3]. This has motivated the creation of the haveibeenpwned.com website where users can search for leaks that might involve them. In particular, it is possible to search for a password into multiple datasets taken from real leaks accounting around 847M passwords [16]. The service is available both online and offline by downloading the full dataset of passwords in hashed form, so to protect passwords containing personal information [15], making it possible to check if a password has been leaked without submitting it to the website. In our opinion, this is a responsible approach that also addresses the three challenges above by offering a stable password dataset that allows for reproducible research results and is not biased to a specific data breach. However, the fact that passwords are hashed limits the analysis and the training, as we will discuss below. Interestingly, this dataset also provides the frequency of the leaked passwords, i.e., the number of occurrences of each (hashed) password in the collected leaks. For future reference, we name this dataset hbp.

There is a very popular password dataset called rockyou, named after a company that suffered a very important data breach in 2009 resulting in the exposure of over 32 million user accounts from partner sites, including Facebook and Myspace. The rockyou dataset is composed of approximately 14M unique passwords and has been publicly available since the data breach. Moreover, Kali Linux provides this dictionary file as part of its standard installation [6]. Thus, we consider this dataset reliable and suitable for research purposes, as it will very likely remain available in the future. Moreover, rockyou has been used in many previous research papers and technical blog posts, because of its effectiveness in dictionary-based attacks.

Recently, another dataset called rockyou2021 has appeared on the Internet [7]. It is a collection of various leaks, including COMB (Combination Of Many Breaches) [22], in a single file containing approximately 8.5 billion unique passwords[1]. The author claims that it is just a wordlist that does not contain usernames or other personal information, and should be used to legally test internal security. The advantages of this dataset with respect to rockyou are: its huge size that makes it very suitable for both training and testing, and its variety of sources that reduces the possible bias, as discussed in item (*iii*) above. However, since this dataset is very recent, and it is not protected by hashes as [16], we cannot be sure it will remain available in the future for further testing and for reproducing experimental results. The author of rockyou2021 makes a claim about passwords included in the dataset that we rephrase as follows:

**Definition 1 (Password well-formedness).** *A well-formed password should be 6–20 characters long and only include printable ASCII characters except space, tab and other control characters. More precisely, the ASCII code of each character should be in the interval 0x21-0x7e.*

Notice that, ASCII codes that are less than or equal 0x20 are control characters including white space, while ASCII codes bigger than or equal to 0x7f are DEL plus values outside the ASCII range. Even if this definition does not apply to all passwords, we found it interesting and useful for our purposes: first of all 6–20 is a reasonable password length limitation as shorter passwords can be cracked without special techniques, and longer passwords are likely more similar to passphrases and are usually out-of-the-scope of tools such as hashcat. Second, restricting to printable ASCII characters solves technical issues related to encoding: if a password dataset mixes passwords with different encodings and foreign charsets it becomes very complicated, if not impossible, to analyze them in a reproducible and deterministic way.

---

[1] The number of 82 billion passwords indicated in [7] is incorrect. We double-checked it, and found the same number already indicated in [23].

In the rest of the paper we will stick to Definition 1. We will also show that author's claim about `rockyou2021` adhering to Definition 1 is not fully accurate.

## 3.1   Dataset Analysis

Since the sources of the available datasets are not clearly stated and/or available, we have analysed and compared them, looking for overlaps. In fact, overlaps would confirm that a password belongs to a popular leak. Notice that, since `hbp` is hashed, we cannot check its inclusion in `rockyou` and `rockyou2021`. Checking the opposite inclusion is possible but resource-intensive. The first natural check was whether `rockyou` ⊆ `rockyou2021`. Thus, we performed a dictionary attack using `hashcat` with `rockyou2021` as dictionary and `rockyou` as target[2]. We found 14161809 out of the 14344392 `rockyou` passwords, i.e., 98.73% of the total, confirming that `rockyou` is almost completely included in `rockyou2021`. The attack took about 63 min on our hardware (cf. Sect. 2).

We analysed the found passwords, and we discovered anomalies with respect to well-formedness. Apart from a few non-ASCII characters we found many short passwords. The explanation is that some passwords of length 5 in `rockyou2021` have the DOS-style newline with the extra carriage-return, which was probably counted reaching the minimum length limit of 6. Interestingly, 635 passwords cracked by `hashcat` could not be found in `rockyou` by our analysis scripts. We realized that this is due to character encoding as all of these passwords contained bytes with values over `0x79`, i.e., out of the ASCII range. This confirms that it is a good idea to restrict datasets to ASCII chars, as done in Definition 1, to avoid encoding issues that would make it difficult to reproduce the results. We also analysed the passwords of `rockyou` not found by `hashcat` and we spotted another anomaly: 5540 well-formed passwords, all containing a column character. Our explanation is that these missing passwords could be due to the output format of `hashcat` that separates hashes and passwords using a column and this might mess up post-processing (in fact we did similar mistakes at some point). In summary, we recovered 97.20% well-formed `rockyou` passwords and all the missing password are either non well-formed or they contain a column character (only 3.02%).

Then, we checked `rockyou2021` ⊆ `hbp` by running `hashcat` over `hbp` using `rockyou2021` as dictionary similarly to what we did before[3]. We faced a technical issue due to the size of the `hbp` (around 847M of passwords), and we had to split the hash file into four parts. As we said, `hbp` also provides the frequency of each hash and the version that we downloaded was already sorted by frequency in decreasing order, i.e., the first hash was the most frequent one. Interestingly, running the cracking on the four parts we obtained a decreasing success rate confirming the consistency of the datasets: since a high frequency `hbp` hash appeared in as many leaks, then it is more likely that it is also covered by `rockyou2021`. Overall, we were able to crack 85.92% of the `hbp` hashes in about

---

[2] Option `-m 99999` does not perform any hash and just looks for plaintext passwords.

[3] Since `hbp` is hashed with NTLM we set the corresponding hash mode with `-m 1000`.

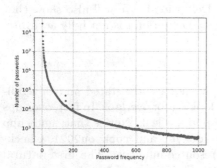

| Password | Frequency |
|---|---|
| 123456 | 37359195 |
| 123456789 | 16629796 |
| qwerty | 10556095 |
| password | 9545824 |
| 12345678 | 5119355 |
| 111111 | 4833228 |
| qwerty123 | 4759446 |
| 1q2w3e | 4456640 |
| 1234567 | 4043126 |
| abc123 | 3891152 |

(a) Passwords of $\mathcal{D}$ with lowest frequency.      (b) Most frequent passwords in $\mathcal{D}$.

**Fig. 1.** Analysis of the dataset $\mathcal{D}$.

30 h, with a best success rate of 96.16% for the first part of the hashes, i.e., the most frequent ones. We also cleaned up the cracked passwords by removing the non well-formed ones, that were only 0.57% of the found passwords, mostly because of the DOS-style newline, as for the previous case. We found another anomaly: some of the passwords were in the format $HEX[...] which is used by hashcat to represent passwords in their hexadecimal representation, e.g., for encoding issues. They are probably in rockyou2021 because, in some cases, the author collected the output of hashcat without reconverting the $HEX[...] notation to actual passwords. Overall, we recovered around 723M well-formed passwords from hbp, i.e., the 85.43% of the entire dataset.

Since hbp provides this very interesting information about hash frequency, that we have already shown to cause variations in cracking success rates, we recomputed the hash of these 723M passwords and searched them in hbp to associate the frequency to the corresponding plaintext password. This has allowed us to build a plaintext dataset of 723M well-formed real passwords with associated frequencies which, to the best of our knowledge, is the biggest one ever analysed in the literature. We name this dataset $\mathcal{D}$ for future reference in the paper. In Fig. 1a we plot the number of passwords in $\mathcal{D}$ that have frequencies in the range $1, \ldots, 1000$, i.e., the 1000 lowest frequencies in the dataset. There are about 286M passwords, i.e., 39.54% of the total, with frequency 1 then the number of passwords decreases quickly, giving 40549 passwords with frequency 100, 1238 passwords with frequency 500 and only 321 passwords with frequency 1000. Even if taken singularly these numbers are just a very small fraction of the whole dataset, their cumulative effect is interesting and we will exploit it in the training phase. For example, if we take the most frequent 13943307 passwords, i.e., the same number as the clean rockyou dataset discussed above, we obtain a set where the lowest password frequency is 30, meaning that all passwords have been seen at least in 30 leaks. On the other side of the range, we have few passwords with a huge frequency. Figure 1b reports the ten most frequent ones.

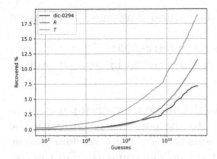
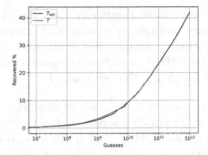

(a) Most frequent passwords $T$ from the training set outperform $R$ and `dic-0294`.

(b) Longer dictionary from $\text{Train}_\mathcal{D}$ cracks 41.94% passwords in about $10^{12}$ guesses.

**Fig. 2.** Comparison between dictionaries using `best64` and `generated2` rules.

We have split $\mathcal{D}$ in two disjoint subsets, $\text{Train}_\mathcal{D}$ for training and $\text{Test}_\mathcal{D}$ for testing, respectively of size 80–20%, using a reproducible pseudorandom sequence with a fixed seed.

## 4  Dictionaries with Off-the-Shelf Rules

In [21] it was suggested to use a training set directly as a dictionary in conjunction with mangling rules to perform attacks which are, in principle, more effective than those based on natural language dictionaries. The training set is simply sorted in descending order of password frequency to prioritize the most likely passwords, so that they are used first in the cracking process. There are two interesting assumptions behind this idea: ($i$) using passwords instead of natural language dictionaries might give better results, and ($ii$) more frequent passwords are more likely to constitute the base of other passwords in mangling attacks. Naturally, if the search space is fully searched all the passwords will be used, so ordering the training set would not affect the final success rate but it would improve the efficiency of the attack by achieving higher cracking rate early. Similar ideas are also present in many blog posts where `rockyou` is used as dictionary together with mangling rules. We observe that ($ii$) makes it possible to build a dictionary that is smaller than the training set by simply sorting it in decreasing password frequency and cutting it to the desired length. This is different from [21] where the whole training set was used and frequency did not change the final success rate. This is particularly useful for getting the experiments to finish in a reasonable time, and for comparing the results on the same search space, as we will see shortly.

In [21] assumptions ($i$) and ($ii$) are not demonstrated experimentally. We decided to perform an experiment to confirm them as they will be very important in the following. We have replicated the test done in [21] with rules `best64` and `generated2` from the `hashcat` distribution, using three different dictionaries:

- A very large commonly used dictionary of natural language words named dic-0294 composed of 869228 unique entries;
- A random sample $R$ of $\text{Train}_D$, the same size as dic-0294;
- The 869228 most frequent passwords in $\text{Train}_D$, sorted in decreasing order of frequency, that we name $T$.

The last one is a variation of what is done in the above mentioned paper, were we cut $\text{Train}_D$ to a desired length in order to compare the results with the ones achieved with a natural language words dictionary and a random sample of $\text{Train}_D$, i.e., the first two dictionaries in the list. The comparison of the last one with the first two dictionaries will respectively check assumptions $(i)$ and $(ii)$. In Fig. 2a we show the results: we clearly see that the most frequent passwords from the training set $T$ outperform both the natural language dictionary dic-0294 and the random password sample $R$ from $\text{Train}_D$. The final success rates are, respectively, 18.96%, 7.17% and 11.5%. We also notice that $R$ outperforms dic-0294 confirming assumption $(i)$: using dictionary of real passwords works better than natural language dictionaries. Moreover, the huge gap between $T$ and the other two confirms assumption $(ii)$: more frequent passwords are even better dictionaries, which means they are more likely to form the basis of other passwords in mangling attacks.

In this experiment, we used the length of dic-0294 to compare the different dictionaries. This gave a search space of about $5.6 \cdot 10^{10}$ passwords, which is the product between the number of dictionary words and the number of rules, since each rule generates one password variation. In the rest of the paper, similarly to [21] we fix the total number of guesses to about $10^{12}$. This provides a reasonable cracking time of 2–3 h on our hardware and allows for experimenting with big dictionaries and rule sets.

In the next experiment we have cut $\text{Train}_D$ so to reach about $10^{12}$ guesses. This new dictionary $T_{ext}$ extends $T$ with extra passwords so it reaches the same performance as $T$, as shown in Fig. 2b. In fact, even if the first part of the dictionaries are exactly the same, there are small variations in the curve due to the parallelism of hashcat that implies some non-determinism in the actual cracking process. Apart from this, the two curves basically overlap. The longer dictionary is able to crack 41.94% of $\text{Test}_D$ which resembles the results of [21] for the Webhost dataset, the only one not subject to password rules. Figure 8(b) in the paper seems to reach a success rate of about 40% which is very close to our result. We will use $T_{ext}$ with best64 and generated2 as our baseline for next experiments and results.

## 5   Training Masks

Mask attacks are brute force attacks on a reduced search space (cf. Sect. 2). Since masks reflect the charset pattern of a password they can be thought as a simple way to analyze how humans choose passwords. For example, when no password policies are in place, a very common pattern would be a sequence

**Algorithm 1.** Simulation of a mask based attack.

---
**for** $m, f \in M_{\text{Test}_{\mathcal{D}}}$ **do**
    $H_{\text{Test}_{\mathcal{D}}}[m] \leftarrow f$
**end for**
Sort $M_{\text{Train}_{\mathcal{D}}}$ by $|m|/f$
$M_L \leftarrow []$
**for** $m, f \in M_{\text{Train}_{\mathcal{D}}}$ **do**
    **if** $m \in H_{\text{Test}_{\mathcal{D}}}$ **then**
        $M_L.\text{append}((m, f, H_{\text{Test}_{\mathcal{D}}}[m]))$
    **else**
        $M_L.\text{append}((m, f, 0))$
    **end if**
**end for**
**for** $(m, f_{\text{Train}_{\mathcal{D}}}, f_{\text{Test}_{\mathcal{D}}}) \in M_L$ **do**
    Plot the cumulative values of $|m|$ and $f_{\text{Test}_{\mathcal{D}}}/|\text{Test}_{\mathcal{D}}|$
    Plot the cumulative values of $|m|$ and $f_{\text{Train}_{\mathcal{D}}}/|\text{Train}_{\mathcal{D}}|$, for reference
**end for**

---

of digits (i.e., a PIN) or a sequence of lowercase characters. With password policies we will have combination of charsets but some combinations might be more likely then others. Following this idea, the statsgen script included in the pack tool [5], computes statistics about a given set of passwords, by generating their masks and computing how effective these masks are in terms of password coverage. Interestingly, by limiting masks to disjoint charsets such as lowercase, uppercase, digits and symbols, noted in hashcat as ?l, ?u, ?d and ?s, each password will be mapped to a unique mask, providing a unique characterization of the password set. For example, if we have passwords: apple456, house123 and houseABC, they will be mapped to masks ?l?l?l?l?l?d?d?d with frequency 2, and ?l?l?l?l?l?u?u?u with frequency 1.

We investigated the use of statsgen to train and test masks without resorting to actual cracking tests. The idea is to compute the masks for $\text{Train}_{\mathcal{D}}$, sort them by efficiency, and simulate their application to $\text{Test}_{\mathcal{D}}$. This simulation can be done by computing the masks for $\text{Test}_{\mathcal{D}}$ and use them to derive the number of password guessed when running an attack based on the trained masks. We let $M_{\text{Train}_{\mathcal{D}}}$ and $M_{\text{Test}_{\mathcal{D}}}$ denote the sets of pairs $(m, f)$ computed respectively by $\text{Train}_{\mathcal{D}}$ and $\text{Test}_{\mathcal{D}}$ using statsgen. Pair $(m, f)$ represents mask $m$ covering exactly $f$ passwords from the originating set. Notice that, $M_{\text{Train}_{\mathcal{D}}}$ and $M_{\text{Test}_{\mathcal{D}}}$ are complete, i.e., they cover all the passwords in $\text{Train}_{\mathcal{D}}$ and $\text{Test}_{\mathcal{D}}$. We also let $|m|$ denote the overall guesses for a given mask $m$ which can be easily computed as the product of the charsets sizes, e.g., $|\text{?l?l?l?l?l?d?d?d}| = 26^5 \cdot 10^3$. Algorithm 1 simulates the attack. To make the computation efficient we use a hashmap $H_{\text{Test}_{\mathcal{D}}}$ to store the mapping between $\text{Test}_{\mathcal{D}}$ masks and their frequency (cf. first for loop). $M_{\text{Train}_{\mathcal{D}}}$ is sorted with respect to a *mask inefficiency* index $|m|/f$ representing the number of guesses per cracked password for a mask $m$, i.e., smaller values correspond to more efficient masks. Then, we build a list $M_L$ that includes tuples $(m, f_{\text{Train}_{\mathcal{D}}}, f_{\text{Test}_{\mathcal{D}}})$ for all $(m, f_{\text{Train}_{\mathcal{D}}}) \in M_{\text{Train}_{\mathcal{D}}}$, where

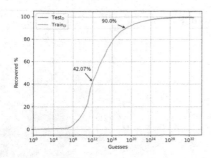
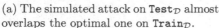
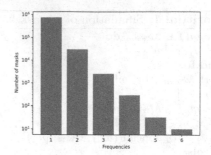

(a) The simulated attack on $\text{Test}_{\mathcal{D}}$ almost overlaps the optimal one on $\text{Train}_{\mathcal{D}}$.

(b) The masks in $M_{\text{Test}_{\mathcal{D}}}$ that are not covered by $M_{\text{Train}_{\mathcal{D}}}$ grouped by frequencies.

**Fig. 3.** Simulation of mask-based attack.

$f_{\text{Test}_{\mathcal{D}}}$ is the frequency of $m$ in $M_{\text{Test}_{\mathcal{D}}}$ which can be efficiently searched in $H_{\text{Test}_{\mathcal{D}}}$ (cf. second for loop). Notice, in particular, that when a $\text{Train}_{\mathcal{D}}$ mask is not found in the $\text{Test}_{\mathcal{D}}$ masks, $f_{\text{Test}_{\mathcal{D}}}$ is set to zero. The cumulative values $|m|$ and $f_{\text{Test}_{\mathcal{D}}}/|\text{Test}_{\mathcal{D}}|$, i.e., the guesses and the success rate, are plotted. We also plot the cumulative values $|m|$ and $f_{\text{Test}_{\mathcal{D}}}/|\text{Test}_{\mathcal{D}}|$ for comparison. Intuitively, this simulates how $M_{\text{Train}_{\mathcal{D}}}$ masks would perform on $\text{Test}_{\mathcal{D}}$ when used in an optimal way, i.e., sorted by their efficiency.

Apart from the clear performance advantage, as statsgen creates the masks starting from the target password set and does not require any brute forcing, this has allowed us to simulate how masks would perform with very high number of guesses, up to exhausting the search space, which would be unfeasible otherwise. The results of testing are impressively good: we could recover 99.44% of $\text{Test}_{\mathcal{D}}$ and the attack progression is almost identical to the trained one, as illustrated in Fig. 3a. We observe that the attack on $\text{Test}_{\mathcal{D}}$ overlaps the one on $\text{Train}_{\mathcal{D}}$, apart from the very end of the attack. Interestingly, 39.11% of the masks in $M_{\text{Test}_{\mathcal{D}}}$ are not covered by $M_{\text{Train}_{\mathcal{D}}}$ but the frequencies of these masks are very small. We report them in Fig. 3b: they only present frequencies in the interval 1 to 6 and 95.83% of these missing masks have frequency 1. Intuitively, although many test masks are not covered by the training ones, they are particularly inefficient, mostly breaking a single password and not affecting the outcome of the attack.

Comparing once more with Fig. 8(b) of [21] the curve we obtain is pretty similar to the ones in the paper. Interestingly, with $10^{12}$ guesses we achieve a success rate of 42.07% with is basically the same that we got with dictionaries and rules, i.e., 41.94% (cf. Fig. 2b). Thus, even with mask attacks we are close to the results of [21], for what concerns password crackers. Moreover, our attack seems slower at the beginning but faster in the second part reaching a success rate of 90% at about $0.8 \cdot 10^{19}$ guesses.

A variant of Algorithm 1 can be used to compute password guessability from $M_{\text{Train}_D}$, once it has been sorted by the mask inefficiency index introduced before. In fact, given a password it is enough to compute its (unique) mask and search it into the sorted list of rules, returning the cumulative value of |m| corresponding to the minimum number of guesses that are necessary before trying the mask that will break the password. We make our masks publicly available, together with the code for Algorithm 1 and an implementation of the password guessability script at [11]. From an ethical perspective, even if they are based on known passwords and capture all $\text{Train}_D$ and $\text{Test}_D$ sets, they do not leak the actual password values but just a distribution of their syntactic structure.

## 6    Training Rules

In Sect. 4, we have used two fixed rule sets best64 and generated2 with a part of $\text{Train}_D$ as dictionary. These two rule sets are part of the ones distributed with hashcat. There are many other rule sets available, some of which built from other existing rule sets through some selection mechanisms. After some sifting through many blogs on the subject and some preliminary experiments, we have placed our attention to two sets: OneRuleToRuleThemAll [3] and pantagrule [4]. They are both based on some form of training. In particular, OneRuleToRuleThemAll considers various existing rule sets, compares their performance, and then selects the best 25% performing rules for each set to create an optimized rule set. Rule performance is collected through a debugging functionality of hashcat that allows for collecting statistics about rule usage during cracking. The most used rules are the most performing ones. pantagrule is a rule set generated using a specific pack utility for automated rule generation [5] starting from datasets of real passwords. The rules were generated based on the number of occurrences, and then filtered using various test data sets, discarding the rules that were not used for cracking or taking the best performing ones. This has led to four quite big rule sets popular.rule, random.rule, hybrid.rule, one.rule.

First of all we have tested these rule sets to compare them with our baseline results of previous sections. Since the size of the rule sets is different, in the experiments we have cut $\text{Train}_D$ so to reach the target guesses of $10^{12}$, i.e., bigger rule sets have been tested with a smaller portion of $\text{Train}_D$. Results are reported in Fig. 4a. We notice that, OneRuleToRuleThemAll outperforms all the other rule sets with a success rate of 51.87%; then popular.rule and random.rule behave similarly and are slightly better than our baseline experiment with best64 and generated2; hybrid.rule, one.rule instead perform very closely to best64 and generated2. Interestingly, popular.rule and random.rule outperform OneRuleToRuleThemAll in the initial phase.

Our idea is to propose a general, repeatable method to train a rule set starting from existing ones. However, instead of producing a rule set that is supposed to be used as a whole, our aim is to sort rules based on their effectiveness, similarly to what we have done with masks, so that it is possible to select the most effective ones combined with a large enough dictionary. In other words, our

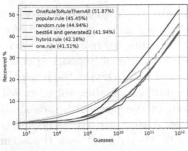
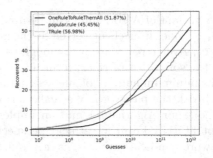
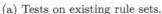

(a) Tests on existing rule sets.     (b) `TRule` outperforms other rule sets.

**Fig. 4.** Training a rule set from existing ones.

training amounts to sorting the rules so that they can be used more efficiently when only subsets are employed. Since we needed to start from a big enough set of rules, we decided to use all the rule sets provided in the `hashcat` distribution plus `OneRuleToRuleThemAll` and the best of `pantagrule`, i.e., `popular.rule`. Interestingly, `pantagrule` rule sets are pretty big so they constitute a good basis for our training. In summary, we started from about $779K$ unique rules.

In order to train rules we needed to actually test them on some passwords. So far, we have used $\text{Train}_D$ as a single dictionary but for mask-based attacks we need to split it in two parts, one part is used as a training dictionary and the other one as a training set of passwords. We randomly split $\text{Train}_D$ in two sets of about equal size that we call $\text{TrainDic}_D$ and $\text{TrainPwd}_D$, and we then run an attack up to $10^{12}$ guesses using a suitable portion of $\text{TrainDic}_D$ and our initial $779K$ unique rules. Using `hashcat` debugging output we collected the frequency of the rules and we sorted the rules by decreasing frequency. We call this rule set `TRule`. Since some of the rules form the initial set are not used the size is decreased to about $641K$ rules. In Fig. 4b we compare `TRule` with `OneRuleToRuleThemAll` and `popular.rule` on $\text{Test}_D$, using the same rule set size of 52014, i.e., the size of `OneRuleToRuleThemAll`, since it was the best performing ones. Recall that `TRule` is sorted by decreasing frequency so we take the most frequent 52014 rules for the experiment. We see that our trained rules outperform `OneRuleToRuleThemAll` by 5.11%. From the shape of the curve we observe that `TRule` got the best of `pantagrule` and `OneRuleToRuleThemAll` by starting as fast as `pantagrule` and by ending up as fast as `OneRuleToRuleThemAll`. In fact, by selecting the most frequent rules we actually take the best of the initial rule set.

We now have a dictionary $\text{Train}_D$ of passwords and a trained rule set `TRule` both sorted by descending frequency. We can thus cut them as necessary to perform tests. A natural question at this point is: what is the best tradeoff? Given a number of target guesses $G$, since rules generate one password variation, we have that the $G = D \cdot R$, where $D$ is the size of the dictionary and $R$ is the size of the rule set. Thus, for a given $G$ we can try different combinations of $D$ and $R$ in order to see how success rate changes. We started from the full `TRule`

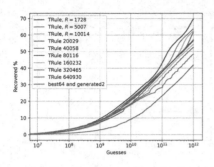 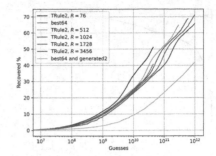

(a) Smaller $R$'s perform better.  (b) `TRule2` reaches 71.11% success rate.

**Fig. 5.** Analysis of rule and dictionary sizes.

rule set of length $R = 640930$ and we performed experiments with $G = 10^{12}$ and decreasing sizes for the rule set $R = \lfloor 640930/2^i \rfloor$ with $i \in [0,7]$, and increasing size for the dictionary $D = \lfloor G/R \rfloor$. Results are reported in Fig. 5a. We can see that the final success rate increases when $R$ decreases and, consequently, $D$ increases. So, in fact, there does not seem to exist a tradeoff, it is always convenient to take the full dictionary and compute $R = \lfloor G/D \rfloor$, which we did with $R = 1728$ achieving our best success rate so far, an impressive 69.67%

We could conclude that with bigger dictionaries (and smaller rule sets) the success rate would increase even more. However, we noticed that, by experimenting with smaller subsets of `TRule` the success rate was not as good as expected. For example, for $R = 76$ which is the actual size of `best64`, the success rate of `TRule` was smaller than `best64`. We decided to try a second round of training starting from the 3726 best rules of `TRule`, which was the biggest $R$ for `TrainDic`$_D$, and we actually improved a lot the results for smaller values of $R$. We call this new rule set `TRule2`. In Fig. 5b we report the results from some values of $R$. In particular, we can see that the result for 1728 improves the previous one getting the new best success rate of 71.11% and smaller values of $R$ show better curves, even if they stop before, due to the maximum size of $D$. In particular, we improve the performance of `best64` of about 10%. The intuitive explanation is that `hashcat` only outputs the first matching rule even if more then one rule would break a given password, so the initial order of rules matters.

Mask and rule based attacks are very different. A natural question is whether or not they complement each other increasing the success rate. Assuming, as usual, a target number of guesses $G$ we need to decide how to split it in favour of the two attacks. Given that we do not know in advance to which extent the two methods overlap in terms of search space (and so cracked passwords), the only chance that we have to maximize success is to maximize the overall cracked passwords. We have computed this tradeoff from training data and we found that if we split $G$ budget into 63.13% guesses for rule based attack and 36.87% guesses for mask attack we maximize the overall number of cracked passwords. We have tried this configuration but the result is clearly showing a huge overlap

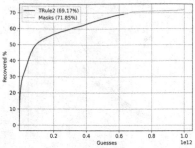
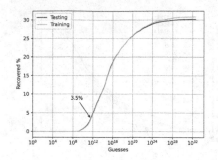

(a) A combined attack giving 71.85%.     (b) Masks trained on uncracked passwords give a 72.67% success rate.

**Fig. 6.** Combining rule based and mask based attacks.

in the search spaces, as reported in Fig. 6a (where we do not use a logarithmic scale to better show the split of the $G$ budget). In particular, we have run the two attacks in sequence increasing a bit the overall success rate to 71.85% but we can see from the figure that mask attack only contributes with a 2.68%.

We have tried to overcome this overlap between the two techniques by training one technique against the passwords that the other did not crack. To this aim, we have taken the passwords not cracked while training rule based attacks for TRule2, and we have used statsgen to create a new set of rules. Then, using Algorithm 1 we have simulated the attack using the same split of $G$ as above to see how effective these rules would possibly be on the passwords missed by TRule2. As shown in Fig. 6b, we obtain a 3.5% success rate in this case that produces the new best results of $69.17 + 3.5 = 72.67\%$. Even if we have slightly improved the previous result, this somehow confirms the poor potential of combined attacks due to overlaps. In the end, we only increase the success rate of 1.56% with respect to a pure rule based attack. Figure 6b also confirms that mask training works very well on tests, even for what concerns uncracked passwords.

## 7   Conclusion

We have done a systematic and in-depth analysis of various cracking strategies using the popular password recovery tool hashcat. Starting from off-the-shelf rules and a dictionary of popular real world passwords, we have investigated various training strategies. We have generated a set of masks covering the entire Train$_\mathcal{D}$ training set, sorted by efficiency, showing strikingly similar behaviour on Test$_\mathcal{D}$ (cf. Fig. 3a), which can be used to simulate an attack and to compute a password guessability value; interestingly, the success rate seems to be quite close to previous results (e.g. [21]). Then, we have trained a frequency-ordered rule set that surpasses previous strategies and we have performed a detailed analysis showing that it is convenient to use a large dictionary with few efficient rules. Following this idea, we have re-trained a smaller set of selected masks using a larger dictionary, further improving the success rate (cf. Fig. 5b). We have combined mask and rule-based attacks, trying to maximize the success rate and, even if we discovered an important overlap, we were able to slightly improve the success rate within the same guess budget. Finally, we have generated a set of masks starting from passwords that were not cracked during the training. This allowed us to achieve our best cracking rate of 72.67% which significantly outperforms the 41.94% success rate of the off-the-shelf configurations.

Our work is the first demonstrating that it is convenient to use a very large dictionary of leaked passwords with few efficient rules. As password leaks are more and more frequent, increasing the size of password dictionaries, we suspect that the success rate may further increase. We leave the verification of this claim as a future work. As discussed in Sect. 6, the initial order of rules matter in the training. This implies that training can be done iteratively, starting from sizes $R$, $D$ and a constant $c$, and then taking the best $R/c$ rules and running the training again with a dictionary of size $D \cdot c$, and so on. Another possibility would be to shuffle the initial set of rules and repeat the training in order to compute an average frequency value for each rule. We did not have time to experiment systematically these techniques and we leave their exploration as future work.

We make masks and rules available together with an implementation of Algorithm 1 and a script to compute password guessability [11]. For ethical and legal issues, we do not make plaintext passwords available.

# References

1. Hashcat. https://hashcat.net/hashcat/
2. John the Ripper. https://www.openwall.com/john/
3. One rule to rule them all. https://notsosecure.com/one-rule-to-rule-them-all
4. Pantagrule. https://github.com/rarecoil/pantagrule
5. Password analysis and cracking kit (PACK). https://github.com/iphelix/pack
6. Rockyou dataset. https://gitlab.com/kalilinux/packages/wordlists
7. Rockyou2021 dataset. https://github.com/ohmybahgosh/RockYou2021.txt
8. Brodkin, J.: 10 (or so) of the worst passwords exposed by the LinkedIn hack. Ars Technica, June 2012
9. de Carné de Carnavalet, X., Mannan, M.: From very weak to very strong: analyzing password-strength meters. In: 21st Annual Network and Distributed System Security Symposium, NDSS 2014. The Internet Society (2014)
10. Cubrilovic, N.: RockYou hack: from bad to worse. TechCrunch, December 2009
11. Di Campi, A.M., Focardi, R., Luccio, F.L.: Automated training of password cracking tools (repository). https://github.com/focardi/PasswordCrackingTraining
12. Duckett, C.: Login duplication allows 20M Alibaba accounts to be attacked. ZDNet, February 2016. https://www.zdnet.com/article/login-duplication-allows-20m-alibaba-accounts-to-be-attacked/
13. Hitaj, B., Gasti, P., Ateniese, G., Perez-Cruz, F.: PassGAN: a deep learning approach for password guessing. In: Deng, R.H., Gauthier-Umaña, V., Ochoa, M., Yung, M. (eds.) ACNS 2019. LNCS, vol. 11464, pp. 217–237. Springer, Cham (2019). https://doi.org/10.1007/978-3-030-21568-2_11

14. Hranický, R., Lištiak, F., Mikuš, D., Ryšavý, O.: On practical aspects of PCFG password cracking. In: Foley, S.N. (ed.) DBSec 2019. LNCS, vol. 11559, pp. 43–60. Springer, Cham (2019). https://doi.org/10.1007/978-3-030-22479-0_3
15. Hunt, T.: Pwned Passwords. https://haveibeenpwned.com/Passwords
16. Hunt, T.: Open source Pwned Passwords with FBI feed and 225M new NCA passwords is now live! December 2021. https://www.troyhunt.com/open-source-pwned-passwords-with-fbi-feed-and-225m-new-nca-passwords-is-now-live/
17. Kelley, P.G., et al.: Guess again (and again and again): measuring password strength by simulating password-cracking algorithms. In: 2012 IEEE Symposium on Security and Privacy, pp. 523–537 (2012)
18. Komanduri, S.: Modeling the adversary to evaluate password strength with limited samples, Ph.D. thesis, CMU-ISR (2016)
19. Liu, E., Nakanishi, A., Golla, M., Cash, D., Ur, B.: Reasoning analytically about password-cracking software. In: 2019 IEEE S&P Symposium, pp. 380–397 (2019)
20. Ma, J., Yang, W., Luo, M., Li, N.: A study of probabilistic password models. In: 2014 IEEE S&P Symposium, pp. 689–704 (2014)
21. Melicher, W., et al.: Fast, lean, and accurate: modeling password guessability using neural networks. In: 25th USENIX Security Symposium, pp. 175–191 (2016)
22. Meyer, B.: COMB: largest breach of all time leaked online with 3.2 billion records. Cybernews, February 2021
23. Mikalauskas, E.: RockYou2021: largest password compilation of all time leaked online with 8.4 billion entries. Cybernews, June 2021
24. Morris, R., Thompson, K.: Password security: a case history. Commun. ACM **22**(11), 594–597 (1979)
25. Narayanan, A., Shmatikov, V.: Fast dictionary attacks on passwords using time-space tradeoff. In: ACM CCS 2005, pp. 364–372 (2005)
26. NIST: Digital Identity Guidelines - Authentication and Lifecycle Management. Special Publication 800-63B (2017)
27. Pasquini, D., Cianfriglia, M., Ateniese, G., Bernaschi, M.: Reducing bias in modeling real-world password strength via deep learning and dynamic dictionaries. In: 30th USENIX Security Symposium, pp. 821–838, August 2021
28. Pasquini, D., Gangwal, A., Ateniese, G., Bernaschi, M., Conti, M.: Improving password guessing via representation learning. In: 42nd IEEE S&P Symposium, pp. 1382–1399 (2021)
29. Ur, B., et al.: Design and evaluation of a data-driven password meter. In: CHI Conference on Human Factors in Computing Systems, pp. 3775–3786. ACM (2017)
30. Ur, B., et al.: How does your password measure up? The effect of strength meters on password creation. In: 21th USENIX Security Symposium, pp. 65–80 (2012)
31. Ur, B., et al.: Measuring real-world accuracies and biases in modeling password guessability. In: 24th USENIX Security Symposium, pp. 463–481 (2015)
32. Weir, M., Aggarwal, S., de Medeiros, B., Glodek, B.: Password cracking using probabilistic context-free grammars. In: 30th IEEE S&P Symposium, pp. 391–405 (2009)

# Fuzzy Authenticated Key Exchange
# with Tight Security

Mingming Jiang[1,2], Shengli Liu[1,2,4]($\boxtimes$), Shuai Han[2,3], and Dawu Gu[1]

[1] Department of Computer Science and Engineering, Shanghai Jiao Tong University,
Shanghai 200240, China
{jiangmingming,slliu,dwgu}@sjtu.edu.cn
[2] State Key Laboratory of Cryptology, P.O. Box 5159, Beijing 100878, China
dalen17@sjtu.edu.cn
[3] School of Cyber Science and Engineering, Shanghai Jiao Tong University,
Shanghai 200240, China
[4] Westone Cryptologic Research Center, Beijing 100070, China

**Abstract.** Fuzzy authenticated key exchange (FAKE) enables two parties to agree on a shared key with the help of their fuzzy sources, like biometric features [3,9], physical unclonable functions (PUFs) [16], etc. In FAKE, each user will generate public strings from its own fuzzy source, and register public strings to the system. In the interactive protocol of FAKE, the user will again employ their own fuzzy sources to accomplish key agreement and achieve authenticity and privacy for the agreed session keys. The advantage of FAKE is that users do not have to store them in the devices, hence do not worry about key leakage due to bad key management in devices.

In this paper, We propose a generic construction of FAKE from three building blocks including secure sketch (SS), key encapsulation scheme (KEM) and a digital signature (SIG). We also define authenticity for users and pseudo-randomness for session keys to formalize the security of FAKE in the multi-user multi-challenge setting. We prove the security of our FAKE construction with tight security reductions to the building blocks in the random oracle model. Given the available choices for SS, tightly secure KEM and tightly secure SIG schemes, we obtain a bunch of FAKE schemes with tight security in the multi-user multi-challenge setting.

**Keywords:** Fuzzy authenticated key exchange · Random oracle · Tight security

## 1 Introduction

Authenticated Key Exchange (AKE) allows two parties to securely share a session key, which can be used for secure communication afterwards. A conventional AKE consists of three stages: system setup, user registration and protocol execution. In AKE, each user will generate its own long-term secret key and public key,

V. Atluri et al. (Eds.): ESORICS 2022, LNCS 13555, pp. 337–360, 2022.
https://doi.org/10.1007/978-3-031-17146-8_17

then register its long-term public key to the system. In the interactive protocol of AKE, users will make use of long-term secret key to implement key agreement and rely on secrecy of long-term keys to accomplish authenticity and security for AKE. Therefore, those long-term secret keys have to be stored locally by users, and the users must run good key management to avoid long-term key leakage. The recent AKE works [6,8,14,15] all need to store long-term secret key, thus have to handle the key storage issue. A natural question arises:

*Can we get rid of the storage of long-term secret key?*

To address this issue, we propose the concept of *Fuzzy Authenticated Key Exchange* (FAKE), where two users take advantage of fuzzy source to agree on a session key. By fuzzy sources, we mean those sources which have high-entropy and the samplings of the same source are very close (though not identical). There are many choices for fuzzy sources, like faces, fingerprint, palm-print, quantum bits, physical unclonable functions, etc. In the registration phase of FAKE, users sample from their fuzzy sources to generate some public information for registration. In the protocol execution, users sample again their fuzzy source so as to agree on a shared key. With FAKE only some public data is stored for each user. By this way, we resolve the issue of long-term secret key storage.

For the security proof, we adapt the strong security model of AKE from [8], where adversaries are allowed to modify, replay, replace, drop or inject arbitrary messages. Besides, adversaries can adaptively corrupt users' secret keys and/or reveal their session keys. Furthermore, they can adaptively reveal user's states between rounds. The security of FAKE is similar to that of AKE, and we consider passive and active attacks in multi-user setting. Besides, adversaries can also corrupt some users to obtain the samplings of their fuzzy sources and/or get some revealed session keys. The security requires that explicit authenticity of users and the pseudo-randomness of the session keys which are not revealed and the involved users are not corrupted. A stronger security for FAKE, similar to AKE is the support of state reveal. This allows the adversary to adaptively reveal round state of users, which has to be transmitted from a round to the next. That is, even the round state is obtained by the adversary, the corresponding session key remains pseudo-random, as long as the involved two users are not corrupted. Note that in FAKE, corrupting a user means obtaining some sampling of the user's fuzzy source.

For security proof, we seek tight security reduction to achieve tight security for FAKE for multiple challenge session keys in multi-user setting. Tight security provides strong security guarantees, as it enables theoretically-sound implementations without the need to compensate security loss, and allows universal key-length recommendations. For AKE, the most challenging work is to design tight AKE supporting state reveal and guarantee pseudorandomness of multi-challenge session keys. This is solved by [8], where the security of AKE is tightly reduced to the public-key primitive, but the reduction to a symmetric key encryption is still lossy. As for FAKE, a similar challenge is:

*How to design tightly secure FAKE supporting state reveal in multi-user multi-challenge setting?*

**Our Contribution.** In this paper, we resort to a Secure Sketch (SS), a signature (SIG) scheme and a Key Encapaulation Mechanism (KEM) to build an FAKE with tight security in the random oracle model. To achieve tight security, we characterize the security requirements for SS, SIG and KEM and prove the tight security of FAKE in the Random Oracle model. Our FAKE is the first AKE that is free of long-term key storage and achieves tight security. Meanwhile, our proposed FAKE is a black-box construction, thus different instantiations of the underlying building blocks admit a variety of specific FAKE schemes. In Table 1, we list some comparisons between existing AKE schemes and our FAKE scheme. Whether GGM is needed in our FAKE depends on the specific instantiations of the underlying building blocks.

**Related Works.** A related notion is biometric AKE (BAKE) proposed in [17]. In BAKE, secret keys are derived from biometric features. Compared to BAKE, our FAKE deals with any fuzzy source including biometric feature, quantum bits, or physical unclonable functions, etc. Therefore, our FAKE is more general than BAKE. We also note that the security of BAKE is weak in the sense that it only considers selective security (the target users are chosen beforehand) in a two-user and single challenge setting. Another related notion is fuzzy Password-based AKE [5], where two parties pre-share a similar (fuzzy) password and agree on a session key later if their passwords are close enough. We note that fuzzy password-based AKE considers a completely different scenario from our FAKE, and our FAKE does not require two parties to pre-share any secret information.

**Table 1.** Comparisons between known (F)AKE.

| Fuzzy? | Schemes | Model | Free of long term key storage | StateReveal | SessionKeyReveal | Corrupt | Multi Challenge | Tight | Authentication |
|---|---|---|---|---|---|---|---|---|---|
| Non | [14] | std | ✗ | ✗ | ✓ | ✓ | ✓ | ✓ | Explicit |
| | [8] | std | ✗ | ✓ | ✓ | ✓ | ✓ | ✓ (almost) | Explicit |
| | [15] | RO+GGM | ✗ | ✗ | ✓ | ✓ | ✓ | ✓ | Explicit |
| Fuzzy | [17] | RO | ✓ | ✓ | ✓ | ✓ | ✗ | ✗ | Implicit |
| | Ours | RO(+GGM) | ✓ | ✓ | ✓ | ✓ | ✓ | ✓ | Explicit |

## 2    Preliminary

Let $[n]$ denote $\{1, 2, \ldots, n\}$. For a set $\mathcal{X}$, let $x \leftarrow_\$ \mathcal{X}$ denote choosing an element $x$ from set $\mathcal{X}$ uniformly at random. If $X$ is a random variable (or a distribution), let $x \leftarrow X$ denote sampling $x$ according to the distribution of $X$. For two random variables $X$ and $Y$, let $H_\infty(X)$ denote the min-entropy of $X$, which is defined by $H_\infty(X) := -\log(\max_x \Pr[X = x])$ and the average conditional entropy is defined by $H_\infty(X|Y) := -\log(\mathbb{E}_{y \leftarrow Y}[2^{-H_\infty(X|Y=y)}])$. Let $\mathcal{M}$ be a metric space. For any $w_1, w_2 \in \mathcal{M}$, let $\mathsf{dis}(w_1, w_2)$ denote the distance between $w_1$ and $w_2$. Next we will introduce the concepts of secure sketch (SS), digital signature (SIG) and key encapsulation mechanism (KEM).

The concept of Secure Sketch (SS) was proposed by Dodis et al. [4]. Secure sketch allows recovery of a sampling $w$ from any distance-close fuzzy samplings from a fuzzy source.

**Definition 1 (Secure Sketch [4]).** *An $(\mathcal{M}, m, \tilde{m}, t)$-secure sketch SS for metric space $\mathcal{M}$ consists of a pair of PPT algorithms (SS.Gen, SS.Rec) with the following specifications:*

- SS.Gen(w): *on input $w \in \mathcal{M}$, the generation algorithm outputs a sketch $s \in \mathcal{S}$.*
- SS.Rec(w', s): *on input $w' \in \mathcal{M}$ and a sketch $s$, the recover algorithm outputs $\hat{w}$.*

*It also satisfies the following properties:*
    **Correctness.** *If $\mathsf{dis}(w, w') \leq t$, then it holds that $w = $ SS.Rec(w', SS.Gen(w)).*
    **Privacy.** *For any distribution $W$ over $\mathcal{M}$, if $H_\infty(W) \geq m$, then $H_\infty(W|\mathsf{SS.Gen}(W)) \geq \tilde{m}$.*

**Definition 2 (Digital signature).** *A signature (SIG) scheme SIG = (SIG.Setup, SIG.Gen, Sign, Ver) is defined by the following four algorithms.*

- SIG.Setup: *The setup algorithm outputs a public parameter $\mathsf{pp}_{\mathsf{SIG}}$, which defines message space $\mathcal{M}$, signature space $\Sigma$, verification key space $\mathcal{VK}$ and signing key space $\mathcal{SK}$.*
- SIG.Gen($\mathsf{pp}_{\mathsf{SIG}}$): *The key generation algorithm takes as input $\mathsf{pp}_{\mathsf{SIG}}$ and outputs a pair of keys $(vk, ssk) \in \mathcal{VK} \times \mathcal{SK}$. For canonical key generation algorithm, $ssk$ is uniformly chosen from $\mathcal{SK}$ and $vk$ is generated by verification generation algorithm VK.Gen($\cdot$), i.e., $vk \leftarrow \mathsf{VK.Gen}(\mathsf{pp}_{\mathsf{SIG}}; ssk)$.*
- Sign($ssk, m$): *Taking as input a signing key $ssk$ and a message $m \in \mathcal{M}$, the signing algorithm outputs a signature $\sigma \in \Sigma$.*
- Ver($vk, m, \sigma$): *Taking as input a verification key $vk$, a message $m$ and a signature $\sigma$, the deterministic verification algorithm outputs a bit indicating whether $\sigma$ is a valid signature or not.*

**Correctness.** *For all $\mathsf{pp}_{\mathsf{SIG}} \in $ SIG.Setup, $(vk, ssk) \in $ SIG.Gen($\mathsf{pp}_{\mathsf{SIG}}$) and $m \in \mathcal{M}$, it holds that Ver($vk, m, $ Sign($ssk, m$)) $= 1$.*

In this paper, we will consider canonical key generation algorithm for SIG.

Now we recall the security notion of unforgeability against chosen message attacks under user corruptions in multi-user settings (MU-EUF-CMA$^{\mathsf{corr}}$) for SIG.

**Definition 3 (MU-EUF-CMA$^{\mathsf{corr}}$ [2]).** *To a digital signature scheme SIG, the number of users $\mu \in \mathbb{N}$ and an adversary $\mathcal{A}$, we associate the advantage function $\mathsf{Adv}^{\mathsf{mu\text{-}corr}}_{\mathsf{SIG}, \mu}(\mathcal{A}) := \Pr[\mathsf{Exp}^{\mathsf{mu\text{-}corr}}_{\mathsf{SIG}, \mu, \mathcal{A}} \Rightarrow 1]$ where $\mathsf{Exp}^{\mathsf{mu\text{-}corr}}_{\mathsf{SIG}, \mu, \mathcal{A}}$ is defined in Fig. 1. SIG is MU-EUF-CMA$^{\mathsf{corr}}$ secure if $\mathsf{Adv}^{\mathsf{mu\text{-}corr}}_{\mathsf{SIG}, \mu}(\mathcal{A}) \leq \mathsf{negl}(\lambda)$ for all $\mu = \mathsf{poly}(\lambda)$ and all PPT $\mathcal{A}$.*

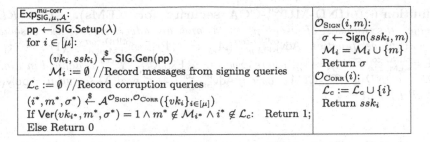

**Fig. 1.** The $\mathsf{Exp}^{\mathsf{mu\text{-}corr}}_{\mathsf{SIG},\mu,\mathcal{A}}$ security experiment for SIG.

**Definition 4 (KEM).** *A key encapsulation mechanism (KEM)* KEM = (KEM. Setup, KEM.Gen, Encap, Decap) *consists of four algorithms:*

- KEM.Setup: *The setup algorithm outputs public parameters* $\mathsf{pp}_{\mathsf{KEM}}$, *which determines encapsulation key space $\mathcal{K}$, public key space $\mathcal{PK}$, secret key space $\mathcal{SK}$, and ciphertext space $\mathcal{CT}$.*
- KEM.Gen($\mathsf{pp}_{\mathsf{KEM}}$): *Taking $\mathsf{pp}_{\mathsf{KEM}}$ as input, it outputs a pair of public key and secret key $(pk, sk) \in \mathcal{PK} \times \mathcal{SK}$. For canonical key generation algorithm, $sk$ is uniformly chosen from $\mathcal{SK}$ and $pk$ is generated by a public-key generation algorithm $\mathsf{PK.Gen}(\cdot)$, i.e., $pk \leftarrow \mathsf{PK.Gen}(\mathsf{pp}_{\mathsf{KEM}}; sk)$.*
- Encap($pk$): *Taking $pk$ as input, it outputs a ciphertext $c \in \mathcal{CT}$ and an encapsulated key $K \in \mathcal{K}$.*
- Decap($sk, c$): *Taking as input $sk$ and $c$, it outputs $K \in \mathcal{K} \cup \{\perp\}$.*

For all $\mathsf{pp}_{\mathsf{KEM}} \in \mathsf{KEM.Setup}$, $sk \in \mathcal{SK}$, $pk \in \mathsf{PK.Gen}(sk)$, $(c, K) \in \mathsf{Encap}(pk)$, it holds that $\mathsf{Decap}(sk, c) = K$. We consider canonical key generation algorithm for KEM in this paper.

**Definition 5 ($\gamma$-diversity of KEM).** *A KEM scheme* KEM *has $\gamma$-diversity if*

$$\Pr\left[ {(pk, sk) \leftarrow \mathsf{KEM.Gen}(\mathsf{pp}_{\mathsf{KEM}}); \atop r, r' \leftarrow_\$ \mathcal{R}; (c, K) \leftarrow \mathsf{Encap}(pk, r); (c', K') \leftarrow \mathsf{Encap}(pk, r')} : K = K' \right] \leq 2^{-\gamma},$$

$$\Pr\left[ {(pk, sk) \leftarrow \mathsf{KEM.Gen}(\mathsf{pp}_{\mathsf{KEM}}); (pk', sk') \leftarrow \mathsf{KEM.Gen}(\mathsf{pp}_{\mathsf{KEM}}) \atop r \leftarrow_\$ \mathcal{R}; (c, K) \leftarrow \mathsf{Encap}(pk, r); (c', K') \leftarrow \mathsf{Encap}(pk', r)} : K = K' \right] \leq 2^{-\gamma}$$

*hold for all* $\mathsf{pp}_{\mathsf{KEM}} \in \mathsf{KEM.Setup}$, *where $\mathcal{R}$ is the randomness space of* Encap.

Now we introduce one-time CCA security for KEMs under user corruptions in multi-user multi-challenge settings, which is named by otIND-MU$^{\mathsf{corr}}$-CCA security. It requires that the adversary asks ENCAP, DECAP, TEST oracles only once per user.

**Definition 6 (otIND-MU$^{\text{corr}}$-CCA security for KEMs).** *To a KEM scheme, the number of users $\mu \in \mathbb{N}$ and an adversary $\mathcal{A}$, we associate the advantage function* $\text{Adv}_{\text{KEM},\mu}^{\text{otIND-corr}}(\mathcal{A}) := |\Pr[\text{Exp}_{\text{KEM},\mu,\mathcal{A}}^{\text{otIND-corr-cca}}(1) \Rightarrow 1] - \Pr[\text{Exp}_{\text{KEM},\mu,\mathcal{A}}^{\text{otIND-corr-cca}}(0) \Rightarrow 1]|$, *where experiment* $\text{Exp}_{\text{KEM},\mu,\mathcal{A}}^{\text{otIND-corr-cca}}$ *is defined in Fig. 2. KEM is otIND-MU$^{\text{corr}}$-CCA secure if* $\text{Adv}_{\text{SIG},\mu}^{\text{mu-corr}}(\mathcal{A}) \leq \text{negl}(\lambda)$ *for all $\mu = \text{poly}(\lambda)$ and all PPT $\mathcal{A}$.*

---

$\text{Exp}_{\text{KEM},\mu,\mathcal{A}}^{\text{otIND-corr-cca}}(\theta), \theta \in \{0,1\}$:

  $\text{pp}_{\text{KEM}} \leftarrow \text{KEM.Setup}$
  For $i \in [\mu]$: $(pk_i, sk_i) \leftarrow \text{KEM.Gen}(\text{pp}_{\text{KEM}})$
  $\mathcal{L}_e = \emptyset, \mathcal{L}_c = \emptyset, \mathcal{L}_t = \emptyset, \mathcal{L}_d = \emptyset$
  $\theta' \leftarrow \mathcal{A}^{\text{Corr}(\cdot),\text{Test}(\cdot,\cdot),\text{Encap}(\cdot),\text{Decap}(\cdot,\cdot)}(pk_1, \ldots, pk_\mu)$
  Return $\theta'$

$\text{Corr}(i)$
  If $i \notin [\mu]$: Return $\perp$
  If $(i, \cdot) \in \mathcal{L}_t$: Return $\perp$
  $\mathcal{L}_c := \mathcal{L}_c \cup \{i\}$
  Return $sk_i$.

$\text{Test}(i,c)$
  If $\nexists(i, c, \cdot) \in \mathcal{L}_e$: Return $\perp$.
  If $(i \in \mathcal{L}_c) \vee ((i, c) \in \mathcal{L}_d)$ : Return $\perp$    //Avoid trivial attack
  $K_1 \leftarrow_\$ K$
  Retrieve $(i, c, K)$ from $\mathcal{L}_e$ and set $K_0 := K$
  $\mathcal{L}_t := \mathcal{L}_t \cup \{(i, c)\}$
  Return $K_\theta$

$\text{Encap}(i)$://at most one time for each $i$
  If $i \notin [\mu]$: Return $\perp$
  If $\exists(i, \cdot, \cdot) \in \mathcal{L}_e$:
    Return $\perp$
  $(c, K) \leftarrow \text{Encap}(pk_i)$
  $\mathcal{L}_e = \mathcal{L}_e \cup \{(i, c, K)\}$
  Return $c$

$\text{Decap}(i,c)$//at most one time for each $i$
  If $i \notin [\mu]$: return $\perp$.
  If $(i, c) \in \mathcal{L}_t$: Return $\perp$    //Avoid trivial attack
  $K/\perp := \text{Decap}(sk_i, c)$;
  If $(i, c, \cdot) \in \mathcal{L}_e$:
    $\mathcal{L}_d := \mathcal{L}_d \cup \{(i, c)\}$
  Return $K/\perp$

---

**Fig. 2.** The one-time $\text{Exp}_{\text{KEM},\mu,\mathcal{A}}^{\text{otIND-corr-cca}}(\theta), \theta \in \{0, 1\}$ security game of KEM.

# 3  Fuzzy Authenticated Key Exchange

Now we show the syntax of FAKE in Subsect. 3.1 and present the security notion for FAKE in Subsect. 3.2. We stress that users utilize fuzzy sources rather than long-term secret key in FAKE.

## 3.1  Definition of Fuzzy Authenticated Key Exchange

Fuzzy Authenticated Key Exchange (FAKE) makes use of users' fuzzy sources to accomplish session key agreement and provide security for FAKE. Below is the formal definition for FAKE.

**Definition 7 (Fuzzy Authenticated Key Exchange).** *A fuzzy authenticated key exchange (FAKE) scheme* FAKE = (FAKE.Setup, FAKE.Gen, FAKE.Protocol) *consists of two probabilistic algorithms and an interactive protocol.*

- FAKE.Setup: *The setup algorithm outputs public parameter* $\text{pp}_{\text{FAKE}}$.
- FAKE.Gen($\text{pp}_{\text{FAKE}}, W_i$): *The generation algorithm computes user-related information with the user's fuzzy source. It takes as input* $\text{pp}_{\text{FAKE}}$ *and a user's fuzzy source $W_i$, and outputs a local string* $\text{local}_i$ *and a public helper string* $\text{pub}_i$.

- FAKE.Protocol($U_i(\text{res}_i) \leftrightarrow U_j(\text{res}_j)$): *The protocol involves two users $U_i$ and $U_j$, who have access to their own resources,* $\text{res}_i := (W_i, \text{local}_i, \{\text{pub}_u\}_{u \in [\mu]}, \text{pp}_{\text{FAKE}})$ *and* $\text{res}_j := (W_j, \text{local}_j, \{\text{pub}_u\}_{u \in [\mu]}, \text{pp}_{\text{FAKE}})$ *respectively. Here $\mu$ is the total number of registered users in the system. After execution, user $U_i$ outputs a flag $\Psi_i \in \{\emptyset, \textbf{accept}, \textbf{reject}\}$ and a session key $k_i$ ($k_i$ might be the empty string $\emptyset$). Similarly, user $U_j$ outputs $\Psi_j, k_j$ respectively.*

**Correctness of FAKE.** For any distinct users $U_i$ and $U_j$, after the execution of FAKE.Protocol $(U_i(\text{res}_i) \leftrightarrow U_j(\text{res}_j))$, they will share the same session key, i.e., $\Psi_i = \Psi_j = \textbf{accept}$ and $k_i = k_j \neq \emptyset$.

## 3.2   Security Model of FAKE

Like the security model of AKE [8], the following attacks are considered in FAKE: user corruptions which allow the adversary to obtain samplings of some users' fuzzy sources; session key reveal which allows the adversary to obtain the session keys of the protocol instances; state reveal which allows the user to obtain the state of a user transmitted between rounds in an instance of FAKE; active attacks which allow the adversary to impersonate users to send messages to other users. The security of FAKE asks the pseudorandomness of multi-challenge session keys under the adversary's attacks, but trivial attacks must be excluded. For instances, the target session keys must not be revealed and the involved users in the target sessions must not be corrupted by the adversary.

We adapt the security model of AKE to FAKE. We also consider pseudorandomness of the target session keys under user corruptions, session key reveal, and state reveal in the multi-user multi-instance settings. The security model is formalized by oracles and $\mathcal{A}$'s queries to oracles.

**Oracles and $\mathcal{A}$'s Queries in the Security Model.** Suppose there are at most $\mu$ users $U_1, U_2, \ldots, U_\mu$ in the system, and each user will involve at most $\ell$ instances. For $i \in \{1, 2, \ldots, \mu\}$, $U_i$'s involvement in a protocol instance is formalized by a series of oracles, $\pi_i^1, \pi_i^2, \ldots, \pi_i^\ell$.

- Oracle $\pi_i^s$ formalizes user $U_i$'s execution of the $s$-th protocol instance.

Each oracle $\pi_i^s$ has access to $U_i$'s resources $\text{res}_i := (W_i, \text{local}_i, \{\text{pub}_u\}_{u \in [\mu]}, \text{pp}_{\text{FAKE}})$ and also has its own variables $\text{var}_i^s := (\text{st}_i^s, \text{Pid}_i^s, k_i^s, \Psi_i^s)$ with initial values $(\emptyset, \emptyset, \emptyset, \emptyset)$.

- $\text{st}_i^s$: State information that has to be stored and transmitted to the next round by $\pi_i^s$ in the execution of one protocol instance.
- $\text{Pid}_i^s$: The intended communication peer's identity.
- $k_i^s \in \mathcal{K}$: The session key computed by $\pi_i^s$. Here $\mathcal{K}$ is the session key space. Assume that $\emptyset \in \mathcal{K}$.
- $\Psi_i^s \in \{\emptyset, \textbf{accept}, \textbf{reject}\}$: $\Psi_i^s$ indicates whether $\pi_i^s$ has completed the protocol and accepted $k_i^s$.

Formally, $\mathcal{A}$ has access to the following oracles via queries.

- $\mathsf{Send}(i, s, j, \mathsf{msg})$. It formalizes active/passive attacks by $\mathcal{A}$. If $\mathsf{msg} = \top$, it means that $\mathcal{A}$ asks oracle $\pi_i^s$ to send the first protocol message to $U_j$. Otherwise, $\mathcal{A}$ impersonates $U_j$ to send message $\mathsf{msg}$ to $\pi_i^s$. Then just like $U_i$ does, $\pi_i^s$ executes the FAKE protocol with $\mathsf{msg}$, outputs message $\mathsf{msg}'$, and updates its own variables $\mathsf{var}_i^s = (\mathsf{st}_i^s, \mathsf{Pid}_i^s, k_i^s, \Psi_i^s)$. The output message $\mathsf{msg}'$ is returned to $\mathcal{A}$. If $\mathsf{Send}(i, s, j, \mathsf{msg})$ is the $\tau$-th query asked by $\mathcal{A}$ and $\pi_i^s$ changes $\Psi_i^s$ to **accept** after that, then we say that $\pi_i^s$ is $\tau$-accepted.
- $\mathsf{Corrupt}(i)$. It formalizes user corruptions by $\mathcal{A}$. Upon query $i$, the challenger $\mathcal{C}$ will send some sampling $w_i$ of $U_i$'s fuzzy source $W_i$. After corruption, $\pi_i^1, \ldots, \pi_i^\ell$ will stop answering any query from $\mathcal{A}$. If $\mathsf{Corrupt}(i)$ is the $\tau$-th query

```
Exp_{FAKE,μ,ℓ,A}
pp_FAKE ← FAKE.Setup
For i ∈ [μ]:
   (pub_i, local_i) ← FAKE.Gen(pp_FAKE, W_i);
   crp_i := false //source Corruption variable
VKList := {pub_i}_{i∈[μ]}
PublicData := {local_i}_{i∈[μ]}
b ←$ {0,1}
For (i, s) ∈ [μ] × [ℓ] :
   var_i^s := (st_i^s, Pid_i^s, k_i^s, Ψ_i^s) := (∅, ∅, ∅, ∅)
   Aflag_i^s := false //Whether Pid_i^s is corrupted when π_i^s accepts
   T_i^s := false; kRev_i^s = false // Test, Key Reveal variables
   stRev_i^s := false, FirstAcc_i^s := ∅
   //State Reveal & First Acceptance variables
b* ← A^{O_FAKE(·)}(pp_FAKE, VKList, PublicData)

Win_Auth := false
Win_Auth := true, If ∃(i, s) ∈ [μ] × [ℓ] s.t.
(1) Ψ_i^s = accept
(2) Aflag_i^s = false
(3) (3.1) ∨ (3.2) ∨ (3.3). Let j := Pid_i^s
   (3.1) ∄t ∈ [ℓ] s.t. Partner(π_i^s ← π_j^t)
   (3.2) ∃t ∈ [ℓ], (j', t') ∈ [μ] × [ℓ] with (j, t) ≠ (j', t') s.t.
         Partner(π_i^s ← π_j^t) ∧ Partner(π_i^s ← π_{j'}^{t'})
   (3.3) ∃t ∈ [ℓ], (i', s') ∈ [μ] × [ℓ] with (i, s) ≠ (i', s') s.t.
         Partner(π_i^s ← π_j^t) ∧ Partner(π_{i'}^{s'} ← π_j^t) //Replay attacks

Win_Ind := false
If b* = b :
   Win_Ind := true; Return 1
Else: Return 0

Partner(π_i^s ← π_j^t) :      //Checking whether Partner(π_i^s ← π_j^t)
If π_i^s sent the first message and k_i^s = K(π_i^s, π_j^t) ≠ ∅ : Return 1
If π_i^s received the first message and k_i^s = K(π_j^t, π_i^s) ≠ ∅ : Return 1
Return 0

O_FAKE(query) :
If query = Test(i, s) :
   If (i, s) ∉ [μ] × [ℓ], Return ⊥
   If Ψ_i^s ≠ accept ∨ Aflag_i^s = true ∨ kRev_i^s = true
    ∨T_i^s = true : Return ⊥ // avoid TA1, TA2, TA3
   If FirstAcc_i^s = false :
      If crp_i = true ∧ stRev_i^s = true :
         Return ⊥ // avoid TA6
   Let j := Pid_i^s
   If ∃t ∈ [ℓ] s.t. Partner(π_i^s ⇔ π_j^t) :
      If kRev_j^t = true ∨ T_j^t = true :
         Return ⊥ // avoid TA4, TA5
   If ∃t ∈ [ℓ] s.t. Partner(π_i^s ← π_j^t) :
      If FirstAcc_j^t = false ∧ crp_j = true
         ∧stRev_j^t = true : Return ⊥ // avoid TA7
   T_i^s := true; k_0 := k_i^s; k_1 ←$ K; Return k_b

π_i^s(msg, j) :
//π_i^s executes FAKE according to the protocol specification
If Pid_i^s = ∅ : Pid_i^s := j
If Pid_i^s = j:
   π_i^s receives msg and uses res_i, var_i^s to generate the next
   message msg' of FAKE, and updates (st_i^s, Pid_i^s, k_i^s, Ψ_i^s);
   If msg = ⊤ : π_i^s generates the first message msg' as initiator;
   If msg is the last message of FAKE : msg' := ∅;
   Return msg' If Pid_i^s ≠ j : Return ⊥

O_FAKE(query) :
If query = Send(i, s, j, msg) :
   If (i, s) ∉ [μ] × [ℓ], Return ⊥
   If Ψ_i^s = accept : Return ⊥
   //msg' ← π_i^s(msg, j)
   If Ψ_i^s = accept :
      If crp_j = true: Aflag_i^s := true;
      // Determine whether π_i^s accepts before its partner
      If crp_j = false ∧ ∃t ∈ [ℓ] s.t. Partner(π_i^s ← π_j^t):
         If Ψ_j^t ≠ accept:
            FirstAcc_i^s := true; FirstAcc_j^t := false
         If Ψ_j^t = accept:
            FirstAcc_i^s := false; FirstAcc_j^t := true
   Return msg'

If query = Corrupt(i) :
   If i ∉ [μ], Return ⊥
   For s ∈ [ℓ]:
      If FirstAcc_i^s = false ∧ stRev_i^s = true :
         If T_i^s = true : Return ⊥ //avoid TA6
         If ∃t ∈ [ℓ] s.t. Partner(π_j^t ← π_i^s) :
            If T_j^t = true : Return ⊥; //avoid TA7
   crp_i := true ; Return W_i

If query = SessionKeyReveal(i, s) :
   If (i, s) ∉ [μ] × [ℓ], Return ⊥
   If Ψ_i^s ≠ accept : Return ⊥
   If T_i^s = true : Return ⊥ // avoid TA2
   Let j := Pid_i^s
   If ∃t ∈ [ℓ] s.t. Partner(π_i^s ⇔ π_j^t) :
      If T_j^t = true : Return ⊥ // avoid TA4
   kRev_i^s := true; Return k_i^s

If query = StateReveal(i, s) :
   If (i, s) ∉ [μ] × [ℓ], Return ⊥
   If FirstAcc_i^s = false ∧ crp_i = true :
      If T_i^s = true : Return ⊥; // avoid TA6
      Let j := Pid_i^s
      If ∃t ∈ [ℓ] s.t. Partner(π_j^t ← π_i^s) :
         If T_j^t = true : Return ⊥ // avoid TA7
   stRev_i^s := true; Return st_i^s
```

**Fig. 3.** The security experiment $\mathsf{Exp}_{\mathsf{FAKE},\mu,\ell,\mathcal{A}}$ for FAKE.

asked by $\mathcal{A}$, we say that $U_i$ is $\tau$-corrupted. If $\mathcal{A}$ has never asked $\mathsf{Corrupt}(i)$, we say that $U_i$ is $\infty$-corrupted.

- $\mathsf{StateReveal}(i, s)$. It formalizes state reveals by $\mathcal{A}$. Upon query $(i, s)$, $\mathcal{C}$ will reply state $\mathsf{st}_i^s$ to $\mathcal{A}$, where $\mathsf{st}_i^s$ is the round state transmitted to the next round during the session execution.
- $\mathsf{SessionKeyReveal}(i, s)$. It formalizes session key reveals query from $\mathcal{A}$, where $\mathcal{A}$ asks $\mathcal{C}$ to reveal $\pi_i^s$'s session key. If $\Psi_i^s \neq \mathbf{accept}$, $\mathcal{C}$ reveals $\perp$. Otherwise, $\mathcal{C}$ replies the session key $k_i^s$ to $\mathcal{A}$.
- $\mathsf{Test}(i, s)$. Via Test queries $(i, s)$, $\mathcal{A}$ designates target sessions for test (challenges). If $\Psi_i^s \neq \mathbf{accept}$, $\mathcal{C}$ returns $\perp$. Otherwise, $\mathcal{C}$ sets $k_0 = k_i^s$, samples $k_1 \leftarrow_\$ \mathcal{K}$, and returns $k_b$ to $\mathcal{A}$. Here $b$ is the random coin chosen by $\mathcal{C}$ and will be fixed once chosen. We require that $\mathcal{A}$ can ask $\mathsf{Test}(i, s)$ to each oracle $\pi_i^s$ only once.

For target sessions, the pseudorandomness of $k_i^s$ requires the hardness for $\mathcal{A}$ to tell whether $k_b$ is the real session key $k_i^s$ or the a truly random element. To precisely characterize pseudorandomness of $k_i^s$, trivial attacks must be identified and forbidden.

**Trivial Attacks** To define trivial attacks, we introduce the concepts of original key and partner.

**Definition 8 (Original Key [13]).** *For two oracles $\pi_i^s$ and $\pi_j^t$, the original key, denoted as $\mathsf{K}(\pi_i^s, \pi_j^t)$ is the session key computed by the two peers of the protocol under a passive adversary only, where $\pi_i^s$ is the initiator.*

*We note that $\mathsf{K}$ is determined by the identities of $U_i$ and $U_j$ and the internal randomness.*

**Definition 9 (Partner [13]).** *Let $\mathsf{K}(\cdot, \cdot)$ denote the original key function. We say that an oracle $\pi_i^s$ is partnered to $\pi_j^t$, denoted as $\mathsf{Partner}(\pi_i^s \leftarrow \pi_j^t)$, if either $\pi_i^s$ has sent the first message and $k_i^s = \mathsf{K}(\pi_i^s, \pi_j^t) \neq \emptyset$, or $\pi_i^s$ has received the first message and $k_i^s = \mathsf{K}(\pi_j^t, \pi_i^s) \neq \emptyset$.*

We write $\mathsf{Partner}(\pi_i^s \leftrightarrow \pi_j^t)$ if $\mathsf{Partner}(\pi_i^s \leftarrow \pi_j^t)$ and $\mathsf{Partner}(\pi_j^t \leftarrow \pi_i^s)$.

To clearly describe trivial attacks, we define the following variables for each user $U_i$ and oracle $\pi_i^s$. $crp_i$: whether $U_i$'s source $W_i$ is corrupted; $\mathsf{Aflag}_i^s$: whether the intended partner is corrupted when $\pi_i^s$ accepts; $T_i^s$: whether $\pi_i^s$ is tested; $kRev_i^s$: whether the session key $k_i^s$ is revealed; $stRev_i^s$: whether the session state $\mathsf{st}_i^s$ is revealed; $FirstAcc_i^s$: whether $U_i$ is the first to accept the key in the session.

Now trivial attacks are listed in Table 2 with descriptions shown in the rightmost column.

**Table 2.** Trivial Attacks **TA1**-**TA7** for security experiments $\mathsf{Exp}_{\mathsf{FAKE},\mu,\ell,\mathcal{A}}$. Note that "Aflag$_i^s$ = **false**" is implicitly contained in **TA2**-**TA7** because of **TA1**.

| Types | Trivial attacks | Explanation |
|---|---|---|
| **TA1** | $T_i^s = \textbf{true} \wedge \text{Aflag}_i^s = \textbf{true}$ | $\pi_i^s$ is tested but $\pi_i^s$'s partner is corrupted when $\pi_i^s$ accepts session key $k_i^s$ |
| **TA2** | $T_i^s = \textbf{true} \wedge kRev_i^s = \textbf{true}$ | $\pi_i^s$ is tested and its session key $k_i^s$ is revealed |
| **TA3** | $T_i^s = \textbf{true}$ when $\mathsf{Test}(i,s)$ is queried | $\mathsf{Test}(i,s)$ is queried at least twice |
| **TA4** | $T_i^s = \textbf{true} \wedge \mathrm{Partner}(\pi_i^s \leftrightarrow \pi_j^t) \wedge kRev_j^t = \textbf{true}$ | $\pi_i^s$ is tested, $\pi_j^t$ and $\pi_i^s$ are partnered to each other, and $\pi_j^t$'s session key is revealed |
| **TA5** | $T_i^s = \textbf{true} \wedge \mathrm{Partner}(\pi_i^s \leftrightarrow \pi_j^t) \wedge T_j^t = \textbf{true}$ | $\pi_i^s$ is tested, $\pi_j^t$ and $\pi_i^s$ are partnered to each other, and $\pi_j^t$ is tested |
| **TA6** | $T_i^s = \textbf{true} \wedge FirstAcc_i^s = \textbf{false}$ $\wedge stRev_i^s = \textbf{true} \wedge crp_i = \textbf{true}$ | $\pi_i^s$ is tested, $\pi_i^s$ accepts its key after its partner, and $\pi_i^s$ is both corrupted and has its state st$_i^s$ revealed |
| **TA7** | $T_i^s = \textbf{true} \wedge \mathrm{Partner}(\pi_i^s \leftrightarrow \pi_j^t)$ $\wedge FirstAcc_j^t = \textbf{false} \wedge stRev_j^t = \textbf{true} \wedge crp_j = \textbf{true}$ | $\pi_i^s$ is tested, $\pi_i^s$ accepts its session key before its partner, but its partner $\pi_j^t$ is both corrupted and state revealed. |

**Security Definition of FAKE.** With the definitions of oracles and trivial attacks, we are ready to give a formal definition for the security of FAKE. The security experiment $\mathsf{Exp}_{\mathsf{FAKE},\mu,\ell,\mathcal{A}}$ played between challenger $\mathcal{C}$ and adversary $\mathcal{A}$ is also presented in Fig. 3.

**Definition 10 (Security of FAKE).** *Let $\mu$ be the number of users and $\ell$ be the maximum number of protocol executions per user. The security experiment $\mathsf{Exp}_{\mathsf{FAKE},\mu,\ell,\mathcal{A}}$ played between challenger $\mathcal{C}$ and adversary $\mathcal{A}$ is described as follows (see also Fig. 3).*

1. *$\mathcal{C}$ invokes $\mathsf{FAKE.Setup}$ to get the public parameter $\mathsf{pp}_{\mathsf{FAKE}}$.*
2. *For each user $U_i$, $\mathcal{C}$ invokes $\mathsf{FAKE.Gen}(\mathsf{pp}_{\mathsf{FAKE}}, W_i)$ to get the public helper string $\mathsf{pub}_i$ and local string $\mathsf{local}_i$. Next $\mathcal{C}$ provides $\mathcal{A}$ with $\mathsf{pp}_{\mathsf{FAKE}}$, local data $\{\mathsf{local}_i\}_{i\in[\mu]}$ and public data $\{\mathsf{pub}_i\}_{i\in[\mu]}$.*
3. *$\mathcal{C}$ chooses a random bit $b \leftarrow_{\$} \{0,1\}$,*
4. *$\mathcal{A}$ adaptively issues queries to oracles $\mathsf{Send}$, $\mathsf{Corrupt}$, $\mathsf{SessionKeyReveal}$, $\mathsf{StateReveal}$ and $\mathsf{Test}$.*
5. *$\mathcal{A}$ terminates with an output $b^*$.*

- ***Strong Authentication.*** *Let $\mathsf{Win}_{\mathsf{Auth}}$ denote the event that $\mathcal{A}$ breaks authentication in the security experiment. $\mathsf{Win}_{\mathsf{Auth}}$ happens iff $\exists (i,s) \in [\mu] \times [\ell]$ s.t.*
  (1) *$\pi_i^s$ is $\tau$-accepted.*
  (2) *$U_j$ is $\hat{\tau}$-corrupted with $j := \mathsf{Pid}_i^s$ and $\hat{\tau} > \tau$.*
  (3) *Either (3.1) or (3.2) or (3.3) happens. Let $j := \mathsf{Pid}_i^s$.*
    (3.1) *There is no oracle $\pi_j^t$ that $\pi_i^s$ is partnered to.*
    (3.2) *There exist two distinct oracles $\pi_j^t$ and $\pi_{j'}^{t'}$, to which $\pi_i^s$ is partnered.*
    (3.3) *There exists two oracles $\pi_{i'}^{s'}$ and $\pi_j^t$ with $(i,s) \neq (i',s')$, such that both $\pi_i^s$ and $\pi_{i'}^{s'}$ are partnered to $\pi_j^t$.*
- ***Indistinguishability.*** *At the end of experiment $\mathsf{Exp}_{\mathsf{FAKE},\mu,\ell,\mathcal{A}}$, $\mathcal{A}$ outputs a bit $b^*$. If $b^* = b$, experiment $\mathsf{Exp}_{\mathsf{FAKE},\mu,\ell,\mathcal{A}}$ outputs 1; otherwise $\mathsf{Exp}_{\mathsf{FAKE},\mu,\ell,\mathcal{A}}$ outputs 0.*

*The security of FAKE requires that for all $\mu = \mathsf{poly}(\lambda)$, $\ell = \mathsf{poly}(\lambda)$, all PPT $\mathcal{A}$, the advantage function of $\mathcal{A}$ satisfies*

$$\mathsf{Adv}_{\mathsf{FAKE},\mu,\ell}(\mathcal{A}) := \max \left\{ \Pr[\mathsf{Win}_{\mathsf{Auth}}], |\Pr[\mathsf{Exp}_{\mathsf{FAKE},\mu,\ell,\mathcal{A}} \Rightarrow 1] - \frac{1}{2}| \right\} \leq \mathsf{negl}(\lambda).$$

Here "strong" authentication also takes into account replay attacks as formalized by (3.3).

## 4   Our FAKE Scheme

We now construct our FAKE scheme from a secure sketch SS, a signature scheme SIG and a key encapsulation mechanism KEM and a hash function H. The details are presented in Fig. 4.

- Let $\mathsf{SS} = (\mathsf{SS.Gen}, \mathsf{SS.Rec})$ be an $(\mathcal{M}, m, \tilde{m}, t)$ secure sketch with distance function dis.
- Let $\mathsf{SIG} = (\mathsf{SIG.Setup}, \mathsf{VK.Gen}, \mathsf{Sign.Ver})$ be a signature scheme with signing key space $\mathcal{R}$.
- Let $\mathsf{KEM} = (\mathsf{KEM.Setup}, \mathsf{PK.Gen}, \mathsf{Encap}, \mathsf{Decap})$ be a KEM scheme with secret key space $\mathcal{R}$.
- Let $\mathsf{H} : \mathcal{M} \times \{0,1\}^\lambda \to \mathcal{R}$ be a hash function.

Intuitively, we rely on SS to make sure that the samplings $w_i'$ of a fuzzy source $W_i$ can be tuned to a unique sampling $w_i$. Then the hash function converts $w_i$ into a signing secret key $ssk_i$. The signatures for each message in FAKE provides authentication of the two peers $U_i$ and $U_j$. The KEM allows the two users to exchange KEM's $pk$ and encapsulation ciphertext $c$ so that the same encapsulated key $k$ can be computed by both $U_i$ and $U_j$ as the session key. The security of KEM can provide the pseudorandomness of session key.

Our FAKE Scheme is described as follows.

- $\mathsf{pp}_{\mathsf{FAKE}} \leftarrow \mathsf{FAKE.Setup}$. The setup algorithm invokes $\mathsf{pp}_{\mathsf{SIG}} \leftarrow \mathsf{SIG.Setup}$ and $\mathsf{pp}_{\mathsf{KEM}} \leftarrow \mathsf{KEM.Setup}$ and returns the public parameters $\mathsf{pp}_{\mathsf{FAKE}} := (\mathsf{pp}_{\mathsf{SIG}}, \mathsf{pp}_{\mathsf{KEM}})$.
- $(\mathsf{pub}_i := vk_i, \mathsf{local}_i := (P_i^{\mathsf{SIG}}, \mathsf{ctr}_i)) \leftarrow \mathsf{FAKE.Gen}(\mathsf{pp}_{\mathsf{FAKE}}, W_i)$. The generation algorithm for user $i$ takes as input the public parameter $\mathsf{pp}_{\mathsf{FAKE}}$ and the user's fuzzy source $W_i$. It first samples the fuzzy source with $w_i \leftarrow W_i$ and invokes $s_i \leftarrow \mathsf{SS.Gen}(w_i)$ to generate sketch $s_i$. Then it chooses a random string $x_i$ uniformly from $\{0,1\}^\lambda$. It computes $ssk_i := \mathsf{H}(w_i, x_i)$ as its signing key, then invokes $vk_i \leftarrow \mathsf{VK.Gen}(\mathsf{pp}_{\mathsf{SIG}}; ssk_i)$ to get $U_i$'s verification key. Meanwhile, for user $U_i$, a counter list $\mathsf{ctr}_i := \{\mathsf{ctr}_i[j]\}_{i \in [\mu]}$ is initialized with 0s and $\mathsf{ctr}_i[j]$ denotes $U_i$'s counter targeting $U_j$. Define $P_i^{\mathsf{SIG}} := (s_i, x_i)$. It returns $\mathsf{pub}_i := vk_i$ and $\mathsf{local}_i := (P_i^{\mathsf{SIG}}, \mathsf{ctr}_i) = ((s_i, x_i), \mathsf{ctr}_i)$.
- $\mathsf{FAKE.Protocol}(U_i(\mathsf{res}_i) \leftrightarrow U_j(\mathsf{res}_j))$. The protocol is executed between two users $U_i$ and $U_j$. Each user has access to their own resources $\mathsf{res}_i = (W_i, (P_i^{\mathsf{SIG}}, \mathsf{ctr}_i), \{vk_u\}_{u \in [\mu]}, (\mathsf{pp}_{\mathsf{SIG}}, \mathsf{pp}_{\mathsf{KEM}}))$ and $\mathsf{res}_j = (W_j, (P_j^{\mathsf{SIG}}, \mathsf{ctr}_j),$

$\{vk_u\}_{u\in[\mu]},(\mathsf{pp}_\mathsf{SIG},\mathsf{pp}_\mathsf{KEM}))$. For example, $\mathsf{res}_i$ contains $U_i$'s fuzzy source $W_i$, its local string $\mathsf{local}_i := (P_i^\mathsf{SIG},\mathsf{ctr}_i) = ((s_i,x_i),\mathsf{ctr}_i)$, verification keys of all users $\{vk_u\}_{u\in[\mu]}$ and public parameter $\mathsf{pp}_\mathsf{FAKE} := (\mathsf{pp}_\mathsf{SIG},\mathsf{pp}_\mathsf{KEM})$. $U_i$ and $U_j$ have their own local variables $(\mathsf{st}_i,\mathsf{Pid}_i,k_i,\Psi_i)$ and $(\mathsf{st}_j,\mathsf{Pid}_j,k_j,\Psi_j)$ respectively, both of which are initialized with empty strings. The execution of FAKE protocol consists of three rounds:

- To initialize a session, the user $U_i$ parses $P_i^\mathsf{SIG}$ as $(s_i,x_i)$, where $s_i$ is the sketch and $x_i$ is the random string. With the help of $(s_i,x_i)$, $U_i$ tries to regenerate its signing key $ssk_i$ as follows. It samples $w_i' \leftarrow W_i$ and invokes $\hat{w}_i \leftarrow \mathsf{SS.Rec}(w_i',s_i)$, trying to reproduce $w_i$. Then it invokes $ssk_i' \leftarrow \mathsf{H}(\hat{w}_i,x_i)$ and $vk_i' \leftarrow \mathsf{VK.Gen}(\mathsf{pp}_\mathsf{SIG};ssk_i')$. Repeat the above procedure by re-sampling $w_i'$ until $vk_i' = vk_i$ so that $ssk_i$ is correctly reproduced.
  
  It then chooses a bit string $x$ from $\{0,1\}^\lambda$ and generates a public and secret key pair $(pk,sk)$ for KEM by invoking $sk_\mathsf{KEM} \leftarrow \mathsf{H}(\hat{w}_i,x)$ and $pk \leftarrow \mathsf{PK.Gen}(\mathsf{pp}_\mathsf{KEM};sk)$. $U_i$ updates its counter $\mathsf{ctr}_i[j]$ with $\mathsf{ctr}_i[j] := \mathsf{ctr}_i[j] + 1$. It then uses $ssk_i'$ to sign the message $m_1 := (U_i,U_j,pk,\mathsf{ctr}_i[j])$ and obtains the corresponding signature $\sigma_1 \leftarrow \mathsf{SIG.Sign}(ssk_i',m_1)$. Then $U_i$ sends $(U_i,U_j,pk,\mathsf{ctr}_i[j],\sigma_1)$ to $U_j$. Define $P_i^\mathsf{KEM} := x$. It stores $\mathsf{st}_i := (P_i^\mathsf{KEM},pk)$ as the round state.

- After $U_j$ receives the message $m_1 = (U_i,U_j,pk,\mathsf{ctr}_i[j])$ and signature $\sigma_1$, it first checks whether $\mathsf{ctr}_i[j] > \mathsf{ctr}_j[i]$ holds and uses $\mathsf{Ver}(vk_i,m_1,\sigma_1)$ to check the validity of $\sigma_1$. If $\mathsf{ctr}_i[j] \leq \mathsf{ctr}_j[i]$ or the verification fails, $U_j$ returns $\Psi_j = \mathbf{reject}$. Otherwise, $U_j$ first updates its counter with $\mathsf{ctr}_j[i]$: $= \mathsf{ctr}_i[j]$. Then $U_j$ encapsulates a key $k_j$ via $(c,k_j) \leftarrow \mathsf{Encap}(pk)$. Next $U_j$ parses its local string $P_j^\mathsf{SIG}$ as $(s_j,x_j)$. It samples $w_j' \leftarrow W_j$ and invokes $\hat{w}_j \leftarrow \mathsf{SS.Rec}(w_j',s_j)$ trying to reproduce $w_j$. Then it computes $vk_j'$ by running $ssk_j' \leftarrow \mathsf{H}(\hat{w}_j,x_j)$ and $vk_j' \leftarrow \mathsf{VK.Gen}(\mathsf{pp}_\mathsf{SIG};ssk_j')$. Repeat the above procedure by re-sampling $w_j'$ until $vk_j' = vk_j$. Then $U_j$ uses $ssk_j'$ to sign message $m_2 = (U_i,U_j,pk,\mathsf{ctr}_j[i],c)$ to obtain the corresponding signature $\sigma_2 \leftarrow \mathsf{SIG.Sign}(ssk_j',m_2)$. It sends $(U_i,U_j,c,\sigma_2)$ to $U_i$. Meanwhile, $U_j$ sets $\Psi_j := \mathbf{accept}$ and accepts $k_j$ as its session key.

- After $U_i$ obtains $(U_i,U_j,c,\sigma_2)$, it sets $m_2 := (U_i,U_j,pk,\mathsf{ctr}_i[j],c)$ and verifies whether $(m_2,\sigma_2)$ is a valid message-signature pair w.r.t. $vk_j$. If invalid, it returns $\Psi := \mathbf{reject}$ and terminates the execution. Otherwise, it parses $P_i^\mathsf{KEM} = x, P_i^\mathsf{SIG} = (s_i,x_i)$ and tries to recover the secret key $sk$ of KEM as follows. It first samples $w_i' \leftarrow W_i$ and invokes $\hat{w}_i \leftarrow \mathsf{SS.Rec}(w_i',s_i)$. Then it computes $pk'$ by running $sk' \leftarrow \mathsf{H}(\hat{w}_i,x)$ and $pk' \leftarrow \mathsf{PK.Gen}(\mathsf{pp}_\mathsf{KEM};sk')$. Repeat the above procedure until $pk' = pk$. Then $U_i$ decapsulates the ciphertext $c$ to obtain $k_i \leftarrow \mathsf{Decap}(sk',c)$. $U_i$ sets $\Psi_i := \mathbf{accept}$ and accepts $k_i$ as its session key.

Our FAKE is only two-round protocol, hence it is round-optimal. Moreover, each user extracts its own long-term secret key and ephemeral key from its fuzzy source. However, these long-term and ephemeral secret keys are never stored locally. Instead, the user will always re-generate them by making use of its own fuzzy source. Consequently, user $U_i$ only stores a local helper string $(s_i, x_i)$ which is used to re-generate its long-term secret key $ssk_i$. Similarly, user $U_i$ only transmits another helper string $x$ so that the ephemeral keys can be recovered in the next round of the protocol. Note that the local information $(s_i, x_i)$ for each user $U_i$ can be publicly stored. This is different from the traditional AKE where long-term secret keys have to be secretly stored by users in AKE.

FAKE.Setup:
$pp_{SIG} \leftarrow$ SIG.Setup
$pp_{KEM} \leftarrow$ KEM.Setup
Return $pp_{FAKE} := (pp_{SIG}, pp_{KEM})$

FAKE.Gen($pp_{FAKE}, W_i$):
$w_i \leftarrow W_i$
$s_i \leftarrow$ SS($w_i$)
$x_i \leftarrow_s \{0,1\}^\lambda$
$ssk_i \leftarrow$ H($w_i, x_i$)
$P_i^{SIG} := (s_i, x_i)$
$vk_i \leftarrow$ VK.Gen($pp_{SIG}; ssk_i$)
for $j \in [\mu]$:
$\quad ctr_i[j] = 0$ //counter
Return $(vk_i, P_i^{SIG})$

FAKE.Protocol($U_i \rightleftharpoons U_j$):

$U_i(res_i)$
$res_i := (W_i, P_i^{SIG}, ctr_i, \{vk_u\}_{u \in [\mu]}, pp_{FAKE})$

$\Psi_i := \emptyset, k_i := \emptyset, st_i := \emptyset$
Parse $P_i^{SIG} = (s_i, x_i)$
Repeat{
$\quad w_i' \leftarrow W_i$
$\quad \hat{w}_i \leftarrow$ SS.Rec($w_i', s_i$)
$\quad ssk_i' \leftarrow$ H($\hat{w}_i, x_i$)
$\quad vk_i' \leftarrow$ VK.Gen($pp_{SIG}; ssk_i'$)}
until $(vk_i' = vk_i)$
$x \leftarrow_s \{0,1\}^\lambda$
$sk \leftarrow$ H($\hat{w}_i, x$)
$pk \leftarrow$ PK.Gen($pp_{KEM}; sk$)
$ctr_i[j]$ ++
$\sigma_1 \leftarrow$ SIG.Sign($ssk_i', (U_i, U_j, pk, ctr_i[j])$)
$P_i^{KEM} := x$
$st_i = (P_i^{KEM}, pk)$

$\downarrow st_i$

$(U_i, U_j, pk, ctr_i[j], \sigma_1) \longrightarrow$

If Ver($vk_j, (U_i, U_j, pk, ctr_i[j], c), \sigma_2) \neq 1$:
$\quad \Psi_i =$ reject
Else:
$\quad$ Parse $P_i^{KEM} = x, P_i^{SIG} = (s_i, x_i)$
$\quad$ Repeat{
$\quad\quad w_i' \leftarrow W_i$
$\quad\quad \hat{w}_i \leftarrow$ SS.Rec($w_i', s_i$)
$\quad\quad sk' \leftarrow$ H($\hat{w}_i, x$)
$\quad\quad pk' \leftarrow$ PK.Gen($pp_{KEM}; sk'$)}
$\quad$ until $(pk' = pk)$
$\quad k_i =$ Decap($sk', c$)
$\quad \Psi_i :=$ accept
Return $(\Psi_i, k_i)$

$\longleftarrow (U_i, U_j, c, \sigma_2)$

$U_j(res_j)$
$res_j := (W_j, P_j^{SIG}, ctr_j, \{vk_u\}_{u \in [\mu]}, pp_{FAKE})$

$\Psi_j := \emptyset, k_j := \emptyset, st_j := \emptyset$
If $ctr_j[i] \geq ctr_i[j] \lor$ Ver($vk_i, (U_i, U_j, pk, ctr_i[j]), \sigma_1) \neq 1$:
$\quad \Psi_j =$ reject
Else:
$\quad ctr_j[i] := ctr_i[j]$
$\quad (c, k_j) \leftarrow$ Encap($pk$)
$\quad$ Parse $P_j^{SIG} = (s_j, x_j)$
$\quad$ Repeat {
$\quad\quad w_j' \leftarrow W_j$
$\quad\quad \hat{w}_j \leftarrow$ SS.Rec($w_j', s_j$)
$\quad\quad ssk_j' \leftarrow$ H($\hat{w}_j, x_j$)
$\quad\quad vk_j' \leftarrow$ VK.Gen($pp_{SIG}; ssk_j'$)}
$\quad$ until $(vk_j' = vk_j)$
$\quad \sigma_2 \leftarrow$ Sign($ssk_j', (U_i, U_j, pk, ctr_j[i], c)$)
$\quad \Psi_j :=$ accept
Return $(\Psi_j, k_j)$

Fig. 4. Construction of FAKE.

# 5  Security Proof of FAKE

Intuitively, we rely on SIG to provide explicit authentication for users in our FAKE, and rely on KEM to guarantee pseudorandomness for the session keys.

If both SIG and KEM have the tight security, and the hash function H is taken as a random oracle, then our PAKE can be proved to be tightly secure, as shown in the following theorem.

**Theorem 1 (Security of** FAKE**).** *Suppose that the samplings of fuzzy sources have min-entropy at least* $m$ *and* SS *is an* $(\mathcal{M}, m, \tilde{m}, t)$ *secure sketch with* $\tilde{m} = \omega(\log \lambda)$. *Suppose that* SIG *is MU-EUF-CMA$^{corr}$ secure, and* KEM *is otIND-MU$^{corr}$-CCA secure and has* $\gamma$-*diversity with* $\gamma = \omega(\log \lambda)$. *Then for any adversary* $\mathcal{A}$ *against* FAKE, *there exist an MU-EUF-CMA$^{corr}$ adversary* $\mathcal{B}_{\mathsf{SIG}}$ *against* SIG *and an otIND-MU$^{corr}$-CCA adversary* $\mathcal{B}_{\mathsf{KEM}}$ *against* KEM, *such that*

$$\mathsf{Adv}_{\mathsf{FAKE},\mu,\ell}(\mathcal{A}) = \max\{\Pr[\mathsf{Win}_{\mathsf{Auth}}], |\Pr[\mathsf{Exp}_{\mathsf{FAKE},\mu,\ell,\mathcal{A}} \Rightarrow 1] - \frac{1}{2}|\} = \max\{2\mathsf{Adv}_{\mathsf{SIG},\mu}^{\mathsf{mu\text{-}corr}}(\mathcal{B}_{\mathsf{SIG}}) + 2^{-\omega(\log\lambda)},$$

$$2\mathsf{Adv}_{\mathsf{SIG},\mu}^{\mathsf{mu\text{-}corr}}(\mathcal{B}_{\mathsf{SIG}}) + \mathsf{Adv}_{\mathsf{KEM},\mu}^{\mathsf{otIND\text{-}corr}}(\mathcal{B}_{\mathsf{KEM}}) + 2^{-\omega(\log\lambda)}\}.$$

$$= 2\mathsf{Adv}_{\mathsf{SIG},\mu}^{\mathsf{mu\text{-}corr}}(\mathcal{B}_{\mathsf{SIG}}) + \mathsf{Adv}_{\mathsf{KEM},\mu}^{\mathsf{otIND\text{-}corr}}(\mathcal{B}_{\mathsf{KEM}}) + 2^{-\omega(\log\lambda)}.$$

**Proof of Theorem 1.** We describe the original experiment $\mathsf{Exp}_{\mathsf{FAKE},\mu,\ell,\mathcal{A}}$ in Fig. 5 in Appendix A. To prove the theorem, we consider a sequence of games $\mathsf{G}_0$-$\mathsf{G}_6$ whose full codes are displayed in Fig. 6 in Appendix B. In the following, we describe the games and show the adjacent games are indistinguishable. Let $\mathsf{Win}_i$ denote the event that $\mathcal{A}$ wins, i.e. $b' = b^*$, in $\mathsf{G}_i$. Hence $\mathsf{Win}_i$ happens iff $\mathsf{G}_i$ returns 1. Let $\mathsf{Win}_{\mathsf{Auth}_i}$ denote the event that $\mathsf{Win}_{\mathsf{Auth}} = \mathbf{true}$ in $\mathsf{G}_i$.

**Game $\mathsf{G}_0$:** $\mathsf{G}_0$ is the same as the original experiment $\mathsf{Exp}_{\mathsf{FAKE},\mu,\ell,\mathcal{A}}$ (see Fig. 5), except that the challenger $\mathcal{C}$ adds the sets $\mathsf{Sent}_i^s$ and $\mathsf{Recv}_i^s$ recording messages. $\mathsf{Sent}_i^s$ records messages sent by $\pi_i^s$, while $\mathsf{Recv}_i^s$ records valid messages received by $\pi_i^s$. The changes are only conceptual. Hence we have

$$\Pr[\mathsf{Win}_{\mathsf{Auth}}] = \Pr[\mathsf{Win}_{\mathsf{Auth}_0}] = \Pr_{\exists(i,s)}[(1) \wedge (2) \wedge ((3.1) \vee (3.2) \vee (3.3))]$$

$$\leq \Pr_{\exists(i,s)}[(1) \wedge (2) \wedge (3.1)] + \Pr_{\exists(i,s)}[(1) \wedge (2) \wedge (3.2)] + \Pr_{\exists(i,s)}[(1) \wedge (2) \wedge (3.3)] \quad (1)$$

$$\Pr[\mathsf{Exp}_{\mathsf{FAKE},\mu,\ell,\mathcal{A}} \Rightarrow 1] = \Pr[\mathsf{Win}_0]. \quad (2)$$

**Game $\mathsf{G}_1$:** $\mathsf{G}_1$ is the same as $\mathsf{G}_0$ except for the way of generating $sk_{i,s}$ and regenerating $ssk_i$ and $sk_{i,s}$ when answering oracle query of $\mathsf{Send}(i, s, j, \mathsf{msg})$ for $\mathcal{A}$. In $\mathsf{G}_1$, the challenger directly obtains the $ssk_i'$ and $sk_{i,s}'$ from the tuple $(w_i, x_i, h)$ recorded in HList, instead of invoking recover algorithm of SS and H function to regenerate $ssk_i$ and $sk_{i,s}$ as in $\mathsf{G}_0$.

We assume that the distance of samples of the same fuzzy source is no more than $t$. Thus, due to the correctness of SS, we have $w_i = \mathsf{SS.Rec}(w_{i,s}', s_i) = \mathsf{SS.Rec}(w_i', s_i)$, so the original sample $w_i$ used in registration can always be correctly recovered in $\mathsf{G}_0$. As a result, we have

$$\Pr[\mathsf{Win}_{\mathsf{Auth}_0}] = \Pr[\mathsf{Win}_{\mathsf{Auth}_1}], \quad \Pr[\mathsf{Win}_0] = \Pr[\mathsf{Win}_1]. \quad (3)$$

**Game $\mathsf{G}_2$:** $\mathsf{G}_2$ is the same as $\mathsf{G}_1$ except for the way of generating Hash values. In $\mathsf{G}_1$, both challenger and adversary ask Random Oracle H to get hash values with input $(w, x)$ and corresponding output $h$ is recorded in HList. Note that Random Oracle H is only needed in three places: the generation of $ssk_i$, the generation of $sk_{i,s}$ and $\mathcal{A}$'s query. Thus, in $G_2$, we add two more lists, namely SIGHList and KEMHList, both of which are initialized to empty sets. Moreover, H oracle is simulated by SIGHList, KEMHList and HList accordingly.

- The challenger's generation of $ssk_i = H(w_i, x_i)$ is simulated with SIGHList in $G_2$.
- The challenger's generation of $sk_{i,s} = H(\hat{w_{i,s}}, x_{i,s})$ is simulated with KEMHList in $G_2$.
- Answers to $\mathcal{A}$'s queries for H oracle are still simulated with HList.

Note that simulation of H oracle with the three lists is perfect, so

$$\Pr[\mathsf{Win}_{\mathsf{Auth}_2}] = \Pr[\mathsf{Win}_{\mathsf{Auth}_1}], \quad \Pr[\mathsf{Win}_2] = \Pr[\mathsf{Win}_1]. \tag{4}$$

**Game $G_3$:** $G_3$ is the same as $G_2$ except for the following two changes.

(1) For all $(i,s) \in [\mu] \times [\ell]$, the challenger randomly generates $ssk_i \leftarrow_\$ \mathcal{R}$ and $sk_{i,s} \leftarrow_\$ \mathcal{R}$ without consistency check among SIGHList, KEMHList and HList. Let $\mathsf{Bad}_1$ denote the event that $\exists i, s$ when $(w, x)$ is sampled to generate $ssk_i$ or $sk_{i,s}$ the sample of $(w, x)$ has already existed in SIGHList, KEMHList or HList during execution.

(2) When adversary makes a query to Hash oracle with input $(w, x)$, for $i \in [\mu]$, if $crp_i = \mathbf{false}$, $\mathcal{C}$ will not check whether $(w, x)$ has appeared in SIGHList and for $s \in [\ell]$, if $stRev_i^s = \mathbf{false} \vee crp_i = \mathbf{false}$, $\mathcal{C}$ will not check whether $(w, x)$ has appeared in KEMHList.

Let $\mathsf{Bad}_2$ denote $(w, x)$ appears in SIGHList with $crp_i = \mathbf{false}$ or KEMHList with $crp_i = \mathbf{false}$ or $stRev_i^s = \mathbf{false}$.

$\mathsf{Bad}_1$ and $\mathsf{Bad}_2$ denotes the collusion among challenger's queries and $\mathcal{A}$'s hash queries in the three lists. According to the definitions of $\mathsf{Bad}_1$ and $\mathsf{Bad}_2$, we know that if $\mathsf{Bad}_1$ and $\mathsf{Bad}_2$ do not occur, $G_2$ is identical to $G_3$. According to the difference lemma [11], we have

$$|\Pr[\mathsf{Win}_{\mathsf{Auth}_3}] - \Pr[\mathsf{Win}_{\mathsf{Auth}_2}]| \leq \Pr[\mathsf{Bad}_1] + \Pr[\mathsf{Bad}_2], \quad |\Pr[\mathsf{Win}_3] - \Pr[\mathsf{Win}_2]| \leq \Pr[\mathsf{Bad}_1] + \Pr[\mathsf{Bad}_2]. \tag{5}$$

Recall that $x_i$ $x_{i,s}$ are randomly chosen for $i \in [\mu], s \in [\ell]$, so distinct $x_i$ and $x_{i,s}$ collides with probability $2^{-\lambda}$. Given $U_i$ is not corrupted, $w_i$ and $w_{i,s}$ has entropy at least $m$, so its guessing probability is at most $2^{-\tilde{m}}$ given the sketch $s_i$. Considering that the number of users and the query number are both polynomials and the fact that $\tilde{m} = \omega(\log \lambda)$, we have

$$\Pr[\mathsf{Bad}_1] \leq \mathsf{poly}(\lambda) \cdot (2^{-\lambda} + 2^{-\tilde{m}}) = 2^{-\omega(\log \lambda)}, \quad \Pr[\mathsf{Bad}_2] \leq \mathsf{poly}(\lambda) \cdot (2^{-\lambda} + 2^{-\tilde{m}}) = 2^{-\omega(\log \lambda)}. \tag{6}$$

According to (5) and (6), we know that

$$|\Pr[\mathsf{Win}_{\mathsf{Auth}_3}] - \Pr[\mathsf{Win}_{\mathsf{Auth}_2}]| \leq \mathsf{poly}(\lambda) \cdot (2^{-\lambda} + 2^{-\tilde{m}}) = 2^{-\omega(\log \lambda)}. \tag{7}$$

$$|\Pr[\mathsf{Win}_3] - \Pr[\mathsf{Win}_2]| \leq \mathsf{poly}(\lambda) \cdot (2^{-\lambda} + 2^{-\tilde{m}}) = 2^{-\omega(\log \lambda)}. \tag{8}$$

Now we analyze $\mathsf{Win}_{\mathsf{Auth}_3}$ in $G_3$ and show a reduction to MU-EUF-CMA$^{\mathsf{corr}}$ security of SIG. For ease of the reduction, We will first introduce the concept of **Message Consistency**.

**Message Consistency.** An oracle $\pi_i^s$ is message-consistent with another oracle $\pi_j^t$ denoted by $\mathsf{MsgCon}(\pi_i^s \leftarrow \pi_j^t)$, if $\mathsf{Pid}_i^s := j$ and $\mathsf{Pid}_j^t := i$ and either

- $\pi_i^s$ has received the first message, and $U_j, U_i, pk, \mathsf{ctr}_j[i]$ is contained in both $\mathsf{Recv}_i^s$ and $\mathsf{Sent}_j^t$,
- or $\pi_i^s$ has sent the first message, and $U_i, U_j, c$ is contained in $\mathsf{Recv}_i^s$ and $\mathsf{Sent}_j^t$ and same message $U_i, U_j, pk, \mathsf{ctr}_i[j]$ is contained in $\mathsf{Sent}_i^s$ and $\mathsf{Recv}_j^t$.

If $\mathsf{MsgCon}(\pi_i^s \leftarrow \pi_j^t)$ and $\mathsf{MsgCon}(\pi_j^t \leftarrow \pi_i^s)$, we say $\pi_i^s$ and $\pi_j^t$ are message-consistent to each other and denoted by $\mathsf{MsgCon}(\pi_i^s \leftrightarrow \pi_j^t)$.

**NoMsgCon.** The event $\mathsf{NoMsgCon}$ happens, if $\exists(i, s)$ with $\mathsf{Pid}_i^s = j$ such that (1) $\pi_i^s$ accepts; (2) $j$ is uncorrupted when $\pi_i^s$ accepts; (4) $\nexists t \in [\ell]$ such that $\pi_i^s$ is message-consistent with $\pi_j^t$.

**Lemma 1.** $\Pr\limits_{\exists(i,s)}[(1) \wedge (2) \wedge (3.1)] \leq \Pr[\mathsf{NoMsgCon}] \leq \mathsf{Adv}_{\mathsf{SIG},\mu}^{\mathsf{mu\text{-}corr}}(\mathcal{B}_{\mathsf{SIG}})$.

*Proof (Proof of Lemma 1).* For an oracle $\pi_i^s$ with $\mathsf{Pid}_i^s = j$, if (1) and (2) hold but $\mathsf{Partner}(\pi_i^s \leftarrow \pi_j^t)$ does not hold for any $t \in [\ell]$, then we have (1) (2) and $\mathsf{MsgCon}(\pi_i^s \leftrightarrow \pi_j^t)$ does not hold for any $t \in [\ell]$. This leads to $\Pr\limits_{\exists(i,s)}[(1) \wedge (2) \wedge (3.1)] \leq \Pr[\mathsf{NoMsgCon}]$.

Next we will prove that if $\mathsf{NoMsgCon}$ happens, a PPT algorithm $\mathcal{B}_{\mathsf{SIG}}$ can be constructed against the MU-EUF-CMA$^{\mathsf{corr}}$ security of SIG such that $\Pr[\mathsf{NoMsgCon}] \leq \mathsf{Adv}_{\mathsf{SIG},\mu}^{\mathsf{mu\text{-}corr}}(\mathcal{B}_{\mathsf{SIG}})$.

$\mathcal{B}_{\mathsf{SIG}}$ is given $(\mathsf{pp}_{\mathsf{SIG}}, \{vk_i\}_{i \in [\mu]})$ and has access to a signing oracle $\mathcal{O}_{\mathsf{SIGN}}(\cdot, \cdot)$ and a corruption oracle $\mathcal{O}_{\mathsf{CORR}}(\cdot)$. Now $\mathcal{B}_{\mathsf{SIG}}$ simulates $\mathsf{G}_3$ for $\mathcal{A}$ as follows.

- $\mathcal{B}_{\mathsf{SIG}}$ invokes $\mathsf{pp}_{\mathsf{KEM}} \leftarrow \mathsf{KEM.Setup}$ and sets $\mathsf{pp}_{\mathsf{FAKE}} := (\mathsf{pp}_{\mathsf{SIG}}, \mathsf{pp}_{\mathsf{KEM}})$ and $\mathsf{VKList} := \{vk_i\}_{i \in [\mu]}$. Then it samples $w_i \leftarrow W_i$ and $x_i \leftarrow_\$ \{0,1\}^\lambda$, and records $(i, w_i, x_i, *)$ in $\mathsf{SIGHList}$, here $*$ is implicitly set to $ssk_i$. Meanwhile, it invokes $P_i^{\mathsf{SIG}} \leftarrow \mathsf{SS.Gen}(w_i)$ and initializes $\mathsf{ctr}_i$ to 0s, then sets $\mathsf{LocalList} := \{(P_i^{\mathsf{SIG}}, \mathsf{ctr}_i)\}_{i \in [\mu]}$. $\mathcal{B}_{\mathsf{SIG}}$ sends $(\mathsf{pp}_{\mathsf{FAKE}}, \mathsf{VKList}, \mathsf{LocalList})$ to $\mathcal{A}$.
- If $\mathcal{A}$ issues $\mathcal{O}_{\mathsf{FAKE}}$ oracle queries, $\mathcal{B}_{\mathsf{SIG}}$ responds the queries as follows.
  - $\mathsf{Send}(i, s, j, \mathsf{msg} = \top)$: $\mathcal{B}_{\mathsf{SIG}}$ retrieves $(i, w_i, x_i, *)$ from $\mathsf{SIGHList}$, samples $x_{i,s} \leftarrow_\$ \{0,1\}^\lambda$, $sk_{i,s} \leftarrow_\$ \mathcal{R}$, and records $(i, s, w_i, x_{i,s}, sk_{i,s})$ in $\mathsf{KEMHList}$. Then it invokes $pk_{i,s} \leftarrow \mathsf{PK.Gen}(\mathsf{pp}_{\mathsf{KEM}}; sk_{i,s})$ and set $P_{i,s}^{\mathsf{KEM}} := x_{i,s}$, $\mathsf{st}_i^s = (P_{i,s}^{\mathsf{KEM}}, pk_{i,s})$. Update $\mathsf{ctr}_i[j] := \mathsf{ctr}_i[j] + 1$. Let $\mathsf{msg}_1 := (U_i, U_j, pk_{i,s}, \mathsf{ctr}_i[j])$. $\mathcal{B}_{\mathsf{SIG}}$ queries its signing oracle $\mathcal{O}_{\mathsf{SIGN}}(i, \mathsf{msg}_1)$ and gets signature $\sigma_1$. Finally, $\mathcal{B}_{\mathsf{SIG}}$ returns $\mathsf{msg}' := (U_i, U_j, pk_{i,s}, \mathsf{ctr}_i[j], \sigma_1)$ to $\mathcal{A}$.
  - $\mathsf{Send}(i, s, j, \mathsf{msg} = (U_j, U_i, pk, \mathsf{ctr}_j[i], \sigma_1))$: $\mathcal{B}_{\mathsf{SIG}}$ checks the validity of counter value and signature $\sigma_1$ as $\mathsf{G}_3$ does. If $\sigma_1$ is invalid for $\mathsf{msg}$, set $\Psi_i^s := \mathbf{reject}$. Otherwise, $\mathcal{B}_{\mathsf{SIG}}$ invokes $(c, k) \leftarrow \mathsf{Encap}(pk_{i,s})$ and updates $\mathsf{ctr}_i[j] := \mathsf{ctr}_j[i]$. $\mathcal{B}_{\mathsf{SIG}}$ sets $\Psi_i^s := \mathbf{accept}$ and $k_i := k$. Let $\mathsf{msg}_2 := (U_j, U_i, pk_{i,s}, \mathsf{ctr}_i[j], c)$, then $\mathcal{B}_{\mathsf{SIG}}$ queries its signing oracle $\mathcal{O}_{\mathsf{SIGN}}(i, \mathsf{msg}_2)$ to obtain $\sigma_2$ and returns $\mathsf{msg}' := (U_j, U_i, c, \sigma_2)$ to $\mathcal{A}$.
  - $\mathsf{Send}(i, s, j, \mathsf{msg} = (U_i, U_j, c, \sigma_2))$: $\mathcal{B}_{\mathsf{SIG}}$ simulates the answer just like $\mathsf{G}_3$ does.

- Corrupt($i$): $\mathcal{B}_{\mathsf{SIG}}$ returns $w_i$ to $\mathcal{A}$ and immediately makes a corruption query to its own oracle $\mathcal{O}_{\mathrm{CORR}}(i)$ to get $ssk_i$. Then $\mathcal{B}_{\mathsf{SIG}}$ replaces $(i, w_i, s_i, *)$ in SIGHList with $(i, w_i, s_i, ssk_i)$.
- All queries H($w, x$), StateReveal($i, s$), SessionKeyReveal($i, s$), Test($i, s$) are simulated as in $G_3$.

During the simulation, $\mathcal{B}_{\mathsf{SIG}}$ checks if NoMsgCon happens. If this is the case, there exists an oracle $\pi_i^s$ with $\Psi_i^s = \mathbf{accept}$ and $j := \mathsf{Pid}_i^s$ is uncorrupted when $\pi_i^s$ accepted. $\mathcal{B}_{\mathsf{SIG}}$ retrieves $(U_i, U_j, pk, \mathsf{ctr}, c, \sigma_2)$ from $\mathsf{Sent}_i^s$ and $\mathsf{Recv}_i^s$. If $\pi_i^s$ is initiator, $\mathcal{B}_{\mathsf{SIG}}$ outputs ($\mathsf{msg}^* = (U_i, U_j, pk, \mathsf{ctr}, c)$, $\sigma^* := \sigma_2$), otherwise $\mathcal{B}_{\mathsf{SIG}}$ outputs ($\mathsf{msg}^* = (U_j, U_i pk, \mathsf{ctr}, c)$, $\sigma^* := \sigma_2$). Event NoMsgCon implies that $\mathsf{msg}^*$ is a fresh message, and $\Psi_i^s = \mathbf{accept}$ implies that $\sigma^*$ is a valid signature for $\mathsf{msg}^*$. Hence $\mathcal{B}_{\mathsf{SIG}}$ succeeds as long as NoMsgCon happens. So $\Pr[\mathsf{NoMsgCon}] \leq \mathsf{Adv}_{\mathsf{SIG},\mu}^{\mathsf{mu\text{-}corr}}(\mathcal{B}_{\mathsf{SIG}})$. This concludes the proof of Lemma 1. □

Next, let us bound $\Pr_{\exists(i,s)}[(1) \wedge (2) \wedge (3.2)]$ and $\Pr_{\exists(i,s)}[(1) \wedge (2) \wedge (3.3)]$ in $G_3$.

Event $(1) \wedge (2) \wedge (3.2)$ happens if there exists any oracle $\pi_i^s$ that has accepted with $\mathsf{Aflag}_i^s = \mathbf{false}$ and has more than one partner oracle. Now we analyze the probability of this event in Lemma 2.

**Lemma 2.** $\Pr_{\exists(i,s)}[(1) \wedge (2) \wedge (3.2) \text{ in } G_3] \leq (\mu\ell)^3 \cdot 2^{-\gamma}$.

*Proof (Proof of Lemma 2).* The session key only depends on the ephemeral public key $pk$ and ciphertext $c$. In the following, we assume that there are two oracles $\pi_j^t$ and $\pi_{j'}^{t'}$, such that $\pi_i^s$ is partnered to both $\pi_j^t$ and $\pi_{j'}^{t'}$. Given $pk, pk' \leftarrow$ KEM.Gen, $(c, K) \leftarrow$ Encap($pk; r$) and $(c', K') \leftarrow$ Encap($pk'; r$), we know that $K = K'$ happens with probability at most $2^{-\gamma}$ according to the $\gamma$-diversity of KEM. If $\pi_i^s$ is partnered to both oracles, then $k_i^s = K = K'$ must happen. As there are $\mu\ell$ sessions and $\binom{\mu\ell}{2}$ choices for $(j, t)$ and $(j', t')$, we can upper bound the probability for event $(1) \wedge (2) \wedge (3.2)$ by $\Pr_{\exists(i,s)}[(1) \wedge (2) \wedge (3.2) \text{ in } G_3] \leq \mu\ell \cdot \binom{\mu\ell}{2} \cdot 2^{-\gamma} \leq (\mu\ell)^3 \cdot 2^{-\gamma}$.
□

**Lemma 3.** $\Pr_{\exists(i,s)}[(1) \wedge (2) \wedge (3.3) \text{ in } G_3] \leq (\mu\ell)^3 \cdot 2^{-\gamma} + \mathsf{Adv}_{\mathsf{SIG},\mu}^{\mathsf{mu\text{-}corr}}(\mathcal{B}_{\mathsf{SIG}})$.

*Proof (Proof of Lemma 3).* To prove this lemma, we need to bound the probability that $\exists \pi_i^s, \pi_{i'}^{s'}, \pi_j^t$, s.t. $\mathsf{Aflag}_i^s = \mathbf{false}$, $\pi_i^s \neq \pi_{i'}^{s'}$, Partner($\pi_i^s \leftarrow \pi_j^t$), and Partner($\pi_{i'}^{s'} \leftarrow \pi_j^t$).

We know that MsgCon($\pi_i^s \leftarrow \pi_j^t$), and MsgCon($\pi_{i'}^{s'} \leftarrow \pi_j^t$) holds except with probability $\Pr[\mathsf{NoMsgCon}]$.

Now we assume $\mathsf{MsgCon}(\pi_i^s \leftarrow \pi_j^t)$ and $\mathsf{MsgCon}(\pi_{i'}^{s'} \leftarrow \pi_j^t)$ hold. If $\pi_i^s$ is the responder, then the message consistence implies $i' = i$ and $\mathsf{ctr}_j[i'] = \mathsf{ctr}_j[i]$. $\pi_i^s \neq \pi_{i'}^{s'}$ and $i' = i$ implies $s \neq s'$, which further implies $\mathsf{ctr}_j[i'] \neq \mathsf{ctr}_j[i]$. This gives a contradiction hence is impossible. If $\pi_i^s$ is the initiator, then $\pi_j^t$ accepts before $\pi_i^s$ and $\pi_{i'}^{s'}$. Therefore, we have $\mathsf{MsgCon}(\pi_j^t \leftarrow \pi_i^s)$, and $\mathsf{MsgCon}(\pi_j^t \leftarrow \pi_{i'}^{s'})$, hence $\mathsf{Partner}(\pi_j^t \leftarrow \pi_i^s)$, and $\mathsf{Partner}(\pi_j^t \leftarrow \pi_{i'}^{s'})$. This implies $(1) \wedge (2) \wedge (3.2)$. Therefore,
$$\Pr_{\exists(i,s)}[(1) \wedge (2) \wedge (3.3) \text{ in } \mathsf{G}_3] \leq \Pr_{\exists(i,s)}[(1) \wedge (2) \wedge (3.2) \text{ in } \mathsf{G}_3] + \Pr[\mathsf{NoMsgCon}] \leq$$
$(\mu\ell)^3 \cdot 2^{-\gamma} + \mathsf{Adv}_{\mathsf{SIG},\mu}^{\mathsf{mu\text{-}corr}}(\mathcal{B}_{\mathsf{SIG}})$. □

By Lemmas 1, 2 and 3, in $\mathsf{G}_3$ we have

$$\Pr[\mathsf{Win}_{\mathsf{Auth}_3}] \leq \Pr_{\exists i,s}[(1) \wedge (2) \wedge (3.1) \text{ in } \mathsf{G}_3] + \Pr_{\exists i,s}[(1) \wedge (2) \wedge (3.2) \text{ in } \mathsf{G}_3] + \Pr_{\exists i,s}[(1) \wedge (2) \wedge (3.3) \text{ in } \mathsf{G}_3]$$

$$\leq 2\mathsf{Adv}_{\mathsf{SIG},\mu}^{\mathsf{mu\text{-}corr}}(\mathcal{B}_{\mathsf{SIG}}) + 2(\mu\ell)^3 \cdot 2^{-\gamma}. \tag{9}$$

According to (1), (3), (4), (7), and (9) and the fact of $\gamma = \omega(\log \lambda)$, we have

$$\Pr[\mathsf{Win}_{\mathsf{Auth}}] = \Pr[\mathsf{Win}_{\mathsf{Auth}_0}] \leq \Pr[\mathsf{Win}_{\mathsf{Auth}_3}] + \sum_{i=0}^{2} |\Pr[\mathsf{Win}_{\mathsf{Auth}_i}] - \Pr[\mathsf{Win}_{\mathsf{Auth}_{i+1}}]|$$

$$\leq 2\mathsf{Adv}_{\mathsf{SIG},\mu}^{\mathsf{mu\text{-}corr}}(\mathcal{B}_{\mathsf{SIG}}) + 2(\mu\ell)^3 \cdot 2^{-\gamma} + 2^{-\omega(\log \lambda)} = 2\mathsf{Adv}_{\mathsf{SIG},\mu}^{\mathsf{mu\text{-}corr}}(\mathcal{B}_{\mathsf{SIG}}) + 2^{-\omega(\log \lambda)}. \tag{10}$$

In the following games, we focus on event $\mathsf{Win}$ and analyze its probability. **Game $\mathsf{G}_4$:** $\mathsf{G}_4$ is identical to $\mathsf{G}_3$ except that in $\mathsf{G}_4$, if event $\mathsf{Win}_{\mathsf{Auth}}$ happens, the game will abort. Due to the difference lemma [11],

$$|\Pr[\mathsf{Win}_3] - \Pr[\mathsf{Win}_4]| \leq \mathsf{Win}_{\mathsf{Auth}_3} \leq 2\mathsf{Adv}_{\mathsf{SIG},\mu}^{\mathsf{mu\text{-}corr}}(\mathcal{B}_{\mathsf{SIG}}) + 2^{-\omega(\log \lambda)}. \tag{11}$$

**Game $\mathsf{G}_5$:** $\mathsf{G}_5$ is identical to $\mathsf{G}_4$ except that in $\mathsf{G}_5$ the partnership is checked by message-consistency $\mathsf{MsgCon}(\pi_i^s \leftarrow \pi_j^t)$, instead of $\mathsf{Partner}(\pi_i^s \leftarrow \pi_j^t)$. By this change, the check of partnership becomes simple and efficient. We claim that Lemma 4 holds.

**Lemma 4.** $|\Pr[\mathsf{Win}_4] - \Pr[\mathsf{Win}_5]| \leq \Pr[\mathsf{NoMsgCon}] \leq \mathsf{Adv}_{\mathsf{SIG},\mu}^{\mathsf{mu\text{-}corr}}(\mathcal{B}_{\mathsf{SIG}})$.

*Proof (Proof of Lemma 4).* Notice that in $\mathsf{G}_5$, for any $(i, s)$ with $\mathsf{Pid}_i^s = j$, the challenger only checks $\mathsf{Partner}(\pi_i^s \leftarrow \pi_j^t)$ for $t \in [\ell]$ when (1) and (2) satisfy. Since $\mathsf{Win}_{\mathsf{Auth}}$ does not happen, (1) and (2) implies that $\exists! \, t \, \text{s.t.} \mathsf{Partner}(\pi_i^s \leftarrow \pi_j^t)$. Then it holds that $\exists! t \text{ s.t.} \mathsf{MsgCon}(\pi_i^s \leftarrow \pi_j^t)$, since otherwise $\mathsf{NoMsgCon}$ must happen, whose probability is upper bounded by $\mathsf{Adv}_{\mathsf{SIG},\mu}^{\mathsf{mu\text{-}corr}}(\mathcal{B}_{\mathsf{SIG}})$ by Lemma 1. □

**Game $G_6$:** In $G_6$, when $T_i^s = \textbf{true}$, the challenger sets $k_0 \leftarrow_\$ \mathcal{K}$ instead of setting $k_0 = k_i^s$. Now $\mathcal{A}$' view is independent of bit $b$. Obviously, $\Pr[\text{Win}_6] = 1/2$.

**Lemma 5.** *There exists an adversary* $\mathcal{B}_{\text{KEM}}$ *against* KEM *s.t.* $|\Pr[\text{Win}_5] - \Pr[\text{Win}_6]| \le \text{Adv}_{\text{KEM},\mu}^{\text{otIND-corr}}(\mathcal{B}_{\text{KEM}})$.

*Proof (Proof of Lemma 5).* For the proof, we construct a PPT algorithm $\mathcal{B}_{\text{KEM}}$ to break KEM's otIND-MU$^{\text{corr}}$-CCA security. $\mathcal{B}_{\text{KEM}}$ is given $\text{pp}_{\text{KEM}}$ and a set of pubic keys $\text{PKList} := \{pk_l\}_{l \in [\mu\ell]}$ from its challenger, and it has access to $\text{CORR}(\cdot)$, $\text{TEST}(\cdot, \cdot)$, $\text{ENCAP}(\cdot)$, $\text{DECAP}(\cdot, \cdot)$ oracles. The task of $\mathcal{B}_{\text{KEM}}$ is to tell whether the output $K^*$ of $\text{TEST}(l, c)$ are the encapsulated keys of $c$ under $pk_l$ or random keys. Then $\mathcal{B}_{\text{KEM}}$ simulates $G_5$ or $G_6$ for $\mathcal{A}$ as follows.

- $\mathcal{B}_{\text{KEM}}$ samples $b, x_i, w_i, ssk_i$, generates $\text{pp}_{\text{FAKE}}$, $s_i, vk_i$, records $(i, w_i, x_i, ssk_i)$ in SIGHList, and sends $(\text{pp}_{\text{FAKE}}, \text{VKList} := \{vk_i\}_{i \in [\mu]}, \text{LocalList} := \{(P_i^{\text{SIG}} = (s_i, x_i), \text{ctr}_i)\}_{i \in [\mu]})$ to $\mathcal{A}$, just like $G_5$.
- $\mathcal{B}_{\text{KEM}}$ maps $\{pk_l\}_{l \in [\mu\ell]}$ into $\mu\ell$ ephemeral public keys $\{pk_{i,s}\}_{i \in [\mu], s \in [\ell]}$ with $l = (i-1)\ell + s$.
- $\mathcal{B}_{\text{KEM}}$'s simulation of output message of initiator oracle $\pi_i^s$ is just $\text{msg}' := (U_i, U_j, pk_{i,s}, \text{ctr}_i[j], \sigma_1)$, just like in $G_5$, but records $(i, s, w_i, x_{i,s}, *)$ in KEMHList since $sk_{i,s}$ is unknown. $\mathcal{B}_{\text{KEM}}$'s simulation of output message of responder oracle $\pi_j^t(\text{msg} = (U_i, U_j, pk_{i,s}, \text{ctr}_i[j], \sigma_1))$ is just $\text{msg}' := (U_i, U_j, c, \sigma_2)$ just like in $G_5$, except that $c$ is obtained by querying its own oracle $\text{ENCAP}(l)$ and $k_j^t := *$ if $pk = pk_l \in \text{PKList}$. $\mathcal{B}_{\text{KEM}}$'s simulation of $\pi_i^s(\text{msg} = (U_i, U_j, c, \sigma_2))$ is just like $G_5$, except that $\mathcal{B}_{\text{KEM}}$ does not decapulate $c$ (since $\mathcal{A}$ does not ask for the encapsulated key here).
- To simulate oracle $\text{SessionKeyReveal}(i, s)$, $\mathcal{B}_{\text{KEM}}$ retrieves ciphertext $c$ and $pk = pk_l \in \text{PKList}$ from the transcript of accepted $\pi_i^s$, then queries its own oracle $\text{DECAP}(l, c)$ to obtain $k_i^s$ for $\mathcal{A}$.
- To simulate oracles $\text{Corrupt}(i)$ and $\text{StateReveal}(i, s)$, $\mathcal{B}_{\text{KEM}}$ does just like $G_5$, except that it also detects whether both $\text{Corrupt}(i)$ and $\text{StateReveal}(i, s)$ are queried w.r.t an initiator $\pi_i^s$. If yes, $\mathcal{B}_{\text{KEM}}$ queries its own oracle $\text{CORR}((i-1)\ell + s)$ to get $sk_{(i-1)\ell+s}$ and updates $(i, s, w_{i,s}, x_{i,s}, *)$ with $(i, s, w_{i,s}, x_{i,s}, sk_{(i-1)\ell+s})$ in KEMHList. Note that $\mathcal{B}_{\text{KEM}}$ is able to perfectly simulate $\text{H}(w, x)$ just like in $G_5$, since $\mathcal{B}_{\text{KEM}}$ knows all $ssk_i$ and already obtains $sk_{(i-1)\ell+s}$ from its own $\text{CORR}$ oracle when $\text{Corrupt}(i)$ and $\text{StateReveal}(i, s)$ are both queried.

– To answer $\mathcal{A}$'s test query $\mathsf{Test}(i, s)$, $\mathcal{B}_{\mathsf{KEM}}$ retrieves ciphertext $c$ and $pk = pk_l \in \mathsf{PKList}$ from the transcript of accepted $\pi_i^s$, and queries its own oracle $\mathrm{TEST}(l, c)$ to get $k$ and sets $k_0 := k$. $\mathcal{B}_{\mathsf{KEM}}$ randomly chooses $k_1 \leftarrow_\$ \mathcal{K}$ and returns $k_b$ to $\mathcal{A}$.

Finally, when $\mathcal{A}$ answers with a bit $b^*$, $\mathcal{B}_{\mathsf{KEM}}$ checks whether $b^* = b$ holds, and returns 1 if $b^* = b$.

For any oracle query $\mathrm{TEST}(l, c)$ from $\mathcal{B}_{\mathsf{KEM}}$, if the answer $k$ is the encapsulated key, $\mathcal{B}_{\mathsf{KEM}}$ perfectly simulates $\mathsf{G}_5$ for $\mathcal{A}$; if the answer $k$ is a random key, $\mathcal{B}_{\mathsf{KEM}}$ perfectly simulates $\mathsf{G}_6$ for $\mathcal{A}$. Therefore, $|\Pr[\mathsf{Win}_5] - \Pr[\mathsf{Win}_6]| \leq \mathsf{Adv}_{\mathsf{KEM},\mu}^{\mathsf{otIND\text{-}corr}}(\mathcal{B}_{\mathsf{KEM}})$. $\qquad\square$

Finally, Theorem 1 follows from (2), (3), (4), (8), (9), (11), Lemmas 4, 5 and $\Pr[\mathsf{Win}_6] = 1/2$.

## 6    Instantiation of Our FAKE Construction

To obtain specific FAKE schemes, we need to instantiate the three underlying building blocks.

**Instantiations of SS.** Secure sketch is an information-theoretical primitive, hence any instantiation works. The popular candidates are error-correction code-based SS [4,10,18,19].

**Instantiations of SIG.** We suggest two choices for SIG. One is the Schnorr signature scheme, which was proved to have MU-EUF-CMA$^{\mathsf{corr}}$ security based ob the DDH & CDH assumptions in the random oracle model with generic group model (GGM). The other choice is the signature scheme proposed in [1], and its MU-EUF-CMA$^{\mathsf{corr}}$ security can be tightly reduced to the SXDH assumption (which is a well-know assumption on pairing group [7]).

**Instantiations of KEM.** The KEM scheme in [12] has tight IND-MU$^{\mathsf{corr}}$-CCA Security. Note that IND-MU$^{\mathsf{corr}}$-CCA Security is stronger than otIND-MU$^{\mathsf{corr}}$-CCA, hence this KEM scheme is a good choice.

**Acknowledgements.** We would like to thank the anonymous reviewers for their helpful comments. Shengli Liu and Mingming Jiang were partially supported by National Natural Science Foundation of China (NSFC No. 61925207) and Guangdong Major Project of Basic and Applied Basic Research (2019B030302008). Shuai Han was partially supported by National Natural Science Foundation of China (Grant No. 62002223), Shanghai Sailing Program (20YF1421100), and Young Elite Scientists Sponsorship Program by China Association for Science and Technology (YESS20200185).

# A    Figure 5: The Security Experiment $\mathsf{Exp}_{\mathsf{FAKE},\mu,\ell,\mathcal{A}}$ for FAKE

$\mathsf{Exp}_{\mathsf{FAKE},\mu,\ell,\mathcal{A}}$:
// $\mathsf{pp}_{\mathsf{FAKE}} \leftarrow \mathsf{FAKE.Setup}$
$\mathsf{pp}_{\mathsf{SIG}} \leftarrow \mathsf{SIG.Setup}$
$\mathsf{pp}_{\mathsf{KEM}} \leftarrow \mathsf{KEM.Setup}$
$\mathsf{pp}_{\mathsf{FAKE}} := (\mathsf{pp}_{\mathsf{SIG}}, \mathsf{pp}_{\mathsf{KEM}})$
$\mathsf{HList} := \emptyset$
For $i \in [\mu]$:
    // $(vk_i, (P_i^{\mathsf{SIG}}, ctr_i)) \leftarrow \mathsf{FAKE.Gen}(\mathsf{pp}_{\mathsf{FAKE}}, W_i)$;
    $crp_i :=$ false //Corruption variable
    $w_i \leftarrow W_i$
    $s_i \leftarrow \mathsf{SS.Gen}(w_i)$
    $x_i \leftarrow_{\$} \{0,1\}^{\lambda}$
    $P_i^{\mathsf{SIG}} := (s_i, x_i)$
    For $j \in [\mu]$:
        $ctr_i[j] = 0$//counter
    $ssk_i \leftarrow \mathsf{H}(w_i, x_i)$
    $vk_i \leftarrow \mathsf{VK.Gen}(\mathsf{pp}_{\mathsf{SIG}}, ssk_i)$
$\mathsf{VKList} := \{vk_i\}_{i \in [\mu]}$
$\mathsf{LocalList} := \{(P_i^{\mathsf{SIG}}, ctr_i)\}_{i \in [\mu]}$
$b \leftarrow_{\$} \{0,1\}$
For $(i,s) \in [\mu] \times [\ell]$:
    $var_i^s := (st_i^s, Pid_i^s, k_i^s, \Psi_i^s) := (\emptyset, \emptyset, \emptyset, \emptyset)$;
    $Aflag_i^s :=$ false//Whether $Pid_i^s$ is corrupted when $\pi_i^s$ accepts
    $T_i^s :=$ false; $kRev_i^s =$ false // Test, Key Reveal variables
    $stRev_i^s :=$ false, $FirstAcc_i^s := \emptyset$ //State Reveal & First Acceptance variables
$b^* \leftarrow \mathcal{A}^{\mathcal{O}_{\mathsf{FAKE}}(\cdot)}(\mathsf{pp}_{\mathsf{FAKE}}, \mathsf{VKList}, \mathsf{LocalList})$

$\mathsf{Win}_{\mathsf{Auth}} :=$ false
$\mathsf{Win}_{\mathsf{Auth}} :=$ true, If $\exists (i,s) \in [\mu] \times [\ell]$ s.t.
(1) $\Psi_i^s \leftarrow$ accept
(2) $Aflag_i^s =$ false
(3) $(3.1) \lor (3.2) \lor (3.3)$. Let $j := Pid_i^s$
    $(3.1)\ \nexists t \in [\ell]$ s.t. $\mathsf{Partner}(\pi_i^s \leftarrow \pi_j^t)$
    $(3.2)\ \exists t \in [\ell], (j', t') \in [\mu] \times [\ell]$ with $(j,t) \neq (j', t')$ s.t.
        $\mathsf{Partner}(\pi_i^s \leftarrow \pi_j^t) \land \mathsf{Partner}(\pi_i^s \leftarrow \pi_{j'}^{t'})$
    $(3.3)\ \exists t \in [\ell], (i', s') \in [\mu] \times [\ell]$ s.t. $(i,s) \neq (i', s')$ s.t.
        $\mathsf{Partner}(\pi_i^s \leftarrow \pi_j^t) \land \mathsf{Partner}(\pi_{i'}^{s'} \leftarrow \pi_j^t)$ //Replay attacks
$\mathsf{Win}_{\mathsf{Ind}} :=$ false
If $b^* = b$:
    $\mathsf{Win}_{\mathsf{Ind}} :=$ true; Return 1
Else: Return 0

$\mathsf{Partner}(\pi_i^s \leftarrow \pi_j^t)$:    //Checking whether $\mathsf{Partner}(\pi_i^s \leftarrow \pi_j^t)$
If $\pi_i^s$ sent the first message and $k_i^s = \mathsf{K}(\pi_i^s, \pi_j^t) \neq \emptyset$ : Return 1
If $\pi_i^s$ received the first message and $k_i^s = \mathsf{K}(\pi_j^t, \pi_i^s) \neq \emptyset$ : Return 1
Return 0

$\mathcal{O}_{\mathsf{FAKE}}(\mathsf{query})$:
If $\mathsf{query} = \mathsf{Corrupt}(i)$:
    If $i \notin [\mu]$, Return $\bot$
    For $s \in [\ell]$:
        If $FirstAcc_i^s =$ false $\land stRev_i^s =$ true :
            If $T_i^s =$ true : Return $\bot$ //avoid TA6
        If $\exists t \in [\ell]$ s.t. $\mathsf{Partner}(\pi_j^t \leftarrow \pi_i^s)$:
            If $T_j^t =$ true : Return $\bot$; //avoid TA7
    $crp_i :=$ true ; Return $W_i$

If $\mathsf{query} = \mathsf{Test}(i,s)$:
    If $(i,s) \notin [\mu] \times [\ell]$, Return $\bot$
    If $\Psi_i^s \neq$ accept $\lor Aflag_i^s =$ true $\lor kRev_i^s =$ true
        $\lor T_i^s =$ true : Return $\bot$ // avoid TA1, TA2, TA3
    If $FirstAcc_i^s =$ false :
        If $crp_i =$ true $\land stRev_i^s =$ true :
            Return $\bot$ // avoid TA6
    Let $j := Pid_i^s$
    If $\exists t \in [\ell]$ s.t. $\mathsf{Partner}(\pi_i^s \leftrightarrow \pi_j^t)$:
        If $kRev_j^t =$ true $\lor T_j^t =$ true:
            Return $\bot$ // avoid TA4, TA5
    If $\exists t \in [\ell]$ s.t. $\mathsf{Partner}(\pi_j^t \leftarrow \pi_i^s)$:
        If $FirstAcc_j^t =$ false $\land crp_j =$ true
            $\land stRev_j^t =$ true : Return $\bot$ // avoid TA7
    $T_i^s :=$ true; $k_0 := k_i^s$;
    $k_1 \leftarrow_{\$} \mathcal{K}$; Return $k_b$

If $\mathsf{query} = \mathsf{H}(w, x)$:
    If $\exists (w', x', h') \in \mathsf{HList}$ s.t. $(w, x) = (w', x')$:
        Return $h'$
    $h \leftarrow_{\$} \mathcal{R}$
    $\mathsf{HList} := \mathsf{HList} \cup \{(w, x, h)\}$
    Return $h$.

$\mathcal{O}_{\mathsf{FAKE}}(\mathsf{query})$:
If $\mathsf{query} = \mathsf{Send}(i, s, j, \mathsf{msg})$:
    If $(i,s) \notin [\mu] \times [\ell]$, Return $\bot$
    If $\Psi_i^s =$ accept : Return $\bot$
    // $\mathsf{msg} = \pi_i^s(\mathsf{msg}, j)$
    If $\mathsf{msg} = \top$//$\pi_i^s$ is the initiator to generate the first message
        $Pid_i^s := j$
        $ctr_i[j] + +$
        Parse $P_i^{\mathsf{SIG}} = (s_i, x_i)$
        Repeat{
            $w_{i,s} \leftarrow W_i$
            $\tilde{w}_{i,s} \leftarrow \mathsf{SS.Rec}(w_{i,s}, s_i)$
            $ssk_i' \leftarrow \mathsf{H}(\tilde{w}_{i,s}, x_i)$
            $vk_i' \leftarrow \mathsf{VK.Gen}(\mathsf{pp}_{\mathsf{SIG}}, ssk_i')$
        until $(vk_i' = vk_i)$
        $x_{i,s} \leftarrow_{\$} \{0,1\}^{\lambda}$
        $sk_{i,s} \leftarrow \mathsf{H}(\tilde{w}_{i,s}, x_{i,s})$
        $pk_{i,s} \leftarrow \mathsf{PK.Gen}(\mathsf{pp}_{\mathsf{KEM}}; sk_{i,s})$
        $P_{i,s}^{\mathsf{KEM}} := x_{i,s}$
        $\sigma_1 \leftarrow \mathsf{SIG.Sign}(\mathsf{pp}_{\mathsf{SIG}}, U_i, U_j, pk, ctr_i[j])$
        $st_i^s := (P_{i,s}^{\mathsf{KEM}}, pk)$
        $\mathsf{msg}' := (U_i, U_j, pk, ctr_i[j], \sigma_1)$

    If $\mathsf{msg} = (U_j, U_i, pk, ctr_j[i], \sigma_1)$://$\mathsf{msg}$ is the first message
        If $(ctr_j[i] \leq ctr_i[j]) \lor \mathsf{Ver}(vk_j, (U_j, U_i, pk, ctr_i[i]), \sigma_1) \neq 1$
            $\Psi_i^s :=$ reject; Return $\bot$
        $ctr_i[j] := ctr_j[i]$
        $(c, k) \leftarrow \mathsf{Encap}(pk)$
        Parse $P_i^{\mathsf{SIG}} = (s_i, x_i)$
        Repeat {
            $w_i' \leftarrow W_i$
            $\tilde{w}_i \leftarrow \mathsf{SS.Rec}(w_i', s_i)$
            $ssk_i' \leftarrow \mathsf{H}(\tilde{w}_i, x_i)$
            $vk_i' \leftarrow \mathsf{VK.Gen}(\mathsf{pp}_{\mathsf{SIG}}, ssk_i')$
        until $(vk_i' = vk_i)$
        $\sigma_2 \leftarrow \mathsf{Sign}(ssk_i', (U_j, U_i, pk, ctr_i[j], c))$
        $\Psi_i :=$ accept; $k_i := k$
        $\mathsf{msg}' := (U_j, U_i, c, \sigma_2)$

    If $\mathsf{msg} = (U_i, U_j, c, \sigma_2)$: //$\mathsf{msg}$ is the second message
        Parse $st_i^s = (pk_{\mathsf{KEM}}, P_{i,s}^{\mathsf{KEM}})$
        If $\mathsf{Ver}(vk_j, (U_i, U_j, pk, ctr_i[j]), \sigma_2) \neq 1$:
            $\Psi_i^s :=$ reject; Return $\bot$
        Parse $st_i^s = (P_{i,s}^{\mathsf{KEM}}, pk_{i,s})$
        Parse $P_{i,s}^{\mathsf{KEM}} = x_{i,s}, \pi_i^{\mathsf{SIG}} := (s_i, x_i)$
        Repeat{
            $w_{i,s}' \leftarrow W_i$
            $\tilde{w}_{i,s} \leftarrow \mathsf{SS.Rec}(w_{i,s}', s_i)$
            $sk_{i,s}' \leftarrow \mathsf{H}(\tilde{w}_{i,s}, x_{i,s})$
            $(pk_{i,s}') \leftarrow \mathsf{PK.Gen}(\mathsf{pp}_{\mathsf{KEM}}; sk_{i,s}')\}$
        until $(pk_{i,s}' = pk_{i,s})$
        $k = \mathsf{Decap}(sk_{i,s}, c)$
        $\Psi_i :=$ accept; $k_i := k$
        $\mathsf{msg}' := \emptyset$

    If $\Psi_i^s =$ accept :
        If $crp_j =$ true : $Aflag_i^s :=$ true;
        // Determine whether $\pi_i^s$ accepts before its partner
        Else if $\exists t \in [\ell]$ s.t. $\mathsf{Partner}(\pi_i^s \leftarrow \pi_j^t)$:
            If $\Psi_j^t \neq$ accept:
                $FirstAcc_j^t :=$ true; $FirstAcc_i^s :=$ false
            If $\Psi_j^t =$ accept:
                $FirstAcc_i^s :=$ false; $FirstAcc_j^t :=$ true
        Return $\mathsf{msg}'$

If $\mathsf{query} = \mathsf{StateReveal}(i, s)$:
    If $(i,s) \notin [\mu] \times [\ell]$, Return $\bot$
    If $FirstAcc_i^s =$ false $\land crp_i =$ true :
        If $T_i^s =$ true : Return $\bot$; // avoid TA6
    Let $j := Pid_i^s$
    If $\exists t \in [\ell]$ s.t. $\mathsf{Partner}(\pi_j^t \leftarrow \pi_i^s)$:
        If $T_j^t =$ true : Return $\bot$ // avoid TA7
    $stRev_i^s :=$ true; Return $st_i^s$

If $\mathsf{query} = \mathsf{SessionKeyReveal}(i, s)$:
    If $(i,s) \notin [\mu] \times [\ell]$, Return $\bot$
    If $\Psi_i^s \neq$ accept : Return $\bot$
    If $T_i^s =$ true : Return $\bot$ // avoid TA2
    Let $j := Pid_i^s$
    If $\exists t \in [\ell]$ s.t. $\mathsf{Partner}(\pi_i^s \leftrightarrow \pi_j^t)$:
        If $T_j^t =$ true : Return $\bot$ // avoid TA4
    $kRev_i^s :=$ true; Return $k_i^s$

**Fig. 5.** The original $\mathsf{Exp}_{\mathsf{FAKE},\mu,\ell,\mathcal{A}}$ for our FAKE scheme, where $\mathsf{Corrupt}(i)$, $\mathsf{StateReveal}(i, s)$ and $\mathsf{SessionKeyReveal}(i, s)$ are the same as in Fig. 3 and omitted here for conciseness.

# B    Figure 6: The Security Games $G_0$-$G_6$ for FAKE

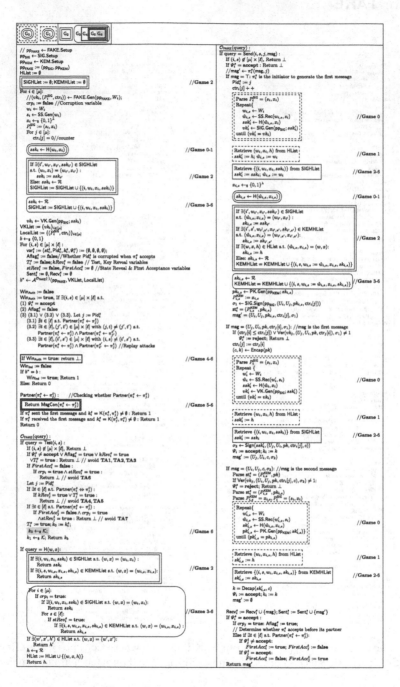

**Fig. 6.** FAKE security games $G_0$-$G_6$.

In Fig. 6, oracles Corrupt$(i)$, StateReveal$(i, s)$ and SessionKeyReveal$(i, s)$ are the same as in Fig. 3 and omitted here for conciseness. Note that $G_0$ contains the plain text, ⌈text⌉ and ⟮text⟯ part. $G_1$ contains the plain text, ⟮text⟯ and ⌈text⌉ part. $G_2$ contains the plain text, ‖text‖ and |text| part. $G_3$ contains the plain text, ⌊text⌋ and |text| part. $G_4$ contains $G_3$ and |text| part. $G_5$ contains $G_4$ and ‖text‖ part. $G_6$ contains $G_5$ and text part.

# References

1. Bader, C.: Efficient signatures with tight real world security in the random-oracle model. In: Gritzalis, D., Kiayias, A., Askoxylakis, I. (eds.) CANS 2014. LNCS, vol. 8813, pp. 370–383. Springer, Cham (2014). https://doi.org/10.1007/978-3-319-12280-9_24

2. Bader, C., Hofheinz, D., Jager, T., Kiltz, E., Li, Y.: Tightly-secure authenticated key exchange. In: Dodis, Y., Nielsen, J.B. (eds.) TCC 2015. LNCS, vol. 9014, pp. 629–658. Springer, Heidelberg (2015). https://doi.org/10.1007/978-3-662-46494-6_26

3. Bedari, A., Wang, S., Yang, J.: A two-stage feature transformation-based fingerprint authentication system for privacy protection in IoT. IEEE Trans. Ind. Informatics 18(4), 2745–2752 (2022)

4. Dodis, Y., Ostrovsky, R., Reyzin, L., Smith, A.D.: Fuzzy extractors: how to generate strong keys from biometrics and other noisy data. SIAM J. Comput. 38(1), 97–139 (2008)

5. Dupont, P.-A., Hesse, J., Pointcheval, D., Reyzin, L., Yakoubov, S.: Fuzzy password-authenticated key exchange. In: Nielsen, J.B., Rijmen, V. (eds.) EUROCRYPT 2018. LNCS, vol. 10822, pp. 393–424. Springer, Cham (2018). https://doi.org/10.1007/978-3-319-78372-7_13

6. Gjøsteen, K., Jager, T.: Practical and tightly-secure digital signatures and authenticated key exchange. In: Shacham, H., Boldyreva, A. (eds.) CRYPTO 2018. LNCS, vol. 10992, pp. 95–125. Springer, Cham (2018). https://doi.org/10.1007/978-3-319-96881-0_4

7. Groth, J., Sahai, A.: Efficient non-interactive proof systems for bilinear groups. In: Smart, N. (ed.) EUROCRYPT 2008. LNCS, vol. 4965, pp. 415–432. Springer, Heidelberg (2008). https://doi.org/10.1007/978-3-540-78967-3_24

8. Han, S., et al.: Authenticated key exchange and signatures with tight security in the standard model. In: Malkin, T., Peikert, C. (eds.) CRYPTO 2021. LNCS, vol. 12828, pp. 670–700. Springer, Cham (2021). https://doi.org/10.1007/978-3-030-84259-8_23

9. Im, J., Jeon, S., Lee, M.: Practical privacy-preserving face authentication for smartphones secure against malicious clients. IEEE Trans. Inf. Forensics Secur. 15, 2386–2401 (2020)

10. Juels, A., Sudan, M.: A fuzzy vault scheme. Des. Codes Cryptogr. 38(2), 237–257 (2006)

11. Katz, J., Lindell, Y.: Introduction to Modern Cryptography, Second Edition. 2nd edn. Chapman & Hall/CRC (2014)

12. Lee, Y., Lee, D.H., Park, J.H.: Tightly CCA-secure encryption scheme in a multi-user setting with corruptions. Des. Codes Cryptogr. **88**(11), 2433–2452 (2020)

13. Li, Y., Schäge, S.: No-match attacks and robust partnering definitions: Defining trivial attacks for security protocols is not trivial. In: Thuraisingham, B.M., Evans, D., Malkin, T., Xu, D. (eds.) CCS 2017, pp. 1343–1360. ACM (2017)

14. Liu, X., Liu, S., Gu, D., Weng, J.: Two-pass authenticated key exchange with explicit authentication and tight security. In: Moriai, S., Wang, H. (eds.) ASIACRYPT 2020. LNCS, vol. 12492, pp. 785–814. Springer, Cham (2020). https://doi.org/10.1007/978-3-030-64834-3_27

15. Pan, J., Qian, C., Ringerud, M.: Signed diffie-hellman key exchange with tight security. In: Paterson, K.G. (ed.) CT-RSA 2021. LNCS, vol. 12704, pp. 201–226. Springer, Cham (2021). https://doi.org/10.1007/978-3-030-75539-3_9

16. Patil, V.C., Kundu, S.: Realizing robust, lightweight strong PUFs for securing smart grids. IEEE Trans. Consumer Electron. **68**(1), 5–13 (2022)

17. Wang, M., He, K., Chen, J., Li, Z., Zhao, W., Du, R.: Biometrics-authenticated key exchange for secure messaging. In: Kim, Y., Kim, J., Vigna, G., Shi, E. (eds.) CCS '21, pp. 2618–2631, ACM (2021)

18. Wen, Y., Liu, S.: Robustly reusable fuzzy extractor from standard assumptions. In: Peyrin, T., Galbraith, S. (eds.) ASIACRYPT 2018. LNCS, vol. 11274, pp. 459–489. Springer, Cham (2018). https://doi.org/10.1007/978-3-030-03332-3_17

19. Woodage, J., Chatterjee, R., Dodis, Y., Juels, A., Ristenpart, T.: A new distribution-sensitive secure sketch and popularity-proportional hashing. In: Katz, J., Shacham, H. (eds.) CRYPTO 2017. LNCS, vol. 10403, pp. 682–710. Springer, Cham (2017). https://doi.org/10.1007/978-3-319-63697-9_23

# Continuous Authentication in Secure Messaging

Benjamin Dowling[1] , Felix Günther[2] , and Alexandre Poirrier[3]([⊠])

[1] University of Sheffield, London, UK
b.dowling@sheffield.ac.uk
[2] ETH Zürich, Zürich, Switzerland
mail@felixguenther.info
[3] École polytechnique and Direction Générale de l'Armement, Paris, France
alexandre.poirrier@polytechnique.org

**Abstract.** Secure messaging schemes such as the Signal protocol rely on out-of-band channels to verify the authenticity of long-running communication. Such out-of-band checks however are only rarely actually performed by users in practice.

In this paper, we propose a new method for performing continuous authentication during a secure messaging session, without the need for an out-of-band channel. Leveraging the users' long-term secrets, our *Authentication Steps* extension guarantees authenticity as long as long-term secrets are not compromised, strengthening Signal's post-compromise security. Our mechanism further allows to detect a potential compromise of long-term secrets after the fact via an out-of-band channel.

Our protocol comes with a novel, formal security definition capturing continuous authentication, a general construction for Signal-like protocols, and a security proof for the proposed instantiation. We further provide a prototype implementation which seamlessly integrates on top of the official Signal Java library, together with bandwidth and storage overhead benchmarks.

**Keywords:** Secure messaging · Authentication · Compromise detection · Post-compromise security.

## 1 Introduction

The Signal end-to-end encrypted messaging protocol [20] is used by billions of people [28], in the Signal app itself and other messengers such as Facebook Messenger [11] and WhatsApp [26]. The security of encryption keys used in the Signal protocol relies on two composed cryptographic protocols. First, a Diffie–Hellman-style key exchange protocol involving long-term asymmetric keys (whose public part is distributed via a central Signal server) is used to derive a shared secret. This initial shared secret is then used by parties in Signal's Double Ratchet protocol [17] to derive symmetric keys, used to encrypt messages between the two communicating parties.

© The Author(s), under exclusive license to Springer Nature Switzerland AG 2022
V. Atluri et al. (Eds.): ESORICS 2022, LNCS 13555, pp. 361–381, 2022.
https://doi.org/10.1007/978-3-031-17146-8_18

**Signal's Security.** There have been numerous analyses of the security of the Signal protocol, as has been recapitulated in [22], which show that security properties for messaging protocols come in a variety of flavours with different adversary powers and strengths.

For these analyses, models separate different types of secrets: *session secrets* (like ephemeral randomness or state), which are used throughout the Double Ratchet protocol, and *long-term secrets*, used only in the initial key agreement. Some [6,7] study the security of the Signal protocol in its entirety, including the X3DH key exchange. Others [1,2,10,13,15,18] focus exclusively on the ratcheting part of the protocol, thus considering only session secrets. Among other security properties, [6] and [1] confirm that against strong adversaries who control the network and can adaptively compromise session and long-term secrets, Signal offers forward secrecy (meaning that the secrecy of messages sent before a secret leakage are still secure) as well as post-compromise security [7] (meaning that after users exchange *unmodified* messages, security is restored or "healed").

As pointed out by [9], the definition of post-compromise security is quite restrictive in the sense that the adversary needs to remain completely passive for security to be restored. Indeed, if the adversary remains active after a state leakage and continuously injects forged messages, authenticity is never restored. [9] instead proposes a protocol relying on an out-of-band channel (like email, SMS, or an in-person meeting) to detect such active adversaries, leveraging additional *fingerprints* computed by the protocol and compared over the out-of-band channel. However, while detection clearly is a good step towards mitigating attacks, it does not prevent the actual attack from continuing.

**Locking Out Active Adversaries.** The question we are interested in for this work goes one step further:

> *Can we, post-compromise, lock out even*
> *an <u>active</u> adversary from a messaging communication?*

Clearly, the answer in general is: No. An active network adversary that fully compromises a user's device, including all session and long-term secrets can, by design, fully impersonate that user subsequently. Our angle to approach the above question is to distinguish (and thus better leverage), the difference between the use of session and long-term secrets in the Signal protocol.

More specifically, what if we can leverage that user long-term secrets are harder to compromise, e.g., due to stronger randomness sources or better protection in hardware? Indeed, messaging services like WhatsApp or Signal are now deployed [27] on devices which have access to secure hardware such as Trusted Platform Modules (TPM) in which long-term secrets can be stored more safely. Phones on the other hand can use smart-cards to store their long-term keys. A typical attack scenario are border searches, where a travelling user would need to give away their phone or laptop for analysis, risking the leak of their session secrets. An adversary could then remain an active Man-in-the-Middle (MitM), possibly on nation-controlled networks, yet long-term keys in smart cards or a

TPM might not have been leaked. Such a breach of authenticity can have a high impact in the case of Signal as sessions are typically months or years long.

We can then ask:

> *Can we, post-compromise, lock out even*
> *an <u>active</u> adversary from a messaging communication*
> *that compromised session, but <u>not</u> long-term secrets?*

Notably, the answer for Signal is still: No. We will show how to, generically, turn this into a Yes.

## 1.1  Contributions

The main contributions of this paper are

1. a formal, game-based definition of *continuous authentication*, a post-compromise security property locking out active adversaries who have not compromised long-term secrets;
2. a demonstration that protocols similar to Signal do not meet the security requirement;
3. a *generic extension* for messaging protocols to provide them with provably-secure continuous authentication;
4. a prototype implementation of our extension for Signal and an *analysis and benchmark* of the overhead it introduces;
5. exposing a discrepancy between the post-compromise security by Signal's official library and what is claimed in the literature.

## 1.2  Further Related Work

The security of real secure messaging implementations is also evaluated in [8], with a focus on (de)synchronization. Somewhat similar to our setting, their analysis involves an adversary trying to break post-compromise security by impersonating a compromised user and finding discrepancies between the implementations and the formal specifications.

Similarly to our approach, [13] proposes a construction for secure messaging by signing message transcripts, focusing though on healing communication under *passive* attacks while we are interested to detect and prevent *active* attacks.

## 2  Continuous Authentication

This section presents what locking out an active adversary from a messaging communication formally means. The basis for this is a formal syntax, following [1], that captures generic *messaging schemes* that operate on an unreliable channel, derive an initial shared session secret using long-term keys and then derive further session secrets from previous state, new randomness and possibly long-term keys. This in particular encompasses the Signal Double Ratchet protocol.

We then put forward a game-based security definition for *continuous authentication*, which guarantees two core properties:

1. An active MitM adversary that compromised a user's communication state gets *locked out* of the communication *unless* it has also compromised the user's long-term secrets.
2. Users can correctly *decide whether* long-term secrets have been compromised in an active attack, via an out-of-band channel.

The first property captures the desired strengthening of messaging protocols. In the Double Ratchet protocol [17], all secrets are derived from prior established secret state (the so-called *root* and *chain* keys) and new randomness generated by the users (the Diffie–Hellman *ratchet* keys). The former is revealed in a full state compromise and the latter are unauthenticated and can hence be impersonated by the adversary. Therefore, an adversary can conserve its Man-in-the-Middle position indefinitely without being detected in-band.

The second property improves on a related issue: If long-term secrets *are* compromised, then security is not restored if users only close their current session and reopen a new one, but users will instead need to generate and distribute new long-term keys. This procedure however is cumbersome and typically involves manual effort, so ideally one would like to better know *when* it is indeed necessary. Continuous authentication offers such a checking mechanism, enabling users to only change their long-term secrets if they have indeed been leaked.

## 2.1 Messaging Schemes

A messaging scheme consists of several algorithms: The core algorithms, following [1], are used to create users (REGISTER), initiate sessions between them (INITSTATE) and let them send and receive messages (SEND and RECV). Our definition supports an arbitrary number of users, but only two-party sessions (*i.e.*, no group chats).

In addition to the four core messaging algorithms, our formalization introduces STARTAUTH, a procedure which can be used to initiate an in-band authentication step[1] and DETECTOOB, a procedure that compares the states of two session participants out-of-band and decides whether an adversary has used a long-term secret to avoid in-band detection.

Moreover, the session state contains an `auth` flag which is initially set to **None**. STARTAUTH is a special procedure which may set this flag to a value other than **None** to indicate that the party is currently performing an authentication step. An authentication step is *passed* once the `auth` flags of both communication parties are back to **None**.

In a session between two parties, we define an *epoch* as a flow of messages, sent by one party without receiving a reply by their peer. Epochs are numbered: even epochs correspond to messages sent by the initiator of the conversation and

---

[1] This procedure can leave the state unchanged if the messaging scheme, like the original Signal protocol, does not support in-band authentication.

odd epochs to messages sent by the responder. Within an epoch, messages are again numbered consecutively.

## 2.2   Security Game

We now present the formal security game capturing continuous authentication, represented in Definition 1.

The security game creates two users, Alice $(A)$ and Bob $(B)$, and lets the adversary interact with them using oracles to simulate a communication. As the final objective is to detect long-term secret compromise, long-term secrets are distributed honestly to parties. In contrast, medium-term secrets are generated by parties, but delivered on the communication channel, allowing the adversary to tamper with them. The adversary is active on the network and can corrupt devices, leaking their current state. The adversary can also compromise long-term secrets, which sets a flag *compromised* in the game, maintaining adversary knowledge within the game. When the adversary terminates, an out-of-band detection step (detectTrial, see Algorithm 1) is triggered.

The adversary breaks continuous authentication (we say the adversary "wins") by (1) fooling the out-of-band detection DETECTOOB to think it compromised the long-term keys when it actually did not, or (2) injecting a message and successfully passing an authentication step ($passinj \neq \emptyset$), without being detected.

Note that our model conservatively grants the adversary more power than may seem reasonable in practice. In particular, the adversary can choose when in-band and out-of-band detection steps happen (by calling STARTAUTH and terminating). In practice, in-band detection steps may follow a predefined schedule, and out-of-band detection steps are performed at the discretion of users.

**Oracles and Security Game.** The adversary has access to the following oracles, with corresponding counterpart oracles for Bob:

- createState-A creates the initial state of Alice given some public information of Bob provided by the adversary.
- transmit-A takes a plaintext as input and simulates Alice sending it.
- deliver-A takes a ciphertext as input and simulates Alice receiving it.
- corruptState-A returns the current state of Alice.
- auth-A makes Alice request authentication.
- corruptLTS-A leaks Alice's long-term secret to the adversary.

For space reasons, we defer their formal definition to Fig. 2 in the appendix.

The security game itself and resulting security notions are defined as follows.

**Definition 1. (Continuous Authentication).** *Let $\mathcal{A}$ be a probabilistic polynomial-time adversary against a messaging scheme MS. It has access to oracles defined above, abbreviated as oracles$_{MS}$. The security game is given in Algorithm 1.*

```
 1  game Detection-Game(A, MS):
 2      (LTI_A, LTS_A, MTI_A, MTS_A) ⭠$ MS.REGISTER()
 3      (LTI_B, LTS_B, MTI_B, MTS_B) ⭠$ MS.REGISTER()
 4      π_A, π_B ← None, None
 5      win ← False, closed ← False, compromised ← False
 6      trans_A, trans_B ← ∅, ∅
 7      inj_A, inj_B, authinj, passinj ← ∅, ∅, ∅, ∅
 8      A^oracles_MS(LTI_A, LTI_B, MTI_A, MTI_B)
 9      detectTrial()
10      return win ∧ ¬closed

11  procedure detectTrial():
12      assert(π_A ∧ π_B ∧ ¬π_A.auth ∧ ¬π_B.auth)
13      d ← DETECTOOB(π_A, π_B)
14      if d ∧ ¬compromised:
15      |   win ← True
16      elif ¬d ∧ passinj ≠ ∅:
17      |   win ← True
```

**Algorithm 1:** Security game capturing continuous authentication.

*The advantage of adversary A against the messaging scheme MS in the detection game is:*

$$\mathrm{Adv}(\mathcal{A}) = Pr[\text{Detection-Game}(\mathcal{A}, \text{MS}) = 1].$$

*The messaging scheme MS is said to provide* continuous authentication *if for all efficient adversaries A, Adv(A) is small.*

The game defines internal variables to keep track of the communication and of the adversary's actions:

- $(LTI_U, LTS_U)$ is the long-term information and secret of user $U$ and $\pi_U$ its state.
- *win* is a flag representing if the adversary has met the winning conditions.
- *closed* is a flag representing the state of the connection (if it is closed or not).
- *compromised* records if the adversary has compromised either of the parties' long-term secrets.
- $trans_U$ is a set holding ciphertexts created by a legitimate user $U$.
- $inj_U$ is a set containing messages injected to user $U$ (which user $U$ accepted) that are yet to be authenticated. *authinj* is a set used during authentication steps which holds all injected messages currently being authenticated. *passinj* is a set containing all injected messages that successfully passed authentication.

**Oracle Details.** (See Appendix, Fig. 2 for the oracles' code-based definition.)

The `transmit-A/B` oracles are a wrapper around SEND, which records ciphertexts created legitimately by users. Similarly, the `deliver-A/B` oracles are a wrapper around RECV which add injected ciphertexts to the *inj* sets.

When Alice starts an authentication step (which happens when she receives an authentication message or when `auth-A` is called), *authinj* is filled with all messages that were injected to her. Authenticated messages will be those she has received in the last epoch and before.

Whenever the adversary calls `deliver-A/B`, a function is called to check if the adversary has successfully injected a message and passed an authentication step. In that case, it adds the injected messages that were successfully authenticated in *passinj* and removes them from *authinj* and *inj* sets.

The *win* flag can only be set to **True** in the `detectTrial` function. This happens either if parties output **True** in the out-of-band detection step but the long-term secret was not compromised (users produced a false positive) or if they output **False** but communication was successfully tampered with and the authentication step passed (the attacker was successful at avoiding detection).

## 3  Introducing Authentication Steps

This section presents our proposed *Authentication Steps* protocol that generically extends messaging schemes to achieve continuous authentication.

Our extension introduces authentication steps that may happen regularly at defined epochs in a session or could be user-triggered. These authentication steps leverage long-term secrets. In Signal, the long-term secret of a user consists of their private identity key, a Diffie–Hellman exponent. The Authentication Steps protocol introduces a new type of long-term secret, which is a signing key $sigk^U$.[2]

The objectives of an authentication step are twofold:

1. to convince parties that they are communicating with the holder of their peer's private key, and
2. to detect tampering with messages since the last authentication step.

To that end, each party sends on the in-band channel their own view of the communication since the last authentication step. These messages are included alongside regular messages exchanged between users; as we will see, this allows the authentication steps to seamlessly be integrated on top of the existing Signal protocol.

In order to maintain forward secrecy, the additional information is derived from the (public) ciphertexts sent. To save space, intermediate computations compress those ciphertexts as they are sent or received. Those intermediate computations and an authentication step are illustrated in Fig. 1.

---

[2] In practice, Signal already re-uses the identity key to sign a user's medium-term public key using the XEdDSA [16] signature scheme; we therefore emphasize that an implementation may similarly reuse that identity key as the signing long-term key for our authentication steps extension. In practice, this means only maintaining a single long-term secret for both Signal and our Authentication Steps protocol.

**Alice**                                        **Bob**

$$H_{0,0}^A \leftarrow \mathtt{H}\left(c_{0,0}^A\right) \xrightarrow{\quad c_{0,0} \quad} H_{0,0}^B \leftarrow \mathtt{H}\left(c_{0,0}^B\right)$$

$$H_{0,1}^A \leftarrow \mathtt{H}\left(c_{0,1}^A\right) \xrightarrow{\ c_{0,1}\ }\!\!\times$$

$$H_{0,2}^A \leftarrow \mathtt{H}\left(c_{0,2}^A\right) \xrightarrow{\quad c_{0,2} \quad} \begin{array}{l} H_{0,2}^B \leftarrow \mathtt{H}\left(c_{0,2}^B\right) \\ SKIP_B = \{(0,1)\} \end{array}$$

$$H_{1,0}^A \leftarrow \mathtt{H}\left(c_{1,0}^A\right) \xleftarrow{\quad c_{1,0} \quad} H_{1,0}^B \leftarrow \mathtt{H}\left(c_{1,0}^B\right)$$

$$H_{2,0}^A \leftarrow \mathtt{H}\left(c_{2,0}^A\right) \xrightarrow{\ c_{2,0}\ }\!\!\times$$

$$H_{1,1}^A \leftarrow \mathtt{H}\left(c_{1,1}^A\right) \xleftarrow{\quad c_{1,1} \quad} H_{1,1}^B \leftarrow \mathtt{H}\left(c_{1,1}^B\right)$$

$$\times\!\!\xleftarrow{\quad c_{1,2} \quad} H_{1,2}^B \leftarrow \mathtt{H}\left(c_{1,2}^B\right)$$

$$H_{2,1}^A \leftarrow \mathtt{H}\left(c_{2,1}^A\right) \xrightarrow{\quad c_{2,1} \quad} \begin{array}{l} H_{2,1}^B \leftarrow \mathtt{H}\left(c_{2,1}^B\right) \\ SKIP_B = \{(0,1),(2,0)\} \end{array}$$

$$\begin{array}{l} H_{3,0}^A \leftarrow \mathtt{H}\left(c_{3,0}^A\right) \\ SKIP_A = \{(1,2)\} \end{array} \xleftarrow{\quad c_{3,0} \quad} H_{3,0}^B \leftarrow \mathtt{H}\left(c_{3,0}^B\right)$$

$$\text{last message: } (3,0) \xrightarrow{\quad c_{4,0} \quad} \mathtt{Vfy}_{sigpk^A}(.,.)$$
$$(\mathbf{3},\mathbf{0}), \{(1,2)\},$$
$$\mathtt{SIG}_{sigk^A}((\mathbf{3},\mathbf{0}),\{(1,2)\})$$

$$\begin{array}{l}\text{[Computation A]} \\ \mathtt{Vfy}_{sigpk^B}(.,.)\end{array} \xleftarrow{\quad c_{5,0} \quad} \begin{array}{l}\{(0,1),(2,0)\}, \\ \text{[Computation B]}\end{array}$$
$$\mathtt{SIG}_{sigk^B}(H_B^{(0)},\{(0,1),(2,0)\})$$

$$\xrightarrow{\quad c_{6,0} \quad} \mathtt{Vfy}_{sigpk^A}(.,.)$$
$$\mathtt{SIG}_{sigk^A}(H_A^{(0)})$$

**Fig. 1.** An example execution of an authentication step. The actual authentication step is performed during epochs **4** to **6**, with authenticated messages from epoch **0** (epoch numbers in **boldface**). Additional data sent for those messages is included below arrows. For epochs **4** to **6**, $H_{i,j}$ hashes are still computed by both parties, but they are omitted in this figure as they concern the next authentication step. [Computation U] for $U \in \{A, B\}$ corresponds to the computation $H_U^{(0)} \leftarrow 0\|\mathtt{H}\left(\varepsilon\|H_{0,0}^U\|H_{0,2}^U\|H_{1,0}^U\|H_{1,1}^U\|H_{2,1}^U\|H_{3,0}^U\right)$.

## 3.1  Recording Ciphertexts

In order to perform authentication steps, parties need to store the transcript of ciphertexts sent and received. The order in which messages are received is not relevant as reordering may be caused by the unreliable channel.

Instead of storing ciphertexts as sent, each party computes digests of those ciphertexts using a hash function and stores those in a dictionary. Concretely, for every sent or received message, each user $U$ computes and stores $H_{i,j}^U = \mathtt{H}\left(c_{i,j}^U\right)$, where $\mathtt{H}$ is a cryptographic hash function and $c_{i,j}^U$ is the ciphertext corresponding to message $j$ sent or received in epoch $i$ by user $U$.

## 3.2  Authentication Steps

The stored (and hashed) ciphertexts are then used in the actual authentication step. An authentication step is a 3-pass message exchange and therefore requires three epochs to complete. In the following, an authentication step is described wlog. with Alice sending the first authentication message. Figure 1 illustrates an authentication step, performed in epochs 4 to 6.

The authentication step information is included in every message of the epoch. That way, the peer receives the authentication information at least once, as if they do not receive it, the epoch number will not increase. If authentication information is missing from a message where it should have been included, then the receiving party should dismiss the message.

In the first epoch, Alice sends the following additional authentication information (encrypted along with actual plaintext):

- the indexes of messages that she should have received from Bob, but did not, denoted $SKIP_A$,
- the index of the most recent message she has received from Bob, denoted $authidx$, and
- a signature $\mathtt{SIG}_{sigk^A}(authidx, SKIP_A)$ over both values.

This allows Bob to know which messages Alice wants to authenticate. When Bob receives this message, he first verifies the signature using Alice's signing public key. In case of success, Bob computes the following hash:

$$H_B^{(n_B)} = n_B \| \mathtt{H}\left(H_B^{(n_B-1)} \| \; \|_{(i,j)\in I_B^{(n_B)}} H_{i,j}^B\right),$$

where $n_B$ is the number of authentication steps Bob has completed and $H_B^{(n_B-1)}$ the hash computed in the previous authentication step (with the convention $H_B^{(-1)} = \varepsilon$ the empty string). The concatenation happens in lexicographic order over $I_B^{(n_B)}$, the set of all messages sent and received by Bob since last authentication step and until message $authidx$, and excluding messages with an index contained in $SKIP_A$.

In the second epoch (with Bob sending messages), Bob sends the following information (along with the regular message plaintexts):

- the indexes of messages that he should have received from Alice, denoted $SKIP_B$, and
- a signature $\mathrm{SIG}_{sigk^B}(H_B^{(n_B)}, SKIP_B)$ over the hash computed and the indexes of missed messages.

When Alice receives Bob's message, she extracts the list $SKIP_B$ and computes the following hash:

$$H_A^{(n_A)} = n_A \| \mathrm{H}\left(H_A^{(n_A-1)} \| \; \|_{(i,j)\in I_A^{(n_A)}} H_{i,j}^A\right),$$

where, like for Bob, $n_A$ is her number of completed authentication steps and $H_A^{(n_A-1)}$ is the previous hash (or $H_A^{(-1)} = \varepsilon$). Alice then checks the signature received from Bob, using Bob's public signing key, on data $(H_A^{(n_A)}, SKIP_B)$.

In the third epoch, Alice sends a signature $\mathrm{SIG}_{sigk^A}(H_A^{(n_A)})$ over her hashed collection of seen messages. When Bob receives it, he verifies the signature's validity on $H_B^{(n_B)}$ using Alice's signing public key.

If at some point a signature verification fails, the verifier closes the connection. Otherwise, Alice and Bob have *passed the authentication step*.

**Deniable Signing.** We emphasize that any unforgeable signature scheme can be used in the authentication step. In particular, to maintain Signal's deniability of the initial key agreement (cf. [25]), signatures can be generated using designated-verifier or 2-user ring signatures [14,19], similarly to their deployment in recent proposals for Signal-like deniable key exchanges [3,12,23,24].

### 3.3   Detecting Compromised Long-Term Secrets

In this setting, we assume that Alice and Bob have passed at least one authentication step. At each authentication step, parties derive a hash $H_A^{(n_A)}$ or $H_B^{(n_B)}$. Authentication steps succeed if the signatures over those hashes match.

On a high-level, users execute the following protocol: Using the out-of-band channel, parties compare the last hash they have computed (which they store in their state until the next authentication step) as well as the number of authentication steps performed. If the hash values and authentication steps counters match, the users output **False**, indicating that they do not detect long-term key compromise, otherwise they output **True**.

If no adversary tampers with the communication, then exchanged hashes would match. Conversely, hashes not matching means that an adversary is present. Moreover, as at least one authentication step has been successful, the adversary must have been able to forge a signature to avoid in-band detection, which indicates they know at least one long-term secret. We will formally prove these two properties of the Authentication Steps protocol next.

# 4    Security of the Authentication Steps Protocol

We now formally establish the continuous authentication security (as per Definition 1) of our Authentication Steps protocol extension given in Sect. 3.

**Theorem 1.** *Assuming a collision resistant hash function* H *and an existentially unforgeable signature scheme* $S$, *the Authentication Steps protocol presented in Sect. 3 provides continuous authentication as per Definition 1.*

*Formally, the advantage of any adversary* $A$ *in the detection game against the Authentication Steps protocol is bounded as follows:*

$$Adv(A) \leq Adv_{B_1}^{coll}(H) + 2 \cdot Adv_{B_2}^{EUF\text{-}CMA}(S),$$

*for reduction adversaries* $B_1$ *and* $B_2$ *given in the proof.*

The proof is separated into two cases:

1. users decide one of their long-term secrets is compromised when that is not the case; and
2. the adversary manages to inject a message and remain undetected.

Due to space restrictions, we defer the detailed proof to Appendix A, and only give a proof sketch here.

In Case 1, the adversary never corrupts the long-term secret, yet the parties decide that their long-term secret is compromised. Thus, the hashes that Alice and Bob exchanged at the end of the game must be different, but both Alice and Bob verified signatures hashes in the last authentication step. It follows then that either Alice or Bob received a signature that was not produced by their peer, and that the adversary must have successfully forged a message under one of their (non-compromised) signing key. This would violate EUF-CMA security of the signature scheme, leading to the $2 \cdot Adv_{B_2}^{EUF\text{-}CMA}(S)$ term in the theorem bound.

In Case 2, the adversary must have injected a message between Alice and Bob, but when Alice and Bob exchanged their hashes at the end of the game, the hash outputs matched. It follows that between Alice's or Bob's computations there must be a hash collision, leading to the $Adv_{B_1}^{coll}(H)$ term in the theorem bound.

# 5    Implementation and Benchmarks

We implemented a prototype of our Authentication Steps protocol which integrates seamlessly *on top* of the official Signal Java library.

Our full implementation can be found on GitHub[3], along with build instructions and our benchmarking tests.

---

[3] https://github.com/apoirrier/libsignal-java-authsteps

**Space and Computation Overhead.** Authentication steps require additional data to be computed and stored, such as the ciphertexts hashes between authentication steps.

The storage and bandwidth overhead is a function of the channel reliability and the average number of messages per authentication step, the latter being the more influential parameter. Indeed, the sender cannot know in advance which messages the peer has received, thus there is no alternative but storing every ciphertext hash individually.

As for computational overhead, computing the ciphertext hashes involves one hash invocation; additionally, at most one signature and one verification operation is performed per epoch. The signature scheme employed by Signal is XEdDSA [16]. Signing and verifying data typically requires the same amount of computation as the Diffie-Hellman key computation happening in asymmetric ratchet steps. Thus, the computational overhead is at most the same magnitude as the original computations in Signal.

**Benchmarking the Space Overhead.** In order to give an estimate on the space overhead induced by the Authentication Steps extension, we performed simulations of communication sessions to evaluate ciphertext size and state sizes. The message inputs for our simulations are taken from the National University of Singapore SMS Corpus [4,5], an SMS dataset composed of English text messages.

At the example of a 95%-reliable channel, our results show a mean increase of 43 bytes ($+39\%$) in ciphertext size and 2.6 KB ($+411\%$) in session state size compared to the unmodified Signal protocol. Overheads increase with longer communication epoch lengths and lower channel reliability.

This overhead can be optimized through the usage of trees (for instance Merkle trees) to store hashes, and compress them if consecutive sequences of messages are received. This optimization would be interesting to implement and benchmark, at the same time it would make the underlying analysis and notions more complex. Furthermore, this optimization can only be performed on the receiver's side, as the sender has no way to know which sent messages will eventually be received. Thus, the compression can only happen on at most half of the conversation, and the space optimisation is bound by a factor 2.

## 6    Observations on the Official Implementation

While implementing the proposed protocol, we found that the state deletion strategy in Signal's official Java implementation [21] is different from the strategy described in the formal analyses in the literature, such as [1] or [6], even if the latter claim to be based on the implementation. The official Signal specification [17] itself is unclear, and the strategy used in the implementation is implied but not made explicit.

In [1] or [6], post-compromise security kicks in after two epochs, which means that after two epochs of untampered communication after a state compromise, security is restored. This happens by the deletion of no longer necessary state once an epoch ends. However, the Signal implementation deletes this state only 5 epochs later, which is a hardcoded value[4].

Based on this, we observe that the following attack is possible which demonstrates that the official Signal implementation achieves only slightly weaker post-compromise security than claimed in the literature. In the middle of a communication between Alice and Bob, an adversary leaks the state of Alice. Assume that during this epoch $i$, Alice sent $n_i$ messages to Bob. The adversary can, by using the leaked state, create a valid ciphertext for message $(i, n_i + 1)$ (and even more messages).

Given the literature definition of post-compromise security, as the adversary remained passive security should be restored at epoch $i + 3$. However, with the Signal implementation, as Bob's state for epoch $i$ is not yet deleted at epoch $i + 3$, the adversary can successfully inject messages (for epoch $i$) to Bob.

Note however that security is restored 5 epochs after compromise, therefore the implementation still guarantees a weaker post-compromise security property.

**An Explanation of this Weaker Property, and Fixing it.** The Signal implementation disregards the total number of messages sent in the previous epoch, which is included alongside messages, and instead keeps the chain key without computing in advance message keys for missed messages. This saves computation time and space as the keys are not computed if those messages never arrive while the immediate decryption property is still valid as the chain key is kept and message keys can be derived if needed.

To fix this, when a new receiving epoch begins, the value of the total number of messages can be used to derive all message keys for this epoch and then delete the chain key from the state. This recovers the strong post-compromise security as claimed in the literature.

# 7   Conclusion

Messaging protocols such as Signal that only use their long-term secrets for session initiation allow for state-compromising adversaries to permanently take over a connection as a Man-in-the-Middle. This paper offers a strengthened security notion, continuous authentication, which locks out an active adversary post-compromise who has not compromised long-term keys, and enables detection of long-term secret compromises using an out-of-band channel. Our Authentication Steps protocol extension generically enables this security in a provably-secure way, adding regular authentication steps in the protocol that leverages long-term keys to authenticate users and ensure no tampering has occurred. Moreover, an out-of-band protocol can be used on top of that to detect adversaries having used long-term secrets to avoid in-band detection.

---

[4] Cf. line 210 in https://github.com/signalapp/libsignal-protocol-java/blob/fde96d22 004f32a391554e4991e4e1f0a14c2d50/java/src/main/java/org/whispersystems/ libsignal/state/SessionState.java#L210.

```
1  procedure createState-A(PI):
2  |  assert(¬π_A)
3  |  π_A ←$ INITSTATE(LTS_A, MTS_A, LTI_B, PI)
```

```
1  procedure transmit-A(m):
2  |  assert(π_A)
3  |  (π_A, c, idx) ←$ SEND(π_A, LTS_A, m)
4  |  if c ∈ inj_B ∪ authinj ∪ passinj :
5  |  |  inj_B ← inj_B \ {c}
6  |  |  authinj ← authinj \ {c}
7  |  |  passinj ← passinj \ {c}
8  |  trans_B.append(c)
9  |  return c
```

```
1  procedure corruptState-A():
2  |  if π_A:
3  |  |  return π_A
4  |  return MTS_A
```

```
1  procedure auth-A():
2  |  assert(lastrecv_A > 0 ∧ ¬π_A.auth ∧ ¬π_B.auth)
3  |  π_A ←$ STARTAUTH(π_A)
4  |  authinj, authidx ← inj_A, lastrecv_A
```

```
1  procedure corruptLTS-A():
2  |  compromised ← True
3  |  return LTS_A
```

```
1  procedure deliver-B(c):
2  |  assert(π_B)
3  |  try:
4  |  |  (π'_B, m, idx) ←$ RECV(π_B, LTS_B, c)
5  |  |  if m ≠ ⊥ ∧ idx > lastrecv_B:
6  |  |  |  lastrecv_B ← idx
7  |  |  if ¬π_B.auth ∧ π'_B.auth :
8  |  |  |  authinj ← authinj ∪ {c ∈ inj_B | c.idx ≤ authidx}
9  |  |  CheckAuthStepPassed()
10 |  |  π_B ← π'_B
11 |  |  if c ∉ trans_B ∧ m ≠ ⊥ :
12 |  |  |  inj_B[idx] ← c
13 |  |  return m
14 |  except Close:
15 |  |  closed ← True
```

```
1  procedure CheckAuthStepPassed():
2  |  if authinj ≠ ∅ ∧ ¬π_A.auth ∧ ¬π_B.auth:
3  |  |  passinj ← passinj ∪ authinj
4  |  |  inj_A ← inj_A \ authinj
5  |  |  inj_B ← inj_B \ authinj
6  |  |  authinj ← ∅
```

**Fig. 2.** Oracles available to the adversary in the continuous authentication security game (cf. Definition 1). The MS. prefixes for functions of the messaging scheme are omitted. The CheckAuthStepPassed function checks if the adversary succeeded in injecting a message which passed an authentication step. Each oracle has a counterpart whose implementation is similar by swapping A and B in the implementation.

We analysed the overhead introduced by authentication steps, benchmarking our prototype implementation which seamlessly integrates on top of the official Signal library. While implementing those benchmarks, we remarked that the official implementation has a weaker post-compromise security property than claimed in the literature.

While this paper focuses mainly on the Signal protocol, the concept of continuous authentication as well as the Authentication Steps protocol is generic. We envision that it can be adapted to other messaging protocols or protocols with long-lived connections, like TLS 1.3 resumption sessions, to provide stronger authenticity guarantees.

The Authentication Steps protocol strongly authenticates the entire transcript, even if the underlying channel is unreliable. Another interesting direction for future work is a conceivable reduced-overhead variant that only authenticates the key material (e.g., the ratchet keys in Signal) in every epoch. Such variant would still strengthen post-compromise security, yet in a weaker sense as it would not necessarily allow to detect the injection of messages at the end of compromised epochs, a property the Authentication Steps protocol provides.

# A    Security of the Authentication Steps Protocol

This section proves Theorem 1, which states that the Authentication Steps protocol is secure given the assumption that the underlying cryptographic primitives are secure, namely the hash function and the signature scheme. We denote $\text{Adv}_{\mathcal{A}}^{coll}(H)$ the advantage of an adversary trying to find a collision for a hash function $H$ and $\text{Adv}_{\mathcal{A}}^{EUF\text{-}CMA}(\mathcal{S})$ the advantage of an adversary in the EUF-CMA (Existential UnForgeability in the Chosen Message Attack setting) game against a signature scheme $\mathcal{S}$.

**False Positives and False Negatives.** Before proving security of the Authentication Steps protocol from Sect. 3, we introduce several useful definitions.

Recall that from the specification, no authentication steps can overlap. Therefore, users will reject messages that start a new authentication step if they are currently performing one. We can thus number authentication steps from a user $U$'s point of view from 1 to $n_U$.

For the actual theorem proof, we split the winning condition into two events, which we denote the false positive case and the false negative case, and use results from Propositions 1 and 2 to give an upper bound on their probability.

**Definition 2.** *Given an adversary $\mathcal{A}$ playing the security game of Definition 1, we define the following events:*

- *W is the event that the $\mathcal{A}$ wins the game,*
- *FP is the event that at the end of the game, $\neg closed \wedge \neg compromise \wedge d$ is true,*
- *FN is the event that at the end of the game, $\neg closed \wedge passinj \neq \emptyset \wedge \neg d$ is true.*

*FP and FN respectively stand for false positive and false negative.*

*Proof (Proof of Theorem 1).* Let $\mathcal{A}$ be an adversary in the game of Definition 1. Because of the implementation of the `detectTrial` function and because the *win* flag is only set in this function, it is immediate that $W = FP \sqcup FN$ which are the events defined in Definition 2.

Therefore:

$$\text{Adv}(\mathcal{A}) = \Pr[W] = \Pr[FP] + \Pr[FN].$$

Moreover, Proposition 2 states that $\Pr[FP] \leq 2 \cdot \text{Adv}_{\mathcal{B}_2}^{EUF\text{-}CMA}(\mathcal{S})$ and Proposition 1 states that $\Pr[FN] \leq \text{Adv}_{\mathcal{B}_1}^{coll}(H)$, which proves the inequality. $\square$

## A.1    Upper Bound for False Negatives

This section gives an upper bound on the probability $\Pr[FN]$ that an adversary produces a false negative in the game. We first introduce Lemma 1 which is used to prove Proposition 2.

**Lemma 1.** *Let $\mathcal{A}$ be an adversary playing the security game of Definition 1 against the Authentication Steps protocol from Sect. 3.*

*If passinj $\neq \emptyset$ at the end of the game, it means that there exists some user $U \in \{A, B\}$, an authentication step $j$ for $U$ and a message index $i \in I_U^{(j)}$ such that $c_i^A \neq c_i^B$ (where one of the ciphertext could be $\perp$ if the corresponding user has sent no ciphertext for index $i$).*

*Proof.* In the following we consider an execution of the game which leads to *passinj* $\neq \emptyset$ at the end of the game.

Let $i$ be the index of a ciphertext in *passinj*. *passinj* is filled only in the `CheckAuthStepPassed` function (see Fig. 2) if *authinj* is not empty.

*authinj* is filled only at two places: at Line 4 of the `auth-A/B` oracle, or at Line 8 of `deliver-A/B` (see Fig. 2). For both cases, this happens when a user $U$ enters an authentication step (wlog. we choose authentication step $j$), and message $i$ comes from $inj_U$.

Message $i$ has already been received because it is in $inj_U$ when added to *authinj*, i.e., when the authentication step begins, so it is not a skipped message. Moreover, $i \leq auth.authidx$ given the implementation of STARTAUTH.

$\pi_U.lastauth$ contains the index of the last message authenticated. As *authinj* is cleared at the end of every authentication step, having the ciphertext corresponding to index $i$ in *authinj* means that it has not been authenticated in a previous authentication step. Moreover, messages coming before the previous authentication step are not decrypted, which means that necessarily $i > \pi_U.lastauth$.

This proves that for this authentication step $j$, $i \in [\pi_U.lastauth, authinfo.authidx]$ and not in $U$'s skipped dictionary, which means $i \in I_U^{(j)}$.

Because $i \in inj_U$, it means $U$ received and accepted ciphertext $c_i^U$ (when it was added to $inj_U$). If $V$ is the peer of $U$, then $c_i^V$ (if it exists) cannot be equal to $c_i^U$ because otherwise it would have been generated honestly by $V$ and therefore removed from injected sets in lines 5 to 7 of `transmit-A/B` in Fig. 2, or never added to $inj_U$ because in $trans_U$ (see Line 8 of `transmit-A` and Line 11 of `deliver-B` in Fig. 2). Therefore, $c_i^A \neq c_i^B$.

The following proposition gives an upper bound on the probability that the adversary produces a false negative.

Note that in the construction given in Sect. 3, hashes are used to save space for ciphertexts. However, if no hashes were used and transcripts of actual ciphertexts were stored instead, false negatives could never happen.

**Proposition 1 (False Negatives).** *Let $\mathcal{A}$ be an adversary in the detection game of Definition 1 playing against the Authentication Steps protocol presented in Section 3.*

*Then $\Pr[\text{FN}] \leq Adv_{\mathcal{B}_1}^{coll}(H)$, for a reduction adversary $\mathcal{B}_1$ constructed in the proof.*

*Proof.* Let $\mathcal{A}$ be an adversary producing event FN. Recall from Definition 2 that $\text{FN} = \neg closed \wedge passinj \neq \emptyset \wedge \neg d$.

In particular, *passinj* is not empty at the end of the game. According to Lemma 1, this implies the existence of an authentication step $j_0$ for user $V \in \{A, B\}$ and some index $i$ such that $i \in I_V^{(j_0)}$ and $c_i^A \neq c_i^B$.

However, $d$ is **False**. Given the computation of $d$ in the DETECTOOB procedure this means that $\pi_A.H_A^{(n_A)} = \pi_B.H_B^{(n_B)}$.

Recall that for any user $U$, $H_U^{(n_U)} = n_U || H_U^{(n_U - 1)}$. In particular $n_A = n_B$ and Alice and Bob have seen the same number of authentication steps.

Hashes $H_U^{(j)}$ are computed as follows: $H_U^{(j)} \leftarrow \text{H}\left(H_U^{(j-1)} \; || \; ||_{k \in \texttt{sorted}(I_U^{(j)})} \pi_U.H_k^U\right)$ for any $j \geq 0$ and with $H_U^{(-1)} = \varepsilon$.

For any $j \geq 0$, if $H_A^{(j)} = H_B^{(j)}$, then there are only two possibilities:

1. either $H_A^{(j-1)} \; || \; ||_{k \in \texttt{sorted}(I_A^{(j)})} \pi_A.H_k^A \neq H_B^{(j-1)} \; || \; ||_{k \in \texttt{sorted}(I_B^{(j)})} \pi_B.H_k^B$;
2. either they are equal.

For the first case, because $H_A^{(j)} = H_B^{(j)}$ but the two inputs to the hash function are different, we have a hash collision.

The second case would induce a propagation property and yield $H_A^{(j-1)} = H_B^{(j-1)}$.

As the equality $H_A^{(j)} = H_B^{(j)}$ is true for the last authentication step, by induction we can deduce that either there is a hash collision or for all authentication step $j$:

$$||_{k \in \texttt{sorted}(I_A^{(j)})} \pi_A.H_k^A = ||_{k \in \texttt{sorted}(I_B^{(j)})} \pi_B.H_k^B.$$

This is true in particular for $j = j_0$. Recall that elements of $\pi_U.H^U$ are hashes of ciphertexts computed on sending and receiving.

As the hash function produces outputs of the same length, it means that there are exactly the same number of hashes in each concatenation. Moreover, $i \in I_V^{(j_0)}$ so one hash corresponds to the ciphertext with index $i$. Let's denote $H_V = \text{H}(c_i^V)$ and $H_W = \text{H}(c^W)$ the corresponding hashes (where $H_W$ is at the same position in the concatenation that $H_V$ but for the other user).

Because the concatenations are equal, $H_V = H_W$. However, $c^W \neq c_i^V$. Indeed, if we had $c^W = c_i^V$, then both would correspond to the same index $i$, but $c^W$ is the version of ciphertext $i$ sent by $W$ and $c_i^V$ is the version received by $V$. However, by definition of $i$, we necessarily have $c_i^A \neq c_i^B$ and therefore the equality is impossible. As $H_V = H_W$ but $c^W \neq c_i^V$, we have a hash collision.

Therefore, any case leading the adversary to a false negative shows that the adversary could produce an explicit hash collision, and therefore the reduction $\mathcal{B}_1$ from the detection game to the hash collision game is immediate.

This shows that $\Pr[\text{FN}] \leq \text{Adv}_{\mathcal{B}_1}^{coll}(H)$.

## A.2    Upper Bound for False Positives

This section gives an upper bound on the probability $\Pr[\text{FP}]$ that the adversary produces a false positive in the game.

**Proposition 2 (False Positives).** *Let $\mathcal{A}$ be an adversary in the detection game of Definition 1 playing against the Authentication Steps protocol of Sect. 3.*
*Then $\Pr[\text{FP}] \leq 2 \cdot \mathbf{Adv}_{\mathcal{B}_2}^{EUF-CMA}(\mathcal{S})$, for a reduction adversary $\mathcal{B}_2$ constructed in the proof.*

*Proof.* Let $\mathcal{A}$ be an adversary producing event FP. Having $\neg compromise$ means that $\mathcal{A}$ never calls the corruptLTS-A/B oracles. Moreover, $\neg closed$ means the communication never closes, which means that signature verifications always succeed. We will build an adversary $\mathcal{B}_2$ for the EUF-CMA game against signature scheme $\mathcal{S}$ as a wrapper around $\mathcal{A}$, which acts as a challenger in the detection game for $\mathcal{A}$.

$\mathcal{B}_2$ creates two users Alice and Bob, but will embed a public key provided by the EUF-CMA challenger into one party's signing key-pair and use the signing oracle to generate signatures.

As user $U_1$ is entirely generated by $\mathcal{B}_2$, the adversary can simulate the oracles concerning $U_1$, and therefore they are similar to the oracles defined in Fig. 2.

$\mathcal{B}_2$ keeps track of signature forgeries. Every time $\mathcal{B}_2$ signs a message using the oracle provided by his challenger, $\mathcal{B}_2$ stores it. Moreover, every time a signature on the signing public key $pk$ given by the EUF-CMA game is verified, $\mathcal{B}_2$ checks if the signature was produced by the signing oracle. If that is not the case, but the verification is successful, $\mathcal{B}_2$ stops and outputs the corresponding pair $m^*, \sigma^*$.

To simulate user $U_0$ whose private key is unknown, $\mathcal{B}_2$ can also use the original oracles, except for transmit$-U_0$ which is the only oracle using $U_0$'s private signing key in the SEND procedure. Recall that the corruptLTS-A/B oracles are not called by adversary $\mathcal{A}$ and therefore $\mathcal{B}_2$ does not need to simulate those oracles when the event FP happens. In order to create the signature, $\mathcal{B}_2$ can query their own challenger with message $\pi_{U_0}.auth$ to get the signature using $U_0$'s private key. Therefore, $\mathcal{B}_2$ is correctly defined and can act as a challenger for $\mathcal{A}$.

Let's now prove that if $\mathcal{A}$ triggers the event FP, then $\mathcal{B}_2$ wins the EUF-CMA game with probability at least $\frac{1}{2}$.

During his last authentication step $n$, $U_1$ verified successfully a signature $\sigma$ on $\pi_{U_1}.auth$ by using $U_0$'s public signing key $sigpk^{U_0}$. $\pi_{U_1}.auth$ contains in particular $n_U = n$ and $H = H_1$ computed by $U_1$. Because $U_0$ and $U_1$ can number their authentication steps, they will produce at most one signature on an $auth$ set having $n_U = n$. At the end of the game, parties output $d = \textbf{True}$. From the implementation of DETECTOOB, this means that $\pi_A.H_A^{(n_A)} \neq \pi_B.H_B^{(n_B)}$. Given the definition of $\pi_U.H_U^{(n_U)}$ this means that during the last authentication step of each party:

$$\pi_A.n_A || \pi_A.auth.H \neq \pi_B.n_B || \pi_B.auth.H.$$

There are two disjoint possibilities:

1. either $\pi_A.n_A = \pi_B.n_B$ but $\pi_A.auth.H \neq \pi_B.auth.H$;
2. either $\pi_A.n_A \neq \pi_B.n_B$;

In Case 1, $\pi_A.n_A = \pi_B.n_B = n$ and $\pi_A.auth.H \neq \pi_B.auth.H$. Yet $U_1$'s verification of $\sigma$ succeeded on the data $\pi_{U_1}.auth$ which contains $n_U = n$ and $H = H_1$. However, as stated above $U_0$ can produce and sign at most one set $auth$ with $n_U = n$, and this set has $H = \pi_{U_0}.auth.H \neq \pi_{U_1}.auth.H = H_1$. Therefore, $\pi_{U_1}.auth$ was not submitted to the signing oracle, and yet $\sigma$ verifies over $\pi_{U_1}.auth$, so $\mathcal{B}_2$ can output this forgery.

In Case 2, $\pi_A.n_A \neq \pi_B.n_B$. Recall that $U_0$ and $U_1$ are chosen uniformly at random at the beginning of the game. Because the signing key-pair and signatures are sampled and created in the same way in the detection game and in the reduction when using the signing oracle, $\mathcal{A}$ cannot distinguish which key-pair is used in the signing game. Therefore, with probability $\frac{1}{2}$, $\pi_{U_0}.n_{U_0} < \pi_{U_1}.n_{U_1}$.

In that case, $U_0$ cannot have signed a set $\pi_{U_0}.auth$ with $n_{U_0} = \pi_{U_1}.n_{U_1}$ as it has not yet reached the correct number of authentication steps. This once again yields a valid signature forgery.

Therefore, with probability at least $\frac{1}{2}$, if $\mathcal{A}$ triggers FP then $\mathcal{B}_2$ wins the EUF-CMA game. This leads to the upper bound $\Pr[\text{FP}] \leq 2 \cdot \text{Adv}_{\mathcal{B}_2}^{EUF\text{-}CMA}(\mathcal{S})$.

# References

1. Alwen, J., Coretti, S., Dodis, Y.: The double ratchet: security notions, proofs, and modularization for the signal protocol. In: Ishai, Y., Rijmen, V. (eds.) EUROCRYPT 2019. LNCS, vol. 11476, pp. 129–158. Springer, Cham (2019). https://doi.org/10.1007/978-3-030-17653-2_5
2. Bellare, M., Singh, A.C., Jaeger, J., Nyayapati, M., Stepanovs, I.: Ratcheted encryption and key exchange: the security of messaging. In: Katz, J., Shacham, H. (eds.) CRYPTO 2017. LNCS, vol. 10403, pp. 619–650. Springer, Cham (2017). https://doi.org/10.1007/978-3-319-63697-9_21
3. Brendel, J., Fiedler, R., Günther, F., Janson, C., Stebila, D.: Post-quantum asynchronous deniable key exchange and the Signal handshake. In: Hanaoka, G., Shikata, J., Watanabe, Y. (eds.) PKC 2022, Part II. LNCS, vol. 13178, pp. 3–34. Springer (2022). https://doi.org/10.1007/978-3-030-97131-1_1
4. Chen, T., Kan, M.Y.: Creating a live, public short message service corpus: the NUS SMS corpus. Lang. Resour. Eval. **47**(2), 299–335 (2013). https://doi.org/10.1007/s10579-012-9197-9
5. Chen, T., Kan, M.Y.: The National University of Singapore SMS Corpus [Dataset] (2015). https://doi.org/10.25540/WVM0-4RNX
6. Cohn-Gordon, K., Cremers, C., Dowling, B., Garratt, L., Stebila, D.: A Formal Security Analysis of the Signal Messaging Protocol. J. Cryptol. **33**(4), 1914–1983 (2020). https://doi.org/10.1007/s00145-020-09360-1
7. Cohn-Gordon, K., Cremers, C.J.F., Garratt, L.: On post-compromise security. In: Hicks, M., Köpf, B. (eds.) CSF 2016 Computer Security Foundations Symposium, pp. 164–178. IEEE Computer Society Press (2016). https://doi.org/10.1109/CSF.2016.19

8. Cremers, C., Fairoze, J., Kiesl, B., Naska, A.: Clone detection in secure messaging: improving post-compromise security in practice. In: Ligatti, J., Ou, X., Katz, J., Vigna, G. (eds.) ACM CCS 2020, pp. 1481–1495. ACM Press, Nov 2020. https://doi.org/10.1145/3372297.3423354

9. Dowling, B., Hale, B.: Secure messaging authentication against active man-in-the-middle attacks. In: 2021 IEEE European Symposium on Security and Privacy (EuroS&P), pp. 54–70 (2021). https://doi.org/10.1109/EuroSP51992.2021.00015

10. Durak, F.B., Vaudenay, S.: Bidirectional asynchronous ratcheted key agreement with linear complexity. In: Attrapadung, N., Yagi, T. (eds.) IWSEC 2019. LNCS, vol. 11689, pp. 343–362. Springer, Cham (2019). https://doi.org/10.1007/978-3-030-26834-3_20

11. Facebook: Messenger Secret Conversation, Technical Whitepaper (2016). https://about.fb.com/wp-content/uploads/2016/07/messenger-secret-conversations-technical-whitepaper.pdf

12. Hashimoto, K., Katsumata, S., Kwiatkowski, K., Prest, T.: An efficient and generic construction for signal's handshake (X3DH): post-quantum, state leakage secure, and deniable. In: Garay, J.A. (ed.) PKC 2021. LNCS, vol. 12711, pp. 410–440. Springer, Cham (2021). https://doi.org/10.1007/978-3-030-75248-4_15

13. Jaeger, J., Stepanovs, I.: Optimal channel security against fine-grained state compromise: The safety of messaging. In: Shacham, H., Boldyreva, A. (eds.) CRYPTO 2018. LNCS, vol. 10991, pp. 33–62. Springer, Cham (2018). https://doi.org/10.1007/978-3-319-96884-1_2

14. Jakobsson, M., Sako, K., Impagliazzo, R.: Designated verifier proofs and their applications. In: Maurer, U. (ed.) EUROCRYPT 1996. LNCS, vol. 1070, pp. 143–154. Springer, Heidelberg (1996). https://doi.org/10.1007/3-540-68339-9_13

15. Jost, D., Maurer, U., Mularczyk, M.: Efficient ratcheting: almost-optimal guarantees for secure messaging. In: Ishai, Y., Rijmen, V. (eds.) EUROCRYPT 2019. LNCS, vol. 11476, pp. 159–188. Springer, Cham (2019). https://doi.org/10.1007/978-3-030-17653-2_6

16. Perrin, T.: The XEdDSA and VXEdDSA signature schemes. Tech. rep., Signal (2016). https://whispersystems.org/docs/specifications/xeddsa/

17. Perrin, T., Marlinspike, M.: The Double Ratchet algorithm (2016). https://whispersystems.org/docs/specifications/doubleratchet/

18. Poettering, B., Rösler, P.: Towards bidirectional ratcheted key exchange. In: Shacham, H., Boldyreva, A. (eds.) CRYPTO 2018. LNCS, vol. 10991, pp. 3–32. Springer, Cham (2018). https://doi.org/10.1007/978-3-319-96884-1_1

19. Rivest, R.L., Shamir, A., Tauman, Y.: How to leak a secret. In: Boyd, C. (ed.) ASIACRYPT 2001. LNCS, vol. 2248, pp. 552–565. Springer, Heidelberg (2001). https://doi.org/10.1007/3-540-45682-1_32

20. Signal: Technical information. https://signal.org/docs/

21. Systems, O.W.: libsignal-protocol-java (2021). https://github.com/signalapp/libsignal-protocol-java

22. Unger, N., et al.: SoK: Secure messaging. In: 2015 IEEE Symposium on Security and Privacy, pp. 232–249 (2015). https://doi.org/10.1109/SP.2015.22

23. Unger, N., Goldberg, I.: Deniable key exchanges for secure messaging. In: Ray, I., Li, N., Kruegel, C. (eds.) ACM CCS 2015, pp. 1211–1223. ACM Press, Oct 2015. https://doi.org/10.1145/2810103.2813616

24. Unger, N., Goldberg, I.: Improved strongly deniable authenticated key exchanges for secure messaging. PoPETs **2018**(1), 21–66 (2018). https://doi.org/10.1515/popets-2018-0003

25. Vatandas, N., Gennaro, R., Ithurburn, B., Krawczyk, H.: On the cryptographic deniability of the signal protocol. In: Conti, M., Zhou, J., Casalicchio, E., Spognardi, A. (eds.) ACNS 2020. LNCS, vol. 12147, pp. 188–209. Springer, Cham (2020). https://doi.org/10.1007/978-3-030-57878-7_10
26. WhatsApp Security. https://www.whatsapp.com/security/
27. How WhatsApp enables multi-device capability (2021). https://engineering.fb.com/2021/07/14/security/whatsapp-multi-device/
28. WhatsApp Security Advisories (2021). https://www.whatsapp.com/security/advisories

# Digital Signatures

# Half-Aggregation of Schnorr Signatures with Tight Reductions

Yanbo Chen and Yunlei Zhao[✉]

Fudan University, Shanghai, China
{ybchen,ylzhao}@fudan.edu.cn

**Abstract.** An aggregate signature (AS) scheme allows an unspecified aggregator to compress many signatures into a short aggregation. AS schemes can save storage costs and accelerate verification. They are desirable for applications where many signatures need to be stored, transferred, or verified together, including blockchain systems, sensor networks, certificate chains, network routing, etc. However, constructing AS schemes based on general groups, only requiring the hardness of the discrete logarithm problem, is quite tricky and has been a long-standing research question. Recently, Chalkias et al. [6] proposed a half-aggregate scheme for Schnorr signatures. We observe the scheme lacks a tight security proof and does not well support incremental aggregation, i.e., adding more signatures into a pre-existing aggregation.

This work's contributions are threefold. We first give a tight security proof for the scheme in [6] in the ROM and the algebraic group model (AGM). Second, we provide a new half-aggregate scheme for Schnorr signatures that perfectly supports incremental aggregation, whose security also tightly reduces to Schnorr's security in the AGM+ROM. Third, we present a Schnorr-based sequential aggregate signature (SAS) scheme that is tightly secure as Schnorr signature scheme in the ROM (without the AGM). Our work may pave the way for applying Schnorr aggregation in real-world cryptographic applications.

## 1 Introduction

The notion of *aggregate signatures* (AS) was proposed by Boneh et al. [5]. As a type of signature scheme, an AS scheme additionally allows an aggregator to compress an arbitrary number of individual signatures into a short aggregation. One can verify the validity of all those individual signatures by verifying the aggregate signature. The signers do not need to interact, and the aggregator can be an arbitrary one. AS schemes are very useful in applications where many signatures need to be stored, transferred, or verified together. Traditional application scenarios of AS schemes include sensor networks, software authentication [1], secure logging [16], etc. They can also be applied to blockchain systems like Bitcoin, e.g., to aggregate the signatures for multiple transactions to an aggregated one for improving throughput and reducing verification time.

Lysyanskaya et al. [19] proposed a useful variant of aggregate signatures, *sequential aggregate signatures* (SAS). In an SAS scheme, the signatures can

© The Author(s), under exclusive license to Springer Nature Switzerland AG 2022
V. Atluri et al. (Eds.): ESORICS 2022, LNCS 13555, pp. 385–404, 2022.
https://doi.org/10.1007/978-3-031-17146-8_19

only be compressed sequentially. Specifically, a signer additionally gets a pre-existing aggregation as its input and directly produces a new aggregation based on the pre-existing one. Unlike traditional AS schemes, the signature aggregation cannot be made publicly by anyone but the signers involved in the SAS scheme. SAS schemes are suitable for applications like certificate chains, routing protocols, and secure logging. In these scenarios, the signatures are produced and passed in order, and a signer always knows the previous aggregation. For example, in a hierarchical public key infrastructure, a certificate on a user's public key consists of a chain of certificates issued by multiple certification authorities (CAs). Each CA certifies the CA at the next level, and the deepest CA directly certifies the user.

Boneh et al. pointed out in their seminal work [5] that the aggregation can be *incrementally* performed in their scheme. That is, the aggregator can add individual signatures into a pre-existing aggregation. In this work, we refer to AS schemes with such a feature as *incremental aggregate signature* (IAS) schemes.

In SAS schemes, the aggregation is naturally performed incrementally one-by-one. However, the feature of incremental aggregation is unspecified in the definition of AS schemes. Hence, AS schemes are not strictly stronger than SAS schemes, but IAS schemes can serve as both of them.

Most of the previous AS/SAS schemes are based on bilinear maps [3,5,17,18] and trapdoor permutations [19]. Some proposals work in the synchronized model [1,11]. Constructing AS/SAS schemes based on general groups, only requiring the hardness of discrete logarithm problem (DLP), is quite tricky and is a long-standing question.

Recently, Chalkias et al. [6] provided an aggregate scheme for Schnorr signatures. We refer to their scheme as ASchnorr and Schnorr signature scheme as Schnorr for presentation simplicity. ASchnorr achieves "half-aggregation" rather than "full-aggregation", i.e., the total size is compressed a half, rather than to a constant size. The authors provided some evidence of the impossibility of fully aggregating Schnorr signatures. Anyhow, half-aggregation of Schnorr signatures still significantly reduces the storage, so it is very useful and timely as Schnorr signature was enforced in Bitcoin (and many other blockchain systems) in November of 2021 with the Taproot update [24].

We observe two problems of ASchnorr. In [6], ASchnorr's security is reduced to Schnorr's security in the random oracle model (ROM), and hence can be further reduced to the hardness of DLP. The first problem is that the reduction has a quadratic loss, due to the reliance on rewinding. The authors suggested ignoring the quadratic loss when setting parameters for ASchnorr in practice, just as people do for Schnorr. But for deploying ASchnorr in reality, particularly in cryptocurrency systems like Bitcoin, we may want more confidence in its security. They also designed another aggregate scheme, referred to as TightASchnorr. TightASchnorr permits a tight security reduction in the ROM but is relatively expensive in both space and time. Specifically, it achieves (half+$\epsilon$)-aggregation rather than half-aggregation, where $\epsilon = \mathcal{O}(\lambda/\log\lambda)$ with $\lambda$ as the security parameter. It also has a costly aggregating procedure and makes the verification slower than verifying the batch of individual signatures one by one. Whether there exists half-aggregate schemes for Schnorr signatures that is tightly secure as Schnorr is a fundamental question to explore.

Second, ASchnorr does not support incremental aggregation well. In particular, it suffers from ambiguity and redundant operations. By "ambiguity" we mean the verifier cannot correctly verify an aggregation without knowing how it was produced (namely, whether and when incremental aggregation happened). Without the feature of incremental aggregation, only when all the signatures are received the aggregator can start the aggregation. In reality, particularly in asynchronous distributed systems, signatures are usually not produced and transferred at the same time. It is more convenient to perform the aggregation with part of the signatures and incrementally aggregate the others when they arrive. Incremental aggregation is especially important for fault tolerance in asynchronous systems. In such applications, there may exist both faulty nodes and delayed honest nodes. An aggregator should not assume that every node will eventually provide a valid signature. It should start aggregating when it receives some signatures rather than keep waiting, but later it may need to add delayed signatures to the aggregation. Moreover, non-incremental AS schemes cannot serve as SAS schemes, so they may not applicable in scenarios like certificate chains and network routing. Hence, incremental aggregation is crucial for practical use. Many schemes based on bilinear maps naturally support incremental aggregation, so the property is rarely mentioned explicitly in the previous works. However, this is not the case for Schnorr signature aggregation.

## 1.1 Contributions

The contributions of this work are threefold. For the first problem of ASchnorr about security tightness, we further justify its security. We reduce the security of ASchnorr to the security of Schnorr with a tight bound in the ROM and the algebraic group model (AGM) [9]. The AGM is similar to while weaker than the generic group model (GGM) [20,23]. In the AGM, we only consider adversaries as algebraic algorithms. This is reasonable, for no attack is so far known to be significantly more efficient than such algorithms on elliptic curve groups. The AGM is widely applied in security proofs for cryptographic schemes, including blind signatures [10] and multi-signatures [2].

For the second problem about incremental aggregation, our solution is a new half-aggregation scheme, referred to as IASchnorr. IASchnorr perfectly supports incremental signature aggregation. It no more suffers from ambiguity and redundant operations. It also permits a tight security reduction in the AGM+ROM.

Our third contribution is an SAS scheme, referred to as SASchnorr. We tightly reduce its security to Schnorr's security in the ROM (without the AGM). Unlike tightASchnorr proposed in [6], our scheme SASchnorr achieves half-aggregation, and it does not increase the verification time. On one hand, SASchnorr is the first to achieve half-aggregation of Schnorr signatures with a tight security proof in the ROM. On the other hand, as ASchnorr cannot serve as an SAS scheme while keeping secure in the ROM, SASchnorr is also the first to achieve sequential half-aggregation of Schnorr signatures with an (even non-tight) security proof in the ROM.

Tight security analysis of ASchnorr and the construction of IASchnorr pave the way for applying Schnorr aggregation in distributed ledger systems like Bitcoin, and IASchnorr may be best applicable in these application scenarios. SASchnorr may not be appropriate directly in so many scenarios as IASchnorr, but it is useful in many other applications like certificate chains, network routing, and secure logging. It achieves (sequential) half-aggregation of Schnorr signatures with a tight security reduction in the ROM, which is of theoretical interest. Meanwhile, getting rid of loose security bounds and the AGM could also be desirable for real-world cryptography.

## 2  Preliminaries

### 2.1  Aggregate Signatures

An aggregate signature (AS) scheme AS consists of five algorithms KGen, Sign, Vf, Agg, and AggVf. The first three algorithms KGen, Sign, and Vf constitute a traditional signature scheme. The signature scheme must be complete for AS to be complete. Algorithm Agg takes as inputs an arbitrary number of signatures $\sigma_1, ..., \sigma_n$, corresponding messages $m_1, ..., m_n$ and public keys $\mathsf{pk}_1, ..., \mathsf{pk}_n$ and outputs an aggregate signature $\tilde{\sigma}$. Algorithm AggVf takes as inputs an aggregate signature $\tilde{\sigma}$, messages $m_1, ..., m_n$, and public keys $\mathsf{pk}_1, ..., \mathsf{pk}_n$ and outputs 0 or 1, representing $\tilde{\sigma}$ is valid or not. The completeness requirement here is that: if some signatures are correctly generated with Sign, then their aggregation must be verified as valid on/under corresponding messages/public keys.

An incremental aggregate signature (IAS) scheme is an AS scheme that additionally contains an algorithm IncrAgg. Algorithm IncrAgg takes as inputs an existing aggregate signature $\tilde{\sigma}$, corresponding messages $m_1, \ldots, m_n$ and public keys $\mathsf{pk}_1, \ldots, \mathsf{pk}_n$, an arbitrary number of individual signatures $\sigma_{n+1}, \ldots, \sigma_{n'}$, and corresponding messages $m_{n+1}, \ldots, m_{n'}$ and public keys $\mathsf{pk}_{n+1}, \ldots, \mathsf{pk}_{n'}$ and outputs a new aggregation $\tilde{\sigma}'$. The completeness requirement here is that: if some signatures are correctly generated with Sign, then their aggregation, no matter how they are aggregated (incrementally or not), must be verified as valid on/under corresponding messages/public keys.

**Security.** Boneh et al. [5] defined the existential unforgeability under chosen-message attacks (EUF-CMA) [12] of AS schemes in the *aggregate chosen-key model*. We abbreviate the EUF-CMA security in this model as CK-AEUF-CMA. The CK-AEUF-CMA game consists of three stages defined as follows:

*Setup.* The forger $\mathcal{F}$ is given a public key $\mathsf{pk}^*$ generated by KGen.

*Queries.* The forger $\mathcal{F}$ has access to a signing oracle. It can adaptively requests signatures under $\mathsf{pk}^*$ on messages of its choice.

*Response.* The forger $\mathcal{F}$ outputs an arbitrary number $n$ of public keys $\mathsf{pk}_1, ..., \mathsf{pk}_n$, $n$ messages $m_1, ..., m_n$, and an aggregate signature $\tilde{\sigma}$ .

We say $\mathcal{F}$ wins this game if $\tilde{\sigma}$ is a valid aggregate signature on $m_1$, ..., $m_n$ under $\mathsf{pk}_1$, ..., $\mathsf{pk}_n$, there exists $k \in \{1, \ldots, n\}$ such that $\mathsf{pk}_k = \mathsf{pk}^*$, and $\mathcal{F}$ has not queried $m_k$ to the signing oracle.

In this work, we only consider the security in the ROM, and the security results for AS schemes in this work are independent of the maximum number of aggregated signatures. We say a forger $\mathcal{F}$ $(t, q_{H_1}, \ldots, q_{H_l}, q_S, \varepsilon)$-breaks the CK-AEUF-CMA security of an AS scheme AS in the ROM if: $\mathcal{F}$ runs in time at most $t$; $\mathcal{F}$ makes at most $q_{H_1}, \ldots, q_{H_l}$ queries respectively to the random oracles $H_1$, ..., $H_l$ modeling the hash functions used in AS; $\mathcal{F}$ makes at most $q_S$ queries to the signing oracle; and $\mathcal{F}$ wins the CK-AEUF-CMA game with probability at least $\varepsilon$.

## 2.2 Sequential Aggregate Signatures

A sequential aggregate signature (SAS) scheme SAS consists of three algorithm KGen, SeqSign, and Vf. Algorithms KGen and Vf are the same as the ones in a normal signature scheme. Algorithm SeqSign takes an existing aggregate signature $\tilde{\sigma}_{n-1}$, corresponding messages $m_1$, ..., $m_{n-1}$ and public keys $\mathsf{pk}_1$, ..., $\mathsf{pk}_{n-1}$, a secret key $\mathsf{sk}_n$, and a message $m_n$ as inputs and outputs a new aggregation $\tilde{\sigma}_n$. With $n = 1$, the behavior of SeqSign is the same as algorithm Sign in a normal signature scheme, and it indeed constitutes a normal scheme together with KGen and Vf. The completeness requirement is that: if a sequential aggregate signature is generated correctly by sequentially running SeqSign multiple times, then it must be verified as valid on/under corresponding messages/public keys.

**Security.** Lysyanskaya et al. [19] defined the EUF-CMA security in the *sequential aggregate chosen-key model* (CK-SAEUF-CMA) for SAS schemes. We introduce the security notion here, while we will prove the security of our scheme in a modified model which we will define later in Sect. 5.2. The three-stage CK-SAEUF-CMA game is defined as follows:

*Setup.* The forger $\mathcal{F}$ is given a public key $\mathsf{pk}^*$ generated by KGen.
*Queries.* The forger $\mathcal{F}$ has access to a signing oracle. It can adaptively requests signatures under $\mathsf{pk}^*$ on messages, existing aggregations, and previous public keys and messages of its choice.
*Response.* The forger $\mathcal{F}$ outputs an arbitrary number $n$ of public keys $\mathsf{pk}_1$, ..., $\mathsf{pk}_n$, $n$ messages $m_1$, ..., $m_n$, and a sequential aggregate signature $\tilde{\sigma}$.

We say $\mathcal{F}$ wins this game if $\tilde{\sigma}$ is a valid aggregate signature on $m_1$, ..., $m_n$ under $\mathsf{pk}_1$, ..., $\mathsf{pk}_n$, there exists $k$ such that $\mathsf{pk}_k = \mathsf{pk}^*$, and $\mathcal{F}$ has not queried $m_k$ together with previous public keys and messages $\{(\mathsf{pk}_1, m_1), \ldots, (\mathsf{pk}_{k-1}, m_{k-1})\}$. Note it is allowed to query $m_k$ with another set of previous public keys and messages.

We say a forger $\mathcal{F}$ $(t, q_{H_1}, \ldots, q_{H_l}, q_S, N, \varepsilon)$-breaks the CK-SAEUF-CMA security of an SAS scheme SAS in the ROM if: $\mathcal{F}$ runs in time at most $t$; $\mathcal{F}$ makes at

| KGen() | Sign(sk, m) | Vf(pk, m, σ) |
|---|---|---|
| $x \leftarrow\$ \mathbb{Z}_p$ | $x := \mathsf{sk}; X := g^x$ | $X := \mathsf{pk}$ |
| $X := g^x$ | $r \leftarrow\$ \mathbb{Z}_p; R := g^r$ | $(c, s) := \sigma$ |
| $\mathsf{sk} := x$ | $c := \mathsf{H}_1(R, m)$ | $R := g^s / X^c$ |
| $\mathsf{pk} := X$ | $s := r + cx$ | **return** $[\![\mathsf{H}_1(R, m) = c]\!]$ |
| **return** $(\mathsf{sk}, \mathsf{pk})$ | **return** $\sigma := (c, s)$ | |

**Fig. 1.** Description of Schnorr signatures. The cyclic group $\mathbb{G}$, of order $p$ with a generator $g$ and the hash functions $\mathsf{H}_1$ are scheme-level parameters.

most $q_{\mathsf{H}_1}, \ldots, q_{\mathsf{H}_l}$ queries respectively to the random oracles $\mathsf{H}_1, \ldots, \mathsf{H}_l$ modeling the hash functions used in SAS; $\mathcal{F}$ makes at most $q_S$ queries to the signing oracle; $\mathcal{F}$ gives a forged sequential aggregate signature of length at most $N$; and $\mathcal{F}$ wins the CK-SAEUF-CMA game with probability at least $\varepsilon$.

### 2.3 Algebraic Group Model

The algebraic group model (AGM) is an ideal model proposed in [9]. In the AGM, we require the adversary to provide the representations of any group elements it outputs as a product of the elements it received. The AGM lies between the generic group model (GGM) [20,23] and the realistic world. While the GGM is useful for proving information-theoretical bounds, the AGM is useful for making reductions.

To be more specific, consider a multiplicative group. Let $X_1, \ldots, X_n$ be group elements provided to the adversary as inputs or from oracles. For any group element $Y$ it outputs or queries to oracles, it also gives a representation of $Y$, i.e., a vector $(\alpha_1, \ldots, \alpha_n)$ satisfying that $Y = \prod_{i=1}^n X_i^{\alpha_i}$.

### 2.4 Schnorr Signatures

In Fig. 1, we present Schnorr signature scheme in its traditional $(c, s)$-format [22], while nowadays it is also common to deploy its $(R, s)$ variant on elliptic groups. For instance, the $(R, s)$ version of Schnorr signature scheme was standardized as EdDSA [4]. Bitcoin also chose the $(R, s)$ version [24].

Schnorr signature in the $(c, s)$-format is more compact than its $(R, s)$-format over integer groups, but the difference is relatively small over elliptic curve groups [14]. Practical elliptic curves of order $p$ with $\log p = 2\lambda$ can offer approximately $\lambda$ bits of security, and the points over these groups can be represented by about $2\lambda$ bits (to be precise, $2\lambda + 1$ bits). In practice, it is safer to use a hash function $\mathsf{H}_1$ with $2\lambda$-bit outputs for $\lambda$-bit security, which avoids some subtle fragile caused by shorter hashes. For example, such a full-length hash function can computationally bind the signature to the corresponding message, which is increasingly important for applications like blockchain [6]. In short, the point $R$, the scalar $s$, and the hash value $c$ all have a size of about $2\lambda$ bits.

| $\mathsf{Agg}(\{(\mathsf{pk}_1, m_1, \sigma_1), \ldots, (\mathsf{pk}_n, m_n, \sigma_n)\})$ | $\mathsf{AggVf}(\{(\mathsf{pk}_1, m_1), \ldots, (\mathsf{pk}_n, m_n)\}, \tilde{\sigma})$ |
|---|---|
| **for** $i = 1, \ldots, n$ **do** | **for** $i = 1, \ldots, n$ **do** |
| $\quad X_i := \mathsf{pk}_i$ | $\quad X_i := \mathsf{pk}_i$ |
| $\quad (c_i, s_i) := \sigma_i$ | $\quad (\{R_1, \ldots, R_n\}, \tilde{s}) := \tilde{\sigma}$ |
| $\quad R_i := g^{s_i}/X^{c_i}$ | $L := \{(R_1, X_1, m_1), \ldots, (R_n, X_n, m_n)\}$ |
| $L := \{(R_1, X_1, m_1), \ldots, (R_n, X_n, m_n)\}$ | **for** $i = 1, \ldots, n$ **do** |
| **for** $i = 1, \ldots, n$ **do** | $\quad c_i := \mathsf{H}_1(R_i, m_i)$ |
| $\quad a_i := \mathsf{H}_2(L, i)$ | $\quad a_i := \mathsf{H}_2(L, i)$ |
| $\tilde{s} := \displaystyle\sum_{i=1}^{n} a_i s_i$ | **return** $[\![ g^{\tilde{s}} = \displaystyle\prod_{i=1}^{n}(R_i X_i^{c_i})^{a_i} ]\!]$ |
| **return** $\tilde{\sigma} := (\{R_1, \ldots, R_n\}, \tilde{s})$ | |

**Fig. 2.** Description of ASchnorr. The cyclic group $\mathbb{G}$, of order $p$ with a generator $g$, and the hash functions $\mathsf{H}_1$ and $\mathsf{H}_2$ are scheme-level parameters. The range of $\mathsf{H}_2$ is denoted by $\mathcal{H}_2$.

# 3  Half-Aggregation of Schnorr Signatures, Revisited

## 3.1  Scheme Description

In this section, we analyze the security of ASchnorr, the half-aggregate scheme for Schnorr signatures in [6], in the AGM+ROM. Figure 2 describes the scheme, with a slight difference that we consider individual signatures in the $(c, s)$-format, as presented in Fig. 1. $\mathsf{H}_1$ and $\mathsf{H}_2$ are hash functions to $\mathbb{Z}_p$, and we use $\mathcal{H}_2$ to denote the range of $\mathsf{H}_2$.

On signatures $(c_1, s_1)$, $\ldots$, $(c_n, s_n)$, respectively on messages $m_1, \ldots, m_n$ under public keys $X_1, \ldots, X_n$, algorithm Agg recovers $R_1, \ldots, R_n$. Then it computes $n$ coefficients $a_1, \ldots, a_n$ and aggregates the responses into $\tilde{s} = \sum_{i=1}^{n} a_i s_i$. In the aggregate signature, $R_1, \ldots, R_n$ replace $c_1, \ldots, c_n$. To verify an aggregate signature, algorithm Vf also computes these coefficients and checks whether $g^{\tilde{s}} = \prod_{i=1}^{n}(R_i X_i^{c_i})^{a_i}$, where $c_i = \mathsf{H}_1(R_i, m_i)$.

The scheme certainly works well with signatures in the $(R, s)$-format. Actually, the two formats are mathematically equivalent, and the scheme essentially recovers $R$ and aggregates the $(R, s)$ signatures.

Let $\lambda$ be the security parameter. As discussed in Sect. 2.4, we consider the case that $R$, $c$, and $s$ are all approximately $2\lambda$-bit long. Then $n$ individual signatures are about $2n \cdot 2\lambda$ bits of total length, while the aggregation of these signatures is only about $(n + 1) \cdot 2\lambda$ bits of length as discussed above. In this case, ASchnorr compresses the signatures to roughly half the original size. For instance, consider the widely applied curve secp256k1 and the hash function SHA256 for about 128 bits of security. The order $p$ of secp256k1 is of 32 bytes. A point over secp256k1 is usually represented by 32 bytes (represent the $x$-ordinate) plus one more bit (indicating the sign of its $y$-coordinate). SHA256 gives 32-byte outputs.

Then ASchnorr compresses $n$ individual signatures, of $64n$ byte length, into $(32(n+1) + n/8)$ byte length.

One needs to compute $2n+1$ exponentiations to verify an aggregate signature, while it takes 2 exponentiations to verify each individual signature. Although we do not reduce the number of exponentiations, AggVf can be significantly speed up by applying the simultaneous exponentiation techniques [8,13,15]. It was estimated in [25] that verifying an aggregate signature using simultaneous exponentiation techniques is about 72% faster than sequentially verifying the individual signatures. The benchmarks in [6] also support this estimation. Note that ASchnorr only reduces the verification time of signatures in the $(c, s)$-format, because $(R, s)$ signatures support batch verification, which is also essentially computing $2n + 1$ simultaneous exponentiations.

## 3.2  Security in the AGM+ROM

We prove the CK-AEUF-CMA security of ASchnorr with a tight bound in the AGM+ROM, where the hash function $H_2$ is modeled as a random oracle, based on the EUF-CMA security of Schnorr. In comparison, the bound in the ROM suffers from a quadratic loss, for the proof is based on rewinding. In the CK-AEUF-CMA game against ASchnorr, a forger has accesses to a signing oracle SIGN and the random oracle $H_2$.

**Theorem 1.** *If there exists a forger that $(t, q_{H_2}, q_S, \varepsilon)$-breaks the CK-AEUF-CMA security of ASchnorr in the AGM+ROM with $H_2$ modeled as a random oracle, then there exists an algorithm that $(t', q_S, \varepsilon')$-breaks the EUF-CMA security of Schnorr with $t' = \mathcal{O}(t)$ and $\varepsilon' \geq \varepsilon - (q_{H_2} + 1)/|\mathcal{H}_2|$.*

*Proof.* Suppose that $\mathcal{F}$ is the forger that $(t, q_{H_2}, q_S, \varepsilon)$-breaks the CK-AEUF-CMA security of ASchnorr. We construct an algorithm $\mathcal{A}$ to break the EUF-CMA security of Schnorr. On the target public key $X^*$, $\mathcal{A}$ first initializes an empty table $T[\cdot, \cdot]$ for simulating random oracle $H_2$. After that, it runs $\mathcal{F}$ with $X^*$ as the target public key. Algorithm $\mathcal{A}$ handles queries from $\mathcal{F}$ as follows:

- Signing queries. On query SIGN$(m)$ from $\mathcal{F}$, $\mathcal{A}$ queries $m$ to its own signing oracle in the EUF-CMA game. It receives a signature $(c, s)$ and returns it to $\mathcal{F}$.
- $H_2$ queries. On query $H_2(L, k)$ from $\mathcal{F}$, $\mathcal{A}$ assigns $T[L, k] \leftarrow_\$ \mathcal{H}_2$ if $T[L, k]$ is undefined and then returns $T[L, k]$ to $\mathcal{F}$.

As the AGM requires, whenever $\mathcal{F}$ queries or outputs a group element, it should also provide the representation of the element as a product of those elements given to it, i.e., the generator $g$ and the target public key $X^*$. We assume $\mathcal{A}$ never gets two different representations of the same element, otherwise it can directly compute the discrete logarithm of $X^*$.

At last, $\mathcal{F}$ outputs a forged aggregate signature $(\{R_1, \ldots, R_n\}, \tilde{s})$ together with the corresponding messages $m_1, \ldots, m_n$ and public keys $X_1, \ldots, X_n$ it chooses. $\mathcal{F}$ also outputs a representation of each group element. Precisely, $\mathcal{A}$ gets $2n$ pairs $(\alpha_{1,1}, \beta_{1,1}), \ldots, (\alpha_{1,n}, \beta_{1,n}), (\alpha_{2,1}, \beta_{2,1}), \ldots, (\alpha_{2,n}, \beta_{2,n})$ satisfying

$$R_i = g^{\alpha_{1,i}} X^{*\beta_{1,i}} \quad \text{and} \quad X_i = g^{\alpha_{2,i}} X^{*\beta_{2,i}}$$

for $i = 1, \ldots, n$. Let $c_i = H_1(R_i, m_i)$ for $i = 1, \ldots, n$.

If there exists $k$ such that $X_k = X^*$ and $\beta_{1,k} + c_k\beta_{2,k} = 0$, which we call Case 1, then we have

$$R_k X^{*c_k} = g^{\alpha_{1,k} + c_k\alpha_{2,k}}.$$

Thus, $\mathcal{A}$ obtains a forged Schnorr signature $(R_k, \alpha_{1,k} + c_k\alpha_{2,k})$ on $m_k$ and wins the EUF-CMA game if $m_k$ is fresh (i.e., has not been queried to the signing oracle).

We further consider the case that $\beta_{1,k} + c_k\beta_{2,k} \neq 0$ for all $k$ that satisfies $X_k = X^*$, which we call Case 2. Let $L = \{(R_1, X_1, m_1), \ldots, (R_n, X_n, m_n)\}$ and $a_i = H_2(L, i)$ for $i = 1, \ldots, n$. It must hold that $g^{\tilde{s}} = \prod_{i=1}^n (R_i X_i^{c_i})^{a_i}$ for $\mathcal{F}$ to win. Let

$$\alpha^* = \sum_{i=1}^n a_i(\alpha_{1,i} + c_i\alpha_{2,i}) \quad \text{and} \quad \beta^* = \sum_{i=1}^n a_i(\beta_{1,i} + c_i\beta_{2,i}).$$

It can be verified that $\prod_{i=1}^n (R_i X_i^{c_i})^{a_i} = g^{\alpha^*} X^{*\beta^*}$, and consequently $g^{\tilde{s}} = g^{\alpha^*} X^{*\beta^*}$. Therefore, $\mathcal{A}$ can extract the discrete logarithm $(\tilde{s} - \alpha^*)/\beta^*$ of $X^*$ as long as $\beta^* \neq 0$. It can further produce signatures on any message it chooses and certainly win the EUF-CMA game.

To be exact, to compute $\alpha^*$ and $\beta^*$, $\mathcal{A}$ only needs to let $a_i = T[L, i]$ for every $i$ satisfying $R_i X_i^{c_i} \neq 1_{\mathbb{G}}$, where $1_{\mathbb{G}}$ denotes the identity in $\mathbb{G}$ (otherwise $a_i$ is irrelevant). If anyone of those items is undefined, then $\mathcal{A}$ just aborts. Here we show that $\mathcal{F}$ is almost impossible to win in such a case. Suppose $T[L, i]$ was undefined when $\mathcal{F}$ decides its forgery. We regard it as the last one to be determined. Since $R_i X_i^{c_i} \neq 1_{\mathbb{G}}$, there is at most one value of $a_i = T[L, i]$ in $\mathcal{H}_2$ can make $g^{\tilde{s}} = \prod_{i=1}^n (R_i X_i^{c_i})^{a_i}$. Hence, $\mathcal{F}$ wins with probability at most $1/|\mathcal{H}_2|$.

Now let us show that $\mathcal{A}$ can win the EUF-CMA game in one of the above two cases (by extracting a forged signature or directly computing the discrete logarithm of $X^*$) with high probability. To do so, we define an event AggElim, explain how it relates to $\mathcal{A}$'s winning, and bound its probability.

We say AggElim occurs if there exists $L = \{(R_1, X_1, m_1), \ldots, (R_n, X_n, m_n)\}$ satisfying the following conditions:

- Let $\mathcal{I}$ be the set of those $i$ satisfying $R_i X_i^{c_i} \neq 1_{\mathbb{G}}$, where $c_i = H_1(R_i, m_i)$. The condition is that for each $i \in \mathcal{I}$, $T[L, i]$ has been defined.
- Let $(\alpha_{1,i}, \beta_{1,i})$ and $(\alpha_{2,i}, \beta_{2,i})$ be the representations of $R_i$ and $X_i$ respectively. Let $\beta_i^* = \beta_{1,i} + c_i\beta_{2,i}$. The condition is that there exists $k \in \mathcal{I}$ such that $\beta_k^* \neq 0$.
- $\sum_{i \in \mathcal{I}} T[L, i]\beta_i^* = 0$.

If $\mathcal{F}$ wins, but $\mathcal{A}$ does not go to Case 1 (and then extract a forged signature), does not abort because of undefined table items, and also does not win in Case 2 (by directly computing the discrete logarithm of $X^*$), then AggElim must happen. Conditioned on $\mathcal{F}$'s winning, there must exist $k$ such that $X^* = X_k$ and $m_k$ is fresh. Since $\mathcal{A}$ does not go to Case 1, it must hold that $\beta_{i,k} + c_k\beta_{2,k} \neq 0$, and hence the second condition holds. That $\mathcal{A}$ does not abort because of undefined table items implies the first condition. Recall the definition of $\beta^*$, and we can see if $\mathcal{A}$ does not win in Case 2 (only when $\beta^* = 0$), the third condition holds.

Among those $i \in \mathcal{I}$ satisfying $\beta_i^* \neq 0$, consider the last $a_i$ to be determined. There is at most one value from $\mathcal{H}_2$ can make $L$ satisfy the third condition. This means AggElim happens with probability at most $1/|\mathcal{H}_2|$ for each $L$ occurring in table $T$. The total probability of AggElim is thus upper bounded by $q_{\mathsf{H}_2}/|\mathcal{H}_2|$.

Now we can bound the probability $\varepsilon'$ that $\mathcal{A}$ wins the EUF-CMA game. Consider the case $\mathcal{F}$ wins. We assume $\mathcal{A}$ does not win in the first way. It then loses the game only if it aborts for undefined table items or $\beta^* = 0$, respectively bounded by $1/|\mathcal{H}_2|$ and $q_{\mathsf{H}_2}/|\mathcal{H}_2|$. Therefore, we have $\varepsilon' \geq \varepsilon - (q_{\mathsf{H}_2} + 1)/|\mathcal{H}_2|$.

It remains to bound the running time $t'$ of $\mathcal{A}$. Except the running time $t$ of $\mathcal{F}$, there are two significant parts of $t'$ we need to consider: maintaining table $T$ and handling $\mathsf{H}_2$ queries and the final forgery. Assuming that a table operation takes constant time, the first part takes $\mathcal{O}(q_{\mathsf{H}_2})$ which is also $\mathcal{O}(t)$. The second part of time is $\mathcal{O}(t)$, for the forger needs to write the queries and the forgery all. In conclusion, we have $t' \leq \mathcal{O}(t)$.  □

*Remark 1 (Security of aggregating signatures in the $(R, s)$-format).* Compared to signatures in the $(R, s)$-format, the $(c, s)$-format slightly simplifies the proof in the AGM, since forger $\mathcal{F}$ does not get other group elements than $g$ and $X^*$. Nevertheless, it is easy to adapt our proof to $(R, s)$ signatures. Let $(\hat{R}_j, \hat{s}_j)$ be the signature that $\mathcal{F}$ receives in the $j$-th signing query $\textsc{Sign}(\hat{m}_j)$. In addition to $g$ and $X^*$, it can also use $\hat{R}_1, \ldots, \hat{R}_{q_S}$ to represent the group elements it queries or outputs. Let $\hat{c}_j = \mathsf{H}_1(\hat{R}_j, \hat{m}_j)$. By the validity of signatures, $\hat{R}_j = g^{\hat{s}_j}/X^{*\hat{c}_j}$ for $j = 1, \ldots, q_S$. Hence, since $\mathcal{A}$ knows how to represent each $\hat{R}_j$ with $g$ and $X^*$, it essentially gets a representation with $g$ and $X^*$ of each group element that $\mathcal{F}$ queries or outputs. The rest of the proof remains.

# 4 Incremental Aggregation of Schnorr Signatures

## 4.1 Scheme Description

In the real world, it is common that we need to store more signatures after we have produced an aggregation, which leads to the demand for incremental aggregation. However, ASchnorr does not support incremental aggregation well. The procedure of incremental aggregating is not explicitly defined at the scheme level. We can implement it by treating a pre-existing aggregation as a normal signature, but this causes ambiguity and redundant operations. We can omit some redundant computations, but the ambiguity comes from the scheme intrinsically. Following ASchnorr, if we aggregate $n'$ signatures, we will compute coefficients $a_1, \ldots, a_{n'}$. If we aggregate the first $n$ signatures among them, we will compute

$$
\begin{array}{l|l}
\hline
\mathsf{IncrAgg}(L, \tilde{\sigma}, L') & \mathsf{AggVf}(\{(\mathsf{pk}_1, m_1), \ldots, (\mathsf{pk}_n, m_n)\}, \tilde{\sigma}) \\
\hline
/\!/\ L = \{(\mathsf{pk}_1, m_1), \ldots, (\mathsf{pk}_n, m_n)\} & \textbf{for } i = 1, \ldots, n \textbf{ do } X_i := \mathsf{pk}_i \\
/\!/\ L' = \{(\mathsf{pk}_{n+1}, m_{n+1}, \sigma_{n+1}), \backslash\backslash & (\{R_1, \ldots, R_n\}, \tilde{s}) := \tilde{\sigma} \\
/\!/\ \quad \ldots, (\mathsf{pk}_{n'}, m_{n'}, \sigma_{n'})\} & a_1 := 1; \quad c_1 := \mathsf{H}_1(R_1, m_1) \\
\textbf{for } i = 1, \ldots, n' \textbf{ do } X_i := \mathsf{pk}_i & \textbf{for } i = 2, \ldots, n \textbf{ do} \\
(\{R_1, \ldots, R_n\}, \tilde{s}) := \tilde{\sigma} & \quad c_i := \mathsf{H}_1(R_i, m_i) \\
\textbf{for } i = n+1, \ldots, n' \textbf{ do} & \quad L_i := \{(R_1, X_1, m_1), \ldots, (R_i, X_i, m_i)\} \\
\quad (c_i, s_i) := \sigma_i & \quad a_i := \mathsf{H}_2(L_i) \\
\quad R_i := g^{s_i}/X_i^{c_i} & \\
\quad L_i := \{(R_1, X_1, m_1), \ldots, (R_i, X_i, m_i)\} & \textbf{return } [\![ g^{\tilde{s}} = \prod_{i=1}^{n}(R_i X_i^{c_i})^{a_i} ]\!] \\
\quad a_i := \mathsf{H}_2(L_i) & \\
\tilde{s}' := \tilde{s} + \sum_{i=n+1}^{n'} a_i s_i & \\
\textbf{return } \tilde{\sigma}' := (\{R_1, \ldots, R_{n'}\}, \tilde{s}') & \\
\hline
\end{array}
$$

**Fig. 3.** Algorithms $\mathsf{IncrAgg}$ and $\mathsf{AggVf}$ of $\mathsf{IASchnorr}$. The cyclic group $\mathbb{G}$, of order $p$ with a generator $g$, and the hash functions $\mathsf{H}_1$ and $\mathsf{H}_2$ are scheme-level parameters. The range of $\mathsf{H}_2$ is denoted by $\mathcal{H}_2$. The aggregate algorithm $\mathsf{Agg}$ is a special case of $\mathsf{IncrAgg}$.

coefficients $a'_1, \ldots, a'_n$. The scheme-level ambiguity is reflected by that usually $a_i \neq a'_i$ for $i = 1, \ldots, n$. Hence, a verifier has to know whether the first $n$ signatures are aggregated first, or aggregated together with the others. Otherwise, it can not correctly verify the aggregation of the $n'$ signatures.

For such a problem, we provide a modified scheme $\mathsf{IASchnorr}$, described in Fig. 3. See how we remove the ambiguity: the coefficient $a_i$ for the $i$-th signature only depends on the first $i$ signatures. As a result, whether the first $n$ signatures are aggregated first or together with the others does not affect the value of the coefficients. The normal scheme $\mathsf{Schnorr}$ (i.e., algorithms $\mathsf{KGen}$, $\mathsf{Sign}$, and $\mathsf{Vf}$) is unchanged, so Fig. 3 only describes algorithms $\mathsf{IncrAgg}$ and $\mathsf{AggVf}$. The aggregate algorithm $\mathsf{Agg}$ can be seen as a special case of $\mathsf{IncrAgg}$ when $n = 0$.

## 4.2 Security

We can easily prove almost the same security result for $\mathsf{IASchnorr}$ as $\mathsf{ASchnorr}$ in the AGM+ROM. The proof is very similar to the one of Theorem 1, so we defer it to the full version of this paper [7].

**Theorem 2.** *If there exists a forger that $(t, q_{\mathsf{H}_2}, q_{\mathsf{S}}, \varepsilon)$-breaks the CK-AEUF-CMA security of aggregate signature scheme $\mathsf{IASchnorr}$ in the AGM+ROM with $\mathsf{H}_2$ modeled as a random oracle, then there exists an algorithm that $(t', q_{\mathsf{S}}, \varepsilon')$-breaks the EUF-CMA security of $\mathsf{Schnorr}$ with $t' = \mathcal{O}(t)$ and $\varepsilon' \geq \varepsilon - (q_{\mathsf{H}_2} + 1)/|\mathcal{H}_2|$.*

| $\mathsf{SeqSign}(L, \tilde{\sigma}_{n-1}, \mathsf{sk}_n, m_n)$ | $\mathsf{Vf}(\{(\mathsf{pk}_1, m_1), \dots, (\mathsf{pk}_n, m_n)\}, \tilde{\sigma}_n)$ |
|---|---|
| $/\!/ \ L = \{(\mathsf{pk}_1, m_1), \dots, (\mathsf{pk}_{n-1}, m_{n-1})\}$ | **for** $i = 1, \dots, n$ **do** $\quad X_i := \mathsf{pk}_i$ |
| **for** $i = 1, \dots, n-1$ **do** $\quad X_i := \mathsf{pk}_i$ | $(\tilde{R}_n, \{s_1, \dots, s_n\}) := \tilde{\sigma}_n$ |
| $(\tilde{R}_{n-1}, \{s_1, \dots, s_{n-1}\}) := \tilde{\sigma}_{n-1}$ | $c_n := \mathsf{H}(\tilde{R}_n, X_n, m_n, s_{n-1}, n)$ |
| $x_n := \mathsf{sk}_n; \quad X_n := g^{x_n}$ | **if** $n = 1$ **then** $\quad$ **return** $[\![g^{s_1} = \tilde{R}_1 X_1^{c_1}]\!]$ |
| $r_n \xleftarrow{\$} \mathbb{Z}_p; \quad R_n := g^{r_n}$ | **else** |
| $\tilde{R}_n = \tilde{R}_{n-1} \cdot R_n$ | $\quad R_n := g^{s_n}/X_n^{c_n}$ |
| $c_n := \mathsf{H}(\tilde{R}_n, X_n, m_n, s_{n-1}, n)$ | $\quad \tilde{R}_{n-1} := \tilde{R}_n/R_n$ |
| $s_n := r_n + c_n x_n$ | $\quad \tilde{\sigma}_{n-1} := (\tilde{R}_{n-1}, \{s_1, \dots, s_{n-1}\})$ |
| **return** $\tilde{\sigma}_n := (\tilde{R}_n, \{s_1, \dots, s_n\})$ | $\quad$ **return** $\mathsf{Vf}(L', \tilde{\sigma}_{n-1})$ |
| | $/\!/ \ L' = \{(\mathsf{pk}_1, m_1), \dots, (\mathsf{pk}_{n-1}, m_{n-1})\}$ |

**Fig. 4.** Description of SASchnorr. The cyclic group $\mathbb{G}$, of order $p$ with a generator $g$, and the hash function $\mathsf{H}$ are scheme-level parameters. The range of $\mathsf{H}$ is denoted by $\mathcal{H}$. The key generation algorithm KGen is the same as Schnorr's, as described in Fig. 2. We define $s_0$ as always 0.

# 5 Sequential Aggregation of Schnorr Signatures with Tight Reduction in the ROM

## 5.1 Scheme Description

We describe SASchnorr in Fig. 4. The aggregation is implemented in a very different way in SASchnorr compared with the other schemes: we aggregate the commitment parts of the individual signatures rather than the response parts. Provided an pre-existing sequential aggregate signature $(\tilde{R}_{n-1}, \{s_1, \dots, s_{n-1}\})$ on messages $m_1, \dots, m_{n-1}$ under public keys $X_1, \dots, X_{n-1}$, what the signer does in SeqSign is basically producing a normal Schnorr signature. The difference is what it hashes to get its challenge $c_n$. Instead of its own commitment $R_n = g^{r_n}$, it hashes the aggregate commitment $\tilde{R}_n = \tilde{R}_{n-1} \cdot R_n$. It additionally hashes its public key $X_n$, the response $s_{n-1}$ from the last signer, and the current length $n$.

To verify an aggregate signature, the verifier sequentially recovers the individual commitments from the $n$-th to the first one. Provided the aggregation of $j$ commitments $\tilde{R}_j$, the verifier can compute $c_j$. It then obtains $R_j$, the $j$-th individual commitment, by $R_j = g^{s_j}/X_j^{c_j}$. After that, it knows $\tilde{R}_{j-1}$ and iteratively continues the procedure.

As ASchnorr and IASchnorr do, SASchnorr achieves about half aggregation in elliptic curve groups. On the other hand, the verification in SASchnorr is similar to a sequence of individual verification. We cannot use simultaneous multiplication techniques to accelerate the verification.

Note that in Fig. 4, we minimize what the signer needs to hash. As a result, many inputs are irrelevant to the signing procedure. There are some potential optimizations can be made in practice. For example, consider the scenario where a fixed destination is public known to all signers, and they do not care the validity of the partial aggregations. A signer can choose to not pass redundant information to the next one. Instead, the $j$-th signer can pass only $\tilde{R}_j$ and $s_j$ to the next signer and directly pass $X_j$, $m_j$, and $s_j$ to the destination. Thus, the total communication complexity is significantly reduced.

For consistency, we require the first signer also hashes $s_0$, which we define as 0, and the current length 1. This can be omitted without ambiguity.

## 5.2   A New Security Model for SAS Schemes

Rather than the security model presented in [19] and Sect. 2.2 for SAS schemes, we analyze the security of SASchnorr in a modified model. There is no essential difference between them. We just adapt the model to fit the fact that in our scheme SASchnorr, algorithm SeqSign takes fewer inputs than the general syntax of SAS schemes defined in [19] and Sect. 2.2. Hence, we still use the term CK-SAEUF-CMA to denote the security notion.

Note that the signature produced by SeqSign only depends on $x_n$, $m_n$, and part of $\tilde{\sigma}_{n-1}$, i.e., $\tilde{R}_{n-1}$ and $s_{n-1}$. We only take them as the arguments of the signing oracle. Precisely, the adversary can query $\text{SIGN}(\tilde{R}_{n-1}, s_{n-1}, m_n, n)$ and receive $(\tilde{R}_n, s_n)$.

The adversary's goal is to forge an aggregation $(\tilde{R}_n, \{s_1, \ldots, s_n\})$ on/under corresponding messages/public keys $m_1, \ldots, m_n$, $\text{pk}_1, \ldots, \text{pk}_n$ on its choice. The adversary is said to win if the forgery is valid, and it has not queried $\text{SIGN}(\cdot, s_{k-1}, m_k, k)$ for some $k$ such that $X_k = X^*$, where $X^*$ is the target public key.

We make some comparisons between the new security model and the original model defined in [19]. On the one hand, the adversary does not need to give a valid aggregation in order to request a subsequent aggregation. Specifically, the signing oracle cannot verify the validity of the previous aggregation, as it doesn't know the corresponding public keys and messages. In this aspect, our model allows for a more powerful adversary. On the other hand, the success conditions of the adversary in our model are also adjusted according to the change of the signing oracle, which makes our model incomparable with the original one.

We underline that the reason why we introduce the new model is not that we cannot achieve security in the original one. Actually, simpler designs can already make the scheme secure in the original model. If we require each signer to verify the previous aggregation, or we let $c_n$ be instead $\text{H}(\tilde{R}_n, X_1, \ldots, X_n, m_1, \ldots, m_n)$, then our scheme can be proved secure in the original model. We introduce our new security model for SAS schemes to show the possibility of signing without knowing so much information. This feature allows essential bandwidth/storage saving.

See the full version of this paper [7] for more discussion. In the full version, we explain our model as a result of a three-step modification on the original model, among which two steps strengthen the model and one weakens it. We also explain how to prove the security of our scheme (with minor modifications as mentioned above) in the original model.

## 5.3   Security

We prove that the security of SASchnorr reduces to the EUF-CMA security of Schnorr in the ROM, with only an additive security loss. Note that we can directly reduce the security of SASchnorr to the DLP based on the forking lemma, but we intentionally avoid doing so. Improving the proof techniques and finding tighter bounds for Schnorr signatures in the ROM are popular research topics, and some great results were achieved in a recent work [21]. We prove a relatively modular result which is compatible with any previous or future improvements on the security results for Schnorr.

**Theorem 3.** *If there exists a forger that $(t, q_H, q_S, N, \varepsilon)$-breaks the CK-SAEUF-CMA security of SASchnorr in the ROM, then there exists an algorithm that $(t', q_H + q_S, q_S, \varepsilon')$-breaks the EUF-CMA security of Schnorr in the ROM, with*

$$t' \leq t + 2Nt_{\exp} + \mathcal{O}\left(q_S + q_H\right)$$

*and*

$$\varepsilon' \geq \varepsilon - \frac{(q_H + q_S)(q_H + 3q_S)}{2p} - \frac{(q_H + q_S + 1)^2 + 1}{2|\mathcal{H}|},$$

*where $t_{\exp}$ is the time of an exponentiation in $\mathbb{G}$.*

We give some intuition before the actual proof. Let $X^*$ be the target public key. In a valid forgery, there must exist a $k \in \{1, \ldots, n\}$ such that $X_k = X^*$, and it holds that $R_k X^{*c_k} = g^{s_k}$. The equality is in form of the verification of an individual signature, so intuitively, we would like to take $(R_k, s_k)$ as a forged Schnorr signature.

Let H and H' denote the random oracles in the CK-SAEUF-CMA game against SASchnorr and the EUF-CMA game against Schnorr, respectively. For the reduction to win the latter game, it should hold that $c_k = H'(R_k, m^*)$ for some $m^*$. On the other hand, $c_k = H(\tilde{R}_k, m_k, X^*, s_{k-1}, k)$ in the former game. Therefore, to use $(R_k, s_k)$ as its own forgery, the reduction has to find out $R_k$ when handling the forger's hash query, given only $\tilde{R}_k$.

The key point is to retrieve $\tilde{R}_{k-1}$ with $s_{k-1}$ (and then obtain $R_k = \tilde{R}_k / \tilde{R}_{k-1}$). We do so by setting the exponent of the expected response $s_n$ as the index of each query $H(\tilde{R}_n, m_n, X_n, s_{n-1}, n)$. It takes most of our effort to show this works. Simply speaking, we present a mathematical induction: we can retrieve unique $\tilde{R}_1$ with $s_1$; given that we can retrieve $\tilde{R}_{i-1}$ with $s_{i-1}$, we can successfully figure out $R_i = \tilde{R}_i / \tilde{R}_{i-1}$ and set the index of query $H(\tilde{R}_i, m_i, X_i, s_{i-1}, i)$, and thus we can retrieve $\tilde{R}_i$ with $s_i$.

Following Fig. 4, we define $s_0$ as always 0. Moreover, we define $\tilde{R}_0$ as $1_{\mathbb{G}}$, which simplifies the discussion a bit.

*Proof. (Theorem 3).* Suppose $\mathcal{F}$ is the forger that breaks the CK-SAEUF-CMA security of SASchnorr. We construct an algorithm $\mathcal{A}$ that breaks the EUF-CMA security of Schnorr. In the EUF-CMA game, it has access to a signing oracle SIGN', and the hash function is modeled as a random oracle H'.

On target public key $X^*$, algorithm $\mathcal{A}$ first initializes an empty table $T[\cdot, \cdot, \cdot, \cdot, \cdot]$ for simulating the random oracle H. Each table item may have an index $I[\cdot, \cdot, \cdot, \cdot, \cdot]$ which is a group element. For any group element, $\mathcal{A}$ can efficiently locate the table item with an index equal to the element. Algorithm $\mathcal{A}$ runs $\mathcal{F}$ with the same target public key. It handles queries from $\mathcal{F}$ as follows:

- Hash queries. On a hash query $H(\tilde{R}_j, X_j, m_j, s_{j-1}, j)$, algorithm $\mathcal{A}$ returns $T[\tilde{R}_j, X_j, m_j, s_{j-1}, j]$. If the item is undefined, $\mathcal{A}$ first defines it as follows. Algorithm $\mathcal{A}$ checks the following two conditions:

  C1 $X_j = X^*$;

  C2 $j = 1$; or among all defined items with the last arguments being $j - 1$, there exists a unique one $T[\tilde{R}_{j-1}, X_{j-1}, m_{j-1}, s_{j-2}, j - 1]$ whose index is $g^{s_{j-1}}$.

  If C2 is not true, $\mathcal{A}$ assigns $c \leftarrow_\$ \mathcal{H}$ to $T[\tilde{R}_j, X_j, m_j, s_{j-1}, j]$. If only C2 is true, $\mathcal{A}$ additionally sets the index

  $$I[\tilde{R}_j, X_j, m_j, s_{j-1}, j] = (\tilde{R}_j/\tilde{R}_{j-1})X_j^c.$$

  If both conditions hold, $\mathcal{A}$ instead assigns $c = H'(\tilde{R}_j/\tilde{R}_{j-1}, m^*)$, with $m^*$ uniformly chosen from $\{0,1\}^{\log p}$, to $T[\tilde{R}_j, X_j, m_j, s_{j-1}, j]$. It sets the index in the same way. We say $\mathcal{A}$ *retrieves* $\tilde{R}_{j-1}$ here.

- Signing queries. To answer a signing query $\text{SIGN}(\tilde{R}_{n-1}, s_{n-1}, m_n, n)$, $\mathcal{A}$ uniformly chooses $m^*$ from $\{0,1\}^{\log p}$ and queries $m^*$ to $\text{SIGN}'$. It receives a Schnorr signature $(R, s)$ on $m^*$ under $X^*$. Let $\tilde{R}_n = \tilde{R}_{n-1} \cdot R$. Algorithm $\mathcal{A}$ aborts if $T[\tilde{R}_n, X^*, m_n, s_{n-1}, n]$ has been defined. Otherwise, $\mathcal{A}$ assigns $H'(R, m^*)$ to $T[\tilde{R}_n, X^*, m_n, s_{n-1}, n]$. It returns $(\tilde{R}_n, s)$ to $\mathcal{F}$. It also checks condition C2 defined above and sets index $I[\tilde{R}_n, X^*, m_n, s_{n-1}, n] = g^s$ if C2 is true.

At last, $\mathcal{F}$ outputs a forgery with messages and public keys it chooses:

$$\{(X_1, m_1), \ldots, (X_n, m_n)\}, (\tilde{R}_n, \{s_1, \ldots, s_n\}).$$

Algorithm $\mathcal{A}$ runs the verification procedure. Namely, for $i = n, \ldots, 2$, it lets $c_i = T[\tilde{R}_i, X_i, m_i, s_{i-1}, i]$ and then computes $\tilde{R}_{i-1} = \tilde{R}_i/(g^{s_i}/X_i^{c_i})$. It finally lets $c_1 = T[\tilde{R}_1, X_1, m_1, 0, 1]$ and determines whether the forgery is valid by checking whether $g^{s_1} = \tilde{R}_1 X_1^{c_1}$. In this verification procedure, $\mathcal{A}$ aborts if it meets an undefined table item. This behavior is different from the verification algorithm Vf, since the item would be defined now if we run Vf. However, we will later show that the forgery is unlikely to be valid with such an undefined table item.

There must exist $k \in \{1, \ldots, n\}$ such that $X_k = X^*$, and $\mathcal{F}$ has not queried $\text{SIGN}(\cdot, s_{k-1}, m_k, k)$ for $\mathcal{F}$ to win the CK-SAEUF-CMA game. From the forgery's validity, we know

$$(\tilde{R}_k/\tilde{R}_{k-1})X^{*c_k} = g^{s_k},$$

where $c_k = T[\tilde{R}_k, X^*, m_k, s_{k-1}, k]$. If $c_k = H'(\tilde{R}_k/\tilde{R}_{k-1}, m^*)$, and $m^*$ is fresh in the EUF-CMA game (i.e., has not queried to the signing oracle $\text{SIGN}'$), then $\mathcal{A}$ wins the game with a forged signature $(\tilde{R}_k/\tilde{R}_{k-1}, s_k)$ on message $m^*$. Our main task below is to prove this is exactly the case with high probability, guaranteed by how $\mathcal{A}$ handles the queries from $\mathcal{F}$.

To do so, we consider a list of events. We define them, explain how they relate to $\mathcal{A}$'s winning, and bound their probabilities. They are defined as follows:

E1 Algorithm $\mathcal{A}$ aborts when handling a signing query. We also use SimFail to denote this event.

E2 Algorithm $\mathcal{A}$ chooses some duplicate random messages from $\{0,1\}^{\log p}$. We also use MsgCol to denote this event.

E3 Forger $\mathcal{F}$ succeeds. We also use $\mathsf{Acc}_\mathcal{F}$ to denote this event.

E4 Algorithm $\mathcal{A}$ meets an undefined table item in the above verification procedure we described. We also use UnDef to denote this event.

E5 When $T[\tilde{R}_k, X^*, m_k, s_{k-1}, k]$ was defined, condition C2 was not true, or the aggregate commitment that $\mathcal{A}$ retrieved was not $\tilde{R}_{k-1}$.

As long as E3 happens while E2, E4, and E5 do not happen, $\mathcal{A}$ finds a forged Schnorr signature $(\tilde{R}_k/\tilde{R}_{k-1}, s_k)$ on a fresh message $m^*$ (for the EUF-CMA game) and wins. Excluding E2 guarantees the freshness of $m^*$, excluding E4 guarantees $\mathcal{A}$ does not abort in the verification procedure, and excluding E5 guarantees $c_k$ was indeed set to $\mathsf{H}'(\tilde{R}_k/\tilde{R}_{k-1}, m^*)$. If E1 and E2 do not happen, then the simulated game is identical to the real CK-SAEUF-CMA game, and we know E3 happens with probability at least $\varepsilon$ on such a condition. Here we also exclude E2 to avoid one hash value $\mathsf{H}'(R, m^*)$ being assigned to different table items. Below we separately consider the probabilities of these events.

*E1* For every signing query from $\mathcal{F}$, $\tilde{R}_n$ to be returned is uniformly distributed on a set of order $p$. This is because $\tilde{R}_n = \tilde{R}_{n-1} \cdot R$ with $R$ uniformly distributed on $\mathbb{G}$, since $R$ is the commitment of a Schnorr signature from $\mathrm{SIGN}'$. This $\tilde{R}_n$ may collide with the at most $q_\mathsf{H} + q_\mathsf{S}$ aggregate commitments occurring in $T$. Hence, SimFail happens in every signing query with probability at most $(q_\mathsf{H} + q_\mathsf{S})/p$. In total, we have $\Pr[\mathsf{SimFail}] \leq q_\mathsf{S}(q_\mathsf{H} + q_\mathsf{S})/p$.

*E2* Algorithm $\mathcal{A}$ needs to choose at most one message from $\{0,1\}^{\log p}$ for every signing query and hash query from $\mathcal{F}$. The total number of the chosen messages is bounded by $q_\mathsf{H} + q_\mathsf{S}$, and it follows that $\Pr[\mathsf{MsgCol}] \leq (q_\mathsf{H} + q_\mathsf{S})^2/(2p)$.

*E4* To bound the probability of this event, we need Lemma 4 below. Note that when one verifies a forgery with Vf, all the recursive calls return equal values. Hence, as long as $\mathcal{A}$ meets an undefined table item, the probability of the whole forgery's validity is bounded by $(q_\mathsf{H} + q_\mathsf{S} + 1)/|\mathcal{H}|$. Namely, we have $\Pr[\mathsf{Acc}_\mathcal{F} \mid \mathsf{UnDefAcc}_\mathcal{F}] \leq (q_\mathsf{H} + q_\mathsf{S} + 1)/|\mathcal{H}|$.

**Lemma 4.** *For any* $\{(X_1, m_1), \ldots, (X_j, m_j)\}, (\tilde{R}_j, \{s_1, \ldots, s_j\})$, *if table item* $T[\tilde{R}_j, X_j, m_j, s_{j-1}, j]$ *is undefined, then the probability that*

$$\mathsf{Vf}(\{(X_1, m_1), \ldots, (X_j, m_j)\}, (\tilde{R}_j, \{s_1, \ldots, s_j\})) = 1$$

*is upper-bounded by* $(q_\mathsf{H} + q_\mathsf{S} + 1)/|\mathcal{H}|$.

*E5* We consider condition C2 in two aspects. First, it requires that there *exists* an item $T[\tilde{R}_{j-1}, X_{j-1}, m_{j-1}, s_{j-2}, j-1]$ with index being $g^{s_{j-1}}$. Second, it requires the item to be *unique*. Lemma 5 and 6 relate to the uniqueness and existence requirements respectively.

**Lemma 5.** *Let $q_j$ be the number of defined entries in $T$ with the last argument being $j$. Define* Dup *as the event that there exist two different table items*

$$T[\tilde{R}_j, X_j, m_j, s_{j-1}, j] \quad and \quad T[\tilde{R}'_j, X'_j, m'_j, s'_{j-1}, j]$$

*with the last arguments being equal, such that*

$$I[\tilde{R}_j, X_j, m_j, s_{j-1}, j] = I[\tilde{R}'_j, X'_j, m'_j, s'_{j-1}, j].$$

*It holds that* $\Pr[\mathsf{Dup}] \leq (\sum_{i=1}^{\infty} q_i^2)/(2|\mathcal{H}|).$

**Lemma 6.** *Let $q_j$ be the number of defined entries in $T$ with the last argument being $j$. Define* BadOrder *as the event that there exists a valid chain in $T$, namely a set of items*

$$c_1 = T[\tilde{R}_1, X_1, m_1, 0, 1], \ldots, c_j = T[\tilde{R}_j, X_j, m_j, s_{j-1}, j]$$

*satisfying $(\tilde{R}_i/\tilde{R}_{i-1})X_j^{c_i} = g^{s_i}$ for $i = 1, \ldots, j-1$, while these items were not defined in order. It holds that* $\Pr[\mathsf{BadOrder} \mid \neg\mathsf{DupBadOrder}] \leq (\sum_{i=1}^{\infty} q_i q_{i+1})/|\mathcal{H}|.$

We now show the link between E5 and these two lemmas. For a valid chain described in Lemma 6, suppose the items in it are defined in order. We use an induction to show the following statement is true for every item in the chain if Dup does not happen: for the item $T[\tilde{R}_i, X_i, m_i, s_{i-1}, i]$ in the chain, condition C2 was true when it is defined, and $\mathcal{A}$ exactly retrieved $\tilde{R}_{i-1}$ at that time.

For the first item in the chain, the statement is true directly from the definition of C2, and its index is $g^{s_1}$ from the validity of the chain. Assume the statement is true for the $(i-1)$-th item, and its index is $g^{s_{i-1}}$. When the $i$-th item in the chain is going to be defined, the $(i-1)$-th has been defined. From the assumption, the index of the $(i-1)$-th item has been defined and equals $g^{s_{i-1}}$. That Dup does not happen guarantees there does not exist another item with the last argument being $i-1$ and equal index. Thus, condition C2 for the $i$-th item holds, and $\mathcal{A}$ retrieves $\tilde{R}_{i-1}$. The index of the $i$-th item is thus $g^{s_i}$ from the validity of the chain. This means that the statement is true for the $i$-th item. By induction, the statement is true for every item in the chain.

Obviously, the forgery must correspond to a valid chain for it to be valid, conditioned on that E4 does not happen. The above statement means that E5 is impossible if none of BadOrder and Dup happen. The probability of E5 is hence bounded by

$$\Pr[\mathsf{Dup} \vee \mathsf{BadOrder}] = \Pr[\mathsf{Dup}] + \Pr[\mathsf{BadOrder} \mid \neg\mathsf{Dup}]$$

$$\leq \frac{\sum_{i=1}^{\infty} q_i^2 + \sum_{i=1}^{\infty} 2q_i q_{i+1}}{2|\mathcal{H}|}$$

$$\leq \frac{(q_{\mathsf{H}} + q_{\mathsf{S}})^2}{2|\mathcal{H}|},$$

where the last inequality follows from $q_H + q_S = \sum_{i=1}^{\infty} q_i$.

Put all these bounds together, and we have

$$\varepsilon' \geq \Pr[\text{Acc}_{\mathcal{F}} \wedge \neg\text{MsgCol} \wedge \neg\text{UnDef} \wedge \neg\text{Dup} \wedge \neg\text{BadOrder}]$$
$$\geq \Pr[\text{Acc}_{\mathcal{F}} \wedge \neg\text{MsgCol}] - \Pr[\text{UnDef}] - \Pr[\text{Dup} \vee \text{BadOrder}]$$
$$\geq \Pr[\text{Acc}_{\mathcal{F}} \wedge \neg\text{SimFail} \wedge \neg\text{MsgCol}]$$
$$\quad - \Pr[\text{Acc}_{\mathcal{F}} \wedge \text{UnDef}] - \Pr[\text{Dup} \vee \text{BadOrder}]$$
$$\geq \Pr[\text{Acc}_{\mathcal{F}} \mid \neg\text{SimFail} \wedge \neg\text{MsgColAcc}_{\mathcal{F}}] \cdot \Pr[\neg\text{SimFail} \wedge \neg\text{MsgCol}]$$
$$\quad - \Pr[\text{Acc}_{\mathcal{F}} \wedge \text{UnDef}] - \Pr[\text{Dup} \vee \text{BadOrder}]$$
$$\geq \Pr[\text{Acc}_{\mathcal{F}} \mid \neg\text{SimFail} \wedge \neg\text{MsgColAcc}_{\mathcal{F}}] - \Pr[\text{SimFail}] - \Pr[\text{MsgCol}]$$
$$\quad - \Pr[\text{Acc}_{\mathcal{F}} \mid \text{UnDefAcc}_{\mathcal{F}}] - \Pr[\text{Dup} \vee \text{BadOrder}]$$
$$\geq \varepsilon - \frac{(q_H + q_S)(q_H + 3q_S)}{2p} - \frac{(q_H + q_S + 1)^2 + 1}{2|\mathcal{H}|}$$

It only remains for us to bound the running time of $\mathcal{A}$. We assume a table operation takes constant time with enough space and a hash table implemented properly. We also assume retrieving a table item as described in condition C2 also takes constant time with an index structure implemented properly. In total, the time $\mathcal{A}$ spends on handling queries from $\mathcal{F}$ and maintaining table $T$ is bounded by $\mathcal{O}(q_S + q_H)$.

Note that $\mathcal{A}$ runs a verification procedure on $\mathcal{F}$'s forgery in order to obtain $\tilde{R}_k / \tilde{R}_{k-1}$, the commitment part of its own forged Schnorr signature. This takes at most $2N$ exponentiation operations. In conclusion, we have

$$t' \leq t + 2Nt_{\text{exp}} + \mathcal{O}(q_S + q_H).$$

$\square$

We defer the proofs of Lemma 4 to 6 to the full version of this paper [7].

**Acknowledgement.** We are grateful to the anonymous reviewers of ESORICS 2022 for their insightful and very helpful comments, and particularly to Yvo Desmedt for shepherding and invaluable advice, which have significantly improved this work.

This work is supported by the following foundation items: The National Natural Science Foundation of China (No. U1536205, No. 61472084), The National Key Research and Development Program of China (No. 2017YFB0802000), Shanghai Innovation Action Project (No. 16DZ1100200), Shanghai Science and Technology Development Funds (No. 16JC1400801), Technical Standard Project of Shanghai Scientific and Technological Committee (No. 21DZ2200500), Shandong Provincial Key Research and Development Program (No. 2017CXG0701, No. 2018CXGC0701).

# References

1. Ahn, J.H., Green, M., Hohenberger, S.: Synchronized aggregate signatures: new definitions, constructions and applications. In: Al-Shaer, E., Keromytis, A.D., Shmatikov, V. (eds.) ACM CCS 2010, pp. 473–484. ACM Press, October 2010. https://doi.org/10.1145/1866307.1866360

2. Kılınç Alper, H., Burdges, J.: Two-round trip Schnorr multi-signatures via delinearized witnesses. In: Malkin, T., Peikert, C. (eds.) CRYPTO 2021, Part I. LNCS, vol. 12825, pp. 157–188. Springer, Cham (2021). https://doi.org/10.1007/978-3-030-84242-0_7

3. Bellare, M., Namprempre, C., Neven, G.: Unrestricted aggregate signatures. In: Arge, L., Cachin, C., Jurdziński, T., Tarlecki, A. (eds.) ICALP 2007. LNCS, vol. 4596, pp. 411–422. Springer, Heidelberg (2007). https://doi.org/10.1007/978-3-540-73420-8_37

4. Bernstein, D.J., Duif, N., Lange, T., Schwabe, P., Yang, B.-Y.: High-speed high-security signatures. In: Preneel, B., Takagi, T. (eds.) CHES 2011. LNCS, vol. 6917, pp. 124–142. Springer, Heidelberg (2011). https://doi.org/10.1007/978-3-642-23951-9_9

5. Boneh, D., Gentry, C., Lynn, B., Shacham, H.: Aggregate and verifiably encrypted signatures from bilinear maps. In: Biham, E. (ed.) EUROCRYPT 2003. LNCS, vol. 2656, pp. 416–432. Springer, Heidelberg (2003). https://doi.org/10.1007/3-540-39200-9_26

6. Chalkias, K., Garillot, F., Kondi, Y., Nikolaenko, V.: Non-interactive half-aggregation of EdDSA and variants of Schnorr signatures. In: Paterson, K.G. (ed.) CT-RSA 2021. LNCS, vol. 12704, pp. 577–608. Springer, Cham (2021). https://doi.org/10.1007/978-3-030-75539-3_24

7. Chen, Y., Zhao, Y.: Half-aggregation of Schnorr signatures with tight reductions. Cryptology ePrint Archive, Report 2022/222 (2022). https://ia.cr/2022/222

8. Dimitrov, V.S., Jullien, G.A., Miller, W.C.: Complexity and fast algorithms for multiexponentiations. IEEE Trans. Comput. **49**(2), 141–147 (2000)

9. Fuchsbauer, G., Kiltz, E., Loss, J.: The algebraic group model and its applications. In: Shacham, H., Boldyreva, A. (eds.) CRYPTO 2018, Part II. LNCS, vol. 10992, pp. 33–62. Springer, Cham (2018). https://doi.org/10.1007/978-3-319-96881-0_2

10. Fuchsbauer, G., Plouviez, A., Seurin, Y.: Blind Schnorr signatures and signed ElGamal encryption in the algebraic group model. In: Canteaut, A., Ishai, Y. (eds.) EUROCRYPT 2020, Part II. LNCS, vol. 12106, pp. 63–95. Springer, Cham (2020). https://doi.org/10.1007/978-3-030-45724-2_3

11. Gentry, C., Ramzan, Z.: Identity-based aggregate signatures. In: Yung, M., Dodis, Y., Kiayias, A., Malkin, T. (eds.) PKC 2006. LNCS, vol. 3958, pp. 257–273. Springer, Heidelberg (2006). https://doi.org/10.1007/11745853_17

12. Goldwasser, S., Micali, S., Rivest, R.L.: A digital signature scheme secure against adaptive chosen-message attacks. SIAM J. Comput. **17**(2), 281–308 (1988)

13. Gordon, D.M.: A survey of fast exponentiation methods. J. Algorithms **27**(1), 129–146 (1998)

14. Hankerson, D., Menezes, A.: Elliptic Curve Signature Schemes, pp. 1–3. Springer, Heidelberg (2019). https://doi.org/10.1007/978-3-642-27739-9_251-2

15. Hankerson, D., Menezes, A.J., Vanstone, S.: Guide to Elliptic Curve Cryptography. Springer, New York (2006)

16. Hartung, G., Kaidel, B., Koch, A., Koch, J., Rupp, A.: Fault-tolerant aggregate signatures. In: Cheng, C.-M., Chung, K.-M., Persiano, G., Yang, B.-Y. (eds.) PKC 2016, Part I. LNCS, vol. 9614, pp. 331–356. Springer, Heidelberg (2016). https://doi.org/10.1007/978-3-662-49384-7_13

17. Lee, K., Lee, D.H., Yung, M.: Sequential aggregate signatures with short public keys: design, analysis and implementation studies. In: Kurosawa, K., Hanaoka, G. (eds.) PKC 2013. LNCS, vol. 7778, pp. 423–442. Springer, Heidelberg (2013). https://doi.org/10.1007/978-3-642-36362-7_26

18. Lu, S., Ostrovsky, R., Sahai, A., Shacham, H., Waters, B.: Sequential aggregate signatures and multisignatures without random oracles. In: Vaudenay, S. (ed.) EUROCRYPT 2006. LNCS, vol. 4004, pp. 465–485. Springer, Heidelberg (2006). https://doi.org/10.1007/11761679_28

19. Lysyanskaya, A., Micali, S., Reyzin, L., Shacham, H.: Sequential aggregate signatures from trapdoor permutations. In: Cachin, C., Camenisch, J.L. (eds.) EURO-CRYPT 2004. LNCS, vol. 3027, pp. 74–90. Springer, Heidelberg (2004). https://doi.org/10.1007/978-3-540-24676-3_5

20. Maurer, U.: Abstract models of computation in cryptography. In: Smart, N.P. (ed.) Cryptography and Coding 2005. LNCS, vol. 3796, pp. 1–12. Springer, Heidelberg (2005). https://doi.org/10.1007/11586821_1

21. Rotem, L., Segev, G.: Tighter security for Schnorr identification and signatures: a high-moment forking lemma for $\Sigma$-protocols. In: Malkin, T., Peikert, C. (eds.) CRYPTO 2021, Part I. LNCS, vol. 12825, pp. 222–250. Springer, Cham (2021). https://doi.org/10.1007/978-3-030-84242-0_9

22. Schnorr, C.P.: Efficient identification and signatures for smart cards. In: Brassard, G. (ed.) CRYPTO 1989. LNCS, vol. 435, pp. 239–252. Springer, New York (1990). https://doi.org/10.1007/0-387-34805-0_22

23. Shoup, V.: Lower bounds for discrete logarithms and related problems. In: Fumy, W. (ed.) EUROCRYPT 1997. LNCS, vol. 1233, pp. 256–266. Springer, Heidelberg (1997). https://doi.org/10.1007/3-540-69053-0_18

24. Wuille, P., Nick, J., Ruffing, T.: Schnorr signatures for secp256k1. https://github.com/bitcoin/bips/blob/master/bip-0340.mediawiki

25. Zhao, Y.: Practical aggregate signature from general elliptic curves, and applications to blockchain. In: Galbraith, S.D., Russello, G., Susilo, W., Gollmann, D., Kirda, E., Liang, Z. (eds.) ASIACCS 19, pp. 529–538. ACM Press, July 2019. https://doi.org/10.1145/3321705.3329826

# Ring Signatures with User-Controlled Linkability

Dario Fiore[1], Lydia Garms[1,2(✉)], Dimitris Kolonelos[1,3], Claudio Soriente[4], and Ida Tucker[5]

[1] IMDEA Software Institute, Madrid, Spain
[2] Keyless Technologies Limited, London, UK
`lydia.garms@keyless.io`
[3] Universidad Politecnica de Madrid, Madrid, Spain
[4] NEC Laboratories Europe, Heidelberg, Germany
[5] Zondax AG, Zug, Switzerland

**Abstract.** Anonymous authentication primitives, e.g., group or ring signatures, allow one to realize privacy-preserving data collection applications, as they strike a balance between authenticity of data being collected and privacy of data providers. At PKC 2021, Diaz and Lehmann defined group signatures with User-Controlled Linkability (UCL) and provided an instantiation based on BBS+ signatures. In a nutshell, a signer of a UCL group signature scheme can link any of her signatures: linking evidence can be produced at signature time, or after signatures have been output, by providing an explicit linking proof.

In this paper, we introduce Ring Signatures with User-Controlled Linkability (RS-UCL). Compared to group signatures with user-controlled linkability, RS-UCL require no group manager and can be instantiated in a completely decentralized manner. We also introduce a variation, User Controlled and Autonomous Linkability (RS-UCAL), which gives the user full control of the linkability of their signatures.

We provide a formal model for both RS-UCL and RS-UCAL and introduce a compiler that can upgrade any ring signature scheme to RS-UCAL. The compiler leverages a new primitive we call Anonymous Key Randomizable Signatures (AKRS)—a signature scheme where the verification key can be randomized—that can be of independent interest. We also provide different instantiations of AKRS based on Schnorr signatures and on lattices. Finally, we show that an AKRS scheme can additionally be used to construct an RS-UCL scheme.

## 1   Introduction

Group signatures [CvH91, BMW03, BSZ05, BCC+16] and ring signatures [RST01] allow users to sign messages, while providing anonymity of signers and unlinkability of signatures. Group signatures require a central entity that manages group membership, whereas ring signatures allow a signer to choose an arbitrary ring of public keys, and sign on behalf of that ring.

© The Author(s), under exclusive license to Springer Nature Switzerland AG 2022
V. Atluri et al. (Eds.): ESORICS 2022, LNCS 13555, pp. 405–426, 2022.
https://doi.org/10.1007/978-3-031-17146-8_20

Many application scenarios do not require full anonymity/unlinkability, and may actually ask for mechanisms to identify the signer or link signatures produced by the same party. Group signatures feature an opening authority that can de-anonymize signers and thereby test if two signatures have the same signer.

Recently, researchers have proposed more flexible linkability options for group signature schemes, where even less power is entrusted to the opener. In [HLC+11, HLC+13, SSU14, KTY04] group signatures with an authority who can test whether two signatures have the same signer but cannot open signatures were introduced. In [GL19, FGL21], group signatures are originally unlinkable, but later on can be converted to linkable signatures by an oblivious "converter". Group signatures with message-dependant opening [SEH+12, OSEH13, LJ14, LMN16] introduce an additional entity, the admitter, who can specify messages such that the corresponding signatures can be opened. Group signatures with certified limited opening [ZWC19] introduce a certifier, instead of an admitter, who can certify a particular opener to allow them to open signatures on messages within a particular context. Abe et al., [ACHO13] use "public-key anonymous tag system" to build a traceable signature scheme. In all these lines of work, linking is performed by a trusted party, and signers have no say in which of their signatures can be linked together. Another line of work [BCC04, BFG+13, CDL16b, CDL16a] considers scenarios where a so-powerful authority is undesirable, and achieves linkability by including a one-way function of the signing key and a "scope" chosen by the signer—also known as "pseudonym"—in each signature, so that two signatures with the same pseudonym can be trivially linked.

Pseudonym-based linkability, however, require signers to decide at signature time whether their signatures should be ever linked: two signatures using different scopes – hence, with different pseudonyms – would be unlinkable by definition. Recently, Diaz and Lehmann [DL21] introduced group signatures with User-Controlled Linkability (UCL) that provide pseudonym-based linkability (labelled "implicit" linkability), but also allow a signer to link any set of her signatures generated with the same linking secret, even if those had different pseudonyms (labelled "explicit" linkability). This linking model turns useful in applications where authenticated data is collected in anonymous fashion but, later on, one may be interested to link specific data items. For example, in smart-metering applications, energy consumptions may be collected in a fully anonymous way, while, at a later time, a user may want to link her measurements to, e.g., receive tailored offers from the energy providers. Similarly, connected vehicles can anonymously report their mobility traces but, at a later time, a driver may want to link her reports so to obtain discounts from insurance companies.

**Our Contributions.** In this paper, we continue the study of UCL but focus on ring signatures. Compared to group signatures, a ring signature scheme enables fully decentralized applications as no group manager is needed. Previous linkable ring signatures [LWW04, SALY17] solely allow anyone to link two signatures by the same signer on the same ring.

Our first contribution is the formalization of UCL in ring signatures. We introduce the first formal model for ring signatures with UCL allowing for both implicit and explicit linkability, as in [DL21]. Next, we introduce ring signatures with *User Controlled Autonomous Linkability* (UCAL) to give signers full control over the linkability of their signatures. Different from UCL, UCAL does not use the signing key to create pseudonyms, but instead uses a "linking secret" which can be re-used or chosen afresh. A fresh linking secret ensures that signatures cannot be linked (i.e., via implicit linkability) even if they have the same scope. Of course, a signer can use the same linking secret on multiple signatures with the same scope so to provide implicit linkability. Ultimately, a signer can prove linkability of any set of her signatures generated with the same linking secret, even if those had different pseudonyms. Further, using different linking secrets ensures that past signatures cannot be linked even if the signer is corrupted, providing a form of forward anonymity.

As a second contribution we propose constructions of UCL and UCAL ring signatures. To do so, we introduce a new cryptographic primitive that we label *Anonymous Key Randomizable Signatures* (AKRS) that may be of independent interest. AKRS is essentially a signature scheme where public keys can be re-randomized, while maintaining the correspondence to the same secret key, so that a randomized public key cannot be linked to the original one. However, by using the secret, the signer can prove that multiple public keys are all randomized versions of the original one. The primitive is in a similar spirit to Signatures with Flexible Public Key [BHKS18], which however is not fully suitable for our requirements. We elaborate more on the differences in Sect. 3.

We show that AKRS can be used to upgrade *any ring signature scheme* to UCAL. In particular, we use an AKRS public key that has been re-randomised with the scope as the pseudonym for the (ring) signature. By using a public key corresponding to the same AKRS secret key and scope, we provide implicit linkability. Otherwise, the signer may use a different AKRS secret key to make two signatures unlinkable even on the same scope. At a later time, the signer can use her AKRS secret key to link the pseudonyms of a set of ring signatures, thereby proving that all such signatures are linked. Notably, our construction does not modify the original ring signature public keys and thus can be used to upgrade to UCAL an already up-and-running system using ring signatures.

We also show how to use AKRS, along with a NIZK, to build a UCL ring signature. The linking mechanism is obtained using the AKRS in a similar way to the UCAL construction. The difference is that, for UCL the AKRS secret key is used as the ring signature secret. Therefore, to sign a message with some scope, in addition to using the AKRS secret key to compute the pseudonym, we also add a non-interactive signature of knowledge [CS97] that the secret used to derive the pseudonym corresponds to one of the public keys in the ring.

Finally, we propose two instantiations of AKRS: one based on Schnorr's signatures in prime order groups, and one based on Lyubashevsky's signatures [Lyu12] on lattices. Compiling our AKRS with a ring signature scheme we get UCAL ring signatures with minimal overhead: one additional Schnorr or Lyubashevsky signature, respectively. In contrast to previous works (on group signatures) [DL21], the constructions are generic and can bootstrap any arbitrary ring signature scheme to a UCAL one. For instance we can achieve UCAL without pairings.

**Related Work.** There is an extensive line of work studying and constructing efficient ring signatures from various settings and assumptions, with the today's state-of-the art achieving signatures of size logarithmic in the size of the ring [GK15, BCC+15, LPQ18, LRR+19, YSL+20, YEL+21].

Park and Sealfon [PS19] proposed the related notions of (un)Claimable and (un)Repudiable Ring Signatures. Claimability states that one can always claim a signature after she signed it, while Repudiability states the opposite, that one can always repudiate a signature she did not sign. Claimability is a notion relevant to user-controlled linkability, although it is weaker: a signer can claim a signature by linking it to a signature of a dummy message on-the-fly. The inverse, achieving user-controlled linkability from claimability, does not apply.

The idea of linking anonymous signatures of a user by using a Pseudorandom Function (PRF) has been used in the past. A user can additionally sign a random value together with its PRF output, where the seed is kept by the signer. Then, a NIZK proving knowledge of the (same) seed can be used to link signatures. However, this linking mechanism provides no succinctness: the linking proof typically grows with the number of linked signatures. AKRS generalizes this linking mechanism and guarantees succinctness; we note that an AKRS may also be instantiated with a PRF and a (succinct) NIZK.

## 2 Ring Signatures with User-Controlled Linkability

### 2.1 Standard Linkability

As in [DL21], we consider two types of linkability:

**Implicit linkability:** Signatures are accompanied by a pseudonym, generated by the user for a particular scope. Re-using the same scope leads to the same pseudonym, making all signatures with the same scope linkable. Signatures with different scopes cannot be linked, except via explicit link proofs.

**Explicit linkability:** A user can prove that she created a set of previously generated signatures, i.e. link the signatures in the set.

**Definition 1 (RS-UCL).** *A ring signature scheme with user controlled linkability (RS-UCL) is a tuple of PPT algorithms* (KGen, Sig, Vf, Link, VerifyLink), *satisfying* correctness, anonymity *(Definition 3),* unforgeability *(Definitions 4 and 6) and* non-frameability *(Definitions 7 and 8); and with the following syntax:*

KGen($1^\lambda$) *on input a security parameter, outputs a signing key* sk *and a verification key* vk.

Sig(sk, $R, m$, scp) *signs a message $m$ w.r.t. scope* scp *via secret signing key* sk *for set of verification keys (called the ring) $R = \{$vk$_1, \ldots,$ vk$_n\}$. The output is a pseudonym* nym *and a ring signature $\sigma$.*

$\mathsf{Vf}(\Sigma)$ *on input a signature tuple* $\Sigma = (m, \mathsf{scp}, R, \sigma, \mathsf{nym})$ *for ring* $R = \{\mathsf{vk}_1, \ldots, \mathsf{vk}_n\}$, *returns 1 if* $\sigma$ *and* $\mathsf{nym}$ *are valid for message* $m$ *and scope* $\mathsf{scp}$ *w.r.t.* $R$, *and 0 otherwise.*

$\mathsf{Link}(\mathsf{sk}, \mathsf{lm}, \boldsymbol{\Sigma})$ *on input a set of signature tuples* $\boldsymbol{\Sigma} = \{\Sigma_i\}_{i \in [n]}$, *a user secret key* $\mathsf{sk}$, *and a linking message* $\mathsf{lm}$ *(can be used to ensure freshness of the proof), outputs a proof* $\pi_l$ *that these signatures are linked, or the error symbol* $\perp$.

$\mathsf{VerifyLink}(\mathsf{lm}, \boldsymbol{\Sigma}, \pi_l)$ *returns 1 if* $\pi_l$ *is a valid proof that* $\boldsymbol{\Sigma} = \{\Sigma_i\}_{i \in [n]}$ *were produced by the same signer for link message* $\mathsf{lm}$, *and 0 otherwise.*

## 2.2 Autonomous Linking

We also introduce the notion of ring signatures with user controlled, and *autonomous* linking (RS-UCAL). This variant allows users to chose the linking secret independently of the signing key. It hence gives users the liberty of choosing which of their signatures should be linkable in the future. We express this feature via an additional algorithm $\mathsf{GenLinkSec}$ which outputs a linking secret $\mathsf{ls}$. Now both the signing algorithm and the linking algorithm should input both the signing secret $\mathsf{sk}$ and the linking secret $\mathsf{ls}$.

**Definition 2.** *A ring signature scheme with user controlled autonomous linking (RS-UCAL) is a tuple of PPT algorithms* $(\mathsf{KGen}, \mathsf{GenLinkSec}, \mathsf{Sig}, \mathsf{Vf}, \mathsf{Link}, \mathsf{VerifyLink})$, *where* $\mathsf{KGen}, \mathsf{Vf}, \mathsf{VerifyLink}$ *have the same syntax as an RS-UCL, and:*

$\mathsf{GenLinkSec}(1^\lambda)$ *takes input a security parameter, and outputs a linking secret* $\mathsf{ls}$.

$\mathsf{Sig}(\mathsf{sk}, \mathsf{ls}, R, m, \mathsf{scp})$ *as in a RS-UCL scheme, only with additional input a linking secret* $\mathsf{ls}$.

$\mathsf{Link}(\mathsf{ls}, \mathsf{lm}, \boldsymbol{\Sigma})$ *as in an RS-UCL scheme, only with input a linking secret* $\mathsf{ls}$ *instead of the secret key.*

*An RS-UCAL scheme satisfies correctness anonymity (Definition 3), unforgeability (Definitions 5 and 6) and non-frameability (Definitions 7 and 8).*

Text which is highlighted in blue only occurs for a RS-UCAL scheme. Text which is highlighted in green only occurs for a RS-UCL scheme.

## 2.3 Correctness

An RS-UC(A)L scheme should satisfy both verification correctness, which is equivalent to correctness for standard ring signatures, and linking correctness which ensures the correctness of the explicit linking algorithm Link. We give the full definitions in the full version of this paper.

## 2.4 Security Model

For privacy, signatures must not reveal anything about the signer's identity beyond what was intended by her (**anonymity**). Security is expressed through both **unforgeability**, which ensures that an adversary cannot forge a signature on behalf of a ring they are not a member of or forge a link proof for signatures they did not generate, and **non-frameability**, which states that an honest user cannot be framed by the adversary, so that signatures of an honest user are (implicitly or explicitly) linkable to signatures that she has not generated.

**Oracles and State.** All oracles are parametrised by a list of keys pairs $\{(\mathsf{pk}_i, \mathsf{sk}_i)\}_{i \in [n]}$ and linking secrets $\{\mathsf{ls}_i\}_{i \in [n]}$, where $n = \mathsf{poly}(\lambda), k = \mathsf{poly}(\lambda)$. In Fig. 1 we describe the global state variables that all oracles can access.

**Corruption oracle** Corr takes as input an index $i \in [n]$, adds $i$ to the list of corrupted indices $I \leftarrow I \cup \{i\}$, and outputs the randomness $w_i$ used to compute key pair $(\mathsf{pk}_i, \mathsf{sk}_i)$.

**Linking secret oracle** OLS takes as input an index $i \in [k]$, adds $i$ to the list of corrupted indices $J \leftarrow J \cup \{i\}$, and outputs the randomness $w'_i$ used to compute linking secret $ls_i$.

**Signing oracle** $\mathsf{OSign}^{\text{ucl-r}}$: takes as input a set $R$, an index $i \in [N]$, an index $j \in [k]$, a message $m$ and a scope scp computes $(\mathsf{nym}, \sigma) \leftarrow \mathsf{Sig}(\mathsf{sk}_i, \mathsf{ls}_j, R \cup \mathsf{vk}_i, m, \mathsf{scp})$, adds $\Sigma := (m, \mathsf{scp}, R, \sigma, \mathsf{nym})$ to the list of signatures signed by user index $i$ with linking secret index $j$: $\mathsf{SIG}[i,j] \leftarrow \mathsf{SIG}[i,j] \cup \{\Sigma\}$, and returns $(\mathsf{nym}, \sigma)$.

**Linking oracle** OLink: Allows the adversary to obtain link proofs for signatures of its choice. On input an index $i \in [n]$, an index $i \in [k]$, a linking message lm and a set of tuples $\Sigma = \{\Sigma = (m, \mathsf{scp}, R, \sigma, \mathsf{nym})\}$, this oracle adds $(\mathsf{lm}, \Sigma)$ to the list of link proofs produced for index $i$: $\mathsf{LNK}[i] \leftarrow \mathsf{LNK}[i] \cup \{(\mathsf{lm}, \Sigma)\}$, and returns $\pi_l \leftarrow \mathsf{Link}(\mathsf{sk}_i, \mathsf{ls}_i, \mathsf{lm}, \Sigma)$.

**Challenge signing oracle** $\mathsf{Ch} - \mathsf{Sign}_b$: Allows $\mathcal{A}$ to get signatures for challenge user index $i_b$ with linking secret index $j_b$. On input a ring $R$, a message $m$, and a scope scp, $\mathsf{Ch} - \mathsf{Sign}_b$ computes $(\mathsf{nym}, \sigma) \leftarrow \mathsf{Sig}(\mathsf{sk}_{i_b}, \mathsf{ls}_{j_b}, R \cup \{\mathsf{vk}_{i_0}, \mathsf{vk}_{i_1}\}, m, \mathsf{scp})$, sets $\Sigma := (m, \mathsf{scp}, R, \sigma, \mathsf{nym})$, adds $\Sigma$ to the list of queried challenge signatures $\mathsf{CSIG} \leftarrow \mathsf{CSIG} \cup \{\Sigma\}$, and returns $(\mathsf{nym}, \sigma)$.

**Challenge linking oracle** $\mathsf{Ch} - \mathsf{Link}_b$: Allows $\mathcal{A}$ to get link proofs for a challenge index $i_b/j_b$. Precisely, on input a linking message lm and a set of tuples $\Sigma = \{\Sigma = (m, \mathsf{scp}, R, \sigma, \mathsf{nym})\}$, it adds $(\mathsf{lm}, \Sigma)$ to the list of challenge link proofs $\mathsf{CLNK} \leftarrow \mathsf{CLNK} \cup \{(\mathsf{lm}, \Sigma)\}$, and returns $\pi_l \leftarrow \mathsf{Link}(\mathsf{sk}_{i_b}, \mathsf{ls}_{j_b}, \mathsf{lm}, \Sigma)$.

| Variable | Content |
|---|---|
| $I$ | List of corrupted indices (queried to Corr) |
| $J$ | List of corrupted indices (queried to OLS) |
| $i_b$ | Challenge user index in **anon-b**. Ignored in the other games |
| $j_b$ | Challenge linking secret index in **anon-b**. Ignored in the other games |
| $\mathsf{SIG}[i]$ | Signature tuples produced by OSign for user index $i$ |
| $\mathsf{CSIG}$ | Signature tuples produced by $\mathsf{Ch} - \mathsf{Sign}_b$ for challenge user index $i_b$ |
| $\mathsf{LNK}[i]$ | Link queries sent to OLink for user index $i$ |
| $\mathsf{CLNK}$ | Link queries made to $\mathsf{Ch} - \mathsf{Link}_b$ |

**Fig. 1.** Global state variables and their contents.

*Helper Algorithm.* As in [DL21], we introduce the helper algorithm Identify. In this case we do not need to require the existence of Identify, because there is no trusted issuer in the ring signature setting. Therefore, user secret keys do not need to be extracted from join protocols as in the group signature setting. Identify here is just defined for notational simplicity, and can be achieved from the user controlled linkability functionality.

---

Identify(sk, pk, ls, $\Sigma = (m, \text{scp}, R, \sigma, \text{nym})$)

---

$(\text{sk}, \text{vk}) \leftarrow \text{KGen}(1^\lambda)$, $(\text{nym}', \sigma') \leftarrow \text{Sig}(\text{sk}, \text{ls}, \{vk\}, m, \text{scp})$

if $\text{nym}' = \text{nym}$   **return** 1   **else return** 0

---

**Anonymity.** Anonymity ensures that an adversary cannot figure out which of two (honest) challenge users generated a given signature. In formalizing this notion, one must be careful to exclude trivial wins leveraging user-controlled linkability (see the comments in the security experiment).

**Definition 3 (Anonymity).**  *An RS-UCAL scheme satisfies adaptive anonymity against adversarially chosen keys if, for any PPT adversary $\mathcal{A} = (\mathcal{A}_1, \mathcal{A}_2)$, and any $n = \text{poly}(\lambda)$, $k = \text{poly}(\lambda)$, it holds that $|\Pr[\text{Exp}_{\text{UCL},\mathcal{A}}^{\text{anon-1}}(1^\lambda, n, k) = 1] - \Pr[\text{Exp}_{\text{UCL},\mathcal{A}}^{\text{anon-0}}(1^\lambda, n, k) = 1]|$ is negligible in $\lambda$.*

---

Experiment : $\text{Exp}_{\text{UCL},\mathcal{A}}^{\text{anon-b}}(1^\lambda, n, k)$

---

1 :   **for** $i = 1, \ldots, n$   $(\text{sk}_i, \text{vk}_i) \leftarrow \text{KGen}(1^\lambda)$

2 :   **for** $i = 1, \ldots, k$   $\text{ls}_i \leftarrow \text{GenLinkSec}(1^\lambda)$

3 :   $(i_0, i_1, j_0, j_1, \text{state}) \leftarrow \mathcal{A}_1^{\text{OSign}^{uc\text{-}r}, \text{OLink}, \text{Corr}, \text{OLS}}(\text{choose}, \text{vk}_1, \ldots, \text{vk}_n)$

4 :   $d \leftarrow \mathcal{A}_2^{\text{OSign}^{uc\text{-}r}, \text{OLink}, \text{Ch}-\text{Sign}_b, \text{Ch}-\text{Link}_b, \text{Corr}, \text{OLS}}(\text{guess}, \text{state})$

5 :   // *Exclude trivial wins via implicit linking: a signature for scope scp was queried to Ch − Sign$_b$ and to OSign for index $i_0$ or $i_1$*

6 :   **if** $\exists \text{scp } s.t. (*, \text{scp}, *, *, *) \in CSIG \wedge (*, \text{scp}, *, *, *) \in SIG[i_0, j_0] \cup SIG[i_1, j_1]$

7 :       **then return** $\perp$

8 :   // *Exclude trivial wins via explicit linking: both challenge and non challenge signatures were queried to Ch − Link$_b$ or to OLink*

9 :   **if** $\exists \Sigma \ s.t. (\Sigma \cap CSIG \neq \emptyset \wedge (*, \Sigma) \in LNK[*])$

10 :     $\vee (\Sigma \cap (SIG[i_0, j_0] \cup SIG[i_1, j_1]) \neq \emptyset \wedge (*, \Sigma) \in CLNK)$   **then return** $\perp$

11 :   **if** $\{i_0, i_1\} \cap I \neq \emptyset$ **then return** $\perp$

12 :   **if** $\{j_0, j_1\} \cap J \neq \emptyset$ **then return** $\perp$

13 :     **else return** $d$

---

**Unforgeability.** For both RS-UCL and RS-UCAL we must ensure that only ring members can sign. However, for RS-UCL, we must also prevent signers from outputting multiple unlinkable signatures on the same scope. For RS-UCL one captures both by defining an attack as the generation of more signatures with different pseudonyms than corrupted users in the ring, using the same scope. This is meaningless for RS-UCAL where a single corrupted user can generate many linking secrets.

**Definition 4 (Signature unforgeability).** *An RS-UCL scheme satisfies signature unforgeability if for any PPT adversary $\mathcal{A}$, and any $n = \text{poly}(\lambda)$, it holds that $\Pr[\text{Exp}_{\text{UCL},\mathcal{A}}^{\text{sig-uf}}(1^\lambda, n) = 1]$ is negligible in $\lambda$.*

Experiment :$\text{Exp}_{\text{UCL},\mathcal{A}}^{\text{sig-uf}}(1^\lambda, n)$

---

1 :  **for** $i = 1, \dots, n$   $(\text{sk}_i, \text{vk}_i) \leftarrow \text{KGen}(1^\lambda)$

2 :  $(\{\Sigma_1^*, \cdots, \Sigma_m^*\}, R^*) \leftarrow \mathcal{A}^{\text{OSign}^{\text{ucl-r}}, \text{OLink}, \text{Corr}}(\text{vk}_1, \dots, \text{vk}_n)$

3 :  *Parse* $\Sigma_j^* = (m_j^*, \text{scp}_j^*, R_j, \sigma_j^*, \text{nym}_j^*)$ *for* $j \in [m]$

4 :  **if** $\exists j \in [m]$ s.t. $R_j \neq R^*$  **return** 0

5 :  $m^* \leftarrow |R^* \backslash \{\text{vk}_i\}_{i \in [n] \backslash I}|$

6 :  **if**  *the following conditions all hold*

7 :     1.$m > m^*$ // *more signatures are output than the corrupted users in the ring*

8 :     2.$\forall j_1, j_2 \in [m]$  $\text{scp}_{j_1}^* = \text{scp}_{j_2}^*$ *and* $\text{nym}_{j_1}^* \neq \text{nym}_{j_2}^*$ // *all signatures are unlinked*

9 :     3.$\forall j \in [m]$  $\text{Vf}(\Sigma_j^*) = 1$

10 :    4.$\forall i \in [n], j \in [m]$  $(m_j^*, \text{scp}_j^*, R^*, *, *) \notin SIG[i]$

11 :       **then return** 1

12 : **else return** 0

---

As mentioned earlier, Definition 4 is too strong for RS-UCAL. Indeed, the autonomous linking property allows parties to change the linking secret as frequently as desired. Hence an adversary which wants to output many unlinkable secrets could simply keep changing the linking secret. For such schemes we adopt a similar notion of (signature) unforgeability as that of standard ring signatures, with the difference that the adversary also has access to a linking oracle. We give the full experiment in Appendix B.

**Definition 5 (Signature unforgeability with autonomous linking).** *An RS-UCAL scheme satisfies signature unforgeability if, for any PPT adversary $\mathcal{A}$, and any $n = \text{poly}(\lambda)$, $k = \text{poly}(\lambda)$, it holds that $\Pr[\text{Exp}_{\text{UCAL},\mathcal{A}}^{\text{sig-uf-al}}(1^\lambda, n, k) = 1]$ is negligible in $\lambda$.*

We additionally define link unforgeability for both the RS-UCL and RS-UCAL schemes, which ensures that the linking proof is unforgeable.

**Definition 6 (Link unforgeability).** *An RS-UCAL scheme satisfies link unforgeability if, for any PPT adversary $\mathcal{A}$, and any $n = \text{poly}(\lambda)$, $k = \text{poly}(\lambda)$, the following is negligible in $\lambda$: $\Pr[\text{Exp}_{\text{UCL},\mathcal{A}}^{\text{link-uf}}(1^\lambda, n, k) = 1]$.*

Experiment :$\text{Exp}_{\text{UCL},\mathcal{A}}^{\text{link-uf}}(1^\lambda, n, k)$

---

1 :  **for** $i = 1, \dots, n$   $(\text{sk}_i, \text{vk}_i) \leftarrow \text{KGen}(1^\lambda)$

2 :  **for** $i = 1, \dots, k$   $\text{ls}_i \leftarrow \text{GenLinkSec}(1^\lambda)$

3 :  $(\text{lm}, \Sigma, \pi_l) \leftarrow \mathcal{A}^{\text{OSign}^{\text{ucl-r}}, \text{OLink}, \text{Corr}, \text{OLS}}(\text{vk}_1, \dots, \text{vk}_n)$

4 :  $\text{VerifyLink}(\text{lm}, \Sigma, \pi_l) = 0$ *or* $\exists i \in [n][k] : (\text{lm}, \Sigma) \in LNK[i]$  **return** 0

5 :  **if** $\exists i \in [n] : \forall \Sigma \in \Sigma : \Sigma \in SIG[i]$ *and* $i \notin I$  **return** 1

6 :  **if** $\exists i \in [k] : \forall \Sigma \in \Sigma : \Sigma \in SIG[\cdot, i]$ *and* $i \notin J$  **return** 1

7 :  **else return** 0

---

**Non-frameability.** Non-frameability guarantees that an honest user cannot be framed by the adversary, such that signatures of an honest user are linkable to signatures that she has not generated. We capture this in the implicit/explicit setting with signature/link non-frameability respectively. We give the full games in Appendix B. Roughly, signature non-frameability ensures that an adversary cannot output a valid signature that links to another signature generated by an uncorrupted user via the signing oracle. Link non-frameability ensures that an adversary cannot explicitly link two signatures that were either from different users or such that one of the two signatures is not from a user in the experiment.

**Definition 7 (Signature non-frameability).** *An RS-UCAL scheme satisfies signature non-frameability if, for any PPT adversary $\mathcal{A}$, and any $n = \mathsf{poly}(\lambda)$, $k = \mathsf{poly}(\lambda)$, the following is negligible in $\lambda$:* $\Pr[\mathsf{Exp}^{sign\text{-}frame}_{UCL,\mathcal{A}}(1^\lambda, n, k) = 1]$.

**Definition 8 (Link non-frameability).** *An RS-UCAL scheme satisfies link non-frameability if, for any PPT adversary $\mathcal{A}$, and any $n = \mathsf{poly}(\lambda)$, $k = \mathsf{poly}(\lambda)$, the following is negligible in $\lambda$:* $\Pr[\mathsf{Exp}^{link\text{-}frame}_{UCL,\mathcal{A}}(1^\lambda, n, k) = 1]$.

## 3  Anonymous Key Randomisable Signatures

We will now give the syntax and security requirements for a new primitive we call Anonymous Key Randomisable Signatures (AKRS), which is closely related to Signatures with Flexible Public Key (SFPK) [BHKS18].

*Intuition.* An SFPK scheme is a standard signature scheme that allows for public and secret keys to be re-randomised. These re-randomised keys are considered to be in the same equivalence class as the original key pair. Such re-randomised public keys, and signatures which verify for them, should not be linkable to the original key pair of their equivalence class. This is formalised by a class hiding requirement. Furthermore, during key generation, a trapdoor can be generated allowing to efficiently decide if public keys are in the same equivalence class.

At first sight, an SFPK scheme seems to allow transforming ring signatures into ring signatures with user controlled and autonomous linking. A user's key pair would be that of a standard ring signature, while their linking secret key would be an SFPK key pair, with the corresponding trapdoor. During signing, the user's pseudonym could be a re-randomisation of the SFPK public key with the randomness set to be the scope, so that the resulting public key is within the same equivalence class as the original keypair in their linking key. The signature should include a standard ring signature to ensure that the signature was output by a ring member and a SFPK signature valid under the public key in the pseudonym to prevent framing attacks.

However, in the SFPK class hiding requirement, which is necessary to ensure anonymity of the ring signature, the adversary does not get to see the randomness used to re-randomise the public key. In their game, the knowledge of this randomness allows to trivially win, as an adversary can re-run the randomisation algorithm itself. For the application to ring signatures described in the previous paragraph, this will not do, since the randomness is a public value: the scope.

On the other hand, in this application, the SFPK's secret key remains hidden: it is part of the linking secret, which is unknown to the anonymity adversary. Therefore, we modify SFPK to ensure that the secret key is necessary to generate public keys in the same equivalence class, thereby avoiding the aforementioned trivial attack, while allowing for the adversary to know the randomness.

A second issue in the above construction, is that signatures can only be explicitly linked by revealing the trapdoor, which would allow *all signatures* under the same linking key to be linked. One way around this is to add an additional functionality, proving, in zero-knowledge, that the pseudonyms in signatures are in the same equivalence class, using the trapdoor in the linking secret key. For efficiency, however, we chose a different approach: we allow for several key pairs in the same equivalence class to be accumulated into one key pair. Then the accumulated secret key could be used to sign a signature valid under the accumulated public key. A verifier can check that this signature is valid under an accumulated public key, resulting from the pseudonyms of all signatures being linked. This means the linking proof is only the size of an SFPK signature. However, explicitly linking signatures requires keeping track of each re-randomised secret key used in the linking key. We overcome this by re-randomising only public keys, but not secret keys, i.e., the secret key remains the same for all public keys in a given equivalence class. An accumulated public key will then correspond to the same secret key as the public keys it was built from, as long as the latter lie in the same equivalence class. Finally, observe that the secret key essentially fulfils the role of the trapdoor, as it allows to link public keys in the same equivalence class. We thus remove the trapdoor from our primitive's syntax.

We now formally define Anonymous Key Randomisable Signatures. The security properties required are given in Sect. 3.1 to 3.3.

**Definition 9 (Anonymous Key Randomisable Signature (AKRS)).** *An* anonymous key randomisable signature scheme *is a tuple of PPT algorithms* (KGen, ChgPK, Sig, Vf, Accum), *satisfying* correctness *(Definition 10),* class hiding *(Definition 11),* existential unforgeability under chosen message attacks *(Definition 12) and* accumulation soundness *(Definition 13); and with the following syntax:*

KGen($1^\lambda$) *on input a security parameter* $1^\lambda$, *outputs a signing key* sk *and a public key* pk.

ChgPK(sk, $t$) *on input a secret key* sk *and a tag* $t$, *outputs a new public key* pk' *in the same equivalence class.*

Sig(sk, pk, $m$) *on input a signing key* sk, *a public key* pk *and a message* $m$, *outputs a signature* $\sigma$.

Vf(pk, $m$, $\sigma$) *on input a public key* pk, *a message* $m$ *and a signature* $\sigma$, *the verification algorithm returns 1 if* $\sigma$ *is a valid signature on* $m$ *w.r.t.* pk, *and 0 otherwise.*

Accum(($t_1$, pk$_1$), $\cdots$, ($t_k$, pk$_k$)) *on input* $k$ *public keys* pk$_1$, $\cdots$, pk$_k$ *with respect to tags* $t_1$, $\cdots$, $t_k$, *outputs an accumulated public key* pk.

**Definition 10 (Correctness).** *Consider any positive integer $k$; any tags [BCC+15] $t_1, \cdots, t_k \in \{0,1\}^*$; let $(\mathsf{sk}, \mathsf{pk}) \leftarrow \mathsf{KGen}(1^\lambda)$, for all $i \in [k]$ $\mathsf{pk}'_i \leftarrow \mathsf{ChgPK}(\mathsf{sk}, t_i)$, and $\tilde{\mathsf{pk}} \leftarrow \mathsf{Accum}((t_1, \mathsf{pk}'_1), \cdots (t_k, \mathsf{pk}'_k))$. An AKRS scheme is correct if for any message $m$, there exists a negligible function $\epsilon$ such that:*

$$\Pr\left[\begin{array}{c} \mathsf{Vf}(\mathsf{pk}, m, \sigma) = 1 \\ \wedge \forall i \in [k], \mathsf{Vf}(\mathsf{pk}'_i, m, \sigma_i) = 1 \\ \wedge \mathsf{Vf}(\tilde{\mathsf{pk}}, m, \tilde{\sigma}) = 1 \end{array} \middle| \begin{array}{c} \sigma \leftarrow \mathsf{Sig}(\mathsf{sk}, \mathsf{pk}, m), \\ \forall i \in [k], \sigma_i \leftarrow \mathsf{Sig}(\mathsf{sk}, \mathsf{pk}'_i, m), \\ \tilde{\sigma} \leftarrow \mathsf{Sig}(\mathsf{sk}, \tilde{\mathsf{pk}}, m) \end{array}\right] = 1 - \epsilon(\lambda).$$

*If $\epsilon = 0$ then* perfect correctness *is satisfied.*

## 3.1 Class Hiding

We ensure that an adversary cannot guess which of two public keys are re-randomised with a tag *chosen by the adversary* (through oracle OChgPK), even while they can obtain signatures on these public keys and the re-randomised keys (via the OSign oracle).

**Definition 11 (Class Hiding).** *An anonymous key randomisable signature scheme satisfies class hiding if for any PPT adversary $\mathcal{A} = (\mathcal{A}_1, \mathcal{A}_2)$, [BCC+15] $\Pr[\mathsf{Exp}_{\mathsf{AKRS},\mathcal{A}}^{class\text{-}hiding}(1^\lambda) = 1]$ is negligible in $\lambda$:*

---

Experiment : $\mathsf{Exp}_{\mathsf{AKRS},\mathcal{A}}^{class\text{-}hiding}(1^\lambda)$

$b^* \leftarrow_\$ \{0,1\}$

**for** $b \in \{0,1\}$ $\quad$ $(\mathsf{sk}_b, \mathsf{pk}_b) \leftarrow \mathsf{KGen}(1^\lambda)$

$\mathsf{sk}_2 \leftarrow \mathsf{sk}_{b^*}, L_1 := \{\}, L_2 := \{\}$

$d \leftarrow \mathcal{A}^{\mathsf{OChgPK}_{L_1,L_2}, \mathsf{OSign}_{L_1,L_2}}(\text{choose}, \mathsf{pk}_0, \mathsf{pk}_1)$

**return** $((d = b^*) \wedge (L_1 \cap L_2 = \emptyset))$

---

$\mathsf{OChgPK}_{L_1,L_2}(a, t)$

1 : **if** $\mathsf{sk}_a =\bot$ **then return** $\bot$

2 : **if** $a \in \{0,1\}$ **then** $L_1 \leftarrow L_1 \cup \{t\}$

3 : **if** $a = 2$ **then** $L_2 \leftarrow L_2 \cup \{t\}$

4 : $\mathsf{pk}' \leftarrow \mathsf{ChgPK}(\mathsf{sk}_a, t)$

5 : **return** $\mathsf{pk}'$

---

$\mathsf{OSign}_{L_1,L_2}(a, m, \mathsf{pk}', \{t_1, \cdots, t_m\})$

1 : **if** $\mathsf{sk}_a =\bot$ **then return** $\bot$

2 : **if** $\{t_1, \cdots, t_m\} \neq *$ **then**

3 : $\quad$ **if** $a \in \{0,1\}$ **then** $L_1 \leftarrow L_1 \cup \{t_1, \cdots, t_m\}$

4 : $\quad$ **if** $a = 2$ **then** $L_2 \leftarrow L_2 \cup \{t_1, \cdots, t_m\}$

5 : $\quad$ **if** $\mathsf{pk}' \neq \mathsf{Accum}((t_1, \mathsf{ChgPK}(\mathsf{sk}_a, t_1)), \cdots, (t_m, \mathsf{ChgPK}(\mathsf{sk}_a, t_m)))$ **then return** $\bot$

6 : $\quad$ $\sigma \leftarrow \mathsf{Sig}(\mathsf{sk}_a, \mathsf{pk}', m)$

7 : **if** $t = *$ **then if** $a = 2$ **then return** $\bot$

8 : $\quad$ **else** $\sigma \leftarrow \mathsf{Sig}(\mathsf{sk}_a, \mathsf{pk}_a, m)$

9 : **return** $\sigma$

---

## 3.2 Existential Unforgeability Under Chosen Message Attacks

We ensure that signatures cannot be forged for a public key in the equivalence class of an honest user, even when they can obtain multiple public keys in that equivalence class on tags of their choice. We give the full game in Appendix A.

**Definition 12 (Existential Unforgeability under Chosen Message Attacks).** *An anonymous key randomisable signature scheme satisfies existential unforgeability under chosen message attacks if for any PPT adversary $\mathcal{A}$,* $\Pr[\mathsf{Exp}_{\mathsf{AKRS},\mathcal{A}}^{\mathsf{euf-cma}}(1^\lambda) = 1]$ *is negligible in* $\lambda$.

### 3.3 Accumulation Soundness

This is a new requirement necessary due to the accumulation functionality. It must not be possible to produce a signature which verifies for an accumulated public key, if the public keys input to the accumulation algorithm do not belong to the same equivalence class.

**Definition 13 (Accumulation Soundness).** *An anonymous key randomisable signature scheme satisfies accumulation soundness if for any PPT adversary $\mathcal{A}$,* $\Pr[\mathsf{Exp}_{\mathsf{AKRS},\mathcal{A}}^{\mathsf{acc-sound}}(1^\lambda) = 1]$ *is negligible in* $\lambda$.

---

Experiment :$\mathsf{Exp}_{\mathsf{AKRS},\mathcal{A}}^{\mathsf{acc-sound}}(1^\lambda)$

1:  **for** $i \in [k]$   $(\mathsf{sk}_i, \mathsf{pk}_i) \leftarrow \mathsf{KGen}(1^\lambda)$

2:  $(\{(\hat{t}_i, \hat{pk}_i, \hat{m}_i, \hat{\sigma}_i)\}_{i \in [k+1, k+l]}, \mathcal{I}, \{t_i\}_{i \in \mathcal{I}}, m, \sigma) \leftarrow \mathcal{A}((\mathsf{sk}_1, \mathsf{pk}_1), \cdots, (\mathsf{sk}_k, \mathsf{pk}_k))$

3:  **if** $\exists (i, j) \in \mathcal{I} \cup [k+1, k+l]$ such that $i \neq j$ and $t_i = t_j$   **return** 0

4:  **if** $\mathcal{I} = \emptyset$   **return** 0

5:  **if** $\exists i \in [k+1, k+l]$ s.t $\mathsf{Vf}(\hat{pk}_i, \hat{m}_i, \hat{\sigma}_i) = 0$   **return** 0

6:  **for** $i \in \mathcal{I}$   $\mathsf{pk}_i' \leftarrow \mathsf{ChgPK}(\mathsf{sk}_i, t_i)$

7:  $\tilde{pk} \leftarrow \mathsf{Accum}(\{(t_i, \mathsf{pk}_i')\}_{i \in \mathcal{I}}, \{(\hat{t}_i, \hat{pk}_i)\}_{i \in [k+1, k+l]})$

8:  **if** $\mathsf{Vf}(\tilde{pk}, m, \sigma) = 0$   **return** 0

9:  **if** $\exists (i, j) \in \mathcal{I}$ s.t. $\mathsf{sk}_i \neq \mathsf{sk}_j \vee \exists i \in [k+1, k+l]$ s.t. $\forall j \in \mathcal{I}, \mathsf{ChgPK}(sk_j, \hat{t}_i) \neq \hat{pk}_i$

10:      **then return** 1

11:  **else return** 0

---

## 4   Constructions for RS-UCL and RS-UCAL

### 4.1   A RS-UCAL Construction

We provide a generic construction, upgrading a standard ring signature scheme to a scheme with user controlled autonomous linking. We build upon a standard ring signature scheme $\mathsf{RS} := (\mathsf{KGen}, \mathsf{Sig}, \mathsf{Vf})$ as described formally in the full version of the paper and an AKRS $\mathsf{AKRS} = (\mathsf{KGen}, \mathsf{ChgPK}, \mathsf{Sig}, \mathsf{Vf}, \mathsf{Accum})$, as defined in Sect. 3.

Our RS-UCAL scheme UCAL, given in Fig. 2, works as follows. Key generation is simply the key generation for a standard ring signature, whereas the linking secret is the secret key for an AKRS. When signing, the pseudonym is the public key corresponding to the linking secret, randomised with respect to the scope, a one way function of the linking secret and scope as desired. We then included a standard ring signature to ensure that a non-member cannot sign on behalf of the ring, i.e. signature unforgeability. In order to prevent a signature non-frameability attack, where an adversary uses the pseudonym of an honest user's signature in their own signature, we also include an AKRS signature with respect to the pseudonym as the public key. In order to explicitly link signatures we make use of the accumulation functionality from AKRS. A set of signatures that were all generated with the same linking secret contain pseudonyms that can be accumulated. This accumulated public key can be used to sign an AKRS signature, which will be the link proof. Due to the accumulation soundness property and unforgeability of AKRS, link non-frameability and link unforgeability are ensured, respectively. Anonymity follows from the anonymity of standard ring signatures, and the class hiding property of the AKRS which ensures AKRS public keys and signatures cannot be linked based on equivalence class, and so UCAL signatures cannot be linked based on the linking secret.

We prove the following theorem that UCAL is a secure UCAL ring signature in the full version of the paper.

**Theorem 1.** *If AKRS is an anonymous key re-randomisable signature scheme and RS is a (standard) ring signature scheme, then UCAL is a ring signature scheme with user controlled autonomous linking.*

---

KGen($1^\lambda$)

1 :   $(\mathsf{sk}, \mathsf{vk}) \leftarrow \mathsf{RS.KGen}(1^\lambda)$
2 :   return $(\mathsf{sk}, \mathsf{vk})$

GenLinkSec($1^\lambda$)

1 :   $(\mathsf{ls}, \cdot) \leftarrow \mathsf{AKRS.KGen}(1^\lambda)$   return $\mathsf{ls}$

Sig($\mathsf{sk}, \mathsf{ls}, R, m, \mathsf{scp}$)

1 :   Parse $(\mathsf{vk}_1, \ldots, \mathsf{vk}_n) \leftarrow R$
2 :   $\mathsf{nym} \leftarrow \mathsf{AKRS.ChgPK}(\mathsf{ls}, \mathsf{scp})$
3 :   $\Omega \leftarrow \mathsf{RS.Sig}(\mathsf{sk}, R, m\|\mathsf{scp}\|\mathsf{nym})$
4 :   $\Psi \leftarrow \mathsf{AKRS.Sig}(\mathsf{ls}, \mathsf{nym}, m\|\mathsf{scp}\|R\|\Omega)$
5 :   $\sigma \leftarrow (\Omega, \Psi)$
6 :   return $(\mathsf{nym}, \sigma)$

Vf($m, \mathsf{scp}, R, (\Omega, \Psi), \mathsf{nym}$)

1 :   Parse $(\mathsf{vk}_1, \ldots, \mathsf{vk}_n) \leftarrow R$
2 :   if $\mathsf{RS.Vf}(\Omega, R, m\|\mathsf{scp}\|\mathsf{nym}) = 0$
3 :       thenreturn 0
4 :   if $\mathsf{AKRS.Vf}(\mathsf{nym}, m\|\mathsf{scp}\|R\|\Omega, \Psi) = 0$
5 :       thenreturn 0
6 :   return 1

Link($\mathsf{ls}, \mathsf{lm}, \Sigma$)

1 :   if Parse $\{(m_i, \mathsf{scp}_i, R_i, \sigma_i, \mathsf{nym}_i)\}_{i \in [k]} \leftarrow \Sigma$
2 :   if $\exists i, j \in [k], (i \neq j) \wedge (\mathsf{scp}_i = \mathsf{scp}_j)$
3 :       thenreturn $\bot$
4 :   if $\exists i \in [k], \mathsf{nym}_i \neq \mathsf{AKRS.ChgPK}(\mathsf{ls}, \mathsf{scp}_i)$
5 :       thenreturn $\bot$
6 :   if $\exists i \in [k], \mathsf{Vf}(m_i, \mathsf{scp}_i, R_i, \sigma_i, \mathsf{nym}_i) = 0$
7 :       thenreturn $\bot$
8 :   $\mathsf{n\tilde{y}m} \leftarrow \mathsf{Accum}(\mathsf{nym}_1, \ldots, \mathsf{nym}_k)$
9 :   $\pi_l \leftarrow \mathsf{AKRS.Sig}(\mathsf{ls}, \mathsf{n\tilde{y}m}, \mathsf{lm}\|\Sigma)$
10 :   return $\pi_l$

VerifyLink($\mathsf{lm}, \Sigma, \pi_l$)

1 :   Parse $\{(m_i, \mathsf{scp}_i, R_i, \sigma_i, \mathsf{nym}_i)\}_{i \in [k]} \leftarrow \Sigma$
2 :   if $\exists i, j \in [k], (i \neq j) \wedge (\mathsf{scp}_i = \mathsf{scp}_j)$
3 :       thenreturn 0
4 :   if $\exists i \in [k], \mathsf{Vf}(m_i, \mathsf{scp}_i, R_i, \sigma_i, \mathsf{nym}_i) = 0$
5 :       thenreturn 0
6 :   $\mathsf{n\tilde{y}m} \leftarrow \mathsf{Accum}(\mathsf{nym}_1, \ldots, \mathsf{nym}_k)$
7 :   return $\mathsf{AKRS.Vf}(\mathsf{n\tilde{y}m}, \mathsf{lm}\|\Sigma, \pi_l)$

**Fig. 2.** RS-UCAL from standard ring signatures and AKRS.

## 4.2   Construction for Ring Signatures with User Controlled Linkability

We provide a generic construction for a ring signature scheme with user controlled linking. We build upon a NIZK for the language $\mathcal{L} = \{(\mathsf{nym}, \mathsf{scp},$

$(\mathsf{vk}_i)_{i \in [n]}; \mathsf{sk}) : \mathsf{nym} = \mathsf{AKRS.ChgPK}(\mathsf{sk}, \mathsf{scp}) \wedge \bigvee_{i \in [n]}(\mathsf{vk}_i, \mathsf{sk}) = \mathsf{AKRS.KGen}(1^\lambda)\}$
and an AKRS AKRS = (KGen, ChgPK, Sig, Vf, Accum), as defined in Sect. 3.

Our RS-UCL scheme UCL, given in Fig. 3, works as follows. Key generation (instead of the linking secret generation) is now identical to key generation for an AKRS. When signing, the pseudonym, similarly to the UCAL construction, is the AKRS public key randomised with the scope and now with the ring signature secret key corresponding to the AKRS secret key. For the RS-UCL model, we additionally need to prove that the pseudonym was generated with a secret key corresponding to one of the public keys in the ring to ensure signature unforgeability. This ensures that if an adversary holds $n$ keys in the ring, they can only generate $n$ different pseudonyms and so output $n$ unlinked signatures. We therefore attach a non-interactive zero-knowledge proof of knowledge that attests to this, which also fulfills the role of the ring signature in the UCAL construction. The AKRS signature from the UCAL construction is now also not needed to ensure signature non-frameability, because it is necessary to know the secret key corresponding to a pseudonym in order to generate the NIZK. Explicit linking can be done in exactly the same way as the UCAL construction with link non-frameability and link unforgeability satisfied in the same way. Anonymity similarly follows from the class hiding property of the AKRS, and now also from the zero knowledge property of the NIZK.

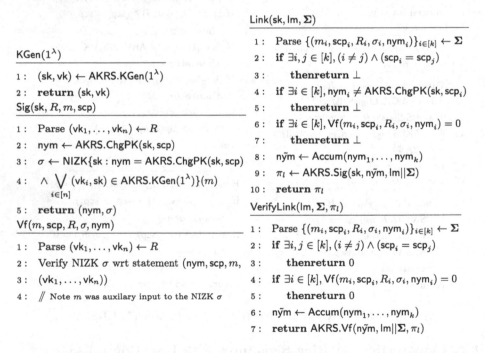

**Fig. 3.** RS-UCL from AKRS and non-interactive zero knowledge proofs of knowledge.

We prove the following theorem that UCL is a secure UCL ring signature in the full version of the paper.

**Theorem 2.** *If* AKRS *is an anonymous key re-randomisable signature scheme and* NIZK *is a non-interactive zero knowledge proof of knowledge satisfying simulation sound extractability, then* UCL *is a UCL ring signature.*

# 5  AKRS Instantiations

## 5.1  Construction from Schnorr Signatures

Consider a group $\mathbb{G}$, of prime order $q$, generated by $g$; and hash functions $H_1 : \{0,1\}^* \to \mathbb{G}$, and $H_2 : \{0,1\}^* \to \mathbb{Z}_q$. In Fig. 4, we recall the standard algorithms of the standard Schnorr signature scheme. We also introduce new algorithms ChgPK and Accum which augment the scheme to an AKRS.

**Security Argument.** We now provide some intuition as to why the augmented Schnorr signature given in Fig. 4 satisfies our requirements for an AKRS. Unforgeability is, modulo minor technical details, inherent from the unforgeability property of Schnorr Signatures. Class hiding follows from the fact that two public keys in the same equivalence class are of the form $(H_1(t), H_1(t)^x)$ and $(H_1(t'), H_1(t')^x)$, which is a DDH tuple. Therefore, linking public keys by equivalence class can be reduced to distinguishing DDH tuples. In the proof, signatures can be simulated without the secret key, assuming that $H_2$ is a random oracle. Accumulation soundness is the property that involves more novel techniques, in the design of our construction and its security analysis. The accumulation algorithm can be seen as a way to batch $\ell$ Schnorr statements with the same witness into a *succinct proof* that, to the best of our knowledge, is new. Roughly, accumulation soundness follows from the fact that signing with respect to an accumulated public key $(\prod \tilde{g}_i, \prod \tilde{h}_i)$ requires knowledge of the discrete logarithm of $\prod \tilde{h}_i$ base $\prod \tilde{g}_i$. Letting $\prod \tilde{g}_i = \prod H_1(t_i) = g^{\sum \tilde{t}_i}$, where $H_1(t_i) = g^{\tilde{t}_i}$ the adversary must know $\frac{\sum \mathsf{sk}_i \tilde{t}_i}{\sum \tilde{t}_i}$, which entails knowledge of the $\tilde{t}_i$, i.e. breaking the discrete logarithm. For lack of space we leave the formal proofs for the full version of the paper.

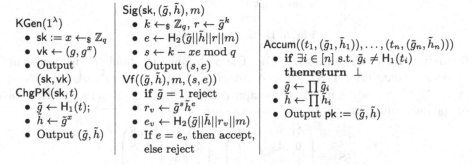

**Fig. 4.** Schnorr AKRS

**Compiling to UCAL and UCL.** Combined with any Ring Signature scheme the above AKRS gives a UCAL-Ring Signature with a very small overhead: for the signature size it is 1 additional Schnorr Signature, while all the extra computational costs are insignificant. Then, linking $\ell$ signatures requires a group multiplication of $\ell$ elements and a Schnorr Signature. Verifying the linking of $\ell$ signatures requires $\ell$ group multiplications and a Schnorr-Signature verification. For UCL the main efficiency overhead comes from the NIZK. Our Schnorr-based AKRS allows for the $k$-out-of-$n$ NIZK by Attema et al. [ACF21] to be used (setting $k = 1$), which gives similar asymptotic performance to the state-of-the-art on Ring Signatures [GK15, BCC+15, LPQ18, LRR+19, YSL+20, YEL+21].

## 5.2 Lattice Construction

Our Lattice-based AKRS is based on the Fiat-Shamir signature scheme by Lyubashevsky [Lyu12], which can be seen as the Lattice analogue of Schnorr signatures. We show how to bootstrap this signature scheme to an AKRS. For the sake of simplicity we describe the scheme w.r.t. integer lattices (based on SIS). However, it extends normally to ideal lattices (based on ring-SIS). The construction is in Fig. 5. where in the above $D_{v,\sigma}^{\mu}(\cdot)$ is the discrete normal distribution over $\mathbb{Z}^{\mu}$ centered around $v \in \mathbb{Z}^{\mu}$ ($D_{\sigma}^{\mu}(\cdot)$ centered around $v = 0$ resp.) with standard deviation $\sigma$ and $n, \mu, k, \sigma, M, \eta, d$ are parameters. We refer to [Lyu12] for details.

**KGen($1^{\lambda}$)**
- $S \leftarrow_\$ [-d, d]^{\mu \times k}$
  sk := $S$
- $A \leftarrow_\$ \mathbb{Z}_q^{n \times \mu}, T = AS$
  vk := $(A, T)$
- Output (sk, vk)

**ChgPK(sk, $t$)**
- $\tilde{A} \leftarrow H_1(t)$;
- $\tilde{T} \leftarrow \tilde{A}S$
- Output $(\tilde{A}, \tilde{T})$

**Sig(sk, $(\tilde{A}, \tilde{T}), m$)**
- $k \leftarrow_\$ D_{\sigma}^{\mu}, r \leftarrow \tilde{A}k$
- $e \leftarrow H_2(\tilde{A}\|\tilde{T}\|r\|m)$
- $s \leftarrow Se + k$
- Output $(s, e)$ with probability
  $$Pr = \min\left\{\frac{D_{\sigma}^{\mu}(z)}{MD_{Se,\sigma}^{\mu}(s)}, 1\right\}$$
- Otherwise repeat.

**Vf($(\tilde{A}, \tilde{T}), m, (s, e)$)**
- Accept if:
  1. $e = H_2(\tilde{A}\|\tilde{T}\|\tilde{A}s - \tilde{T}e\|m)$
  2. $\|s\| \le \eta\sigma\sqrt{\mu}$
- else reject

**Accum$\left(\left(t_i, (\tilde{A}_i, \tilde{T}_i)\right)_{i=1}^{\ell}\right)$**
- if $\tilde{A}_i \ne H_1(t_i)$
  thenreturn $\perp$
- $\tilde{A} \leftarrow \sum_i \tilde{A}_i$
- $\tilde{T} \leftarrow \prod_i \tilde{T}_i$
- Output pk := $(\tilde{A}, \tilde{T})$

**Fig. 5.** Lattice-based AKRS

**Security and Parameters.** For Class hiding to hold it is sufficient to show that $(\tilde{A}_1, \tilde{A}_1 S) \approx (\tilde{A}_2, \tilde{A}_2 S) \approx \ldots \approx (\tilde{A}_\ell, \tilde{A}_\ell S)$, where $\tilde{A}_i \leftarrow_\$ \mathbb{Z}_q^{n \times \mu}, S \leftarrow_\$ [-d, d]^{\mu \times k}$. If we apply the Leftover hash lemma [HILL99] to the hash function:

$$f(S) = \begin{pmatrix} \tilde{A}_1 & 0 & \ldots & 0 \\ 0 & \tilde{A}_2 & \ldots & 0 \\ \vdots & \vdots & \ddots & \vdots \\ 0 & 0 & \ldots & \tilde{A}_\ell \end{pmatrix} \cdot \begin{pmatrix} S \\ S \\ \vdots \\ S \end{pmatrix} = \begin{pmatrix} \tilde{A}_1 S \\ \tilde{A}_2 S \\ \vdots \\ \tilde{A}_\ell S \end{pmatrix}$$

then the statistical distance of $f(\boldsymbol{S})$ from the uniform over $\mathbb{Z}_q^{n \times k}$ is negligible $(2^{-\lambda})$ if $\mu \log(2d+1) \geq k\ell n + 2\lambda$. So if we set $\ell_{\mathsf{max}}$ to be the maximum number of re-randomizations of the public key and $\mu \geq (k\ell_{\mathsf{max}} n + 2\lambda)/\log(2d+1)$ then we get class-hiding. The rest of the lattice parameters are set according to [Lyu12].

Unforgeability then comes directly from the unforgeability of [Lyu12] signatures and Accumulation Soundness is analogous to the Schnorr Signatures AKRS construction. Due to space limitations we postpone the detailed proofs for the full version.

**Compiling to UCL and UCAL.** As in the Schnorr signatures case, the overhead of bootstrapping a ring signature scheme to a UCAL one with the above AKRS is minimal. We further note that concrete costs of our AKRS (and thus the compilation to UCAL) can be optimized using follow-up optimizations on the Lyubashevsky signatures [DDLL13]. For UCL any general purpose NIZK for lattice relations can be used; our AKRS language is a basic lattice one.

# 6 Conclusions

In this paper, we have introduced Ring Signatures (RS) with User-Controlled Linkability (UCL) and User-Controlled Autonomous Linkability (UCAL). RS-UCL allows for both implicit and explicit linkability of signatures. Thus, signers can decide to make their signatures linkable either when issuing the signatures (by using the same scope in all signatures to be linked) or at a later time (by providing an explicit linking proof). We note that UCL was recently defined for group signatures. However, we argue that ring signatures are better suited for distributed applications, as no group manager is necessary. As such RS-UCL finds direct applicability in smart metering or smart mobility applications as argued in Sect. 1. Also, RS-UCL may be used in e-voting protocols where each election could use a different scope so that (i) double-voting in the same election round would be detected by implicit linkability, and (ii) voters can use the same (registered) key across election rounds.

RS-UCAL gives even more power to signers as they now can ensure unlinkability of their signatures, even if signatures use the same scope. Still, at a later time signers can prove linkability with an explicit linking proof.

We show how to upgrade *any* RS to RS-UCAL by means of a new cryptographic primitive that we have introduced in this paper and that we have labelled Anonymous Key Randomisable Signatures (AKRS). We have also shown how AKRS can be used to instantiate RS-UCL. We note that AKRS may be of independent interest and we have introduced two AKRS instantiations, one in prime-order groups and one based on lattices.

**Acknowledgements.** his work has received funding from the European Research Council (ERC) under the European Union's Horizon 2020 research and innovation program under projects PICOCRYPT (grant agreement No. 101001283), and TER-MINET (grant agreement No. 957406), by the Spanish Government under projects SCUM (ref. RTI2018-102043-B-I00), and RED2018-102321-T, by the Madrid Regional

Government under project BLOQUES (ref. S2018/TCS-4339). This work is also supported by a grant from Nomadic Labs and the Tezos foundation.

## A    Full Definitions for our AKRS Model

We here provide the full experiment for our AKRS existential unforgeability under chosen message attacks requirement.

Experiment :$\mathsf{Exp}_{\mathsf{AKRS},\mathcal{A}}^{\mathsf{euf-cma}}(1^\lambda)$

1 : $Q \leftarrow \{\}, (\mathsf{sk}, \mathsf{pk}) \leftarrow \mathsf{KGen}(1^\lambda)$

2 : $(\mathsf{pk}', \{t_1, \cdots, t_m\}, m, \sigma) \leftarrow \mathcal{A}^{\mathsf{OChgPK},\mathsf{OSign}}(\mathsf{pk})$

3 : if $\mathsf{Vf}(\mathsf{pk}', m, \sigma) = 1 \wedge (m, \{t_1, \cdots, t_m\},) \notin Q$

4 : $\wedge\ \mathsf{pk}' = \mathsf{Accum}((t_1, \mathsf{ChgPK}(\mathsf{sk}, t_1)), \cdots, (t_m, \mathsf{ChgPK}(\mathsf{sk}, t_m)))$

5 :        **thenreturn** 1

6 : **else return** 0

OChgPK($t$)

1 : $\mathsf{pk}' \leftarrow \mathsf{ChgPK}(\mathsf{sk}, t)$

2 : **return** $\mathsf{pk}'$

$\mathsf{OSign}_Q(m, \mathsf{pk}', \{t_1, \cdots, t_m\})$

1 : **if** $t \neq *$ **then**

2 :    **if** $\mathsf{pk}' \neq \mathsf{Accum}((t_1, \mathsf{ChgPK}(\mathsf{sk}, t_1)), \cdots, (t_m, \mathsf{ChgPK}(\mathsf{sk}, t_m)))$

3 :        **thenreturn** $\perp$

4 :    $\sigma \leftarrow \mathsf{Sig}(\mathsf{sk}, \mathsf{pk}', m)$

5 : **if** $t = *$ **then**$\sigma \leftarrow \mathsf{Sig}(\mathsf{sk}, \mathsf{pk}, m)$

6 : $Q \leftarrow Q \cup \{(m, t)\}$

7 : **return** $\sigma$

## B    Full Definitions for our Ring Signature Models

We here provide the full definitions for ring signatures with user controlled (autonomous) linking that were omitted from the main body of the paper.

*Signature Unforgeability for RS-UCAL.* We next provide the full experiment for the signature unforgeability requirement in the RS-UCAL model.

Experiment :$\mathsf{Exp}_{\mathsf{UCAL},\mathcal{A}}^{\mathsf{sig-uf-al}}(1^\lambda, n, k)$

1 : **for** $i = 1, \ldots, n$

2 :    $(\mathsf{sk}_i, \mathsf{vk}_i) \leftarrow \mathsf{KGen}(1^\lambda)$

3 : **for** $i = 1, \ldots, k$   $\mathsf{ls}_i \leftarrow \mathsf{GenLinkSec}(1^\lambda)$

4 : $\Sigma^* := (m^*, \mathsf{scp}^*, R, \sigma^*, \mathsf{nym}^*) \leftarrow \mathcal{A}^{\mathsf{OSign}^{\mathsf{ucl-r}},\mathsf{OLink},\mathsf{Corr},\mathsf{OLS}}(\mathsf{vk}_1, \ldots, \mathsf{vk}_n)$

5 : **if** $\mathsf{Vf}(\Sigma^*) = 0$ **thenreturn** 0

6 : **if** $R^* \subseteq \{\mathsf{vk}_i\}_{i \in [n] \setminus I}$   // none of the keys in $R^*$ were corrupted

7 :    **thenif** $\forall i \in [n], (m^*, \mathsf{scp}^*, R^*, *, *) \notin \mathsf{SIG}[i, \cdot]$

8 :        **thenreturn** 1

9 : **else return** 0

*Non-Frameability.* We now provide the full experiments for both the signature non-frameability and link non-frameability requirements in the RS-UC AL model.

Experiment :$\mathsf{Exp}_{\mathsf{UCL},\mathcal{A}}^{\mathsf{sign\text{-}frame}}(1^\lambda, n, k)$

1 : **for** $i = 1, \ldots, n$   $(\mathsf{sk}_i, \mathsf{vk}_i) \leftarrow \mathsf{KGen}(1^\lambda)$

2 : **for** $i = 1, \ldots, k$   $\mathsf{ls}_i \leftarrow \mathsf{GenLinkSec}(1^\lambda)$

3 : $\Sigma := (m, \mathsf{scp}, R, \sigma, \mathsf{nym}) \leftarrow \mathcal{A}^{\mathsf{OSign}^{\mathsf{ucl\text{-}r}}, \mathsf{OLink}, \mathsf{Corr}, \mathsf{OLS}}(\mathsf{vk}_1, \ldots, \mathsf{vk}_n)$

4 : **return** 1  **if** :

5 :     $\mathsf{Vf}(\Sigma) = 1$ and

6 :     $\exists i \in [n] : (m, \mathsf{scp}, R, \mathsf{nym}, \cdot) \notin \mathsf{SIG}[i] \wedge i \notin I \wedge (\cdot, \mathsf{scp}, \cdot, \cdot, \mathsf{nym}) \in \mathsf{SIG}[i]$

7 :     $\exists i \in [k] : \Sigma \notin \mathsf{SIG}[\cdot, i] \wedge i \notin J \wedge (\cdot, \mathsf{scp}, \cdot, \cdot, \mathsf{nym}) \in \mathsf{SIG}[\cdot, i]$

8 : **else return** 0

Experiment :$\mathsf{Exp}_{\mathsf{UCL},\mathcal{A}}^{\mathsf{link\text{-}frame}}(1^\lambda, n, k)$

1 : **for** $i = 1, \ldots, n$   $(\mathsf{sk}_i, \mathsf{vk}_i) \leftarrow \mathsf{KGen}(1^\lambda)$

2 : **for** $i = 1, \ldots, k$   $\mathsf{ls}_i \leftarrow \mathsf{GenLinkSec}(1^\lambda)$

3 : $(\mathsf{lm}, \boldsymbol{\Sigma}, \pi_l) \leftarrow \mathcal{A}^{\mathsf{OSign}^{\mathsf{ucl\text{-}r}}, \mathsf{OLink}, \mathsf{Corr}, \mathsf{OLS}}(\mathsf{vk}_1, \ldots, \mathsf{vk}_N)$

4 : **if** $\mathsf{VerifyLink}(\mathsf{lm}, \boldsymbol{\Sigma}, \pi_l) = 0$  **return** 0

5 : Parse $\boldsymbol{\Sigma} = \{\Sigma_1, \cdots \Sigma_m\}$

6 : $\forall j \in [m]$

7 :     **if** $\exists i \in [n] : \Sigma_j \in \mathsf{SIG}[i]$ **then** $i_j \leftarrow i$

8 :     **if** $\exists i \in [k] : \Sigma_j \in \mathsf{SIG}[\cdot, i]$ **then** $i_j \leftarrow i$

9 :     **elseif** $\exists i \in [n] : \mathsf{Identify}(\mathsf{sk}_i, \mathsf{vk}_i, \Sigma_j) = 1$ **then** $i_j \leftarrow i$

10 :     **elseif** $\exists i \in [k] : \mathsf{Identify}(\mathsf{ls}_i, \Sigma_j) = 1$ **then** $i_j \leftarrow i$

11 :     **else** $i_j \leftarrow n + 1$

12 : **if** $\exists j_1, j_2 \in [m]$   $i_{j_1} \neq i_{j_2}$   **return** 1

13 : **else return** 0

# References

[ACF21]  Attema, T., Cramer, R., Fehr, S.: Compressing proofs of $k$-out-of-$n$ partial knowledge. In: Malkin, T., Peikert, C. (eds.) CRYPTO 2021. LNCS, vol. 12828, pp. 65–91. Springer, Cham (2021). https://doi.org/10.1007/978-3-030-84259-8_3

[ACHO13]  Abe, M., Chow, S.S.M., Haralambiev, K., Ohkubo, M.: Double-trapdoor anonymous tags for traceable signatures. Int. J. Inf. Secur. **12**(1), 19–31 (2013)

[BCC04]  Brickell, E.F., Camenisch, J., Chen, L.: Direct anonymous attestation. In: ACM CCS (2004)

[BCC+15]  Bootle, J., Cerulli, A., Chaidos, P., Ghadafi, E., Groth, J., Petit, C.: Short accountable ring signatures based on DDH. In: Pernul, G., Ryan, P.Y.A., Weippl, E. (eds.) ESORICS 2015. LNCS, vol. 9326, pp. 243–265. Springer, Cham (2015). https://doi.org/10.1007/978-3-319-24174-6_13

424     D. Fiore et al.

[BCC+16]  Bootle, J., Cerulli, A., Chaidos, P., Ghadafi, E., Groth, J.: Foundations of fully dynamic group signatures. In: ACNS (2016)

[BFG+13]  Bernhard, D., Fuchsbauer, G., Ghadafi, E., Smart, N.P., Warinschi, B.: Anonymous attestation with user-controlled linkability. Int. J. Inf. Secur. **12**(3), 219–249 (2013)

[BHKS18]  Backes, M., Hanzlik, L., Kluczniak, K., Schneider, J.: Signatures with flexible public key: introducing equivalence classes for public keys. In: Peyrin, T., Galbraith, S. (eds.) ASIACRYPT 2018. LNCS, vol. 11273, pp. 405–434. Springer, Cham (2018). https://doi.org/10.1007/978-3-030-03329-3_14

[BMW03]  Bellare, M., Micciancio, D., Warinschi, B.: Foundations of group signatures: formal definitions, simplified requirements, and a construction based on general assumptions. In: Biham, E. (ed.) EUROCRYPT 2003. LNCS, vol. 2656, pp. 614–629. Springer, Heidelberg (2003). https://doi.org/10.1007/3-540-39200-9_38

[BSZ05]  Bellare, M., Shi, H., Zhang, C.: Foundations of group signatures: the case of dynamic groups. In: Menezes, A. (ed.) CT-RSA 2005. LNCS, vol. 3376, pp. 136–153. Springer, Heidelberg (2005). https://doi.org/10.1007/978-3-540-30574-3_11

[CDL16a]  Camenisch, J., Drijvers, M., Lehmann, A.: Anonymous attestation using the strong Diffie Hellman assumption revisited. In: Franz, M., Papadimitratos, P. (eds.) Trust 2016. LNCS, vol. 9824, pp. 1–20. Springer, Cham (2016). https://doi.org/10.1007/978-3-319-45572-3_1

[CDL16b]  Camenisch, J., Drijvers, M., Lehmann, A.: Universally composable direct anonymous attestation. In: Cheng, C.-M., Chung, K.-M., Persiano, G., Yang, B.-Y. (eds.) PKC 2016. LNCS, vol. 9615, pp. 234–264. Springer, Heidelberg (2016). https://doi.org/10.1007/978-3-662-49387-8_10

[CS97]  Camenisch, J., Stadler, M.: Efficient group signature schemes for large groups. In: Kaliski, B.S. (ed.) CRYPTO 1997. LNCS, vol. 1294, pp. 410–424. Springer, Heidelberg (1997). https://doi.org/10.1007/BFb0052252

[CvH91]  Chaum, D., van Heyst, E.: Group signatures. In: Davies, D.W. (ed.) EUROCRYPT 1991. LNCS, vol. 547, pp. 257–265. Springer, Heidelberg (1991). https://doi.org/10.1007/3-540-46416-6_22

[DDLL13]  Ducas, L., Durmus, A., Lepoint, T., Lyubashevsky, V.: Lattice signatures and bimodal gaussians. In: Canetti, R., Garay, J.A. (eds.) CRYPTO 2013. LNCS, vol. 8042, pp. 40–56. Springer, Heidelberg (2013). https://doi.org/10.1007/978-3-642-40041-4_3

[DL21]  Diaz, J., Lehmann, A.: Group signatures with user-controlled and sequential linkability. In: Garay, J.A. (ed.) PKC 2021. LNCS, vol. 12710, pp. 360–388. Springer, Cham (2021). https://doi.org/10.1007/978-3-030-75245-3_14

[FGL21]  Fraser, A., Garms, L., Lehmann, A.: Selectively linkable group signatures—stronger security and preserved verifiability. In: Conti, M., Stevens, M., Krenn, S. (eds.) CANS 2021. LNCS, vol. 13099, pp. 200–221. Springer, Cham (2021). https://doi.org/10.1007/978-3-030-92548-2_11

[GK15]  Groth, J., Kohlweiss, M.: One-out-of-many proofs: or how to leak a secret and spend a coin. In: Oswald, E., Fischlin, M. (eds.) EUROCRYPT 2015. LNCS, vol. 9057, pp. 253–280. Springer, Heidelberg (2015). https://doi.org/10.1007/978-3-662-46803-6_9

[GL19]  Garms, L., Lehmann, A.: Group signatures with selective linkability. In: PKC (2019)

[HILL99] Håstad, J., Impagliazzo, R., Levin, L.A., Luby, M.: A pseudorandom generator from any one-way function. SIAM J. Comput. **28**(4), 1364–1396 (1999)

[HLC+11] Hwang, J.Y., Lee, S., Chung, B.-H., Cho, H. S., Nyang, D.: Short group signatures with controllable linkability. In: Workshop on Lightweight Security & Privacy: (LightSec) (2011)

[HLC+13] Hwang, J.Y., Lee, S., Chung, B.-H., Cho, H.S., Nyang, D.H.: Group signatures with controllable linkability for dynamic membership. Inf. Sci. **222**, 761–778 (2013)

[KTY04] Kiayias, A., Tsiounis, Y., Yung, M.: Traceable signatures. In: Cachin, C., Camenisch, J.L. (eds.) EUROCRYPT 2004. LNCS, vol. 3027, pp. 571–589. Springer, Heidelberg (2004). https://doi.org/10.1007/978-3-540-24676-3_34

[LJ14] Libert, B., Joye, M.: Group signatures with message-dependent opening in the standard model. In: Benaloh, J. (ed.) CT-RSA 2014. LNCS, vol. 8366, pp. 286–306. Springer, Cham (2014). https://doi.org/10.1007/978-3-319-04852-9_15

[LMN16] Libert, B., Mouhartem, F., Nguyen, K.: A lattice-based group signature scheme with message-dependent opening. In: Manulis, M., Sadeghi, A.-R., Schneider, S. (eds.) ACNS 2016. LNCS, vol. 9696, pp. 137–155. Springer, Cham (2016). https://doi.org/10.1007/978-3-319-39555-5_8

[LPQ18] Libert, B., Peters, T., Qian, C.: Logarithmic-size ring signatures with tight security from the DDH assumption. In: Lopez, J., Zhou, J., Soriano, M. (eds.) ESORICS 2018. LNCS, vol. 11099, pp. 288–308. Springer, Cham (2018). https://doi.org/10.1007/978-3-319-98989-1_15

[LRR+19] Lai, R.W.F., Ronge, V., Ruffing, T., Schröder, D., Thyagarajan, S.A.K., Wang, J.: Omniring: scaling private payments without trusted setup. In: Proceedings of the 2019 ACM SIGSAC Conference on Computer and Communications Security, pp. 31–48 (2019)

[LWW04] Liu, J.K., Wei, V.K., Wong, D.S.: Linkable spontaneous anonymous group signature for ad hoc groups. In: Wang, H., Pieprzyk, J., Varadharajan, V. (eds.) ACISP 2004. LNCS, vol. 3108, pp. 325–335. Springer, Heidelberg (2004). https://doi.org/10.1007/978-3-540-27800-9_28

[Lyu12] Lyubashevsky, V.: Lattice signatures without trapdoors. In: Pointcheval, D., Johansson, T. (eds.) EUROCRYPT 2012. LNCS, vol. 7237, pp. 738–755. Springer, Heidelberg (2012). https://doi.org/10.1007/978-3-642-29011-4_43

[OSEH13] Ohara, K., Sakai, Y., Emura, K., Hanaoka, G.: A group signature scheme with unbounded message-dependent opening. In: ASIA-CCS (2013)

[PS19] Park, S., Sealfon, A.: It wasn't me! In: Boldyreva, A., Micciancio, D. (eds.) CRYPTO 2019. LNCS, vol. 11694, pp. 159–190. Springer, Cham (2019). https://doi.org/10.1007/978-3-030-26954-8_6

[RST01] Rivest, R.L., Shamir, A., Tauman, Y.: How to leak a secret. In: Boyd, C. (ed.) ASIACRYPT 2001. LNCS, vol. 2248, pp. 552–565. Springer, Heidelberg (2001). https://doi.org/10.1007/3-540-45682-1_32

[SALY17] Sun, S.-F., Au, M.H., Liu, J.K., Yuen, T.H.: RingCT 2.0: a compact accumulator-based (linkable ring signature) protocol for blockchain cryptocurrency Monero. In: Foley, S.N., Gollmann, D., Snekkenes, E. (eds.) ESORICS 2017. LNCS, vol. 10493, pp. 456–474. Springer, Cham (2017). https://doi.org/10.1007/978-3-319-66399-9_25

[SEH+12] Sakai, Y., Emura, K., Hanaoka, G., Kawai, Y., Matsuda, T., Omote, K.: Group signatures with message-dependent opening. In: Abdalla, M., Lange, T. (eds.) Pairing 2012. LNCS, vol. 7708, pp. 270–294. Springer, Heidelberg (2013). https://doi.org/10.1007/978-3-642-36334-4_18

[SSU14] Slamanig, D., Spreitzer, R., Unterluggauer, T.: Adding controllable linkability to pairing-based group signatures for free. In: Chow, S.S.M., Camenisch, J., Hui, L.C.K., Yiu, S.M. (eds.) ISC 2014. LNCS, vol. 8783, pp. 388–400. Springer, Cham (2014). https://doi.org/10.1007/978-3-319-13257-0_23

[YEL+21] Yuen, T.H., Esgin, M.F., Liu, J.K., Au, M.H., Ding, Z.: *DualRing*: generic construction of ring signatures with efficient instantiations. In: Malkin, T., Peikert, C. (eds.) CRYPTO 2021. LNCS, vol. 12825, pp. 251–281. Springer, Cham (2021). https://doi.org/10.1007/978-3-030-84242-0_10

[YSL+20] Yuen, T.H., et al.: RingCT 3.0 for blockchain confidential transaction: shorter size and stronger security. In: Bonneau, J., Heninger, N. (eds.) FC 2020. LNCS, vol. 12059, pp. 464–483. Springer, Cham (2020). https://doi.org/10.1007/978-3-030-51280-4_25

[ZWC19] Zhang, T., Wu, H., Chow, S.S.M.: Structure-preserving certificateless encryption and its application. In: Matsui, M. (ed.) CT-RSA 2019. LNCS, vol. 11405, pp. 1–22. Springer, Cham (2019). https://doi.org/10.1007/978-3-030-12612-4_1

# DualDory: Logarithmic-Verifier Linkable Ring Signatures Through Preprocessing

Jonathan Bootle[1], Kaoutar Elkhiyaoui[1], Julia Hesse[1(✉)], and Yacov Manevich[2]

[1] IBM Research - Zurich, Rüschlikon, Switzerland
{jbt,kao,jhs}@zurich.ibm.com
[2] IBM Research - Haifa, Haifa, Israel
yacovm@il.ibm.com

**Abstract.** A linkable ring signature allows a user to sign anonymously on behalf of a group while ensuring that multiple signatures from the same user are detected. Applications such as privacy-preserving e-voting and e-cash can leverage linkable ring signatures to significantly improve privacy and anonymity guarantees. To scale to systems involving large numbers of users, short signatures with fast verification are a must. Concretely efficient ring signatures currently rely on a trusted authority maintaining a master secret, or follow an accumulator-based approach that requires a trusted setup.

In this work, we construct the first linkable ring signature with both logarithmic signature size and verification that does not require any trusted mechanism. Our scheme, which relies on discrete-log type assumptions and bilinear maps, improves upon a recent concise ring signature called DualRing by integrating improved preprocessing arguments to reduce the verification time from linear to logarithmic in the size of the ring. Our ring signature allows signatures to be linked based on what message is signed, ranging from linking signatures on any message to only signatures on the same message.

We provide benchmarks for our scheme and prove its security under standard assumptions. The proposed linkable ring signature is particularly relevant to use cases that require privacy-preserving enforcement of threshold policies in a fully decentralized context, and e-voting.

## 1 Introduction

Group signatures [18] and ring signatures [20] enable members of a group to sign messages anonymously. That is, a verifier of a valid signature only learns that the signature was produced by a member of the group and nothing else; in particular, the verifier cannot tell if two signatures were produced by the same party or not. The main difference between group and ring signatures is that group signatures rely on a designated group manager to maintain group membership for the purposes of accountability. More specifically, the group manager is responsible for user enrollment and revocation so that later it can de-anonymize signatures. On the other hand, ring signatures allow for a spontaneous group formation, where a user signs anonymously by creating a group that contains its public key and the public keys of others. The absence of a group manager, ensures that ring signatures can never be de-anonymized; a property that is crucial in

© The Author(s), under exclusive license to Springer Nature Switzerland AG 2022
V. Atluri et al. (Eds.): ESORICS 2022, LNCS 13555, pp. 427–446, 2022.
https://doi.org/10.1007/978-3-031-17146-8_21

applications where unconditional anonymity is desired, e.g., whistle blowing and secret ballot. It also allows ring signatures to be used in decentralized applications without additional setup or assumptions.

A useful extension to ring signatures is *linkability*, which ensures that a signer cannot sign twice without being detected. A prominent application of linkability is e-voting where a voter should not cast a vote more than once, and linkability allows easy detection. Linkability can also be leveraged to obtain threshold ring signatures by simply concatenating the required threshold of individual signatures. Threshold ring signatures are useful for regulated and decentralized e-cash where transactions exceeding a certain amount can only be committed if $t$ *independent* endorsers approve the transaction. The identities of the endorsers should not be disclosed as that may leak information about the origin of the transaction, and thus, calling for privacy-preserving threshold policy enforcement[1].

To scale to applications with large rings, we need linkable ring signatures with fast verification. Currently, linkable ring signatures with constant-time verifier [7,12,20] require either the RSA setting or q-type assumptions, and rely hence, on trusted parameter generation. Accordingly, applications depending on these constructions cannot be fully decentralized. In this paper, we investigate the construction of *efficient* linkable ring signatures with *transparent setup*, where the system parameters are generated without a secret trapdoor, making the scheme amenable to decentralization. We introduce DualDory, a linkable ring signature with a logarithmic verifier and transparent setup.

*DualDory.* DualDory is based on the ring signature scheme DualRing [31] and the preprocessing argument Dory [23]. DualRing is a ring signature that incorporates discrete-logarithm-based interactive arguments building on [13,15] to obtain logarithmic-size ring signatures, albeit with a linear verifier. Dory is a pairing-based interactive argument similar to [13,15] which achieves logarithmic verifier time thanks to a one-time offline preprocessing phase. DualDory replaces techniques from [13,15] with Dory and brings the linear verification cost of DualRing [31] down to logarithmic. When applied to DualRing, Dory's preprocessing phase involves computing a succinct commitment to the ring of users included in the signature. To avoid repeated preprocessing for signatures with respect to rings which are only used once, we recommend DualDory for rings that are either *static*, which are relevant to regulated and decentralized e-cash, or *updatable* with a subset of signers joining or leaving, which are well-suited for e-voting. To give a concrete example, DualDory is well-suited for e-cash transaction audits that require a threshold policy such as, e.g., "a transaction exceeding 10K USD should be signed by at least two banks before it is confirmed". The choice of banks in this scenario may leak information about the origin of the transaction, for example, if users select always the same banks.

We further enhance DualDory with linkability through *deterministic* tags. More precisely, we combine Pedersen commitments and signatures of knowledge to show that the tag is computed using one of the secret keys in the ring. As a positive side effect,

---

[1] Note that multi-signatures [25] cannot be used because they reveal the identity of the signer. Threshold signatures [29] are not suitable either since they require coordination of key material among voters or auditing authorities.

we are able to precompute the linear work of signing, leaving only a constant number of operations to be performed when messages are known.

*Contributions.* Our contributions can be summarized as follows.

- With DualDory we give the first (linkable) ring signature that combines transparent setup, logarithmic signature size *and* logarithmic verification time. We leverage an argument of knowledge of bilinear pairing products [23], which thanks to a *one-time offline preprocessing* phase gives us a logarithmic verifier.
- While signature generation in DualDory is linear in the size of the ring, most of the work can be precomputed before knowing the message.
- We equip DualDory with "fine-tuned" linkability that allows linkability for signatures on either arbitrary messages, or on the same messages only, or anything in between. We extend the security notions of linkable ring signatures from the literature to this configurable linkability notion, which we call *prefix linkability*.
- We conduct a performance evaluation that demonstrates the practicality of Dual-Dory.
- We provide a full formal security analysis showing that DualDory is a secure linkable ring signature under the SXDH assumption, in the random oracle model.

*Related Work on Signatures.* Group and ring signatures have been extensively studied since the early nineties [6,7,12,16,18,20–22,24,26,31], with ongoing attempts to reduce signature sizes and computational complexity. We give an overview in Table 1 of which works offered significant improvements in these regards. It can be noted that constant size and complexity [7,30] is currently only achievable if there is an authority which issues an RSA group setup, which anybody can use to generate their own keys and form ad-hoc groups referred to as *rings* [26]. Another line of work is schemes that maintain their security in the presence of maliciously chosen public keys [16,21,22][2]. Recently, research has focused on improving efficiency also for ring signatures based on discrete-log-type assumptions. These schemes do not rely on any authority and can be deployed in elliptic curve groups which are about 10 times smaller than RSA groups. Unfortunately, it has proven to be difficult to achieve competitive signing and verification time for discrete-log-based ring signatures (see Table 1 for references). Chandran et al. [16] were the first to achieve sublinear signature sizes, namely $O(\sqrt{n})$. Subsequently, Groth and Kohlweiss [22] achieved logarithmic signature sizes through concise one-out-of-many proofs, inspiring subsequent works such as DualRing [31], which we describe in more detail in Sect. 2.1. Note that while our scheme achieves logarithmic signature sizes like [22,31], it does so in the bilinear group setting rather than the standard discrete logarithm setting, incurring higher concrete costs. However, all of the aforementioned schemes take linear time to verify a signature. Lastly, we mention that the fine-tuning of linkability has already been discussed in the group signature setting [32].

---

[2] Security against maliciously chosen public keys can be added to schemes such as DualRing or our scheme by appending a non-interactive proof of correct key computation to the public key, at the cost of increased public key sizes and verification time. Note that it suffices to verify validity of each public key only once, hence the overhead is negligible when considering verifications of many signatures under the same public key.

**Table 1.** Development of the asymptotic efficiency of practical RSA- and DLOG-based signature schemes that allow signing on behalf of a group with $n$ members. Costs depict exponentiations in the group for Sign and Verify, and number of group elements for Signature size. In DualDory, verification time is split into preprocessing effort per group ("offl."), plus verification effort per signature ("onl."). ● means applicable/required, ○ means not applicable/required. (●) means linkable only by the key generation authority.

| | Sign | Verification | | Signature size | Assumptions and model | KGen Authority | Transparent setup | Malicious pk | Linkable |
|---|---|---|---|---|---|---|---|---|---|
| | | offl. | onl. | | | | | | |
| Ateniese et al. [6] | $O(1)$ | – | $O(1)$ | $O(1)$ | strong RSA, DDH | RO | ● | ○ | ○ | (●) |
| Rivest et al. [26] | $O(n)$ | – | $O(n)$ | $O(n)$ | TD-OWP | RO | ○ | ● | ○ | ○ |
| Liu et al. [24] | $O(n)$ | – | $O(n)$ | $O(n)$ | DDH | RO | ○ | ● | ○ | ● |
| BBS Signatures [12] | $O(1)$ | – | $O(1)$ | $O(1)$ | q-SDH, DLin | RO | ● | ○ | ○ | (●) |
| Dodis et al. [20] | $O(1)$ | – | $O(1)$ | $O(1)$ | strong RSA | RO | ○ | ○ | ○ | ○ |
| Au et al. [7] | $O(1)$ | – | $O(1)$ | $O(1)$ | strong RSA, DDH, LD-RSA | RO | ○ | ○ | ○ | ● |
| Chandran et al. [16] | $O(n)$ | – | $O(n)$ | $O(\sqrt{n})$ | strong DDH, SUB | CRS | ○ | ○ | ● | ○ |
| Groth et al. [22] | $O(n\log n)$ | – | $O(n)$ | $O(\log n)$ | DLOG | RO | ○ | ● | ● | ○ |
| CLSAG [21] | $O(n)$ | – | $O(n)$ | $O(n)$ | OM-LC-DLOG, DDH | RO | ○ | ● | ● | ● |
| DualRing-EC [31] | $O(n)$ | – | $O(n)$ | $O(\log n)$ | DLOG | RO | ○ | ● | ○ | ○ |
| DualDory, **this work** | $O(n)$ | $O(n)$ | $O(\log n)$ | $O(\log n)$ | SXDH | RO | ○ | ● | ○ | ● |

*Related Work on Succinct Arguments.* DualRing [31] uses split-and-fold techniques to construct a succinct argument of knowledge which is used to compress signature sizes from $O(n)$ to $O(\log n)$. This is based on techniques first introduced in the discrete logarithm setting in [13,15], with succinct proofs but linear verification time. Later, Dory [23] introduced a preprocessing argument using similar techniques but using a one-time preprocessing phase to reduce verifier complexity to logarithmic.

*Paper Organization.* The paper is organized as follows. Section 2 provides an overview of DualDory and the techniques used to achieve linkability and logarithmic verification. Section 3 introduces the cryptographic assumptions and building blocks. Section 4 formalizes the security of linkable ring signatures. Section 5 describes DualDory and analyzes its security. Section 6 evaluates the performance of DualDory.

## 2 Technical Overview

In this section, we explain our new construction of a linkable ring signature. We obtain our construction by using the basic DualRing ring signature of [31] as a starting point, and modifying it in two ways.

1. We make the scheme *prefix linkable* as described in Sect. 2.2 by adding tags to signatures and using extra 'tag proofs' to show that the tags were computed correctly.
2. We simultaneously improve the proof size and online signature verification time of the basic signature scheme in [31] to logarithmic in the number of users using Dory [23].

## 2.1   Overview of Dualring

DualRing [31] is a generic ring signature construction with both efficient discrete-logarithm and lattice-based instantiations. The construction has two parts. The first part is a basic signature scheme which builds on the classic construction of ring signatures from [5]. For a ring of $n$ users, basic signatures have size $O(n)$. The second part is a "sum argument" which compresses basic signatures to size $O(\log n)$, by proving knowledge of values satisfying the basic signature verification procedure.

In this paper, we focus on the discrete-logarithm instantiation of DualRing, which works over a group $\mathbb{G} = \langle P \rangle$ of prime order $p$, and user public keys $pk_1, \ldots, pk_n \in \mathbb{G}$. A basic DualRing signature is a zero-knowledge proof that the signer knows a private key $sk_j \in \mathbb{Z}_p$ satisfying $pk_j = P^{sk_j}$, without leaking $sk_j$ or the index $j \in [n]$. The signature is based on an interactive proof made non-interactive via the Fiat-Shamir transformation, using a hash function $H$. Basic signatures on a message $m$ consist of elements $X \in \mathbb{G}$ and $c_1, \ldots, c_n, y \in \mathbb{Z}_p$ satisfying the following equations:

$$H(pk_1, \ldots, pk_n, X, m) = \sum_{i=1}^{n} c_i \tag{1}$$

$$P^y / X = \prod_{i=1}^{n} pk_i^{c_i} \tag{2}$$

Checking Eq. 1 and Eq. 2 involves calculations on all $n$ user public keys $pk_1, \ldots, pk_n \in \mathbb{G}$ and all $n$ challenges $c_1, \ldots, c_n \in \mathbb{Z}_p$, leading to signature sizes and verification time of $O(n)$. In [31], the authors observed that $P^y / X$ is a Pedersen commitment to $(c_1, \ldots, c_n)$ under commitment key $(pk_1, \ldots, pk_n)$, and used a *sum argument* to prove that Eq. 1 was satisfied using the committed values.

The sum argument is based on split-and-fold zero-knowledge arguments such as [13,15], which can prove that Eq. 1 is satisfied with proof sizes of $O(\log n)$, but still require the verifier to perform a multi-exponentiation in $(pk_1, \ldots, pk_n)$, which costs at best $O(n/\log n)$ operations using Pippenger's algorithm. Further, the construction does not have any linkability properties.

## 2.2   Adding Linkability

In this section, we explain the prefix-linkability notion that our scheme satisfies, and the tagging technique used to achieve it. The original notion of linkability for ring signature schemes uses a linking algorithm to determine whether two signatures were created by the same user. We introduce *prefix linkability*, where the string to be signed is split into two parts: a prefix prfx and a message $m$. Two signatures can be linked if they were created by the same user, and sign messages with the same prefix prfx. For example, in e-voting, setting prfx to the unique identifier of the bill being voted on, and $m$ to the value of the vote, the linking algorithm would be able to detect that a user had tried to vote twice.

To make our construction prefix-linkable, we ask the signer to compute a tag $H'(\text{prfx})^{sk}$, based on the user's secret key $sk$, the prefix prfx and a hash function $H'$, following a similar strategy to [24]. The tag is uniquely determined by the user's secret key $sk$ and the prefix prfx, which allows an efficient linking algorithm. To ensure that the tag is computed correctly using the same secret key as the rest of the signature, we have the signer produce a Pedersen commitment $\text{com} = P^{sk}Q^r$ to their secret key, and use a 'tag proof' based on standard sigma protocols to show that com and tag both use the same secret key. Note that we cannot perform this consistency check on the user's public key, since this would leak the identity of the user.

This leaves us with a further problem. A signer can use DualRing to prove that they know a secret key $sk_i$ corresponding to public key $pk_i$ from a list $(pk_1, \ldots, pk_n)$, but this proof is not connected with tag or com. To solve this problem, we use an idea from [22]. Since the signer knows an opening $sk, r \in \mathbb{Z}_p$ to com satisfying $\text{com} = P^{sk}Q^r$, they know how to open exactly one of the commitments $(\text{com}/pk_1, \ldots, \text{com}/pk_n)$ to zero, i.e. they know a discrete logarithm $r \in \mathbb{Z}_p$ satisfying $\text{com}/pk_i = Q^r$.

Applying DualRing to $\text{com}/pk_1, \ldots, \text{com}/pk_n$ and adding the tag proof produces a linkable RS where the verifier checks the tag proof and the following equations:

$$H(\text{com}/pk_1, \ldots, \text{com}/pk_n, X, m) = \sum_{i=1}^{n} c_i \ , \tag{3}$$

$$P^y/X = \prod_{i=1}^{n} (\text{com}/pk_i)^{c_i} \ . \tag{4}$$

The size of this signature could be reduced to $O(\log n)$ using the same sum argument as [31]. However, the verification time would still be $O(n)$.

## 2.3   Reducing Signature Size and Verification Time Simultaneously

Our ring signatures consist of 7 elements of $\mathbb{G}_1$, 2 elements of $\mathbb{G}_2$, and $18 \log(n)$ elements of $\mathbb{G}_T$. We can achieve a logarithmic verification time by replacing the sum argument with an argument with lower verification costs.

The sum argument is based on split-and-fold zero-knowledge arguments such as [13,15]. Dory [23] extends [13,15] to the setting of bilinear pairings. This setting uses a pairing-based commitment scheme which commits to a message $\underline{\Omega} \in \mathbb{G}_1^n$ with commitment key $\underline{\tilde{\Gamma}} \in \mathbb{G}_2^n$ using the commitment $\mathbf{A} = \prod_{i=1}^{n} e(\underline{\Omega}_i, \underline{\tilde{\Gamma}}_i)$ (and similarly for messages $\underline{\tilde{\Omega}} \in \mathbb{G}_2^n$ and keys in $\underline{\Gamma} \in \mathbb{G}_1^n$). Dory allows the prover to prove knowledge of $\underline{\Omega} \in \mathbb{G}_1^n$ and $\underline{\tilde{\Omega}} \in \mathbb{G}_2^n$ satisfying $\mathbf{A} = e(\underline{\Omega}, \underline{\tilde{\Gamma}})$, $\mathbf{B} = e(\underline{\Gamma}, \underline{\tilde{\Omega}})$ and $\mathbf{C} = e(\underline{\Omega}, \underline{\tilde{\Omega}})$, for publicly known commitment keys $\underline{\Gamma} \in \mathbb{G}_1^n$, $\underline{\tilde{\Gamma}} \in \mathbb{G}_2^n$ and target values $\mathbf{A}$, $\mathbf{B}$ and $\mathbf{C} \in \mathbb{G}_T$.

When proving statements of this form, the verifier must perform operations on each of the $n$-dimensional commitment keys, leading to $O(n)$ verification costs. However, unlike [13, 15], in which calculations on keys must be done online, Dory allows preprocessing of commitment keys once and for all in an offline phase. Thereafter, the verifier need only use succinct commitments to these keys and incurs $O(\log n)$ costs.

Now, we explain how to apply Dory to Eq. 3 and Eq. 4. First, we map Eq. 3 and Eq. 4 to equations over bilinear groups. Imagine that the DualRing scheme has been executed over $\mathbb{G}_1$ of the bilinear group . Consider group element $e(P, \tilde{P})$ (where $P \in \mathbb{G}_1$ and $\tilde{P} \in \mathbb{G}_2$). Exponentiate using the left and right hand sides of Eq. 3, using the bilinearity of $e$, to get

$$e\left(P^{H(\text{com}/pk_1,\ldots,\text{com}/pk_n,X,m)}, \tilde{P}\right) = \prod_{i=1}^{n} e(P, \tilde{P}^{c_i}) \tag{5}$$

In a similar way, Eq. 6 can be paired with $\tilde{P}$ and rearranged to obtain

$$e(P^y/X, \tilde{P}) = \prod_{i=1}^{n} e(\text{com}/pk_i, \tilde{P}^{c_i}) \tag{6}$$

Since the exponentiation and pairing maps are injective, Eq. 5 and Eq. 6 imply Eq. 3 and Eq. 4. Thus, given commitments to $(P, \ldots, P) \in \mathbb{G}_1^n$, $(\tilde{P}^{c_1}, \ldots, \tilde{P}^{c_n}) \in \mathbb{G}_2^n$, and $(\text{com}/pk_i)_{i=1}^n \in \mathbb{G}_1^n$, the signer can apply Dory to prove that Eq. 5 and Eq. 6 hold with the left hand side of each equation as target values. Note that the target value from Eq. 5 involves $n$ values, so to avoid $O(n)$ verifier costs here, we replace these values with the commitment to $(\text{com}/pk_1, \ldots, \text{com}/pk_n)$. This is still sufficient for security of DualRing as long as the commitment scheme is binding.

Dory relies on the SXDH assumption for security, which implies the hardness of the discrete logarithm assumption over $\mathbb{G}_1$, and therefore the security of DualRing over $\mathbb{G}_1$.

Fast online verification time relies on the verifier being able to compute a commitment to $(\text{com}/pk_1, \ldots, \text{com}/pk_n) \in \mathbb{G}_1^n$ using $O(n)$ offline operations and $O(\log n)$ online operations. Since com depends on randomness $r$, it is different for every signature, so it is impossible for the verifier to compute this commitment once and for all independently of any signatures. Instead, the verifier computes $\tilde{\Gamma} := \prod_{i=1}^n \tilde{\Gamma}_i$, and a commitment $\mathbf{A}_0 := \prod_{i=1}^n e(pk_i, \tilde{\Gamma}_i)$ to $(pk_1, \ldots, pk_n)$ offline, which costs $O(n)$ operations. Unlike in [31], this does not depend on any part of the signature and can be computed once "offline" for each ring and then reused in "online" signature verification. Note that the length $n$ of the commitment keys gives an upper bound on the number of user public keys that can be committed to. When verifying a signature, the verifier can compute a commitment to $(\text{com}/pk_1, \ldots, \text{com}/pk_n)$ as $e(\text{com}, \tilde{\Gamma})/\mathbf{A}_0$.

*On Logarithmic Verification Time.* The construction described above achieves logarithmic online verification time when the list of user public keys in the ring signature is read just once and used to compute a succinct commitment. Logarithmic verification time is achieved in an amortised sense, when verifying many signatures with respect to the same set of users. This is the best one can hope for, as verifying signatures with respect to many different sets of users requires the verifier to read the set of users each time, and perform operations on each user public key. If not, and it was possible to verify a signature without reading every public key, then a signature might verify with respect to a different, unintended group of users in which some of the unread public keys had been replaced by others, facilitating forgeries. Our construction avoids this issue as the commitment acts as a succinct representation of the user public keys, and binds a signature to that collection of users.

Since the commitment to the set of user public keys is of the form $\prod_{i=1}^{n} e(pk_i, \tilde{\Gamma}_i)$, given a commitment to a large group of users, it is also easy to update the commitment to include new users by multiplying the commitment by $e(pk_{n+1}, \tilde{\Gamma}_{n+1})$, or remove existing users by dividing by a suitable value. This means that logarithmic verifier complexity can be maintained up to small changes in the set of users.

*Comparison with Accumulator-Based Approaches.* In our construction, the commitment to the set of public keys related to a given signature acts like an accumulator for those public keys. However, prior accumulator-based approaches rely on either $q$-type assumptions over bilinear groups, or RSA groups. Both approaches have trapdoors. This means that the public parameters for group and ring signature schemes based on these approaches must be generated by a trusted party or via a secure multiparty computation protocol. By contrast, the public parameters for our scheme can be generated without a trusted setup.

# 3 Preliminaries

On input the security parameter $1^\lambda$, a *group generator* G.Gen($1^\lambda$) produces public parameters Gpp $= (p, \mathbb{G}, P)$, where $p$ is a prime of bitlength $\lambda$, and $\mathbb{G}$ is a cyclic group of order $p$ with generator $P$. Similarly, a *bilinear group generator* BG.Gen($1^\lambda$) produces public parameters BGpp $= (p, \mathbb{G}_1, \mathbb{G}_2, \mathbb{G}_T, e, P, \tilde{P})$ where $\mathbb{G}_1 = \langle P \rangle$, $\mathbb{G}_2 = \langle \tilde{P} \rangle$, $\mathbb{G}_T$ are groups of order $p$. The map $e : \mathbb{G}_1 \times \mathbb{G}_2 \to \mathbb{G}_T$ is *bilinear* (for all $u, v \in \mathbb{Z}_p$, $e(P^u, \tilde{P}^v) = e(P, \tilde{P})^{uv}$ and non-degenerate (for all generators $P$ of $\mathbb{G}_1$, $\tilde{P}$ of $\mathbb{G}_2$, $\mathbb{G}_T = \langle e(P, \tilde{P}) \rangle$). For $\underline{P} \in \mathbb{G}_1^n$ and $\underline{\tilde{P}} \in \mathbb{G}_2^n$, let $e(\underline{P}, \underline{\tilde{P}}) := \prod_{i=1}^{n} e(P_i, \tilde{P}_i)$.

**Notations.** We refer to group elements with upper-case letters. Elements in $\mathbb{Z}_p$ are referred to using lower-case letters. We use $\tilde{\ast}$ to denote elements in $\mathbb{G}_2$ and bold font to denote elements in $\mathbb{G}_T$. Vectors are denoted by $\underline{\ast}$.

**Definition 1 (SXDH assumption).** *Let* $(p, \mathbb{G}_1, \mathbb{G}_2, \mathbb{G}_T, e, P, \tilde{P}) \leftarrow$ BG.Gen($1^\lambda$) *be a bilinear group generator. The SXDH assumption holds for* BG.Gen *if the DDH assumption holds for* $\mathbb{G}_1$ *and* $\mathbb{G}_2$ *(replacing* G.Gen *and tuple* $(p, \mathbb{G}, P)$ *with* BG.Gen *and tuple* $(p, \mathbb{G}_1, \mathbb{G}_2, \mathbb{G}_T, e, P, \tilde{P})$*).*

**Definition 2 (DPair assumption).** *Let* $(p, \mathbb{G}_1, \mathbb{G}_2, \mathbb{G}_T, e, P, \tilde{P}) \leftarrow$ BG.Gen($1^\lambda$) *be a bilinear group generator, and let* $n = poly(\lambda)$. *The double-pairing (DPair) assumption holds for* BG.Gen *if for all probabilistic polynomial time adversaries* $\mathcal{A}$, *for* $\underline{P} \leftarrow \mathbb{G}_1^n$, *the probability that* $\mathcal{A}$ *can produce* $\underline{\tilde{P}} \in \mathbb{G}_2^n$ *such that* $e(\underline{P}, \underline{\tilde{P}}) = 1$ *is negligible.*

The DPair assumption is first introduced in [4], where it is shown to be implied by the SXDH assumption.

## 3.1 Arguments of Knowledge

**Definition 3.** *A relation $\mathcal{R}$ is a set of tuples $(\mathsf{pp}, \mathrm{x}, \mathrm{w})$ where $\mathsf{pp}$ is called the public parameters, $\mathrm{x}$ is called the instance and $\mathrm{w}$ is called the witness. The language $\mathcal{L}_{\mathcal{R}}$ corresponding to $\mathcal{R}$ is the set of pairs $(\mathsf{pp}, \mathrm{x})$ such that there exists a witness $\mathrm{w}$ with $(\mathsf{pp}, \mathrm{x}, \mathrm{w}) \in \mathcal{R}$.*

**Definition 4.** *An interactive argument is a tuple of three algorithms $(\mathsf{G}, \mathsf{P}, \mathsf{V})$ with the following syntax.*

- $\mathsf{G}(1^{\lambda}, n) \to \mathsf{pp}$. *The generator $\mathsf{G}$ is a p.p.t. algorithm which takes the security parameter $\lambda$ and instance size $n$ as input and outputs public parameters $\mathsf{pp}$.*
- *The prover $\mathsf{P}$ and verifier $\mathsf{V}$ are p.p.t. interactive algorithms. The prover takes $\mathsf{pp}$, $\mathrm{x}$ and $\mathrm{w}$ as inputs. The verifier takes $\mathsf{pp}$ and $\mathrm{x}$ as inputs. An interaction between $\mathsf{P}$ and $\mathsf{V}$ on inputs $s$ and $t$, producing transcript $\mathsf{tr}$ is denoted by $\mathsf{tr} \leftarrow \langle \mathsf{P}(s), \mathsf{V}(t) \rangle$. The output of $\mathsf{V}$ at the end of an interaction is denoted by $\langle \mathsf{P}(s), \mathsf{V}(t) \rangle = b$. If $b = 1$, we say that the transcript is* accepted *by the verifier, and if $b = 0$, it is* rejected.

We say that $(\mathsf{G}, \mathsf{P}, \mathsf{V})$ is an argument of knowledge for a relation $\mathcal{R}$ if it satisfies the following completeness and knowledge soundness definitions.

- **Completeness.** For all $\lambda, n \in \mathbb{N}$ and all adversaries $\mathcal{A}$,

$$\Pr\left[ \begin{array}{c} (\mathsf{pp}, \mathrm{x}, \mathrm{w}) \in \mathcal{R} \\ \wedge \\ \langle \mathsf{P}(\mathsf{pp}, \mathrm{x}, \mathrm{w}), \mathsf{V}(\mathsf{pp}, \mathrm{x}) \rangle = 1 \end{array} \;\middle|\; \begin{array}{c} \mathsf{pp} \leftarrow \mathsf{G}(1^{\lambda}, n) \\ (\mathrm{x}, \mathrm{w}) \leftarrow \mathcal{A}(\mathsf{pp}) \end{array} \right] = 1 \;.$$

- **Knowledge soundness.** For all $\lambda, n \in \mathbb{N}$, there exists an expected polynomial time emulator $\mathsf{E}$ such that for all efficient adversaries $\mathcal{A}$, we have

$$\Pr\left[ \mathcal{A}(\mathsf{st}, \mathsf{tr}) = 1 \;\middle|\; \begin{array}{c} \mathsf{pp} \leftarrow \mathsf{G}(1^{\lambda}, n) \\ (\mathrm{x}, \mathsf{st}) \leftarrow \mathcal{A}(\mathsf{pp}) \\ \mathsf{tr} \leftarrow \langle \mathcal{A}(\mathsf{st}), \mathsf{V}(\mathsf{pp}, \mathrm{x}) \rangle \end{array} \right]$$

$$\approx \Pr\left[ \begin{array}{c} \mathcal{A}(\mathsf{st}, \mathsf{tr}) = 1 \quad \wedge \\ (\mathsf{tr} \text{ is accepting} \to (\mathsf{pp}, \mathrm{x}, \mathrm{w}) \in \mathcal{R}) \end{array} \;\middle|\; \begin{array}{c} \mathsf{pp} \leftarrow \mathsf{G}(1^{\lambda}, n) \\ (\mathrm{x}, \mathsf{st}) \leftarrow \mathcal{A}(\mathsf{pp}) \\ (\mathsf{tr}, \mathrm{w}) \leftarrow \mathsf{E}^{\mathcal{A}(\mathsf{st})}(\mathsf{pp}, \mathrm{x}) \end{array} \right] \;.$$

**Argument of Knowledge for Pairing Products**

**Definition 5.** *Define the relation $\mathcal{R}^n_{\mathsf{PProd}}$ as the set of tuples $(\mathsf{pp}, \mathrm{x}, \mathrm{w})$ satisfying $\mathbf{A} = e(\underline{\Omega}, \underline{\tilde{\Gamma}})$, $\mathbf{B} = e(\underline{\Gamma}, \underline{\tilde{\Omega}})$ and $\mathbf{C} = e(\underline{\Omega}, \underline{\tilde{\Omega}})$, where*

- $\mathsf{pp} = ((p, \mathbb{G}_1, \mathbb{G}_2, \mathbb{G}_T, e, P, \tilde{P}), (\underline{\Gamma}, \underline{\tilde{\Gamma}}))$ *where $(p, \mathbb{G}_1, \mathbb{G}_2, \mathbb{G}_T, e, P, \tilde{P}) \leftarrow \mathsf{BG.Gen}(1^{\lambda})$, $\underline{\Gamma} \in \mathbb{G}_1^n$ and $\underline{\tilde{\Gamma}} \in \mathbb{G}_2^n$;*

- $x = (A, B, C) \in \mathbb{G}_T^3$; and
- $w = (\underline{\Omega}, \underline{\tilde{\Omega}})$ where $\underline{\Omega} \in \mathbb{G}_1^n, \underline{\tilde{\Omega}} \in \mathbb{G}_2^n$.

**Theorem 1** ([23]). *Assuming that SXDH holds for* BG.Gen, *then there is a preprocessing argument of knowledge* $(\mathsf{G_{PProd}}, \mathsf{P_{PProd}}, \mathsf{V_{PProd}})$ *for* $\mathcal{R}_{\mathrm{PProd}}^n$, *for every* $n \in \mathbb{N}$, *with the following performance parameters:*

- *prover time dominated by* $O(n)$ *pairing operations and* $\mathbb{G}_1$, $\mathbb{G}_2$ *and* $\mathbb{G}_T$ *operations;*
- *offline verifier time dominated by* $O(n)$ *pairing operations and* $\mathbb{G}_T$ *operations in a one-time preprocessing phase; and*
- *online verifier time dominated by* $O(\log n)$ *pairing operations and* $\mathbb{G}_T$ *operations.*

### 3.2  Signatures of Knowledge

We describe here signatures of knowledge following the definitions in [17]. In a nutshell, a signature of knowledge generalizes the concept of public key signatures to NP statements. Such a signature proves that "a person holding a witness $w$ to a statement $x$ has signed a message $m$".

**Definition 6.** *A signature of knowledge (SoK) is a tuple of three algorithms* $(\mathsf{G}, \mathsf{S}, \mathsf{V})$ *with the following syntax.*

- $\mathsf{G}(1^\lambda) \to \mathsf{pp}$. *The generator* $\mathsf{G}$ *is a p.p.t. algorithm which takes the security parameter* $\lambda$ *as input and produces public parameters* $\mathsf{pp}$ *as output.*
- *The signer* $\mathsf{S}$ *is a p.p.t. algorithm that takes* $\mathsf{pp}$, $x$, $w$ *and a message* $m$ *as inputs and produces a signature* $\sigma$.
- *The verifier* $\mathsf{V}$ *is a p.p.t. algorithm that takes as input* $\mathsf{pp}$, $x$, *message* $m$ *and signature* $\sigma$, *and outputs a bit* $b$. *If* $b = 1$, *we say that* $\sigma$ *is a valid signature on message* $m$ *relative to* $\mathsf{pp}$ *and* $x$.

We say that $(\mathsf{G}, \mathsf{S}, \mathsf{V})$ is a signature of knowledge for a relation $\mathcal{R}$ if it satisfies the following properties.

- **Completeness.** For all $\lambda, n \in \mathbb{N}$, $m \in \{0, 1\}^*$ and all adversaries $\mathcal{A}$

$$\Pr\begin{bmatrix} (\mathsf{pp}, x, w) \in \mathcal{R} \wedge \\ \sigma \leftarrow \mathsf{S}(\mathsf{pp}, x, w, m) \wedge \\ \mathsf{V}(\mathsf{pp}, x, m, \sigma) = 1 \end{bmatrix} \begin{matrix} \mathsf{pp} \leftarrow \mathsf{G}(1^\lambda, n) \\ (x, w) \leftarrow \mathcal{A}(\mathsf{pp}) \end{matrix} = 1 .$$

- **Simulatability.** There exists a polynomial-time simulator Sim that runs two algorithms
  - $\mathsf{SimG}(1^\lambda) \to (\mathsf{pp}, \tau)$: The generator $\mathsf{SimG}$ is a p.p.t. algorithm which takes the security parameter $\lambda$ as input and produces public parameters $\mathsf{pp}$ and trapdoor $\tau$ as output.
  - $\mathsf{SimS}$ is a p.p.t. algorithm that takes $\mathsf{pp}$, trapdoor $\tau$, $x$ and a message $m$ as inputs and produces a simulated signature $\sigma$.

such that Sim receives values $(x, w, m)$ as inputs, checks whether $w$ is valid and outputs $SimS(pp, \tau, x, m)$, and for all p.p.t. adversaries $\mathcal{A}$ with oracle access to simulator Sim and SoK signer S

$$\Pr\left[1 \leftarrow \mathcal{A}^{Sim}(pp) \,\middle|\, (pp, \tau) \leftarrow SimG(1^\lambda, n)\right] \approx \Pr\left[1 \leftarrow \mathcal{A}^{S}(pp) \,\middle|\, pp \leftarrow G(1^\lambda, n)\right] .$$

– **Simulation Extractability.** These exists a polynomial time extractor Extractor such that for all p.p.t adversaries $\mathcal{A}$

$$\Pr\left[\begin{array}{cc|c} (pp, x, w) \in \mathcal{R} & \vee & (pp, \tau) \leftarrow SimG(1^\lambda) \\ (x, w, m) \in Queries & \vee & (x, m, \sigma) \leftarrow \mathcal{A}^{Sim}(pp) \\ V(pp, x, w, m) = 0 & & w \leftarrow Extractor(pp, \tau, x, m, \sigma) \end{array}\right] \approx 1 .$$

where Queries denotes all queries $(x, w, m)$ that Sim receives from $\mathcal{A}$.

## 4  Prefix-Linkable Ring Signature Schemes

We now give a definition of prefix-linkable ring signatures. We follow [7] and [8], and modify their definitions by splitting strings to be signed into message and prefix[3], and link only with respect to the prefix (but not the message).

**Definition 7 (Prefix-linkable ring signature scheme).** *A prefix-linkable ring signature (PLRS) scheme is a tuple of algorithms* RS $=$ (Gen, KeyGen, Sign, Verify, Link) *with message space* $\mathcal{M}$ *and prefix space* $\mathcal{P}$ *where*

– pp $\leftarrow$ RS.Gen$(1^\lambda)$ *produces public parameters* pp, *which we assume to be available to all the algorithms below.*
– $(sk, pk) \leftarrow$ RS.KeyGen(pp) *produces a key pair.*
– $\sigma \leftarrow$ RS.Sign($\underline{pk}, sk, m, prfx$), *where* $m$ *is a message,* prfx *is a prefix, and* $\underline{pk}$ *is a vector of public keys produced by* RS.KeyGen *that includes the public key* pk *corresponding to secret key sk.*
– $0/1 \leftarrow$ RS.Verify($\underline{pk}, m, prfx, \sigma$).
– $0/1 \leftarrow$ RS.Link($\underline{pk}, \sigma, m, \sigma', m', prfx$).

*We require that the scheme is* correct; *that is, for any* $m, m' \in \mathcal{M}$, *any* prfx $\in \mathcal{P}$, *any* $(sk, pk), (sk', pk')$ *produced by* RS.Gen$(1^\lambda)$ *with* $pk \neq pk'$ *and any* $\underline{pk}$ *of public keys produced by* RS.KeyGen *that includes pk and pk'*:

– RS.Verify($\underline{pk}, m, prfx, RS.Sign(\underline{pk}, sk, m, prfx)$) $= 1$.
– RS.Link($\underline{pk}, RS.Sign(\underline{pk}, sk, m, prfx), m, RS.Sign(\underline{pk}, sk, m', prfx), m', prfx$) $= 1$.
– RS.Link($\underline{pk}, m, RS.Sign(\underline{pk}, sk, m, prfx), m', RS.Sign(\underline{pk}, sk', m', prfx), prfx$) $= 0$ *except with negligible probability.*

---

[3] A synonym for prefix used in the literature is *event identity* [19]. We use the term prefix for brevity.

We now define various security properties. First, unforgeability demands that an adversary cannot produce a valid signature for any message-prefix pair, for a ring for which the adversary does not know any secret key, even when equipped with a signing oracle for that ring. Forgeries need to verify with respect to the ring generated by the experiment. All our notions below are in the "honest ring with insider corruption" setting [11], i.e., all the games sample $\mathsf{pp} \leftarrow \mathsf{RS.Gen}(1^\lambda)$, $(sk_i, pk_i) \leftarrow \mathsf{RS.KeyGen}(\mathsf{pp})$, $i \in [n]$ and set $\underline{pk} := (pk_1, \ldots, pk_n)$.

**Definition 8 (Corruption oracle).** *Given a well-formed public key pk produced by* RS.KeyGen, *the* corruption oracle CO *returns the corresponding sk.*

**Definition 9 (Signing oracle).** *Given a well-formed set of public keys $\underline{pk}$, on input $pk \in \underline{pk}$, a message m, and a prefix* prfx, *the signing oracle* $\mathsf{SO}_{\underline{pk}}$ *returns a signature $\sigma$ whose distribution is comp. indistinguishable from the output of* $\mathsf{RS.Sign}(\mathsf{pp}, \underline{pk}, sk, m, \mathsf{prfx})$, *where sk corresponds to pk.*

**Definition 10 (Unforgeability).** *A PLRS is* unforgeable *if for all efficient adversaries* $\mathcal{A}^{\mathsf{SO}_{\underline{pk}}}(\mathsf{pp}, \underline{pk})$ *outputting $(m, \mathsf{prfx}, \sigma)$, the probability that $\sigma$ was not produced by* $\mathsf{SO}_{\underline{pk}}$ *on any input $(m, \mathsf{prfx})$ and* $\mathsf{RS.Verify}(\mathsf{pp}, \underline{pk}, m, \mathsf{prfx}, \sigma) = 1$ *is negligible.*

Next, we define anonymity, which demands that an adversary cannot tell which of a ring's secret keys was used to produce a signature.

**Definition 11 (Anonymity).** *A PLRS is* anonymous *if for all efficient stateful adversaries $\mathcal{A}$, the probability of winning the following game is negligibly close to $1/2$.*

- $(m, \mathsf{prfx}, pk_0, pk_1) \leftarrow \mathcal{A}^{\mathsf{CO}, \mathsf{SO}_{\underline{pk}}}(\mathsf{pp}, \underline{pk})$
- $b \leftarrow \{0, 1\}$;
- $\sigma \leftarrow \mathsf{RS.Sign}(\mathsf{pp}, \underline{pk}, sk_b, m, \mathsf{prfx})$;
- $b' \leftarrow \mathcal{A}(\sigma)$.

$\mathcal{A}$ *wins if all of the following hold:*
- $b = b'$;
- $pk_0, pk_1 \in \underline{pk}$ *and* $pk_0 \neq pk_1$;
- $pk_0, pk_1$ *were never queried to* CO;
- $(pk_0, \mathsf{prfx})$ *and* $(pk_1, \mathsf{prfx})$ *were never used in any* $\mathsf{SO}_{\underline{pk}}$ *query.*

Next, we demand that it must be hard to bypass the linking property of the signature scheme. For standard linkable ring signatures, i.e., ones that link with respect to any message, this property simply ensures that it is hard to create two signatures from the same secret key that do not link with each other. Here, we additionally require the adversary to create such non-linking signatures with respect to the same prefix, as otherwise the game would be trivial to win. As in [8], the adversary can use all of the secret keys in the ring to achieve this goal.

**Definition 12 (Prefix linkability).** *A PLRS is* prefix-linkable *if for all efficient adversaries $\mathcal{A}$, the probability of winning the following game is negligible.*

- $(m_i, \mathsf{prfx}, \sigma_i)_{i \in [n+1]} \leftarrow \mathcal{A}^{\mathsf{CO}, \mathsf{SO}_{\underline{pk}}}(\mathsf{pp}, \underline{pk})$

$\mathcal{A}$ *wins if all of the following hold:*
- $\mathsf{RS.Verify}(\mathsf{pp}, \underline{pk}, m_i, \mathsf{prfx}, \sigma_i) = 1$ *for all $i \in [n+1]$;*
- $\mathsf{RS.Link}(\mathsf{pp}, \underline{pk}, \sigma_i, m_i, \sigma_j, m_j, \mathsf{prfx}) = 0$ *for all $i, j \in [n+1], i \neq j$.*

Finally, we demand that it must be hard to create a signature that links to one of the honest signers. We follow the 2-staged definition of [8] and grant the adversary access to all of secret keys in the ring only after producing the "slandering" signature $\sigma'$.

**Definition 13 (Non-slanderability).** *A PLRS is non-slanderable if for all efficient adversaries $\mathcal{A}$, the probability of winning the following game is negligible.*

- $(m', \text{prfx}', \sigma') \leftarrow \mathcal{A}^{\text{SO}_{\underline{pk}}}(\text{pp}, \underline{pk})$
- $(m, \sigma) \leftarrow \mathcal{A}^{\text{CO}, \text{SO}_{\underline{pk}}}$

*$\mathcal{A}$ wins if all of the following hold:*
- RS.Verify$(\text{pp}, \underline{pk}, m, \text{prfx}', \sigma) = 1$
- RS.Verify$(\text{pp}, \underline{pk}, m', \text{prfx}', \sigma') = 1$;
- RS.Link$(\underline{pk}, \sigma, m, \sigma', m', \text{prfx}') = 1$;
- $\sigma'$ *was not received from* $\text{SO}_{\underline{pk}}$.

*Discussion.* In case prfx is the empty string, the definitions in this section define a linkable ring signature with message space $\mathcal{M}$. Dropping prfx from them leads the anonymity game (Definition 11) to forbid usage of signing oracles with respect to $pk_0, pk_1$ completely. The definitions then become equivalent to the definition of Au et al. [7]. In case $m$ is the empty string, the definitions in this section define a "same-message" linkable RS with message space $\mathcal{P}$, where linking of signatures is only possible if a signer signs the same message more than once. Hence, our notion of prefix linkability is a generalization that allows fine-tuned linkability for ring signatures.

## 5   Our Construction

**Definition 14.** *The relation $\mathcal{R}_{\text{Tag}}$ consists of tuples*

$$(\text{pp}_{\text{Tag}}, \mathbb{x}, \mathbb{w}) = \big((p, \mathbb{G}, P, Q, H, H'), (\text{prfx}, \text{tag}, \text{com}), (sk, r)\big)$$

*such that $\mathbb{G}$ is a group of prime order $p$ with generators $P$ and $Q$, $H: \{0,1\}^* \to \mathbb{Z}_p$ and $H': \{0,1\}^* \to \mathbb{G}$ are two hash functions, $\text{com}, \text{tag} \in \mathbb{G}$, $\text{prfx} \in \{0,1\}^*$, and $sk, r \in \mathbb{Z}_p$, satisfy $\text{com} = P^{sk}Q^r$ and $\text{tag} = H'(\text{prfx})^{sk}$.*

**Construction 1.** *Let $\lambda \in \mathbb{N}$ be a security parameter and G.Gen be a group generator. Our tag proof scheme is a tuple of algorithms $(\mathsf{G}_{\text{Tag}}, \mathsf{S}_{\text{Tag}}, \mathsf{V}_{\text{Tag}})$ defined as follows.*

| $\text{pp}_{\text{Tag}} \leftarrow \mathsf{G}_{\text{Tag}}(1^\lambda)$: | $\sigma_{\text{Tag}} \leftarrow \mathsf{S}_{\text{Tag}}(\text{pp}_{\text{Tag}}, \mathbb{x}, \mathbb{w}, m)$: |
|---|---|
| $(p, \mathbb{G}, P) \leftarrow \text{G.Gen}(1^\lambda)$ | $(\text{prfx}, \text{tag}, \text{com}) := \mathbb{x}$ and $(sk, r) := \mathbb{w}$ |
| $Q \leftarrow \mathbb{G}$ | $a, b \leftarrow_s \mathbb{Z}_p$ |
| *define hash functions* | $A := H'(\text{prfx})^a \in \mathbb{G}, \ B := P^a Q^b \in \mathbb{G}$ |
| $\quad H: \{0,1\}^* \to \mathbb{Z}_p$ *and* | $c = H(\text{prfx}, \text{com}, \text{tag}, A, B, m) \in \mathbb{Z}_p$ |
| $\quad H': \{0,1\}^* \to \mathbb{G}$ | $\bar{a} := a + c \cdot sk \in \mathbb{Z}_p, \ \bar{b} := b + c \cdot r \in \mathbb{Z}_p$ |
| *output* $\text{pp}_{\text{Tag}} := (p, \mathbb{G}, P, Q, H, H')$. | *output* $\sigma_{\text{Tag}} := (A, B, \bar{a}, \bar{b}) \in \mathbb{G}^2 \times \mathbb{Z}_p^2$. |

| $b \leftarrow \mathsf{V}_{\text{Tag}}(\text{pp}_{\text{Tag}}, \mathbb{x}, \sigma_{\text{Tag}}, m)$: |
|---|
| $(\text{prfx}, \text{tag}, \text{com}) := \mathbb{x}, \ (A, B, \bar{a}, \bar{b}) := \sigma_{\text{Tag}} \in \mathbb{G}^2 \times \mathbb{Z}_p^2$ |
| $c = H(\text{prfx}, \text{com}, \text{tag}, A, B, m) \in \mathbb{Z}_p$ |
| *if* $H'(\text{prfx})^{\bar{a}} = A \cdot \text{tag}^c$ *and* $P^{\bar{a}}Q^{\bar{b}} = B \cdot \text{com}^c$ *then output* 1, *else output* 0. |

**Theorem 2.** *Tag proof (Construction 1) is a signature of knowledge for* $\mathcal{R}_{\mathrm{Tag}}$.

*Proof (Sketch).* Tag proof is a non-interactive zero-knowledge proof of knowledge for $\mathcal{R}_{\mathrm{Tag}}$ made up of two simple zero-knowledge proofs:

- one Schnorr proof-of-knowledge of the discrete logarithm $sk$ of $A$ to base $H'(\mathrm{prfx})$ (see e.g. [28, Fig. 4.3]); and
- one Okamoto proof of knowledge of exponents $sk, r$ such that com $= P^{sk}Q^r$ for $P, Q, \mathrm{com} \in \mathbb{G}$ (see e.g. [28, Fig. 4.5]).

The proofs are combined using an EQ transformation in which parts of the Schnorr proof (such as $a, \bar{a}$) are reused in the Okamoto proof (see [28, Section 5.2.2]), before making the resulting proof non-interactive using the Fiat-Shamir heuristic. If $H$ takes also message $m$ as input, this results in a signature of knowledge for $(\mathrm{x}, \mathrm{w}) = ((\mathrm{prfx}, \mathrm{tag}, \mathrm{com}), (sk, r))$. First, given that Schnorr and Okamoto proofs are simulatable [27], the corresponding signature is also simulatable in the random oracle model [10]. Second, applying the forking lemma to $H$, one can successfully extract a valid witness from a valid forgery [10].

**Construction 2.** *Let* $\lambda \in \mathbb{N}$ *denote a security parameter and* $n \in \mathbb{N}$ *an upper bound on the ring size. Let* BG.Gen *a bilinear group generator,* $(\mathrm{G}_{\mathrm{Tag}}, \mathrm{S}_{\mathrm{Tag}}, \mathrm{V}_{\mathrm{Tag}})$ *the tag proof scheme of Construction 1,* $\mathcal{R}^n_{\mathrm{PProd}}$ *the relation w.r.t* BG.Gen *as in Definition 5, and* $(\mathrm{G}_{\mathrm{PProd}}, \mathrm{P}_{\mathrm{PProd}}, \mathrm{V}_{\mathrm{PProd}})$ *a preprocessing argument of knowledge for* $\mathcal{R}^n_{\mathrm{PProd}}$.
  *Then* DualDory *is defined by the set of procedures in Fig. 1.*

**Theorem 3.** *DualDory (Construction 2) is an unforgeable, anonymous, prefix-linkable and non-slanderable PLRS scheme with the following complexity parameters:*

- *public parameter size* $O(n)$ *elements of* $\mathbb{G}_1$ *and* $\mathbb{G}_2$;
- *signature size* $O(\log n)$ $\mathbb{G}_T$-*elements,* $O(1)$ $\mathbb{G}_1$-*elements and* $O(1)$ $\mathbb{Z}_p$-*elements;*
- *signing complexity dominated by* $O(n)$ *pairing operations;*
- *online verification complexity dominated by* $O(\log n)$ *pairing operations;*
- *offline verification complexity dominated by* $O(n)$ *pairing operations;*

*Proof.* The proof follows from a straightforward inspection of the complexity of the procedures, and from Theorems 4-7. Due to space limitations, these theorems and their proofs are deferred to Appendix A.

## 6   Evaluation

We implement our linkable ring signature in $\approx 1,500$ lines of Go. Our implementation is publicly available [1] and open source. We use the BN254 [9] elliptic curve implementation of gnark-crypto [14]. We evaluate the performance by running 100 independent trials for each measured operation on an Ubuntu 22.04 AWS c5a.xlarge machine equipped with 4 2.8 Ghz CPUs with 8 GB RAM. We compare our results with the implementation [2] of DualRing [31] evaluated on the same machine.

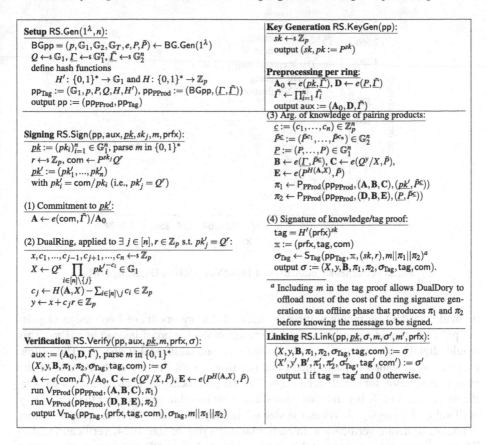

**Setup RS.Gen$(1^\lambda, n)$:**

$BGpp = (p, \mathbb{G}_1, \mathbb{G}_2, \mathbb{G}_T, e, P, \tilde{P}) \leftarrow BG.Gen(1^\lambda)$
$Q \leftarrow_\$ \mathbb{G}_1, \Gamma \leftarrow_\$ \mathbb{G}_1^n, \tilde{\Gamma} \leftarrow_\$ \mathbb{G}_2^n$
define hash functions
$\quad H': \{0,1\}^* \to \mathbb{G}_1$ and $H: \{0,1\}^* \to \mathbb{Z}_p$
$pp_{Tag} := (\mathbb{G}_1, p, P, Q, H, H')$, $pp_{PProd} := (BGpp, (\Gamma, \tilde{\Gamma}))$
output $pp := (pp_{PProd}, pp_{Tag})$

**Signing RS.Sign$(pp, aux, \underline{pk}, sk_j, m, prfx)$:**

$\underline{pk} := (pk_i)_{i=1}^n \in \mathbb{G}_1^n$, parse $m$ in $\{0,1\}^*$
$r \leftarrow_\$ \mathbb{Z}_p$, $com \leftarrow P^{sk_j}Q^r$
$\underline{pk'} := (pk'_1, ..., pk'_n)$
with $pk'_i = com/pk_i$ (i.e., $pk'_j = Q^r$)

(1) Commitment to $\underline{pk'}$:

$\mathbf{A} \leftarrow e(com, \tilde{\Gamma})/\mathbf{A}_0$

(2) DualRing, applied to $\exists\, j \in [n], r \in \mathbb{Z}_p$ s.t. $pk'_j = Q^r$:

$x, c_1, ..., c_{j-1}, c_{j+1}, ..., c_n \leftarrow_\$ \mathbb{Z}_p$
$X \leftarrow Q^x \prod_{i \in [n]\setminus\{j\}} pk'^{-c_i}_i \in \mathbb{G}_1$
$c_j \leftarrow H(\mathbf{A}, X) - \Sigma_{i \in [n]\setminus j}\, c_i \in \mathbb{Z}_p$
$y \leftarrow x + c_j r \in \mathbb{Z}_p$

**Verification RS.Verify$(pp, aux, \underline{pk}, m, prfx, \sigma)$:**

$aux := (\mathbf{A}_0, \mathbf{D}, \tilde{\Gamma})$, parse $m$ in $\{0,1\}^*$
$(X, y, \mathbf{B}, \pi_1, \pi_2, \sigma_{Tag}, tag, com) := \sigma$
$\mathbf{A} \leftarrow e(com, \tilde{\Gamma})/\mathbf{A}_0$, $\mathbf{C} \leftarrow e(Q^y/X, \tilde{P})$, $\mathbf{E} \leftarrow e(P^{H(\mathbf{A},X)}, \tilde{P})$
run $V_{PProd}(pp_{PProd}, (\mathbf{A}, \mathbf{B}, \mathbf{C}), \pi_1)$
run $V_{PProd}(pp_{PProd}, (\mathbf{D}, \mathbf{B}, \mathbf{E}), \pi_2)$
output $V_{Tag}(pp_{Tag}, (prfx, tag, com), \sigma_{Tag}, m||\pi_1||\pi_2)$

**Key Generation RS.KeyGen(pp):**

$sk \leftarrow_\$ \mathbb{Z}_p$
output $(sk, pk := P^{sk})$

**Preprocessing per ring:**

$\mathbf{A}_0 \leftarrow e(\underline{pk}, \tilde{\Gamma})$, $\mathbf{D} \leftarrow e(P, \tilde{\Gamma})$
$\tilde{\Gamma} \leftarrow \prod_{i=1}^n \tilde{\Gamma}_i$
output $aux := (\mathbf{A}_0, \mathbf{D}, \tilde{\Gamma})$

(3) Arg. of knowledge of pairing products:

$\underline{c} := (c_1, ..., c_n) \in \mathbb{Z}_p^n$
$\tilde{P}^{\underline{c}} := (\tilde{P}^{c_1}, ..., \tilde{P}^{c_n}) \in \mathbb{G}_2^n$
$\underline{P} := (P, ..., P) \in \mathbb{G}_1^n$
$\mathbf{B} \leftarrow e(\Gamma, \tilde{P}^{\underline{c}})$, $\mathbf{C} \leftarrow e(Q^y/X, \tilde{P})$,
$\mathbf{E} \leftarrow e(P^{H(\mathbf{A},X)}, \tilde{P})$
$\pi_1 \leftarrow P_{PProd}(pp_{PProd}, (\mathbf{A}, \mathbf{B}, \mathbf{C}), (\underline{pk'}, \tilde{P}^{\underline{c}}))$
$\pi_2 \leftarrow P_{PProd}(pp_{PProd}, (\mathbf{D}, \mathbf{B}, \mathbf{E}), (\underline{P}, \tilde{P}^{\underline{c}}))$

(4) Signature of knowledge/tag proof:

$tag = H'(prfx)^{sk}$
$\mathbb{x} := (prfx, tag, com)$
$\sigma_{Tag} \leftarrow S_{Tag}(pp_{Tag}, \mathbb{x}, (sk, r), m||\pi_1||\pi_2)^a$
output $\sigma := (X, y, \mathbf{B}, \pi_1, \pi_2, \sigma_{Tag}, tag, com)$.

---

[a] Including $m$ in the tag proof allows DualDory to offload most of the cost of the ring signature generation to an offline phase that produces $\pi_1$ and $\pi_2$ before knowing the message to be signed.

**Linking RS.Link$(pp, \underline{pk}, \sigma, m, \sigma', m', prfx)$:**

$(X, y, \mathbf{B}, \pi_1, \pi_2, \sigma_{Tag}, tag, com) := \sigma$
$(X', y', \mathbf{B}', \pi'_1, \pi'_2, \sigma'_{Tag}, tag', com') := \sigma'$
output 1 if $tag = tag'$ and 0 otherwise.

**Fig. 1.** The DualDory linkable ring signature scheme. Note that the parameter generation $\mathbb{G}_{Tag}$ is not used, and instead tag proof is run on the pairing source group $\mathbb{G}_1$ produced by BG.Gen.

Figure 2 shows the time it takes to produce and verify a DualDory signature and a DualRing signature and the cost of the DualDory offline preprocessing in relation to the size of the ring. We note that although DualDory appears to be faster than DualRing, one needs to take into consideration that DualRing [2] is a single-threaded Python program while Dory is a Go program which runs each argument of knowledge of pairing products ($\pi_1$, $\pi_2$) in a different thread. We draw three conclusions from the empirical results of DualDuary: (1) As expected, the verification speed of our linkable ring signature is logarithmic in the size of the ring, and scales well even for large rings. (2) The time it takes to generate a ring signature is linear in the size of the ring. For a ring of size 1024, signing takes 3.53 s. Fortunately, most of the signature work, which corresponds to the prover computation of DualRing and the argument of knowledge of bilinear pairing products, can be precomputed by the signer before knowing either the message or the prefix. This leaves only the tag proof to be generated online (i.e., when the message and the prefix are known). Our benchmarks show that the time it takes to compute the tag proof is less than 1ms for a ring of size 1024. The cost of tag proof generation can

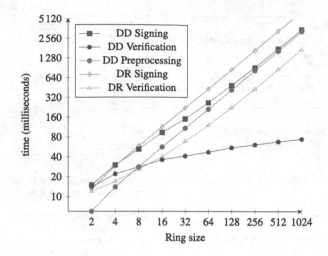

**Fig. 2.** Performance evaluation of DualDory (DD) vs DualRing (DR)

be made constant by precomputing the hash of the arguments of knowledge of pairing products $\pi_1$ and $\pi_2$ and including the result in the tag proof instead of $\pi_1 \| \pi_2$. This would slightly increase the cost of verification (one additional hash). (3) The offline preprocessing, which is performed once per ring, grows linearly with the size of the ring. Furthermore, for small-sized rings $\leq 8$, the preprocessing is cheaper than the verification, which probably indicates that there is no tangible gain yet and that DualDory is ill-suited for rings $\leq 8$. When the size of the ring increases $\geq 16$, the preprocessing overtakes signature verification. In particular, for a ring of size 1024, verification takes 74 ms, whereas preprocessing takes 3.31 s. Although the offline preprocessing is not too expensive, it is desirable to amortize its cost over multiple verifications. Thus, we recommend DualDory for settings with static or incrementally-updatable rings.

## A    Security Analysis

Due to space limitations, we only provide proof sketches to the main theorems of the paper. The full proofs are deferred to an extended version that can be found here [3].

**Theorem 4 (Correctness).** *DualDory satisfies correctness (Definition 7).*

*Proof (Sketch).* We show that $\mathsf{RS.Verify}(\underline{pk}, m, \mathsf{prfx}, \mathsf{RS.Sign}(\underline{pk}, sk, m, \mathsf{prfx})) = 1$. Let $\underline{pk}' = (\mathsf{com}/pk_i)_{i=1}^n$ and recall that $\mathbf{A} = e(\mathsf{com}, \tilde{\Gamma})/A_0 = e(\underline{pk}', \tilde{\Gamma})$, $\mathbf{B} = e(\Gamma, \tilde{P}^c)$, $\mathbf{C} = e(Q^y/X, \tilde{P})$, $\mathbf{D} = e(\underline{P}, \tilde{\Gamma})$ and $\mathbf{E} = e(P^{H(\mathbf{A}, X)}, \tilde{P})$. Parse the last input element as $(X, y, \mathbf{B}, \pi_1, \pi_2, \sigma_{\mathsf{Tag}}, \mathsf{tag}, \mathsf{com})$. Following DualRing: $Q^y/X = \prod_{i=1}^n pk_i'^{c_i}$ and $\sum_{i=1}^n c_i = H(\mathbf{A}, X)$. Therefore, $\mathbf{C} = e(\underline{pk}', \tilde{P}^c)$ and $\mathbf{E} = e(\underline{P}, \tilde{P}^c)$.

$\mathsf{V_{PProd}}(\mathsf{pp_{PProd}}, (\mathbf{A}, \mathbf{B}, \mathbf{C}), \pi_1) = 1$ because $\pi_1 \leftarrow \mathsf{P_{PProd}}(\mathsf{pp_{PProd}}, (\mathbf{A}, \mathbf{B}, \mathbf{C}), (\underline{pk}', \tilde{P}^c))$. Similarly, $\pi_2 \leftarrow \mathsf{P_{PProd}}(\mathsf{pp_{PProd}}, (\mathbf{D}, \mathbf{B}, \mathbf{E}), (\underline{P}, \tilde{P}^c))$ and $\mathsf{V_{PProd}}(\mathsf{pp_{PProd}}, (\mathbf{D}, \mathbf{B}, \mathbf{E}), \pi_2) = 1$. Finally, $\sigma_{\mathsf{Tag}} \leftarrow \mathsf{S_{Tag}}(\mathsf{pp_{Tag}}, (\mathsf{prfx}, \mathsf{tag}, \mathsf{com}), (sk, r), m \| \pi_1 \| \pi_2)$, which means that

$V_{Tag}(pp_{Tag}, (prfx, tag, com), \sigma_{Tag}, m||\pi_1||\pi_2) = 1$.

The correctness properties related to linking are straightforward.

**Theorem 5.** *DualDory is anonymous (Definition 11) in the random oracle model under the DDH assumption.*

*Proof (Sketch).* Given an adversary $\mathcal{A}$ which wins the anonymity game (Definition 11) with non-negligible advantage. We show that there is a distinguisher $\mathcal{D}$, which leverages $\mathcal{A}$ to break the DDH assumption in $\mathbb{G}_1$ in the random oracle model.

Let $BGpp := (p, \mathbb{G}_1, \mathbb{G}_2, \mathbb{G}_T, e, P, \tilde{P}) \leftarrow BG.Gen(1^{\lambda})$, and let $(U, V, W) \in \mathbb{G}_1^3$ be sampled either as a DDH tuple or uniformly at random. The distinguisher $\mathcal{D}$ receives $BGpp$ and $(U, V, W)$ as input. $\mathcal{D}$ then sets the public key $pk_j$ of one the signers to $U$ while computing the public keys of the remaining signers honestly. To simulate the output of signature queries $(pk_j, m, prfx)$ without knowledge of the secret key $sk_j$ matching $pk_j$, $\mathcal{D}$ programs random oracle $H'$ such that $H'(prfx) = V^{r'}$ for $r' \leftarrow \mathbb{Z}_p$ and computes $tag = W^{r'}$. $\mathcal{D}$ also programs random oracle $H$ in such a way that it is able to produce a tag proof that verifies correctly. Note that the DualRing and the arguments of knowledge of bilinear pairing product parts in DualDory can be computed honestly by $\mathcal{D}$ ($\mathcal{D}$ does not need $sk_j$). Now if $(U, V, W)$ is a DDH tuple, then the simulated signature is statistically indistinguishable from a signature generated following DualDory. If not, then $\mathcal{A}$ cannot tell the difference thanks to DDH assumption, given that the simulated signature verifies correctly.

At the end of the anonymity game, $\mathcal{A}$ outputs two public keys $\{pk_0^*, pk_1^*\}$. If we assume that $\mathcal{A}$ issues $n - 2$ corruption queries where $pk_j$ does not show, then $pk_j \in \{pk_0^*, pk_1^*\}$. Let $pk_j = pk_0^*$. $\mathcal{D}$ then simulates a signature using public key $pk_0^*$ and outputs the result to $\mathcal{A}$. $\mathcal{A}$ accordingly, outputs its guess $b$. To break DDH, $\mathcal{D}$ returns $1 - b$.

Note that if $(U, V, W)$ is a DDH tuple, then $\mathcal{A}$ will output the correct guess $b = 0$ with a non-negligible advantage, and $\mathcal{D}$ breaks DDH by outputting 1. If not, then $\mathcal{A}$ will perform no better than a random guess, and so will $\mathcal{D}$. Actually, tuple $(com, tag, \sigma_{Tag})$ in the signature leaks no information whatsoever about the underlying secret key – com is perfectly hiding, $tag = W^r$ is a random group element and $\sigma_{Tag}$ is computed without using any secret keys.

**Theorem 6.** *DualDory is prefix linkable (Definition 12) in the random oracle model under the SXDH assumption.*

*Proof (Sketch).* Assume there is an adversary $\mathcal{A}$ which breaks the prefix linkability of DualDory. We construct an adversary $\mathcal{B}$ which uses $\mathcal{A}$ to break the DPair assumption with two generators which is implied by SXDH. Let $BGpp := (p, \mathbb{G}_1, \mathbb{G}_2, \mathbb{G}_T, e, P, \tilde{P}) \leftarrow BG.Gen(1^{\lambda})$, and let $(P_1, P_2)$ be two additional generators of $\mathbb{G}_1$. Adversary $\mathcal{B}$ receives $BGpp$ and $(P_1, P_2)$ as input. $\mathcal{B}$'s goal is to output two generators $(\tilde{P}_1, \tilde{P}_2) \in \mathbb{G}_2^2$ such that $e(P_1, \tilde{P}_1)e(P_2, \tilde{P}_2) = 1$. To that end, $\mathcal{B}$ computes $n$ pairs $(sk_i, pk_i) = (sk_i, P_1^{sk_i}), i \in [n]$, sets Pedersen commitment generators to $(P_1, P_2)$ and simulates the prefix linkability game honestly. At the end of the game, $\mathcal{A}$ outputs $n + 1$ tuples $(m_i, prfx, \sigma_i)$ for $i \in [n+1]$. We parse $\sigma_i$ as $(X_i, y_i, \mathbf{B}_i, \pi_{1,i}, \pi_{2,i}, \sigma_{Tag,i}, tag_i, com_i)$. If $\mathcal{A}$ wins the prefix linkability game, then $tag_i, tag_j$ are all pairwise distinct for $i \neq j \in [n + 1]$. By the soundness of tag proof, this implies that $\text{tag}_i = H'(\text{prfx})^{sk'_i} \neq \text{tag}_j = H'(\text{prfx})^{sk'_j}$. In particular, using the simulation extractability of tag proof, $\mathcal{B}$ is able to extract $n+1$ pairs $(sk'_i, r_i), i \in [n]$ that satisfy $\mathcal{R}_{\text{Tag}}$. It follows that there is $sk'_i \notin \{sk_1, ..., sk_n\}, i \in [n+1]$. Assume that $sk'_{n+1} \notin \{sk_1, ..., sk_n\}$. Applying the knowledge soundness of arguments of knowledge of bilinear pairing products (Theorem 1) to $\pi_{1,n+1}$ allows us to extract $\tilde{\underline{\Omega}}$ such that

$$e\left(\left(\frac{\text{com}_{n+1}}{pk_i}\right)_{i=1}^n, \tilde{\underline{\Omega}}\right) = e\left(\frac{P_2^{y_{n+1}}}{X_{n+1}}, \tilde{P}\right) \text{ and } e(\underline{P}, \tilde{\underline{\Omega}}) = e(P, \tilde{P}^c) \text{ with } c = H(\mathbf{A}, X_{n+1}).$$ Now to break the DPair assumption, we use the forking lemma on hash $H(\mathbf{A}, X_{n+1})$ to extract

another witness $\tilde{\underline{\Omega}}'$ such that $e\left(\left(\frac{\text{com}_{n+1}}{pk_i}\right)_{i=1}^n, \tilde{\underline{\Omega}}'\right) = e\left(\frac{P_2^{y'_{n+1}}}{X_{n+1}}, \tilde{P}\right)$ and $e(\underline{P}, \tilde{\underline{\Omega}}') = e(P, \tilde{P}^{c'})$ with $c' = H(\mathbf{A}, X_{n+1})$. Replacing $\text{com}_{n+1}$ with $P_1^{sk'_{n+1}} P_2^{r_{n+1}}$ and $pk_i$ with $P_1^{sk_i}$, and using the bilinearity of $e$, we get: $e\left(P_1, \prod_{i=1}^n \left(\frac{\tilde{\Omega}_i}{\tilde{\Omega}'_i}\right)^{(sk'_{n+1}-sk_i)}\right) e\left(P_2, \frac{P_2^{y'_{n+1}}}{P_2^{y_{n+1}}} \prod_{i=1}^n \left(\frac{\tilde{\Omega}_i}{\tilde{\Omega}'_i}\right)^{r_{n+1}}\right) = 1.$

$\mathcal{B}$ breaks DPair by outputting $\tilde{P}_1 = \prod_{i=1}^n \left(\frac{\tilde{\Omega}_i}{\tilde{\Omega}'_i}\right)^{(sk'_{n+1}-sk_i)}$ and $\tilde{P}_2 = \frac{P_2^{y'_{n+1}}}{P_2^{y_{n+1}}} \prod_{i=1}^n \left(\frac{\tilde{\Omega}_i}{\tilde{\Omega}'_i}\right)^{r_{n+1}} = \frac{P_2^{y'_{n+1}}}{P_2^{y_{n+1}}} \tilde{P}^{(c-c')r_{n+1}}$. Thanks to the Schwartz-Zippel lemma, we show that $\tilde{P}_1$ and $\tilde{P}_2$ are generators of $\mathbb{G}_2$ with probability $1 - 1/p$.

**Theorem 7.** *DualDory is prefix non-slanderable (Definition 13) in the random oracle model under the SXDH assumption.*

*Proof (Sketch).* Suppose there is an adversary $\mathcal{A}$ that breaks the prefix non-slanderability of DualDory. We construct, in the random oracle model, an adversary $\mathcal{B}$ which uses $\mathcal{A}$ to break the discrete logarithm in $\mathbb{G}_1$, which is implied by the SXDH assumption. Assume that $\mathcal{B}$ would like to compute $u = \log_P(U)$. Accordingly, $\mathcal{B}$ sets one of the signers' public key to $pk_j = U$, while generating the rest of the public keys honestly. To simulate answers to signing queries $(pk_j, m, \text{prfx})$ to oracle $\text{SO}_{pk}$ in the non-slanderability experiment, $\mathcal{B}$ programs $H'$ to return $P^{r'}$ as $H'(\text{prfx})$. This allows $\mathcal{B}$ to compute $\text{tag} = pk_j^{r'} = H'(\text{prfx})^{sk_j}$. $\mathcal{B}$ then leverages the simulatability of signatures of knowledge to simulate a tag proof that verifies correctly. Before any corruption query, $\mathcal{A}$ outputs forgery $(m', \text{prfx}', \sigma')$. $\mathcal{B}$ using random oracle $H'$ checks if the corresponding $\text{tag}' = pk_j^{r'}$ for some $r' \leftarrow \mathbb{Z}_p$. If so, then thanks to simulation extractability of tag proof, $\mathcal{B}$ extracts $sk_j = \log_P(U)$.

**Theorem 8.** *If a ring signature RS is prefix-linkable (Definition 12) and non-slanderable (Definition 13), then it is also unforgeable (Definition 10).*

*Proof (Sketch).* Assume that a ring signature RS is prefix linkable. We show in what follows that if there is an adversary $\mathcal{A}$ that wins the unforgeability game, then there is another adversary $\mathcal{B}$ that breaks non-slanderability. The intuition is that $\mathcal{B}$ simulates the unforgeability game for $\mathcal{A}$ using the game for non-slanderability. At the end of the simulated unforgeability game, $\mathcal{A}$ outputs a forgery $(m', \text{prfx}', \sigma')$, which $\mathcal{B}$ returns as the first forgery in the non-slanderability game (i.e., before any corruption query). $\mathcal{B}$ then queries signing oracle $\text{SO}_{pk}$ in the non-slanderability game with $n$ signing queries $(pk_i, m_i, \text{prfx}')$ for $i \in [n]$. Given the prefix linkability of RS, there exists $j \in [n]$ such that $\text{RS.Link}(\underline{pk}, m_j, \sigma_j, m', \sigma', \text{prfx}') = 1$, breaking thus non-slanderability. Similarly, we can show that if RS is non-slanderable, then $\mathcal{B}$ can break prefix linkability with the help of an adversary $\mathcal{A}$ that wins the unforgeability game.

# References

1. Dualdory implementation. https://github.com/yacovm/DualDory
2. Dualring implementation. https://github.com/DualDory/dualring
3. Full version of this work. https://dualdory.github.io/
4. Abe, M., Fuchsbauer, G., Groth, J., Haralambiev, K., Ohkubo, M.: Structure-preserving signatures and commitments to group elements. In: Rabin, T. (ed.) CRYPTO 2010. LNCS, vol. 6223, pp. 209–236. Springer, Heidelberg (2010). https://doi.org/10.1007/978-3-642-14623-7_12
5. Abe, M., Ohkubo, M., Suzuki, K.: 1-out-of-n signatures from a variety of keys, pp. 131–140 (2004)
6. Ateniese, G., Camenisch, J., Joye, M., Tsudik, G.: A practical and provably secure coalition-resistant group signature scheme. In: Bellare, M. (ed.) CRYPTO 2000. LNCS, vol. 1880, pp. 255–270. Springer, Heidelberg (2000). https://doi.org/10.1007/3-540-44598-6_16
7. Au, M.H., Chow, S.S.M., Susilo, W., Tsang, P.P.: Short linkable ring signatures revisited. In: Atzeni, A.S., Lioy, A. (eds.) EuroPKI 2006. LNCS, vol. 4043, pp. 101–115. Springer, Heidelberg (2006). https://doi.org/10.1007/11774716_9
8. Backes, M., Döttling, N., Hanzlik, L., Kluczniak, K., Schneider, J.: Ring signatures: logarithmic-size, no setup—from standard assumptions. In: Ishai, Y., Rijmen, V. (eds.) EUROCRYPT 2019. LNCS, vol. 11478, pp. 281–311. Springer, Cham (2019). https://doi.org/10.1007/978-3-030-17659-4_10
9. Barreto, P.S.L.M., Naehrig, M.: Pairing-friendly elliptic curves of prime order. In: Preneel, B., Tavares, S. (eds.) SAC 2005. LNCS, vol. 3897, pp. 319–331. Springer, Heidelberg (2006). https://doi.org/10.1007/11693383_22
10. Bellare, M., Neven, G.: New multi-signature schemes and a general forking lemma (2005)
11. Bender, A., Katz, J., Morselli, R.: Ring signatures: stronger definitions, and constructions without random oracles. In: Halevi, S., Rabin, T. (eds.) TCC 2006. LNCS, vol. 3876, pp. 60–79. Springer, Heidelberg (2006). https://doi.org/10.1007/11681878_4
12. Boneh, D., Boyen, X., Shacham, H.: Short group signatures. In: Franklin, M. (ed.) CRYPTO 2004. LNCS, vol. 3152, pp. 41–55. Springer, Heidelberg (2004). https://doi.org/10.1007/978-3-540-28628-8_3
13. Bootle, J., Cerulli, A., Chaidos, P., Groth, J., Petit, C.: Efficient zero-knowledge arguments for arithmetic circuits in the discrete log setting. In: Fischlin, M., Coron, J.-S. (eds.) EUROCRYPT 2016. LNCS, vol. 9666, pp. 327–357. Springer, Heidelberg (2016). https://doi.org/10.1007/978-3-662-49896-5_12
14. Botrel, G., Piellard, T., El Housni, Y., Tabaie, A., Kubjas, I.: Consensys/gnark-crypto: v0.6.1, February 2022
15. Bünz, B., Bootle, J., Boneh, D., Poelstra, A., Wuille, P., Maxwell, G.: Bulletproofs: short proofs for confidential transactions and more. In: IEEE Security & Privacy, pp. 315–334 (2018)
16. Chandran, N., Groth, J., Sahai, A.: Ring signatures of sub-linear size without random oracles. In: Arge, L., Cachin, C., Jurdziński, T., Tarlecki, A. (eds.) ICALP 2007. LNCS, vol. 4596, pp. 423–434. Springer, Heidelberg (2007). https://doi.org/10.1007/978-3-540-73420-8_38
17. Chase, M., Lysyanskaya, A.: On signatures of knowledge. In: Dwork, C. (ed.) CRYPTO 2006. LNCS, vol. 4117, pp. 78–96. Springer, Heidelberg (2006). https://doi.org/10.1007/11818175_5

18. Chaum, D., van Heyst, E.: Group signatures. In: Davies, D.W. (ed.) EUROCRYPT 1991. LNCS, vol. 547, pp. 257–265. Springer, Heidelberg (1991). https://doi.org/10.1007/3-540-46416-6_22

19. Chow, S.S.M., Susilo, W., Yuen, T.H.: Escrowed linkability of ring signatures and its applications. In: Nguyen, P.Q. (ed.) VIETCRYPT 2006. LNCS, vol. 4341, pp. 175–192. Springer, Heidelberg (2006). https://doi.org/10.1007/11958239_12

20. Dodis, Y., Kiayias, A., Nicolosi, A., Shoup, V.: Anonymous identification in *ad hoc* groups. In: Cachin, C., Camenisch, J.L. (eds.) EUROCRYPT 2004. LNCS, vol. 3027, pp. 609–626. Springer, Heidelberg (2004). https://doi.org/10.1007/978-3-540-24676-3_36

21. Goodell, B., Noether, S., RandomRun: Concise linkable ring signatures and forgery against adversarial keys. IACR Cryptol. ePrint Arch. (2019). https://ia.cr/2019/654

22. Groth, J., Kohlweiss, M.: One-out-of-many proofs: or how to leak a secret and spend a coin. In: Oswald, E., Fischlin, M. (eds.) EUROCRYPT 2015. LNCS, vol. 9057, pp. 253–280. Springer, Heidelberg (2015). https://doi.org/10.1007/978-3-662-46803-6_9

23. Lee, J.: Dory: efficient, transparent arguments for generalised inner products and polynomial commitments. In: Nissim, K., Waters, B. (eds.) TCC 2021. LNCS, vol. 13043, pp. 1–34. Springer, Cham (2021). https://doi.org/10.1007/978-3-030-90453-1_1

24. Liu, J.K., Wei, V.K., Wong, D.S.: Linkable spontaneous anonymous group signature for ad hoc groups. In: Wang, H., Pieprzyk, J., Varadharajan, V. (eds.) ACISP 2004. LNCS, vol. 3108, pp. 325–335. Springer, Heidelberg (2004). https://doi.org/10.1007/978-3-540-27800-9_28

25. Pointcheval, D., Sanders, O.: Short randomizable signatures. In: Sako, K. (ed.) CT-RSA 2016. LNCS, vol. 9610, pp. 111–126. Springer, Cham (2016). https://doi.org/10.1007/978-3-319-29485-8_7

26. Rivest, R.L., Shamir, A., Tauman, Y.: How to leak a secret. In: Boyd, C. (ed.) ASIACRYPT 2001. LNCS, vol. 2248, pp. 552–565. Springer, Heidelberg (2001). https://doi.org/10.1007/3-540-45682-1_32

27. Rotem, L., Segev, G.: Tighter security for Schnorr identification and signatures: a high-moment forking lemma for $\Sigma$-protocols. In: Malkin, T., Peikert, C. (eds.) CRYPTO 2021. LNCS, vol. 12825, pp. 222–250. Springer, Cham (2021). https://doi.org/10.1007/978-3-030-84242-0_9

28. Schoenmakers, B.: Lecture notes cryptographic protocols (2021). https://www.win.tue.nl/berry/2WC13/LectureNotes.pdf

29. Shoup, V.: Practical threshold signatures. In: Preneel, B. (ed.) EUROCRYPT 2000. LNCS, vol. 1807, pp. 207–220. Springer, Heidelberg (2000). https://doi.org/10.1007/3-540-45539-6_15

30. Tsang, P.P., Wei, V.K.: Short linkable ring signatures for E-voting, E-cash and attestation. In: Deng, R.H., Bao, F., Pang, H.H., Zhou, J. (eds.) ISPEC 2005. LNCS, vol. 3439, pp. 48–60. Springer, Heidelberg (2005). https://doi.org/10.1007/978-3-540-31979-5_5

31. Yuen, T.H., Esgin, M.F., Liu, J.K., Au, M.H., Ding, Z.: *DualRing*: generic construction of ring signatures with efficient instantiations. In: Malkin, T., Peikert, C. (eds.) CRYPTO 2021. LNCS, vol. 12825, pp. 251–281. Springer, Cham (2021). https://doi.org/10.1007/978-3-030-84242-0_10

32. Zhang, T., Wu, H., Chow, S.S.M.: Structure-preserving certificateless encryption and its application. In: Matsui, M. (ed.) CT-RSA 2019. LNCS, vol. 11405, pp. 1–22. Springer, Cham (2019). https://doi.org/10.1007/978-3-030-12612-4_1

# Efficient Unique Ring Signatures
# from Lattices

Tuong Ngoc Nguyen[1]([✉])[iD], Anh The Ta[3][iD], Huy Quoc Le[1,2][iD],
Dung Hoang Duong[1][iD], Willy Susilo[1][iD], Fuchun Guo[1][iD],
Kazuhide Fukushima[4][iD], and Shinsaku Kiyomoto[4][iD]

[1] School of Computing and Information Technology, University of Wollongong,
Northfields Avenue, Wollongong, NSW 2522, Australia
{ntn807,qhl576}@uowmail.edu.au, {hduong,wsusilo,fuchun}@uow.edu.au
[2] CSIRO Data61, Sydney, NSW, Australia
[3] AI Lab, FPT Software Ltd., Ho Chi Minh City, Vietnam
[4] Information Security Laboratory, KDDI Research, Inc., 2-1-15 Ohara, Fujimino-shi,
Saitama 356-8502, Japan
{ka-fukushima,kiyomoto}@kddi-research.jp

**Abstract.** Unique ring signatures (URS) were introduced by Franklin
and Zhang (FC 2012) as a unification of linkable and traceable ring signatures. In URS, each member within a ring can only produce, on behalf
of the ring, at most one signature for a message.

Applications of URS potentially are e–voting systems and e–token
systems. In blockchain technology, URS have been implemented for mixing contract. However, existing URS schemes are based on the Discrete
Logarithm Problem, which is insecure in the post-quantum setting.

In this paper, we design a new lattice-based URS scheme where the
signature size is logarithmic in number of ring members. The proposed
URS exploits a Merkle tree-based accumulator as building block in the
lattice setting. Our scheme is secure under the Short Integer Solution
and Learning With Rounding assumptions in the random oracle model.

**Keywords:** Unique ring signatures · Lattice-based cryptography ·
Merkle tree accumulator · Zero knowledge argument of knowledge

## 1 Introduction

Ring signatures (RS) were firstly introduced by Rivest, Shamir, and Tauman [16].
An RS of a group of signers (called the *ring*) is designed in such a way that any
member in the group can sign messages on behalf of the group, but no one
can tell who the real signer is. The ring can be dynamically formed by a signer
without the need of agreement from other members. Thus, besides *unforgeability*,
RS schemes offer the *anonymity* property.

© The Author(s), under exclusive license to Springer Nature Switzerland AG 2022
V. Atluri et al. (Eds.): ESORICS 2022, LNCS 13555, pp. 447–466, 2022.
https://doi.org/10.1007/978-3-031-17146-8_22

Unique ring signatures (URS) was firstly proposed by Franklin and Zhang [7, 8]. A URS signature has a part called *unique identifier*. A URS offers anonymity, unforgeability, and the so-called *uniqueness* property. The uniqueness property guarantees that $k$ colluding signers in the same ring cannot produce *more than* $k$ valid signatures for *the same* message. Compared to Linkable ring signature (LRS) firstly proposed [14], while in LRS two signatures are linked if they are signed with respect to the same ring, in URS, two signatures are linked if they are signed with respect to the same ring AND the same message. Informally speaking, In a URS, the anonymity of an uncorrupted user should be preserved as long as he/she does not issue 2 signatures with respect to the same pair (*message, ring*). It is not the case with LRS, since any 2 signatures of the same user are linked.

URS schemes are potentially used in the e-voting systems, e-token systems and $k$-times anonymous authentication applications mentioned above. Moreover, in the blockchain technology, Mercer proposed a mixing contract based on the URS. The author implemented the Franklin– Zhang URS protocol using the secp256k1 elliptic curve (EC). The implementation makes URS compatible with Bitcoin and Ethereum's EC libraries [15].

The rapid development of quantum algorithms, as well as the remarkable realization of quantum computers, not only offer more powerful computational devices but may also lead to severe threats to many modern cryptography schemes and protocols. Indeed, from a cryptographic point of view, Peter Shor [17] showed that all cryptosystems, which are based on the hardness of classical (number-theoretic) assumptions, e.g., the Integer Factorization Problem and the Discrete Logarithm Problem (DLP), will be broken as soon as large-scale quantum computers realized. To address this issue, there have been many proposed alternative hard problems that are believed to be quantum-resistant. Among others, lattice-based cryptography, firstly introduced by Ajtai [1], is emerging as a promising direction as it has better asymptotic efficiency than others and supports many advanced functionalities.

There exist several RS schemes in the literature over lattices regarding ring signatures [2,5,6,12]. However, there have been only URS constructions [7,8] that all base their security on the Computational Diffie-Hellman (CDH) and/or Decisional Diffie-Hellman (DDH) assumptions. The CDH and DDH, in turn, rely on the difficulty of the DLP problem. Hence, these schemes would be no longer secure in the quantum era. Moreover, these URS schemes, unfortunately, have the signature size of $\mathcal{O}(\lambda N)$ which is linear in $N$, where $\lambda$ is the security parameter, and $N$ is the number of members in the corresponding ring. Ta *et al.* [19] addressed this issue by proposing a URS scheme with logarithmic size. However, the signature scheme is only based on DDH and DLP problems. Therefore, it is essential to design new URS schemes that are not only based on alternative hard problems offering quantum safety but also more efficient in terms of signature size.

## 1.1   Contributions

We propose a logarithmic size URS scheme based on the hardness of the Short Integer Solution (SIS) and the Learning With Rounding (LWR) problems in lattices. The construction exploits the accumulator technique introduced by Libert et al. [12]. However, in order to obtain the uniqueness property, we add a *unique tag* to every node of the Merkle tree. Since the tag only needs to be computed once and then appended to every node, the extra computation cost is insignificant. Specifically, the signature size of the proposed URS scheme is $\mathcal{O}(\lambda \log N)$ where $\lambda$ is the security parameter, and $N$ is the number of members in the ring, versus $\mathcal{O}(\lambda N)$ in the schemes of Franklin and Zhang [8]. To the best of our knowledge, the scheme is the *first* lattice-based unique ring signature. Thus, the scheme is the first that is secure against classical adversaries basing the security proofs on post-quantum assumptions. Moreover, in comparison with most of existing URS schemes, our signature size is much smaller since it is logarithmic in the number of ring members. In Table 1, we make a comparison of existing URS schemes with ours.

**Table 1.** Comparison our URS with the [7,8] URSs

| URS schemes | Assumptions | Security model | Signature size | Based on post-quantum assumptions? |
|---|---|---|---|---|
| Franklin and Zhang [7] | CDH + DDH | ROM/SDM | Linear | ✗ |
| Franklin and Zhang [8] | DDH | ROM | Linear | ✗ |
| Ta et al. [19] | DDH + DLP | ROM | Logarithmic | ✗ |
| **Ours** | SIS + LWR | ROM | Logarithmic | ✓ |

## 1.2   Overview of the Results

Our key idea is to transform lattice-based ring signatures with logarithmic size to get the desired unique ring signatures. To this end, we embed the so-called *unique tag* (a.k.a., *unique identifier*) into the ring signature schemes. A unique tag corresponding to a signer can be computed using a weak pseudorandom function. Namely, if we denote the hash function (modelled as a random oracle) being used here by $H_{\mathsf{UT}}$, a weak pseudorandom function $\mathsf{F}$, a message by $\mu$, a ring of signers by $R$, and the secret key for a signer by $sk$, then the uniqueness tag for the signer is of the form $\mathbf{t} := \mathsf{F}_{sk}(H_{\mathsf{UT}}(\mu, R))$. Our starting point is a Merkle tree-based accumulator used in the LLNW ring signature in lattices [12]. Intuitively, the Merkle tree there looks like a binary tree but travelling via the bottom-up direction. The leaves' values are ones that we want to accumulate, while the root corresponds to the accumulator value. See Fig. 1 for an illustration of how data values $\mathbf{p}_0, \cdots, \mathbf{p}_7$ are accumulated into the value $\mathbf{v}_\epsilon$. The associated hash function used to accumulate is denoted by $h_\mathbf{A}$, being indicated by a random matrix $\mathbf{A} := [\mathbf{A}_0|\mathbf{A}_1] \in \mathbb{Z}_q^{n \times m/2} \times \in \mathbb{Z}_q^{n \times m/2}$. Formally, $h_\mathbf{A}(\mathbf{v}) := \mathsf{bin}(\mathbf{A}_0\mathbf{v}_0 + \mathbf{A}_1\mathbf{v}_1 \pmod{q}) \in \{0,1\}^{m/2}$, for any vector $\mathbf{v} := (\mathbf{v}_0, \mathbf{v}_1) \in \{0,1\}^{m/2} \times \{0,1\}^{m/2}$. Here, bin denotes the binary decomposition operation. Such a hash function is proved to be collision-resistant under the hardness of the Short Integer Solution (SIS) problem.

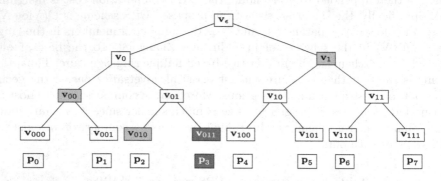

**Fig. 1.** An illustration for Merkle tree-based accumulator in [12], in which $2^3$ data values $\mathbf{p}_0, \cdots, \mathbf{p}_7$ are accumulated into the value $\mathbf{v}_\epsilon$. It works as follows. First, it assigns data values $\mathbf{p}_i$'s to the leaves of the tree (at depth 3) and re-names it as $\mathbf{v}_{i_1,i_2,i_3}$ where $(i_1, i_2, i_3) = \mathsf{bin}_3(i) \in \{0,1\}^3$, i.e., $\mathbf{v}_{i_1,i_2,i_3} \leftarrow \mathbf{p}_i$. At depth 3, it accumulates the pair $(\mathbf{v}_{000} := \mathbf{p}_0, \mathbf{v}_{001} := \mathbf{p}_1)$ to get $\mathbf{v}_{00}$. Similarly for $(\mathbf{v}_{010} := \mathbf{p}_2, \mathbf{v}_{011} := \mathbf{p}_3)$, $(\mathbf{v}_{010} := \mathbf{p}_4, \mathbf{v}_{011} := \mathbf{p}_5)$, $(\mathbf{v}_{010} := \mathbf{p}_6, \mathbf{v}_{011} := \mathbf{p}_7)$ to get $\mathbf{v}_{01}, \mathbf{v}_{10}, \mathbf{v}_{11}$, respectively. At depth 2, it continues to accumulate two pairs $(\mathbf{v}_{00}, \mathbf{v}_{01})$, $(\mathbf{v}_{10}, \mathbf{v}_{11})$ to get $\mathbf{v}_0$ and $\mathbf{v}_1$, respectively. Finally, at depth 3, $(\mathbf{v}_0, \mathbf{v}_1)$ is accumulated to $\mathbf{v}_\epsilon$ located at the root of the tree. The witness for the fact that $\mathbf{p}_3$ (i.e., $\mathbf{v}_{011}$) (dark grey-filled boxes) has been accumulated is wit $= \{011, \{\mathbf{v}_{010}, \mathbf{v}_{00}, \mathbf{v}_1\}\}$ (light grey-filled boxes).

To transform the ring signature in [12] to a URS, we modify the Merkle tree and the corresponding hash function. The modified Merke tree will also allow to accumulate the uniqueness tag $\mathbf{t}$. Specifically, for each hashing time in the modified Merkle tree, each of two inputs is also appended to the uniqueness tag $\mathbf{t}$. For instance, the inputs now are $(\mathbf{v}_0^\top|\mathbf{t}^\top)$, $(\mathbf{v}_1^\top|\mathbf{t}^\top)$ instead of $(\mathbf{v}_0, \mathbf{v}_1)$. (See Fig. 2 for the modified Merkle tree illustration used in our URS.) Accordingly, the hash function $h_\mathbf{A}$ will be changed to be

$$h_{\mathbf{A},\mathbf{B},\mathbf{t}}(\mathbf{v}_0, \mathbf{v}_1) := \mathsf{bin}(\mathbf{A}_0\mathbf{v}_0 + \mathbf{A}_1\mathbf{v}_1 + \mathbf{B}_0\mathbf{t} + \mathbf{B}_1\mathbf{t} \pmod{q}) \in \{0,1\}^{nk},$$

where $\mathbf{B} = [\mathbf{B}_0|\mathbf{B}_1] \leftarrow H_{\mathsf{UT}}(\mu, R)$. Since $\mathbf{B}$ and $\mathbf{t}$ are fixed as constants then by a simple reduction, we can prove that $h_{\mathbf{A},\mathbf{B},\mathbf{t}}$ is also collision-resistant assuming the hardness of the average case SIS assumption in lattices.

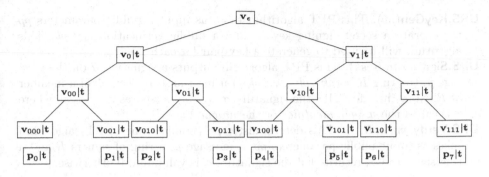

**Fig. 2.** The modified Merkle tree-based accumulator for our unique ring signatures.

In this paper, we consider the following relation:

$$\mathcal{R}_{\mathsf{URS}} := \{(\mathbf{A}, \mathbf{B}, \mathbf{v}) \in \mathbb{Z}_q^{n \times m} \times \mathbb{Z}_q^{n \times m} \times \{0,1\}^{nk};$$
$$\mathbf{x} \in \{0,1\}^m, \mathbf{p} \in \{0,1\}^{nk}, \mathbf{t} \in \{0,1\}^{nk}, \mathsf{wit} \in \{0,1\}^{\ell} \times (\{0,1\}^{nk})^{\ell} :$$
$$\mathsf{ACC.Verify}_{\mathbf{A}}(\mathbf{B}, \mathbf{t}, \mathbf{v}, \mathbf{p}, \mathsf{wit}) = 1 \wedge \mathbf{A}\mathbf{x} = \mathbf{G}\mathbf{p} \wedge \mathsf{F}_{\mathbf{x}}(\mathbf{B}) = \mathbf{G}\mathbf{t}\}.$$

Here, the *gadget matrix* $\mathbf{G}$ is a special matrix with property that $\mathbf{G} \cdot \mathsf{bin}(\mathbf{a}) = \mathbf{a}$. We are therefore able to utilize the same "extend-then-permute" technique done for $\mathcal{R}_{\mathsf{ring}}$ to handle the ZKAoK for $\mathcal{R}_{\mathsf{URS}}$. The details of the induced URS will be presented in Sect. 4. Due to space limitation, we omit the proofs for lemmata and theorems in the paper. We provide these proofs in the full version.

## 2 Preliminaries

**Notation.** Throughout this work, all vectors are in column form unless otherwise stated. A vector is written in bold-face small letter, e.g., $\mathbf{v}$, while a matrix in bold-face capital letter, e.g., $\mathbf{A}$. The transpose operation of a vector or a matrix denoted by the superscript $\top$; e.g., transpose of vector $\mathbf{v}$ is $\mathbf{v}^{\top}$. For $k \in \mathbb{N}$, the notation $[k]$ means $\{1, \ldots, k\}$. We denote by $|S|$ the cardinality of a discrete set $S$.

### 2.1 Framework of Unique Ring Signatures

We first recall the framework of URS as introduced by Franklin and Zhang in [7,8].

**Syntax.** A URS scheme consists of four algorithms URS = (URS.Setup, URS.KeyGen, URS.Sign, URS.Verify) described as follows.

**URS.Setup$(1^{\lambda})$.** This probabilistic polynomial time (PPT) algorithm takes as input a security parameter $\lambda$ to output public parameters $pp$.

**URS.KeyGen**$(pp)$. This PPT algorithm takes as input a public parameters $pp$ to generate a secret signing key $sk$ and a public verification key $pk$. This algorithm will be used to generate a key pair for each user.

**URS.Sign**$(pp, \mu, R, sk)$. This PPT algorithm outputs a signature $\sigma$ on the message $\mu$, the ring $R = (pk_1, pk_2, \ldots, pk_N)$ using the secret key $sk$ of a member of $R$. Note that, for URS the signature $\sigma$ can be parsed as $\sigma = (\tau, \pi)$ where $\tau$ is called the *unique identifier* or the *unique tag*.

**URS.Verify**$(pp, \mu, R, \sigma)$. This deterministic polynomial time (DPT) algorithm takes as input public parameters $pp$, a message $\mu$, a ring of signers $R$ and a ring signature $\sigma$, returns 1 if the signature $\sigma$ is valid, and 0 otherwise.

**Definition 1 (Correctness).** *For any $pp \leftarrow$ URS.Setup$(1^\lambda)$, any integer $N$, $i = 1, 2, \ldots, N : (pk_i, sk_i) \leftarrow$ URS.KeyGen$(pp)$, and $R = \{pk_1, pk_2, \ldots, pk_N\}$, for any message $\mu$ and any member $(pk_j, sk_j)$ of $R$, the correctness of a URS holds that*

$$\text{URS.Verify}(pp, \mu, R, \text{URS.Sign}(pp, \mu, R, sk_j)) = 1.$$

In order to formally define the security notions, we need some further definitions.

**Queried Oracles.** Given $\{(pk_i, sk_i)\}_{i=1}^N$ and a ring $S = \{pk_i\}_{i=1}^N$ for reference, the adversaries can have access to one or more of the following oracles depending the security they involve:

- **The user secret key oracle** $\mathcal{O}_{sk}(i)$: Output the secret key $sk_i$ of some member $i$ in $R$.
- **The ring signature oracle** $\mathcal{O}_{Sign}(i, R, \mu)$: Output the ring signature on message $\mu$ respective to a subring $R \subseteq S$, in which $pk_i \in R$ is the real signer.

In addition to the above oracles, we need some more notations below.

- SIGNER$_{R,\mu}$ denotes a set of users (i.e., secret keys) that have been queried to $\mathcal{O}_{Sign}(\cdot, R, \mu)$ by the adversary.
- $\overrightarrow{\text{SIGNER}}_{\mathcal{R},\mathcal{M}} := \{\text{SIGNER}_{R,\mu} : R \in \mathcal{R}, \mu \in \mathcal{M}\}$ where $\mathcal{R}$ is a set of rings and $\mathcal{M}$ a set of messages.
- Corrupt denotes the set of all users whose secret keys are given to the adversary.
- Also, Corrupt$_R$ denotes the set of all users *in the ring $R$*, whose secret keys are given to the adversary.

We now give formal definitions for the URS security notions.

---

$\underline{\text{URS}_{\mathcal{A},N}^{\text{Anom}}}$:

**Setup.** The challenger $\mathcal{C}$ runs URS.Setup($1^\lambda$) on input a security parameter $\lambda$, to get public parameters $pp$. Now, the challenger runs URS.KeyGen($pp$) to get a key pair $(pk_i, sk_i) \leftarrow$ URS.KeyGen($pp$) for each user $i = 1, 2, \ldots, N$. Then $\mathcal{C}$ sets $S = \{pk_i\}_{i=1}^N$ and hands $(pp, S)$ to $\mathcal{A}$. The challenger also sets Corrupt $\leftarrow \emptyset$ and $\overrightarrow{\text{SIGNER}}_{\mathcal{R},\mathcal{M}} \leftarrow \emptyset$.

**Query 1.** $\mathcal{A}$ may make polynomially bounded number of queries to the oracles $\mathcal{O}_{sk}$ and $\mathcal{O}_{Sign}$, and $\mathcal{C}$ responses it in the way mentioned above. Meanwhile, $\mathcal{C}$ updates the sets Corrupt and $\overrightarrow{\text{SIGNER}}_{\mathcal{R},\mathcal{M}}$.

**Challenge.** $\mathcal{A}$ chooses two indices $i_0, i_1$ together with a message $\mu^*$ and a ring $R^* \subseteq S$ such that $i_0, i_1 \notin$ Corrupt and $i_0, i_1 \notin$ SIGNER$_{R^*,\mu^*}$, and sends the tuple $(i_0, i_1, \mu^*, R^*)$ to $\mathcal{C}$. Then $\mathcal{C}$ choosed uniformly at random a bit $b \leftarrow \{0, 1\}$ and runs $\sigma \leftarrow$ URS.Sign($\mu^*, R^*, sk_{i_b}$). The challenger returns $\sigma$ to $\mathcal{A}$.

**Query 2.** Same as **Query 1**, with restriction that $\mathcal{A}$ is not allowed to query to $\mathcal{O}_{sk}(i_0)$, $\mathcal{O}_{sk}(i_1)$, and signing queries $\mathcal{O}_{Sign}(i_0, \mu^*, R^*)$, $\mathcal{O}_{Sign}(i_1, \mu^*, R^*)$.

**Guess.** $\mathcal{A}$ outputs a guess $b'$ for $b$. $\mathcal{A}$ wins if and only if $b' = b$.

**Fig. 3.** Anonymity experiment for URS

---

$\underline{\text{URS}_{\mathcal{A},N}^{\text{Unforge}}}$:

**Setup.** Same as **Setup** of URS$_{\mathcal{A},N}^{\text{Anom}}$.
**Query.** Same as **Query 1** of URS$_{\mathcal{A},N}^{\text{Anom}}$.
**Forge.** The adversary $\mathcal{A}$ outputs a ring signature $\sigma^*$ on a message $\mu^*$ and a ring $R^* \subseteq S$, with the condition that $R^*$ does not contain corrupted users (i.e., $R^* \subseteq S \setminus$ Corrupt), and $\mathcal{A}$ has never made queries $\mathcal{O}_{Sign}(\cdot, R^*, \mu^*)$ before. $\mathcal{A}$ wins the game if and only if URS.Verify($\mu^*, R^*, \sigma^*$) = 1.

**Fig. 4.** Unforgeability experiment for URS

**Definition 2 (Anonymity).** *A URS is called anonymous if for any polynomial-time adversary $\mathcal{A}$, the advantage $\text{Adv}_{\mathcal{A},N}^{\text{URS,Anom}}(\lambda)$ of $\mathcal{A}$ in the Anonymity experiment* URS$_{\mathcal{A},N}^{\text{Anom}}$ *presented in Fig. 3 is negligible. That is,* $\text{Adv}_{\mathcal{A},N}^{\text{URS,Anom}}(\lambda) := 2 |\Pr[b' = b] - 1/2| = \text{negl}(\lambda)$.

**Definition 3 (Unforgeability).** *A URS is called unforgeable under adaptive chosen-message attacks if for any PPT adversary $\mathcal{A}$, the advantage* $\text{Adv}_{\mathcal{A},N}^{\text{URS,Unforge}}(\lambda)$ *of $\mathcal{A}$ in the Unforgeability experiment* URS$_{\mathcal{A},N}^{\text{Unforge}}$ *presented in Fig. 4 is negligible. That is,*

$$\text{Adv}_{\mathcal{A},N}^{\text{URS,Unforge}}(\lambda) := \Pr[\mathcal{A} \text{ wins}] = \text{negl}(\lambda).$$

---

$\underline{\mathsf{URS}^{\mathsf{Unique}}_{\mathcal{A},N}}:$

**Setup.** Same as **Setup** of $\mathsf{URS}^{\mathsf{Anom}}_{\mathcal{A},N}$.

**Query.** Same as **Query 1** of $\mathsf{URS}^{\mathsf{Anom}}_{\mathcal{A},N}$.

**Forge.** The adversary $\mathcal{A}$ outputs $t := |\mathsf{Corrupt}_{R^*} \cup \mathsf{SIGNER}_{R^*,\mu^*}| + 1$ different valid signatures $\sigma_1, \ldots, \sigma_t$ on the same message $\mu^*$ in regards the same ring $R^*$. The challenger parses the signatures as $\sigma_j = (\tau_j, \pi_j)$, and checks whether the unique tags $\tau_k$, $k = 1, 2, \ldots, t$, are pairwise distinct. If this is the case, then the challenger returns 1 and $\mathcal{A}$ wins; otherwise, returns 0 and $\mathcal{A}$ loses.

---

**Fig. 5.** Uniqueness experiment for URS

**Definition 4 (Uniqueness).** *A URS is called unique if for any PPT adversary $\mathcal{A}$, the advantage $\mathsf{Adv}^{\mathsf{URS},\mathsf{Unique}}_{\mathcal{A},N}(\lambda)$ of $\mathcal{A}$ in the Uniqueness experiment $\mathsf{URS}^{\mathsf{Unique}}_{\mathcal{A},N}$ presented in Fig. 5 is negligible. That is,*

$$\mathsf{Adv}^{\mathsf{URS},\mathsf{Unique}}_{\mathcal{A},N}(\lambda) := \Pr[\mathcal{A} \ wins] = \mathsf{negl}(\lambda).$$

Additionally, a URS is also required to satisfy the *non-colliding property*. Note that the non-colliding property is not a security requirement.

**Definition 5 (Non-colliding property).** *For all $i \neq j$, a URS scheme is non-colliding when the probability*

$$\Pr[\sigma_i = (\tau_i, \pi_i) \leftarrow \mathsf{URS.Sign}(\mu, R, sk_i), \sigma_j = (\tau_j, \pi_j) \leftarrow \mathsf{URS.Sign}(\mu, R, sk_j) : \tau_i = \tau_j]$$

*is negligible to the security parameter $\lambda$.*

**Definition 6 (Security of URS).** *A URS is called secure if it satisfies the correctness and the non-colliding property, and it is unforgeable, anonymous as well as unique.*

## 2.2 Lattices and Hardness Assumptions

An integer lattice $\mathcal{L}$ is a discrete subgroup which can be represented as $\mathcal{L} = \mathcal{L}(\mathbf{B}) := \{\mathbf{Bx} : \mathbf{x} \in \mathbb{Z}^m\}$, where $\mathbf{B} \in \mathbb{Z}^{n \times m}$ is a basis of $\mathcal{L}$. The lattice $\mathcal{L}$ is called *full-rank* if $n = m$.

**Definition 7 (SIS, [1,9]).** *Short Integer Solution problem $\mathsf{SIS}^{\infty}_{m,n,q,\theta}$ is, given matrix $\mathbf{A} \xleftarrow{\$} \mathbb{Z}^{n \times m}_q$, to find $\mathbf{x} \in \mathbb{Z}^m$ such that $\mathbf{Ax} = 0 \pmod{q}$ and $0 < \|\mathbf{x}\|_\infty \leq \theta$.*

**Definition 8 (Decision-LWR, [3]).** *For a vector $\mathbf{s} \in \mathbb{Z}^n_q$, define the LWR distribution $\mathcal{L}_s$ to be the distribuiton over $\mathbb{Z}^n_q \times \mathbb{Z}_p$ obtained by choosing a vector $\mathbf{a} \xleftarrow{\$} \mathbb{Z}^n_q$ and outputting $(\mathbf{a}, b = \lfloor \langle \mathbf{a} \cdot \mathbf{s} \rangle \rceil_p)$. The decision-$\mathsf{LWR}_{n,m,q,p}$ is to distinguish between $m$ independent samples $(\mathbf{a}_i, b_i) \leftarrow \mathcal{L}_s$, and $m$ samples drawn uniformly and independently from $\mathbb{Z}^n_q \times \mathbb{Z}_p$. We denote the advanatge of an LWR solver $\mathcal{S}$ by $\mathsf{Adv}^{\mathsf{LWR}}(\mathcal{S})$.*

**Lemma 1 (Leftover Hash Lemma).** *Given $m, n$ are positive integers, $q \geq 2$ is a prime such that $m \geq 2n \log q$, and that $\mathbf{x} \xleftarrow{\$} \{0,1\}^m, \mathbf{A} \xleftarrow{\$} \mathbb{Z}_q^{n \times m}, \mathbf{y} \xleftarrow{\$} \mathbb{Z}_q^n$, the distribution $(\mathbf{A}, \mathbf{A} \cdot \mathbf{x})$ is statistically close to the distribution $(\mathbf{A}, \mathbf{y})$.*

*Proof.* An unbounded adversary $\mathcal{A}$ can guess $\mathbf{x}$ correctly with the probability $v = 1/2^m \leq 1/(2^{2n \log q})$. Because the range size is $|\Omega| = q^n = 2^{n \log q}$, the distinguishing advantage of $\mathcal{A}$ is bounded by $v \cdot |\Omega| = 1/q^n = \mathsf{negl}(n)$.

## 2.3 Accumulator Schemes

**Syntax.** An accumulator consists of the following algorithms:

$pp \leftarrow$ **ACC.Setup**$(1^\lambda)$: It takes as input a security parameter $\lambda$ to output public parameters $pp$.

$\mathbf{v} \leftarrow$ **ACC.Acc**$(pp, R)$: It takes as input public parameters pp, a list of $N$ data values $R = (\mathbf{p}_1, \cdots, \mathbf{p}_{N-1})$ to output an accumulator value $\mathbf{v}$ for $R$.

**wit** $\leftarrow$ **ACC.Witness**$(pp, R, \mathbf{p})$: It takes as input public parameters pp, a list of $N$ data values $R = (\mathbf{p}_1, \cdots, \mathbf{p}_{N-1})$ and a data value $\mathbf{p}$. It outputs $\perp$ if $\mathbf{p} \notin R$. Otherwise, it outputs a witness wit proving that $\mathbf{p}$ has been accumulated in ACC.Acc.

$0/1 \leftarrow$ **ACC.Verify**$(pp, \mathbf{v}, \mathbf{p}, \mathbf{wit})$: It takes as input public parameters $pp$, a pair $(\mathbf{p}, \mathbf{wit})$. It outputs 1 if $(\mathbf{p}, \mathbf{wit})$ is valid for the accumulator value $\mathbf{v}$ and outputs 0 otherwise.

**Correctness.** It is required for ACC that for all $pp \leftarrow$ ACC.Setup$(1^\lambda)$, $\mathbf{v} \leftarrow$ ACC.Acc$(pp, R)$, wit $\leftarrow$ ACC.Witness$(pp, R, \mathbf{p})$, it holds that

$$\mathbf{ACC.Verify}(pp, \mathbf{v}, \mathbf{p}, \mathsf{wit}) = 1, \text{ for all } \mathbf{p} \in R.$$

**Security.** An accumulator scheme is called secure if for all PPT adversaries $\mathcal{A}$:

$$\Pr[pp \leftarrow \mathsf{ACC.Setup}(1^\lambda); (R, \mathbf{p}^*, \mathsf{wit}^*) \leftarrow \mathcal{A}(pp) :$$
$$\mathbf{p}^* \notin R \wedge \mathsf{ACC.Verify}(pp, \mathsf{ACC.Acc}(pp, R), \mathbf{p}^*, \mathsf{wit}^*) = 1] = \mathsf{negl}(\lambda).$$

## 2.4 String Commitment Schemes

In this work, we also exploit the so-called *string commitment function*. We need it to be *statistically hiding* and *computationally binding*. The first property ensures that any computationally unbounded adversarial receiver cannot distinguish two commitment strings generated from two distinct strings. The second property says that no polynomial-time algorithm can change the committed string after sending the commitment. See [10,11] for more details.

In lattices, such a string commitment scheme comes from Kawachi et al. [11]. It is statistically hiding and computationally binding if the $\mathsf{SIS}_{m,n,q,\theta}^\infty$ problem is hard. We will denote it by $\mathsf{COM} : \{0,1\}^* \times \{0,1\}^m \rightarrow \mathbb{Z}_q^n$ and use it for the ZKAoK, which is generally described later in Sect. 2.5.

## 2.5   Zero Knowledge Arguments of Knowledge (ZKAoK)

Let $\mathcal{R} := \{(\mathsf{stm}, \mathsf{wit}) \in \{0,1\}^* \times \{0,1\}^*\}$ be a polynomial time decidable binary relation for a language $\mathcal{L}$ in the NP class. We call $\mathsf{wit}$ a witness for a statement $\mathsf{stm} \in \mathcal{L}$ if $(\mathsf{stm}, \mathsf{wit}) \in \mathcal{R}$.

A *statistical* zero knowledge arguments (ZKA) system for the relation $\mathcal{R}$ with soundness error $\epsilon$ is an interactive system $(\mathcal{P}, \mathcal{V})$ between a prover $\mathcal{P}$ and a verifier $\mathcal{V}$ endowed with the following properties:

1. **Completeness:** If $(\mathsf{stm}, \mathsf{wit}) \in \mathcal{R}$ then $\Pr[(\mathcal{P}(\mathsf{stm}, \mathsf{wit}), \mathcal{V}(\mathsf{stm})) = 1] = 1$.
2. **$\epsilon$-Soundness:** If $(\mathsf{stm}, \mathsf{wit}) \notin \mathcal{R}$ then for all PPT $\mathcal{P}^*$, $\mathsf{Adv}_{(\mathcal{P}, \mathcal{V})}^{\mathsf{sound}}(\mathcal{P}^*) :=$ $\Pr[(\mathcal{P}^*(\mathsf{stm}, \mathsf{wit}), \mathcal{V}(\mathsf{stm})) = 1] \leq \epsilon$. Here, note that $\mathcal{P}^*$ is a *computationally bounded* cheating prover.
3. **Statistical zero-knowledge:** For any $\mathcal{V}^*(\mathsf{stm})$, there exists a PPT simulator $\mathcal{S}(\mathsf{stm}))$ who is able to simulate a transcript[1] statistically close to the transcript produced by the real interaction between $\mathcal{P}$ and $\mathcal{V}^*$. We define the advantage of $\mathcal{V}^*$ who can break the statistical zero-knowledge by $\mathsf{Adv}_{(\mathcal{P}, \mathcal{V})}^{\mathsf{zk}}(\mathcal{V}^*)$.

The notion of *Argument of Knowledge* is related to the so-called witness-extended emulation [13]. Informally stating, the witness-extended emulation requires that given an adversary that produces an acceptable argument with some probability, there exists an emulator that produces a similar argument with the same probability together with a witness $\mathsf{wit}$. Note that the emulator can rewind the prover and verifier's interaction to any previous move. See [4, Def. 7] for a formal definition.

## 2.6   Weak Pseudorandom Function (wPRF)

In [20], a weak pseudorandom function under the LWR hardness assumtion was proposed. More precisely, let $n, m, p, q$ are positive integers, $p \geq 2, \gamma = q/p$ is an odd integer and $m \geq n(\log q + 1)(\log p - 1)$, a wPRF $\mathsf{F}$ is described as below:

- KeyGen($1^\lambda$). The algorithm takes as input a security parameter $\lambda$, and outputs $\mathbf{x} \xleftarrow{\$} \mathbb{Z}_q^m$.
- Eval($\mathbf{x}, \mathbf{A}$). The algorithm takes as input $\mathbf{A} \xleftarrow{\$} \mathbb{Z}_q^{n \times m}$, and outputs $\mathsf{F}_{\mathbf{x}}(\mathbf{A}) = \lfloor \mathbf{A}\mathbf{x} \rfloor_p$.

**Lemma 2** ([20]). *If the $LWR_{n,p,q}$ assumption holds, and $m \geq n(\log q + 1)(\log p - 1)$, then $\mathsf{F}$ is a secure wPRF.*

We adapt the domain of $\mathbf{x}$ to $\{0,1\}^m$ in this paper. A wRPF $\mathsf{F}$ has the following properties:

---

[1] Roughly speaking, transcript is what the prover and the verifier have exchanged in a complete interaction.

- Weak Pseudorandomness. Let $\mathbf{x}_1 \leftarrow \mathsf{KeyGen}(1^\lambda)$, $\mathbf{A} \xleftarrow{\$} \mathbb{Z}_q^{n\times m}$, $\mathbf{y}_1 = F_{\mathbf{x}}(\mathbf{A})$ and $\mathbf{x}_2 \xleftarrow{\$} \{0,1\}^m$, $\mathbf{y}_2 \xleftarrow{\$} \mathbb{Z}_p^n$, any PPT adversary $\mathcal{A}$ successfully distinguishes $(\mathbf{x}_1, \mathbf{y}_1)$ and $(\mathbf{x}_2, \mathbf{y}_2)$ with negligible probability.
- Strong Uniqueness. Let $\mathbf{x}_1, \mathbf{x}_2 \leftarrow \mathsf{KeyGen}(1^\lambda)$ be two secret keys, and two random matrices $\mathbf{A}_1, \mathbf{A}_2 \xleftarrow{\$} \mathbb{Z}_q^{n\times m}$, if we require $m \geq 2n(\log q + 1)(\log p - 1)$, we have:

$$\Pr[\exists \mathbf{x}_1, \mathbf{x}_2, \mathbf{x}_1 \neq \mathbf{x}_2 \wedge F_{\mathbf{x}_1}(\mathbf{A}_1) = F_{\mathbf{x}_2}(\mathbf{A}_2)] \leq \mathsf{negl}(\lambda).$$

# 3   The Underlying Accumulator for Our URS

Aiming to apply the lattice-based accumulator to constructing a unique ring signature, we will build a modified Merkle tree and a corresponding family of hash functions. Now the Merkle tree also allows us to accumulate the unique tag $\mathbf{t} := \mathsf{bin}(H_{\mathsf{UT}}(\mu, R) \cdot \mathbf{x})$, where $\mu$ is a message, $R$ is a ring of signers and $\mathbf{x}$ is the secret key for the real signer (see Fig. 2 for the modified Merkle tree used in our URS). Accordingly, we take into account the family of hash functions formally defined in Definition 9 below.

**Definition 9.** *Let* $k := \lceil \log q \rceil$, *and* $m := 2nk$. *Fix a message* $M$ *and a ring* $R$, *we define a family of hash functions as follows:*

$$\mathcal{H}_{\mathbf{B},\mathbf{t}} = \{h_{\mathbf{A},\mathbf{B},\mathbf{t}} : \mathbf{A} := [\mathbf{A}_0|\mathbf{A}_1] \xleftarrow{\$} \mathbb{Z}_q^{n\times nk} \times \mathbb{Z}_q^{n\times nk}, \mathbf{B} := [\mathbf{B}_0|\mathbf{B}_1] \in \mathbb{Z}_q^{n\times nk} \times$$
$$\mathbb{Z}_q^{n\times nk}, \mathbf{t} \in \{0,1\}^{nk}\} \text{ mapping from } \{0,1\}^{nk} \times \{0,1\}^{nk} \text{ to } \{0,1\}^{nk} \text{ such that}$$

$$h_{\mathbf{A},\mathbf{B},\mathbf{t}}(\mathbf{v}_0, \mathbf{v}_1) := \mathsf{bin}(\mathbf{A}_0\mathbf{v}_0 + \mathbf{A}_1\mathbf{v}_1 + \mathbf{B}_0\mathbf{t} + \mathbf{B}_1\mathbf{t} \pmod{q}) \in \{0,1\}^{nk}.$$

*Note that* $h_{\mathbf{A},\mathbf{B},\mathbf{t}}(\mathbf{v}_0, \mathbf{v}_1) = \mathbf{v}$ *is equivalent to* $\mathbf{A}_0\mathbf{v}_0 + \mathbf{A}_1\mathbf{v}_1 + \mathbf{B}_0\mathbf{t} + \mathbf{B}_1\mathbf{t} = \mathbf{G}\mathbf{v} \pmod{q}$.

**Lemma 3.** *The family* $\mathcal{H}_{\mathbf{B},\mathbf{t}}$ *defined in Definition 9 is collision-resistant assuming the hardness of the* $\mathsf{SIS}_{m,n,q,\theta}^\infty$.

## 3.1   The Parameterized Lattice-Based Accumulator Scheme

Let $N = 2^\ell$ be a positive integer for some $\ell \in \mathbb{N}$. Let $\mathsf{bin}_\ell(\cdot)$ be the binary decomposition mapping an integer $i \in 0, \cdots, 2^\ell - 1$ to a bit string in $\{0,1\}^\ell$. For example, $011 \leftarrow \mathsf{bin}_3(3)$, while $11 \leftarrow \mathsf{bin}_2(3)$.

The accumulator we consider in this work is parametrized by a matrix $\mathbf{B} \in \mathbb{Z}_q^{n\times 2nk}$ and a vector $\mathbf{t} \in \{0,1\}^{nk}$, where $k = \lceil \log q \rceil$. We call it the *parameterized accumulator* (or PACC for short). The PACC works as follows:

$pp \leftarrow$ **PACC.Setup**$(n)$**:** On input a security parameter $n$, do:
  1. Choose $q$. Let $k := \lceil \log_2 q \rceil$, $m := 2nk$, $N = 2^\ell$.
  2. Sample $\mathbf{A} \xleftarrow{\$} \mathbb{Z}_q^{n\times m}$ and output $pp := \mathbf{A}$.

$\mathbf{v} \leftarrow$ **PACC.Acc**$_{pp}(\mathbf{B}, \mathbf{t}, R)$: On input public parameters $pp$ and a list $R :=$ $\{\mathbf{p}_0, \cdots, \mathbf{p}_{N-1}\}$ with $N = 2^\ell$ for some $\ell$, do:

1. For $i \in \{0, N-1\}$, assign $\mathbf{v}_{i_1, \cdots, i_\ell} \leftarrow \mathbf{p}_i$, where $(i_1, \cdots, i_\ell) \in \{0, 1\}^\ell \leftarrow$ $\text{bin}_\ell(i)$.
2. Build a Merkle tree of depth $\ell$ whose leaves are $\mathbf{v}_{0,0,\cdots,0}, \cdots, \mathbf{v}_{1,1,\cdots,1}$.
3. At depth $i \in [\ell]$, for $j \in \{0, i-1\}$, the value of the $(j+1)$-th node denoted by $\mathbf{v}_{j_1, \cdots, j_i}$, where $(j_1, \cdots, j_i) \in \{0, 1\}^i \leftarrow \text{bin}_i(j)$, can be computed as

$$\mathbf{v}_{j_1, \cdots, j_i} \leftarrow h_{\mathbf{A}, \mathbf{B}, \mathbf{t}}(\mathbf{v}_{j_1, \cdots, j_i, 0}, \mathbf{v}_{j_1, \cdots, j_i, 1}).$$

4. At depth 0, the root $\mathbf{v} := \mathbf{v}_\epsilon \leftarrow h_{\mathbf{A}, \mathbf{B}, \mathbf{t}}(\mathbf{v}_0, \mathbf{v}_1)$.
5. Output the accumulator value $\mathbf{v}$.

$\text{wit} \leftarrow$ **PACC.Witness**$_{pp}(\mathbf{B}, \mathbf{t}, R, \mathbf{p})$: On input public parameters $pp$, a ring $R :=$ $\{\mathbf{p}_0, \cdots, \mathbf{p}_{N-1}\}$, and $\mathbf{p}$, perform:

1. If $\mathbf{p} \notin R$, return $\perp$. Otherwise, we have $\mathbf{p} = \mathbf{p}_i$ for some $i \in \{0, \cdots, N-1\}$. Now, let $(i_1, \cdots, i_\ell) \in \{0, 1\}^\ell \leftarrow \text{bin}_\ell(i)$.
2. The witness for the fact $\mathbf{p} \in R$ is

$$\text{wit} := \{(i_1, \cdots, i_\ell), (\mathbf{v}_{i_1, \cdots, i_{\ell-1}, \overline{i_\ell}}, \cdots, \mathbf{v}_{i_1, \overline{i_2}}, \mathbf{v}_{\overline{i_1}})\},$$

where $\mathbf{v}_{i_1, \cdots, i_{\ell-1}, \overline{i_\ell}}, \cdots, \mathbf{v}_{i_1, \overline{i_2}}, \mathbf{v}_{\overline{i_1}}$ are computed using $\text{PACC.Acc}_{pp}(\mathbf{B}, \mathbf{t}, R)$.

$0/1 \leftarrow$ **PACC.Verify**$_{pp}(\mathbf{B}, \mathbf{v}, \mathbf{t}, \mathbf{p}, \text{wit})$: On input public parameters $pp$, an accumulator value, a witness $\text{wit} := \{(i_1, \cdots, i_\ell), (\mathbf{w}_\ell, \cdots, \mathbf{w}_1)\}$ for $\mathbf{p}$, compute:

1. Assign $\mathbf{z}_\ell \leftarrow \mathbf{p}$. For $j \in \{\ell-1, \cdots, 0\}$, compute

$$\mathbf{z}_j := \overline{i_{j+1}} \cdot h_{\mathbf{A}, \mathbf{B}, \mathbf{t}}(\mathbf{z}_{j+1}, \mathbf{w}_{j+1}) + i_{j+1} \cdot h_{\mathbf{A}, \mathbf{B}, \mathbf{t}}(\mathbf{w}_{j+1}, \mathbf{z}_{j+1}). \qquad (1)$$

2. If $\mathbf{z}_0 = \mathbf{v}$, return 1. Otherwise, return 0.

The following theorem guarantees the security of the PACC.

**Theorem 1.** *Provided the hardness of the* $\text{sda}_{\tilde{\mathcal{O}}(n)}$ *problem, the accumulator scheme* PACC *is secure.*

*Proof.* Suppose by contradiction that there is a PPT adversary $\mathcal{A}$ such that the probablity of the following event is non-negligible:

$$\mathbf{A} \leftarrow \text{PACC.Setup}(1^\lambda); (R, \mathbf{p}^*, \text{wit}^*) \leftarrow \mathcal{A}(\mathbf{A}):$$

$$\mathbf{p}^* \notin R \wedge \text{PACC.Verify}_{pp}(\mathbf{B}, \text{PACC.Acc}_{pp}(\mathbf{B}, \mathbf{t}, R), \mathbf{t}, \mathbf{p}^*, \text{wit}^*) = 1.$$

Here matrix $\mathbf{B}$ and vector $\mathbf{t}$ parametrise the PACC. Now, we construct an algorithm $\mathcal{B}$ that can break an SIS instance and hence break the $\text{as}_{\tilde{\mathcal{O}}(n)}$ problem. Assume that $\mathcal{B}$ wants to solve the SIS instance given by matrix $\mathbf{A} \in \mathbb{Z}_q^{n \times m}$. Now $\mathcal{B}$ sets $\mathbf{A}$ as the output of PACC.Setup$(1^\lambda)$ then sends it to $\mathcal{A}$. Finaly $\mathcal{A}$ returns $(R, \mathbf{p}^*, \text{wit}^*)$. Here, the witness $\text{wit}^* := \{(i_1^*, \cdots, i_\ell^*), (\mathbf{w}_\ell, \cdots, \mathbf{w}_1)\}$ in which $(i_1^*, \cdots, i_\ell^*)$ is the binary expansion of some integer $i^* \in \{0, \cdots N-1\}$.

Let $\mathbf{v}^* := \mathsf{PACC.Acc}_{pp}(\mathbf{B}, \mathbf{t}, R)$. Accordingly, we will have a path $[\mathbf{v}_{i_1^*, \cdots, i_\ell^*} = \mathbf{p}_{i^*} \to \mathbf{v}_{i_1^*, \cdots, i_{\ell-1}^*} \to \cdots \to \mathbf{v}_{i_1^*} \to \mathbf{v}^*]$ from the leave $\mathbf{p}_{i^*}$ to the root $\mathbf{v}^*$ of the Merkle tree formed through the execution of $\mathbf{v}^* \leftarrow \mathsf{PACC.Acc}_{pp}(\mathbf{B}, \mathbf{t}, R)$. However, through the execution of $\mathsf{PACC.Verify}_{pp}(\mathbf{B}, \mathbf{v}^*, \mathbf{t}, \mathbf{p}^*, \mathsf{wit}^*) = 1$, we will have the path $[\mathbf{z}_\ell = \mathbf{p}^* \to \mathbf{z}_{\ell-1} \to \cdots \to \mathbf{z}_1 \to \mathbf{z}_0 = \mathbf{v}^*]$. Notice that $\mathbf{p}^* \notin R$. Thus, $\mathbf{p}^* \neq \mathbf{p}_{i^*}$. This implies by comparing these above two paths that there is the smallest integer $k \in [\ell]$ satisfying that $\mathbf{z}_k \neq \mathbf{v}_{i_1^*, \cdots, i_k^*}$. Therefore, there will be a collision for the hash function $h_{\mathbf{A}, \mathbf{B}, \mathbf{t}}$ at the parent node of $\mathbf{v}_{i_1^*, \cdots, i_k^*}$. At this point, the theorem follows from Lemma 3. $\qquad\square$

## 4  Lattice-Based Unique Ring Signature from Accumulator

### 4.1  The Unique Ring Signature Construction

We present a construction of URS from ring signatures based on accumulators described as below.

$urs.pp \leftarrow$ **URS.Setup**$(n)$: On input a security parameter $n$, do:
1. Choose $q$. Let $k := \lceil \log_2 q \rceil$, $m = 2nk$.
2. Sample $\mathbf{A} \xleftarrow{\$} \mathbb{Z}_q^{n \times m}$, choose hash functions $H_{\mathsf{UT}}$ and $H_{\mathsf{FS}}$, and output

$$urs.pp := ((n, m, q, k, \mathbf{A}), H_{\mathsf{UT}}, H_{\mathsf{FS}}).$$

Here, $H_{\mathsf{UT}} : \{0,1\}^* \to \mathbb{Z}_q^{n \times m}$ which will be modeled as a random orcale.
3. Consider the weak pseudorandom function $\mathsf{F}$ presented in Sect. 2.6.

$(\mathbf{x}, \mathbf{p}) \leftarrow$ **URS.Key**$(urs.pp)$: On input public parameters $urs.pp$, choose $\mathbf{x} \xleftarrow{\$} \{0,1\}^m$ then compute $\mathbf{p} = \mathsf{bin}(\mathbf{A}\mathbf{x} \pmod{q}) \in \{0,1\}^{nk}$, and output $(sk, pk) = (\mathbf{x}, \mathbf{p})$.

**sig** $\leftarrow$ **URS.Sign**$(urs.pp, sk, \mu, R)$: On input public parameters $urs.pp := \mathbf{A}$, the secret key $\mathsf{sk} = \mathbf{x}$ for the real signer (with respect to the public key $\mathbf{p} := \mathsf{bin}(\mathbf{A}\mathbf{x} \pmod{q})$) belonging to the ring $R := \{\mathbf{p}_1, \cdots, \mathbf{p}_{N-1}\}$, a message $\mu$, perform:
1. Compute $\mathbf{B} = [\mathbf{B}_0 | \mathbf{B}_1] \leftarrow H_{\mathsf{UT}}(\mu, R)$.
2. Compute the unique tag $\mathbf{t} := \mathsf{bin}(\mathsf{F}_\mathbf{x}(\mathbf{B}) \pmod{p})$.
3. Let $acc.pp := \mathbf{A}$.
4. Run $\mathbf{v} \leftarrow \mathsf{PACC.Acc}_{acc.pp}(\mathbf{B}, \mathbf{t}, R)$ using the hash function $h_{\mathbf{A}, \mathbf{B}}$.
5. Run $\mathsf{wit} \leftarrow \mathsf{PACC.Witness}_{acc.pp}(\mathbf{B}, \mathbf{t}, R, \mathbf{p})$ where

$$\mathsf{wit} := \{(i_1, \cdots, i_\ell) \in \{0,1\}^\ell, (\mathbf{w}_\ell, \cdots, \mathbf{w}_1) \in (\{0,1\}^{nk})^\ell\}.$$

6. Use the Fiat-Shamir Heuristic with the hash function $H_{\mathsf{FS}}$ to transform the ZKAoK in Fig. 6 to a non-interactive ZKAoK protocol NIZKAoK. The NIZKAoK protocol is repeated up to $\kappa = \omega(\log n)$ (to get a negligible soundness error) on input $(\mathbf{A}, \mathbf{B}, \mathbf{v}, \mathbf{t})$ and the prover's witness $(\mathbf{x}, \mathbf{p}, \mathsf{wit})$ to produce a transcript $\Pi_{\mathsf{urs}} := (\{\mathsf{CMT}_j\}_{j=1}^\kappa, \{\mathsf{CH}_j\}_{j=1}^\kappa, \{\mathsf{RSP}_j\}_{j=1}^\kappa, \mathbf{t})$, where

$$\mathsf{CH}_j := H_{\mathsf{FS}}(\mu, \mathsf{CMT}_j, \mathbf{A}, \mathbf{v}, R, \mathbf{B}, \mathbf{t}) \in \{1, 2, 3\}.$$

7. Output sig := $\Pi_{\mathsf{urs}}$.

$0/1 \leftarrow$ **URS.Verify**$(urs.pp, \mu, R, \mathbf{sig})$: On input public parameters urs.pp, a message $\mu$, a ring of signers $R$ and a signature sig, compute:

1. Compute $\mathbf{B} = [\mathbf{B}_0|\mathbf{B}_1] \leftarrow H_{\mathsf{UT}}(\mu, R)$. Let $acc.pp := (n, m, q, k, \mathbf{A})$.
2. Run $\mathbf{v} \leftarrow \mathsf{PACC.Acc}_{acc.pp}(\mathbf{B}, \mathbf{t}, R)$ using the hash function $h_{\mathbf{A},\mathbf{B},\mathbf{t}}$.
3. Parse sig $= \Pi_{\mathsf{urs}} := (\{\mathsf{CMT}_j\}_{j=1}^\kappa, \{\mathsf{CH}_j\}_{j=1}^\kappa, \{\mathsf{RSP}_j\}_{j=1}^\kappa, \mathbf{t})$.
   Return 0 if $\{\mathsf{CH}_j\}_{j=1}^\kappa \neq H_{\mathsf{FS}}(\mu, \{\mathsf{CMT}_j\}_{j=1}^\kappa, \mathbf{A}, \mathbf{v}, R, \mathbf{B}, \mathbf{t})$.
4. Run ZKAoK.Verify to check the validity of each tuple $(\mathsf{CMT}_j, \mathsf{CH}_j, \mathsf{RSP}_j)_{j=1}^\kappa$. If any of them does not hold then return 0. Otherwise, return 1.

## 4.2   A ZKAoK for the Unique Ring Signatures

For the accumulator-based unique ring signatures from lattices, we consider the following relation:

$$\mathcal{R}_{\mathsf{URS}} := \{(\mathbf{A}, \mathbf{B}, \mathbf{v}, \mathbf{t}) \in \mathbb{Z}_q^{n \times m} \times \mathbb{Z}_q^{n \times m} \times \{0,1\}^{nk} \times \{0,1\}^{nk};$$

$$\mathbf{x} \in \{0,1\}^m, \mathbf{p} \in \{0,1\}^{nk}, \mathsf{wit} \in \{0,1\}^\ell \times (\{0,1\}^{nk})^\ell :$$

$$\mathsf{PACC.Verify}_{\mathbf{A}}(\mathbf{B}, \mathbf{v}, \mathbf{t}, \mathbf{p}, \mathsf{wit}) = 1 \,\wedge\, \mathbf{A}\mathbf{x} = \mathbf{G}\mathbf{p} \,\wedge\, \mathsf{F}_{\mathbf{x}}(\mathbf{B}) = \mathbf{G}\mathbf{t}\}.$$

We will design a ZKAoK for the relation $\mathcal{R}_{\mathsf{URS}}$. That is, the ZKAoK is to prove that a prover $\mathcal{P}$ knows a witness $(\mathbf{x}, \mathbf{p}, \mathsf{wit})$ for a given statement $(\mathbf{A}, \mathbf{B}, \mathbf{v}, \mathbf{t})$ such that $((\mathbf{A}, \mathbf{B}, \mathbf{v}, \mathbf{t}); \mathbf{x}, \mathbf{p}, \mathsf{wit}) \in \mathcal{R}_{\mathsf{URS}}$. Note that $\mathbf{v} = \mathbf{z}_0$, and $\mathbf{p} = \mathbf{z}_\ell$.

We introduce here some new notations:

- Let $\mathcal{B}_m^{nk} := \{\mathbf{x} = (x_1, \cdots, x_m) : \mathbf{x} \in \{0,1\}^m \wedge \|\mathbf{x}\|_1 = nk\}$ be the set of vectors in $\{0,1\}^m$ having Hamming weight $nk$. Here $\|\mathbf{x}\|_1 := \sum_{i=1}^m |x_i|$.
- Let $\mathcal{S}_m$ be the set of all permutations of $m$ elements.
- Let $\mathsf{ext}(b, \mathbf{z}) := \begin{pmatrix} \overline{b} \cdot \mathbf{z} \\ b \cdot \mathbf{z} \end{pmatrix}$, and $\mathsf{dbl}(\mathbf{t}) := \begin{pmatrix} \mathbf{t} \\ \mathbf{t} \end{pmatrix}$.
- For $b \in \{0,1\}, \pi \in \mathcal{S}_m$, we denote by $T_{b,\pi}$ the permutation that transforms $\mathbf{w} = \begin{pmatrix} \mathbf{y}_0 \\ \mathbf{y}_1 \end{pmatrix}$, where $\mathbf{y}_i \in \mathbb{Z}_q^m$, into $T_{b,\pi}(\mathbf{y}) = \begin{pmatrix} \pi(\mathbf{y}_b) \\ \pi(\mathbf{y}_{\overline{b}}) \end{pmatrix}$, where $\mathbf{z}_i \in \mathbb{Z}_q^m$.

Note that, for all $b, c \in \{0,1\}, \pi, \phi \in \mathcal{S}_m$ and all $\mathbf{z}, \mathbf{w} \in \{0,1\}^m$, the following equivalences hold:

$$\begin{cases} \widehat{\mathbf{z}} := \mathsf{ext}(c, \mathbf{z}) \wedge \mathbf{z} \in \mathcal{B}_m^{nk} & \Longleftrightarrow T_{b,\pi}(\widehat{\mathbf{z}}) = \mathsf{ext}(c \oplus b, \pi(\mathbf{z})) \wedge \pi(\mathbf{z}) \in \mathcal{B}_m^{nk}; \\ \widehat{\mathbf{w}} := \mathsf{ext}(c, \mathbf{w}) \wedge \mathbf{w} \in \mathcal{B}_m^{nk} & \Longleftrightarrow T_{b,\pi}(\widehat{\mathbf{w}}) = \mathsf{ext}(c \oplus b, \phi(\mathbf{w})) \wedge \phi(\mathbf{w}) \in \mathcal{B}_m^{nk}. \end{cases}$$

Now, we analyze the relation $\mathcal{R}_{\mathsf{URS}}$. We start with the condition

$$\mathsf{PACC.Verify}_{\mathbf{A}}(\mathbf{B}, \mathbf{v}, \mathbf{t}, \mathbf{p}, \mathsf{wit}) = 1.$$

From Eq. (1), we have

$$\mathbf{G}\mathbf{z}_j := \overline{i_{j+1}} \cdot (\mathbf{A}_0 \mathbf{z}_{j+1} + \mathbf{A}_1 \mathbf{w}_{j+1} + \mathbf{B}_0 \mathbf{t} + \mathbf{B}_1 \mathbf{t}) + i_{j+1} \cdot (\mathbf{A}_0 \mathbf{w}_{j+1} + \mathbf{A}_1 \mathbf{z}_{j+1} + \mathbf{B}_0 \mathbf{t} + \mathbf{B}_1 \mathbf{t}),$$

which is equivalent to $\mathbf{Gz}_j := \mathbf{A} \cdot \text{ext}(i_{j+1}, \mathbf{z}_{j+1}) + \mathbf{A} \cdot \text{ext}(\overline{i_{j+1}}, \mathbf{w}_{j+1}) + \mathbf{B} \cdot \text{dbl}(\mathbf{t})$.
Let $\widehat{\mathbf{z}}_{j+1} := \text{ext}(i_{j+1}, \mathbf{z}_{j+1})$, $\widehat{\mathbf{w}}_{j+1} := \text{ext}(\overline{i_{j+1}}, \mathbf{w}_{j+1})$, and $\widehat{\mathbf{t}} := \text{dbl}(\mathbf{t})$ we have

$$
\begin{cases}
\mathbf{Gz}_j & = \mathbf{A} \cdot \widehat{\mathbf{z}}_{j+1} + \mathbf{A} \cdot \widehat{\mathbf{w}}_{j+1} + \mathbf{B} \cdot \widehat{\mathbf{t}}, \forall j \in [\ell - 1] \\
\mathbf{Gv} & = \mathbf{A} \cdot \widehat{\mathbf{z}}_1 + \mathbf{A} \cdot \widehat{\mathbf{w}}_1 + \mathbf{B} \cdot \widehat{\mathbf{t}}
\end{cases}.
$$

We exploit the "extend-then-permute" technique for the ZKAoK. For doing that, we

- extend $\mathbf{A} = [\mathbf{A}_0|\mathbf{A}_1]$ to $\mathbf{A}^* = [\mathbf{A}_0|0_{n \times nk}|\mathbf{A}_1|0_{n \times nk}]$, $\mathbf{A}$ to $\widehat{\mathbf{A}} := [\mathbf{A}|0_{n \times m}]$, $\mathbf{B}$ to $\widehat{\mathbf{B}} := [\mathbf{B}|0_{n \times m}]$, $\mathbf{G}$ to $\mathbf{G}^* := [\mathbf{G}|0_{n \times nk}]$
- extend $\mathbf{z}_1, \cdots, \mathbf{z}_\ell, \mathbf{w}_1, \cdots, \mathbf{w}_\ell$ to $\mathbf{z}_1^*, \cdots, \mathbf{z}_\ell^*, \mathbf{w}_1^*, \cdots, \mathbf{w}_\ell^* \in \mathcal{B}_m^{nk}$, respectively. These vectors are extended by concatenating a length-$nk$ vector of suitable Hamming weight.
- also, extend $\mathbf{x}, \widehat{\mathbf{t}}$ to $\mathbf{x}^*, \widehat{\mathbf{t}}^*$ by appending vector $\{0\}^m$, respectively.

We will a brief description of the ZAKoK for $\mathcal{R}_{\mathsf{URS}}$ aiming to the goals and the strategies that a prover $\mathcal{P}$ would like to perform.

**Common inputs:** $(\mathbf{A}, \mathbf{B}, \mathbf{v}, \mathbf{t})$, where $\mathbf{A}$ is extended to $\mathbf{A}^*$ and $\widehat{\mathbf{A}}$, while $\mathbf{B}$ is extended to $\widehat{\mathbf{B}}$ as above.
$\mathcal{P}$'s inputs: $(\mathbf{x}, \mathbf{p}, \text{wit})$, where wit $:= \{(i_1, \cdots, i_\ell), (\mathbf{w}_\ell, \cdots, \mathbf{w}_1))\}$.
$\mathcal{P}$'s goal: $\mathcal{P}$ proves in zero knowledge that it knows that
**Goal 1.** $\mathbf{z}_i^*, \mathbf{w}_i^* \in \mathcal{B}_m^{nk}$, $\widehat{\mathbf{z}}_j^* = \text{ext}(i_j, \mathbf{z}_j^*)$, $\widehat{\mathbf{w}}_j^* = \text{ext}(\overline{i_j}, \mathbf{w}_j^*)$ for all $i \in [\ell]$; and that
**Goal 2.** the following equations hold:

$$
\begin{cases}
\forall j \in [\ell - 1], \mathbf{A}^* \cdot \widehat{\mathbf{z}}_{j+1}^* + \mathbf{A}^* \cdot \widehat{\mathbf{w}}_{j+1}^* + \mathbf{B} \cdot \widehat{\mathbf{t}} & = \mathbf{G}^* \mathbf{z}_j^* \pmod{q} \\
\mathbf{A}^* \cdot \widehat{\mathbf{z}}_1^* + \mathbf{A}^* \cdot \widehat{\mathbf{w}}_1^* + \mathbf{B} \cdot \widehat{\mathbf{t}} & = \mathbf{Gv} \pmod{q} \\
\widehat{\mathbf{A}} \cdot \mathbf{x}^* & = \mathbf{G}^* \mathbf{z}_\ell^* = \mathbf{Gp} \pmod{q} \\
F_{\mathbf{x}^*}(\widehat{\mathbf{B}}) & = \mathbf{Gt} \pmod{p}
\end{cases}
$$
(2)

**Techniques/Strategies for Prover $\mathcal{P}$:**

**For Goal 1:** For each $j \in [\ell]$, $\mathcal{P}$ samples permutations $\pi_j, \phi_j \xleftarrow{\$} \mathcal{S}_m$ and $b_j \xleftarrow{\$} \{0, 1\}$ then it shows that

$$
\pi_j(\mathbf{z}_j^*) \in \mathcal{B}_m^{nk} \wedge T_{b_j, \pi_j}(\widehat{\mathbf{z}}_j^*) = \text{ext}(i_j \oplus b_j, \pi_j(\mathbf{z}_j^*))
$$
$$
\phi_i(\mathbf{w}_j^*) \in \mathcal{B}_m^{nk} \wedge T_{b_j, \pi_j}(\widehat{\mathbf{w}}_j^*) = \text{ext}(i_j \oplus b_j, \phi_j(\mathbf{w}_j^*))
$$

**For Goal 2:** $\mathcal{P}$ uniformly samples random masking vectors $\mathbf{r}_{\mathbf{z}}^{(1)}, \cdots, \mathbf{r}_{\mathbf{z}}^{(\ell)}, \xleftarrow{\$} \mathbb{Z}_q^m$;
$\mathbf{r}_{\widehat{\mathbf{z}}}^{(1)}, \cdots, \mathbf{r}_{\widehat{\mathbf{z}}}^{(\ell)}; \mathbf{r}_{\widehat{\mathbf{w}}}^{(1)}, \cdots, \mathbf{r}_{\widehat{\mathbf{w}}}^{(\ell)}; \mathbf{r}_{\mathbf{x}}^{(A)}; \mathbf{r}_{\mathbf{x}}^{(B)} \xleftarrow{\$} \mathbb{Z}_q^{2m}; \mathbf{r}_{\mathbf{e}}^{(B)} \xleftarrow{\$} \mathbb{Z}_q^n$.

We can transform last equation in Eq. (2) as $\lfloor \widehat{\mathbf{B}} \mathbf{x}^* \rfloor_p = \mathbf{G} \mathbf{t} \pmod{p}$. Given $\gamma = p/q$, let $\mathbf{e} = \gamma \cdot \mathbf{G} \mathbf{t} - \widehat{\mathbf{B}} \mathbf{x}^*$, we have $\widehat{\mathbf{B}} \mathbf{x}^* + \mathbf{e} = \gamma \cdot \mathbf{G} \mathbf{t} \pmod{q}$, or equivalently

$$\widehat{\mathbf{B}}(\mathbf{x}^* + \mathbf{r}_{\mathbf{x}}^{(B)}) + (\mathbf{e} + \mathbf{r}_{\mathbf{e}}^{(B)}) = \gamma \cdot \mathbf{G} \mathbf{t} + \widehat{\mathbf{B}} \mathbf{r}_{\mathbf{x}}^{(B)} + \mathbf{r}_{\mathbf{e}}^{(B)} \pmod{q}.$$

That is, $\mathcal{P}$ proves $\mathcal{V}$ that

$$\begin{cases} \mathbf{A}^*(\widehat{\mathbf{z}}_1^* + \mathbf{r}_{\widehat{\mathbf{z}}}^{(1)}) + \mathbf{A}^*(\widehat{\mathbf{w}}_1^* + \mathbf{r}_{\widehat{\mathbf{w}}}^{(1)}) - \mathbf{G}\mathbf{v} + \mathbf{B} \cdot \widehat{\mathbf{t}} = \mathbf{A}^*\mathbf{r}_{\widehat{\mathbf{z}}}^{(1)} + \mathbf{A}^*\mathbf{r}_{\widehat{\mathbf{w}}}^{(1)} \pmod{q}; \\ \forall j \in [\ell - 1], \mathbf{A}^*(\widehat{\mathbf{z}}_{j+1} + \mathbf{r}_{\widehat{\mathbf{z}}}^{(j+1)}) + \mathbf{A}^*(\widehat{\mathbf{w}}_{j+1} + \mathbf{r}_{\widehat{\mathbf{w}}}^{(j+1)}) + \mathbf{B} \cdot \widehat{\mathbf{t}} - \mathbf{G}^*(\mathbf{z}_j^* + \mathbf{r}_{\mathbf{z}}^{(j+1)}) \\ \quad = \mathbf{A}^*\mathbf{r}_{\widehat{\mathbf{z}}}^{(j+1)} + \mathbf{A}^*\mathbf{r}_{\widehat{\mathbf{w}}}^{(j+1)} - \mathbf{G}^*\mathbf{r}_{\mathbf{z}}^{(j)} \pmod{q}; \\ \widehat{\mathbf{A}}(\mathbf{x}^* + \mathbf{r}_{\mathbf{x}}^{(A)}) - \mathbf{G}^*(\mathbf{z}_\ell^* + \mathbf{r}_{\mathbf{z}}^{(\ell)}) = \widehat{\mathbf{A}}\mathbf{r}_{\mathbf{x}}^{(A)} - \mathbf{G}^*\mathbf{r}_{\mathbf{z}}^{(\ell)} \pmod{q}; \\ \widehat{\mathbf{B}}(\mathbf{x}^* + \mathbf{r}_{\mathbf{x}}^{(B)}) + (\mathbf{e} + \mathbf{r}_{\mathbf{e}}^{(B)}) = \gamma \cdot \mathbf{G} \mathbf{t} + \widehat{\mathbf{B}} \mathbf{r}_{\mathbf{x}}^{(B)} + \mathbf{r}_{\mathbf{e}}^{(B)} \pmod{q}. \end{cases}$$

The following lemma says that there exists a ZKAoK for the relation $\mathcal{R}_{\mathsf{URS}}$. The ZKAoK given in Fig. 6 is a Stern type one [18] which is a 2-Sigma protocol enjoying 3-special soundness. That is, we need up to 3 transcripts in order to be able to extract the witness.

**Lemma 4.** *Assume that the* $\mathsf{SIS}_{m,n,q,\theta}^\infty$ *problem is hard. Then there exists a statistical ZKAoK for the relation* $\mathcal{R}_{\mathsf{URS}}$ *with perfect completeness and communication cost* $\tilde{O}(\ell \cdot n)$. *In particular:*

- *There exists an efficient simulator that, on input* $(\mathbf{A}, \mathbf{v})$, *outputs an accepting transcript which is statistically close to that produced by the real prover.*
- *There exists an efficient knowledge extractor that, on input 3 valid responses* $(\mathsf{RSP}_1, \mathsf{RSP}_2, \mathsf{RSP}_3)$ *to the same commitment* $\mathsf{CMT}$, *outputs* $(\mathbf{x}', \mathbf{p}', \mathsf{wit}')$ *such that* $((\mathbf{A}, \mathbf{B}, \mathbf{v}, \mathbf{t}), \mathbf{x}', \mathbf{p}', \mathsf{wit}') \in \mathcal{R}_{\mathsf{URS}}$.

## 4.3  Analysis of the ZKAoK for the Relation $\mathcal{R}_{\mathsf{URS}}$

**Theorem 2 (Completeness and Communication Cost).** *The interactive protocol described in Fig. 6 is perfectly complete and costs* $\tilde{O}(\ell \cdot n)$ *bits for communication. It is a statistical zero-knowledge argument of knowledge if the string commitment* $\mathsf{COM}$ *is statistically hiding and computationally binding.*

Follows Sect. 3.1, one can easiely check that:

$$\Pr[\mathcal{P}((\mathbf{A}, \mathbf{B}, \mathbf{v}, \mathbf{t}), \mathbf{x}, \mathbf{p}, \mathsf{wit}), \mathcal{V}(\mathbf{B}, \mathbf{v}, \mathbf{t}, \mathbf{p}, \mathsf{wit}) = 1] = 1,$$

where $((\mathbf{A}, \mathbf{B}, \mathbf{v}, \mathbf{t}), \mathbf{x}, \mathbf{p}, \mathsf{wit}) \in \mathcal{R}_{\mathsf{URS}}$, that means an honest the prover $\mathcal{P}$ always successfully convinces the verifier $\mathcal{V}$. To compare to the accumulator in [12], our approach adds extra information of $(\eta, \mathbf{r}_{\mathbf{x}}^{(B)}, \mathbf{B}, \mathbf{t})$ which just costs marginally larger. Hence, the communication cost of our protocol is of order $\tilde{O}(\ell \cdot m \cdot \log_q) = \tilde{O}(\ell \cdot n)$ bits.

**Commitment.** $\mathcal{P}$ performs:

1. Samples randomnesses $\rho_1, \rho_2, \rho_3$ for COM
2. For $j \in [\ell]$, sample $\pi_j, \phi_j \xleftarrow{\$} \mathcal{S}_m; \tau, \eta \xleftarrow{\$} \mathcal{S}_{2m}; \zeta \xleftarrow{\$} \mathcal{S}_n; b_j \xleftarrow{\$} \{0,1\}$.
3. Sample random masking vectors $\mathbf{r}_{\mathbf{z}}^{(1)}, \cdots, \mathbf{r}_{\mathbf{z}}^{(\ell)} \xleftarrow{\$} \mathbb{Z}_q^m$;
   $\mathbf{r}_{\widehat{\mathbf{z}}}^{(1)}, \cdots, \mathbf{r}_{\widehat{\mathbf{z}}}^{(\ell)}; \mathbf{r}_{\widehat{\mathbf{w}}}^{(1)}, \cdots, \mathbf{r}_{\widehat{\mathbf{w}}}^{(\ell)}; \mathbf{r}_{\mathbf{x}}^{(A)}; \mathbf{r}_{\mathbf{x}}^{(B)} \xleftarrow{\$} \mathbb{Z}_q^{2m}; \mathbf{r}_{\mathbf{e}}^{(B)} \xleftarrow{\$} \mathbb{Z}_q^n$.
4. Compute commitment $\mathsf{CMT} = (C_1, C_2, C_3)$, where
   
   (i) $C_1 := \mathsf{COM}(\{b_j, \pi_j, \phi_j\}_{j=1}^{\ell}; \tau; \eta; \mathbf{A}^* \mathbf{r}_{\mathbf{z}}^{(1)} + \mathbf{A}^* \mathbf{r}_{\widehat{\mathbf{w}}}^{(1)}; \widehat{\mathbf{A}} \mathbf{r}_{\mathbf{x}}^{(A)} - \mathbf{G}^* \mathbf{r}_{\mathbf{z}}^{(\ell)};$
   $\gamma \cdot \mathbf{G} \mathbf{t} + \widehat{\mathbf{B}} \mathbf{r}_{\mathbf{x}}^{(B)} + \mathbf{r}_{\mathbf{e}}^{(B)}; \{\mathbf{A}^* \mathbf{r}_{\mathbf{z}}^{(j+1)} + \mathbf{A}^* \mathbf{r}_{\widehat{\mathbf{w}}}^{(j+1)} - \mathbf{G}^* \mathbf{r}_{\mathbf{z}}^{(j+1)}\}_{j=1}^{\ell-1}; \rho_1)$
   
   (ii) $C_2 := \mathsf{COM}(\{\pi_j(\mathbf{r}_{\mathbf{z}}^{(j)}); T_{b_j, \pi_j}(\mathbf{r}_{\widehat{\mathbf{w}}}^{(j)}); T_{\overline{b}_j, \phi_j}(\mathbf{r}_{\widehat{\mathbf{z}}}^{(j)})\}_{j=1}^{\ell}; \tau(\mathbf{r}_{\mathbf{x}}^{(A)}), \eta(\mathbf{r}_{\mathbf{x}}^{(B)}),$
   $\zeta(\mathbf{r}_{\mathbf{e}}^{(B)}); \rho_2)$
   
   (iii) $C_3 := \mathsf{COM}(\{\pi_j(\mathbf{z}_j^* + \mathbf{r}_{\mathbf{z}}^{(j)}); T_{b_j, \pi_j}(\widehat{\mathbf{z}_j}^* + \mathbf{r}_{\widehat{\mathbf{z}}}^{(j)}); T_{\overline{b}_j, \phi_j}(\widehat{\mathbf{w}_j}^* + \mathbf{r}_{\widehat{\mathbf{w}}}^{(j)})\}_{j=1}^{\ell};$
   $\tau(\mathbf{r}_{\mathbf{x}}^{(A)} + \mathbf{x}^*); \eta(\mathbf{r}_{\mathbf{x}}^{(B)} + \mathbf{x}^*); \zeta(\mathbf{r}_{\mathbf{e}}^{(B)} + \mathbf{e}); \rho_3)$

**Challenge.** $\mathcal{V}$ chooses a challenge $\mathsf{CH} \xleftarrow{\$} \{1, 2, 3\}$ and sends back to $\mathcal{P}$.

**Response.** What $\mathcal{P}$ responds will depend on the value of $\mathsf{CH}$. Namely,

1. If $\mathsf{CH} = 1$: Let $\mathbf{a}_{\mathbf{x}}^{(A)} := \tau(\mathbf{x}^*), \mathbf{a}_{\mathbf{x}}^{(B)} := \eta(\mathbf{x}^*), \mathbf{b}_{\mathbf{x}}^{(A)} := \tau(\mathbf{r}_{\mathbf{x}}^{(A)}), \mathbf{b}_{\mathbf{x}}^{(B)} :=$
   $\eta(\mathbf{r}_{\mathbf{x}}^{(B)}), \mathbf{a}_{\mathbf{e}}^{(B)} := \zeta(\mathbf{e}); \mathbf{b}_{\mathbf{e}}^{(B)} := \zeta(\mathbf{r}_{\mathbf{e}}^{(B)})$ and for each $j \in [\ell]$, compute:
   $$\begin{cases} a_j := i_j \oplus b_j; \mathbf{a}_{\mathbf{z}}^{(j)} := \pi_j(\mathbf{z}_j^*); \mathbf{a}_{\mathbf{w}}^{(j)} := \phi_j(\mathbf{w}_j^*); \\ \mathbf{b}_{\mathbf{z}}^{(j)} := \pi_j(\mathbf{r}_{\mathbf{z}}^{(j)}); \mathbf{b}_{\widehat{\mathbf{z}}}^{(j)} := T_{b_j, \pi_j}(\mathbf{r}_{\widehat{\mathbf{z}}}^{(j)}); \mathbf{b}_{\widehat{\mathbf{w}}}^{(j)} := T_{\overline{b}_j, \phi_j}(\mathbf{r}_{\widehat{\mathbf{w}}}^{(j)}). \end{cases}$$
   Set $\mathsf{RSP} := (\{a_j; \mathbf{a}_{\mathbf{z}}^{(j)}; \mathbf{a}_{\mathbf{w}}^{(j)}; \mathbf{b}_{\mathbf{z}}^{(j)}; \mathbf{b}_{\widehat{\mathbf{z}}}^{(j)}; \mathbf{b}_{\widehat{\mathbf{w}}}^{(j)}\}_{j=1}^{\ell}; \mathbf{a}_{\mathbf{x}}^{(A)}; \mathbf{b}_{\mathbf{x}}^{(A)}; \mathbf{a}_{\mathbf{x}}^{(B)}; \mathbf{b}_{\mathbf{x}}^{(B)};$
   $\mathbf{a}_{\mathbf{e}}^{(B)}, \mathbf{b}_{\mathbf{e}}^{(B)}; \rho_2; \rho_3)$.

2. If $\mathsf{CH} = 2$: Let $\hat{\tau} := \tau; \hat{\eta} := \eta; \hat{\zeta} := \zeta; \mathbf{c}_{\mathbf{x}}^{(A)} := \mathbf{x}^* + \mathbf{r}_{\mathbf{x}}^{(A)}; \mathbf{c}_{\mathbf{x}}^{(B)} := \mathbf{x}^* +$
   $\mathbf{r}_{\mathbf{x}}^{(B)}; \mathbf{c}_{\mathbf{e}}^{(B)} := \mathbf{e} + \mathbf{r}_{\mathbf{e}}^{(B)}$ and for each $j \in [\ell]$, compute:
   $c_j = b_j; \hat{\pi}_j := \pi_j; \hat{\phi}_j := \phi_j; \mathbf{c}_{\mathbf{z}}^{(j)} := \mathbf{z}_j^* + \mathbf{r}_{\mathbf{z}}^{(j)}; \mathbf{c}_{\widehat{\mathbf{z}}}^{(j)} := \widehat{\mathbf{z}}_j^* + \mathbf{r}_{\widehat{\mathbf{z}}}^{(j)};$
   $\mathbf{c}_{\widehat{\mathbf{w}}}^{(j)} := \widehat{\mathbf{w}}_j^* + \mathbf{r}_{\widehat{\mathbf{w}}}^{(j)}.$
   Set $\mathsf{RSP} := (\{c_j; \hat{\pi}_j; \hat{\phi}_j; \mathbf{c}_{\mathbf{z}}^{(j)}; \mathbf{c}_{\widehat{\mathbf{z}}}^{(j)}; \mathbf{c}_{\widehat{\mathbf{w}}}^{(j)}\}_{j=1}^{\ell}; \hat{\tau}; \mathbf{c}_{\mathbf{x}}^{(A)}; \hat{\eta}; \mathbf{c}_{\mathbf{x}}^{(B)}; \hat{\zeta}; \mathbf{c}_{\mathbf{e}}^{(B)}; \rho_1; \rho_3)$.

3. If $\mathsf{CH} = 3$ Let $\tilde{\tau} := \tau; \tilde{\eta} := \eta; \tilde{\zeta} := \zeta; \mathbf{g}_{\mathbf{x}}^{(A)} := \mathbf{r}_{\mathbf{x}}^{(A)}; \mathbf{g}_{\mathbf{x}}^{(B)} := \mathbf{r}_{\mathbf{x}}^{(B)};$
   $\mathbf{g}_{\mathbf{e}}^{(B)} := \mathbf{r}_{\mathbf{e}}^{(B)}$ and for each $j \in [\ell]$, compute:
   $g_j := b_j; \tilde{\pi}_j := \pi_j; \tilde{\phi}_j := \phi_j; \mathbf{g}_{\mathbf{z}}^{(j)} := \mathbf{r}_{\mathbf{z}}^{(j)}; \mathbf{g}_{\widehat{\mathbf{z}}}^{(j)} := \mathbf{r}_{\widehat{\mathbf{z}}}^{(j)}; \mathbf{g}_{\widehat{\mathbf{w}}}^{(j)} := \mathbf{r}_{\widehat{\mathbf{w}}}^{(j)};$
   Set $\mathsf{RSP} := (\{g_j; \tilde{\pi}_j; \tilde{\phi}_j; \mathbf{g}_{\mathbf{z}}^{(j)}; \mathbf{g}_{\widehat{\mathbf{z}}}^{(j)}; \mathbf{g}_{\widehat{\mathbf{w}}}^{(j)}\}_{j=1}^{\ell}; \tilde{\tau}; \mathbf{g}_{\mathbf{x}}^{(A)}; \tilde{\eta}; \mathbf{g}_{\mathbf{x}}^{(B)}; \tilde{\zeta}; \mathbf{g}_{\mathbf{e}}^{(B)}; \rho_1; \rho_2)$.

**ZKAoK.Verify.** Upon receiving $\mathsf{RSP}$, $\mathcal{V}$ verifies it following below cases:

1. If $\mathsf{CH} = 1$: Parse $\mathsf{RSP}$. Check that $\mathbf{a}_{\mathbf{x}}^{(A)} \in \mathcal{B}_{2m}^m; \mathbf{a}_{\mathbf{x}}^{(B)} \in \mathcal{B}_{2m}^m$. Check that:
   (i) $C_2 := \mathsf{COM}(\{\mathbf{b}_{\mathbf{z}}^{(j)}; \mathbf{b}_{\widehat{\mathbf{z}}}^{(j)}; \mathbf{b}_{\widehat{\mathbf{w}}}^{(j)}\}_{j=1}^{\ell}; \mathbf{b}_{\mathbf{x}}^{(A)}; \mathbf{b}_{\mathbf{x}}^{(B)}; \mathbf{b}_{\mathbf{e}}^{(B)}; \rho_2)$
   (ii) $C_3 := \mathsf{COM}(\{\mathbf{a}_{\mathbf{z}}^{(j)} + \mathbf{b}_{\mathbf{z}}^{(j)}; \mathbf{a}_{\widehat{\mathbf{z}}}^{(j)} + \mathbf{b}_{\widehat{\mathbf{z}}}^{(j)}; \mathbf{a}_{\widehat{\mathbf{w}}}^{(j)} + \mathbf{b}_{\widehat{\mathbf{w}}}^{(j)}\}_{j=1}^{\ell}; \mathbf{a}_{\mathbf{x}}^{(A)} + \mathbf{b}_{\mathbf{x}}^{(A)};$
   $\mathbf{a}_{\mathbf{x}}^{(B)} + \mathbf{b}_{\mathbf{x}}^{(B)}; \mathbf{a}_{\mathbf{e}}^{(B)} + \mathbf{b}_{\mathbf{e}}^{(B)}; \rho_3)$

2. If $\mathsf{CH} = 2$ Parse $\mathsf{RSP}$. Check that:
   (i) $C_1 := \mathsf{COM}(\{c_j, \hat{\pi}_j, \hat{\phi}_j\}_{j=1}^{\ell}; \hat{\tau}; \hat{\eta}; \mathbf{A}^* \mathbf{c}_{\mathbf{z}}^{(1)} + \mathbf{A}^* \mathbf{c}_{\widehat{\mathbf{w}}}^{(1)} - \mathbf{G} \mathbf{v} + \widehat{\mathbf{B}} \mathbf{t};$
   $\{\mathbf{A}^* \mathbf{c}_{\mathbf{z}}^{(j+1)} + \mathbf{A}^* \mathbf{c}_{\widehat{\mathbf{w}}}^{(j+1)} - \mathbf{G}^* \mathbf{c}_{\mathbf{z}}^{(j+1)}\}_{j=1}^{\ell-1}; \widehat{\mathbf{A}} \mathbf{c}_{\mathbf{x}}^{(A)} - \mathbf{G}^* \mathbf{c}_{\mathbf{z}}^{(\ell)}; \widehat{\mathbf{B}} \mathbf{c}_{\mathbf{x}}^{(B)} +$
   $\mathbf{c}_{\mathbf{e}}^{(B)}; \rho_1)$
   (ii) $C_3 := \mathsf{COM}(\{\hat{\pi}_j(\mathbf{c}_{\mathbf{z}}^{(j)}); T_{c_j, \hat{\pi}_j}(\mathbf{c}_{\widehat{\mathbf{z}}}^{(j)}); T_{\overline{c}_j, \hat{\phi}_j}(\mathbf{c}_{\widehat{\mathbf{w}}}^{(j)})\}_{j=1}^{\ell}; \hat{\tau}(\mathbf{c}_{\mathbf{x}}^{(A)}); \hat{\eta}(\mathbf{c}_{\mathbf{x}}^{(B)});$
   $\hat{\zeta}(\mathbf{c}_{\mathbf{e}}^{(B)}); \rho_3)$

3. If $\mathsf{CH} = 3$ Parse $\mathsf{RSP}$. Check that:
   (i) $C_1 := \mathsf{COM}(\{g_j; \tilde{\pi}_j; \tilde{\phi}_j\}_{j=1}^{\ell}; \tilde{\tau}; \tilde{\eta}; \mathbf{A}^* \mathbf{g}_{\mathbf{z}}^{(1)} + \mathbf{A}^* \mathbf{g}_{\widehat{\mathbf{w}}}^{(1)};$
   $\{\mathbf{A}^* \mathbf{g}_{\widehat{\mathbf{z}}}^{(j+1)} + \mathbf{A}^* \mathbf{g}_{\widehat{\mathbf{w}}}^{(i+1)} - \mathbf{G}^* \mathbf{g}_{\mathbf{z}}^{(j)}\}_{j=1}^{\ell-1}; \widehat{\mathbf{A}} \mathbf{g}_{\mathbf{x}}^{(A)} - \mathbf{G}^* \mathbf{g}_{\mathbf{z}}^{(\ell)}; \gamma \cdot \mathbf{G} \mathbf{t} + \widehat{\mathbf{B}} \mathbf{g}_{\mathbf{x}}^{(B)} +$
   $\mathbf{g}_{\mathbf{e}}^{(B)}; \rho_1)$
   (ii) $C_2 := \mathsf{COM}(\{\hat{\pi}_j(\mathbf{g}_{\mathbf{z}}^{(j)}); T_{g_j, \hat{\pi}_j}(\mathbf{g}_{\widehat{\mathbf{z}}}^{(j)}); T_{\overline{g}_j, \hat{\phi}_j}(\mathbf{g}_{\widehat{\mathbf{w}}}^{(j)})\}_{j=1}^{\ell}; \tilde{\tau}(\mathbf{g}_{\mathbf{x}}^{(A)}); \tilde{\eta}(\mathbf{g}_{\mathbf{x}}^{(B)});$
   $\tilde{\zeta}(\mathbf{g}_{\mathbf{e}}^{(B)}); \rho_2)$

If all conditions hold, $\mathcal{V}$ returns *accepted*. Otherwise, $\mathcal{V}$ returns *rejected*.

**Fig. 6.** The ZKAoK for the relation $\mathcal{R}_{\mathsf{URS}}$. Here COM is the string commitment scheme introduced in Sect. 2.4

**Lemma 5 (Zero-Knowledge Property).** *The interactive protocol described in Fig. 6 is a statistical zero-knowledge argument, that is* $\mathsf{Adv}^{\mathsf{zk}}_{(\mathcal{P},\mathcal{V})}(\mathcal{V}^*) \leq \mathsf{negl}(\lambda)$, *if the string commitment* COM *is statistically hiding.*

**Lemma 6 (Argument of Knowledge (i.e., Soundness)).** *Suppose the string commitment* COM *is computationally biding, there exists a knowledge extractor* $\mathcal{K}$ *that takes input as a commitment* CMT *and its valid reponses* $(\mathsf{RSP}_1, \mathsf{RSP}_2, \mathsf{RSP}_3)$ *then outputs* $(\mathbf{x}^*, \mathbf{p}^*, \mathsf{wit}^*)$ *such that* $((\mathbf{A}, \mathbf{B}, \mathbf{v}, \mathbf{t}), \mathbf{x}^*, \mathbf{p}^*, \mathsf{wit}^*) \in \mathcal{R}_{\mathsf{URS}}$. *That is,* $\mathsf{Adv}^{\mathsf{sound}}_{(\mathcal{P},\mathcal{V})}(\mathcal{P}^*) \leq \mathsf{negl}(\lambda)$.

### 4.4 Analysis of the Unique Ring Signature Scheme

**Correctness.** The completeness of the underlying ZKAoK protocol described in Fig. 6 directly implies the correctness of the corresponding unique ring signature. An honest ring member's signature is always accepted by the verification algorithm since he can efficiently produce a tuple $(\mathbf{x}, \mathbf{p}, \mathsf{wit})$ such that

$$((\mathbf{A}, \mathbf{B}, \mathbf{v}, \mathbf{t}), \mathbf{x}, \mathbf{p}, \mathsf{wit}) \in \mathcal{R}_{\mathsf{URS}}.$$

**Efficiency.** The signature bit-size of the given unique ring signature is of order $\tilde{\mathcal{O}}(\log N \cdot n)$ as the communication cost of the underlying ZKAoK protocol is of order $\tilde{\mathcal{O}}(\ell \cdot n)$.

**Theorem 3 (Unforgeability).** *In the random oracle model, the unique ring signature scheme given in Sect. 4 is unforgeable with respect to insider corruption under the hardness of the* $\mathsf{SIS}^{\infty}_{m,n,q,\theta}$ *problem.*

**Theorem 4 (Anonymity).** *In the random oracle model, the unique ring signature scheme is statistically anonymous under the zero-knowledge of the underlying ZKAoK protocol and the hardness of the decision-*$\mathsf{LWR}_{n,m,q,p}$ *problem.*

**Theorem 5 (Uniqueness).** *In the random oracle model, the unique ring signature scheme provides uniqueness against a probabilistic polynomially bounded adversary under the zero-knowledge property, the soundness of the underlying ZKAoK protocol, and the hardness of the decision-*$\mathsf{LWR}_{n,m,q,p}$ *problem.*

**Theorem 6 (Non-colliding property).** *The unique ring signature scheme given in Sect. 4 is non-colliding under the hardness of decisional-*$\mathsf{LWR}_{n,q,p}$ *problem with* $m \geq n(\log q + 1)(\log p - 1)$.

## 5   Concrete Parameters

We choose the parameters $m, n, q, p$ such that $m \geq n(\log q + 1)(\log p - 1)$ and $\theta = 1$ to ensure that the SIS and LWR problems are computationally hard. The security level for all parameter sets is for the root Hermite factor $\delta \approx 1.007$.

The concrete parameters for our URS scheme are provided in Table 2. Since our URS scheme has a signature size that is logarithmic to the number of ring members, the signature size gradually grows when this number increases.

**Table 2.** Concrete instantiations of URS scheme.

| Number of ring users ($N$) | Parameters | | | | | Size in MB | |
|---|---|---|---|---|---|---|---|
| | $m$ | $n$ | $q$ | $\theta$ | $p$ | Public key | Signature |
| 16 | 4608 | 128 | $2^{18}$ | 1 | 4 | 2.4 | 7.85 |
| 32 | 4608 | 128 | $2^{18}$ | 1 | 4 | 2.4 | 9.53 |
| 64 | 4608 | 128 | $2^{18}$ | 1 | 4 | 2.4 | 11.2 |
| 128 | 4608 | 128 | $2^{18}$ | 1 | 4 | 2.4 | 12.89 |
| 256 | 4608 | 128 | $2^{18}$ | 1 | 4 | 2.4 | 14.56 |

# 6   Conclusions

In this paper, we present the first URS based on post-quantum hardness assumptions with logarithmic signature size. We showed that our scheme enjoys anonymity, unforgeability and unique properties in the random oracle model under the SIS and LWR assumptions. Since we only prove our URS scheme in ROM, we leave the proof in the quantum random oracle model as an open problem.

**Acknowledgements.** We are grateful to the ESORICS 2022 anonymous reviewers for their helpful comments. This work is partially supported by the Australian Research Council Linkage Project LP190100984. Dung Duong is also partially suported by the RevITAlise (RITA) Research Grants from University of Wollongong. Huy Quoc Le has been sponsored by a CSIRO Data61 PhD Scholarship and CSIRO Data61 Top-up Scholarship.

# References

1. Ajtai, M.: Generating hard instances of lattice problems (extended abstract). In: Proceedings of the Twenty-Eighth Annual ACM Symposium on Theory of Computing, STOC 1996, pp. 99–108. ACM, New York (1996)
2. Backes, M., Döttling, N., Hanzlik, L., Kluczniak, K., Schneider, J.: Ring signatures: logarithmic-size, no setup—from standard assumptions. In: Ishai, Y., Rijmen, V. (eds.) EUROCRYPT 2019. LNCS, vol. 11478, pp. 281–311. Springer, Cham (2019). https://doi.org/10.1007/978-3-030-17659-4_10
3. Banerjee, A., Peikert, C., Rosen, A.: Pseudorandom functions and lattices. In: Pointcheval, D., Johansson, T. (eds.) EUROCRYPT 2012. LNCS, vol. 7237, pp. 719–737. Springer, Heidelberg (2012). https://doi.org/10.1007/978-3-642-29011-4_42
4. Bootle, J., Cerulli, A., Chaidos, P., Groth, J., Petit, C.: Efficient zero-knowledge arguments for arithmetic circuits in the discrete log setting. In: Fischlin, M., Coron, J.-S. (eds.) EUROCRYPT 2016. LNCS, vol. 9666, pp. 327–357. Springer, Heidelberg (2016). https://doi.org/10.1007/978-3-662-49896-5_12
5. Chatterjee, R., et al.: Compact ring signatures from learning with errors. In: Malkin, T., Peikert, C. (eds.) CRYPTO 2021. LNCS, vol. 12825, pp. 282–312. Springer, Cham (2021). https://doi.org/10.1007/978-3-030-84242-0_11

6. Esgin, M.F., Steinfeld, R., Sakzad, A., Liu, J.K., Liu, D.: Short lattice-based one-out-of-many proofs and applications to ring signatures. In: Deng, R.H., Gauthier-Umaña, V., Ochoa, M., Yung, M. (eds.) ACNS 2019. LNCS, vol. 11464, pp. 67–88. Springer, Cham (2019). https://doi.org/10.1007/978-3-030-21568-2_4

7. Franklin, M., Zhang, H.: A framework for unique ring signatures. IACR Cryptology ePrint Archive 2012:577 (2012)

8. Franklin, M., Zhang, H.: Unique ring signatures: a practical construction. In: Sadeghi, A.-R. (ed.) FC 2013. LNCS, vol. 7859, pp. 162–170. Springer, Heidelberg (2013). https://doi.org/10.1007/978-3-642-39884-1_13

9. Gentry, C., Peikert, C., Vaikuntanathan, V.: Trapdoors for hard lattices and new cryptographic constructions. In: Proceedings of the Fortieth Annual ACM Symposium on Theory of Computing, STOC 2008, pp. 197–206. ACM, New York (2008)

10. Halevi, S., Micali, S.: Practical and provably-secure commitment schemes from collision-free hashing. In: Koblitz, N. (ed.) CRYPTO 1996. LNCS, vol. 1109, pp. 201–215. Springer, Heidelberg (1996). https://doi.org/10.1007/3-540-68697-5_16

11. Kawachi, A., Tanaka, K., Xagawa, K.: Concurrently secure identification schemes based on the worst-case hardness of lattice problems. In: Pieprzyk, J. (ed.) ASIACRYPT 2008. LNCS, vol. 5350, pp. 372–389. Springer, Heidelberg (2008). https://doi.org/10.1007/978-3-540-89255-7_23

12. Libert, B., Ling, S., Nguyen, K., Wang, H.: Zero-knowledge arguments for lattice-based accumulators: logarithmic-size ring signatures and group signatures without trapdoors. In: Fischlin, M., Coron, J.-S. (eds.) EUROCRYPT 2016. LNCS, vol. 9666, pp. 1–31. Springer, Heidelberg (2016). https://doi.org/10.1007/978-3-662-49896-5_1

13. Lindell, Y.: Parallel coin-tossing and constant-round secure two-party computation. J. Cryptol. **16**, 143–184 (2003)

14. Liu, J.K., Wei, V.K., Wong, D.S.: Linkable spontaneous anonymous group signature for ad hoc groups. In: Wang, H., Pieprzyk, J., Varadharajan, V. (eds.) ACISP 2004. LNCS, vol. 3108, pp. 325–335. Springer, Heidelberg (2004). https://doi.org/10.1007/978-3-540-27800-9_28

15. Mercer, R.: Privacy on the blockchain: unique ring signatures (2016)

16. Rivest, R.L., Shamir, A., Tauman, Y.: How to leak a secret. In: Boyd, C. (ed.) ASIACRYPT 2001. LNCS, vol. 2248, pp. 552–565. Springer, Heidelberg (2001). https://doi.org/10.1007/3-540-45682-1_32

17. Shor, P.W.: Algorithms for quantum computation: discrete logarithms and factoring. In: Proceedings 35th Annual Symposium on Foundations of Computer Science, pp. 124–134, November 1994

18. Stern, J.: A new paradigm for public key identification. IEEE Trans. Inf. Theory **42**(6), 1757–1768 (1996)

19. Ta, A.T., et al.: Efficient unique ring signature for blockchain privacy protection. In: Baek, J., Ruj, S. (eds.) ACISP 2021. LNCS, vol. 13083, pp. 391–407. Springer, Cham (2021). https://doi.org/10.1007/978-3-030-90567-5_20

20. Yang, R., Au, M.H., Lai, J., Xu, Q., Yu, Z.: Lattice-based techniques for accountable anonymity: Composition of abstract stern's protocols and weak PRF with efficient protocols from LWR. Cryptology ePrint Archive, Report 2017/781 (2017). https://ia.cr/2017/781

# Verifiable Timed Linkable Ring Signatures for Scalable Payments for Monero

Sri AravindaKrishnan Thyagarajan[1]([✉]), Giulio Malavolta[2], Fritz Schmid[3], and Dominique Schröder[3]

[1] Carnegie Mellon University, Pittsburgh, USA
t.srikrishnan@gmail.com
[2] Max Planck Institute for Security and Privacy, Bochum, Germany
[3] Friedrich Alexander Universität Erlangen-Nürnberg, Erlangen, Germany
{fritz.schmid,dominique.schroeder}@fau.edu

**Abstract.** Decentralized cryptocurrencies still suffer from three interrelated weaknesses: Low transaction rates, high transaction fees, and long confirmation times. Payment Channels promise to be a solution to these issues, and many constructions for cryptocurrencies, such as Bitcoin and Ethereuem, are known. Somewhat surprisingly, no solution is known for Monero, the largest privacy-preserving cryptocurrency, without requiring system-wide changes like a hard-fork of its blockchain like prior solutions.

In this work, we close this gap for Monero by presenting the first provably secure payment channel protocol that is fully compatible with Monero's transaction scheme. Notably, the payment channel related transactions are identical to standard transactions in Monero, therefore not hampering the coins' fungibility. With standard techniques, our payment channels can be extended to support atomic swap of tokens in Monero with tokens of several other major currencies like Bitcoin, Ethereum, Ripple, etc., in a fungible and privacy-preserving manner.

Our main technical contribution is a new cryptographic tool called verifiable timed linkable ring signatures (VTLRS), where linkable ring signatures can be hidden for a pre-determined amount of time in a verifiable way. We present a practically efficient construction of VTLRS which is fully compatible with the transaction scheme of Monero, and allows for users to make timed payments to the future which might be of independent interest to develop other applications on Monero.

Our implementation results show that even with high network latency and with a single CPU core, two regular users can perform up to 93500 payments over 2 min (the block production rate of Monero). This is approximately five orders of magnitude improvement over the current payment rate of Monero.

**Keywords:** Timed signatures · Time-lock puzzles · Payment channels

## 1 Introduction

Modern cryptocurrencies, such as Bitcoin or Monero, realize the digital analog of a fiat currency without a trusted central authority. They typically consist of

V. Atluri et al. (Eds.): ESORICS 2022, LNCS 13555, pp. 467–486, 2022.
https://doi.org/10.1007/978-3-031-17146-8_23

two main components: (i) A public ledger that publishes all transactions and (ii) a transaction scheme that describes the structure and validity of transactions. Compared to traditional centralized solutions, decentralized cryptocurrencies suffer from three weaknesses: First, they have a relatively low transaction rate; for example, the current transaction rate of Bitcoin is about four transactions per second while it is 0.1 transactions per second in case of Monero [1]. Second, the transaction fees are relatively high, about 0,60$ per transaction in the case of Bitcoin and about 0.25$ in Monero [2]. Third, the confirmation of a transaction takes (on average) one hour in the case of Bitcoin and 20 min in the case of Monero. Payment Channels (PC) [27], and its generalization Payment Channel Networks (PCN) [15,22,23,27] have emerged as one of the most promising solutions to mitigate these issues and have been widely deployed to scale payment in major cryptocurrencies, such as Bitcoin [5], Ethereum [7] or Ripple [6]. These solutions are commonly referred to as *layer 2* or *off-chain* solutions.

A PC allows a pair of users to perform multiple payments without committing every intermediate payment to the blockchain. Abstractly, a PC consists of three phases: (i) Two users Alice and Bob, open a payment channel or a *joint address* by adding a single transaction to the blockchain. This transaction is a promise from Alice that she may pay up to a certain amount of coins to Bob, which he must claim before a certain time $T$. (ii) Within this time window, Alice may send coins from the joint address to Bob by sending a corresponding transaction to the other user. (iii) The channel closes when one of those payment transactions is posted on the chain, thus spending coins from the joint address. *Bi-directional* payment channels allow for payments to be made from the joint address to either users. While realizing PCs for Bitcoin is an established task due to the functionality available in the Bitcoin scripting language, several challenges arise when considering privacy-preserving cryptocurrencies like Monero or Zcash [11]. Bolt [18] is a PC proposal for Zcash while Moreno-Sanchez et al. [26] developed a PC protocol for Monero. However, their proposal has various shortcomings (see below for more details) and, as a consequence, is unlikely to be integrated into Monero. In this work, we aim to close this gap by constructing a PC protocol that is fully compatible with the transaction scheme of Monero and can be used to make off-chain transactions.

**Brief Look into Monero.** Monero is the largest privacy-preserving cryptocurrency. The notion of privacy it offers is that: Any external observer cannot learn who the sender or the receiver of a transaction is and the number of coins being transferred. Monero achieves these properties with Ring Confidential Transactions (RingCT) as its cryptographic bedrock. Briefly, a RingCT is a transaction scheme where the sender of the transaction 'hides' his key in an anonymity set (ring). Comparing with Bitcoin, where transactions have typically one source address, the amount in plain, one or two recipient address(es), and a simple signature (ECDSA), Monero transactions contain a ring of addresses, destination addresses, commitments to amounts, related consistency proofs, and a (linkable ring) signature, making the transactions considerably larger. Moreover, the size of a Monero transaction grows linearly with the size of the anonymity set. This results in a major setback to the scalability of Monero and often requires users to make tough choices between better privacy (high transaction fee) and smaller transactions (lower transaction fees). There has been a line of research [20, 36] that proposes new and efficient RingCT constructions that result in smaller transaction sizes. These approaches help to increase privacy because they support larger ring sizes and therefore do not increase the transaction fees. However, the central three issues that PCs are addressing remain open: Increasing the transaction rate, reducing the transaction fees in general, and therefore supporting fast micro-payments, as well as fast verification time. Moreover, all these on-chain solutions require system-wide changes in the Monero protocol, and it is unclear if Monero will fork and adapt to one of these schemes. Unfortunately, layer two solutions (such as PCs) proposed for Bitcoin do not extend to Monero as they require scripting features that are absent in Monero.

## 1.1 Our Contribution

The contributions of this work can be summarized as follows.

- We propose PAYMO, the first payment channel protocol that is fully compatible with the transaction scheme of Monero (Appendix B). A notable feature of our solution is that PC transactions are syntactically identical to standard transactions in Monero, thus retaining the *fungibility*[1] of the Monero coins. Following the work from [23], we can also extend PAYMOto have the first secure *scriptless* atomic-swap for Monero with many other major currencies.
- At the heart of our proposal is a new cryptographic primitive, called *verifiable timed linkable ring signatures* (VTLRS), that we define and construct (Sect. 3). Our solution relies on well-established cryptographic assumptions, and VTLRS can be of interest for other applications on Monero.
- We demonstrate the practicality of our approach by benchmarking PAYMO (Sect. 4). Our analysis shows that PAYMO can be used on today's hardware by Monero's users. In terms of performance, at its full power, PAYMO supports close to 93500 payments for 2 min between two regular users with one CPU core each. Here 2 min is the block production rate of Monero. This is a significant increase in payments in Monero, which currently supports only one payment from an address per 2 min.

## 1.2 Related Work and Discussion

In the following, we compare our approach with existing systems, and we discuss some of the choices behind practical aspects of our design.

The first PC proposal for Monero was recently put forth by Moreno-Sanchez et al. [26], however, their solution requires a hard fork with major changes to the

---

[1] Fungibility is a property of a currency whereby two units can be substituted in place of one another: no coins are special irrespective of transactions acting on them.

Monero transaction scheme and is *not* backward compatible. Specifically, a joint address of their comprises of two public keys where the secret keys of both keys are shared among the users, and they also require an explicit time-lock script for the joint address. Both of the above requirements are not supported in Monero.

We stress that even assuming that Monero will fork in the near future to integrate their scheme, the adoption procedure still requires one to solve some challenges: Since the tag generation in [26] is different from the currently used algorithm, one needs to perform massive system-wide changes to the Monero protocol itself, requiring *every* Monero user to spend from their existing, unspent keys (with old tag generation) to a new key (with the new tag generation) during a specific time interval. This is highly undesirable as it requires *every* Monero user to be online and make transactions, and any user unable to make this switch during this time interval loses his coins permanently. An additional limitation of their proposal in terms of transaction privacy where the time-lock information which is public can lead to on-chain censorship from miners and other users.

On the contrary, PAYMO does not require any changes to the transaction scheme of Monero, nor it needs to add any functionality to the scripting language. Any interested pair of users can run PAYMO without the knowledge of any other user in the Monero system. Furthermore, any PAYMO related transaction posted on-chain is *identical* to posting any other regular transaction in Monero. However, PAYMOusers need to run a background computation in the form of time-lock puzzle solving [28]. We discuss how to mitigate this computational load with batching techniques and outsourcing the solving to a decentralized service [34].

Payment Channels and Payment Channel Networks [22,27] have been proposed as solutions for Bitcoin's scalabiltiy problem. They rely on the special script *Hash Time-Lock Contract (HTLC)* that lets a user get paid if he produces a pre-image of a certain hash value before a specific time, referred to as the time-lock of the payment. Bolt [18] is a payment channel protocol specially tailored for Zcash [11] which uses zk-SNARKs [17], and is not compatible with the transaction scheme of Monero, which is the focus of this work. A generalisation of a payment channel with complex conditional payments is a *state channel* [14] that requires highly expressive scripting functionalities from the underlying blockchain, that are not available in Monero. Recently Gugger [19] proposed a mechanism for atomic swaps between Bitcoin and Monero. However their swap protocol is only semi-scriptless because they require a hash function verification from the bitcoin script. On the other hand, all PAYMO requires signature verification from the Bitcoin and Monero and, therefore, improves both the coins' fungibility in their respective chains.

## 2   Technical Overview

We first introduce the notion of *Verifiable Timed Linkable Ring Signature* (VTLRS) that is fully compatible with the transaction scheme in Monero. Then we describe how to leverage VTLRS to construct payment channels (PCs) for Monero. Finally, we discuss how to extend our protocol to support atomic swaps with tokens from other currencies and how to integrate our approach in the current implementation of Monero.

For ease of presentation, we consider a simplified view of a transaction in Monero consisting of: A ring of one-time public keys (addresses) $\mathcal{R}$, a linkability tag $tag$ (for double-spend protection against same key spending twice), a signature $\sigma$ and the target public key (recipient). We omit other components of a Monero transaction as our tools and techniques only deal with the above components and it can be naturally extended to the current transaction scheme of Monero with all components in place[2].

## 2.1 VTLRS for Monero

On a high-level, a VTLRS lets a user create a timed commitment of a linkable ring signature on a message (transaction) such that the recipient of the commitment can force open the commitment and learn the signature only after a pre-specified time $\mathbf{T}$. The recipient also receives a proof that convinces him that the force opening would indeed reveal the valid linkable ring signature on the message. Our construction of VTLRS is compatible with the linkable ring signature transaction scheme that is currently implemented in Monero, where the message is now a Monero transaction.

On a high-level, to commit to a VTLRS, the committer takes a (linkable ring) signature on a transaction $tx$ and *encodes* it into a time-lock puzzle [28], which keeps it hidden until time $\mathbf{T}$. To convince the verifier that the puzzle contains a valid signature on the transaction $tx$, the committer also computes a non-interactive zero-knowledge (NIZK) proof for such a statement. The challenge here is to design an efficient NIZK proof that certifies the validity of the encoded signature. General solutions exist [32] only for common signature schemes, like Schnorr, ECDSA, and BLS.

**Efficient NIZKs.** To design an efficient NIZK, we adopt a cut-and-choose approach. The basic idea of this approach is to encode the signature into many puzzles redundantly. The validity can be checked by revealing the random coins corresponding to a subset of them. If implemented naïvely, this could compromise the privacy of the signature. Instead, we harness the structural properties of signatures in Monero to reveal only isolated components while at the same time keeping the signature hidden. More specifically, the committer computes a $t$-out-of-$n$ secret sharing of a particular component of the signature. Given a $t-1$ subset of the shares (which are revealed by the cut-and-choose), the verifier can check the validity of the puzzles and that these opened shares are valid shares of the signature component. If the check is successful, then the verifier is convinced that *at least one* of the unopened puzzles contains a valid share, which is enough to reconstruct a valid signature. The scheme is made non-interactive using the Fiat-Shamir transformation [16].

---

[2] A Monero transaction is based on RingCT [20] which additionally consists of commitments to hide the amounts and range proofs to prove that they are well-formed.

**Time-Lock Puzzles.** We then instantiate the time-lock puzzles with [24,33] and use the homomorphic properties of such a scheme to combine puzzles in such a way that the computation needed to force open is the same as that to force open *a single puzzle*. We stress that the use of homomorphism is crucial for the solver's efficiency (verifier) and also for security. Without the homomorphism, a user with $\tilde{n} = n - (t-1)$ processors can solve $\tilde{n}$ puzzles in parallel and in total time $\mathbf{T}$. On the other hand, users with fewer processors will have to solve the puzzles one after another, thereby spending more time than $\mathbf{T}$ time. This could lead to scenarios in PCs where an adversarial party has an unfair advantage with respect to an honest user and could post a valid transaction ahead of time, effectively stealing coins.

## 2.2 (Uni-directional) Payment Channels in Monero

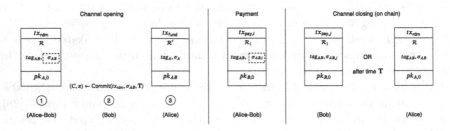

**Fig. 1.** Three phases to a (uni-directional) payment channel protocol between Alice and Bob in PayMo. The channel opening phase has three steps. Steps run individually and jointly through interaction are denoted with (Alice) or (Bob) and (Alice-Bob) respectively. Signature $\sigma_{AB}$ inside a dotted box indicates that only Bob learns the signature after interaction with Alice.

Equipped with our efficient VTLRS scheme, we show how Alice and Bob can run a payment channel protocol to make payments (i.e., an address whose secret key is shared between Alice and Bob, and both of them have to agree on a payment). A pictorial description of our PC protocol (PayMo) is given in Fig. 1 and its three main subroutines (channel opening, payment, and channel closing) are discussed below briefly. Due to space constraints, we defer the complete formal description to the full version [35] along with full security analysis.

**Channel Opening.** Alice and Bob jointly generate a spending key $pk_{AB}$ (the corresponding secret key is additively shared between Alice and Bob) and a redeem transaction $tx_{rdm}$ (containing the joint tag $tag_{AB}$) that spends the coins from $pk_{AB}$ (belonging to some ring $\mathcal{R}$) to some address of Alice $pk_{A,0}$. Note that $pk_{AB}$ is an address that is not yet present on the chain. Bob then generates a VTLRS of the signature $\sigma_{AB}$ on $tx_{rdm}$ with timing hardness $\mathbf{T}$. Bob gives the VTLRS commitment and proof (generated using $\mathsf{Com}(tx_{rdm}, \sigma_{AB}, \mathbf{T})$ in Fig. 1) to Alice, who then posts the transaction $tx_{fund}$ on the Monero blockchain. Such a transaction initializes the channel by sending funds from one of her addresses $pk_A$ to the joint key $pk_{AB}$. The channel is now created and initialized on-chain, and its expiry time is set to **T** (via the VTLRS). Note that after time **T** Alice will be able to recover the signature $tx_{rdm}$ and redeem the remaining funds in the address $pk_{AB}$ if any.

**Payment.** When Alice wishes to pay Bob, they jointly generate a transaction $tx_{pay,i}$ for the $i$-th payment. $tx_{pay,i}$ spends from $pk_{AB}$ (in some ring $\mathcal{R}_1$) and sends it to some address of Bob $pk_{B,0}$. They jointly generate a signature $\sigma_{AB,i}$ on $tx_{pay,i}$ (as the secret key for $pk_{AB}$ was shared among the users), in such a way that only Bob learns the signature $\sigma_{AB,i}$. Importantly, the transaction $tx_{pay,i}$ is not posted on the blockchain. Alice and Bob can continue making further payments this way.

**Channel Closing.** If Bob wishes to close the channel, he takes the last exchanged transaction payment $tx_{pay,j}$ with Alice and posts it along with $\sigma_{AB,j}$ on the Monero blockchain. In case Bob has not posted any such payment and time **T** has passed, Alice by then learns $\sigma_{AB}$ from the VTLRS on $tx_{rdm}$ (that was given by Bob during channel opening). Alice can now post $tx_{rdm}$ and $\sigma_{AB}$ on the Monero blockchain and redeem all the coins from the channel. In either case, once a transaction spending from $pk_{AB}$ is posted on-chain, the payment channel is considered closed.

**Integration in Monero.** An additional challenge stems from the fact that each public key in the ring used in a transaction is associated with a `key_offset` field [3] in the current implementation of Monero. This field stores the index of the key with respect to the global set of public keys as a way to optimise the look up of keys during transaction verification. Recall that, during channel opening, Alice and Bob need to generate the redeem transaction $tx_{rdm}$ that spends from the payment channel key $pk_{AB}$ before $tx_{fund}$ (that spends to $pk_{AB}$) is posted on the blockchain. This means that, in order to sign a correctly formed transaction $tx_{rdm}$, one needs to guess ahead of time the offset position of $pk_{AB}$.

There are two ways to bypass this obstacle. (1) Modify the current implementation (not the transaction scheme) to adopt a different look up strategy for public keys, that allows users to sign transactions that spend from a key that is not posted on the blockchain yet. (2) Instead of generating a VTLRS commitment of a signature on $tx_{rdm}$, Bob can generate a timed commitment to his share of the joint secret key $sk_{AB}$, for time **T**. After force opening the commitment, Alice learns $sk_{AB}$ and can use it to correctly sign $tx_{rdm}$, since the offset of $pk_{AB}$ is fixed at this point. Clearly, one needs an efficient mechanism to ensure that the timed commitment of Bob indeed contains a valid share of $sk_{AB}$. This can be realized using a verifiable timed discrete-log (VTDlog) scheme, and an efficient instantiation was recently proposed in [32].

While using VTDlog is a viable option to construct Monero-compatible PCs, we argue that VTLRS is a more desirable solution, since it enables the usage of stealth addresses [20]. Stealth addressing reduces interaction between the sender and the receiver of a payment in the following way: Alice (sender) generates a one-time public key $\mathsf{opk}_B$ for Bob (recipient) given access to Bob's master public key $\mathsf{mpk}_B$, and then sends coins to $\mathsf{opk}_B$. Bob can later spend from $\mathsf{opk}_B$ by generating the one time secret key $\mathsf{osk}_B$ using his master secret key $\mathsf{msk}_B$. This way the receiver is not required to send a recipient key to the sender every time he wishes to receive funds. Since the VTD-based solution leaks information about the long term secret key of a party, stealth addressing scheme used currently in Monero, is no longer a viable option, as one could link all future transactions of Bob once $\mathsf{osk}_B$ is disclosed [30]. Note that this issue does not arise in the VTLRS-based scheme, since neither user learns the secret key shares of the other user involved. More details can be found in [35].

**Outsource Computation.** Notice that Alice is required to perform persistent computation to open her VTLRS commitments. This could limit the number of channels that Alice can operate simultaneously. However, the persistent computation of opening a VTLRS commitment can be securely outsourced to a decentralized service [34] at a market determined cost. This relieves Alice of any potentially heavy computation related to VTLRS opening, provided she has enough funds to outsource using the service from [34]. Therefore the number of channels Alice operates is no longer limited by her computational power.

**Extending to Bi-directional Payments.** PAYMO supports payment channels with uni-directional payments. A payment channel with bi-directional payments allows both Alice and Bob to make payments to each other using their channel. A recent work [10] proposed *Sleepy Channels*, the first bi-directional payment channel protocol compatible with Monero. However, the key tools that they require to achieve this, are based on our work. Specifically, they crucially rely on VTLRS and the channel operations of PAYMO, to realise timed payments and payment revocation, which are essential for bi-directional payment channels.

## 3    Verifiable Timed Linkable Ring Signature

In the following we define and construct a *Verifiable Timed Linkable Ring Signature* (VTLRS) transaction scheme. We introduce some notation that we use extensively in this paper. We denote by $\lambda \in \mathbb{N}$ the security parameter and by $x \leftarrow \mathcal{A}(\mathsf{in}; r)$ the output of the algorithm $\mathcal{A}$ on input in using $r \leftarrow \{0,1\}^*$ as its randomness. We omit this randomness and only mention it explicitly when required. We denote the set $\{1, \ldots, n\}$ by $[n]$. We model parallel algorithms as Parallel Random Access Machines (PRAM) and *probabilistic polynomial time* (PPT) machines as efficient algorithms.

### 3.1    Definition

A VTLRS is a linkable ring signature based transaction scheme (see Appendix B) where one commits to such a signature in a *verifiable* and *extractable* way.

**Definition 1 (VTLRS).** *A Verifiable Timed Linkable Ring Signature Transaction Scheme* $\Pi_{\mathsf{VTLRS}}$, *for a LRS transaction scheme* $\Sigma$ := (Setup, OTKGen, TgGen, Spend, Vf) *is a tuple of five algorithms* (Setup, Com, Vfy, Op, FOp) *where:*

$crs \leftarrow \mathsf{Setup}(1^{\lambda})$: *the setup algorithm outputs a common reference string crs which is implicitly taken as input in all other algorithms.*

$(C, \pi) \leftarrow \mathsf{Com}(\sigma, tx, \mathbf{T}; r)$: *the commit algorithm takes as input a signature* $\sigma$, *the transaction tx, a hiding time* $\mathbf{T}$ *and randomness r. It outputs a commitment C and a proof* $\pi$.

$0/1 \leftarrow \mathsf{Vfy}(tx, C, \pi)$: *the verify algorithm takes as input a transaction m, a commitment C of hardness* $\mathbf{T}$ *and a proof* $\pi$ *and accepts the proof if and only if, the value* $\sigma$ *embedded in C is a valid signature on the transaction tx (i.e.,* $\mathsf{LRS.Vf}(tx, \sigma) = 1$). *Else it outputs 0.*

$(\sigma, r) \leftarrow \mathsf{Op}(C; r)$: *the opening algorithm is run by the committer that as input a commitment C and outputs the committed signature* $\sigma$ *and the randomness r used in generating the commitment C.*

$\sigma \leftarrow \mathsf{FOp}(C)$: *the deterministic* FOp *algorithm takes as input the commitment C and outputs a signature* $\sigma$.

We require standard notion of correctness that is formalized in the full version [35]. In terms of security, a VTLRS must satisfy the notions of *timed privacy* and *soundness*, defined below.

**Timed Privacy.** This notion requires that all PRAM algorithms whose running time is at most $t$ (where $t < \mathbf{T}$), succeed in extracting $\sigma$ from the commitment $C$ and $\pi$ with at most negligible probability. The adversary is given the spending public key and the tag as input, and gets access to a spending oracle. The challenge for the adversary here is to distinguish (within time $\mathbf{T}$ even with parallelism) a commitment from being a commitment to a valid LRS signature with the above attributes, to a simulated commitment.

**Definition 2 (Timed Privacy).** *A VTLRS scheme* $\Pi_{\mathsf{VTLRS}} =$ (Setup, Com, Vfy, Op, FOp) *for a LRS transaction scheme* $\Sigma$ *is timed private if there exists a PPT simulator* $\mathcal{S}$, *a negligible function* negl, *and a polynomial* $\tilde{\mathbf{T}}$ *such that for all polynomials* $\mathbf{T} > \tilde{\mathbf{T}}$, *all algorithms* $\mathcal{A} = (\mathcal{A}_1, \mathcal{A}_2)$ *where* $\mathcal{A}_1$ *is PPT and* $\mathcal{A}_2$ *is a PRAM whose running time is at most* $t < \mathbf{T}$, *and all* $\lambda \in \mathbb{N}$ *it holds that*

$$\Pr\left[b = b' \left| \begin{array}{c} (pk, sk) \leftarrow \mathsf{LRS.OTKGen}(pp) \\ tag \leftarrow \mathsf{TgGen}(sk) \\ (\mathcal{R}, \mathcal{O}, \mu) \leftarrow \mathcal{A}_1^{\mathsf{Spend}\mathcal{O}}(pk, tag, pp) \\ s.t.\ pk = pk_{|\mathcal{R}|}\ and\ tx := \{\mathcal{R}, tag, \mathcal{O}, \mu\} \\ b \leftarrow \{0, 1\},\ b' \leftarrow \mathcal{A}_2^{\mathsf{Spend}\mathcal{O}}(tx, C_b, \pi_b) \end{array} \right. \right] \leq \mathsf{negl}\,(\lambda)$$

*where,* $pp \leftarrow \mathsf{LRS.Setup}(1^{\lambda})$, $crs \leftarrow \mathsf{Setup}(1^{\lambda})$ *and if* $b = 0$, *then* $(C_0, \pi_0) \leftarrow \mathsf{Com}(\sigma, tx, \mathbf{T})$ *where* $\sigma \leftarrow \mathsf{LRS.Spend}(\mathcal{R}, (|\mathcal{R}|, sk, tag), \mathcal{O}, \mu)$ *and if* $b = 1$, $(C_1, \pi_1) \leftarrow \mathcal{S}(pk, tx, \mathbf{T})$.

**Soundness.** This says that the accepting verifier is convinced that given $C$, the FOp algorithm will return a valid signature $\sigma$ on transaction $tx$ in time $\mathbf{T}$. A VTLRS is *simulation-sound* if it is sound even when the prover has access to simulated proofs for (possibly false) statements of his choice; i.e., the prover must not be able to compute a valid proof for a fresh false statement of his choice.

**Definition 3 (Soundness).** *A VTLRS scheme $\Pi_{\text{VTLRS}} = (\text{Setup}, \text{Com}, \text{Vfy}, \text{Op}, \text{FOp})$ for a LRS transaction scheme $\Sigma$ is sound if there is a negligible function* negl *such that for all PPT adversaries $\mathcal{A}$ and all $\lambda \in \mathbb{N}$, we have:*

$$
\Pr\left[ b_1 = 1 \wedge b_2 = 0 \,\middle|\, 
\begin{array}{l}
crs \leftarrow \text{Setup}(1^\lambda) \\
(tx, C, \pi, \mathbf{T}) \leftarrow \mathcal{A}(crs) \\
(\sigma, r) \leftarrow \text{FOp}(C) \\
b_1 := \text{Vfy}(tx, C, \pi) \\
b_2 := \text{LRS.Vf}(tx, \sigma)
\end{array}
\right] \leq \text{negl}(\lambda) .
$$

## 3.2 Our VTLRS Construction

We give a construction of VTLRS transaction scheme for the LRS-TS transaction scheme used in Monero.

**LRS-TS Construction in Monero.** We give a formal description of the LRS-TS scheme deployed in Monero. We do not consider the "confidential transaction" part, and only focus on the signature of the transaction scheme, for conceptual simplicity. The scheme (Fig. 2) is defined over a cyclic group $\mathbb{G}$ of prime order $q$ with generator $G$ and uses two different hash functions $H_P : \mathbb{G} \to \mathbb{G}, H_S : \{0,1\}^* \to \mathbb{Z}_q^*$. The private-public key pair is the tuple $(x, G^x) \in \mathbb{Z}_q^* \times \mathbb{G}$. Each secret key is associated with a unique linkability tag that is set as $tag := H_P(pk)^{sk}$. For ease of understanding we make the assumption that the spending public key is always $pk_{|\mathcal{R}|}$ (as shown in Fig. 2). The spend algorithm samples $(s_0', s_1, \ldots, s_D) \leftarrow \mathbb{Z}_q^*$ and computes $L_0, R_0, h_0$ and $L_i, R_i, h_i$ for each index $i \in [D]$ (as shown in Fig. 2). The algorithm finally sets $s_0 := s_0' - h_D \cdot sk$ and the signature consists of $\sigma := (s_0, s_1, \ldots, s_D, h_0)$. Note that $s_0$ is reminiscent of how signing is done in Schnorr signatures. The verification algorithm runs the same loop as in the spend algorithm (except that it now ranges over the full ring) to obtain $h_{|\mathcal{R}|}$ and it accepts only if $h_0 = h_{|\mathcal{R}|}$. For brevity, we denote $D = |\mathcal{R}| - 1$.

Throughout the following overview, we describe the VTLRS as an interactive protocol between a committer and a verifier, which can be made non-interactive using the Fiat-Shamir transformation [16]. A formal description of our VTLRS is given in Figs. 3 and 4, where hash function $H' : \{0,1\}^* \to J$, with $J$ being a set of indices in $[n]$ such that $|J| = t - 1$, is used used to implement the Fiat-Shamir transformation.

**High-Level Overview.** The commit algorithm proceeds as follows: Consider a signature $\sigma := (s_0, s_1, \ldots, s_D, h_0)$ (where $D = |\mathcal{R}| - 1$) generated by Spend algorithm of Fig. 2 on a transaction $tx := \left( \{pk_i\}_{i=1}^{|\mathcal{R}|}, tag, \mathcal{O}, \mu \right)$. Let $pk_{|\mathcal{R}|}$ be

| Setup$(1^\lambda, 1^\alpha)$ | Spend$(\mathcal{R}, \mathcal{I}, \mathcal{O}, \mu)$ | Vf$(tx, \sigma)$ |
|---|---|---|
| $H_P : \mathbb{G} \to \mathbb{G}$ | $\mathcal{R} := (pk_1, \dots, pk_{|\mathcal{R}|})$ | $tx := (\mathcal{R}, tag, \mathcal{O}, \mu)$ |
| $H_S : \{0,1\}^* \to \mathbb{Z}_q^*$ | $\mathcal{I} := (j, sk, tag)$, s.t. | $\mathcal{R} := (pk_1, \dots, pk_{|\mathcal{R}|})$ |
| $pp := (\mathbb{G}, q, G, H_P, H_S)$ | $\quad j = |\mathcal{R}|$ and $pk_{|\mathcal{R}|} = G^{sk}$ | $\sigma := (s_0, \dots, s_D, h_0)$ |
| **return** $pp$ | $tx := tx(\mathcal{R}, \mathcal{I}, \mathcal{O}, \mu)$ | **set** $s_{|\mathcal{R}|} := s_0$ |
| | $(s'_0, s_1, \dots, s_D) \leftarrow \mathbb{Z}_q^*$ | **for** $i \in [|\mathcal{R}|]$ **do** |
| OTKGen$(pp)$ | $L_0 := G^{s'_0}, R_0 := H_P(pk_{|\mathcal{R}|})^{s'_0}$ | $\quad L_i := G^{s_i} pk_i^{h_{i-1}}$ |
| $x \leftarrow \mathbb{Z}_q^*$ | $h_0 := H_S(tx \| L_0 \| R_0)$ | $\quad R_i := H_P(pk_i)^{s_i} tag^{h_{i-1}}$ |
| $sk := x$ | **for** $i \in [D]$ **do** | $\quad h_i := H_S(tx \| L_i \| R_i)$ |
| $pk := G^x$ | $\quad L_i := G^{s_i} pk_i^{h_{i-1}},$ | **endfor** |
| **return** $(pk, sk)$ | $\quad R_i := H_P(pk_i)^{s_i} tag^{h_{i-1}}$ | **return** $(h_0 = h_{|\mathcal{R}|})$ |
| | $\quad h_i := H_S(tx \| L_i \| R_i)$ | |
| TgGen$(sk)$ | **endfor** | |
| $tag := H_P \left( G^{sk} \right)^{sk}$ | $s_0 := s'_0 - h_D \cdot sk$ | |
| **return** $tag$ | $\sigma := (s_0, s_1, \dots, s_D, h_0)$ | |
| | **return** $(tx, \sigma)$ | |

**Fig. 2.** LRS-TS $\Sigma := ($Setup, OTKGen, TgGen, Spend, Vf$)$ used in Monero.

the spending key. The commit algorithm takes as input this transaction $tx$, signature $\sigma$ and the hiding time **T**. To generate a VTLRS on transaction $tx$, the committer secret shares the values in $sc := (s_0, G^{s_0}, H_P(pk_{|\mathcal{R}|})^{s_0})$ using a $t$-out-of-$n$ threshold sharing scheme:

1. For the first $t - 1$ shares, choose $\alpha_i \in \mathbb{Z}_q$ uniformly at random and set $K_i := G^{\alpha_i}$ and $Y_i := H_P(pk_{|\mathcal{R}|})^{\alpha_i}$, respectively.
2. For the remaining $n - (t - 1)$ shares, use Lagrange interpolation in the exponent, i.e., for $i \in \{t, t+1, \dots, n\}$ set $\alpha_i, K_i, Y_i$ as

$$\left( s_0 - \sum_{j \in [t-1]} \alpha_j^{\ell_j(0)} \right)^{\ell_i(0)^{-1}}, \quad \left( \frac{G^{s_0}}{\prod_{j \in [t-1]} K_j^{\ell_j(0)}} \right)^{\ell_i(0)^{-1}},$$

$$\left( \frac{H_P(pk_{|\mathcal{R}|})^{s_0}}{\prod_{j \in [t-1]} Y_j^{\ell_j(0)}} \right)^{\ell_i(0)^{-1}},$$

respectively, where $\ell_i(\cdot)$ is the $i$-th Lagrange polynomial basis.

The $K$ and $Y$ elements ensure verifiability, that is we can indeed reconstruct (via Lagrange interpolation) the value $s_0$ that is part of the signature $\sigma$ from *any* $t$-sized set of shares of $sc$.

The committer then computes a time-lock puzzle $Z_i$ (using LHTLP.PGen) with time parameter $\mathbf{T}$ for each share $\alpha_i$ separately. The first message consists of all puzzles $(Z_1, \ldots, Z_n)$ together with $G^{s_0}, H_P(pk_{|\mathcal{R}|})^{s_0}$ and all $(K_i, Y_i)$ as defined above.

After receiving the above first message, the verifier chooses a random set $I$ of size $(t-1)$ as the challenge set. For this set, the committer opens the time-lock puzzles $\{Z_i\}_{i \in I}$ and reveals the underlying value $\alpha_i$ (together with the corresponding random coins) that it committed to. The verifier wants to ensure that, (i) the puzzles are indeed generated for the correct timing hardness $\mathbf{T}$ and can be successfully solved in that time and (ii) as long as at least one of the shares in the *unopened* puzzles $(\{Z_i\}_{i \in [n]/I})$ is consistent with respect to the corresponding partial commitments $(K_i, Y_i)$, then we can use it to reconstruct $s_0$ and therefore a valid $\sigma$. To do this, the verifier performs the following checks and accepts the commitment as legitimate only if they are all successful: (1) All puzzles $\{Z_i\}_{i \in I}$ are correctly generated using $\alpha_i$ and the corresponding randomness (which was also revealed above) with timing hardness $\mathbf{T}$, (2) All $\{\alpha_i\}_{i \in I}$ are consistent with the corresponding $K_i, Y_i$, i.e., $K_i = G^{\alpha_i}, Y_i = H_P(pk_{|\mathcal{R}|})^{\alpha_i}$ and (3) All $K_i, Y_i$ are valid shares of $G^{s_0}$ and $H_P(pk_{|\mathcal{R}|})^{s_0}$ respectively, i.e., $K_i^{\ell_i(0)} \cdot \prod_{j \in I} K_j^{\ell_j(0)} = G^{s_0}$ and $Y_i^{\ell_i(0)} \cdot \prod_{j \in I} Y_j^{\ell_j(0)} = H_P(pk_{|\mathcal{R}|})^{s_0}$.

Consequently, to fool a verifier, a malicious prover has to guess the challenge set $I$ ahead of time to pass the above checks without actually committing a valid $s_0$ (signature $\sigma$). Setting the parameters appropriately, we can guarantee that this happens only with negligible probability.

**Signature Recovery via Homomorphic Packing.** To recover $s_0$ and the valid signature, the verifier has to solve $\tilde{n} = (n - t + 1)$ puzzles to force the opening of a VTLRS. To close the gap between honest and malicious verifiers, we would like to reduce his workload to the minimal one of solving a single puzzle. To achieve this goal, we use the linearly homomorphic time-lock puzzle construction from [24] or [33] (for a transparent setup), combined with standard packing techniques to compress $\tilde{n}$ puzzles into a single one. Concretely, the verifier, on input $(Z_1, \ldots, Z_{\tilde{n}})$ homomorphically evaluates the linear function $f(x_1, \ldots, x_{\tilde{n}}) = \sum_{i=1}^{\tilde{n}} 2^{(i-1) \cdot \lambda} \cdot x_i$ to obtain a single puzzle $\tilde{Z}$, which he can solve in time $\mathbf{T}$. Observe that, once the puzzle is solved, all signatures can be decoded from the bit-representations of the resulting message. However we need to ensure that: (1) The message space of the homomorphic time-lock puzzle must be large enough to accommodate all $\tilde{n}$ signatures and (2) The values $\alpha_i$ encoded in the the input puzzles must not exceed the maximum size of a signature (say $\lambda$ bits).

Condition (1) can be satisfied instantiating the linearly homomorphic time-lock puzzles with a large enough message space. On the other hand, condition (2) is enforced by including a range NIZK $(\mathcal{P}_{\mathsf{NIZK}, \mathcal{L}_{\mathsf{rng}}}, \mathcal{V}_{\mathsf{NIZK}, \mathcal{L}_{\mathsf{rng}}})$ for the language $\mathcal{L}_{\mathsf{rng}} := \{(Z, 0, 2^\lambda, \mathbf{T}) : \exists w = (\alpha, r), s.t., (Z = \mathsf{LHTLP.PGen}(pp, \alpha; r)) \wedge (\alpha \in [0, 2^\lambda])\}$, which certifies that the message of each time-lock puzzles falls into the range $[0, 2^\lambda]$. We instantiate the range proof with the recently introduced protocol [32].

The following theorem states the security of our VTLRS construction and the formal proof is deferred to the full version [35].

**Theorem 1 (Timed Privacy, Soundness).** *Let* $(\mathsf{Setup}_{\mathsf{NIZK},\mathcal{L}_{\mathsf{rng}}}, \mathcal{P}_{\mathsf{NIZK},\mathcal{L}_{\mathsf{rng}}}, \mathcal{V}_{\mathsf{NIZK},\mathcal{L}_{\mathsf{rng}}})$ *be a NIZK for* $\mathcal{L}_{\mathsf{rng}}$ *and let* LHTLP *be a secure time-lock puzzle with perfect correctness. Then the protocol satisfies timed privacy (Definition 2) and soundness (Definition 3) in the ROM.*

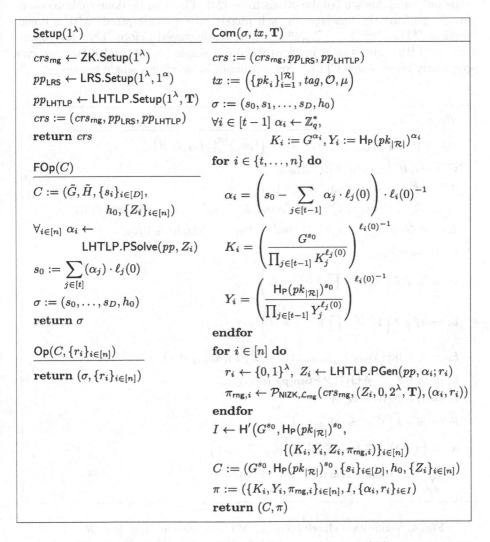

**Fig. 3.** Algorithms of our VTLRS Scheme. Here $D = |\mathcal{R}| - 1$.

**Instantiating** LHTLP. We can instantiate the LHTLP with the RSA based construction from [24] or the class group based construction from [33]. In the former we can let the committer run the setup while additionally proving the well-formedness, and in the latter we have a transparent setup which can be run by any party. Notice that one-time setup for VTLRS other than LHTLP, can be instantiated in the ROM without any trust.

**Batch Force-Opening of VTLRS Commitments.** We observe that assuming (i) a large enough message space of the time-lock puzzles and (ii) global public parameters $pp$, one can batch the solutions of different puzzles into a single one using known constructions from [24]. This can be done by homomorphically packing the messages in each puzzle into a single puzzle with a linear function $f(x_1, \ldots, x_{\tilde{n}}) = \sum_{i=1}^{\tilde{n}} 2^{(i-1)\cdot\lambda} \cdot x_i$ as discussed before. Therefore opening a VTLRS commitment involves solving a single puzzle, and infact, we can potentially open many VTLRS commitments by solving a single puzzle.

---

$\mathsf{Vfy}(tx, C, \pi)$

---

$crs := (crs_{\mathsf{rng}}, pp_{\mathsf{LRS}}, pp_{\mathsf{LHTLP}}), \quad tx := \left( \{pk_i\}_{i=1}^{|\mathcal{R}|}, tag, \mathcal{O}, \mu \right)$

$C := (\tilde{G}, \tilde{H}, \{s_i\}_{i \in [D]}, h_0, \{Z_i\}_{i \in [n]})$

$\pi := (\{K_i, Y_i, \pi_{\mathsf{rng},i}\}_{i \in [n]}, I, \{\alpha_i, r_i\}_{i \in I})$

$\forall i \in [D], \quad L_i := G^{s_i} pk_i^{h_{i-1}}, \quad R_i := \mathsf{H_P}(pk_i)^{s_i} tag^{h_{i-1}}, h_i := \mathsf{H_S}(tx\|L_i\|R_i)$

$L_{|\mathcal{R}|} := \tilde{G} \cdot pk_{|\mathcal{R}|}^{h_D}, \quad R_{|\mathcal{R}|} := \tilde{H} \cdot tag^{h_D}, \quad h_{|\mathcal{R}|} := \mathsf{H_S}(tx\|L_{|\mathcal{R}|}\|R_{|\mathcal{R}|})$

$b_1 := (h_0 \neq h_{|\mathcal{R}|})$

$b_2 := \exists j \notin I \left( K_j^{\ell_j(0)} \cdot \prod_{i \in I} K_i^{\ell_i(0)} \neq \tilde{G} \right)$

$b_3 := \exists j \notin I \left( Y_j^{\ell_j(0)} \cdot \prod_{i \in I} Y_i^{\ell_i(0)} \neq \tilde{H} \right)$

$b_4 := \exists i \in [n] \left( \mathcal{V}_{\mathsf{NIZK},\mathcal{L}_{\mathsf{rng}}}(crs_{\mathsf{rng}}, (Z_i, 0, 2^\lambda, \mathbf{T}), \pi_{\mathsf{rng},i}) \neq 1 \right)$

$b_5 := \exists i \in I \left( Z_i \neq \mathsf{LHTLP.PGen}(pp, \alpha_i; r_i) \right)$

$b_6 := \exists i \in I \left( K_i \neq G^{\alpha_i} \right)$

$b_7 := \exists i \in I \left( Y_i \neq \mathsf{H_P}(pk_{|\mathcal{R}|})^{\alpha_i} \right)$

$b_8 := \left( I \neq \mathsf{H'} \left( \tilde{G}, \tilde{H}, \{(K_i, Y_i, Z_i, \pi_{\mathsf{rng},i})\}_{i \in [n]} \right) \right)$

**if** $\bigvee_{i \in [8]} b_i = 1$ **thenreturn** 0     **else return** 1

---

**Fig. 4.** Verification algorithm of our VTLRS scheme. Here $D = |\mathcal{R}| - 1$.

# 4   Benchmarking

We implement prototypes of our VTLRS construction and PayMo. We build our VTLRS prototype with rust using the curve25519-dalek [8] library with security parameter $\lambda = 128$. All measurements were done on on a single CPU core of an AWS t2 micro instance for easier comparison with the following specifications: 1 core of a Intel Xeon E5-2676 v3 @ 2.40 Ghz, 1 GB of RAM, Ubuntu Linux 18.04.2 LTS (4.15.0-1045-aws) and rust 1.41. Our measurements are reported as a median over 1000 executions.

All hashing operations ($H_S$, $H_P$, $H$ and $H'$) are implemented using SHA-512 or the Keccak variant used in Monero. For all Elliptic Curve Operations the Curve25519 implementation from curve25519-dalek [8] in Ristretto form [9] was used. We implemented the NIZK proof from [12] for $\mathcal{L}_{eqdl}$ and the NIZK proof for $\mathcal{L}_{rng}$ from [32]. The prover and verifier times for the NIZK proof for $\mathcal{L}_{eqdl}$ is 0.079 ms and 0.143 ms, respectively. For the NIZK for $\mathcal{L}_{rng}$, for statistical soundness parameter $k = 64$, the prover and verifier times are 258.66 ms and 289.56 ms, respectively. We implemented the LHTLP construction [24] for time-lock puzzles, with a 1024 bit RSA modulus $N$. In our benchmark, the time taken for PSetup (including prime generation) is 730.43 ms, and the time taken for PGen is 3.557 ms. And the time taken by PSolve for timing hardness $\mathbf{T} := 1024, 2048$ and 4096 is 2.708 ms, 4.070 ms and 6.795 ms, respectively.

**VTLRS.** We evaluated our VTLRS construction by setting the parameters as $n = 80$ and $t = 40$ (probability of adversary breaking soundness is $9.3 \times 10^{-24}$). Our results show that Com and Vfy algorithms of our VTLRS construction take 586.76 ms and 467.84 ms in CPU time, respectively. We implemented the LRS transaction scheme of Monero with a ring size of 10 keys (which is the common size used in Monero today [4]), with one spending key and one recipient.

**Evaluation of PayMo.** We consider two different measurements: (i) Only the computation operations and not the cost of serialisation and network transmission in PayMo. This shows the performance of the protocol on the sender and receiver side of a PayMo channel. (ii) Total time taken by operations including network operations and latency. To show the impact of network transmission in this measurement, two settings with different network latency are considered. We focus only on LRS-TS of Monero and omit other confidential transactions related operations. A possible future work is to have a complete prototype that is executable on the Monero network.

We consider Alice and Bob who share a payment channel. To evaluate the performance of PayMo, we measure the computation time of both users during the channel opening and payment phase. We also measure the total time taken for PayMo operations that includes network latency between parties. Our results from Table 1 show that the time taken for finishing a single payment is less a third of second even under high latency scenarios.

**Table 1.** PAYMO operations for Alice and Bob excluding network overhead. PC operations for both parties including network latency, with low latency setup **S1** (Alice and Bob) and high latency setup **S2** (Alice and Bob) with Round Trip Times between the two users of 0.3 ms and 144 ms, respectively. All measurements are reported in milliseconds (ms).

|                          | Alice | Bob   | Setup S1 | Setup S2 |
|--------------------------|-------|-------|----------|----------|
| Joint key/Tag generation | 0.13  | 0.31  | 1.85     | 440.7    |
| PC opening               | 468.1 | 588.4 | 1060     | 1351     |
| PC payment               | 1.30  | 1.28  | 3.61     | 297.9    |

**Interpretation.** Our results from Table 1 show that by exploiting parallel request processing, the receiver of one or more channel(s) can process around 780 payments per second per CPU core, while the sender of one of more channel(s) can process around 770 payments per second per CPU core. The parties can scale up their processing power if they spawn more PC nodes (or cores) as done in the Lightning Network.

For instance, for a payment service provider (recipient) who has payment channels with several users, it can accept more than 93600 payments per CPU core over a span of 2 min (average block production rate in Monero), from users with PAYMO channels with the service provider. In this case, only the receiver's CPU time for payments is considered, excluding the overhead for serialization and network.

Alice and Bob can process close to 93500 payments per CPU core (with acknowledgement of payment) over a span of 2 min even with a round trip latency time of 144 ms per message. This is because during message transmission, parties do not stay idle but instead spawn new payments in parallel. In case the parties only make sequential payments, Alice can still make more than 400 payments over the span of 2 min.

## 5    Conclusions

We presented verifaible timed linkable ring signatures a new cryptographic tool and PAYMO, which is the first payment channel protocol that is fully compatible with Monero, the largest privacy-preserving cryptocurrency. Our results show an increase in the transaction throughput of several orders of magnitudes when compared with the current implementation of Monero. As an exciting next step, we plan to work on large scale adoption of PAYMO in Monero.

**Acknowledgements.** The work was in part supported by THE DAVID AND LUCILLE PACKARD FOUNDATION - Award #202071730, SRI INTERNATIONAL - Award #53978 / Prime: DEFENSE ADVANCED RESEARCH PROJECTS AGENCY - Award #HR00110C0086 and NATIONAL SCIENCE FOUNDATION - Award #2212746. This work is also partially supported by Deutsche Forschungsgemeinschaft (DFG, German Research Foundation) as part of the Research and Training Group 2475 "Cybercrime and Forensic Computing" (grant number 393541319/GRK2475/1-2019), and by the grant 442893093, and by the state of Bavaria at the Nuremberg Campus of Technology (NCT). NCT is a research cooperation between the Friedrich-Alexander-Universität Erlangen-Nürnberg (FAU) and the Technische Hochschule Nürnberg Georg Simon Ohm (THN).

## A   Preliminaries

**Time-Lock Puzzles.** Time-lock puzzles [28] allow one to conceal a secret for a certain amount of time $\mathbf{T}$. *Homomorphic Time-Lock Puzzles (HTLPs)* [24] allow one to perform homomorphic computation on honestly generated puzzles. It consists of a setup algorithm (PSetup), that takes as input a time hardness parameter $\mathbf{T}$ and outputs public parameters of the system $pp$, a puzzle generation algorithm (PGen) that, on input a message, generates the corresponding puzzle. One can then evaluate homomorphically functions over encrypted messages (PEval) and solve the resulting puzzle in time $\mathbf{T}$ (PSolve). The security requirement is that for every PRAM adversary $\mathcal{A}$ of running time $\leq \mathbf{T}^\varepsilon(\lambda)$ the messages encrypted are computationally hidden. Malavolta and Thyagarajan [24] show an efficient construction that is linearly homomorphic over the ring $\mathbb{Z}_{N^s}$, where $N$ is an RSA modulus and $s$ is any positive integer. The scheme is perfectly correct and is secure under the sequential squaring assumption [28].

**Non-interactive Zero-Knowledge.** Let $R : \{0,1\}^* \times \{0,1\}^* \to \{0,1\}$ be an NP relation with corresponding NP-language $\mathcal{L} := \{stmt : \exists w \ s.t. \ R(stmt, w) = 1\}$. A non-interactive zero-knowledge proof (NIZK) [13] system for $\mathcal{L}$ is initialized with a setup algorithm $\mathsf{Setup}(1^\lambda)$ that outputs a common reference string $crs$. A prover can show the validity of a statement $stmt$ with a witness $w$ by invoking $\mathcal{P}_{\mathsf{NIZK},\mathcal{L}}(crs, stmt, w)$, which outputs a proof $\pi$. The proof $\pi$ can be efficiently checked by the verification algorithm $\mathcal{V}_{\mathsf{NIZK},\mathcal{L}}(crs, stmt, \pi)$. A NIZK proof for language $\mathcal{L}$ is simulation extractable if one can extract a valid $w$ from adversarially generated proofs, even if the adversary sees arbitrarily many simulated proofs. A NIZK must also be zero knowledge in the sense that nothing beyond the validity of the statement is leaked to the verifier.

**Threshold Secret Sharing.** Secret sharing is a method of creating shares of a given secret and later reconstructing the secret itself only if given a threshold number of shares. Shamir [31] proposed a threshold secret sharing scheme where the sharing algorithm takes a secret $s \in \mathbb{Z}_q$ and generates shares $(s_1, \ldots, s_n)$ each in $\mathbb{Z}_q$. The reconstruction algorithm takes as input at least $t$ shares and outputs a secret $s$. The security demands that knowing only a set of shares smaller than the threshold size does *not* reveal any information about $s$.

## B   Transaction Scheme of Monero

We review the basic definitions of Linkable Ring Signatures (LRS) following Lai et al. [20]. In contrast to their work, our definitions do not consider the "confidential transaction" part, and only focus on the signature of the transaction scheme, for conceptual simplicity.

## B.1   Definition

A ring signature [29] scheme allows to sign messages such that the signer is anonymous within a set a possible signers, called the ring. The members associated to the ring are chosen "on-the-fly" by the signer using their public-keys. Linkability [21] means that anonymity is retained unless the same user signing key is used to sign twice. This is achieved by associating a unique linkability tag to each signing key that is revealed while generating a signature.

In a transaction scheme, we have a block of data referred to as a transaction, that determines the amount of coins transferred from one user address (source) to another user address (target) and it is accompanied by an authentication token (signature) of the sending user. Since the sending user is represented through the source address in the transaction, the signature is checked for validity with respect to the source account. Combining linkable ring signatures and a transaction scheme, we have a linkable ring signature based transaction scheme (LRS-TS), where the message signed is the transaction which consists of: A ring of addresses (LRS public keys) and their associated coins (out of which one of the addresses is the source account), and one or more target addresses. The authentication token of the transaction is a linkable ring signature on the transaction (as message), with the ring of addresses as the ring, and the secret authentication key of the source address as the signing key of the linkable ring signature scheme. To prevent leakage of the source address it is assumed that each address in the ring of addresses have the same amount of associated coins[3].

**Definition 4.** *A* Linkable Ring Signature (LRS) *transaction scheme $\Sigma$ consists of the* PPT *algorithms* (Setup, OTKGen, TgGen, Spend, Vf) *which are defined as follows:*

$pp \leftarrow$ Setup($1^\lambda$): *outputs the public parameter pp.*

$(pk, sk) \leftarrow$ OTKGen($pp$): *The* one-time *key generation algorithm outputs a public-secret key-pair $(pk, sk)$.*

$tag \leftarrow$ TgGen($sk$): *The* tag-generation *algorithm takes as input a secret key sk. It outputs a tag tag.*

$(tx, \sigma) \leftarrow$ Spend($\mathcal{R}, \mathcal{I}, \mathcal{O}, \mu$): *The spend algorithm takes as input a set $\mathcal{R}$ of public keys with each key associated with c coins, a tuple $I = (j, sk, tag)$ consisting of an index j, a secret key sk, and a tag tag, a set $\mathcal{O}$ consisting of target public keys and some metadata $\mu$. It outputs a transaction $tx := (\mathcal{R}, tag, \mathcal{O}, \mu)$ and a signature $\sigma$.*

$b \leftarrow$ Vf($tx, \sigma$): *The verify algorithm inputs a transaction tx and a signature $\sigma$. It outputs a bit b denoting the validity of $\sigma$.*

**Security.** We have three properties of LRS-TS, namely (1) *Privacy:* LRS-TS should ensure privacy of the source account, meaning an adversarial observer on the blockchain should not learn any information about the source address from a transaction other than the fact that it is a member of the ring of one-time

---

[3] This assumption can be relaxed with the use of confidential transactions [25] where an account's associated amount is hidden using commitments.

addresses, (2) *Non-Slanderability (Unforgeability)*: LRS-TS must ensure that an adversarial user cannot steal the coins of an honest user (unforgeability) or spend coins on behalf of an honest user (non-slanderability), and (3) *Linkability*: LRS-TS must ensure that an adversary cannot double spend his coins and any such attempts must be linkable. We refer the reader to [35] for the formal definitions.

# References

1. https://www.blockchain.com/en/charts/transactions-per-second
2. https://bitinfocharts.com/comparison/transactionfees-btc-xmr.html
3. https://tinyurl.com/sujsu369
4. https://moneroblocks.info/block/2047966
5. Lightning Network. https://lightning.network/
6. Payment Channels in Ripple. https://xrpl.org/use-payment-channels.html
7. Raiden Network. https://raiden.network/
8. curve25519-dalek (2019). https://tinyurl.com/rb3pnfvm
9. Arcieri, T., de Valence, H., Lovecruft, I.: The ristretto group (2019). https://ristretto.group/ristretto.html
10. Aumayr, L., Thyagarajan, S.A., Malavolta, G., Monero-Sánchez, P., Maffei, M.: Sleepy channels: bitcoin-compatible bi-directional payment channels without watchtowers (2021). (To Appear at ACM CCS 2022)
11. Ben-Sasson, E., et al.: Zerocash: decentralized anonymous payments from bitcoin. In: 2014 S&P, pp. 459–474. IEEE (2014). https://doi.org/10.1109/SP.2014.36
12. Camenisch, J., Stadler, M.: Proof systems for general statements about discrete logarithms. Technical report/Department of Computer Science, ETH Zürich 260 (1997)
13. De Santis, A., Micali, S., Persiano, G.: Non-interactive zero-knowledge proof systems. In: Pomerance, C. (ed.) CRYPTO 1987. LNCS, vol. 293, pp. 52–72. Springer, Heidelberg (1988). https://doi.org/10.1007/3-540-48184-2_5
14. Dziembowski, S., Eckcy, L., Faust, S., Malinowski, D.: Perun: virtual payment hubs over cryptocurrencies. In: 2019 S&P, pp. 106–123. IEEE (2019). https://doi.org/10.1109/SP.2019.00020
15. Egger, C., Moreno-Sanchez, P., Maffei, M.: Atomic multi-channel updates with constant collateral in bitcoin-compatible payment-channel networks. In: ACM CCS 2019, pp. 801–815. ACM Press (2019). https://doi.org/10.1145/3319535.3345666
16. Fiat, A., Shamir, A.: How to prove yourself: Practical solutions to identification and signature problems. In: Odlyzko, A.M. (ed.) CRYPTO 1986. LNCS, vol. 263, pp. 186–194 (1987). https://doi.org/10.1007/3-540-47721-7_12
17. Gennaro, R., Gentry, C., Parno, B., Raykova, M.: Quadratic span programs and succinct NIZKs without PCPs. In: Johansson, T., Nguyen, P.Q. (eds.) EUROCRYPT 2013. LNCS, vol. 7881, pp. 626–645. Springer, Heidelberg (2013). https://doi.org/10.1007/978-3-642-38348-9_37
18. Green, M., Miers, I.: Bolt: anonymous payment channels for decentralized currencies. In: ACM CCS 2017, pp. 473–489. ACM Press (2017). https://doi.org/10.1145/3133956.3134093
19. Gugger, J.: Bitcoin-monero cross-chain atomic swap. Cryptology ePrint Archive, Report 2020/1126 (2020). https://eprint.iacr.org/2020/1126
20. Lai, R.W.F., Ronge, V., Ruffing, T., Schröder, D., Thyagarajan, S.A.K., Wang, J.: Omniring: scaling private payments without trusted setup. In: ACM CCS 2019, pp. 31–48. ACM Press (2019). https://doi.org/10.1145/3319535.3345655

21. Liu, J.K., Wei, V.K., Wong, D.S.: Linkable spontaneous anonymous group signature for Ad Hoc groups. In: Wang, H., Pieprzyk, J., Varadharajan, V. (eds.) ACISP 2004. LNCS, vol. 3108, pp. 325–335. Springer, Heidelberg (2004). https://doi.org/10.1007/978-3-540-27800-9_28

22. Malavolta, G., Moreno-Sanchez, P., Kate, A., Maffei, M., Ravi, S.: Concurrency and privacy with payment-channel networks. In: ACM CCS 2017, pp. 455–471. ACM Press (2017). https://doi.org/10.1145/3133956.3134096

23. Malavolta, G., Moreno-Sanchez, P., Schneidewind, C., Kate, A., Maffei, M.: Anonymous multi-hop locks for blockchain scalability and interoperability. In: NDSS 2019. ISOC (2019)

24. Malavolta, G., Thyagarajan, S.A.K.: Homomorphic time-lock puzzles and applications. In: Boldyreva, A., Micciancio, D. (eds.) CRYPTO 2019. LNCS, vol. 11692, pp. 620–649. Springer, Cham (2019). https://doi.org/10.1007/978-3-030-26948-7_22

25. Maxwell, G.: Confidential transactions (2015). https://people.xiph.org/~greg/confidential_values.txt

26. Moreno-Sanchez, P., Le, D.V., Noether, S., Goodell, B., Kate, A.: Dlsag: non-interactive refund transactions for interoperable payment channels in Monero. Tech. rep., Cryptology ePrint Archive, Report 2019/595 (2019)

27. Poon, J., Dryja, T.: The bitcoin lightning network: Scalable off-chain instant payments (2016)

28. Rivest, R.L., Shamir, A., Wagner, D.A.: Time-lock puzzles and timed-release crypto. Tech. rep. (1996)

29. Rivest, R.L., Shamir, A., Tauman, Y.: How to leak a secret. In: Boyd, C. (ed.) ASIACRYPT 2001. LNCS, vol. 2248, pp. 552–565. Springer, Heidelberg (2001). https://doi.org/10.1007/3-540-45682-1_32

30. van Saberhagen, N.: Cryptonote v 2.0 (2013)

31. Shamir, A.: How to share a secret. Commun. ACM 22(11), 612–613 (1979)

32. Thyagarajan, S.A.K., Bhat, A., Malavolta, G., Döttling, N., Kate, A., Schröder, D.: Verifiable Timed Signatures Made Practical, CCS 2020. Association for Computing Machinery (2020)

33. Thyagarajan, S.A.K., Castagnos, G., Laguillaumie, F., Malavolta, G.: Efficient CCA Timed Commitments in Class Groups. ACM CCS (2021)

34. Thyagarajan, S.A.K., Gong, T., Bhat, A., Kate, A., Schröder, D.: Opensquare: Decentralized Repeated Modular Squaring Service, CCS 2021 (2021)

35. Thyagarajan, S.A.K., Malavolta, G., Schmidt, F., Schröder, D.: Paymo: payment channels for monero. Cryptology ePrint Archive, Report 2020/1441 (2020)

36. Yuen, T.H., et al.: RingCT 3.0 for blockchain confidential transaction: shorter size and stronger security. Cryptology ePrint Archive, Report 2019/508 (2019). https://eprint.iacr.org/2019/508

# Deterministic Wallets for Adaptor Signatures

Andreas Erwig[✉] and Siavash Riahi

Technische Universität Darmstadt, Darmstadt, Germany
{andreas.erwig,siavash.riahi}@tu-darmstadt.de

**Abstract.** *Adaptor signatures* are a new cryptographic primitive that binds the authentication of a message to the revelation of a secret value. In recent years, this primitive has gained increasing popularity both in academia and practice due to its versatile use-cases in different Blockchain applications such as atomic swaps and payment channels. The security of these applications, however, crucially relies on users storing and maintaining the secret values used by adaptor signatures in a secure way. For standard digital signature schemes, cryptographic wallets have been introduced to guarantee secure storage of keys and execution of the signing procedure. However, no prior work has considered cryptographic wallets for adaptor signatures.

In this work, we introduce the notion of *adaptor wallets*. Adaptor wallets allow parties to securely use and maintain adaptor signatures in the Blockchain setting. Our adaptor wallets are both deterministic and operate in the hot/cold paradigm, which was first formalized by Das et al. (CCS 2019) for standard signature schemes. We introduce a new cryptographic primitive called *adaptor signatures with rerandomizable keys*, and use it to generically construct adaptor wallets. We further show how to instantiate adaptor signatures with rerandomizable keys from the ECDSA signature scheme and discuss that they can likely be built for Schnorr and Katz-Wang schemes as well. Finally, we discuss the limitations of the existing ECDSA- and Schnorr-based adaptor signatures w.r.t. deterministic wallets in the hot/cold setting and prove that it is impossible to overcome these drawbacks given the current state-of-the-art design of adaptor signatures.

## 1 Introduction

Blockchains have gained huge popularity in the past decade as they provide a decentralized infrastructure that allows not only to make simple payments but also to execute applications in a secure way. However, most Blockchains, including Bitcoin, only support the execution of simple applications while others, such as Monero or Zcash, are even more restrictive in their functionality and only support simple payments [20,25]. Nevertheless, virtually all Blockchains rely on digital signatures in order to authenticate the origin of a transaction. While the functionality of Blockchains can be extended by appropriately adjusting the mining algorithms, this requires a hard fork of the Blockchain code which can take

© The Author(s), under exclusive license to Springer Nature Switzerland AG 2022
V. Atluri et al. (Eds.): ESORICS 2022, LNCS 13555, pp. 487–506, 2022.
https://doi.org/10.1007/978-3-031-17146-8_24

several years to complete in practice. In order to improve the restricted functionality of many Blockchains without having to change the Blockchain implementation and to allow for the execution of a larger class of applications, a new type of signature scheme called *adaptor signatures* was introduced by the cryptocurrency community [19] and first formally analyzed by Aumayr et al. [3]. At a high level, adaptor signatures allow two parties, say a *signer* and a *publisher* to trade a signature in exchange for a secret, i.e., if the publisher publishes a signature under the signer's secret key on the Blockchain, a secret value is leaked to the signer. More concretely, the publisher first generates an instance of a hard relation, i.e., a statement and witness pair and sends the statement to the signer. Using its secret key and the statement, the signer generates an incomplete signature called *pre-signature* which can be *adapted* by the publisher to a full valid signature using the witness. Once the adapted full signature is published, the signer can *extract* the witness given the pre- and full signature.

Adaptor signatures have proven to be extremely versatile for Blockchain applications. They allow for efficient constructions of two important categories of applications, namely payment channels (e.g., [3,22]) and atomic swaps (e.g., [7,24]), while requiring only a minimal functionality from the underlying Blockchain. Payment channels are a so-called off-chain solution, which allows two parties to issue many micropayments to each other without incurring fees for each transaction. Atomic swaps, on the other hand, allow two (or more) parties to atomically exchange tokens, i.e., either the exchange terminates and both parties obtain the other party's token or none does. Both of these applications rely on a technique that allows exchanging a secret value for a signature, which is exactly the functionality that adaptor signatures provide.

As the security of a user's funds in a Blockchain network depends solely on the secure storage of this user's signing secret key (and witnesses of adaptor signatures), it is of utmost importance how users store these secret values. Unfortunately, despite the increasing popularity of adaptor signatures, no prior work tried to address this issue. In other words we would like to answer the following question:

*How can parties in practice employ adaptor signatures securely?*

A concept known as *cryptographic wallets* has been introduced to use standard signature schemes securely in Blockchain networks. However, it has never been investigated if this concept can be extended to adaptor signatures.

*Deterministic Wallets.* One of the most promising proposals for cryptographic wallets are so-called deterministic wallets, which at a high level store a master signing key pair from which session key pairs are deterministically derived. Das et al. [6] gave the first formalization of such deterministic wallets in the hot/cold setting and later extended their model [5] to incorporate hierarchical wallets. In a bit more detail, a wallet scheme in the hot/cold setting consists of two separate devices, a hot and a cold wallet, that store the public and secret key respectively. The cold wallet is kept mostly offline and is only used to generate a new signature, whereas the hot wallet is constantly online to receive new transactions. This wallet structure ensures that it is inherently difficult for an attacker to steal the wallet's secret key, as it is stored in the offline cold wallet. Besides a standard unforgeability notion, wallet schemes should typically also satisfy an *unlinkability* property, which ensures that a third party cannot link two transactions issued to the same wallet. A naïve approach to achieve unlinkability is to let the wallet generate a fresh key pair for each transaction. This, however, requires the wallet to store all key pairs, which is not efficient, especially since cold wallets sometimes require special hardware (with limited storage) to securely store the secret keys. As such, deterministic wallets were introduced where the unlinkable keys are deterministically derived from a master key pair. This allows the wallet to derive new keys on the fly when they are needed instead of storing them indefinitely.

To date deterministic wallets have only been analyzed for digital signature schemes (e.g., [6]). Considering that the security of adaptor signatures does not only depend on the secure storage of the secret key but also on the secure handling of witnesses, designing a secure wallet scheme for adaptor signatures becomes even more pressing.

## 1.1 Our Contribution

In this work, we initiate the study of deterministic wallets in the hot/cold setting for adaptor signatures following the approach of Das et al. [6]. To this end, we first introduce a new notion of adaptor signatures, which we call *adaptor signature with rerandomizable keys*. This primitive extends regular adaptor signatures by key rerandomization algorithms. That is, given an adaptor signature key pair $(sk, pk)$ and some randomness $\rho$, an adaptor signature with rerandomizable keys allows to deterministically and independently rerandomize $sk$ and $pk$ using $\rho$ to obtain a new key pair $(sk', pk')$ such that (1) $(sk', pk')$ constitutes a valid signing key pair, and (2) $(sk', pk')$ is indistinguishable from a freshly generated key pair. We formally define this primitive and show how to instantiate it by transforming the existing ECDSA-adaptor signature scheme [3,18] into an adaptor signature with rerandomizable keys.

We provide a formal model for adaptor wallets (in the full version of this paper[1]). Our adaptor wallets are the first cryptographic wallets that are deterministic, in the hot/cold setting and support the use of adaptor signatures. While the hot/cold wallet setting allows to provide strong security guarantees, it is not suitable for all applications in practice. Payment channels, for instance, have a short life span but require a frequent exchange of signatures. As such, storing the secret key in an offline cold wallet seems counterintuitive. Instead, for such applications our model allows to store secret values on one online device while guaranteeing that even if this device gets corrupted, the master key pair and other keys derived from the master key pair remain secure. To achieve this feature, we use the idea of hardened/non-hardened wallets as defined in [5] and adjust it for adaptor wallets (see Sect. 4.1 for more details).

---

[1] The full version will be published on the IACR Cryptology ePrint Archive.

We then show how to generically construct adaptor wallets from *any* adaptor signature scheme with rerandomizable keys where the hard relation is *witness rerandomizable* and further show how to initiate such a relation for ECDSA-adaptor signatures. Witness rerandomizability of a hard relation $R$ essentially means that for any statement/witness pair $(Y, y) \in R$ the witness $y$ can be rerandomized deterministically using some randomness $\rho$ to a witness $y'$ with corresponding statement $Y'$ such that $(Y', y') \in R$. We require this property to alleviate the storage constraints on the cold wallet, i.e., as explained above, the cold wallet is often a storage restricted device and hence deterministic rerandomization can be useful to generate required values on the fly instead of storing them long-term. Although we do not formally show how adaptor wallets can be instantiated from Schnorr and Katz-Wang signature schemes [13,21], it seems that our approach can be used in order to transform these schemes to adaptor signatures with rerandomizable keys and use them to instantiate adaptor wallets.

Our final contribution is closely related to witness rerandomizable hard relations. Surprisingly, we show that it is *impossible* to construct an adaptor wallet from fully rerandomizable hard relations, i.e., hard relations where the statement and witness can be rerandomized independently using the same randomness. This is in stark contrast to the secret and public keys which can be rerandomized independently. We believe that our work paves the way for mainstreaming the usage of adaptor signatures by providing a secure and efficient deterministic wallet framework in the hot/cold setting.

## 1.2   Related Work

We divide the related work into adaptor signatures and deterministic wallets.

*Adaptor Signatures.* After being first introduced by Poelstra [19], adaptor signatures have been used in many Blockchain related applications, such as atomic swaps [7], payment channel networks [17] and payment channel hubs [22]. Aumayr et al. [3] later provided a standalone formalization of this primitive. Shortly after, Esgin et al. and Tairi et al. [9,23] provided instantiations of adaptor signatures in the post-quantum setting where the adversary has access to a quantum computer while the end users do not. Finally, Erwig et al. [8] showed how to generically transform signature schemes built from identification schemes which satisfy certain properties, into single party and two party adaptor signatures. There have been several other recent works on adaptor signatures (e.g., [16,24]) which used or extended this primitive to build more complex applications.

*Deterministic Wallets.* There have been many recent works formalizing and analyzing cryptographic wallets, such as [2,12,14,15]. The concept of deterministic wallets in the hot/cold setting was first formalized and instantiated by Das et al. [6]. Alkadri et al. [1] later showed how to realize such wallets with security in the post-quantum setting. In a follow-up work, Das et al. [5] extended the original model by allowing hierarchical derivation of new wallets. In order to guarantee security even in case one of such wallets is corrupted, e.g., when a wallet is not implemented in the hot/cold setting, the authors introduced two different key derivation mechanisms, namely hardened key derivation for keys that might be leaked to the adversary and non-hardened key derivation for keys that are stored securely via the hot/cold wallet paradigm. Later, Yin et al. [26] introduced hierarchical deterministic wallets that support stealth addresses. However, none of these works have considered adaptor signature support for deterministic wallets.

## 2    Preliminaries

**Notation.** We denote by $s \leftarrow_\$ H$ the uniform random sampling of a value $s$ from the set $H$. For an integer $l$, the notation $[l]$ denotes the set of integers $\{1, \cdots, l\}$ and for a randomized algorithm $A$, we denote by $y \leftarrow_\$ A(x)$ the execution of $A$ on input $x$ that outputs $y$. For a deterministic algorithm $B$, we write $y \leftarrow B(x, \rho)$ to denote the execution of $B$ on input $x$ and $\rho$ that outputs $y$. By $y \in A(x)$ we denote that $y$ is an element in the set of possible outputs of an execution of $A$ on input $x$. Throughout our paper, we assume that public parameters par can be used as input to all algorithms. For two strings $a$ and $b$, we write $a = (b, \cdot)$ if $b$ is a prefix of $a$. We abbreviate the expressions *deterministic polynomial time* and *probabilistic polynomial time* by DPT and PPT respectively.

### 2.1    Non-interactive Zero-Knowledge Proofs

A non-interactive zero knowledge proof (NIZK) [4] with respect to a polynomial-time recognizable binary relation $R$ is given by the following tuple of algorithms $\mathsf{NIZK} := (\mathsf{Setup}_R, \mathsf{P}, \mathsf{V})$, where (i) $\mathsf{Setup}_R(1^n)$ outputs a common reference string crs; (ii) $\mathsf{P}(\mathsf{crs}, (Y, y))$ outputs a proof $\pi$ for $(Y, y) \in R$; (iii) $\mathsf{V}(\mathsf{crs}, Y, \pi)$ outputs a bit $b \in \{0, 1\}$. Further, the NIZK proof of knowledge w.r.t. $R$ should satisfy the properties *completeness*, *soundness*, and *zero knowledge*. We do not go into the details of these properties here.

### 2.2    (Witness Rerandomizable) Hard Relation

**Definition 1 (Hard Relation).** *Let $R \subseteq \mathcal{D}_Y \times \mathcal{D}_w$ be a relation with statement/witness pairs $(Y, y) \in \mathcal{D}_Y \times \mathcal{D}_w$ and let the language $L_R \subseteq \mathcal{D}_Y$ associated to $R$ be defined as $L_R := \{Y \in \mathcal{D}_Y \mid \exists y \in \mathcal{D}_w \text{ s.t. } (Y, y) \in R\}$. We say that $R$ is a* hard relation *if: (i) There exists a PPT sampling algorithm $\mathsf{GenR}(1^n)$ that on input the security parameter outputs a pair $(Y, y) \in R$; (ii) There exists a PPT algorithm $\mathsf{WitToSt}(y)$ that on input a witness $y$ outputs a statement $Y$, s.t. $(Y, y) \in R$; (iii) The relation $R$ is poly-time decidable; (iv) For all PPT adversaries $\mathcal{A}$, the probability that $\mathcal{A}$ outputs a valid witness $y \in \mathcal{D}_w$ for $Y \in L_R$ is negligible.*

In this work we require a stronger notion of hard relation namely hard relations that are witness rerandomizable.

**Definition 2 (Witness Rerandomizable Hard Relation).** *Let* $R \subseteq \mathcal{D}_Y \times \mathcal{D}_w$ *be a hard relation with statement/witness pairs* $(Y, y) \in \mathcal{D}_Y \times \mathcal{D}_w$ *and let the public parameters* par *define a randomness space* $X := X(\mathsf{par})$. *Further, let* RandWit *be a DPT algorithm which is defined as follows:*

RandWit$(y, \rho)$: *The deterministic witness randomization algorithm takes as input a witness* $y \in \mathcal{D}_w$, *a randomness* $\rho \in X$ *and outputs a rerandomized witness* $y'$.

*We say that* $R$ *is* perfectly witness rerandomizable *if for all* $(\cdot, y) \in \mathsf{GenR}(1^n)$ *and all* $\rho \leftarrow_\$ X$ *the distributions of* $(Y', y')$ *and* $(Y'', y'')$ *are identical, where:*

$$(Y', y') \leftarrow (\mathsf{WitToSt}(\mathsf{RandWit}(y, \rho)), \mathsf{RandWit}(y, \rho))$$
$$(Y'', y'') \leftarrow \mathsf{GenR}(1^n)$$

### 2.3  Adaptor Signatures

We recall the definition of an adaptor signature scheme by Aumayr et al. [3].

**Definition 3 (Adaptor Signature Scheme).** *An adaptor signature scheme w.r.t. a hard relation* $R$ *and a signature scheme* $\Sigma = (\mathsf{Gen}, \mathsf{Sign}, \mathsf{Verify})$ *consists of four algorithms* $\mathsf{ASig}_{R, \Sigma} = (\mathsf{pSign}, \mathsf{Adapt}, \mathsf{pVrfy}, \mathsf{Ext})$ *with the following syntax:* $\mathsf{pSign}(sk, m, Y)$ *is a PPT algorithm that on input a secret key* $sk$, *message* $m \in \{0, 1\}^*$ *and statement* $Y \in L_R$, *outputs a pre-signature* $\tilde{\sigma}$; $\mathsf{pVrfy}(pk, m, Y, \tilde{\sigma})$ *is a DPT algorithm that on input a public key* $pk$, *message* $m \in \{0, 1\}^*$, *statement* $Y \in L_R$ *and pre-signature* $\tilde{\sigma}$, *outputs a bit* $b$; $\mathsf{Adapt}(\tilde{\sigma}, y)$ *is a DPT algorithm that on input a pre-signature* $\tilde{\sigma}$ *and witness* $y$, *outputs a signature* $\sigma$; *and* $\mathsf{Ext}(\sigma, \tilde{\sigma}, Y)$ *is a DPT algorithm that on input a signature* $\sigma$, *pre-signature* $\tilde{\sigma}$ *and statement* $Y \in L_R$, *outputs a witness* $y$ *such that* $(Y, y) \in R$, *or* $\perp$.

An adaptor signature scheme $\mathsf{ASig}_{R, \Sigma}$ must satisfy *pre-signature correctness* stating that for every $m \in \{0, 1\}^*$ and every $(Y, y) \in R$, the following holds:

$$\Pr\left[\begin{matrix} \mathsf{pVrfy}(pk, m, Y, \tilde{\sigma}) = 1, \\ \mathsf{Verify}(pk, m, \sigma) = 1, (Y, y') \in R \end{matrix} \;\middle|\; \begin{matrix} (sk, pk) \leftarrow \mathsf{Gen}(1^n), \quad \tilde{\sigma} \leftarrow \mathsf{pSign}(sk, m, Y), \\ \sigma := \mathsf{Adapt}_{pk}(\tilde{\sigma}, y), \quad y' := \mathsf{Ext}(pk, \sigma, \tilde{\sigma}, Y) \end{matrix}\right] = 1.$$

An adaptor signature scheme has to satisfy the following properties.

**Definition 4 (Existential Unforgeability).** *An adaptor signature scheme* $\mathsf{ASig}_{R, \Sigma}$ *is unforgeable if for every PPT adversary* $\mathcal{A} = (\mathcal{A}_1, \mathcal{A}_2)$ *there exists a negligible function* $\nu$ *such that:* $\Pr[\mathsf{aSigForge}_{\mathcal{A}, \mathsf{ASig}_{R, \Sigma}}(n) = 1] \leq \nu(n)$, *where the experiment* $\mathsf{aSigForge}_{\mathcal{A}, \mathsf{ASig}_{R, \Sigma}}$ *is defined as in Fig. 1.*

**Definition 5 (Pre-signature Adaptability).** *An adaptor signature scheme* $\mathsf{ASig}_{R, \Sigma}$ *satisfies pre-signature adaptability if for any message* $m \in \{0, 1\}^*$, *any statement/witness pair* $(Y, y) \in R$, *any public key* $pk$ *and any pre-signature* $\tilde{\sigma} \in \{0, 1\}^*$ *with* $\mathsf{pVrfy}(pk, m, Y, \tilde{\sigma}) = 1$, *we have* $\mathsf{Verify}(pk, m, \mathsf{Adapt}(\tilde{\sigma}, y)) = 1$.

**Definition 6 (Witness Extractability).**  *An adaptor signature scheme* $\mathsf{ASig}_{R,\Sigma}$ *is witness extractable if for every PPT adversary* $\mathcal{A} = (\mathcal{A}_1, \mathcal{A}_2)$, *there exists a negligible function* $\nu$ *such that the following holds:* $\Pr[\mathsf{aWitExt}_{\mathcal{A},\mathsf{ASig}_{R,\Sigma}}(n) = 1] \le \nu(n)$, *where the experiment* $\mathsf{aWitExt}_{\mathcal{A},\mathsf{ASig}_{R,\Sigma}}$ *is defined as in Fig. 1.*

**Definition 7.** *An adaptor signature scheme* $\mathsf{ASig}_{R,\Sigma}$ *is secure, if it is unforgeable, pre-signature adaptable and witness extractable.*

---

$\mathsf{aWitExt}(n)$
00  $\mathcal{Q} := \emptyset, (sk, pk) \leftarrow \mathsf{Gen}(1^n)$
01  $(m^*, Y^*, \mathsf{st}) \leftarrow \mathcal{A}_1^{\mathsf{SignO}(\cdot), \mathsf{PreSignO}(\cdot, \cdot)}(pk)$
02  $\tilde{\sigma}^* \leftarrow \mathsf{pSign}(sk, m^*, Y^*)$
03  $\sigma^* \leftarrow \mathcal{A}_2^{\mathsf{SignO}, \mathsf{PreSignO}}(\tilde{\sigma}^*, \mathsf{st})$
04  $b_1 \leftarrow (Y^*, \mathsf{Ext}(\sigma^*, \tilde{\sigma}^*, Y^*)) \notin R$
05  $b_2 \leftarrow m^* \notin \mathcal{Q}$
06  $b_3 \leftarrow \mathsf{Verify}(pk, m^*, \sigma^*)$
07  $b_4 \leftarrow Y^* \in L_R$
08  Return $(b_1 \wedge b_2 \wedge b_3 \wedge b_4)$

Oracle $\mathsf{PreSignO}(m, Y)$
09  $\tilde{\sigma} \leftarrow \mathsf{pSign}(sk, m, Y)$
10  $\mathcal{Q} := \mathcal{Q} \cup \{m\}$
11  Return $\tilde{\sigma}$

$\mathsf{aSigForge}(n)$
12  $\mathcal{Q} := \emptyset, (sk, pk) \leftarrow \mathsf{Gen}(1^n)$
13  $(Y, y) \leftarrow \mathsf{GenR}(1^n)$
14  $(m^*, \mathsf{st}) \leftarrow \mathcal{A}_1^{\mathsf{SignO}, \mathsf{PreSignO}}(pk, Y)$
15  $\tilde{\sigma}^* \leftarrow \mathsf{pSign}(sk, m^*, Y)$
16  $\sigma^* \leftarrow \mathcal{A}_2^{\mathsf{SignO}, \mathsf{PreSignO}}(\tilde{\sigma}^*, \mathsf{st})$
17  Return
    $(m^* \notin \mathcal{Q} \wedge \mathsf{Verify}(pk, m^*, \sigma^*))$

Oracle $\mathsf{SignO}(m)$
18  $\sigma \leftarrow \mathsf{Sign}(sk, m)$
19  $\mathcal{Q} := \mathcal{Q} \cup \{m\}$
20  Return $\sigma$

---

**Fig. 1.** aSigForge and aWitExt games for an adaptor signature scheme ASig.

## 2.4  ECDSA-Based Adaptor Signature

We briefly recall the ECDSA-based adaptor signature scheme $\mathsf{EC}_{R_g, \mathsf{PEC}}[\mathsf{H}] = (\mathsf{pSign}, \mathsf{Adapt}, \mathsf{pVrfy}, \mathsf{Ext})$ as presented by Aumayr et al. [3], which is defined w.r.t. the positive ECDSA signature scheme $\mathsf{PEC} = (\mathsf{Gen}, \mathsf{Sign}, \mathsf{Verify})$ and a hard relation $R_g$. Recall that the positive ECDSA scheme operates over a cyclic group $\mathbb{G} = \langle g \rangle$ of prime order $p$ and that the key generation outputs a key pair $(sk, pk)$ with $sk \leftarrow_\$ \mathbb{Z}_p$ and $pk \leftarrow g^{sk}$. A message $m \in \{0,1\}^*$ is then signed by first sampling $k \leftarrow_\$ \mathbb{Z}_p$, setting $r \leftarrow f(g^k)$ and computing $s := k^{-1}(\mathsf{H}(m) + r \cdot sk)$, where $\mathsf{H} : \{0,1\} \rightarrow \mathbb{Z}_p$ is a hash function and $f : \mathbb{G} \rightarrow \mathbb{Z}_p$. The signature is then $\sigma := (r, s)$, which can be verified by checking if $f(g^{s^{-1}\mathsf{H}(m)} pk^{s^{-1}r}) = r$. The hard relation $R_g$ is defined as $R_g := \{((Y, \pi), y) | Y = g^y \wedge \mathsf{V}(Y, \pi) = 1\}$, i.e., it is the standard dlog relation with an additional non-interactive zero knowledge (NIZK) proof, which proves knowledge of the witness. The additional NIZK proof is required for technical reasons which we do not discuss here. Apart from the NIZK proof for relation $R_g$, the $\mathsf{EC}_{R_g, \mathsf{PEC}}[\mathsf{H}]$ construction also includes a NIZK proof for another relation $R_Y := \{((\tilde{K}, K), k) | \tilde{K} = g^k \wedge K = Y^k\}$. For further details we refer to [3]. The construction of $\mathsf{EC}_{R_g, \mathsf{PEC}}[\mathsf{H}]$ is depicted in Fig. 2.

# 3    Adaptor Signatures with Rerandomizable Keys

In this section we define the notion of adaptor signatures with rerandomizable keys and show how to instantiate it. Later in Sect. 4.1 we will use this primitive to generically construct adaptor wallets.

## 3.1    Definition

The notion of signature schemes with rerandomizable keys has first been introduced by Fleischhacker et al. [11] and has since been proven to be useful for the construction of deterministic wallet schemes (e.g., [5,6]). Essentially, a signature scheme with rerandomizable keys extends regular signature schemes by two deterministic algorithms, a public key and a secret key rerandomization algorithm, which on input a public key or a secret key respectively and a randomness, output rerandomized keys. Such keys, if rerandomized with the same randomness, constitute a new signing key pair, which is distributed identically to a freshly and independently generated signing key pair. These properties and the deterministic nature of the rerandomization make such signature schemes good candidates for the construction of deterministic wallets. In our work, we are concerned with adaptor signatures. Therefore, we define in the following the notion of adaptor signatures with rerandomizable keys.

| $\mathsf{pSign}(sk, m, I_Y)$ | $\mathsf{pVrfy}(pk, m, I_Y, \tilde{\sigma})$ | $\mathsf{Adapt}(\tilde{\sigma}, y)$ | $\mathsf{Ext}(\sigma, \tilde{\sigma}, I_Y)$ |
|---|---|---|---|
| $x := sk, (Y, \pi_Y) := I_Y$ | $X := pk, (Y, \pi_Y) := I_Y$ | $(r, \tilde{s}, K, \pi) := \tilde{\sigma}$ | $(r, s) := \sigma$ |
| $k \leftarrow_\$ \mathbb{Z}_q, \tilde{K} := g^k$ | $(r, \tilde{s}, K, \pi) := \tilde{\sigma}$ | $s := \tilde{s} \cdot y^{-1}$ | $(\tilde{r}, \tilde{s}, K, \pi) := \tilde{\sigma}$ |
| $K := Y^k, r := f(K)$ | $u := \mathsf{H}(m) \cdot \tilde{s}^{-1}$ | $\mathbf{return}\ (r, s)$ | $y' := s^{-1} \cdot \tilde{s}$ |
| $\tilde{s} := k^{-1}(\mathsf{H}(m) + rx)$ | $v := r \cdot \tilde{s}^{-1}, K' := g^u X^v$ | | $\mathbf{if}\ (I_Y, y') \in R_g$ |
| $\pi \leftarrow \mathsf{P}_Y((\tilde{K}, K), k)$ | $\mathbf{return}\ (I_Y \in L_R$ | | $\quad\mathbf{then\ return}\ y'$ |
| $\mathbf{return}\ (r, \tilde{s}, K, \pi)$ | $\quad \wedge\ (r = f(K)) \wedge \mathsf{V}_Y((K', K), \pi))$ | | $\quad\mathbf{else\ return}\ \perp$ |

**Fig. 2.** ECDSA-based adaptor signature scheme $\mathsf{EC}_{R_g, \mathsf{PEC}}[\mathsf{H}]$ instantiated with a hash function $\mathsf{H} : \{0,1\}^* \to \mathbb{Z}_p$.

**Definition 8 (Adaptor Signature Scheme with Rerandomizable Keys).** *An adaptor signature scheme with rerandomizable keys w.r.t. a hard relation R and a signature scheme $\Sigma = (\mathsf{Gen}, \mathsf{Sign}, \mathsf{Verify})$ consists of six algorithms $\mathsf{RASig}_{R,\Sigma} = (\mathsf{RandSK}, \mathsf{RandPK}, \mathsf{pSign}, \mathsf{Adapt}, \mathsf{pVrfy}, \mathsf{Ext})$ where $(\mathsf{pSign}, \mathsf{Adapt}, \mathsf{pVrfy}, \mathsf{Ext})$ are the same algorithms as defined for adaptor signatures (cf. Definition 3). Assuming that the public parameters par define a randomness space $X := X(\mathsf{par})$, the remaining algorithms are defined as follows:*

$\mathsf{RandSK}(sk, \rho)$: *The deterministic secret key rerandomization algorithm takes as input a secret key sk and a randomness $\rho \in X$ and outputs a rerandomized secret key sk'.*

RandPK$(pk, \rho)$: *The deterministic public key rerandomization algorithm takes as input a public key pk and a randomness $\rho \in X$ and outputs a rerandomized public key pk'.*

An adaptor signature scheme with rerandomizable keys $\mathsf{RASig}_{R,\Sigma}$ must satisfy the following two correctness properties:

1. Pre-signature correctness *stating that for all* $(sk, pk) \leftarrow \mathsf{Gen}(1^n)$, *all* $m \in \{0,1\}^*$, *all* $\rho \in X$ *and all* $(Y, y) \in R$, *the rerandomized keys* $sk' \leftarrow$ RandSK$(sk, \rho)$ *and* $pk' \leftarrow$ RandPK$(pk, \rho)$ *satisfy:*

$$\Pr\left[\begin{array}{l} \mathsf{pVrfy}(pk', m, Y, \tilde{\sigma}) = 1, \\ \mathsf{Verify}(pk', m, \sigma) = 1, (Y, y') \in R \end{array} \middle| \begin{array}{l} \tilde{\sigma} \leftarrow \mathsf{pSign}(sk', m, Y), \\ \sigma := \mathsf{Adapt}(\tilde{\sigma}, y), \end{array} y' := \mathsf{Ext}(\sigma, \tilde{\sigma}, Y)\right] = 1.$$

2. (Perfect) rerandomizability of keys: *For all* $(sk, pk) \in \mathsf{Gen}(1^n)$ *and* $\rho \leftarrow_\$ X$, *the distributions of* $(sk', pk')$ *and* $(sk'', pk'')$ *are identical, where:*

$$(sk', pk') \leftarrow (\mathsf{RandSK}(sk, \rho), \mathsf{RandPK}(pk, \rho)),$$
$$(sk'', pk'') \leftarrow_\$ \mathsf{Gen}(1^n).$$

Like adaptor signatures, an $\mathsf{RASig}_{R,\Sigma}$ scheme must satisfy pre-signature adaptability.

**Definition 9 (Pre-signature adaptability).** *An adaptor signature scheme with perfectly rerandomizable keys $\mathsf{RASig}_{R,\Sigma}$ satisfies pre-signature adaptability if for any message $m \in \{0,1\}^*$, any statement/witness pair $(Y, y) \in R$, any public key pk and any pre-signature $\tilde{\sigma} \in \{0,1\}^*$ with $\mathsf{pVrfy}(pk, m, Y, \tilde{\sigma}) = 1$, we have $\mathsf{Verify}(pk, m, \mathsf{Adapt}(\tilde{\sigma}, y)) = 1$.*

For adaptor signatures with rerandomizable keys, we introduce the notions of *existential unforgeability under honestly rerandomizable keys* and *witness extractability under honestly rerandomizable keys*. These notions extend the respective security notions of adaptor signatures by allowing the adversary to not only obtain (pre-)signatures under $sk$ but also under secret keys that constitute honest rerandomizations of $sk$. An honest rerandomization is one where the randomness has been chosen uniformly at random from the randomness space $X$. Further, in our security notions the adversary can win the game by providing a forgery either under $sk$ or under any honestly rerandomized key. We formally describe these security notions in Fig. 3.

**Definition 10 (Existential Unforgeability Under Honestly Rerandomizable Keys).** *An adaptor signature scheme with rerandomizable keys $\mathsf{RASig}_{R,\Sigma}$ is unforgeable if for every PPT adversary $\mathcal{A} = (\mathcal{A}_1, \mathcal{A}_2)$ there exists a negligible function $\nu$ such that:* $\Pr[\mathsf{aSigForge-hrk}_{\mathcal{A},\mathsf{RASig}_{R,\Sigma}}(n) = 1] \leq \nu(n)$, *where the experiment* $\mathsf{aSigForge-hrk}_{\mathcal{A},\mathsf{RASig}_{R,\Sigma}}$ *is defined as in Fig. 3.*

**Definition 11 (Witness Extractability Under Honestly Rerandomizable Keys).** *An adaptor signature scheme with rerandomizable keys $\mathsf{RASig}_{R,\Sigma}$ is witness extractable if for every PPT adversary $\mathcal{A} = (\mathcal{A}_1, \mathcal{A}_2)$, there exists a negligible function $\nu$ such that the following holds:* $\Pr[\mathsf{aWitExt-hrk}_{\mathcal{A},\mathsf{RASig}_{R,\Sigma}}(n) = 1] \leq \nu(n)$, *where the experiment* $\mathsf{aWitExt-hrk}_{\mathcal{A},\mathsf{RASig}_{R,\Sigma}}$ *is defined as in Fig. 3.*

## 3.2   Construction

In Fig. 4, we present an adaptor signature with rerandomizable keys $\mathsf{REC}_{R,\mathsf{PEC}}[\mathsf{H}]$ from the ECDSA-based adaptor signature $\mathsf{EC}_{R_g,\mathsf{PEC}}[\mathsf{H}]$ from Fig. 2. Similar to the rerandomizable ECDSA construction of Das et al. [6], we use public key-prefixed messages in our construction which is required to ensure security (see the proof sketch of Thm. 1) and we use a hash function $\mathsf{H}\colon \{0,1\}^* \to \mathbb{Z}_p$.

To prove the security of our construction, we follow the approach of Das et al. [6], who presented a security proof of the plain ECDSA signature scheme with rerandomizable keys via a reduction to the (non-rerandomizable) ECDSA signature scheme. The main ingredient in their security proof is a related key attack which allows to transform a signature on message $m_1$ under public key $pk_1$ to a signature for message $m_0$ under a related public key $pk_0$. We recall their transformation in the following (and formally in Lemma 1 and Fig. 5).

| aSigForge$-$hrk$_{\mathcal{A},\mathsf{RASig}_{R,\Sigma}}(n)$ | aWitExt$-$hrk$_{\mathcal{A},\mathsf{RASig}_{R,\Sigma}}(n)$ | Oracle RSignO$(m,\rho)$ |
|---|---|---|
| 00 $\mathcal{Q} := \emptyset, \mathcal{R} := \emptyset$ | 00 $\mathcal{Q} := \emptyset, \mathcal{R} := \emptyset$ | 00 If $\rho \notin \mathcal{R}$ : return 0 |
| 01 $(sk, pk) \leftarrow \mathsf{Gen}(1^n)$ | 01 $(sk, pk) \leftarrow \mathsf{Gen}(1^n)$ | 01 $sk' \leftarrow \mathsf{RandSK}(sk, \rho)$ |
| 02 $(Y, y) \leftarrow \mathsf{GenR}(1^n)$ | 02 $(m^*, \rho^*, Y^*, \mathsf{st}) \leftarrow \mathcal{A}_1^{\mathcal{O}}(pk)$ | 02 $\sigma \leftarrow \mathsf{Sign}(sk', m)$ |
| 03 $(m^*, \rho^*, \mathsf{st}) \leftarrow \mathcal{A}_1^{\mathcal{O}}(pk, Y)$ | 03 $sk^* \leftarrow \mathsf{RandSK}(sk, \rho^*)$ | 03 $\mathcal{Q} := \mathcal{Q} \cup \{m\}$ |
| 04 $sk^* \leftarrow \mathsf{RandSK}(sk, \rho^*)$ | 04 $pk^* \leftarrow \mathsf{RandPK}(pk, \rho^*)$ | 04 Return $\sigma$ |
| 05 $pk^* \leftarrow \mathsf{RandPK}(pk, \rho^*)$ | 05 $\tilde{\sigma}^* \leftarrow \mathsf{pSign}(sk^*, m^*, Y^*)$ | Oracle PreSignO$(m, Y, \rho)$ |
| 06 $\tilde{\sigma}^* \leftarrow \mathsf{pSign}(sk^*, m^*, Y)$ | 06 $\sigma^* \leftarrow \mathcal{A}_2^{\mathcal{O}}(\tilde{\sigma}^*, \mathsf{st})$ | 05 If $\rho \notin \mathcal{R}$ : return 0 |
| 07 $\sigma^* \leftarrow \mathcal{A}_2^{\mathcal{O}}(\tilde{\sigma}^*, \mathsf{st})$ | 07 $b_1 \leftarrow (Y^*, \mathsf{Ext}(\sigma^*, \tilde{\sigma}^*, Y^*)) \notin R$ | 06 $sk' \leftarrow \mathsf{RandSK}(sk, \rho)$ |
| 08 $b_1 \leftarrow m^* \notin \mathcal{Q}$ | 08 $b_2 \leftarrow m^* \notin \mathcal{Q}$ | 07 $\tilde{\sigma} \leftarrow \mathsf{pSign}(sk', m, Y)$ |
| 09 $b_2 \leftarrow \mathsf{Verify}(pk^*, m^*, \sigma)$ | 09 $b_3 \leftarrow \mathsf{Verify}(pk^*, m^*, \sigma^*)$ | 08 $\mathcal{Q} := \mathcal{Q} \cup \{m\}$ |
| 10 $b_3 \leftarrow \rho^* \in \mathcal{R}$ | 10 $b_4 \leftarrow \rho^* \in \mathcal{R}$ | 09 Return $\tilde{\sigma}$ |
| 11 Return $(b_1 \wedge b_2 \wedge b_3)$ | 11 $b_5 \leftarrow Y^* \in L_R$ | Oracle RandO |
| | 12 Return $(b_1 \wedge b_2 \wedge b_3 \wedge b_4 \wedge b_5)$ | 10 $\rho \leftarrow_\$ X$ |
| | | 11 $\mathcal{R} := \mathcal{R} \cup \{\rho\}$ |
| | | 12 Return $\rho$ |

**Fig. 3.** aSigForge$-$hrk and aWitExt$-$hrk games for an adaptor signature scheme with rerandomizable keys $\mathsf{RASig}_{R,\Sigma}$. In the above games we have $\mathcal{O} := \{\mathsf{RSignO}, \mathsf{PreSignO}, \mathsf{RandO}\}$.

Let $\mathsf{PEC}[\mathsf{H}_0]$ and $\mathsf{PEC}[\mathsf{H}_1]$ denote two (positive) ECDSA signature schemes instantiated with hash functions $\mathsf{H}_0$ and $\mathsf{H}_1$ respectively. Then the authors show that if $pk_1 = (pk_0)^\rho$ where $\rho = \frac{\mathsf{H}_1(m_1)}{\mathsf{H}_0(m_0)} \in \mathbb{Z}_p$ and given a valid signature $\sigma_1$ (i.e., $\mathsf{PEC}[\mathsf{H}_1].\mathsf{Verify}(pk_1, m_1, \sigma_1) = 1$), the algorithm $\mathsf{Trf}[\mathsf{H}_0, \mathsf{H}_1](m_0, m_1, \sigma_1, \rho, pk_0, pk_1)$ returns a valid signature $\sigma_0$ under $pk_0$ and $m_0$, i.e., $\mathsf{PEC}[\mathsf{H}_0].\mathsf{Verify}(pk_0, m_0, \sigma_0) = 1$. For this transformation, Das et al. state and prove the following lemma.

**Lemma 1.** *Consider the algorithm* $\mathsf{Trf}[\mathsf{H}_0, \mathsf{H}_1]$ *in Fig. 5. Suppose that:*

$- \rho = \frac{\mathsf{H}_1(m_1)}{\mathsf{H}_0(m_0)} \in \mathbb{Z}_p,\ pk_0, pk_1 \in \mathbb{G}\ s.t.\ pk_0 = g^{x_0}\ and\ pk_1 = pk_0^\rho,$

– $\mathsf{PEC}[\mathsf{H}_1].\mathsf{Verify}(pk_1, m_1, \sigma_1) = 1$, $\sigma_0 \leftarrow \mathsf{Trf}[\mathsf{H}_0, \mathsf{H}_1](m_0, m_1, \sigma_1, \rho, pk_0, pk_1)$.

Then $\mathsf{PEC}[\mathsf{H}_0].\mathsf{Verify}(pk_0, m_0, \sigma_0) = 1$.

We show that a similar transformation can be applied to the ECDSA-based adaptor signature scheme $\mathsf{EC}_{R_g, \mathsf{PEC}}[\mathsf{H}]$ to transform pre-signatures. Since pre-signatures in this scheme include a zero-knowledge proof, it is not immediately clear that such a transformation goes through. We next give the lemma for the pre-signature transformation as well as the proof for the lemma.

**Lemma 2.** *Let* $\mathsf{EC}_{R_g, \mathsf{PEC}}[\mathsf{H}_0]$ *and* $\mathsf{EC}_{R_g, \mathsf{PEC}}[\mathsf{H}_1]$ *denote two ECDSA-based adaptor signature schemes according to Fig. 2 instantiated with hash functions* $\mathsf{H}_0$ *and* $\mathsf{H}_1$. *Consider the algorithm* $\mathsf{ATrf}[\mathsf{H}_0, \mathsf{H}_1]$ *in Fig. 5. Suppose that:*

| Algorithm $\mathsf{REC}_{R,\mathsf{PEC}}[\mathsf{H}].\mathsf{pSign}\,(sk, m, Y)$ | Algorithm $\mathsf{REC}_{R,\mathsf{PEC}}[\mathsf{H}].\mathsf{Sign}\,(sk, m)$ |
|---|---|
| 00 $\mathsf{pm} \leftarrow (pk, m)$ | 08 $\mathsf{pm} \leftarrow (pk, m)$ |
| 01 $\tilde{\sigma} \leftarrow \mathsf{EC}_{R_g, \mathsf{PEC}}[\mathsf{H}].\mathsf{pSign}\,(sk, \mathsf{pm}, Y)$ | 09 $\sigma \leftarrow \mathsf{EC}_{R_g, \mathsf{PEC}}[\mathsf{H}].\mathsf{Sign}\,(sk, \mathsf{pm})$ |
| 02 Return $\tilde{\sigma}$ | 10 Return $\sigma$ |
| Algorithm $\mathsf{REC}_{R,\mathsf{PEC}}[\mathsf{H}].\mathsf{pVrfy}\,(pk, m, Y, \tilde{\sigma})$ | Algorithm $\mathsf{REC}_{R,\mathsf{PEC}}[\mathsf{H}].\mathsf{Verify}\,(pk, \sigma, m)$ |
| 03 $\mathsf{pm} \leftarrow (pk, m)$ | 11 $\mathsf{pm} \leftarrow (pk, m)$ |
| 04 Return $\mathsf{EC}_{R_g, \mathsf{PEC}}[\mathsf{H}].\mathsf{pVrfy}\,(pk, \mathsf{pm}, Y, \tilde{\sigma})$ | 12 Return $\mathsf{EC}_{R_g, \mathsf{PEC}}[\mathsf{H}].\mathsf{Verify}\,(pk, \sigma', \mathsf{pm})$ |
| Algorithm $\mathsf{REC}_{R,\mathsf{PEC}}[\mathsf{H}].\mathsf{Adapt}\,(\tilde{\sigma}, y)$ | Algorithm $\mathsf{REC}_{R,\mathsf{PEC}}[\mathsf{H}].\mathsf{Ext}\,(\sigma, \tilde{\sigma}, Y)$ |
| 05 Return $\mathsf{EC}_{R_g, \mathsf{PEC}}[\mathsf{H}].\mathsf{Adapt}\,(\tilde{\sigma}, y)$ | 13 Return $\mathsf{EC}_{R_g, \mathsf{PEC}}[\mathsf{H}].\mathsf{Ext}\,(\sigma, \tilde{\sigma}, Y)$ |
| Algorithm $\mathsf{REC}_{R,\mathsf{PEC}}[\mathsf{H}].\mathsf{RandSK}\,(sk, \rho)$ | Algorithm $\mathsf{REC}_{R,\mathsf{PEC}}[\mathsf{H}].\mathsf{RandPK}\,(pk, \rho)$ |
| 06 $sk' \leftarrow sk \cdot \rho \bmod p$ | 14 $pk' \leftarrow pk^\rho$ |
| 07 Return $sk'$ | 15 Return $pk'$ |

**Fig. 4.** Construction of a key-prefixed ECDSA-based adaptor signature scheme with perfectly rerandomizable keys $\mathsf{REC}_{R,\mathsf{PEC}}[\mathsf{H}]$ from the ECDSA-based adaptor signature scheme $\mathsf{EC}_{R_g, \mathsf{PEC}}[\mathsf{H}]$ as described in Fig. 2. Both schemes are instantiated with a hash function $\mathsf{H} \colon \{0,1\}^* \to \mathbb{Z}_p$.

| $\mathsf{Trf}[\mathsf{H}_0, \mathsf{H}_1](m_0, m_1, \sigma_1, \rho, pk_0, pk_1)$ | $\mathsf{ATrf}[\mathsf{H}_0, \mathsf{H}_1](m_0, m_1, \tilde{\sigma}_1, \rho, pk_0, pk_1, I_Y)$ |
|---|---|
| 00 $z_0 \leftarrow \mathsf{H}_0(m_0)$ | 00 $z_0 \leftarrow \mathsf{H}_0(m_0)$ |
| 01 $z_1 \leftarrow \mathsf{H}_1(m_1)$ | 01 $z_1 \leftarrow \mathsf{H}_1(m_1)$ |
| 02 If $(\mathsf{PEC}_{R_g, \mathsf{PEC}}[\mathsf{H}_1].\mathsf{Verify}(pk_1, \sigma_1, m_1) = 0)$ | 02 If $(\mathsf{EC}_{R_g, \mathsf{PEC}}[\mathsf{H}_1].\mathsf{pVrfy}(pk_1, m_1, I_Y, \tilde{\sigma}_1)\vee$ |
| $\vee \left(\rho \neq \frac{z_1}{z_0} \vee pk_1 \neq pk_0^\rho\right):$ | $\left(\rho \neq \frac{z_1}{z_0} \vee pk_1 \neq pk_0^\rho \vee I_Y \notin L_R\right):$ |
| 03    Return $\perp$ | 03    Return $\perp$ |
| 04 $(r, s_1) \leftarrow \sigma_1$ | 04 $(r, \tilde{s}_1, K, \pi) \leftarrow \tilde{\sigma}_1$ |
| 05 $s_0 \leftarrow \frac{s_1}{\rho} \bmod p$ | 05 $\tilde{s}_0 \leftarrow \frac{\tilde{s}_1}{\rho} \bmod p$ |
| 06 $\sigma_0 \leftarrow (r, s_0)$ | 06 $\tilde{\sigma}_0 \leftarrow (r, \tilde{s}_0, K, \pi)$ |
| 07 Return $\sigma_0$ | 07 Return $\tilde{\sigma}_0$ |

**Fig. 5.** Figure shows the $\mathsf{Trf}[\mathsf{H}_0, \mathsf{H}_1]$ and $\mathsf{ATrf}[\mathsf{H}_0, \mathsf{H}_1]$ algorithms for hash functions $\mathsf{H}_0, \mathsf{H}_1 \colon \{0,1\}^* \to \mathbb{Z}_p$.

- $I_Y \in L_{R_Y}$, $\rho = \frac{H_1(m_1)}{H_0(m_0)} \in \mathbb{Z}_p$,
- $pk_0, pk_1 \in \mathbb{G}$ s.t. $pk_0 = g^{x_0}$ and $pk_1 = pk_0^\rho$,
- $EC_{R_g,PEC}[H_1].pVrfy(pk_1, m_1, I_Y, \tilde{\sigma}_1) = 1$,
- $\tilde{\sigma}_0 \leftarrow ATrf[H_0, H_1](m_0, m_1, \tilde{\sigma}_1, \rho, pk_0, pk_1, I_Y)$.

*Then* $EC_{R_g,PEC}[H_0].pVrfy(pk_0, m_0, I_Y, \tilde{\sigma}_0) = 1$.

We would like to point out that Lemma 2 requires that after the transformation, the new pre-signature $\tilde{\sigma}_0$ is indeed valid with respect to the same statement $I_Y$. In other words, given the witness $y$, both $\tilde{\sigma}_0$ and $\tilde{\sigma}_1$ can be adapted into full signatures under $pk_0$ and $pk_1$ respectively.

*Proof.* The proof of this lemma is similar to the proof of Lemma 1 from [6]. To prove the lemma, we have to show that given a statement $I_Y := (Y, \pi_Y) \in L_R$, a public key $pk_1 = pk_0^\rho$ where $\rho = \frac{H_1(m_1)}{H_0(m_0)}$ and a pre-signature $\tilde{\sigma}_1$ such that $EC_{R_g,PEC}[H_1].pVrfy(pk_1, m_1, I_Y, \tilde{\sigma}_1) = 1$, $ATrf[H_0, H_1]$ outputs a pre-signature $\tilde{\sigma}_0$ such that $EC_{R_g,PEC}[H_0].pVrfy(pk_0, m_0, I_Y, \tilde{\sigma}_0) = 1$. Recall that for the pre-signature $\tilde{\sigma}_1 := (r, \tilde{s}_1, K, \pi)$ it holds that $\tilde{s}_1 = k^{-1}(H_1(m) + r \cdot sk_1)$, $r := f(K)$, $K := Y^k$ and $\pi$ is a valid proof that $(\tilde{K}, K)$ is a valid statement in $R_Y$. Then $EC_{R_g,PEC}[H_0].pVrfy(pk_0, m_0, Y, \tilde{\sigma}_0)$ computes the following:

$$K' = g^u \cdot pk_0^v = g^{(H_0(m_0) \cdot \tilde{s}_0^{-1})} \cdot pk_0^{r \cdot \tilde{s}_0^{-1}} = g^{\tilde{s}_0^{-1} \cdot (H_0(m_0) + x_0 \cdot r)}$$

$$= g^{\frac{\rho}{\tilde{s}_1} \cdot (H_1(m_1) \cdot \rho^{-1} + x_1 \cdot \rho^{-1} \cdot r)} = g^{\frac{\rho}{k^{-1}(H_1(m_1) + x_1 \cdot r)} \cdot (H_1(m_1) + x_1 \cdot r) \cdot \rho^{-1}} = g^{\frac{\rho \cdot \rho^{-1}}{k^{-1}}} = g^k$$

Therefore, the zero-knowledge proof $\pi$ is valid w.r.t. the statement $(K', K)$ where $K' = g^k$ and $K = Y^k$. We can conclude that the pre-signature $\tilde{\sigma}_0 \leftarrow ATrf[H_0, H_1](m_0, m_1, \tilde{\sigma}_1, \rho, pk_0, pk_1, I_Y)$ with $\tilde{\sigma}_0 := (r, \frac{\tilde{s}_1}{\rho}, K, \pi)$ constitutes a valid pre-signature w.r.t. public key $pk_0$, message $m_0$ and statement $I_Y$.

**Theorem 1.** *Let* $H_0 \colon \{0,1\}^* \to \mathbb{Z}_p$, $H_1 \colon \{0,1\}^* \to \mathbb{Z}_p$ *be hash functions modeled as random oracle and let* $EC_{R_g,PEC}[H_0]$ *be the secure ECDSA-based adaptor signature as per Fig. 2. Then the construction* $REC_{R_g,PEC}[H_1]$ *as described in Fig. 4 is existentially unforgeable under honestly rerandomizable keys as per Definition 10.*

*Proof (Sketch).* The proof of this theorem is similar to the proof of the multiplicatively rerandomizable ECDSA signature scheme as provided by Das et al. [6]. In their proof, the authors show unforgeability of an ECDSA scheme with rerandomizable keys by exhibiting a reduction to the unforgeability of the regular ECDSA signature scheme. The proof of Das et al. relies crucially on the related key attack as depicted by the algorithm $Trf[H_0, H_1]$ in Fig. 5, which allows to transform a signature under a public key $pk$ to a valid signature under a related public key $pk' \leftarrow pk^{\rho'}$, if $\rho'$ has a certain structure. In more details, Das et al. instantiate the ECDSA scheme with a hash function $H_0$ and the ECDSA scheme with rerandomizable keys with a hash function $H_1$ (both hash functions are modeled as random oracles). They then program the random oracle $H_1$ in such a way that on input $m' = (pk', m)$, where $pk'$ is a public key rerandomized with randomness $\rho'$ (i.e., $pk' = pk^{\rho'}$), it holds $H_1(m') = H_0(m) \cdot \rho'$. This allows the reduction to transform signatures for rerandomized public keys to signatures for the original public key and vice versa using algorithm $\mathsf{Trf}[H_0, H_1]$.

In our proof, we can show unforgeability of the $\mathsf{REC}_{R_g, \mathsf{PEC}}[H_1]$ scheme via a reduction to the unforgeability of the ECDSA-based adaptor signature scheme $\mathsf{EC}_{R_g, \mathsf{PEC}}[H_0]$. The main difference in our proof as compared to the proof of Das et al. arises from the fact that we need to apply the related key attack on pre-signatures as well. This transformation requires us to use the algorithm $\mathsf{ATrf}[H_0, H_1]$ as described in Fig. 5. To apply this transformation, we program the random oracle $H_1$ in exactly the same way as is done in the proof of Das et al. and hence, the programming of $H_1$ is consistent for signatures and pre-signatures.

**Theorem 2.** *Let $H_0 \colon \{0,1\}^* \to \mathbb{Z}_p$, $H_1 \colon \{0,1\}^* \to \mathbb{Z}_p$ be hash functions modeled as random oracle and let $\mathsf{EC}_{R_g, \mathsf{PEC}}[H_0]$ be the secure ECDSA-based adaptor signature as per Fig. 2. Then the construction $\mathsf{REC}_{R_g, \mathsf{PEC}}[H_1]$ as described in Fig. 4 is witness extractable under honestly rerandomizable keys as per Definition 11.*

*Proof (Sketch).* The proof of this theorem is similar to the proof of Theorem 1. Here we must provide a reduction to the witness extractability property aWitExt of the ECDSA-based adaptor signature scheme $\mathsf{EC}_{R_g, \mathsf{PEC}}[H_0]$. However, here we have to show that a valid forgery in game aWitExt$-$hrk for scheme $\mathsf{REC}_{R_g, \mathsf{PEC}}[H_1]$ can be transformed into a valid forgery in game aWitExt for scheme $\mathsf{EC}_{R_g, \mathsf{PEC}}[H_0]$. Recall that for a valid forgery $\sigma^*$ in game aWitExt$-$hrk and given the corresponding pre-signature $\tilde{\sigma}^*$, it must hold that $(I_Y^*, \mathsf{REC}_{R_g, \mathsf{PEC}}[H_1].\mathsf{Ext}(\sigma^*, \tilde{\sigma}^*, I_Y^*)) \notin R_g$. Therefore, we must show that applying the transformations $\mathsf{Trf}[H_0, H_1]$ and $\mathsf{ATrf}[H_0, H_1]$ from Fig. 5 on $\sigma^*$ and $\tilde{\sigma}^*$ respectively preserves the above condition w.r.t. scheme $\mathsf{REC}_{R_g, \mathsf{PEC}}[H_0]$. We show this via the following claim, for which we assume that $m_0, m_1 \in \{0,1\}^*$ are two messages, $\rho^* = \frac{H_1(m_1)}{H_0(m_0)} \in \mathbb{Z}_p$ and $pk^* = pk_{\mathsf{aWitExt}}^{\rho^*}$, where $pk_{\mathsf{aWitExt}}$ is the public key in game aWitExt.

**Claim 1.** *If it holds that $(I_Y^*, \mathsf{REC}_{R_g, \mathsf{PEC}}[H_1].\mathsf{Ext}(\sigma^*, \tilde{\sigma}^*, I_Y^*)) \notin R_g$ then we have $(I_Y^*, \mathsf{EC}_{R_g, \mathsf{PEC}}[H_0].\mathsf{Ext}(\sigma', \tilde{\sigma}', I_Y^*)) \notin R_g$, where*

$$\sigma' \leftarrow \mathsf{Trf}[H_0, H_1](m_0, m_1, \sigma^*, \rho^*, pk_{\mathsf{aWitExt}}, pk^*)$$

$$\tilde{\sigma}' \leftarrow \mathsf{ATrf}[H_0, H_1](m_0, m_1, \tilde{\sigma}^*, \rho^*, pk_{\mathsf{aWitExt}}, pk^*, I_Y^*).$$

Let $\sigma^* = (r, s)$ and $\tilde{\sigma}^* = (r, \tilde{s}, K, \pi)$, then we have: $\sigma' := (r, \frac{s}{\rho^*}), \tilde{\sigma}' := (r, \frac{\tilde{s}}{\rho^*}, K, \pi)$. Therefore, we can conclude that:

$$\mathsf{REC}_{R_g, \mathsf{PEC}}[H_1].\mathsf{Ext}(\sigma^*, \tilde{\sigma}^*, I_Y^*) = s^{-1}\tilde{s} = \left(\frac{s}{\rho^*}\right)^{-1}\frac{\tilde{s}}{\rho^*} = \mathsf{EC}_{R_g, \mathsf{PEC}}[H_0].\mathsf{Ext}(\sigma', \tilde{\sigma}', I_Y^*)$$

Hence, we can conclude that if $(I_Y^*, \mathsf{REC}_{R_g, \mathsf{PEC}}[H_1].\mathsf{Ext}(\sigma^*, \tilde{\sigma}^*, I_Y^*)) \notin R_g$ then $(I_Y^*, \mathsf{EC}_{R_g, \mathsf{PEC}}[H_0].\mathsf{Ext}(\sigma', \tilde{\sigma}', I_Y^*)) \notin R_g$. And thus, a forgery in game aWitExt$-$hrk can be transformed into a valid forgery in game aWitExt.

We note that pre-signature adaptability (cf. Definition 9) of $\mathsf{REC}_{R_g, \mathsf{PEC}}$ follows immediately from the pre-signature adaptability property of $\mathsf{EC}_{R_g, \mathsf{PEC}}$.

## 3.3    Discussion

Note that our ECDSA-based instantiation of an adaptor signature with rerandomizable keys is compatible with a plethora of cryptocurrencies, since many
cryptocurrency networks, including Bitcoin and Ethereum, rely on the ECDSA
signature scheme. In our instantiation, we use a multiplicative key rerandomization instead of an additive one. This seemingly insignificant difference has a
crucial impact on the security of the resulting scheme as shown by Das et al. [5].
More concretely, Das et al. presented an ECDSA scheme with additive key rerandomization, which incurred a security loss in the number of rerandomized keys,
whereas the ECDSA scheme with multiplicative rerandomization from [6] does
not incur such a loss.[2]. In a nutshell, this security loss stems from the related key
attack that is required to prove security of the additively rerandomizable scheme.
Since the security proof for ECDSA-based adaptor signatures with rerandomizable keys would rely on the same related key attack, a similar security loss can
be expected for the additively rerandomizable ECDSA-based adaptor signature.
Worse yet, the related key attack for additively rerandomizable ECDSA allows to
prove only *one-per-message unforgeability* [10], which is a weaker security notion
than standard unforgeability. Therefore, we used multiplicative rerandomization
in our instantiation.

   While we did not work out the details, it is likely that adaptor signatures
with rerandomizable keys can be constructed from Schnorr and Katz-Wang-
based adaptor signatures [8] (due to the existing related key attack for Schnorr
signatures as presented in [11]). Finally, we believe that it would be an interesting
future work to extend the notion of two-party adaptor signatures as presented
in [8] to two-party adaptor signatures with rerandomizable keys.

# 4    Adaptor Wallets

In this section, we introduce the idea of adaptor wallets, which securely maintain
and operate adaptor signature schemes in a cryptocurrency network. We first
provide a high level overview of our model and then provide a generic wallet
construction from any adaptor signature scheme with rerandomizable keys and
witness rerandomizable hard relation. Finally, we show that it is impossible to
achieve deterministic and independent statement/witness rerandomization in our
model. Due to space limitations, we defer the full formal model and the security
arguments for our generic construction to the full version of this paper.

## 4.1    Model and Construction

We now describe a model for adaptor wallets and we discuss how adaptor signature schemes with rerandomizable keys can be used to instantiate such a wallet.
Our notion of adaptor wallets resembles the notion of hierarchical deterministic

---

[2] Das et al. show that this loss results in 20 bits less security for certain parameters.
   We refer the reader to [5] for details.

wallets by Das et al. [5], however, extending their notion to support adaptor signature operations such as pre-signing. We describe our model here informally and show a construction from adaptor signatures with rerandomizable keys.

An adaptor wallet considers one *master wallet*, which is used to deterministically initialize new wallets, so-called *child wallets*. Such child wallets are then used to generate (adaptor) signatures and are identified in our model by an identifier ID. In more detail, the master wallet generates and stores a master key pair $(\mathsf{msk}, \mathsf{mpk})$, a state $\mathsf{St}$ and a master statement/witness pair $(Y_m, y_m)$ of a witness rerandomizable hard relation (cf. Definition 2). However, the master wallet is not used to generate signatures, but only to deterministically initialize child wallets, i.e., in order to initialize a child wallet with identifier ID, the master wallet deterministically derives a new key pair $(sk^{\mathsf{ID}}, pk^{\mathsf{ID}})$ from $(\mathsf{msk}, \mathsf{mpk})$, and a new statement/witness pair $(Y^{\mathsf{ID}}, y^{\mathsf{ID}})$ from $(Y_m, y_m)$. The child wallet can then use its key pair $(sk^{\mathsf{ID}}, pk^{\mathsf{ID}})$ to generate signatures and use its statement/witness pair $(Y^{\mathsf{ID}}, y^{\mathsf{ID}})$ and a counter $\mathsf{ctr}$ to deterministically derive further statement/witness pairs. To keep our model simple, we do not allow child wallets to initialize further child wallets (as is done in the fully hierarchical setting [5]). We note, however, that our model can be extended to the fully hierarchical setting.

Similarly to the model of hierarchical deterministic wallets [5], we consider two kinds of child wallets, namely (1) non-hardened wallets, and (2) hardened wallets. Broadly speaking, the difference between these two is that we allow full corruption of hardened wallets, i.e., in our security games we allow the adversary to learn all secret values stored in a hardened wallet, including the session secret key $sk^{\mathsf{ID}}$. For non-hardened wallets, on the other hand, we allow the adversary to only learn the session public key $pk^{\mathsf{ID}}$ and statement $Y^{\mathsf{ID}}$. As a motivation for these two kinds of child wallets, recall the main applications of adaptor signatures as mentioned in the Introduction, namely payment channels and atomic swaps. A payment channel is typically used for frequent micropayments, i.e., users deposit only small amounts of money in a channel and use it often to sign transactions. In this case, it would be sensible to assume that the user operates the corresponding wallet on a mobile device, as it has to sign many transactions (possibly at a remote locations) and the impact of a wallet corruption is limited. Such a wallet would be represented by a hardened wallet in our model. On the other hand, atomic swaps are used, e.g., to swap coins of one cryptocurrency with coins of another currency. Such swaps are often one-time transactions of large amounts of funds or valuable tokens. In this example, it seems reasonable to implement the corresponding wallet as a hot/cold wallet, as it is crucial to secure such large amounts of funds or valuable tokens in the best possible way. The security goal for an adaptor wallet scheme is that the full corruption of hardened wallets does not compromise the security of any other (child or master) wallet. Additionally, we require that for all uncorrupted wallets, the derived public keys and statement/witness pairs are indistinguishable from freshly generated public keys and statement/witness pairs. Lastly, adaptor wallets must satisfy security notions similar to witness extractability under honestly rerandomizable keys (cf. Definition 11) and pre-signature adaptability (cf.

Definition 9) of adaptor signatures with rerandomizable keys. Figure 6 gives an illustration of our wallet model.

*Statement/Witness Rerandomization.* According to the hot/cold wallet setting, it would be ideal if the deterministic derivation of statements and witnesses can be done independently. That is, we would like to store and derive statements exclusively on the hot wallet and witnesses only on the cold wallet. This would allow the cold wallet to stay entirely inactive (and therefore secure) in applications where it suffices to derive statements first and the corresponding witnesses only at a later time. Surprisingly, we show in Sect. 4.2 that for any multiplicative or additive statement/witness derivation, such an independent derivation is impossible. In our model and construction, we therefore resort to a joint statement/witness derivation.

An adaptor wallet scheme consists of a Setup algorithm, which initializes the master wallet, derivation algorithms for hardened and non-hardened keys (SKDer$_H$, PKDer$_H$, SKDer$_{NH}$, PKDer$_{NH}$) as well as for statement/witness pairs RDer, adaptor signature algorithms (pSign, pVrfy, Adapt, Ext) and signing and verification algorithms (Sign, Verify).

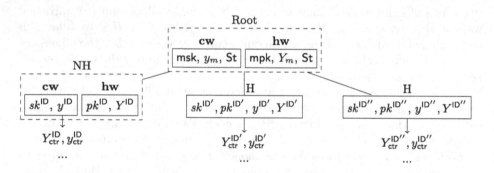

**Fig. 6.** Exemplatory design of our adaptor wallet scheme with three child wallets. H and NH denote hardened and non-hardened nodes respectively, **cw** and **hw** denote cold and hot wallets respectively and the values below the child wallets (e.g. $y_{ctr}^{ID}, Y_{ctr}^{ID}$) illustrate the statement/witness pairs that are being derived within each child wallet.

We now provide our generic construction of adaptor wallets, from an adaptor signature scheme with rerandomizable keys RASig$_{R,\Sigma}$ = (RandSK, RandPK, pSign, Adapt, pVrfy, Ext). This construction uses a hash function H : $\{0,1\}^* \to X$ and we require that the hard relation $R$ is witness rerandomizable as per Definition 2. Our construction can be found in Fig. 7.

### 4.2   Impossibility of Independent Statement/Witness Derivation

As mentioned above, one main question that arises when modeling derivation of statement/witness pairs in a deterministic fashion is whether an independent derivation of statement/witness pairs in hot and cold wallets respectively is possible. Surprisingly, unlike the secret and public key derivation mechanism, we show that this is not necessarily the case. At a high level, this is because unlike session secret keys, derived witnesses do not remain secret but are typically revealed in adaptor signature applications. More formally, we say that a hard relation $R \subseteq \mathcal{D}_Y \times \mathcal{D}_w$ has independently rerandomizable statement/witness pairs, if there exist two functions $f_{\mathsf{STDer}} : \mathcal{D}_Y \times \{0,1\}^* \to \mathcal{D}_Y$ and $f_{\mathsf{WitDer}} : \mathcal{D}_w \times \{0,1\}^* \to \mathcal{D}_w$ where for any $\rho \in \{0,1\}^*$ and any $(Y,y) \in R$ we have: $Y' \leftarrow f_{\mathsf{STDer}}(Y,\rho)$, $y' \leftarrow f_{\mathsf{WitDer}}(y,\rho)$, and $(Y',y') \in R$.

Translating the above to the hot/cold wallet setting, means that the cold wallet executes function $f_{\mathsf{WitDer}}$ and the hot wallet function $f_{\mathsf{STDer}}$. An adversary in this setting can corrupt the hot wallet but not the cold wallet, and hence can learn the statements $Y$ and $Y'$ as well as the respective randomness $\rho$. In addition, as required by certain adaptor signature applications, the adversary eventually learns a derived witness $y' \leftarrow f_{\mathsf{WitDer}}(y,\rho)$. Therefore, if there exists a function $f^{-1} : \mathcal{D}_w \times \{0,1\}^* \to \mathcal{D}_w$ which on input $y', \rho$ returns $y$, i.e., $y \leftarrow f^{-1}(y',\rho)$, then we cannot construct deterministic and independent statement/witness derivation from $f_{\mathsf{WitDer}}$ and $f_{\mathsf{STDer}}$. This is, because an adversary

---

Algorithm Setup($1^n$)
00  St $\leftarrow_\$ \{0,1\}^n$
01  $(Y_m, y_m) \leftarrow R.\mathsf{GenR}(1^n)$
02  $(\mathsf{msk}, \mathsf{mpk}) \leftarrow \mathsf{RASig}_{R,\Sigma}.\mathsf{Gen}(1^n)$
03  Return $(\mathsf{msk}, \mathsf{mpk}, \mathsf{St}, Y_m, y_m)$

Algorithm pSign($sk^{\mathsf{ID}}, m, Y$)
04  $\tilde{\sigma} \leftarrow \mathsf{RASig}_{R,\Sigma}.\mathsf{pSign}(sk^{\mathsf{ID}}, m, Y)$
05  Return $\tilde{\sigma}$

Algorithm pVrfy($pk^{\mathsf{ID}}, m, Y, \tilde{\sigma}$)
06  Return $\mathsf{RASig}_{R,\Sigma}.\mathsf{pVrfy}(pk^{\mathsf{ID}}, m, Y, \tilde{\sigma})$

Algorithm Adapt($\tilde{\sigma}, y_{\mathsf{ctr}}^{\mathsf{ID}}$)
07  $\sigma \leftarrow \mathsf{RASig}_{R,\Sigma}.\mathsf{Adapt}(\tilde{\sigma}, y_{\mathsf{ctr}}^{\mathsf{ID}})$
08  Return $\sigma$

Algorithm Ext($\sigma, \tilde{\sigma}, Y_{\mathsf{ctr}}^{\mathsf{ID}}$)
09  Return $\mathsf{RASig}_{R,\Sigma}.\mathsf{Ext}(\sigma, \tilde{\sigma}, Y_{\mathsf{ctr}}^{\mathsf{ID}})$

Algorithm Sign($sk^{\mathsf{ID}}, m$)
10  $\sigma \leftarrow \mathsf{RASig}_{R,\Sigma}.\mathsf{Sign}(sk^{\mathsf{ID}}, m)$
11  Return $\sigma$

Algorithm Verify($pk^{\mathsf{ID}}, m, \sigma$)
12  Return $\mathsf{RASig}_{R,\Sigma}.\mathsf{Verify}(pk^{\mathsf{ID}}, m, \sigma)$

Algorithm $\mathsf{SKDer}_{\mathsf{H}}(\mathsf{msk}, \mathsf{St}, \mathsf{ID})$
13  $\rho \leftarrow \mathsf{H}(\mathsf{msk}, \mathsf{St}, \mathsf{ID})$
14  $sk^{\mathsf{ID}} \leftarrow \mathsf{RASig}_{R,\Sigma}.\mathsf{RandSK}(\mathsf{msk}, \rho)$
15  Return $sk^{\mathsf{ID}}$

Algorithm $\mathsf{SKDer}_{\mathsf{NH}}(\mathsf{msk}, \mathsf{mpk}, \mathsf{St}, \mathsf{ID})$
16  $\rho \leftarrow \mathsf{H}(\mathsf{mpk}, \mathsf{St}, \mathsf{ID})$
17  $sk^{\mathsf{ID}} \leftarrow \mathsf{RASig}_{R,\Sigma}.\mathsf{RandSK}(\mathsf{msk}, \rho)$
18  Return $sk^{\mathsf{ID}}$

Algorithm $\mathsf{PKDer}_{\mathsf{H}}(\mathsf{msk}, \mathsf{mpk}, \mathsf{St}, \mathsf{ID})$
19  $\rho \leftarrow \mathsf{H}(\mathsf{msk}, \mathsf{St}, \mathsf{ID})$
20  $pk^{\mathsf{ID}} \leftarrow \mathsf{RASig}_{R,\Sigma}.\mathsf{RandPK}(\mathsf{mpk}, \rho)$
21  Return $pk^{\mathsf{ID}}$

Algorithm $\mathsf{PKDer}_{\mathsf{NH}}(\mathsf{mpk}, \mathsf{St}, \mathsf{ID})$
22  $\rho \leftarrow \mathsf{H}(\mathsf{mpk}, \mathsf{St}, \mathsf{ID})$
23  $pk^{\mathsf{ID}} \leftarrow \mathsf{RASig}_{R,\Sigma}.\mathsf{RandPK}(\mathsf{mpk}, \rho)$
24  Return $pk^{\mathsf{ID}}$

Algorithm RDer($Y, y, \mathsf{ctr}, \mathsf{ID}$)
25  $\rho \leftarrow \mathsf{H}(y, \mathsf{ctr}, \mathsf{ID})$
26  $y_{\mathsf{ctr}}^{\mathsf{ID}} \leftarrow R.\mathsf{RandWit}(y, \rho)$
27  $Y_{\mathsf{ctr}}^{\mathsf{ID}} \leftarrow R.\mathsf{WitToSt}(y_{\mathsf{ctr}}^{\mathsf{ID}})$
28  Return $(Y_{\mathsf{ctr}}^{\mathsf{ID}}, y_{\mathsf{ctr}}^{\mathsf{ID}})$

**Fig. 7.** Generic construction of adaptor wallets w.r.t. an adaptor signature scheme with rerandomizable keys $\mathsf{RASig}_{R,\Sigma}$, where $R$ is a witness rerandomizable hard relation as per Definition 2 and a hash function $\mathsf{H} : \{0,1\}^* \to X$.

could compute $y$ and thereby break unforgeability of the adaptor wallet scheme. In the full version of this paper, we formalize this claim and prove it.

Let us now see how this result affects existing adaptor signature constructions. For the ECDSA-based adaptor signature construction $EC_{R_g,PEC}[H]$ as described in Sect. 2.4 it is not possible to define $f_{STDer}$ without providing the witness as input. This is mainly because the hard relation $R_g := \{((Y, \pi), y) \mid Y = g^y \wedge V_g(Y, \pi) = 1\}$ requires a zero-knowledge proof alongside the statement $Y$, that proves knowledge of the witness $y$. Naturally, generating this proof without the witness is not possible. Now consider the "pure" dlog hard relation $R^{dlog} := \{(Y, y) \mid Y = g^y\}$, which is required for adaptor signature schemes based on Schnorr and Katz-Wang [8]. The statement/witness pairs for this relation can be rerandomized either multiplicatively or additively. Both of these operations, however, can easily be inverted. For instance, for a statement/witness pair $(g^y, y) \in R^{dlog}$, an additive rerandomization would instantiate the functions $f_{STDer}$ and $f_{WitDer}$ as $f_{STDer}(g^y, \rho) := g^y \cdot g^\rho = Y'$ and $f_{WitDer}(y, \rho) := y + \rho = y'$. Naturally, the function $f^{-1}$ can simply be instantiated as $f^{-1}(y', \rho) := y' - \rho = y$.

*Impact of the Impossibility Result.* Due to the above impossibility result of independent statement/witness derivation we cannot construct an adaptor wallet scheme with statement derivation in the hot wallet. However, for certain applications of adaptor signatures, this restriction is tolerable as the cold wallet does not need to generate many signatures and/or statement/witness pairs and therefore does not need to be activated frequently. Further, in practice one can minimize the number of times a cold wallet must be activated by batching the generation of statement/witness pairs, i.e., the cold wallet can generate multiple pairs and send all statements at once to the hot wallet. For other applications with frequent transactions, such as payment channels, an adaptor wallet user can use a hardened wallet as explained in Sect. 4.1.

**Acknowledgments.** This work is supported by the German Research Foundation DFG - SFB 1119 - 236615297 (CROSSING Project S7), by the German Federal Ministry of Education and Research (BMBF) *iBlockchain Project* (grant nr. 16KIS0902), by the German Federal Ministry of Education and Research and the Hessen State Ministry for Higher Education, Research and the Arts within their joint support of the *National Research Center for Applied Cybersecurity ATHENE*.

# References

1. Alkeilani Alkadri, N., et al.: Deterministic wallets in a quantum world. In: Ligatti, J., Ou, X., Katz, J., Vigna, G. (eds.) ACM CCS 2020, November 2020, pp. 1017–1031. ACM Press (2020). https://doi.org/10.1145/3372297.3423361
2. Atallah, M.J., Blanton, M., Fazio, N., Frikken, K.B.: Dynamic and efficient key management for access hierarchies. ACM Trans. Inf. Syst. Secur. **12**, 3 (2009). https://doi.org/10.1145/1455526.1455531

3. Aumayr, L., et al.: Generalized channels from limited blockchain scripts and adaptor signatures. In: Tibouchi, M., Wang, H. (eds.) ASIACRYPT 2021. LNCS, vol. 13091, pp. 635–664. Springer, Cham (2021). https://doi.org/10.1007/978-3-030-92075-3_22

4. Blum, M., Feldman, P., Micali, S.: Non-interactive zero-knowledge and its applications. In: Proceedings of the Twentieth Annual ACM Symposium on Theory of Computing, STOC 1988. Chicago, pp. 103–112. Association for Computing Machinery (1988). https://doi.org/10.1145/62212.62222

5. Das, P., Erwig, A., Faust, S., Loss, J., Riahi, S.: The exact security of BIP32 wallets. In: Vigna, G., Shi, E. (eds.) ACM CCS 2021, pp. 1020–1042. ACM Press (2021). https://doi.org/10.1145/3460120.3484807

6. Das, P., Faust, S., Loss, J.: A formal treatment of deterministic wallets. In: Cavallaro, L., Kinder, J., Wang, X., Katz, J. (eds.) ACM CCS 2019, pp. 651–668. ACM Press (2019). https://doi.org/10.1145/3319535

7. Deshpande, A., Herlihy, M.: Privacy-preserving cross-chain atomic swaps. In: Bernhard, M., et al. (eds.) FC 2020. LNCS, vol. 12063, pp. 540–549. Springer, Cham (2020). https://doi.org/10.1007/978-3-030-54455-3_38

8. Erwig, A., Faust, S., Hostáková, K., Maitra, M., Riahi, S.: Two-party adaptor signatures from identification schemes. In: Garay, J.A. (ed.) PKC 2021. LNCS, vol. 12710, pp. 451–480. Springer, Cham (2021). https://doi.org/10.1007/978-3-030-75245-3_17

9. Esgin, M.F., Ersoy, O., Erkin, Z.: Post-quantum adaptor signatures and payment channel networks. In: Chen, L., Li, N., Liang, K., Schneider, S. (eds.) ESORICS 2020. LNCS, vol. 12309, pp. 378–397. Springer, Cham (2020). https://doi.org/10.1007/978-3-030-59013-0_19

10. Fersch, M., Kiltz, E., Poettering, B.: On the one-per-message unforgeability of (EC)DSA and its variants. In: Kalai, Y., Reyzin, L. (eds.) TCC 2017. LNCS, vol. 10678, pp. 519–534. Springer, Cham (2017). https://doi.org/10.1007/978-3-319-70503-3_17

11. Fleischhacker, N., et al.: Efficient unlinkable sanitizable signatures from signatures with re-randomizable keys. In: Cheng, C.-M., Chung, K.-M., Persiano, G., Yang, B.-Y. (eds.) PKC 2016. LNCS, vol. 9614, pp. 301–330. Springer, Heidelberg (2016). https://doi.org/10.1007/978-3-662-49384-7_12

12. Gutoski, G., Stebila, D.: Hierarchical deterministic bitcoin wallets that tolerate key leakage. In: Böhme, R., Okamoto, T. (eds.) FC 2015. LNCS, vol. 8975, pp. 497–504. Springer, Heidelberg (2015). https://doi.org/10.1007/978-3-662-47854-7_31

13. Katz, J., Wang, N.: Efficiency improvements for signature schemes with tight security reductions. In: Jajodia, S., Atluri, V., Jaeger, T. (eds.) ACM CCS 2003, pp. 155–164. ACM Press (2003). https://doi.org/10.1145/948109.948132

14. Kondi, Y., Magri, B., Orlandi, C., Shlomovits, O.: Refresh when you wake up: proactive threshold wallets with offline devices. In: 2021 IEEE Symposium on Security and Privacy (SP), pp. 608–625 (2021) https://doi.org/10.1109/SP40001.2021.00067

15. Di Luzio, A., Francati, D., Ateniese, G.: Arcula: a secure hierarchical deterministic wallet for multi-asset blockchains. In: Krenn, S., Shulman, H., Vaudenay, S. (eds.) CANS 2020. LNCS, vol. 12579, pp. 323–343. Springer, Cham (2020). https://doi.org/10.1007/978-3-030-65411-5_16

16. Madathil, V., Thyagarajan, S.A., Vasilopoulos, D., Fournier, L., Malavolta, G., Moreno-Sanchez, P.: Practical Decentralized Oracle Contracts for Cryptocurrencies. Cryptology ePrint Archive, Report 2022/499 (2022). https://ia.cr/2022/499. 2022

17. Malavolta, G., Moreno-Sanchez, P., Schneidewind, C., Kate, A., Maffei, M.: Anonymous multi-hop locks for blockchain scalability and interoperability. In: NDSS 2019. The Internet Society (2019)

18. Moreno-Sanchez, P., Kate, A.: Scriptless Scripts with ECDSA (2018). https://lists.linuxfoundation.org/pipermail/lightning-dev/attachments/20180426/fe978423/attachment-0001.pdf

19. Poelstra, A.: Scriptless scripts (2017). https://download.wpsoftware.net/bitcoin/wizardry/mw-slides/2017-03-mit-bitcoin-expo/slides.pdf. Accessed Oct 2020

20. Sasson, E.B., et al.: Zerocash: decentralized anonymous payments from bitcoin. IEEE Symp. Secur. Privacy **2014**, 459–474 (2014)

21. Schnorr, C.P.: Efficient signature generation by smart cards. J. Cryptol. **4**(3), 161–174 (1991). https://doi.org/10.1007/BF00196725

22. Tairi, E., Moreno-Sanchez, P., Maffei, M.: $A^2L$: anonymous atomic locks for scalability in payment channel hubs. In: 2021 IEEE Symposium on Security and Privacy, pp. 1834–1851. IEEE Computer Society Press (2021). https://doi.org/10.1109/SP40001.2021.00111

23. Tairi, E., Moreno-Sanchez, P., Maffei, M.: Post-quantum adaptor signature for privacy-preserving off-chain payments". In: Borisov, N., Diaz, C. (eds.) Financial Cryptography and Data Security, pp. 131–150. Springer, Heidelberg (2021). ISBN:978-3-662-64331-0

24. Thyagarajan, S.A., Malavolta, G., Moreno-Sánchez, P.: Universal Atomic Swaps: Secure Exchange of Coins Across All Blockchains. Cryptology ePrint Archive, Report 2021/1612 (2021). https://ia.cr/2021/1612.2021

25. Van Saberhagen, N.: CryptoNote v 2.0 (2013)

26. Yin, X., Liu, Z., Yang, G., Chen, G., Zhu, H.: Secure Hierarchical Deterministic Wallet Supporting Stealth Address. Cryptology ePrint Archive, Paper 2022/627 (2022). https://eprint.iacr.org/2022/627

# Puncturable Signature: A Generic Construction and Instantiations

Mei Jiang$^{(\boxtimes)}$ , Dung Hoang Duong , and Willy Susilo

Institute of Cybersecurity and Cryptology, School of Computing and Information Technology, University of Wollongong, Northfields Avenue, Wollongong, NSW 2522, Australia
mj847@uowmail.edu.au, {hduong,wsusilo}@uow.edu.au

**Abstract.** Puncturable signature (PS), proposed by Bellare, Stepanovs and Waters at EUROCRYPT 2016, is a special kind of digital signature that supports a fine-grained revocation of signing capacity by updating the secret key with selective messages. Puncturable signature has many usages like asynchronous transaction data signing services and proof-of-stake blockchain protocols. Meanwhile, it is an essential building block in constructing disappearing signatures in the bounded storage model. In this paper, we propose the first generic construction of puncturable signature from identity-based signature by treating identities as prefixes. With the help of our generic framework, we present different puncturable signature instantiations over lattices, bilinear maps, and multivariate public key cryptography (MPKC). Specifically, the lattice-based instantiation is based on the short integer solution (SIS) assumption and is proven secure in the random oracle model. Besides, the pairing-based instantiation is based on the computational Diffie-Hellman (CDH) assumption and is proven secure in the standard model. In addition, we show that the instantiation over MPKC is secure under current attacks.

**Keywords:** Puncturable signature · Generic construction · Lattices · Bilinear maps · Multivariate public key cryptography

## 1 Introduction

Digital signature is one of the most important cryptographic primitives for protecting the integrity and authenticity of messages transmitted over insecure communication channels. It has been commonly used in software distribution, financial transactions, contract management software, and blockchains. *Puncturable signature* (PS) is a special kind of digital signature that provides a fine-grained revocation of signing capacity by updating the secret key selectively. Compared with a general digital signature, it contains an additional algorithm named **Puncture**, where the signer could update the secret key with messages chosen by himself. More specifically, with a punctured secret key $sk'$ punctured at the message $\mu$, the signer can sign on any message except for the punctured message $\mu$. In 2020, Li *et al.* [15] extended the definition of puncturable signature by changing the punctured message from the whole message to a certain part of it (e.g. its prefix), which speeds up the revocation of authentication for messages with the same prefix.[1] Generally speaking, a punctured secret key could be updated sequentially with different prefixes many times.

Puncturable signature has many usages like asynchronous transaction data signing services and proof-of-stake blockchain protocols. Besides, puncturable signature provides forward secrecy at a fine-grained level. Forward secrecy is a promising approach to mitigating the key exposure issue by updating the secret key periodically. In forward-secure signature schemes, the time is divided into multiple time intervals in advance, and the secret key is updated at each time interval. Forward secrecy preserves the validity of past signatures since a forger cannot forge any signature in past time intervals even if the current secret key has been compromised. In contrast with puncturable signatures, forward-secure signatures provide a limited (only for past messages) revocation of signing capacity. It is difficult for forward-secure signatures to revoke the signing capacity for any individual message or a class of messages with particular features at a specific time interval, but it is easy for puncturable signatures.

Meanwhile, puncturable signature is an indispensable building block in the construction of *disappearing signature* [11] in the bounded storage model. The bounded storage model [17] is an approach to enabling secure applications by leveraging the storage bounds of the adversary. More precisely, the transmitted signature is streamed bit by bit, and the stream is so long that the adversary cannot record it entirely. In the bounded storage model, the signature can only be verified online since it will *disappear* once the stream stops. The security of disappearing signatures requires that the forger cannot forge a signature on any message, even for those messages that he has seen the corresponding signatures previously. In [11], Guan and Zhandry proposed a disappearing signature construction by combining the online obfuscation with a puncturable signature, where the puncturable signature guarantees the security of the resulting scheme.

## 1.1 Related Work

In 2016, Bellare *et al.* [5] proposed the notion of puncturable signature and presented an impractical puncturable signature scheme. The scheme was based on indistinguishability obfuscation, which brought prohibitive computational overhead in practice. One year later, Halevi *et al.* [12] proposed a puncturable signature scheme by combining a statistically binding commitment scheme with *non-interactive zero-knowledge* (NIZK) proofs. The scheme was slightly different from the general puncturable signature since it updated the public key instead of the secret key during each puncture operation. Although such a scheme had some theoretical merits, it was hard to deploy in real-world applications since repeatedly

---

[1] Throughout the paper, we focus on the extended puncturable signature introduced in [12]. It is also called *prefix puncturable signature* in [11].

updating the public key was impractical. In 2020, Li *et al.* [15] proposed a puncturable signature scheme combined with the bloom filter, which outperformed previous schemes in terms of signature size and algorithm efficiency, especially for the key puncture efficiency. The scheme was based on the strong Diffie-Hellman assumption in bilinear maps and was proven secure in the random oracle model. But it suffered from non-negligible false-positive errors due to the probabilistic bloom filter data structure. As the number of puncture operations increases, the false-positive probability would increase, leading to much business cost. In blockchains, causing false-positive errors is economically beneficial for attackers.

To the best of our knowledge, there has been no specific puncturable signature scheme that simultaneously enjoys post-quantum security and eliminates false-positive errors until now.

## 1.2    Overview of Technique

The core of puncturable signatures is to bind the punctured secret key with punctured prefixes such that the updated secret key cannot sign on any message with a punctured prefix. That is why few puncturable signature schemes exist, especially for efficient constructions. In [15], Li *et al.* presented a simple way to generate the punctured secret key with the bloom filter which is a tool solving the approximate set membership problem. The bloom filter contains multiple hash functions and a bit-array $T$ with the pre-determined size. The punctured secret key and punctured prefixes in [15] are connected in the following way. For each bit in $T$, the signer generates a corresponding key randomly and stores it in a set $S$. The initial secret key in puncturable signatures consists of the bit-array $T$ and the set $S$. With a non-punctured prefix, the signer updates the bloom filter and deletes the corresponding keys in $S$. After that, the punctured secret key contains an updated bit-array $T$ and an updated set $S$. The signer cannot sign on any message with a punctured prefix since all related keys have been deleted already.

By observation, we find that the bloom filter in [15] was for testing whether a prefix has been punctured, which is independent of protecting the secret key. Besides, it didn't take advantage of its space-efficient feature here since the signer had to store all related keys in the set $S$. On the other hand, the bloom filter brought two downsides due to its inherent structure. One was the false-positive error due to the collisions of hash functions such that the signer cannot sign on the message even with a non-punctured prefix. The probability of false-positive errors is non-negligible and increases as the times of key puncture increase. Although we can decrease them by choosing reasonable parameters or puncturing fewer times, it is impossible to eliminate false-positive errors. Another drawback was that the security proof became more complicated since there were several different keys related to one prefix. Therefore, the security proof in [15] had to be divided into two steps since it constructed another adversary with a fixed position which helped the challenger attack the strong Diffie-Hellman assumption.

Motivated by eliminating the above drawbacks, we use a one-dimensional array to represent the bloom filter. Inspired by [15], we propose a generic construction of puncturable signature from *identity-based signature* (IBS). More specifically, we assume that the identity space is bounded and treated as the prefix space in puncturable signatures. In the Setup algorithm, the signer generates the key pair of IBS, where the public parameter is regarded as the public key in PS. For each valid identity, the signer computes a related secret key using the Extract algorithm and stores it in the one-dimensional array which is the initial secret key in PS. In the Puncture algorithm, the signer converts the non-punctured prefix (a binary string) to a decimal integer and deletes the corresponding key. Without the related key, the signer cannot sign on any message with a punctured prefix, which achieves the puncturable functionality easily. The Sign and Verify algorithms are similar between IBS and PS if we treat each identity as a prefix.

## 1.3    Our Contribution

In this paper, we first propose a *generic* construction of puncturable signature from identity-based signature by treating identities as prefixes. With the help of our generic construction, we present different puncturable signature instantiations based on lattices, bilinear maps, and multivariate public key cryptography, respectively. More precisely, the lattice-based instantiation is based on the efficient identity-based signature scheme proposed by Tian and Huang [21], which is an identity-based version of Lyubashevsky's signature [16]. Our instantiation is based on the short integer solution assumption and is proven secure in the random oracle model. Besides, the pairing-based instantiation comes from the novel identity-based signature scheme [22], which improved Paterson's signature [20]. Our instantiation is based on the computational Diffie-Hellman assumption in bilinear maps and is proven secure in the standard model. In addition, the multivariate-based instantiation is based on the ID-based Rainbow signature [7], and we show it is secure under current attacks. Our instantiations have the following characteristics:

- They work for a pre-determined time of key punctures since the range of prefix space is fixed in advance. The size of the punctured secret key decreases linearly as the times of key puncture increase.
- They support efficient puncture operations that only contain a conversion from a bit string to a decimal integer and the deletion of a certain part in the current secret key.
- They eliminate false-positive errors.
- The schemes over lattices and MPKC enjoy post-quantum security.

As shown in Table 1, we compare our instantiations with previous puncturable signature schemes. Our lattice-based and multivariate-based instantiations enjoy post-quantum security without false-positive errors. Although the scheme [15] and our pairing-based instantiaition depend on bilinear maps, our scheme is secure in the standard model and eliminates false-positive errors.

**Table 1.** Comparison of the existing puncturable signature schemes

| Instantiation | Assumption | Security model | Post-quantum | False-positive errors |
|---|---|---|---|---|
| Li [15] | $\tau$-SDH | ROM | ✗ | ✓ |
| **Lattice Ins.** | SIS | ROM | ✓ | ✗ |
| **Pairing Ins.** | CDH | SDM | ✗ | ✗ |
| **MPKC Ins.** | MQ | | ✓ | ✗ |

## 1.4 Organization

This paper is organized as follows. In Sect. 2, we introduce relevant notations, definitions and theorems. In Sect. 3, we review the definition and security model of identity-based signatures and give a generic construction of puncturable signature from identity-based signature. In Sect. 4, we propose puncturable signature instantiations over lattices, bilinear maps, and multivariate public key cryptography respectively. In Sect. 5, we conclude our work and present open problems.

## 2 Preliminary

Throughout the paper, vectors are in column forms and denoted by lower-case bold letters (e.g. $\mathbf{v}$). Matrices are denoted by upper-case bold letters (e.g. $\mathbf{M}$) and treated interchangeably as an ordered set of its column vectors. For a vector $\mathbf{v}$, $\|\mathbf{v}\|$ denotes its $\ell_2$ norm. For a matrix $\mathbf{M}$, $\|\mathbf{M}\|$ denotes the $\ell_2$ norm of the longest column vector in $\mathbf{M}$, and $\mathbf{M}_{\mathrm{GS}}$ denotes the Gram-Schmidt orthogonalization of $\mathbf{M}$. $(n)_2$ denotes a binary string converted from the integer $n$, while $(s)_{10}$ denotes a decimal integer converted from the binary string $s$. A negligible function is generically denoted by $\mathrm{negl}(n)$. We say that a probability is overwhelming if it is $1 - \mathrm{negl}(n)$. The *statistical distance* between two distributions $\mathbf{X}$ and $\mathbf{Y}$ over a countable domain $\Omega$ is defined as $\frac{1}{2} \sum_{w \in \Omega} |\Pr[\mathbf{X} = w] - \Pr[\mathbf{Y} = w]|$. We say that two distributions are *statistically close* if their statistical distance is negligible.

### 2.1 Puncturable Signature

Let $\mathcal{M}$ and $\mathcal{P}$ denote the message and prefix space respectively. In general, a puncturable signature scheme $\mathcal{PS} = (\mathbf{Setup}, \mathbf{Puncture}, \mathbf{Sign}, \mathbf{Verify})$ consists of the following four algorithms.

- **Setup**$(1^\lambda) \to (PK, SK)$: On input the security parameter $\lambda$, it outputs the public key $PK$ and the initial secret key $SK$.
- **Puncture**$(SK, p) \to SK'$: On input the current secret key $SK$ and a prefix $p \in \mathcal{P}$, it outputs the punctured secret key $SK'$. Meanwhile, the prefix $p$ is regarded as a punctured prefix.

- **Sign**$(SK, \mu) \to \sigma$ *or* $\perp$: On input the secret key $SK$ and a message $\mu \in \mathcal{M}$, it outputs a signature $\sigma$ if the prefix $p^2$ has not been punctured. Otherwise, it returns $\perp$.
- **Verify**$(PK, \mu, \sigma) \to 1$ *or* 0: On input the public key $PK$, a message $\mu$ and a signature $\sigma$, it returns 1 if $\sigma$ is a valid signature for $\mu$ and 0 otherwise.

**Correctness.** The correctness of puncturable signatures requires that (1) any signature under any message could be generated with the initial (non-punctured) secret key, and (2) signing fails if the prefix of a to-be-signed message has been punctured. Formally, a puncturable signature scheme verifies successfully for the message space $\mathcal{M}$ and prefix space $\mathcal{P}$ if:

- **Verify**$(PK, \mu, \textbf{Sign}(SK_0, \mu)) = 1$, where $SK_0$ is the initial secret key.
- **Verify**$(PK, \mu, \textbf{Sign}(SK', \mu)) = 0$, where $SK' \leftarrow \textbf{Puncture}(SK, p)$ and $p \in \mathcal{P}$ is the prefix of $\mu \in \mathcal{M}$.
- **Verify**$(PK, \mu, \textbf{Sign}(SK', \mu)) = 1$, where $SK' \leftarrow \textbf{Puncture}(SK, p)$, $p' \in \mathcal{P}$ is the prefix of $\mu \in \mathcal{M}$ and $p \neq p'$.

**Security Model.** The security of puncturable signatures requires that the forger cannot forge any signature on any message with a punctured prefix even if the current secret key is compromised. Formally, the security experiment $\text{Exp}_{\mathcal{F}}^{\text{PS}}(1^\lambda)$ between the forger $\mathcal{F}$ and the challenger $\mathcal{C}$ is described as follows.

- **Setup.** The challenger $\mathcal{C}$ computes $(PK, SK) \leftarrow \textbf{Setup}(1^\lambda)$ and sends $PK$ to the forger $\mathcal{F}$. Then $\mathcal{C}$ initializes two empty sets $Q_{sig}$ and $Q_{pun}$ for signed messages and punctured prefixes respectively.
- **Query.** The forger $\mathcal{F}$ adaptively issues the following queries many times.

- **Puncture Query**: After receiving a prefix $p$, $\mathcal{C}$ generates a punctured secret key by running **Puncture**$(SK, p)$ and updates $Q_{pun} = Q_{pun} \cup \{p\}$.
- **Signature Query**: After receiving a message $\mu$, the challenger $\mathcal{C}$ checks whether $p \in Q_{pun}$, where $p$ is implicit in $\mu$. If $p \in Q_{pun}$, $\mathcal{C}$ returns $\perp$. Otherwise, $\mathcal{C}$ generates the signature $\sigma \leftarrow \textbf{Sign}(SK, \mu)$, updates $Q_{sig} = Q_{sig} \cup \{\mu\}$, and returns $\sigma$ to $\mathcal{F}$.

- **Challenge.** The forger $\mathcal{F}$ sends a target prefix $p^*$ to the challenger $\mathcal{C}$ and issues additional puncture and signature queries as described in the **Query** phase.
- **Corruption Query.** The challenger $\mathcal{C}$ returns the current secret key $SK$ if $p^* \in Q_{pun}$ and $\perp$ otherwise.
- **Forgery.** The forger $\mathcal{F}$ outputs a forgery signature $\sigma^*$ on a message $\mu^*$ with the prefix $p^*$. We say that $\mathcal{F}$ wins the security experiment $\text{Exp}_{\mathcal{F}}^{\text{PS}}(1^\lambda)$ if $p^* \in Q_{pun}$, $\mu^* \notin Q_{sig}$ and Verify$(PK, \mu^*, \sigma^*) = 1$.

**Definition 1.** *A puncturable signature scheme is existential unforgeability under chosen message attacks with adaptive puncturing, if any PPT forger $\mathcal{F}$ wins the security experiment* $\text{Exp}_{\mathcal{F}}^{\text{PS}}(1^\lambda)$ *with at most a negligible probability, where the probability is over the randomness of the challenger and forger.*

---

[2] We assume that the prefix $p$ is implicitly contained in the message $\mu$.

## 2.2   Lattices

An $m$-dimensional lattice $\Lambda$ is a discrete additive subgroup of $\mathbb{R}^m$. Specifically, a lattice $\Lambda$ with the basis $\mathbf{B} = [\mathbf{b}_1|\cdots|\mathbf{b}_n] \in \mathbb{R}^{m \times n}$, is defined as $\Lambda := \{\sum_{i=1}^n \mathbf{b}_i x_i | x_i \in \mathbb{Z}, \forall i = 1, \ldots, n\} \subseteq \mathbb{R}^m$. In this paper, we mainly consider $q$-ary lattices defined as follows. Given $\mathbf{A} \in \mathbb{Z}_q^{n \times m}$ and $\mathbf{u} \in \mathbb{Z}_q^n$,

$$\Lambda_q(\mathbf{A}) = \{\mathbf{z} \in \mathbb{Z}^m : \exists\, \mathbf{s} \in \mathbb{Z}_q^n \text{ s.t. } \mathbf{z} = \mathbf{A}^\top \mathbf{s} \bmod q\},$$

$$\Lambda_q^\perp(\mathbf{A}) = \{\mathbf{z} \in \mathbb{Z}^m : \mathbf{A}\mathbf{z} = 0 \bmod q\},$$

$$\Lambda_q^{\mathbf{u}}(\mathbf{A}) = \{\mathbf{z} \in \mathbb{Z}^m : \mathbf{A}\mathbf{z} = \mathbf{u} \bmod q\}.$$

**Gaussians on Lattices.** For any $s > 0$, the Gaussian function on $\mathbb{R}^m$ centered at $\mathbf{c}$ with $s$ is defined as $\rho_{s,\mathbf{c}}(\mathbf{x}) = \exp(-\pi \|\mathbf{x} - \mathbf{c}\|^2 / s^2)$ for each $\mathbf{x} \in \mathbb{R}^m$. The subscript $s$ and $\mathbf{c}$ are taken to be 1 and 0 respectively when they are omitted. For any $\mathbf{c} \in \mathbb{R}^n$, real $s > 0$ and $m$-dimensional lattice $\Lambda$, the *discrete Gaussian distribution over* $\Lambda$ is defined as

$$\forall\, \mathbf{x} \in \Lambda, D_{\Lambda,s,\mathbf{c}}(\mathbf{x}) = \frac{\rho_{s,\mathbf{c}}(\mathbf{x})}{\rho_{s,\mathbf{c}}(\Lambda)}.$$

Note that the denominator in above expression is merely a normalization factor, and the probability $D_{\Lambda,s,\mathbf{c}}(\mathbf{x})$ is simply proportional to $\rho_{s,\mathbf{c}}(\mathbf{x})$.

The following lemma shows some basic facts about the discrete Gaussian distribution over $\mathbb{Z}^m$ from [3,18,20].

**Lemma 1.** *For any $\sigma > 0$ and positive integer $m$, we have:*

1. $Pr[|z| > \omega(\sigma\sqrt{\log m}); z \leftarrow D_\sigma^1] = 2^{-\omega(\log m)}$, *and more specifically,* $Pr[|z| > 12\sigma; z \leftarrow D_\sigma^1] = 2^{-100}$.
2. *For any* $\mathbf{z} \in \mathbb{Z}^m$, *and* $\sigma \geq \sqrt{\log 3m}$, $D_\sigma^m(\mathbf{z}) \leq 2^{-m+1}$.
3. $Pr[\|\mathbf{z}\| > 2\sigma\sqrt{m}; \mathbf{z} \leftarrow D_\sigma^m] < 2^{-m}$.

**Definition 2 (Short Integer Solution (SIS) [1]).** *Given a positive integer $q$, a real $\beta$ and a matrix $\mathbf{A} \in \mathbb{Z}_q^{n \times m}$, the goal of the SIS problem is to find a non-zero vector $\mathbf{v} \in \mathbb{Z}^m$ such that $\mathbf{A}\mathbf{v} = 0 \bmod q$ and $\|\mathbf{v}\| \leq \beta$.*

For the hardness of SIS assumption, Micciancio and Regev [18] showed that for any polynomial-bounded $m, \beta$ and any prime $q \geq \beta \cdot \omega(\sqrt{n \log n})$, solving SIS on average-case is as hard as approximating some intractable lattice problems like the shortest independent vectors problem (SIVP) in worst-case.

**Theorem 1 ([2]).** *Let $n > 0$, $q$ be a prime, and $m = O(n \log q)$. There exists a probabilistic polynomial-time algorithm* TrapGen$(q, n)$ *that outputs a matrix $\mathbf{A} \in \mathbb{Z}_q^{n \times m}$, and a basis $\mathbf{T_A}$ of $\Lambda_q^\perp(\mathbf{A})$ such that $\mathbf{A}$ is statistical close to uniform, $\|\mathbf{T_A}\| \leq O(n \log q)$, and $\|\mathbf{T_A}\|_{\mathrm{GS}} \leq O(\sqrt{n \log q})$ with overwhelming probability.*

**Theorem 2 ([10]).** *Let $m \geq n$ be an integer and $q$ be a prime. Let $\mathbf{A} \in \mathbb{Z}_q^{n \times m}$ and $\mathbf{T_A} \in \mathbb{Z}^{m \times m}$ be a basis of $\Lambda_q^\perp(\mathbf{A})$. If $\sigma \geq \|\mathbf{T_A}\|_{\mathrm{GS}} \cdot \omega(\sqrt{\log n})$ then for each $\mathbf{U} \in \mathbb{Z}_q^{n \times d}$, there is a PPT algorithm* SamplePre$(\mathbf{A}, \mathbf{T_A}, \sigma, \mathbf{U})$ *that outputs a sample $\mathbf{X}$ from a distribution that is statistically close to $D_\sigma(\Lambda_q^{\mathbf{U}}(\mathbf{A}))$.*

## 2.3   Bilinear Maps and CDH Assumption

Let $\mathbb{G}$ and $\mathbb{G}_T$ be cyclic groups of prime order $q$. Let $g$ be a generator of the cyclic group $\mathbb{G}$. The map $e : \mathbb{G} \times \mathbb{G} \leftarrow \mathbb{G}_T$ is said to be an admissible map if the following three conditions hold true:

- Bilinearity: For any $a, b \in \mathbb{Z}_q^*$, $e(g^a, g^b) = e(g, g)^{ab}$ holds.
- Non-degenerate: $e(g, g) \neq 1_{\mathbb{G}_T}$, where $1_{\mathbb{G}_T}$ is the unit of $\mathbb{G}_T$.
- Computability: For any $g, h \in \mathbb{G}$, there are effecitve algorithms to calculate $e(g, h)$.

**Definition 3 (Computational Diffie-Hellman Assumption (CDH)).** *Given a group $\mathbb{G}$ of prime order $q$ with the generator $g$ and elements $g^a, g^b \in \mathbb{G}$ where $a, b$ are selected uniformly at random from $\mathbb{Z}_q^*$, the goal of the CDH problem in $\mathbb{G}$ is to compute $g^{ab}$.*

## 2.4   Multivariate Public Key Cryptography

Multivariate public key cryptography is one of the widely accepted post-quantum candidates, and is viewed as the most promising candidate for RSA algorithm. The security of MPKC is based on solving a set of random quadratic multivariate equations on a finite field (MQ problem), which is NP-hard. In general, a MPKC scheme over the finite field $\mathbb{F}_q$ is built as $P = L_1 \circ F \circ L_2$, where $F$ is a set of $m$ quadratic multivariate equations in $n$ variables, $L_1$ is an affine transformation from $\mathbb{F}_q^m$ to $\mathbb{F}_q^m$, and $L_2$ is an affine transformation from $\mathbb{F}_q^n$ to $\mathbb{F}_q^n$.

Unbalanced Oil and Vinegar (UOV) [13] is a seminal MPKC signature scheme. The central map $F$ of UOV contains a set of Oil-Vinegar polynomials with the form

$$\sum_{i=1}^{o}\sum_{j=1}^{v} a_{i,j} x_i x_j' + \sum_{i=1}^{v}\sum_{j=1}^{v} b_{i,j} x_i' x_j' + \sum_{i=1}^{o} c_i x_i + \sum_{j=1}^{v} d_j x_j' + e$$

In this polynomial, there are two kinds of variables: Oil variables $(x_i)$ and Vinegar variables $(x_j')$, where $o$ and $v$ denote the number of oil and vinegar variables respectively. Once we assign random values for vinegar variables, $F$ becomes a set of linear polynomials and could be easily inverted. In UOV, there are more vinegar variables than oil variables in each polynomial of $F$.

Rainbow [9] could be viewed as a multi-layer UOV signature scheme with better efficiency. In the Rainbow scheme, each layer is an independent UOV and all variables (including oil and vinegar) in each layer become vinegar variables in the next layer.

## 3   Generic PS Construction from IBS

In this section, we first review the definition and security model of identity-based signatures. Then we provide a generic construction of puncturable signature from identity-based signature by treating identities as prefixes.

## 3.1  Identity-Based Signature

Identity-based signature is an efficient alternative of public-key signature since the public keys are derived from identities without digital certificates. The secret key of each user is generated by a trusted third party named private key generator (PKG). Let $\mathcal{M}$ and $\mathcal{ID}$ denote the message and identity space. In general, an identity-based signature scheme $\mathcal{IBS} = (\textbf{Setup}, \textbf{Extract}, \textbf{Sign}, \textbf{Verify})$ contains the following algorithms.

- **Setup**$(1^\lambda) \to (pp, msk)$: On input the security parameter $\lambda$, PKG outputs a public parameter $pp$ and the master secret key $msk$.
- **Extract**$(pp, msk, id) \to sk_{id}$: On input the public parameter $pp$, the master secret key $msk$ and an identity $id \in \mathcal{ID}$, PKG outputs a secret key $sk_{id}$ which implicitly contains the identity $id$.
- **Sign**$(pp, sk_{id}, \mu) \to \sigma$: On input the public parameter $pp$, the secret key $sk_{id}$ and a message $\mu \in \mathcal{M}$, the signer outputs a signature $\sigma$.
- **Verify**$(pp, id, \mu, \sigma) \to 1$ *or* $0$: On input the public parameter $pp$, an identity $id \in \mathcal{ID}$, a message $\mu \in \mathcal{M}$ and a signature $\sigma$, it outputs 1 if $\sigma$ is a valid signature for message $\mu$ and identity $id$. Otherwise, it outputs 0.

**Correctness.** For correctness, the IBS scheme requires that the following equation holds

$$\textbf{Verify}(pp, id, \mu, \textbf{Sign}(pp, sk_{id}, \mu)) = 1$$

for each $\mu \in \mathcal{M}$ and $id \in \mathcal{ID}$.

**Security Model.** For security, we consider the notion of existential unforgeability under chosen message attacks and adaptive identity, which allows the forger to adaptively issue queries on any identity. A weaker selective-identity model requires the forger to announce the target identity before seeing the public parameter. Formally, the security experiment $\text{Exp}_{\mathcal{F}}^{\text{IBS}}(1^\lambda)$ between the forger $\mathcal{F}$ and the challenger $\mathcal{C}$ is described as follows.

  - **Setup.** The challenger $\mathcal{C}$ computes $(pp, msk) \leftarrow \textbf{Setup}(1^\lambda)$ and sends the public parameter $pp$ to $\mathcal{F}$.
  - **Query.** The forger $\mathcal{F}$ adaptively issues the following queries many times.

- **Extract Query**: After receiving an identity $id$, the challenger $\mathcal{C}$ generates the secret key $sk_{id} \leftarrow \textbf{Extract}(pp, msk, id)$ and returns it to $\mathcal{F}$.
- **Signature Query**: After receiving a message $\mu$ and an identity $id$, $\mathcal{C}$ checks whether the secret key for $id$ has been defined. If not, it generates the secret key $sk_{id}$, computes the signature $\sigma \leftarrow \textbf{Sign}(pp, sk_{id}, \mu)$ and returns it to $\mathcal{F}$.

  - **Forgery.** The forger $\mathcal{F}$ outputs a forgery signature $\sigma^*$ based on the message $\mu^*$ and identity $id^*$. We say that $\mathcal{F}$ wins the security experiment $\text{Exp}_{\mathcal{F}}^{\text{IBS}}(1^\lambda)$ if $\textbf{Verify}(pp, id^*, \mu^*, \sigma^*) = 1$, and $\mathcal{F}$ never queried $\textbf{Extract}(id^*)$ and $\textbf{Sign}(id^*, \mu^*)$.

**Definition 4.** *An identity-based signature scheme is existential unforgeability under chosen message attacks with adaptive identity, if any PPT forger $\mathcal{F}$ wins the security experiment $\text{Exp}_{\mathcal{F}}^{\text{IBS}}(1^\lambda)$ with at most a negligible probability, where the probability is over the randomness of the challenger and forger.*

## 3.2   Generic Construction

The main idea behind our generic construction of puncturable signature from identity-based signature is to treat identities as prefixes. Moreover, the puncture operation is achieved by a conversion from a bit string to a decimal integer and the deletion of a corresponding part in the initial secret key. Let $\Pi = (\mathcal{IBS}.\mathbf{Setup}, \mathcal{IBS}.\mathbf{Extract}, \mathcal{IBS}.\mathbf{Sign}, \mathcal{IBS}.\mathbf{Verify})$ denote an identity-based signature scheme with the message space $\mathcal{M} = \{0,1\}^*$ and a bounded identity space $\mathcal{ID} = \{0,1\}^\ell \subseteq \mathcal{M}$. With the help of $\Pi$, we could construct a puncturable signature scheme $\Phi = (\mathbf{Setup}, \mathbf{Puncture}, \mathbf{Sign}, \mathbf{Verify})$ with the prefix space $\mathcal{P} = \mathcal{ID}$. The construction of $\Phi$ is described as follows.

- **Setup**$(1^\lambda)$: On input the security parameter $\lambda$, it computes the key pair $(pp, msk) \leftarrow \mathcal{IBS}.\mathbf{Setup}(1^\lambda)$. For each prefix $p \in \mathcal{P}$, it generates the key $sk_p \leftarrow \mathcal{IBS}.\mathbf{Extract}(pp, msk, p)$ and stores it in the array $T$ by setting $T[i] = sk_p$ where $i = (p)_{10}$. Finally, it outputs the key pair $(PK, SK) = (pp, T)$.
- **Puncture**$(SK, p)$: On input the current secret key $SK$ and a prefix $p \in \mathcal{P}$, it computes $i = (p)_{10}$, sets $T[i] = 0$ and returns the punctured secret key $SK = T$.
- **Sign**$(SK, \mu)$: On input the current secret key $SK$ and a message $\mu \in \mathcal{M}$, it computes $i = (p)_{10}$ and returns $\perp$ if $T[i] = 0$, where $p$ is implicitly contained in $\mu$. Otherwise, it returns a signature $\sigma \leftarrow \mathcal{IBS}.\mathbf{Sign}(PK, T[i], \mu)$.
- **Verify**$(PK, \mu, \sigma)$: On input the public key $PK$, a message $\mu$ with an implicit prefix $p$ and a signature $\sigma$, it returns the output of $\mathcal{IBS}.\mathbf{Verify}(PK, p, \mu, \sigma)$.

**Correctness.** The correctness of PS scheme requires that (1) the initial secret key $SK$ can sign on any message, and (2) a punctured secret key is used to generate signatures on any message with a non-punctured prefix. Both conditions hold by the correctness of the underlying IBS scheme.

**Theorem 3.** *The resulting PS construction $\Phi$ is existential unforgeability under chosen message attacks with adaptive puncturing assuming that the underlying IBS construction $\Pi$ is existential unforgeability under chosen message attacks with adaptive identity.*

*Proof.* Assume that there exists a forger $\mathcal{F}$ who breaks the security of $\Phi$ with probability $\delta$. We construct a simulator $\mathcal{S}$ who simulates the setting for $\mathcal{F}$, takes advantage of $\mathcal{F}$ and breaks the security of $\Pi$ with the same probability. Let $\mathcal{C}$ denote the challenger of $\Pi$.

- **Setup.** The challenger $\mathcal{C}$ computes $(pp, msk) \leftarrow \mathcal{IBS}.\mathbf{Setup}(1^\lambda)$ and returns $pp$ to the simulator $\mathcal{S}$. For each $id \in \mathcal{ID}$, $\mathcal{C}$ generates the key $sk_{id} \leftarrow \mathcal{IBS}.\mathbf{Extract}(pp, msk, id)$ and sets $T[i] = sk_{id}$, where $i = (id)_{10}$. After receiving $pp$, $\mathcal{S}$ forwards it to $\mathcal{F}$, and initializes two empty sets $Q_{pun}$ and $Q_{sig}$ for punctured prefixes and signed messages respectively.
- **Query.** The forger $\mathcal{F}$ adaptively issues puncture and signature queries many times. After receiving a prefix $p$, the simulator $\mathcal{S}$ updates $Q_{pun} = Q_{pun} \cup \{p\}$. After receiving a message $\mu$, $\mathcal{S}$ checks whether $p \in Q_{pun}$, where $p$ is implicitly included in $\mu$. If $p \in Q_{pun}$, $\mathcal{S}$ returns $\perp$. Otherwise, $\mathcal{S}$ issues a signature query with message $\mu$ and identity $p$ to $\mathcal{C}$, and forwards the reply from $\mathcal{C}$ to $\mathcal{F}$.

- **Challenge.** The forger $\mathcal{F}$ sends a target prefix $p^*$ to $\mathcal{S}$, and $\mathcal{S}$ forwards $p^*$ as the target identity to $\mathcal{C}$. Then $\mathcal{F}$ issues additional puncture and signature queries as described in the **Query** phase.
- **Corruption Query.** After receiving a corruption query, the simulator $\mathcal{S}$ returns $\perp$ if $p^* \notin Q_{pun}$. Otherwise, $\mathcal{S}$ issues **Extract**$(p)$ for each $p \in \mathcal{P} \setminus \{p^*\}$ and stores it in an array $SK$ by setting $SK[i] = sk_p$ where $i = (p)_{10}$. For each $p \in Q_{pun}$, the simulator $\mathcal{S}$ deletes the related key by setting $SK[j] = 0$ where $j = (p)_{10}$, and returns the current secret key $SK$ to $\mathcal{F}$.
- **Forgery.** The forger $\mathcal{F}$ outputs a forgery $\sigma^*$ based on a message $\mu^*$ with prefix $p^*$, while the simulator $\mathcal{S}$ uses $\mathcal{F}$'s output as its forgery in IBS.

As the simulation for $\mathcal{F}$ is perfect, we can conclude that if the underlying IBS scheme is existential unforgeability under chosen message attacks with adaptive identity, then the resulting PS scheme is existential unforgeability under chosen message attacks with adaptive puncturing.

## 4    Instantiations of Puncturable Signature

In this section, we present three puncturable signature instantiations derived from the existing identity-based signature schemes over lattices, bilinear maps, and multivariate public key cryptography by using our generic construction.

### 4.1    Lattice-Based Instantiation

The lattice-based instantiation is derived from an efficient identity-based signature scheme [21], which is an identity-version of Lyubashvesky's signature [16]. The underlying identity-based signature scheme has been provably secure in the random oracle model based on the short integer solution assumption.

**Description.** Let $\mathcal{M} = \{0,1\}^*$ and $\mathcal{P} = \{0,1\}^\ell \subseteq \mathcal{M}$ denote the message and prefix space respectively. Consider two cryptographic hash functions $H_0 : \{0,1\}^\ell \rightarrow \mathbb{Z}_q^{n \times d}$ and $H_1 : \{0,1\}^* \rightarrow \left\{ v : v \in \{-1,0,1\}^d, \|v\|_1 \leq \theta \right\}$. Our scheme is described as follows.

**Setup**$(n, q)$:

- Run TrapGen$(n, q)$ to generate a uniform matrix $\mathbf{A} \in \mathbb{Z}_q^{n \times m}$ along with its trapdoor $\mathbf{T_A}$, which is a basis of the q-ary lattice $\Lambda_q^\perp(\mathbf{A})$.
- For each prefix $p \in \mathcal{P}$, compute the index by a conversion from a binary string to a decimal integer $i = (p)_{10}$. Generate $s_i \leftarrow$ SamplePre$(\mathbf{A}, H_0(p), \mathbf{T_A}, \sigma_0)$ such that $\mathbf{A} \cdot s_i = H_0(p)$ and store it in the array $T$ by setting $T[i] = s_i$.
- Output the public key $pk = \mathbf{A}$ and the initial secret key $sk = T$.

**Puncture**$(sk, p)$:

- Compute $i = (p)_{10}$ and set $T[i] = 0$. The remaining keys in $T$ are unchanged.
- Output the punctured secret key $sk = T$.

**Sign**$(pk, sk, \mu)$:

- Compute $j = (p)_{10}$ and returns $\perp$ if $T[j] = 0$, where $p$ is the prefix of $\mu$.
- Otherwise, choose a random vector $\mathbf{y} \leftarrow D_{\sigma_1}^m$ and compute $\mathbf{h} = H_1(\mathbf{Ay}, \mu)$. Compute $\mathbf{z} = s_j\mathbf{h}+\mathbf{y}$ where $s_j = T[j]$ and output $sig = (\mathbf{h}, \mathbf{z})$ with probability $\min(\frac{D_{\sigma_1}^m(\mathbf{z})}{MD_{\sigma_1, s_j\mathbf{h}}^m(\mathbf{z})}, 1)$. Repeat it if the output is empty.

**Verify**$(pk, sig, \mu)$:

- Output 1 if and only if $\mathbf{h} = H_1(\mathbf{Az} - H_0(p)\mathbf{h}, \mu)$ and $\|\mathbf{z}\| \leq 2\sigma_1\sqrt{m}$, where $p$ is the prefix of message $\mu$. Otherwise, return 0.

**Correctness and Parameters.** The correctness follows the underlying identity-based signature scheme [21]. Given the public key $pk = \mathbf{A}$, the signature $sig = (\mathbf{h}, \mathbf{z})$, and the message $\mu$ with a prefix $p$, we have

$$\mathbf{Az} - H_0(p)\mathbf{h} = \mathbf{A}(s_j\mathbf{h} + \mathbf{y}) - (\mathbf{A} \cdot s_j)\mathbf{h} = \mathbf{Ay}$$

where $j = (p)_{10}$. Therefore, we have $H_1(\mathbf{Az} - H_0(p)\mathbf{h}, \mu) = H_1(\mathbf{Ay}, \mu) = \mathbf{h}$. From the rejection sampling technique, we find that the distribution of $\mathbf{z}$ is very close to $D_{\sigma_1}^m$. Therefore, $\|\mathbf{z}\| \leq 2\sigma_1\sqrt{m}$ with a probability at least $1 - 2^{-m}$ from Lemma 1.

Following [2,16,18,21], we choose parameters for our puncturable signature scheme with a slight modification. For the construction to work correctly, we need to ensure:

- that the TrapGen algorithm can operate, i.e., $m > (5 + 3\delta)n \lceil \log q \rceil^3$, where $\delta$ could be any positive constant,
- that $\sigma_0$ is large enough for the SamplePre algorithm, i.e., $\sigma_0 \geq \|\mathbf{T_A}\|_{\mathrm{GS}} \cdot \omega(\sqrt{\log n})$,
- that $\theta$ is large enough to hold the security of $H_1$ such that $2^\theta \cdot \binom{n}{\theta} \geq 2^{80}$ if $H_1$ is 80-bit secure,
- that if $\sigma_1 = \omega(K\sqrt{\log m})$ where $K = 2\sigma_0\sqrt{m}$, then the signature will be output with probability $1/M$ according to the rejection sampling technique, where $M = exp(\frac{12}{\sigma_1/K} + \frac{1}{2(\sigma_1/K)^2})$,
- that solving SIS on average-case is as hard as approximating SIVP in worst-case, i.e., $q \geq \beta \cdot \omega(\sqrt{n \log n})$, where $\beta = (4\sigma_1 + 2\sigma_0\theta)\sqrt{m}$ in our scheme.

**Security.** The proposed instantiation is existential unforgeability under chosen message attacks with adaptive puncturing in the random oracle model based on the SIS assumption. It follows the proof of the underlying identity-based scheme in [21]. The full version of the security proof could be found in Appendix A.

---

[3] The bound of the parameter $m$ comes from Theorem 3.2 in [2].

## 4.2   Pairing-Based Instantiation

The pairing-based instantiation is derived from a novel identity-based signature scheme [22], which improved Paterson's signature [19]. The underlying identity-based signature scheme is based on bilinear maps and its security has been reduced to the hardness of the CDH problem in the standard model.

**Description.** Let $\mathcal{M} = \{0,1\}^{\ell_\mu}$ and $\mathcal{P} = \{0,1\}^{\ell} \subseteq \mathcal{M}$ denote the message and prefix space, respectively. Our construction is described as follows.

**Setup**$(q)$:

- Choose two groups $\mathbb{G}$ and $\mathbb{G}_T$ of prime order $q$ such that an admissible pairing $e : \mathbb{G} \times \mathbb{G} \to \mathbb{G}_T$ can be constructed and pick a generator $g$ from $\mathbb{G}$.
- Choose a random element $a \in \mathbb{Z}_q^*$ and compute $g_1 = g^a$.
- Choose an element $g_2 \in \mathbb{G}$ and two integers $c, d \in \mathbb{Z}_q^*$ randomly.
- Define two random vectors $\mathbf{u} = (u_i)$ and $\mathbf{v} = (v_i)$ of length $\ell_\mu$ and $\ell$ respectively, where $u_i \in \mathbb{Z}_q^*$ and $v_i \in \mathbb{Z}_q^*$.
- For each prefix $p \in \mathcal{P}$, let $P \subseteq \{1, 2, \cdots, \ell\}$ denote the set of position $i$ such that $p[i] = 1$, where $p[i]$ is the $i$-th bit of prefix $p$. Choose a random element $b \in \mathbb{Z}_q^*$, compute $s_j = ((g_2^a)^{1+b(c+\sum_{i \in P} v_i)}, e(g_2, g_1)^b)$, and store it in the array $T$ by setting $T[j] = s_j$ for $j \in [2^\ell]$.
- Output the public key $pk = (\mathbb{G}, \mathbb{G}_T, e, g, g_1, g_2, c, d, \mathbf{u}, \mathbf{v})$ and the initial secret key $sk = T$.

**Puncture**$(sk, p)$:

- Compute $i = (p)_{10}$ and set $T[i] = 0$. Other keys in $T$ remain the same.
- Output the punctured secret key $sk = T$.

**Sign**$(pk, sk, \mu)$:

- Compute $j = (p)_{10}$ and abort if $T[j] = 0$, where $p$ is the prefix of message $\mu$.
- Otherwise, parse the corresponding key $T[j] = ((g_2^a)^{1+b(c+\sum_{i \in P} v_i)}, e(g_2, g_1)^b)$. Let $U \subseteq \{1, 2, \cdots, \ell_\mu\}$ be the set of position $i$ such that $\mu[i] = 1$, where $\mu[i]$ is the $i$-th bit of message $\mu$. Choose a random element $r \in \mathbb{Z}_q^*$ and output the signature $\sigma = (z_1, z_2, z_3) = ((g_2^a)^{1+b(c+\sum_{i \in P} v_i)} \cdot (g_2^r)^{d+\sum_{j \in U} u_j}, e(g_2, g)^r, e(g_2, g_1)^b)$.

**Verify**$(pk, \sigma, \mu)$:

- Parse the signature $\sigma = (z_1, z_2, z_3)$.
- Output 1 if and only if $e(z_1, g) = e(g_2, g_1) \cdot z_2^{d+\sum_{j \in U} u_j} \cdot z_3^{c+\sum_{i \in P} v_i}$. Otherwise, return 0.

**Correctness.** The correctness follows the underlying identity-based siganture scheme [22]. Given the public key $pk = (\mathbb{G}, \mathbb{G}_T, e, g, g_1, g_2, c, d, \mathbf{u}, \mathbf{v})$, the signature $\sigma = (z_1, z_2, z_3) = ((g_2^a)^{1+b(c+\sum_{i \in P} v_i)} \cdot (g_2^r)^{d+\sum_{j \in U} u_j}, e(g_2, g)^r, e(g_2, g_1)^b)$ and the message $\mu$ with a prefix $p$, we have

$$e(z_1, g) = e((g_2^a)^{1+b(c+\sum_{i \in P} v_i)} \cdot (g_2^r)^{d+\sum_{j \in U} u_j}, g)$$

$$= e(g_2^a \cdot (g_2^a)^{b(c+\sum_{i \in P} v_i)} \cdot (g_2^r)^{d+\sum_{j \in U} u_j}, g)$$

$$= e(g_2^a, g) \cdot e((g_2^a)^{b(c+\sum_{i \in P} v_i)}, g) \cdot e((g_2^r)^{d+\sum_{j \in U} u_j}, g)$$

$$= e(g_2, g_1) \cdot e(g_2, g_1)^{b(c+\sum_{i \in P} v_i)} \cdot e(g_2, g)^{r(d+\sum_{j \in U} u_j)}$$

$$= e(g_2, g_1) \cdot z_3^{c+\sum_{i \in P} v_i} \cdot z_2^{d+\sum_{j \in U} u_j}$$

where $g_1 = g^a$, $P$ is the set of positions such that the $i$-th bit of prefix $p$ is 1, $U$ is the set of positions such that the $i$-th bit of message $\mu$ is 1.

**Security.** Our instantiation is existential unforgeability under chosen message attacks with adaptive puncturing in the standard model based on the CDH assumption. It follows the proof of the underlying identity-based scheme in [22].

### 4.3 Multivariate-Based Instantiation

The multivariate-based instantiation is derived from the identity-based Rainbow signature [7] over multivariate public key cryptography. Although the underlying identity-based Rainbow signature cannot be provable secure, it is secure under the identity attack and other current attacks on MPKC schemes.

**Description.** Let $M = \mathbb{F}_q^m$ and $P = \mathbb{F}_q^d$ denote the message and prefix space respectively, where $\mathbb{F}$ is a finite field of order $q$. A prefix $p = (p_1, \cdots, p_d) \in \mathbb{F}_q^d$ is implicitly contained in messages. Our construction is described as follows.

**Setup**$(n, m, d, q)$:

- Let $L_1(x_1, \cdots, x_m) = (L_{1,1}(x_1, \cdots, x_m), \cdots, L_{1,m}(x_1, \cdots, x_m))$. For each $i \in [1, m]$, $L_{1,i}(x_1, \cdots, x_m) = \sum L_{(1,i,j)}(p_1, \cdots, p_d)x_j + L_{(1,i,0)}(p_1, \cdots, p_d)$, where each $L_{(1,i,j)}(p_1, \cdots, p_d)$ is a linear function of $p_1, \cdots, p_d$. Choose random coefficients $L_{(1,i,j)}$ and $L_{(1,i,0)}$ such that $L_1$ is a random affine transformation from $\mathbb{F}_q^m$ to $\mathbb{F}_q^m$.
- Let $L_2(x_1, \cdots, x_n) = (L_{2,1}(x_1, \cdots, x_n), \cdots, L_{2,n}(x_1, \cdots, x_n))$. For each $i \in [1, n]$, $L_{2,i}(x_1, \cdots, x_n) = \sum L_{(2,i,j)}(p_1, \cdots, p_d)x_j + L_{(2,i,0)}(p_1, \cdots, p_d)$, where each $L_{(2,i,j)}(p_1, \cdots, p_d)$ is a linear function of $p_1, \cdots, p_d$. Choose random coefficients $L_{(2,i,j)}$ and $L_{(2,i,0)}$ such that $L_2$ is a random affine transformation from $\mathbb{F}_q^n$ to $\mathbb{F}_q^n$.
- Let $F(x_1, \cdots, x_n) = (F_1(x_1, \cdots, x_n), \cdots, F_m(x_1, \cdots, x_n))$. For $\ell \in [1, m]$, $F_\ell(x_1, \cdots, x_n) = \sum \alpha_{\ell_{i,j}}(p_1, \cdots, p_d)x_i x_j + \sum \beta_{\ell_i}(p_1, \cdots, p_d)x_i + \gamma_\ell(p_1, \cdots, p_d)$, where $\alpha_{\ell_{i,j}}(p_1, \cdots, p_d)$, $\beta_{\ell_i}(p_1, \cdots, p_d)$ and $\gamma_\ell(p_1, \cdots, p_d)$ are all linear functions of $p_1, \cdots, p_d$. Choose random coefficients $\alpha_{\ell_{i,j}}$, $\beta_{\ell_i}$ and $\gamma_\ell$ such that $F$ is a set of random $m$ quadratic multivariate polynomials in $n$ variables.
- Choose two random linear transformations $L_1'$ and $L_2'$ such that the map $L_1' \circ F \circ L_2'$ can still be easily inverted.
- For each prefix $p = (p_1, \cdots, p_d) \in P$, compute $L_{1,p} = L_1 \circ L_1'^{-1}$, $F_p = L_1' \circ F \circ L_2'$, and $L_{2,p} = L_2'^{-1} \circ L_2$. Compute $i = ((p_1)_2 || \cdots || (p_d)_2)_{10}$ and set $T[i] = (L_{1,p}, F_p, L_{2,p})$.

- Output the public key $pk = L_1 \circ F \circ L_2$ and the initial secret key $sk = T$.

**Puncture**$(sk, p)$:

- Given a prefix $p = (p_1, \cdots, p_d)$, compute $i = ((p_1)_2 || \cdots || (p_d)_2)_{10}$ and set $T[i] = \bot$.
- Output the punctured secret key $sk = T$.

**Sign**$(sk, \mu)$:

- Compute $j = ((p_1)_2 || \cdots || (p_d)_2)_{10}$ and abort if $T[j] = \bot$, where $p = (p_1, \cdots, p_d)$ is the prefix of message $\mu = (\mu_1, \cdots, \mu_m)$.
- Otherwise, parse the corresponding key as $T[j] = (L_{1,p}, F_p, L_{2,p})$ and compute $x = L_{1,p}^{-1}(\mu)$. Solve the equation $x = F_p(y)$ to get $y$ and output the signature $\sigma = L_{2,p}^{-1}(y)$.

**Verify**$(pk, \sigma, \mu)$:

- Substitute $p$ to the public key $pk$ and check whether $pk(\sigma) = \mu$, where $p$ is the prefix of message $\mu$. Output 1 if it is true. Otherwise, return 0.

**Correctness.** The correctness follows from the underlying ID-based Rainbow signature [7]. Given the public key $pk = L_1 \circ F \circ L_2$, the signature $\sigma$ and the message $\mu$ with a prefix $p$, we have

$$
\begin{aligned}
pk(\sigma) &= L_1 \circ F \circ L_2(\sigma) \\
&= L_1 \circ F \circ L_2 \circ L_{2,p}^{-1}(y) \\
&= L_1 \circ F \circ L_2 \circ L_{2,p}^{-1} \circ F_p^{-1}(x) \\
&= L_1 \circ F \circ L_2 \circ L_{2,p}^{-1} \circ F_p^{-1} \circ L_{1,p}^{-1}(\mu) \\
&= L_1 \circ F \circ L_2 \circ L_2^{-1} \circ L_2' \circ L_2'^{-1} \circ F^{-1} \circ L_1'^{-1} \circ L_1' \circ L_1^{-1}(\mu) \\
&= \mu
\end{aligned}
$$

where $\sigma = L_{2,p}^{-1}(y)$, $x = F_p(y)$, $x = L_{1,p}^{-1}(\mu)$, $L_{1,p} = L_1 \circ L_1'^{-1}$, $F_p = L_1' \circ F \circ L_2'$, and $L_{2,p} = L_2'^{-1} \circ L_2$.

**Security.** As long as the underlying ID-based Rainbow signature is secure under the current attacks over MPKC, the proposed puncturable signature scheme will satisfy the security requirement. We show our instantiation is secure under current attacks in Appendices since the underlying ID-based Rainbow signature is secure [7].

## 5    Conclusion

Puncturable signature is a special kind of digital signature which provides the forward security in a fine-grained level. It allows the signer to selectively revoke his signing capacity by updating the secret key with special prefixes. In this paper, we propose the first generic construction of puncturable signature from identity-based signature by treating identities as prefixes. From the generic construction, we present puncturable signature instantiations based on lattices, bilinear maps, and multivariate quadratic polynomials respectively. All of them support pre-determined puncture times and efficient key puncture operations. For further research, it is interesting to construct puncturable signature schemes supporting unbounded key punctures. How to construct lattice-based puncturable signatures in the standard model also needs further research.

**Acknowledgements.** This work is partially supported by the Australian Research Council Linkage Project LP190100984. Mei Jiang has been sponsored by the CSC scholarship from China and the CSC Top-Up scholarship from the University of Wollongong.

## A    Proof for Lattice-Based Instantiation

**Theorem 4.** *In the random oracle model, suppose that exists a PPT forger $\mathcal{F}$ who makes at most $q_H$ random oracle queries $H_1$, initiates at most $q_S$ signing queries, and succeeds in providing a forgery signature with probability $\delta$. Then there exists a PPT challenger $\mathcal{C}$ that for a given $\mathbf{A} \xleftarrow{\$} \mathbb{Z}_q^{n \times m}$ finds a non-zero $\mathbf{v} \in \mathbb{Z}^m$ such that $\mathbf{Av} = 0$ and $\|\mathbf{v}\| \leq (4\sigma_1 + 2\sigma_0\theta)\sqrt{m}$ with probability at least*

$$(\frac{1}{2} - 2^{-100})(\delta - 2^{-100})(\frac{\delta - 2^{-100}}{q_H + q_S} - 2^{-100})$$

*Proof.* The theorem is proved in two steps. First we show that the real signing algorithm could be replaced by a hybrid algorithm and random oracle programming. That is why it needs the rejection sampling technique. With the forking lemma [4], we prove that the challenger $\mathcal{C}$ could use the valid forgery signature to find a non-zero short vector $\mathbf{v} \in \mathbb{Z}^m$ such that $\mathbf{Av} = 0$ for a given matrix $\mathbf{A} \in \mathbb{Z}_q^{n \times m}$.

**Lemma 2.** *Let $\mathcal{D}$ be a distinguisher who can query the random oracle $H_1$ and either the real signing algorithm or Hybrid 2 in Fig. 1. If $\mathcal{D}$ makes at most $q_H$ random oracle queries $H_1$ and at most $q_S$ signing queries, then for all but a $e^{-\Omega(n)}$ fraction of all possible $\mathbf{A}$, his advantage of distinguishing the real signing algorithm from the Hybrid 2 is at most $q_S(q_H + q_S) \cdot 2^{-n+1} + q_S \cdot \frac{2^{-\omega(\log m)}}{M}$.*

*Proof.* The difference between the real signing algorithm and Hybrid 1 is the output of random oracle $H_1$. In Hybrid 1, the output of $H_1$ is chosen randomly from $\left\{ v : v \in \{-1, 0, 1\}^d, \|v\|_1 \leq \theta \right\}$ and then programmed as $H_1(\mathbf{Az} - H_0(p)\mathbf{h}, \mu) = H_1(\mathbf{Ay}, \mu)$. There are at most $q_S + q_H$ values of $(\mathbf{Ay}, \mu)$ since $\mathcal{D}$ issues $H_1$ and signing queries at most $q_H$ and $q_S$ times respectively. With Lemma 1, the probability of generating a $\mathbf{y}$ such that $\mathbf{Ay}$ is equal to a queried value is at most $2^{-n+1}$. Thus the probability that a collision occurs after running Hybrid 1 $q_S$ times is at most $q_S(q_S + q_H)2^{-n+1}$. From the rejection sampling technique, the statistical distance between the outputs of Hybrid 1 and Hybrid 2 is at most $\frac{2^{-\omega \log m}}{M}$. More details could be found in [16].

Sign$(pk, sk, \mu)$:
1: $j = (p)_{10}$, where $p$ is the prefix of $\mu$
2: Return $\perp$ if $T[j] = 0$
3: $\mathbf{y} \leftarrow D_{\sigma_1}^m$
4: $\mathbf{h} \xleftarrow{\$} \left\{ v : v \in \{-1, 0, 1\}^d, \|v\|_1 \le \theta \right\}$
5: $\mathbf{z} = s_j \mathbf{h} + \mathbf{y}$
6: Output $sig = (\mathbf{h}, \mathbf{z})$ with probability
$\min(\frac{D_{\sigma_1}^m(\mathbf{z})}{M D_{\sigma_1, s_j \mathbf{h}}^m(\mathbf{z})}, 1)$
7: Program $H_1(\mathbf{Az} - H_0(p)\mathbf{h}, \mu) = \mathbf{h}$

(a) Hybrid 1

Sign$(pk, sk, \mu)$:
1: $j = (p)_{10}$, where $p$ is the prefix of $\mu$
2: Return $\perp$ if $T[j] = 0$
3: $\mathbf{h} \xleftarrow{\$} \left\{ v : v \in \{-1, 0, 1\}^d, \|v\|_1 \le \theta \right\}$
4: $\mathbf{z} \leftarrow D_{\sigma_1}^m$
5: Output $sig = (\mathbf{h}, \mathbf{z})$ with probability $1/M$
6: Program $H_1(\mathbf{Az} - H_0(p)\mathbf{h}, \mu) = \mathbf{h}$

(b) Hybrid 2

**Fig. 1.** Signing hybrids

**Lemma 3.** *Assume that exists a PPT forger $\mathcal{F}$ who makes at most $q_H$ random oracle queries $H_1$, initiates at most $q_S$ signing queries to the signer in Hybrid 2, and succeeds in providing a forgery signature with probability $\delta$. Then there exists a PPT challenger $\mathcal{C}$ that for a given $\mathbf{A} \xleftarrow{\$} \mathbb{Z}_q^{n \times m}$ finds a non-zero $\mathbf{v} \in \mathbb{Z}^m$ such that $\mathbf{Av} = 0$ and $\|\mathbf{v}\| \le (4\sigma_1 + 2\sigma_0 \theta)\sqrt{m}$ with probability at least*

$$\left(\frac{1}{2} - 2^{-100}\right)(\delta - 2^{-100})\left(\frac{\delta - 2^{-100}}{q_H + q_S} - 2^{-100}\right)$$

*Proof.* Given an SIS instance $\mathbf{A} \xleftarrow{\$} \mathbb{Z}_q^{n \times m}$, the challenger $\mathcal{C}$ simulates the signature setting for the forger $\mathcal{F}$ as follows.

**Setup.** The challenger $\mathcal{C}$ initializes two empty sets $Q_{pun}$ and $Q_{sig}$ for punctured prefixes and queried messages respectively. Then it initializes two empty lists $L_0$ and $L_1$ for the output of $H_0$ and $H_1$ queries. After that, the challenger $\mathcal{C}$ sets $pk = \mathbf{A}$ and returns it to $\mathcal{F}$. Finally, $\mathcal{C}$ generates the key related to each prefix $p \in \mathcal{P}$ as follows. Specifically, it randomly chooses matrices $s_0, \cdots, s_{2^\ell - 1}$ from $\mathbb{Z}^{m \times d}$ such that each column of $s_i$ is chosen from $D_{\mathbb{Z}^m, \sigma}$ for $i \in [2^\ell]$, and stores them in the array $T$. For each prefix $p \in \mathcal{P}$, $\mathcal{C}$ computes $H_0(p) = \mathbf{A} \cdot s_i \mod q$ and stores $(i, s_i, H_0(p))$ in $L_0[\cdot]$, where $i = (p)_{10}$.

**Query.** The forger $\mathcal{F}$ adaptively issues the following queries for polynomial times. For simplicity, we assume that $\mathcal{F}$ makes $H_0(p)$ queries before any query involving the same prefix $p$.

– $H_0(p)$ **Query.** The challenger $\mathcal{C}$ checks the list $L_0[\cdot]$ and returns $H_0(p)$ to $\mathcal{F}$.
– $H_1(\mathbf{Ay}, \mu)$ **Query.** The challenger $\mathcal{C}$ checks the list $L_1[\cdot]$. If $H_1(\mathbf{Ay}, \mu)$ is not defined, $\mathcal{C}$ chooses a random value from $\left\{ v : v \in \{-1, 0, 1\}^d, \|v\|_1 \le \theta \right\}$ and stores $((\mathbf{Ay}, \mu), H_1(\mathbf{Ay}, \mu))$ in $L_1$. Then $\mathcal{C}$ returns $H_1(\mathbf{Ay}, \mu)$ to $\mathcal{F}$.

- **Puncture Query**. After receiving a prefix $p$, $\mathcal{C}$ sets $T[j] = 0$ and $Q_{pun} = Q_{pun} \cup \{p\}$, where $j = (p)_{10}$. Other positions in $T$ remain the same.
- **Signature Query**. After receiving a message $\mu$, the challenger $\mathcal{C}$ generates a puncturable signature according to Hybrid 2 and returns it to $\mathcal{F}$. Then $\mathcal{C}$ stores $H_1(\mathbf{A}\mathbf{y}, \mu)$ in list $L_1[\cdot]$ and sets $Q_{sig} = Q_{sig} \cup \{\mu\}$.

**Challenge.** The forger $\mathcal{F}$ sends a target prefix $p^*$ to $\mathcal{C}$ and issues additional queries as described in the **Query** phase with a condition that $\mathcal{F}$ cannot make any signature query on messages with the prefix $p^*$.

**Corruption.** The challenger $\mathcal{C}$ returns the current secret key $sk = T$ if $p^* \in \mathcal{P}$ and $\perp$ otherwise.

**Forgery.** Without loss of generality, assume that the forger $\mathcal{F}$ issued the $H_1$ query on $\mu$ before outputting the forgery on message $\mu$. If $\mathcal{F}$ returns $\perp$, the challenger $\mathcal{C}$ outputs $\perp$ as well. Otherwise, $\mathcal{F}$ outputs a puncturable signature $sig = (\mathbf{z}, \mathbf{h})$ on message $\mu$ with the punctured prefix $p^*$. Then $\mathcal{C}$ checks whether $\mathbf{h} = H_1(\mathbf{A}\mathbf{z} - H_0(p)\mathbf{h}, \mu)$, $\|\mathbf{z}\| \leq 2\sigma_1\sqrt{m}$ and $\mu \notin Q_{sig}$. If those conditions hold, then the forgery signature generated by $\mathcal{F}$ is valid.

With the forking lemma [4], the challenger $\mathcal{C}$ rewinds $\mathcal{F}$ with the same random tape but different outputs for $H_1$ queries. Therefore, $\mathcal{F}$ forge a new signature $sig' = (\mathbf{z}', \mathbf{h}')$ on the same message $\mu$ with prefix $p^*$ such that

$$\mathbf{A}\mathbf{z} - H_0(p^*) \cdot \mathbf{h} = \mathbf{A}\mathbf{y} = \mathbf{A}\mathbf{z}' - H_0(p^*) \cdot \mathbf{h}'. \tag{1}$$

By plugging $H_0(p^*) = \mathbf{A} \cdot s_{i^*}$ and $i^* = (p^*)_{10}$ into the above equality, we have

$$\mathbf{A}[\mathbf{z} - \mathbf{z}' + s_{i^*}(\mathbf{h}' - \mathbf{h})] = 0. \tag{2}$$

Due to $\|\mathbf{z}\|, \|\mathbf{z}'\| \leq 2\sigma_1\sqrt{m}$ and $\|s_{i^*}\mathbf{h}\|, \|s_{i^*}\mathbf{h}'\| \leq \sigma_0\lambda\sqrt{m}$ with overwhelming probability, then we have

$$\|\mathbf{z} - \mathbf{z}' + s_{i^*}(\mathbf{h}' - \mathbf{h})\| \leq (4\sigma_1 + 2\sigma_0\lambda)\sqrt{m}.$$

Now we show that $\mathbf{z} - \mathbf{z}' + s_{i^*}(\mathbf{h}' - \mathbf{h}) \neq 0$. According to the preimage min-entropy property [10], there exists another key $s'_{i^*}$ such that $\mathbf{A}s_{i^*} = \mathbf{A}s'_{i^*} = H_0(i^*)$. If $\mathbf{z} - \mathbf{z}' + s_{i^*}(\mathbf{h}' - \mathbf{h}) = 0$, then we have $\mathbf{z} - \mathbf{z}' + s'_{i^*}(\mathbf{h}' - \mathbf{h}) \neq 0$. Since the signature is independent of both keys, $\mathcal{F}$ cannot know which key is used in the simulation. Therefore, we can get a non-zero solution with probability at least $\frac{1}{2}$, since each key has an equal possibility of being chosen. It means that $\mathcal{C}$ solves an SIS instance for $\beta \leq (4\sigma_1 + 2\sigma_0\lambda)\sqrt{m}$, which is assumed to be hard.

## B     Security Analysis for Multivariate-Based Instantiation

We will describe the current attacks of MPKC on our multivariate-based instantiation and show that the proposed scheme is secure.

**The Kipnis and Shamir Attack.** The Kipnis and Shamir attack [14] is to attack the balanced Oil and Vinegar scheme which contains $o$ oil variables and $v$ vinegar variables. The aim of this attack is to find the pre-image of the Oil subspace $O = \{x \in K_n : x_1 = \cdots = x_v = 0\}$ under the affine invertible transformation $T$. To achieve this, it forms a random linear combination $P = \sum_{j=1}^{o} \beta_j H_j$, multiplies it with the inverse of one of $H_i$ and figures out the invariant subspaces of this matrix.

As mentioned in [6], the Kipnis and Shamir attacks takes the time about $O(q^{v-o-1}o^4)$ to break a $(q, v, o)$ unbalanced Oil and Vinegar (UOV) scheme. The Rainbow scheme could be regarded as a multi-layer UOV scheme, where the number of vinegar variables at the $\ell$ layer is the sum of oil and vinegar variable at the $(\ell - 1)$ layer. When apply such an attack to identity-based Rainbow scheme, it treats all polynomials as the polynomials at the last layer which contains $v_\ell$ vinegar variables and $o_\ell$ oil variables. And its complexity is $q^{n-2o_\ell-1}o_\ell^4$, where $n = v_\ell + o_\ell$. For our instantiation over MPKC, it cannot lead to any security threats and enjoys the same complexity as the underlying identity-based Rainbow Signature.

**MinRank Attack.** The MinRank attack is based on the MinRank problem [8] which asks to find a linear (or affine) combination of given matrices that has a small rank. Let $H_i$ be the symmetric matrix representing the homogenous quadratic part of the $i$th public polynomial. In the MinRank attack, one tries to find linear combinations $H = \sum_{i=1}^{m} \alpha_i H_i$ of the matrices representing the homogeneous quadratic parts of the public polynomials such that $\text{rank}(H) = r < n$.

For identity-based Rainbow, the first layer has the possible minimum rank $v_1 + o_1$, where $v_1$ and $o_1$ denotes the the number of vinegar and oil variables respectively. Assume that the matrices related to the public key are $Q_1, \cdots, Q_m$, the MinRank attack is to find the linear combination $M = \sum_{k-1}^{m} \lambda_k Q_k$ with a minimum rank $r$. Following the analysis in [7], the total complexity of MinRank attack on identity-based Rainbow is estimated by $q^{r+1} \times m^3$. For our puncturable scheme, it keeps the same complexity as identity-based Rainbow since construction of public key are identical.

# References

1. Ajtai, M.: Generating hard instances of lattice problems. In: Proceedings of the Twenty-Eighth Annual ACM Symposium on Theory of Computing, pp. 99–108 (1996)
2. Alwen, J., Peikert, C.: Generating shorter bases for hard random lattices. In: 26th International Symposium on Theoretical Aspects of Computer Science STACS 2009, pp. 75–86. IBFI Schloss Dagstuhl (2009)
3. Banaszczyk, W.: New bounds in some transference theorems in the geometry of numbers. Math. Annal. **296**(1), 625–635 (1993)

4. Bellare, M., Neven, G.: Multi-signatures in the plain public-key model and a general forking lemma. In: Proceedings of the 13th ACM Conference on Computer and Communications Security, pp. 390–399 (2006)
5. Bellare, M., Stepanovs, I., Waters, B.: New negative results on differing-inputs obfuscation. In: Fischlin, M., Coron, J.-S. (eds.) EUROCRYPT 2016. LNCS, vol. 9666, pp. 792–821. Springer, Heidelberg (2016). https://doi.org/10.1007/978-3-662-49896-5_28
6. Cao, W., Hu, L., Ding, J., Yin, Z.: Kipnis-Shamir attack on unbalanced oil-vinegar scheme. In: Bao, F., Weng, J. (eds.) ISPEC 2011. LNCS, vol. 6672, pp. 168–180. Springer, Heidelberg (2011). https://doi.org/10.1007/978-3-642-21031-0_13
7. Chen, J., Ling, J., Ning, J., Ding, J.: Identity-based signature schemes for multivariate public key cryptosystems. Comput. J. **62**(8), 1132–1147 (2019)
8. Courtois, N.T.: Efficient zero-knowledge authentication based on a linear algebra problem MinRank. In: Boyd, C. (ed.) ASIACRYPT 2001. LNCS, vol. 2248, pp. 402–421. Springer, Heidelberg (2001). https://doi.org/10.1007/3-540-45682-1_24
9. Ding, J., Schmidt, D.: Rainbow, a new multivariable polynomial signature scheme. In: Ioannidis, J., Keromytis, A., Yung, M. (eds.) ACNS 2005. LNCS, vol. 3531, pp. 164–175. Springer, Heidelberg (2005). https://doi.org/10.1007/11496137_12
10. Gentry, C., Peikert, C., Vaikuntanathan, V.: Trapdoors for hard lattices and new cryptographic constructions. In: Proceedings of the Fortieth Annual ACM Symposium on Theory of Computing, pp. 197–206 (2008)
11. Guan, J., Zhandry, M.: Disappearing cryptography in the bounded storage model. In: Nissim, K., Waters, B. (eds.) TCC 2021. LNCS, vol. 13043, pp. 365–396. Springer, Cham (2021). https://doi.org/10.1007/978-3-030-90453-1_13
12. Halevi, S., Ishai, Y., Jain, A., Komargodski, I., Sahai, A., Yogev, E.: Non-interactive multiparty computation without correlated randomness. In: Takagi, T., Peyrin, T. (eds.) ASIACRYPT 2017. LNCS, vol. 10626, pp. 181–211. Springer, Cham (2017). https://doi.org/10.1007/978-3-319-70700-6_7
13. Kipnis, A., Patarin, J., Goubin, L.: Unbalanced oil and vinegar signature schemes. In: Stern, J. (ed.) EUROCRYPT 1999. LNCS, vol. 1592, pp. 206–222. Springer, Heidelberg (1999). https://doi.org/10.1007/3-540-48910-X_15
14. Kipnis, A., Shamir, A.: Cryptanalysis of the oil and vinegar signature scheme. In: Krawczyk, H. (ed.) CRYPTO 1998. LNCS, vol. 1462, pp. 257–266. Springer, Heidelberg (1998). https://doi.org/10.1007/BFb0055733
15. Li, X., Xu, J., Fan, X., Wang, Y., Zhang, Z.: Puncturable signatures and applications in proof-of-stake blockchain protocols. IEEE Trans. Inf. Forens. Secur. **15**, 3872–3885 (2020)
16. Lyubashevsky, V.: Lattice signatures without trapdoors. In: Pointcheval, D., Johansson, T. (eds.) EUROCRYPT 2012. LNCS, vol. 7237, pp. 738–755. Springer, Heidelberg (2012). https://doi.org/10.1007/978-3-642-29011-4_43
17. Maurer, U.M.: Conditionally-perfect secrecy and a provably-secure randomized cipher. J. Cryptol. **5**(1), 53–66 (1992). https://doi.org/10.1007/BF00191321
18. Micciancio, D., Regev, O.: Worst-case to average-case reductions based on gaussian measures. SIAM J. Comput. **37**(1), 267–302 (2007)
19. Paterson, K.G., Schuldt, J.C.N.: Efficient identity-based signatures secure in the standard model. In: Batten, L.M., Safavi-Naini, R. (eds.) ACISP 2006. LNCS, vol. 4058, pp. 207–222. Springer, Heidelberg (2006). https://doi.org/10.1007/11780656_18
20. Peikert, C., Rosen, A.: Efficient collision-resistant hashing from worst-case assumptions on cyclic lattices. In: Halevi, S., Rabin, T. (eds.) TCC 2006. LNCS, vol. 3876, pp. 145–166. Springer, Heidelberg (2006). https://doi.org/10.1007/11681878_8

21. Tian, M., Huang, L.: Identity-based signatures from lattices: simpler, faster, shorter. Fundam. Inf. **145**(2), 171–187 (2016)
22. Yi, P., et al.: An efficient identity-based signature scheme with provable security. Inf. Sci. **576**, 790–799 (2021)

# IoT Security

# fASLR: Function-Based ASLR for Resource-Constrained IoT Systems

Xinhui Shao[1], Lan Luo[3], Zhen Ling[2(✉)], Huaiyu Yan[2], Yumeng Wei[1], and Xinwen Fu[3,4]

[1] School of Cyber Science and Engineering, Southeast University, Nanjing, China
{xinhuishao,yumeng5}@seu.edu.cn
[2] School of Computer Science and Engineering, Southeast University, Nanjing, China
{zhenling,huaiyu_yan}@seu.edu.cn
[3] University of Central Florida, Orlando, USA
lukachan@knights.ucf.edu
[4] University of Massachusetts Lowell, Lowell, USA
xinwen_fu@uml.edu

**Abstract.** The address space layout randomization (ASLR) has been widely deployed on modern operating systems against code reuse attacks (CRAs) such as return-oriented programming (ROP) and return-to-libc. However, porting ASLR to resource-constrained IoT devices is a great challenge due to the limited memory space. We propose a function-based ASLR scheme (fASLR) for IoT runtime security utilizing the ARM TrustZone-M technique and the memory protection unit (MPU). fASLR loads a function from the flash and randomizes its entry address in a randomization region in RAM when the function is called. We design novel mechanisms on cleaning up finished functions from the RAM and memory addressing to deal with the complexity of function relocation and randomization. Compared with related work, a prominent advantage of fASLR is that fASLR can run an application even if the application code cannot be completely loaded into RAM for execution. We test fASLR with 21 applications. fASLR achieves high randomization entropy and incurs runtime overhead of less than 10%.

**Keywords:** Function-based randomization · IoT · ASLR · CRA · ROP

## 1 Introduction

With the booming IoT industry, there are rising concerns on the security and privacy of IoT devices. IoT application code is often written in unsafe programming languages such as C and C++, and is vulnerable to memory corruption attacks [5]. One typical memory corruption attack is the code reuse attack (CRA), which hijacks the control flow and reuses the application code [3]. Memory corruption

---

X. Shao and L. Luo—Contribute equally to this work.

© The Author(s), under exclusive license to Springer Nature Switzerland AG 2022
V. Atluri et al. (Eds.): ESORICS 2022, LNCS 13555, pp. 531–548, 2022.
https://doi.org/10.1007/978-3-031-17146-8_26

attacks and defenses have been actively studied for mainstream operating systems such as Windows, macOS, Lniux, Android and iOS.

In this paper, we focus on defending against memory corruption attacks for resource-constrained IoT devices, particularly those running on micrcontrollers (MCUs). It is an intuitive idea to port existing security schemes to IoT platforms. We study the use of ASLR in memory-constrained IoT devices to mitigate CRAs such as the return-oriented programming (ROP) by randomizing the memory layout of code and data. Modern operating systems often implement the following ASLR scheme. When an executable is loaded into RAM, its base (start) address is randomly chosen while the executable structure is kept almost intact. Fine-grained ASLR strategies have been proposed and randomize executable code at fine levels of basic blocks, functions, or instructions [20] within a loaded application image. However, porting ASLR to resource-constrained IoT devices is a great challenge due to the limited memory space.

We propose a function-based ASLR scheme (fASLR) based on the ARM Cortex-M processor with TrustZone-M enabled [2] to protect MCU-based IoT devices from code reuse attacks that require knowledge of locations of executable code snippets, such as ROP and JOP. The runtime fASLR is located in the Secure World (SW) of TrustZone-M. The application is in the Non-secure World (NSW) flash and denoted as the NS app, which is protected by the memory protection unit (MPU). When a function call occurs, MPU redirects the function call to the runtime fASLR for callee randomization. Compared to the most recent related work [19] that requires loading the whole application code into RAM, fASLR can run an application even if the application on flash is too large to be completely loaded into RAM.

Our major contributions are summarized as follows. (i) We propose a *function-based ASLR* scheme for resource-constrained IoT devices with limited RAM and flash. fASLR dynamically loads only needed functions into RAM and randomizes their entry addresses so as to achieve large randomization entropy. (ii) Novel schemes are designed for fASLR to perform memory management and addressing. Finished functions are efficiently removed from RAM when there is no RAM for storing more functions. We carefully address the issue of addressing since functions are randomly moved around. (iii) We implement fASLR with a TrustZone-M enabled MCU, SAM L11, and validate the feasibility and performance of fASLR with 21 applications. fASLR incurs a runtime overhead of less than 10% for all the applications.

## 2    Related Work

Compared to conventional ASLR which rebases the whole executable, fine-grained ASLR strategies achieve higher randomization entropy, change the structure of the executable, and thereby are considered to be more effective against CRAs and brute-force attacks. Code randomization can have different granularities [14] based on what is diversified. ASLP [12] is a code permutation scheme which applies function level permutation to the code segment and object permutation to the data segment without knowledge of source code. In [22], the original binary code is partitioned into small blocks of which the addresses are decided when the application is loaded. Xifer [8] achieves fine-grained randomization by splitting code into arbitrary small pieces, spreading the code pieces within the address space, and rewriting the code to preserve its semantics. ILR [11] is an instruction-based randomization scheme which relocates every instruction thereby achieving high randomization entropy.

Snow et al. [20] introduce an attack framework which bypasses fine-grained randomization via just-in-time code reuse (JIT-ROP). With the knowledge of a single memory disclosure, the framework is able to excavate memory contents of multiple memory pages at runtime, search and assemble gadgets on-the-fly, and then launch code reuse attack. Accordingly a fine-grained randomization approach named Isomeron [7] is proposed as the countermeasure to JIT-ROP attacks. Combining fine-grained ASLR with execution path randomization, Isomeron makes any gadgets unpredictable. Related research has been performed to overcome newly emerging code reuse attacks and meet increasing compatibility requirements [13,17,21,23].

Shi et al. [19] leverage the TrustZone-M hardware extension to enable a function-level ASLR scheme for ARM-based MCUs. The proposed system loads the NS code to NS RAM and periodically reordering all functions at runtime. Compared with our work, this scheme loads the whole application code to RAM. Instead of loading the whole NS app code, our mechanism—fASLR—only loads functions in use and promptly cleans up finished functions from RAM at runtime. fASLR requires smaller RAM and achieves larger randomization entropy for resource constrained IoT devices. [19] rewrites binaries of the NS code offline and introduces a code size overhead of about 10%–15%, while fASLR has a code size overhead below 5%.

## 3    System Architecture

In this section, we first present the threat model and design goals of our ASLR scheme—fASLR. We then introduce the architecture of a fASLR-enabled system and the workflow of fASLR. At last, we discuss challenges for implementing a practical fASLR.

### 3.1    Threat Model

fASLR leverages ARM Cortex-M processors and hardware-based techniques including TrustZone-M, memory protection unit (MPU), and exception handling mechanism. Based on the hardware isolation provided by TrustZone-M, on-device system resources are divided into two worlds, namely the Secure World (SW) and the Non-secure World (NSW).

We assume a TrustZone-M enabled device has the following security features. (i) Main components of fASLR reside in the SW and can be fully trusted. The application (denoted as NS app) is located in the NSW and may be vulnerable. (ii) The NS app is located at a fixed address in the NS flash and is executed from the flash (instead of RAM) by default. (iii) The device supports the memory protection mechanisms such as the MPU.

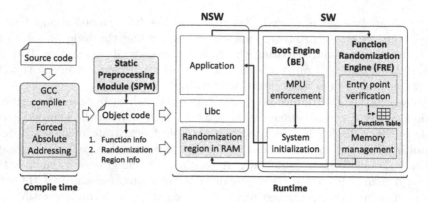

Fig. 1. fASLR architecture.

We assume an adversary has the following capabilities. (i) The NS app may be subject to CRAs such as the ROP attack. (ii) The adversary can obtain the binary of the NS app, disassemble the binary, and obtain code gadgets for CRAs.

### 3.2   Design Goals

fASLR is designed to achieve the following goals.

- **Mitigating CRAs**. The scheme shall provide dynamic function-level code randomization for resource-constraint IoT devices to mitigate CRAs, which require a certain chain of gadgets found in the NS app. The randomization shall achieve high entropy to defeat brute-force guessing attacks.
- **Usability**. The scheme shall be user-friendly and will not add much burden of programming.
- **Low overhead**. The proposed scheme cannot introduce large overhead in terms of time and space and affect the NS app performance much.

### 3.3   System Architecture

As illustrated in Fig. 1, fASLR has three key components. (i) the ***Static Preprocessing Module (SPM)*** for compilation time preparation, (ii) The ***Boot Engine (BE)*** for boot time configuration, and (iii) The ***Function Randomization Engine (FRE)*** for runtime function-level randomization.

**Static Preprocessing Module (SPM).** The *SPM* serves two major purposes: (i) Creating the *Function Table*. Once the NS app code is compiled via a GCC compiler, the SPM tries to extract needed information of all functions in the ELF object file, including function entry point addresses and function sizes from the symbol table, and function stack frame sizes from .debug_frame section of the ELF file. Function information is recorded in a data structure called *Function Table*. (ii) Profiling randomization region. Extracting RAM usage information from the compiler output file, the *SPM* determines the size and location of the largest unused RAM space as the *randomization region*. Users can also set a smaller randomization region by manually modifying related configurations.

**Boot Engine (BE).** When a TrustZone-M enabled device boots, the boot flow is the Secure bootloader, Secure app, and then the NS app. The NS app starts with the `reset` handler that calls the first function, e.g., `main()`. The *BE* is a part of the Secure bootloader stored in the SW flash. It configures and enables the MPU to mark the NS app code in the flash as non-executable for two purposes: (i) MPU prevents the NS app in the NS flash from being exploited by CRAs. (ii) Once the NS code is set as non-executable, any attempt to execute the NS code triggers a hardware exception, which is handled by the `HardFault` exception handler in the SW [1].

**Function Randomization Engine (FRE).** The *FRE* is a part of the `HardFault` exception handler and handles invoked functions in the NSW flash protected by the MPU. It serves two purposes, i.e., **function entry point verification** and **memory management**.

When a `HardFault` exception occurs, the *FRE* fetches the return address of the exception, which is the entry point of the invoked function, through the NSW exception stack frame. Then the **function entry point verification** is performed by comparing the return address to all legitimate function entry point addresses in the *Function Table* until there is a match. After a match, the *FRE* obtains the size of the corresponding function from the *Function Table* for later use in randomization. A `HardFault` exception may be caused by other reasons, for instance, memory access violation when an adversary launches CRAs trying to execute an instruction not at legitimate function entry points. In such a case, a security alert shall be raised.

After the function entry point verification, **memory management** is performed. Specifically, the invoked function is randomly relocated to a RAM region within the *randomization region*. After the function randomization, we need to carefully handover the control flow from the exception handler to the relocated function. We overwrite the return address of the exception handler on stack with the new function entry point so that the execution mode will change back to the mode of the NS app with correct privileges.

### 3.4   Workflow

**Offline—Compilation and Flashing.** After the NS app is compiled and linked by the GCC compiler at compile time, the *SPM* creates the *Function Table* offline according to the NS app ELF file. The *Function Table* and NS app image are then flashed to the SW and NSW flash respectively. The *BE* and *FRE* are also flashed to the SW flash.

**Runtime.** Figure 2 shows the program flow, which is an iterative sequence of function calls (e.g., ① and ❹), MPU violation exception (e.g., ② and ❺), runtime function randomization, function execution (e.g., ③ and ❻), and function return (e.g., ❼ and ⑧).

Once we turn on the device power supply, the *BE* boots the system and then the NS app initiates the `reset` handler [24]. After a sequence of initialization operations, the `reset` handler branches to the main application code, i.e., *main()*. Both attempts of executing the reset handler and *main()* trigger runtime fASLR, and their code is loaded by the *FRE* to the *randomization region* in the RAM for execution. During the execution of *main()* function, the control flow can divert to a callee on the MPU-protected flash only if the callee is invoked by *main()*.

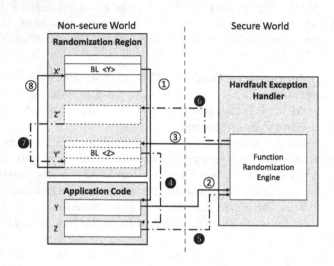

**Fig. 2.** Program flow of function $X$, $Y$ and $Z$. For any function $F$ in the NS app, we use $F'$ to represent its corresponding copy in the randomization region.

In a fASLR-enabled system, when a function call occurs in the randomization region, it jumps to the entry point of the callee in the original MPU-protected application, and thus triggers the MPU violation exception. The *FRE* then conducts runtime function randomization for the callee and diverts the control flow to the callee relocated in the RAM. During the execution of the callee, any function call in the callee can also trigger a MPU violation exception. The *FRE* handles function calls and randomization in such an iterative way above. The control flow returns to the caller in the RAM once its callee is finished. fASLR does not interfere with the function return mechanism, and the function in the RAM returns normally as functions in a system without fASLR do. Note that in a fASLR enabled system, a callee returns to the relocated caller in the randomization region since that is where the function call really occurs.

Figure 2 presents an exemplary program flow for the call path $X \rightarrow Y \rightarrow Z$ of functions $X$, $Y$ and $Z$. A call path illustrates the calling relationship. Starting from the leftmost one, each function in the path calls the function right after it. Suppose that function $X$ has been loaded to the randomization region and the program flow starts from the relocated function $X'$. When $X'$ calls $Y$, the attempt of executing $Y$ (①) results in a MPU violation exception (②), handled by the *FRE* inside the `HardFault` exception handler. $Y$ is then relocated to the randomization region as $Y'$ and consequently, the control flow is redirected to $Y'$ (③). During the execution of $Y'$, $Y'$ attempts to call $Z$ (❹), and the MPU violation exception (❺) is triggered again and is then handled by the *FRE* (❻). Finally, the control flow returns from $Z'$ to $Y'$ (❼) and $Y'$ to $X'$ (⑧) when $Z'$ and $Y'$ finish execution.

### 3.5   Challenges

A practical fASLR faces the following challenges. We address these challenges in detail in Sect. 4.

**Memory Management.** We target MCUs with limited RAM and the whole NS app may not be loaded into the RAM for execution. Therefore, a memory management strategy is needed to dynamically trim finished functions. *Ancestor functions* are defined as direct or indirect callers of the current running function. Such functions are awaiting returns from some ongoing function calls, and shall not be trimmed before their descendants return. *Finished functions* are those that have finished execution and are not ancestors of any running function. They can be disposed safely. The runtime *FRE* needs to distinguish finished functions and select an appropriate timing to trim them from the randomization region.

**Memory Addressing.** A function in the randomization region may contain branches that use absolute or relative addresses. All absolute branches in the ARMv8-M architecture compiled by GCC are function calls, which would not be affected by the relocation and will function normally. Relative branches within a function can work normally as well since a relative position would not change when the function is relocated as a whole. However, relative branches may be used to jump between functions. In a fASLR-enabled system, those relative branches can lead the control flow to branch to an unexpected destination as function-based randomization changes the relative position of two functions.

## 4   Memory Management and Addressing

In this section, we discuss the challenges of fASLR and present our key memory management and addressing schemes.

### 4.1   Memory Management

We devise a function cleaning scheme that dynamically cleans up finished functions from the *randomization region* with the following mechanisms: (i) *Call stack unwinding.* Finished functions are found through unwinding the Non-secure call stack. (ii) *Cleaning on demand.* Finished functions are cleaned up only if the available randomization region space is not large enough for the callee. (iii) *Call instruction rewriting.* We further reduce the runtime overhead by overwriting a call instruction in a loaded function if the callee of that call instruction has already been loaded into RAM.

**Call Stack Unwinding.** The key of function cleaning is to distinguish finished functions from all loaded functions in RAM. However, it is difficult to trace all finished functions at runtime because fASLR runtime does not capture any function return information. Instead, our approach finds ancestor functions of the current callee, and records all loaded functions. *Any function that is a loaded function but not an ancestor function is a finished function that can be disposed.* Now the problem is decomposed to record all loaded functions and find all ancestor functions.

---

**Algorithm 1.** Call Stack Unwinding

$nsSp = getNSSp()$
$returnAddress = readExceptionStackFrame(nsSp)$
$funcSp = nsSp + sizeof(ExceptionStackFrame)$
**for** $i = 1; i < loadingQueue.size; i + +$ **do**
    **if** $(returnAddress \leq loadingQueue[i].endAddress)$ & $(returnAddress \geq loadingQueue[i].loadAddress)$ **then**
        $funcRecord = loadingQueue[i]$
        $funcRecord.state = UNFINISHED$
        $funcSp = funcSp + funcRecord.callFrameSize$
        $returnAddress = getReturnAddress(funcSp)$
    **end if**
**end for**

---

A queue structure named *Loading Queue* is used to store meta data, denoted as function record, of all loaded functions in the RAM. The *FRE* pushes a function record into the *Loading Queue* when an unloaded function is called. A function record includes the following information of the callee, (i) *loadAddress*– the new entry point of the callee in the randomization region, (ii) *size* of the callee, and (iii) *stack frame size* of the callee.

We also need to find out all ancestor functions. Modern computer system uses the call stack to retain return addresses of functions that have been called but have not returned yet. Such functions are direct or indirect callers of the current running function, which is also the callee when program execution is trapped in the *FRE* in our system. Therefore, functions which have their stack frames in the call stack are ancestor functions of the callee. To figure out all functions in the call stack, **stack unwinding** is needed. Basically, stack unwinding helps to locate **all return addresses in the call stack**. A return address then tells where the caller is within the RAM. If we can obtain all return addresses on the call stack, by comparing each return address with the function records in the *Loading Queue*, we are able to identify all ancestor functions.

Frame pointer is an intuitive approach of unwinding the call stack [10]. However, the Armv8-M architecture only implements the Thumb instruction set, which does not support the frame pointer mechanism. To achieve stack unwinding without frame pointers, we devise a stack unwinding method utilizing the stack top address and the stack frame sizes of all functions to resolve return addresses on the call stack. Recall that the stack frame size of each function is extracted offline by the *SPM* from `.debug_frame` section of the ELF file and stored in the *Function Table*.

In ARM, by convention return address is the first object pushed onto the stack when there is a function call, and is at the bottom of the callee's stack frame. Once a function call triggers the `HardFault` exception and the program execution is trapped by the *FRE*, the top stack frame is the exception stack frame of the `HardFault` exception handler and has a fixed length $s_e$. The current stack top can be obtained through the SP register of the NSW. The frame top of the first function $f_1$ (namely the current caller) is $T_1 = SP + s_e$. According to the LR register, which stores an address within $f_1$, *FRE* is able to search the frame size $s_1$ of $f_1$ from the function records in the *Loading Queue*. To access the return address of $f_1$, the frame bottom $B_1$ is calculated by $B_1 = T_1 + s_1$. Following this procedure, the *FRE* is able to resolve return address of every stack frame from the stack top to bottom. Algorithm 1 presents our stack unwinding procedure.

Note that recursion is compatible with our function cleaning strategy. A recursive function is the function that calls itself. In our compilation environment, a recursive function uses a relative branch instruction. Therefore, when a recursive function is loaded to the randomization region, it can still call itself with the relative branch without triggering the MPU violation exception.

**Cleaning on Demand.** The *FRE* removes functions only when the randomization region does not have enough space to load a new function. Before loading a function to RAM, the *FRE* checks if there is enough memory space for it. If not, the *FRE* first recovers rewritten call instructions in the loaded functions as introduced below. It then unwinds the call stack, finds out all ancestor functions, and marks those functions in the *Loading Queue* as unfinished. According to the marked *Loading Queue*, the *FRE* disposes all finished functions and updates the *Loading Queue*. The call instruction rewriting mechanism, which will be introduced next, ensures that any function pointers pointing to a trimmed function will be restored to point to the original function in flash.

**Call Instruction Rewriting.** Function call rewriting optimizes the memory management scheme so that finished but not disposed functions in RAM can be called again without triggering the `HardFault` exception. Specifically, when a function call occurs and the control flow is trapped in the `HardFault` exception handler, the *FRE* overwrites that call instruction (in the loaded caller) to change the destination address of the call (i.e., the entry point of the callee in flash) with the entry of the loaded callee in RAM. Thus, the caller will directly jump to the loaded callee next time this call instruction executes. The rewriting history, including which instruction is rewritten and what the original instruction is, is recorded in the *Rewriting List*. Such records are used to recover the call instructions with callees' original flash entry points before function cleaning, since the loaded callees of those call instructions might be disposed.

**Memory Fragmentation Management.** In the randomization region, each loaded function occupies a function block. A disposed function block becomes a free block. If there are any adjacent free blocks, the *FRE* merges them into one big free block. All free blocks are managed by a linked list. A function block, as presented in Fig. 3 (a), consists of a two-word metadata, a payload and padding bytes for memory alignment. The metadata contains the size of the block and the pointer which points the next free block. The payload region is used to stores the randomized function.

When the system starts, fASLR initializes the whole randomization region as a big free block since no function has been allocated yet. Once a function is called in the NSW, the *FRE* allocates a function block for the target function. Specifically, it first scans the linked list and finds out all free blocks larger than the target function in the payload region. The *FRE* randomly selects one block among the discovered free blocks and then randomly allocates the target function to the selected free block. After the allocation, new free blocks may be generated and the linked list will be updated accordingly. Figure 3 (a) and (b) illustrate the case of randomizing Function 2 when there are two free blocks. Function 2 is consequently allocated to the middle of free block 1. The new free block 1 and free block 2 are then formed.

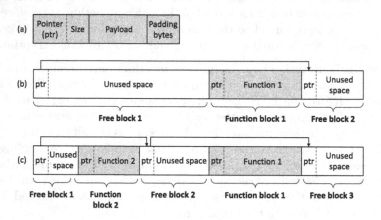

**Fig. 3.** Memory management. (a) Structure of the randomization region; (b) Memory layout before loading Function 2; (c) Memory layout after loading and randomizing Function 2

## 4.2   Memory Addressing

Control flow instructions using relative addresses in the ARMv8-M instruction set include *B* (branch), *BL* (branch with link), and *CBNZ/CBZ* (conditional branches), among which the *BL* (branch with link) is used to branch between functions. It is difficult for fASLR to handle such relative addressing without instruction patching, namely runtime instruction update. Note that the relative positions of two functions change after function randomization. Recalculating all the relative addresses used in the randomized function and updating the related instructions with the new relative addresses will result in unacceptable overhead in performance.

fASLR eradicates relative addressing at compile time. A user needs to access the source code of the app (including libraries) and compile the app with specific compilation flags (i.e., *-mlong-calls*, *-fno-jump-tables*). As a result, original relative function calls now use absolute addressing. It is worth noting that compiling with such flags would not break the normal build process or affect runtime behavior of the original program.

## 5  Security and Performance Analysis

In this section, we analyze the effectiveness of fASLR against ROP, a representative code reuse attack. Entropy is computed to quantify the randomness of gadgets required for the ROP attack, which indicates the difficulty of guessing the gadget locations in a brute-force way. We also study time and memory overheads introduced by fASLR.

### 5.1  Effectiveness Against ROP

The prerequisite of ROP is that the adversary knows where the ROP gadgets are. In a fASLR enabled system, an adversary can only use ROP gadgets in randomized functions relocated to the randomization region. Gadgets in the NS app stored in flash are non-executable, so it is hard for adversaries to use them. Recall that any MPU violation triggers the HardFault exception. As discussed in Sect. 3.3, the *FRE* validates the return address of the exception by using the *Function Table*. Therefore, the *FRE* is incapable of identifying exceptions triggered by a ROP attack if the adversary targets the entry point of a function since normal function calls will trigger such exceptions as well. In other words, the adversary will succeed in reusing a whole function as a gadget for ROP attack. However, such gadgets are often of very low quality [4,9] containing too many instructions. It is almost impossible for an adversary to assemble a chain of gadgets with such low quality gadgets to achieve certain malicious goal.

An adversary may also guess the addresses of randomized functions in a brute-force way. However, our runtime randomization approach rebases a function every time as long as it has not been loaded into RAM and achieves high randomization entropy as analyzed below.

### 5.2  Randomization Entropy

fASLR mitigates the brute-force guessing attack as follows. (i) fASLR restricts the number of functions that can be reused at a time. This is achieved by configuring the whole app image as non-executable. The only code snippets that can be utilized are functions relocated to the randomization region in the RAM. (ii) Even if all the required gadgets can be found from the relocated functions, the adversary has to guess locations of all those functions at once. Formula (1) gives the total number (denoted as $C$) of possible function layouts in the randomization region.

$$C = k! \binom{V + k}{k}, \tag{1}$$

where $k$ is the number of functions in the randomization region, and $V$ is the size of unused randomization space divided by two since the ARMv8-M architecture only allows even function addresses. Note the ARMv8-M architecture only allows an function to be loaded to an even address. Thus the randomization space can be treated as $V$ free randomization units and each unit is 2 bytes. We assume the randomization region is large enough to accommodate $k$ functions. If all free blocks are too small to fit the upcoming function, defragmentation can be applied. We calculate the maximum possibility of arranging $k$ distinguished functions among $V$ free units since from an attacker's perspective, any combination of $k$ functions and $V$ free units is possible. The combinations can be counted by the binomial coefficient $\binom{V+k}{k}$ multiplied by $k!$ because the $k$ functions are distinguished. For example, if $k = 5$ and $V = 100$, there are $5!\binom{100+5}{5} = 1.159\mathrm{e}{+10}$ combinations in total.

The probability of a layout is the reciprocal of C, i.e., $P = 1/C$. Formula (2) gives the entropy $H$ of function randomization.

$$H = -\sum_{i_1=1}^{C} P \log_2 P = -\sum_{i_1=1}^{C} \frac{1}{C} \log_2 \frac{1}{C} = \log_2 C \tag{2}$$

## 5.3   Time Overhead

fASLR introduces runtime overhead when it hijacks a function call for function randomization via hardware exception. According to fASLR runtime mechanism, we consider three factors that affect the program runtime performance, namely the number of function calls $N_c$ that trigger HardFault exceptions, function randomization processing time for the $i$th function call denoted as $T_R(i)$, and hardware exception processing time $T_E$. Formula (3) gives the relationship between the time overhead $TO$ and the three factors.

$$TO = \sum_{i=1}^{N_c} (T_R(i) + T_E). \tag{3}$$

Intuitively, $T_R(i)$ would be much larger than $T_E$ since $T_R$ involves several time-consuming operations such as memory write and table scanning, while $T_E$ is accomplished by hardware. The overhead from the function randomization process primarily comes from the following aspects: (i) address verification, which involves looking up the *Function Table*; (ii) function cleaning on demand, which looks up the call stack and cleans up finished functions; (iii) randomization, which selects a free block to rebase the callee; (iv) function loading, which reads and writes the function body; (v) function rewriting, which overwrites the destination of the call instruction with the entry point of loaded function.

## 5.4   Memory Overhead

The components of fASLR deployed in the SW include the *BE* code, *FRE* code, *Function Table*, *Loading Queue*, and *Rewriting List*. The *Function Table* is a static table with three 4-byte attributes and its size is linear to the total number of functions in the NS app. The *Loading Queue* and *Rewriting List* are dynamic data structures that contain function records and rewriting records respectively. Each function record has three 4-bytes metadata and a rewriting record contains double 4-bytes data. The maximum number of records that the *Loading Queue* may contain at runtime is equal to the number of functions in the NS app, while the maximum number of rewriting records in the *Rewriting List* is the total number of call instructions. Formula (4) presents the size of the *Function Table* (i.e., $MO_t$), *Loading Queue* (i.e., $MO_q$), and *Rewriting List* (i.e., $MO_l$),

$$MO_t = N_f \times 3 \times 4 = 12N_f, \tag{4}$$

$$MO_q = N_f \times 3 \times 4 = 12N_f, \tag{5}$$

$$MO_l = N_c \times 2 \times 4 = 8N_c, \tag{6}$$

where $N_f$ is the number of functions in the NS app, and $N_c$ is the number of function calls in the NS app.

## 5.5   Size Requirement of the Randomization Region

fASLR will run out of memory (OOM) if a new function cannot fit into the randomization region and no function can be trimmed. To avoid such an OOM issue, there is a size requirement of the randomization region for a certain application. We define call path size as the total size of all functions on a call path. The randomization region should be no less than the largest call path of the application when fragmentation compaction is applied by the memory management scheme. We can calculate the size requirement by statically analyzing the application code and perform defragmentation to the randomization region if needed.

# 6   Evaluation

In this section, we first present the experiment setup. We then present evaluation of randomization entropy, runtime overhead and memory overhead.

## 6.1   Experiment Setup

fASLR is implemented and deployed on the SAM L11 Xplained Pro Evaluation Kit, a MCU development board using the ARM Cortex-M23 core with TrustZone-M enabled. SAM L11 has a 64 KB flash and a 16 KB SRAM.

Software in SAM L11 is built with the GNU Arm Embedded Toolchain. User code, namely the NS app code, is compiled with two flags, *-mlong-calls* and

*-fno-jump-tables*, to eliminate instructions using relative addressing. We recompile the C library with the same compiler flags to make C functions compatible with fASLR. A Python script runs during the compilation time to collect function metadata and saves them in the *Function Table*. fASLR program and the *Function Table* are part of the Secure application placed in the SW flash, while the user app is deployed in the NSW flash.

We evaluate the performance of fASLR with 21 applications, including our own air quality monitoring system *(AirQualityMonitor)*. The air quality monitoring device, as shown in Fig. 4, consists of a SAM L11 development board, a PMSA003 air quality sensor module, and a SIM7000 cellular module. The NS app in SAM L11 periodically receives air quality data from PMSA003 and sends the data to SIM7000, which then transfers the data to the AWS IoT platform via secure MQTT protocol. The other twenty apps including the CoreMark benchmark [6], two micro benchmarks *Cache Test* and *Matrix Multiply* created based on [18], nine benchmarks of BEEBS [16], and eight SAM L11 demo apps obtained from Atmel Start [15].

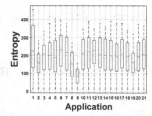
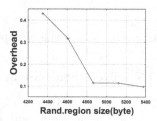

**Fig. 4.** Our air quality monitoring device developed with SAML11

**Fig. 5.** Entropy distribution

**Fig. 6.** Time overhead of *TrustRAM* application vs. randomization region size

## 6.2   Randomization Entropy

The entropy of function randomization changes dynamically when a function call occurs. We explore the entropy for all test applications. For each measured pair of $k$ and $V$, we calculate the corresponding entropy of function randomization according to Formulas (1) and (2). Figure 5 is the box plot demonstrating the entropy distribution for each app. The smallest average entropy is around 80 which is still considered to be large enough to defend against brute-force guessing.

## 6.3   Runtime Overhead

fASLR introduces runtime overhead since it intercepts every non-rewritten function call of the NS app for function randomization. We evaluate the time overhead by measuring and comparing the execution time of an application with and without fASLR. We use the internal `systick` timer of the Cortex-M core to record the execution time with precision of 0.01s. Since the main program of an

IoT application is usually a big loop, in the experiments we measure the execution time of 1000 loops for each testing application. We comment out all `delay` functions inside the loop for better estimation of time overhead introduced by fASLR. Table 1 presents the total execution time of 1000 loops for each application. The runtime overhead of fASLR is less than 10% for all apps, and 14 apps achieve time overheads below 5%. We also count for the occurrence of function cleaning for each app. The result shows that 19 apps have exhausted memory space during execution and triggered at least one function cleaning.

We also evaluate the influence of the randomization region size on time overhead with *TrustRAM*, the app with the largest time overhead in Table 1. Figure 6 illustrates that fASLR tends to perform better with a larger randomization region. This is mainly because fASLR with a larger randomization region will less likely apply function cleaning and function loading during program execution.

**Table 1.** Total execution time (in second) of 1000 loops and overheads.

| Application | # of cleanings | Baseline | with fASLR | Overhead |
|---|---|---|---|---|
| AirQualityMonitor | 1 | 324.79 | 327.50 | 0.83% |
| CoreMark | 4 | 15.62 | 15.78 | 1.02% |
| Cache test | 2 | 2.13 | 2.26 | 6.10% |
| Matrix multiply | 1 | 24.47 | 26.13 | 6.78% |
| SecureDriver | 1 | 12.56 | 12.64 | 0.64% |
| ADC event system | 2 | 12.41 | 12.54 | 1.04% |
| Calendar | 0 | 50.36 | 50.33 | −0.06% |
| Light sensor | 1 | 24.77 | 25.36 | 2.38% |
| Low power | 0 | 14.60 | 14.60 | 0% |
| ADP Hello | 1 | 9.93 | 10.88 | 9.57% |
| CRYA | 1 | 6.79 | 7.35 | 8.25% |
| TrustRAM | 1 | 1.14 | 1.25 | 9.65% |
| Beebs-crc | 1 | 7.44 | 7.73 | 3.90% |
| Beebs-aha-mont64 | 1 | 7.30 | 7.56 | 3.56% |
| Beebs-aha-compress | 1 | 4.50 | 4.67 | 3.78% |
| Beebs-bs | 1 | 0.28 | 0.29 | 3.57% |
| Beebs-bubblesort | 1 | 0.33 | 0.35 | 6.06% |
| Beebs-compress | 2 | 2.02 | 2.18 | 7.92% |
| Beebs-md5 | 2 | 0.42 | 0.44 | 4.76% |
| Beebs-levenshtein | 1 | 17.42 | 17.97 | 3.16% |
| Beebs-edn | 2 | 15.96 | 16.24 | 1.75% |

## 6.4   Memory Overhead

For each tested application, we measure the total number of functions and the memory overhead of NS apps before and after deploying fASLR, as illustrated in Table 2. In the SW, the code overhead is caused by the program of fASLR with a fixed code size of 3.45 KB, and the data overhead is mainly introduced by the static *Function Table*, dynamic *Loading Queue* and *Rewriting List*, and thus depends on the number of functions in the NS app. The size of the NS app is changed because of the compilation with specific compiler flags. Table 2 shows little memory overhead below 5% for all tests. It can be observed the app sizes in Table 2 are larger than the RAM size (16 KB). This shows the strength of fASLR, which can run an applications that is too large to be completely loaded into RAM compared with related work [19].

**Table 2.** NS app size (in byte) and overheads.

| Application | # of Functions | Size of rand. region | App size (baseline) | App size with fALSR | Overhead |
|---|---|---|---|---|---|
| AirQualityMonitor | 148 | 6144 | 41092 | 43036 | 4.73% |
| CoreMark | 174 | 6144 | 46048 | 47648 | 3.47% |
| Cache Test | 140 | 5632 | 40228 | 41844 | 4.02% |
| Matrix Multiply | 145 | 6144 | 40728 | 42404 | 4.12% |
| SecureDriver | 139 | 6144 | 39544 | 41184 | 4.15% |
| ADC Event System | 173 | 6144 | 43036 | 44640 | 3.73% |
| Calendar | 97 | 6144 | 36780 | 36808 | 0.08% |
| Light Sensor | 132 | 6144 | 40496 | 40528 | 0.08% |
| Low Power | 67 | 6144 | 34136 | 34164 | 0.08% |
| ADP Hello | 99 | 6144 | 38072 | 38316 | 0.64% |
| CRYA | 143 | 7168 | 41368 | 43012 | 3.97% |
| TrustRAM | 142 | 6144 | 39896 | 41500 | 4.02% |
| Beebs-crc | 138 | 6144 | 39944 | 41492 | 3.88% |
| Beebs-aha-mont64 | 142 | 6144 | 40476 | 42028 | 3.83% |
| Beebs-aha-compress | 140 | 6144 | 39944 | 41492 | 3.88% |
| Beebs-bs | 137 | 6144 | 39344 | 40896 | 3.94% |
| Beebs-bubblesort | 137 | 6144 | 39932 | 40892 | 2.40% |
| Beebs-compress | 143 | 5632 | 40808 | 42360 | 3.80% |
| Beebs-md5 | 137 | 6144 | 41552 | 43100 | 3.73% |
| Beebs-levenshiein | 138 | 6144 | 39708 | 41348 | 4.13% |
| Beebs-edn | 144 | 6144 | 42112 | 43736 | 3.86% |

## 7   Conclusion

In this paper, we propose fASLR, a function-based ASLR scheme for runtime software security of resource-constrained IoT devices, particularly those based on microcontrollers. fASLR leverages hardware-based security provided by the

TrustZone-M technique as the trust anchor. It uses MPU and prevents direct code execution of the application image in the Non-secure world flash. Instead, it traps control flow in an exception handler and relocates functions to be executed to a randomly selected location within the RAM. A memory management strategy is designed for allocating and cleaning up functions in the randomization region. fASLR is user friendly and only requires a user compiling the app with specific flags. We implement fASLR with a TrustZone-M enabled MCU—SAM L11. fASLR achieves high randomization entropy with acceptable overheads. We will release fASLR to GitHub for broad adoption and refine the implementation to further reduce the overhead.

**Acknowledgment.** This research was supported in part by National Key R&D Program of China 2018YFB2100300, National Natural Science Foundation of China Grant Nos. 62022024, 61972088, 62072103, 62102084, 62072102, 62072098, and 61972083, by US National Science Foundation (NSF) Awards 1931871, 1915780, and US Department of Energy (DOE) Award DE-EE0009152, by Jiangsu Provincial Natural Science Foundation for Excellent Young Scholars Grant No. BK20190060, Jiangsu Provincial Natural Science Foundation of China Grant No. BK20190340, Jiangsu Provincial Key Laboratory of Network and Information Security Grant No. BM2003201, Key Laboratory of Computer Network and Information Integration of Ministry of Education of China Grant Nos. 93K-9, and Collaborative Innovation Center of Novel Software Technology and Industrialization. Any opinions, findings, conclusions, and recommendations in this paper are those of the authors and do not necessarily reflect the views of the funding agencies.

# References

1. ARM. Armv8-m fault handling and detection
2. ARM. Trustzone for cortex-m
3. Bletsch, T.K., Jiang, X., Freeh, V.W.: Mitigating code-reuse attacks with control-flow locking. In: Zakon, R.H., McDermott, J.P., Locasto, M.E. (eds.) Twenty-Seventh Annual Computer Security Applications Conference, ACSAC 2011, Orlando, FL, USA, 5–9 December 2011, pp. 353–362. ACM (2011)
4. Brown, M.D., Pande, S.: Is less really more? Why reducing code reuse gadget counts via software debloating doesn't necessarily indicate improved security. arXiv preprint arXiv:1902.10880 (2019)
5. Chen, S., Xu, J., Nakka, N., Kalbarczyk, Z., Iyer, R.K.: Defeating memory corruption attacks via pointer taintedness detection. In: 2005 International Conference on Dependable Systems and Networks (DSN 2005), 28 June–1 July 2005, Yokohama, Japan, Proceedings, pp. 378–387. IEEE Computer Society (2005)
6. EEMBC Embedded Microprocessor Benchmark Consortium. Cpu benchmark–mcu benchmark–coremark
7. Davi, L., Liebchen, C., Sadeghi, A.R., Snow, K.Z., Monrose, F.: Code randomization resilient to (just-in-time) return-oriented programming. In: NDSS (2015)
8. Davi, L.V., Dmitrienko, A., Nünberger, S., Sadeghi, A.R.: Gadge me if you can: secure and efficient ad-hoc instruction-level randomization for x86 and arm. In: 8th ACM SIGSAC Symposium on Information, Computer and Communications Security, pp. 299–310 (2013)

9. Follner, A., Bartel, A., Bodden, E.: Analyzing the gadgets. In: International Symposium on Engineering Secure Software and Systems, pp. 155–172 (2016)

10. Hejazi, S.M., Talhi, C., Debbabi, M.: Extraction of forensically sensitive information from windows physical memory. Digit. Investig. **6**, S121–S131 (2009). The Proceedings of the Ninth Annual DFRWS Conference

11. Hiser, J., Nguyen-Tuong, A., Co, M., Hall, M., Davidson, J.W.: Ilr: where'd my gadgets go? In: 2012 IEEE Symposium on Security and Privacy, pp. 571–585. IEEE (2012)

12. Kil, C., Jun, J., Bookholt, C., Xu, J., Ning, P.: Address space layout permutation (ASLP): towards fine-grained randomization of commodity software. In: 2006 22nd Annual Computer Security Applications Conference (ACSAC 2006), pp. 339–348. IEEE (2006)

13. Koo, H., Chen, Y., Lu, L., Kemerlis, V.P., Polychronakis, M.: Compiler-assisted code randomization. In: 2018 IEEE Symposium on Security and Privacy (SP), pp. 461–477. IEEE (2018)

14. Larsen, P., Homescu, A., Brunthaler, S., Franz, M.: SoK: automated software diversity. In: 2014 IEEE Symposium on Security and Privacy, pp. 276–291. IEEE (2014)

15. Microchip. Atmel start

16. Pallister, J., Hollis, S., Bennett, J.: BEEBS: open benchmarks for energy measurements on embedded platforms. arXiv preprint arXiv:1308.5174 (2013)

17. Priyadarshan, S., Nguyen, H., Sekar, R.: Practical fine-grained binary code randomization. In: Annual Computer Security Applications Conference, pp. 401–414 (2020)

18. Quinn, H.: Microcontroller benchmark codes for radiation testing

19. Shi, J., Guan, L., Li, W., Zhang, D., Chen, P., Zhang, N.: Harm: hardware-assisted continuous re-randomization for microcontrollers. In: 2022 IEEE European Symposium on Security and Privacy (EuroS P) (2022)

20. Snow, K.Z., Monrose, F., Davi, L., Dmitrienko, A., Liebchen, C., Sadeghi, A.R.: Just-in-time code reuse: on the effectiveness of fine-grained address space layout randomization. In: 2013 IEEE Symposium on Security and Privacy, SP 2013, Berkeley, CA, USA, 19–22 May 2013, pp. 574–588. IEEE Computer Society (2013)

21. Wang, X., Yeoh, S., Lyerly, R., Olivier, P., Kim, S.H., Ravindran, B.: A framework for software diversification with {ISA} heterogeneity. In: 23rd International Symposium on Research in Attacks, Intrusions and Defenses ({RAID} 2020), pp. 427–442 (2020)

22. Wartell, R., Mohan, V., Hamlen, K.W., Lin, Z.: Binary stirring: self-randomizing instruction addresses of legacy x86 binary code. In: 2012 ACM Conference on Computer and Communications Security, pp. 157–168 (2012)

23. Feng, X., Wang, D., Lin, Z., Kuang, X., Zhao, G.: Enhancing randomization entropy of x86–64 code while preserving semantic consistency. In: 2020 IEEE 19th International Conference on Trust, Security and Privacy in Computing and Communications (TrustCom), pp. 1–12. IEEE (2020)

24. Yiu, J.: Chapter 2–getting started with cortex-m programming. In: Yiu, J. (ed.) Definitive Guide to Arm®Cortex®-M23 and Cortex-M33 Processors, pp. 19–51. Newnes (2021)

# An Infection-Identifying and Self-Evolving System for IoT Early Defense from Multi-Step Attacks

Hyunwoo Lee[1(✉)], Anand Mudgerikar[1], Ashish Kundu[2], Ninghui Li[1], and Elisa Bertino[1]

[1] Purdue University, West Lafayette, IN, USA
{lee3816,amudgeri,ninghui,bertino}@purdue.edu
[2] Cisco Research, San Jose, CA, USA
{ashkundu@cisco.com}

**Abstract.** Internet-of-Things (IoT) cyber threats such as jackware [14] and cryptomining [33] show that insecure IoT devices can be exploited by attackers with different goals. As many such attacks are multi-steps, early detection is critical. Early detection enables early attack containment and response, and prevention of malware propagation. However, it is challenging to detect early-phase attacks with both high precision and high recall as attackers typically attempt to evade the detection systems with stealthy or zero-day attacks. To enhance the security of IoT devices, we propose IoTEDEF, a deep learning-based system able to identify the infection events and evolve with the identified infections. IoTEDEF understands multi-step attacks based on cyber kill chains and maintains detectors for each step. When it detects anomalies related to a later stage of the kill chain, IoTEDEF backtracks the log of events and analyzes these events to identify infection events. Then, IoTEDEF updates its infection detector with the identified events. IoTEDEF can be used for threat hunting as well as the generation of indicators of compromise and attacks. To show its feasibility, we implement a prototype of the system and evaluate it against the Mirai botnet campaign [2] and the multi-step attack that exploits the Log4j vulnerability [36] to infect the IoT devices. Our results show that the F1-score of our evolved infection detector in IoTEDEF, instantiated with long short-term memory (LSTM) and the attention mechanism, increases from 0.31 to 0.87. We also show that existing attention-based NIDSes can benefit from our approach.

**Keywords:** Internet of things · Multi-step attacks · Infection identification · Threat hunting · Attention mechanism

## 1 Introduction

The Internet of Things (IoT) is the network of physical objects (or "things"), embedding electronics, software, and network connectivity, which enable these objects to collect and exchange data. IoT allows objects to be sensed and controlled

© The Author(s), under exclusive license to Springer Nature Switzerland AG 2022
V. Atluri et al. (Eds.): ESORICS 2022, LNCS 13555, pp. 549–568, 2022.
https://doi.org/10.1007/978-3-031-17146-8_27

remotely across existing network infrastructure, creating opportunities for more direct integration between the physical world and computer-based systems. IoT technology thus enables many novel applications and business opportunities [1].

However, IoT devices are at higher security risks than conventional computer systems [4]. Such devices often have access to attackers' targets such as sensitive data, cyber-physical systems, and/or user credentials [9]. Coming up with security techniques for IoT devices is challenging because these devices are often resource-constrained and thus hardly able to defend themselves. Often they are not appropriately hardened, nor regularly patched, and not even managed according to security best practices, leading them to become easy targets for attackers.

Very often, attack campaigns aiming at compromising IoT devices include multiple steps to acquire a foothold in a targeted system. For example, recent botnet campaigns, such as Reaper [26] or Mozi [38], scan ports to find any vulnerable entry points of the target device and attempt to take over it by performing telnet dictionary attacks or zero-day attacks. Once such a foothold is established, the attacker maintains persistence in the system, spreading malware to other devices, ex-filtrating confidential data, or stealing credentials. Therefore, detecting attacks at an early stage and identifying infection vectors are critical in order to contain and respond to the attacks, prevent re-infection, and fully remove the attacker's footholds.

However, it is challenging to detect early-phase attacks with both high precision and high recall. The reason is that to acquire a foothold in a target system, an attacker typically attempts to evade the detection systems by performing stealthy attacks (e.g., stealthy, distributed SSH brute-forcing [22]) or exploiting completely unknown device vulnerabilities (i.e., zero-day attacks) [26,39,40]. To detect such attacks, the detectors may classify all the suspicious or unknown patterns as anomalies, but it results in a high number of false positives [21].

In this paper, we propose IoTEDEF, an anomaly-based network intrusion detection system (NIDS) tailored for IoT devices, which is *kill chain-based*, *infection-identifying*, and *self-evolving*. As IoTEDEF is *network-based*, it supports resource-constrained IoT devices without requiring additional computation or networking by these devices. We design IoTEDEF to be *anomaly-based* because anomaly detection is able to detect unknown patterns [10] and is effective for IoT networks that have simple communication patterns [18]. Building on the concept of a *cyber kill chain*, which is a framework for understanding multi-step attacks [13,20,43], IoTEDEF uses several detectors – one for each step, and detects abnormal traffic based on results from these detectors. IoT-EDEF focuses on the steps of a kill chain where networking communication is involved and models the attack's structure. We refer to the steps executed by the attacker to gain a foothold in the targeted system as *early* stages and the other steps as *later* stages. With such knowledge, IoTEDEF backward traverses the log of the events upon detecting anomalies related to a later stage of the kill chain, and analyzes these events to identify infection events. IoTEDEF updates the system based on the identified events to improve the performance of its infection detector. Essentially, IoTEDEF gives up precise detection of unknown patterns of an early stage attack when IoTEDEF faces an unknown attack for the first time. Instead, after IoTEDef recognizes that there has been an early stage attack through known patterns of the later stage attack, IoTEDef identifies the corresponding early stage attack patterns and makes its early detector learn the patterns. Then, IoTEDef can detect such an early stage attack with high precision later on.

Implementing such a strategy is, however, challenging as IoTEDef needs to correlate adversarial and separate events in two different steps (e.g., UDP flooding in the action step and dictionary attack packets in the infection step), where the interval between them can be long. Solving the problem requires mapping diverse networking patterns into kill chain steps and backtracking from later events to earlier events. We note that similar challenges also exist in the area of language translation, and many techniques have been developed to address these challenges [5]. Therefore, we model the problem as a language translation problem by introducing a novel *probability-based embedding* to encode past events into steps that the events belong to and a *attention-based infection identification algorithm* to correlate the encoded events with long-term dependencies in different steps. The algorithm we use helps identify infection events that lead to action events. Finally, we use the identified infection events to improve the performance of the infection detector.

Our systematic and automated method for early detection and self-evolution is beneficial to organizations that perform threat hunting [42]. According to a survey [7], many organizations value threat hunting as it is helpful for early detection and faster repair of vulnerabilities. However, 88% of the respondents say their current systems for threat hunting are immature in terms of formal processes and automation. It shows the value of IoTEDef since it meets such requirements.

To summarize, we make the following contributions:

- We propose IoTEDef, an NIDS that prevents persistent attacks in IoT environments at an early stage.
- We design an attention mechanism-based algorithm to identify infection events from past events.
- We implement a proof-of-concept of IoTEDef and release it on a publicly available repository.
- We carry out comprehensive experiments to assess the accuracy of IoTEDef. Our results show that our approach is feasible and effective.

## 2    Background

### 2.1   Cyber Kill Chains

The term 'kill chain' has been coined in the military domain to describe the steps an attacker should complete one by one to achieve its malicious objectives. There are several frameworks [13,20,43] proposed to apply this concept to the area of information security. These frameworks understand the structure of attacks as many attacks are multi-steps. Although the number and the name of steps vary, these kill chains commonly break down an attack into the following five steps:

- **Reconnaissance:** the attacker collects information about the target. The attacker may perform social engineering or port scanning.
- **Infection:** the attacker exploits vulnerabilities of the target to take over it and installs malware binaries required to launch attacks. The attacker may launch dictionary attacks or zero-day attacks for this purpose.
- **Lateral movement:** once the attacker has access to the target, the attacker may move laterally to other devices to gain more leverage. The attacker may perform scanning activities or propagate malware in the internal domain.
- **Obfuscation:** the attacker hides its tracks. This step may involve laying false trails and clearing logs.
- **Action:** the attacker launches the attack. For example, in botnets, the attacker directs bots to perform a DDoS attack such as UDP flooding.

We focus on the three steps – *Reconnaissance*, *Infection*, and *Action* – in our NIDS to model the multi-step attacks. The reason is that NIDS can issue the alarms for the reconnaissance and infection steps with the higher priority [32] and can also detect networking attacks, such as DDoS, of the action step.

## 2.2   Attention Mechanism

The goal of the attention mechanism [3,30] in deep learning is to pay greater attention to certain factors when classifying data. It was introduced in the natural language processing field to address the problem of *long-term dependencies* in the sequence-to-sequence model that consists of the encoder and the decoder [44]. The encoder compresses a sentence in one language into a fixed-length vector (called a *context vector*). With the vector, the decoder generates a sentence in the other language. Both the encoder and the decoder are recurrent neural networks (RNNs) with long short-term memory (LSTM) units, and the final hidden state of the encoder is provided to the decoder as a context vector. However, Cho *et al.* [6] have shown that the performance of the model degrades as the length of the sentences increases, which is called the bottleneck problem. It is mainly because information loss occurs in the context vector due to its fixed size. Specifically, it often cannot capture interdependence between words far apart in sentences.

With the attention mechanism, the decoder not only refers to the final hidden state of the encoder but also checks all the hidden states of the encoder. In generating a translated sentence, the decoder outputs the next word focusing more on certain hidden states related to the decoder's current state. To this end, each hidden state of the encoder is associated with a weight per state of the decoder, called an *attention weight*. It is determined by the *alignment score* that quantifies the amount of attention. The most widely used scoring function is a *dot product* by which the score is obtained by multiplying the hidden states of the encoder with the state of the decoder.

## 3   Architecture of IoTEDEF

This section presents the design of IoTEDEF. We first provide the threat model and the main properties, then describe the architecture of IoTEDEF.

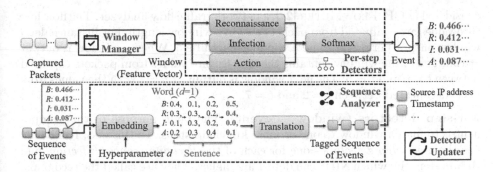

**Fig. 1.** Architecture of IoTEDEF and infection identification flow.

## 3.1  Design Principles

**Threat Model.** IoTEDEF analyzes network packets exchanged between the network (where it aims to protect) and the Internet. We assume that IoTEDEF is not compromised; thus, it does not manipulate the exchanged packets. Also, we assume that an attack is always initiated from the Internet by using remote network access. IoT devices when initially deployed in the network are not compromised; however, they can be compromised later on.

**Main Properties.** IoTEDEF is designed to adhere to the following properties:

- **Network-based:** it works with network packets; thus, it does not impose any computation overhead on IoT devices, and is immediately deployable as it does not require any change on IoT devices.
- **Anomaly-based:** it is able to detect unknown patterns and it is also appropriate for the simple communication behavior of IoT devices.
- **Kill chain-based:** it understands multi-step attacks based on a kill chain and deploys classifiers specialized for the steps.
- **Infection-identifying:** it backtracks past events to identify infection events when it detects known events of later stages.
- **Self-evolving:** it updates the infection detector with the identified events.

## 3.2  Overview

IoTEDEF consists of four main components: *window manager, per-step detectors, sequence analyzer*, and *detector updater* (see Fig. 1)

**Window Manager (packets → window).** IoTEDEF works on a *flow-based window* where a *flow* is defined as a 5-tuple – the protocol in use, source/destination IP addresses, and source/destination ports. A window manager collects packets per flow and runs a sliding window based on two parameters – a *window output period* and a *window length*. On every window output period, the window manager outputs a *window* in the form of a vector that consists of the 84 flow feature values considered in CICFLOWMETER [28], a network traffic flow analyzer. The flow feature values are evaluated from packets within a window length. For instance, let a window output period be 2 and a window length be 5. When a window is output at time $t = 5$, the window contains the flow feature values from packets captured between $t = 0$ and $t = 5$. The next window is output at $t = 7$ with the values from packets captured between $t = 2$ and $t = 7$.

**Per-step detectors (window → event).** The main purpose of this component is to map a window to one or more kill chain steps. To this end, IOTEDEF has three *per-step detectors* - one for each of the *Reconnaissance*, *Infection*, and *Action* steps, by which NIDS can detect anomalies. They are called the reconnaissance detector, the infection detector, and the action detector, respectively. Each detector has its classifier learned from networking patterns of the corresponding step. Once a window is given to IOTEDEF, each per-step detector takes it as input and determines if it contains any anomalous pattern for the corresponding step. If so, IOTEDEF labels the window with the name of the corresponding step. For example, we call a given window a reconnaissance window if the reconnaissance detector detects anomalies from the window. This process provides a precedence relation between windows according to the kill chain steps.

A window may belong to multiple steps. For example, the window can be classified as *Reconnaissance* and *Infection* by the reconnaissance and the infection detectors. We call such a window both a reconnaissance window and an infection window. As the results of per-step detectors can be false positives, we make our per-step detectors return confidence scores as well as the results. IOTEDEF applies the softmax function to normalize the confidence scores from per-step detectors, resulting in a probability distribution. The probability distribution is used to correct false positives by the infection identification algorithm. We call an output of per-step detectors an *event* that contains a window, three labels (i.e., whether the window belongs to each step respectively), and four probabilities (i.e., normalized confidence scores).

**Sequence Analyzer (sequence of events → identified infection events).** This module runs the infection identification algorithm to find the infection events that lead to the action event. The algorithm takes a sequence of past events, each of which has a probability distribution assigned by per-step detectors. Then, the algorithm analyzes the sequence and determines only one kill chain step for each event according to the entire context. To this end, we develop an identification algorithm based on the attention mechanism in deep learning techniques, which considers all the (hidden) states when producing the next state. Finally, the algorithm returns the infection events from the resulting sequence.

**Detector Updater (identified infection events → updated infection detector).** The detector updater is responsible for updating the classifier of the infection detector. The module labels the identified infection events as *Infection* and re-trains a new classifier with the training set and the events.

# 4    Detail of IoTEDef

This section provides IoTEDef in detail. We first formally define the problem to be solved and present our solution with the probability-based embedding and the attention-based translation. Finally, we discuss our update strategies.

## 4.1    Problem Definition

We begin with the notions of a tag and an event. Our formal definitions include notation $a.b$ to indicate an attribute $b$ of $a$.

**Definition 1 (tag).** A set $\mathcal{L} = \{B, R, I, A\}$ is a collection of tags that an event can be labeled with, where $B, R, I, A$ denote *Benign, Reconnaissance, Infection*, and *Action*, respectively.

**Definition 2 (event).** An event $e = (w, l, p, t)$ is a tuple of four attributes. $e.w$ is a window. $e.l = (r, i, a)$ is a tuple of three attributes where $e.l.r, e.l.i, e.l.a \in \{0, 1\}$ and each indicates whether the window $(e.w)$ is labeled by each step detector. $e.p = (b, r, i, a)$ is a tuple of four attributes $(0 \leq e.p.b, e.p.r, e.p.i, e.p.a \leq 1, e.p.b + e.p.r + e.p.i + e.p.a = 1)$, which are the probabilities of the window belonging to the class *Benign, Reconnaissance, Infection*, and *Action*, respectively. $e.t \in \mathcal{L}$ is a tag that will be finally assigned by the identification algorithm.

In what follows, $\mathcal{E}$ denotes the set of events. Recall that our goal is to identify infection events by backtracking the past events (or an input sequence of events) based on anomalies in the action step. We model the process of backtracking as an event tagging problem described as follows:

**Problem 1 (event tagging problem).** Let $\mathbf{e} = \{e_1, e_2, \cdots, e_n\}$ be an input sequence that belongs to $\mathcal{E}^*$ and let $\mathbf{y} = \{y_1, y_2, \cdots, y_n\}$ be an output sequence that belongs to $\mathcal{L}^*$, where $\mathcal{E}^*$ is a set of all sequences over the set of events $\mathcal{E}$ and $\mathcal{L}^*$ is a set of all sequences over an output space $\mathcal{L}$. Our goal is to design a function $g : \mathcal{E}^* \to \mathcal{L}^*$ that takes an input sequence $\mathbf{e}$ and outputs $\mathbf{y}$.

While solving the problem, we face the challenge of long-term dependency between events. As an example, an infection event always precedes an action event, but the time interval between those two events can be long. For instance, in Mirai [2], a device is infected by an attacker's dictionary attack (an infection step). Then, the device launches the UDP flooding attack (an action step), possibly a long time after the infection event. In this example, the role of IoTEDef is to identify events that contain dictionary attack patterns when IoTEDef detects a UDP flooding pattern. Therefore, IoTEDef should be able to correlate distant events.

To address such an issue, we review language translation techniques in natural language processing as even words that appear far apart can have a significant relationship in natural language. There have been many techniques to capture such dependencies [5]. Our idea is that if we are able to model an event as a word in a language and a sequence as a sentence in a language, we can achieve the goal by using language translation techniques. To this end, we should resolve the two challenges: 1) *how to model an event as a word in the language* and 2) *what technique we use to translate an input sequence to an output sequence.*

Modeling an event as a word in a language requires defining the word sets of input and output sequences. For an output word set, we can use $\mathcal{L}$. However, it is challenging to define an input word set to represent each in a sequence of events. One important requirement is that our encoding scheme should be able to model long-term dependency. For example, using the one-hot encoding is inappropriate in our scheme since it cannot capture the informative relations between different categorical variables [16] (see Subsect. 5.2).

Another challenge is what technique to use for translating an input sequence to an output sequence. There are traditional sequence labeling or decoding algorithms from observations, such as an episode-tree-based model [41] or the Viterbi algorithm [11]. However, they are ineffective as they cannot model long-term dependency (see Subsect. 5.4).

Therefore, we divide Problem 1 into the following two subproblems.

**Subproblem 1 (embedding).** Let $\mathbf{e} = \{e_1, e_2, \cdots, e_n\}$ be an input sequence of length $n$ that belongs to $\mathcal{E}^*$ and let $\mathbf{x} = \{x_1, x_2, \cdots, x_n\}$ be an *input sentence* that belongs to $\mathcal{X}^*$, where $\mathcal{X}^*$ is a set of all sentences over an input word set $\mathcal{X}$. Our goal is to define an input word set $\mathcal{X}$ and an embedding function $e : \mathcal{E} \to \mathcal{X}$ that takes an event $e$ as an input and outputs an input word $x$ to finally convert $\mathbf{e}$ to $\mathbf{x}$.

**Subproblem 2 (translation).** Let $\mathbf{x} = \{x_1, x_2, \cdots, x_n\}$ be an input sentence that belongs to $\mathcal{X}^*$ and let $\mathbf{y} = \{y_1, y_2, \cdots, y_n\}$ be an output sentence that belongs to $\mathcal{L}^*$. Our goal is to design a translation function $t : \mathcal{X}^* \to \mathcal{L}^*$ that takes $\mathbf{x}$ as an input, tags all the embedded windows in $\mathbf{x}$, and outputs $\mathbf{y} = \{y_1, y_2, \cdots, y_n\}$.

Our solution to the problem consists of the following three steps (see Fig. 1):

**1. Probability distribution assignment:** an event is assigned a probability distribution $(e.p)$ that shows how much a window $(e.w)$ belongs to a class.
**2. Probability-based embedding:** the probability distribution of an event is encoded into a word in a language.
**3. Attention-based translation.** A series of embedded words are translated into tagged ones each of which has only one label.

## 4.2   Probability Distribution Assignment

Per-step detectors are responsible for this step. Recall that the per-step detectors detect reconnaissance, infection, and action patterns in a given window. Each detector has its own classifier trained with packets of the corresponding step and detects anomalies according to the classification results. For example, the classifier of the infection detector is generated from the network patterns of the telnet dictionary attack, the Log4j attack, or other attacks aiming to infect IoT devices. For a classifier of each per-step detector, any algorithm can be used. However, the performance of IoTEDEF depends on the characteristics of the classification algorithm as the infection identification algorithm runs over the detection result. Our result shows that the class of recurrent neural networks (RNN) with long short-term memory (LSTM) units is most effective (Subsect. 5.3).

Each detector evaluates the probability of the window belonging to its corresponding step. For instance, the reconnaissance detector may label the window as *Reconnaissance* with a probability of 0.68 and the infection detector may classify the window as *Infection* with a probability of 0.53. We convert the probabilities into one probability distribution using the softmax function and finally output the distribution as an event. As an example, an event may be associated with a probability distribution $(0.46, 0.31, 0.11, 0.12)$, which means that the probability that the corresponding window belongs to *Benign* is 0.46, *Reconnaissance* is 0.31, *Infection* is 0.11, and *Action* is 0.12.

---

**Algorithm 1.** Probability-based Embedding $e$

---

**Input:** Sequence of events $\mathbf{s} = (e_1, \cdots, e_n)$ and $d$
**Output:** Sequence of words (Sentence) $\mathbf{x} = (x_1, \cdots, x_n)$
**Initialize:** $\mathbf{x}[:] = []$
1: **for** $k = 1, 2, \ldots, n$ **do**
2:    sort $e_k.p.b, e_k.p.r, e_k.p.i, e_k.p.a$ by the decimal part to be rounded off in descending order
3:    **if** more than two decimal parts are larger than 5 **then**
4:       Round down the last one or two probabilities to ensure $sum = 1$
5:       Round off the rest of the probabilities
6:    **else if** more than two decimal parts are smaller than 5 **then**
7:       Round up the first one or two probabilities to ensure $sum = 1$
8:       Round off the rest of the probabilities
9:    **else**
10:       Round off the probabilities
11:    **end if**
12:    ▷ $\mathbf{r}(a, b)$: the result of rounding up/down/off $a$ to $b$ of decimal places
13:    $x_k = (\mathbf{r}(e_k.p.b, d), \mathbf{r}(e_k.p.r, d), \mathbf{r}(e_k.p.i, d), \mathbf{r}(e_k.p.a, d))$
14:    Add a word $x_k$ to Sequence $\mathbf{x}$
15: **end for**

---

## 4.3    Probability-Based Embedding

To solve Subproblem 1, we design a novel probability-based embedding algorithm (see Algorithm 1). We represent input words as a vector of four probabilities (for each step) - the sum of which is 1.

**Hyperparameter $d$.** One issue is that the above input word set is infinite, which would be inappropriate for a language translation model based on finite input word sets. Thus, we change the input set to be finite. To this end, we introduce a hyper-parameter $d$, which is the number of decimal places to round off the probabilities. Given $d \in \mathbb{N}$, let $\mathcal{P}$ be $\{p|p = \text{round}(q, d), 0 \leq q \leq 1\}$, where $\text{round}(a, b)$ is a function that rounds off $a$ to $b$ of decimal places. With $d$, the input set is changed to $\mathcal{X} = \{(b, r, i, a)|b, r, i, a \in \mathcal{P} \text{ and } b + r + i + a = 1\}$. However, rounding off does not guarantee that the sum of the rounded probabilities is always one. To avoid the case that the sum is not one, we first sort the probabilities by the decimal part to be rounded off. Then, we round up the first one or two probabilities or down the last one or two to ensure the sum of the resulting probabilities is one. For example, $(0.466 \cdots, 0.412 \cdots, 0.031 \cdots, 0.087 \cdots)$ became $(0.5, 0.4, 0.0, 0.1)$ when $d = 1$ (see bolded numbers in Fig. 1). Note that $d$ determines the number of input words in the word set.

---

**Algorithm 2.** Attention-based Translation $t$

---

**Input:** Sequence $s_i = (e_1, \cdots, e_n)$, Decimal Place $d$
**Output:** Sequence $s_o$
**Initialize:** $s_o[:] = 0$
1: $s_e = \texttt{ProbabilityBasedEmbedding}(s_i, d)$
2: $r_{lstm} = \texttt{LSTM}(s_e)$
3: $r_{attention} = \texttt{Attention}(r_{lstm})$
4: $r_{ff} = \texttt{Feedforward}(r_{attention})$
5: $r_{sm} = \texttt{Softmax}(r_{ff})$
6: $\triangleright r_{sm} = (p_{b_1}, p_{r_1}, p_{i_1}, p_{a_1}), \cdots, (p_{b_n}, p_{r_n}, p_{i_n}, p_{a_n})$
7: **for** $k = 1, 2, \ldots, n$ **do**
8:     $e_k.t = \texttt{argmax}((p_{b_k}, p_{r_k}, p_{i_k}, p_{a_k}))$
9:     Add $e_k$ to sequence $s_o$
10: **end for**

---

### 4.4 Attention-Based Translation

To solve Subproblem 2, we apply the attention mechanism to our neural network classifier that has been introduced to address the long-term dependency problem in language translation. The flow of infection identification with the multi-classification neural network is as follows (see Algorithm 2):

- **Input:** an input sequence is a series of events, each of which has a probability distribution assigned by the per-step detectors.
- **Embedding:** the events in an input sequence are converted to a sentence of input words, each of which consists of four probabilities.
- **Long short term memory (LSTM):** after the embedding, a sequence of input words passes through an LSTM layer. The layer outputs vectors considering the context of each input word.
- **Attention:** we add an attention layer after the LSTM layer. It calculates correlation scores between events and assigns attention weights.

- **Feedforward & Softmax:** we add a feedforward layer and a softmax layer. They output four probabilities for each input word. Each probability represents the degree that an input word is translated into an output word.
- **Output:** finally, each input word in the input sequence is translated into the output word with the highest probability.

With the attention mechanism, IoTEDef analyzes a given sequence in the context between events. As words of the same form may have different meanings in the context of the sentence, events with the same distribution may also belong to different steps in the context of the sequence. For example, some events with the same distribution may belong to *Benign* or *Infection*, depending on whether an action event is in the sequence or not. In the attention mechanism, the attention weights are evaluated with respect to different steps and positions in sequences. Thus, it helps to distinguish the differences between the events that have the same distribution but belong to different steps and identify infection events related to an action event in the sequence.

### 4.5 Self-Evolving Strategies

The detector updater updates the classifier of the infection detector with the identified infection events. We consider three different strategies. Let $\mathcal{A}$ be a set of events having the highest probability of *Infection* after passing through the per-step detectors and let $\mathcal{B}$ be a set of infection events tagged by the attention-based translation. We denote the difference between the two sets by $\mathcal{C}$ (i.e., $\mathcal{A} \backslash \mathcal{B}$).

- **Strategy 1:** a new infection classifier is generated over a training set, all the events in $\mathcal{B}$ as *Infection*, and all the events in $\mathcal{C}$ as *Benign*. For example, let say there are 5 events $e_1, e_2, e_3, e_4, e_5 \in \mathcal{A}$ (i.e., $e_i.l.i = 1$ for $i = \{1, 2, 3, 4, 5\}$) and the attention-based algorithm provides the information that $e_1, e_2, e_4$ ($\mathcal{B}$) are infection events (i.e., $e_1.t = e_2.t = e_4.t = I$). Then, IoTEDef updates the classifier with $e_1.w, e_2.w, e_4.w$ labeled as *Infection* and $e_3.w, e_5.w$ labeled as *Benign*.
- **Strategy 2:** this strategy is similar to the first one except that it only uses a training set and all the events in $\mathcal{B}$ (not the events in $\mathcal{C}$). It adds information about the true positives to the updated model. In our example, $e_1.w, e_2.w, e_4.w$ labeled as *Infection* are used to update the model.
- **Strategy 3:** this strategy is similar to the first one, but it uses a training set and all the events in $\mathcal{C}$ (not the events in $\mathcal{B}$). It aims to reduce the false positives of the updated model. In our example, $e_3.w, e_5.w$ labeled as *Benign* are used to update the model.

## 5    Evaluation

This section provides an experimental analysis of IoTEDef. We implement a proof-of-concept prototype and build a testbed for evaluation using a dataset related to the Mirai botnet [2] and the Log4j attack [36]. We release the dataset, the scripts, and the implementation source codes at https://github.com/iotedef.

## 5.1    Experimental Setting

**Implementation.** We use the PCAPY library [8] to capture packets and the *keras* library [24] to implement neural networks and other machine learning-related functions. The LSTM layer consists of 100 units for our attention-based neural network with 0.5 for the dropout rate and 0.2 for the recurrent dropout rate. The subsequent attention layer uses a dot-product as a scoring function. Finally, the feedforward layer consists of 64 units. We use *sparse categorical cross entropy* as loss function.

**Datasets.** We generate datasets considering the following two scenarios.

– **Mirai botnet campaign** [2]: it includes the telnet dictionary attack as an infection activity. We use a publicly available IoT intrusion dataset from academia [23]. It contains captured packets from the real-world and consists of diverse types of packets including benign packets, port scanning packets, telnet dictionary attack packets, and flooding packets, as separate files. We extract packets from the files and combine them into one dataset. We label port scanning packets to *Reconnaissance*, the telnet dictionary attack packets to *Infection*, and the flooding packets to *Action*. We add benign telnet login packets to degrade the performance of the infection detector.

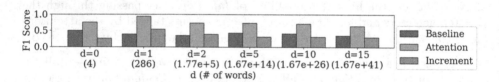

**Fig. 2.** Impact of the probability-based embedding.

– **Log4j attack** [36]: it includes the Log4j attack as an adversary's infection activity. We build our testbed based on Mininet [27], run multi-step attacks, and capture the packets. The resulting dataset includes the port scanning packets as *Reconnaissance*, the Log4j attack packets as *Infection*, and the flooding packets as *Action*. The dataset also contains benign HTTP POST packets from which the Log4Shell attack packets are difficult to tell.

We generate several datasets per scenario, each of which has a different number of packets corresponding to the step and time intervals between different events. The detail of the dataset generation algorithm is described in Sect. A.

**Testbed.** We perform our experiments in one machine with i7-4700 CPU @ 3.60 GHz 8 core processors and 16 GB RAM. To evaluate the performance of IoTEDEF with the practical scenarios, we replay the packets from the above dataset with *Tcpreplay* [25]. The generated packets are captured by IoTEDEF.

**Experiments.** We measure the performance for the following three cases for a given test set. We report averaged results of 30 trials per scenario.

- **Baseline:** We see how many infection events can be correctly detected with the infection detector learned only with the training set.
- **Attention:** We evaluate how well our attention-based infection identification algorithm (ATTENTION) works over a sequence of events.
- **Update:** We measure the performance of the infection detector evolved with the identified infection events on a different test set.

## 5.2    Impact of Probability-based Embedding

We assess the impact of our probability-based embedding on the performance of our attention-based translation by varying the value of the hyper-parameter $d$ (see Fig. 2). Overall, the F1-score increases from BASELINE when ATTENTION is used. Furthermore, we see that ATTENTION works best with $d = 1$. Note that the larger the value of $d$ is, the higher the number of elements in the set is. For $d > 1$, the number of elements is higher than $10^5$, which we believe is too large to map to only four variables in the output word set. The worst increment is at $d = 0$, where the one-hot encoding is used. The result shows that the one-hot encoding is ineffective for ATTENTION as it cannot capture dependency between words. Hereafter, we fix $d = 1$ in the other experiments.

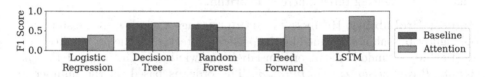

**Fig. 3.** Compatibility with the detector classifiers. Note that "LSTM" in the figure is a classifier in the infection detector, not an encoder layer before the attention layer in ATTENTION.

## 5.3    Impact of Classifiers of Per-step Detectors

As ATTENTION relies on probabilities assigned by per-step detectors (see Fig. 1), we experiment to understand the impact of different types of classifiers for the per-step detectors on the performance of ATTENTION. As classifiers, we use LOGISTIC REGRESSION, DECISION TREE, RANDOM FOREST, the FEEDFORWARD neural network, and LSTM. We evaluate each classifier with and without ATTENTION and calculate the F1-score.

We find that the neural networks are compatible with ATTENTION (see Fig. 3). The increments of the F1-score for both neural network algorithms are 0.29 (FEEDFORWARD) and 0.48 (LSTM), respectively, while for other algorithms is less than 0.08. Notably, LSTM is the one classifier that works best with ATTENTION. Compared with other algorithms, LSTM is the only algorithm that considers the context of windows, which explains the result. After breaking down the result of the neural networks, we find that ATTENTION contributes to increasing precision while maintaining recall. This result shows that the attention mechanism assigns higher weights to features that are useful to find false positive results in the detectors.

The reason why non-neural network algorithms show worse performance is because of their assumption. LOGISTIC REGRESSION shows poor performance due to its linear boundary assumption. DECISION TREE shows high precision with low recall, which means it is over-fitted. Furthermore, the difference in F1-score between DECISION TREE with and without ATTENTION is only 0.01. It is because DECISION TREE does not produce a probability and thus is not compatible with our embedding scheme. Also, DECISION TREE has high variance and is very sensitive to small changes in the input, which makes it highly deterministic. It results in loss of information when encoding different steps of the attack. Although the problem is alleviated by using RANDOM FOREST, we find that RANDOM FOREST also does not perform well with ATTENTION for similar reasons. Therefore, we use LSTM for our classifiers of the per-step detectors hereafter.

### 5.4    Other Identification Algorithms

We compare ATTENTION with other traditional algorithms for sequences. We consider the following three different algorithms:

**Highest Probability.** HIGHEST PROBABILITY tags a window to the step with the highest probability assigned by the per-step detectors. If the probabilities are identical for a window, the algorithm labels the window in the order of *Benign*, *Action*, *Reconnaissance*, and *Infection*. The order is based on the number of samples in our dataset.

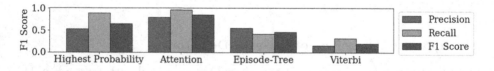

**Fig. 4.** Comparison with other algorithms.

**Fig. 5.** Self-evolving strategies.

**Viterbi.** VITERBI [11] is based on a hidden Markov model and estimates a sequence of hidden states from an observed sequence with memory-less noise.

**Episode-tree.** An episode-tree is a collection of window sequences. Based on the training set, we build an episode-tree using the tree generation algorithm by Mannila *et al.* [31]. EPISODE-TREE identifies infection windows if a given window sequence matches a branch of the episode-tree, which contains infection windows.

The result (see Fig. 4) shows that the attention-based algorithm outperforms the other algorithms. The F1-score of the attention-based algorithm is 0.85. The performance of EPISODE-TREE (0.46) and VITERBI (0.20) are even worse than HIGHEST PROBABILITY (0.65). EPISODE-TREE is a simple pattern matching algorithm; thus, it depends on how many patterns are captured from the training set. Therefore, EPISODE-TREE can be easily over-fitted, which accounts for high precision and low recall of its result. VITERBI shows the worst performance due to its memory-less assumption that makes the algorithm unable to capture long-term dependencies.

## 5.5 Self-Evolving Strategies

We carry out an experiment to assess the impact of the three strategies discussed in Sect. 4. We compare the performance of the baseline with the performance of the updated model according to the strategies. STRATEGY 1 is the strategy that uses both identified infection and benign events, STRATEGY 2 is the strategy that only uses identified infection events, and STRATEGY 3 is the strategy that only uses benign events.

Our results (see Fig. 5) show that all the updated models outperform the baseline regardless of the strategy. Compared with other strategies, STRATEGY 2 works best (an F1-score of 0.87) with the highest precision (0.82). STRATEGY 1 has an F1-score of 0.82 and a precision of 0.77, and STRATEGY 3 has an F1-score of 0.72 and a precision of 0.64. We conclude that the self-evolving strategy affects the performance of the models. The results show that many anomalous samples are classified as *Benign* under STRATEGY 1 and STRATEGY 3, resulting in worse performance compared to STRATEGY 2.

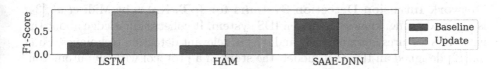

**Fig. 6.** Comparison with attention-based NIDSes.

## 5.6 Comparison with Attention-based NIDSes

Although our approach is orthogonal to the detection algorithm, we compare ATTENTION with existing attention-based NIDSes with respect to two aspects. First, we see if the performance of LSTM after being evolved is comparable to the performance of those IDSes. Second, we assess whether ATTENTION is also beneficial to them. In our analysis, the following two systems are considered:

**Hierarchical Attention Model (HAM).** HAM [29] is based on two attention layers, namely the feature-based attention layer and the slice-based attention layer. The former weighs the features and the latter calculates an attention score for a time window considering a specific number of previous windows. Finally, the NIDS predicts the next window with the neural network.

**SAAE-DNN.** SAAE-DNN [45] is based on a stacked autoencoder with the attention mechanism. It consists of two autoencoders. In-between an encoder layer and a latent layer of each autoencoder, an attention layer is inserted. The latent nodes of the second autoencoder are connected to the four-layer neural network, which finally outputs the classification result.

In the experiment, we use two test sets (referred to as $set_1$ and $set_2$) with different networking patterns. First, we evaluate the F1-score of LSTM, HAM, and SAAE-DNN on both $set_1$ and $set_2$. Then, we apply our self-evolving STRATEGY 2 to update the models based on the result on $set_1$. We refer to the updated models as UPDATED LSTM, UPDATED HAM, and UPDATED SAAE-DNN, respectively. Finally, we measure the F1-score of the updated models on $set_2$. We compare the results of LSTM, HAM, SAAE-DNN, and their updated models on $set_2$ (see Fig. 6).

Our conclusions are as follows. First, UPDATED LSTM outperforms HAM and SAAE-DNN. The F1-score of the original LSTM is only 0.14, which is lower than the scores of HAM (0.19) and SAAE-DNN (0.77). However, the F1-score of LSTM became the highest (0.92) after being evolved. It shows that our self-evolving strategy can make the performance of the classifier comparable to existing systems. Second, existing NIDSes can benefit from our approach. After being evolved, the F1-scores of HAM and SAAE-DNN increases from 0.19 to 0.42 and from 0.77 to 0.86 respectively.

# 6   Related Work

**Network Intrusion Detection Systems for IoT.** KALIS by Midi *et al.* [34] is a self-adapting, knowledge-driven IDS system. It collects knowledge about the network's features autonomously and selects relevant detection techniques. Fu *et al.* [12] designed an IDS that models the steps of a protocol with an automaton. Upon receiving a packet, the automaton corresponding to the packet protocol executes a transition. If there is any deviation in the execution of a protocol, the IDS raises the alarm. DÏoT by Nguyen *et al.* [37] is a federated self-learning anomaly detection system. It builds on device-type-specific communication profiles and raises an alarm upon detecting deviations with respect to these profiles. To capture diverse device-type-specific communication profiles, it uses a federated learning approach for aggregating profiles from large numbers of clients. Unlike the above systems, the focus of IoTEDEF is to identify infection events from an attacker's actions, which is orthogonal to the goals of those systems.

**Multi-step Attack Detection.** Gu *et al.* [15] present BOTHUNTER that detects successful malware infection by tracking communication flows between internal assets and external entities, and applying their dialog-based correlation. Haas and Fischer *et al.* [17] propose GAC, a graph-based approach for correlation. They apply the graph-based clustering algorithm to the alarms to cluster them based on their similarity. Then, each cluster is labeled considering the communications between attackers and victims within the cluster. Finally, the clusters are correlated based on the labels. Sadegh *et al.* [35] suggest HOLMES that models the attacks with a kill chain. From audit logs, they generate a provenance graph, find adversarial activities based on predefined rules, and map the activities to the corresponding kill chain step. Xueyuan *et al.* [19] propose UNICORN that detects the APT attacks by leveraging provenance graphs to detect anomalies with no prior knowledge of the APT attack patterns by using the clustering approach.

Our work differs from those approaches in three aspects: (1) *Goals:* they use correlation algorithms to *automatically detect* multi-step attacks. On the other hand, our approach aims to *automatically identify* the infection vectors and *update* the IDS after seeing anomalies in the action step (or other steps). (2) *Logs:* although one can identify infection windows using their correlation algorithms, such approaches mostly rely on host events (e.g., process-related events). Applying such approaches would require extensions of IoT devices, which we want to avoid. (3) *Used techniques:* the above approaches rely on graphs to analyze the causality between events. Unlike them, IoTEDEF uses the attention mechanism with the neural network to associate the event windows.

**NIDS Based on the Attention Mechanism.** We have discussed HAM [29] and SAAE-DNN [45] in Subsect. 5.6.

# 7    Conclusion

In this paper, we have introduced IoTEDEF, a kill chain-based approach for early detection of persistent attacks against IoT devices. To improve the accuracy of the infection detector, IoTEDEF adopts a feedback strategy that backtracks past events to identify infection events when anomalies at the later steps of a kill chain are detected.

We plan to enhance our approach with host information, such as system calls and CPU/memory and resource usage, and more steps of the cyber kill chain, such as lateral movement and obfuscation, as part of future work.

**Acknowledgement.** The work reported in this paper has been supported by Cisco Research and by NSF under grant 2112471.

# A    Dataset Generation

In our experiment, we use the dataset from [23]. It consists of several files that capture packets related to the Mirai botnet. In detail, it includes the ARP spoofing packets, host discovery packets, or other flooding packets. Among them, we use the following packets in our experiment:

- **Benign:** these packets are normal packets exchanged between benign entities.
- **Port scanning:** these packets are simple SYN packets to scan open ports at a targeted device. These packets are labeled as *Reconnaissance*.
- **Brute force:** these packets are used to perform dictionary attacks with pre-defined credentials to infiltrate into a target device. We label these packets as *Infection*.
- **Flooding:** these packets are SYN/ACK/HTTP/UDP flooding packets to cause a DoS condition to a victim. These packets are tagged as *Action*.

Due to the limited number of datasets, we manipulate the existing dataset to create new diverse scenarios. For example, we want to generate a dataset with a specified number of infection packets at a certain time and a number of UDP flooding packets for a particular time. To this end, we implement a data manipulation script, which works as follows:

1. A new scenario file is created. The starting time of the scenario is 0.
2. A list of files that contain interesting packets is specified with the starting time and the duration. In detail, the list consists of a number of pairs (*<file name>* *<starting time>* *<duration>*), which means that the packets are randomly extracted from *<file name>* and inserted into the new scenario file at time *<starting time>* for *<duration>*. For example, `bruteforce.pcap 10 2` means that the packets from `bruteforce.pcap` are inserted into the new scenario at time 10 for 2 s.
3. All the packets are extracted from the files in the list and put into the new scenario file appropriately. We allow overlaps between different packets.
4. Finally, the IP addresses of the packets are modified to the loopback addresses.

This way, we can flexibly generate a new dataset. The dataset generation script is available at https://github.com/iotedef.

# References

1. Andrea, H.: 10 benefits of internet of things (iot) in our lives and businesses (2021). https://www.tech21century.com/internet-of-things-iot-benefits/. Accessed 13 Sep 2021
2. Antonakakis, M., et al.: Understanding the mirai botnet. In: 26th USENIX Security Symposium (2017)
3. Bahdanau, D., Cho, K., Bengio, Y.: Neural machine translation by jointly learning to align and translate. In: International Conference on Learning Representations (2015)
4. Bertino, E., Islam, N.: Botnets and internet of things security. IEEE Comput. **50**(2), 76–79 (2017)
5. Chaudhari, S., Mithal, V., Polatkan, G., Ramanath, R.: An attentive survey of attention models. ACM Trans. Intell. Syst. Technol. (TIST) **12**(5), 1–32 (2021)

6. Cho, K., Merriënboer, B.V., Bahdanau, D., Bengio, Y.: On the properties of neural machine translation: encoder-decoder approaches (2014)
7. Cole, E.: Threat hunting: Open season on the adversary (2016). https://de.malwarebytes.com/pdf/white-papers/Survey_Threat-Hunting-2016_Malwarebytes.pdf. Accessed 31 Jan 2022
8. CoreSecurity: Pcapy (2014). Accessed 15 Oct 2021
9. Dingee, D.: Iot, not people, now the weakest link in security, January 2019. https://devops.com/iot-not-people-now-the-weakest-link-in-security/. Accessed 13 May 2021
10. Eskandari, M., Janjua, Z.H., Vecchio, M., Antonelli, F.: Passban IDS: an intelligent anomaly-based intrusion detection system for IoT edge devices. IEEE Internet Things J. **7**(8), 6882–6897 (2020)
11. Forney, G.D.: The viterbi algorithm. Proc. IEEE **61**(3), 268–278 (1973)
12. Fu, Y., Yan, Z., Cao, J., Koné, O., Cao, X.: An automata based intrusion detection method for internet of things. Mob. Inf. Syst. **2017**, 1750637:1–1750637:13 (2017)
13. Gartner: Addressing the cyber kill chain: Full gartner research report and looking-glass perspectives (2016). Accessed 06 Mar 2021
14. Glassberg, J.: Jackware: a new type of ransomware could be 10 times as dangerous (2021). https://finance.yahoo.com/news/ransomware-jackware-115229732.html. Accessed 12 June 2021
15. Gu, G., Porras, P.A., Yegneswaran, V., Fong, M.W., Lee, W.: Bothunter: detecting malware infection through ids-driven dialog correlation. In: USENIX Security Symposium, vol. 7, pp. 1–16 (2007)
16. Guo, C., Berkhahn, F.: Entity embeddings of categorical variables. arXiv preprint arXiv:1604.06737 (2016)
17. Haas, S., Fischer, M.: GAC: graph-based alert correlation for the detection of distributed multi-step attacks. In: Proceedings of the 33rd Annual ACM Symposium on Applied Computing, pp. 979–988 (2018)
18. Habibi, J., Midi, D., Mudgerikar, A., Bertino, E.: Heimdall: mitigating the internet of insecure things. IEEE Internet Things J. **4**(4), 968–978 (2017)
19. Han, X., Pasquier, T., Bates, A., Mickens, J., Seltzer, M.: Unicorn: runtime provenance-based detector for advanced persistent threats. In: Proceedings of the Network and Distributed System Security Symposium (NDSS) (2020)
20. Hutchins, E.M., Cloppert, M.J., Amin, R.M., et al.: Intelligence-driven computer network defense informed by analysis of adversary campaigns and intrusion kill chains. Lead. Issues Inf. Warfare Secur. Res. **1**(1), 80 (2011)
21. Jallad, K.A., Aljnidi, M., Desouki, M.S.: Anomaly detection optimization using big data and deep learning to reduce false-positive. J. Big Data **7**(1) (2020)
22. Javed, M., Paxson, V.: Detecting stealthy, distributed SSH brute-forcing. In: Proceedings of the 2013 ACM SIGSAC Conference on Computer & Communications Security, pp. 85–96 (2013)
23. Kang, H., Ahn, D., Lee, G., Yoo, J., Park, K., Kim, H.: Iot network intrusion dataset (2019). https://ieee-dataport.org/open-access/iot-network-intrusion-dataset. Accessed 06 Mar 2021
24. Keras: Keras (2016). https://keras.io/. Accessed 15 Oct 2021
25. Klassen, F.: AppNeta: Tcpreplay (2018). https://tcpreplay.appneta.com/. Accessed 06 Mar 2021
26. Krebs, B.: Reaper: calm before the iot security storm?, October 2017. https://krebsonsecurity.com/2017/10/reaper-calm-before-the-iot-security-storm/. Accessed 05 July 2021

27. Lantz, B., Heller, B., McKeown, N.: A network in a laptop: rapid prototyping for software-defined networks. In: Proceedings of the 9th ACM SIGCOMM Workshop on Hot Topics in Networks, pp. 1–6 (2010)
28. Lashkari, A.H.: Cicflowmeter features (2018). https://github.com/ahlashkari/CICFlowMeter/blob/master/ReadMe.txt. Accessed 19 May 2022
29. Liu, C., Liu, Y., Yan, Y., Wang, J.: An intrusion detection model with hierarchical attention mechanism. IEEE Access **8**, 67542–67554 (2020)
30. Luong, M.T., Pham, H., Manning, C.D.: Effective approaches to attention-based neural machine translation. In: The 2015 Conference on Empirical Methods in Natural Language Processing (EMNLP 2015) (2015)
31. Mannila, H., Toivonen, H., Verkamo, A.I.: Discovery of frequent episodes in event sequences. Data Min. Knowl. Disc. **1**(3), 259–289 (1997)
32. Martin, L.: Seven ways to apply the cyber kill chain with a threat intelligence platform (2015). lockheed martin corporation
33. McMillen, D., Alvarez, M.: Mirai iot botnet: mining for bitcoins?, April 2017. https://securityintelligence.com/mirai-iot-botnet-mining-for-bitcoins/. Accessed 05 July 2021
34. Midi, D., Rullo, A., Mudgerikar, A., Bertino, E.: Kalis-a system for knowledge-driven adaptable intrusion detection for the internet of things. In: 2017 IEEE 37th International Conference on Distributed Computing Systems (ICDCS), pp. 656–666. IEEE (2017)
35. Milajerdi, S.M., Gjomemo, R., Eshete, B., Sekar, R., Venkatakrishnan, V.: Holmes: real-time apt detection through correlation of suspicious information flows. In: 2019 IEEE Symposium on Security and Privacy (S&P), pp. 1137–1152. IEEE (2019)
36. Msehgal: Protect your iot devices from log4j 2 vulnerability (2021). https://live.paloaltonetworks.com/t5/blogs/protect-your-iot-devices-from-log4j-2-vulnerability/ba-p/453381. Accessed 14 Jan 2022
37. Nguyen, T.D., Marchal, S., Miettinen, M., Fereidooni, H., Asokan, N., Sadeghi, A.R.: Dïot: a federated self-learning anomaly detection system for IoT. In: 2019 IEEE 39th International Conference on Distributed Computing Systems (ICDCS), pp. 756–767. IEEE (2019)
38. Osborne, C.: This is why the mozi botnet will linger on (2021). https://www.zdnet.com/article/this-is-why-the-mozi-botnet-will-linger-on/. Accessed 27 Jan 2022
39. Palmer, D.: This sneaky hacking group hid inside networks for 18 months without being detected (2022). https://www.zdnet.com/article/this-sneaky-hacking-group-hid-inside-networks-for-18-months-without-being-detected/. Accessed 18 May 2022
40. Research, C.P.: Iotroop botnet: the full investigation, March 2017. https://research.checkpoint.com/2017/iotroop-botnet-full-investigation/. Accessed 05 July 2021
41. Soleimani, M., Ghorbani, A.A.: Multi-layer episode filtering for the multi-step attack detection. Comput. Commun. **35**(11), 1368–1379 (2012)
42. Sqrrl Data, I.: A framework for cyber threat hunting (2018). https://www.threathunting.net/files/framework-for-threat-hunting-whitepaper.pdf. Accessed 31 Jan 2022
43. Storm, B.E., Applebaum, A., Miller, D.P., Nickels, K.C., Pennington, A.G., Thomas, C.B.: Mitre att&ck: design and philosophy (2018). Accessed 06 Mar 2021
44. Sutskever, I., Vinyals, O., Le, Q.V.: Sequence to sequence learning with neural networks. In: Proceedings of the 27th International Conference on Neural Information Processing Systems, vol. 2, pp. 3104–3112 (2014)
45. Tang, C., Luktarhan, N., Zhao, Y.: SAAE-DNN: deep learning method on intrusion detection. Symmetry **12**(10), 1695 (2020)

# IoTEnsemble: Detection of Botnet Attacks on Internet of Things

Ruoyu Li[1,2], Qing Li[2]($\boxtimes$), Yucheng Huang[1,2], Wenbin Zhang[3], Peican Zhu[4], and Yong Jiang[1,2]

[1] Shenzhen International Graduate School, Tsinghua University, Shenzhen, China
`{liry19,huangyc20}@mails.tsinghua.edu.cn`
`jiangy@sz.tsinghua.edu.cn`
[2] Peng Cheng Laboratory, Shenzhen, China
`liq@pcl.ac.cn`
[3] Xidian University, Xi'an, China
`wbzhang_2@stu.xidian.edu.cn`
[4] Northwestern Polytechnical University, Xi'an, China
`ericcan@nwpu.edu.cn`

**Abstract.** As the Internet of Things (IoT) plays an increasingly important role in real life, the concern about IoT malware and botnet attacks is considerably growing. Meanwhile, with new techniques such as edge computing and artificial intelligence applied to IoT networks, these devices nowadays become more functional than ever before, which challenges many existing network anomaly detection systems due to the lack of generalization ability to profile diverse activities.

To address it, this paper proposes IoTEnsemble, an ensemble network anomaly detection framework. We propose a tree-based activity clustering method that aggregates network flows dedicated to the same activity so that their traffic patterns remain identical. Based on the clustering result, we implement an ensemble model in which each submodel only needs to profile a specific activity, which highly reduces the burden of a single model's generalization ability. For evaluation, we build a 57.1 GB IoT dataset collected in 9 months composed of comprehensive normal and malicious traffic. Our evaluation proves that IoTEnsemble possesses a state-of-the-art detection performance on various IoT botnet malware and attack traffic, exhibiting a significantly better result than other baselines in a more intelligent and functional IoT network.

**Keywords:** Internet of Things · Network anomaly detection · Malware detection · Botnet

---

This work is supported by the National Key Research and Development Project of China under grant No. 2020AAA0107704, National Natural Science Foundation of China under grant No. 61972189 and 62073263, Shenzhen Key Lab of Software Defined Networking under grant No. ZDSYS20140509172959989, and Research Center for Computer Network (Shenzhen) Ministry of Education.

V. Atluri et al. (Eds.): ESORICS 2022, LNCS 13555, pp. 569–588, 2022.
https://doi.org/10.1007/978-3-031-17146-8_28

# 1    Introduction

The number of the Internet of Things (IoT) connections worldwide will reach 5.8 billion by 2029 [5]. Nevertheless, IoT security issues remain severe, such as insecure communications, lack of timely firmware updates, and weak configurations by consumers, which highly increase the risk of being attacked [1].

The network anomaly detection system (NADS) is a promising solution, which learns the pattern of normal traffic and can detect known and unknown attack traffic by deviation from the normality. Since IoT devices are typically low-functional, their traffic is relatively easy to model, and many studies have proposed effective NADS solutions for IoT networks [12,26,28,37].

However, due to emerging technologies applied to IoT networks like edge/fog computing and Artificial Intelligence of Things (AIoT), IoT devices are becoming more functional than ever before [4], and thus the scope of "normal" network activities becomes harder to define. Technically, different activities are far from conforming to an independent identical distribution (i.i.d.), which challenges the fundamental assumption of many algorithms [12,26,31,37]. Besides, the amount and frequency of activities greatly depend on the user's habits, such as a smart camera barely connecting to a command server unless a user opens its app. As a result, a NADS might produce inaccurate results on infrequent functions. These facts are challenging the practicality of existing NADS.

To address them, a conceivable method is to "divide and conquer": instead of building a single comprehensive model, we cluster the traffic for each activity and build multiple fine-grained *submodels* into an *ensemble model*, which reduces the difficulty for one model to learn with a more specific pattern of normality. However, to achieve it, the following challenges should be resolved:

1) **Activity clustering.** Many IoT devices use non-standard domain resolution, dynamic ports or no certificates, possibly making rule-based clustering methods [10,13] unreliable. Besides, statistical clustering like K-Means usually needs a priori like the number of clusters. Too coarse-grained clustering has little significance, while too fine-grained clustering leads to excessive loads.
2) **Heterogeneous IoT traffic.** A variety of network protocols is used for IoT communications, such as HTTP, MQTT, XMPP, CoAP and even many proprietary protocols. This fact invalidates many proposed traffic representation methods since they only focus on specific protocols [10,29,34] or rely on deep packet inspection [38] which is incapable of handling encrypted traffic.
3) **Nontrivial overhead.** Running an ensemble of detection submodels simultaneously might be unrealistic for some deployment positions, such as a home router or a gateway [28,37]. Also, since a NADS aims to treat all incoming traffic suspicious and inspect each traffic flow, the mapping process from a 5-tuple flow to an activity cluster must be efficient to avoid extra processing delay.

Toward this end, this paper proposes IoTEnsemble, which resolves the challenges above by the following design: 1) We propose a tree-based activity clustering algorithm that combines traffic rules and traffic statistics to produce a reliable clustering result. 2) We design a preprocessing pipeline that transforms any raw IP traffic into a data representation that only requires the first few packets of a flow. 3) The clustering tree generates a set of rules that fast maps a 5-tuple flow to an activity and provides a *trigger-action* mechanism for only limited number of submodels being awakened during the execution.

We configure a real-world IoT testbed composed of 28 IoT devices running for 9 months. The experiment shows that IoTEnsemble outperforms the state-of-the-art NADS in the detection of botnet-related attacks. In particular, while other baselines are greatly affected by the increasing activities, IoTEnsemble shows extremely little reduction in effectiveness, which demonstrates its feasibility to secure a more diverse IoT ecosystem in the future.

We summarize our contributions as follows: 1) A reliable and efficient clustering algorithm for device activities; 2) A state-of-the-art NADS that uses an ensemble of autoencoders to profile diverse activities of increasingly functional IoT networks; 3) A real-world IoT testbed with a diversity of devices and activities, contributing a 57.1 GB dataset as a benchmark for IoT networks.[1]

## 2   Related Work

### 2.1   IoT Security, Malware and Botnet

A report in 2016 gives a detailed summary of IoT threats, including vulnerabilities, insecure communications, data leaks, malware, service disruption, persistence of these problems and "disposable" devices [1]. Among these threats, malware is a persistently annoying issue, mainly because IoT devices have relatively weak protections and improper configurations. Mirai, one of the most notorious IoT malware that compromised over 600,000 devices and launched a 620 Gbps DDoS attack in 2016, has been studied by many researchers [6,17]. Its infrastructure includes a report server, a loader server and a command and control (C&C) server. As its source code was somehow released [11], Mirai becomes a paradigm for many variations [3,24,27]. Infected bots can be used for DDoS attacks, scanning, spamming, data leaking or even cryptomining [2].

### 2.2   Network Anomaly Detection System

The network anomaly detection system (NADS) is commonly used against botnet and other network attacks. Bhuyan et al. summarize over 200 related works and categorize NADS into seven classes [9]. Among these classes, many machine learning-based (ML) methods are used, such as KNN, SVM, decision tree and neural network. Recently, the community turns to deep learning (DL) for its great generalization ability [20,25]. Compared to traditional ML, an advantage of DL is to automate the feature extraction from raw traffic to reduce the reliance on feature engineering. Tang et al. propose a seq2seq model to detect zero-day attacks after a web application firewall [33]. However, it can only parse HTTP packets, which is not suitable for heterogeneous IoT traffic. Marín et al. propose

---

[1] Our datasets are made public: https://github.com/HeliosHuang/ESORICS.

a DL-based malware traffic detection method relying on no handcrafted feature engineering but using raw bytes as data representation [23]. Despite achieving high accuracy, it lacks interpretability on encrypted traffic and may cause privacy violations in IoT scenarios. Mirsky et al. propose Kitsune, an unsupervised NADS using an ensemble architecture similar to ours and achieving a state-of-art performance [28], but it does not separate a device's entire activity into multiple specific activities. We will use Kitsune as a baseline in the evaluation to highlight the advantage of IoTEnsemble.

### 2.3   Activity Clustering

Activity clustering is a technique to group the traffic dedicated to the same activity. It can be primarily divided into rule-based methods and statistical methods. Rule-based methods identify the flows with the same or a certain range of domain names [10], destination ports [15] or TLS/SSL certificates [13] as the same activity, which has great interpretability. However, simply matching the rules with IoT traffic may cause unreliable clustering results since many IoT devices are not manufactured to use fixed domains and ports. On the other hand, statistical methods typically use statistical features of traffic along with ML algorithms for clustering, such as packet size and flow rate [14,29]. The disadvantage of these methods includes relatively weak interpretability and unstable validity due to high sensitivity to the fluctuation of the statistical features. Other applications like device identification [22,34] and app fingerprinting [10,13] also use activity clustering techniques, but their design goal is different from ours as they can ignore the commonly used activities between devices or apps and only identifies a small proportion of unique activities for fingerprinting, whereas a NADS needs to handle all traffic efficiently because it treats every flow as a suspicious target.

## 3   Threat Model

In this paper, adversaries are the people who infect and compromise IoT devices as part of a botnet. They are assumed to have the following capabilities: 1) they can infect a device by known or unknown exploits, which means zero-day attacks are possible; 2) they can either be located in the same local area network (LAN) as IoT devices or outside the LAN; 3) after infecting a device, they can command the victim device to take malicious actions, such as data leaking, cryptomining, spamming or attacking other devices and websites.

Our system is positioned inside the same LAN as the IoT devices to be protected. The deployment could be on a home gateway or a computer that is able to sniff all the traffic from and to the IoT devices, including the traffic across the devices inside the LAN, which can be realized by mirroring the traffic through the LAN interface on the home gateway to our system. Besides, we assume that a newly connected device can be simply identified by its DHCP messages and MAC addresses so that the traffic can be separated.

To define a clear scope of this paper, we also make the following assumptions: 1) IoT vendors are not adversaries; in other words, IoT devices are not manufactured initially to be malicious and no backdoors are pre-installed; 2) the malicious activities launched by adversaries leave a trace on L3 network layer. This paper does not consider the attacks on L1 and L2 network layers, such as spoofing attacks on Bluetooth Low Energy (BLE).

# 4 Flow Clustering by Activity

## 4.1 IoT Network

Recent years have witnessed IoT's astonishing promotion in functions, such as AI-based functions like movement detection and face recognition in IP cameras. In addition, many IoT vendors like Samsung SmartThings are building an ecosystem for easy communications between devices. Accordingly, these functions are reflected on the network by a variety of connections.

Although IoT devices are becoming more intelligent, they are still far from general-purpose devices as most of their network communications are pre-set by their vendors. This paper uses the expression *network activity* or simply *activity* referring to a purpose that the network communications are dedicated to.

## 4.2 Design Goal

In this paper, the ultimate purpose of clustering is to group the traffic flows for the same activity so that a submodel can easily learn each activity's normal pattern. Given this purpose and the condition of IoT networks, we list three design goals for the clustering algorithm: 1) It has good interpretability for network administrators to understand; 2) It needs as little prior knowledge as possible, such as what protocols to use or the number of clusters; 3) It has an appropriate granularity with as few numbers of clusters as possible and meanwhile still achieves a reliable clustering validity.

To achieve these goals is not easy. For one thing, most ML-based clustering methods disobey them. For another, rule-based methods usually cannot satisfy the requirement of reliability due to the unstable IoT traffic rules deriving from the use of non-standard domain resolution, dynamic ports, no TLS/SSL authentication and proprietary protocols [15]. To propose a proper method, we firstly give a motivating case about our observations on IoT traffic and activities.

## 4.3 A Motivating Case: TP-Link Camera

We manually traverse the functions of a TP-Link camera and monitor its network activities by Wireshark. By associating the traffic with the triggered functions, we notice seven activities (Table 1) including device status reporting (dev), API call (api), business (biz, related to cloud service), stream relaying (relay), UPnP broadcasting (UPnP), streaming to local apps (local) and request for public IP (STUN) with their traffic characteristics, where $\mathbb{S}_{ps}$ is the set of packet sizes (TLS handshakes in bold) and $\Delta t$ is the mean of packet inter-arrival time in two directions. We present our three observations on these activities:

**Table 1.** Traffic characteristics of seven activities

| Activity | Domain/IP | Protocol (port) | Period | TLS/SSL? | $S_{ps}$ | $\Delta t^{out}$ | $\Delta t^{in}$ |
|---|---|---|---|---|---|---|---|
| dev | n-device-api.; dynamic IP | TCP (50443) | 30 s | ✓ | 153, 37, 52 | 0.25 | 0.042 |
| api | n-devs-ipc | TCP (443) | 3600 s | ✓ | **134**, **873**, **319**, **143**, 457, 329, 121 | 12.59 | 0.12 |
| biz | biz-ipc | TCP (443) | – | ✓ | **122**, **849**, **307**, **131**, 333, 141, 301, 237, 109 | 0.021 | 0.039 |
| relay | n-txc-relay-ipc-nj | TCP (443) | 900 s | ✓ | **122**, **857**, **307**, **131**, 237, 381, 109 | 0.024 | 0.052 |
| UPnP | 255.255.255.255; local IP | UDP (5001) | 20 s | ✗ | 278 | 20.0 | – |
| local | local IP | UDP (dynamic) | – | ✗ | 48, 69, 92, 1476 | 0.15 | 0.15 |
| STUN | dynamic IP | UDP (dynamic) | – | ✗ | 56, 96 | 0.097 | 0.024 |

**Observation 1:** *A device could contain multiple activities that show greatly different traffic patterns.* For example, some of the activities in Table 1 use encryption protocols, which clearly present distinct traffic patterns from the other plaintext traffic. Also, these highly asynchronous activities due to diverse periods result in different patterns of the device traffic in different time. These facts challenge the generalization ability of training a single model to profile the complex characteristics of the mixed traffic by diverse activities.

**Observation 2:** *Rules like domains, protocols and ports are still effective for preliminary clustering but do not always work.* For example, the "dev" activity contacts dynamic IP addresses not in any of its DNS answers (we did power off, reset and reboot the device before the experiment to clear the cached domain resolutions). Some ports like 443 and 5001 are stably used by certain activities, but activities like local streaming and STUN always use random dynamic ports.

**Observation 3:** *The set of packet sizes and inter-arrival time are surprisingly helpful for distinguishing the activities.* In fact, Trimananda et al. have found a similar observation on the packet size of a request-reply packet sequence[34], but it only works for TCP connections. We extend this observation by finding that the request-reply sequence is not necessary – instead, a limited set of packet sizes has identical efficacy, which also works with UDP activities. To the best of our knowledge, it is the first time to find such an easy but effective observation for activity clustering. We explain this observation by two points: 1) TLS provides a stable and differential certificate exchange process (packet size in bold); 2) IoT communications comply with strict data formatting.

We also analyze the traffic from other types of devices such as plugs and speakers and find consistent observations. We attribute these observations to the typically purpose-driven design of IoT devices – though a device may contain a diverse set of functions, each of them is pre-set by the firmware for a specific purpose and hardly changes its traffic patterns. This preliminary analysis suggests a possibility to combine traffic rules with spatial and temporal statistics for reliable activity clustering.

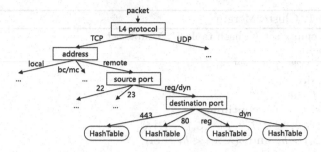

**Fig. 1.** An illustration of the tree-based activity clustering; bc/mc: broadcasting/multicasting; sys: system port (0-1023); reg: registration port (1024-32767 in Linux); dyn: dynamic port (32768-65535 in Linux).

## 4.4   Clustering Method

We present a tree-based clustering method for IoT traffic activity as Fig. 1 illustrates. Given Observation 2, a packet belonging to a bidirectional flow $f :=$ (device-IP, dst-domain/IP, src-port, dst-port, protocol) goes through the four-level hierarchical rules for a preliminary clustering: 1) L4 protocol: protocol is TCP or UDP; 2) address: dst-domain/IP is a specific domain, a remote IP address, a local IP address or a broadcasting/multicasting address; 3) src-port is a specific system port, or in registration/dynamic port range; 4) destination port: dst-port is a specific system port, in registration port range or in dynamic port range.

Note that the use of each system port has an individual tree path as it typically indicates a specific service. Since IoT devices are at the client end, the source port is usually useless for clustering (unless it is a system port like 22 for SSH, 23 for Telnet, etc.) while the destination port in registration range reveals some commonly used IoT services, such as 1900 for SSDP, 3478 for STUN, etc.

At the end of the tree, each leaf node is a hash table in which the key is $f$ and the value is an incremental statistical structure. This structure is defined by a five tuple $IS := (N^{in}, N^{out}, T^{in}, T^{out}, \mathbb{S})$, where $N$ is the number of packets, $T$ is the sum of packet inter-arrival time, $in$ and $out$ indicate the direction, $\mathbb{S}$ is the set of packet sizes. The advantage of $IS$ is its constant storage complexity no matter how many packets a flow has. When a packet with direction $d$, packet size $s$ and inter-arrival time $\Delta t$ arrives at a leaf node, $IS$ is updated by:

$$N^{in} \leftarrow N^{in} + 1 \text{ if } d = in \text{ else } N^{out} \leftarrow N^{out} + 1$$
$$T^{in} \leftarrow T^{in} + \Delta t \text{ if } d = in \text{ else } T^{out} \leftarrow T^{out} + \Delta t \qquad (1)$$
$$\mathbb{S}.add(s)$$

For each leaf node, a more abstract flow rule can be obtained by merging the flows on the leaf node to reduce the final number of clusters. Each two flows $f_1$, $f_2$ with their incremental statistics $IS_1$, $IS_2$ are compared by two aspects:

---

**Algorithm 1.** ClusterMerging

---

    **Input**: An empty set $K$, hash table $H$, 5-tuple set $L$

1   $f \leftarrow L.Pop()$;

2   $IS := (N^{in}, N^{out}, T^{in}, T^{out}, \mathbb{S}) \leftarrow H[f]$;

3   **for** $f_i$ in $L$ **do**

4      **if** $f_i \subseteq f$ **then**

5         |   $L.remove(f_i)$; **continue**;

6      $IS_i := (N_i^{in}, N_i^{out}, T_i^{in}, T_i^{out}, \mathbb{S}_i) \leftarrow H[f_i]$;

7      **if** $J(\mathbb{S}, \mathbb{S}_i) > h_s$ **and** $b(\lambda, \lambda_i) < h_t$ **then**

8         |   $L.remove(f_i)$; $f \leftarrow merge(f, f_i)$;

9   **end for**

10   $K.add(f)$;

11   ClusterMerging($K$, $H$, $L$);

---

**Spatial Correlation.** $\mathbb{S}_1$, $\mathbb{S}_2$ are compared by the Jaccard index: $J(\mathbb{S}_1, \mathbb{S}_2) = \frac{|\mathbb{S}_1 \cap \mathbb{S}_2|}{|\mathbb{S}_1 \cup \mathbb{S}_2|}$. If the result surpasses a threshold $h_s$, $f_1$ and $f_2$ are believed to be spatially correlated.

**Temporal Correlation.** Packet inter-arrival time is typically modelled by a Poisson process [7], which conforms to an exponential distribution $f(t) = \lambda e^{-\lambda t}$. By a set of observations $t_1, t_2, ..., t_N$, parameter $\lambda$ can be calculated by maximum likelihood estimation: $\lambda = \frac{N}{T}$. The theoretical derivation of the estimation is in Appendix A. Accordingly, $\lambda_1$ and $\lambda_2$ can be derived from $IS_1$ and $IS_2$ to determine their distributions. We separately calculate the difference between two parameters for two directions: $b(\lambda_1, \lambda_2) = \frac{|\lambda_1 - \lambda_2|}{max(\lambda_1, \lambda_2)}$. If any of the results is below a threshold $h_t$, $f_1$ and $f_2$ are believed to be temporally correlated.

For each hash table $H$ at a leaf node and the set of its 5-tuple keys $L$, we use a greedy strategy to compare and merge the flow rules as Algorithm 1 describes. In line 8, if two flows are correlated, they are merged into a new five tuple where the new address and port will be their path name in the clustering tree (e.g., "local", "reg/dyn", "dyn"). If the merged destination domains have a common secondary-level domain, the new address will use a wildcard (e.g., *.tplink.com). The symbol of subset in line 4 means that $f$ has a more abstract expression that contains $f_i$ (e.g., src-port is 29983 in $f_i$ and "reg/dyn" in $f$). This algorithm is recursive that has an average complexity of $O(n\log n)$. By using the Depth-First-Search (DFS) on the entire tree, the tuple sets on each leaf node are finally merged into a single set $K$. We call the tuples in this set *activity keys* as each of them indicates a rule for one activity. The next section presents the use of activity keys for the construction of our framework.

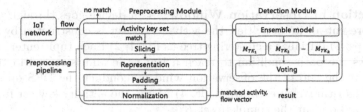

**Fig. 2.** An overview of IoTEnsemble's architecture.

## 5 IoTEnsemble Design

### 5.1 Overview

IoTEnsemble is an anomaly detection framework designed for current increasingly intelligent and functional IoT networks. Generally, it is a combination of two detection stages:

**Rule matching** by activity keys that efficiently filters out the extremely anomalous traffic flows with unknown domain, address or port range.

**Ensemble model** that learns each activity and detects anomalies by the deviation from the normal traffic pattern.

Figure 2 illustrates IoTEnsemble's overview. The preprocessing module firstly handles the IoT network traffic and matches 5-tuple flows to activity keys. Subsequently, it processes the first $r$ packets of each flow into a numerical data representation, where $r$ is the fixed length of a packet window. The detection module is composed of multiple submodels that profile one activity respectively. It follows a *trigger-action* mechanism which only awakens the submodels with similar activities to the flow for the inspection, and the final detection result is voted only by the awakened submodels. Compared to the basic ensemble architecture, this mechanism reduces the overhead of multiple submodels' simultaneous execution. Since IoTEnsemble is neither privacy-intrusive nor protocol-specific, it is trusty and practical for wide usage scenarios. For example, the preprocessing module can be deployed on a home router and the detection module can be executed on a router, a personal computer or an edge server.

IoTEnsemble has two phases during the operation. The *learning phase* starts with a new device joining the network and assumes that it will not be compromised in an initial time window (e.g., one or two hours). During this period, IoTEnsemble generates the activity key set and trains an ensemble model using the observed network traffic. Then the framework enters the *detection phase* in which the internal parameters of IoTEnsemble are fixed for inference. We discuss how each component works in greater detail in the following subsections.

### 5.2 Preprocessing Module

**Activity Key Set.** As assumed in Sect. 3, all traffic is considered benign during an initial observation window. Hence, we generate an activity key set and use this set as a profile of normal activities for rule matching.

**Construction in Observation Window:** As a device goes through its functions to present all its activities, the activity key set is constructed by the following steps: 1) Initialize a clustering tree as Fig. 1; 2) Each tuple enters the tree and follows the path condition to reach a leaf node and is stored in the hash table; 3) At the end of the observation window, conduct the DFS on the tree and run Algorithm 1 on each leaf node; 4) Merge the activity key set from each leaf node and output the complete set $K$.

**Utilization in Detection Phase:** An incoming 5-tuple flow is mapped to activity keys, which is simply a matching process with at most $O(n)$ complexity and is practical for online use. Given the abstract address and port range indicators in an activity key (e.g., wildcard domains, "local", "reg/dyn", etc.), it is a relaxed matching process and may result in multiple matches, which gives a chance of further inspection to every possible activity key to reduce false positives. However, if a flow cannot match any of the activity keys, it will be directly labeled as malicious traffic.

**Preprocessing Pipeline.** A traffic flow that matches activity keys will enter the second detection stage by the ensemble model. To make a network flow processible by an ML model, a preprocessing pipeline is built to convert a flow of packets into a numerical vector. Formally, given a flow $f$ and its packets by an ordered list $\mathbf{p}_f = [p_1, p_2, ..., p_l]$, it follows a pipeline of functions $\{\mathcal{S}(Slicing), \mathcal{R}(Representation), \mathcal{P}(Padding), \mathcal{N}(Normalization)\}$ to generate a representation that describes the underlying characteristics of the flow.

**Slicing:** Some IoT flows last extremely long or even never end, such as keepalive traffic with the server. To deal with this, we use a time window to slice a flow into multiple small flows with equal intervals. We set two time windows separately for TCP and UDP denoted by $t_T$ and $t_U$.

**Representation:** The data representation derives from the sequential relationship of IP packet size and inter-arrival time between packets in a flow. It is motivated by the characteristics of botnets that generate sequential small packets when searching for susceptible hosts and follow a uniform pattern throughout C&C life-cycle to reduce their observability on the network [36]. Packet size and inter-arrival time form two ordered lists that only preserve the first $r$ packets. Based on our preliminary experiment, the first 100 packets have sufficed an effective representation for the entire flow.

**Padding:** A list with less than $r$ items is zero-padded to satisfy a fixed-length input for an ML algorithm. Another use of padding is to reveal the length of a flow – a long flow has more values in a list compared to short flows.

**Normalization:** We adopt the L2 norm to make each value in a list between 0 and 1 and stack two lists into a two-dimensional sequential data sample.

### 5.3    Anomaly Detection Module

**Ensemble Architecture.** Figure 3 illustrates the overall architecture, which is a combination of multiple unsupervised learning submodels that learn normal activity's traffic pattern. The advantages of using an unsupervised learning algorithm include 1) no need for malicious traffic data for training; 2) the capability of discovering zero-day attacks. We believe that such an ensemble architecture is a good solution to an increasingly functional IoT network given a submodel only learns a specific activity which better conforms to an i.i.d.

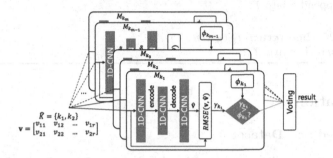

**Fig. 3.** An illustration of our ensemble model; only the submodels with matched activity keys engage in the execution.

A submodel is constructed by a one-dimensional Convolutional Neural Network autoencoder (1D-CNN AE) [18]. It is an unsupervised model that brings CNN's invariant feature extraction to sequential data. It learns the latent distribution of the training data and adjusts its parameters to minimize the reconstruction error between the input and output measured by root mean squared error (RMSE). In the detection phase, a data sample inconsistent with the learned distribution produces a higher reconstruction error and thus can be detected.

**Learning Phase.** The training of an ensemble model starts by the end of the construction of activity key set $K$. A device's network flows processed by the pipeline $\{\mathcal{S}, \mathcal{R}, \mathcal{P}, \mathcal{N}\}$ compose the training dataset denoted by $\mathbf{X} = \{\mathbf{X}_{k_1}, \mathbf{X}_{k_2}, ..., \mathbf{X}_{k_m}\}$, where $\mathbf{X}_{k_i}$ represents the traffic data belonging to the activity with activity key $k_i$. Each dataset is then split into a training subset for training a submodel's parameter $\theta$ and a validation subset for the determination of a hyperparameter $\phi$, i.e., the threshold of RMSE. It is determined by a quantile of order $q$, which can also be interpreted as the setting of true negative rate (TNR) on the validation subset. Finally, an ensemble model $\mathbf{M}$ can be described as a set of submodels: $\mathbf{M} = \{M_{k_1}, M_{k_2}, ..., M_{k_m}\}$ where $M_{k_i} = \{\theta_{k_i}, \phi_{k_i}\}, m = |K|$.

**Detection Phase.** When a flow passes the rule matching, the matched activity key set $\hat{K}$ awakens the corresponding submodels in $\mathbf{M}$ and each of them parallelly inspects the feature vector $\mathbf{v}$ by comparing the reconstruction error to its threshold, which is called the *trigger-action* mechanism. A flow is judged as normal if any of the awakened submodels claims it is normal. The process of detection phase is described by Algorithm 2.

---

**Algorithm 2:** Ensemble Model Detection

---

**Input:** Ensemble model $\mathbf{M}$, feature vector $\mathbf{v}$, matched activity key set $\hat{K}$
**Output:** Detection result and failed activity key set $\varUpsilon$
1 Initialize an empty set $\varUpsilon$;
2 **for** $k$ **in** $\hat{K}$ **do**
3      Awaken submodel $M_k = \{\theta, \phi\}$ from $\mathbf{M}$;
4      $\hat{\mathbf{v}} \leftarrow h_\theta(\mathbf{v})$;
5      $\gamma \leftarrow RMSE(\mathbf{v}, \hat{\mathbf{v}})$;
6      **if** $\gamma > \phi$ **then**
7          | Append $k$ into $\varUpsilon$;
8 **end for**
9 **if** $|\varUpsilon| < |\hat{K}|$ **then return** (Negative, $\varUpsilon$);
10 **else return** (Positive, $\varUpsilon$);

---

# 6 Evaluation

## 6.1 Testbed and Dataset

To demonstrate a realistic and functional IoT network, we set up a real-world testbed consisting of 28 popular IoT devices that cover most mainstream IoT vendors in China and diverse device types. We basically categorize them into *camera, sound box, gateway* and *appliance*. Figure 4 illustrates the network topology of our testbed. To present each device's activity, we consider both manual and automated interaction as follows: 1) we explore each device's functions by instructions and app UI and make a list of functions for our researchers to trigger at least once a day, such as pressing physical buttons, walking before a camera or talking to a sound box; besides, the testbed is located in a public location for free use; 2) we configure a laptop with Android Debug Bridge (ADB) and an emulator installed with 19 apps for all devices, and run a Python script to trigger their functions by app and voice commands (to four sound boxes) at regular intervals; for example, a smart camera is requested for streaming or a sound box plays a song at 2pm every day. This testbed has been run for 9 months and contributed over 57 GB data. Given that IoTEnsemble does not require a large amount of data for training, we use the data of the first week for training and the rest for testing. We also use two benchmark datasets: one from UNSW collected in a lab environment [32] and one from NEU collected in an idle status of IoT devices [30]. As synthesized without heterogeneous activities, they are used to compare the performance between functional and low-functional IoT networks.

We make two Raspberry Pi boards infected by IoT malware (Mirai, BASH-LITE [11]) and a C&C server (in WAN) for malware traffic collection. We modify the packet header information like IP address to make it consistent with the IoT devices. We also replay some public IoT botnet attack datasets as supplementary [2,8,19]. All traffic is collected by a computer via port mirroring by the router, making it a comprehensive IoT traffic dataset for evaluation.

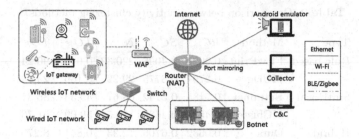

**Fig. 4.** Network topology of our testbed

## 6.2 Metrics

The detection performance of an IDS is typically evaluated by true positives $(TP)$, true negatives $(TN)$, false positives $(FP)$, false negatives $(FN)$ and their tradeoff. In our evaluations, we fix the true negative rate $(TNR = \frac{TN}{TN+FP})$ by adjusting the threshold $\phi$ and measure the true positive rate $(TPR = \frac{TP}{TP+FN})$. For our framework, each sample in the dataset is considered benign only if it passes the inspection of both the detection stages.

The validity of activity clustering, however, is harder to evaluate as the target of clustering is more subjective and therefore it lacks a general metric [16]. For a fair and comprehensive comparison with both previous rule-based methods and statistical methods, we propose a network-specific metric called *cohesion index*, which is the mean of the standard deviation of the distance between every two 5-tuple flows within each cluster. It is further divided into *rule cohesion* $(RC)$ and *statistical cohesion* $(SC)$. In $RC$, the distance is measured by the header information: 1) add 1 if two destination IP addresses are not in the same range (i.e., local, external, multicasting); 2) add 1 if two ports are not in the same range (i.e., system port, register port, dynamic port); 3) add 1 if two L4 protocols are different (i.e., TCP, UDP, ICMP). In $SC$, the distance is measured by the vector distance composed of five commonly used statistical features for traffic profiling (mean and variance of packet size, mean and variance of inter-arrival time, inbound/outbound ratio). We also include the number of clusters $(N_c)$ in the metrics. To present the tradeoff between the cluster number and the validity, which is one of our design goals, we multiple the two cohesion indexes (after normalization) and the cluster number to form $TO_R$ and $TO_S$. A method with smaller cohesion and tradeoff indexes is better for our design goal.

## 6.3 Validity of Activity Clustering

Firstly, our method clearly satisfies the first two goals because: 1) it generates a set of rules by the tree paths with good interpretability; 2) it does not assume any prior knowledge about the traffic. As for the third goal, we compare our method with four baselines, including two rule-based methods: 1) FlowPrint [13] that uses destination and port numbers along with TLS certificates for clustering;

**Table 2.** Comparison between activity clustering methods.

| Type | Method | $RC$ | $SC$ | $N_c$ | $TO_R$ | $TO_S$ |
|------|--------|------|------|-------|--------|--------|
| Rule-based | FlowPrint | 0.0029 | 0.4096 | 220.33 | 0.6407 | 90.24 |
| | MUDgee | 0.2791 | 0.8775 | 29.22 | 8.156 | 25.64 |
| Statistical | Botminer | 0.7185 | 0.5142 | 68.67 | 49.34 | 35.31 |
| | MCluster | 0.4531 | 0.4682 | 110.56 | 50.09 | 51.76 |
| Hybrid | Ours | 0.0682 | 0.6706 | 12.33 | 0.8414 | 8.270 |

2) MUDgee [15] that uses the rules upon the YANG model (RFC 6020) to separate network activities; and two statistical methods: 3) Botminer [14], a two-stage clustering framework using X-Means; 4) MCluster [29], a network-level behavioral clustering system for malware detection.

We use a one-week dataset of normal device traffic for the evaluation. Table 2 shows the result. It can be seen that the rule-based methods have lower $RC$ and higher $SC$, and vice versa for the statistical methods, which is in line with their design. Besides, we notice that the methods with the lowest $RC$ (FlowPrint) and the lowest $SC$ (MCluster) result in a great number of clusters. It is reasonable since more fine-grained clustering generally owns better cohesion inside each cluster, while it does not accord with our design goal to reduce the overhead of cluster numbers. Note that a high $RC$ suggests the possibility of obviously wrong clustering, such as treating a TCP flow and a UDP flow as the same activity just because they are coincidentally similar in statistics. In contrast, our method combines both of the advantages, using heuristic rules for preliminary clustering and statistics for cluster merging, which demonstrates a better tradeoff between the validity and the number of clusters. It proves that our method outperforms previous works in the case of our design goal.

We also measure the observation window for a device to present all its activities. Before the experiment, we power off the devices and reset them to make sure the cached configurations are cleared. The manual interaction and automated interaction methods mentioned above are separately adopted to traverse the device's activities. It shows that the average time of exhibiting all activities by manual use is 20 days, whereas the average time of exhibiting all activities by our automated script is only 100 min. It implies that the activity key set can be reliably generated only within one or two hours after the connection, which is practical for real use. The full result can be found in Appendix B.

### 6.4   Overall Performance

We train IoTEnsemble and evaluate its detection performance on four categories of attacks: C&C, DDoS, Scan and Leakage. We empirically set $h_s$ and $h_t$ to 0.4 and 0.5, resulting in a stable number of clusters. The time window for both UDP and TCP flows is set to 30 s. The sequence length $r$ is 100. For each submodel, the total amount of trainable parameters is 10530. We set two

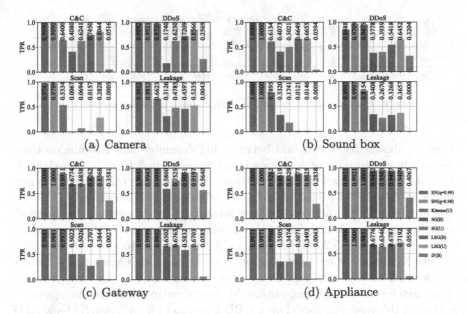

**Fig. 5.** Detection performance of IoTEnsemble ($q = 0.99$ and $q = 0.98$) and five baselines on four categories of attacks.

thresholds: $q = 0.99$ and $q = 0.98$, which means the FPR is set to be 0.01 and 0.02 on the validation dataset. To demonstrate the advantage of IoTEnsemble over a single model's architecture, six unsupervised baseline NADS are used: 1) Kitsune [28], a state-of-the-art unsupervised NADS using an ensemble model of multiple autoencoders; 2) *SG(U)*, a single 1D-CNN AE model identical to the submodel in IoTEnsemble trained without balanced data from different activities (unbalanced training); 3) *SG(B)* a single model identical to *SG(U)* trained with balanced data from different activities by oversampling (balanced training); 4) *LSG(U)*, a large single 1D-CNN AE model with approximately 16 times trainable parameters as *SG(U)* by unbalanced training; 5) a large single model identical to *LSG(U)* by balanced training; 6) *IF(B)* [21], an isolation forest by balanced training. The threshold of the baselines is uniformly set by an FPR of 0.02.

Figure 5 illustrates the experiment result. Detailed results of each device are in Appendix B. It shows that IoTEnsemble outperforms Kitsune and other baselines in all four attacks, suggesting that IoTEnsemble achieves a state-of-the-art detection performance. We attribute the advantage to our reliable activity clustering that makes the pattern of traffic better conform to an i.i.d. Besides, *LSG* exhibits insignificant superiority over *SG* compared to the large difference between their scales, showing that a single model's generalization ability is challenged by the variety of activities. Another finding is that all baselines including Kitsune exhibit worse detection performance on complex devices like cameras and sound boxes, while IoTEnsemble shows little difference.

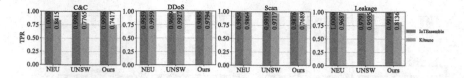

**Fig. 6.** Comparison of detection performance on three datasets.

Figure 6 shows the comparison between IoTEnsemble and Kitsune on three datasets, whose diversity of activities is getting enriched from left to right. It again proves that the variety of device functionality apparently affects the performance of Kitsune and meanwhile barely influences IoTEnsemble.

We highlight IoTEnsemble's runtime advantage by its average 2.1 submodels simultaneously awakened during the execution (camera: 1.7/11.3, sound box: 3.9/12.7, gateway: 1.4/5.2, appliance: 1.4/5.7). Compared to a normal ensemble model like Kitsune that has over 20 submodels for parallel inference, IoTEnsemble is more efficient thanks to the trigger-action mechanism that only awakens the best match submodels for execution. Moreover, we measure the average inference time of the ensemble model on a CPU computer (Intel Xeon(R) Gold 5117 @ 2.00 GHz with one single core used), resulting in about 244.59 µs, which is extremely trivial compared to the time window of a sliced flow (30 s).

## 6.5   Discussion

**Possible Attacks.** It is possible that malware bypasses the first detection stage by disguising the C&C channel as a normal service like HTTP. To assess its impact, we modify half of the C&C traffic of four malware by encapsulation with HTTP headers and ports. We choose part of the devices that normally use HTTP traffic as victims so that the disguised C&C traffic can bypass their rules. As Table 3 shows, even if they evade the first detection stage, most malware traffic can still be detected by the second detection stage, which presents the robustness of IoTEnsemble. As for evasive attacks [35], given the trigger-action mechanism, it is difficult to find a perturbation for a dynamic combination of submodels while maintain the malicious function. IoTEnsemble may be susceptible to *poisoning attacks* that spoil the training data. However, it is not easy for an adversary to compromise a device so fast considering our short observation window, and afterwards most of the poisoning traffic can be easily filtered out.

**Limitations.** One limitation of IoTEnsemble is the false positive caused by normal but unseen activities, which is also an inherent drawback of unsupervised learning-based methods. Nevertheless, as we have shown in the experiment, a deliberately designed script can reduce the trigger time of complete device activities from days to minutes, which suggests a trivial probability of missing learning from existing activities. Meanwhile, we believe that this limitation can be more highlighted when new functions are induced by IoT firmware/software updates.

**Table 3.** Detection on modified malware that bypasses the first detection stage.

| Malware | Camera | Soundbox | Gateway | Appliance |
|---------|--------|----------|---------|-----------|
| Aidra | 0.647 | 0.873 | 0.987 | 0.873 |
| BASHLITE | 0.958 | 1.00 | 1.00 | 1.00 |
| Mirai | 1.00 | 0.985 | 0.596 | 0.985 |
| Xbash | 1.00 | 1.00 | 1.00 | 1.00 |

To address it, a solution is to add a feedback function to IoTEnsemble by developing a controller app on the cellphone or the PC. An unseen activity is reported to the app for a manual decision from the administrator, so that a corresponding rule can be added to the first detection stage of IoTEnsemble to avoid the same false positives. We consider the development of this function as part of our future work.

## 7   Conclusion and Future Work

This paper presents IoTEnsemble, an anomaly detection framework against IoT botnet attacks. It is designed to accommodate current increasingly functional IoT devices with a variety of activities. It contains a two-stage detection process of rule matching by a tree-based clustering algorithm and an ensemble model. We set up a real-world testbed to generate a dataset that reveals the diversity of IoT activities. The experiment result shows that, no matter how many activities an IoT network exhibits, IoTEnsemble obtains a state-of-the-art performance on botnet attacks. Our future work is to design and implement a plug-and-play programmable home router that secures an IoT network based on IoTEnsemble. To fulfill this goal, we are trying to transform IoTEnsemble into a more lightweight model that consumes fewer resources while still maintains its effectiveness.

## A   Maximum Likelihood Estimation

Suppose $N$ observations of packet inter-arrival time $t_1, t_2, ..., t_N$ that conform to an exponential distribution $f(t) = \lambda e^{-\lambda t}$ are sampled. $T$ represents the sum of each observation, i.e., $T = \sum_{i=1}^{N} t_i$. The maximum likelihood estimation of the parameter $\lambda$ is derived as follow:

$$\lambda = \arg\max_{\lambda} \prod_{i=1}^{N} \lambda e^{-\lambda t_i} = \arg\max_{\lambda} \sum_{i=1}^{N} \ln \lambda e^{-\lambda t_i}$$

$$= \arg\max_{\lambda} N \ln \lambda - \sum_{i=1}^{N} \lambda t_i$$

$$= \frac{N}{\sum_{i=1}^{N} t_i} = \frac{N}{T}$$

## B    Complete Dataset Information and Evaluation Result

See Table 4.

**Table 4.** Complete experimental result of each device in the testbed; $N_c$ is the number of activity clusters; $t_0$ and $t_1$ are required time to observe all activities of a device by manual use and automated script; the last 8 devices are not IP-enabled and they are connected to the corresponding gateways.

| Device | Size | $N_c$ | $t_0$ | $t_1$ | C&C | DDoS | Scan | Leakage | C&C | DDoS | Scan | Leakage |
|---|---|---|---|---|---|---|---|---|---|---|---|---|
| | | | (day) | (min) | $q = 0.99$ | | | | $q = 0.98$ | | | |
| 360-camera | 4.7 GB | 13 | 6 | 150 | 1.0 | 1.0 | 0.992 | 1.0 | 1.0 | 1.0 | 0.992 | 1.0 |
| 360-doorbell | 6.5 GB | 17 | 6 | 100 | 1.0 | 0.956 | 1.0 | 1.0 | 1.0 | 0.976 | 1.0 | 1.0 |
| EZVIZ-camera | 2.9 GB | 14 | 5 | 50 | 1.0 | 0.998 | 0.958 | 0.999 | 1.0 | 1.0 | 0.958 | 0.999 |
| Hichip-camera | 320 MB | 7 | 1 | 50 | 1.0 | 0.973 | 0.998 | 0.835 | 1.0 | 0.976 | 1.0 | 0.835 |
| Mercury-camera | 2.5 GB | 13 | 13 | 100 | 0.993 | 1.0 | 0.992 | 1.0 | 0.993 | 1.0 | 0.992 | 1.0 |
| Philips-camera | 7.0 GB | 6 | 2 | 80 | 1.0 | 1.0 | 0.951 | 1.0 | 1.0 | 1.0 | 0.951 | 1.0 |
| Skyworth-camera | 1.2 GB | 7 | 6 | 100 | 0.998 | 1.0 | 0.942 | 0.997 | 0.998 | 1.0 | 0.994 | 0.997 |
| TPLink-camera | 3.8 GB | 11 | 9 | 100 | 1.0 | 1.0 | 1.0 | 1.0 | 1.0 | 1.0 | 1.0 | 1.0 |
| Xiaomi-camera | 4.7 GB | 14 | 13 | 120 | 1.0 | 0.976 | 0.933 | 1.0 | 1.0 | 0.976 | 0.933 | 1.0 |
| Biu-speaker | 3.4 GB | 6 | 5 | 240 | 1.0 | 0.999 | 1.0 | 1.0 | 1.0 | 1.0 | 1.0 | 1.0 |
| Xiaomi-soundbox | 9.5 GB | 23 | 7 | 390 | 1.0 | 0.913 | 1.0 | 0.999 | 1.0 | 0.927 | 1.0 | 0.999 |
| Xiaodu-audio | 7.7 GB | 9 | 3 | 280 | 1.0 | 0.635 | 1.0 | 1.0 | 1.0 | 0.986 | 1.0 | 1.0 |
| Aqara-gateway | 366 MB | 5 | 7 | 30 | 1.0 | 0.962 | 0.941 | 1.0 | 1.0 | 0.995 | 0.941 | 1.0 |
| Gree-gateway | 242 MB | 5 | 1 | 30 | 1.0 | 1.0 | 1.0 | 1.0 | 1.0 | 1.0 | 1.0 | 1.0 |
| TCL-gateway | 903 MB | 4 | 1 | 30 | 1.0 | 1.0 | 1.0 | 1.0 | 1.0 | 1.0 | 1.0 | 1.0 |
| iHORN-gateway | 241 MB | 3 | 1 | 20 | 1.0 | 1.0 | 1.0 | 0.999 | 1.0 | 1.0 | 1.0 | 0.999 |
| Xiaomi-gateway | 594 MB | 9 | 3 | 40 | 1.0 | 0.960 | 1.0 | 1.0 | 1.0 | 0.976 | 1.0 | 1.0 |
| HONYAR-strip | 211 MB | 5 | 1 | 40 | 1.0 | 1.0 | 0.991 | 1.0 | 1.0 | 1.0 | 0.991 | 1.0 |
| WiZ-LED | 221 MB | 5 | 3 | 20 | 1.0 | 0.976 | 1.0 | 1.0 | 1.0 | 0.976 | 1.0 | 1.0 |
| Xiaomi-plug | 208 MB | 7 | 5 | 30 | 1.0 | 1.0 | 1.0 | 1.0 | 1.0 | 1.0 | 1.0 | 1.0 |
| iHorn-temperature | \ | \ | \ | \ | \ | \ | \ | \ | \ | \ | \ | \ |
| iHorn-door sensor | \ | \ | \ | \ | \ | \ | \ | \ | \ | \ | \ | \ |
| iHorn-body sensor | \ | \ | \ | \ | \ | \ | \ | \ | \ | \ | \ | \ |
| Xiaomi-light sensor | \ | \ | \ | \ | \ | \ | \ | \ | \ | \ | \ | \ |
| Xiaomi-temperature | \ | \ | \ | \ | \ | \ | \ | \ | \ | \ | \ | \ |
| Xiaodu-doorbell | \ | \ | \ | \ | \ | \ | \ | \ | \ | \ | \ | \ |
| Aqara-water sensor | \ | \ | \ | \ | \ | \ | \ | \ | \ | \ | \ | \ |
| TCL-body sensor | \ | \ | \ | \ | \ | \ | \ | \ | \ | \ | \ | \ |

## References

1. Internet of things security and privacy recommendations (2016). http://www.bitag.org/documents/BITAG_Report_-_Internet_of_Things_(IoT)_Security_and_Privacy_Recommendations.pdf (2016)
2. IoT malware dataset (2018). https://www.stratosphereips.org/datasets-iot
3. The ransomware tsunami (2019). https://www.pandasecurity.com/en/mediacenter/security/2019-the-ransomware-tsunami/
4. AIoT (2020). http://report.iresearch.cn/report_pdf.aspx?id=3529

5. IoT forecast: connections, revenue and technology trends 2020–2029 (2021). https://www.analysys.com/research/content/regional-forecasts-/iot-worldwide-forecast-rdme0

6. Antonakakis, M., et al.: Understanding the Mirai botnet. In: 26th USENIX Security Symposium, USENIX Security (2017)

7. Bertsekas, D.P., Gallager, R.G.: Data Networks. Prentice Hall, Hoboken (1992)

8. Bezerra, V., Turrisi da Costa, V., Martins, R., Barbon, S., Miani, R., Bogaz Zarpelo, B.: Providing IoT host-based datasets for intrusion detection research. In: Simpósio Brasileiro em Seguran ça da Informa ção e de Sistemas Computacionais (SBSeg) (2018)

9. Bhuyan, M.H., Bhattacharyya, D.K., Kalita, J.K.: Network anomaly detection: methods, systems and tools. IEEE Commun. Surv. Tutorials **16**(1), 303–336 (2014)

10. Dai, S., Tongaonkar, A., Wang, X., Nucci, A., Song, D.: NetworkProfiler: towards automatic fingerprinting of Android apps. In: Proceedings of the IEEE INFOCOM (2013)

11. Ding, F.: IoT malware (2017). https://github.com/ifding/iot-malware

12. Doshi, R., Apthorpe, N.J., Feamster, N.: Machine learning DDoS detection for consumer Internet of Things devices. In: 2018 IEEE Security and Privacy Workshops, SP Workshops (2018)

13. van Ede, T., et al.: FlowPrint: semi-supervised mobile-app fingerprinting on encrypted network traffic. In: 27th Annual Network and Distributed System Security Symposium, NDSS (2020)

14. Gu, G., Perdisci, R., Zhang, J., Lee, W.: BotMiner: clustering analysis of network traffic for protocol- and structure-independent botnet detection. In: Proceedings of the 17th USENIX Security Symposium (2008)

15. Hamza, A., Ranathunga, D., Gharakheili, H.H., Roughan, M., Sivaraman, V.: Clear as MUD: generating, validating and applying IoT behavioral profiles. In: Proceedings of the 2018 Workshop on IoT Security and Privacy, IoT S&P@SIGCOMM (2018)

16. Jain, A.K., Dubes, R.C.: Algorithms for Clustering Data. Prentice-Hall, Hoboken (1988)

17. Kambourakis, G., Kolias, C., Stavrou, A.: The Mirai botnet and the IoT zombie armies. In: 2017 IEEE Military Communications Conference, MILCOM (2017)

18. Kiranyaz, S., Avci, O., Abdeljaber, O., Ince, T., Gabbouj, M., Inman, D.J.: 1D convolutional neural networks and applications: a survey. CoRR (2019)

19. Koroniotis, N., Moustafa, N., Sitnikova, E., Turnbull, B.: Towards the development of realistic botnet dataset in the Internet of Things for network forensic analytics: Bot-IoT dataset. Future Gener. Comput. Syst. **100**, 779–796 (2019)

20. Li, R., Li, Q., Zhou, J., Jiang, Y.: ADRIoT: an edge-assisted anomaly detection framework against IoT-based network attacks. IEEE Internet Things J. **9**(13), 10576–10587 (2022)

21. Liu, F.T., Ting, K.M., Zhou, Z.: Isolation forest. In: Proceedings of the 8th IEEE International Conference on Data Mining (ICDM) (2008)

22. Ma, X., Qu, J., Li, J., Lui, J.C.S., Li, Z., Guan, X.: Pinpointing hidden IoT devices via spatial-temporal traffic fingerprinting. In: 39th IEEE Conference on Computer Communications, INFOCOM (2020)

23. Marín, G., Casas, P., Capdehourat, G.: Deep in the dark - deep learning-based malware traffic detection without expert knowledge. In: 2019 IEEE Security and Privacy Workshops, SP Workshops (2019)

24. Marzano, A., et al.: The evolution of Bashlite and Mirai IoT botnets. In: 2018 IEEE Symposium on Computers and Communications, ISCC (2018)

25. McDermott, C.D., Majdani, F., Petrovski, A.: Botnet detection in the internet of things using deep learning approaches. In: 2018 International Joint Conference on Neural Networks, IJCNN (2018)

26. Miettinen, M., Marchal, S., Hafeez, I., Asokan, N., Sadeghi, A., Tarkoma, S.: IoT SENTINEL: automated device-type identification for security enforcement in IoT. In: 37th IEEE International Conference on Distributed Computing Systems, ICDCS (2017)

27. Mimoso, M.: New IoT botnet malware borrows from Mirai (2016). https://threatpost.com/new-iot-botnet-malware-borrows-from-mirai/121705

28. Mirsky, Y., Doitshman, T., Elovici, Y., Shabtai, A.: Kitsune: an ensemble of autoencoders for online network intrusion detection. In: 25th Annual Network and Distributed System Security Symposium, NDSS (2018)

29. Perdisci, R., Lee, W., Feamster, N.: Behavioral clustering of http-based malware and signature generation using malicious network traces. In: Proceedings of the 7th USENIX Symposium on Networked Systems Design and Implementation, NSDI (2010)

30. Ren, J., Dubois, D.J., Choffnes, D.R., Mandalari, A.M., Kolcun, R., Haddadi, H.: Information exposure from consumer IoT devices: a multidimensional, network-informed measurement approach. In: Proceedings of the Internet Measurement Conference, IMC (2019)

31. Singh, A., et al.: HANZO: collaborative network defense for connected things. In: 2018 Principles, Systems and Applications of IP Telecommunications, IPTComm (2018)

32. Sivanathan, A., et al.: Classifying IoT devices in smart environments using network traffic characteristics. IEEE Trans. Mob. Comput. **18**, 1745–1759 (2019)

33. Tang, R., et al.: ZeroWall: detecting zero-day web attacks through encoder-decoder recurrent neural networks. In: 39th IEEE Conference on Computer Communications, INFOCOM (2020)

34. Trimananda, R., Varmarken, J., Markopoulou, A., Demsky, B.: Packet-level signatures for smart home devices. In: 27th Annual Network and Distributed System Security Symposium, NDSS (2020)

35. Usama, M., Asim, M., Latif, S., Qadir, J., Al-Fuqaha, A.I.: Generative adversarial networks for launching and thwarting adversarial attacks on network intrusion detection systems. In: 15th International Wireless Communications & Mobile Computing Conference, IWCMC (2019)

36. Venkatesh, G.K., Anitha, R.: Botnet detection via mining of traffic flow characteristics. Comput. Electr. Eng. **50**, 91–101 (2016)

37. Wan, Y., Xu, K., Xue, G., Wang, F.: IoTArgos: a multi-layer security monitoring system for Internet-of-Things in smart homes. In: 39th IEEE Conference on Computer Communications, INFOCOM (2020)

38. Yao, H., Ranjan, G., Tongaonkar, A., Liao, Y., Mao, Z.M.: SAMPLES: self adaptive mining of persistent lexical snippets for classifying mobile application traffic. In: Proceedings of the 21st Annual International Conference on Mobile Computing and Networking, MobiCom (2015)

# IoTPrivComp: A Measurement Study of Privacy Compliance in IoT Apps

Javaria Ahmad, Fengjun Li, and Bo Luo[✉]

Department of Electrical Engineering and Computer Science, Center for High
Assurance and Secure Systems (HASS), Institute of Information Sciences (I2S),
The University of Kansas, Lawrence, KS, USA
{javaria.ahmad,fli,bluo}@ku.edu

**Abstract.** The growth of IoT apps poses increasing concerns about sensitive data leaks. While privacy policies are required to describe how IoT apps use private user data (i.e., data practice), problems such as missing, inaccurate, and inconsistent policies have been repeatedly reported. Therefore, it is important to assess the actual data practice in IoT apps and identify the potential gaps between the actual and declared data usage. In this work, we conducted a measurement study using our framework called IoTPrivComp, which applies an automated analysis of IoT apps' code and privacy policies to identify compliance gaps. We collected 1,489 IoT apps with English privacy policies from the Play Store. IoTPrivComp found 532 apps with sensitive external data flows, among which 408 (76.7%) apps had undisclosed data leaks. Moreover, 63.4% of the data flows that involved health and wellness data was inconsistent with the practices disclosed in the apps' privacy policies.

**Keywords:** IoT · Compliance · Security · Privacy

## 1 Introduction

Regulations such as EU General Data Protection Regulation (GDPR) [43] and the California Online Privacy Protection Act require a service provider (e.g., websites or mobile apps) who collects personally identifiable data from users to disclose its actions with the collected data in the privacy policy. Therefore, privacy policies nowadays become a standard practice to notify users about the necessary data collection, management, and/or sharing operations that a mobile or IoT app requests to perform. However, the state-of-the-art (SOTA) implementations of privacy policies face two main challenges: (i) the privacy policies are often difficult to comprehend [17,29], while the users are unwilling to spend the time and effort necessary to understand the policies; and (ii) while the vendors should disclose user-data-related practices in privacy policies, recent studies [4,37,46,49,52] uncovered various issues showing the policies were incomplete or inconsistent with the actual practices.

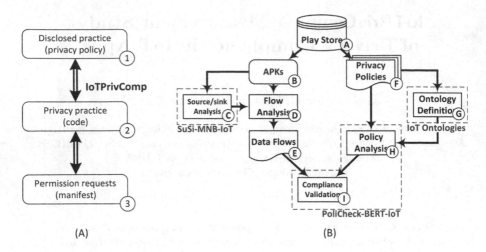

**Fig. 1.** (A) Privacy compliance measurement for mobile/IoT apps.; (B) The flowchart and key contributions of IoTPrivComp.

Such challenges motivate researchers to study privacy policies and practices. Based on their objectives and methodologies, SOTA research efforts can be categorized into three directions: (1) *privacy policy comprehension* (Fig. 1-A ①) that focuses on facilitating the (automated) understanding of privacy policies [22,42]; (2) *privacy threat detection* (Fig. 1-A ② and ③) that aims to examine app code and behaviors to identify potential privacy threats [23,35]; and (3) *privacy compliance gap detection* (Fig. 1-A ① and ②), which studies the gaps between privacy policies and data practices [4,13,21,27,31,51,52].

In this paper, we present a measurement study to investigate the privacy compliance gaps in *IoT apps*, which are mobile applications interacting with or managing IoT devices. With the rapid deployment of IoT technologies in our daily life, the IoT devices collect personal data such as heart rate, pulse, voice, biometrics, and location, which raise increasing privacy concerns [25]. Therefore, it is important to understand the privacy practices of IoT apps, as they often access more sensitive data than general mobile apps. However, **the compliance gap between privacy policies and privacy practices in IoT apps is yet to be investigated**. Our initial exploration shows that the off-the-shelf (OTS) tools for IoT code and privacy policy analysis provide insufficient performance. Therefore, we first developed IoTPrivComp, a framework for IoT code and policy consistency analysis. IoTPrivComp consists of five main components as shown in Fig. 1-B: (1) a new ontology to represent entity and data object relationships in privacy policies; (2) the SuSi-MNB-IoT sink analysis module that uses a Multinomial Naive Bayesian (MNB) classifier to analyze data flows and identify sinks; (3) a static code analysis module to identify leaks of sensitive information through external data flows; (4) a model based on Bidirectional Encoder Representations from Transformers (BERT) to identify entity and data objects from IoT privacy policies; and (5) the PoliCheck-BERT-IoT compliance analysis module that finally identifies the inconsistent privacy disclosures.

With IoTPrivComp, we further present a large-scale measurement study of the inconsistencies between the practices disclosed in privacy policies (Fig. 1-A ①) and the privacy practices implemented in app code (Fig. 1-A ②). In particular, we aim to answer the following questions: *(1) what does the landscape of IoT app privacy compliance look like?* While we are interested in the current practices that IoT apps take to be compliant with privacy regulations, there lacks such an overview in the literature. *(2) Which privacy compliance gaps exist in IoT apps?* Compliance issues exist when an app's actual practices are not consistent with the practices disclosed in its privacy policy. For example, does the privacy policy of an app fully disclose all types of private data transmitted to the first and third parties? And *(3) does there exist any patterns in privacy compliance gaps?* For example, are certain types of IoT data more commonly associated with compliance issues? Our primary contributions are three-fold:

**1.** We conduct a measurement study to identify the privacy gaps between the privacy practices and disclosures in 1,951 IoT apps. IoTPrivComp is the first attempt to autonomously validate privacy compliance of IoT apps at this scale.
**2.** We show that simply assembling OTS tools only provides limited performance for IoT compliance validation and non-trivial modifications/ enhancements are necessary. We developed an automated privacy compliance analysis tool for IoT apps, called IoTPrivComp, with a new SuSi-MNB-IoT mechanism for sink identification and a new PoliCheck-BERT-IoT mechanism for privacy policy analysis, and open-sourced it[1]. With all the novel improvements, IoTPrivComp achieves significantly better performance (94% accuracy) than the OTS baseline.
**3.** We examined 1,951 IoT apps from Google Play Store and analyzed the privacy disclosure gaps. For instance, out of 532 apps with sensitive data flows, we identified compliance violations in 408 (76.7%) apps. We further provided a comprehensive analysis of the inconsistent disclosures and the leaked data.

**Ethics:** This study did not involve any human subjects. All the data analyzed in this work was collected from the publicly available data in the Play Store.

## 2    The Problem and Baseline Solution

### 2.1    Problem Statement

Our objectives are two-fold: (1) we conducted a large-scale measurement study to examine the (in)consistencies between the privacy practices implemented in IoT apps and the privacy disclosures released in privacy policies. In particular, we focus on answering key questions about the current state of IoT privacy policy usage, compliance gaps, and potential compliance patterns, e.g., *how many apps provide available privacy policies to the users, what type of private data is transmitted to first/third-party entities, which of the practices are disclosed in*

---

[1] https://github.com/IoTPrivComp.

*privacy policies?* (2) Since existing OTS tools are unable to provide satisfactory performance for IoT apps, we propose the IoTPrivComp framework to perform app code analysis, privacy policy analysis, and compliance gap analysis.

In privacy practices and disclosures, we focus on information *collection* and *sharing*. "Collection" means that certain (private) data is accessed by the app and transmitted out of the app's memory space to a first-party entity, e.g., the app's cloud server, while "sharing" takes place when the data is transmitted to a third party, e.g., the app sends payment information to PayPal. The collection and sharing practices take place as a result of certain API executions [5,51]. In both cases, the data accessed is transferred externally, either outside the app or out of the device. We refer to these leaks as *external data flows*. Some of the external data flow scenarios that we have identified include sending the data to an external server, sending the text messages and emails, sending the log data outside the app, and sharing data with another app using exported components.

The problem of IoT privacy compliance analysis is challenging. Data leaks are usually found by analyzing the APIs, permissions, and protected resources [16, 19,52], but identifying data sources and sinks is not straightforward as many permission-protected methods are not source nor sink [34]. Moreover, like other static flow analyzers for mobile apps, we assume the code is not obfuscated. Privacy policy analysis approaches usually rely on a hand-annotated corpus [42, 51,52] but they are limited due to the manual effort. It is also difficult to identify contradictory statements in the policies [3]. NLP still has limited capabilities in analyzing statements that span multiple sentences and that use confusing language [4].

Finally, we would like to note that our focus in this work is not on detecting unknown privacy threats or providing security evaluations. This aspect of IoT app security has been extensively studied in the literature. Instead, we aim to understand the landscape of IoT app privacy compliance. While our findings can be used to improve future privacy policies, we consider privacy policy comprehension or enforcement out of the scope of this work.

## 2.2   The Baseline Solution Using Off-the-Shelf Tools

Privacy policy compliance in mobile applications has been extensively studied. As shown in Fig. 1-B, it consists of three main tasks, i.e., *app flow analysis* (Ⓒ and Ⓓ), *privacy policy analysis* (Ⓖ and Ⓗ), and *flow-to-policy consistency analysis* (Ⓘ). To avoid re-inventing the wheel, we examined several existing tools and tested their effectiveness in identifying privacy gaps in IoT apps.

**Tools and Implementation.** First, we studied PoliCheck [4], which implements an automated, entity-sensitive privacy policy consistency analysis for mobile apps. It employed AppCensus [16] for data flow analysis and PolicyLint [3] for privacy policy analysis. Unfortunately, AppCensus was commercialized and unavailable to the research community. Hence, we replaced the data flow analysis module of PoliCheck with two other open-source tools, i.e., SuSi [34] and AndroShield [2]. SuSi was used to identify Android source and sink methods, while AndroShield was used to extract the paths between the identified sources and sinks. In this baseline approach, we modified the interface to feed flow data from AndroShield to PoliCheck and also implemented the necessary interfaces to assemble all the off-the-shelf tools together.

**Table 1.** Sample IoT devices from four popular IoT platforms.

| | |
|---|---|
| IFTTT | Ai-Sync, Iotics, Lexi, LIFX, AirTouch, Arlo, Neato, Neo Smart |
| SmartThings | Ring, Belkin, Leviton, Yeelight, Blaze, Awair, Danalock, Connected |
| OpenHAB | Netatmo, BenQ, Nest, Nanaleaf, Ecobee, Nuki, Onkyo, OpenGarage |
| Zapier | Phillips Hue, Luxafor, Flic, Kisi, bttn, Amazon Alexa, Tap NFC |

**Evaluation and Results.** We extracted external data flows from 68 IoT apps and manually verified them. Then, we randomly selected 100 external data flows for evaluation. The baseline approach discovered only 64 external data flows and correctly reported only 29 privacy disclosures including 2 clear disclosures and 27 omitted disclosures (see Sect. 3.4 for privacy disclosure definitions). Therefore, it achieved an overall accuracy of 29%. In comparison, IoTPrivComp identified all the external data flows and correctly reported 94 (consistent and inconsistent) privacy disclosures, achieving a 94% overall accuracy. IoTPrivComp failed in 6 cases because the corresponding privacy policies did not include clear statements about their privacy practices.

The baseline's low performance may be caused by three issues. First, SuSi and AndroShield were implemented over Android 4.2, which cannot correctly handle new Android APIs (e.g., Android 29) and IoT-specific data flows. Second, SuSi and PoliCheck adopted conventional machine learning models with limited performance for classification and NLP tasks. Finally, PolicyLint used spaCy's NER engine (en_core_web_lg model) for entity and data object identification. Its outdated ontology cannot correctly handle the IoT-specific terminologies in the privacy policies. In recognizing the root causes of the low performance, we propose to revamp the baseline approach by tackling these three issues.

## 3    IoTPrivComp: Privacy Compliance for IoT Apps

In this section, we present IoTPrivComp, an automated privacy compliance verification framework for IoT apps. As shown in Fig. 1-B (our primary contributions are highlighted), the IoTPrivComp framework consists of four key components: data collection (Sect. 3.1), ontology definition (Sect. 3.2), data flow analysis (Sect. 3.3), privacy policy analysis, and compliance validation (Sect. 3.4).

### 3.1    Data Collection

There is no clear or authoritative definition for IoT apps. In this work, we consider all the mobile applications that control, manage, and/or interact with IoT devices as *IoT apps*. According to [25], IoT devices are low-cost devices with sensors and/or actuators that generate sensing data and offer various services to their users. Therefore, smartphones, laptops, and PCs are controller devices that interact with IoT devices but they are not considered IoT devices themselves.

**IoT Apps.** To recognize the loosely-defined IoT apps from the Play Store, we considered the popular IoT platforms studied in the literature [8,20,24,33,36, 48], e.g., IFTTT (If-This-Then-That), SmartThings, openHAB, and Zapier, and identified IoT devices from each platform, as shown in Table 1. We also added wearable devices that directly connect to smartphones using WiFi/Bluetooth to this seed set. Next, we wrote a Scrapy script to collect the most relevant Play Store apps for the seed devices and identified 543 unique app manufacturers from the apps, for which we further scraped all their free IoT apps. Finally, we employed a pattern matching approach to identify and remove any non-IoT apps based on their names and descriptions. Our final dataset has 1,951 IoT apps. We downloaded the original APK files of 1,915 IoT apps from the Google Play Store, where 36 APKs failed to download.

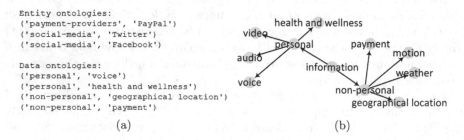

Fig. 2. (a) Examples of entity and data ontologies; (b) A part of data ontology graph.

**Privacy Policies.** For each crawled app, we followed the embedded link to retrieve its full policy page including the dynamically loaded contents, and then converted it into a text file. Among 1,951 IoT apps, 234 apps did not have an available privacy policy due to missing or broken links and 228 apps had non-English policies (discussed in Sect. 4). Finally, we obtained the privacy policies of 1,489 apps and used them in our privacy compliance analysis.

### 3.2   Ontology Definition for IoT App Privacy Policies

Ontologies are used to represent "is-a" relationships among the terms in privacy policies, which enable a semantic analysis of privacy policies. Since there is no ontology for IoT privacy policies, we created our own in this work by manually annotating 134 policies with *entity objects* and *data objects* and their subsumptive ("is-a") relationships and splitting the annotated data for training, validation, and testing. We trained a Tok2Vec relation classifier with 81% precision. Next, we extracted entity/data objects with a BERT model that is fine-tuned on a privacy policy corpus. BERT was introduced in [14] to fine-tune the pre-trained models for accomplishing various tasks without changing the architecture significantly for each task. Then, we applied the Tok2Vec classifier to the extracted objects and retained only the predictions with a confidence score of 90% or higher. For example, for the below sentence, our model generated the relation as (`information`, `location`):

We collect information about you, including location.

We further extracted two types of ontology graphs from the relationships, *entity ontologies*, and *data ontologies*, which represent the relationships between entities and data objects, respectively. Figure 2(a) shows a few examples of the extracted data and entity ontologies, while Fig. 2(b) shows a subset of the data ontology graph. A few more ontology examples can be found in Appendix A. Using the relationships found from ontology extraction, we also identified the synonyms, i.e., functionally equivalent/similar entities and data objects. For example, **payment transaction** and **payment processing** are identified as synonyms of **payment**. Finally, the ontologies were fed into PoliCheck-BERT-IoT.

### 3.3 SuSi-MNB-IoT: Analyzing Sinks and Data Flows in IoT Apps

To extract the app code, we reverse-engineered the downloaded APK files. In particular, we obtained the DEX (Dalvik Executable) files from the APKs using Apkanalyzer [39] and converted them to Jimple files using the Soot program analysis framework [38]. Then, we extracted the manifest files in binary format and converted them into XML. The extracted Android code is analyzed to identify *sources* that are associated with the collection of sensitive data, *sinks* that transmit that data external to app/device, and *data flows* from the sources to the sinks. Manually classifying the sources and sinks is a costly task due to a large number of supported methods. To tackle the challenge, automated code analyzers such as SuSi [34] and AndroShield [2] proposed machine-learning-based approaches to conduct flow analysis in three steps, i.e., source and sink identification, data flow tracing, and sink categorization. However, our baseline study showed that 71% of flows were missed or incorrectly reported when directly applying Susi for IoT app analysis. Inspired by Susi, we developed a code analysis module, called SuSi-MNB-IoT, which introduced non-trivial modifications as follows to improve sink and data flow identification for Android code analysis.

**Customization for IoT Devices/Apps.** IoT apps collect new types of data that are rarely accessed by general mobile apps. Therefore, existing code analyzers fall short in identifying these sensitive data. In SuSi-MNB-IoT, we defined several new sink categories pertaining to sensitive data types, including Geolocation, Health_wellness, Motion, Socialmedia_activity, Music, Payment, and Video. A detailed list of sink categories is shown in Table 2.

**Advanced Machine Learning Approach.** The Support Vector Machine (SVM) model performs poorly when the training data is small [45]. To improve the performance in text snippet classification, we built a Multinomial Naive

Bayesian (MNB) classifier in SuSi-MNB-IoT. MNB is a probabilistic classifier based on Bayes' theorem that predicts using previous and current knowledge [15]. Compared with SVM, our MNB model is two to six times faster [28].

**Adding Support for Android 29.** As most of the IoT apps in our dataset use Android 29, we added a mechanism to handle the new API methods and identified the new sinks from Android 29 API methods.

**Adding Support for Exported Components.** Exported components in Android facilitate permissioned data sharing *between apps*. In SuSi-MNB-IoT, we included exported components along with other data flows.

With the sources and sinks identified by SuSi-MNB-IoT, we traced data flows and identified data leaks through Android API sinks. In particular, we followed the AndroShield approach [2], which is based on FlowDroid [5], to construct call graphs. The APIs and methods involved in sensitive data flows are identified as nodes of the call graph. Then, we extracted tainted paths from the sources to the sinks by traversing the call graph with a Depth-First Search (DFS) algorithm. Sensitive data travels through these paths and is finally sent out through the sinks. Next, we manually annotated 2,450 data flows (1,960 for training, 490 for testing) across various sink categories. Using this dataset, we finally trained an MNB classifier for automated app analysis, which categorizes data flows based on their classes and sink methods.

**Table 2.** Sink categories and SuSi-MNB-IoT's classification performance. R: Recall (%); P: Precision (%).

| Category | R | P | Category | R | P | Category | R | P | Category | R | P |
|---|---|---|---|---|---|---|---|---|---|---|---|
| AAID | 100 | 98 | Audio | 100 | 88 | Calendar | 100 | 98 | Camera | 81 | 94 |
| Email | 100 | 95 | Gallery | 96 | 96 | Geolocation | 97 | 92 | Health_Wellness | 92 | 97 |
| Motion | 100 | 98 | Music | 100 | 97 | NFC | 97 | 97 | Payment | 100 | 95 |
| Phone | 92 | 98 | Router | 100 | 95 | SIMID | 100 | 100 | Socialmedia_Activity | 96 | 94 |
| SMS | 100 | 100 | Sound | 100 | 97 | Video | 69 | 98 | Weather | 100 | 95 |
| Voice | 98 | 92 | Weighted Average: Recall: 96%; Precision: 96% | | | | | | | | |

## 3.4   PoliCheck-BERT-IoT: Policy and Consistency Analysis

To detect the inconsistencies between apps' data flows and the disclosed privacy practices, we developed a new policy analyzer, called PoliCheck-BERT-IoT, which followed the PoliCheck approach [4] originally developed for mobile privacy policy analysis. Compared with PoliCheck, PoliCheck-BERT-IoT introduced two improvements to capture IoT-specific data practice statements.

**IoT-Specific Ontology.** PoliCheck uses PolicyLint [3] to identify entities and objects in privacy policies. To process IoT policies, PoliCheck-BERT-IoT extended PolicyLint to capture the IoT-specific ontologies developed in Sect. 3.2. It can recognize the synonyms for entities and data objects and the IoT-specific relationship mappings. With domain adaptation, the improved PolicyLint module achieved an 89.6% precision and a 73.3% recall in identifying data objects, and an 88.5% precision and a 69.5% recall in identifying entities, respectively.

**Adapting State-of-the-Art NLP Model.** PoliCheck/PolicyLint uses spaCy's NER engine with the en_core_web_lg model, which is based on Convolutional Neural Networks (CNN). To improve NER performance, we replaced the CNN-based model with a transformer-based BERT model. Transformers enable downstream tasks to fine-tune a pre-trained model to a specific domain without incurring the resource-intensive training process of complex models [47].

Based on the policy analysis results and the sensitive data flows obtained in Sect. 3.3, PoliCheck-BERT-IoT performs a consistency analysis. It extracts sentences about the app's data practice from its privacy policy. Each statement is then matched with the identified sensitive data flows to determine the type of privacy disclosures. Data flows of the same data type and the same root domain are combined to output unique data flows. For example, two flows <com.samsung.auth, music.activity.SoundPickerActivity> and <com.samsung.report, music.activity.SoundPlayerActivity> are considered the same flow in consistency analysis since they have the same data type (i.e., music) and the same root domain.

**Table 3.** Privacy policies of IoT apps under study: (left) policy availability; (right) External Data Flows (EDF).

| App category | # of apps | % of apps | App category | # of apps | % of apps |
|---|---|---|---|---|---|
| All crawled apps | 1,951 | 100 | Apps w. sensitive EDFs | 623 | 100 |
| Missing policy | 234 | 12.0 | Missing policy | 33 | 5.3 |
| Non-English policy | 228 | 11.7 | Non-English policy | 58 | 9.3 |
| Available policy | 1,489 | 76.3 | Available policy | 532 | 85.4 |

PoliCheck-BERT-IoT identifies five types of privacy disclosures: **(i) clear disclosures**, in which the privacy policy precisely states that the data is being disclosed to the entity involved in the flow. **(ii) vague disclosures**, in which the privacy policies use vague or broad terms to describe data types and/or entities, e.g., stating that the app "collects your data" instead of "collects your fingerprint and voice data", or the app "shares data with social networks", instead of "shares data with Facebook and Twitter". **(iii) omitted disclosures**, where the privacy policy fails to disclose the data flow, e.g., sharing data with Facebook without mentioning it in the privacy policy. **(iv) incorrect disclosures**, in which the privacy policy statement incorrectly states that the practice will not take place, e.g., collecting camera information while the privacy policy states not collecting such data. And **(v) contradictory disclosures**, where the flow matches more than one privacy statement and the statements contradict each other. We consider the privacy practice and disclosure as *consistent* in case of clear and vague disclosures, whereas, *inconsistent* disclosures refer to omitted, incorrect and contradictory cases. Moreover, when the entity names match with the app package names or a part of the privacy policy link, the flow is considered *first-party*. Otherwise, the flow is considered *third-party*.

## 4   Evaluation and Analysis

In this section, we first evaluate the performance of IoTPrivComp in identifying the inconsistencies between privacy disclosures and privacy practices and then employ IoTPrivComp to measure the privacy compliance status of the IoT apps and answer the research questions presented in Sect. 1.

### 4.1   Performance Evaluation of IoTPrivComp

We first evaluated the performance of the key components of IoTPrivComp. In particular, SuSi-MNB-IoT achieved an average precision and recall of 96% for sensitive sink identification, as shown in Table 2. For PoliCheck-BERT-IoT, we manually annotated 50 privacy policies of IoT apps. We extracted the dictionary of annotations and applied them to the large corpus of 2,050 policies (1,640 policies for fine-tuning and 410 policies for validation). The training process took 2 h on an NVIDIA Tesla P100 GPU (PCI-E 16GB). The final model achieved an 87.94% precision and an 88.09% recall for identifying data objects from privacy policies, and a 90.89% precision and a 91.05% recall for identifying entities. The performance is significantly improved over the CNN-based model.

**Table 4.** Number of flows and apps associated with different privacy disclosure types.

| Privacy disclosures | | IoT 1st-party | | IoT 3rd-party | | Wearable 1st-party | | Wearable 3rd-party | |
|---|---|---|---|---|---|---|---|---|---|
| | | Flows | Apps | Flows | Apps | Flows | Apps | Flows | Apps |
| Consistent | Clear | 12 | 12 | 0 | 0 | 9 | 8 | 0 | 0 |
| | Vague | 92 | 75 | 72 | 63 | 22 | 19 | 28 | 21 |
| Inconsistent | Omitted | 171 | 136 | 253 | 203 | 52 | 46 | 98 | 61 |
| | Incorrect | 1 | 1 | 1 | 1 | 0 | 0 | 0 | 0 |
| | Contradictory | 1 | 1 | 4 | 3 | 0 | 0 | 0 | 0 |
| Total # | | 277 | 225 | 330 | 270 | 83 | 73 | 126 | 82 |
| Total Inconsistent | | 173 | 138 | 258 | 207 | 52 | 46 | 98 | 61 |
| Inconsistent rate (%) | | 62.5 | 61.3 | 78.2 | 76.7 | 62.7 | 63.0 | 77.8 | 74.4 |

Next, we validated the overall performance of IoTPrivComp by sampling 68 IoT apps and manually analyzing their data flows. We read the corresponding privacy policies to verify the disclosure types and consistency results reported by IoTPriv-Comp. If IoTPrivComp extracts a data flow and classifies the corresponding policy statement correctly, the result is marked as true positive. In particular, IoT-PrivComp reported 100 sensitive data flows and labeled 18, 38, and 44 flows as "clear disclosures", "vague disclosures", and "omitted disclosures", respectively.

There were no incorrect and contradictory disclosures, as they are very rare. We found that 94 out of the 100 reported flows were true positives, indicating an overall accuracy of 94%. Moreover, all the "clear disclosures" were correctly reported, while 5 "vague disclosures" and one "omitted disclosure" were incorrect. The discrepancies occur because of the confusing language of privacy policies that do not state clearly the collection and sharing practices.

## 4.2   Policy and Data Flow Analysis

In this study, we identified a total of 1,951 unique IoT apps and retrieved 1,489 privacy policies written in English and 1,825 APKs, where 36 APKs failed to download and 90 apps failed during static analysis.

**Missing Privacy Policies.** As shown in Table 3, 234 (12%) apps did not have available privacy policies. Among them, 188 apps did not provide any policy URL, while 46 apps provided invalid URLs. The number of apps with missing policies reported in this study was non-trivial, as these apps may have potentially undisclosed data leakages. The result highlights the need for strict and continuous enforcement of regulations. Meanwhile, there were 228 (11.7%) apps with non-English privacy policies. Among them, 160 had app descriptions in English, which indicates that they were intended for English-speaking users but their privacy policies fell short in disclosing the app practices to the users.

**Data Flows and Sinks.** IoTPrivComp extracted a total of 23,959 *external data flows* from 1,825 APKs, from which information flows out of the device or the app's memory space through first- or third-party code. Among them, 1,782 external data flows disclosed *sensitive information* of 21 categories defined in Table 2. These sensitive data flows involved 623 IoT apps and 1,075 distinct Android APIs. `com.facebook`, `com.samsung`, and `com.amazon` are the most frequently used APIs, which appeared in multiple flow categories, e.g., payment, social media activity, voice, and video. Finally, we found 33 apps with missing policies and 58 apps with non-English policies, which is 14.6% of all apps that disclose sensitive data.

**Table 5.** Privacy disclosures of IoT-specific practices.

| Privacy disclosures | Clear | Vague | Omitted | Total |
|---|---|---|---|---|
| # of flows | 10 | 37 (26.4%) | 93 (66.4%) | 140 |
| # of apps | 10 | 37 (27.2%) | 89 (65.4%) | 136 |

## 4.3   IoT Privacy Compliance Analysis

Next, we conducted a privacy compliance analysis at the flow level and app level of 532 apps with available privacy policies. As wearable devices collect more sensitive data such as biometrics and physical activities than general IoT devices, we reported the results for wearable apps separately.

**Flow-Level Compliance Analysis.** IoTPrivComp extracted 6,823 sentences with the positive or negative sentiment about the apps' data practices and associated them with 816 unique data flows. Each flow has a unique data type and disclosure type. The results of the flow-level compliance analysis are summarized in Table 4. For *IoT apps*, 173 (62.5%) first-party data flows and 258 (78.2%) third-party flows were reported with inconsistent privacy disclosures, where most of them had "omitted disclosures", indicating a direct compliance violation in apps' data practices. Similarly, for wearable apps, 52 (62.7%) and 98 (77.8%) inconsistent disclosures were detected in the first-party and third-party flows, respectively. Overall, a total of 581 (i.e., 173+258+52+98) inconsistent disclosures were reported, among which 574 (i.e., 171+253+52+98) were omitted disclosures.

IoT apps often collect personal data that are rarely accessed by conventional mobile apps. For example, among the 21 data categories defined in Table 2, health and wellness, motion, and voice data are often collected by IoT apps. Therefore, we further analyzed the flow-level compliance gaps specifically in the IoT data practices. We extracted data flows to these three sink categories and measured the number of flows with clear, vague, and omitted disclosures. As shown in Table 5, 92.8% of IoT-specific data flows had vague or inconsistent disclosures (26.4% vague and 66.4% omitted disclosures).

**App-Level Compliance Analysis.** 816 unique flows were associated with 411 IoT apps and 121 wearable apps. Table 4 summarizes apps with different types of privacy disclosures. It is worth noting that an app may be counted more than once if it has multiple flows with different types of disclosures. To understand the disclosure behavior of individual apps, we further calculate the number of apps with at least one disclosure of each type. As shown in Table 6, only 12 (2.9%) of the 411 IoT apps clearly disclosed their data collection practices, while 123 (30%) IoT apps disclosed the data practices in vague terms. The majority of the apps (74.5%) failed to disclose their privacy practices (omitted disclosures). The situation is worse for wearable apps. Only 8 (6.6%) apps clearly disclosed the data practices, while 36 (29.8%) apps disclosed the practices in vague terms and 96 (79.3%) apps did not disclose the practice at all.

**Table 6.** Apps' privacy compliance; TP: Third Party, SMA: Social Media Activity.

| App category | # of IoT | # of Wearable | Total # | % of apps |
|---|---|---|---|---|
| Apps analyzed for privacy disclosures | 411 | 121 | 532 | 100 |
| At least one clear disclosure | 12 | 8 | 20 | 3.8 |
| At least one vague disclosure | 123 | 36 | 159 | 30.0 |
| At least one omitted disclosure | 306 | 96 | 402 | 75.6 |
| At least one incorrect disclosure | 2 | 0 | 2 | 0.4 |
| At least one contradictory disclosure | 4 | 0 | 4 | 0.8 |
| At least one inconsistent disclosure | 312 | 96 | 408 | 76.7 |
| At least one omitted TP disclosure | 203 | 61 | 264 | 49.6 |
| Omitted disclosure about TP SMA | 45 | 19 | 64 | 12.0 |

*In summary*, we have the following observations regarding the privacy disclosures and privacy compliance gaps in IoT and wearable apps.

(1) *Very few IoT apps clearly disclosed their data collection practices.* Among all the apps analyzed in this work, only 3.8% clearly stated their practices of first-party data collection, while none of them clearly disclosed third-party data sharing actions. Figure 3(a) shows the breakdown of clear disclosures across different data types. Most of the clear disclosures belong to the health and wellness category, but only 8 out of 101 health and wellness flows were disclosed.

(2) *30% of IoT apps had vague disclosures in their privacy policies.* They often use vague language or broad terms to describe data types (e.g., "your data" instead of "voice data") or the third-party entities (e.g., "social networks", "platforms" "service providers", "vendors", "contractors", and "sponsors"). Such disclosures are considered consistent from the compliance perspective, however, the practice is concerning because agreeing to the blanket policies puts the users in a very vulnerable situation. Figure 3(b) shows vague disclosures of various data types. Health and wellness and social media information are the most common data types with vague disclosure in first- and third-party data access. Moreover, 3.7% and 10.3% of vague disclosure flows are associated with voice data and payment information, which are sensitive in IoT applications.

(3) *76.7% of the analyzed apps had at least one inconsistent data collection or sharing practice.* That is, they collected or shared at least one sensitive data item that was incorrectly or contradictorily disclosed, or not disclosed at all.

(4) *75.6% of the apps contained at least one undisclosed sensitive data collection or sharing practices.* The most common type of inconsistent disclosure is *omitted*, where the privacy policies did *not* mention the data collection and data sharing practice at all. As compared to the first-party data collection practices, it is more common for the app privacy policies to not disclose the third-party data sharing practices, as shown in Fig. 3(c).

(5) *35.5% of all the flows with omitted disclosure involved personal data* including audio, photo, health and wellness, video, and voice data. Meanwhile, *12.0% of the apps shared social media information with third-party platforms without disclosing the practice.* There were only five social media omitted disclosure flows for the first party but 65 omitted disclosures for the third party.

(6) *49.6% of the apps had at least one data sharing practice with third parties that were not disclosed in privacy policies.* The third-party omitted flows made up a surprisingly high (43.0%) percentage of all the flows. Incorrect and contradictory disclosures were less frequent, as shown in Fig. 3(d) and (e).

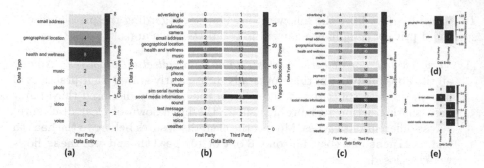

**Fig. 3.** Statistics of flows for (a) clear disclosures, (b) vague disclosures, (c) omitted disclosures, (d) incorrect disclosures, and (e) contradictory disclosures.

## 5   Case Studies

We present our case studies of real-world apps and use them as examples to demonstrate the capability of IoTPrivComp in our measurement study. In particular, we examined 2 wearable apps ("Your Fitness" and "Fitness Tracker by Echoronics") and 3 IoT apps ("Ahome Light", "Hager Coviva", and "My Leviton"), Two of them ("Your Fitness" and "Ahome Light") were selected from the manual evaluation set (in Sect. 2.2). In Table 7, we list the privacy policy and the APIs used by each app to collect/share personal data. IoTPrivComp reported different types of vague and/or inconsistent privacy disclosures for each app, which help to raise awareness among users and provide useful information for developers and regulators to identify and address the compliance issues.

**Case 1: Your Fitness** (`com.yc.yourfitness`) works with smart-bracelet devices to manage daily exercise and sleep activities. IoTPrivComp identified multiple APIs in the code that collected data about the steps taken by the user. However, the privacy policy only vaguely mentioned the collection and disclosure of "personal information", for which IoTPrivComp identified as a *vague disclosure*. It also used the `com.baidu.location` API for the third-party access of the location data but did not disclose this practice in the privacy policy at all. Therefore, it was reported by IoTPrivComp as an *omitted disclosure*.

**Case 2: Fitness Tracker by Echoronics** (`com.mevofit.fitness.fitness` `tracker.walkingjogginghrbp.echotrackers`) manages Echoronics wearable devices and tracks fitness-related information. Its privacy policy identifies specific types of personal data collected by the app, however, it does not mention ECG (e.g., heart rate, rhythm, etc.) data and geolocation data. However, IoT-PrivComp identified three APIs that were used for third-party sharing of ECG and geolocation data, and therefore reported corresponding omitted disclosures.

**Case 3: Hager Coviva** (`com.hager.koala.android`) is used with a home controller to monitor and control alarms, lights, and shutters that are deployed in smart homes. Its privacy policy describes multiple types of personal data collected by the Coviva controller, but does not mention any personal data collected

**Table 7.** Case studies: apps' privacy policies and APIs for data access/sharing.

| | | |
|---|---|---|
| Case 1 | Privacy policy | "Your Fitness will disclose all or part of your personal information in accordance with your personal wishes or legal provisions in the following circumstances: To provide the products and services you require, you must share your personal information with third parties" |
| | APIs | `com.yc.pedometer.MainActivity`, `com.yc.pedometer.SplashActivity`, `com.yc.pedometer.service.MessageAccessibilityService`, `com.yc.pedometer.wxapi.WXEntryActivity`, `com.yc.pedometer.service.StatusbarMsgNotificationListener` |
| Case 2 | Privacy policy | "When you use our services, the personal data that is collected includes - your email address, name, gender, age, height, and weight. Depending on your use of application we may collect data like calorie intake, weight loss goal, lifestyle, and body measurements.", "Personal information about you, such as your gender, birthday, zip code, country, height, weight, lifestyle and exercise frequency" |
| | APIs | `com.ecgview.EcgReportActivity`, `com.ecgview.EcgReportView`, `com.gpstracker.GPSTrackerSummeryActivity` |
| Case 3 | Privacy policy | "Data which you make available to Hager: When you register, you provide us with certain data, to be specific your name and email address.", "Data which is automatically collected and saved in the system: Every time you log in, you use and we collect your IP source address to allow the Coviva controller to communicate with your mobile device.", "Data which is collected during installation: Further information on the installer, product-related information (serial number and MAC address), and the status of the installation ('system consigned/not consigned to customer') is recorded" |
| | APIs | `com.hager.koala.android.activitys.motiondetector.ImageViewerForHistoryMotionDetectorScreen`, `com.hager.koala.android.activitys.motiondetector.ImageViewerMotionDetectorS`, `com.hager.koala.android.activitys.motiondetector.LastIntrusionsMotionDetector`, `com.hager.koala.android.activitys.motiondetector.UpdateInovaMotionDetectorS` |
| Case 4 | Privacy policy | "Specifically, the App and the related Product(s) have collected the following categories of Personal Information ("PI") from its consumers, as defined by the California Privacy Laws: Genetic, physiological, behavioral, and biological characteristics, or activity patterns used to extract a template or other identifier or identifying information, such as fingerprints, faceprints, and voiceprints, iris or retina scans, keystroke, gait, or other physical patterns, and sleep, health, or exercise data." |
| | APIs | `de.niklasmerz.cordova.biometric.BiometricActivity` |
| Case 5 | Privacy policy | "The information and materials about you collected by this application will be stored on the server of this application and/or its affiliates." |
| | APIs | `wl.smartled.service.AudioRecorderService` |

by its sensors. In fact, IoTPrivComp identified 4 APIs that collected the motion sensor data, which is considered private. IoTPrivComp reported several *omitted disclosures* of the app. Meanwhile, from the app descriptions, we did not notice any functionality associated with user tracking. However, from the data flows, the app appears to trace the users using its own APIs, which could be a serious privacy violation that warrants further investigation.

**Case 4: My Leviton** (`com.leviton.home`) manages Leviton's Decora smart Wi-Fi devices, such as dimmers, switches, and smart plugs. Its privacy policy mentions the collection of biometric data by the first party, while IoT-PrivComp reported that this app also shared the collected biometric data with a third-party `niklasmerz` using the `de.niklasmerz.cordova.biometric.BiometricActivity` API. We researched the third party and found the cordova plugin that works with the biometric sensor data. This case is an example of the *omitted* disclosure of sensitive personal information.

**Case 5: Ahome Light** (`wl.smartled.rgb.ahomelight`) allows users to control smart LED lights. IoTPrivComp found that the app collects audio data (through the microphone) using the `wl.smartled.service.AudioRecorderService` API. However, this practice is not disclosed in its privacy policy. Instead, it makes very broad references to the collected data as the "information and materials about you", which vaguely covers the voice data. This was reported by IoTPrivComp as a *vague* disclosure. In fact, collecting or sharing the audio data without properly disclosing it in the privacy policy is quite concerning.

# 6    Discussions and Future Work

With IoTPrivComp, we conducted a measurement study over 1,489 IoT applications and discovered several types of compliance issues in a significant number of IoT apps, whose privacy practices (such as collecting and sharing of private data) are not properly disclosed in their privacy policies. Our results help to answer the research questions raised in Sect. 1.

1. *What does the landscape of IoT app privacy compliance look like?*
*Answer:* Our literature review shows that little effort has been devoted to IoT privacy compliance issues in the research community. Our results show that even with the privacy regulations in place, a significant gap still exists between the apps' privacy practices and their disclosures of such practices to the users.

2. *Which privacy compliance gaps exist in IoT apps?*
*Answer:* The compliance gaps include policies that are unavailable or difficult to comprehend and inconsistent disclosures. For instance, 12% of 1,951 apps do not have any privacy policies, while 8.2% of them have English app descriptions but non-English privacy policies. 75.6% (402/532) of the analyzed apps have omitted disclosures for sensitive data flows, while none of the third-party sensitive data flows is clearly disclosed.

3. *Does there exist any patterns in privacy compliance gaps?*
*Answer:* Some patterns could be observed from the identified compliance gaps. For instance, the vast majority (574 out of 581) of inconsistent disclosures are omitted disclosures, while incorrect and contradictory disclosures are very rare. Certain types of data are more frequently involved in undisclosed data collection/sharing than others. While one may expect the developers to be more cautious in properly disclosing the practice with more sensitive data, we do not observe such a pattern. In statistics, 237 (40.8%) of all the 581 inconsistent flows are related to personal data such as audio, email address, health and wellness, video, voice, and social media information, while 63.4% of the 101 health and wellness data flows are inconsistent with disclosure.

Our findings call for stricter control from regulations regarding the violations of sensitive data leaks. In particular, there should be regulations enforcing controls to address the leak of Protected Health Information (PHI) and Personally Identifiable Information (PII) data from the IoT apps. Therefore, IoTPrivComp can be used as a policy compliance verification tool to automatically check if an IoT application's data practice follows its privacy policy. It can help app users, app markets, and regulators efficiently detect privacy violations. Meanwhile, app developers could leverage it to identify unintended data use or inappropriate privacy policies.

For future work, we recognize that different types of privacy information pose different levels of risk. For instance, sharing weather data is significantly less risky than sharing heath-related sensor data. Therefore, we will consider the risk levels and generate comprehensive compliance and risk profiles for IoT apps.

# 7   Related Work

Our work is related to three research directions in the literature, i.e., IoT app security, app code analysis, and privacy policy analysis.

**IoT App Security and Privacy.** Most of the existing work focuses on identifying security vulnerabilities in IoT applications. For example, Celik et al. discovered privacy leaks in IoT apps [10] and proposed mechanisms to verify or enforce security policies [11,12]. Another research direction is to discover side-channel privacy leaks [41,44]. [9] identified privacy leakage in SmartThings apps and [6] proposed to alert the user when the privacy preferences are violated. Finally, some recent work proposed to capture IoT traffic to validate compliance of data disclosure to the privacy policy [40] or check IoT app descriptions against the data practices described in privacy policies [26]. While they are related to our work, they either took manual analysis approaches or focused on one aspect of private information (e.g., 11 apps in [40] and [26] studied voice assistants only).

**App Code Analysis.** Code analysis has been widely used to study Android app permissions, such as mapping API calls to permissions to analyze the access control models [7,50] and identify the overprivileged apps [1,18], locating potential data leaks by analyzing the APIs, permissions, and protected resources [19,52], etc. SuSi [34] proposed a machine learning approach to identify the sources of sensitive data and sinks. Code analysis tools (e.g., AndroShield [2]) constructed tainted paths from the identified sources to sinks. Recently, AppCensus [16] and Han [21] proposed to identify sensitive data flows based on sensitive resources protected by permissions. These app code analysis approaches adopt static [32,51,52], dynamic [30], and hybrid analysis [16].

**Privacy Policy Analysis.** Existing works on privacy policy analysis such as MAPS [51], PolicyLint [3] and PoliCheck [4] focused mainly on mobile applications. IoTPrivComp is among the first to study privacy compliance gaps in IoT applications. As reported in [3], prior approaches using bigrams [51] or regular expressions [31] for policy analysis struggled with the accurate detection of negative statements. Similar to PolicyLint [3], IoTPrivComp uses sentence-level NLP and ontologies to detect negations in complex sentences. Finally, previous works mostly rely on hand-annotated corpora datasets and rules [22,42,51,52], which have limited coverage and scalability. IoTPrivComp leverages state-of-the-art machine learning methods to automatically annotate data and entity objects in a large corpus of 2,050 privacy policies.

# 8    Conclusion

In this paper, we present a large-scale measurement study on the privacy compliance of IoT apps. To conduct this measurement study, we first develop IoT-PrivComp, which analyzes the code and privacy policies of IoT apps to find compliance gaps between the actual and declared data practices. The IoTPrivComp framework consists of a new ontology for IoT app privacy policies, a new sink identification module SuSi-MNB-IoT, a data flow analysis module, and a new consistency analysis module PoliCheck-BERT-IoT for detecting inconsistent privacy disclosures.

Using IoTPrivComp, we found that a vast majority of the analyzed apps had data practices that were inconsistent with their privacy disclosures. The most common inconsistencies are the omitted disclosures where the privacy policy does not mention the privacy practice. Despite the privacy regulations in place, we still found significant compliance gaps. Our results show that there is a strong need for strict regulations that are thoroughly enforced in the app stores.

**Acknowledgements.** The authors were sponsored in part by NSF IIS-2014552, DGE-1565570, DGE-1922649, and the Ripple University Blockchain Research Initiative. The authors would like to thank the anonymous reviewers for their valuable comments and suggestions.

# A    Ontologies

We have 121 entity ontology pairs, 52 data ontology pairs, and 7,592 synonyms in the IoT-specific ontology. Table 8 shows parts of the data and entity ontologies.

**Table 8.** Examples from the Data and Entity Ontologies.

| Data ontology |
| --- |
| ('information', 'personal'), ('information', 'non-personal'), ('personal', 'email address'), |
| ('personal', 'account user info'), ('personal', 'phone'), ('personal', 'address') |
| ('personal', 'voice'), ('personal', 'photo'), ('personal', 'social media information'), |
| ('personal', 'audio'), ('personal', 'video'), ('personal', 'account details'), |
| ('personal', 'health and wellness'), ('non-personal', 'music'), ('non-personal', 'router'), |
| ('non-personal', 'sound'), ('non-personal', 'payment'), ('non-personal', 'motion'), |
| ('non-personal', 'geographical location'), ('non-personal', 'user patterns and usage'), |
| ('non-personal', 'weather'), ('non-personal', 'calendar'), ('non-personal', 'camera'), |
| ('non-personal', 'organization info'), ('non-personal', 'sim serial number') |
| ('non-personal', 'device info'), ('non-personal', 'nfc'), ('non-personal', 'text message') |
| **Entity ontology** |
| ('entity', 'third-party'), ('entity', 'we'), ('third-party', 'social-media') |
| ('third-party', 'service-providers'), ('third-party', 'payment-providers'), |
| ('social-media', 'LinkedIn'), ('social-media', 'Twitter'), ('social-media', 'Facebook'), |
| ('third-party', 'analytic-service'), ('service-providers', 'Microsoft'), |
| ('payment-providers', 'PayPal'), ('analytic-service', 'google') |

# References

1. Aafer, Y., Tao, G., Huang, J., Zhang, X., Li, N.: Precise android API protection mapping derivation and reasoning. In: ACM CCS, pp. 1151–1164 (2018)
2. Amin, A., Eldessouki, A., Magdy, M.T., Abdeen, N., Hindy, H., Hegazy, I.: Androshield: automated android applications vulnerability detection, a hybrid static and dynamic analysis approach. Information 10(10), 326 (2019)
3. Andow, B., et al.: Policylint: investigating internal privacy policy contradictions on google play. In: USENIX Security, pp. 585–602 (2019)
4. Andow, B.,et al.: Actions speak louder than words: entity-sensitive privacy policy and data flow analysis with policheck. In: USENIX Security, pp. 985–1002 (2020)
5. Arzt, S., et al.: Flowdroid: precise context, flow, field, object-sensitive and lifecycle-aware taint analysis for android apps. ACM Sigplan. Notice. 49(6), 259–269 (2014)
6. Babun, L., Celik, Z.B., McDaniel, P., Uluagac, A.S.: Real-time analysis of privacy-(un) aware IoT applications. Proc. Privacy Enhanc. Technol. 2021(1), 145–166 (2021)
7. Backes, M., Bugiel, S., Derr, E., McDaniel, P., Octeau, D., Weisgerber, S.: On demystifying the android application framework: re-visiting android permission specification analysis. In: USENIX Security, pp. 1101–1118 (2016)
8. Bastys, I., Balliu, M., Sabelfeld, A.: If this then what? controlling flows in IoT apps. In: ACM CCS, pp. 1102–1119 (2018)
9. Celik, Z.B., et al.: Sensitive information tracking in commodity IoT. In: USENIX Security, pp. 1687–1704 (2018)
10. Celik, Z.B., Fernandes, E., Pauley, E., Tan, G., McDaniel, P.: Program analysis of commodity IoT applications for security and privacy: challenges and opportunities. ACM Comput. Surv. 52(4), 1–30 (2019)
11. Celik, Z.B., McDaniel, P., Tan, G.: Soteria: automated IoT safety and security analysis. In: USENIX ATC, pp. 147–158 (2018)
12. Celik, Z.B., Tan, G., McDaniel, P.D.: Iotguard: dynamic enforcement of security and safety policy in commodity IoT. In: NDSS (2019)
13. Degeling, M., Utz, C., Lentzsch, C., Hosseini, H., Schaub, F., Holz, T.: We value your privacy... now take some cookies: measuring the gdpr's impact on web privacy. arXiv preprint arXiv:1808.05096 (2018)
14. Devlin, J., Chang, M., Lee, K., Toutanova, K.: BERT: pre-training of deep bidirectional transformers for language understanding. arXiv preprint arXiv:1810.04805 (2018)
15. Efron, B.: Bayes' theorem in the 21st century. Science 340(6137), 1177–1178 (2013)
16. Egelman, S.: Taking responsibility for someone else's code: studying the privacy behaviors of mobile apps at scale. In: USENIX PEPR (2020)
17. Ermakova, T., Fabian, B., Babina, E.: Readability of privacy policies of healthcare websites. Wirtschaftsinformatik 15, 1–15 (2015)
18. Felt, A.P., Chin, E., Hanna, S., Song, D., Wagner, D.: Android permissions demystified. In: Proceedings of the 18th ACM Conference on Computer and Communications Security, pp. 627–638 (2011)
19. Gibler, C., Crussell, J., Erickson, J., Chen, H.: AndroidLeaks: automatically detecting potential pivacy leaks in android applications on a large scale. In: Katzenbeisser, S., Weippl, E., Camp, L.J., Volkamer, M., Reiter, M., Zhang, X. (eds.) Trust 2012. LNCS, vol. 7344, pp. 291–307. Springer, Heidelberg (2012). https://doi.org/10.1007/978-3-642-30921-2_17

20. Gyory, N., Chuah, M.: Iotone: integrated platform for heterogeneous IoT devices. In: 2017 International Conference on Computing, Networking and Communications (ICNC), pp. 783–787. IEEE (2017)
21. Han, C., et al.: The price is (not) right: comparing privacy in free and paid apps. Proc. Privacy Enhanc. Technol. **2020**(3), 222–242 (2020)
22. Harkous, H., Fawaz, K., Lebret, R., Schaub, F., Shin, K.G., Aberer, K.: Polisis: automated analysis and presentation of privacy policies using deep learning. In: USENIX Security, pp. 531–548 (2018)
23. Hatamian, M., Serna, J., Rannenberg, K.: Revealing the unrevealed: mining smartphone users privacy perception on app markets. Comput. Secur. **83**, 332–353 (2019)
24. Jia, Y.J., et al.: Contexlot: towards providing contextual integrity to appified IoT platforms. In: 24th Annual Network and Distributed System Security Symposium, San Diego, CA (2017)
25. Kumar, A.: Internet of things for smart cities. IEEE Internet Things J. **1**(1) (2014)
26. Liao, S., Wilson, C., Cheng, L., Hu, H., Deng, H.: Measuring the effectiveness of privacy policies for voice assistant applications. In: Annual Computer Security Applications Conference, pp. 856–869 (2020)
27. Libert, T.: An automated approach to auditing disclosure of third-party data collection in website privacy policies. In: World Wide Web Conference, pp. 207–216 (2018)
28. Matwin, S., Sazonova, V.: Direct comparison between support vector machine and multinomial Naive Bayes algorithms for medical abstract classification. J. Am. Med. Inf. Assoc. **19**(5), 917–917 (2012)
29. McDonald, A.M., Cranor, L.F.: The cost of reading privacy policies. ISJLP **4**, 543 (2008)
30. Monkey. Google, inc. ui/application exerciser monkey. https://developer.android.com/tools/help/monkey.html. Accessed Aug 2021
31. Okoyomon, E., et al.: On the ridiculousness of notice and consent: contradictions in app privacy policies. In: Workshop on Technology and Consumer Protection (ConPro 2019), in Conjunction with the 39th IEEE Symposium on Security and Privacy (2019)
32. Qark. Tool to look for several security related android application vulnerabilities. https://github.com/linkedin/qark. Accessed Aug 2021
33. Rahmati, A., Fernandes, E., Jung, J., Prakash, A.: Ifttt vs. zapier: a comparative study of trigger-action programming frameworks. arXiv preprint arXiv:1709.02788 (2017)
34. Rasthofer, S., Arzt, S., Bodden, E.: A machine-learning approach for classifying and categorizing android sources and sinks. In: NDSS, vol. 14, p. 1125 (2014)
35. Rosen, S., Qian, Z., Mao, Z.M.: Appprofiler: a flexible method of exposing privacy-related behavior in android applications to end users. In: ACM CODASPY, pp. 221–232 (2013)
36. Schmeidl, F., Nazzal, B., Alalfi, M.H.: Security analysis for smart things IoT applications. In: 2019 IEEE/ACM 6th International Conference on Mobile Software Engineering and Systems (MOBILESoft), pp. 25–29. IEEE (2019)
37. Slavin, R., et al.: Toward a framework for detecting privacy policy violations in android application code. In: Proceedings of the 38th International Conference on Software Engineering, pp. 25–36 (2016)
38. StevenArzt. Soot-a java optimization framework (2021). https://github.com/Sable/soot. Accessed Aug 2021
39. A. STUDIO. Apkanalyzer (2020). https://developer.android.com/studio/command-line/apkanalyzer. Accessed Aug 2021

40. Subahi, A., Theodorakopoulos, G.: Ensuring compliance of IoT devices with their privacy policy agreement. In: 2018 IEEE 6th International Conference on Future Internet of Things and Cloud (FiCloud), pp. 100–107. IEEE (2018)
41. Subahi, A., Theodorakopoulos, G.: Detecting IoT user behavior and sensitive information in encrypted IoT-app traffic. Sensors **19**(21), 4777 (2019)
42. Tesfay, W.B., Hofmann, P., Nakamura, T., Kiyomoto, S., Serna, J.: Privacyguide: towards an implementation of the EU GDPR on internet privacy policy evaluation. In: ACM Workshop on Security and Privacy Analytics, pp. 15–21 (2018)
43. Voigt, P., von dem Bussche, A.: The EU General Data Protection Regulation (GDPR). Springer, Cham (2017). https://doi.org/10.1007/978-3-319-57959-7
44. Wang, H., Lai, T. T.-T., Roy Choudhury, R.: Mole: Motion leaks through smartwatch sensors. In: Proceedings of the 21st Annual International Conference on Mobile Computing and Networking, pp. 155–166 (2015)
45. Wang, S.I., Manning, C.D.: Baselines and bigrams: simple, good sentiment and topic classification. In: Proceedings of the 50th Annual Meeting of the Association for Computational Linguistics (Volume 2: Short Papers), pp. 90–94 (2012)
46. Wang, X., Qin, X., Hosseini, M.B., Slavin, R., Breaux, T.D., Niu, J.: Guileak: tracing privacy policy claims on user input data for android applications. In: Proceedings of the 40th International Conference on Software Engineering, pp. 37–47 (2018)
47. Wolf, T., et al.: Transformers: state-of-the-art natural language processing. In: Proceedings of the 2020 Conference on Empirical Methods in Natural Language Processing: System Demonstrations, pp. 38–45 (2020)
48. Yu, H., Hua, J., Julien, C.: Dataset: analysis of IFTTT recipes to study how humans use internet-of-things (IOT) devices. arXiv preprint arXiv:2110.00068 (2021)
49. Yu, L., Luo, X., Liu, X., Zhang, T.: Can we trust the privacy policies of android apps? In: 2016 46th Annual IEEE/IFIP International Conference on Dependable Systems and Networks (DSN), pp. 538–549. IEEE (2016)
50. Yu, L., Zhang, T., Luo, X., Xue, L., Chang, H.: Toward automatically generating privacy policy for android apps. IEEE Trans. Inf. Forens. Secur. **12**(4), 865–880 (2016)
51. Zimmeck, S., et al.: Maps: scaling privacy compliance analysis to a million apps. Proc. Priv. Enhancing Tech. **2019**, 66 (2019)
52. Zimmeck, S., et al.: Automated analysis of privacy requirements for mobile apps. In: AAAI Fall Symposium (2016)

# No-Label User-Level Membership Inference for ASR Model Auditing

Yuantian Miao[1], Chao Chen[2(✉)], Lei Pan[3], Shigang Liu[4], Seyit Camtepe[5],
Jun Zhang[4], and Yang Xiang[4]

[1] University of Newcastle, Callaghan, NSW 2308, Australia
`chao.chen@jcu.edu.au`
[2] James Cook University, Townsville, QLD 4811, Australia
[3] Deakin University, Geelong, VIC 3220, Australia
[4] Swinburne University of Technology, Hawthorn, VIC 3122, Australia
[5] CSIRO Data61, Marsfield, NSW 2122, Australia

**Abstract.** With the advancement of speech recognition techniques, AI-powered voice assistants become ubiquitous. However, it also increases privacy concerns regarding users' voice recordings. User-level membership inference detects whether a service provider misused users' audio to build its Automatic Speech Recognition (ASR) model without users' consent. Previous research assumes the model's outputs, including its label (i.e., transcription) and confidence score, are available for security auditing. However, the model's outputs are unavailable in many real-world cases, i.e., no-label black-box scenarios, which is a big challenge. We propose a substitute model analysis to transfer the knowledge of the service system to that of its built-in ASR model's behavior with semantic analysis techniques. Based on this analysis, our auditor can determine the user-level membership with high accuracy (~80%) by utilizing a shadow system technique and a gap inference method. The gap inference-based auditor is generic and independent of ASR models.

**Keywords:** IoT privacy · Membership inference attack · Automated speech recognition

## 1 Introduction

With the increasing public awareness of audio privacy, some laws and regulations (i.e. General Data Protection Regulation (GDPR) [15,24], Children's Online Privacy Protection Act (COPPA) [11], California Consumer Privacy Act (CCPA) [1], etc.) are enforced by governments. Thus, an audio auditor is required for law enforcement agencies to verify whether some services are leaking individuals' audio privacy and for companies to check their service's potential breach of customers' privacy. Membership Inference Attack (MIA) has been intensively studied to infer whether a data record has been used to train a specific machine learning model [3,5,9,10,17,21,23]. Previous works [12,18] have demonstrated that the ASR model is vulnerable to MIA and reveals users' spoken information and their identity. However, the existing investigations focus on the model itself [3,21,22] without considering the impact of its production system, implying that the ASR model's information could be obtained from real-world applications. We define this scenario as no-label black-box access, while our auditor allows users to verify their privacy leakage issue with limited accessibility. We conduct MIA against an ASR model for our auditor's verification task.

Under no-label black-box access, the output label of an ASR model (a.k.a. the translated text) is implicit, while the black-box access requires no prior knowledge about the model's structure information and the output's confidence score. This setting releases the state-of-art MIA research's restrictions, as the success of MIA relies on the model's translation accuracy being unobservable. To overcome the issue of unobservable accuracy, we unfold the internal structure of an ASR system, analyze the relationship between components within the system, and introduce a substitute model analysis method. Specifically, by learning another relevant model's behavior in the same system, the target model's performance can be inferred accordingly. In a voice service system, we find another model closely related to the embedded ASR model—the system's default search engine, as it provides search results based on the ASR model's implicit translation result. We conduct a feature analysis with various semantic analysis techniques to measure the degree of relationship between the search engine's behavior and the ASR model's performance.

In addition, our auditor aims to audit a user's data privacy leakage at the user level. It is impractical to reproduce an audio recording that is identical to another with the same tone, same speed, and same words. That is, it is challenging in theory to reliably determine a newly produced audio clip as a member of the target ASR model's training set. Thus, instead of auditing the record-level privacy leakage, we extract the user-level information from audio recordings and conduct a user-level membership inference for our auditing task. Similar to [12], the user-level membership inference can be referred to as querying a user's audio recording and determining whether any audio within the target model's training set belongs to this user.

Incorporating the substitute model analysis, we propose two techniques for the user-level membership inference task. One is a shadow system method, and the other is a gap inference method. Our shadow system extends the shadow model technique proposed by Shokri et al. [21]. Instead of mimicking the target model's behavior, we mimic a system's behavior. More specifically, our shadow system simulates the substitute model's behavior in a simple version of the target voice service system. Our gap inference method learns the gap between a member sample and a non-member sample based on the substitute model's analysis results. Our empirical studies show that the gap inference method is fast and generic.

In summary, with a given voice service system, we design and evaluate an audio auditor under no-label black-box access to help users verify its ASR model's trustworthiness regarding audio data protection. The contributions of this work are listed as follows:

- We innovatively investigate the MIA problem in a system instead of a single model. We unfold an ASR system and firstly disclose the effect of the response module within the system on its user-level MIA performance. We further release the restriction of available resources from the given system with no-label black-box access. To deal with this challenge, we propose a substitute model analysis method to learn the target ASR model's behavior indirectly from the system's default search engine reactions.
- We propose a new shadow system method by integrating a substitute model analysis method. Our shadow system simplifies the target voice service system and mimics the system's responses. The highest accuracy can reach up to 79.90%, which outperforms previous user-level membership inference results [12].
- We propose a gap inference method to construct an auditor based on the substitute model analysis results. It is more generic than the shadow system method and independent of the ASR model's algorithms. The highest accuracy achieved is 80% (similar to our shadow system method).

The rest of this paper is organized as follows: Sect. 2 illustrates the details of no-label user-level membership inference as our auditors. Section 3 shows the setup and the results of our experiments. Section 4 discusses the limitations of our method and future work. Finally, Sect. 5 concludes the paper.

## 2    No-Label Audio Auditor

This section formalizes our research problem before introducing our user-level audio auditors under no-label black-box access. Our two audio auditors are constructed on top of shadow systems and gap inferences, respectively.

### 2.1    Problem Statement

A voice assistance service processes and reacts to users' voice requests. Taking the Amazon voice assistant service architecture as a reference [8,27], we generalize the process of a generic voice assistant service processing a user's voice request. As shown in Fig. 1, the system is made up of three modules—an ASR module, a Natural Language Understanding (NLU) module, and a response module. The ASR model, as a built-in service, translates the voice into a text request. The NLU module analyzes the text request and customizes the machine understanding for the follow-up response module [25,27]. The response module reacts to the delivered machine understanding request. The reaction usually invokes three kinds of functionalities, including third-party applications interaction with dialog style, web search, and chat for fun [7]. Herein, the web search outputs are a list of websites, while we only focus on the websites' titles and short descriptions displayed on the list, which shows the relevance of the ASR model's output in text.

We define a *no-label black-box access* as querying an audio record with the voice service such that the system response is the only observable information.

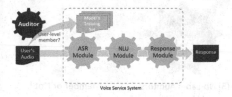

**Fig. 1.** A voice service reacts to a user's voice request.

**Fig. 2.** Data collection. Query audio is selected if it triggers the web search function via a voice service system.

Our audio auditors aim to reveal whether a specific user has audio samples contributed to the ASR model in the voice assistance service system. We refer to this process as a *user-level membership inference*: querying a user's audio and determining whether any audio within the target ASR model's training set belongs to the user.

**Prior Knowledge.** Let $(x, y) \in \mathbb{X} \times \mathbb{Y}$ denote an audio sample, where $x$ represents the audio component, and $y$ is the actual text of $x$. An ASR model is expressed as a function $\mathcal{F} : \mathbb{X} \to \mathbb{Y}$. The ASR module's output of querying $x$ is denoted as $y' = \mathcal{F}(x)$. With an intent analysis performed by the NLU module, the response module invokes a function $\mathcal{R}(\cdot)$. The response is denoted as $r^{y'} = \mathcal{R}(y') = \mathcal{R}(\mathcal{F}(x))$. Undertaking user-level membership inference against the built-in ASR model, our prior knowledge with no-label black-box access is as listed below:

- *User-level information:* Since the query audios are selected or generated by the auditor, the number of speakers and their corresponding audio samples are known.
- *Query records:* The query audio clip $x$ and its true transcription $y$ are known.
- *Response function:* The response reacted on the true text is obtained as $r^y = \mathcal{R}(y)$.
- *Response results:* The system reacts to the ASR model's query audio and returns the response $r^{y'}$.

**Task Formalization.** Assume that the built-in ASR model $\mathcal{F}_A$ is trained on a set of audio clips $A$ of size $N$. Let $U$ of size $M$ be the speaker set of the audio set $A$ ($U \leftarrow A$, $M \leq N$). When $\mathcal{A}$ is our no-label audio auditor, its auditing process can be formalized as follows:

- A speaker $u$ has $S = \bigcup_{i=1}^{n}(x_i, y_i)$, where $S$ is a set of audio samples corresponding to the speaker $u$ ($u \leftarrow S$).
- Let $R^Y = \bigcup_{i=1}^{n} r^{y_i}$ and $R^{Y'} = \bigcup_{i=1}^{n} r^{y'_i}$.
- Set $b =$ "*member*" if $u \in U$, or $b =$ "*nonmember*" if $u \notin U$.
- The auditor is successful if $\mathcal{A}(u, S, R^Y, R^{Y'}) == b$; otherwise it fails.

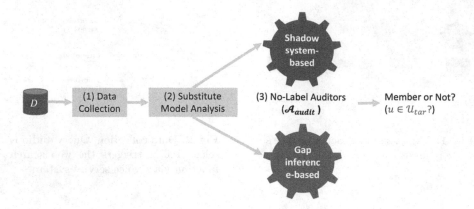

**Fig. 3.** The overall process of our audio auditors performing user-level membership inference under no-label black-box access. The gray box refers to the data collection step in Fig. 2. The blue block is illustrated in Fig. 4 and the green block in Fig. 5. (Color figure online)

## 2.2   No-Label User-Level Membership Inference

Membership inference [21] observes the difference between a model fed with samples it knows (training data) and it does not know (unknown samples). User-level membership inference needs a higher level of robustness to learn the relationship between the model's behavior and the speaker's characteristics. Further, targeting a built-in ASR model in a voice service system, the no-label black-box access needs to transfer knowledge of behaviors between the voice service system and the ASR model. Therefore, we learn this knowledge through a substitute model analysis.

Figure 3 illustrates the entire process of our audio auditors. The process consists of three steps: data collection, substitute model analysis, and no-label auditors' construction. Audio clips and their transcriptions are collected during data collection, after which a substitute model analysis extracts features representing the ASR model's behavior. Finally, the no-label auditor processes the collected data with particular features to determine whether a specific user is a member of the target ASR model's training set or not. Our auditor $\mathcal{A}_{audit}$ infers a user's $(u)$ membership, if $u \in U_{tar} \leftarrow A_{tar}$ holds.

**Data Collection.** With no-label black-box access, the voice service system returns the reaction results to the user's audio request. The system's reaction results are reacted to the built-in ASR model's transcription results. Thus, we introduce a substitute model to imitate the remaining two modules of the voice service system. Among various reaction functions, the web search reaction is the simplest option to construct a substitute model simulating the corresponding NLU and response modules. Specifically, the substitute model acts as the system's default search engine.

As shown in Fig. 2, focusing on the voice service system's web search results, the query audio clip $x$ is selected for data collection based on its true transcription $y$. To ensure that the web search returns valid results, $y$ should satisfy a few conditions: 1) $y$ should not contain any voice commands which would invoke other apps like "set the alarm at [time]" and many alike; 2) $y$ should not start a conversation like asking any questions, greetings, and many alike; and 3) $y$ should avoid long phrases. To satisfy the first two conditions, we choose the audio clips from book reading recordings (i.e., the LibriSpeech dataset). For the third condition, we filter out the records without any semantically meaningful search results after querying the voice assistant.

Having prepared the audio clips and the search results, we query the voice service system with an audio request $x$ and the substitute model with $x$'s true transcription $y$, respectively. The web search usually returns a list of pages, but we merely retain the results' titles and short descriptions. Voice service systems restrict the number of returned pages at different levels. For instance, Apple Siri returns the top three, and Google Assistant returns up to ten pages. Therefore, only the top three page titles and short descriptions are collected in this work.

To sum up, for each input audio clip $x$ and its true transcription $y$, our collected reaction outcomes are denoted as $(r^{y',titles}, r^{y',doc}, r^{y,titles}, r^{y,doc})$. Herein, $r^{y',titles}$ and $r^{y',doc}$ respectively represent a string list of the returned websites' titles and a document including the returned websites' short descriptions based on the searching query $y'$.

**Substitute Model Analysis.** With the help of carefully selected query audio samples, a search engine can substitute the NLU and response modules in the target voice service system. The substitute model allows us to transfer the knowledge of the system's behavior to its built-in ASR model's behavior, before categorizing the ASR model's training set according to the system's behavior. Analyzing our substitute model, the system's behavior is recorded in a list of search results, while the ASR model's behavior is recorded in a sentence. The latter behavior is measurable from the impact of an ASR model's performance to the search engine results. That is, we obtain the semantic and lexical similarities between two search results ($r^y$ and $r^{y'}$) for measuring the system's and the ASR model's behaviors, respectively. Intuitively, the better the ASR model behaves, the smaller the differences are between the true text $y$ and the translated text $y'$, as well as their search results $R = \{r^{y'}, r^y\} = \{r^{y',titles}, r^{y',doc}, r^{y,titles}, r^{y,doc}\}$. Table 1 summarizes the NLU techniques that we applied to analyze the relationships and extract model-specific features. We divide the model-specific features into two groups.

One group compares two correlations. One correlation is the syntactic similarity score between the true transcription $y$ and the substitute model's web search results $r^y$, while the other correlation is the semantic similarity score between $y$ and the system's web search results $r^{y'}$. Specifically, the TF-IDF method ($f_{\text{tf-idf}}$) with semantic similarity measures the importance of $y$ regarding different $r$

**Table 1.** Model-specific feature extraction methods ('na': no methods applied.)

|  | $r^{y,titles}$ | $r^{y',titles}$ | $r^{y,doc}$ | $r^{y',doc}$ |
|---|---|---|---|---|
| $y$ | $f_{\text{tf-idf}}, f_{\text{fuzzy}}$ | $f_{\text{tf-idf}}, f_{\text{fuzzy}}$ | $f_{\text{tf-idf}}, f_{\text{fuzzy}}$ | $f_{\text{tf-idf}}, f_{\text{fuzzy}}$ |
| $r^{y,titles}$ | na | $f_{\text{fuzzy}}, f_{\text{nlp}}, f_{\text{w2v}}$ | na | na |
| $r^{y,doc}$ | na | na | na | $f_{\text{fuzzy}}, f_{\text{nlp}}, f_{\text{w2v}}$ |

settings, while the fuzzy string matching method ($f_{\text{fuzzy}}$) calculates their lexical similarity [16].

The other group calculates the similarity distance between the true transcription and the predicted transcription via their web search results ($r^y$ vs. $r^{y'}$). Apart from $f_{\text{fuzzy}}$ used for the lexical similarity, we use two word embedding methods for the semantic similarity analysis. One method is a trained pipeline *en_core_web_sm* (denoted as $f_{\text{nlp}}$) that lemmatizes each token in every sentence, removes stop words, and calculates two sentences' semantic similarity. The other is a customized Word2Vec model [13] trained with the LibriSpeech textual dataset and our research results (denoted as $f_{\text{w2v}}$).

Apart from the model-specific features, a set of audio-specific features contribute to our user-level membership inference task. It mainly reveals the user's speaking habits, such as speed, high pitch, and many alike. In this work, we only consider the speed, while others like high pitch or low pitch is left as future work. For all these features, record-level features are extracted before user-level features are derived using statistical methods, such as sum, maximum, minimum, mean, average, standard deviation, and variance.

Upon completion of extracting features, different feature selection strategies are evaluated according to our substitute model analysis results. Specifically, we classify those model-specific features as high-relevant features, medium-relevant features, and low-relevant features (Sect. 3.2). Data with the selected feature set are prepared to be fed into our audio auditors. As shown in Table 2, a medium-above feature set is the best choice for our shadow system-based auditor, while the top two features are sufficient for our gap inference-based auditor.

**Shadow System-Based Auditor.** Our shadow system-based auditor performs the user-level membership inference task through a shadow system. The shadow system mimics the target voice service system's behavior on the audio requested web search reactions. The NLU and response modules within the system can be substituted by a search engine ($\mathcal{R}$). We train a shadow ASR model ($\mathcal{F}_{shd}$) to mimic its built-in ASR module.

As shown in Fig. 4, we need to sample the training and testing sets for the shadow ASR model from an auxiliary reference dataset $D_{ref}$. We assume all the recordings within $D_{ref}$ request the web search results in the voice service system. The samples in the training set $A_{shd}^{train}$ are selected according to their web search results querying the target voice service system. Intuitively, we consider an audio sample as a training sample of $\mathcal{F}_{shd}$, where its web search results and its

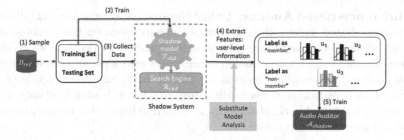

**Fig. 4.** The training process of a shadow system-based auditor. The substitute model analysis (from Fig. 3) guide feature extraction for the shadow system-based auditor.

request context are highly consistent. Specifically, TF-IDF is used to identify the relevance as $d_{tar}$. We define a close correlation if $d_{tar} \geq 0.5$. The data sampling process for the shadow model is illustrated in Algorithm 1.

In the data collection step, we query our shadow model $\mathcal{F}_{shd}$ and the search engine $\mathcal{R}$ with $A_{shd}^{test}$ and $A_{shd}^{train}$. As described in Sect. 2.2, we collect the information of $(x_{shd}, y_{shd}, r^{y_{shd}},$ and $r^{y'_{shd}})$. Subsequently, various user-level features are extracted, and three feature selection strategies are evaluated for different qualities of the model-specific features (Sect. 2.2). Specifically, Strategy One aims to obtain all features including all model-specific features and the audio-specific features; Strategy Two aims to obtain a medium and above feature set that includes medium-relevant and high-relevant model-specific features and the audio-specific features; and Strategy Three aims to obtain high-relevant feature set that include high-relevant model-specific features and the audio-specific features. The three strategies are evaluated so that the best strategy is applied in the auditor's training and auditing processes. We label the user $u_{shd}$'s record with selected features as "member" if $(x_{shd}, y_{shd}) \in A_{shd}^{train}$, otherwise as "nonmember". Repeating the label assignment process, we create a training data set, from which a binary classification model is trained as our shadow system-based auditor $\mathcal{A}_{shadow}$.

---

**Algorithm 1.** Data Sampling for the Shadow ASR Model

---

**Input:** Auxiliary reference dataset $D_{ref}$
**Output:** Shadow ASR model dataset $A_{shd}$
    *Initialisation* : *The target ASR model $\mathcal{F}_{tar}$; The target system reaction function $\mathcal{R}$; Randomly sampled $A_{ref}$ and $A_{shd}^{test}$, where $D_{ref} = A_{ref} \cap A_{shd}^{test}$.*
1: **for** each audio, $(x, y) \in A_{ref}$ **do**
2:    $r^{y'}_{tar} = \mathcal{R}(\mathcal{F}_{tar}(x))$
3:    $d_{tar} = f_{\text{tf-idf}}(y, r^{y'}_{tar})$
4:    **if** $(d_{tar} \geq 0.5)$ **then**
5:       $A_{shd}^{train} \leftarrow (x, y)$
6:    **end if**
7: **end for**
8: **return** $A_{shd} = A_{shd}^{train} \cap A_{shd}^{test}$

---

**Gap Inference-Based Auditor.** Unlike the shadow system-based auditor, our gap inference-based auditor directly learns the gap based on the target system's reactions without the assistance of a shadow system. To do this, we construct two sets of audio samples as a pseudo member set and a pseudo nonmember set. Similar to the data sampling process in Algorithm 1, an audio sample $(x, y)$ is considered as a pseudo member audio sample if its web search results and its query context are highly consistent $(d_{tar} \geq 0.5)$; otherwise it is considered as a pseudo nonmember audio sample.

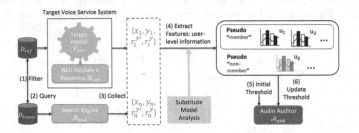

**Fig. 5.** The training process of a gap inference-based auditor. The substitute model analysis (from Fig. 3) guides feature extraction for the gap inference-based auditor.

Figure 5 depicts our gap inference-based auditor's training process by updating the thresholds. The first three steps are identical to the data collection phase described in Sect. 2.2. Then we extract user-level features as demonstrated in Sect. 2.2. Based on the substitute model analysis, we primarily examine the high-relevant features and use the top two for our gap inference. Herein, we aggregate each user's audio query information according to their user-level records. Since our model-related features are all similarity scores, 100% means the highest similarity while 0% means no similarity. The threshold to explore the gap is initialized as 50% and gradually updated by increasing 10% each step until the auditor's performance decreases. Specifically, when both of the top two user-level features reach this threshold, our gap inference-based auditor $\mathcal{A}_{gap}$ considers this user as "*member*", otherwise as "*nonmember*".

To update the threshold and maximize the performance of $\mathcal{A}_{gap}$, we query the target system and its default search engine with a pseudo member set and a pseudo nonmember set. Then these pseudo labeled queries are collected, while the top two high-relevant features are extracted and processed at the user-level. We update the threshold by evaluating the current $\mathcal{A}_{gap}$ with the pseudo labeled data.

## 3   Experimental Setup and Evaluation

In this section, we describe the dataset and target system architecture to set up our experiments, along with evaluations of the auditors.

## 3.1  Experimental Setup

**Datasets and Target System Architecture Datasets.** The **LibriSpeech** corpora is a standard speech corpus to calibrate and evaluate ASR systems. The corpus includes 1000 h of English speech sampled at 16 kHz, mostly audiobooks [14].

**Target System Architecture.** A typical voice service system consists of three modules (Fig. 1). We construct a target voice service system by training an ASR model and introducing a search engine to represent the functionalities of the NLU module and the response module. The ASR model is trained with a four-layer LSTM network with one Softmax layer, and the search engine is Google accessed through ChromeDriver version 88.0.4324.96. We denote this ASR model as an *LSTM-ASR* model and the target system as an *LSTM-ASR-Google* system.

## 3.2  Experimental Evaluation

The random guessing method [9,17,21] is considered as our baseline for comparison. Further, five metrics are used to evaluate the auditor's performance, including Accuracy, Precision, Recall, ROC curve, and AUC. We pose the following research questions.

RQ1 *What features does a system's reaction represent its built-in ASR model's behavior?* We analyze the system's reaction and the substitute model's results to extract the model-specific features with various semantic analysis methods as presented in Sect. 2.2.

RQ2 *How effective are the two auditors in auditing an ASR system?* We explore two auditors with the best performance. Then we study a user-friendly setting of querying audio per user, including the number of audio samples and their lengths.

RQ3 *What are the differences between the two auditors?* We compare our shadow system-based auditor and gap inference-based auditor from four perspectives—the auditing performance, robustness, time consumption, and computing resource.

**System Reaction Versus ASR Model's Behavior.** For RQ1, various model-specific feature extraction methods listed in Table 1 are analyzed for the best reflection of the target ASR model's behavior. As demonstrated in Sect. 2.2, we divide those features into two groups to explore the relationship between the system reaction and its built-in ASR model's behavior. The character error rate (CER) between the true transcription and the predicted transcription is calculated with Levenshtein distance. Theoretically, the better the ASR model behaves, the smaller the CER. The higher the similarity between the predicted transcription $y'$ and the true text $y$, the higher the probability between the similarity distances within two comparison groups.

As presented in Appendix, the CER distributions in those relationships support our observation. For the first group features, we consider $f_{\text{tf-idf}}(y, r^{y',doc})$ as one high-relevant feature, $f_{\text{tf-idf}}(y, r^{y,titles})$ and $f_{\text{tf-idf}}(y, r^{y',titles})$ as two medium-relevant features, and the rest as low-relevant features. For the second group, we consider $f_{\text{fuzzy}}(r^{y,titles}, r^{y',titles})$, $f_{\text{fuzzy}}(r^{y,doc}, r^{y',doc})$, $f_{\text{nlp}}(r^{y,titles}, r^{y',titles})$, $f_{\text{nlp}}(r^{y,doc}, r^{y',doc})$, and $f_{\text{w2v}}(r^{y,titles}, r^{y',titles})$ as high-relevant features, while the rest are considered as low-relevant features.

Our experiments in Appendix show that model-specific features well represent the ASR model's behavior, even though neither the transcription nor the predicted probability is known under the no-label black-box access.

**A Shadow System-Based Auditor's Performance.** Based on the methodology described in Sect. 2.2, we train shadow system-based auditors with three feature selection strategies and with four ML algorithms to analyze their effectiveness (RQ2).

As described in Sect. 3.1, we target an *LSTM-ASR-Google* system. When the shadow system is constructed alternatively to *LSTM-ASR-Google* with a different dataset, we explain the user-level auditor's importance and show the advantages of the user-level auditors over the record-level auditors. To avoid imbalanced bias, all auditors' training sets in this work have the same number of "member" and "nonmember" samples. Each experiment configuration repeats 100 times, and the averaged performance results are reported.

**Table 2.** Three feature selection strategies are used to train the user-level and record-level shadow system-based auditors. The best performance results are highlighted.

| Auditor & Strategy | Accuracy (%) | Precision (%) | Recall (%) |
|---|---|---|---|
| User-level & Strategy One | 62.46 | 61.67 | 65.85 |
| User-level & Strategy Two | **65.10** | 63.00 | **73.24** |
| User-level & Strategy Three | 64.80 | **63.08** | 71.44 |
| Record-level & Strategy One | 56.54 | 52.55 | 57.11 |
| Record-level & Strategy Two | 56.22 | 56.69 | 52.70 |
| Record-level & Strategy Three | 56.13 | 56.48 | 53.45 |

Table 2 compares the user-level and record-level shadow system-based auditors' performances, showing Strategy Two with medium-above feature set as the best choice for the user-level auditor. Further, the user-level auditor's ability significantly surpasses the record-level auditor's because a well-performed ASR model is only required to translate the input audio into textual correctness. However, one sentence could be uttered in different ways, resulting in different transcriptions provided by the ASR model and by a human being.

Then we explore the best fit algorithm with Strategy Two. The user-level shadow system-based auditor is trained with four popular ML algorithms— Decision Tree (DT), Random Forest (RF), $k$-Nearest Neighbor with $k = 3$ (3-NN), and Naive Bayes (NB). Since our shadow system is *LSTM-ASR-Google*, we denote our auditors as the *LSTM-DT* auditor, *LSTM-RF* auditor, *LSTM-kNN* auditor, and *LSTM-NB* auditor.

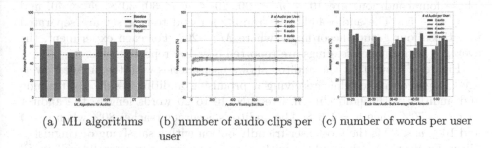

(a) ML algorithms      (b) number of audio clips per     (c) number of words per user
                           user

**Fig. 6.** The performance of user-level shadow system-based auditors.

As shown in Fig. 6a, the *LSTM-RF* auditor and the *LSTM-kNN* auditor perform better than *LSTM-DT* and *LSTM-NB*, while all of their accuracy rates are above the baseline performance (50%). *LSTM-RF* and *LSTM-kNN* perform similarly (both above 60%), with the *LSTM-RF* auditor being slightly better. Therefore, we consider the RF algorithm as the best algorithm among the four choices to train our shadow system-based classifier for user-level membership inference in a voice service system's auditing task.

When the input audio length is fixed, the number of audio samples per user is varied to analyze its impact on the auditor's performance on the target *LSTM-ASR-Google* system. We assume that a user $u$ has $n$ audio recordings querying the shadow *LSTM-ASR-Google* system. Following feature selection Strategy Two, we construct one training sample set for our shadow system-based auditor. We generated the training set of our auditor with $n$ audio samples per user, while the testing set are also generated with $n$ samples per user. We evaluate the performance by varying the number of samples per user and per set $n = 2, 4, 6, 8, 10$. The impact of multiple training set sizes $M$ is evaluated as well. As such, $M \times n$ audio clips were sampled to query the shadow system for our *LSTM-RF* auditor's training set. We trained the audit model with a small set of users ($M = 10, 20, 40, 60, 80, 100$) and a relatively large set of users ($M = 150, 200, 400, 600, 800, 1000$), which are sampled randomly. We repeated each experiment 100 times and reported the averaged results.

Figure 6b shows that the more audio clips for each user are used to audit their membership, the more accurate our shadow system-based auditor performs in general. However, when the training set is large enough, the auditor generates eight samples per user and surpasses the auditor with ten samples per user. The best configuration is eight samples per user, while two samples per user and four samples per user are much more user-friendly. In addition, no matter how many audio records are queried by each user, the performance of the audio auditor becomes more stable as the training set expands in size.

We set $M = 200$ to further explore the impact of the query audio's length. Herein, we use the average number of words to represent the length of each user's query audio set. We set $w_i$ to represent the number of words within one audio clip. Then the length of $u$'s query audio set is $\hat{w} = \frac{\sum^n (w_i)}{n}$. We separate the length of query audio into four groups where $\hat{w}$ satisfies different conditions. Those four conditions are $10 \leq \hat{w} < 20$, $20 \leq \hat{w} < 30$, $30 \leq \hat{w} < 40$, and $40 \leq \hat{w} \leq 50$. The audio auditor's training set and testing set are separated into those four groups accordingly where $M = 200$. For each experiment, the averaged performance readings are reported over 100 repeated runs.

Figure 6c shows that the auditor allows user queries with the smallest averaged length of audio while receiving a promising auditing result. By training and auditing with audio clips in averaged 10 to 20 words length, the auditor surpasses 70% when $n = 4, 6, 8$. The auditor's accuracy reaches 80% when $n = 4$ and $10 \leq \hat{w} < 20$ is the most user-friendly option with a satisfying distinguishability. Furthermore, the auditor with $n = 8$ performs consistently well in all ranges of the query audio length.

Our shadow system-based auditor is effective in the auditing task, which is trained with an RF algorithm with feature selection Strategy Two. Its training set is generated with four audio samples per user by querying with short audio, otherwise eight audio samples per user is a better choice.

**A Gap Inference-Based Auditor's Performance.** Moreover, we train a gap inference-based auditor with top two features as $f_{\text{fuzzy}}(r^{y,titles}, r^{y',titles})$ and $f_{\text{fuzzy}}(r^{y,doc}, r^{y',doc})$, and try to find the best-fit threshold. Unlike the shadow system-based auditor, the gap inference-based auditor is independent of shadow system simulation results except for the substitute model analysis.

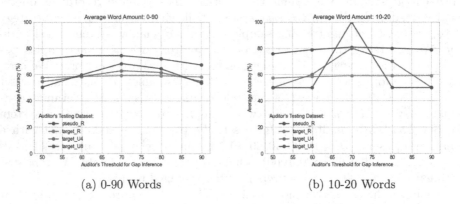

(a) 0-90 Words          (b) 10-20 Words

**Fig. 7.** The performance of gap inference-based auditors trained with various thresholds. Each user's querying audio in (a) and (b) are in different arranges.

A proper threshold is essential to a gap inference-based auditor for our target *LSTM-ASR-Google* system. We initialize the threshold as 50% and gradually increase it to 90% by 10%. The pseudo dataset (*pseudo_R*) described in Sect. 5 is labeled according to the target system's results. According to the shadow system-based auditor's results, we focus on querying audios belonging to users whose $\hat{w}$ is within 0 to 90 (Fig. 7a) and within 10 to 20 (Fig. 7b). Herein, user-level datasets for auditing the target system's membership are generated by querying the system with four and eight audio records per user (*target_U4* and *target_U8*). The record-level dataset for auditing is marked as *target_R*. As shown in Fig. 7, neither a high nor a low threshold makes an auditor perform at high accuracy. When the *pseudo_R*'s auditing result reaches the highest accuracy, the auditor with that threshold can perform the best in the target system's membership inference task. Specifically, when the threshold of our gap inference-based auditor is 70%, the highest accuracy of auditing results in *target_U8* are 68.34% and 100% with different $\hat{w}$. The more audio per user, the more accurate the user-level auditor can perform for the best threshold.

The pseudo dataset helps us find the best threshold for a gap inference-based auditor auditing a voice service system. For our target *LSTM-ASR-Google* system, our gap inference-based auditor with a 70% threshold toward two model-specific features can effectively audit users' audio privacy in the target system.

**Two Auditors' Comparison.** To compare two auditors under no-label black-box access (RQ3), our shadow system-based auditor should be compatible with different systems' architectures. That is, when the target system is a *LSTM-ASR-Google* system, we analyze the performance of auditors trained with a *RNN-ASR-Google* system and a *GRU-ASR-Google* system.

To generalize across different training sets, we use the training set of the *LSTM-ASR* shadow model to train the *RNN-ASR* model and the *GRU-ASR* model within two different shadow systems. Three types of auditors, including an *LSTM-ASR-RF* auditor, an *RNN-ASR-RF* auditor, and a *GRU-ASR-RF* auditor, are constructed accordingly. Further, we combine all types of these shadow systems' output as an *LRG-RF* auditor's training set to mitigate the negative effects.

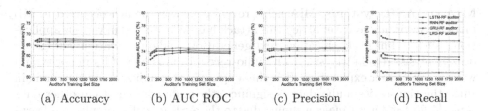

(a) Accuracy        (b) AUC ROC        (c) Precision        (d) Recall

**Fig. 8.** Shadow system-based auditors' performance trained various shadow systems

As shown in Fig. 8, the performances of different auditors follow the same trend in auditing user-level membership, while different ASR models significantly affect the audio auditor's performance. Specifically, the larger the training set size, the more stable the auditors performed. Their AUC ROC scores are comparatively high (reaching up to 74.53%). Based on the accuracy performance in

Fig. 8a, the *LSTM-RF* auditor trained with the same type of the shadow system as the target system. With different system types, the accuracy drops by almost 4% auditing the *GRU-RF* auditor. The reason is that the *GRU-RF* auditor shows a high precision performance but with a low recall performance. The final accuracy and AUC ROC results prove the efficiency of the *LRG-RF* auditor. As shown in Fig. 8c and Fig. 8d, the combined method smooths the deviation caused by different ASR models.

Based on the results in Sect. 3.2, "four audio clips per user with 10 to 20 words of input audio length" and "eight audio per user with 0 to 90 words of query audio length" are the best two effective settings. Table 3 shows the performance of different auditing methods from accuracy, precision, and recall under these two settings. The gap inference auditor with a 70% threshold and the *LRG-RF* auditor significantly outperform the baseline method. Further, the gap inference auditor yields the best performance with a promising result of 80% accuracy that is significantly higher than our shadow system-based auditor (71.30%).

**Table 3.** Comparison of the auditors' performance in our work and the baseline.

| Methods | # words(w); # audio/user(a/u) | Accuracy (%) | Precision (%) | Recall (%) |
|---------|-------------------------------|--------------|---------------|------------|
| LRG-RF Auditor | 10–20 w; 4 a/u | 71.30 | **72.75** | 71.30 |
| | 0–90 w; 8 a/u | 66.82 | 67.63 | 66.82 |
| Gap Infer Auditor | 10–20 w; 4 a/u | **80.00** | 71.42 | **100.00** |
| | 0–90 w; 8 a/u | 68.34 | 65.67 | 76.86 |
| Random Guess | 10–20 w; 4 a/u | 49.10 | 47.94 | 47.60 |
| | 0–90 w; 8 a/u | 50.12 | 50.12 | 50.46 |

## 4    Related Work and Discussion

**MIA on ASR Systems.** MIA helps reveal a privacy breach occurred in ML models. According to Hu et al. [6], this attack has been studied in various applications, such as image classification, text generation, audio recognition, and graph data analysis. Herein, the study on audio recognition is one of its minority and waiting for further exploration. It is challenging in the audio recognition domain since the time-series audio data is significantly more complex than other data types [4,20], and it is time-consuming due to the ASR model's complicated learning architectures [2]. Shah et al. [18] conduct a general record-level membership inference and a user-level membership inference for a specific speaker against an end-to-end ASR model. Similar to our observations, their results show that the end-to-end ASR model is vulnerable to a specific user's membership inference. Miao et al. [12] investigate a user-level membership inference attack against the two most popular ASR models—one hybrid ASR model and one end-to-end ASR model, when the highest performance reached 78.81%. All previous membership inference studies on ASR models are conducted with black-box access. Our work further relaxes the access restriction to the ASR model as no-label black-box access, which is more realistic than the previous works in the real-world voice service scenario. Meanwhile, a semantic analysis is applied to demonstrate the ASR model's behavior, resulting in a high performance of the membership inference (around 80%).

**Limitations and Future Work.** Although our auditor provides a promising result, a few limitations require further research. Firstly, since our auditor is built upon the semantic analysis results, we only consider the audio set that activates the voice service's specific response, that is, web search. Most of those audio sets' contents are longer than our daily audio commands. If the ASR model is trained with other data distribution (i.e., all common commands), the performance of our auditor remains unknown. In this case, further research is required to study whether the semantic analysis represents the model's behavior well or not. Additionally, the relationship between the search results and the ASR system's built-in model's transcriptions might be different with different search engines. In this work, we disclose the effect of the syntactic-based search engine— Google on our auditors' performance. The effect of semantic-based search engines like Bing and DuckDuckGo on the performance of user-level membership inference remains unknown. Secondly, our semantic analysis studied the relationship between the input audio's true text, the translated text's web search results, and the true text's web search result. The method relies on the voice service's web search results. However, the voice service's response functions are diverse. How to utilize other response function's results remains an open research question. Finally, our auditors are evaluated on a hybrid ASR model—the Pytorch-Kaldi ASR model. There are other popular ASR architectures on the market, like the end-to-end ASR model [4] and Wav2Vec ASR model [26]. It would be valuable to evaluate the auditor's robustness further against additional architectures.

## 5   Conclusion

This paper proposes audio auditors for the built-in ASR model in IoT voice services under no-label black-box access. We investigate the user-level membership inference assuming that the translated text is not available explicitly. Our auditor extends the boundary of membership inference by releasing the label-only membership inference assumption [9]. With the substitute model analysis, our auditors learn the ASR model's behavior indirectly. Accordingly, the shadow system-based auditor and the gap inference-based auditor perform well on our task. Both methods achieve high performance for model-independent auditing tasks. Specifically, the highest accuracy score reaches 80% accuracy by our gap inference-based auditor. Examining other factors on performance and extending possible defences against audit are all worth further exploration.

**Acknowledgement.** This research was supported by Data61 and DST Group under the Next Generation Technologies Fund initiative. We especially thank Dr. Paul Montague and Dr. Tamas Abraham for their valuable suggestions.

# A  Appendix

Various model-specific feature extraction methods listed in Table 1 are compared for the best reflection of the target ASR model's behavior. Those features are divided into two groups to explore the relationship between the system reaction and its built-in ASR model's behavior.

The first group compares two correlations, including the similarity distance of $y$ and $r^y$ and that of $y$ and $r^{y'}$. According to search engine optimization, the query sentence should have a close relationship to the search results, indicating semantic relevance ($f_{\text{tf-idf}}$) or lexical relevance ($f_{\text{fuzzy}}$). Intuitively, the better the ASR model behaves, the more similar the $y$ is to $y'$, and the more similar the $y$ and $r^y$ are to $y$ and $r^{y'}$. Therefore, the two correlations in the first group are positive.

As shown in Fig. 9, most of the semantic similarities $f_{\text{tf-idf}}$ faithfully represents the ASR model's transcription performance. With the increasing similarity distance between $y$ and $r^{y',doc}$, the similarity distance between $y$ and $r^{y,doc}$ increases as well (Fig. 9d). However, the relationship between $f_{\text{tf-idf}}(y, r^{y,titles})$ and $f_{\text{tf-idf}}(y, r^{y',titles})$ is not strongly positively correlated. Thus, we consider the $f_{\text{tf-idf}}(y, r^{y',doc})$ as one high-relevant feature, $f_{\text{tf-idf}}(y, r^{y,titles})$ and $f_{\text{tf-idf}}(y, r^{y',titles})$ as two medium-relevant features, and the rest as low-relevant features. Additionally, the distributions of their CER shown in those relationships prove our observation.

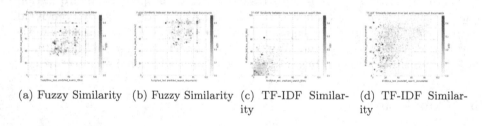

(a) Fuzzy Similarity  (b) Fuzzy Similarity  (c) TF-IDF Similarity  (d) TF-IDF Similarity

**Fig. 9.** The relationship of two correlations including the similarity of the true transcription $y$ within the substitute model's web search results $r^y$ and that of the $y$ within the system's web search results $r^{y'}$.

The second group reflects the ASR model's performance by comparing search results' similarity distance ($r^y$ vs $r^{y'}$) between the true transcription and the predicted transcription. Similarly, the two correlations in the second group should be in a positive correlation. Figure 10 shows the lexical similarities $f_{\text{fuzzy}}$ in this group comparison representing the best relevant relationship. We choose to use Google search as the substitute model, which is syntactic search engine [19]. The syntactic search engine relies more than a semantic search engine on the keywords extracted from the query text. Thus, we mark $f_{\text{fuzzy}}(r^{y,titles}, r^{y',titles})$, $f_{\text{fuzzy}}(r^{y,doc}, r^{y',doc})$, $f_{\text{nlp}}(r^{y,titles}, r^{y',titles})$, $f_{\text{nlp}}(r^{y,doc}, r^{y',doc})$, and $f_{\text{w2v}}(r^{y,titles}, r^{y',titles})$ as high-relevant features, while the rest are considered as low-relevant features. The CER analysis shows the same result for evaluation.

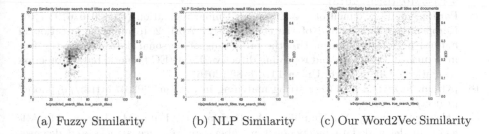

(a) Fuzzy Similarity     (b) NLP Similarity     (c) Our Word2Vec Similarity

**Fig. 10.** The similarity between the substitute model's web search results $r^y$ and the system's web search results $r^{y'}$.

# References

1. CCPA, D.U.: California consumer privacy act (ccpa) website policy (2020)
2. Chen, Y., et al.: Devil's whisper: A general approach for physical adversarial attacks against commercial black-box speech recognition devices. In: Proceedings of the 29th USENIX Security Symposium (USENIX Security 20) (2020)
3. Choo, C.A.C., Tramer, F., Carlini, N., Papernot, N.: Label-only membership inference attacks. arXiv preprint arXiv:2007.14321 (2020)
4. Du, T., Ji, S., Li, J., Gu, Q., Wang, T., Beyah, R.: Sirenattack: generating adversarial audio for end-to-end acoustic systems. arXiv preprint arXiv:1901.07846 (2019)
5. Hayes, J., Melis, L., Danezis, G., De Cristofaro, E.: Logan: membership inference attacks against generative models. Proc. Privacy Enhan. Technol. **2019**(1), 133–152 (2019)
6. Hu, H., Salcic, Z., Dobbie, G., Zhang, X.: Membership inference attacks on machine learning: a survey. arXiv preprint arXiv:2103.07853 (2021)
7. Jiang, J., et al.: Automatic online evaluation of intelligent assistants. In: Proceedings of the 24th International Conference on World Wide Web. pp. 506–516 (2015)
8. Kim, T.K.: Short research on voice control system based on artificial intelligence assistant. In: 2020 International Conference on Electronics, Information, and Communication (ICEIC). pp. 1–2. IEEE (2020)
9. Li, Z., Zhang, Y.: Label-leaks: membership inference attack with label. arXiv preprint arXiv:2007.15528 (2020)
10. Liu, G., Wang, C., Peng, K., Huang, H., Li, Y., Cheng, W.: Socinf: membership inference attacks on social media health data with machine learning. IEEE Trans. Comput. Soc. Syst. **6**(5), 907–921 (2019)
11. McReynolds, E., Hubbard, S., Lau, T., Saraf, A., Cakmak, M., Roesner, F.: Toys that listen: a study of parents, children, and Internet-connected toys. In: Proceedings of the 2017 CHI Conference on Human Factors in Computing Systems. pp. 5197–5207. ACM (2017)
12. Miao, Y., et al.: The audio auditor: user-level membership inference in internet of things voice services. Proc. Privacy Enhan. Technol. **2021**, 209–228 (2021)
13. Mikolov, T., Chen, K., Corrado, G., Dean, J.: Efficient estimation of word representations in vector space. arXiv preprint arXiv:1301.3781 (2013)

14. Panayotov, V., Chen, G., Povey, D., Khudanpur, S.: Librispeech: an ASR corpus based on public domain audio books. In: Proceedings of the 2015 IEEE International Conference on Acoustics, Speech and Signal Processing (ICASSP). pp. 5206–5210. IEEE (2015)
15. Parliament, E.: Council of the European Union: regulation (eu) 2016/679 of the European parliament and of the council of 27 April 2016 on the protection of natural persons with regard to the processing of personal data and on the free movement of such data and repealing directive 95/46/EC (general data protection regulation). Off. J. Euro. Union **119**, 1–88 (2016)
16. python: Fuzzywuzzy: Fuzzy string matching in python (2020). https://pypi.org/project/fuzzywuzzy/
17. Salem, A., Zhang, Y., Humbert, M., Berrang, P., Fritz, M., Backes, M.: Ml-leaks: model and data independent membership inference attacks and defenses on machine learning models. In: Proceedings of the 26th Annual Network and Distributed System Security Symposium (NDSS) (2019)
18. Shah, M.A., Szurley, J., Mueller, M., Mouchtaris, A., Droppo, J.: Evaluating the vulnerability of end-to-end automatic speech recognition models to membership inference attacks. In: Proceedings Interspeech. pp. 891–895 (2021)
19. Sheela, A.S., Jayakumar, C.: Comparative study of syntactic search engine and semantic search engine: a survey. In: Proceedings of the 2019 Fifth International Conference on Science Technology Engineering and Mathematics (ICONSTEM). vol. 1, pp. 1–4. IEEE (2019)
20. Shokoohi-Yekta, M., Chen, Y., Campana, B., Hu, B., Zakaria, J., Keogh, E.: Discovery of meaningful rules in time series. In: Proceedings of the 21th ACM SIGKDD International Conference on Knowledge Discovery and Data Mining (KDD). pp. 1085–1094. ACM (2015)
21. Shokri, R., Song, M.S., Shmatikov, V.: Membership inference attacks against machine learning models. In: Proceedings of the 2017 IEEE Symposium on Security and Privacy (S&P). pp. 3–18. IEEE (2017)
22. Song, C., Shmatikov, V.: Auditing data provenance in text-generation models. In: Proceedings of the 25th ACM SIGKDD International Conference on Knowledge Discovery & Data Mining (KDD). pp. 196–206 (2019)
23. Song, L., Shokri, R., Mittal, P.: Privacy risks of securing machine learning models against adversarial examples. In: Proceedings of the 2019 ACM SIGSAC Conference on Computer and Communications Security (CCS). pp. 241–257 (2019)
24. Xue, M., Magno, G., Cunha, E., Almeida, V., Ross, K.W.: The right to be forgotten in the media: a data-driven study. Proc. Privacy Enhan. Technol. **2016**(4), 389–402 (2016)
25. Yerukola, A., Bretan, M., Jin, H.: Data augmentation for voice-assistant NLU using bert-based interchangeable rephrase. arXiv preprint arXiv:2104.08268 (2021)
26. Yuan, Y., Xun, G., Suo, Q., Jia, K., Zhang, A.: Wave2vec: Learning deep representations for biosignals. In: 2017 IEEE International Conference on Data Mining (ICDM). pp. 1159–1164. IEEE (2017)
27. Zhang, Y., Xu, L., Mendoza, A., Yang, G., Chinprutthiwong, P., Gu, G.: Life after speech recognition: fuzzing semantic misinterpretation for voice assistant applications. In: Proceedings of the Network and Distributed System Security Symposium (NDSS'19) (2019)

# Applications

# A Toolbox for Verifiable Tally-Hiding E-Voting Systems

Véronique Cortier, Pierrick Gaudry[(✉)], and Quentin Yang

Université de Lorraine, CNRS, Inria, Metz, France
`pierrick.gaudry@loria.fr`

**Abstract.** In most verifiable electronic voting schemes, one key step is the tally phase, where the election result is computed from the encrypted ballots. A generic technique consists in first applying (verifiable) mixnets to the ballots and then revealing all the votes in the clear. This however discloses much more information than the result of the election itself (that is, the winners, plus possibly some information required by law) and may offer the possibility to coerce voters.

In this paper, we present a collection of building blocks for designing tally-hiding schemes based on multi-party computations. From these building blocks, we design a fully tally-hiding scheme for Condorcet elections. Our implementation shows that the approach is practical, at least for medium-size elections. Similarly, we provide the first tally-hiding schemes with no leakage for three important counting functions: D'Hondt, STV, and Majority Judgment. We prove that they can be used to design a private and verifiable voting scheme. We also unveil unknown flaws or leakage in some previously proposed tally-hiding schemes.

## 1 Introduction

Electronic voting is used in many countries and various contexts, from major politically binding elections to small elections among scientific councils. It allows voters to vote from any place and is often used as a replacement for postal voting. Moreover, it enables complex tally processes where voters express their preference by ranking their candidates (preferential voting). In such cases, the votes are counted using the prescribed procedure (*e.g.* Single Transferable Vote or Condorcet), which is tedious by hand but easy for a computer.

Numerous electronic voting protocols have been proposed such as Helios [6], Civitas [15], or CHVote [21]. They all intend to guarantee at least two security properties: *vote secrecy* (no one should know how I voted) and *verifiability*. Vote secrecy is typically achieved through asymmetric encryption: election trustees jointly compute an election public key that is used to encrypt the votes. The trustees take part in the tally, to compute the election result. Only a coalition of dishonest trustees (set to some threshold) can decrypt a ballot and violate vote secrecy. Verifiability typically guarantees that a voter can check that her vote has been properly recorded and that an external auditor can check that the result corresponds to the received votes. Then, depending on the protocol, additional properties can be achieved such as coercion-resistance or cast-as-intended.

© The Author(s), under exclusive license to Springer Nature Switzerland AG 2022
V. Atluri et al. (Eds.): ESORICS 2022, LNCS 13555, pp. 631–652, 2022.
https://doi.org/10.1007/978-3-031-17146-8_31

Various techniques are used to achieve such properties but one common key step is the tally: from the set of encrypted ballots, it is necessary to compute the result of the election, in a verifiable manner.

There are two main approaches for tallying an election. The first one is the *homomorphic tally*. Thanks to the homomorphic property of the encryption scheme (typically ElGamal), the ballots are combined to compute the (encrypted) sum of the votes. Then only the resulting ciphertext is decrypted to reveal the election result, without leaking the individual votes. For verifiability, each trustee produces a zero-knowledge proof of correct (partial) decryption so that anyone can check that the result indeed corresponds to the encrypted ballots. The second main approach is based on *verifiable re-encryption mixnets*. The encrypted ballots are shuffled and re-randomized such that the resulting ballots cannot be linked to the original ones [21,40]. A zero-knowledge proof of correct mixing is produced to guarantee that no ballot has been removed nor added. Several mixers are successively used and then each (rerandomized) ballot is decrypted, yielding the original votes in clear, in a random order.

Homomorphic tally can only be applied to simple vote counting functions, where voters select one or several candidates among a list and the result of the election is the sum of the votes, for each candidate. We note that even in this simple case, the tally reveals more information than just the winner(s) of the election. Mixnet-based tally can be used for any vote counting function since it reveals the (multi)set of the initial votes. On the other hand, this is much more information than the result itself, and such systems can be subject to Italian attacks. Indeed, when voters rank their candidates by order of preference, the number of possible choices can be higher than the number of voters. Hence a voter can be coerced to vote in a certain way by first selecting the first candidates as desired by the coercer and then "signing" her ballot with some very particular order of candidates, as prescribed by the coercer. The coercer will check at the end of the election that such a ballot appears.

Recent work have explored the possibility to design tally-hiding schemes, that compute the result of the election from a set of encrypted ballots, without leaking any other information. This can be seen as an instance of Multi-Party Computation (MPC), but the context of voting adds some constraints. First, a voter should only produce one encrypted ballot that should remain of reasonable size and be computed with low resources (*e.g.* in JavaScript). The trustees can be assumed to have more resources. Yet, it is important to minimize the number of communications and the computation cost, whenever possible. In particular, voters should not wait for weeks before obtaining the result. Moreover, all proofs produced by the authorities need to be downloaded and verified by external, independent auditors. It is important that verifying an election remains affordable.

*Related Work.* Even when the winner(s) of the election is simply the one(s) that received the most votes, leaking the scores of each candidate can be embarrassing and even lower vote privacy. This is discussed in [25] where the authors propose a protocol called Ordinos that computes the candidate who received the most votes, without any extra information. In case of preferential voting, where voters rank candidates, several methods can be applied to determine the winner(s). Two popular methods are Single Transferable Vote (STV) and Condorcet. STV is used in politically binding elections in several countries, including Australia, Ireland or UK. Condorcet has several variants and the Schulze variant is popular among several associations like Ubuntu or GnuGP. These are the counting methods offered by the voting platform CIVS [1] and used in many elections. Literature for tally-hiding schemes includes [22] which shows how to compute the result in Condorcet, while [37] and [9] provide several methods for STV. They all leak some partial information, but much less than the complete set of votes. Ordinos has been extended [24] to cover various counting functions that include Borda, Hare-Niemeyer, Condorcet, and Instant-Runoff Voting (IRV, which is STV with only one seat). This shows the flexibility of Ordinos, yet at a cost: ballots are of size cubic in the number of candidates for Condorcet-Schulze and even super-exponential for IRV. The last system we study, Majority Judgment (MJ) is a vote system where voters give a grade to each candidate (typically between 1 and 6). The winner is, roughly, the candidate with the highest median rating. Since typically several candidates have the same median, the winner is determined by a complex algorithm that iteratively compares the highest median, then the second one and so on (see [7] for the full details). In [12], the authors show how to compute Majority Judgment in MPC. All these approaches except [22] rely on Paillier encryption since it is better suited than ElGamal for the arithmetic comparison of the content of two ciphertexts.

*Our Contributions.* First, we revisit the existing work, exhibiting weaknesses and even flaws for some of them. For example, we discovered that the scheme proposed in [22] for Condorcet breaks vote privacy for each voter that voted blank. Moreover, we found out that the approach developed in [12] for Majority Judgement fails in not-so-rare cases.

Our second and main contribution is the design of a toolbox of MPC primitives well suited for tally-hiding schemes. We provide a precise cost analysis, with various tradeoffs in terms of message size, number of communications, and computational costs. We believe this study could be useful in other settings. As an application of our toolbox, we provide new algorithms for computing vote counting functions, decreasing both the complexity and the leakage or proposing other trade-offs regarding the load for the voters and the trustees. One of our first findings is that even for complex counting functions, it is possible to use Exponential ElGamal encryption instead of Paillier. This offers a much better tool support as well as new tradeoffs in terms of computational costs.

As counting functions, we first consider Condorcet-Schulze and propose the first tally-hiding scheme that allows candidates to be ranked at equality, with a quasi-linear complexity for voters (vs cubic in [24]). We also devise several efficiency/leakage compromises. We continue by considering three major counting functions: D'Hondt, Majority Judgment, and STV. For each of them, we propose the first tally-hiding schemes with no leakage.

*Security Proof and Implementation.* The Paillier setting of our toolbox builds upon the same low-level primitive as previous works. However, in the ElGamal setting that we found to be highly relevant, the core ingredient is the `CGate` protocol (that conditionally sets a component to 0). An important contribution of our work is to formally prove that this primitive is UC-secure and verifiable. Concentrating on this ElGamal setting, this allows us to prove vote secrecy and verifiability of a voting scheme that embeds our tally-hiding protocol.

With the same goal of validating our ElGamal approach, we have implemented our building blocks in a library in this setting. As a proof of concept, we have combined them to form the tally-hiding scheme that corresponds to Condorcet-Schulze. Our experiments show a reasonable execution time. Authorities need a couple of minutes to perform the tally for 5 candidates, and about 9 h for 20 candidates (and 1024 voters). In contrast, the code [24] developed in the Paillier setting, needed more than 9 days for 20 candidates (and was almost insensitive to the number of voters).

Finally, we emphasize that our toolbox should be suitable to implement any realistic counting method. For example, we assumed here that the desired result of the election is exactly the set of winners but our toolbox could be used to reveal more information if needed (for example, it could tell that candidate A receives between 55% and 60% of the votes).

*Outline of the Paper.* We start (Sect. 2) by explaining how to obtain all basic arithmetic operations in MPC on encrypted integers, using El Gamal encryption and we show that it is UC-secure. Figure 1 in Appendix provides the cost of each basic function, that allows to derive the cost of any complex function, obtained by composition. In Sect. 3, we apply our toolbox to the Condorcet-Schulze tally function and we provide a detailed computational cost analysis, and compare it with previous approaches (one of them suffering from a privacy breach). Due to space constraints, we overview in Sect. 4 how our toolbox can be applied to single voting, STV and Majority judgement, again comparing our approach to previous techniques. The exact cost of each tally function is given in Appendix. We show in Sect. 5 that, in all these cases, we can derive a privacy preserving voting protocol.

A companion report [18] provides a more detailed overview on how our toolbox can be applied to build MPC secure tally functions for Condorcet, single voting, STV, and Majority judgement. It also contains all the detailed algorithms and security proofs. Our source code for the implementation is available in [4].

## 2   Description of the Tally-Hiding Toolbox

We focus on the tally phase, common to most voting schemes. We assume a public ballot box that contains the list of encrypted ballots where all the traditional issues up to here have been handled: eligibility, validity of ballots, revoting policy if applicable, and so on. We concentrate on the counted-as-recorded property.

Our goal is to compute the winners of the election, while preserving the privacy of the voters, namely with no additional leakage of information about the tally. The decryption key is assumed to be shared among $a$ trustees, with a threshold scheme, and we wish the procedure to produce a transcript such that: 1) if at least a threshold of $t+1$ trustees is honest, the result will be obtained; 2) if at most $t$ trustees are corrupted, only the result is known (no side-information is leaked); 3) even if all $a$ trustees are dishonest, if the transcript is valid then the result is guaranteed to be correct.

## 2.1   Encryption Scheme: Paillier vs ElGamal

Paillier and Exponential ElGamal are the most popular asymmetric encryption schemes that are homomorphic, where multiplication or division of ciphertexts correspond to addition or subtraction of the corresponding cleartexts. They therefore allow re-encryption, by multiplying by an encryption of 0. These are properties at the heart of the MPC protocols.

When Exponential ElGamal encryption can be used, it offers several advantages over Paillier. First, popular elliptic curves like NIST P-256 or Curve25519 are now ubiquitous in cryptographic libraries, while there is in general no support for Paillier. Moreover, in our context, it is important to split the decryption key among several trustees so that no single authority can break vote privacy. It is easy to set up threshold decryption in ElGamal, with an arbitrary threshold of trustees [16]. The situation is more complex in Paillier. The general threshold key distribution scheme [23] is of high complexity. A more efficient scheme exists [29], but only with a honest majority. Another reason for preferring ElGamal is that the underlying security assumption (Decisional Diffie Hellman) can be considered as more standard than the one for Paillier (Decisional $n$-Residuosity).

On the other hand, Paillier offers more possibilities when it comes to MPC. Therefore, in general, an algorithm based on the Paillier scheme requires less exponentiations than when based on ElGamal; however, exponentiations are more costly. Later on, we will provide the complexities of our algorithms measured by the number of exponentiations. When comparing these figures, one should remember the respective costs in ElGamal and in Paillier, that we estimate now.

**Table 1.** Estimation of the number of exponentiations per second in Paillier and ElGamal settings.

|                        | Paillier | Elliptic ElGamal | Ratio |
|------------------------|----------|------------------|-------|
| Native (server-side)   | 200      | 10,000           | 50    |
| In browser (voter-side)| 2        | 5,000            | 2,500 |

**Parameter Sizes and Cost of Operations.** For a voting system, a 128-bit level of security seems to be a reasonable choice. While 112-bit level is probably acceptable for the next decade, many certification bodies will ask for 128 bits or more. In the case of an elliptic ElGamal this translates readily into a curve over a base field of 256 bits, and usually prime files are preferred.

For the Paillier scheme, the security relies on a problem that is not harder than integer factorization of an RSA number $n$. Since the complexity of the best known factoring algorithm is hard to evaluate, there is no strict consensus about the size of $n$ for a 128-bit security level. Generally, this goes around 3072 bits. In Table 1, we estimate the number of exponentiations per second, based on a medium level of optimization, for a native implementation on a modern processor (based on OpenSSL, using RSA for Paillier emulation), and for a JavaScript implementation in a browser (based on `libsodium.js` and JavaScript BigInt).

## 2.2   Key Elements of ElGamal-Based MPC

Our toolbox contains subroutines for both ElGamal and Paillier, but in this description, we concentrate on ElGamal, since in the end we find it more suitable for e-voting. In ElGamal-based MPC, some operations seem to be impossible to be performed efficiently, for instance comparing two encrypted integers. In order to evaluate any counting function, we will therefore restrict ourselves to manipulating encrypted bits. By the homomorphic property, dividing an encryption of 1 by a ciphertext provides an easy and cheap Not gate. The main workhorse of our toolbox is a primitive from [32] called conditional gate, that provides an And gate. We readily deduce that a Nand gate is available, which is complete, and therefore any function can be implemented by working on encrypted bits.

---

**Algorithm 1:** CGate

**Require:** $X, Y$ such that $X, Y$ are encryptions of $x, y \in \{0,1\}$
**Ensure:** $Z = \text{Enc}(xy)$
1  Compute $Y_0 = \text{Enc}(-1)Y^2$, set $X_0$ to $X$
2  **for** $i = 1$ to $a$, for the authority $i$, **do**
3    |   Choose $r_1, r_2 \in_r \mathbb{Z}_q$ and $s \in_r \{-1, 1\}$
4    |   Compute $X_i = \text{ReEnc}(X_{i-1}^s, r_1)$ and $Y_i = \text{ReEnc}(Y_{i-1}^s, r_2)$
5    |   Reveal $X_i, Y_i$ and a ZKP that $X_i$ and $Y_i$ are well formed
6  Each authority verifies the proof of the other authorities
7  They collectively rerandomize $X_a$ and $Y_a$ into $X'$ and $Y'$
8  They collectively compute $y_a = \text{Dec}(Y')$
9  Return $Z = (XX'^{y_a})^{\frac{1}{2}}$

---

**Conditional Gates.** A conditional gate [32] is a protocol which allows to compute, from two encryptions of $x$ and $y$, an encryption of $xy$. It is named this way because $y$ needs to lie in a known binary domain. We propose the CGate protocol (Algorithm 1), adapted from [32] so that we could prove its security in the SUC framework (see Sect. 2.4). This protocol is the main building block of our MPC protocols, which consist of CGate protocols and homomorphic operations. Note that each participant of a CGate protocol produces a Zero Knowledge Proof (ZKP) that guarantees that the correct computations were performed (including at steps 7 and 8 for example). Those ZKP can later form a transcript which can be used to verify the output of the protocol. Their exact description can be found in [18]. By concatenating the transcripts of all the CGate subprotocols, a transcript for verifiability can be obtained for all our MPC protocols.

**Encrypting an Integer.** When ElGamal is used for a homomorphic tally, the result is an integer that is directly encrypted thanks to a *natural encoding*. We can still add and subtract encrypted values, but most other operations (comparison, multiplication, ...) are more difficult, or even impossible. Therefore, in our protocol we will keep intermediate integer values encrypted in the *bit-encoding*, where each bit of the integer is separately encrypted. We denote it $X^{\text{bits}} = (X_0, \dots, X_{m-1})$, where $2^m$ is a bound on the integer represented by $X$, and $X_i$ is the encryption of the $i$-th bit of the binary expansion (index 0 for the least significant bit). Converting an integer in bit-encoding to natural encoding is done using the homomorphic property and the Horner scheme. The other direction is impossible in the ElGamal setting. However, if the Paillier scheme is used, converting from the natural to the bit-encoding is still possible [33].

## 2.3 MPC Toolbox

We now present the building blocks that constitute our toolbox, such as addition, multiplication and comparison. Those building blocks can be combined to evaluate any counting function without leaking anything but the result. For each of them, we study their cost, which are summarized in the Fig. 1 of the Appendix. The computation cost is the number of exponentiations, but for the communications, we distinguish the broadcast and the rounds of communications. An important information is also the size of the transcript that is created during the process and that should be checked, for example by auditors, to guarantee that the result is correct.

We believe that this toolbox is of independent interest and could be used in contexts beyond tally-hiding protocols. This gathers results from various domains, first on ZKP [11,27,30,40] and MPC [8,19,28,32–34] but also on hardware circuits [10]. We distinguish between the functionality (*e.g.* addition) and the protocol that realizes it since different options may be considered, leading to different trade-offs in terms of communications and computations. For some building blocks, we propose our own protocols, improving existing propositions.

**Branch-Free Tools.** In MPC, the algorithms must be implemented in a branch-free setting, because the result of a test cannot be revealed. We consider the following conditional operations, where $B$ is an encrypted bit.

- CondSetZero$(X, B)$, CondSetZero$^{\text{bits}}(X^{\text{bits}}, B)$: conditionally sets to zero by outputting a re-encryption of $X$ if $B$ is an encryption of 1, or of Enc(0) otherwise. In the bit-encoding setting, each bit of $X$ is treated separately.
- Select$(X, Y, B)$, Select$^{\text{bits}}(X^{\text{bits}}, Y^{\text{bits}}, B)$: selects according to bit by outputting a re-encryption of $X$ if $B$ is an encryption of 0, or of $Y$ otherwise.

- SelectInd($[X_i], [B_i]$): selects in array according to bits by outputting a re-encryption of $X_i$ for the $i$ such that $B_i$ is an encryption of 1. This requires that $[B_i]$ is such that there is only one index $i$ for which $B_i$ is Enc(1).

The CondSetZero functionality is essentially just the CGate protocol. The other functionalities can be easily derived using the homomorphic property. If the Paillier setting is used, a more efficient realization is possible [19,34]. More details can be found in [18].

**Arithmetic.** Thanks to the homomorphic property, additions and subtractions are easily handled with the natural encoding. However, they are more involved with the bit-encoding [32]. We denote the corresponding functionalities Add and Sub. They can be implemented as we would do for binary circuits.

Comparison of two integers is denoted by LT. In bit-encoding, it can be seen as a subtraction where only the final borrow bit is needed. Similarly, we define the Mul functionality that can be applied to integers in the bit-encoding, following the schoolbook algorithm for bit-wise encoded integers. Finally, a frequent operation is to compute the sum of many encrypted binary values, typically to get the total number of votes for a given option. We call this operation Aggreg. If this is the final result before decryption, the homomorphic property is enough, but in general the result is needed in the bit-encoding format. We therefore designed a dedicated tree-based algorithm with variable precision, which improves the complexity compared to a naive approach.

The cost of many variants of all of these, with different trade-offs, are given in Appendix. We also include algorithms in the Paillier setting for which more operations are available in the natural encoding.

**Shuffle and Mixnet.** A tool that is of great use in our context is the verifiable shuffle [39,40], leading to mixnets. In electronic voting, the typical use of a mixnet is during the tally phase, just before decrypting all the ballots, one by one. Our tally-hiding schemes actually makes a thorough use of shuffle, not only on the trustees side but also on the voter's side, as shown in Sect. 3.

## 2.4   Security

We consider the well-known UC-framework [13] to prove security. A composable framework is particularly suitable to analyze the security of our MPC protocols since we provide building blocks that we combine. We actually use the composition framework from [14], which is a Simpler version of the Universally Composable framework (SUC), shown to imply UC-security. Participants of a protocol $P$ are modeled as Polynomial Probabilistic Turing Machines (PPT). Each of the $a$ participants has a single input and output communication tape, and interacts with a router, which in turn interacts with an adversary $\mathbb{A}$. The adversary interacts with the router and the environment $\mathcal{Z}$. It can corrupt a subset $C$ of participants of size at most $t$, where $t \leq a$ is some threshold. Non-corrupted participants are honest and follow the protocol, while corrupted participants are fully impersonated by the adversary and give away any secret they have. The process terminates when $\mathcal{Z}$ writes on its output tape. We denote $\mathsf{REAL}_{P,\mathbb{A},\mathcal{Z}}(\kappa, z)$ the output, where $\kappa$ is a security parameter and $z$ is an arbitrary auxiliary input.

The security of the process is guaranteed by a comparison with an ideal one, in which each party hands over their inputs to a trusted party $T$ which honestly performs the desired computation. Corrupted parties may send arbitrary outputs as instructed by the adversary, and the adversary can block or delay communications with the trusted party. Intuitively, $T$ computes some ideal function $f$, such as Add but it cannot be just a function. Indeed, $T$ additionally takes care of failure cases (for example, when too many parties return inconsistent data). We denote $\mathsf{IDEAL}_{T,\mathcal{S},\mathcal{Z}}(\kappa, z)$ the output of the environment in the ideal process, when it interacts with the adversary $\mathcal{S}$. Intuitively, a protocol is SUC-secure if, for all adversary $\mathbb{A}$ in the real process, there exists a simulator $\mathcal{S}$ in the ideal process such that no PPT environment $\mathcal{Z}$ can tell whether they are interacting with the adversary in the real process or with the simulator in the ideal process.

**Definition 1 (Secure computation [14]).** *Let $P$ be a protocol, $T$ some trusted party. We say that $P$ securely computes $T$ if, for all PPT $\mathbb{A}$, there exists a PPT $\mathcal{S}$ such that, for all PPT $\mathcal{Z}$, there exists a negligible function $\mu$ such that for all $\kappa$ and all $z$ polynomial in $\kappa$,*

$$| \Pr(\mathit{IDEAL}_{T,\mathcal{S},\mathcal{Z}}(\kappa, z) = 1) - \Pr(\mathit{REAL}_{P,\mathbb{A},\mathcal{Z}}(\kappa, z) = 1)| \leq \mu(\kappa).$$

All our building blocks (except shuffle and mixnets, that are handled separately) rely on CondSetZero in the sense that they can all be derived as composition of this function, possibly with intermediate operations using only the homomorphic property. To compute CondSetZero, we consider the MPC protocol CGate [32] based on ElGamal, and we adapt it in order to prove, in the SUC framework, that CGate securely computes the trusted party $T_{\mathsf{CGate}}$, that behaves as CondSetZero except when parties do not answer, in which case it returns an error. The CGate protocol also produces a transcript which acts as a ZKP that the protocol was performed correctly. The SUC security of the other building blocks then follows by composition. Actually, as detailed in [14], SUC-security is not directly composable but instead requires to introduce intermediary (composable) hybrid models, where participants have an oracle access to some ideal trusted parties. We could prove by composition of the hybrid models that each of our building blocks securely computes its corresponding ideal trusted party. However, this would require some extra work since our building blocks compute a re-encryption of the desired function (*e.g.* addition) and hence is not a deterministic function. Instead, we use a different proof strategy: we show that any composition of CGate, followed by a final decryption, is SUC-secure, which corresponds exactly to our needs when applied to tally-hiding schemes. All the precise definitions and proofs are provided in the full version of this paper [18].

# 3   Tally-Hiding Schemes for Condorcet-Schulze

The Condorcet approach is a popular technique to determine a winner when voters rank candidates by order of preference, possibly with equalities. A Condorcet winner is a candidate that is preferred to every other candidate by a majority of voters. More formally, we consider the *matrix of pairwise preferences d* where $d_{i,j}$ is the number of voters that prefer (strictly) candidate $i$ over $j$. Then a Condorcet winner is a candidate $i$ such that $d_{i,j} > d_{j,i}$ for all $j \neq i$. Such a candidate may not exist. In that case, several variants can be applied to compute the winner. We focus here on the Schulze method, used for example for Ubuntu elections [5]. It first considers by "how much" a candidate is preferred, which can be reflected into the *adjacency matrix a* defined as

$$a_{i,j} = \begin{cases} d_{i,j} - d_{j,i} & \text{if } d_{i,j} > d_{j,i}, \\ 0 & \text{otherwise.} \end{cases}$$

Then a weighted directed graph is derived from the adjacency matrix, where each candidate $i$ is associated to a node and there is an edge from $i$ to $j$ with weight $a_{i,j}$. This itself induces an order relation between the candidates by comparing the "strength" of the paths between $i$ and $j$. The exact algorithm can be found in [35]. Note that there may be several winners according to Condorcet-Schulze. We denote by $f_{\text{Cond}}$ the function that returns the winners.

We propose several MPC implementations of Condorcet-Schulze, depending on the accepted leakage and on the load balance between the voters and the authorities. The different approaches are summarized in Table 2.

**Table 2.** Leading terms of the cost of MPC implementations for Condorcet-Schulze. $n$: number of voters, $m = \lceil \log(n+1) \rceil$, $k$: number of candidates, $a$: number of authorities.

| Version | Leakage | EG/P | Voters | Authorities | | Size of the transcript |
|---------|---------|------|--------|-------------|---|------------------------|
| | | | # exp. | # exp. | # comm. | |
| [22] | Adj. matrix privacy breach [i] | EG | $5k^2$ | $18nak^2$ | 2 | $13nak^2$ |
| [24] [ii][iii] | ∅ | P | $5k^3$ | $6nak^3 + (54m+292\log m)ak^3$ | $4k\log m$ | $9nk^3 + (56m +100\log m)ak^3$ |
| Ballots as list of integers (partial MPC) | Adj. matrix | EG | $8k\log k$ | $\frac{87}{2}nak^2\log k$ | $2\log k$ | $\frac{93}{2}nak^2\log k$ |
| Ballots as list of integers (full MPC) | ∅ | EG | $8k\log k$ | $\frac{29}{2}nak^2(3\log k+5m) + 174mak^3$ | $m(m+4k)$ | $\frac{31}{4}nak^2(3\log k+5m) + 186mak^3$ |
| Ballots as matrices | Adj. matrix | EG | $\frac{43}{2}k^2$ | $\frac{47}{2}nk^2$ | 0 | $\frac{85}{2}nk^2$ |

i [22] leaks, for each ballot, the number of candidates ranked at equality. In particular, who voted blank is known to everyone.

ii [24] does not allow voters to give the same rank to several candidates.

iii [24] originally does not take into account the cost of verifying the ZKP from the voters.

## 3.1   Ballots as Matrices

A first approach is to encode the vote as a *preference matrix m*. For each candidate $i$, let $c_i$ be its rank, possibly with equality. Then $m_{i,j}$ is set to 1 if $c_i < c_j$, 0 if $c_i = c_j$ and $-1$ otherwise. The voters then encode their ballot as an encrypted preference matrix $M$. They also need to prove that $M$ is well-formed, that is, corresponds to a total order (with equalities). This requires e.g. to prove that if the voter prefers $i$ over $j$ and $j$ over $k$ then she prefers $i$ over $k$:

$$(m_{i,j} = 1) \wedge (m_{j,k} = 1) \Rightarrow (m_{i,k} = 1)$$

and similar relations when $m_{i,j}$ and $m_{j,k}$ are equal to $0$ or $-1$.

To discharge the voter from such a proof effort, in [22] the authorities shuffle each preference matrix in blocks and then decrypt them to check that it was indeed well formed. However, this yields a privacy breach, unnoted in [22]: for each voter, everyone learns the number of candidates placed at equality. In particular, everyone learns who voted blank since in that case all candidates are placed at equality. A costly way to repair [22] is to let the voters prove the relations with a ZKP, with a cost of $O(k^3)$ exponentiations to build and to check a ballot, where $k$ is the number of candidates. This is the approach of [24], that also assumes that voters do not place candidates at equality (the case $c_i = c_j$ is forbidden).

We propose an alternative approach in $O(k^2)$ exponentiations for both the voter and the verifier. Assume first that a voter prefers candidate 1 over candidate 2, that is preferred over candidate 3 and so on. Then the corresponding preference matrix is $m^{\text{init}}$. We consider a fixed encryption $M^{\text{init}}$ of this matrix, where $E_\alpha$ is the ElGamal encryption of $\alpha$ with "randomness" 0. Everyone can check that $M^{\text{init}}$ is formed as prescribed, at no cost, since we use a constant "randomness":

$$m^{\text{init}} = \begin{pmatrix} 0 & 1 & \cdots & 1 \\ -1 & 0 & \ddots & \vdots \\ \vdots & \ddots & \ddots & 1 \\ -1 & \cdots & -1 & 0 \end{pmatrix} \qquad M_{i,j}^{\text{init}} = \begin{cases} E_1 & \text{if } i < j \\ E_0 & \text{if } i = j \\ E_{-1} & \text{otherwise.} \end{cases}$$

Assume now that a voter wishes to rank the candidates in some order, which is a permutation $\sigma$ of $1, 2, \ldots, k$. Then the voter can simply shuffle $M^{\text{init}}$ using $\sigma$. The associated proofs of a shuffle guarantee that the resulting matrix is indeed a permutation of $M^{\text{init}}$, hence is well formed. Interestingly the secret vote $\sigma$ is not encoded in the initial matrix but in the permutation used to shuffle it. Applying [40], this requires $O(k^2)$ exponentiations for the voter. To account for candidates that have an equal rank, the voter still shuffles $M^{\text{init}}$ according to a permutation $\sigma$ consistent with her preference order, that is such that $\sigma(i) < \sigma(j)$ implies that $c_i \leq c_j$. But beforehand, she sends an additional vector $B$ of encrypted bits $(b_i)$, where $b_i = 1$ if candidates $\sigma^{-1}(i)$ and $\sigma^{-1}(i+1)$ have equal rank and $b_i = 0$ otherwise. The voter will then modify the matrix $M^{\text{init}}$ into a transformed matrix $M'$, using $B$, so that $M'$ corresponds to her preference matrix. The resulting cost is still in $O(k^2)$ (since $k^2$ coefficients need to be updated) instead of $O(k^3)$ for [24] (that, yet, does not consider equalities).

Then the (encrypted) adjacency matrix can be computed by simply multiplying all ballots. This matrix is then (provably) decrypted by the authorities and Condorcet-Schulze as well as many variants can be applied. The main cost for the authorities lies in the verification of the proofs for each ballot. We could also avoid leaking the adjacency matrix by computing the Condorcet-Schulze winner(s) in MPC. However, the cost for the authorities would be in $O(k^3)$. If this is considered affordable, then we can further alleviate the charge of the voters, as we shall explain now.

### 3.2   Ballots as List of Integers

To minimize computations on the voter's side, we simply ask them to encrypt the list of integers $(c_i)$ representing their preference. In the ElGamal setting, we directly use the bit representation of each integer and encrypt each bit separately. If there are $k$ candidates, we need $\log k$ bits to encode each candidate, hence a ballot will contain $k \log k$ ciphertexts, together with ZKP which prove that they encrypt only 0 or 1. This is to be compared with the $k^2$ encryptions when ballots are encoded as a preference matrix. To apply the Schulze method, the authorities transform back each ballot into a preference matrix. We consider the *positive preference matrix*, obtained from the preference matrix by setting negative coefficients to 0. If $C_i$ denotes the encryption of $c_i$ then the encrypted positive preference matrix $M$ are computed by the authorities as $M_{i,j} = \mathrm{LT}^{\mathrm{bits}}(C_i, C_j)$.

Summing up the (encrypted) matrix $M_v$ for each voter $v$, we obtain the (encrypted) pairwise positive preferences matrix $D$. Then the authorities can apply the Schulze method in MPC from $D$, which can be implemented from the Floyd-Warshall algorithm [20,36]. Indeed, the latter mostly consists in computations of min/max, and translates into an MPC algorithm using the building blocks presented in Sect. 2. We denote by $P_{\mathrm{Cond}}$ the corresponding MPC protocol.

The advantage of this solution is that the load for voters remains minimal, with $O(k \log k)$ exponentiations in total. However, for the authorities, transforming each ballot into a preference matrix costs $O(k^2 \log k)$ per voter, while computing the Floyd-Warshall algorithm requires $O(k^3)$ exponentiations.

To summarize, when the number of candidates and voters remain reasonable, it is actually possible to compute the Condorcet winners with no leakage. Interestingly, the costly operations performed by the trustees can be done on-the-fly, while voters submit their ballots. Note that unless the number of candidates is really large w.r.t. the number of voters, a fully-hiding tally scheme is not really more expensive than schemes leaking the adjacency matrix.

**Security.** We denote by $T_{\mathrm{Cond}}$ the trusted party that implements $f_{\mathrm{Cond}}$ in the SUC framework. We show that $P_{\mathrm{Cond}}$ securely computes $T_{\mathrm{Cond}}$ (proof in [18]).

**Theorem 1.** *$P_{Cond}$ securely computes $T_{Cond}$ under the DDH assumption and the random oracle model (ROM).*

### 3.3   Implementation

In order to validate our approach, we have written a prototype implementation. In the literature, most of such prototypes are based on Paillier encryption. Here, we concentrate on the ElGamal setting, in order to evaluate its practical feasibility. The `libsodium` library is used for randomness and all elliptic curve and hashing operations. The rest is implemented as a standalone C++ program. It is available as a companion artifact of this paper [4] and is published as free software. Most of the primitives of our toolbox have been implemented, and as a proof of concept, we have written a fully tally-hiding protocol for Condorcet-Schulze (ballots as list of integers, and no leakage, in Table 2).

We ran our software on various sets of parameters. In order to compare to [24], we also consider 3 trustees (and no threshold). Our experimental setting is a single server hosting two 16-core AMD EPYC 7282 processors and 128 GB of RAM. Each of the 3 trustees runs 4 computing threads and a few scheduling and I/O threads. The communication between the trustees is emulated via the loopback network interface. Thus, all the network system calls are indeed performed by the program, even though this is just a simulation. The verification of the validity of the ballots is a non-MPC computation that takes a negligible time, compared to the tally. In Table 3, we summarize the cost in terms of wall-clock time and the size of the transcript, measured by the program.

**Table 3.** Benchmark (wall-clock time and transcript size) of fully tally-hiding Condorcet-Schulze MPC computation.

| Voters | 5 candidates | 10 candidates | 20 candidates |
|---|---|---|---|
| 64 | 1 min 50 s/49 MB | 8 min 30 s/0.30 GB | 45 min/1.8 GB |
| 128 | 2 min 40 s/87 MB | 12 m/0.51 GB | 1 h 27 min/2.9 GB |
| 256 | 4 min 35 s/160 MB | 20 m/0.88 GB | 2 h 37 min/4.8 GB |
| 512 | 8 min 10 s/305 MB | 34 min/1.6 GB | 4 h 43 min/8.6 GB |
| 1024 | 15 min/595 MB | 1 h 05 min/3.1 GB | 8 h 50 min/16 GB |

This experiment demonstrates that the approach is sound and in the realm of practicability, for moderate-sized elections. With this choice of ballot representation, which is very cheap from the voter's point of view, the agglomeration of the preference matrices has to be done in MPC, and therefore the cost for the trustees grows quasi-linearly in the number of voters. Therefore, at some point, the approach of [24] using Paillier encryption becomes preferable, since the aggregation is for free, and the MPC cost is essentially independent of the number of voters. Still, their benchmark gives more than 9 days of MPC computation for tallying a 20-candidates Condorcet-Schulze election, which is more than what we provide for 1024 voters.

# 4  Other Counting Methods

We also provide fully leakage-free tally protocols for D'Hondt, Majority Judgment and Single Transferable Vote. We survey our findings and encodings for each counting functions. Full details are available in [18]. In particular, we prove that our tally protocols are SUC-secure by providing analogs of Theorem 1.

## 4.1  Single Vote

A first class of counting functions applies to the case where voters simply select some candidate(s). The typical way to determine the $s$ winners is to count the number of votes for each candidate and select the $s$ ones with the most votes. This is the case covered by Ordinos [25], which however suffers from a shortcoming in case of equalities: it may return more winners than the number of seats. We correct this and we show that it is possible to rely on ElGamal, thanks to an adapted algorithm. This lowers the size of a ballot for voters at a higher cost for the authorities, which can be preferred in practice.

Things get more complex when voters select a candidate list instead of a single candidate. Indeed, the seats need to be shared among the candidates of the different lists, according to the number of votes received. One popular technique is the D'Hondt method, which is used in practice for politically-binding elections. We extend the approach initiated by Ordinos to the case of D'Hondt, building on two main ideas: the use of a more advanced algorithm and a more efficient primitive for comparison, inspired from circuits. In this case, ElGamal is a key ingredient for designing a practical tally-hiding scheme. The analysis in terms of cost is displayed in Fig. 2 of the appendix.

## 4.2  Majority Judgment

Majority Judgment (MJ) [7] is a method in which candidates are each given a grade, such as Excellent, Good, Poor, *etc.* Then the candidates are compared based on the sequence formed by their median grades *i.e.* the median grade, then the median obtained when the median grade is removed, and so on. It has been recently used by more than 400 000 voters in French primary elections [2]. In [12], an MPC protocol is proposed to realize MJ, but we discovered that it only implements a simplified version, called majority gauge. When the majority gauge returns a winner, then it is indeed a MJ winner but, in small elections, there is a rather high probability that the simplified algorithm does not provide any result. For example, in an election with 100 voters, [12] can fail with probability 20% [18], which not only is inconvenient (imagine an election that must be canceled because no winner is declared!) but also leaks some information (there is no winner according to the majority gauge).

To repair the approach, one issue is that the complexity of the MJ algorithm depends (linearly) on the number of voters, which may be large. Hence, [7] devises an alternative (complex) algorithm that no longer depends on the number of voters. We propose a variant of this algorithm and use it as a basis to derive a tally-hiding procedure. Our algorithm has a similar complexity to [12] while they implement a much simpler algorithm. Then we show that it is possible to adapt our algorithm to ElGamal encryption. Interestingly, the format remains unchanged for the voter (hence the resulting ballot is even easier to compute). The resulting computational costs are displayed in Fig. 3 in appendix. This is a good example where working with bit-encoded integers allowed to perform all the needed operations in MPC. The load for the trustees increases but our study shows that it remains reasonable since the extra operations are more or less compensated by the fact that computations are faster in ElGamal.

### 4.3 Single Transferable Vote

In Single Transferable Vote (STV), each voter must give a strict ordering of a subset of candidates. It consists of several rounds, during which each ballot grants a (weighted) number of votes to its first candidate. If a candidate has more votes than a quota, she is selected and any exceeding votes are transferred to the next candidate in each ballot (*i.e.* the weight of the ballot is multiplied by a transfer coefficient and the candidate is removed from all ballots). Otherwise, the candidate with the least votes is eliminated. Many variants of STV exist, depending on the way in which the votes are transferred. We took advise from Australian academics to choose an ideal version of STV, which is easy to analyze.

We discovered that even without any cryptography, the ideal STV algorithm is exponential and far from being practical. The reason is that the numerators and denominators of the fractions grow exponentially with the number of seats. On real data elections from the South New Wales election in Australia [3], it would take about one month on a personal computer to compute the result, and about 30 GB of central memory to store all the fractions.

Given that ideal STV cannot be efficiently computed in the clear, we considered a variant with rounding. In [9,37], there are three techniques to compute the STV winners, all with some leakage. Note that [37] computes the ideal STV (with no rounding) but probably because the authors did not realize that it would quickly be impractical. [24,31] cover a particular case where only one candidate is elected (IRV). Note that [24] uses a naive encoding of the possible choices: if there are $c$ candidates, they view the $c!$ possible orders as $c!$ possible "candidates" from which a voter makes a selection, yielding a ballot of super-exponential size, while the ballot size is $O(c^2)$ in [31]. We propose a fully tally-hiding algorithm for STV, with no leakage, at a cost similar to [9,37], as displayed in Fig. 4 in appendix. To keep the cost reasonable, we re-used techniques of hardware circuits to implement efficiently the arithmetic functions.

## 5    Application to E-Voting Security

We show that our tally-hiding schemes can be used for e-voting, preserving vote secrecy and verifiability. We consider a mini-voting scheme, TH-voting, where we assume that voters have an authenticated channel with the voting server.

Similarly to Ordinos [25], voters simply encrypt their vote following the expected format and the MPC protocol is used for tallying.

## 5.1   Definitions

A *voting scheme* consists of four algorithms and one MPC protocol (Setup, vote, isValid, $P_{tally}$, Verify) where:

- Setup$(\kappa, a, t)$ takes as input the security parameter $\kappa$, the number of authorities $a$ and a threshold $t$. It returns $sk, pk, (s_i, h_i)_{i=1}^{a}$, respectively a key pair $sk, pk$ and the corresponding private and public shares $s_i, h_i$ for each authorities.
- vote$(pk, v)$ takes a public key $pk$, a vote $v$, and returns a ballot.
- isValid$(BB, B)$ takes as input a ballot $B$ and a ballot box $BB$ and returns a boolean that states whether $B$ is valid w.r.t. $BB$.
- $P_{tally}(a, t) = P_1, \cdots, P_a$ is an MPC protocol to compute the tally.
- Verify$(r, \Pi, BB)$ takes as input a result $r$, a transcript $\Pi$ and a ballot box $BB$ and returns a boolean that states whether $r$ is correct w.r.t. $BB$ and $\Pi$. This check is typically run by external auditors.

In [26], a quantitative definition of privacy is proposed, where a voting system is said $\delta$-private for some $\delta$. This definition can be turned into a qualitative one when $\delta$ is shown to be minimal, in a sense that an ideal protocol achieves $\delta'$-privacy with a negligible $|\delta - \delta'|$. Hence, a natural definition of privacy is to compare the probability of success of the adversary in a real and in an ideal protocol, and to show that the difference is negligible. Just as in [26], we consider a definition where the adversary tries to guess the vote of a single voter. We consider a fixed set $V$ of valid *voting options* and the games defined respectively in Algorithms 2 and 3, where the differences are highlighted in blue.

**Definition 2 (vote privacy).** *We say that a voting protocol (Setup, vote, isValid, $P_{tally}$, Verify) guarantees vote privacy w.r.t a result function tally if, for all parameters $t, a, n, n_c$ with $t < a$ and $n_c \leq n$, for all $C \subset [1, a]$ of size at most $t$, for all adversary $\mathbb{A}$, there exists an adversary $\mathbb{B}$ and a negligible function $\mu$ such that for all voting options $v_2, \cdots, v_n \in V$,*

$$|Pr(\textbf{Real}^{Priv}_{\mathbb{A}, P_{tally}}(\kappa, n, n_c, a, t, C, V, v_2, \cdots, v_n) = 1)$$
$$- Pr(\textbf{Ideal}^{Priv}_{\mathbb{B}, tally}(\kappa, n, n_c, a, t, C, V, v_2, \cdots, v_n) = 1)| \leq \mu(\kappa).$$

| **Algorithm 2:** $\text{Real}^{\text{Priv}}_{\mathbb{A}, P_{tally}}$ | **Algorithm 3:** $\text{Ideal}^{\text{Priv}}_{\mathbb{B}, tally}$ |
|---|---|
| **Require:** $\kappa, n, n_c, a, t, C, V, v_2, \cdots, v_n$ | **Require:** $\kappa, n, n_c, a, t, C, V, v_2, \cdots, v_n$ |
| 1 $sk, pk, (s_i, h_i)_{i=1}^{a} :=$ $\quad$ $\text{Setup}(\kappa, a, t)$ | 1 $sk, pk, (s_i, h_i)_{i=1}^{a} := \text{Setup}(\kappa, a, t)$ |
| 2 $b \in_r \{0, 1\}; par = pk, h_1, \cdots, h_a$ | 2 $b \in_r \{0, 1\}; par = pk, h_1, \cdots, h_a$ |
| 3 $v_0, v_1 := \mathbb{A}(\kappa, par, (s_i)_{i \in C})$ | 3 $v_0, v_1 := \mathbb{B}(\kappa, par, (s_i)_{i \in C})$ |
| 4 $BB := \{\text{vote}(pk, v_b)\}$ | 4 $BB := \{\text{vote}(pk, v_b)\}$ |
| 5 **for** $i = 2$ **to** $n - n_c$ **do** $\quad$ $BB := BB \bigcup \{\text{vote}(pk, v_i)\}$ | 5 **for** $i = 2$ **to** $n - n_c$ **do** $\quad$ $BB := BB \bigcup \{\text{vote}(pk, v_i)\}$ |
| 6 $(X_i)_{i > n - n_c} := \mathbb{A}(BB)$ | 6 $(X_i)_{i > n - n_c} := \mathbb{B}()$ |
| 7 **for** $i > n - n_c$ **do** | 7 **for** $i > n - n_c$ **do** |
| 8 $\quad$ **if** $\text{isValid}(BB, X_i)$ **then** $\quad\quad$ $BB := BB \bigcup \{X_i\}$ | 8 $\quad$ **if** $\text{isValid}(BB, X_i)$ **then** $\quad\quad$ $BB := BB \bigcup \{X_i\}$ |
| 9 $r := \mathbb{A}\|_{i \in [1,a] \backslash C} P_i(s_i, par, BB)$ | 9 $r := \text{tally}((\text{Extract}_{sk}(B))_{B \in BB})$ |
| 10 $b' := \mathbb{A}()$ | 10 $b' := \mathbb{B}(r)$ |
| 11 Return $(b == b') \wedge (v_0, v_1 \in V)$ | 11 Return $(b == b') \wedge (v_0, v_1 \in V)$ |

## 5.2   TH-voting

We define a voting protocol $V_{\text{tally}}$ for each tally function $\text{tally}$ covered in our work (D'Hondt, Majority Judgment, Condorcet-Schulze, and STV), with $P_{\text{tally}}$ the corresponding tally-hiding protocol, in the ElGamal setting. The algorithm $\text{vote}_{\text{tally}}$ returns an encrypted ballot following the devised encoding, and a ZKP that the ballot is correctly formed. The algorithm $\text{isValid}_{\text{tally}}$ checks the ZKP and additionally ensures that the ballot is not already on the board. As explained in Sect. 2, the CGate protocol produces a transcript which acts as a ZKP that the protocol was performed correctly. By concatenating the transcripts of all CGate and the transcript of the threshold decryption, the participants produce a ZKP $\Pi$ that $P_{\text{tally}}$ has been performed correctly. This also defines a $\text{Verify}_{\text{tally}}$ algorithm which simply consists of verifying all the ZKP. Finally, we consider an ideal $\text{Setup}(\kappa, a, t)$ that picks a group $G$ corresponding to the security parameter $\kappa$, picks randomly a generator $g$ and returns $sk, pk, s_1, h_1, \cdots, s_a, h_a$ where the $(s_i, h_i)$ are distributed following Shamir's scheme with $a$ authorities and a threshold $t$; $sk$ is the corresponding secret key and $pk = (g, g^{sk})$. The setup can be further refined with a UC-secure DKG (see *e.g.* [38]).

**Theorem 2.** *Let* $\text{tally}$ *be one of the previously defined tally functions (D'Hondt, Majority Judgment, Condorcet-Schulze, and STV). Assuming DDH,* $V_{\text{tally}}$ *is private w.r.t.* $\text{tally}$.

The proof can be found in [18]. We also prove that $V_{\text{tally}}$ is verifiable for a notion of verifiability similar to [17]. Note that the key step is the fact that our tally-hiding schemes guarantees universal verifiability: auditors can check that the result is valid. Individual verifiability is straightforward in our setting since we implicitly assume that all voters verify their vote. How to achieve individual verifiability in practice is beyond the scope of this work.

# Appendix

| Functionality | Option | Algorithm | Exp per trustee | Comm. cost | Transcript size |
|---|---|---|---|---|---|
| Dec | P/EG | Dec | $5a$ | $B$ | $4a$ |
| RandBit | P/EG | RandBit | $3a+2$ | $R$ | $6a$ |
| CSZ | EG | CGate [32] | $29a$ | $R+4B$ | $31a$ |
| | P | Mul [34] | $10a$ | $2B$ | $11a$ |
| Select | P/EG | Select | CSZ | CSZ | CSZ |
| SelectInd | P/EG | SelectInd | $n$CSZ | CSZ | $n$CSZ |
| Neg$^{\text{bits}}$ | P/EG | Neg$^{\text{bits}}$ | $(m-1)$CSZ | $(m-1)$CSZ | $(m-1)$CSZ |
| Add$^{\text{bits}}$ | P/EG | Add$^{\text{bits}}$ [32] | $(2m-1)$CSZ | $(2m-1)$CSZ | $(2m-1)$CSZ |
| | Sublinear P/EG | UFCAdd$^{\text{bits}}$ | $m(\frac{3}{2}\log m+2)$CSZ | $2(\log m+1)$CSZ | $m(\frac{3}{2}\log m+2)$CSZ |
| Sub$^{\text{bits}}$ | P/EG | Sub$^{\text{bits}}$ | $(2m-1)$CSZ | $(2m-1)$CSZ | $(2m-1)$CSZ |
| | LT P/EG | SubLT$^{\text{bits}}$ | $(2m-1)$CSZ | $(2m-1)$CSZ | $(2m-1)$CSZ |
| | LT+EQ P/EG | SubLT$^{\text{bits}}$ | $(3m-2)$CSZ | $(2m+\log m)$CSZ | $(3m-2)$CSZ |
| | Sublinear P/EG | UFCSub$^{\text{bits}}$ | $m(\frac{3}{2}\log m+2)$CSZ | $2(\log m+1)$CSZ | $m(\frac{3}{2}\log m+2)$CSZ |
| LT$^{\text{bits}}$ | LT P/EG | SubLT$^{\text{bits}}$ | $(2m-1)$CSZ | $(2m-1)$CSZ | $(2m-1)$CSZ |
| | LT+EQ P/EG | SubLT$^{\text{bits}}$ | $(3m-2)$CSZ | $(2m+\log m)$CSZ | $(3m-2)$CSZ |
| | Sublinear P/EG | CLT$^{\text{bits}}$ | $(4m-3)$CSZ | $2(\log m+1)$CSZ | $(4m-3)$CSZ |
| | Sublinear+EQ P/EG | CLT$^{\text{bits}}$ | $(5m-4)$CSZ | $2(\log m+1)$CSZ | $(5m-4)$CSZ |
| EQ$^{\text{bits}}$ | P/EG | EQ$^{\text{bits}}$ | $(2m-1)$CSZ | $(\log m+1)$CSZ | $(2m-1)$CSZ |
| EQ | Precomp P | EQH [28] | $21ma+75a$ $+4(m+1)$ | $R+8B$ | $(22m+28)a$ |
| GT | Precomp P | GTH [28] | $(27m+146\log m)a$ $+8m+9a+5\log m$ | $(2R+13B)\log m$ | $(28m+50\log m)a$ $+6a$ |
| BinExpand | P | BinExpand [33] | $12ma+53a+3m$ | $R+2mB$ | $(17m+21)a$ |
| Aggreg$^{\text{bits}}$ | EG | Aggreg$^{\text{bits}}$ | $3n$CSZ | $(\log n+1)\log n$CSZ | $3n$CSZ |
| Mul$^{\text{bits}}$ | P/EG | Mul$^{\text{bits}}$ | $3m^2$CSZ | $2m^2$CSZ | $3m^2$CSZ |
| Div$^{\text{bits}}$ | P/EG | Div$^{\text{bits}}$ | $(3m-1)r$CSZ | $2mr$CSZ | $(3m-1)r$CSZ |
| MinMax$^{\text{bits}}$ | naive P/EG | MinMax$^{\text{bits}}$ | $(8m-2)n$CSZ | $2m\log n$CSZ | $(8m-2)n$CSZ |
| | sublinear P/EG | MinMax$^{\text{bits}}$ | $(12m-6)n$CSZ | $2\log n(\log m+2)$CSZ | $(12m-6)n$CSZ |
| Mixnet | EG | [40] | $(9n+11)a$ $+n-6$ | $R$ | $10(n+1)a$ |
| | P | [40] | $(8n+10)a$ | $R$ | $10(n+1)a$ |

**Fig. 1.** Cost of various MPC primitives: basic functionalities for logic, integer arithmetic, and a few advanced functions. The Option column includes whether this is available in Paillier (P) or ElGamal (EG). The notations are $a$ for the number of authorities, $m$ for the bit-length of the operands, $n$ for the number of operands, $r$ for the precision (in the division). All logarithms are in base 2. The communication costs are expressed in terms of broadcast (denoted $B$) and full-rounds (denoted $R$). The unit of the transcript size is the key length. This corresponds to half the size of a ciphertext in both Paillier (typically 3072 bits) and ElGamal (typically 256 bits) settings.

**Fig. 2.** Leading terms of the cost of tally-hiding for single choice systems. $s$: # seats, $k$: # lists, $\alpha$: # authorities, $n$: # voters, $m = \lceil\log(n + 1)\rceil$, $m_1 = m+\log k$, $m_2 = m+\log(sk)$, $m_3 = m_1+\log(\mathrm{lcm}(2,\cdots ,s))$, $R$: round of comm., $B$: broadcasts.

| Version | Leak-age | EG/P | Voters #exp. | Authorities #exp. | #comm. | Transcript size |
|---|---|---|---|---|---|---|
| Basic counting [25] | [i] | P | $5k$ | $4kn + (27m + 146\log m)k^2a$ | $(4R + 26B)\log m$ | $6kn + (28m + 50\log m)k^2a$ |
| ours (exact winners) | ∅ | P | $5k$ | $4kn + (\frac{27}{2}m_2 + 73\log m_1)k^2a$ | $(4R + 26B)\log m_1$ | $6kn + (14m_1 + 25\log m_1)k^2a$ |
| ours (exact winners) | ∅ | EG | $8k$ | $87(nk + m_1(2k - s)a$ | $(m^2 + 2sm_1\log m_1)R$ | $93(nk + m_1(2k - s)s)a$ |
| D'Hondt (comm.) | ∅ | P | $5k$ | $4kn + (27m_2 + 146\log m_2)(ks)^2a$ | $(4R + 26B)\log m_2$ | $6kn + (28m_2 + 50\log m_2)a(ks)^2$ |
| D'Hondt (comm.) | ∅ | EG | $8k$ | $29ka(3n + 2m_2ks^2)$ | $(m(m + \log s) + \log(ks)^2)R$ | $93nak + 62m_2(ks)^2a$ |
| D'Hondt (comp.) | ∅ | EG | $8k$ | $29ka(3n + mss' + 6m_3s^2)$ | $(m^2 + ms^3 + 2s\log(ks)\log m_3)R$ | $31ka(3n + mss' + 6m_3s^2)$ |

[i] More than $s$ winners can be output in case of tie.

**Fig. 3.** Leading terms of the cost of tally-hiding for MJ. $n$: # voters, $m = \lceil\log(n + 1)\rceil$, $k$: # candidates, $d$: # grades, $\alpha$: # authorities.

| Version | Leak-age | Voters #exp. | Authorities #exp. | #comm. | Transcript size |
|---|---|---|---|---|---|
| [12] | [i] | $5kd$ | $4nkd + krma(224k + 58d)$ | $(4m + d)R$ | $6nkd + krma(280k + 62d)$ |
| ours (P) | ∅ | $5kd$ | $4nkd + kda(75m + 146\log m + 20d)$ | $d(2R + 13B)\log m\log k$ | $6nkd + kda(78m + 50\log m + 22d)$ |
| ours (EG) | ∅ | $8kd$ | $87nkda+ 58kmda(10 + d)$ | $m^2 + d(6m + 2\log k\log m)$ | $31kda(3n + (20 + 2d)m)$ |

[i] [12] leaks whether the winner can be determined with the simplified algorithm.

**Fig. 4.** Leading terms of the cost of tally-hiding for STV. $n$: # voters, $k$: # candidates, $m = \lceil\log(n + 1)\rceil$, $a$: # authorities, $r$: precision in power of 2, $m' = m + r$, $k' = k + r$.

| Version | Leakage | P/EG | Voters #exp. | Authorities #exp. | #comm. | Transcript size |
|---|---|---|---|---|---|---|
| [9, Sec. II] [37] | [i] | EG | $10k^2$ | $62nak^2$ | $9kR$ | $19nak^2$ |
| [9, Sec. II] [37] | [ii] | P | $5k^2$ | $22nk^2am$ | $2nkrmR$ | $11nak^2m$ |
| [9, Sec. III.B] | [iii] | EG | $10k^2$ | $62nak^2$ | $9kR$ | N/A |
| ours (naive arith.) | ∅ | EG | $9k\log k$ | $29nak^2(4\log k + 3m(r + 1))$ | $k(2m'(m + 2r + \log k) + k\log\log k)R$ | $31nak^2(4\log k + 3m(r + 1))$ |
| ours (optimized arith.) | ∅ | EG | $9k\log k$ | $\frac{29}{2}nak^2(9\log k + 3m(r + 1)\log m')$ | $k(2m'(\log k + 2\log m') + (\log k)^2)R$ | $\frac{31}{2}nak(9k\log k + 3m'(r + 1)\log m')$ |

[i] Score of selected candidates at each turn   [ii] Score of all candidates at each turn   [iii] Selected or eliminated candidates and approximation of transfer coefficient at each turn. Trustees learn the score of all candidates at each turn

# References

1. Condorcet Internet Voting Service (CIVS). https://civs.cs.cornell.edu/
2. The Guardian, 30 January. https://www.theguardian.com/world/2022/jan/30/peoples-primary-backs-as-taubira-as-unity-candidate-of-french-left
3. NSWEC - Election results. NSW Electoral Commision. https://pastvtr.elections.nsw.gov.au/SG1901/LC/State/preferences
4. Source code of prototype implementation of Section 3. https://gitlab.inria.fr/gaudry/THproto
5. Ubuntu IRC council position. https://lists.ubuntu.com/archives/ubuntu-irc/2012-May/001538.html
6. Adida, B.: Helios: Web-based Open-Audit Voting. In: USENIX (2008)
7. Balinski, M., Laraki, R.: Majority Judgment: Measuring Ranking and Electing. MIT Press (2010)
8. Bar-Ilan, J., Beaver, D.: Non-cryptographic fault-tolerant computing in constant number of rounds of interaction. In: PODC. ACM (1989)
9. Benaloh, J., Moran, T., Naish, L., Ramchen, K., Teague, V.: Shuffle-Sum: coercion-resistant verifiable tallying for STV voting. IEEE Trans. Inf. Forensics Secur. **4**, 685–698 (2010)
10. Brent, R., Kung, H.: A regular layout for parallel adders. IEEE Trans. Comput. **C-31**(3), 260–264 (1982)
11. Bünz, B., Bootle, J., Boneh, D., Poelstra, A., Wuille, P., Maxwell, G.: Bulletproofs: Short Proofs for Confidential Transactions and More. In: S&P 2018 (2018)
12. Canard, S., Pointcheval, D., Santos, Q., Traoré, J.: Practical strategy-resistant privacy-preserving elections. In: Lopez, J., Zhou, J., Soriano, M. (eds.) ESORICS 2018. LNCS, vol. 11099, pp. 331–349. Springer, Cham (2018). https://doi.org/10.1007/978-3-319-98989-1_17
13. Canetti, R.: Universally composable security: a new paradigm for cryptographic protocols. In: FOCS (2001)
14. Canetti, R., Cohen, A., Lindell, Y.: A simpler variant of universally composable security for standard multiparty computation. In: CRYPTO (2015)
15. Clarkson, M.R., Chong, S., Myers, A.C.: Civitas: toward a Secure Voting System. In: S&P (2008)
16. Cortier, V., Galindo, D., Glondu, S., Izabachene, M.: Distributed ElGamal à la Pedersen - application to helios. In: WPES (2013)
17. Cortier, V., Galindo, D., Glondu, S., Izabachène, M.: Election verifiability for Helios under weaker trust assumptions. In: Kutyłowski, M., Vaidya, J. (eds.) ESORICS 2014. LNCS, vol. 8713, pp. 327–344. Springer, Cham (2014). https://doi.org/10.1007/978-3-319-11212-1_19
18. Cortier, V., Gaudry, P., Yang, Q.: A toolbox for verifiable tally-hiding e-voting systems. Cryptology ePrint Archive, Report 2021/491 (2021)
19. Cramer, R., Damgård, I., Nielsen, J.B.: Multiparty computation from threshold homomorphic encryption. In: Pfitzmann, B. (ed.) EUROCRYPT 2001. LNCS, vol. 2045, pp. 280–300. Springer, Heidelberg (2001). https://doi.org/10.1007/3-540-44987-6_18
20. Floyd, R.W.: Algorithm 97: shortest path. Commun. ACM **5**, 345 (1962)
21. Haenni, R., Koenig, R.E., Locher, P., Dubuis, E.: CHVote System Specification. Cryptology ePrint Archive, Report 2017/325 (2017)

22. Haines, T., Pattinson, D., Tiwari, M.: Verifiable homomorphic tallying for the Schulze vote counting scheme. In: Chakraborty, S., Navas, J.A. (eds.) VSTTE 2019. LNCS, vol. 12031, pp. 36–53. Springer, Cham (2020). https://doi.org/10.1007/978-3-030-41600-3_4

23. Hazay, C., Mikkelsen, G.L., Rabin, T., Toft, T., Nicolosi, A.A.: Efficient RSA Key generation and threshold Paillier in the two-party setting. J. Cryptol. 32(2), 265–323 (2018). https://doi.org/10.1007/s00145-017-9275-7

24. Hertel, F., Huber, N., Kittelberger, J., Kuesters, R., Liedtke, J., Rausch, D.: Extending the tally-hiding ordinos system: implementations for Borda, Hare-Niemeyer, Condorcet, and instant-runoff voting. In: Proceedings E-Vote-ID 2021. University of Tartu Press (2021)

25. Kuesters, R., Liedtke, J., Mueller, J., Rausch, D., Vogt, A.: Ordinos: a verifiable tally-hiding e-voting system. In: EuroS&P (2020)

26. Küsters, R., Truderung, T., Vogt, A.: Verifiability, privacy, and coercion-resistance: new insights from a case study. In: S&P (2011)

27. Lipmaa, H.: On Diophantine complexity and statistical zero-knowledge arguments. In: Laih, C.-S. (ed.) ASIACRYPT 2003. LNCS, vol. 2894, pp. 398–415. Springer, Heidelberg (2003). https://doi.org/10.1007/978-3-540-40061-5_26

28. Lipmaa, H., Toft, T.: Secure equality and greater-than tests with sublinear online complexity. In: Fomin, F.V., Freivalds, R., Kwiatkowska, M., Peleg, D. (eds.) ICALP 2013. LNCS, vol. 7966, pp. 645–656. Springer, Heidelberg (2013). https://doi.org/10.1007/978-3-642-39212-2_56

29. Nishide, T., Sakurai, K.: Distributed Paillier cryptosystem without trusted dealer. In: Chung, Y., Yung, M. (eds.) WISA 2010. LNCS, vol. 6513, pp. 44–60. Springer, Heidelberg (2011). https://doi.org/10.1007/978-3-642-17955-6_4

30. Poupard, G., Stern, J.: Security analysis of a practical "on the fly" authentication and signature generation. In: Nyberg, K. (ed.) EUROCRYPT 1998. LNCS, vol. 1403, pp. 422–436. Springer, Heidelberg (1998). https://doi.org/10.1007/BFb0054143

31. Ramchen, K., Culnane, C., Pereira, O., Teague, V.: Universally verifiable MPC and IRV ballot counting. In: Goldberg, I., Moore, T. (eds.) FC 2019. LNCS, vol. 11598, pp. 301–319. Springer, Cham (2019). https://doi.org/10.1007/978-3-030-32101-7_19

32. Schoenmakers, B., Tuyls, P.: Practical two-party computation based on the conditional gate. In: Lee, P.J. (ed.) ASIACRYPT 2004. LNCS, vol. 3329, pp. 119–136. Springer, Heidelberg (2004). https://doi.org/10.1007/978-3-540-30539-2_10

33. Schoenmakers, B., Tuyls, P.: Efficient binary conversion for Paillier encrypted values. In: Vaudenay, S. (ed.) EUROCRYPT 2006. LNCS, vol. 4004, pp. 522–537. Springer, Heidelberg (2006). https://doi.org/10.1007/11761679_31

34. Schoenmakers, B., Veeningen, M.: Universally verifiable multiparty computation from threshold homomorphic cryptosystems. In: Malkin, T., Kolesnikov, V., Lewko, A.B., Polychronakis, M. (eds.) ACNS 2015. LNCS, vol. 9092, pp. 3–22. Springer, Cham (2015). https://doi.org/10.1007/978-3-319-28166-7_1

35. Schulze, M.: A new monotonic, clone-independent, reversal symmetric, and condorcet-consistent single-winner election method. Soc. Choice Welf. 36, 267–303 (2011). https://doi.org/10.1007/s00355-010-0475-4

36. Warshall, S.: A theorem on Boolean matrices. J. ACM 9, 11–12 (1962)

37. Wen, R., Buckland, R.: Mix and Test Counting in Preferential Electoral Systems. University of New South Wales, Technical report (2008)

38. Wikström, D.: Universally composable DKG with linear number of exponentiations. In: Blundo, C., Cimato, S. (eds.) SCN 2004. LNCS, vol. 3352, pp. 263–277. Springer, Heidelberg (2005). https://doi.org/10.1007/978-3-540-30598-9_19
39. Wikström, D.: A sender verifiable mix-net and a new proof of a shuffle. In: Roy, B. (ed.) ASIACRYPT 2005. LNCS, vol. 3788, pp. 273–292. Springer, Heidelberg (2005). https://doi.org/10.1007/11593447_15
40. Wikström, D.: A commitment-consistent proof of a shuffle. In: Boyd, C., González Nieto, J. (eds.) ACISP 2009. LNCS, vol. 5594, pp. 407–421. Springer, Heidelberg (2009). https://doi.org/10.1007/978-3-642-02620-1_28

# How to Verifiably Encrypt Many Bits for an Election?

Henri Devillez[✉], Olivier Pereira, and Thomas Peters

ICTEAM, UCLouvain, 1348 Louvain-la-Neuve, Belgium
{henri.devillez,olivier.pereira,thomas.peters}@uclouvain.be

**Abstract.** The verifiable encryption of bits is the main computational step that is needed to prepare ballots in many practical voting protocols. Its computational load can also be a practical bottleneck, preventing the deployment of some protocols or requiring the use of computing clusters. We investigate the question of producing many verifiably encrypted bits in an efficient and portable way, using as a baseline the protocol that is in use in essentially all modern voting systems and libraries supporting homomorphic voting, including ElectionGuard, a state-of-the-art open source voting SDK deployed in government elections. Combining fixed base exponentiation techniques and new encryption and ZK proof mechanisms, we obtain speed-ups by more than one order of magnitude against standard implementations. Our exploration requires balancing conflicting optimization strategies, and the use of asymptotically less efficient protocols that turn out to be very effective in practice. Several of our proposed improvements are now on the ElectionGuard roadmap.

## 1 Introduction

*Verifiable Encryption of Bits.* Encrypting bits is the main computational step that is needed in order to prepare a ballot in numerous voting protocols [5, 10–12] and systems, including VoteBox, Helios, STAR-Vote, Belenios, Strobe and ElectionGuard for instance [1, 3, 4, 8, 13, 22]. In these protocols, which follow the general approach pioneered by Benaloh [5], voters compute one additively homomorphic ciphertext per candidate on the ballot, and prove (in zero-knowledge) that each of these ciphertexts encrypts a bit, expressing whether the voter supports the candidate or not. Thanks to the homomorphic property, the ciphertexts submitted by the voters can be combined candidate-wise, resulting in a vector of ciphertexts encrypting the number of votes that each candidate received, and these ciphertexts can then be verifiably decrypted in order to obtain the election result.

The blueprint that we just described is adequate for approval voting, where voters are allowed to support as many candidates as they want. Different ballot completion rules may require additional verifiable bit encryptions. For example, if voters can support at most $k$ candidates out of $n$, one common approach to proving the validity of ballots, based on the addition of dummy candidates, requires to compute the verifiable encryption of $k + n$ bits [11,13]. For Instant-Runoff voting (IRV), some protocols require to produce a number of verifiably encrypted bits that is equal to the square of the number of candidates [21].

© The Author(s), under exclusive license to Springer Nature Switzerland AG 2022
V. Atluri et al. (Eds.): ESORICS 2022, LNCS 13555, pp. 653–671, 2022.
https://doi.org/10.1007/978-3-031-17146-8_32

Apart from voting applications, which are our main focus here, the verifiable encryption of bits is also a central component of other protocols. A prominent example is the computation of range proofs: there, one of the standard approaches to prove that a ciphertext encrypts a value $v$ less than $2^n$ consists in producing $n$ verifiable encryptions of each of the bits of $v$ [2], and arbitrary ranges can be supported with $2n$ verifiable bit encryptions [23].

*The Computational Cost of Encrypting Bits.* All recent voting protocol with homomorphic tallying implementations encrypt bits using exponential ElGamal, that is, a bit $v$ is encrypted as a pair $(g^r, g^v h^r)$, and the proof that a ciphertext encrypts a bit is computed as a disjunctive Chaum-Pedersen proof [7,9].

The choice of ElGamal over Paillier encryption and its variants [11,12] is motivated by the simplicity to generate keys for a distributed or threshold variant of ElGamal [19], compared to the challenges of generating an RSA modulus in a distributed way [14]. The disjunctive Chaum-Pedersen proof was adopted and used in virtually every system since the initial proposal by Cramer et al. [10]. In this approach, the cost of verifiably encrypting a bit is largely dominated by 7 modular exponentiations: 2 for the ElGamal encryption, and 5 for the proof. This cost can quickly become limiting in practice.

Let us consider, as a motivating example, the state-of-the-art ElectionGuard SDK developed by Microsoft, which has been used in various public elections since 2020 [13]. When ElectionGuard was deployed for a Risk Limiting Audit in Inyo County, the encryption of a single ballot took around 6 s, the exponentiations being reported as the bottleneck [4]. In the context of such an audit, thousands and possibly millions of ballots have to be verifiably encrypted, which led to the deployment of a cluster, raising numerous practical challenges and requiring a significant expertise [24].

As a second example, we can turn to the Verificatum JavaScript Cryptographic Library [25], which is a state-of-the-art crypto library supporting various ElGamal-related operations. A library benchmark shows that a modular exponentiation computed in the group used in ElectionGuard takes around 37 ms. on a 2020 laptop. Encrypting a ballot with 100 candidates, a size that is typical in many countries, would then require around 26 s. This may create important usability issues on a laptop, and would just be unbearable on a slow lower-end smartphone.

## 1.1 Contributions

Taking the state-of-the art ElectionGuard SDK as our baseline, we show how to considerably improve the speed at which bits can be verifiably encrypted, with a focus on the constraints from voting applications.

We proceed in 4 steps:

1. We observe that verifiable bit encryption can take advantage of fixed base encryption techniques, something that is not accounted for in existing libraries. Taking into account that fairly large amounts of memory (at least a few MB) are available on voting devices, we depart from standard techniques

that focus on memory constrained environments and explore the use of a fast and memory-intensive approach.

2. We explore the use of multi-ElGamal encryption, that reduces the number of exponentiations at the cost of requiring a larger number of bases. We show that this approach offer benefits when the precomputation time does not need to be accounted for when preparing a ballot, or when the number of public keys remains relatively low.

3. We propose a switch from the traditional disjunctive Chaum-Pedersen proofs to product proofs. We show that, within the space of protocol design strategies that keep a linear number of multiplication operations (in the number of encrypted bits), the proof computational effort can be halved for multi-ElGamal ciphertexts, and an extra halving can be obtained when many proofs need to be computed, taking the cost of the proof close to 1 exponentiation per encrypted bit.

4. Eventually, we explore the impact of recent developments that aim at providing short proofs. The use of these techniques is intriguing because the proof size is not our primary goal, and the number of multiplications required to compute these proofs is typically super-linear (typically in $\mathcal{O}(n \log^d(n))$) with $d \geq 1$), compared to the linear cost of the Chaum-Pedersen and product proofs. Nevertheless, we propose a new protocol that offers speed improvements for any practical number of proofs to be computed, including by a factor up to 70 for a few thousand proofs.

We benchmark our solutions against our baseline protocol and confirm their benefits. Several of our improvements are now on the ElectionGuard 2.0 roadmap.

## 2   The Baseline

In all the voting systems based on homomorphic tallying that we examined, including [1,8,13,22], the verifiable encryption of bits is performed as in the original protocol of Cramer et al. [10], which can be described as follows.

1. A group $\mathbb{G}$ is chosen as a subgroup of prime order $q$ of a group $\mathbb{Z}_p^*$, with $|q| = 256$ and $2048 \leq |p| \leq 4096$ depending on the implementation. A generator $g$ of $\mathbb{G}$ is also chosen. Then, an ElGamal public key $h \in \mathbb{G}$ is selected, with the corresponding secret key $x : h = g^x$ being kept secret by a group of trustees. (Distributed key generation protocols are used for that.)

2. A bit $v$ is encrypted as an exponential ElGamal pair $(g^r, g^v h^r)$ for a random $r \leftarrow \mathbb{Z}_q$.

3. A disjunctive Chaum-Pedersen proof [7,9] is computed in order to demonstrate that $v \in \{0, 1\}$. Given a ciphertext $(A, B) = (g^r, g^v h^r)$ as above, a commitment is computed as a pair of ciphertexts $(A_0', B_0') = (g^s, g^{vw} h^s)$ and $(A_1', B_1') = (g^t, g^{(1-v)w} h^t)$ where $s, t, w \leftarrow_\$ \mathbb{Z}_q$. Then a random challenge $e \in \mathbb{Z}_q$ is obtained using the Fiat-Shamir transform. Eventually, the sub-challenges $e_0 = (1 - v)e - w$ and $e_1 = ve + w$ are computed, as well

as the responses $f_0 = s + e_0 r$ and $f_1 = t + e_1 r$. The proof is made of $(A'_0, B'_0, A'_1, B'_1, e_0, e_1, f_0, f_1)$.

In real-world implementations, the choice of a subgroup of $\mathbb{Z}_p^*$ is preferred over a group on elliptic curves, motivated by the desire to keep the implementation of a verifier as accessible as possible: the basics of modular arithmetic are part of any CS curriculum, which is not the case of elliptic curves. Exponential ElGamal is preferred over Paillier, which is also additively homomorphic and has a more efficient decryption process, because ElGamal comes with efficient threshold key generation protocols. The disjunctive Chaum-Pedersen proof can be described in various ways. Here, we follow ElectionGuard, whose specification can be accessed for further details [13]. Numerous other descriptions exist and lead to equally or less efficient implementations.

We observe that the verifiable encryption of a bit requires 2 exponentiations for the ciphertext and 5 more exponentiations for the proof. In terms of storage, the ciphertext takes 2 elements in $\mathbb{Z}_p^*$, and the proof takes 4 elements in $\mathbb{Z}_p^*$ and 4 elements in $\mathbb{Z}_q$. Using the ElectionGuard parameters with $|p| = 4096$, we see that each verifiably encrypted bit requires 25600 bits $\approx 3\,\mathrm{KB}$. However (and even though this is usually not the case in practice), the proof size can be much reduced by omitting the 4 elements in $\mathbb{Z}_p^*$, which can be recomputed from the other ones, taking the size down to about $1\,\mathrm{KB}$.

## 3   Fixed-Base Exponentiation

Existing implementations of homomorphic voting schemes (e.g., VoteBox, Helios, Belenios, ElectionGuard...) make use of the exponentiation function of standard Multi-Precision arithmetic libraries for computing modular exponentiations, including gmpy2 [15] in Python and jsbn [26] in JavaScript. These libraries support the computation of modular exponentiations as a stateless operation.

Numerous techniques however exist that make it possible to compute multiple exponentiations w.r.t. a single base much faster than independently [6,18]. This is precisely our case here: we only use bases $g$ and $h$.

The design of most fixed base exponentiation algorithms was however guided by constraints that are quite different of those of voting exponentiations: while these algorithms behave very well when a small amount of memory is available to store the result of precomputation, voting applications can typically dedicate several MB, and possibly even GB of memory to precomputation storage.

It is tempting to consider such an option, given that we may need to compute a lot of exponentiations: a single race with half a dozen candidates will already require a few dozens exponentiation, and a full ballot, which can often contain one or two hundreds choices, can take a thousand exponentiations. Even more challenging is the encryption of all the ballots cast in an election, as needed for a privacy preserving publicly verifiable risk limiting audit, which may require millions of exponentiations. Based on these observations, we explore the use of a simple precomputation approach based on the standard right-to-left $k$-ary exponentiation algorithm, aiming at minimizing the number of multiplications needed per exponentiation. We will compare it to other traditional approaches below.

*Precomputation.* Suppose that we are willing to compute a lot of exponentiations in base $g$, with exponents of at most $\ell$ bits. We select a parameter $k$, and precompute a table of $t = \lceil \ell/k \rceil$ lines and $2^k$ columns, in which $table[i][j] \leftarrow g^{2^i \cdot j}$. Such a table can be computed using $t \cdot (2^k - 1)$ multiplications as the first column of "1"'s, for $j = 0$, requires no computation. As an example, for $\ell = 6$ and $k = 2$, the table looks as follows:

| 1 | $g$ | $g^2$ | $g^3$ |
|---|-----|-------|-------|
| 1 | $g^4$ | $g^8$ | $g^{12}$ |
| 1 | $g^{16}$ | $g^{32}$ | $g^{48}$ |

*Computation.* Computing $g^e$ for $e = (e_{t-1} \ldots e_0)_{2^k}$ with $e_i \in \{0, \ldots, 2^k - 1\}$ is now immediate: we just need to pick the correct element on each line of the table, and multiply them together: $g^e = \prod_{i=0}^{t-1} table[i][e_i]$.

This algorithm requires $t-1$ multiplications, and makes use of the first column of the table in order to deal with the cases where some $e_i = 0$. An alternative would be to simply exclude these terms from the product but, since we intend to use relatively large values of $k$, this strategy would only save us a marginal amount of memory and computation, while adding a test on each $e_i$ value.

*How to Choose $k$?* We see that, for a fixed exponent size, the number of multiplications and the storage that are required for the precomputation grow like $2^k/k$, while the online computation decreases like $1/k$.

Obviously, if the precomputation time does not matter (because it can be performed well in advance), choosing a value of $k$ as large as the memory can fit would lead to the fastest online exponentiations. If we would like to minimize the total computation time, then the right balance needs to be found between the time spent on precomputation and the time spent on computation: for $n$ exponentiations in base $g$, the total number of multiplications is $\lceil \ell/k \rceil (2^k - 1) + (\lceil \ell/k \rceil - 1)n$. When $n \gg 1$, this expression is minimum when $n \approx (\ln(2)k - 1)2^k$.

For the sake of concreteness, we explore these values in the group used in ElectionGuard, that is $\ell = |q| = 256$. Table 1 contains the maximum value of $n$ until which various choices of $k$ are optimal, based on the multiplication count made above. We may observe that $k = 15$ and $k = 17$ are never optimal choices.

The storage that is required for the precomputation table grows relatively fast: if we ignore the first column that only contains "1", we need to store $t \cdot (2^k - 1)$ group elements. Table 1 also shows these volumes for various values of $k$. Even if this grows fast, the volumes remain lower than 100 MB for values of $k$ up to 13, which should be within reach of any modern computer. The table also shows that the benefits of increasing the value of $k$ for such values also starts plummeting: moving from $k = 7$ to $k = 10$ gives a speedup by a factor $36/25 = 1.44$ for an extra 11.6 MB of storage, while moving from $k = 10$ to $k = 13$ only gives an extra factor $25/19 = 1.31$ for an extra 70 MB of storage.

**Table 1.** The $n$ line gives an estimation of the maximum value of $n$ for which choices of $k$ are optimal. For instance, $k = 8$ is the best choice for $n \in [693, 2219]$. We also give the precomputation storage volume and the online computation work for various parameters of $k$.

| $k$ | 3 | 4 | 5 | 6 | 7 | 8 | 9 |
|---|---|---|---|---|---|---|---|
| $n$ | 16 | 54 | 121 | 332 | 692 | 2219 | 3926 |
| Table size (MB) | 0.3 | 0.5 | 0.8 | 1.4 | 2.4 | 4.2 | 7.6 |
| $t - 1$ (online mult.) | 85 | 63 | 51 | 42 | 36 | 31 | 28 |
| $k$ | 10 | 11 | 12 | 13 | 14 | 16 | 18 |
| $n$ | 11265 | 20481 | 36865 | 147457 | 245761 | 2883585 | 3407873 |
| Table size (MB) | 14 | 25 | 46 | 84 | 159 | 537 | 2013 |
| $t - 1$ (online mult.) | 25 | 23 | 21 | 19 | 18 | 15 | 14 |

Overall, we observe a few "sweet spots" in this table: in a low-memory setting, we see that computational gains remain fairly high until we reach $k = 8$ and $t - 1 = 31$, which still comes with a very small memory requirement of 4 MB. The value $k = 13$ and $t - 1 = 19$ is the second-to-last that saves at least 2 online multiplications compared to the previous value of $k$ and keeps memory requirements below 100 MB. As we will see in our benchmarks in Sect. 7.1, all these values offer important speed improvements over the standard exponentiation function of big integer libraries.

*What About Other Fixed-Base Exponentiation Methods?* The method that is described above is demanding in terms of precomputation table size, compared to traditional solutions. Nevertheless, we see that, when aiming for very fast exponentiations, it is quite competitive, and remarkably simple. To offer some points of comparison, we consider the classical methods as described in [18] for the parameters listed above.

- The fixed-base windowing method (Algo. 3.41) is expected to require $2^k + t - 3$ multiplications/exponentiation and the storage of $t$ values. This is minimum for $k = 4$ in our case, and requires 77 multiplications per exponentiation and the storage of 63 group elements. So, our method leads to faster exponentiations as soon as $k > 4$.
- The fixed-base comb method (Algo. 3.44) is expected to require $2t - 2$ multiplications per exponentiation, and the storage of $2^k$ precomputed values. If we aim for the same number of multiplications/exponentiation (meaning that $k$ needs to be approximately twice as big for the comb method compared to our method), our method is more efficient as soon as $k > 5$.
- The two-table fixed-base comb method (Algo 3.45) is expected to require $3t/2 - 2$ multiplications/exponentiation, and the storage of $2^{k+1}$ precomputed values. Here, our method is more efficient as soon as $k > 7$.

So, it seems that, apart from its extreme simplicity, the method we described also offers important speed-ups. Our estimates only focus on the number of multiplications, being the bulk of the work here. More sophisticated methods focusing on the efficient computation of short multiplication chains, for example Pippenger's [20], may require a smaller number of multiplications. However, they also require more bit-by-bit inspection in the exponents, and create multiplication chains that combine all the exponents, which requires additional book keeping.

## 4   Multi-ElGamal

The implementation improvement discussed above does not touch the voting protocol itself, easing its integration in an existing system. Nevertheless, it is appealing to explore whether the use of other cryptographic mechanisms would reduce the efforts needed to verifiably encrypt a bit. We start by exploring the case of ElGamal encryption, and will turn to the ZK proof in the next sections.

ElGamal encryption requires 2 exponentiations per bit. But ElGamal encryptions can be easily batched if we have multiple public keys $(h_1, \ldots, h_m) = (g^{x_1}, \ldots, g^{x_m})$ with each $x_i \leftarrow \mathbb{Z}_q$: we can encrypt $m$ bits $(v_0, \ldots, v_m)$ as $(g^r, g^{v_1} h_1^r, \ldots, g^{v_m} h_m^r)$ – the security of this multi-ElGamal scheme can be reduced to the one of the original ElGamal encryption scheme. We can now encrypt $m$ bits with $m + 1$ exponentiations, compared to $2m$ with plain ElGamal, leading to a speed-up by a factor close to 2 even for relatively low values of $m$.

However, exponentiations are now computed w.r.t. $m + 1$ bases instead of 2, which may require more efforts of precomputation if we want to use fixed-base exponentiation methods. If the precomputation is taken offline, and in the absence of memory concerns, multi-ElGamal will always be more efficient.

But if the precomputation needs to be made online, then what we gain on one side may be lost on the other side. We can estimate this by exploring a few values by multiplication counts. If $n = 1000$, the two exponentiations of plain ElGamal (i.e., $m = 1$) require an optimal effort of 78320 multiplications for $k = 8$ (including precomputation), and a storage of 8 MB. The use of multi-ElGamal can offer some benefits: we reach 66045 multiplications for $m = 4$ and $k = 6$, and a slightly lower precomputation volume of 7 MB. If $n = 100000$, plain ElGamal requires an optimal effort of 4.13 million multiplications for $k = 13$. If we switch to multi-ElGamal, we can for instance obtain 3.06 millions multiplications for $m = 5$ and $k = 11$. The storage needed for the tables again slightly decreases from 168 MB to 151 MB. Overall, we observe that the benefits increase when we have more votes to encrypt. But they remain well below the factor $\approx 2$ that was hoped for a large $m$.

The adoption of multi-ElGamal may also be complicated by extra validity requirements on ballots. It is for instance quite common to require that a maximum number of candidates are selected within a single race. This is typically handled by computing an encryption of the number of candidates selected within the race as the homomorphic sum of the ciphertexts computed for each choice, and proving that this sum is within the expected range. However, this homomorphic addition won't work if the choices within a race are encrypted with a different public key $h_i$. Nevertheless, it remains an option to use multi-ElGamal in an election with multiple races, and to use one public key $h_i$ per race.

## 5   Adapting the ZK 0-1 Proofs – Linear Techniques

The disjunctive version of the Chaum-Pedersen protocol described in Sect. 2, requires 5 modular exponentiations: 3 in base $g$, and 2 in base $h$, and makes most of the computational effort.

We will first see how a simple change in the ElGamal encryption process makes it possible to save 1 exponentiation in base $g$, down to a total of 4 exponentiations. As a second step, we will turn to proofs for multi-ElGamal ciphertexts, and show how to compute the proof with $3m + 1$ exponentiations for an $m$-key multi-ElGamal ciphertext. Eventually, using batching techniques, we will show how to compute a proof for $\ell$ multi-ElGamal ciphertexts with $\ell \cdot m + \ell + m + 1$ exponentiations, bringing the cost of the proof down to almost 1 exponentiation per encrypted bit.

### 5.1   From 5 to 4 Exponentiations

Looking back at the disjunctive Chaum-Pedersen proof as it is described in Sect. 2, we can observe that the computation of $(A'_0, B'_0) = (g^s, g^{vw}h^s)$ and $(A'_1, B'_1) = (g^t, g^{(1-v)w}h^t)$ requires a total of 3 exponentiations when $v$ is 0 or 1.

We observe that exponential ElGamal encryption works just as well, and may be slightly more efficient by saving one multiplication, if bits are encrypted as a $(g^r, h^{v+r})$ pair. Now, the commitment of the proof can be computed with a pair of ciphertexts $(A'_0, B'_0) = (g^s, h^{vw+s})$ and $(A'_1, B'_1) = (g^t, h^{(1-v)w+t})$, and the rest of the proof can remain unchanged. This saves 1 exponentiation in base $g$, taking the cost of computing a proof from 5 to 4 exponentiations.

### 5.2   A 0-1 Product Proof

The adaptation of the disjunctive Chaum-Pedersen proof to multi-ElGamal ciphertexts does not offer any particular benefit, unfortunately: one basically needs to compute one full proof for each $(A, B_j) = (g^r, h_j^{v_j + r})$ pair, keeping a cost of 4 exponentiations per encrypted bit.

In Table 2, we describe another proof approach, that consists in proving that $v_j(1 - v_j) = 0$, adapting a classical approach described in [17] for instance, and see that it makes it possible to take the cost of the 0-1 proof for a multi-ElGamal ciphertext down to $3m + 1$ exponentiations.

### 5.3   Batching the Product Proof

Another advantage of the product proof is that it becomes compatible with batching techniques. To compress the proof further and save the computation of some exponentiations, and even more when we have $\ell$ multi-ElGamal ciphertexts, we consider a batching process. More precisely, when we have $\ell$ ciphertexts of the form $(A_i, \{B_{ij}\}_{j=1}^m) = (g^{r_i}, \{h_j^{v_{ij}+r_i}\}_{j=1}^m)$, for $i \in [\ell]$, we seek to prove that $\sum_{ij} v_{ij}(1-v_{ij}) \cdot \alpha^{(i-1)m+j-1} = 0$, where $\alpha \in \mathbb{Z}_q$ is a random value. As long as $\alpha$ is

**Table 2.** Proof of 0-1 encryption for multi-ElGamal ciphertexts.

---

**Commitment** The prover computes: $A' = g^s$, $B'_j = h_j^{w_j+s}$, $C_j = g^{t_j}$, $D_j = h_j^{w_j v_j + t_j}$, where $s, w_j, t_j \leftarrow\!\!\$\ \mathbb{Z}_q$ and $j \in [m]$.

**Challenge** The verifier sends a challenge $e \leftarrow\!\!\$\ \mathbb{Z}_q$.

**Response** The prover computes the response, for $j \in [m]$:
$$f_r = s + er, \qquad f_{v_j} = w_j + e v_j, \qquad f_{u_j} = t_j + r(e - f_{v_j}).$$

**Verification** The verification proceeds by checking that, for every $j \in [m]$:
$$A^e A' = g^{f_r}, \qquad B_j^e \bar{B}'_j = h_j^{f_{v_j}+f_r}, \qquad A^{e-f_{v_j}} C_j = g^{f_{u_j}}, \qquad B_j^{e-f_{v_j}} D_j = h_j^{f_{u_j}}.$$

---

independent of the statements to be proven, the Schwartz-Zippel lemma implies that the above equation (seen as the evaluation of a polynomial at the random point $\alpha$) ensures $v_{ij} \in \{0,1\}$, for all $i \in [\ell]$ and $j \in [m]$, with overwhelming probability $1 - \ell m/q$.

Our protocol is in Table 3. In the commit phase, we provide the $A'$ and $B'$ elements from which we can extract all the $r_i$ and $v_{ij}$ exponents, as in our previous protocol. This makes it possible to isolate all these exponents from each other before starting the batching.

Now, the batching proceeds by picking a random exponent $\alpha$ after all the ciphertexts have been chosen and compressing the $C$ and $D$ terms of our previous proof: using $\alpha$, the $\ell m$ $C_{ij}$ terms can be compressed into a single group element $C_0$ and the $\ell m$ $D_{ij}$ terms can be compressed into $m$ group elements, one per $h_j$ base. With respect to $\ell$ parallel executions of the first protocol, we would have the relation $C_0 = \prod_{i \in [\ell], j \in [m]} C_{ij}^{\alpha^{(i-1)m+j-1}}$ and $D_{0j} = \prod_{i \in [\ell]} D_{ij}^{\alpha^{(i-1)m+j-1}}$.

It would be tempting to further compress our $D_{0j}$'s into a single $D_0$ as we do for $C_0$, but the special-soundness would then have to rely on the hardness of computing the discrete logarithms of the $h_j$'s in basis $g$. While the security of the encryption implies this hardness, the authorities that know the secret key would have the possibility to cheat when colliding with corrupted users/provers. This is the reason why we keep our $m$ values.

We prove the special-soundness of our protocol below – the other standard properties of $\Sigma$-protocols come by inspection.

**Theorem 1.** *The protocol in Table 3 has special soundness.*

*Proof.* From any two transcripts of this protocol with identical $\alpha$ and commitments $(A'_i, \{B'_{ij}\}_{j=1}^m)_{i=1}^\ell, C_0, \{D_{0j}\}_{j=1}^m$ different challenges $e$ and $e'$ and responses $(f_{r_i}, \{f_{v_{ij}}\}_{j=1}^m, \{f_{u_{ij}}\}_{j=1}^m)_{i=1}^\ell$ and $(f'_{r_i}, \{f'_{v_{ij}}\}_{j=1}^m, \{f'_{u_{ij}}\}_{j=1}^m)_{i=1}^\ell$, we can extract, for all $i \in [\ell]$ and $j \in [m]$,

$$r_i = \frac{f_{r_i} - f'_{r_i}}{e - e'}, \qquad v_{ij} = \frac{f_{v_{ij}} - f'_{v_{ij}}}{e - e'}, \qquad u_{ij} = \frac{f_{u_{ij}} - f'_{u_{ij}}}{e - e'},$$

**Table 3.** Batch proof of 0-1 encryption for multi-ElGamal ciphertexts.

---

**Statement** Given the statement $A_i = g^{r_i}$, $\{B_{ij} = h_j^{v_{ij}+r_i}\}_{j=1}^m$, for $i \in [\ell]$, the verifier generates and sends $\alpha \leftarrow\!\!\$\, \mathbb{Z}_q$ to the prover.

**Commitment** The prover computes $A_i' = g^{s_i}$, $B_{ij}' = h_j^{w_{ij}+s_i}$ for proving openings,

$$C_0 = g^{\sum_{i\in[\ell],j\in[m]} t_{ij}\cdot\alpha^{(i-1)m+j-1}} , \qquad D_{0j} = h_j^{\sum_{i\in[\ell]}(v_{ij}w_{ij}+t_{ij})\cdot\alpha^{(i-1)m+j-1}}$$

for proving the relations, where $s_i, w_{ij}, t_{ij} \leftarrow\!\!\$\, \mathbb{Z}_q$, for all $i \in [n], j \in [m]$.

**Challenge** The verifier sends a challenge $e \leftarrow\!\!\$\, \mathbb{Z}_q$.

**Response** The prover computes the response for all $i \in [\ell], j \in [m]$:

$$f_{r_i} = er_i + s_i , \qquad f_{v_{ij}} = ev_{ij} + w_{ij} , \qquad f_{u_{ij}} = r_i(e - f_{v_{ij}}) + t_{ij} .$$

**Verification** The verification proceeds by checking that, for all $i \in [\ell], j \in [m]$:

$$A_i^e A_i' = g^{f_{r_i}} , \qquad\qquad B_{ij}^e B_{ij}' = h_j^{f_{v_{ij}}+f_{r_i}} ,$$

$$\prod_{i\in[n],j\in[m]} A_i^{(e-f_{v_{ij}})\cdot\alpha^{(i-1)m+j-1}} \quad C_0 = g^{\sum_{i\in[n],j\in[m]} f_{u_{ij}}\cdot\alpha^{(i-1)m+j-1}} ,$$

$$\prod_{i\in[n]} B_{ij}^{(e-f_{v_{ij}})\cdot\alpha^{(i-1)m+j-1}} \quad D_{0j} = y_j^{\sum_{i\in[n]} f_{u_{ij}}\cdot\alpha^{(i-1)m+j-1}} .$$

---

where $(r_i, \{v_{ij}\}_{j=1}^m)_{i=1}^\ell$ are the exponents of the ciphertexts, since dividing the first two verification equations gives $A_i^{e-e'} = g^{f_{r_i}-f_{r_i}'}$ and $B_{ij}^{e-e'} = h_j^{(f_{v_{ij}}-f_{v_{ij}}')+(f_{r_i}-f_{r_i}')}$, and the encryption scheme is perfectly binding.

It remains to show that $v_{ij} \in \{0,1\}$, for $i \in [\ell], j \in [m]$. If we divide the remaining verification equations of the two transcripts by corresponding equations, and raise them all to the power $(e - e')^{-1} \bmod q$, then take the discrete logarithms in their respective basis, we get:

$$\sum_{i\in[\ell],j\in[m]} r_i(1 - v_{ij}) \cdot \alpha^{(i-1)\ell+j-1} = \sum_{i\in[\ell],j\in[m]} u_{ij} \cdot \alpha^{(i-1)\ell+j-1} ,$$

$$\sum_{i\in[\ell]} (v_{ij} + r_i)(1 - v_{ij}) \cdot \alpha^{(i-1)\ell+j-1} = \sum_{i\in[\ell]} u_{ij} \cdot \alpha^{(i-1)\ell+j-1} ,$$

for all $j \in [m]$. By injecting the values of the right-hand side member of the last equations for $j \in [m]$ into the one above we find

$$\sum_{i\in[\ell],j\in[m]} r_i(1 - v_{ij}) \cdot \alpha^{(i-1)\ell+j-1} = \sum_{i\in[\ell],j\in[m]} (v_{ij} + r_i)(1 - v_{ij}) \cdot \alpha^{(i-1)\ell+j-1} ,$$

where the constants in front of the powers of $\alpha$ are uniquely determined by the statement. Since $\alpha$ was generated after the verifier received the statement, we have $r_i(1 - v_{ij}) = (v_{ij} + r_i)(1 - v_{ij})$, for all $i \in [\ell], j \in [m]$, due to the Schwartz-Zippel lemma, which implies that $0 = v_{ij}(1 - v_{ij}) \bmod q$.

*Efficiency.* Computing the proof in Table 3 requires $(\ell + 1)(m + 1)$ exponentiations. The number of multiplications in the exponents increases to $4\ell m + \ell$ multiplications, but this will remain negligible in the group we consider where $|p| = 16|q|$. We can make a few more observations:

- If we need to compute $n = \ell \cdot m$ 0-1 proofs and if there is no precomputation, then picking $m \approx \ell$ is the best choice. In this case, when $n$ is large, the cost of the proof comes close to 1 exponentiation per encrypted bit.
- However, when precomputation is used, and since the number of exponentiations in each base is well-balanced, the remarks made for the choice of $m$ in the multi-ElGamal encryption still apply: we can expect only marginal benefits when increasing $m$ above 4, for most values of $n$.
- While our basic product proof did not offer any benefit for a regular ElGamal ciphertext ($m = 1$), the batching process helps quite a bit in that case: we move from $4n$ exponentiations down to $2n + 2$.

## 6    Adapting the ZK 0-1 Proofs - Logarithmic Batching

We propose a shorter proof system showing that $n = 2^\tau$ ElGamal ciphertexts encrypt bits. Our system shares similarities with a protocol due to Groth [16] that was described recursively as a subroutine of a bigger protocol. Here, we give an iterative description which *halves* the number of rounds of [16] to prove that $n$ pairs of commitments $\{(c_i, d_i)\}_{i=0}^{n-1}$, for any homomorphic commitment Com (ElGamal encryption in our case), satisfy $\sum_{i=0}^{n-1} x_i y_i = 0$, where $c_i = \mathsf{Com}(x_i; r_i)$ and $d_i = \mathsf{Com}(y_i; s_i)$ for some coins $r_i, s_i \in \mathbb{Z}_q$, for all $i = 0, \ldots, n - 1$. That is, we prove that the inner product is null. We then show how to turn our protocol into our desired proof system and analyze the efficiency.

### 6.1    Notations

We identify the index $i = \sum_{k=1}^{\tau} i_k 2^{k-1}$ with the $\tau$-bit string multi-index $i_1 \ldots i_\tau$ so that $x_i = x_{i_1 \cdots i_\tau}$, for all $0 \leq i \leq 2^\tau - 1$, and conversely for all $0 \leq i_1, \ldots, i_\tau \leq 1$. To get a shortened form of $x_{i_1 \cdots i_{k-1} i_k i_{k+1} \cdots i_\tau}$, we write $x_{i_k^- i_k i_k^+}$ with $i_k^- = i_1 \cdots i_{k-1}$ and $i_k^+ = i_{k+1} \cdots i_\tau$ when $\tau$ is implicit. By convention $i_1^-$ and $i_\tau^+$ are empty strings so that we have $x_{i_1^- i_1 i_1^+} = x_{i_1 i_1^+}$ as well as $x_{i_\tau^- i_\tau i_\tau^+} = x_{i_\tau^- i_\tau}$. In the same spirit, we set $x_{i_0^+} = x_{i_1 \cdots i_\tau}$. For the sake of readability, we often do not specify the values taken by the multi-indexes in the summation

$$\sum_{i_k^- i_k i_k^+} = \sum_{i_k^- \in \{0,1\}^{k-1}} \sum_{i_k \in \{0,1\}} \sum_{i_k^+ \in \{0,1\}^{\tau-k}}$$

since the bit-strings take all their possible values determined by the bit-size.

Similarly for exponents, we use a notation to compress the product $\alpha_1^{i_1} \cdots \alpha_\tau^{i_\tau}$ over $\mathbb{Z}_q$ as $\alpha^I$ when $\alpha = (\alpha_1, \ldots, \alpha_\tau)$ and $I = i_1 \cdots i_\tau$. For the product of the first $k - 1$ factors, with $\alpha_{<k} = (\alpha_1, \ldots, \alpha_{k-1})$, we naturally write $\alpha_{<k}^{i_k^-} = \alpha_1^{i_1} \cdots \alpha_{k-1}^{i_{k-1}}$. By convention $\alpha_{<1} = ()$ and $\alpha_{<1}^{i_1^-} = 1$. We also see $k$-bit strings as tuples of $\mathbb{Z}^k$ so that, component-wise, $i_k^- - j_k^-$ is well defined. Finally, $x_I = x_{i_1 \cdots i_\tau}$.

## 6.2  Intuition

Assuming that the prover receives $\tau \in \mathcal{O}(\log n)$ unpredictable scalars $\alpha_1, \ldots, \alpha_\tau$ of $\mathbb{Z}_q$ from the verifier, both parties can efficiently compute

$$C = \prod_{i_1,\ldots,i_\tau=0}^{1} c_{i_1 \ldots i_\tau}^{\alpha_1^{i_1} \cdots \alpha_\tau^{i_\tau}} = \prod_{I \in \{0,1\}^\tau} c_I^{\alpha^I} = \mathsf{Com}\left(\sum_I x_I \alpha^I; \sum_I r_I \alpha^I\right)$$

as well as

$$D = \prod_{i_1,\ldots,i_\tau=0}^{1} d_{i_1 \ldots i_\tau}^{\alpha_1^{-i_1} \cdots \alpha_n^{-i_\tau}} = \mathsf{Com}\left(\sum_I y_I \alpha^{-I}; \sum_I s_I \alpha^{-I}\right).$$

Letting zero-knowledge apart for now, the prover can send the opening $(X, R)$ of $C = \mathsf{Com}(X, R)$ to the verifier so that both parties can also compute the commitment $D^X = \mathsf{Com}(Y; S)^X = \mathsf{Com}(XY; XS) = \mathsf{Com}(Z, T)$ where $Z = XY = \sum_{I,J} x_I y_J \alpha^{I-J}$.

Viewed as a rational fraction over $\mathbb{Z}_q(\alpha)$ with $\tau$ indeterminates $\alpha = (\alpha_1, \ldots, \alpha_\tau)$, the prover has to ensure that the constant term of $Z(\alpha)$ is $\sum_I x_I y_I = 0$. To get a proof of size in $\mathcal{O}(\tau)$ we rely on the following observation:

$$Z(\alpha) = \underbrace{\left( \sum_{i_{\bar{\tau}}, j_{\bar{\tau}}} x_{i_{\bar{\tau}} 0} \cdot y_{j_{\bar{\tau}} 1} \cdot \alpha_{<\tau}^{i_{\bar{\tau}} - j_{\bar{\tau}}} \right) \cdot \alpha_\tau^{-1}}_{U_{\tau-1}}$$

$$+ \underbrace{\sum_{i_{\bar{\tau}}, j_{\bar{\tau}}, i_\tau} x_{i_{\bar{\tau}} i_\tau} \cdot y_{j_{\bar{\tau}} i_\tau} \cdot \alpha_{<\tau}^{i_{\bar{\tau}} - j_{\bar{\tau}}}}_{V_{\tau-1}} + \underbrace{\left( \sum_{i_{\bar{\tau}}, j_{\bar{\tau}}} x_{i_{\bar{\tau}} 1} \cdot y_{j_{\bar{\tau}} 0} \cdot \alpha_{<\tau}^{i_{\bar{\tau}} - j_{\bar{\tau}}} \right) \cdot \alpha_\tau}_{W_{\tau-1}},$$

where the terms $U_{\tau-1}, V_{\tau-1}, W_{\tau-1}$ no more depend on $\alpha_\tau$. By iterating this process with the middle term we find

$$Z(\alpha) = U_{\tau-1} \alpha_\tau^{-1} + \cdots + U_0 \alpha_1^{-1} + V_0 + W_0 \alpha_1 + \cdots + W_{\tau-1} \alpha_\tau,$$

for $V_0 = \sum_I x_I y_I$ and some $U_0, W_0, \ldots, U_{\tau-1}, W_{\tau-1} \in \mathbb{Z}_q(\alpha)$, where for each $k = 1, \ldots, \tau$, the terms $U_{k-1}, W_{k-1}$ only depends on $\alpha_{<k} = (\alpha_1, \ldots, \alpha_{k-1})$. This means that we can gradually build $V_k \in \mathbb{Z}_q(\alpha_{<k})(\alpha_k)$ as

$$V_k = U_{k-1} \cdot \alpha_k^{-1} + V_{k-1} + W_{k-1} \cdot \alpha_k,$$

for all $k = 1, \ldots, \tau$, from $k = 1$, with $V_0 = \sum_I x_I y_I = 0$, to $V_\tau = Z(\alpha)$.

Therefore, the special-soundness may use the Schwartz-Zippel lemma since the prover can *first* compute and send commitments[1]

$$c_{u_{k-1}} \in \mathsf{Com}(U_{k-1}) \qquad c_{v_{k-1}} \in \mathsf{Com}(V_{k-1}) \qquad c_{w_{k-1}} \in \mathsf{Com}(W_{k-1})$$

---

[1] Actually, the verifier can compute the commitment of $V_{k-1}$ itself.

to the verifier *before* receiving back the next scalar $\alpha_k \leftarrow_{\$} \mathbb{Z}_q$ and iterating with

$$c_{v_k} = c_{u_{k-1}}^{\alpha_k^{-1}} \cdot c_{v_{k-1}} \cdot c_{w_{k-1}}^{\alpha_k} \in \mathsf{Com}(V_k)$$

which can also be computed by the verifier. Starting from $1 = \mathsf{Com}(V_0; 0)$ the process stops with $c_{v_\tau} = \mathsf{Com}(Z) =: E$ after $\tau$ iterations. The prover and the verifier then engage in a simple proof for a product relation between $C, D$ and $E$ ensuring $XY = Z$.

For the extraction of the witness, since the protocol reveals only one opening related to $\{c_i\}_{i=0}^{n-1}$ and one opening related to $\{d_i\}_{i=0}^{n-1}$ we cannot hope to extract the witness in less than $2^\tau \approx n$ rewinds in the proof of special-soundness. Fortunately, we only need less than $2n$ rewinds to extract the witness.

## 6.3   Proof of Inner Product

**Common Reference String:** ck, where ck $\leftarrow \mathsf{Gen}(1^\lambda)$. It will be implicit in every use of Com.

**Statement:** $\{(c_i, d_i)\}_{i=0}^{n-1}$, where $c_i, d_i \in \mathcal{C}_{\mathsf{ck}}$, for all $i = 0$ to $n-1$, and $n = 2^\tau$.

**Prover's Witness:** openings $\{(x_i, r_i), (y_i, s_i)\}_{i=0}^{n-1}$ such that $c_i = \mathsf{Com}(x_i, r_i)$ and $d_i = \mathsf{Com}(y_i, s_i)$, for all $i = 0$ to $n-1$, and satisfying $\sum_{i=0}^{n-1} x_i y_i = 0$.

**Initial Round:** common inputs are ck and the statement.

$\mathcal{P} \rightarrow \mathcal{V}$: Pick $\mu_0, \nu_0 \leftarrow_{\$} \mathbb{Z}_q$ and compute

$$c_{u_0} = \mathsf{Com}(U_0, \mu_0), \qquad U_0 = \sum_{i_1^+ \in \{0,1\}^{\tau-1}} x_{0i_1^+} \cdot y_{1i_1^+},$$

$$c_{w_0} = \mathsf{Com}(W_0, \nu_0), \qquad W_0 = \sum_{i_1^+ \in \{0,1\}^{\tau-1}} x_{1i_1^+} \cdot y_{0i_1^+}.$$

Send $c_{u_0}$ and $c_{w_0}$. (We set $V_0 = 0$, $\rho_0 = 0$ so that $c_{v_0} = \mathsf{Com}(V_0, \rho_0) = 1$)

$\mathcal{V} \rightarrow \mathcal{P}$: If $c_{u_0}, c_{w_0} \in \mathcal{C}_{\mathsf{ck}}$, pick and send $\alpha_1 \leftarrow_{\$} \mathbb{Z}_q$, else abort and output 0.

For later use, already compute $c_{v_1} = c_{u_0}^{\alpha_1^{-1}} \cdot c_{v_0} \cdot c_{w_0}^{\alpha_1}$.

**Iterative Round:** in the $k$-th round the common inputs are ck, the statement as well as the values generated in the previous rounds $\{(c_{u_{k-2}}, c_{w_{i-2}}, \alpha_{i-1})\}_{i=2}^k$ and the private prover's inputs are the witness and $\{(\mu_{i-2}, \rho_{i-2}, \nu_{i-2})\}_{i=2}^k$.

$\mathcal{P} \rightarrow \mathcal{V}$: Pick $\mu_{k-1}, \nu_{k-1} \leftarrow_{\$} \mathbb{Z}_q$ and compute

$$c_{u_{k-1}} = \mathsf{Com}(U_{k-1}, \mu_{k-1}) , \qquad U_{k-1} = \sum_{i_k^-, i_k^+, j_k^-} x_{i_k^- 0 i_k^+} \cdot y_{j_k^- 1 i_k^+} \cdot \alpha_{<k}^{i_k^- - j_k^-} ,$$

$$c_{w_{k-1}} = \mathsf{Com}(W_{k-1}, \nu_{k-1}) , \qquad W_{k-1} = \sum_{i_k^-, i_k^+, j_k^-} x_{i_k^- 1 i_k^+} \cdot y_{j_k^- 0 i_k^+} \cdot \alpha_{<k}^{i_k^- - j_k^-} .$$

Send $c_{u_{k-1}}$ and $c_{w_{k-1}}$. (Compute $\rho_{k-1} = \mu_{k-2}\alpha_{k-1}^{-1} + \rho_{k-2} + \nu_{k-2}\alpha_{k-1}$.)

$\mathcal{V} \rightarrow \mathcal{P}$: If $c_{u_{k-1}}, c_{w_{k-1}} \in \mathcal{C}_{\mathsf{ck}}$, pick and send $\alpha_k \leftarrow_{\$} \mathbb{Z}_q$, else abort and output 0.

For later use, already compute $c_{v_k} = c_{u_{k-1}}^{\alpha_k^{-1}} c_{v_{k-1}} c_{w_{k-1}}^{\alpha_k}$.

**Penultimate Round:** $((\tau + 1)$-th round) after the first $\tau$ rounds the common inputs are ck, the statement as well as $\{(c_{u_{i-1}}, c_{w_{i-1}}, \alpha_i)\}_{i=1}^{\tau}$ and the private prover's inputs are the witness and $\{(\mu_{i-1}, \rho_{i-1}, \nu_{i-1})\}_{i=1}^{\tau}$. From that point, both $\mathcal{P}$ and $\mathcal{V}$ can deterministically compute

$$C = \prod_I c_I^{\alpha^I} = \mathsf{Com}\left(\sum_I x_I \alpha^I; \sum_I r_I \alpha^I\right) = \mathsf{Com}(X, R),$$

$$D = \prod_I d_I^{\alpha^{-I}} = \mathsf{Com}\left(\sum_I y_I \alpha^{-I}; \sum_I s_I \alpha^{-I}\right) = \mathsf{Com}(Y, S),$$

and $c_{v_\tau} = \mathsf{Com}(V_\tau, \rho_\tau)$ iteratively, as $\mathcal{V}$ already did. It remains to ensure that $XY = V_\tau$ using a standard protocol.

$\mathcal{P} \to \mathcal{V}$: First, compute $\rho_\tau = \mu_{\tau-1}\alpha_\tau^{-1} + \rho_{\tau-1} + \nu_{\tau-1}\alpha_\tau$ and $T = \rho_\tau - SX$ such that $E := c_{v_\tau} = D^X \cdot \mathsf{Com}_{\mathrm{ck}}(0, T)$. Then, pick $X', Y', R', S', T' \leftarrow_\$ \mathbb{Z}_q$ and compute the commitments

$$C' = \mathsf{Com}(X', R'), \quad D' = \mathsf{Com}(Y', S'), \quad E' = \mathsf{Com}(YX', SX' + T'),$$

so that $E' = D^{X'} \cdot \mathsf{Com}(0, T')$. Send $C', D'$ and $E'$.

$\mathcal{V} \to \mathcal{P}$: If $C', D', E' \in \mathcal{C}_{\mathrm{ck}}$, pick and send $\beta \leftarrow_\$ \mathbb{Z}_q$, else abort and output 0.

**Final Round:** the common inputs are ck, the statement, $\{(c_{u_{k-1}}, c_{w_{i-1}}, \alpha_i)\}_{i=1}^{\tau}$ as well as $(C', D', E')$ and the private prover's inputs are the witness, the $\tau$ triples $\{(\mu_{i-1}, \rho_{i-1}, \nu_{i-1})\}_{i=1}^{\tau}$, the opening values $(X, Y, R, S, T)$ and $\rho_\tau$ as well as the random scalars $(X', Y', R', S', T')$ and $\beta$.

$\mathcal{P} \to \mathcal{V}$: Compute and send the final response as

$$z_x = \beta X + X', \qquad z_y = \beta Y + Y',$$
$$z_r = \beta R + R', \qquad z_s = \beta S + S', \qquad z_t = \beta T + T'.$$

Note that $X$ and $Y$ have been computed in the previous round.

$\mathcal{V} \to \mathcal{P}$: If $z_x, z_y, z_r, z_s, z_t \in \mathbb{Z}_q$ does not hold, output 0, else perform the last verification: from $\alpha = (\alpha_1, \ldots, \alpha_\tau)$, compute $C = \prod_I c_I^{\alpha^I}$ and $D = \prod_I d_I^{\alpha^{-I}}$, and check whether

$$C^\beta C' = \mathsf{Com}(z_x, z_r), \quad D^\beta D' = \mathsf{Com}(z_y, z_s), \quad E^\beta E' = D^{z_x} \mathsf{Com}(0, z_t),$$

holds or not. If so, output 1, otherwise, output 0.

*Efficiency.* The communication complexity of the interactive protocol is $2\tau + 3$ commitments and 5 scalars of $\mathbb{Z}_q$ for the prover and $\tau + 1$ scalars for the verifier. The size of the transcript $\langle c_{u_0}, c_{w_0}, \alpha_1, \ldots, c_{u_{\tau-1}}, c_{w_{\tau-1}}, \alpha_\tau, C', D', E', \beta, z_x, z_y, z_r, z_s, z_t \rangle$ is $2\tau + 3$ commitments and $\tau + 6$ scalars. The non interactive version of this $\tau + 2$-round protocol based on the Fiat-Shamir heuristic saves the 3 last commitments of the transcript and the $\tau$ scalars of the challenge tuple $(\alpha_1, \ldots, \alpha_\tau)$.

## 6.4   The Many-Bits Case

We turn the proof of inner-product into a proof that $n$ ElGamal ciphertexts $\{(g^{r_i}, h^{v_i + r_i})\}_{i=0}^{n-1}$ encrypt $v_i \in \{0, 1\}$, for all $i + 1 \in [n]$. Since the ElGamal encryption is homomorphic, we have $c_i = \mathsf{Com}(v_i; r_i)$ in the previous notation. Also, $d_i := \mathsf{Com}(1; 0)\, c_i^{-1} = \mathsf{Com}(1 - v_i, -r_i)$ is a publicly computable ElGamal encryption of $1 - v_i$, so that $x_i = v_i$ and $y_i = 1 - v_i$ in the previous notation.

Assuming that $n = 2^\tau$, a direct application of the inner product proof only ensures $\sum_{i=0}^{n-1} v_i(1 - v_i) = 0$ while our goal is $v_i(1 - v_i) = 0$, for all $i + 1 \in [n]$, and not their sum. Fortunately, by applying the Schwartz-Zippel technique to $y_i' = y_i \cdot \gamma^i$ over $d_i' = d_i^{\gamma^i}$, we see that $\sum_{i=0}^{n-1} v_i(1 - v_i)\gamma^i = 0$ implies, for all $i + 1 \in [n]$, $v_i(1 - v_i) = 0$, but with negligible probability $n/q$. In the case that $n$ is not a power of two, we can still pad $x$ and $y'$ with 0's using dummy ElGamal ciphertext $c_i = \mathsf{Com}(0, 0)$ and $d_i' = \mathsf{Com}(0, 0)$. Note that we can ignore these terms when computing the $X$, $Y$, $U_k$ and $W_k$ sums in the proof as they will always result in a 0 value. Therefore, the padding does not increase the cost of the proof. Finally, note that we drop the $D', z_s$ and $z_s$ entries in the proof for the many-bits case. They are used to prove the knowledge of $y$, but here $y$ is directly derived from $x$.

*Efficiency.* Computing the log-based proof requires $4 \log n + 4$ exponentiations in $\mathbb{Z}_p^*$: 4 in each round to compute $c_u$ and $c_w$ and 4 to compute $C'$ and $E'$. However, we now need to compute $n(\tau + 8) + 2\tau + 7$ multiplications and $n(\tau + 5) + 4\tau + 8$ additions in $\mathbb{Z}_q$, which now dominate the cost asymptotically since $\tau = \log n$. Finally, the size of the proof is $4\tau$ elements in $\mathbb{Z}_p^*$ and 4 elements in $\mathbb{Z}_q$.

# 7   Benchmarking

We implemented the algorithms described above in Python, and executed them on an AMD 3990X processor with the turbo boost technology disabled, using the Python 3.8.10 interpreter, and gmpy2 2.1.0. All the running times listed below are in milliseconds. The implementation of the schemes and the benchmarks can be found on this repository: https://github.com/uclcrypto/many01proofs.

## 7.1   Precomputation and Exponentiations

We first tested the time needed to precompute and compute 1000 exponentiations in the ElectionGuard default group ($|p| = 4096$, $|q| = 256$).

As a baseline, computing 1000 modular exponentiations using gmpy2.powmod takes 1560 ms. Figure 1(a) shows the precomputation and computation time for various values of the precomputation parameter $k$. The speed-up factors of the exponentiation, compared to gmpy2.powmod are quite important: they range from a factor 4 when $k = 4$ to a factor 12 when $k = 13$.

Depending on the application context, the precomputation time may need to be taken into account. This question is particularly interesting in the case of

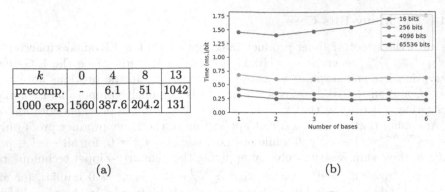

| $k$ | 0 | 4 | 8 | 13 |
|---|---|---|---|---|
| precomp. | - | 6.1 | 51 | 1042 |
| 1000 exp | 1560 | 387.6 | 204.2 | 131 |

(a)                                                    (b)

**Fig. 1.** (a) Precomputation time and time to compute 1000 exponentiations. (b): evolution of the time needed to encrypt votes with optimal choice of $k$ and various choices of the number of multi-ElGamal bases.

multi-ElGamal encryption where, for a given number of bits to verifiably encrypt, we may wonder which $(k, m)$ pair leads to an optimal running time, as discussed in Sect. 4.

This is explored in Fig. 1(b), in which we show, for a number $n$ of bits to be encrypted with $n \in \{2^4, 2^8, 2^{12}, 2^{16}\}$, the computation time/bit for $m \in [1, 6]$, selecting the optimal $k$ every time. The lines are surprisingly flat: what is gained by multi-ElGamal is lost in the fixed-base exponentiations. The maximum benefits of multi-ElGamal are around 25%, much lower than the factor of almost 2 that was hoped for, and this gain is reached around $m = 4$ for our 3 highest values of $n$. So, picking $m = 4$ independently of $n$ might be a reasonable choice, should multi-ElGamal encryption be adopted. The picture is of course different is the precomputation time does not need to be taken into account: there, multi-ElGamal keeps its expected efficiency benefits.

### 7.2   Verifiable Bit Encryption Using Linear Techniques

As a second step, we explore in Fig. 2(a) the efficiency of our proof techniques with linear complexity. For the same values of $n$ as above, a choice of $m = 4$ for the multi-ElGamal encryption, and optimal values of $k$, we explore the time needed for performing the precomputation, encryption, product proof (from Table 2), and batch proof (from Table 3). We can make a few observations from this figure: (i) As expected, the optimal $k$ grows with $n$, and so does the time spent in precomputation. But the proportion of the time spent in precomputation decreases when $n$ increases, which illustrates the decreasing returns of increasing $k$. (ii) While $n$ is multiplied by a factor 16 from line to line, the computation time is only multiplied by a factor around 10, thanks to the amortization coming from an increased amount of precomputation. (iii) The cost of our batch proof is essentially equal to the cost of the multi-ElGamal encryption.

| $n$ | $k$ | Pre. | Multi-ElGamal | Prod. Proof | Batch Proof |
|---|---|---|---|---|---|
| 16 | 2 | 12 | 13 | 33 | 16 |
| 256 | 5 | 51 | 103 | 270 | 107 |
| 4096 | 7 | 150 | 1214 | 3187 | 1256 |
| 65536 | 11 | 1573 | 13022 | 34353 | 13605 |

(a)

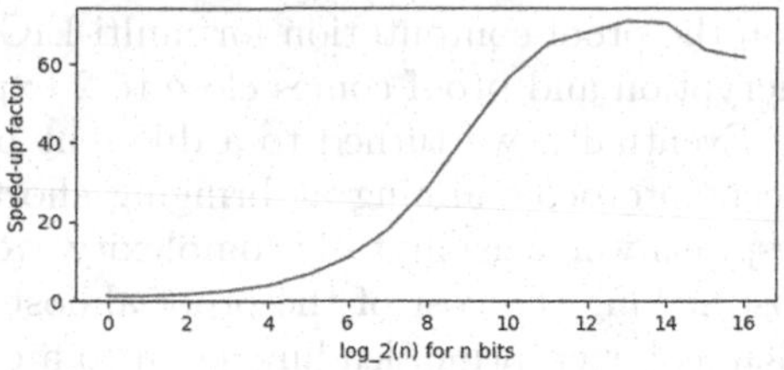

(b)

Fig. 2. (a) Running time with linear techniques. (b) Speed-up given by the log proof for $n \in \{2^i | i \in [16]\}$.

## 7.3 Verifiable Bit Encryption Using Logarithmic Proof Techniques

Eventually, Fig. 2(b) shows the speed-ups obtained in an implementation of our logarithmic proof of Sect. 6, compared to the baseline Chaum-Pedersen disjunctive proof (the batched proof is faster by a factor $\approx 2.5$ when $n$ is big enough). Both proofs take advantage of the fixed base precomputation, which is needed for the ElGamal encryption.

Here, and despite a higher asymptotic complexity due to the $n \log(n)$ multiplications needed in $\mathbb{Z}_q$, the log proof provides dramatic speed improvements, by a factor up to 70 when around 8000 proofs need to be computed, making the cost of the proof computation negligible compared to the one of encryption. The gains are already there for a small number of proofs: we obtain a speedup by a factor 2.5 for 8 proofs and a factor 18 for 128 proofs, about the size of a ballot. If one needs to compute a large number of 0-1 proofs, it may be more convenient and efficient to compute many logarithmic proofs by batches of a size between $2^{10}$ and $2^{14}$ for instance.

## 8 Conclusions

We proposed various techniques that could be used to increase the speed of verifiably encrypting bits, both at the arithmetic level (modular exponentiations) and at the protocol level (encryption and ZK proofs), compared to the usual implementation of the protocol of Cramer et al. [10].

Fixed base exponentiation techniques showed dramatic speed improvements. But, interestingly, these techniques reduced the potential benefits associated to the use of multi-ElGamal encryption, which requires fewer exponentiations but more bases: when the precomputation time is accounted for, we observe essentially no benefit in using more than $m = 4$ ElGamal public keys.

We then turned to the ZK proofs. First, we observed that changing a base in the ElGamal encryption, which is of no consequence there, brings a 25% speed-up on the traditional proof of Cramer et al. Switching to product proofs rather than disjunctive proofs, we observed no benefit for a single ElGamal ciphertext, but new possibilities for batching that brought a speed-up by a factor close to

3 on the proof computation for multi-ElGamal ciphertexts: the total cost of the encryption and proof comes close to 2 exponentiations per encrypted bit.

Eventually, we turned to a different proof strategy, in the line of the many recent protocols aiming at bringing short (logarithmic size) proofs. Here, and despite a worse asymptotic complexity, we again observed very important speed-ups, making the cost of the proof almost negligible compared to the cost of an ElGamal encryption, leading again to a cost close to 2 exp./encrypted bit.

This leaves a natural question for further works: can we go below a complexity of around 2 exp./bit for DL based protocols and parameters useful for an election? Another question comes from the choice of the group, $\mathbb{Z}_p^*$, which is by far the most common choice in current voting system implementations: how would our benchmarks evolve if ECC were considered?

**Acknowledgements.** This research was supported in part by the FNRS project SeVote and by a Microsoft Research Award. Henri Devillez is supported by a FRIA grant and Thomas Peters is a research associate of the FNRS. We thank Josh Benaloh, Michael Naehrig and Dan Wallach for numerous interesting discussions and useful feedback about this work.

# References

1. Adida, B., de Marneffe, O., Pereira, O., Quisquater, J.: Electing a university president using open-audit voting: analysis of real-world use of Helios. In: 2009 Electronic Voting Technology Workshop/Workshop on Trustworthy Elections, EVT/WOTE 2009. USENIX Association (2009)
2. Bellare, M., Goldwasser, S.: Verifiable partial key escrow. In: Proceedings of the 4th ACM Conference on Computer and Communications Security, CCS 1997, pp. 78–91. ACM (1997)
3. Benaloh, J., et al.: Star-vote: a secure, transparent, auditable, and reliable voting system. In: 2013 Electronic Voting Technology Workshop/Workshop on Trustworthy Elections, EVT/WOTE 2013. USENIX Association (2013)
4. Benaloh, J., Foote, K., Stark, P.B., Teague, V., Wallach, D.S.: VAULT-style risk-limiting audits and the Inyo county pilot. IEEE Secur. Priv. **19**(4), 8–18 (2021)
5. Benaloh, J.C., Yung, M.: Distributing the power of a government to enhance the privacy of voters (extended abstract). In: Proceedings of the 5th Annual ACM Symposium on Principles of Distributed Computing, pp. 52–62. ACM (1986)
6. Bernstein, D.J.: Pippenger's exponentiation algorithm, January 2002. http://cr.yp.to/papers/pippenger.pdf
7. Chaum, D., Pedersen, T.P.: Wallet databases with observers. In: Brickell, E.F. (ed.) CRYPTO 1992. LNCS, vol. 740, pp. 89–105. Springer, Heidelberg (1993). https://doi.org/10.1007/3-540-48071-4_7
8. Cortier, V., Gaudry, P., Glondu, S.: Belenios: a simple private and verifiable electronic voting system. In: Guttman, J.D., Landwehr, C.E., Meseguer, J., Pavlovic, D. (eds.) Foundations of Security, Protocols, and Equational Reasoning. LNCS, vol. 11565, pp. 214–238. Springer, Cham (2019). https://doi.org/10.1007/978-3-030-19052-1_14
9. Cramer, R., Damgård, I., Schoenmakers, B.: Proofs of partial knowledge and simplified design of witness hiding protocols. In: Desmedt, Y.G. (ed.) CRYPTO 1994. LNCS, vol. 839, pp. 174–187. Springer, Heidelberg (1994). https://doi.org/10.1007/3-540-48658-5_19

10. Cramer, R., Gennaro, R., Schoenmakers, B.: A secure and optimally efficient multi-authority election scheme. In: Fumy, W. (ed.) EUROCRYPT 1997. LNCS, vol. 1233, pp. 103–118. Springer, Heidelberg (1997). https://doi.org/10.1007/3-540-69053-0_9

11. Damgård, I., Jurik, M.: A generalisation, a simplification and some applications of Paillier's probabilistic public-key system. In: Kim, K. (ed.) PKC 2001. LNCS, vol. 1992, pp. 119–136. Springer, Heidelberg (2001). https://doi.org/10.1007/3-540-44586-2_9

12. Damgård, I., Jurik, M.: A length-flexible threshold cryptosystem with applications. In: Safavi-Naini, R., Seberry, J. (eds.) ACISP 2003. LNCS, vol. 2727, pp. 350–364. Springer, Heidelberg (2003). https://doi.org/10.1007/3-540-45067-X_30

13. ElectionGuard, May 2022. http://www.electionguard.vote/

14. Frederiksen, T.K., Lindell, Y., Osheter, V., Pinkas, B.: Fast distributed RSA key generation for semi-honest and malicious adversaries. In: Shacham, H., Boldyreva, A. (eds.) CRYPTO 2018. LNCS, vol. 10992, pp. 331–361. Springer, Cham (2018). https://doi.org/10.1007/978-3-319-96881-0_12

15. gmpy: gmpy2 module. http://github.com/aleaxit/gmpy

16. Groth, J.: Linear algebra with sub-linear zero-knowledge arguments. In: Halevi, S. (ed.) CRYPTO 2009. LNCS, vol. 5677, pp. 192–208. Springer, Heidelberg (2009). https://doi.org/10.1007/978-3-642-03356-8_12

17. Groth, J., Kohlweiss, M.: One-out-of-many proofs: or how to leak a secret and spend a coin. In: Oswald, E., Fischlin, M. (eds.) EUROCRYPT 2015. LNCS, vol. 9057, pp. 253–280. Springer, Heidelberg (2015). https://doi.org/10.1007/978-3-662-46803-6_9

18. Hankerson, D., Menezes, A.J., Vanstone, S.: Guide to Elliptic Curve Cryptography. SPC, Springer, Heidelberg (2003). https://doi.org/10.1007/b97644

19. Pedersen, T.P.: A threshold cryptosystem without a trusted party. In: Davies, D.W. (ed.) EUROCRYPT 1991. LNCS, vol. 547, pp. 522–526. Springer, Heidelberg (1991). https://doi.org/10.1007/3-540-46416-6_47

20. Pippenger, N.: On the evaluation of powers and related problems (preliminary version). In: 1976 17th Annual Symposium on Foundations of Computer Science, pp. 258–263. IEEE Computer Society (1976)

21. Ramchen, K., Culnane, C., Pereira, O., Teague, V.: Universally verifiable MPC and IRV ballot counting. In: Goldberg, I., Moore, T. (eds.) FC 2019. LNCS, vol. 11598, pp. 301–319. Springer, Cham (2019). https://doi.org/10.1007/978-3-030-32101-7_19

22. Sandler, D., Derr, K., Wallach, D.S.: VoteBox: a tamper-evident, verifiable electronic voting system. In: van Oorschot, P.C. (ed.) Proceedings of the 17th USENIX Security Symposium, pp. 349–364. USENIX Association (2008)

23. Schoenmakers, B.: Some efficient zeroknowledge proof techniques. In: Workshop on Cryptographic Protocols (2001)

24. Wallach, D.: Anyscale connect: encrypting and tabulating big elections, December 2020. http://www.youtube.com/watch?v=m7r33EuN6Zw

25. Wikström, D.: Verificatum, May 2022. http://www.verificatum.org/

26. Wu, T.: RSA and ECC in JavaScript (2009). http://www-cs-students.stanford.edu/~tjw/jsbn/

# A Framework for Constructing Single Secret Leader Election from MPC

Michael Backes[1], Pascal Berrang[2], Lucjan Hanzlik[1], and Ivan Pryvalov[1,3(✉)]

[1] CISPA Helmholz Center for Information Security, Saarbrücken, Germany
{backes,hanzlik}@cispa.de
[2] University of Birmingham, Birmingham, UK
P.P.Berrang@bham.ac.uk
[3] University of Luxembourg, Esch-sur-Alzette, Luxembourg
ivan.pryvalov@uni.lu

**Abstract.** The emergence of distributed digital currencies has raised the need for a reliable consensus mechanism. In proof-of-stake cryptocurrencies, the participants periodically choose a closed set of validators, who can vote and append transactions to the blockchain. Each validator can become a leader with the probability proportional to its stake. Keeping the leader private yet unique until it publishes a new block can significantly reduce the attack vector of an adversary and improve the throughput of the network. The problem of Single Secret Leader Election (SSLE) was first formally defined by Boneh et al. in 2020.

In this work, we propose a novel framework for constructing SSLE protocols, which relies on secure multi-party computation (MPC) and satisfies the desired security properties. Our framework does not use any shuffle or sort operations and has a computational cost for $N$ parties as low as $O(N)$ of basic MPC operations per party. We improve the state-of-the-art for SSLE protocols that do not assume a trusted setup. Moreover, our SSLE scheme efficiently handles weighted elections. That is, for a total weight $S$ of $N$ parties, the associated costs are only increased by a factor of $\log S$. When the MPC layer is instantiated with techniques based on Shamir's secret-sharing, our SSLE has a communication cost of $O(N^2)$ which is spread over $O(\log N)$ rounds, can tolerate up to $t < N/2$ of faulty nodes without restarting the protocol, and its security relies on DDH in the random oracle model. When the MPC layer is instantiated with more efficient techniques based on garbled circuits, our SSLE requires all parties to participate, up to $N-1$ of which can be malicious, and its security is based on the random oracle model.

## 1 Introduction

In 2008, Bitcoin [21] laid the foundation for the increasingly important areas of cryptocurrencies and distributed ledgers. One of the main advantages of distributed ledgers is that there is no single central authority that controls the transaction flow (*censorship resistance*). Anyone can access the public ledger, which is a sequence of blocks that contains transactions. For example, in Bitcoin, participants called "miners" are randomly selected to produce and append

V. Atluri et al. (Eds.): ESORICS 2022, LNCS 13555, pp. 672–691, 2022.
https://doi.org/10.1007/978-3-031-17146-8_33

a new block to the chain. This selection process relies on the "proof-of-work" concept (PoW). To append a block to the chain, the participant has to find a value, such that a cryptographic hash function is evaluated below some threshold.

To avoid extreme energy consumption induced by PoW protocols [22], an alternative approach, "proof-of-stake" (PoS), has been proposed. Here, the probability of being selected for appending the chain depends on the stake (i.e., coins) a party owns. It does not matter whether the party owns an account with some stake $v$, or several accounts whose accumulated stake amounts to $v$. The protocol consensus works as long as the majority of all stake is controlled by honest users.

In cryptocurrencies based on proof-of-stake [15,16,19,20], a single party that produces a block is chosen randomly from a set of participants, called validators (which is the equivalent to miners in a PoW protocol). In a PoS cryptocurrency there could be potentially thousands or millions users, who may come and go. It is up to a PoS protocol to determine and fix a relatively small (typically tens or hundreds) set of validators [19] from which a validator is selected that can append a block within a given time frame. To create a consistent picture for all validators, this selection has to be deterministic, but pseudo-random – properties often achieved by relying on Verifiable Random Functions (VRF). However, if an adversary knows in advance which of the validators is selected, it can launch a targeted attack and cause a denial-of-service.

Previous approaches to solving this issue aim to run the selection process in private, with the selected participant publishing a proof alongside the block. Until recently, these approaches failed to guarantee only a single participant to be chosen [19]. After much interest in a solution that provides such a guarantee [25], Boneh et al. proposed a formal definition and several instantiations of a Single Secret Leader Election [4].

The primary motivation of having a single leader is a simple consensus design, as there are no forks in the blockchain (assuming some reasonable connectivity between parties). This property encourages the leader to solely perform heavy computations, which may even exceed the running time of SSLE and/or require multiple cores. For example, the leader's task may consist of prover-heavy computations, whereas verification is very fast (SNARKs). Many protocols (e.g., [15,20]) assume uniqueness, and it is easy to update them with a SSLE solution. They may require a full redesign if the uniqueness assumption no longer holds.

## 1.1  Our Contribution

1. In this work, we propose a framework for constructing an efficient Single Secret Leader Election (SSLE), which relies on secure multi-party computation (MPC). We formulate a simulation-based definition of the SSLE problem.
2. We present two instantiations of our framework, which improve the state-of-the-art for SSLE protocols that do not require a trusted setup. The first instantiation a $t$-threshold SSLE scheme that is based on Shamir's secret sharing in the random oracle model. We prove that our construction is secure in the honest-but-curious and malicious adversary models. For the latter, we additionally assume DDH. For $N$ parties, the leader election requires $O(\log N)$

communication rounds and $O(N)$ of basic operations on the underlying primitives. Furthermore, we instantiate our SSLE scheme using the MPC framework by Wang et al. [29], which is secure against any number of malicious parties and is more scalable, but requires all parties to be online.

3. Our SSLE framework can efficiently handle arbitrary stake distributions. For $N$ parties and the overall sum of their stake units $S$, our construction achieves $O(N \log S)$ cost of the election. Compared with a standard multi-registration technique, in which a party registers multiple times for the election proportionally to her stake, this cost may go up to $O(S)$, which makes our solution exceptionally efficient if $N << S$.

4. We implemented and microbenchmarked our solution using two different MPC frameworks. The performance evaluation indicates that our DDH-based SSLE protocol can be used in practical scenarios up to 30–40 parties when instantiated with the textbook $O(N^2)$ techniques using the verifiable secret sharing scheme (VSS). Furthermore, we implemented our SSLE in the MPC framework based on garbled circuits [29]. The overall time to set up and complete the protocol for 128 parties in a practical scenario is less than 7 min.

Note that, due to space limitations, we refer to the full-version [3] for most proofs. Only the security analysis can be found in the appendix.

## 1.2 Background

The idea of proof-of-stake was first discussed on the Bitcoin forum[1] in 2011. Kiayaias et al. presented a provably-secure PoS protocol "Ouroboros" at CRYPTO 2017 [20], in which the participants that produce the blocks are elected publically. Such a leader election may be public as in Ouroboros or private as in Algorand [19]. In a private leader election, each node needs to check whether it will be the next leader using its private information but then can prove to others using only public information that it is indeed the next leader. Such a design makes it impossible for others to predict and carry out DoS attacks against the next leader until it is too late.

Algorand achieves this private leader election using Verifiable Random Functions, for which a participant has to prove the outcome to be below a certain threshold. This, however, can result in either no participant or multiple participants being elected. Another protocol employing a private leader election has been formalized by Ganesh et al., whose protocol Ouroboros Praos [16] does not guarantee existence and uniqueness of the leader either.

To mitigate these shortcomings of previous private leader elections, a problem statement of a single secret leader election was first posed at a GitHub page [25] in the form of a research proposal in the context of the Filecoin cryptocurrency. The protocol's goal is to elect a *single* leader among a finite set of participants. Moreover, the protocol should be reasonably efficient, i.e., on-chain $O(\log n)$ bits per block, $O(n)$ communication complexity (per active party).

---

[1] https://bitcointalk.org/index.php?topic=27787.0 (accessed 31.01.2022).

**Table 1.** Comparison of SSLE protocols, assuming all $N$ users participate in election, amortized per one election. On-chain asymptotics include a security parameter $\lambda$; PEKS-based on-chain asymptotic is shown assuming the parameter choice suggested in [7].

| Construction | Assumptions | Security notion | Setup | Rounds | Computation/ Communication | On-chain |
|---|---|---|---|---|---|---|
| Obfuscation-based [4] | iO | Game-based | Trusted | 0 + beacon | $O(\lambda)$, feasibility result | $O(1)$ |
| TFHE-based [4] | TFHE, weak PRF | Game-based, $t$-threshold | Trusted | 1 + beacon | Depends on a particular instance | $O(N)$ |
| Shuffle-based [4] | ROM, DDH | Game-based, *weak unpredictability* | – | 1 + beacon | $O(\sqrt{N})$ pub./group el. | $O(\sqrt{N})$ |
| Shuffle-based [4] | ROM, DDH | Game-based | – | 1 + beacon | $O(N)$ pub./group el | $O(N)$ |
| PEKS-based [7] | ROM, SXDH | UC, $t$-threshold | Trusted | $\leq 2$ + beacon | $O(N)$ pub./group el | $O(\log^2 N)$ |
| Our Construction 1 | ROM, DDH | UC, $t$-threshold | – | $O(\log N)$ | $O(N)$ MPC op. | $O(1)$ |
| Our Construction 2 | ROM | UC | – | $O(\log N)$ | $O(N)$ MPC op. | $O(1)$ |

## 1.3 Related Work

Following this call, Boneh et al. [4] formalized the problem of Single Secret Leader Election (SSLE) and presented three constructions: 1) a feasibility result based on indistinguishability obfuscation, 2) a construction based on threshold fully homomorphic encryption (TFHE), and 3) a construction based on DDH that achieves a weaker notion of security. Subsequently, Catalano et al. [7] proposed a UC-secure SSLE based on public key encryption with keyword search (PEKS).

We begin by first comparing how arbitrary stake distributions are handled in previous and our work. While a scenario with equal stakes is easier to analyze, in practice one has to also account for arbitrary stake distributions and how they affect the overall performance of the scheme. Boneh et al. [4] suggest a multi-registration technique (one registration corresponds to one unit of stake) to address arbitrary stake distributions, which makes the associated costs grow linearly with the user's stake. In contrast, our construction offers a more efficient tree-based solution to this setting with the associated costs grow logarithmically in the total stake $S$ of participating parties.

We compare our constructions with Boneh et al. [4] and Catalano et al. [7] in Table 1. By *pub.* we denote the number of public key operations such as exponentiation, by *MPC op.* we denote basic MPC operations such as multiplication. The most notable differences are that (1) our scheme does require neither a trusted setup nor a randomness beacon, and (2) requires only a constant amount of data to be posted on-chain.

In the discussed schemes except for iO- and PEKS-based the leader has to re-register before next election, since she reveals a secret that was generated and used for the registration.

Concurrently to our work, Catalano et al. [8] revisit the shuffle-based SSLE realization from [4] and propose two UC-secure SSLE constructions from DDH.

Their first construction is secure against static adversaries and their second achieves adaptive security with erasures.

**On the Practicality of Our SSLE Framework.** The number of validators depends on the PoS protocol and can vary from dozens to a few hundred and in limited cases thousands. It does not necessarily correlate with the total number of users. Stake disbalances also vary, and therefore they need to be approximated in our framework by a tree of a sufficient height (Sect. 7.1). Our tree optimization technique has a better effect when applied to a smaller set of validators.

In our SSLE framework, we rely on existing MPC techniques. If a more efficient MPC protocol than the ones used in our constructions emerges, it will help to further improve the running time of the SSLE.

## 2 Definitions

### 2.1 Preliminaries

*DDH Assumption* [13]. Let $g$ be a generator of a group $G$ of a prime order $q$. For any probabilistic polynomial time (PPT) machine $\mathcal{A}$ and $(x, y, z) \leftarrow (\mathbb{Z}_q)^3$, $|Pr[\mathcal{A}(g, g^x, g^y, g^{xy}) = 1] - Pr[\mathcal{A}(g, g^x, g^y, g^z) = 1]| \leq negl(\lambda)$.

*Secret Sharing.* Secret sharing schemes allow a dealer to share a secret $s$ among parties such that later a qualified set of parties can jointly reconstruct $s$, whereas a non-qualified set of parties learns no information about it. We use Shamir's Secret Sharing [27], which is a $t$-threshold scheme. We denote Share a protocol to share a secret $x$ as $[x]$, and Rec to reconstruct $x$ from $[x]$. Whereas Shamir's Secret Sharing is only secure against passive adversaries, Verifiable Secret Share (VSS) schemes [23] can protect against active.

*Communication and Adversary Models.* We assume secure point-to-point communication channels between parties. An adversary is allowed to corrupt up to $t < N$ parties. We consider two models of adversaries: honest-but-curious and malicious. In the honest-but-curious model, adversaries follow the protocol honestly and try to learn as much as possible from observed communication by corrupted parties. In the malicious model, the parties controlled by an adversary can stop communicating or send arbitrary messages to other parties, not necessarily following the prescribed protocols.

*Secure Multi-Party Computation (MPC).* MPC allows a set of parties $\mathcal{P} = \{P_1, ..., P_N\}$ to jointly compute a function on their private inputs in a privacy-preserving manner [30]. Our SSLE scheme is based on MPC.

We borrow the standard definitions of *VIEW* and $t$-Privacy from [1].

We instantiate our SSLE scheme using the following underlying protocols:

1. The VSS-based MPC protocols [9,12,17,18,23,24], in which secrets are shared between the parties using Shamir's secret sharing scheme:
   - Protocols for adding shares, subtracting, and multiplying by a scalar: $[x] + [y], [x] - [y], [\alpha \cdot x]$,

- RndFld to generate a share of a random field element in $\mathbb{Z}_p$,
- RndBit to generate a share of a random bit,
- Mul to compute $[x \cdot y]$ given $[x]$ and $[y]$.

2. Garbled circuit based MPC [29] on boolean circuits, where each party can privately input her input to a computing circuit.

## 2.2 Single Secret Leader Election

We consider the following problem. Given a set of $N$ parties. The parties do some interactive pre-computation. Then, each party can run a local function that takes the transcript as input to determine whether it is the leader or not. The leader can show a proof that it is the leader.

*Game-Based Formulation of the SSLE Problem.* Our syntax and security properties of SSLE are based on that of [4], with a slight difference that we do not have an external source of randomness (random beacon) and we allow multiple rounds of communication between the parties during the election, whereas the definition of SSLE in [4] allows a single round of communication.

Informally, we capture the following security properties:

1. **Uniqueness** – an adversary wins this experiment if in at least one election in a series of consecutive elections there is more than one verifiable leader.
2. **Unpredictability** – the adversary asks for a challenge election after a series of elections. The challenger does not send to the adversary the outcome of this election. The adversary has to guess the leader in this challenge election. If some honest party is the leader, the adversarial chances to correctly guess the leader should not be significantly greater than pure guessing.
3. **Fairness** – the adversary asks for a challenge election after a series of elections. The probability of winning this challenge election by one of the corrupted parties should not be significantly greater than $c/n$, where $c$ is the number of corrupted parties, and $n$ is the number of parties registered for the challenge election.

Due to page limits, we postpone the formal game-based definition to the full version of this paper [3].

*Simulation-Based Definition of the SSLE Problem.* We now formulate the SSLE problem as an ideal functionality $\mathcal{F}_{\mathsf{SSLE}}^{N,\ell,c}$, which is presented in Fig. 1. In the description of the ideal functionality, we denote election id as *eid*, and registration numbers as $C_i$. We then show that the simulation-based definition implies the game-based one.

Our modeling of the ideal functionality $\mathcal{F}_{\mathsf{SSLE}}^{N,\ell,c}$ for $N$ parties with an adversary statically corrupting up to $t$ of them is influenced by the corresponding game-based definition, which defines the registration and verification algorithms that surround the election itself. We follow the same approach and define messages in the ideal functionality for registration, election, and their verification.

In $\mathcal{F}_{\mathsf{SSLE}}^{N,\ell,c}$, the parties send messages to the ideal functionality that correspond to a specific stage of the election. First, the parties register for an election with

---

$\mathcal{F}_{\mathsf{SSLE}}^{N,\ell,c}$ for a set of parties $\mathcal{P} = \{P_1, \ldots, P_N\}$, $c$ of which are corrupted by an adversary, consists of the following steps:

- Upon receiving a message $(eid, \mathsf{register}, C)$ from $P_i$, check if $(eid, P_i, \cdot)$ or $(eid, elected, \cdot, \cdot)$ is stored. If so, ignore the message. Otherwise, store $(eid, P_i, C)$. When storing tuples, we write $P_i$ to denote the party's unique identifier. Send $(eid, registered, P_i)$ to all parties and the environment.

- Upon receiving a message $(eid, \mathsf{regVerify})$ from $P_i$, reply 0 if there exist two stored tuples $(eid, P_j, C_j)$ and $(eid, P_k, C_k)$ such that $j \neq k$ and $C_j = C_k$. Otherwise, reply 1.

- Upon receiving a message $(eid, \mathsf{elect})$ from $P_i$, check if there are at least $\ell$ registered parties that have corresponding stored tuples $(eid, \cdot, \cdot)$. If not, ignore the message, otherwise proceed. Check if $(eid, elected, P_u, C_u)$ is stored. If not, pick one of the stored tuples $(eid, \cdot, \cdot)$ uniformly at random as $(eid, P_u, C_u)$, append it as $(eid, elected, P_u, C_u)$, and send $(eid, elected, C_u)$ to the environment. Send $(eid, elected, C_u)$ to $P_i$.

- Upon receiving a message $(eid, \mathsf{verify}, P_j, C)$ from $P_i$, check if $(eid, elected, P_u, C_u)$ is stored. If such a tuple exists, reply 1 if $P_u = P_j$ and $C_u = C$. In all other cases, reply 0.

**Fig. 1.** Ideal functionality $\mathcal{F}_{\mathsf{SSLE}}^{N,\ell,c}$.

id $eid$ via sending $\mathsf{register}$ messages containing the registration number $C$. They receive notifications from the ideal functionality for every registered party. To verify registration, the parties send messages $\mathsf{regVerify}$ to the ideal functionality, which outputs 1 if all registered numbers are distinct, otherwise it outputs 0 and the execution of $\mathcal{F}_{\mathsf{SSLE}}^{N,\ell,c}$ stops. If $\mathsf{regVerify}$ returned 1, the parties participate in the election by sending messages $\mathsf{elect}$ to $\mathcal{F}_{\mathsf{SSLE}}^{N,\ell,c}$, which returns one of the registered numbers as the elected number. Finally, the parties can verify whether some party $P_i$ is the elected leader by sending a message $\mathsf{verify}$ with the identifier for $P_i$ and the elected number.

Next, we discuss some of the design choices that we made in $\mathcal{F}_{\mathsf{SSLE}}^{N,\ell,c}$:

1. With the explicit inputs associated to parties, the definition naturally captures the adversarial ability to register multiple parties using the same private material and thereby break the uniqueness property.
2. The result of the election is returned to the parties as one of the numbers, used for the registration. In this way we model the information leakage, which suggests an efficient way of running multiple elections by the same parties. To run a subsequent election, the leader has to simply re-register, while other parties can keep their previously registered numbers.

Intuitively, the security properties from the game-based definitions are captured in the ideal functionality $\mathcal{F}_{\mathsf{SSLE}}^{N,\ell,c}$ as follows:

1. **Uniqueness** – provided by answering $\mathsf{regVerify}$ messages, which excludes the case that two parties register the same number, and $\mathsf{elect}$ messages are answered with exactly one number.
2. **Unpredictability**– provided by answering $\mathsf{elect}$ messages with one of $n$ registered numbers, which are known only to the respective parties. In the beginning, party $P_i$ sends her input $C_i$ only to the ideal functionality and never

discloses $C_i$ to other parties until the election is finished. $P_i$ discloses her registered number only when $P_i$ is the elected leader.

3. **Fairness** – provided by answering elect messages by *uniformly at random* selecting one of $n$ registered distinct numbers as the elected value.

We formally prove that the ideal functionality implies the game-based definitions by showing the non-existence of a simulator given any of the game-based attackers.

**Proposition 1.** *The ideal functionality* $\mathcal{F}_{SSLE}^{N,\ell,c}$ *implies the game-based definitions for uniqueness, unpredictability, and fairness.*

Due to space limitations, we refer to the full-version [3] for the proof of Proposition 1 and subsequent theorems. Only the security analysis can be found in the appendix.

In this work, we only consider SSLE schemes with *expiring registration*. In such schemes, in a single SSLE instance elections are run sequentially and the eventual leader has to re-register for subsequent elections. In the remainder of the paper we will only consider the modified ideal functionality that ensures sequentiality. To this end, the ideal functionality keeps track of the current election id $eid^*$. As soon as it receives a message with $eid' \neq eid^*$, it stops responding to any further messages with $eid^*$ and updates the current election id to $eid'$. In contrast to the real world, in the ideal world non-leaders have to register for subsequent elections explicitly using the same registration number $C$.

# 3    (Non-secret) Single Leader Election Constructions

In this section, we start by discussing how naive solutions to the problem of SSLE fail in keeping the leader secret. We then gradually introduce the basis for our final SSLE protocol. Note that, while the constructions in this section do not yet meet our requirements and are considered non-secret, they will form the basis of the protocol presented in Sect. 4.

**Oblivious Select.** We begin by defining a *two-party Oblivious Select* (OSelect) protocol, whose goal is to secretly select one out of two commitments. Once the commitment is selected, the parties can open the selected commitment. Let PSwap be an algorithm that on input commitments $C_0$ and $C_1$ computes $(C_i' = \mathsf{Com}(C_i, r_i))_{i \in \{0,1\}}$ and outputs $(C_b', C_{1-b}')$ for a random bit $b$. Let PSelect be an algorithm that on input commitments $C_0$ and $C_1$ outputs $C' = \mathsf{Com}(C_b, r)$. It is easy to see that if the commitment scheme is hiding, then an adversary cannot find the value of $b$ significantly better than pure guessing.

We now describe OSelect between Alice and Bob. The protocol consists of the select and the opening phases. In the select phase, Alice publishes her commitment $C_A$ and Bob $C_B$, then Alice performs PSwap on $(C_A, C_B)$ and sends the result $(C_0, C_1)$ to Bob; Bob now performs PSelect on those values and outputs $C'$. In the opening phase, the two parties reveal their randomness so that the complete transcript of computing $C'$ could be reconstructed by anyone.

The protocol can be naturally extended to $N$ parties, where $N$ is a power of two; let us call the resulting protocol $\mathsf{OSelect}_N$. It consists of $(\log N)$ rounds; in the first round $N/2$ pairs of parties are formed that run $\mathsf{OSelect}$, thereby reducing two commitments into one. In the following round, $N/4$ pairs of parties are formed, etc., until there is a single commitment left. We will use the logical tree-like structure used in $\mathsf{OSelect}_N$ as the basis for our final SSLE construction.

**Leader Election Based on Oblivious Select.** We define LeaderElection, our intermediate non-secret protocol, which essentially uses $\mathsf{OSelect}_N$ in a black-box manner. In the selection phase, each user $U_i$ initially holds a distinct number $m_i$ and commits to it as $C_i = \mathsf{Com}(m_i; r_i)$. Then, the users run $\mathsf{OSelect}_N$. Thanks to the properties of $\mathsf{OSelect}_N$, its output $\bar{C}$ is a commitment to one of the user's inputs. If $\bar{C}$ is a commitment to $m_i$, then $U_i$ is the elected user. Since there are in total $N - 1$ calls to $\mathsf{OSelect}$, we achieve an amortized cost $O(1)$ per party. In the opening phase, all users broadcast their input message and randomness, so that the execution of $\mathsf{OSelect}_N$ could be verified by anyone.

*Problem.* The resulting protocol is still a *non-secret* leader election, as the leader does not learn the output of the protocol exclusively. Moreover, the *unpredictability* property does not hold: an adversary controlling two parties in a single instance of $\mathsf{OSelect}$ can exclude certain parties as potential leaders. Lastly, all parties are required to participate in the protocol in at least one instance of $\mathsf{OSelect}$, which makes it impossible to tolerate a single faulty party. In the next section, we will address these problems and present our secure SSLE protocol.

**Upgrading to Secret Leader.** We now modify LeaderElection by adding an intermediate representation layer in order to let the secret leader actually check whether she is the elected leader. Here, we make use of a distributed key generation and threshold decryption. The resulting secret leader election protocol does not satisfy all our requirements to SSLE but serves as an intermediate point towards our final construction in Sect. 4.

*Distributed Key Generation (DKG)* [23] allows several parties to agree on a joint secret key. The corresponding public key is computed and published jointly by the honest majority of the parties. In a $t$-out-of-$N$ DKG protocol [17], the secret key is shared according to Shamir's secret sharing scheme. The protocol can be efficiently simulated against passive and active adversaries, which can corrupt up to $t$ parties. In *threshold cryptography*, parties jointly generate a group public key to encrypt messages and a qualified subset of parties can collaboratively decrypt ciphertexts encrypted using that key. We consider Shamir's $t$-out-of-$N$ threshold ElGamal-based decryption schemes, for which any coalition of $t$ parties cannot decrypt a given ciphertext or learn any information about the plaintext, whereas any coalition of $t + 1$ parties can recover it, even if the remaining $N - t - 1$ parties stop communicating.

Let $g$ be a generator of a group $G$ of a prime order $\mathbb{Z}_p$. User $U_i$ registers for the election by generating a registration key $k_i \in \mathbb{Z}_p$ and computing a registration token as $e_i \leftarrow (g^r, g^{k_i \cdot r})$ for some random $r$. The values $k_i$ are $e_i$ are kept private. Next, the users generate a temporary shared public key using as $t$-out-of-$N$ DKG protocol, $pk_{\mathcal{G}} = g^{sk_{\mathcal{G}}}$. The corresponding group secret key, $sk_{\mathcal{G}}$, is shared between $N$ parties, such that $t + 1$ parties have to collaborate to decrypt a ciphertext $C$.

Instead of OSelect, we use a new subroutine OSelectD, which is a two-party verifiable oblivious select protocol in the discrete log setting. Unlike OSelect, the users can publicly verify that a OSelectD instance was executed correctly without learning which input was selected. The input to OSelectD is an Elgamal encryption of two group elements $e_i := (g^r, g^{k_i \cdot r})$ under a group public key $y_{\mathcal{G}}$ for some user's registration key $k_i$ and randomness $r$; these two encryptions can be represented as a tuple $(g^{r'}, (y_{\mathcal{G}})^{r'} \cdot g^r, (y_{\mathcal{G}})^{r'} \cdot g^{k_i \cdot r}) \in (G_q)^3$, for some $r'$, and we will call such tuples *valid*. OSelectD relies on the discrete log variants of PSwap and PSelect, which we call PSwapD and PSelectD. Let PSwapD be an algorithm that on input two tuples $C_0$ and $C_1$ computes $C'_0 = (C_0)^{r_0}$, $C'_1 = (C_1)^{r_1}$ and outputs $(C'_b, C'_{1-b})$ for a random bit $b$, accompanied with appropriate NIZK proofs that computation is done correctly. Let PSelectD be an algorithm that on input two tuples $C_0$ and $C_1$ outputs $C' = (C_b)^r$ and appropriate NIZK proofs. These proofs are generalizations [5,11] of Schnorr signature [26] and can be efficiently instantiated in the random oracle model using the Fiat-Shamir transform [14]. It is straightforward to see that if the inputs to OSelectD are valid tuples w.r.t. $k_i$ and $k_j$, then so is the output of OSelectD w.r.t. $k \in \{k_i, k_j\}$.

Expanding OSelectD to $N$ users, we get $\mathsf{OSelectD_N}$. Users jointly run $\mathsf{OSelectD_N}$ and decrypt its output to obtain $\bar{C}$. There will be a unique pair $(e_i, \bar{e})$, which forms a valid DDH tuple, for which the elected leader knows an exponent; all other pairs $(e_j, \bar{e})$, where $j \neq i$, are random tuples. The leader presents the exponent as proof of leadership. She will have to re-register to get a fresh $k_i$ before participating in another election.

*Problem.* While the leader can learn the outcome of the election in private, there remain several problems to address. First, an adversary can run a *duplicate key* attack [4], where she obtains multiple registration tokens that correspond to a single registration key, and thus break fairness. The mitigation measures proposed in [4] work in our setting, too. Second, a malicious adversary can use biased coins when computing OSelectD. If both parties are under her control, she can break the obliviousness of OSelectD and, in turn, the unpredictability and fairness of the SSLE. Finally, even an *honest-but-curious* adversary, who controls both parties in OSelectD and follows the protocol, exactly knows which input has been selected, thus *breaking* unpredictability of SSLE. Since our goal is to satisfy *all* the three properties (uniqueness, unpredictability, and fairness), we will need one more modification to our current construction, which we present in the following section.

## 4  Our SSLE from DDH

In this section, we define our full SSLE construction; to this end we modify the secret leader election from Sect. 3 by replacing OSelect with its MPC variant, OSelectM. Thereby we ensure that no adversary in our model can learn

OSelectM($[C_A]$, $[C_B]$)

---

$[b] \leftarrow$ RandBit()

   **do**   // run in parallel

      $[b \cdot C_A] \leftarrow$ Mul($[b]$, $[C_A]$)

      $[(1 - b) \cdot C_B] \leftarrow$ Mul($[1 - b]$, $[C_B]$)

   $[C'] \leftarrow [b \cdot C_A] + [(1 - b) \cdot C_B]$

   **output** $[C']$

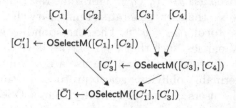

**Fig. 2.** OSelectM: Oblivious Select in the MPC setting.

**Fig. 3.** OSelectM$_N$: Extension OSelectM to $N$ inputs. Example for $N = 4$.

the outcome of a OSelectM protocol instance. The extension of OSelectM to $N$ inputs, which we call OSelectM$_N$, retains the (binary) tree layout of inputs and outputs. Each OSelectM instance is now executed by all parties simultaneously. This modification incurs additional communication costs compared to the previous (insecure) version of our SSLE construction. Fortunately, the number of communication rounds needed for a leader election remains $O(\log N)$, as OSelectM instances on the same level in the tree can run in parallel.

OSelectM is an oblivious select protocol in the MPC setting, which can be completed as long as at least $t + 1$ parties remain online and honestly execute the protocol. It takes two secret shares $[C_A]$, $[C_B]$ as input and outputs a new secret share $[C']$ such that the output secret $C'$ is either $C_A$ or $C_B$ with equal probability, depending on the selection bit $b$. The description of OSelectM protocol is shown in Fig. 2. OSelectM extension to $N$ inputs, called OSelectM$_N$, follows a binary-tree structure of inputs and outputs to OSelectM; see Fig. 3.

To prevent duplicate key attacks, we incorporate into our SSLE scheme a technique used in [4]. The technique works as follow. The registration key $k_i$ is now used to produce a secret part $k_{iL}$ and a public fingerprint $k_{iR}$ using a cryptographic hash function $H$, where $(k_{iL}, k_{iR}) \leftarrow H(k_i)$. Before the election starts, each user verifies that there are no duplicate fingerprints in the public state $st$. The security properties of the hash function ensure that chances for an adversary to succeed in a duplicate key attack are negligible.

The election proceeds as follows. For each $i \in \{1, \ldots, N\}$, the parties jointly generate $[C_i]$, a MPC version of the secret part $k_{iL}$ of the registration key $k_i$, which is $[k_{iL}]$. In the MPC setting we do not need to additionally hide the key using Elgamal encryption, since secret sharing already hides the results of the computation.

The parties then proceed with OSelectM$_N$ and obtain $[\bar{C}]$, which is a secret share of one of the secret inputs to OSelectM$_N$. The parties jointly reconstruct two group elements $(\bar{e}_1, \bar{e}_2)$ from $[\bar{C}]$, which turn out to be a randomization of the secret part of a party participated in the election, which we denote $\bar{k}_L$. If $P_i$ is the elected leader, the following equation will hold $\bar{k}_L = k_{iL}$, i.e. each party learns the secret key $k_{iL}$ of the leader, but does not know which one. The leader $P_i$ sends the registration key $k_i$ as a proof of leadership. To verify a proof $\pi$, one recomputes the secret part $\pi_L$ of the registration key and its fingerprint $\pi_R$ and checks that the computed fingerprint matches the one stored as $st_i$, and that the equation $\pi_L = \bar{k}_L$ holds.

In the malicious adversary model, we can use standard techniques [10,18] to protect the underlying MPC primitives used in the scheme against active adversaries.

We now formally define our fully-fledged SSLE construction.

**Construction 1 (Single secret leader election (SSLE).** *Our $(N, N, t)$-SSLE scheme is a tuple of PPT algorithms SSLE = (Setup, Register, RegisterVerify, Elect, Verify) that use a group $G$ of a prime order $p$. Let $g$ be a generator of $G$, let $H$ be a function that maps $\{0,1\}^\lambda$ to $\mathbb{Z}_p \times \{0,1\}^{r(\lambda)}$. The description of the algorithms is shown in Fig. 4.*

---

Setup($1^\lambda, t, N$)

1:   $p, g \leftarrow$ FindParam($1^\lambda$)
2:   **for** $i \in 1..N$
3:      $st_i \leftarrow \perp$
4:   **return** $p, g, st_1, ..., st_N$

Register($i$)

1:   $k_i \leftarrow \mathbb{Z}_p$
2:   $k_{iL}, k_{iR} \leftarrow H(k_i)$
3:   $st_i \leftarrow k_{iR}$
4:   $[k_{iL}] \leftarrow$ Share($k_{iL}$)
5:   **return** $k_i$

RegisterVerify($i, k_i$)

1:   **for** $j_1 \in 1..(N-1)$
2:      **for** $j_2 \in (j_1 + 1)..N$
3:         **if** $st_{j_1} = st_{j_2} \neq \perp$
4:            **return** 0
5:   $k_{iL}, k_{iR} \leftarrow H(k_i)$
6:   **if** $k_{iR} \neq st_i$
7:      **return** 0
8:   **return** 1

Verify($i, \pi$)

1:   $\pi_L, \pi_R \leftarrow H(\pi)$
2:   **if** $\pi_L = \bar{k}_L$ **and** $\pi_R = st_i$
3:      **return** 1
4:   **return** 0

Elect($i, k_i$)

1:   **for** $i \in 1..N$
2:      $[C_i] := [k_{iL}]$
3:   $[\bar{C}] \leftarrow$ OSelectM$_N$($[C_1],$
4:      $..., [C_N]$)
5:   $\bar{k}_L \leftarrow$ Rec($[\bar{C}]$)
6:   **if** $\bar{k}_L \neq k_{iL}$
7:      **return** $\perp$
8:   **return** $\pi := k_i$

**Fig. 4.** Single Secret Leader Election construction SSLE instantiated with OSelectM$_N$.

**Theorem 1.** *Assuming the underlying MPC primitives are secure in the honest-but-curious adversary model, $H$ is a random oracle, then Construction 1 implements functionality $\mathcal{F}_{SSLE}$.*

## 5   Our SSLE Based on Garbled Circuits

In this section, we present our SSLE protocol, instantiated in the MPC framework by Wang et al. [29], which can tolerate up to $N - 1$ corrupted parties.

We use the MPC protocol [29] to instantiate our SSLE in a black-box manner. The SSLE construction shown in Fig. 4 needs to be updated to account for the technical details specific to the MPC part in the Elect algorithm.

To implement the Oblivious Select, we use a part of the input as selection bits. Each party contributes to these bits, via bitwise-xor; the selection bits are therefore secret-shared. The modified version of the Elect algorithm and a pseudocode of OSelectM instantiated in the framework [29] are shown in the full version [3].

**Construction 2 (Single secret leader election (SSLE)).** *Our SSLE scheme is a tuple of PPT algorithms SSLE = (Setup, Register, RegisterVerify, Elect, Verify). Let H be a function that maps* $\{0,1\}^\lambda$ *to* $\{0,1\}^{l(\lambda)} \times \{0,1\}^{r(\lambda)}$. *The description of the algorithms is shown in fig.4, and Elect is appropriately modified.*

**Theorem 2.** *Assuming the underlying MPC primitives are secure in the malicious adversary model, H is a random oracle, then Construction 2 implements functionality* $\mathcal{F}_{SSLE}$.

# 6   Evaluation

## 6.1   Experimental Setup

We evaluate our SSLE framework, we implemented Constructions 1 and 2 and ran two kind of tests: in a local setting (LAN) and in a global setting (WAN). In the LAN setting, we used machines located in the same Amazon EC2 region. In the WAN setting, we used machines located in four different regions (Europe, North America, South America, and Asia). If not specified otherwise, each machine is a t2.large instance with 2 cores Intel Xeon E5-2686v4 2.3 GHz, 8 Gb of RAM, and installed Ubuntu 20.04. In some regions t2.large instances are not available; instead we used t3.large instances with 2 cores Xeon Platinum 8175 2.5 GHz, 8 Gb of RAM.

In our experiments, we evaluate a complete OSelect tree in our SSLE framework, that is the number of users being a power of two, starting from 8 parties, and each party holding one unit of stake. For each experiment we take average of 10 runs, except that for lengthy experiments with a running time more than 1 min we perform a single run. Next, we present implementation details and the evaluation results individually for each construction.

## 6.2   Construction 1 (Sect. 4)

*Implementation Details.* We implemented our Construction 1 in C++ in the honest-but-curious and malicious adversary models. We implemented the underlying MPC primitives for secret sharing, adding shares, substracting, multiplying by a scalar: $[x] + [y]$, $[x] - [y]$, $[\alpha \cdot x]$, protocols RndFld, RndBit, Mul [9,12,17,18,23,24]. In the malicious adversary model, these primitives are accompanied with verifiable secret sharing (VSS). We set the threshold $t = N/2 - 1$ in all experiments. Our implementation uses the Relic toolkit [2] for operations on elliptic curves in groups of a prime order of 256 bits, the Boost and OpenSSL libraries for secure communication.

**Table 2.** Experimental results for Construction 1 in the honest-but-curious and malicious adversary models (left), and for Construction 2 in the malicious adversary model (right).

| N | t | Algorithm | HbC time, sec. | Mal. time, sec. |
|---|---|---|---|---|
| 8 | 3 | Register | <0.01 | 0.11 |
| | | RegisterVerify | <0.01 | <0.01 |
| | | Elect | 0.1 | 3.56 |
| | | Verify | <0.01 | <0.01 |
| 16 | 7 | Register | 0.01 | 0.56 |
| | | RegisterVerify | <0.01 | <0.01 |
| | | Elect | 0.34 | 28.1 |
| | | Verify | <0.01 | <0.01 |
| 32 | 15 | Register | 0.02 | 3.83 |
| | | RegisterVerify | <0.01 | <0.01 |
| | | Elect | 1.45 | 356.6 |
| | | Verify | <0.01 | <0.01 |
| 64 | 31 | Register | 0.08 | n.a. |
| | | RegisterVerify | <0.01 | |
| | | Elect | 7.63 | |
| | | Verify | <0.01 | |
| 128 | 63 | Register | 0.21 | n.a. |
| | | RegisterVerify | <0.01 | |
| | | Elect | 54.4 | |
| | | Verify | <0.01 | |

| N | $l(\lambda)$ | LAN time, sec. | WAN time, sec. |
|---|---|---|---|
| 8 | 48 | 2.73 | 23.42 |
| | 64 | 2.76 | 24.03 |
| | 80 | 2.80 | 24.27 |
| 16 | 48 | 4.28 | 38.95 |
| | 64 | 4.50 | 39.92 |
| | 80 | 4.86 | 40.61 |
| 32 | 48 | 8.25 | 73.34 |
| | 64 | 8.35 | 75.93 |
| | 80 | 8.80 | 77.81 |
| 64 | 48 | 17.64 | 145.87 |
| | 64 | 18.62 | 153.34 |
| | 80 | 23.90 | 150.67 |
| 128 | 48 | 64.33 | 300.77 |
| | 64 | 74.54 | 326.09 |
| | 80 | 83.54 | 317.46 |

*Experimental Results.* We performed LAN tests for up to 128 parties in the honest-but-curious adversary model, and up to 32 parties in the malicious model. Timings are shown in Table 2.

*Analysis.* The experimental results show that up to 128 parties can complete Elect protocol in under a minute. The running time grows rapidly as the number of parties increases. This is due to expensive public key operations for generating and reconstructing Shamir's secret shares. The explosion of running time is more visible in the malicious adversary model. In order to protect against such adversaries, we have to use verifiable secret sharing, which requires $O(N^2)$ public key operations in the textbook implementation. While Elect is the most heavy algorithm, the rest of the SSLE protocol is essentially for free. We conclude that Construction 1 offers a practical $t$-robust solution to the SSLE problem for a small number of parties (up to 32, according to our evaluation).

## 6.3 Construction 2 (Sect. 5)

*Implementation Details.* We implemented and evaluated Oblivious Select part of the Elect algorithm, as it is the most heavy part of the SSLE protocol (see experimental results for Construction 1 in the honest-but-curious adversary model in Sect. 6.2). Our implementation fully relies on the implementation of the MPC framework by Wang et at. [29], which is available as [28]. We can trade-off security for efficiency by controlling how many bits each party inputs to Oblivious Select.

*Experimental Results.* In the MPC framework, the evaluator of the garbled global circuit requires more RAM than any other party. Therefore, we set up

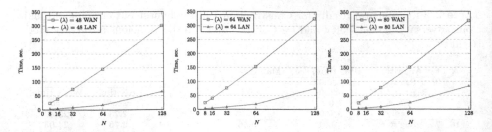

**Fig. 5.** Comparison of timings for Oblivious Select in Construction 2 in the LAN and WAN settings.

one machine as a m5a.4xlarge instance with 16 cores and 64G of RAM, while the rest of machines remain t2.large or t3.large instances. We run experiments for each $N$ up to 128. For the trade-off, we choose the length of user inputs to Oblivious Select, $l(\lambda)$, as 48, 64, and 80 bits. Additionally, each party provides 8 bits of selection bits, which satisfies the constraint that it should be at least as big as $\log(N)$ in all test cases. Timings the LAN and WAN settings are shown in Table 2 and in Fig. 5.

*Analysis.* The experimental results show that the running time of Oblivious Select algorithm (and in turn, Elect) grows almost linearly as the number of parties gets increased. As we ran only 1 iteration for long test cases, we can see some unexpected fluctuations in the running time, which we think are caused by fluctuations in the network and normally should be eliminated after averaging multiple iterations.

The LAN and WAN settings have identical computational and communication cost, as they only differ in the location of machines. We suspect that higher latency between machines in the WAN settings accounts for the increased running time. In the LAN setting, 128 parties can compute a leader in under 1.5 min, where as in the WAN setting, this number approaches 7 min.

# 7    Practical Considerations

There are several constraints in Constructions 1 and 2 that affect its practicality. First, the definition of SSLE says that the probability for a party being elected should be equal among all participants. In practice, the stakeholders may have different stakes, and the probability for a party to be elected should be proportional to her stake. A straightforward solution to this constraint would be to adapt our SSLE construction to work with stake units and let each party control several units. If implemented naively, this approach results in a linear blow-up in computation and required storage (in the number of stake units). In the following, we will show an efficient technique to extend Construction 1 to support arbitrary (non-uniform) probability distributions in the election.

Second, we assumed the number of parties to be a power of two, in order to construct a complete binary tree in Oblivious Select. However, if the number of parties is arbitrary, the tree structure will likely unbalance the tree leaves, as some inputs will not be matched on the first level with other inputs. Therefore, such inputs would proceed to the next round without competition, i.e., with the probability of 1, whereas input $C_i$ in a binary tree will proceed with the probability of $1/2$. We will show that the technique from the previous point addresses this concern, too.

## 7.1  Non-uniform Distributions

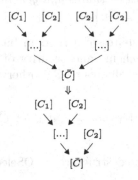

We observe that it is possible to unbalance almost-for-free the probability of being selected (among two parties) if the sum of the weights is a *power of two*. To illustrate this idea, assume that the weights are $(1,3)$, i.e., the probabilities for two parties being selected are determined by the ratio 1:3. We can construct a tree-structure with the probabilities $1/4$ and $3/4$, as shown in Fig. 6.

Basically, we introduce a special case for OSelectM when handling shares of the same secret for free, OSelectM(ShareC, $[C]$) → $[C]$. The resulting tree can be optimized significantly by dropping the nodes with the same inputs.

**Fig. 6.** Tree optimization technique. Example OSelectM$_N$ for $P_1$ and $P_2$ with stakes $(1,3)$.

Using this technique, we can handle weights of the form $(w, 2^L - w)$ with a logarithmic overhead, for some $L \geq 1$ and $1 \leq w < 2^L$. However, we cannot naturally handle arbitrary weight ratios. For example, weights such as $(1,2)$ are problematic. Nevertheless, we can approximate the probabilities in the election according to any weights $(a, b)$ by having a tree of sufficient depth.

*Arbitrary $N$ and Stakes.* Let $N$ be the number of parties participating in the election with their stakes $(s_1, ..., s_N)$, and let $S = \sum_{i=1}^{N} s_i$ be the sum of parties' stakes. The multi-registration solution may lead to $O(S)$ complexity of the election algorithm. We extend our technique to an arbitrary number of users.

We start with a similar idea: each party has a sequence of stake units on the first level in a OSelectM$_N$ tree. If $N \ll S$, there will be many pairs of inputs that represent the same party. We observe that in this case, there is no need to run OSelectM on such inputs. Instead, we can pick any input and advance it to the next level in the tree. The worst case complexity (the number of OSelectM instances) of this technique is $O(N \log S)$, since each party $P_i$'s inputs will be matched in a tree of depth $O(\log S)$ at most two times, against $P_{i-1}$ and $P_{i+1}$. With a tree of depth $L$ we can get the absolute precision up to $2^{-L} \cdot S$.

**Acknowledgements.** We thank anonymous reviewers for their helpful reviews. This work has received funding from the European Research Council under the European Union's Seventh Framework Programme (FP7/2007-2013)/ERC grant agreement no. 610150-imPACT, was supported by the German Federal Ministry of Education and

Research (BMBF) through funding for CISPA and the CISPA-Stanford Center for Cybersecurity (FKZ: 16KIS0762), and by the Luxembourg National Research Fund (FNR) under the CORE Junior project FP2 (C20/IS/14698166/FP2/Mueller).

# A     Security Analysis

**Lemma 1.** *Let $[C_A]$ and $[C_B]$ be the inputs to OSelectM protocol, and let $[C']$ be the output. Then, assuming the underlying secret sharing scheme is linearly homomorphic and the primitives for multiplication secret shares and generating a random shared bit are secure, it holds that $C' \in \{C_A, C_B\}$.*

*Proof.* The underlying RandBit primitive produces shares of a random bit $[b]$. By homomorphic properties of the secret sharing scheme and security of the multiplication primitive, it follows that, if $b = 0$, $C'$ evaluates to $C_A$, otherwise, if $b = 1$, $C'$ evaluates to $C_B$.

**Lemma 2.** *Let $[C_1], ..., [C_N]$ be the inputs to OSelectM$_N$ protocol, and let $[\bar{C}]$ be the output. Then, it holds that $\bar{C} \in \{C_1, ..., C_N\}$.*

*Proof.* It follows from Lemma 1 and the binary tree structure of OSelectM instances in OSelectM$_N$.

**Lemma 3.** *Assuming secret sharing is secure, algorithm Register in Construction 1 called by some party, securely implements sending a (register) message in the ideal model.*

*Proof.* The party uses the output value from Register as input to the (register) message in the ideal model. The proof follows from simulatability of the secret sharing scheme.

**Lemma 4.** *Assuming $H$ is a random oracle, algorithm RegisterVerify in Construction 1 securely implements sending a (regVerify) message in the ideal model.*

*Proof.* By the properties of the random oracle, we have that the probability that $C_i \neq C_j$ in the ideal model and $k_{iR} = k_{jR}$ is $1/2^\lambda$, which is negligible in $\lambda$.

**Lemma 5.** *Algorithm Elect in Construction 1 securely implements sending a (elect) message in the ideal model.*

*Proof.* We construct a simulator $S$ for an ideal adversary $A$. $S$ recovers the adversarial input from party $P_i$ by reconstructing it from the shares available to the simulator ($S$ controls enough honest parties to reconstruct any shared secret).

$S$ sends all inputs from honest parties and the recovered adversarial inputs and receives $C_{U_1^N}$ from the ideal functionality as the result of the election. It is the same for all parties, including those controlled by the adversaries, so the simulator forwards this value to $A$. In order to let the adversary believe it interacts with the real protocol, the simulator has to produce a transcript of the OSelectM$_N$ protocol that will result in a specific value $U_N$ to be chosen and output. To do that, the simulator fixes the shares of the honest parties for random bits $[b]$ in OSelectM instances so that the reconstruction would output the specific fixed $b$, that will result OSelectM$_N$ to select precisely the $U_N$-th element of the sequence $(st_1, \ldots, st_N)$. The underlying secret sharing scheme allows to simulate the transcripts for the honest parties that share a simulator-chosen secret.

In the real protocol, it is possible that for some $i \neq j$, $k_{iL} = k_{jL}$, while $k_{iR} \neq k_{jR}$ and so the parties would pass the registration. However, this only happens with a low probability that we can control.

**Lemma 6.** *Assuming $H$ is a random oracle, Construction 1 produces a unique leader with the probability at least $1 - e^{-\frac{N(N-1)}{2p}}$.*

*Proof.* The probability that there exist two parties $P_i$ and $P_j$ such that $k_{iL} = k_{jL}$ and $k_{iR} \neq k_{jR}$ can be estimated by the birthday paradox. Specifically, this probability is bounded by $e^{-\frac{N(N-1)}{2p}}$.

**Lemma 7.** *Algorithm Verify in Construction 1 securely implements sending a (verify) message in the ideal model.*

*Proof.* It follows by a similar argument as in the proof of Lemma 4.

*Proof (Proof of Theorem 1).* Since we only consider sequential execution, we need to show that the adversarial view in the real and the ideal worlds is indistinguishable for one instance of the protocol, and the security of the whole protocol will follow by Canetti's composition theorem [6]. To this end, we construct a simulator for a real-world adversary as follows.

- For the registration, the real-world adversary and honest users use a call to the random oracle $H$ for some (random) input and then share a string. Sharing algorithm can be simulated by a secure secret sharing scheme. Moreover, a $t$-private secret sharing scheme for $t < N$ allows $S$ to reconstruct the input used by the corrupted user. Hence, all the numbers shared by the corrupted and honest users during registration are known to $S$.
- To simulate the verification of registration, $S$ verifies that there is no duplicate numbers recorded during registration. If this is the case, it outputs 1, otherwise 0.
- To simulate the election, $S$ first consults the ideal functionality to elect the leader and then we use Lemma 5 to simulate the corresponding transcript.
- To simulate the verify algorithm, $S$ compares the elected number with the number registered by the user (honest or malicious) and outputs 1 if the numbers are equal, otherwise it outputs 0.

We argue that any PPT environment $Z$ cannot distinguish between the ideal world and the real world significantly better than negligible probability via a series or games.

Due to space limits, we complete the proof in the full version.

*Proof (Proof of Theorem 2.).* Since both our constructions Construction 1 and Construction 2 rely on secure MPC primitives and differ only in specifics of the used MPC frameworks, we simply follow the steps in the proof of Theorem 1 to prove the theorem.

# References

1. Aliasgari, M., Blanton, M., Zhang, Y., Steele, A.: Secure computation on floating point numbers. In: NDSS (2013)
2. Aranha, D.F., Gouvêa, C.P.L., Markmann, T., Wahby, R.S., Liao, K.: RELIC is an Efficient LIbrary for Cryptography (2014). https://github.com/relic-toolkit/relic
3. Backes, M., Berrang, P., Hanzlik, L., Pryvalov, I.: A framework for constructing single secret leader election from MPC (full version). eprint 2022/1040 (2022)
4. Boneh, D., Eskandarian, S., Hanzlik, L., Greco, N.: Single secret leader election. In: Proceedings of the 2nd ACM Conference on Advances in Financial Technologies, pp. 12–24 (2020)
5. Camenisch, J., Stadler, M.: Proof systems for general statements about discrete logarithms. Technical report/Department of Computer Science, ETH Zürich 260 (1997)
6. Canetti, R.: Security and composition of multiparty cryptographic protocols. J. Cryptol. **13**(1), 143–202 (2000)
7. Catalano, D., Fiore, D., Giunta, E.: Efficient and universally composable single secret leader election from pairings. IACR Cryptol. ePrint Arch. 2021/344 (2021)
8. Catalano, D., Fiore, D., Giunta, E.: Adaptively secure single secret leader election from DDH. In: ACM PODC 2022, pp. 430–439 (2022)
9. Catrina, O., Saxena, A.: Secure computation with fixed-point numbers. In: Sion, R. (ed.) FC 2010. LNCS, vol. 6052, pp. 35–50. Springer, Heidelberg (2010). https://doi.org/10.1007/978-3-642-14577-3_6
10. Cramer, R., Damgård, I., Maurer, U.: General secure multi-party computation from any linear secret-sharing scheme. In: Preneel, B. (ed.) EUROCRYPT 2000. LNCS, vol. 1807, pp. 316–334. Springer, Heidelberg (2000). https://doi.org/10.1007/3-540-45539-6_22
11. Cramer, R., Damgård, I., Schoenmakers, B.: Proofs of partial knowledge and simplified design of witness hiding protocols. In: Desmedt, Y.G. (ed.) CRYPTO 1994. LNCS, vol. 839, pp. 174–187. Springer, Heidelberg (1994). https://doi.org/10.1007/3-540-48658-5_19
12. Damgård, I., Fitzi, M., Kiltz, E., Nielsen, J.B., Toft, T.: Unconditionally secure constant-rounds multi-party computation for equality, comparison, bits and exponentiation. In: Halevi, S., Rabin, T. (eds.) TCC 2006. LNCS, vol. 3876, pp. 285–304. Springer, Heidelberg (2006). https://doi.org/10.1007/11681878_15
13. Diffie, W., Hellman, M.: New directions in cryptography. IEEE Trans. Inf. Theory **22**(6), 644–654 (1976)
14. Fiat, A., Shamir, A.: How to prove yourself: practical solutions to identification and signature problems. In: Odlyzko, A.M. (ed.) CRYPTO 1986. LNCS, vol. 263, pp. 186–194. Springer, Heidelberg (1987). https://doi.org/10.1007/3-540-47721-7_12
15. França, B., Wissfeld, M., Berrang, P., von Styp-Rekowsky, P., Trinkler, R.: Albatross: an optimistic consensus algorithm. arXiv preprint arXiv:1903.01589 (2019)

16. Ganesh, C., Orlandi, C., Tschudi, D.: Proof-of-stake protocols for privacy-aware blockchains. In: Ishai, Y., Rijmen, V. (eds.) EUROCRYPT 2019. LNCS, vol. 11476, pp. 690–719. Springer, Cham (2019). https://doi.org/10.1007/978-3-030-17653-2_23

17. Gennaro, R., Jarecki, S., Krawczyk, H., Rabin, T.: Secure distributed key generation for discrete-log based cryptosystems. J. Cryptol. **20**(1), 51–83 (2007)

18. Gennaro, R., Rabin, M.O., Rabin, T.: Simplified VSS and fast-track multiparty computations with applications to threshold cryptography. In: PODC 1998, pp. 101–111 (1998)

19. Gilad, Y., Hemo, R., Micali, S., Vlachos, G., Zeldovich, N.: Algorand: Scaling byzantine agreements for cryptocurrencies. In: Proceedings of the 26th Symposium on Operating Systems Principles (SOSP), pp. 51–68 (2017)

20. Kiayias, A., Russell, A., David, B., Oliynykov, R.: Ouroboros: a provably secure proof-of-stake blockchain protocol. In: Katz, J., Shacham, H. (eds.) CRYPTO 2017. LNCS, vol. 10401, pp. 357–388. Springer, Cham (2017). https://doi.org/10.1007/978-3-319-63688-7_12

21. Nakamoto, S.: Bitcoin: a peer-to-peer electronic cash system (2008). https://bitcoin.org/bitcoin.pdf

22. O'Dwyer, K.J., Malone, D.: Bitcoin mining and its energy footprint. In: InISSC 2014/CIICT 2014, pp. 280–285. IET (2014)

23. Pedersen, T.P.: Non-interactive and information-theoretic secure verifiable secret sharing. In: Feigenbaum, J. (ed.) CRYPTO 1991. LNCS, vol. 576, pp. 129–140. Springer, Heidelberg (1992). https://doi.org/10.1007/3-540-46766-1_9

24. Rabin, T., Ben-Or, M.: Verifiable secret sharing and multiparty protocols with honest majority. In: Proceedings of the Twenty-First Annual ACM Symposium on Theory of Computing (STOC), pp. 73–85 (1989)

25. Single-Leader Election (SSLE) (2019). https://github.com/protocol/research-grants/blob/master/RFPs/rfp-006-SSLE.md

26. Schnorr, C.P.: Efficient identification and signatures for smart cards. In: Brassard, G. (ed.) CRYPTO 1989. LNCS, vol. 435, pp. 239–252. Springer, New York (1990). https://doi.org/10.1007/0-387-34805-0_22

27. Shamir, A.: How to share a secret. Commun. ACM **22**(11), 612–613 (1979)

28. Wang, X., Malozemoff, A.J., Katz, J.: EMP-toolkit: efficient MultiParty computation toolkit (2016). https://github.com/emp-toolkit

29. Wang, X., Ranellucci, S., Katz, J.: Global-scale secure multiparty computation. In: CCS 2017, pp. 39–56 (2017)

30. Yao, A.C.: Protocols for secure computations. In: 23rd Annual Symposium on Foundations of Computer Science (SFCS), pp. 160–164 (1982)

# AppBastion: Protection from Untrusted Apps and OSes on ARM

Darius Suciu[✉], Radu Sion, and Michael Ferdman

Stony Brook University, Stony Brook, NY 11794, USA
`dsuciu@cs.stonybrook.edu`

**Abstract.** ARM-based (mobile) devices are more popular than ever. They are used to access, process, and store confidential information and participate in sensitive authentication protocols, making them extremely attractive targets. Many attacks focus on compromising the primary operating system – for example, by convincing the user to download OS rootkits concealed within seemingly innocent apps. To partially mitigate the impact, device manufacturers responded by offering hardware-rooted trusted environments (TEEs). Yet, making use of TEEs (e.g., by securely porting existing apps) is not easy. Only a small number of security-critical applications make use of TEEs, leaving all others to run on a potentially vulnerable OS, under the control of users that all too often fall prey to cleverly disguised malware.

AppBastion is a general-purpose platform that leverages the now ubiquitous ARM TrustZone TEE to secure application data from untrusted OSes. AppBastion enables applications to maintain confidential data in memory regions protected even from a compromised OS. Only approved, signed applications can access their associated protected memory regions. Data never leaves protected regions unencrypted and applications can communicate or declassify protected data only through explicit AppBastion channels. AppBastion ensures that application confidential data cannot be accessed, spoofed, or leaked by the OS.

## 1 Introduction

ARM devices have become a prime target for attackers that can employ a wide range of compromising techniques to obtain access and control over confidential data. Rootkits and general software vulnerabilities are exploited to obtain access to application data or illicitly escalate privileges.

To minimize the impact of such attacks, the multiple privilege layers provided by modern CPUs enable hypervisors and other monitors to isolate applications and OSes from each other. For example, Overshadow [10] is a hypervisor that protects applications running on a hostile OS. The OS can access only encrypted application resources. Further, newer hardware provides hardware-backed mechanisms for constructing mutually-isolated environments, wherein confidential data can be stored and processed (e.g., TrustZone [3], SGX [12]). For example, TrustZone isolates security-sensitive applications ("TAs") in a Trusted Execution

ⓒ The Author(s), under exclusive license to Springer Nature Switzerland AG 2022
V. Atluri et al. (Eds.): ESORICS 2022, LNCS 13555, pp. 692–715, 2022.
https://doi.org/10.1007/978-3-031-17146-8_34

Environment ("Secure World" – implemented as a special CPU operating mode of higher privilege), outside the reach of vulnerable OSes.

Secure World TAs are processes that execute in memory isolated from the Normal World OS and applications, often under their own small Secure World OS or micro-kernel. The TAs typically provide security-critical services to the Normal World, exposed through APIs. Normal World applications can access these APIs by sending requests to the OS, which are forwarded to the Secure World in the form of Secure Monitor Calls (SMCs). Usually, the Secure World OS is designed to forward SMCs to appropriate TAs. This SMC-based communication between applications and TAs also represents the main attack vector for Normal World adversaries to escalate privileges to the level of TAs or even the Secure World OS.

Secure World OS and TA security is highly dependent on the size of its Trusted Computing Base (TCB). Access to the Secure World is tightly controlled by the device manufacturer, which typically only allows small, verifiable TA and kernel code to execute inside Secure World. Complex OS functionality (e.g., networking, filesystems, I/O drivers) are typically not provided inside Secure World to TAs, due to the impact on the Secure World TCB. *Further, each TA introduced increases Secure World TCB and can be leveraged to compromise Secure World security.* In practice, Secure World TAs and OS written by major manufacturers have been shown vulnerable to privilege escalation [23,24] and leaking Secure World data [32]. Further, Secure World TCB restrictions on OS-provided functionality and TAs severely limit the number of applications that can benefit from the TrustZone TEE. As a result, in commercial TrustZone-enabled devices most applications are constrained to run under a more vulnerable TCB inside Normal World and have to rely on isolation provided by a more vulnerable rich OS.

In this work, we introduce AppBastion, a new platform that (i) enabled sensitive applications to run protected from the OS and from peer applications inside the Normal World, while still benefiting from the rich Normal World OS capabilities, and (ii) enables security-critical applications to run as Secure World TAs isolated from the Normal World OS.

AppBastion runs only a small amount of critical logic in TrustZone's Secure Monitor Mode. This logic ensures code integrity of both the Normal World OS and a set of protected sensitive applications dubbed "Shielded Apps". Further, it ensures confidential data inside Shielded Apps are protected from unauthorized accesses within special address spaces that are isolated from all other Normal World applications and from the OS. This isolation is maintained even in the presence of a compromised OS or peer applications. AppBastion orchestrates these special address spaces as private application memory regions, wherein all data are automatically encrypted and decrypted only upon access by its corresponding verified application code.

Inside the Normal World, each AppBastion-protected application can specify which data pages to protect, ensuring only verified application code can access those pages throughout the application life-cycle. Further, these data can be communicated to trusted remote entities or I/O devices through AppBastion channels that prevent data leakage (even under a compromised OS) or declassified for use by other applications.

AppBastion relies only on the execution integrity of a small amount of critical logic running at Secure Monitor Mode level and is independent of the complexity of application and OS code that executes at lower privilege levels inside the Normal or Secure World. *Crucially, the AppBastion TCB does not increase when additional applications are protected or OS functionality is introduced.*

AppBastion contributions include:

(i)   data confidentiality and integrity for apps running under an untrusted OS, through TEE-based OS instrumentation and process monitoring;
(ii)  TEE-based app code concealment and randomization;
(iii) Secure sensitive data exchange with trusted remote servers and peripherals.

# 2 Threat Model

Software may contain vulnerabilities and be prone to compromise. Attackers can obtain control over all Normal World applications not protected by AppBastion and the Normal World OS itself. Using compromised applications and OS, attackers can attempt to launch various software attacks (e.g., confused deputy attacks, SMC hijacking, execution hijacking, etc.) on TAs and apps protected by AppBastion (Shielded Apps). A number of assumptions underlie this work:

**Hardware and Secure Monitor Mode is Trusted.** TrustZone and Memory Management Unit (MMU) hardware are free from defects. Software cannot bypass either TrustZone hardware isolation, privilege levels or MMU-imposed restrictions. Code running at the Secure Monitor Mode privilege level (I.e. secure monitor and Secure World OS under ARMv7) is outside of the attacker's reach and free of exploitable vulnerabilities. Secure World OS also is trusted to isolate and protect its own TAs and assumed out of reach of attackers.

**No Denial of Service Attacks.** SMCs entering and leaving the Secure World can be intercepted and altered by the OS. Similarly, both local (e.g., OS) and on-the-wire attackers can intercept Shielded App network communication. In both cases, AppBastion protects against man-in-the-middle attacks. However, denial-of-service attacks need to be handled separately.

**Shielded App Code Is Position-Independent and Supports Execute-Only.** AppBastion requires Shielded App code to be position-independent and not be mixed with data such that it can be randomized at runtime and made execute-only. Further, we assume adversaries can not bypass either ASLR or the execute-only memory (XOM) restrictions enforced by either hardware or software (such attacks need to be handled separately).

**No Blind Control Flow Hijacking.** Shielded App execution may be altered either directly by the OS or through vulnerabilities within its own code. Blind alteration of Shielded App code pages is assumed to lead to execution failure, effectively a denial of service attack. We assume that without knowing the location of useful gadgets inside randomized unreadable (execute-only) execute-only code the adversaries cannot meaningfully hijack Shielded App execution.

**Correct Shielded App Logic.** AppBastion assumes Shielded Apps are properly designed to store and process confidential data in protected memory regions only and only share it with trusted parties (e.g., remote servers, Shielded Apps or trusted I/O devices) without undergoing declassification for public access.

**No Side-Channels.** AppBastion assumes that cache timing or access-based monitoring side-channels cannot be used by used by the untrusted OS or other applications to infer some information about the confidential data. Additionally, we assume Shielded Apps will not change public data or issue IPCs or syscalls in a manner that leaks confidential data state. Mitigating such side-channels is not addressed under the current AppBastion design and would require handing separately.

## 3  Overview

AppBastion provides protected regions inside Normal World memory for use by Normal World Shielded Apps. These regions are managed by a small Secure Monitor Mode TCB that guarantees their confidentiality and integrity, even when Shielded Apps execute under an untrusted OS. AppBastion ensures that protected region data can be accessed (in clear-text) only by their corresponding verified Shielded App code.

Importantly, AppBastion protects Shielded Apps *without altering the interaction between the (instrumented) Normal World OS kernel and regular applications or the software stack composed of TAs and Secure World OS that execute inside the Secure World.* Changes required to Normal World and Secure World code consist of inserting several AppBastion-specific SMCs in strategic kernel locations to perform additional verifications. These SMCs are directly processed by the AppBastion monitor, replace security-critical privileged instructions inside the OS and provide AppBastion-specific system calls to applications. Any SMCs not introduced by AppBastion are forwarded by the monitor to the Secure World OS, retaining the standard SMC-based communication across worlds.

AppBastion-imposed changes do not affect benign kernel operations or standard communication between Normal and Secure World software. AppBastion memory management, SMC processing, and page fault verification are done transparently from the OS. Normal World OS functionality that requires issuing privileged instructions are intercepted and performed by the monitor, provided

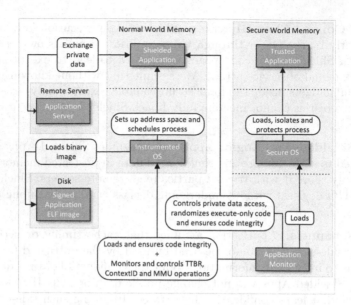

**Fig. 1.** Relationship between the AppBastion monitor, the two OSes, Shielded Apps, and TAs.

the operations do not threaten kernel code integrity or protected memory regions. At the application level, the monitor only affects the operations of Shielded Apps requiring AppBastion protection and does not impact the benign functionality of either unprotected Normal World applications or Secure World TAs.

Figure 1 illustrates the AppBastion framework, highlighting the interactions between AppBastion, the OSes, and a Shielded App running in the Normal World. By instrumenting the Normal World OS kernel, the monitor intercepts all page table updates and active address space changes, effectively taking control over the MMU. Using this control, the monitor tracks and manages all Normal World virtual memory operations, tracking every Normal World executed process and context switch. Additionally, MMU control ensures that the Normal World OS can only map physical memory with monitor verification and approval. Effectively, AppBastion leverages the power and isolation of Secure Monitor Mode, running at the highest privilege level inside the Secure World, to protect Shielded App confidential data, ensure Shielded App and OS code integrity, mitigate control flow hijacking of Shielded Apps, and protect confidential data exchanged with trusted remote servers and I/O devices. A comparison between the protection provided by AppBastion to Shielded Apps and standard Secure World executing TAs is presented in Sect. 3.1. Section 4 details each aspect of AppBastion.

## 3.1   Shielded Apps

Inside Normal World, only Shielded Apps are protected by AppBastion. Any application can become a Shielded App, provided that its binary is signed and verifiable by AppBastion. Developers can run their apps as Shielded Apps by including a new meta-information region in the app signed binary with the following details: (i) which memory segments store confidential data; (ii) a cryptographic hash of Shielded App code authorized to access them; (iii) a set of remote server and dynamic library certificates and (iv) where to map DMA buffers. The effort of turning apps into Shielded Apps is largely dependant on their complexity. For example, to protect a cryptographic key developers only have to specify (inside the signed binary) the memory segment containing it and introduce code that requests AppBastion protection prior to generating/decrypting the key contents inside that memory. Note, developers have to also ensure the app uses this key directly from the protected segment as AppBastion automatically encrypts it when moved out (e.g., heap, stack).

AppBastion instruments the OS binary loader and forces it to pass to the monitor each binary through an SMC. Once the monitor verifies the binary signature, it uses the presented details to determine the confidential data ranges and verify the loaded Shielded App code integrity. In the following, we describe the trade-offs between protected Shielded Apps and Secure World TAs.

**Attack Surface.** TAs run under a trusted Secure World OS, while Shielded Apps are loaded and managed by the untrusted Normal World OS. As a result, while TA execution is isolated from direct untrusted OS access, Shielded Apps can only be hardened against malicious Normal World execution manipulation, as described in Sect. 4.4. Further, the execution inside Normal World also exposes Shielded Apps to more side-channel attacks due to the Normal World hardware shared with untrusted peer applications and OS.

**TCB.** Both TAs and Shielded Apps only contain Secure Monitor Mode and Secure OS code running at the highest privilege level as part of their TCB.

**Device Security Impact.** TAs running in Secure World impact the security of both Normal and Secure World due to their direct access to Secure OS APIs. In contrast, Shielded Apps only have regular Normal World application permissions and do not require direct manufacturer verification.

Overall, Shielded Apps are exposed to a larger attack surface and do not benefit the Secure World execution isolation. Instead, they represent an alternative solution between an isolated TAs and unprotected application. Under AppBastion, the most security-critical applications that require TEE-execution isolation would execute as TAs, while the rest could run protected inside Normal World as Shielded Apps.

# 4    Details

Under AppBastion, Secure Monitor Mode code is responsible for setting up both the Secure and Normal World resources prior to loading the Normal World OS kernel. The Secure World monitor integrity (both data and code) alongside with encryption keys maintained inside the Secure World are protected using Secure Boot [16].

**Monitor Setup.** The boot loader starts and loads the AppBastion monitor code, which starts with full control over the TrustZone security registers. The monitor sets up the Normal and Secure World resources and OSes. First, a secure memory region is set up for the Secure World OS and monitor code and data. Next, the security-sensitive registers are configured for only Secure World access and Secure World OS is loaded. Finally, the monitor loads and executes the Normal World OS kernel code.

AppBastion relies on TrustZone and privilege level isolation to prevent Normal World code from compromising the Secure World monitor. In turn, the monitor identifies, tracks and protects the address spaces of Normal World Shielded Apps from untrusted apps and the OS. Figure 2 depicts key AppBastion components and their interaction. Each component is detailed in the following. Section 4.1 details how AppBastion takes over key OS operations. Section 4.2 describes how the monitor leverages its control over the OS to verify both Shielded App and OS code and ensure its integrity. Section 4.3 details the process of constructing and protecting confidential memory regions inside Shielded Apps which can only be accessed by the protected Shielded App code. Section 4.4 presents how the monitor mitigates Shielded App control-flow-hijacking by randomizing its code prior to making it execute-only. Finally, Sect. 4.5 and Sect. 4.6 describe how the protected confidential data can be communicated between Shielded Apps and trusted remote servers or DMA-capable I/O devices.

## 4.1    Normal World OS Instrumentation

The TrustZone architecture only allows access to the security-sensitive registers through MCR instructions. AppBastion enforces supervision of Normal World memory management by replacing all such MCR instructions (inside the kernel binary) that perform security-sensitive operations (e.g., changing MMU state) with SMCs calling into the AppBastion monitor. The instrumented code is "locked" by preventing additional mapping of kernel executable pages and ensuring the physical code pages are never made writable. As a result, all OS security sensitive operations are only performed by the AppBastion monitor in the Secure World.

**Replacing Security-Sensitive Instructions.** The MCR instructions have special OP codes and have the same format under both ARM and Thumb [1]

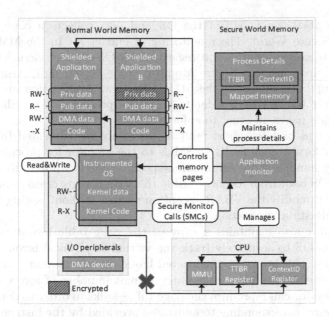

**Fig. 2.** Key AppBastion components and their interaction. Shielded Application A is depicted processing confidential data, while Shielded Application B is processing public data. The AppBastion monitor sets up and controls the access permissions of data and code memory pages belonging to applications, Shielded Apps and the instrumented OS, enforcing the illustrated read/write/execute access permissions. The illustrated DMA device represents an I/O device that is temporary locked for Application A usage by the monitor.

mode. Thus, they are easy to identify and instrument due to the fixed length and alignment of ARM ISA instructions.

The monitor substitutes with SMCs (calling into the AppBastion monitor) all MCR instructions used for accessing the following registers: (i) Translation Table Base Control Register; (ii) Translation Table Base Register 0 (TTBR 0); (iii) Cache operations Register; (iv) ContextID Register; (v) Vector Base Address Register (VBAR). The untrusted OS kernel is thus prevented from making any unauthorized change to its address space or ContextIDs. As a result, the OS can only use the provided SMCs to perform MMU operations or update Translations Table Base Registers (TTBR). This ensures that AppBastion monitor has a consistent and uncompromised view of the memory.

**Overseeing OS Memory Operations.** The AppBastion monitor enables the MMU prior to OS boot. This prevents Normal World software from directly manipulating physical memory. Instead, the OS can only access physical memory through the MMU, which is under AppBastion control. To set Normal World memory page in the MMU, the instrumented OS is forced to issue an SMCs to the AppBastion monitor. For each such SMC, the monitor sets the corresponding entry in the MMU on behalf of the OS and also collects a copy of the set page inside Secure World. The monitoring of entries set in the MMU enables the monitor to collect information regarding all OS-specific virtual-to-physical memory mappings inside a Secure Monitor Mode-hosted data structure. This structure is updated alongside the MMU. Further, AppBastion also leverages its control over the MMU in order to clear the present bits on Shielded App executable code pages, in order to enforce XOM [7].

The data and prefetch abort fault handlers are instrumented by introducing code that forwards all faults as SMCs to the monitor for processing, which automatically handles those AppBastion-specific. The location of the handler is identified at OS boot from its entry inside the VBAR register exception vectors. The OS cannot modify the VBAR exception vectors without issuing SMCs that undergo AppBastion verification.

The monitor also maintains a copy of the page table layout used by the Normal World OS to accurately track the virtual-to-physical layout of Normal World memory. This layout is constructed based on information extracted from the signed kernel binary (e.g., page entry format, number of levels, etc.). As a result, the monitor can reproduce the page table walks in order to determine the physical memory corresponding to addresses provided by the instrumented OS.

The monitor also ensures the page table of processes do not overlap by controlling TTBR0 register assignments. Additionally, the Normal World memory containing all page tables is made read-only by the monitor. As a consequence, the OS cannot modify its page tables directly. Instead it has to issue the appropriate SMC to the monitor – this is done automatically through instrumentation.

The control over physical memory mapping and TTBR0 register enables the monitor to analyze all Normal World mapped physical pages. The monitor prevents malicious manipulation of physical memory mapping, such as mapping physical pages containing Shielded App code as writable, or mapping physical memory used by one process into the address space of another process.

**Tracking Running Processes.** To protect Shielded Apps, AppBastion needs to track executed processes and (re)identify them reliably over time. The monitor can not rely on Normal World OS controlled and maintained data structures for identifying processes. Instead, it uses the TTBR and ContextID registers for this purpose.

Each process has their own page table. The ARM processors MMU loads page tables using their TTBR register written base address. This address is unique for each running process. Additionally, each ARM processor core stores a 8-bit "Address Space Identifier" (ASID) and a 24-bit "Process Identifier" (PROCID) inside the ContextID register. The ASID values are used for marking Translation Lookaside Buffer (TLB) entries.

The instrumented OS is compelled to rely on the monitor for switching page tables on context switches. This allows the monitor to identify both the previously running process (by reading the ContextID) and the newly scheduled one (by its TTBR). The monitor completes a context switch by setting the OS-provided TTBR value and writing its corresponding ASID and PROCID inside the ContextID register.

On each page table change, the monitor logs its corresponding base address inside the Secure World. For each base address it also generates, associates and maintains unique PROCID and ASID values inside Secure World. On each context switch the monitor updates both the TTBR and ContextID registers. The page table address recieved from Normal World is written into the TTBR, while the PROCID and ASID inside the ContextID register are replaced with monitor maintained values. Using the TTBR, PROCID and ASID values maintained inside Secure World AppBastion prevents the OS from loading malicious TTBR values and context switching into writable page tables that are not controlled by the monitor.

The values maintained inside both TTBR and ContextID registers can not be changed by the instrumented OS. *Controlling both registers is necessary for managing context switches.* The control over TTBR ensures the monitor is notified of each context switch, while ContextID management ensures that ASID values are appropriately changed alongside with the TTBR. Note, tracking ASIDs is critical in order to ensure all TLB caches are flushed correctly. Otherwise, a malicious OS could write spoofed ASIDs in order to trick the MMU into not flushing Shielded App pages from the TLB caches.

## 4.2   Protecting App and OS Code Integrity

Hooks inside the Normal World OS boot sequence and binary loader enable the monitor to verify and lock all Normal World pages pertaining to Shielded Apps or the kernel code. These pages can only be mapped inside Normal World once they have undergone monitor verification and instrumentation. Further, the monitor tracks all Normal World processes and ensures correct context switching. The monitor also sets the Privileged Execute-Never bit on all process executable pages to ensure they cannot be mapped into kernel space. This prevents attackers from inserting code containing privileged instructions in attempts to bypass AppBastion control.

**Verifying and Locking Code Pages.** The OS kernel code integrity verification is triggered by SMC calls inserted in the OS boot-sequence and binary loader. AppBastion verifies code integrity of each kernel and Shielded App code page by comparing its cryptographic hash against those provided inside the signed kernel binaries forwarded by the instrumented OS. Using the page table location provided inside the TTBR register, the monitor traverses each page table and verifies each executable page. The verified pages are then made read-only prior to the execution of the first process.

The integrity of kernel code pages is verified and they are made read-only post OS instrumentation. The OS can only load additional kernel code (e.g., kernel modules) by issuing SMC requests (this is instrumented transparently). Upon receiving such requests, the monitor only loads the respective code after passing it through an appropriate instrumentation step (e.g., to replace privileged instructions with SMC calls, etc.) and making it read-only.

AppBastion only allows loading of additional Normal World kernel code through an SMC provided for runtime kernel module loading. Before mapping these modules, however – similarly to OS boot-sequence code instrumentation – AppBastion substitutes privileged instructions that can bypass AppBastion protection with SMCs. Similarly, eBPF [2] JIT compilation can be supported to allow introducing instrumented signed user-space code in the kernel space.

When a Shielded App is executed, an SMC inside the instrumented OS binary loader notifies AppBastion. The monitor verifies the Shielded App's code integrity (similar to kernel pages), randomizes its pages and makes them execute-only. Further, the monitor prevents additional pages from being mapped as executable inside the Shielded App's address space.

### 4.3    Protecting Confidential App Data

For each Shielded App, the monitor sets up a *confidential data region* in memory. At runtime, access into these regions is managed by the monitor in order to ensure that only Shielded App code has access to confidential data. Prior to unauthorized access from the OS or other apps, the confidential data pages of each Shielded App process are encrypted using a unique key generated by the monitor and stored in Secure World memory. This key is generated from a Device Unique Secret Key (DUSK) using a HKDF key derivation function that uses the HMAC-SHA256 algorithm and a salt randomly-generated inside Secure World. In turn, the DUSK is provided by the device manufacturer in a read-only e-fuse. Note, the Normal World OS and apps can't access the DUSK or generated keys and salts. The monitor restricts all memory not marked as confidential to be read-only while Shielded Apps process confidential data. This prevents Shielded App from accidentally transferring confidential data outside memory protected by the monitor.

**Confidential Data Memory Regions.** When a Shielded App is loaded, the monitor initially marks the memory pages inside confidential data regions as not present, without read or write permissions. When the Shielded App attempts to access these pages, it triggers a page fault, which can not be resolved by the instrumented OS. Instead, the respective fault is forwarded to the monitor, which uses it to restore permissions only when Shielded App code requires access.

**Run-Time Data Page Protection.** During execution, the Shielded App code can either process (i) confidential data inside the confidential data regions or (ii) public data located outside. When the Shielded App attempts access to confidential data inside AppBastion protected pages, the monitor receives a fault due to the no-read constraint. As a result, the monitor first makes all public Shielded App pages read-only. Next, it changes confidential data pages access permissions to read-write. This process allows the Shielded App code to transparently copy data from public pages into AppBastion protected pages. When the Shielded App attempts to write in read-only public data pages, the confidential data pages are encrypted and made read-only. At this point, all public data pages permissions are restored to read&write. The confidential data pages are only decrypted and made writable when Shielded App code tries again to write data in confidential data pages.

When a Shielded App tries to write data in read-only pages, a page fault is triggered. This page fault triggers a context switch into the OS fault handler. The first line of the instrumented fault handler issues an SMC, passing the fault details to the monitor. At this point, the permissions of Shielded App data pages are changed depending on the Shielded App's current state. Additionally, confidential data pages are encrypted or decrypted as described previously. On confidential data encryption, the monitor additionally encrypts the general-purpose registers.

The dynamic change of page permissions enables the monitor to transparently protect Shielded App confidential data, while allowing the OS and other processes to access Shielded App public data when needed (e.g., IPCs, signals, shared memory pages, etc.). The encrypted data inside the read-only confidential pages can also be used transparently by the OS while the Shielded App is running (e.g., saved to disk, sent through the network, etc.). Further, Shielded Apps can exchange their public and encrypted confidential data freely with remote servers and peer applications.

**Re-Mapping Protection.** Only controlling confidential page permissions is not sufficient against attacks from inside the OS. The monitor also ensures these physical pages can not be allocated in other address spaces or with different permissions (e.g., double-mapping). Further, all access permissions (read and write) are removed from these pages once the Shielded App is de-scheduled. This prevents untrusted Normal World software from directly accessing the contents within and protects the content integrity and confidentially. The permissions are restored upon Shielded App execution.

**Confidential Data Persistence.** Shielded App persistence encryption key can also be generated by AppBastion from the DUSK and signed Shielded App code hashes. In contrast to the unique per-process Shielded App keys, these persistence keys are only unique across Shielded App binaries and can always re-derived from the persistent signed binaries and DUSK key.

A Shielded App can request AppBastion to encrypt some confidential data pages using its persistence key. The encrypted confidential data can then be declassified as detailed in Appendix 2 and stored safely inside Normal World persistent storage. This data is later only decrypted inside confidential data pages of Shielded Apps loaded from the same signed binary by AppBastion, upon Shielded App decryption request.

**Declassifying Data.** AppBastion prevents the Shielded App from directly disclosing the content of confidential code pages to the untrusted applications or OS. However, some Shielded Apps might require the declassification of confidential information (similar to TAs). In consequence, AppBastion provides a well-defined process for requesting the disclosure of confidential information. This process is detailed in Appendix 2 and ensures that declassification requests cannot be spoofed or replayed by the OS or other apps.

### 4.4 Hardening App Control Flow

Shielded Apps execute inside the Normal World, under the untrusted OS. Moreover, they can contain vulnerabilities which could be leveraged by attackers into hijacking the Shielded App control flow. To mitigate such attacks, the AppBastion monitor verifies Shielded App code integrity prior to setting up the protected address space regions. Upon successful verification, it randomizes the corresponding code using fine-grained ASLR (e.g., [27]), locks its memory pages and makes them execute-only (XOM). From that point, neither the OS or applications can change these permissions or read contents of Shielded App code pages. XOM in conjunction with ASLR hides the layout of the Shielded App executing code. In other words, malicious applications and the OS itself have a much more difficult time locating useful gadgets, which are required for control-flow hijacking attacks.

**Enforcing XOM.** The current AppBastion design uses the approach introduced by XnR [7] to make code pages XOM. From the Secure World, the monitor controls both the MMU and all privileged instructions through instrumentation, as described in Sect. 4.1. This enables AppBastion to mark Shielded App executable pages as not present. Through instrumentation, the monitor intercepts all page faults and ensures that only a Shielded App code page is made present on instruction fetches that originate from Shielded App code. Once another page fault or context switch is triggered, the respective page is again set as not present. XOM ensures that Shielded App code pages are hidden from reads, as detailed in XnR.

### 4.5 Protecting Network Communication

AppBastion provides a protocol for Shielded Apps and trusted remote servers to establish trust and exchange encrypted messages without requiring the introduction of a full network stack inside Secure World. The protocol protects confidential data of Shielded Apps both from remote and local adversaries and prevents replay-attacks using nonces. Next we present the protocol's key aspects. The full protocol is detailed in Appendix 1.

During execution Shielded Apps can request the monitor to establish a secure connection with a remote server. Connections between Shielded Apps and trusted servers are established by using the Secure World monitor as an intermediary.

The monitor verifies the server identity and provides it with the keys required for decrypting Shielded App data. Once the monitor and remote server setup a shared encryption key, Shielded app confidential data is re-encrypted under the shared key, enabling the Shielded App and server to exchange confidential data using the data exchange process described in Appendix 1.

### 4.6   Trusted I/O Paths

I/O devices capable of native encryption (e.g., Bluetooth devices) can participate in the remote communication protocol described in Appendix 1. They can setup connections through attestation and key exchange with AppBastion, similar to remote servers. For DMA devices, AppBastion provides a faster alternative for secure communication.

**Protecting DMA I/O.** AppBastion enables DMA-capable I/O devices to directly read or write content inside Shielded App memory. Through OS instrumentation, the monitor takes control over the DMA controllers of Normal World I/O devices inside Secure World. Using its control over DMA mapping, the monitor provides exclusive DMA access to Shielded App when necessary. First, the monitor maps the memory mapped register corresponding to the DMA controller inside Secure World memory. Then, the monitor replaces the accesses inside OS code inside Normal World with SMCs. As a result, the monitor takes control over the DMA controller of the device. From this point, trusted I/O device can only be accessed under the supervision of AppBastion.

A Shielded App can request access to a trusted I/O device by issuing an SMC to the monitor. Upon receiving such a request, the monitor sets up a new memory region inside the Shielded App's address space, the *SecIO* region. This region operates a set of special rules and cannot contain either public or confidential data pages. Similar to confidential pages, AppBastion only allows the DMA buffers to be mapped inside the SecIO region. Pages inside this region are granted read&write permissions alongside the confidential pages, in order to enable direct transfer of data (without encryption). However, both read and write permissions are removed from SecIO region pages when the confidential data pages are encrypted and made read-only. This difference is necessary because the I/O devices would not be able to handle the encryption of data. Instead, the content of SecIO pages is always cleartext that can only be copied inside confidential code pages directly. Once inside confidential code pages, it can be exchanged similar to other content located inside.

**Protecting DMA Transfers.** The I/O device DMA buffers are mapped by into the SecIO region during Shielded App execution. The monitor will refuse any requests to map DMA buffers of the respective I/O device into other locations. This prevents other apps or the OS from obtaining access to the DMA channel used by the Shielded App. Once a SecIO memory region is mapped to the DMA buffers of an I/O device, Shielded App and I/O device can transfer data directly. AppBastion can (optionally) notify the user (e.g., using a Secure World reserved LED) whenever the trusted I/O device is reserved for Shielded App usage. Additionally, AppBastion only allows configuring the DMA devices to use a fixed predefined physical memory, reserved for mapping their DMA buffers. This prevents the OS or applications from using DMA access to change code pages or leak and alter confidential data of Shielded Apps.

## 5    Evaluation

We implemented and evaluated AppBastion on an i.MX6 Nitrogen6X Max board. This board features a hardware configuration similar to a typical mobile device, comprising an ARMv7 Cortex-A9 CPU and 4GB of DDR3 memory. On device boot, the AppBastion monitor is loaded in the Secure World by the U-boot [17] boot loader. Next, the monitor sets up the Secure and Normal World configuration and loads the Secure World OS alongside an instrumented 32-bit Linux 4.1.15 OS in the Normal World.

AppBastion's TCB consists of approximately 3.6K code running in the Secure World. Additionally, approximately 150 LOC inside the Normal World OS kernel are instrumented. The instrumentation replaces security-critical operations with SMC calls to the AppBastion monitor as described in the previous section. The 150 LOC also includes the syscalls introduced to allow Shielded Apps to issue AppBastion-specific SMC requests.

**Table 1.** LMBench micro-benchmark results ($\mu$s)

| | Null | Open Close | Mmap | Read | Write | Fork | Fork exec | Page fault | Signal handler | | Context switch | |
| --- | --- | --- | --- | --- | --- | --- | --- | --- | --- | --- | --- | --- |
| | | | | | | | | | Install | Delivery | 2p 0k | 100p 0k |
| Linux | 1.02 | 21.25 | 4093 | 0.80 | 1.52 | 1066 | 1166 | 1.41 | 1.60 | 42.46 | 19.95 | 20.56 |
| AppBastion | 1.02 | 21.25 | 15380 | 0.80 | 1.52 | 5842 | 5596 | 16.70 | 1.60 | 42.46 | 24.64 | 29.50 |
| Overhead | 0% | 0% | 275% | 0% | 0% | 448% | 401% | 1084% | 0% | 0% | 23% | 43% |

**System Benchmarks.** Under AppBastion, OS page fault handling and virtual memory management require monitor verification. This process introduces additional context switches and affects the performance of kernel memory management.

We evaluate the impact of introducing context switches and Secure World verification on the key OS operations performance (memory operations, file I/O, signal handling). We issue system calls and measure their latency using the LMBench 3.0 [22] micro-benchmarks. Table 1 presents a comparison between various native Linux 4.1.15 system services and their AppBastion instrumented versions on our platform. For context switching, the latency of switching between processes that do no work is measured. To minimize this latency AppBastion maintains each process metadata (e.g., PROCID, ASID) inside hash tables with TTBR values as keys. This metadata is accessed in $O(1)$ on context switches using instrumented OS-passed TTBR values, which are also written in the TTBR register by AppBastion. Context switching between large numbers of processes is more affected under AppBastion due to introduced data/instructions that cause more cache misses and time spent on switching between worlds. Note, maliciously passed TTBR values only lead to context switching to different processes or denial of service.

Table 1 results indicate that the security checks introduced by AppBastion mainly impact memory operations, specifically those requiring additional Secure World inspection (i.e., page faults and memory mapping). The highest impact, observed on page fault handling, is due to the page permission checks that ensure physical memory containing Shielded App confidential data are only mapped in the Shielded App's address space. *Critically, AppBastion overheads are incurred only on infrequent operations* – large mmap operations, fork, and exec calls, which typically typically happen during application startup, where delays on the order of hundreds of milliseconds are not critical.

Although LMBench micro-benchmarks permit the precise identification of overheads, they can obscure practical considerations. From a practical perspective, Table 2 presents several realistic application benchmarks drawn from Geekbench [29] 4.3.0 and the Phoronix Test Suite [28]. *These benchmark results indicate that the performance of applications running under an AppBastion-protected OS is minimally affected.*

**Table 2.** Application benchmark results

|  | PostgreSQL 10.3 (TPS) | PHPBench 0.8.1 (Score) | Optcarrot 1.0 (FPS) | OpenSSL 1.1.1 (Signs/s) | Java-JMH 1.1.2 (Score) | Geekbench 4.3 (Score) |
|---|---|---|---|---|---|---|
| Linux | 116.28 | 29797 | 6.36 | 8.10 | 218M | 872 |
| AppBastion | 112.89 | 29713 | 6.36 | 8.10 | 217M | 851 |
| Overhead | 2.9% | 0.2% | 0% | 0% | 0.3% | 2.4% |

**Table 3.** Lite Bitcoin wallet benchmark (msec)

| Command | Linux | AppBastion Application | Overhead | AppBastion Shielded App | Overhead |
|---|---|---|---|---|---|
| Check Balance | 8.55 | 8.87 | 3.7% | 8.95 | 4.6% |
| Send money to 1 account | 73.19 | 74.3 | 1.52% | 74.71 | 2.0% |
| Send money to 10 accounts | 94.63 | 95.72 | 1.15% | 96.83 | 2.3% |
| Encrypt wallet | 40238.44 | 40483.02 | 0.6% | 40634.22 | 0.9% |

**Bitcoin Wallet Performance Analysis.** As a showcase for AppBastion, We evaluated the impact of protecting a security-critical Bitcoin [25] wallet app, Bitcoin Knots 0.16.3 [14]. We configured the Bitcoin Knots binary to request protection of all its sensitive data sections. These sections contain eleven 4KB-sized pages. We then evaluated key wallet operations by running the wallet in regression test mode. The resulting execution times for common commands are presented in Table 3. The commands are sent from the command line, eliminating variability and delays introduced when using a GUI. In each test, the operations are performed on a freshly-generated wallet containing 1000 blocks and the average execution time of 1000 runs is presented. Results indicate that most wallet commands (e.g., checking balance, sending money) are executed approximately one millisecond slower. Such an effect is likely not noticeable to the user, especially in a GUI.

Our experiments indicate that applications like Bitcoin Knots are minimally slowed down under an AppBastion-instrumented OS. The simpler operations (checking balance, sending money) are most affected (1.15–3.7%), while impact on the CPU-intensive operations (e.g., encryption) are essentially not noticeable. The evaluation of this application suggests that AppBastion can harden the security of Normal World applications simply by introducing a few lines of code and paying only a minor (1%) performance degradation.

## 6    Discussion

This section analyzes AppBastion's protection against some typical attack vectors.

**Hijacking Shielded App Control Flow.** In an AppBastion-protected system, a malicious app or OS might attempt to use Shielded App code vulnerabilities to hijack its execution and trick it into leaking sensitive information. To prevent such attacks, AppBastion hardens Shielded App control flow against such manipulation by randomizing the Shielded App code and making is code pages execute-only when the Shielded App starts. AppBastion also prevents a malicious OS from jumping Shielded App execution into gadgets located in libraries (e.g., libc) by ensuring all Shielded App libraries are randomized alongside Shielded App code. Blind control-flow hijacking is assumed to not be sufficient for compromising or leaking Shielded App's confidential data.

**Disclosing Execute-Only Memory Contents.** Enforcing XOM from Secure World ensures that attackers can not directly read gadget locations from memory by disabling the MMU or introducing malicious DMA mappings (e.g., mapping physical memory made execute-only for DMA). Thus, under AppBastion, even OS vulnerabilities would not enable disabling the execute-only restriction imposed by the monitor. Further, all key memory management operations are under monitor control, allowing the detection of aggressive monitoring techniques such as single step debugging, forced context switches, etc.

**Malicious Memory Mapping.** Under a vanilla compromised OS, attackers can map physical memory pages belonging to target applications into the address space of other processes or the kernel, a process named "double-mapping". Such attacks are stopped under the AppBastion instrumented OS. Here, all memory operations are verified by the Secure World monitor. AppBastion ensures physical pages containing Shielded App code and confidential data are only ever mapped into Shielded App address spaces, with the correct permissions. Swapped out pages are also monitored by AppBastion through tags maintained inside Secure World.

**Malicious DMA Mapping.** AppBastion monitors the DMA mappings and does not allow DMA mappings into code pages or unauthorized DMA mappings into Shielded App confidential data pages. Thus, Direct Memory Access (DMA) of peripheral devices can not be leveraged to read or modify AppBastion protected memory pages.

# 7   Related Work

## 7.1   Protecting the OS

**Intel.** On Intel processors, SGX enclaves can run isolated applications and protect them from other host software. However, code running in SGX enclaves still relies on a extensive interaction with an untrusted OS to perform various tasks (e.g. I/O, thread management, fault handling). Recent SGX research (Haven [8], Graphene-SGX [33], and SCONE [4]) has focused on reducing reliance on the untrusted host OS by inserting components (small OS, C Standard library) inside the enclaves. However, such approaches significantly enlarge the enclave TCB.

**TrustZone.** The TrustZone-provided TEE can also be used to improve the security of Normal World software. SProbes [18] and TZ-RKP [6] discuss protecting OS code integrity, while [11] shows how to introduce additional memory separation layers, orthogonal to the application/kernel separation. Kenali [31], SKEE [5], PerspicuOS [15] propose leveraging MMU control to isolate a portion of the kernel's address space from application and kernel access.

TZ-RKP and SProbes ensure OS code integrity by taking over the MMU and TTBR registers through OS code instrumentation. AppBastion is inspired by TZ-RKP in particular when ensuring instrumented OS code integrity. However, in AppBastion OS code integrity only represents the first step towards protecting Shielded Apps. The main challenge in protecting Shielded App data represents introducing the monitoring mechanism that automatically encrypts and decrypts memory containing confidential data data while it is executed under an untrusted OS, while also allowing it to be securely communicated with trusted remote servers and I/O devices. To introduce this mechanism AppBastion has to prevent all malicious OS operations that could leak or compromise Shield App confidential data by carefully taking control over DMA mapping, context switching and app memory management. Overall, while TZ-RKP and Sprobes operations protect the OS code from untrusted apps, **AppBastion protects the apps from untrusted OSes**.

## 7.2   Protecting Apps Running Under Untrusted OSes

**Virtualization Based Approaches.** Virtual machines built using hypervisors (VMMs) aim to constrain vulnerable OSes from accessing the entire device, protecting user data in smaller, more secure environments. However, anecdotal evidence [30] indicates that commercial hypervisors like VMware [34] maintain huge TCBs and CVE reports [26] indicate exploitable vulnerabilities are periodically introduced and fixed.

InkTag [19] relies on a hypervisor to isolate application contexts from an untrusted OS. Virtual Ghost [13] provides trusted services for apps. These services include performing operations like memory management, encryption and key management. Overshadow [10] proposes using the hypervisor to protect application data from a hostile OS using a shim running in the application address space. to cooperate with a hypervisor to enforce the encryption. Similar to AppBastion, Overshadow uses the shim to automatically encrypts application data upon OS access. To bypass Overshadow protection, attackers can either compromise the underlying hypervisor or the shim (containing above 1.3 KLOC) introduced by Overshadow in the address space. In contrast, AppBastion protects Shielded App data confidentiality using only Secure World Monitor Mode code and non-bypassable kernel hooks.

vTZ [20] and PrivateZone [21] provide entire isolated, Normal World execution environments for applications and OSes running them. However, these isolated execution environments still expose vulnerabilities in application and kernel code executing within though various communication channels (e.g., IPC, memory sharing, remote communication, etc.). In AppBastion, applications can still run isolated as TAs inside Secure World. However, AppBastion also focuses on hardening the applications that can only execute under the rich OS and protects their confidential data.

**TrustZone Enclaves.** Recent work has also focused on building isolated environments similar to SGX enclaves on ARM processors. To this end, SecTEE [35] leverages TrustZone isolation, the Secure World OS and a cache coloring-mechanism that imposes over a over 40X performance overhead. In contrast, AppBastion provides code and data protection to sensitive applications that do not need to be (or can not be) ported inside Secure World enclaves (or as TAs) and has a minimal impact on system performance and Secure World TCB.

Sanctuary [9] cleverly leverages TZC-400 hardware features to partition memory across cores and create enclaves inside Normal World that are isolated from each other and the Normal World OS and applications, similar to TAs. Sanctuary enclave isolation is more powerfull than Shielded App protection provided through OS instrumentation. However, enforcing Sanctuary enclave isolation also presents significant drawbacks. First, each executing enclave requires an exclusive CPU core during its lifetime. Second, enclaves require setting up shared memory with TAs and untrusted Normal World apps to access I/O devices, storage, networking, etc. Third, porting complex applications into enclaves implies a difficult development process of partitioning the app into unprotected Normal

World components, the enclave and TAs. In contrast, AppBastion focuses on general applications designed to run under the untrusted OS.

# 8   Conclusions

In TrustZone-based commercial devices, only a small set of security-sensitive TAs are protected by the Secure World. Most applications run unprotected on the Normal World OS, which is relatively easy prey for rootkits and malware. AppBastion provides a Secure Monitor Mode-hosted protection mechanism for Normal World applications to directly protect sensitive data from a compromised OS in special memory regions accessible only to their corresponding signed application code. Sensitive application data can only be communicated or declassified through AppBastion-protected channels to/from peripherals or authorized remote parties.

**Acknowledgments.** We would like to thank our anonymous reviewers for their helpful feedback. This work has been supported in part through NSF award 2052951 and ONR award N000142112407.

# Appendix 1 Remote Communication Protocol

AppBastion allows Shielded Apps to exchange confidential information with trusted remote servers. In this Appendix we first describe and discuss the process through which a shared encryption key can be setup ( through an authenticated Diffie-Hellman key exchange) between a remote server and the AppBastion monitor and show how it enables confidential data transfers between the server and Shielded App.

**Establishing Connections.** The key exchange protocol contains three parties: the remote server, the Shielded App and the AppBastion monitor. In the key exchange context, the Shielded App only initiates the connection to the remote server and forwards messages between the monitor and respective server.

First, the Remote Server sends its certificate alongside a nonce to the monitor when a Shielded App initiates a connection. Once the monitor receives a server certificate, it first verifies it against its list of trusted server certificates. If the verification passes, it constructs an attestation proof. This proof consists of cryptographic hashes of the code belonging to the Shielded App, Normal World OS and the monitor itself. The proof is signed using a device private key. This key is burned by the manufacturer in an e-fuse available only to the Secure World. The manufacturer also publishes a certificate containing the public counterpart to the respective key.

Next, the monitor builds a response to the server by encrypting the signed proof alongside the received nonce and public components of a Diffie-Hellman key exchange (e.g., public key "A", modulus "p" and base "g"). The monitor encrypts its response using the public key included in the certificate provided by the server and sends the encrypted response through the Shielded App.

Finally, The server uses its private key to decrypts the monitor response. The response is then processed by using the device public key located in the certificate it already has to decrypt the signed attestation proof and verify it alongside the received nonce. If the verifications succeed, the server finishes the key exchange by sending its signed public key "B". Once "B" is received and verified, a shared symmetric encryption key can derived on both sides, completing the Diffie-Hellman key exchange.

**Exchanging Data.** On each completed key exchange, the monitor and server end up with a shared symmetric key. In order to enable confidential data key exchange under this key, the monitor first has to decrypt the data from under the existing Shielded App key and re-encrypt it under new one shared with the Server. Confidential data can only be exchanged after it is moved under the new key.

For data transfers, lets assume first a Shielded App requests data from the server. First it needs to send a nonce to the server (to detect replay attacks). In response, the server encrypts data alongside the received nonce using the Shielded App key. The resulting ciphertext is then provided to the Shielded App. However, the Shielded App does not have the key required for decryption. Instead, it can only rely on the monitor. Thus, in order to decrypt the received ciphertext, the Shielded App must copy it first into confidential data pages. Then, an SMC can be issued to the monitor in order to request its decryption. Finally, the Shielded App can verify the freshness of received data using the included nonce. Note, the monitor only decrypts data located inside confidential data pages. This ensures that at no point the exchanged data and nonce can be accessed in clear text by untrusted Normal World software.

The Shielded App can also leverage the monitor in order to send its own confidential data to the server. There exist two scenarios, based on the confidential data state. (a) public pages are writable and confidential data is already encrypted by the monitor. In this case, the Shielded App only needs to provide the encrypted data to the server. (b) Public pages are read-only and confidential data is not encrypted. In this case, the Shielded App must first copy the data into public pages (which are read-only). This triggers a page fault, which arrives at the monitor. At this point, the monitor encrypts data using the key shared with the server, restoring the write permissions to public pages. Finally, similar the Shielded App can sent the encrypted data to the server.

# Appendix 2 Confidential Data Disclosure

**Declassification Request.** Shielded Apps can only declassify contents from confidential code pages using the following AppBastion provided steps:

(i) The Shielded App must issue a new declassification request by sending an SMC to the monitor, through the Normal World OS. This SMC forwards to the monitor the address of a 64-bit empty space inside a confidential page. Upon receiving such a request, the monitor first verifies if the address provided is located inside a confidential data page. Then, a unique 64-bit number (nonce) is generated by the monitor and written at the respective address. This nonce is also maintained inside Secure World and associated with the Shielded App. At this point the execution returns to the Shielded App.

(ii) The Shielded App must construct a special declassification header inside its confidential data pages. The nonce received from the monitor must be copied inside this header. The header must also specify the location of the confidential data ciphertext that requires declassification. This location must be inside public memory, otherwise the request is denied (in order to not disrupt the automatic process used for protecting confidential data).

(iii) The Shielded app must copy the confidential data to declassify into the public range specified inside the declassification header. This data is automatically encrypted by the monitor, as per Sect. 4.3.

(iv) Finally, Shielded App can start sending the declassification header to the monitor. This header can only be sent by first copying it into a public page and passing the resulting ciphertext to the monitor through another SMC. Note, the header is automatically encrypted by the monitor when it is copied into the public page. Thus, the untrusted OS can not change the parameters located inside (e.g., locations, nonces, etc.).

**Declassification.** Upon receiving an SMC containing declassification request, the monitor will first decrypt it using the encryption key of the Shielded App. This key is already maintained inside Secure World by the monitor. Next the monitor will check against replay attacks by verifying the unique number freshness. The check is performed by comparing against value maintained inside Secure World. If the verification passes, the monitor will then decrypt the content inside indicated public pages using the Shielded App's encryption key.

In order to simplify subsequent declassification requests, the monitor monotonically increases the nonce maintained inside Secure World after each declassification request. In turn the Shielded App must also increase its provided nonce. This allows future declassification to proceed only using steps (ii-iv).

# References

1. The Thumb instruction set. https://developer.arm.com/documentation/den0013/d/Introduction-to-Assembly-Language/The-ARM-instruction-sets?lang=en
2. A thorough introduction to ebpf. https://lwn.net/Articles/740157/ (2007)
3. ARM: Bulding a secure system using trustzone technology. ARM Technical White Paper (2009)
4. Arnautov, S., et al.: SCONE: Secure linux containers with intel SGX. In: 12th USENIX Symposium on Operating Systems Design and Implementation (OSDI 16) pp. 689–703, USENIX Association, Savannah, GA (2016)

5. Azab, A., et al.: SKEE: A lightweight secure kernel-level execution environment for ARM. In: Proceedings 2016 Network and Distributed System Security Symposium. Internet Society (2016)

6. Azab, A.M., et al.: Hypervision across worlds: Real-time kernel protection from the arm trustzone secure world. In: Proceedings of the 2014 ACM SIGSAC Conference on Computer and Communications Security, pp. 90–102. CCS '14, ACM, New York, NY, USA (2014)

7. Backes, M., Holz, T., Kollenda, B., Koppe, P., Nürnberger, S., Pewny, J.: You can run but you can't read: Preventing disclosure exploits in executable code. In: Proceedings of the 2014 ACM SIGSAC Conference on Computer and Communications Security, pp. 1342–1353 (2014)

8. Baumann, A., Peinado, M., Hunt, G.: ACM Trans. Comput. Syst. Shielding applications from an untrusted cloud with haven 33(3), 1–26 (2015)

9. Brasser, F., Gens, D., Jauernig, P., Sadeghi, A.R., Stapf, E.: SANCTUARY: ARM-ing TrustZone with user-space enclaves. In: Proceedings 2019 Network and Distributed System Security Symposium. Internet Society (2019)

10. Chen, X., et al.: Overshadow: a virtualization-based approach to retrofitting protection in commodity operating systems. SIGPLAN Not. 43(3), 2–13 (2008)

11. Cho, Y., Kwon, D., Yi, H., Paek, Y.: Dynamic virtual address range adjustment for intra-level privilege separation on ARM. In: Proceedings 2017 Network and Distributed System Security Symposium. Internet Society (2017)

12. Costan, V., Devadas, S.: Intel sgx explained. IACR Cryptology ePrint (2016)

13. Criswell, J., Dautenhahn, N., Adve, V.: Virtual ghost: Protecting applications from hostile operating systems. In: Proceedings of the 19th International Conference on Architectural Support for Programming Languages and Operating Systems, pp. 81–96. ASPLOS '14, ACM, New York, NY, USA (2014)

14. Dashjr, L.: Bitcoin knots. https://bitcoinknots.org/ (2011)

15. Dautenhahn, N., Kasampalis, T., Dietz, W., Criswell, J., Adve, V.: Nested kernel. In: Proceedings of the Twentieth International Conference on Architectural Support for Programming Languages and Operating Systems - ASPLOS (2015)

16. Davis, D.L.: Secure boot , US Patent 5,937,063 (1999)

17. Denk, W., et al.: Das u-boot-the universal boot loader. https://www.denx.de/wiki/U-Boot (2013)

18. Ge, X., Vijayakumar, H., Jaeger, T.: Sprobes: Enforcing kernel code integrity on the trustzone architecture. CoRR (2014), arxiv.org/abs/1410.7747

19. Hofmann, O.S., Kim, S., Dunn, A.M., Lee, M.Z., Witchel, E.: Inktag: Secure applications on an untrusted operating system. In: Proceedings of the Eighteenth International Conference on Architectural Support for Programming Languages and Operating Systems. pp. 265–278. ASPLOS '13, ACM, New York, NY, USA (2013)

20. Hua, Z., Gu, J., Xia, Y., Chen, H., Zang, B., Guan, H.: vTZ: Virtualizing ARM trustzone. In: 26th USENIX Security Symposium (USENIX Security 17), pp. 541–556, USENIX Association, Vancouver, BC (2017)

21. Jang, J., et al.: PrivateZone: Providing a private execution environment using ARM TrustZone. IEEE Transactions on Dependable and Secure Computing (2018)

22. McVoy, L.W., Staelin, C., et al.: lmbench: Portable tools for performance analysis. In: USENIX annual technical conference, pp. 279–294, San Diego, CA, USA (1996)

23. MITRE: Cve-2015-6639. https://nvd.nist.gov/vuln/detail/CVE-2015-6639 (2016)

24. MITRE: Cve-2016-2431. https://nvd.nist.gov/vuln/detail/CVE-2016-2431 (2016)

25. Nakamoto, S.: Bitcoin: A peer-to-peer electronic cash system. Cryptography Mailing list at https://www.metzdowd.com (2009)

26. Özkan, S.: Cve details. https://www.cvedetails.com/ (2010)
27. Pappas, V., Polychronakis, M., Keromytis, A.D.: Smashing the gadgets: Hindering return-oriented programming using in-place code randomization. In: 2012 IEEE Symposium on Security and Privacy, pp. 601–615, IEEE (2012)
28. Phoronix: Phoronix test suite. Online at https://www.phoronix-test-suite.com/
29. PrimateLabs: Geekbench. Online at http://primatelabs.ca/geekbench/index.html
30. Rippleweb: VMware vs KVM. http://www.rippleweb.com/vmware-vs-kvm/ (2017)
31. Song, C., Lee, B., Lu, K., Harris, W., Kim, T., Lee, W.: Enforcing kernel security invariants with data flow integrity. In: Proceedings 2016 Network and Distributed System Security Symposium. Internet Society (2016)
32. Suciu, D., McLaughlin, S., Simon, L., Sion, R.: Horizontal privilege escalation in trusted applications. In: 29th {USENIX} Security Symposium ({USENIX} Security 20) (2020)
33. che Tsai, C., Porter, D.E., Vij, M.: Graphene-SGX: A practical library OS for unmodified applications on SGX. In: 2017 USENIX Annual Technical Conference (USENIX ATC 17), pp. 645–658, USENIX Association, Santa Clara, CA (2017)
34. Walters, B.: VMware virtual platform. Linux journal (1999)
35. Zhao, S., Zhang, Q., Qin, Y., Feng, W., Feng, D.: SectEE: A software-based approach to secure enclave architecture using tEE. In: Proceedings of the 2019 ACM SIGSAC Conference on Computer and Communications Security, pp. 1723–1740, CCS '19, Association for Computing Machinery, New York, NY, USA (2019)

# Collaborative Anomaly Detection System for Charging Stations

Jesus Cumplido, Cristina Alcaraz$^{(\boxtimes)}$, and Javier Lopez

Computer Science Department, University of Malaga, Campus de Teatinos s/n, 29071 Malaga, Spain
{cumplido,alcaraz,jlm}@lcc.uma.es

**Abstract.** In recent years, the deployment of charging infrastructures has been increasing exponentially due to the high energy demand of electric vehicles, forming complex charging networks. These networks pave the way for the emergence of new unknown threats in both the energy and transportation sectors. Economic damages and energy theft are the most frequent risks in these environments. Thus, this paper aims to present a solution capable of accurately detecting unforeseen events and possible fraud threats that arise during charging sessions at charging stations through the current capabilities of the Machine Learning (ML) algorithms. However, these algorithms have the drawback of not fitting well in large networks and generating a high number of false positives and negatives, mainly due to the mismatch with the distribution of data over time. For that reason, a Collaborative Anomaly Detection System for Charging Stations (here referred to as CADS4CS) is proposed as an optimization measure. CADS4CS has a central analysis unit that coordinates a group of independent anomaly detection systems to provide greater accuracy using a voting algorithm. In addition, CADS4CS has the feature of continuously retraining ML models in a collaborative manner to ensure that they are adjusted to the distribution of the data. To validate the approach, different use cases and practical studies are addressed to demonstrate the effectiveness and efficiency of the solution.

**Keywords:** Collaborative anomaly detection · Charging station · Machine Learning · Voting system

## 1 Introduction

According to studies carried out in [13], more than 30 million Electric Vehicles (EVs) are predicted to be on the roads by 2030. This encourages organizations to deploy a large number of charging infrastructures in order to meet the energy demand expected from EV batteries. Charging infrastructures are commonly composed of a set of interconnected Charging Stations (CSs), which are remotely controlled by a control system, called CS Management System (CSMS) [5]. These infrastructures often use Information Technologies (ITs) as well as Operational Technologies (OTs) to provide the system with greater functionality and

V. Atluri et al. (Eds.): ESORICS 2022, LNCS 13555, pp. 716–736, 2022.
https://doi.org/10.1007/978-3-031-17146-8_35

intelligence, such as online reservations, payments through bank entities and monitoring of charging profiles from external entities, known as Energy Management Systems (EMSs). Further details about the design of charging station infrastructure can be found in Appendix A. However, this convergence of ITs and OTs to create complex networks leads to new cybersecurity risks in power systems [34]. Standards institutions, such as the National Institute of Standards and Technology (NIST), and other governmental organizations of interest, such as the United States (US) Department of Energy, Transportation and Defense, are raising concerns about these new environments under development [25]. In this report, NIST highlighted how CSs are bringing two critical sectors together for the first time: energy and transportation, which have never been electronically connected before. This implies new potential attacks that could directly impact financial terms, business continuity and human safety.

This concern is accompanied by the observed increase in cybercrime attacks on critical infrastructures according to the latest European Union Agency for Cybersecurity (ENISA) threat landscape report [15], where the major critical infrastructure sectors being impacted are healthcare, transportation and energy. Recently, several researchers have developed a novel attack called BrokenWire [21] against rapid chargers with the ability to wirelessly send malicious signals to the targeted vehicle in order to cause electromagnetic interference and disrupt the charging session. In [19], a botnet of compromised EVs and CSs is also launched to simultaneously attack the proper functioning of the power grid by increasing its load in an uncontrolled manner; consequently provoking a Denial of Service (DoS). Also, the authors of [8] show the feasibility of extracting charging session attributes and creating large datasets to lead privacy issues. Many of these threats are also contemplated in [5,34,36,38], where the authors show how charging infrastructures are susceptible to diverse threats. To clarify the influence of these attacks and its impact to the sector, Appendix A details the most common threats to CS components and communications, as well as the highest risk impacts, corresponding to economic damage and energy theft. As stated in [3], the main security weakness is due to the type of CS deployment in public environments and the type of communication, which can be wireless. Consequently, different cybersecurity expert organizations have been working to provide solutions to these threats. Most organizations rely on frameworks and standards to help ensure a structured defense of control systems [9], where detection is a core element.

One of the most widespread detection solutions in the literature is the Anomaly Detection System (ADS) based on Machine Learning (ML) algorithms [43]. These systems are responsible for identifying deviations or outliers, denominated as anomalies, and launch an early alert when these are detected. One of the main advantages of these algorithms is their ability to learn and adapt to the data distribution, thanks to their ability to recognize both known events and unknown anomalies (e.g. those caused by zero-day vulnerabilities). However, in systems such as charging infrastructures, the distribution of data tends to vary rapidly over time due to their continuous increase in energy demand and the improvements in EV batteries and charging speed. This causes an increase in the False Positive (FP) and False Negative (FN) ratio in ML models by mismatching with the distribution of the data. In addition, charging networks are currently composed of groups of interconnected CSs building up a complex network, usually distributed by zone and managed locally by a CSMS. This distribution also presents the challenge of sharing anomalies and alerts between the independent charging infrastructures, for the purpose of detecting distributed attacks and obtaining global information on the situational awareness of the charging network.

To provide a suitable solution to these challenges, researchers apply Collaborative ADS (CADS) as a protection measure of large networks and large IT ecosystems [40]. CADS is based on the cooperation of different monitors distributed in the system, which act as sensors and collect data. It also contains one or more analysis units that are responsible for intrusion detection by correlating data obtained from sensors. These defensive supports have encouraged us to **contribute with** a novel approach using a centralized CADS – referred to here as CADS for CSs (CADS4CS) – as an optimization measure to adjust detection algorithms according to the real conditions of charging networks. To do so, CADS4CS is composed of a central analysis unit, referred to here as a coordinator, which coordinates a distributed group of standalone ML-based ADSs to: (1) *obtain higher accuracy in anomaly detection using a voting algorithm*; and (2) *continuously retrain ML models in a collaborative and secure manner to ensure that they are always adjusted to the data distribution*. To provide an optimal voting system for CSs, we designed three types of coordinators with three voting algorithms based on: (1) average; (2) weighted average; and (3) mode. Based on this, we conducted several experiments representing various anomaly detection scenarios in charging networks. These scenarios correspond to the use of: (1) a single charging session dataset, which includes the same type of threats and is shared between the different ADSs to validate the performance of ML models; and (2) different datasets, each of which contemplates different anomalies in order for each ADS to validate the effectiveness of the voting algorithms.

This paper is organized as follows. Section 2 summarizes all work related to ML-based anomaly detection on energy consumption in CSs. Section 3 describes the structure and functionality of CADS4Cs. More specifically, Subsect. 3.1 defines the open charging session datasets and the types of anomalies, while Subsect. 3.2 establishes the design of the central coordinator together with the types of voting algorithms proposed. Subsequently, Sect. 4 shows the results of different analyses and experiments on various use cases. Finally, Sect. 5 draws the conclusion from the results obtained and describes future work.

## 2 Related Work

In the literature, there are several recent scientific works proposing different solutions for ADSs in industrial and cyber-physical environments. Table 1 shows a summary of the related works, which are associated with ML-based ADSs in energy environments, such as anomalies in energy consumption or CSs.

In [18], Janetzko et al. introduce an anomaly detection algorithm based on time series to detect and visualize unexpected power consumptions in commercial

**Table 1.** Related work on Machine Learning-based anomaly detection systems

| Reference (year) | Applied technique | Learning process | Method | Scenario | Dataset | Energy consumption-based | Collaborative |
|---|---|---|---|---|---|---|---|
| [18] (2014) | Time series | Unsupervised | Clustering | Building energy consumption | Real data | ✓ | X |
| [17] (2019) | RNN | Deep Learning | Regression | Tennessee Valley Authority | Data provided by 30 power meters | ✓ | X |
| [35] (2018) | SVM, KNN, Random Forest | Supervised | Classification | Water supply system | Testbed | ✓ | X |
| [31] (2018) | TMSE | Supervised | Classification | Industrial Internet of Things | Dataset offered by State Grid of China | ✓ | X |
| [20] (2020) | Regression trees | Supervised | Regression | Smart Grid AMI | Experiment | ✓ | X |
| [11] (2020) | K-means LSTM | Unsupervised, Deep Learning | Clustering, forecasting | User power consumption | Dataport, a public dataset | ✓ | X |
| [12] (2020) | KNN | Supervised | Classification | Charging Station | - | X | X |
| [39] (2019) | Moving Average, DBSCAN | Unsupervised | Clustering | Charging Station | High frequency harmonic data | X | X |
| [6] (2020) | Neural Networks, LSTM | Supervised, Deep Learning | Classification | Charging Station | CICIDS 2018 DoS dataset | X | X |
| [24] (2021) | MHA | Supervised, Deep Learning | Classification | Charging Station | Laboratory, network traffic | X | X |
| [23] (2021) | KNN, SVM, Random Forest | Supervised | Classification | Charging Station | Experiment | ✓ | X |
| CADS4CS (our approach) | Collaborative System | Supervised, Deep Learning | Classification | Charging Station | Open data | ✓ | ✓ |

buildings, and then use clustering techniques to classify them. Similarly in [17], the authors study the use of deep learning algorithms, such as Recurrent Neural Networks (RNNs), to remove trend and seasonality from time series data and predict the power anomalies. Other works, related to energy anomaly monitoring and detection, are [31,35]. Robles-Durazno et al. in [35] propose a supervised learning model for energy monitoring and anomaly detection in a clean water supply system, using classifiers such as Support Vector Machine (SVM), K-Nearest Neighbors (KNN) and Random Forest. In [31], another ML model for detecting energy anomalies is studied by Ouyang et al., where the Three-stage Multi-view Stacking Ensemble (TMSE) model is proposed to detect anomalous power consumption in industrial devices. In addition, other works comprise the ability to predict outliers in the energy. For instance, in [20] a two-level anomaly detection framework based on regression decision trees is proposed with the objective of predicting unexpected power consumption in an Advanced Metering Infrastructure (AMI). The combination of clustering and prediction techniques, such as the K-Means and Long-Short Term Memory (LSTM) techniques, is even analyzed in [11] to predict the power consumption of users in the next hour.

There are also several recent studies on the use of ADSs in CS scenarios. In [12] and [24], anomalous traffic data within the network is identified. An invariant-correlation network and a multivariate time-series segmentation method using the KNN classifier is used in [12], while a Multi-Head Attentions (MHA) model is used in [24] to correlate the network traffic. As an alternative, Streubel et al. in [39] adapt the identification of irregular patterns in the high harmonic frequency spectrum, described by the CS supraharmonic emissions, and group the detected anomalies according to similar characteristics using the technique known as Density-Based Spatial Clustering of Applications with Noise (DBSCAN). Deep learning models have also been considered in [6] for early detection of DoS attacks against CSs.

Finally, the work in [23] performs a threat detection analysis based on power consumption through ML techniques, which are able to classify three types of states in each CS: normal, risk or accident. As can be seen in the Table 1, [23] is the only work that addresses an ADS based on the CS energy consumption. It is focused on the detection of malfunctioning attacks in the CSs that may lead to a DoS of these systems. In contrast, our approach differs from these works in the use of a collaborative system as an optimization measure for intrusion detection in complex charging networks. Although collaborative intrusion detection systems is not a novel approach [22,40,44], its applicability in charging infrastructure environments is. CADS4CS has the ability to detect and learn from different types of power consumption anomalies at CSs, specifically those related to consumption energy deviations in the charging sessions.

# 3   CADS4CS: Datasets and Architecture

This section covers the functionalities of the CADS4CS, starting with the definition of the datasets and types of anomalies used in each of the ADSs, and ends with the CADS4CS design and the types of voting algorithms of the coordinator.

## 3.1   Data Models, Datasets and Anomalies

To gain a correct understanding of the energy data, it is necessary to analyze the behavior of the data distribution and features of the user charging sessions, which usually include the following attributes: (i) total energy consumed (in kWh), (ii) cost or fee, (iii) charge duration, (iv) session duration, (v) type of connector used and (vi) charging speed. Different data models, with derived attributes, have been created from these attributes to train ML models and obtain a high accuracy of anomaly detection at CSs, regardless of their manufacturing model, configuration or the region in which they are located.

We have considered several open charging session databases (dated between 2017 and 2022), whose information comes from different geographic locations and charging networks. These databases correspond with: Boulder [30] and Palo Alto [32] cities in the US; Dundee city [14] and Perth and Kinross council [33] in Scotland, United Kingdom (UK); and charging sessions from the ElaadNL network in the Netherlands [29]. For each of these, the data have been processed and cleaned to a common format, maintaining the aforementioned attributes. In addition to this, we have generated charging session anomalies related to errors or intentional attacks on energy consumption values in the datasets mentioned, which could have a significant impact on the meaning of the monitoring actions and decision-making. To establish these anomalies, we identified two types of perturbations that affect to the charging session data: *measurement reading errors* or *deliberated attacks* such as *false data injection* or *modification*. These anomalies can influence the following attributes: (1) energy consumed, (2) session duration, (3) charge duration, (4) average power, (5) total cost and (6) no charge (energy consumed is 0); note that these attributes have been considered according to the common charging session features of all selected datasets. In order to understand the perturbation procedure, the anomalies were intentionally injected into the datasets following a random strategy. That is, for each dataset, approximately 20% of samples were extracted, which were intentionally perturbed in some of their attributes in a random manner. Therefore, normal and anomalous samples have been explicitly labeled by us for subsequent studies.

In turn, the previous datasets are applied to form a network of distributed CS clusters, as illustrated in Fig. 1. Each cluster contains its own dataset and ADS for local anomaly detection. However, these ADSs have the added problem of being susceptible to increasing the number of FPs and FNs over time due to their mismatch with the data distribution, or due to their inability to detect some unknown or stealthy threats [10]. To avoid this issue, CADS4CS deals with a solution based on a higher-level CADS, which is defined below.

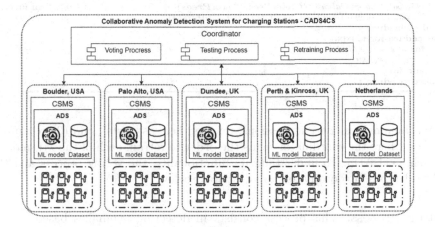

**Fig. 1.** CADS4CS design

## 3.2   Collaborative Anomaly Detection System

CADS4CS is based on establishing a centralized node in the CS network that acts as coordinator of the entire charging network. This coordinator is in charge of communicating with each of the ADSs in each CS cluster and collecting predictions, alerts and performance information from each of them. Therefore, the main goal of these coordinators is to detect anomalies at a global level through a simple voting system based on the local predictions, thereby achieving a lower FP and FN ratio than the local ADSs. To do this, another objective is to develop continuous retraining measures in a collaborative manner to optimize the performance of the ML models of each local ADS.

These two objectives are carried out thanks to three processes incorporated in the coordinator (as defined in Algorithm 1): (1) *voting process*, where the coordinator evaluates the predictions of each local ADS on an unknown anomaly triggered by one of them, thereby deriving a global prediction using a statistical function, as detailed below; (2) *testing process*, where the coordinator evaluates the performance of each local ADS after generating different samples of

---

**Algorithm 1.** Coordinator Model: voting, testing and retraining

---

**Require:** $adsModels$
  **procedure** VOTING($Xsamples$)            ▷ Unknown charging session samples
    $yLocalPreds \Leftarrow EmptyList()$
    **for** $ads \leftarrow adsModels$ **do**
      $yLocalPreds.add(ads.\text{PREDICT}(Xsamples))$
    **end for**
    $yGlobalPred \Leftarrow CalculateGlobalPrediction(yLocalPreds)$     ▷ Statistical function
    **for** $ads \leftarrow adsModels$ **do**    ▷ Add Xsamples and yGlobalPred as label to the train dataset
      $ads.\text{ADDSAMPLE}(Xsamples, yGlobalPred))$
    **end for**
  **end procedure**
  **procedure** TESTING($Xsamples, Ysamples$)       ▷ Known charging session samples
    $yLocalPreds \Leftarrow EmptyList()$
    **for** $ads \leftarrow adsModels$ **do**
      $yLocalPreds.add(ads.\text{PREDICT}(Xsamples))$
      $ads.\text{EVALUATELOCALPREDICTION}(yLocalPred, Ysamples)$
      $ads.\text{ADDSAMPLE}(Xsamples, Ysamples)$     ▷ Add samples to the train dataset
    **end for**
    $yGlobalPred \Leftarrow CalculateGlobalPred(yLocalPreds)$     ▷ Statistical function
    EVALUATEGLOBALPREDICTION($yGlobalPred, Ysamples$)
  **end procedure**
  **procedure** RETRAINING
    **for** $ads \leftarrow adsModels$ **do**
      $ads.\text{RETRAIN}$
    **end for**
  **end procedure**

---

normal/anomalous charging sessions, referred here as "tests"; and (3) *retraining process*, where the coordinator sends the order to retrain each of the ML models of each local ADS. To understand its functionality, the voting process and the different types of coordinators are described below.

**Voting Process:** This process consists in detecting anomalies based on the predictions made by each of the local ADSs, thus obtaining a global prediction from a statistical function (average, weighted-average or mode), as specified in Algorithm 1 (VOTING procedure). Initially, each local ADS individually predicts the charging session samples that are recorded in its CSs. After a local ADS predicts a possible anomaly, it is notified to the coordinator who is in charge of starting the voting phase. The coordinator forwards the received sample to the other local ADSs to make their own local prediction. Note that these ADSs do not know the origin of the sample or whether it corresponds to a sample from another local ADS, or if it is a test generated by the coordinator. The predictions made by the local ADSs are returned to the coordinator, which calculates a global prediction from a statistical function. Finally, the global prediction serves as a labeled sample that is stored in the ADS datasets for future retraining.

Three types of coordinators have been implemented according to the statistical function used to calculate the global prediction.

– **Average Coordinator (ACoord.):** the global prediction is calculated as the arithmetic average of the local probability predictions together with a predefined threshold ($\alpha$). If the average probability obtained is greater than $\alpha$, the sample is considered to be an anomaly.

- **Weighted-Average Coordinator (WACoord.)**: similarly, the global prediction is calculated as the weighted average of the local probability predictions together with an $\alpha$. The weights of each local prediction are determined by the F1-score performance metric of each ADS obtained in its last evaluation. Thus, ADSs with optimal ML models will be more heavily weighted than ADSs with worse performing ML models.
- **Mode Coordinator (MCoord.)**: in this case, the thresholds are automatically defined by each ML model and they directly return a discrete prediction, which corresponds to the label 0 if it is considered a normal sample, or 1 if it is an anomaly. This coordinator simply considers the label that appears most often (i.e. the absolute majority) to be the global prediction.

Note that the average and weighted average have been selected based on the correlation of opinions established in [37]. In addition, we have extended the research by also using the mode as a correlation function, which computes discrete values and does not require defining the prediction threshold (alpha) by the coordinator. Following the classification given in [44] and [40], our approach corresponds to a mix between the similarity-based and filter-based approaches. In the remaining sections, we therefore provide a comprehensive analysis, showing the behavior of these types of correlations for different use cases.

## 4   Analyses, Experiments and Results

Based on the aforementioned open datasets and the possible charging session anomalies described in Sect. 3.1, two types of practical analysis are carried out on the CADS4CS:

- **Analysis 1 (A1) – using a shared dataset**: this corresponds to using the same training and testing dataset shared between the different ADSs, with the objective of analyzing the performance of each ML model and the coordinator to detect known anomalies in all ADSs. Note that the shared dataset contains all types of charging session anomalies proposed in Sect. 3.1. In a real environment, this analysis is useful in scenarios where the same charging network with a centralized and shared dataset incorporates different ADSs to detect possible anomalies.
- **Analysis 2 (A2) – using incomplete datasets**: consists in using different training and test datasets for each of the ADSs of the collaborative system. This analysis simulates the use case of a real scenario where one or more charging networks separate the management and anomaly detection by groups of CSs, where each group contains its own charging session database and ADS (see Fig. 1). In addition, each one may be prone to certain types of anomalies and may be unaware of the anomalies of other CS clusters. To achieve this, we have desegregated each dataset to be incomplete, not incorporating all the types of anomalies, as shown in Table 2.

In order to make a comprehensive study of the performance of the coordinators in different situations, we performed two types of experiments for each of the analyses. These experiments are as follows:

**Table 2.** Summary of known anomalies in each dataset for **A2**

| Dataset / Anomaly | Energy | Charge Duration | Session Duration | Power | Cost | No Charge |
|---|---|---|---|---|---|---|
| Boulder, US | ✓ | X | X | ✓ | ✓ | X |
| Palo Alto, US | ✓ | ✓ | ✓ | X | X | X |
| Dundee, UK | X | ✓ | ✓ | X | X | ✓ |
| Perth and Kinross, UK | ✓ | X | X | ✓ | ✓ | ✓ |
| Netherlands | X | ✓ | ✓ | ✓ | ✓ | X |

- **Experiment 1 (E1)** – **based on three sequential phases**: this is a simple procedure to evaluate the performance of each type of coordinator before and after a retraining of the ML models. For this purpose, a set of charging session samples (including all types of anomalies and ordered chronologically) is initially split into 150 sets. After each split (each subset of samples), F1-score metric of each of the ADSs and coordinators is calculated in order to discern the most optimal algorithm.

For **E1**, we consider three application phases, as shown in Algorithm 2 – EXPERIMENT 1 procedure: (1) *pre-retraining voting phase*, where each ADS predicts the first 50 splits and the coordinators, based on the predictions of the

---

**Algorithm 2.** Experiments: **E1** and **E2**

---

**Require:** *coord, X, Y*
$X splits, Y splits \Leftarrow$ SPLIT$(X, Y, 150)$
**procedure** EXPERIMENT 1
   **for** $i \leftarrow 1$ to 50 **do**           ▷ Pre-Retraining Voting Phase
      $X samples, Y samples \leftarrow X split[i], Y split[i]$
      $yGlobalPred \leftarrow coord.$VOTING$(X samples)$
      EVALUATEF1SCORE
   **end for**
   **for** $i \leftarrow 51$ to 100 **do**           ▷ Retraining Phase
      $X samples, Y samples \leftarrow X split[i], Y split[i]$
      $yGlobalPred \leftarrow coord.$TESTING$(X samples, Y samples)$
      EVALUATEF1SCORE
      $coord.$RETRAINING
   **end for**
   **for** $i \leftarrow 51$ to 150 **do**           ▷ Post-Retraining Voting Phase
      $X samples, Y samples \leftarrow X split[i], Y split[i]$
      $yGlobalPred \leftarrow coord.$VOTING$(X samples)$
      EVALUATEF1SCORE
   **end for**
**end procedure**
**procedure** EXPERIMENT 2
   **for** $i \leftarrow 1$ to 150 **do**
      $X samples, Y samples \leftarrow X split[i], Y split[i]$
      **if** $i$ is *odd* **then**           ▷ Voting Phase
         $yGlobalPred \leftarrow coord.$VOTING$(X samples)$
      **else**           ▷ Testing Phase
         $yGlobalPred \leftarrow coord.$TESTING$(X samples, Y samples)$
      **end if**
      EVALUATEF1SCORE
      $coord.$RETRAINING
   **end for**
**end procedure**

---

ADSs, compute their global predictions using their corresponding statistical function; (2) *retraining phase*, during the next 50 splits, each ADS predicts the samples, adds the sample to its dataset and retrains its ML model with the training dataset updated so far; and (3) *post-retraining voting phase*, where again the last 50 splits are predicted locally by the ADSs and the coordinators compute the global predictions.

- **Experiment 2 (E2) – based on two cyclic phases**: this is a methodology where voting, testing and retraining processes are continuously executed. It is based on two cyclic phases, which alternate during the 150 sets of samples splits, as shown in Algorithm 2 – EXPERIMENT 2 procedure.

More specifically, **E2** includes: (1) *voting phase*, where each ADS and the coordinator collaboratively predict a subset of samples that is finally added to the training set of each ML model, using the coordinator's global predictions as labels (as indicated in the VOTING procedure of Algorithm 1); and (2) *testing phase*, where each ADS predicts a subset of samples again, but this time adds the original samples, with the real labels, to the training set (as indicated in the TESTING procedure of Algorithm 1). After the completion of each phase, the ML models are retrained using their own updated training dataset (with global prediction labels and real test labels). Note that **E2** aims to assess whether continuous retraining of the ML models is required, interleaving the voting process and the testing process.

## 4.1    A1: Analyzing CADS4CS Using a Shared Dataset

**A1** intends to validate the behavior of the coordinators and ADSs when databases are shared for **E1** and **E2**, in addition to plotting the learning result of ML models that best fit the types of perturbations. Table 3 shows the ML classifiers chosen for each ADS: Decision Trees (DT), Random Forest (RF); CatBoost [42], eXtreme Gradient Boosting (XGBoost) [41], and Multi-Layer Perceptron (MLP). We have chosen these classifiers because they have shown the best results in terms of efficiency and accuracy, as also reflected in the following studies [1] [2], [26] and [27]. It is important to note that for **A1** and **A2**, we have established $\alpha = 0.4$ as the anomaly probability threshold. This value is pre-established as the optimum found after several studies with different thresholds.

**Table 3.** Features of the ADSs in **A1** and **A2**

| | Analysis 1 | | Analysis 2 | | Machine Learning |
|---|---|---|---|---|---|
| | Dataset (full) | Size | Dataset (incomplete) | Size | |
| **ADS1** | | | Boulder | 40K | CatBoost |
| **ADS2** | | | Dundee | 180K | DT |
| **ADS3** | Dundee | 200K | Netherlands | 12K | MLP |
| **ADS4** | | | Palo Alto | 200K | RF |
| **ADS5** | | | Perth & Kinross | 80K | XGBoost |

**E1 - Based on Three Sequential Phases:** Figures 2 and 3 show the evolution of the F1-score metric for both individual ADSs and for each of the coordinator classes. The results clearly illustrate the best ML models with higher precision and recall, as well as the usefulness of the coordinators in this type of scenario. More specifically, after the retraining phase, slight improvements (approximately an increase of F1 score between 0.01 and 0.04) can be observed in the performance of the ADSs and coordinators, due to the fact that the ADSs have been initially trained with a shared dataset with all anomalies (cf. Sect. 3.1).

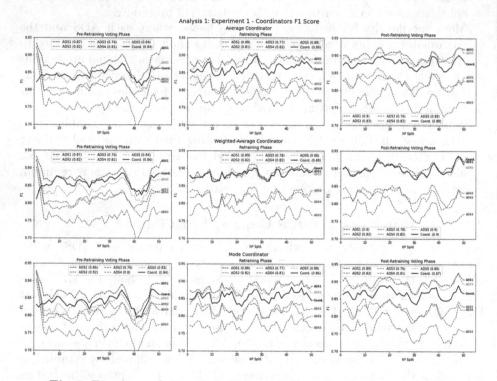

**Fig. 2.** F1-score evolution of all ADSs in each coordinator during **A1–E1**

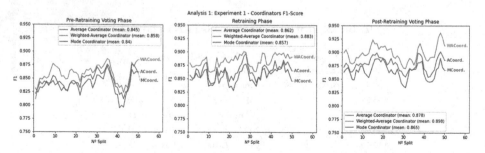

**Fig. 3.** F1-score evolution in each coordinator during **A1–E1**

From Fig. 2, we highlight how the ML models of ADS1 and ADS5, corresponding to the Catboost and XGBoost, show significantly better results providing a 0.9 F1 score in the best case. This is followed by ADS2 and ADS4, corresponding to the use of DT and RF classifiers, with a 0.82 score, and finally ADS3 (corresponding to the MLP model) presents the worst results with a 0.78 score. In this first experiment, we can observe how the ML models based on decision trees, such as DT, RF, CatBoost and XGBoost, are good classifiers for the aforementioned dataset and the perturbations given in it. They are able to train and quickly detect large deviations in the normal distribution of the dataset, as stated in [2]. Moreover, the CatBoost and XGBoost models are even better since they share the use of an efficient and effective implementation of the gradient boosting algorithm to obtain an optimal classifier based on decision trees. In contrast, the neural network used by the MLP classifier has not been able to fit correctly with the data distribution, resulting in a high number of FPs and FNs.

As can be seen in Fig. 2, the types of coordinators present similar results to the ADSs. ACoord. and MCoord. return an evolution curve slightly inferior to ADS1 and ADS5. While WACoord, which uses the F1-score metric of the ADSs as weights, performs similarly to the best ADSs, such as ADS1 and ADS5. For such scenarios, WACoord. can be useful to ensure that the coordinator's detection has as low an FP and FN ratio as possible.

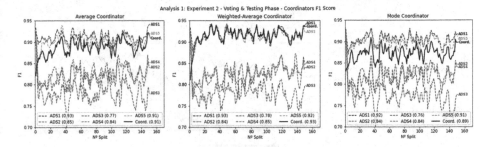

**Fig. 4.** F1-score evolution of all ADSs in each coordinator during **A1–E2**

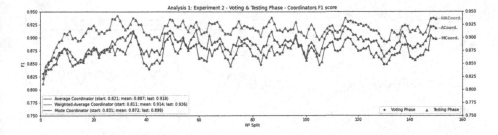

**Fig. 5.** F1-score evolution in each coordinator during **A1–E2**

**E2 - Based on Two Cyclic Phases:** In this experiment, we can observe results very similar to those obtained in **E1**, but with slight improvements, as shown in Figs. 4 and 5 (from 0.81 to 0.93 F1-score). Both ADSs and coordinators achieve an increase in the mean F1-score by approximately 3 hundredths with respect to the **E1** results, particularly in the case of the coordinators. For each type of coordinator, as shown in Fig. 5, there is a slight positive trend in the evolution of F1 over time (splits), which implies a continuous improvement and adjustment of the ML models with the distribution of the dataset. This means that the use of the combination of global predictions with the tests generated by the coordinator as new training samples are useful for detecting future known and unknown anomalies.

## 4.2    A2: Analyzing CADS4CS Using Incomplete Datasets

In this second analysis, each ADS has a different and incomplete dataset, as shown in Table 3. This scenario corresponds to more faithful use cases in practice in real environments, where a charging network is further divided into different groups of CSs according to certain parameters, such as location, model or manufacturer. This distribution facilitates the management of each group, which would have their own CSMS, EMS, security policies, protocols and, above all, their own charging session dataset and ADS. Therefore, the aim of this analysis

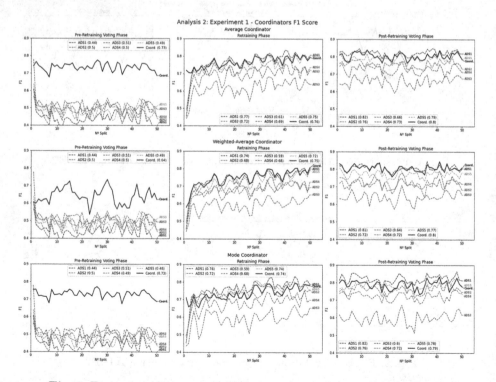

**Fig. 6.** F1-score evolution of all ADSs in each coordinator during **A2–E1**

is to check if the coordinator succeeds in detecting any type of anomaly, which may be unknown to some of the ML models.

**E1 - Based on Three Sequential Phases:** As shown in Fig. 6, in the pre-retraining voting phase, ADSs present results with low precision (F1-score below 0.5), which suggests the detection of a large number of FPs and FNs. This is because the ADSs have initially been trained with incomplete datasets and their ML models are unable to detect certain types of unknown anomalies. However, the different types of coordinators are able to unify the individual detections of the ADSs and provide more accurate predictions, thus obtaining a higher F1-score evolution than the ADSs. In this case, as shown in Fig. 7, ACoord. and MCoord. present better results (above 0.7); while WACoord., due to its high dependence on the F1-score of the ADSs that are used as weights in the weighted average, results in a higher number of FPs and FNs.

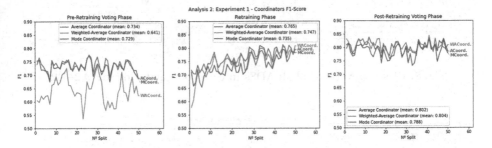

**Fig. 7.** F1-score evolution in each coordinator during **A2–E1**

However, these results change completely at the end of the retraining phase, where in this case, all ML models are retrained with the samples obtained by the coordinators' global prediction during the pre-retraining voting phase and the tests generated by the coordinators during the retraining phase. Therefore, in the last phase (post-retraining voting phase), a significant improvement in the F1-score evolution of the ADSs and coordinators is evident, since the ML models are now able to detect unknown anomalies from their datasets. After the retraining, ADS1 and ADS5, corresponding to the Catboost and XGBoost ML models, remain optimal models with mean F1 scores of 0.82 and 0.78, respectively. This is followed by ADS2 (using DT classifier) and ADS4 (using RF classifier) with scores of 0.76 and 0.72. Finally, ADS3, which uses a Deep Learning model such as MLP, presents significantly lower precision and recall than the rest with an average F1 score of 0.64. As in the previous analysis, the three types of coordinators present similar results to the best ADSs, where ACoord. and WACoord. are the optimum. This feature is also depicted in Fig. 7.

**E2 - Based on Two Cyclic Phases:** In this experiment, a continuous retraining is again performed combining the voting and testing phases. The purpose of this experiment is to observe whether the ADSs succeed in optimizing their ML parameters in a collaborative way, thanks to the global predictions and tests generated by the coordinator. As shown in Fig. 8 and 9, an F1-score evolution with positive trend is achieved for both local ADSs and the various coordinators. With this, we observe that the results obtained are significantly higher than the **E1** results after the retraining phase, especially for the ACoord. and WACoord., which achieve an F1-score of almost 0.85 in the last splits.

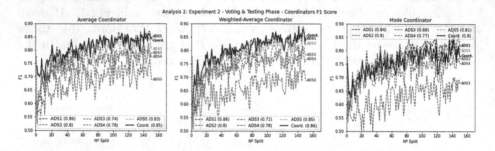

**Fig. 8.** F1-score evolution of all ADSs in each coordinator during **A2–E2**

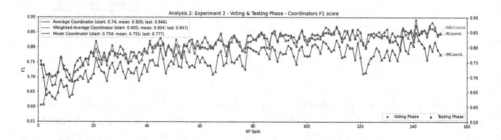

**Fig. 9.** F1-score evolution in each coordinator during **A2–E2**

## 4.3    Discussions: A1 vs A2

Table 4 summarizes the mean F1-score for each ADS and coordinator and for each analysis and experiment. From this table, we first observe that ML models generated using the gradient boosting technique (such as CatBoost and XGBoost) correspond to the optimal ML models. These models show high precision in detecting the types of charging session anomalies discussed in this paper. Specifically, the Catboost algorithm, used in **ADS1**, corresponds to the optimum ML model, achieving an F1-score of up to 0.93 in **A1–E2**.

On the other hand, we can see how the suggested types of coordinators can be useful in certain use cases. ACoord. and MCoord. are quite useful in scenarios where the performance of each ADS is unknown or their ML models are incapable of detecting certain types of unknown anomalies, as occurs in **A2–E1** in the pre-retraining voting phase (Fig. 6); while WACoord. is particularly useful when combined with a continuous retraining of the ML models and testing phases, as also observed in **A1–E2** and **A2–E2**. In Table 4, we can appreciate how WACoord. presents the optimal F1-scores reaching the value of 0.936 in **A1–E2**. This coordinator presents better results compared to the average and mode coordinators, because its correlation prioritizes the predictions of the ADSs with greater precision. Thus, the rate of FPs and FNs is reduced.

Finally, from this table we can also conclude that **E2** offers better performance compared to **E1**. This means that it is advisable in these use cases to follow a continuous retraining methodology where voting and testing processes are alternately combined. This allows the ML models to dynamically adjust to the data distribution, obtaining higher precision over time. However, looking at the results in Table 4 we also highlight that there are still too many FPs and FNs in this scenario, which can saturate human operators. This implies that it is still necessary to advance in this line of research, addressing new solutions to classify anomalies by optimizing existing detection methods.

Table 4. Summary of F1-score results

|    |    | ADS1 | ADS2 | ADS3 | ADS4 | ADS5 | ACoord. | WACoord. | MCoord. |
|----|----|------|------|------|------|------|---------|----------|---------|
| A1 | E1 | **0.90** | 0.82 | 0.78 | 0.82 | **0.90** | 0.878 | **0.898** | 0.865 |
|    | E2 | **0.93** | 0.84 | 0.78 | 0.85 | 0.92 | 0.918 | **0.936** | 0.898 |
| A2 | E1 | **0.82** | 0.76 | 0.64 | 0.72 | 0.78 | 0.802 | **0.804** | 0.788 |
|    | E2 | **0.86** | 0.8 | 0.72 | 0.78 | 0.85 | 0.846 | **0.847** | 0.777 |

The best performing method in every experiment is marked in bold

## 5 Conclusion and Future Work

In this paper, we have carried out a comprehensive analysis of the detection of charging session anomalies in different types of charging stations (slow, fast and rapid charging mode). Firstly, we have collected different open data of charging sessions to later simulate various errors and threats, generating anomalies and deviations in different attributes of the sessions. We have then defined a collaborative anomaly detection system capable of coordinating and retraining a group of independent Machine Learning models. Finally, after performing different analyses and experiments, we have observed how in certain scenarios the collaborative system is successful in achieving a high F1-score with a low false positive and negative ratio, and in establishing an effective procedure for continuous retraining of the ML models. Of all the ML models trained and evaluated, decision tree variants – such as random forest classifier and gradient boosting techniques (CatBoost and XGBoost algorithms) – are the optimal models in these cases. As future work, we intend to extend the approach considering the actual drawbacks of the collaborative detection systems, such as data privacy and trust as stated in [22] and [44]; and integrate the approach in a real charging infrastructure within the "Smart and Secure EV Urban Lab II" project.

**Acknowledgements.** This work has been supported by the "Smart and Secure EV Urban Lab II" through the Second Own Plan of Smart-Campus of the University of Malaga, by the EC under the SealedGRID project (H2020-MSCA-RISE-2017) with GA no. 777996, by the Ministry of Science and Innovation under SECUREDGE project (PID2019-110565RB-I00 − AEI/10.13039/501100011033/), and by the Andalusian Government under the SAVE project (P18-TP-3724).

# A    Design and threats of a public charging infrastructure

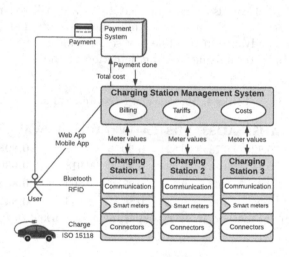

**Fig. 10.** Deployment diagram of a public charging infrastructure

This appendix provides an overview of the components that compose a charging infrastructure and clarifies the level of susceptibility of these infrastructures to attacks according to the state of the art. Public CSs are usually managed by a CSMS, which has the ability to use ITs and OTs to efficiently control each CS and its charging sessions initialized by the users. Specifically, this control center is in charge of authenticating, authorizing and billing users, and diagnosing. Figure 10 shows a generic public charging infrastructure based on the Open Charge Point Protocol (OCPP) standard [4].

The combination of ITs and OTs in these cyber-physical systems leads to new security risks that must be considered right from the design stage. Above all, the addition of new functionalities, communications and external actors in the charging infrastructures open the door to new threats to the system. For this reason, we include in this appendix a high-level review of the state of the art [7,16,28] to show the susceptibility of this infrastructure to attacks and their impact on the end user and the power grid. Among the most common threats are: (T1) natural disasters, (T2) physical damage, (T3) DoS, (T4) identity theft or spoofing, (T5) malware injection, (T6) false data injection, (T7) tampering and (T8) sniffing or information disclosure.

Table 5 shows a summary of these threats with their corresponding environmental, social and economic impacts. As can be seen in the table, blackouts, economic damages and energy theft correspond to the impacts with the greatest likelihood and risk in a public charging infrastructure. This work therefore aims to mitigate these impacts through the use of Machine Learning techniques for anomaly detection. Its scope has been limited to the detection of threats related to T6 and T7, and focuses on studying the normal behavior of energy consumption data.

**Table 5.** Summary of threats and impacts on a public charging infrastructure

| Impact \ Threat | Blackout | Energy theft | Equipment damage | Economic damage | Data leak |
|---|---|---|---|---|---|
| T1 | ✓ | X | ✓ | ✓ | X |
| T2 | ✓ | X | ✓ | ✓ | X |
| T3 | ✓ | X | X | ✓ | X |
| T4 | X | ✓ | X | ✓ | ✓ |
| T5 | ✓ | ✓ | ✓ | ✓ | ✓ |
| T6 | X | ✓ | X | ✓ | X |
| T7 | ✓ | ✓ | ✓ | ✓ | X |
| T8 | X | X | X | X | ✓ |

# References

1. Abdar, M., Yen, N.Y., Hung, J.C.S.: Improving the diagnosis of liver disease using multilayer perceptron neural network and boosted decision trees. J. Med. Biol. Eng. **38**(6), 953–965 (2018)
2. Alcaraz, C., Cazorla, L., Fernandez, G.: Context-awareness using anomaly-based detectors for smart grid domains. In: Lopez, J., Ray, I., Crispo, B. (eds.) CRiSIS 2014. LNCS, vol. 8924, pp. 17–34. Springer, Cham (2015). https://doi.org/10.1007/978-3-319-17127-2_2
3. Alcaraz, C., Lopez, J., Wolthusen, S.: OCPP protocol: security threats and challenges. IEEE Trans. Smart Grid **8**(5), 2452–2459 (2017)
4. Open Charge Alliance: OCPP 2.0.1 (2020). https://www.openchargealliance.org/protocols/ocpp-201/. Accessed 24 May 2022
5. Antoun, J., Kabir, M.E., Moussa, B., Atallah, R., Assi, C.: A detailed security assessment of the EV charging ecosystem. IEEE Netw. **34**(3), 200–207 (2020)
6. Basnet, M., Ali, M.H.: Deep learning-based intrusion detection system for electric vehicle charging station. In: 2nd International Conference on Smart Power and Internet Energy Systems, SPIES, pp. 408–413 (2020)

7. Bhusal, N., Gautam, M., Benidris, M.: Cybersecurity of electric vehicle smart charging management systems. In: 52nd North American Power Symposium, NAPS (2020)

8. Brighente, A., Conti, M., Donadel, D., Turrin, F.: EVScout2. 0: electric vehicle profiling through charging profile. arXiv preprint arXiv:2106.16016 (2021)

9. Bristow, M.: A SANS survey: OT/ICS cybersecurity, pp. 1–23 (2021). www.cisa.gov/critical-infrastructure-sectors

10. Cazorla, L., Alcaraz, C., Lopez, J.: Cyber stealth attacks in critical information infrastructures. IEEE Syst. J. **12**, 1778–1792 (2018)

11. Chahla, C., Snoussi, H., Merghem, L., Esseghir, M.: A deep learning approach for anomaly detection and prediction in power consumption data. Energ. Effi. **13**(8), 1633–1651 (2020). https://doi.org/10.1007/s12053-020-09884-2

12. Chung, Y.W., et al.: The framework of invariant electric vehicle charging network for anomaly detection. In: IEEE Transportation Electrification Conference and Expo, ITEC, pp. 631–636 (2020)

13. Deloitte: Electric vehicle trends | Deloitte Insights. https://www2.deloitte.com/us/en/insights/focus/future-of-mobility/electric-vehicle-trends-2030.html. Accessed 18 May 2022

14. Drive Dundee Electric: Electric Vehicle Charging Sessions Dundee - Datasets (2019). https://data.dundeecity.gov.uk/dataset/ev-charging-data. Accessed 08 May 2022

15. ENISA: ENISA Threat Landscape 2021 (2021). https://doi.org/10.2824/324797, https://www.enisa.europa.eu/news/enisa-news/enisa-threat-landscape-2021

16. Gottumukkala, R., Merchant, R., Tauzin, A., Leon, K., Roche, A., Darby, P.: Cyber-physical system security of vehicle charging stations. In: IEEE Green Technologies Conference (2019)

17. Hollingsworth, K., et al.: Energy anomaly detection with forecasting and deep learning. In: Proceedings of the IEEE International Conference on Big Data, Big Data, pp. 4921–4925 (2018)

18. Janetzko, H., Stoffel, F., Mittelstädt, S., Keim, D.A.: Anomaly detection for visual analytics of power consumption data. Comput. Graph. (Pergamon) **38**(1), 27–37 (2014)

19. Khan, O.G.M., El-Saadany, E., Youssef, A., Shaaban, M.: Impact of electric vehicles botnets on the power grid. In: IEEE Electrical Power and Energy Conference, pp. 1–5. IEEE (2019)

20. Amara Korba, A., Tamani, N., Ghamri-Doudane, Y., karabadji, N.E.I.: Anomaly-based framework for detecting power overloading cyberattacks in smart grid AMI. Comput. Secur. **96**, 101896 (2020)

21. Köhler, S., Baker, R., Strohmeier, M., Martinovic, I.: BROKENWIRE: wireless disruption of CCS electric vehicle charging (2022). https://www.brokenwire.fail/. Accessed 25 May 2022

22. Li, W., Meng, W., Kwok, L.F.: Surveying trust-based collaborative intrusion detection: state-of-the-art, challenges and future directions. IEEE Commun. Surv. Tut. **24**(1), 280–305 (2021)

23. Li, Y., Ji, X., Jiang, D., Meng, T.: Abnormal detection system design of charging pile based on machine learning. IOP Conf. Ser. Earth Environ. Sci. **772**(1), 012058 (2021)

24. Li, Y., Zhang, L., Lv, Z., Wang, W.: Detecting anomalies in intelligent vehicle charging and station power supply systems with multi-head attention models. IEEE Trans. Intell. Transp. Syst. **22**(1), 555–564 (2021)

25. Lightman, S., Brewer, T.: Symposium on Federally Funded Research on Cyberse-curity of Electric Vehicle Supply Equipment (EVSE) (2020). https://doi.org/10.6028/NIST.IR.8294

26. Mishra, M.K., Dash, R.: A comparative study of chebyshev functional link artificial neural network, multi-layer perceptron and decision tree for credit card fraud detection. In: 2014 International Conference on Information Technology, pp. 228–233 (2014)

27. Mokhtari, S., Abbaspour, A., Yen, K.K., Sargolzaei, A.: A machine learning approach for anomaly detection in industrial control systems based on measurement data. Electronics 10(4), 407 (2021)

28. Nejabatkhah, F., Li, Y.W., Liang, H., Reza Ahrabi, R.: Cyber-security of smart microgrids: a survey. Energies 14(1), 27 (2020)

29. ElaadNL: Data delen @ Elaad NL (2021), https://platform.elaad.io/download-data/. Accessed 08 May 2022

30. Open-Data Boulder Colorado: Electric Vehicle Charging Station Energy Consumption (2021). https://open-data.bouldercolorado.gov/datasets/183adc24880b41c4be9fd6a14eb6165f_0/explore. Accessed 08 May 2022

31. Ouyang, Z., Sun, X., Chen, J., Yue, D., Zhang, T.: Multi-view stacking ensemble for power consumption anomaly detection in the context of industrial internet of things. IEEE Access 6, 9623–9631 (2018)

32. City of Palo Alto: Electric Vehicle Charging Station Usage (July 2011–Dec 2020) · Open Data · City of Palo Alto (2021). https://data.cityofpaloalto.org/dataviews/257812/electric-vehicle-charging-station-usage-july-2011-dec-2020/. Accessed 08 May 2022

33. Perth & Kinross Council: Electric Vehicle Charging Station Usage - Datasets - Perth and Kinross - Open Data (2021). https://data.pkc.gov.uk/dataset/ev-charging-data. Accessed 08 May 2022

34. Pourmirza, Z., Walker, S.: Electric vehicle charging station: cyber security challenges and perspective. In: 9th IEEE International Conference on Smart Energy Grid Engineering, SEGE, pp. 111–116 (2021)

35. Robles-Durazno, A., Moradpoor, N., McWhinnie, J., Russell, G.: A supervised energy monitoring-based machine learning approach for anomaly detection in a clean water supply system. In: International Conference on Cyber Security and Protection of Digital Services, Cyber Security, pp. 1–8 (2018)

36. Rubio, J.E., Alcaraz, C., Lopez, J.: Addressing security in OCPP: protection against man-in-the-middle attacks. In: 9th IFIP International Conference on New Technologies, Mobility and Security, NTMS 2018 - Proceedings, pp. 1–5 (2018)

37. Rubio, J.E., Manulis, M., Alcaraz, C., Lopez, J.: Enhancing security and dependability of industrial networks with opinion dynamics. In: Sako, K., Schneider, S., Ryan, P.Y.A. (eds.) ESORICS 2019. LNCS, vol. 11736, pp. 263–280. Springer, Cham (2019). https://doi.org/10.1007/978-3-030-29962-0_13

38. Panda Security: Electric vehicle charging stations are vulnerable to hacker attacks (2022). https://www.pandasecurity.com/en/mediacenter/security/ev-charging-stations/. Accepted 03 May 2022

39. Streubel, T., Kattmann, C., Eisenmann, A., Rudion, K.: Detection and monitoring of supraharmonic anomalies of an electric vehicle charging station. In: IEEE Milan PowerTech, PowerTech, pp. 1–5 (2019)

40. Vasilomanolakis, E., Karuppayah, S., Muhlhauser, M., Fischer, M.: Taxonomy and survey of collaborative intrusion detection. ACM Comput. Surv. 47(4), 1–33 (2015)

41. XGBoost: XGBoost Documentation - xgboost 1.6.0 documentation. https://xgboost.readthedocs.io/en/stable/. Accessed 22 May 2022

42. Yandex: CatBoost - open-source gradient boosting library. https://catboost.ai/. Accessed 22 May 2022
43. Zhang, W., Yang, Q., Geng, Y.: A survey of anomaly detection methods in networks. In: Proceedings of the 1st International Symposium on Computer Network and Multimedia Technology, CNMT, pp. 10–12 (2009)
44. Zhou, C.V., Leckie, C., Karunasekera, S.: A survey of coordinated attacks and collaborative intrusion detection. Comput. Secur. **29**(1), 124–140 (2010)

# Correction to: Real-Time Policy Enforcement with Metric First-Order Temporal Logic

François Hublet⬤, David Basin⬤, and Srđan Krstić⬤

**Correction to:**
**Chapter "Real-Time Policy Enforcement with Metric**
**First-Order Temporal Logic" in: V. Atluri et al. (Eds.):**
*Computer Security – ESORICS 2022*, **LNCS 13555,**
**https://doi.org/10.1007/978-3-031-17146-8_11**

The original version of this chapter was revised. The original figure-1 was loaded.

---

The updated original version of this chapter can be found at
https://doi.org/10.1007/978-3-031-17146-8_11

# Author Index

Printed in the United States
by Baker & Taylor Publisher Services

Printed in the United States
by Baker & Taylor Publisher Services